IRB Inter...
Rugby Yearbook
2001-02

John Griffiths
Mick Cleary

CollinsWillow

An Imprint of HarperCollins*Publishers*

First published in Great Britain in 2001 by
CollinsWillow an imprint of
HarperCollins*Publishers* London

1 3 5 7 9 8 6 4 2

The views expressed in this book are not necessarily
the views of the IRB

A CIP catalogue record for this book is available
from the British Library

The HarperCollins website address is:
www.fireandwater.com

ISBN 0 00 712285 3

Typeset by Letterpart Ltd, Reigate, Surrey

Printed and bound Clays Ltd, St Ives plc.

Picture acknowledgements

All photographs courtesy of Allsport

CONTENTS

ABBREVIATIONS USED IN THIS YEARBOOK

International Teams

A – Australia; Arg – Argentina; AW – Anglo-Welsh; B – British Forces and Home Unions teams; Bb – Barbarians; Be – Belgium; BI – British/Irish teams; Bu – Bulgaria; C – Canada; Ch – Chile; Cr – Croatia; Cv – New Zealand Cavaliers; Cz – Czechoslovakia; E – England; F – France; Fj – Fiji; Gg – Georgia; H – Netherlands; HK – Hong Kong; I – Ireland; It – Italy; Iv – Ivory Coast; J – Japan; K – New Zealand Services; M – Maoris; Mo – Morocco; NAm – North America; Nm – Namibia; NZ – New Zealand; NZA – New Zealand Army; P – President's XV; Pg – Paraguay; Po – Poland; Pt – Portugal; R – Romania; Ru – Russia; S – Scotland; SA – South Africa; SAm – South America; SK – South Korea; Sm – Samoa; Sp – Spain; Tg – Tonga; U – Uruguay; US – United States; W – Wales; Wld – World Invitation XV; WS – Western Samoa; Y – Yugoslavia; Z – Zimbabwe.

Other Abbreviations used in the International Listings

(R) – Replacement or substitute; (t) – temporary replacement; [ ] – Rugby World Cup appearances.

NB: When a series has taken place, figures are used to denote the particular matches in which players have featured. Thus NZ 1,3, would indicate that a player has appeared in the First and Third Tests of the relevant series against New Zealand.

Irish Clubs

CIYMS – Church of Ireland Young Men's Society; KCH – King's College Hospital; NIFC – North of Ireland Football Club.

French Clubs

ASF – Association Sportive Française; BEC – Bordeaux Etudiants Club; CASG – Club Athlétique des Sports Generaux; PUC – Paris Université Club; RCF – Racing Club de France; SB – Stade Bordelais; SBUC – Stade Bordelais Université; SCUF – Sporting Club Universitaire de France; SF – Stade Français; SOE – Stade Olympien des Etudiants; TOEC – Toulouse Olympique Employés Club.

South African Provinces

BB – Blue Bulls; Bol – Boland; Bor – Border; EP – Eastern Province; GL – Gauteng Lions; GW – Griqualand West; Mp – Mpumulanga N – Natal; NT – Northern Transvaal; OFS – Free State; R – Rhodesia; SET – South-East Transvaal; SWA – South-West Africa; SWD – South-West Districts; Tvl – Transvaal; WP – Western Province; WT – Western Transvaal; Z–R – Zimbabwe–Rhodesia.

Australian States

ACT – Australian Capital Territory; NSW – New South Wales; Q – Queensland; V – Victoria; WA – Western Australia.

PREFACE

This first edition of the *IRB International Rugby Yearbook* has two aims: to comment on and record the major events world-wide from September 1st 2000 up to the end of the recent Six Nations Championship, and to provide the practical facts and figures of rugby's distinguished history.

The book's appearance has been timed to coincide with the inaugural IRB Awards ceremony to be held in London on November 11th, when the International Player of the Year (in association with Heineken) will be announced from the five nominated in our special features section. The cosmopolitan voting panel who drew up the short-list was convened by Gerald Davies and comprised Paul Ackford, Sean Fitzpatrick, Simon Poidevin, Hugo Porta, Gareth Rees, Philippe Sella, Fergus Slattery, David Sole and Chester Williams – rugby legends with the collective expertise to run the rule over every playing position.

Lock forwards, the unsung heroes of the game, feature in two of our other special articles: the late Gordon Brown of Scotland and the great John Eales of Australia. Norman Mair, former Scotland hooker and the best rugby union writer in the business, pens a warm tribute to a compatriot who died from cancer earlier this year, while Peter Jenkins in Australia, who saw every one of the 86 Tests that Eales played in, contributes a memoir on the recently retired Wallaby captain. Our final feature article is an illuminating contribution on the strength of rugby in Eastern Europe by Chris Thau, whose knowledge of the game in those parts (and many others for that matter) is unrivalled.

Our thanks go to our team of correspondents who have contributed from all the major rugby-playing nations. In the Home Unions, Terry Cooper, Peter O'Reilly and David Llewellyn deserve particular mention for meeting very tight deadlines when the elongated Six Nations Championship eventually reached its conclusion.

Assembling the statistics for this first edition has been a major undertaking that could not have been achieved without the wholehearted support of an experienced team. New Zealanders have long led the way in the presentation of the game's facts and figures and in Geoff Miller of Hamilton we were fortunate to find a resourceful statistician who, for this edition, has brought many details to print for the first time. Others who patiently answered questions were Michelle Treacy at the International Board in Dublin, Chris Rhys (tours), Matthew Alvarez (Australia), Brian Newth (Japan), Michel Breton (France), Walter Pigatto, Matteo Silini (both Italy), Doug Sturrock, Keith Wilkinson (both Canada) and Frankie Deges, who put at our disposal his magnificent database of Argentine Test records.

On the production side our thanks go to the in-house team. Michael Doggart, Tarda Davison-Aitkins and Tom Whiting at HarperCollins carefully edited the work, while Chris Leggatt at Letterpart skilfully prepared our copy for printing.

Last, but not least by way of introduction, we suggest that the game should be grateful to the IRB's Vernon Pugh and Chris Rea for commissioning this title and thus ensuring that International Rugby has an annual reference book that, we hope, will run and run and be worthy of the sport's rich history.

Dublin, 21st October 2001
Mick Cleary & John Griffiths

Owing to the late completion of the 2001 Six Nations, the international match statistics in this edition are complete up to **21st October 2001**. Elsewhere, statistics relating to the representative and domestic sections are complete to the start of the 2001-02 Northern Hemisphere season.

MESSAGE FROM THE CHAIRMAN OF THE IRB

This new publication fills a major gap in the World of Rugby literature. *The IRB Yearbook* will, we hope, become an established feature and an essential companion to the rugby and sports enthusiast.

We would like to thank the editors for their magnificent work and also the correspondents worldwide who have made contributions to the first edition of this new work. The intention is to provide an authoritative record, a global perspective of our expanding sport, and interesting independent contributions from leading rugby writers.

We do hope that you will find interest and pleasure in the following pages.

Vernon Pugh QC, IRB Chairman

IRB
Huguenot House
35–38 St Stephen's Green
Dublin 2
Tel: +353 1 2409 200
Fax: +353 1 2409 201
Email: irb@irb.ie
Website: www.irb.org

EDITORIAL

The Year of the Pip-Squeak
Mick Cleary

It was the year of the pip-squeak. Only Leicester threatened to spoil the show. In an elongated season of close finishes only those single-minded curmudgeons from the Midlands would not fall quite into step with all the others. They were in a class of their own in so many matters. Elsewhere it was a different story.

The Tri Nations went the way of Australia only in the dying seconds when Wallaby No 8 Toutai Kefu smashed his way over for the try that broke New Zealand hearts and, as it was to turn out, probably cost All Black coach, Wayne Smith, his job. Australia did a similar number on the British/Irish Lions. A riveting series, full of internal tensions and external dramas, was only finally nailed down when a last-gasp, desperate Lions attack was bundled into touch at Stadium Australia one Saturday evening in July. The Wallaby supporters, strangers in their own homeland for the previous three weeks as thousands of British and Irish supporters flooded into the country, were able to breathe a sigh of relief as referee Paddy O'Brien blew the final whistle to confirm the 29-23 victory.

John Eales received the Tom Richards trophy, named after one of the sport's finest, a rugby footballer who played for both the Wallabies and the Lions, a gold medallist in the 1908 Olympics, and one of the original Anzacs who went on to be awarded the Military Cross on the Western Front. Eales would know all about Richards's qualities as a man for he too has shown them – nobility, decency, composure – in a sporting context throughout a distinguished career that came to a fitting climax in that Tri Nations thriller. Eales's athletic involvement may have waned by a fraction. His presence, his reassuring aura, never dimmed.

The Tigers themselves were forced to play to the thrills n' spills script in an enthralling Heineken Cup final won only at the death by virtue of a typically audacious break from Austin Healey that sent Leon Lloyd diving into the corner of the Parc des Princes to secure a 34-30 win over Stade Français. On the English domestic front, however, it was a different story as Leicester were far and away the dominant side in the Zurich Premiership, leading by 18 points at one stage before being hauled back to an eight point margin by Wasps. We reverted to the season's norm in the last ever Tetley's Bitter Cup final, only resolved in the dying seconds, when Newcastle's Dave Walder crashed through to score and help his side to a 30-27 victory over Harlequins, a match watched by a crowd of over 70,000. Somebody, somewhere must be doing something right.

And what does all this suggest? Good things in essence. Namely, that standards are rising around planet rugby, that no one side in whatever territory – Leicester, perhaps, excepted – has really managed to steal away from the field. Munster can lay claim to considerable status themselves after landing their third consecutive Irish inter-provincial title and also reaching the semi-final stages of the Heineken Cup, 12 months after just losing out to Northampton in the final itself. Ulster, however, with their own Heineken Cup success, and the recent resurgence of Leinster, should ensure that Munster will be kept on their toes.

There was a more public and fervent display of the Irish revival. It came on a delirious autumnal day at Lansdowne Road, the old stadium bearing witness to a famous 20-14 victory that denied England the fabled Grand Slam for the third year in succession. The win also confirmed that Irish rugby has laid down solid foundations for its professional future. The four provinces are flourishing on all fronts, be it Celtic League, Heineken Cup or Parker Pen European Shield. And the national team – eventually – came through to pronounce its hand by finishing level on points at the top of the reconvened Six Nations Championship. The title itself went to England for the second year in a row. Ireland needed to beat England by a margin of 61 points to claim the crown for themselves, a feat that, if it had come to pass, would have seen religious historians scurrying to the pulpit to declare another miracle in the land. It didn't happen, of course, but victory itself was sweet enough.

Quite what might have happened if the Championship had been played according to the original schedule is a matter only for late-night pub talk, of what might have been and even what should have been. England, in their pomp before the foot-and-mouth epidemic ravaged livelihoods and decimated the calendar, were obliged to wait until late October before they had a tilt, yet again, at the Grand Slam. Before then they had shredded the record books, scoring 215 points and 28 tries in their four games, all of them notable for seeing various records eclipsed.

Should the games have been postponed? Should the tournament have been held over? That was a matter for political conscience with the Irish government under grievous pressure to make sure that its borders were guarded against the disease. They, in turn, put pressure on governing bodies to be seen to be doing the decent thing. The logic seemed perverse to some of us, wondering how games in Cardiff and Edinburgh might involve more risk to the farming community than did the human flow of traffic through Dublin Airport on any normal day. The England game at Lansdowne Road was, admittedly, on a different scale. It was political expedience at work. However, that not one case of foot-and-mouth was recorded in Ireland, in an economy so much more dependent on farming, is justification enough for such stringent measures.

Was there a need to extend the tournament? Could it not just have been wiped from the slate, a historical footnote detailing the exceptional circumstances? In amateur days, that might well have been the outcome. In the professional era there are other factors to consider, the most pressing of which is a need to fill the coffers. Ironically, it was probably the Irish union that was best placed for any financial downturn. However, all the unions have a pressing need to pay the bills. The games had to go on for that reason alone.

Spare a thought for international players who had to rouse themselves early in the 2001-02 season for such a stringent examination of their talent. Small wonder that there was such seeming discrepancy in the form of sides.

Ireland had three matches to navigate, Scotland and Wales away from home before a potential Grand Slam showdown with England. The games had been rescheduled in a different order in order to tee up that possible climax. The prospect did not last long as Ireland slumped to a humiliating 32-10 defeat at Murrayfield. Then came an about-turn at Cardiff, where Ireland had not lost since 1983. History duly served up another Irish win, 36-6. And so to Lansdowne Road and a day of tumult for all those sporting Irish colours, not to mention the 10,000 or so wearing Keith Wood masks. 'I've never seen an uglier-looking crowd,' said Ireland's captain on the day that he led his country for the 24th time, equalling Tom Kiernan's national record.

England trudged over to collect the Lloyds TSB Six Nations trophy looking forlorn and downcast. They were champions for the season but losers on the day, a reminder that sport has that wonderful capacity to go from fair to foul in the blink of an eye.

England may not appreciate the fact but Ireland's victory was a boon for the game in the northern hemisphere. England have raised the bar to admirable heights in the past few years, setting standards for all the others to aspire to. Their infrastructure is sound, their back-up support staff without equal, their investment lavish, their forward-planning imaginative and detailed. They have forced the other countries to sit up and take notice, to plan and invest in like manner. This does not mean copying what England has done. The RFU themselves made that mistake in trying to ape the southern hemisphere in the early days of professionalism. Now they do their own thing and others are looking how to emulate them. Each to their own. England's rise is good news for the European game. In its wake has come the Irish resurgence. Scotland are to introduce a third provincial team in the Borders next year. Only Wales still seems to be blighted by suspicion and in-fighting. It is time for them to take stock or get left behind.

There is a sense of optimism and good cheer about in the sport, on and off the field. For the first time since the game changed its amateur ways back in 1995, there is a positive mood to report on the political front in England. The deal signed between the clubs and the RFU in late July 2001 is a major breakthrough. For too many years the scribes have had to chronicle the turmoil within the English game as the two sides wrestled for control. There have been any number of doomsday scenarios mapped out as the clubs veered away from the governing bodies and made noises about going their own way.

They never truly did. Nor did the RFU ever wash its hands of them even though there were many times when the divisions between the two camps were alarmingly deep and seemingly unbridgeable. Indeed, it appeared that way at various times in the course of the season. So poor was the relationship between the elite players and the RFU that the England squad went on strike just a few days prior to the game against Argentina in November 2000. The face-off lasted no more than 24 hours, although it took longer than that for the wounds between Clive Woodward and his players to fully heal. Woodward lambasted them for their stance. There was little of substance between the two sides in that dispute. In fact, the money itself boiled down to no more than £25 a man. However, in terms of trust and empathy, there was a chasm. The players felt shunned.

Small wonder then that they were to willingly fall in behind their clubs when the call came for solidarity in spring 2001. The clubs had the platinum-edged chips as a new alliance was formed. There was a veiled threat to the RFU that if they did not come to the negotiating table with something considered worthwhile by the clubs then the players would be withheld from England's summer tour to North America. The clubs had pledged that they would not interfere with the Lions tour. It was touch and go as to whether Clive Woodward's resources would be thinned out even more.

The players went, the tour was a great success as England extended their record-breaking run of wins to 11, and political harmony duly followed. The two sides are henceforth to trade as England Rugby Ltd with a £1.9m payment per club to come from central funding. There was an agreement to limit the number of games played by the top players to 32 a season, although we'll see how binding that figure is when it comes to crunch time.

However, all credit to the two sides for finally getting there. The club game in England is slowly pulling itself together. Crowds are inching their way upwards while, for the second year in succession, Leicester were able to declare a healthy operating profit (£346,000), thereby proving that you don't have to break the bank to get success. Northampton officially opened a refurbished Franklin's Gardens in October 2001, a significant multi-million pound investment that lifts capacity to 11,500.

It's about time that green shoots began to appear across rugby's landscape, parched and bare these last few years as clubs battled to cope with the strains of a fledgling professional business. Several leading lights – notably Richmond, London Scottish, West Hartlepool, Moseley, Coventry, Bristol – all flirted with or went into administration. The bad news bulletins in England are no longer a monthly issue.

There are always going to be wrangles. The build-up to the 2003 World Cup has been pock-marked by administrative tussles. The broad impression, though, is that the sport is shaping up. The calendar still needs to be organised more logically and cogently, and not just to suit the southern hemisphere. The calls from that end of the globe for a global season are disingenuous. They mean a southern hemisphere season, aligned to the natural order of events down there with games played between February and December. It should be resisted.

By far the most uplifting sight of the year was the ranks of red replica-shirted Lions supporters that swarmed into Brisbane for the first of the three Tests against the Wallabies. We expected 10,000 – an inflated estimate was the view of some sceptics. They were wrong, so were we. Some 20,000 turned up drawn from all quarters of the globe, all classes and all ages. It made for a wonderful backdrop and even spurred the Aussies into retaliatory action, the ARU being forced to invest £40,000 over the next two Tests kitting out its own fans with yellow scarves. The Brits and Irish showed the way. And that should not be forgotten.

Here was a potent reminder to the game's authorities of just how important Lions tours are, in a sporting as well as a commercial sense. They excite interest because of their rarity value, another timely dig-in-the-ribs for those that would have every international team touring endlessly to the same countries. They stimulate players and fans alike. The decks have to be cleared around a Lions year, only once every four years. Somehow the season must be clipped to enable players to have a proper build-up. Everyone benefits. If the Lions are successful the spin-offs are felt at every level.

The Lions' ten-match tour was not without controversy. Matt Dawson's mid-tour diary of disaffection caused no end of ructions, likewise Austin Healey's end-of tour ghosted column. Dawson was fined £5,000 at the time, Healey £2,000 at a disciplinary hearing held in Dublin two months after the tour ended. Dawson admitted that the timing of his remarks was wrong, while no-one was ever sure whether ghost (Eddie Butler) or player was responsible for slighting the entire Australian nation and Wallaby lock Justin Harrison in particular, labelled 'a plod' and 'a plank' by Healey.

One consequence is bound to be that player columns are banned for future Lions tours. No matter. There could be no disguising the simmering discontent among certain parts of the squad. This was not caused solely by players not being selected; more that they were being marginalized and put-upon. It was not a happy trip. Did it make a difference? Six points was all that divided the teams in the third Test. Who knows? Fatigue and injury were what really did for the Lions in that last game in Sydney. However, the Home Unions Committee need to take stock of the signals coming from the Lions camp. It's too easy to blame the ills on Dawson and Healey. They voiced the issues; they did not necessarily cause them.

The Wallabies did have their colours lowered in the northern hemisphere in November 2000, Dan Luger's late, late try accounting for them at Twickenham. Wales let slip a glorious chance to do a similar number on the Springboks only to see their hopes fade away after the ill-judged substitution of fly-half Neil Jenkins. The French did their usual Jekyll and Hyde act in the autumn series of games with New Zealand, losing lamely in Paris, 39-26, before turning events on their head in Marseilles the following week winning a wonderful game, 42-33. Their topsy-turvy fortunes carried right through the year, enduring a distinctly humdrum Six Nations, beating Italy and Scotland, but losing to Ireland, England and, at home, to Wales. Their record at the Stade de France is truly dreadful. They eventually finished last but one in the Six Nations with Italy bringing up the rear.

The Heineken Cup went from strength-to-strength, a not inconsiderable achievement given that the competition had already acquired a Herculean reputation in its six years of existence. Attendances continue to rise across the various territories. Such is the elite nature of qualifying for the knockout stages that it came down to a matter of tries scored over the last couple of days of competition before the final names could be inked in. Wisely, the organisers have recognised that games should kick-off as far as is possible at the same time on that final weekend.

Leicester came through to take the ultimate honour before a full house of 44,000 at the Parc des Princes, no more than a decent punt away from Stade Français's home ground at Jean Bouin. Such familiarity with the surroundings was not enough for the Parisians.

The European Shield also gave us a classic final the following day, Harlequins only coming through to win, 42-33, against Narbonne in extra-time. The spur of guaranteed entry for the Heineken Cup gave the competition a real boost in the final stages.

Leicester also won the inaugural Zurich play-off championship, an end-of-season money-spinner between the top eight Premiership clubs. There were over 30,000 at Twickenham for the final against Bath but many of us have to be convinced of the competition's worth.

In the Welsh-Scottish League Swansea came through to take the title after a poor start while Newport confirmed their rediscovered status with a 13-8 win over Neath in the final of the Principality Cup. The Black and Ambers said farewell to Gary Teichmann, the former Springbok captain who led the Welsh club with equal distinction.

In France it was yet again Toulouse who won the coveted championship for a record 16th time beating Montferrand 34-22 in front of a capacity crowd. Benetton Treviso achieved their fourth Italian championship title in five years, defeating Amatori Calvisano 33-13 in the final play-off.

Australia dominated south of the equator. At international level the Wallabies reign as World Cup, Tri Nations and Tom Richards trophy holders, while it was the ACT Brumbies who took the Super 12 honours beating the Sharks 36-6. South Africa, who finished bottom of the pile in the Tri Nations for the second season running, had two teams in the last four in the Super 12s. For the first time in the competition's brief history, no New Zealand side made it through to the semi-finals.

The appointment of John Mitchell to succeed Wayne Smith illustrates that New Zealand rugby is sending out a public signal that it wants to see a return to the classic virtues of All Black rugby. Whether they are still there for Mitchell to exploit is another matter. However, the former Waikato captain and later coach, who spent almost three years alongside Clive Woodward as England forwards coach, has shown that he knows how to lick a side into shape.

As if it couldn't get much worse, there was a rare defeat for the all-conquering New Zealand women's team, beaten 22-17 by England – their first defeat in 24 matches. At least All Black supporters had the consolation of seeing their team, spearheaded by Jonah Lomu, win the Rugby World Cup Sevens crown in Mar del Plata in Argentina and later retain their IRB World Sevens Series title.

In the second tier of international competition it was heartening to see the resurgence of the Fijians. They won a thriving Pacific Rim tournament that reached its climax in a knock-out competition in Japan and were inaugural winners of the Rugby Sevens event staged at the Akita World Games, also in Japan, in August. The IRB nurses ambitions for Rugby Union to be an Olympic Sport again, as it last was in 1924. The sport's successful debut at the World Games will have given huge impetus to Olympic hopes.

Elsewhere at international level, Georgia relieved Romania of the European Nations Cup in an IRB tournament that underpins the Six Nations Championship and is accompanied by competitions for the European Plate and Bowl titles. In Asia, Japan finished top in a similar series of IRB Tri Nations tournaments, while Morocco and South Africa under-23 were about to play out the final of the second African Nations tournament as this Yearbook went to press.

As the sport gears up towards the next World Cup, it's heartening to reflect that it seems to have come to terms with professionalism. There are still concerns, though, with the second tier of international rugby.

The Canadian players, for instance, have gone on strike over a dispute concerning the sacking of coach Dave Clark. The real cause of the bust-up is the relationship between players and union, the level of empowerment that passes from one to the other. Then consider the case of Argentina. Quarter finalists at the last Rugby World Cup tournament, they still have no meaningful annual international competition to act as a focus for their team's development.

While the IRB clearly does a splendid job in nurturing the far-flung grass-roots, it needs to keep a wary eye on this level. The game is neither big enough nor robust enough for the likes of Argentina, Canada or the Pacific Islands to fall off the pace set by the leading countries.

That is the challenge for the game's administrators. They were in form, eventually, in England. Let's hope that they continue to govern wisely and sympathetically. As the Lions fans showed in Australia, there are good times to be had.

Enough said.

FIVE OF THE BEST

Mick Cleary

George Gregan (Australia)

The tackle still lives in the mind, George Gregan's calling card on the world stage as he somehow managed to smash Jeff Wilson away from the Wallaby try-line as the All Black wing arrowed in for what seemed to be a certain score.

Gregan has done so much more since, now an established part of the Wallaby act, their new captain as they look to extend their successful run in the wake of the retirement of John Eales. Gregan has all the attributes to succeed: a proven, polished performer, a resilient presence, an articulate, prominent public figure and a damn fine scrum-half.

He is Australia's most capped scrum-half with 68 caps and has scored 11 tries in Test matches. His game has adapted to the modern era with his sharp eye for the way play unfolds. His quick-fire flick passes, or behind-the-back feints and feeds, keep his men on the move and the defence on the back foot. His partnership with Stephen Larkham is based on an innate understanding of how each of them operate. It has been cultivated down the years for province and for country, the pair of them challenging the gain line at all times.

Gregan has had a clean sweep of honours this year – Super 12, Tom Richards trophy and Tri Nations. He has been the backbone of the Wallaby surge to honours in the past two years, as influential in his day as former Wallaby captain Nick Farr-Jones was in his day. The decision to pass on the captain's armband to Gregan must have been one of the easiest selection matters ever discussed. Gregan has been groomed alongside Eales, fully immersed in the culture of professionalism and thorough preparation that is the hallmark of Wallaby rugby.

Gregan, 28, has been vice-captain since 1997. He knows how it works for the Wallabies, inside and outside the camp.

'The captain has to be a player who is considered a virtual automatic selection and George is certainly that,' said Australian Rugby Union chief executive, John O'Neill, when announcing the appointment. 'He has shown tremendous leadership in guiding the Brumbies to their breakthrough Super 12 triumph and his unwavering support for John Eales was crucial during probably the toughest domestic season that Australia has ever had.'

And for Gregan himself ? He's already a master of media-speak, versed in the art of the diplomatic nicety. Just like Eales before him, you can expect

George Gregan gees-up his forwards during the first Test of the Australia-Lions series in Brisbane in June. Gregan recently succeeded John Eales as captain of the Wallabies.

the man to play a good game but just don't expect him to reveal any insider information or shattering truths when talking about it. Articulate, yes; controversial, no.

'Being Wallaby captain is truly a great honour. It's a job that comes with enormous responsibility but, like the smooth transition of coaches this year, I believe that the team can also carry on without much disruption.'

Gregan himself looks set too to carry on through to the 2003 World Cup and beyond, the only disruption being to opposition back-row defences.

Brian O'Driscoll (Ireland)

The bewitching hat-trick, the solo break from half-way, the blind-side dart to score or tee up tries for others – there are already enough images in the mind's eye to persuade even the sceptic that Brian O'Driscoll has genius in the soles of his shoes. What is more he doesn't look to be too deficient in the head department either. Hype has swirled around his chunky shoulders since he first pulled on the emerald shirt of Ireland against Australia in 1999. It has pursued him relentlessly since, most recently back down to Australia with the British and Irish Lions. This would be the big test for him. This would be the time when we found out whether the big fish in the small pond could cope with choppier waters and vicious predators. He could and he did.

Little seemed to faze him. He delivered on all fronts. His stunning try in the opening seconds of the second half of the first Test in Brisbane left experienced Wallabies such as Matt Burke flat on their backside and sent the thousands of red-shirted Lions fans at the Gabba into raptures.

O'Driscoll has that precious ability to make opposition defences think twice about what he is going to do. He has such natural short-burst speed and strength, that he needs little space in which to operate. He has an eye for the gap too, a pretty useful asset given that so many midfields these days might as well be inhabited with those carrying white sticks. Balance ? He's got that. Nerve ? He's got that too.

Does he lack anything, then ? There are some that question his ability to find others around him, pointing out that he has a tendency to close down the movement if his own audacious break does not come off. Well, given that the breaks so often do turn into something of substance, it's little reason for him to concern himself too much with calls for him to be less selfless.

If his technical passing skills do need more work, then there is little to suggest that O'Driscoll will not be putting in those extra hours on the training field. He knows only too well that he is now a marked man, that the element of surprise in his repertoire has long gone. He is also aware, though, that if defences focus on him, then there will be opportunities for others.

O'Driscoll, 22, was schooled at that famous old rugby academy in Dublin, Blackrock College. He was a keen footballer too, a midfield player, and a more than useful golfer playing off a nine handicap. He played rugby for Ireland at under 19 level helping them to take the title at the Junior

Brian O'Driscoll exploits a gap in the French defence during the Six Nations match with France at Lansdowne Road in February.

World Cup in 1998. He made his full debut that same year, really coming to prominence when he cut the French to shreds a few months later, scoring a hat-trick to help Ireland to their first win in Paris since 1972.

O'Driscoll became a hot property. He had a host of commercial deals put his way as well as offers from clubs all around Europe. He has stayed loyal to Leinster and the Irish Rugby Football Union. He could name his price if he chose to move. The only moving he's doing at present is past opposition defences. There's much more to come yet.

George Smith (Australia)

Rives was blond, Slattery was curly, Back was small, Michael Jones was just, er Michael Jones while George Smith is the dreadlocked one, the Wallaby wonder who played a key role in winning the Tom Richards trophy for Australia last summer against the Lions. It helps to be distinctive when you're an open-side flanker, though appearances are but a minute part of the whole. If there is no substance there, then you'll soon be found out.

There were times during that astonishing first Test at the Gabba when we wondered if Smith's reputation had been overstated. But then came the two remaining Tests – played for the most part without Richard Hill, another outstanding model of the trade, in opposition – and Smith came into his own as a scavenger and destroyer of quick ball. With his straight back and prodigious strength and balance at full extension, he is a priceless asset at the breakdown as he leans in to snaffle opposition ball.

Perhaps he does not yet show the creative flair of a Rives or even Back. But he'll get there. He was a 20-year-old when he made his debut against France in 2000 and now has ten caps to his name. He has been a crucial element in the Wallabies' continuing success. It was felt that the retirement of David Wilson was sure to leave a void in a key part of the field. Wilson had won 79 caps and had been the mainstay of the Wallaby pack. Along came Smith and all anxieties were eased.

He was the outstanding performer for his province, ACT Brumbies, in this year's Super 12 helping them to their first title. Time and again, his suffocating defence nullified the threat of opposition attack while his cleverly judged angles of running enabled him to be in the right place at the right time to maximise the work of half-backs George Gregan and Stephen Larkham.

Smith, 21 on the day of the triumphant third Test in Sydney, does not come from typical Australian stock. He did not go through the public school system. He is the son of a concrete-mixing builder and Tongan mother, one of seven brothers and two sisters who grew up in Sydney's northern suburbs around Manly, playing league as well as union.

His mentor in those early years was Ian MacDonald, a local coach who used to do the circuit in Brookvale to ferry George and his Tongan mates to their weekend rugby.

George Smith, the dreadlocked one. The Wallaby open-side fends off an All Black during Australia's 29-26 win in the Tri Nations decider in Sydney.

'The key thing about George is his timing,' says MacDonald. 'He knows how and when to tackle, regain his feet, rip the ball and move on.'

Smith was credited with no fewer than 12 turnovers in this year's Super 12 semi-final against Queensland. His radar is pinpoint when it comes to locating the action.

'The great open-side flankers of the past all had an ability to be where the ball is,' says the man who introduced Smith to Test rugby, former Wallaby coach, Rod Macqueen. 'I suspect that George Smith has got something that we haven't seen yet.'

Jonny Wilkinson (England)

He's a familiar sight if you happen to be strolling past any sports ground long after the morning bedlam has died away and the throng of players are soaking themselves in a hot tub. No matter the weather or the time, there will be the slightly round-shouldered figure of Jonny Wilkinson teeing up, taking aim, focusing, visualising and swinging that deadly boot. The end-result is invariably a ball sailing high through the distant posts.

As Gary Player once remarked of another sport: 'The more I practise, the luckier I get.'

It's an adage that Wilkinson has lived by throughout what is still a fledgling career. He is only 22 yet already a trail of shattered records lies in his wake. He made his international debut as a substitute against Ireland in 1998 when he became the youngest to play for England since Henri Laird, a fly-half, against Wales in 1927. He was brought to Newcastle as a teenager by Rob Andrew, the man whose points record he broke recently. After the game against Ireland, Wilkinson had 416 points beating his boss's mark of 396. Against Italy in the 2001 Six Nations he scored 35 points, a championship landmark as is his overall points haul for the season's elongated competition.

Wilkinson is far more than a points accumulator, invaluable as that role is. He has matured into a consummate fly-half, mastering the strategic as well as the individual game. As he has matured as a man, so too has he as a player, becoming more self-assured and dominant. It shows in his play. Gone is that diffidence of his early years, when others set the tone and took games by the scruff of the neck. Mind you, it could never be said that he was backward in coming forward in defence. His tackling has always been devastating. His big hit on Frenchman Emile Ntamack in Paris was a symbolic moment for England as they went on to record victory.

Fly-half is so often one of the channels targeted by opposition coaches who sense that they can exploit a potential weakness. In Wilkinson's case that route of attack is a dead-end. Over the last 12 months Wilkinson has brought all his skills to bear on the England midfield, striking up a flourishing relationship with Mike Catt alongside. England have shredded opposition defences as the pair mix up their game, from hand or foot.

A study in concentration. Jonny Wilkinson kicks another goal on his way to a record Six Nations haul of 35 points against Italy at Twickenham in February.

Wilkinson has never been the fastest thing on two legs. No matter. He has worked on ways of beating people by hand or by rolling out of the tackle. He has also worked on a foot-shuffling break that gains precious yards and allows his backs to run off him.

His Lions tour was not the most fruitful as he fell below his high standards of place-kicking success. However, his reputation is ensured. He is the fulcrum of England's attack and defence, a gutsy and gifted individual.

Keith Wood (Ireland)

He came from good rugby stock and there's every reason to hope that the genes of future Woods will be similarly well-endowed with humour, grace, intelligence and courage, if not a bit more hair. It's rare to travel the rugby world and not meet someone who has a carping word about some player or other. Their reputations may be good and strong nearer home, but once on the road you meet all manner of people ready, perhaps legitimately so, to give the myth a dent or two.

In the case of Keith Wood, we've yet to encounter the disbeliever. Wood, 29, may have his flaws – a wonky throwing action on occasions being the most notable – but no-one ever questions his worth in the game. He is an honest citizen away from the field and an engaging presence on it. He has been first-choice Lions hooker in successive tours, following in the footsteps of his late father, Gordon, who represented the Lions on the 1959 tour to Australia and New Zealand. He has led Ireland a record-equalling 24 times, although it's true to say that his spirited leadership has not delivered success in huge abundance. In fact they didn't win a game for his first 10 matches in charge. But he's rolled with the punches, a rallying point for any team under strain.

'You learn an awful lot for losing,' says Wood. 'In those early days in particular, the Ireland team was immature. We didn't have a lot of decision-makers out there. We've grown since then.'

Wood himself has grown in all senses since he first came to international notice when sitting on the Irish bench in 1992. His early career was bedevilled by injury, forcing him to miss large chunks of seasons up until 1996. 'Touch wood, I've not had a bad one since,' he says.

He has spent much of the last five years in England with Harlequins. It was perhaps a surprising choice for one reared and revered in that hot-bed of Irish rugby in Limerick. But Wood has always known his own mind and never been afraid to reveal it in public. He took a year's break from his 'Quins contract to return home to Munster. If he was hoping for a quiet year, he didn't get much of one as Munster embarked on the glorious Heineken Cup run that took them through to their final against Northampton.

Wood's appeal is enduring, a whole-hearted asset to any team in which he plays.

Keith Wood leading from the front against the Italians in the opening match of this year's Six Nations. Ireland won 41-22 and went to finish second in the Championship.

GORDON BROWN

Norman Mair

Broon from Troon . . . It was Chris Rea, a comrade-in-arms for club, country and the Lions, who put it best. To wit, that it was a measure of the extraordinary impact which Gordon Brown had made in both hemispheres that the little Ayrshire town came to connote, for so many of the sporting fraternity, not just golf and a famed Open championship links but rugby football and the particular brand of camaraderie that unique game had engendered for so long.

Brown was not just a great player but very much a product of the television age – a period when, for the first time in traditionally soccer-mad Scotland, rugby players became household names.

Add the arguably even greater exposure which, when his playing days were over, Broon from Troon enjoyed as a television pundit and much sought after postprandial orator and it was perhaps no surprise that his death in March at the age of 53 commanded even more newspaper column inches, and radio and TV time, than the similarly early passing of the former Rangers and Scotland football idol, Jim Baxter.

Before the kick-off in the Welsh match at Murrayfield, the SRU screened a brief but spectacular TV extract of Brown in action in South Africa in 1974 while, in the days after his death, teams all over Scotland, at the Union's behest, stood in silence in honour of his memory. His daughter Mardi's six-year-old son, Zac, proudly led out the team mascots on the day of the Scotland – Barbarians match, the SRU having already announced that the profits from the game would go to the memorial trust newly established in Gordon Brown's name. All of which was largely unprecedented in Scottish rugby.

On the day of Brown's funeral, the 'gate', as he would have put it, greatly tickled, was reckoned to be around 1400. Many among the cosmopolitan congregation had come from far afield and there were so many Lions present that it would have been possible to pick not just a Test XV but a seven-strong bench into the bargain.

Gordon's wife Linda, and his son, Rory, with laughter or a smile never far away, ensured that the occasion played havoc with the word funereal. They had requested that those attending eschew dark suits and black ties. Instead they were to favour bright colours, club ties and so forth.

'The genial giant' – as he was referred to in tribute after tribute though, at 6ft 5in and 16st 12lbs, he would have been dwarfed by some of today's international locks – had himself chosen the hymns and readings. In fact, he had issued such a stream of instructions to the Reverend Howard Haslett, an old friend and erstwhile rugby player, that Haslett had been moved to protest that maybe it would be simpler if he were to get into the box and leave Brown to conduct the service!

Brown had wanted to record one last speech to be played at the funeral service but he was thwarted by the speed with which the end came. Haslett, though, suggested that he should not be denied one last ovation, the rapturous applause raising the rafters of Troon's Old Parish Church. In the hands of many another man of the cloth, that digression might have turned out an embarrassing misjudgement, prompting little more than a spatter of self-conscious clapping. But Haslett had the gathering – which included the like of Ally McCoist and Kenny Dalglish – hanging on his every word.

Haslett told again the G L Brown signature story – how he had phoned his brother Peter to tell him that he, Gordon, was back in the Scotland side. 'Who's out,' asked Peter, delighted at the news. 'You are!' came the ultimate in fraternal sucker punches. The minister even produced a new Brown anecdote. To wit, how Gordon had remarked ruminatively on how both of them as small boys had dreamed of one day being British Lions. 'I got to be a Lion,' Brown had pointed out, teeing up the clergyman for the *coup de grâce*. 'You only got to be the bleeding Christian!'

Brown was a larger than life personality whose highly public battle against Non-Hodgkins lymphoma, and bone cancer in his thigh, had been followed with an affectionate anxiety by not just the rugby community but sundry folk who had never been to a game in their lives.

He had been born into sport with a goalkeeping father, Jock Brown, who had been capped by Scotland, making his international debut against Wales alongside Bill Shankly. When he was 16, Gordon himself kept goal for Troon Juniors and it was certainly true that there was about his lineout jumping echoes of the goalkeeper's art with the ball at times being cut out of the air rather as a goalkeeper cuts out a cross. Much the same applied to his brother, Peter, who captained Scotland with rare panache from No 8.

One of the great strengths of Gordon as a lineout jumper was that he could be cast, in the Lions' Test XV, as the primary jumper alongside the archetypal core forward that was Willie-John McBride or, in a Scotland context, as the broad-shouldered, hefty henchman needed to partner the spring-heeled but irrepressibly nomadic lock that was Alastair McHarg.

A question which is frequently asked is how Brown would have fared in the modern game with its emphasis on lineout lifting. His own preference might well have been for a straight contest between rival jumpers but he was such an adaptable, ball-playing lineout lock that he would surely have taken due advantage of this latter-day alteration in technique. As a scrummager, Brown was described by Ian McLauchlan – an outstanding technician on the loose-head and the man behind whom Brown packed for Scotland and the Lions – as 'quite simply, the best left-side lock in the business.'

Though he was a member of a West of Scotland side which won the unofficial Scottish club championship, Brown, as a club player, was not infrequently somewhat lack-lustre against the lesser opposition. Nonetheless,

The late, lamented Gordon Brown takes a breather during the 1974 Lions tour of South Africa.

Quintin Dunlop, West's international hooker, had a high opinion of him. 'It must often have been damned uncomfortable for Big Broonie,' reflected Dunlop, 'but, for all his height and bulk, he would always get as low as I wanted and, in order to help me strike against the head – as hookers did in those days – get his right shoulder hard into my left buttock. "Come on Quintin," he would urge, "we want that little egg." '

Though Brown was the extrovert's extrovert, Dunlop was at pains to point out that in the most secretive recesses of the set scrum, Brown would strain every nerve and sinew, at least in the more important matches. 'He may have loved the limelight,' said Dunlop, 'but I never felt he was playing for himself.'

When fully fit as he was on a Lions' tour – all told he played in eight Tests – Brown was eagerly mobile with adhesive hands befitting his genes and the ability to give a pass as well as take one. He totalled eight tries on the Lions' unbeaten tour of South Africa in 1974 and yet for Scotland, admittedly in rather less exalted company, he managed not one.

Though Brown much enjoyed his early tag of The Baby-faced Assassin, the hard man in the Scotland pack, by common consent, was McLauchlan. But Brown, in the time-honoured euphemism, could look after himself all right. One never thought of him as a dirty player but circumstances cruelly conspired to ensure that, after the lengthy suspension he received for his retaliatory action in the 1976 Glasgow v North & Midlands match at Murrayfield, he was never to play for Scotland again.

The Lions' selectors, however, having watched him in an offbeat floodlit game at Hughenden, picked him for the 1977 tour of New Zealand – Brown, amid much publicity, even enlisting at Ibrox in his bid to be appropriately restored in wind and limb.

By his own admission, he was, in his native land, never the most assiduous or enthusiastic of trainers. Nevertheless, one has only to look at the record book to appreciate the validity of Jim Telfer's assertion that Brown, in conjunction with McLauchlan, was the man around whom the more successful Scotland packs of the Seventies were built. In a sentence, Scotland won 14 of the 30 internationals in which he featured but only two of their next 19 matches.

Aside from his major role in the victorious Lions' tours of 1971 and 1974, he was on the winning side in six of his eight encounters with England. The most fondly remembered, of course, was the laying of the Twickenham bogey in 1971. Years later, that team had a reunion in Edinburgh on the night of the England match, the sole absentee being McHarg who was in India on business. 'I always knew,' said John Mackay, of the Post Office, the organisers of the dinner, 'that lock forwards were apt to be none too cerebral but Alastair McHarg has to be the first one to travel to India for the Calcutta Cup!'

Brown loved that crack and vowed to add it to his own fund of rugby anecdotes though, actually, it tended to be the old favourites in his repertoire, stories they had heard many times before, which really had his audiences roaring with laughter. So well did he tell 'em . . .

Having found himself in great demand, Brown, an insatiable raconteur, had retired from his career in a building society to become a full-time professional speaker. Many of his engagements were decidedly lucrative while, to my knowledge, he once contrived to 'do' six pre-match luncheons on the day of an international. But he would speak for nothing if the cause was right as witness his response to the ladies' playing section of a rugby club.

At first he declined but eventually he relented, promising that if they could raise a hundred pounds for a charity of his choice, he would make the main speech at their annual dinner. Like many of Broon from Troon's own stories, it may well have grown in the telling but, allegedly, one of the girls promptly grabbed a collection bucket while another stripped to the buff and sped down the crowded touchline awaiting the men's match. Legend has it that they had the hundred quid long before the runner had – metaphorically – breasted the tape.

In his last days, Brown flew South in a friend's private jet, determined, weak though he was, to attend the dinner being staged in London's Grosvenor Hotel in his honour. He had to be helped to his seat but just as he had met every twist and turn in his life with a jest so this bravest of troupers faced the final whistle. 'The last supper,' he murmured, not blasphemously but because, even at the last, the wag in him could not resist a good one-liner.

JOHN EALES

Peter Jenkins

As John Eales prepares for life after rugby, he explains that the transition will not be difficult. There are, after all, more important things than sport.

The image remains engraved on his mind and will still be with him in vivid clarity long after memories of his sporting exploits have clouded over with age: John Eales and immediate family, standing by the bedside of his ailing sister Carmel, as she lost her year-long battle with cancer. It was more than a decade ago. Carmel was just 20, and 16 months older than her gangly brother, the future captain of the world champion Wallabies.

But what stays with Eales – and in some subtle way has helped shape his outlook on life – is the snapshot of a single teardrop escaping from his sister's left eye and rolling down her cheek as she silently slipped away. As Eales – whose great career has reached its dusk – explains it, he found the scene both shattering and consoling. From a deeply religious family – his grandmother used to bless him before games and encourage him to pray to St Anthony for protection – the two metre tall second-rower, one of six children and now father to toddler Elijah, is proud yet protective of his staunch Catholic faith.

'We were all there as she was dying,' he recalled softly. 'And the tear . . . it was her saying goodbye. It was one of those special moments. You knew she was going to a good place but it was also so sad she was leaving. I have a very strong belief that our time here on earth is just a prelude to what comes after. Being a Catholic, having the upbringing I did with my mum and dad, it helps explain a lot of things. It helps explain why people die young, and why good people suffer bad circumstances. That's why things like Carmel's death make you sit up and take stock of your life. It says how lucky you are that you're still around and that you have the love of your family. I do believe in life after death, only I don't know what form it takes. But I am loath to speak openly about religion because people immediately think when you do, that you somehow think you're perfect. I know I'm not.'

'Nobody' they tagged him. As in nobody's perfect. A throwaway line from a team-mate on a rugby tour a few years back. The media embraced it and suddenly Eales was wearing a label he abhors.

A multi-skilled player of rare talent, he has been acknowledged as the greatest forward Australia has produced. Eales was just out of his teens when he won the 1990 Rothmans Medal for the best and fairest player in the Brisbane club competition. It was his first season of senior rugby. And when Queensland coach John Connolly sent the rookie into a match against Canterbury in Christchurch just three months into that debut winter, he wondered whether he was sacrificing a child in the homeland of All Black

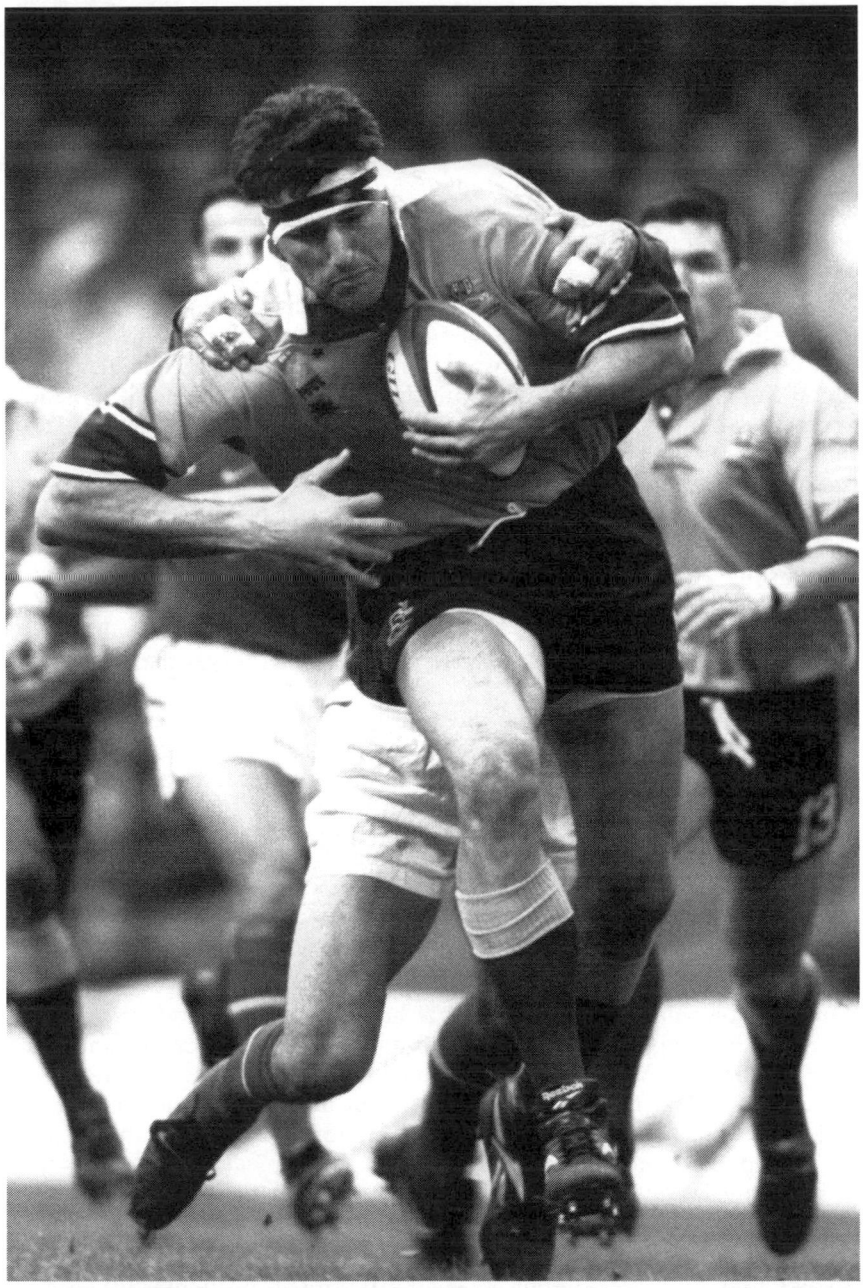

One of the many fine hours enjoyed by John Eales as captain of the Wallabies. Here he is seen escaping a tackle during the 1999 Rugby World Cup final against France.

hard heads. But in the first lineout, Eales soared and stole the ball from New Zealand Test second rower Albert Anderson. 'I'll never forget it,' says Connolly. 'It was as if he had played 20 Tests and 50 games for Queensland. He was that composed.'

The following season, Eales was playing in a club match for Brothers against Teachers-Norths. He fielded an opposition kick on halfway, standing near the sideline. He steadied himself and calmly launched a drop kick between the posts. Eales could not understand the fuss that followed. 'Nobody would have said anything if I'd scored a try and that's worth more points,' was his logic.

The humility that still stamps his character today was evident even then. But the Eales legend was already taking shape. Later that year he made his Test debut against Wales and was a dominant figure in Australia's first World Cup triumph. The finest All Black forward of all time, Colin Meads, tipped the young Aussie to dominate the game world-wide for the next 10 years. He was, in the end, pinpoint accurate with Eales recently bringing down the curtain on his career.

He had 86 Tests to his credit after the recent Tri Nations series and had captained Australia on a record 55 occasions. He led the Wallabies to the 1999 World Cup title in Europe, to three successive Bledisloe Cup series wins – a strike from his own right boot landed the penalty that won the trophy in 2000 – and through victorious Tri Nations campaigns in 2000 and 2001. 'I have never felt, and never will, that any one person is bigger than the team,' he said.

But there were two occasions when the Wallabies were forced to consider a future minus Eales when he suffered career-threatening shoulder injuries at the end of the 1992 season while on tour in Wales, and again in 1999, when his World Cup participation was left in doubt. 'I remember thinking "if this is it, then it's been fantastic," ' Eales says. 'I've enjoyed the game so much but there comes a time when you have to move on, and you can't dwell on things. I like to look on the bright side because there are so many uncertainties in life. But playing the game still means as much to me now as it ever did.'

There are, however, other priorities. Fatherhood has changed him. Eales found leaving wife Lara and their son at home while he took on the persona of a travelling rugby troubador to be a wrench. Training camps and tours have taken him away for months each year. 'Still, once you retire it's something you can't go back to,' he says. 'But there will be more challenges and more goals to set in life. I'd like to study for an MBA, do a bit of work in the media, go into the business world.'

But politics is out. 'The thing that turns me off is that the whole focus of politics is so negative,' he says. 'A guy might be doing a good job, being productive, but for want of a better word, he'll be sledged by other parties because they want to be in power. There's too much wasted energy.'

He does, however, hold statesman-like status within the Wallabies. Coach Rod Macqueen was asked for one word to describe how the Australian team view their skipper. 'Respect,' he replied. 'Mentally, he's very strong. I saw him get frustrated in the World Cup final when the French were eye gouging, but he handled the situation so calmly (he told the referee he would take his team off the field if the foul play did not stop). In the quarter final against Wales, to see who went on to the semi finals in London, there was a lot of dirt in that game too. At one stage one of their forwards had our prop Andrew Blades in a headlock and said: "Where do you think you're going boyo?" John leaned over to him and simply said: "To Twickenham my friend, to Twickenham". But I see the true demeanour of John when we have meetings before every Test. He's always excited about playing rather than being nervous or just wanting it to be over, which can be a common feeling for an elite athlete.'

It is another pointer to the Eales psyche. Sport has become an occupation for him and has helped bring, in the professional era, a more than comfortable lifestyle. But, to Eales, it is not life or death. 'People look at us as Test footballers, they see you lifting the World Cup over your head, they see you holding aloft the Bledisloe Cup, and wonder what it must be like,' he says. 'It is a great feeling but, for me, the greatest joy you can have in your life is to be at the birth of your own child.'

Family is the axis on which Eales's life turns. When he went on an end of season pub crawl with team-mates several years back, he took a lunch box with him, packed by his mother. When he realised at one hotel he had left the lunch box at another, he ran back to retrieve it to save her feelings. His grandmother, too, was a central figure before her death in 2000, a week before her 97th birthday. Nonna had an altar in the Eales family home dominated by a statue of St Anthony. Before he left for a game or a tour, Eales would stand with her, place his hand on the head of St Anthony and say a prayer. Even now, with Nonna gone, the ritual continues. 'My grandmother never watched a game, she was too nervous,' laughs Eales. 'I'll bet she's been watching from heaven though.'

His final remark brings back memories of the 1999 World Cup final when, in the aftermath to the win over France, Eales told me in the cavernous corridor under the Millennium Stadium in Cardiff: 'I saw my dad and my wife down near the fence. My mother, three sisters and my brother were in the crowd as well. And my sister, who passed away, she'll be here somewhere too.'

EASTERN EUROPE ON THE MARCH

Chris Thau

One of the beneficial effects of the collapse of the Soviet Union has been the birth of a host of rugby nations, of which Georgia, Russia, Ukraine, Latvia, Moldova, Kazakhstan, Lithuania and Uzbekistan, are – in this order – the most active and indeed successful. By 1988, as Gorbachev's Perestroika was losing steam, the Georgians had sensed, earlier than any Soviet nation, that the days when they could play as free men representing their free country, were not too far off.

The then Secretary of the Georgian Union, David Kilasonia, approached the IRB seeking membership for his yet-to-become-independent Union. A year later he managed, through an international network of like-minded friends, the seemingly impossible task of bringing Zimbabwe to Tbilisi for what historically is the first ever Test match of the newly born rugby nation. The resourceful and hospitable Georgians secured the invitation for the return visit to Harare in 1990, but the plans for expansion had to be postponed owing to the complex and confusing political climate of post-Soviet Georgia. In 1992, two years after the Zimbabwe tour, Georgia's yearly fixture list was still limited to a couple of encounters against Ukraine, another by-product of the break-up of the old Soviet Empire. However a year later Georgia was able to join the IRB, having meanwhile become an independent republic.

The 1993 qualifying Tournament for the 1995 Rugby World Cup held in the Northern Polish city of Sopot, where Georgia lost to both Russia and Poland, is regarded as a watershed in the recent history of Georgian rugby. Nearly three years of isolation and civil war led to a temporary decline in playing standards, reflected in the performance of the team in the Sopot qualifier. Georgia's clash with Russia in 1993, an encounter which, during the subsequent decade acquired similar significance to the Wales v England rivalry, was a hard yet cleanly fought affair, with the two sides tackling each other to a standstill. Only two years earlier some of the veterans on the Georgian side Alexander Hvedelidze, Nugzar Dzagnidze, Zaza Bakuradze and Tomas Quade were still playing together with some of their Russian opponents Igor Kuperman, Vladislav Voropaiev, Yuri Nikolaev, Igor Frantzusov, Vladimir Negodin and Nicolai Kiseliov, under the flag of convenience of the Soviet Commonwealth CIS.

The Georgians, though disappointed, were not disheartened and having understood the meritocratic nature of the Rugby World Cup competition went back to the drawing board. They changed the coaching set up and decided to target the next World Cup cycle to make an impact. Under a new President, Bidzina Geghidze, working in tandem with his French-based Vice-President Zaza Kasashvili, the Georgian Union adopted a new policy designed to maximise the limited resources of Georgian rugby, while fast-tracking Georgia among the continental elite.

One of the earliest decisions of the new administration was to employ former Béziers flank-forward Claude Saurel and his team of French advisors to prepare the National Teams and help Georgian coaches update and improve their know-how. In parallel, the most promising Georgian players were sent to the West, mainly to France, to help them develop their talent within a demanding rugby environment. The gradual approach of Kasashvili – a businessman in Montpellier in the South West of France – who advised the players to go for part-time contracts with clubs in the second and third division, to enable them to learn the 'trade', establish their credentials and identify their 'market value' has certainly paid off. In addition Kasashvili strongly supported Saurel's argument – against some strong opposition from the more traditionalist Georgian coaches – that the formation of a sevens squad to play in the newly formed IRB Sevens Grand Prix would significantly contribute to the development of Georgian rugby. The players, either in their new French clubs or in the intensely competitive IRB Sevens circuit, absorbed the rugby culture like sponges and made vast progress in very short time. That enabled the more talented of the 40-odd Georgians playing in the lower divisions of the highly competitive French Championship to move up the ranks and land some lucrative professional contracts in France.

The evolution of Levan Tsabadze, the current skipper of the Georgian National Team, and a member of the front-row fraternity at Bègles-Bordeaux is edifying. Tsabadze, a former Olympic wrestler in his native Georgia, was playing for a third division club in France, when, at Kasashvili's suggestion, Pierre Berbizier brought him to Narbonne on a short-term contract. Within a couple of seasons, the athletic and highly mobile giant had established himself as one of the top prop forwards in the French Premiership and was offered a contract with Bègles.

The progress of the Georgians could be chartered in their results against the, until recently, leader of the East European pack, Romania. After the narrow defeat at the hands of the Oaks in Dublin in the qualifying rounds of the 1999 Rugby World Cup, when Georgia showed their considerable potential, Tsabadze led Georgia to an unexpected and immensely satisfying win against the Romanians in Bucharest to acquire the coveted European Nations Cup last season. Georgia's seemingly miraculous progress from the dungeons of European rugby to winners of the European Nations Cup in 2001 is a by-product of the twin-track programme of Kasashvili and Geghidze. The aim of the duo is now to strengthen the domestic structure in Georgia to sustain the ever-expanding international programme.

However, unlike Georgia, Russia – somehow reflecting the political ambiguity that followed the disintegration of the Soviet Union – failed to grasp the opportunities offered by the 'rugby revolution'. The break up of the country into several independent republics, the economic crisis and the end of the state subsidies led to a reduction in the number of clubs from about 100 during the 1980s to 16 in 1993. The number has been further reduced during the subsequent years, when the domestic scene stabilised to about 12 clubs and about 1200 players – of all ages – equally divided between Siberia, the new centre of power of Russian rugby, and the Moscow region.

Significantly, although the postal address of the Russian Federation is nominally in Moscow, the *de facto* centre of Russian Rugby is nowadays Krasnoyarsk, residence of the President of the Russian Federation, Yuri Nikolaev, and of Russia's champion club Krasny-Yar. The man who masterminded this transfer is an unassuming 50 year-old Siberian by the name of Vladimir Grachev, who recently stepped down as coach of the national team. Moscow has remained the centre of the self-styled Russian Federation for seven-a-side rugby, but there is no doubt that the reins of power are in the hands of the Siberian establishment, who underwrite the costs of Russia's international programme in its entirety and fund the budding professional structure.

During the last decade – initially at the instigation of Naas Botha, who had a number of business contacts in Russia – the Russians developed strong ties with Northern Transvaal. In 1993, after their success against Georgia and Poland in Sopot, the Russians toured Southern Africa to prepare for the 1995 Rugby World Cup qualifying tournament in Romania. During their stay in Namibia and South Africa in particular, they benefited from an injection of South African technical expertise and arrived in Bucharest full of confidence. Alas, their dreams of glory were short-lived as the Romanians, still a force to be reckoned with, inflicted the heaviest defeat in the short history of international exchanges between the two countries. The Russians failed again in their bid for the finals of the 1999 World Cup, this time at the hands of Georgia, who derailed the Russian armoured train amid scenes of wild enthusiasm in Tbilisi.

The defeats at the hands of Georgia convinced Nikolaev, a former international fly-half, to emulate the example of their opponents by combining an import of foreign expertise with a forced policy of talent export, to improve both the standard of the domestic game and of the national team. They used sevens as a testing ground and Jim Stonehouse, the affable and extremely capable Blue Bulls Academy coach, took the Russians to the final of the Plate at the 2001 Rugby World Cup Sevens. They not only won it, finishing ninth in the world hierarchy after virtually no prior preparation, but also had the satisfaction of defeating their Georgian tormentors in the final.

In March 2001, the Russians appointed former Western Transvaal and Cats coach James Stoffberg as national director of coaching with special responsibility for the national side, and started sending players to France. The first to go, at the beginning of the year, was the then captain of the national team, the abrasive Krasny-Yar wing-forward Viacheslav Grachev, who joined Montauban, and others will follow soon. Stoffberg's first assignment was against Romania in the European Nations Cup. Although defeated, the Russians put up a brave fight and showed, in patches, that Stoffberg's expertise coupled with their natural athleticism could produce the goods. Evidence is emerging that Russia has managed to arrest the decline and is on its way to reclaiming a respectable position in the continental hierarchy.

RUGBY WORLD CUP 2003

The Story So Far

Brendan Gallagher

Like painting the Severn Bridge, qualification for the World Cup never seems to stop and the process for 2003 has been well underway since 23 September, 2000, when Luxembourg defeated Norway 41-9 in Stavanger. In total, 82 nations from the Five Continents are chasing the 20 places available in Australia and New Zealand in 2003. In past tournaments only the winners, runners-up and third-placed side have been spared the task of qualifying, but the IRB have had a rethink this time around and the top eight from Wales in 1999 – Australia, France, South Africa, New Zealand, Argentina, England, Wales and Scotland – will have automatic passage to the final stages, thus easing their already congested playing schedules.

Qualification is most advanced in Europe where the three pools of Round One have all been completed. In Pool One Belgium, former FIRA Division One contenders, moved smoothly through to Round Two. Among Belgium's opponents were Malta, making their tournament debut, who searched far and wide for qualified players. The selectorial eye eventually fell on Ray Watts, 45, who was quietly minding his own business playing second team rugby for Welsh village side Nantyffyllon.

Watts, who qualified through his Maltese mother Doris, travelled to La Valetta for a trial where New Zealand born coach Len Ethell soon installed him at hooker, Watts making his international debut in the unlikely venue of Chisinau where Malta were demolished 58-8. Unfortunately for Watts he cracked three ribs in the first half and was forced off, but he has no regrets.

'It was a wonderful experience, but I had absolutely no idea of the interest my appearance would generate,' said Watts. 'Of course, I never thought I would participate in the World Cup and nobody can take that away from me now.' Having established the link with Malta, it soon became a family affair for Watts with his 20-year-old nephew Thomas, who plays for the Coventry Development team and Warwickshire U21, being called up at fly-half against Monaco.

From Pool Two, Switzerland squeezed through with an outstanding 90-9 win in Bulgaria, while there were two qualifiers for the second round from Pool Three. Sweden, coached by Guy Deanwoody of the Scottish Rugby Union, powered through in impressive fashion and those doughty fighters, Latvia, progressed as the best runners-up.

Belgium and Switzerland now join Ukraine, Croatia and the Czech Republic in pool A of round two while in pool B, Sweden and Latvia will grapple with Poland, Germany and Denmark. Only the winners of these pools will progress to Round Three.

Elsewhere, the Rugby World Cup qualifying process is well under way in the Pacific with the Western and Eastern zones of the 'small Islands' group going very much according to plan. In the Western zone, the Cook Islands, with their strong contingent of players with experience in New Zealand, were much too powerful when they played Tahiti in Rarotonga, cruising home 86-0.

The small island nation of Niue, making their debut in the tournament, recorded a memorable 41-6 win over Tahiti in Papeete and offered serious resistance in their home match – top marks to anybody who knows that it was played at the island's capital Paliati – before going down 28-8 to Cook Islands. In the Eastern zone Papua New Guinea – who could really challenge the established Pacific island sides if they could harness their Rugby League stars – overcame the challenge of Solomon Island and Vanuatu to join the Cook Islands, Fiji, Tonga and Samoa for the second round of qualifying from the Oceania group next July.

Rugby World Cup 2003 qualifying results (up to 28 July, 2001)

Europe

Round 1

Pool 1: Monaco 15, Moldova 17 (Menton); Belgium 24, Slovenia 10 (Brussels); Slovenia 19, Lithuania 19 (Ljubljana); Moldova 58, Malta 8 (Chisinau); Malta 0, Belgium 26 (Marsa); Monaco 8, Slovenia 13 (Monte Carlo); Malta 3, Monaco 9 (Marsa); Monaco 12, Belgium 18 (St Laurent du Var); Belgium 26, Moldova 10 (Brussels); Slovenia 30, Moldova 15 (Ljubljana); Malta 11, Lithuania 39 (Marsa); Belgium 29, Lithuania 20 (Laakdal); Slovenia 45, Malta 5 (Ljubljana); Lithuania 33, Monaco 10 (Vilnius); Moldova 20, Lithuania 16 (Chisinau).

Belgium qualify for round 2

Pool 2: Bosnia 13, Hungary 12 (Zenica); Switzerland 43, Bosnia 6 (Geneva); Andorra 12, Yugoslavia 9 (Andorra); Bulgaria 9, Switzerland 90 (Pernik); Hungary 27, Andorra 21 (Százhalombatta); Yugoslavia 46, Bulgaria 6 (Dimitrovgrad); Yugoslavia 25, Hungary 10 (Dimitrovgrad); Switzerland 38, Andorra 25 (Lausanne); Bulgaria 30, Bosnia 8 (Pernik); Switzerland 61, Hungary 23 (Basle); Bosnia 23, Yugoslavia 13 (Zenica); Andorra 59, Bulgaria 10 (Andorra); Hungary 46, Bulgaria 7 (Százhalombatta); Yugoslavia 13, Switzerland 10 (Gornji); Andorra 23, Bosnia 13 (Andorra).

Switzerland qualify for Round 2

Pool 3: Norway 9, Luxembourg 41 (Stavanger); Austria 10, Sweden 42 (Vienna); Latvia 24, Luxembourg 19 (Riga); Sweden 44, Norway 3 (Enköping); Latvia 38, Austria 12 (Riga); Luxembourg 3, Israel 62 (Cessange); Israel 3, Latvia 21 (Herzliyya); Israel 43, Norway 3 (Tel Aviv); Luxembourg 3, Sweden 116

(Cessange); Austria 77, Luxembourg 0 (Vienna); Sweden 35, Israel 20 (Växjö); Latvia 37, Norway 0 (Riga); Austria 21, Israel 6 (Vienna); Norway 7, Austria 51 (Horten); Sweden 17, Latvia 10 (Enköping).

Sweden and Latvia (best runners-up) qualify for Round 2.

Round 2 (October 2001-March 2002)

Pool A: Ukraine, Croatia, Czech Republic, Belgium, Switzerland.

Pool B: Poland, Germany, Denmark, Sweden, Latvia

Round 3 (5, 19 May & 2 June 2002)

Six teams in two pools of three

Bottom four teams from European Nations Cup Division A (positions to be determined by results in both seasons 2001 and 2002) plus two qualifying teams from Round B (winners of groups).

Pool winners qualify for Round Four

Round 4

Two pools of three.

Ireland and Italy automatically qualify for Round Four. They will be joined by the top two teams from the European Nations Cup (based on results in season 2001 and 2002) and the two pool winners from Round Three.

The first two teams from both pools to qualify automatically for RWC 2003.

Third placed sides contest a repechage for one place in RWC 2003 Finals.

Oceania ('Small Islands Group')

Round 1

Eastern Zone Pool A: Cook Islands 86, Tahiti 0 (Rarotonga); Tahiti 6, Niue Island 41 (Papeete); Niue Island 8 Cook Islands 28 (Paliati).

Cook Islands qualify for Round 2.

Western Zone Pool B: Papua New Guinea 32, Solomon Islands 10 (Port Moresby); Vanuatu 10, Papua New Guinea 32 (Port Vila); Solomon Islands 11, Vanuatu 3 (Honiara).

Papua New Guinea qualify for Round 2.

Round 2: (July 2002, format to be decided).

Teams that have qualified for the pool: Fiji, Manu Samoa, Tonga, Cook Islands; Papua New Guinea. First two teams to qualify automatically for RWC 2003, third place team goes into repechage.

Africa

Round 1 (July to September 2001)

Pool A: Cameroon, Uganda, Zambia

Pool B: Botswana, Madagascar, Swaziland

Round 2 (November 2001)
Kenya, winner of Pool A, winner of Pool B.

Round 3 (2002)
North: Cote d'Ivoire, Morocco, Tunisia
South: Namibia, Zimbabwe, winner round 2

Round 4
Winner North plays Winner South over two legs. Loser goes into repechage.

Americas

Round 1 (Autumn 2001)
Caribbean Championships: Bahamas, Barbados, Bermuda,Cayman Islands, Guyana, Jamaica, St Lucia, Trinidad & Tobago.
CONSUR Division Two: Brazil, Colombia, Peru, Venezuela.

Round 2 (December 2001)
Winners of Caribbean championship v winner of CONSUR Division Two Championship (home and away).

Round 3 (May/June 2002)
Winners of round three, Chile, Paraguay.

Round 4 (Oct/Nov 2002)
Winner Round 3, Canada, Uruguay, USA. Top two qualify for RWC 2003, third placed goes into repechage.

Asia

Round 1 (2002)
Pool A: Taiwan, Asia Plate 3rd, Asia Shield 3rd
Pool B: Asia Plate 1st, Asia Shield 2nd, Asia Bowl 3rd
Pool C: Asia Plate 2nd; Asia Shield 2nd, Asia Bowl 2nd.
Asia Plate/Shield/Bowl competition will include Arabian Gulf, China, Hong Kong, India, Kazakhstan, Malaysia, Singapore, Sri Lanka, Thailand.

Round 2
Winner A, Winner B, Winner C.

Round 3
Winner Round 2, Japan, Korea.

RUGBY WORLD CUP RECORDS

(Final stages only)

Overall Records

Most Overall Points in Final Stages

227	A G Hastings	Scotland	1987–95
195	M P Lynagh	Australia	1987–95
170	G J Fox	New Zealand	1987–91

Most Overall Tries in Final Stages

15	J T Lomu	New Zealand	1995–99
11	R Underwood	England	1987–95
10	D I Campese	Australia	1987–95

Leading Scorers

Most Points in One Competition

126	G J Fox	New Zealand	1987
112	T Lacroix	France	1995
104	A G Hastings	Scotland	1995
102	G Quesada	Argentina	1999
101	M Burke	Australia	1999

Most Tries in One Competition

8	J T Lomu	New Zealand	1999
7	M C G Ellis	New Zealand	1995
7	J T Lomu	New Zealand	1995

Most Conversions in One Competition

30	G J Fox	New Zealand	1987
20	S D Culhane	New Zealand	1995
20	M P Lynagh	Australia	1987

Most Penalty Goals in One Competition

31	G Quesada	Argentina	1999
26	T Lacroix	France	1995
21	G J Fox	New Zealand	1987
20	C R Andrew	England	1995

Most Dropped Goals in One Competition

6	J H de Beer	South Africa	1999
3	G P J Townsend	Scotland	1999
3	A P Mehrtens	New Zealand	1995
3	J T Stransky	South Africa	1995
3	C R Andrew	England	1995
3	J Davies	Wales	1987

Most Points in a Match

by a team

145	New Zealand v Japan	1995
101	New Zealand v Italy	1999
101	England v Tonga	1999
89	Scotland v Ivory Coast	1995
74	New Zealand v Fiji	1987
72	Canada v Namibia	1999

by a player

45	S D Culhane	New Zealand v Japan	1995
44	A G Hastings	Scotland v Ivory Coast	1995
36	T E Brown	New Zealand v Italy	1999
36	P J Grayson	England v Tonga	1999
34	J H de Beer	South Africa v England	1999
32	J P Wilkinson	England v Italy	1999

Most Tries in a Match

by a team

21	New Zealand v Japan	1995
14	New Zealand v Italy	1999
13	England v Tonga	1999
13	Scotland v Ivory Coast	1995
13	France v Zimbabwe	1987

by a player

6	M C G Ellis	New Zealand v Japan	1995
4	K G M Wood	Ireland v United States	1999
4	A G Hastings	Scotland v Ivory Coast	1995
4	C M Williams	South Africa v Western Samoa	1995
4	J T Lomu	New Zealand v England	1995
4	B F Robinson	Ireland v Zimbabwe	1991
4	I C Evans	Wales v Canada	1987
4	C I Green	New Zealand v Fiji	1987
4	J A Gallagher	New Zealand v Fiji	1987

Most Conversions in a Match
by a team

20	New Zealand v Japan	1995
12	England v Tonga	1999
11	New Zealand v Italy	1999
10	New Zealand v Fiji	1987
9	Canada v Namibia	1999
9	Scotland v Ivory Coast	1995
9	France v Zimbabwe	1987

by a player

20	S D Culhane	New Zealand v Japan	1995
12	P J Grayson	England v Tonga	1999
11	T E Brown	New Zealand v Italy	1999
10	G J Fox	New Zealand v Fiji	1987
9	G L Rees	Canada v Namibia	1999
9	A G Hastings	Scotland v Ivory Coast	1995
9	D Camberabero	France v Zimbabwe	1987

Most Penalty Goals in a Match
by a team

8	Australia v South Africa	1999
8	Argentina v Samoa	1999
8	Scotland v Tonga	1995
8	France v Ireland	1995

by a player

8	M Burke	Australia v South Africa	1999
8	G Quesada	Argentina v Samoa	1999
8	A G Hastings	Scotland v Tonga	1995
8	T Lacroix	France v Ireland	1995

Most Dropped Goals in a Match
by a team

5	South Africa v England	1999
3	Fiji v Romania	1991

by a player

5	J H de Beer	South Africa v England	1999
2	P C Montgomery	South Africa v New Zealand	1999
2	J T Stransky	South Africa v New Zealand	1995
2	C R Andrew	England v Argentina	1995
2	T Rabaka	Fiji v Romania	1991
2	L Arbizu	Argentina v Australia	1991
2	J Davies	Wales v Ireland	1987

Rugby World Cup Tournaments: 1987 to 1999

First Tournament: 1987 in Australia & New Zealand

Pool 1

Australia	19	England	6
USA	21	Japan	18
England	60	Japan	7
Australia	47	USA	12
England	34	USA	6
Australia	42	Japan	23

	P	W	D	L	F	A	Pts
Australia	3	3	0	0	108	41	6
England	3	2	0	1	100	32	4
USA	3	1	0	2	39	99	2
Japan	3	0	0	3	48	123	0

Pool 2

Canada	37	Tonga	4
Wales	13	Ireland	6
Wales	29	Tonga	16
Ireland	46	Canada	19
Wales	40	Canada	9
Ireland	32	Tonga	9

	P	W	D	L	F	A	Pts
Wales	3	3	0	0	82	31	6
Ireland	3	2	0	1	84	41	4
Canada	3	1	0	2	65	90	2
Tonga	3	0	0	3	29	98	0

Pool 3

New Zealand	70	Italy	6
Fiji	28	Argentina	9
New Zealand	74	Fiji	13
Argentina	25	Italy	16
Italy	18	Fiji	15
New Zealand	46	Argentina	15

	P	W	D	L	F	A	Pts
New Zealand	3	3	0	0	190	34	6
Fiji	3	1	0	2	56	101	2
Argentina	3	1	0	2	49	90	2
Italy	3	1	0	2	40	110	2

Pool 4

Romania	21	Zimbabwe	20
France	20	Scotland	20
France	55	Romania	12
Scotland	60	Zimbabwe	21
France	70	Zimbabwe	12
Scotland	55	Romania	28

	P	W	D	L	F	A	Pts
France	3	2	1	0	145	44	5
Scotland	3	2	1	0	135	69	5
Romania	3	1	0	2	61	130	2
Zimbabwe	3	0	0	3	53	151	0

Quarter-finals

New Zealand	30	Scotland	3
France	31	Fiji	16
Australia	33	Ireland	15
Wales	16	England	3

Semi-finals

France	30	Australia	24
New Zealand	49	Wales	6

Third Place match

Wales	22	Australia	21

First World Cup Final, Eden Park, Auckland, 20 June 1987

New Zealand 29 *Tries:* Jones, Kirk, Kirwan *Conversion:* Fox *Penalty Goals:* Fox (4) *Drop Goal:* Fox
France 9 *Try:* Berbizier *Conversion:* Camberabero *Penalty Goal:* Camberabero
Attendance: 48,350

Second Tournament: 1991 in Britain, Ireland & France

Pool 1

New Zealand	18	England	12
Italy	30	USA	9
New Zealand	46	USA	6
England	36	Italy	6
England	37	USA	9
New Zealand	31	Italy	21

	P	W	D	L	F	A	Pts
New Zealand	3	3	0	0	95	39	9
England	3	2	0	1	85	33	7
Italy	3	1	0	2	57	76	5
USA	3	0	0	3	24	113	3

Pool 2

Scotland	47	Japan	9
Ireland	55	Zimbabwe	11
Ireland	32	Japan	16
Scotland	51	Zimbabwe	12
Scotland	24	Ireland	15
Japan	52	Zimbabwe	8

	P	W	D	L	F	A	Pts
Scotland	3	3	0	0	122	36	9
Ireland	3	2	0	1	102	51	7
Japan	3	1	0	2	77	87	5
Zimbabwe	3	0	0	3	31	158	3

Pool 3

Australia	32	Argentina	19
Western Samoa	16	Wales	13
Australia	9	Western Samoa	3
Wales	16	Argentina	7
Australia	38	Wales	3
Western Samoa	35	Argentina	12

	P	W	D	L	F	A	Pts
Australia	3	3	0	0	79	25	9
Western Samoa	3	2	0	1	54	34	7
Wales	3	1	0	2	32	61	5
Argentina	3	0	0	3	38	83	3

Pool 4

France	30	Romania	3
Canada	13	Fiji	3
France	33	Fiji	9
Canada	19	Romania	11
Romania	17	Fiji	15
France	19	Canada	13

	P	W	D	L	F	A	Pts
France	3	3	0	0	82	25	9
Canada	3	2	0	1	45	33	7
Romania	3	1	0	2	31	64	5
Fiji	3	0	0	3	27	63	3

Quarter-finals

England	19	France	10
Scotland	28	Western Samoa	6
Australia	19	Ireland	18
New Zealand	29	Canada	13

Semi-finals

| England | 9 | Scotland | 6 |
| Australia | 16 | New Zealand | 6 |

Third Place match

| New Zealand | 13 | Scotland | 6 |

Second World Cup Final, Twickenham, 2 November 1991

Australia 12 *Try:* Daly *Conversion:* Lynagh *Penalty Goals:* Lynagh (2)
England 6 *Penalty Goals:* Webb (2)
Attendance: 60,000

Third Tournament: 1995 in South Africa

Pool A

South Africa	27		Australia			18
Canada	34		Romania			3
South Africa	21		Romania			8
Australia	27		Canada			11
Australia	42		Romania			3
South Africa	20		Canada			0

	P	W	D	L	F	A	Pts
South Africa	3	3	0	0	68	26	9
Australia	3	2	0	1	87	41	7
Canada	3	1	0	2	45	50	5
Romania	3	0	0	3	14	97	3

Pool B

Western Samoa	42	Italy		18
England	24	Argentina		18
Western Samoa	32	Argentina		26
England	27	Italy		20
Italy	31	Argentina		25
England	44	Western Samoa		22

	P	W	D	L	F	A	Pts
England	3	3	0	0	95	60	9
Western Samoa	3	2	0	1	96	88	7
Italy	3	1	0	2	69	94	5
Argentina	3	0	0	3	69	87	3

Pool C

Wales	57	Japan	10
New Zealand	43	Ireland	19
Ireland	50	Japan	28
New Zealand	34	Wales	9
New Zealand	145	Japan	17
Ireland	24	Wales	23

	P	W	D	L	F	A	Pts
New Zealand	3	3	0	0	222	45	9
Ireland	3	2	0	1	93	94	7
Wales	3	1	0	2	89	68	5
Japan	3	0	0	3	55	252	3

Pool D

Scotland	89	Ivory Coast	0
France	38	Tonga	10
France	54	Ivory Coast	18
Scotland	41	Tonga	5
Tonga	29	Ivory Coast	11
France	22	Scotland	19

	P	W	D	L	F	A	Pts
France	3	3	0	0	114	47	9
Scotland	3	2	0	1	149	27	7
Tonga	3	1	0	2	44	90	5
Ivory Coast	3	0	0	3	29	172	3

Quarter-finals

France	36	Ireland	12
South Africa	42	Western Samoa	14
England	25	Australia	22
New Zealand	48	Scotland	30

Semi-finals

South Africa	19	France	15
New Zealand	45	England	29

Third Place match

France	19	England	9

Third World Cup Final, Ellis Park, Johannesburg, 24 June 1995

South Africa 15 * *Penalty Goals:* Stransky (3) *Drop Goals:* Stransky (2)
New Zealand 12 *Penalty Goals:* Mehrtens (3) *Drop Goal:* Mehrtens
Attendance: 63,000
* *after extra time: 9-9 after normal time*

Fourth Tournament: 1999 in Britain, Ireland & France

Pool A

Spain	15	Uruguay	27
South Africa	46	Scotland	29
Scotland	43	Uruguay	12
South Africa	47	Spain	3
South Africa	39	Uruguay	3
Scotland	48	Spain	0

	P	W	D	L	F	A	Pts
South Africa	3	3	0	0	132	35	9
Scotland	3	2	0	1	120	58	7
Uruguay	3	1	0	2	42	97	5
Spain	3	0	0	3	18	122	3

Pool B

England	67	Italy	7
New Zealand	45	Tonga	9
England	16	New Zealand	30
Italy	25	Tonga	28
New Zealand	101	Italy	3
England	101	Tonga	10

	P	W	D	L	F	A	Pts
New Zealand	3	3	0	0	176	28	9
England	3	2	0	1	184	47	7
Tonga	3	1	0	2	47	171	5
Italy	3	0	0	3	35	196	3

Pool C

Fiji	67	Namibia	18
France	33	Canada	20
France	47	Namibia	13
Fiji	38	Canada	22
Canada	72	Namibia	11
France	28	Fiji	19

	P	W	D	L	F	A	Pts
France	3	3	0	0	108	52	9
Fiji	3	2	0	1	124	68	7
Canada	3	1	0	2	114	82	5
Namibia	3	0	0	3	42	186	3

Pool D

Wales	23	Argentina	18
Samoa	43	Japan	9
Wales	64	Japan	15
Argentina	32	Samoa	16
Wales	31	Samoa	38
Argentina	33	Japan	12

	P	W	D	L	F	A	Pts
Wales	3	2	0	1	118	71	7
Samoa	3	2	0	1	97	72	7
Argentina	3	2	0	1	83	51	7
Japan	3	0	0	3	36	140	3

Pool E

Ireland	53	United States	8
Australia	57	Romania	9
United States	25	Romania	27
Ireland	3	Australia	23
Australia	55	United States	19
Ireland	44	Romania	14

	P	W	D	L	F	A	Pts
Australia	3	3	0	0	135	31	9
Ireland	3	2	0	1	100	45	7
Romania	3	1	0	2	50	126	5
United States	3	0	0	3	52	135	3

Play-offs for quarter-final places

England	45	Fiji	24
Scotland	35	Samoa	20
Ireland	24	Argentina	28

Quarter-finals

Wales	9	Australia	24
South Africa	44	England	21
France	47	Argentina	26
Scotland	18	New Zealand	30

Semi-finals

| South Africa | 21 | Australia | 27 |
| New Zealand | 31 | France | 43 |

Third Place match

| South Africa | 22 | New Zealand | 18 |

Fourth World Cup Final, Millennium Stadium, Cardiff Arms Park, 6 November 1999

Australia 35 *Tries:* Tune, Finegan *Conversions:* Burke (2) *Penalty Goals:* Burke (7)
France 12 *Penalty Goals:* Lamaison (4)
Attendance: 72,500

THE 2001 SIX NATIONS

A Celtic Triple Crown

Terry Cooper

James Bond was once told by Auric Goldfinger: 'Once is happenstance, twice is coincidence – the third time is enemy action.' Now we all understand exactly what Ian Fleming's villain was on about after England's hat-trick of losses in Grand Slam shoot-outs. Matt Dawson twice and Lawrence Dallglio once have been the dejected England captains who stood on the verge of rugby fame only to have the unfancied outsiders send them home to think bitter thoughts of what might have been.

There will be massive self-doubts the next time England reach their last Six Nations match with four wins in the bank. The other home nations always talk about England being the enemy, and beating the white shirts – whatever their previous results – is the highlight of the season. Starting at Wembley in 1999, continuing at Murrayfield in 2000 and finishing – Clive Woodward sincerely hopes – at Lansdowne Road in 2001, England have collapsed in a heap at the final fence when all the hard work of winning a Grand Slam had been done. A Celtic Triple Crown. And let's not forget Murrayfield 1990. All those four flops were failures away from home. After being the losing captain in 1990, Will Carling knew what he was doing when he persuaded the Five Nations Fixtures Committee to allow him to complete the Grand Slams of 1991, 1992 and 1995 at dear old Twickenham.

England's squad pathetically hung around as losers on 20th October collecting the Six Nations trophy and their medals when they really wanted to hide away and let Ireland enjoy their moment of glory. There can be no argument that England were the superior side in the Championship, setting team records for points and tries, while there was an individual scoring record for Jonny Wilkinson. They played rugby that touched perfection in carving up Wales, Italy, Scotland and France.

But the Dublin failure meant that this Championship was not the hopeless, two-season, cobbled-together effort that it seemed might be the case in spring 2001 when foot-and-mouth forced Ireland to postpone their final three fixtures. When 12 matches were completed, it appeared that England were as good as crowned champions, and even more so when Ireland were pitiful in the first of their rearranged fixtures in Scotland. But, just think. If Ireland had managed a decent performance at Murrayfield they would now be champions.

In the end, England won the title on points-difference by the tradesman's entrance, losing – like the Lions – to a couple of penalties when a place in history beckoned. France were the major failures, struggling to put away

Scotland at home and losing to England, Wales and Ireland. Wales had their day of delight with 43 points in Paris. Italy found life tough at the top, enduring a whitewash, while Scotland scrambled five points from a draw and two wins at Murrayfield.

Six Nations 2001: Final Table

	P	W	D	L	F	A	Pts
England	5	4	0	1	229	80	8
Ireland	5	4	0	1	129	89	8
Scotland	5	2	1	2	92	116	5
Wales	5	2	1	2	125	166	5
France	5	2	0	3	115	138	4
Italy	5	0	0	5	106	207	0

Points: win 2; draw 1; defeat 0.

There were 796 points scored at an average of 53.1 a match. The Championship record (803 points at an average of 53.5 a match) was set in 2000. England set a new record for a season, scoring 229 points. Jonny Wilkinson was the leading individual points scorer (89 – a new Championship record) and Will Greenwood scored most tries (six – two short of the all time record).

3 February, Stadio Flaminio, Rome
Italy 22 (2G 1PG 1T)   Ireland 41 (2G 4PG 3T)

The 2001 Championship hinted that it might be unique with two rare events in the opener when Rob Henderson ran all over Rome for a hat-trick and Alessandro Troncon was sent off for flattening his fellow-scrum-half Peter Stringer with the game beyond rescue in the 76th minute. The talented Troncon seemed to have turned up in a bad mood, having spear-tackled Stringer before the sending-off offence against his opponent, who had indulged in fierce rucking that his assailant took exception to. However, Italy had handicapped themselves earlier by poor goal-kicking in the absence of injured expert Diego Dominguez, and having prop Andrea Muraro sin-binned just before half-time. While Muraro reflected on his offence Ireland amassed 17 points.

Ireland's mediocre record in recent Championships was highlighted by the fact that this was a first success in their opening fixture since 1988. After the routine exchange of penalties, Italy scored the first of their three tries when wing Corrado Pilat completed a crunching break by his full-back Cristian Stoica. Ireland shrugged off their deficit during a decisive mid-match spell, with Ronan O'Gara, in an authoritative display, continuing to land goals and Henderson galloping in for his rapid three-timer between the 39th and 58th minutes. Henderson sat back content, his afternoon's contribution having brought a lead of 31-15, while Shane Horgan and O'Gara worked through Italy's increasingly frail defence. Still, Italy cheered their supporters with tries in injury-time of each half from back-row forwards

Carlo Checchinato and Mauro Bergamasco. They might have counted for more if four promising kicks at goal had not flown wide.

Italy: C Stoica; C Pilat, L Martin, G Raineri, D Dallan; R Pez, A Troncon; A Lo Cicero, A Moscardi (*captain*), A Muraro, W Visser, C Checchinato, C Caione, D Dal Maso, M Bergamasco *Substitutions:* E Galon for Pilat (29 mins); G P de Carli for Dal Maso (temp 39 mins to 46 mins) and for Muraro (59 mins); W Pozzebon for Martin (60 mins); G Lanzi for Checchinato (71 mins); F Frati for Dal Maso (79 mins)

Scorers *Tries:* Pilat, Checchinato, Bergamasco *Conversions:* Pez (2) *Penalty Goal:* Pilat

Ireland: G T Dempsey; S P Horgan, M J Mullins, R A J Henderson, T G Howe; R J R O'Gara, P A Stringer; P M Clohessy, K G M Wood (*captain*), J J Hayes, M J Galwey, M E O'Kelly, A Quinlan, A G Foley, D P Wallace *Substitutions:* J W Davidson for Galwey (65 mins); A J Ward for Foley (65 mins); E Byrne for Hayes (68 mins); K M Maggs for Mullins (68 mins); D G Humphreys for Howe (71 mins); Hayes for Quinlan (74 mins); B T O'Meara for Stringer 78 mins); F J Sheahan for Wood (80 mins)

Scorers *Tries:* Henderson (3), Horgan, O'Gara *Conversions:* O'Gara (2) *Penalties:* O'Gara (4)

Referee J Kaplan (South Africa)

3 February, Millennium Stadium, Cardiff Arms Park
Wales 15 (1G 1PG 1T)   England 44 (4G 2PG 2T)

Anything a Wasp can do a Harlequin can match seemed Will Greenwood's attitude when England kicked-off at tea-time in Cardiff after Henderson's post-lunch activities in Rome. Greenwood would not have been informed of Henderson's triple, but he crisply ensured that his club – and country – emerged one-all in the try-hat-trick stakes. Like Henderson, he had the job done in a sharp burst between the 12th and 41st minutes, by which time the result was in the bank at 37-8.

England took about ten minutes to reconnoitre a new venue, and, significantly for the rest of the Championship, show what defence at this level is all about, before carving Wales to shreds and scoring six tries before "declaring" on the hour. England even coped smoothly with Dan Luger's serious neck injury after a mere seven minutes, caused when he tackled solid Scott Gibbs. Austin Healey bounced on and began an excellent personal Championship.

Greenwood collaborated intuitively with, successively, Jonny Wilkinson, Iain Balshaw and Healey in the build-up to his scores. Rob Howley made a marvellous solo break to give Wales false hope at 15-8 at the start of the second quarter. England's own scrum-half, Matt Dawson, took ten minutes to think about this insult before dotting down two tries before the interval that resulted from his supreme eye for the gap. Ben Cohen banged through a faltering defence and there was no relevance to Scott Quinnell's try. Neil Jenkins went past the 1,000 mark in internationals, but walked off dejected with a goal-kicking record of two from five. Wilkinson, the new maestro,

Rob Howley on his hypnotic 75-metre run for the try that galvanised Wales in Paris and set up their first back-to-back wins there since the 1950s.

managed five from seven. Despite England's slow start and their unproductive finish, Welsh coach Graham Henry rated their performance the best he had seen by a European side.

Wales: S M Jones; G Thomas, M Taylor, I S Gibbs, D R James; N R Jenkins, R Howley; D R Morris, R C McBryde, D Young (*captain*), I M Gough, C P Wyatt, C L Charvis, L S Quinnell, M E Williams *Substitutions:* A P Moore for Wyatt (45 mins); M A Jones for Thomas (54 mins); A G Bateman for Taylor (64 mins); S C John for Morris (64 mins); R H StJ B Moon for Howley (80 mins)

Scorers *Tries:* Howley, Quinnell *Conversion:* Jenkins *Penalty Goal:* Jenkins

England: I R Balshaw; B C Cohen, W J H Greenwood, M J Catt, D D Luger; J P Wilkinson, M J S Dawson; J Leonard, D E West, P J Vickery, M O Johnson (*captain*), D J Grewcock, R A Hill, L B N Dallaglio, N A Back *Substitutions:* A S Healey for Luger (7 mins); T J Woodman for Leonard (59 mins); M B Perry for Balshaw (59 mins); M E Corry for Dallaglio (69 mins); M J Tindall for Catt (69 mins)

Scorers *Tries:* Greenwood (3), Dawson (2), Cohen *Conversions:* Wilkinson (4) *Penalty Goals:* Wilkinson (2)

Referee J Dumé (France)

4 February, Stade de France, Paris
France 16 (1G 3PG)   Scotland 6 (2PG)

France's indifferent form since moving from the south-west to toe north of Paris continued, though they at least cobbled together a victory over a Scottish side that perversely refused their hosts' offer to make themselves at home. Obviously Scotland were undermined when the attacking skills of Gregor Townsend were eliminated by a knee injury as early as the fourth minute. But a restructured back division, with Duncan Hodge replacing Townsend, had plenty of opportunities to level, at the very least, from a 13-6 scoreline that was locked solid between Philippe Bernat-Salles's 42nd-minute try and Christophe Lamaison's clinching 80th-minute penalty. Scotland were deeply frustrated at failing to emulate their two 1990s wins in Paris and, of course, the hypercritical home supporters whistled derisively at their players' ineptitude.

Often a deadlocked first half will lead to a second-half thriller. Not this time. Kenny Logan and Lamaison kicked a couple of penalties each in the opening period. Andy Nicol escaped solo twice and searched fruitlessly for colleagues. Bernat-Salles's finishing potential was becoming a significant factor even before his score. A double tackle by Logan and James McLaren, plus the video referee, denied him a first-half try and Martin Leslie was binned for a high tackle on him. While one man light, Scotland conceded the important try. Franck Comba gave Bernat-Salles space and he beat defenders on the outside and inside. It was a gem and worth waiting for. Scotland absorbed the attacks from a briefly galvanised French team and dominated the final quarter – unfortunately lacking that necessary ingredient of a score by any means. Four glimpses of the French line were sighted, but never a close-up. Jon Petrie's dropped pass was the most bitter lapse.

France: X Garbajosa; P Bernat-Salles, R Dourthe, F Comba, D Bory; C Lamaison, F Galthié; S Marconnet, R Ibanez, P de Villiers, D Auradou, F Pelous (*captain*), C Moni, C Juillet, O Magne *Substitutions:* C Califano for Marconnet (50 mins); A Benazzi for Auradou (50 mins); S Betsen for Moni (50 mins); G Merceron for Dourthe (71 mins)

Scorers *Try:* Bernat-Salles *Conversion:* Lamaison *Penalty Goals:* Lamaison (3)

Scotland: C D Paterson; C A Murray, J G McLaren, J A Leslie, K M Logan; G P J Townsend, A D Nicol (*captain*); T J Smith, G C Bulloch, M J Stewart, S Murray, R Metcalfe, M D Leslie, J M Petrie, A C Pountney *Substitutions:* D W Hodge for Townsend (4 mins); S B Grimes for Metcalfe (22 mins); A J Bulloch for J Leslie (temp 27 mins to 33 mins) and for McLaren (68 mins); G R McIlwham for Stewart (53 mins); R R Russell for G Bulloch (66 mins); B W Redpath for Nicol (67 mins); J P R White for Petrie (74 mins)

Scorer *Penalty Goals:* Logan (2)

Referee S J Dickinson (Australia)

17 February, Lansdowne Road, Dublin
Ireland 22 (1G 5PG)   France 15 (1G 1PG 1T)

The Lansdowne Road loyalists could not help talking about taking the Championship after their first win over the French since 1983, a season when they also began with two successes. With an hour gone, Ireland had the contest satisfactorily under control at 22-3. Then France belatedly pulled themselves together with a couple of tries that resulted in a frantic final eight minutes, when Ireland needed to find a touch of steel. The Irish fans saw the full flowering of Brian O'Driscoll, who produced an all-round, world-class game. Malcolm O'Kelly was a line-out giant and a major figure in Ireland pinching six French throws.

Before O'Driscoll tilted the match decisively Ireland's way in the 48th minute, France had typically given the opposition too many penalties. Ronan O'Gara, during an authoritative display, cashed in four chances, while Ireland's discipline permitted Christophe Lamaison, a tepid figure in midfield, a mere single penalty. The only doubt surrounding O'Driscoll's master-class was the legality of his score. Rob Henderson and David Wallace made the initial dents, but O'Driscoll still had plenty of work to do. The defenders were favourites, but O'Driscoll's pace took him beyond the first and second waves of cover. Xavier Garbajosa at least got a tackle in, forcing O'Driscoll to twist and stretch for the corner. Video scrutiny followed and Brian Campsall took four long minutes before convincing himself that hand, ball and turf were briefly in conjunction.

The French revival began when Fabien Pelous was driven over from a penalty and ended when a scrum ball was moved swiftly enough to give Philippe Bernat-Salles just enough space.

Ireland: G T Dempsey; D A Hickie, B G O'Driscoll, R A J Henderson, T G Howe; R J R O'Gara, P A Stringer; P M Clohessy, K G M Wood (*captain*), J J Hayes, M J Galwey, M E O'Kelly, A Quinlan, A G Foley, D P Wallace *Substitutions:* E Byrne for Clohessy (72 mins); G W Longwell for Galwey (72 mins); A J Ward for Quinlan (72 mins); K M Maggs for Henderson (73 mins)

Scorers *Try:* O'Driscoll *Conversion:* O'Gara *Penalty Goals:* O'Gara (5)

France: X Garbajosa; P Bernat-Salles, R Dourthe, F Comba, D Bory; C Lamaison, P Carbonneau; S Marconnet, R Ibanez, P de Villiers, D Auradou, F Pelous (*captain*), C Moni, C Juillet, O Magne *Substitutions:* C Califano for Marconnet (63 mins); A Benazzi for Pelous (temp 16 mins to 23 mins) and for Auradou (63 mins); S Betsen for Moni (70 mins); C Dominici for Bory (70 mins)

Scorers *Tries:* Pelous, Bernat-Salles *Conversion:* Lamaison *Penalty Goal:* Lamaison

Referee S J Young (Australia)

17 February, Twickenham
England 80 (9G 4PG 1T)   Italy 23 (2G 3PG)

For the second match in succession England simply swamped the opposition after a tentative start. But whereas Wales had achieved nothing from their early burst, Italy scored five times before hitting a brick wall as they trotted on to the turf after the interval. There were no more Italian scores, while England added 47 points for yet more records: highest score and tallest margin in the Championship and an individual landmark of 35 points for Jonny Wilkinson, leaving Ronan O'Gara's 30 against Italy in 2000 a fair way adrift.

In the opening half it was fascinating to observe how England coped with enterprising, productive attack. Italy created blind-side tries for wing Denis Dallan and No 8 Carlo Checchinato. Andrea Scanavacca backed up his try-scorers with Dominguez-style accuracy – a perfect five from his only available chances. Italy led twice and levelled twice. It was a quality, gutsy performance against the odds and England were grateful when inevitably the Italians began offending towards the interval and Wilkinson picked up three quick penalties to allow a ten-points cushion, which soon extended to the dimensions of a barrage-balloon.

England were stung but never wounded as Austin Healey kept matters balanced with two tries. Coach Clive Woodward sent on substitutes regularly – including a cap for Rugby League-convert, Jason Robinson, the first significant rung on the ladder to becoming an inked-in certainty by the end of the Lions tour a few months later. He had one touch, but England's backs' coach, Brian Ashton, said: 'There were a dozen situations that involved him and he was in the correct position every time. The ball failed to flow his way, but just watch him when he is finally delivered the ball.' Good call, Brian.

Making more impact as a sub was Joe Worsley, who burst on to Iain Balshaw's scoring-pass. Balshaw provided the outstanding spectacle of England's seven second-half tries with an 80-yard sprint. If Wilkinson had not failed with the last of his 14 kicks, after an immaculate display, he would have overtaken Paul Grayson's all-time England record of 36.

England: I R Balshaw; A S Healey, W J H Greenwood, M J Catt, B C Cohen; J P Wilkinson, M J S Dawson; J Leonard, D E West, P J Vickery, M O Johnson

(*captain*), D J Grewcock, R A Hill, L B N Dallaglio, N A Back *Substitutions:*
M P Regan for West (50 mins); J P R Worsley for Back (50 mins); J Robinson for
Cohen (50 mins); K P P Bracken for Dawson (57 mins); T J Woodman for
Leonard (68 mins); M E Corry for Grewcock (73 mins)

Scorers *Tries:* Healey (2), Balshaw (2), Cohen, Regan, Worsley, Greenwood,
Wilkinson, Dallaglio *Conversions:* Wilkinson (9) *Penalty Goals:* Wilkinson (4)

Italy: A Scanavacca; L Martin, C Stoica, W Pozzebon, D Dallan; G Raineri,
J-M Queirolo; A Lo Cicero, A Moscardi (*captain*), A Muraro, A Gritti, W Visser,
C Caione, C Checchinato, M Bergamasco *Substitutions:* G P de Carli for Muraro
(49 mins); M Rivaro for Pozzebon (66 mins); D Dal Maso for Caione (68 mins)

Scorers *Tries:* Dallan, Checchinato *Conversions:* Scanavacca (2) *Penalty Goals:*
Scanavacca (3)

Referee S J Dickinson (Australia)

17 February, Murrayfield
Scotland 28 (2G 3PG 1T)   Wales 28 (1G 4PG 3DG)

A most entertaining spectacle for any neutral – but maddeningly frustrating
for both participants. As they shook hands on the draw, every player
believed that he should have been on the victorious side. Wales collapsed
from an apparently invincible scoreline of 25-6 shortly after half-time, while
Scotland's controversial nomination of Kenny Logan as their starting kicker
lived down to the pessimists' forecasts. Logan banked only four of his eight
shots, but two of his errors were, in golfing terms, six-inch putts.

Scotland had recourse to Duncan Hodge's boot – he had ended the
match against France as kicker – to save the game with the final
conversion. At the other end, of course, Jenkins was in customary kicking
form with five goals from six place kicks and the first ever hat-trick of
drop-goals by a Welshman in a Test. Those drop-kicks – he took that
option twice more unsuccessfully – implied a lack of confidence in Welsh
attacking potential. As Scottish offences mounted in the opening spell,
Jenkins also collected three penalties.

After Mark Taylor had gratefully crossed from half-way in the 43rd
minute by intercepting John Leslie's long pass, the doubts about the Welsh
defence began to become reality. Scotland's response began almost instantly,
Colin Paterson scoring after a curving run that took him through a weak
tackle by Rhys Williams. Despite losing the command of Rob Howley with
a wrist injury around the hour, Wales could still read the maker's name on
the finishing-tape when they had held on to lead 28-16 with five minutes
remaining. Naturally, it was a case for relentless attack by the Scots and they
succeeded gloriously when James McLaren broke for an unconverted try
and prop Tom Smith, showing the finishing skills of a back, dummied and
darted for the critical try in the final minute. Hodge's nerves stood up to the
test of making the conversion that yielded the first stalemate of the series
since 1922, the first between the nations at Murrayfield, and the highest
score draw in Championship history.

Scotland: C D Paterson; C A Murray, J G McLaren, J A Leslie, K M Logan; D W Hodge, A D Nicol (*captain*); T J Smith, G C Bulloch, M J Stewart, S Murray, R Metcalfe, M D Leslie, J M Petrie, A C Pountney *Substitutions:* G R McIlwham for Stewart (49 mins); S B Grimes for Metcalfe (66 mins); J M Craig for C Murray (69 mins)

Scorers *Tries:* Paterson, McLaren, Smith *Conversions:* Logan, Hodge *Penalty Goals:* Logan (3)

Wales: G R Williams; M A Jones, M Taylor, I S Gibbs, D R James; N R Jenkins, R Howley; D R Morris, R C McBryde, D Young (*captain*), I M Gough, A P Moore, C L Charvis, L S Quinnell, M E Williams *Substitutions:* R H StJ B Moon for Howley (62 mins); J C Quinnell for Gough (62 mins); S C John for Young (80 mins)

Scorers *Try:* Taylor *Conversion:* Jenkins *Penalty Goals:* Jenkins (4) *Drop Goals:* Jenkins (3)

Referee S J Lander (England)

3 March, Stadio Flaminio, Rome
Italy 19 (1G 4PG)   France 30 (3G 3PG)

Jean-Luc Sadourny, one of the most watchable players of his generation, produced an unexpected airing of his arts in an influential afternoon. Sadourny, 34, had twice tried to retire from international action during the previous 18 months, but in a French injury crisis coach Bernard Laporte wisely went for the experience of Sadourny's 68 caps and was rewarded when the maestro scored an early opener and had talented hands in the other two tries. 'I play for pleasure and will always be available for France,' he said. He's certainly given Championship-followers plenty of pleasurable watching.

Sadourny's speed enabled him to pluck Christophe Lamaison's chip from Cristian Stoica's hopeful grab for a try in the 14th minute. Diego Dominguez, restored after a year out of the international scene, had given Italy the lead with the first of four opening-half penalties, though it was Italy who, with unfortunately characteristic illegalities, gave away a total of 20 penalties – tantamount to handicapping themselves out of the match. Lamaison's erratic kicking almost made it worthwhile for Italy to concede him penalties. He landed a mere five of his 11 shots and a touch of the Dominguez certainty from him would have eliminated French anxiety in the later stages.

Still, France took a 14-9 advantage into half-time, Sadourny linking between scorer Philippe Bernat-Salles and blind-side breaker Fabien Galthié in the 24th minute. Lamaison found a rare fertile spell with his three penalties between the 46th and 65th minutes, but France were still vulnerable when Dominguez and Denis Dallan carved out a converted try for wing Massimiliano Perziano. At only 19-23 down with eight minutes available, the crowd screamed for just two more kicks from Dominguez or even an elusive try.

Philippe Bernat-Salles scores against Italy on his way to becoming the first player to cross for tries in every match of a Six Nations season.

But the Italian push faded against a French defence far too rigid to allow an upset, and there was relief in the French camp when Sadourny re-entered the activity by scooping in a misdirected chip from Dominguez. He counter-attacked and the try-scoring beneficiary was debutant centre Sébastien Bonetti.

Italy: C Stoica; M Perziano, W Pozzebon, M Dallan, D Dallan; D Dominguez, A Troncon; A Lo Cicero, A Moscardi (*captain*), C Paoletti, W Visser, A Gritti, A Persico, C Checchinato, M Bergamasco *Substitutions:* F Properzi Curti for Paoletti (46 mins); J-M Queirolo for Troncon (67 mins)

Scorers *Try:* Perziano *Conversion:* Dominguez *Penalty Goals:* Dominguez (4)

France: J-L Sadourny; P Bernat-Salles, S Bonetti, T Lombard, C Dominici; C Lamaison, F Galthié; C Califano, R Ibanez, P de Villiers, D Auradou, F Pelous (*captain*), C Moni, C Juillet, O Magne *Substitutions:* S Betsen for Moni (40 mins); S Marconnet for Califano (53 mins)

Scorers *Tries:* Sadourny, Bernat-Salles, Bonetti *Conversions:* Lamaison (3) *Penalty Goals:* Lamaison (3)

Referee C White (England)

3 March, Twickenham
England 43 (5G 1PG 1T)   Scotland 3 (1PG)

You learned as much about England's overwhelming superiority over Scotland from reactions to the event as from studying the game. England grumbled about missed chances and line-out problems, while Scotland's analysts found their opponents' rugby breathtaking, pioneering.

'The easiest winning game of all,' said Scotland's coach Ian McGeechan, who has been linked with so many England men during his Lions tours, 'is to win in every part of the pitch. England did just that. Rugby is the best it's ever been' – and he meant the way England were leading the way, ahead of at least the other European nations.

England continued to mince the record-books: the highest score and margin in Calcutta Cup combats, with six tries hoisting them to 22 in this Championship, surpassing Wales's 1910 mark. It was significant that the back-row shared the tries with the outside backs. Duncan Hodge's solitary penalty score for Scotland was over and done with by the 14th minute and there was every chance that the Scottish side of the scoreboard would rust over.

Lawrence Dallaglio, of course, relished the occasion, as did all his colleagues who had been humiliated, out-thought and out-played in the Murrayfield swamp a year before. Dallaglio careered over for the opening try in the seventh minute. He received from Danny Grewcock, whose handling during that one movement symbolised the dextrous ability lately developed by the tight forwards. Phil Vickery, Dorian West and then on to try-scorer Richard Hill maintained the theme of English forwards being able to look after themselves in the open spaces. Dallaglio's second score made the second half a sit-back exercise for the spectators, but Scotland did not capitulate. There was skill, fortitude and dignity as they lost, even denying England a score when Budge Pountney was sin-binned for putting his toe on club colleague Matt Dawson. England needed something inventive to make their scores. Scotland were equal to anything trite. England managed the necessary quirky touches. Will Greenwood delivered a behind-the-back flip for Balshaw, whose second score resulted from a full-toss catch of Mike Catt's cross-field kick. Jason Robinson – starting to make a real impact – showed his unique footwork before gifting the sixth try to Greenwood.

England: I R Balshaw; A S Healey, W J H Greenwood, M J Catt, B C Cohen; J P Wilkinson, M J S Dawson; J Leonard, D E West, P J Vickery, M O Johnson (*captain*), D J Grewcock, R A Hill, L B N Dallaglio, N A Back *Substitutions:* M P Regan for West (40 mins); J Robinson for Catt (62 mins); J P R Worsley for Back (68 mins); K P P Bracken for Dawson (73 mins)

Scorers *Tries:* Dallaglio (2), Balshaw (2), Hill, Greenwood *Conversions:* Wilkinson (5) *Penalty Goal:* Wilkinson

Scotland: C D Paterson; C A Murray, A J Bulloch, J A Leslie, K M Logan; D W Hodge, A D Nicol (*captain*); T J Smith, G C Bulloch, M J Stewart, S Murray, R Metcalfe, M D Leslie, S M Taylor, A C Pountney *Substitutions:* G R McIlwham for Stewart (45 mins); S B Grimes for Metcalfe (46 mins); B W Redpath for Nicol (60 mins); J M Craig for C Murray (70 mins); J G McLaren for A Bulloch (75 mins)

Scorer *Penalty Goal:* Hodge

Referee R Davies (Wales)

17 March, Stade de France, Paris
France 35 (2G 7PG)   Wales 43 (4G 3PG 2DG)

All international wins are a cause for deep-down satisfaction, but Dai Young's squad approached the zenith of sporting joy when Neil Jenkins stole this win by completing a rare full-house of scores. At 35-33 down with two minutes of normal time left, he stated that Wales were not going to lose. His boot and hands put his thoughts into effect on the scoreboard with a winning drop-goal and his own converted try. Ten points. Job done. It was a marvellous example of a great international hijacking a game

His 28 points lifted him beyond 1,000 points for Wales and set a new individual Championship-match record for his nation. What sent the Valley loyalists off into the Paris night with extra glee was that France should have won. The French, screaming with nerves, squandered opportunities that must have taken them beyond 50 points. The goal-kickers were exceptions to the second-hand finishing that the rest of their colleagues manifested. Gérald Merceron and Christophe Lamaison were faultless.

The Stade de France has been an unhappy venue, with only four wins for France from 14 fixtures, and this time the crowd and officials turned on the players in a manner that British and Irish under-staters can only aspire to. 'It was humiliating,' raged Federation President, Bernard Lapasset. 'French rugby was murdered and sinned against.' Hooker Raphael Ibanez confessed: 'We lost our honour on that pitch.'

France controlled the opening period with an early score from Sébastien Bonetti and four penalties from Merceron. Wales hung on with the team and Jenkins hinting that it might be their day when Rob Howley's long-range, solo converted try just before the interval tugged the score back to 19-16.

Jenkins then upped the productivity, converting tries from Scott Quinnell and Dafydd James. A drop-kick made it 17 points in six minutes, bringing a Welsh lead of 33-22. It seemed merely a gesture as France regained the lead with Philippe Bernat-Salles's converted try and a penalty from Lamaison. This simply invited Jenkins to intensify his output and he struck the triumphant drop-goal before the clinching flourish of his own try. It was the first back-to-back success for Wales in Paris since 1955/57 and admiring coach Graham Henry, who had not seen every touch during Jenkins's career, wondered: 'He can't have had a better 40 minutes than that second half.'

France: J-L Sadourny; P Bernat-Salles, S Bonetti, T Lombard, C Dominici; G Merceron, F Galthié; C Califano, R Ibanez, P de Villiers, D Auradou, F Pelous (*captain*), C Moni, C Juillet, O Magne *Substitutions:* C Lamaison for Merceron (42 mins); S Betsen for Moni (59 mins); S Marconnet for Califano (70 mins)

Scorers *Tries:* Bonetti, Bernat-Salles *Conversions:* Merceron, Lamaison *Penalty Goals:* Merceron (4), Lamaison (3)

Wales: G R Williams; G Thomas, M Taylor, I S Gibbs, D R James; N R Jenkins, R Howley; D R Morris, R C McBryde, D Young (*captain*), I M Gough, A P Moore, C L Charvis, L S Quinnell, M E Williams *Substitutions:* S M Jones for Gibbs (51 mins); G Lewis for Charvis (63 mins); A L P Lewis for Morris (73 mins); J C Quinnell for Gough (76 mins)

Scorers *Tries:* Howley, S Quinnell, James, Jenkins *Conversions:* Jenkins (4) *Penalty Goals:* Jenkins (3) *Drop Goals:* Jenkins (2)

Referee A Lewis (Ireland)

17 March, Murrayfield
Scotland 23 (5PG 1DG 1T)　Italy 19 (1G 4PG)

Mauro Bergamasco streamed in for one of the supreme tries in Championship history. It was a diamond among dross and deserved to be the centre-piece of an Italian win. Instead, persistent infringements were a lamentable let-down for a side otherwise proving again the wisdom of inviting them into the Six Nations.

Italy donated 19 penalties, including just enough kicks at goal for Duncan Hodge, restored as chief kicker, to scrape Scotland to an unconvincing win. Tom Smith's try – his second decisive strike of this Championship – was a prosaic affair compared with Bergamasco's wonder-try.

Bergamasco, a mere 21, but virtually the complete open-side flanker in defence and attack, illuminated gloomy Murrayfield in the 27th minute. He received from Filippo Frati deep in Italian territory. 'My only thought was to run, run, run,' he recalled. Run is an understatement. He flew outside Gregor Townsend and accelerated away from the back-tracking potential tacklers. Chris Paterson, the last obstacle, was left cold by Bergamasco's hint at coming inside before the gas was applied on a final surge outside and towards the corner. The speediest wing in the world would rate such a score a career highlight. That made it 6-7 after Hodge's early kicks. Diego Dominguez, predictably flawless with his cultured right boot, landed his four penalties between the 34th and 64th minutes, leaving Italy 19-17 in front, Hodge having collected three of his five penalties by then. But there was, regrettably for them, ample time for Italy to give away two more penalties within Hodge's range and he stepped up for the winner, in the 66th minute, and a late clincher. Scotland's handling was far too slipshod to allow any momentum and their backs were comfortably held.

Scotland: C D Paterson; J M Craig, G P J Townsend, J A Leslie, K M Logan; D W Hodge, B W Redpath; T J Smith, G C Bulloch, M J Stewart, S Murray, S B Grimes, M D Leslie, S M Taylor, A C Pountney (*captain*) *Substitutions:* G R McIlwham for Stewart (40 mins); C A Murray for Craig (45 mins); J M Petrie for Taylor (74 mins); S Scott for G Bulloch (77 mins)

Scorers *Try:* Smith *Penalty Goals:* Hodge (5) *Drop Goal:* Hodge

Italy: C Stoica; M Perziano, W Pozzebon, M Dallan, L Martin; D Dominguez, F Frati; A Lo Cicero, A Moscardi (*captain*), F Properzi Curti, W Visser, A Gritti, A Persico, C Checchinato, M Bergamasco *Substitutions:* M Mazzantini for Frati (30 mins); 3 Perugini for Properzi Curti (40 mins); G Raineri for Dallan (46 mins); C Caione for Gritti (59 mins)

Scorers *Try:* Bergamasco *Conversion:* Dominguez *Penalty Goals:* Dominguez (4)

Referee J Dumé (France)

7 April, Twickenham
England 48 (6G 2PG)   France 19 (1G 3PG 1DG)

In the pre-Woodward era it was feasible for dedicated supporters to recall every England try of recent seasons – like an action-replay running through the mind. Now tries flood the eyes and the scoreboard, and the memory-bank can retain only the outstanding efforts. Six more against a side that seemed to have slipped back in Anglo-French terms.

French try-scoring capacity was burned out by the 13th minute, when at least Philippe Bernat-Salles had the distinction of becoming the first player to score a try in every Six Nations game, though there were near things including two thumbs-down from the video referee.

There were two important figures when the squeeze was so tightly exerted on France with a second-half imbalance of 32 points to three. Richard Hill, so often the true man-of-the-match, raced with the focus and swiftness of a wing from 40 yards immediately after the interval to take England clear. And Iain Balshaw effected try-saving tackles on Bernat-Salles and Christophe Dominici – two of the slipperiest customers in the business – as well as claiming a score for himself at the other end that signalled England hitting the pedal from 20-19 ahead. Matt Dawson took a quick penalty – disregarding a gift three points – and Jonny Wilkinson sent Balshaw diving in. Further audacity at a close-range penalty position came from Austin Healey, who, facing away from the French goal, chipped over his head and Mike Catt read his intentions perfectly. Jason Robinson's ability to operate in a confined space was the genesis of Phil Greening's score.

Wilkinson, as remorseless as a Jenkins, chewed up more records, going past Rob Andrew's English mark of 396 career points and his 80 thus far in this Championship was two more, after just four fixtures, than his record in 2000. With Wilkinson in such form – eight goals from nine shots – England went past their own 2000 Championship record of 183 points.

Again England's technical analysts were underwhelmed, but again the opposition lavished praise. 'England played with the same tempo and rhythm throughout,' observed Raphael Ibanez.

England: I R Balshaw; A S Healey, W J H Greenwood, M J Catt, B C Cohen; J P Wilkinson, M J S Dawson; J Leonard, P B T Greening, J M White, M O Johnson (*captain*), S W Borthwick, R A Hill, L B N Dallaglio, N A Back *Substitutions:* D E West for Greening (temp 19 mins to 28 mins); M E Corry for Borthwick (temp 30 mins to 78 mins); D L Flatman for Leonard (temp 38 mins to 40 mins); J Robinson for Cohen (62 mins); J P R Worsley for Hill (77 mins); M B Perry for Balshaw (77 mins); K P P Bracken for Dawson (80 mins);

Scorers *Tries:* Balshaw, Hill, Greenwood, Greening, Catt, Perry *Conversions:* Wilkinson (6) *Penalty Goals:* Wilkinson (2)

France: J-L Sadourny; P Bernat-Salles, S Glas, X Garbajosa, C Dominici; G Merceron, F Galthié; S Marconnet, R Ibanez, P de Villiers, L Nallet, A Benazzi, C Milhères, F Pelous (*captain*), O Magne *Substitutions:* D Auradou for Benazzi (45 mins); T Lièvremont for Nallet (45 mins); F Landreau for Ibanez (56 mins); A Galasso for de Villiers (81 mins)

Scorers *Try:* Bernat-Salles *Conversion:* Merceron *Penalty Goals:* Merceron (3) *Drop Goal:* Merceron

Referee W T S Henning (South Africa) replaced by D T M McHugh (Ireland)

8 April, Stadio Flaminio, Rome
Italy 23 (5PG 1DG 1T)   Wales 33 (3G 4PG)

Wales were always masters of their own destiny once the game had settled. They scored tries at important times and Diego Dominguez was not able to keep pace with his penalties. Scott Gibbs's double gave Wales leads of 17-6 and 27-15, but there was some serious defending to be undertaken when Carlo Checchinato nipped in for Italy's solitary try with four minutes remaining.

Italy's loss made them wooden-spoonists in their second Six Nations experience. That was predictable. They scored plenty of points with the boot, not enough tries and, of course, gave some of the greatest goal-kickers in the modern game far too many "thank-you-very-much" penalties.

Late on, when they were a converted try down, Italy attempted something that they have repeatedly failed to achieve – a sustained burst of scoring. But instead, a fractious second half boiled over. Cristian Stoica and Craig Quinnell were yellow-carded and there could have been others, particularly Italy's gifted flanker Mauro Bergamasco, who plays on the edge and endured a mixed afternoon. He galvanised the move for Checchinato's score, but knocked on the pass for a certain try at 12-20. In his anger he tangled with Charvis and then pushed touch-judge Alan Lewis.

Gareth Cooper, a late stand-in for Rob Howley, placed himself high on the list of early debutant try-scorers with his effort after a mere seven minutes. Gibbs proved unstoppable from close range in the 30th and 50th minutes.

Italy: C Stoica; M Perziano, W Pozzebon, G Raineri, D Dallan; D Dominguez, M Mazzantini; A Lo Cicero, A Moscardi (*captain*), F Properzi Curti, W Visser, A Gritti, A Persico, C Checchinato, M Bergamasco *Substitutions:* S Perugini for Properzi Curti (46 mins); C Pilat for Raineri (50 mins); M Zaffiri for Gritti (63 mins); G P de Carli for Lo Cicero (77 mins); L Martin for Pozzebon (81 mins)

Scorers *Try:* Checchinato *Penalty Goals:* Dominguez (5) *Drop Goal:* Dominguez

Wales: G R Williams; G Thomas, M Taylor, I S Gibbs, D R James; N R Jenkins, G J Cooper; D R Morris, R C McBryde, D Young (*captain*), I M Gough, A P Moore, C L Charvis, L S Quinnell, M E Williams *Substitutions:* A G Bateman for Taylor (temp 33 mins to 40 mins); J C Quinnell for Gough (49 mins)

Scorers *Tries:* Gibbs (2), Cooper *Conversions:* Jenkins (3) *Penalty Goals:* Jenkins (4)

Referee P G Honiss (New Zealand)

22 September, Murrayfield
Scotland 32 (3G 2PG 1T)   Ireland 10 (1G 1PG)

Not even world-championship heavyweight fights enjoy six-months' hype. But since Ireland's spring sprint was abruptly halted after defeating Continental opposition, there was juicy speculation and anticipation. Even during the Lions tour, the phrase 'Grand Slam decider' became a summer 2001 cliché. The sceptics who doubted Ireland's capacity to see off all three UK nations were proved right as Keith Wood's team approached the first hurdle of their Autumn Treble in Scotland like clumsy cart-horses.

The long delay since their last Six Nations fixtures meant that both sides changed almost half their personnel. The winner's start was worse than the loser's. Gregor Townsend missed two routine penalties and a drop-kick, while Ronan O'Gara's failure-rate was a mere couple of penalties. That established a pattern for most of the players to perform miles below their known skill levels in a passionless encounter.

Townsend compensated for a rough kicking display – not for the first time in the Championship Scotland changed their kicker during a match – with deft handling that was instrumental in all Scottish tries.

The first try was worth sitting through 23 minutes of ineptitude. John Leslie made the important first few yards and Chris Paterson – the relief goal-kicker – strode an extraordinary cross-field path as Ireland's tacklers let themselves down before feeding Budge Pountney for a help-yourself. By half-time, prop Tom Smith had muscled in from close range for his third try of the tournament – the sort of return that makes famous wings salivate.

Ireland belatedly made an indentation on the score-board when O'Gara collected a penalty in the 49th minute. A 17-3 deficit might just have been a platform, but not, on this day, for an Irish side out-paced in the back-row and way behind the Scots' backs in exploiting the interesting gap.

Townsend set up Leslie for the third try and a diagonal kick enabled new cap Andrew Henderson to score the fourth. Girvan Dempsey's injury-time try for Ireland was meaningless, as coach Warren Gatland acknowledged when he intoned: 'It was shattering. We were thoroughly outplayed.' So, no green Grand Slam, and Ireland remained winless at Murrayfield since 1985.

Scotland: G H Metcalfe; J F Steel, J G McLaren, J A Leslie, C D Paterson; G P J Townsend, B W Redpath; T J Smith, G C Bulloch, M J Stewart, J P R White, S Murray, G L Simpson, S M Taylor, A C Pountney (*captain*) *Substitutions:* G Graham for Stewart (63 mins); A Henderson for Leslie (63 mins); S B Grimes for White (71 mins); J M Petrie for Simpson (75 mins); S Scott for Bulloch (79 mins); D W Hodge for Townsend (79 mins); A D Nicol for Redpath (79 mins)

Scorers *Tries:* Pountney, Smith, Leslie, Henderson *Conversions:* Paterson (2), Townsend *Penalty Goals:* Paterson (2)

Ireland: G T Dempsey; G E A Murphy, B G O'Driscoll, S P Horgan, D A Hickie; R J R O'Gara, G Easterby; P M Clohessy, K G M Wood (*captain*), J J Hayes, J W Davidson, M E O'Kelly, S H Easterby, A G Foley, K Dawson *Substitutions:* K M Maggs for Murphy (22 mins); E Byrne for Hayes (34 mins); P A Stringer for G Easterby (53 mins); D G Humphreys for O'Gara (63 mins); D P Wallace for Foley (63 mins); G W Longwell for Davidson (73 mins)

Scorers *Try:* Dempsey *Conversion:* Humphreys *Penalty Goal:* O'Gara

Referee C White (England)

13 October, Millennium Stadium, Cardiff Arms Park
Wales 6 (2PG)   Ireland 36 (3G 5PG)

This tournament is supposed to be unpredictable, but woeful Wales collaborated in maintaining at least one long-established tradition – Ireland don't lose in Cardiff.

Ireland reached back into the legion of the multi-capped, making seven changes, and all the recalled men justified Warren Gatland's choice by transforming the team into game-controllers, especially the king of the work-rate, flanker David Wallace. Ireland proved an amazing contrast compared with Murrayfield, where they had been tormented. Another returnee, David Humphreys, nonchalantly landed five first-half penalties as the flow of the match was set early. Ireland simply produced efficient, powerful rugby, and it was far too good for Wales. By the end, when Ireland were finally putting away the tries, the crowd were either voting with their feet and off to drown sorrows or jeering their inadequate squad.

Wales were without the experience of Neil Jenkins and Scott Quinnell. The stats rubbed in the dejection and humiliation suffered by Wales – 27 tackles missed, 17 handling errors and endless kicks of all types being misdirected. Graham Henry accepted 'personal responsibility,' but when allegedly quality players operate like second-teamers, the coach can't catch, kick or pass for them. Basic stuff. Wales did manage just enough in defence to earn the video verdict twice towards half-time and they kept the score locked at 15-6 for half an hour. The final eight minutes was classic floodgates time. Keith Wood's long pass helped release Denis Hickie from half-way. Brian O'Driscoll scooped up Shane Williams's optimistic grubber and Shane Horgan was left with the right hand half of the pitch to himself.

Assuming toddlers were not admitted in 1983, when Wales last won this fixture at home, there is a generation of Welshmen aged almost 30 that has never witnessed the green shirts being sent back as losers. Nine matches (including Wembley two years ago), eight Irish wins and a draw.

Wales: K A Morgan; D R James, A G Bateman, L B Davies, S M Williams; S M Jones, R Howley; I D Thomas, R C McBryde, D Young (*captain*), C P Wyatt, A P Moore, C L Charvis, G Lewis, B D Sinkinson *Substitutions:* B H Williams for McBryde (53 mins); Gavin Thomas for Charvis (53 mins); C T Anthony for Young (64 mins); G R Williams for Morgan (77 mins); J C Quinnell for Moore (80 mins)

Scorer *Penalty Goals:* Jones (2)

Ireland: G T Dempsey; S P Horgan, B G O'Driscoll, K M Maggs, D A Hickie; D G Humphreys, P A Stringer; P M Clohessy, K G M Wood (*captain*), J J Hayes, M J Galwey, M E O'Kelly, E R P Miller, A G Foley, D P Wallace *Substitutions:* T Brennan for Galwey (56 mins); E Byrne for Clohessy (62 mins); R J R O'Gara for Humphreys (77 mins); F J Sheahan for Wood (77 mins); K Dawson for Wallace (80 mins); G Easterby for Stringer (83 mins); M J Mullins for Hickie (83 mins)

Scorers *Tries:* Hickie, O'Driscoll, Horgan *Conversions:* Humphreys (2), O'Gara *Penalty Goals:* Humphreys (5)

Referee J Kaplan (South Africa)

20 October, Lansdowne Road, Dublin
Ireland 20 (5PG 1T) England 14 (3PG 1T)

In countless interviews leading up to the Dublin decider, England's senior players insisted that they were light years away from the vulnerable weaklings who had tamely surrendered inviting Grand Slam chances in the previous two seasons. They were deceiving themselves. At least at Wembley in 1999 and at Murrayfield 2000 England were ambushed late on. This time the Irish were masters from the first kick and even when England attacked with frantic desperation, finally believing that they were going to lose, Ireland retained enough nerve and defensive skill. They permitted just one try when England required two.

English supporters had to have doubts when first Lawrence Dallaglio, then, crucially, Martin Johnson and finally Phil Vickery were extracted from England's scrum by injury. Then emergency captain Matt Dawson went off before the interval. Talk of strength in depth was revealed to be a myth. The scrum was ineffective, the line-out an embarrassment and the back-row mere shadows. The backs, moreover, went backwards.

But which Irish side were going to turn up? The under-performers of Murrayfield or the superb attackers from the final stages in Cardiff? In fact, it was a Dublin display – supremely organised and efficient, striking at the heart of the opposition when it really mattered.

The amazing Keith Wood scored Ireland's only try and it was probably unique in international rugby. He threw the ball into a line-out and never stopped running as Mick Galwey and Anthony Foley caught and handled expertly. Galloping round the back of the line-out, Wood carved through feeble English tackling. 11-6 down at half-time was not badly damaging for England, though the sceptics had a shrewd idea of the outcome from the opening minutes. Nor was 14-9 as the kickers exchanged penalties. It seemed that the equalising score was imminent when Dan Luger broke from just outside his 22. He sprinted 45 metres before Peter Stringer achieved the considerable feat of first missing Luger and then catching him to make a tap-tackle from behind.

England were then destroyed when Ronan O'Gara, substituting for David Humphreys, who had been England's tormentor, kicked a couple of penalties. Austin Healey, substituting for Luger, knifed in with five minutes left, but Ireland were in no mood to waste 75 minutes of effort.

England's ultimate captain Neil Back said that he and his troops were failures. Coach Clive Woodward was angry and Healey called losing a third Grand Slam horrendous. Wood summed up Ireland's autumn: 'We were a total mess in Scotland, but managed to make Wales and England look dull tactically.'

Ireland: G T Dempsey; S P Horgan, B G O'Driscoll, K M Maggs, D A Hickie; D G Humphreys, P A Stringer; P M Clohessy, K G M Wood (*captain*), J J Hayes, M J Galwey, M E O'Kelly, E R P Miller, A G Foley, D P Wallace *Substitutions:* R J R O'Gara for Humphreys (59 mins); T Brennan for Galwey (66 mins); E Byrne for Clohessy (66 mins); K Dawson for Foley (77 mins); M J Mullins for O'Driscoll (77 mins)

Scorers *Try:* Wood *Penalty Goals:* Humphreys (3), O'Gara (2)

England: I R Balshaw; D D Luger, W J H Greenwood, M J Catt, J Robinson; J P Wilkinson, M J S Dawson (*captain*); J Leonard, P B T Greening, J M White, S D Shaw, D J Grewcock, M E Corry, R A Hill, N A Back *Substitutions:* K P P Bracken for Dawson (37 mins); D E West for Greening (40 mins); A S Healey for Luger (60 mins); L W Moody for Corry (75 mins); G C Rowntree for White (75 mins)

Scorers *Try:* Healey *Penalty Goals:* Wilkinson (3)

Referee P G Honiss (New Zealand)

INTERNATIONAL CHAMPIONSHIP RECORDS 1883-2001

Previous winners:

1883 England; 1884 England; 1885 Not completed; 1886 England & Scotland; 1887 Scotland; 1888 Not completed; 1889 Not completed; 1890 England & Scotland; 1891 Scotland; 1892 England; 1893 Wales; 1894 Ireland; 1895 Scotland; 1896 Ireland; 1897 Not completed; 1898 Not completed; 1899 Ireland; 1900 Wales; 1901 Scotland; 1902 Wales; 1903 Scotland; 1904 Scotland; 1905 Wales; 1906 Ireland & Wales; 1907 Scotland; 1908 Wales; 1909 Wales; 1910 England; 1911 Wales; 1912 England & Ireland; 1913 England; 1914 England; 1920 England & Scotland & Wales; 1921 England; 1922 Wales; 1923 England; 1924 England; 1925 Scotland; 1926 Scotland & Ireland; 1927 Scotland & Ireland; 1928 England; 1929 Scotland; 1930 England; 1931 Wales; 1932 England & Ireland & Wales; 1933 Scotland; 1934 England; 1935 Ireland; 1936 Wales; 1937 England; 1938 Scotland; 1939 England & Ireland & Wales; 1947 England & Wales; 1948 Ireland; 1949 Ireland; 1950 Wales; 1951 Ireland; 1952 Wales; 1953 England; 1954 England & Wales & France; 1955 Wales & France; 1956 Wales; 1957 England; 1958 England; 1959 France; 1960 England & France; 1961 France; 1962 France; 1963 England; 1964 Scotland & Wales; 1965 Wales; 1966 Wales; 1967 France; 1968 France; 1969 Wales; 1970 Wales & France; 1971 Wales; 1972 Not completed; 1973 Five Nations tie; 1974 Ireland; 1975 Wales; 1976 Wales; 1977 France; 1978 Wales; 1979 Wales; 1980 England; 1981 France; 1982 Ireland; 1983 Ireland & France; 1984 Scotland; 1985 Ireland; 1986 Scotland & France; 1987 France; 1988 Wales & France; 1989 France; 1990 Scotland; 1991 England; 1992 England; 1993 France; 1994 Wales; 1995 England; 1996 England; 1997 France; 1998 France; 1999 Scotland; 2000 England; 2001 England

England have the title outright 24 times; Wales 22; Scotland 14; France 12; Ireland 10; Italy 0.

Triple Crown winners:

England (21 times) 1883, 1884, 1892, 1913, 1914, 1921, 1923, 1924, 1928, 1934, 1937, 1954, 1957, 1960, 1980, 1991, 1992, 1995, 1996, 1997, 1998.

Wales (17 times) 1893, 1900, 1902, 1905, 1908, 1909, 1911, 1950, 1952, 1965, 1969, 1971, 1976, 1977, 1978, 1979, 1988.

Scotland (10 times) 1891, 1895, 1901, 1903, 1907, 1925, 1933, 1938, 1984, 1990.

Ireland (Six times) 1894, 1899, 1948, 1949, 1982, 1985.

Grand Slam winners:

England (11 times) 1913, 1914, 1921, 1923, 1924, 1928, 1957, 1980, 1991, 1992, 1995.

Wales (Eight times) 1908, 1909, 1911, 1950, 1952, 1971, 1976, 1978.

France (Six times) 1968, 1977, 1981, 1987, 1997, 1998.

Scotland (Three times) 1925, 1984, 1990.

Ireland (Once) 1948.

Chief Records

Record	Detail		Set
Most team points in season	229 by England	in five matches	2001
Most team tries in season	29 by England	in five matches	2001
Highest team score	80 by England	80-23 v Italy	2001
Biggest team win	57 by England	80-23 v Italy	2001
Most team tries in match	12 by Scotland	v Wales	1887
Most appearances	56 for Ireland	C M H Gibson	1964 – 1979
Most points in matches	406 for Wales	N R Jenkins	1991 – 2001
Most points in season	89 for England	J P Wilkinson	2001
Most points in match	35 for England	J P Wilkinson	v Italy, 2001
Most tries in matches	24 for Scotland	I S Smith	1924 – 1933
Most tries in season	8 for England	C N Lowe	1914
	8 for Scotland	I S Smith	1925
Most tries in match	5 for Scotland	G C Lindsay	v Wales, 1887
Most cons in matches	41 for Wales	N R Jenkins	1991 – 2001
Most cons in season	24 for England	J P Wilkinson	2001
Most cons in match	9 for England	J P Wilkinson	v Italy, 2001
Most pens in matches	93 for Wales	N R Jenkins	1991 – 2001
Most pens in season	18 for England	S D Hodgkinson	1991
	18 for England	J P Wilkinson	2000
Most pens in match	7 for England	S D Hodgkinson	v Wales, 1991
	7 for England	C R Andrew	v Scotland, 1995
	7 for England	J P Wilkinson	v France, 1999
	7 for Wales	N R Jenkins	v Italy, 2000
Most drops in matches	9 for France	J-P Lescarboura	1982 – 1988
	9 for England	C R Andrew	1985 – 1997
Most drops in season	5 for France	G Camberabero	1967
	5 for Italy	D Dominguez	2000
	5 for Wales	N R Jenkins	2001
Most drops in match	3 for France	P Albaladejo	v Ireland, 1960
	3 for France	J-P Lescarboura	v England, 1985
	3 for Italy	D Dominguez	v Scotland 2000
	3 for Wales	N R Jenkins	v Scotland 2001

THE 2001 TRI NATIONS

Australia Retain the Title

Paul Dobson

After Australia's win against New Zealand to clinch the Tri Nations title in the magnificent Stadium Australia on 1st September, Peter Crittle, former Australian lock and present President of the Australian Rugby Union, called it the end to the greatest season in Australian rugby. The team, he said, was the greatest ever to represent Australia, and he added several superlatives to describe the retiring captain, John Eales.

The last-minute victory at home to the All Blacks meant that in 2001 Australia had won the Super 12 through the Brumbies, the series against the Lions, and retained both the Bledisloe Cup and the Tri Nations championship. Over two years they have proved their worth as winners of the World Cup and holders of the unofficial title of World Champions.

No team really dominated the 2001 Tri Nations. South Africa, bottom on the table for the third successive year, were unbeaten in their two matches against the winners, Australia, whose five tries was the lowest number of tries by a winning team in the Tri Nations. Indeed, this year the Tri Nations suffered its worst try-drought with only 13 scored in the six matches. No side picked up a bonus point for scoring four tries in a match.

There was much debate about the dominance of defence over attack and many complaints by Eddie Jones, Australia's new coach, about the laws and refereeing, particularly when officials from the Northern Hemisphere were in charge.

New Zealand scored one more try in the series than Australia and conceded two fewer, but were not wholly convincing. Their best performance was against South Africa on wet Eden Park and in the first 25 minutes of the second half in the decider at Stadium Australia. They had the best back line in the competition but the weakest forwards, let down above all at line-out time.

South Africa had the strongest pack in the competition and, as always, defended with astonishing grit. They conceded only three tries, but their attacking skills were limited to individual thrusts, and they ended with only two tries from their four matches. The Springboks threw away their very first match, against the All Blacks in the Newlands rain, for want of a reliable goal-kicker, yet stayed in contention until their Eden Park encounter with the All Blacks.

Tri Nations 2001: Final Table

	P	W	D	L	F	A	Bonus Points	Pts
Australia	4	2	1	1	81	75	1	11
New Zealand	4	2	0	2	79	70	1	9
South Africa	4	1	1	2	52	67	0	6

Points: win 4; draw 2; four or more tries, or defeat by seven or fewer points 1

21 July, Newlands, Cape Town
South Africa 3 (1PG)   New Zealand 12 (4PG)

What a difference a boot makes. Percy Montgomery missed three goal kicks and Butch James one for South Africa. Tony Brown missed none for New Zealand. And with waning confidence in the boot, South Africa attempted to score tries in kickable positions on three occasions. That could have harvested 21 points. The match's final action was a missed kick, when, in search of a bonus point, James kicked high and straight to the left of the posts.

Jonah Lomu provided the turning point in the match, though not with an inspired run, as yet again he failed to score a try against the Springboks. This time his tackling was telling. In the space of a minute he brought off two try-saving tackles with bulky power. First he held up big Dean Hall at the line and then he stopped a low-diving Mark Andrews on the line when a try seemed inevitable. On another occasion Robbie Fleck sniped through and flicked a pass to captain Bob Skinstad who was heading for the welcoming line. Skinstad knocked on.

Tana Umaga, Leon MacDonald, Doug Howlett and, once, Jonah Lomu ran well for the All Blacks, but they were coming mainly from defensive positions. Afterwards Wayne Smith, their coach, praised their adamantine defence for the victory.

The day was cold after a week of rain, and rain fell for the last quarter of the game. After a week of criticism of the Springboks – in the media, from the Minister of Sport and from much of the public for selections – for some the performance was better than expected. It could have been still better, for they could and should have won for all the possession and territory they enjoyed. For one thing the Springbok line-outs were the best they have ever been in the modern era, and the country hailed a new hero – a rampaging bullet of a hooker, Lukas van Biljon. For New Zealand their performance was more controlled and more cohesive. Justin Marshall had much to do with his team's control. The half-time score was also 12-3.

South Africa: P C Montgomery; B J Paulse, M C Joubert, R F Fleck, D B Hall; A D James, J H van der Westhuizen; R B Kempson, L van Biljon, I J Visagie, V Matfield, M G Andrews, A N Vos, R B Skinstad (*captain*), A G Venter
Substitutions: D J Kayser for Joubert (21 mins); A-H le Roux for Kempson (61 mins); J N Ackermann for Matfield (62 mins); J W Smit for Van Biljon (63 mins); J C van Niekerk for Vos (72 mins)
Scorer *Penalty Goal:* Montgomery

New Zealand: J W Wilson; D C Howlett, J F Umaga, P P F Alatini, J T Lomu;
T E Brown, J W Marshall; C H Hoeft, A D Oliver (*captain*), G M Somerville,
N M C Maxwell, T V Flavell, R D Thorne, R T Cribb, T C Randell *Substitutions:*
L R MacDonald for Wilson (40 mins); C R Jack for Maxwell (63 mins);
M R Holah for Cribb (75 mins)

Scorer *Penalty Goals:* Brown (4)

Referee S Young (Australia)

28 July, Loftus Versfeld, Pretoria
South Africa 20 (5PG 1T)   Australia 15 (5PG)

For South Africa, the boot was on the other foot. After missing many kicks
against the All Blacks at Newlands the week before, they kicked three
penalty goals out of three this week while Australia missed two. This gave
the South Africans a 9-0 lead till they scored a try just before half-time. As
the Springboks had been forced to play catch-up against the All Blacks, so
the Wallabies were forced to play catch-up this time.

The man who made the difference was Braam van Straaten. After an
acrimonious week in the wake of the Newlands defeat, when provincialism
became hysteria and the weight of criticism almost led to the resignation of
coach Harry Viljoen, the pressure on van Straaten was intense as he lined up
his first shot at goal. The previous week's defeat had been blamed in part on
the lack of a kicker. For van Straaten to miss would have been unbearable.

He did not miss. He kicked five penalty goals and missed only the
conversion of Bob Skinstad's try. There was more to the Springbok victory
than just the boot. Their lighter pack dominated the Wallabies in all phases,
including the line-outs where the Australians had ruled the world.

The South African try came when David Giffin was lured out of his
channel. He went off to elbow Robbie Fleck, leaving a gap close to the
post-tackle situation for Skinstad to race to the corner. Giffin was later cited
by the New Zealand match commissioner and suspended for three weeks.

The half-time score was 14-0 to South Africa, but early in the second half
Matthew Burke started finding the target. The man who kept the Springboks
ahead was van Straaten. Australia came close to scoring when a clearing
kick by Conrad Jantjes was charged down. Andrew Walker led the chase to
the ball but was eventually adjudged to have knocked on after the matter
had been referred to the television match official, Brian Stirling.

There was much Australian acrimony directed at referee David McHugh,
during the match and afterwards. One advance of 10 metres for dissent in
the first half moved the place of the penalty to just inside the Springbok
half, from which van Straaten goaled.

South Africa: C A Jantjes; B J Paulse, R F Fleck, A J J van Straaten, D B Hall;
A D James, J H van der Westhuizen; R B Kempson, L van Biljon, I J Visagie,
J N Ackermann, M G Andrews, A N Vos, R B Skinstad (*captain*), A G Venter
Substitutions: C P J Krige for Vos (temp 39 to 40 mins and 56 mins); A-H le Roux
for Kempson (65 mins); J W Smit for Van Biljon (69 mins); J C van Niekerk for
Ackermann (69 mins)

Joe Roff passes Conrad Jantjes in the Tri Nations match in Pretoria. Roff, who will be plying his trade in Europe in 2001-02 at Serge Blanco's old club, Biarritz, has appeared in 58 successive Tests for Australia.

Scorers *Try:* Skinstad *Penalty Goals:* van Straaten (5)

Australia: M C Burke; A M Walker, D J Herbert, N P Grey, J W C Roff; E J Flatley, G M Gregan; N B Stiles, M A Foley, R S Moore, D T Giffin, J A Eales (*captain*), O D A Finegan, R S T Kefu, G B Smith *Substitutions:* M J Cockbain for Giffin (56 mins); B J Darwin for Moore (59 mins); M H M Edmonds for Flatley (70 mins); D J Lyons for Kefu (74 mins); C E Latham for Burke (74 mins)

Scorers *Penalty Goals:* Burke (4), Edmonds

Referee D T M McHugh (Ireland)

11 August, Carisbrook, Dunedin
New Zealand 15 (1G 1PG 1T)   Australia 23 (2G 3PG)

After a week of increasing fervour in Dunedin and high expectation of victory throughout New Zealand, it was cold and wet at Carisbrook with an occasional outburst of sun. In winning for the first time in Dunedin, the Wallabies retained the Bledisloe Cup.

The All Blacks started with promise. The Wallabies attacked but a grubber by Stephen Larkham in the opening seconds ricocheted off Jeff Wilson's legs. He footed downfield and only a desperate flykick by Matthew Burke saved the situation. From the ensuing line-out, Tana Umaga slipped a diagonal kick ahead. Jonah Lomu beat Joe Roff to the ball for a try on the right. Lomu was playing his 50th Test match for New Zealand.

There were two kicks in the opening minute setting the tenor for the game. The kicking meant over 30 lineouts in the match. Surprisingly the All Blacks, whose lineout work was considered poor, made four takes against the throw in the match. The Wallabies kicked much better than the All Blacks – at kick-offs, at goal, where Tony Brown missed three attempts, and from the hand where the Australians either kicked along the ground or low and hard into unguarded areas.

Both Wallaby tries came from kicks. Owen Finegan drove and then Burke kicked, chased, swooped and slid over for a try, which he converted. In the second half, with the score 10-8 to the Wallabies, Larkham stabbed a rolling kick ahead into the All Blacks' in-goal. Roff chased and was clearly winning the race for the inviting ball. Ron Cribb tackled him from behind. The referee awarded an indisputable penalty try – the first awarded against the All Blacks in a Test.

With six minutes to go and the Wallabies 23-8 ahead the All Blacks scored the try of the match from within their own half. Tana Umaga punched a gap and fed Lomu on the wing. The big man charged down the touch-line and then fed inside to Jeff Wilson who skated over for his 50th try for New Zealand and 44th in Tests, the New Zealand record.

New Zealand: J W Wilson; D C Howlett, J F Umaga, P P F Alatini, J T Lomu; T E Brown, J W Marshall; C H Hoeft, A D Oliver (*captain*), G M Somerville, N M C Maxwell, T V Flavell, R D Thorne, R T Cribb, T C Randell *Substitutions:* M S B Cooksley for Maxwell (50 mins); C J Hayman for Somerville (55 mins);

L R MacDonald for Howlett (63 mins); B T Kelleher for Marshall (63 mins);
A P Mehrtens for Brown (69 mins); M R Holah for Randell (75 mins)

Scorers *Tries:* Lomu, Wilson *Conversion:* Mehrtens *Penalty Goal:* Brown

Australia: M C Burke; A M Walker, D J Herbert, N P Grey, J W C Roff;
S J Larkham, G M Gregan; N B Stiles, M A Foley, R S Moore, J B G Harrison,
J A Eales (*captain*), O D A Finegan, R S T Kefu, G B Smith *Substitutions:*
B J Darwin for Moore (55 mins); M J Cockbain for Finegan (59 mins);
P R Waugh for Smith (63 mins); C E Latham for Burke (74 mins); B J Cannon for
Foley (74 mins); E J Flatley for Larkham (77 mins)

Scorers *Tries:* Burke, penalty try (Roff) *Conversions:* Burke (2) *Penalty Goals:*
Burke (3)

Referee S J Lander (England).

18 August, Subiaco Oval, Perth
Australia 14 (3PG 1T)   South Africa 14 (3PG 1T)

For the first time in 47 matches between the two countries Australia and
South Africa drew. It probably was a worthy draw. South Africa dominated
most of the game, thanks to their stronger pack which won the line-outs,
were better in the scrums and surprisingly sharper in the loose.

The ball used, a Summit ball, had been the subject of controversy in the
run-up to the Test. The kickers, Matthew Burke for Australia and Braam van
Straaten for South Africa, managed a meagre 50% success rate, which may
have been a commentary on the ball or caused by the awkward breezes at
the ground. Burke missed two simple kicks.

South Africa scored an excellent try, which was also the subject of
controversy. They counterattacked down the left against a Burke chip and
then swung it to the right-hand touch-line where Mark Andrews went over
for his twelfth Test try. Television replays suggested that his right foot may
have touched the touch-line before he scored, but the matter was not
referred to the television match official.

That was not the only controversy in the match. Butch James, the
Springbok fly-half, was sent to the sin-bin for tackling recklessly and later
Bob Skinstad, the Springbok captain, went to the side line for repeatedly
slowing down the Wallaby ball at the tackle.

At half-time the Springboks led 8-3. With 12 minutes to go they led 11-6.
Then the Wallabies mounted attack after attack as the Springboks tackled
and tackled. John Eales opted for kicks to touch in search of a try rather
than at goal. The try eventually came when Nathan Grey burst over from
close quarters. Burke missed a relatively easy conversion.

Straight after that the Springboks took the lead again when the Wallabies
were penalised for a high tackle. When the Springboks played the ball
illegally in a tackle, Matthew Burke levelled the scores. The Wallabies
attacked towards the end against a defence which stood firm. The last act of
the match was an attempted dropped goal by Stephen Larkham, which went
astray.

Australia: M C Burke; C E Latham, D J Herbert, N P Grey, J W C Roff; S J Larkham, G M Gregan; N B Stiles, M A Foley, R S Moore, J B G Harrison, J A Eales (*captain*), O D A Finegan, R S T Kefu, G B Smith *Substitutions:* P R Waugh for Smith (54 mins); B J Darwin for Moore (60 mins); M J Cockbain for Harrison (61 mins); G S G Bond for Latham (65 mins)

Scorers *Try:* Grey *Penalty Goals:* Burke (3)

South Africa: C A Jantjes; B J Paulse, R F Fleck, A J J van Straaten, D B Hall; A D James, J H van der Westhuizen; R B Kempson, L van Biljon, I J Visagie, V Matfield, M G Andrews, A N Vos, R B Skinstad (*captain*), A G Venter *Substitutions:* D J Kayser for Fleck (20 mins); A-H le Roux for Kempson (60 mins); P A van den Berg for Andrews (60 mins); J W Smit for Van Biljon (65 mins)

Scorers *Try:* Andrews *Penalty Goals:* van Straaten (3)

Referee S R Walsh (New Zealand)

25 August, Eden Park, Auckland
New Zealand 26 (2G 4PG)   South Africa 15 (5PG)

In the end the score flattered South Africa as New Zealand outplayed them in all but the scrums and line-outs. The Springboks never looked as if they seriously considered their own avowed intent of going for four tries and the bonus point. They kicked into the wind and they kicked with the wind, and the All Blacks, playing with the ball in hand, made them suffer and tackle till the final whistle.

The match was played in rain on a soggy field. The weather actually deteriorated as the match wore on. Nonetheless it was entertaining as both sides clearly wanted to adopt a positive attitude. New Zealand's ball-in-hand method of doing so was more entertaining than the Springboks' repeated hoofing, though that too produced some entertaining moments as Jonah Lomu charged at them on the counter.

For the All Blacks, returnee fly-half Andrew Mehrtens was imperious and Tana Umaga constructive whenever he had the ball. In the first half, New Zealand played with the wind and lost a golden chance to score when Jonah Lomu dropped Ron Cribb's pass close to the corner. They did score after a multi phased attack which ended with a dart and thrust for a try by inside centre Pita Alatini. That was in only the eighth minute of the match. Mehrtens kicked two penalties and a conversion but missed two attempts at penalties. Braam van Straaten kicked three penalties, missing none, so that at the break New Zealand led 13-9.

The All Blacks had one real chance of scoring a try in the second half, when Mehrtens darted through a gap and sent out a sympathetic pass to full-back Leon MacDonald who was on the right wing. The Springbok hooker Lukas van Biljon tackled MacDonald before the ball got to him, and the referee Peter Marshall, who refereed the match splendidly, awarded a penalty try.

The match had its querulous moments, set going by some rugged All Black footwork at tackle time, but it was worthy of a Test between the two countries. Certainly the All Blacks were far better than they had been in the

Joost van der Westhuizen hands-off his opposite number, Byron Kelleher, in the New Zealand – South Africa Test at Eden Park, Auckland, in August. Defeat for the Springboks left them holding the Tri Nations wooden spoon for the second successive season.

first match at Newlands. The result eliminated South Africa from Tri Nations contention leaving New Zealand to face Australia in what in effect was a final in Sydney.

New Zealand: L R MacDonald; J W Wilson, J F Umaga, P P F Alatini, J T Lomu; A P Mehrtens, B T Kelleher; C H Hoeft, A D Oliver (*captain*), G M Somerville, N M C Maxwell, C R Jack, T V Flavell, R T Cribb, T C Randell *Substitutions:* M S B Cooksley for Maxwell (temp 37 to 40 mins) and for Jack (76 mins); M R Holah for Cribb (50 mins); C J Hayman for Somerville (58 mins)

Scorers *Tries:* Alatini, penalty try (MacDonald) *Conversions:* Mehrtens (2) *Penalty Goals:* Mehrtens (4)

South Africa: C A Jantjes; B J Paulse, A H Snyman, A J J van Straaten, D B Hall; A D James, J H van der Westhuizen; R B Kempson, L van Biljon, I J Visagie, V Matfield, M G Andrews, A N Vos, R B Skinstad (*captain*), A G Venter *Substitutions:* J C van Niekerk for Skinstad (temp 21 to 30 mins) and for Vos (64 mins); A-H le Roux for Kempson (61 mins); J W Smit for Van Biljon (61 mins); P A van den Berg for Andrews (61 mins); D J Kayser for Snyman (76 mins)

Scorer *Penalty Goals:* van Straaten (5)

Referee P L Marshall (Australia)

1 September, Stadium Australia, Sydney
Australia 29 (2G 5PG)   New Zealand 26 (2G 4PG)

Australia were in command throughout the first half and built up a 19-6 lead. They scored a wonderful try when Chris Latham leapt high to catch a diagonal kick which Stephen Larkham had lobbed behind Jonah Lomu. In addition, Matthew Burke landed four penalty goals to become the highest points scorer ever in Tests against New Zealand, while Andrew Mehrtens missed two which were comparatively straightforward. Ten of Australia's points came during the ten minutes that New Zealand's Norm Maxwell was absent, sent to the sin-bin on a touch judge's report.

The first 25 minutes of the second half belonged to New Zealand, who scored 20 points without reply. Pita Alatini broke marvellously, danced past two defenders and sent Doug Howlett skating in for a try to open the half. New Zealand's second try was also brilliant as Jonah Lomu staggered over people on the left-hand touch line and flipped a pass inside to Leon MacDonald who fed Alatini. The centre spurted over to take New Zealand ahead.

Rod Moore became the second player in the sin-bin, but the All Blacks failed to score points while he was off. Mehrtens, however, did increase their lead later with a penalty for an infringement at a tackle. Then, after Byron Kelleher was substituted, came the period of Wallaby resurgence. First Andrew Walker kicked a simple penalty to make the score 26-22. Then Australia attacked over and over again. New Zealand defended grimly but gave away several penalties. The Wallabies eschewed kicks at goal, preferring to seek close-in line-outs.

Line-outs were New Zealand's Achilles' heel. They lost nine of their 14 throws and it was a line-out which finally destroyed them. Anton Oliver failed to find his jumper and in the mess which ensued the All Blacks were penalised. Walker kicked out, the Wallabies won their line-out ball, and Toutai Kefu drove at the All Blacks. He managed to barrel ahead and somehow reach out an arm to score at the posts.

There was much elation in the sell-out crowd of over 91,000, much disappointment from the many Kiwis present, but everybody joined in the emotional applause when Peter Crittle, President of the Australian Rugby Union, said: 'Thank you, John Eales.'

Australia: M C Burke; C E Latham, D J Herbert, N P Grey, J W C Roff; S J Larkham, G M Gregan; N B Stiles, M A Foley, R S Moore, D T Giffin, J A Eales (*captain*), O D A Finegan, R S T Kefu, G B Smith *Substitutions:* P R Waugh for Smith (52 mins); B J Darwin for Finegan (temp 53 to 57 mins) and for Moore (57 mins); A M Walker for Burke (65 mins); M J Cockbain for Giffin (68 mins); E J Flatley for Grey (68 mins)

Scorers *Tries:* Latham, Kefu *Conversions:* Burke, Flatley *Penalty Goals:* Burke (4), Walker

New Zealand: L R MacDonald; D C Howlett, J F Umaga, P P F Alatini, J T Lomu; A P Mehrtens, B T Kelleher; C H Hoeft, A D Oliver (*captain*), G M Somerville, N M C Maxwell, C R Jack, T V Flavell, R T Cribb, T C Randell *Substitutions:* M R Holah for Randell (32 mins); C M Cullen for Howlett (60 mins); J W Marshall for Kelleher (64 mins); C J Hayman for Somerville (68 mins)

Scorers *Tries:* Howlett, Alatini *Conversions:* Mehrtens (2) *Penalty Goals:* Mehrtens (4)

Referee W T S Henning (South Africa)

THE TRI NATIONS RECORDS 1996-2001

Previous winners: 1996 New Zealand; 1997 New Zealand; 1998 South Africa; 1999 New Zealand; 2000 Australia; 2001 Australia
Grand Slam winners: New Zealand (Twice) 1996, 1997; South Africa (Once) 1998

Record	Detail		Set
Most team points in season	159 by N Zealand	in four matches	1997
Most team tries in season	18 by S Africa	in four matches	1997
Highest team score	61 by S Africa	61-22 v Australia (h)	1997
Biggest team win	39 by S Africa	61-22 v Australia (h)	1997
Most team tries in match	8 by S Africa	v Australia	1997
Most appearances	24 for Australia	J W C Roff	1996 to 2001
Most points in matches	262 for N Zealand	A P Mehrtens	1996 to 2001
Most points in season	84 for N Zealand	C J Spencer	1997
Most points in match	29 for N Zealand	A P Mehrtens	v Australia (h) 1999
Most tries in matches	16 for N Zealand	C M Cullen	1996 to 2001
Most tries in season	7 for N Zealand	C M Cullen	2000
Most tries in match	3 for S Africa	P C Montgomery	v Australia (h),1997
Most cons in matches	28 for N Zealand	A P Mehrtens	1996 to 2001
Most cons in season	13 for N Zealand	C J Spencer	1997
Most cons in match	6 for S Africa	J H de Beer	v Australia (h),1997
Most pens in matches	65 for N Zealand	A P Mehrtens	1996 to 2001
Most pens in season	19 for N Zealand	A P Mehrtens	1996
	19 for N Zealand	A P Mehrtens	1999
Most pens in match	9 for N Zealand	A P Mehrtens	v Australia (h) 1999

THE 2001 PACIFIC RIM CHAMPIONSHIP

A New Format and a New Winner

Geoff Miller & John Griffiths

Pacific Rim
CHAMPIONSHIP

The Qualifiers

The Pacific Rim Championship is the third most important tournament behind the Six and Tri Nations events on the annual international rugby calendar. It gives the Pacific Rim nations the opportunity of regularly measuring their playing development and, as a measure of the strength of the nations taking part in the competition, all six of the competing sides in the 1999 event qualified for that year's Rugby World Cup finals in Britain, Ireland and France.

As part of an evolving plan to expand the competition to embrace more nations, the structure of the 2001 tournament provided for regional matches to determine qualifiers for a play-off among the leading four nations in Japan in early July. Canada and the United States played their qualifier in Canada in May and the South Pacific powers, Fiji, Tonga and Samoa, staged a home-and-away round-robin in June to determine winners and runners-up who went forward to the play-offs.

The Can-Am match was a part of the opening round of the Pan-American Championship and saw Canada take the Can-Am Cup from their neighbours for the first time since 1998. The match was a defensive battle in which the place-kicking of veteran Scott Stewart played a decisive part. He kicked two first-half penalties and converted a try scored by John Thiel who had pounced on the ball as it squirted out of a ruck on the American Eagles' goal line to give the Canadians a 13-7 lead at the break. For the Eagles, Kevin Dalzell ran 55 metres from an interception for a try that Grant Wells converted. Two more penalties by Stewart and one by Wells completed the scoring in the second half. Dave Clark, the Canadian coach, was pleased with the performances of his three new caps, Jeff Williams, Ed Fairhurst and John Cannon. His counterpart Duncan Hall, a former Wallaby forward, felt that his inexperienced front-row had struggled against the Canadian front three. 'All the players here tried their hardest,' he said, 'but unfortunately we don't have a lot of depth.'

The Oceania tournament that began a week later was packed with the brand of enterprising rugby from the Islanders that spectators all over the world have warmed to for nearly fifty years. All of the matches were close with never more than nine points separating winner from loser, and the six matches yielded an average of more than five tries a game.

Tonga, performing in front of King Taufa'ahau Tupou IV, sprang a surprise in the opening match by beating Fiji 31-26 to register a first win against their old rivals for five years. In a match packed with clattering tackles, the Tongans were almost always in front and the Fijians had to rely on the goal kicking of Nicky Little to keep alive their chances of winning. It was not until the final five minutes, when replacement flanker Jope Tuikabe crossed at the corner, that Fiji scored a try. That brought them back to 26-28, but Little failed to convert and a late penalty goal by full-back Kusitafu Tonga, whose goal kicking was otherwise indifferent, sealed victory for the Tongans. 'We expected Fiji to be much tougher,' said Tu'ivaita Ueleni after his first match as coach of the Tongan side.

Samoa entered the lists a week later with a narrow two-point win over the Tongans in Apia and when Fiji crashed at home to the Samoans in the match that marked the half-way stage of the qualifiers, their chances of reaching the finals in Japan looked remote.

Fiji enjoyed an excellent first half, however, in the return against Tonga and with a lead of 25-3 looked certain to close the gap on their rivals. But to the annoyance of their coach, Greg Smith, the Fijians failed to capitalise on their strong position, sacrificed the chance to pick up a bonus point for an extra try, and let the Tongans score 17 points unanswered in the second half. With Samoa at the head of the table, Tonga and Fiji thus shared second place with one match each against the Samoans to play.

Given that Fiji had to travel to Samoa while the Tongans would be the hosts in the final match of the qualifiers, the favourites for the Tokyo play-offs were Tonga and Samoa. Yet despite heavy rain, Greg Smith's side pulled off a remarkable win in front of 10,000 spectators in Apia – their first there since 1986 – to keep alive their hopes of reaching the finals. Smith was delighted and singled out the athletic Fijian pack for praise.

The last qualifying match kept everyone on tenterhooks until the 80th minute. Samoa were leading only 16-14 as the Tongans threw everything into all-out attack in a late attempt to claim a qualifying place. But a try on the bell by Terry Fanolua, converted by Silao Leaega, carried Samoa forward with Fiji to join Canada and hosts, Japan, in the finals in Tokyo a week later.

Pacific Rim Championship Results 2001

Preliminary Rounds

Can-Am Match

19 May 2001 Richardson Stadium, Kingston, Ontario
Canada 19 (1G 4PG) **United States 10** (1G 1PG)

Canada Scorers *Try:* J Thiel *Conversion:* D S Stewart *Penalty Goals:* D S Stewart (4)
United States Scorers *Try:* K Dalzell *Conversion:* G Wells *Penalty Goal:* G Wells
Referee S Borsani (Argentina)
Canada qualified

South Pacific Qualifying Championship

25 May 2001 Teufaiva Stadium, Nuku'alofa, Tonga
Tonga 31 (2G 4PG 1T) Fiji 26 (6PG 1DG 1T)

Tonga Scorers *Tries:* A Havili (2), T Fifita *Conversions:* K Tonga (2) *Penalty Goals:* K Tonga (4)

Fiji Scorers *Try:* J Tuikabe *Penalty Goals:* N Little (6) *Dropped Goal:* N Little

Referee F Tapunu'u (Samoa)

2 June 2001 Apia Park, Apia, Samoa
Samoa 20 (2G 2PG) Tonga 18 (1G 2PG 1T)

Samoa Scorers *Tries:* E Seveali'i, penalty try *Conversions:* S Leaega (2) *Penalty Goals:* S Leaega (2)

Tonga Scorers *Tries:* T Fainganuku, E Vunipola *Conversion:* S Tu'ihalamaka *Penalty Goals:* S Tu'ihalamaka (2)

Referee S Tativetua (Fiji)

9 June 2001 National Stadium, Suva, Fiji
Fiji 27 (2G 1PG 2T) Samoa 36 (4G 1PG 1T)

Fiji Scorers *Tries:* V Satala (2), J Rauluni, N Ligairi *Conversions:* N Little (2) *Penalty Goal:* N Little

Samoa Scorers *Tries:* J Paramore (2), A So'oalo (2), E Va'a *Conversions:* S Leaega (4) *Penalty Goal:* S Leaega

Referee P G Honiss (New Zealand)

16 June 2001 Churchill Park, Lautoka, Fiji
Fiji 25 (2G 2PG 1T) Tonga 20 (2G 2PG)

Fiji Scorers *Tries:* N Ligairi (2), V Delasau *Conversions:* N Little (2) *Penalty Goals:* N Little (2)

Tonga Scorers *Tries:* S Matangi (2) *Conversions:* S Tu'ihalamaka (2) *Penalty Goals:* S Tu'ihalamaka (2)

Referee M Talapari (Samoa)

23 June 2001 Apia Park, Apia, Samoa
Samoa 19 (3PG 2T) Fiji 22 (2G 1PG 1T)

Samoa Scorers *Tries:* B Lima (2) *Penalty Goals:* S Leaega (3)

Fiji Scorers *Tries:* V Delasau (2), I Male *Conversions:* N Little (2) *Penalty Goal:* N Little

Referee P D O'Brien (New Zealand)

30 June 2001 Teufaiva Stadium, Nuku'alofa, Tonga
Tonga 14 (2G)   **Samoa 23** (2G 3PG)

Tonga Scorers *Tries:* V Ma'asi, S Matangi *Conversions:* K Tonga (2)
Samoa Scorers *Tries:* S Sititi, T Fanolua *Conversions:* S Leaega (2) *Penalty Goals:*
S Leaega (3)
Referee S Vuki (Fiji)

Final South Pacific Championship Qualifying Table

	P	*W*	*D*	*L*	*For*	*Against*	*Bonus*	*Pts*
Samoa	4	3	0	1	98	81	2	14
Fiji	4	2	0	2	100	106	2	10
Tonga	4	1	0	3	83	94	2	6

Note: Four points for a win; two for a draw; one bonus point for scoring four or
more tries in a match; one bonus point for losing by 7 points or less.
Samoa and Fiji qualified

The Finals

The Fijian squad arrived in Japan for the finals with a caretaker coach. Greg
Smith, the former Australian coach who had steered Fiji to victory seven
times in 10 Tests since taking charge 15 months earlier, resigned a week after
guiding the side to their victory in Apia. Whether he jumped or was pushed
was a talking point for no more than 24 hours as former Fiji lock, Ifereimi
Tawaki, stepped in to make preparations to take the side to Japan.

There, the Fijians were reinforced by their former full-back, Alfred
Uluinayau, who was playing under contract at centre alongside the former
All Black, Alama Ieremia, for the leading Japanese club side, Suntory. He
played a cameo role in Fiji's decisive 52-23 win against Canada in the first of
the semi-finals, scoring one of the tries and setting up one for winger
Vilimoni Delasau, who grabbed a hat trick of tries after the interval. When
Samoa beat Japan 47-8 later the same afternoon, there was the juicy
prospect of a South Seas final to follow four days later.

First semi-final

4 July 2001 Tokyo Stadium, Chofu City, Japan
Fiji 52 (5G 4PG 1T)   **Canada 23** (4PG 2DG 1T)

Fiji: N Ligairi; A Rinakawa, S Rokini, D Baleinadogo, V Delasau; N Little,
J Rauluni; H Qiodravu, G Smith (*captain*), V Cavubati, A Naevo, S Raiwalui,
A Doviverata, S Koyamaibole, J Tuikabe *Substitutions:* A Uluinayau for Ligairi;
V Satala for Baleinadogo; S Rabaka for Rauluni; P Damu for Qiodravu; I Rasila
for Cavubati; E Katalau for Naevo; I Male for Koyamaibole
Scorers *Tries:* Delasau (3), Satala, Uluinayau, Doviverata *Conversions:* Little (4),
Uluinayau *Penalty Goals:* Little (4)

Canada: J Williams; F Asselin, J Cannon, K Nichols, S Fauth; R Ross, M Williams; R Snow, P Dunkley (*captain*), G Cooke, E Knaggs, R Johnstone, R Banks, P Murphy, C Yukes *Substitutions:* S Thompson for Asselin; H Toews for Snow; K Tkachuk for Dunkley; K Wirachowski for Cooke; B Major for Banks
Scorers *Try:* Fauth *Penalty Goals:* Ross (4) *Dropped Goals:* Ross (2)
Referee A Aiolupo (Samoa)

Second semi-final

4 July 2001 Tokyo Stadium, Chofu City, Japan
Japan 8 (1PG 1T)   Samoa 47 (6G 1T)

Japan: H Onozawa; T Kurihara, H Yoshida, Y Motoki, T Masuho; K Iwabuchi, W Murata; S Hasegawa, M Sakata, M Toyoyama, L Vatuvei, H Tanuma, K Kubo, Y Saito, T Ito *Substitutions:* T Hirao for Masuho; N Oto for Iwabuchi; R Yamamura for Toyoyama; K Koizumi for Ito (*temp*)
Scorers *Try:* Onozawa *Penalty Goal:* Kurihara
Samoa: T Vili; E Seveali'i, T Fanolua, V Tuigamala, A So'oalo; E Va'a, J Filemu; M Luafalealo, T Leota, K Lealamanua, O Palepoi, L Tone, S Sititi (*captain*), A To'oala, P Segi *Substitutions:* F So'olefai for Fanolua; T Vaega for Tuigamala; S So'oialo for Filemu; A Tiatia for Leota; H Williams for Lealamanua; J Paramore for Sititi; S Ta'ala for To'oala
Scorers *Tries:* So'oalo (2), Seveali'i (2), Fanolua, Segi, Vili *Conversions:* Va'a (6)
Referee B Kuklinski (Canada)

In the Prince Chichibu Stadium, Uluinayau was in the Fijian starting line-up for the final and fired the side with their only try, early in the second half. The Fijians led from early in the match and never looked likely to relinquish their lead. Nicky Little accumulated their remaining 23 points through accurate goal kicking as Fiji powered to a convincing 28-17 win in a physical battle between two evenly-matched sides. It was the third time that the two islands had met in the space of five weeks and the result left Fiji undisputed kings of the Pacific.

In the curtain-raiser to the final, wing Toru Kurihara scored 24 points including two tries in Japan's 39-7 win against Canada to give his country third place in the Championship.

Final

8 July 2001 Prince Chichibu Stadium, Tokyo
Fiji 28 (1G 7PG)   Samoa 17 (4PG 1T)

Fiji: N Ligairi; A Rinakama, V Satala, A Uluinayau, V Delasau; N Little, J Rauluni; H Qiodravu, G Smith (*captain*),V Cavubati, A Naevo, S Raiwalui, J Tuikabe, I Male, A Doviverata *Substitutions:* S Rokini for Rinakama; D Baleinadogo for Satala; S Rabaka for Rauluni; P Damu for Qiodravu; I Rasila for Cavubati; S Koyamaibole for Naevo

Scorers *Try:* Uluinayau *Conversion:* Little *Penalty Goals:* Little (7)

Samoa: T Vili; B Lima, T Vaega, V Tuigamala, E Seveali'i; E Va'a, S So'oialo; K Lealamanua, A Tiatia, P Asi, O Palepoi, L Tone, S Sititi (*captain*), J Paramore, C Glendinning *Substitutions:* T Fanolua for Vaega; S Leaega for Seveali'i; A To'oala for Va'a; M Luafalealo for Tiatia; T Leota for Tone

Scorers *Try:* So'oialo *Penalty Goals:* Va'a (3), Leaega

Referee B Kuklinski (Canada)

Third/Fourth play-off

8 July 2001 Prince Chichibu Stadium, Tokyo
Japan 39 (4G 2PG 1T)   Canada 7 (1G)

Japan: H Onozawa; T Kurihara, H Namba, Y Motoki, T Masuho; S Onishi, Y Sonoda; S Hasegawa, M Sakata (*captain*), R Yamamura, L Vatuvei, H Tanuma, K Kubo, Y Saito, T Ito *Substitutions:* T Hirao for Masuho; H Yoshida for Onishi; S Tsukita for Sonoda; M Toyoyama for Yamamura; J Akune for Tanuma; K Koizumi for Kuho

Scorers *Tries:* Kurihara (2), Saito, Namba, Vatuvei *Conversions:* Kurihara (4) *Penalty Goals:* Kurihara (2)

Canada: J Williams; J Cordle, S Thompson, J Cannon, S Fauth; R Ross, M Williams; R Snow (*captain*), H Toews, K Wirachowski, E Knaggs, R Johnstone, B Major, P Murphy, C Yukes *Substitutions:* K Nichols for Cannon; M Danskin for Ross; K Tkachuk for Snow; P Dunkley for Toews; G Cooke for Wirachowski; R Banks for Major

Scorers *Try:* Murphy *Conversion:* Ross

Referee A Aiolupo (Samoa)

Previous Pacific Rim Champions: 1996 Canada; 1997 Canada; 1998 Canada; 1999 Japan; 2000 Samoa; 2001 Fiji

PACIFIC RIM CHAMPIONSHIP RECORDS 1996–2001

Record	Detail		Set
Most team points in season	207 by Canada	in six matches	1996
Most team tries in season	25 by Samoa	in five matches	2000
Highest team score	74 by United States	74–5 v Japan	1996
Biggest team win	69 by United States	74–5 v Japan	1996
Most team tries in match	11 by United States	v Japan	1996
Most points in matches	234 for Canada	R Ross	1996–2001
Most points in season	105 for Canada	R Ross	1996
Most points in match	34 for Japan	K Hirose v Tonga	1999
Most tries in matches	13 for United States	V Anitoni	1996–2000
Most tries in season	10 for United States	V Anitoni	1996
Most tries in match	4 for United States	B Hightower v Japan	1996
	4 for Canada	K Nichols v Japan	2000
	4 for Samoa	E Seveali'i v Japan	2000
Most cons in matches	36 for Samoa	N T Little	1999–2001
Most cons in season	17 for Samoa	N T Little	2000
Most cons in match	8 for United States	M Alexander v Japan	1996
	8 for Canada	J Barker v Japan	2000
Most pens in matches	43 for Canada	R Ross	1996–2001
Most pens in season	22 for Canada	R Ross	1996
Most pens in match	9 for Japan	K Hirose v Tonga	1999
Most drops in matches	7 for Canada	R Ross	1996–2001
Most drops in season	3 for Canada	R Ross	1997
Most drops in match	2 for Canada	R Ross v Hong Kong	1997
	2 for Canada	R Ross v Fiji	2001

THE 2001 LIONS IN AUSTRALIA

First Series Victory for the Wallabies

Mick Cleary

They gathered in good heart and wide-eyed innocence at Tylney Hall in Hamsphire. Seven weeks later they went their separate ways and at varying times from Sydney, worn-out and crestfallen. There is always a lot of life to be lived within a Lions tour, a crash-course in sporting highs and lows, an existence that invariably begins in hope, travels through all manner of experiences, and ends either in joy or sorrow. The 2001 Lions ran the gamut of emotions, even breathing in the rarefied air of the victorious summit in Brisbane, yet were ultimately brought down to earth. They lost the third and decisive Test in Sydney, 29-23, to give the Wallabies their first ever series victory against the Lions.

It was a gripping tale from first to last. It was not always the most savoury of stories, as Matt Dawson's provocative mid-tour diary made only too plain. It touched tragic depths, too, when the Lions Australian Rugby Union liaison man, Anton Toia, suffered a suspected heart attack while swimming near the team hotel in Coffs Harbour and died. At such moments a fixation on sport can seem misplaced.

There were many upbeat moments, too, as Toia, a charming, open man would have been the first to tell you. The early opposition was taken apart, as well it should have been, the Lions racking up 199 points in their first two games against Western Australia and the Queensland President's XV. Former rugby league wing, Jason Robinson, scored five second-half tries in that second match as the Lions piled on 73 points without reply after the half-time interval. That was the night that Robinson began to shake off that irritating tag once and for all: no more 'Mister Former Rugby League'. He came into his own on the tour and proved, particularly with his sensational contribution to the first Test victory at the Gabba, that he was a fine rugby union player above all else.

The tour, though, was defined by adversity. The Lions rarely found any clear water, a time when they were free of injury or internal scandal. Eight players – Simon Taylor (knee), Phil Greening (knee), Mike Catt (calf), Dan Luger (fractured eye-socket), Lawrence Dallaglio (knee), Robin McBryde (thigh), Robert Howley (cracked ribs) and Richard Hill (concussion) were forced out of the tour. Seven players were called in as replacements at various points – Martin Corry, Gordon Bulloch, Scott Gibbs, Tyrone Howe, David Wallace, Dorian West and, in a bizarre twist on the morning of the final test, Andy Nicol. Austin Healey had fallen prey to a bulging disc and was forced to withdraw. The Lions had not bothered to call for a replacement for Howley figuring that, with no midweek game, they had adequate resources in Matt Dawson and Austin Healey. It was a misguided assessment. Nicol was summoned to the team hotel at 10.30 on Saturday morning for a cramming session on moves and calls.

During that final week it was evident that the Lions were pretty much played out, battered in body if not in spirit. They were never able to run their first XV in training in the build-up to the Sydney Test, with both centres, Brian O'Driscoll and Rob Henderson, hampered as was No 8 Scott Quinnell. Small wonder that he only made it to half-time.

Are these excuses to be trotted out ? No, for the players themselves do not make them on their own behalf. As Lions captain, Martin Johnson, put it after the Sydney defeat: 'From the moment the first whistle blows to the moment the last whistle sounds it is the players' game. It is the players' fault that we came up short.'

Not quite their responsibility alone. The management team of Graham Henry, Andy Robinson and Donal Lenihan, have to look within and consider whether they handled the squad in the right fashion, whether training was too onerous and whether their relationship with the players was as it should have been. Difficult questions with no easy answers. Hindsight, with a series lost, invariably throws a very critical eye over proceedings.

The self-evaluation process must not duck issues. The squad first. It was the largest ever assembled with 37 players selected for duty on the 10-match tour: 18 players from England, ten from Wales, six from Ireland and three from Scotland. There were surprise omissions: no Scott Gibbs and no Gregor Townsend. No place either for Martin Corry (to be rectified in spectacular fashion), Kyran Bracken, Julian White or Budge Pountney. There were call-ups though for Jason Robinson, who had not made the long list of 67 names, as well as 21 year-old Scotland No 8, Simon Taylor.

It was a big squad and it was obvious that several players would not see much action. And they didn't, hence the mid-tour grumbles. 'You'll always get players grizzling and it's usually those that don't make the Test team,' said Henry at the end of the tour.

Easy to say. Too easy. Henry has never been one to molly-coddle players. They are selected or they are not. He doesn't bother much with explanations. If that's his way, then that's his way. It's a harsh stance and it came back to bite him, all the more so when he publicly abandoned the midweek side to their own fate after the 28-25 loss to Australia A at Gosford. 'We'll just have to prioritise the Test team,' said Henry.

And he did. It was too stark a divide. Of course it's difficult to give adequate time to the midweek side but that is the special challenge of Lions tours – making it all work. One feeds off the other, both in personnel and spirit. It's too convenient to ditch them and should not have happened.

There were complaints from players also that they felt the Test team had been chosen before they left England. That is the way it always is. Selectors have to have a firm idea of who they want where in order to be able to forge

Jason Robinson, one of the successes of the Lions tour to Australia, dives beneath George Gregan's despairing tackle to score near the corner at Stadium Australia, Sydney, in the third and final Test of the series.

the appropriate style. Again, it is a question of manner, of what vibes are given off to the whole squad. Again, it looks as if the management did not hit the mark.

The selectors did mix and match for the early couple of games. The real problem confronting them was that the opposition was so weak. How could they put players through their paces if their opponents bore no resemblance whatsoever to the standard they might expect during the business end of the tour.

Brian O'Driscoll had an outing at full-back against Western Australia as the Lions swept home at the WACA by a record score 116-10. This eclipsed the mark set by the 1974 Lions. Simon Taylor gave a promising 40 minute display as a replacement but by the following day was off the tour.

Across the other side of Australia four days later the President's XV were beaten 83-6. Now came the big test with three tough matches in eight days, against Queensland Reds, Australia A and then New South Wales Waratahs. The Lions had mixed fortunes. The Reds were soundly beaten at Ballymore, 42-8, owing largely to an impressive first-half showing. Rob Henderson had a terrific game at centre. It was a wholly different story three days later on the New South Wales Central Coast. Australia A, coached by Wallaby coach-elect, Eddie Jones, were too sharp and too smart for the Lions. The margin was only three points but that was thanks to two late tries by the Lions. Mike Catt failed to go the distance.

The injuries were mounting. Phil Greening was gone and by the end of the week so too was Dan Luger whose eye-socket was fractured after a collision in training with Neil Back. That weekend the Lions were put through the mincer by the Waratahs, coming through a stormy, ill-tempered match, 41-24. The game was marred by scuffles. There were five yellow cards and one red one for Waratahs full-back, Duncan McRae. The former Saracens player was sent off in the second-half for belting the living daylights out of a prostrate Ronan O'Gara. McRae was suspended for seven weeks. Waratahs lock, Tom Bowman, was sin-binned after just four seconds. Danny Grewcock and Phil Vickery for the Lions and NSW's Brendan Cannon and Cameron Blades all did a spell in the sin-bin at the same time in the second-half. 'A black night for rugby,' is how Henry described it.

The build-up to the first test was savagely interrupted by the death of Anton Toia. It was no surprise that the game the following afternoon, against NSW Cockatoos, was a shabby, misshapen affair, the Lions winning 46-3. David Wallace and Dorian West only arrived in Australia that morning but took up a place on the bench.

The high of the first Test victory at the Gabba was offset by the Dawson diary that appeared in the *Daily Telegraph* that morning. He castigated the management for being too regimented and heavy-handed. He was fined for his views and had an uncomfortable few days in the spotlight until, in dramatic fashion, he landed the conversion, the last kick of the match, to see his side through 30-28 against ACT Brumbies the following Tuesday.

The Lions were in seemingly good order for the second Test in Melbourne. They intended to delay naming their team until the Friday but were forced to comply with IB regulations that state that sides must be announced 48 hours before kick-off. The Lions had ample opportunity to prevail but were unstitched by two errors early in the second-half and conceded a record score against Australia, 35-14.

On to Sydney, without the injured trio of Rob Howley, Richard Hill and Jonny Wilkinson. Only Wilkinson was fit to play in the third Test. 'Sydney will be a lottery,' said Henry before the second Test. 'We have to wrap it up in Melbourne.'

And so it proved.

Tour party

Full backs: I R Balshaw (Bath & England), M B Perry (Bath & England)

Threequarters: B C Cohen (Northampton & England), D R James (Llanelli & Wales), D D Luger (Saracens & England), J Robinson (Sale & England), M J Catt (Bath & England), W J H Greenwood (Harlequins & England), R A J Henderson (London Wasps & Ireland), B G O'Driscoll (Blackrock College & Ireland), M Taylor (Swansea & Wales), *I S Gibbs (Swansea & Wales), *T G Howe (Dungannon & Ireland)

Half-backs: N R Jenkins (Cardiff & Wales), R J R O'Gara (Cork Constitution & Ireland), J P Wilkinson (Newcastle & England), M J S Dawson (Northampton & England), A S Healey (Leicester & England), R Howley (Cardiff & Wales), *A D Nicol (Glasgow Caledonians & Scotland)

Forwards: P B T Greening (London Wasps & England), R C McBryde (Llanelli & Wales), K G M Wood (Harlequins & Ireland), *G C Bulloch (Glasgow Caledonians & Scotland), *D E West (Leicester & England), J Leonard (Harlequins & England), D R Morris (Swansea & Wales), T J Smith (Brive, Fra & Scotland), P J Vickery (Gloucester & England), D Young (Cardiff & Wales), M O Johnson (Leicester & England) (*captain*), D J Grewcock (Saracens & England), S Murray (Saracens & Scotland), M E O'Kelly (St Mary's College & Ireland), J W Davidson (Castres, Fra & Ireland), N A Back (Leicester & England), C L Charvis (Swansea & Wales), L B N Dallaglio (London Wasps & England), R A Hill (Saracens & England), L S Quinnell (Llanelli & Wales), S M Taylor (Edinburgh Reivers & Scotland), M E Williams (Cardiff & Wales), *M E Corry (Leicester & England), *D P Wallace (Garryowen & Ireland)

* Replacement on tour

Manager D G Lenihan **Coach** G W Henry **Assistant coach** R A Robinson

Tour record P 10 W 7 L 3 For 449 Against 184

8 June Won 116-10 v Western Australia (Perth)

12 June Won 83-6 v Queensland President's XV (Townsville)

16 June Won 42-8 v Queensland Reds (Brisbane)

19 June Lost 25-28 v Australia A (Gosford)

23 June Won 41-24 v NSW Waratahs (Sydney)

26 June Won 46-3 v NSW Country Cockatoos XV (Coffs Harbour)

30 June Won 29-13 v AUSTRALIA (Brisbane)

3 July Won 30-28 v ACT Brumbies (Canberra)
7 July Lost 14-35 v AUSTRALIA (Melbourne)
14 July Lost 23-29 v AUSTRALIA (Sydney)

Details

8 June, WACA Stadium, Perth
Western Australia 10 (2T)   British and Irish Lions XV 116 (13G 5T)

Western Australia: S Apaapa; M Gardiner, A Broughton, H Waldin, B Becroft; T Feather, M Fleet; T Stevens, C Duff, A New, N Hollis, T Thomas (*captain*), H Grace, A Brain, R Coney *Substitutions:* P Noriega for New (15 mins); D McRae for Feather (20 mins); R Barugh for Fleet (53 mins); R Cameron for Hollis (61 mins); R Kellam for Duff (64 mins); M Harrington for Waldin (67 mins); G Plimmer for Coney (68 mins); Feather and Coney back for Apaapa and Brain (72 mins)

Scorers *Tries:* Becroft, Barugh

British & Irish Lions XV: B O'Driscoll; B Cohen, W Greenwood, M Taylor, D Luger; R O'Gara, R Howley; D Morris, K Wood (*captain*), P Vickery, D Grewcock, M O'Kelly, R Hill, S Quinnell, N Back *Substitutions:* S Taylor for Hill (40 mins); J Davidson for Quinnell (temp 42 46 mins) and for Grewcock (71 mins); A Healey for Howley (57 mins); I Balshaw for Greenwood (59 mins); J Leonard for Vickery (60 mins); R Henderson for Cohen (64 mins); R McBryde for Wood (71 mins); Howley back for Balshaw (79 mins)

Scorers *Tries:* Luger (3), Quinnell (3), Back (2), Howley (2), Balshaw (2),Greenwood, M Taylor, Grewcock, S Taylor, Healey, O'Driscoll *Conversions:* O'Gara (13)

Referee W J Erickson (ARU)

12 June, Dairy Farmers Stadium, Townsville
Queensland President's XV 6 (2PG)   British and Irish Lions XV 83 (9G 4T)

Queensland President's XV: N Williams; D McCallum, J Pelesasa, J Ramsamy, S Barton; S Drahm, B Wakely; R Tyrell, S Hardman (*captain*), F Dyson, N Mitchell, R Vedelago, S Fava, J Roe, T McVerry *Substitutions:* S Kerr for Dyson (10 mins); M Tabrett for Williams (40 mins); A Scotney for Drahm (55 mins); Williams back for Barton (70 mins); S Berry for Wakely (73 mins)

Scorer Penalty goals: Drahm (2)

British and Irish Lions XV: M Perry; D James, W Greenwood, R Henderson, J Robinson; N Jenkins, M Dawson; T Smith, R McBryde, D Young (*captain*), J Davidson, S Murray, C Charvis, M Corry, M Williams *Substitutions:* G Bulloch for McBryde (10 mins); J Leonard for Smith (59 mins); A Healey and M Taylor for Jenkins and Greenwood (65 mins); M O'Kelly for Davidson (68 mins)

Scorers *Tries:* Robinson (5), Henderson (3), Charvis (2), Young, O'Kelly, penalty try *Conversions:* Jenkins (5), Perry (4)

Referee G J Ayoub (ARU)

16 June, Ballymore, Brisbane
Queensland Reds 8 (1PG 1T)   British and Irish Lions XV 42 (4G 3PG 1T)

Queensland Reds: M Tabrett; J Pelesasa, D Herbert (*captain*), S Kefu, D McCallum; E Flatley, S Cordingley; N Stiles, M Foley, G Panoho, N Sharpe, M Connors, M Cockbain, T Kefu, D Croft *Substitutions:* A Scotney for Flatley (40 mins); J Ramsamy for S Kefu (53 mins); S Hardman for Foley (64 mins); S Kerr for Stiles (66 mins); N Mitchell for Sharpe (71 mins); J Roe for Cockbain (79 mins); B Wakely for Cordingley (80 mins)

Scorers *Try:* Cordingley *Penalty Goal:* Flatley

British and Irish Lions XV: I Balshaw; D James, B O'Driscoll, R Henderson, D Luger; J Wilkinson, R Howley; T Smith, K Wood, P Vickery, M Johnson (*captain*), D Grewcock, R Hill, M Corry, N Back *Substitutions:* M Dawson for Howley (48 mins); J Robinson for O'Driscoll (60 mins); C Charvis for Back (77 mins); S Murray for Johnson (80 mins)

Scorers *Tries:* Luger, Henderson, James, Hill, O'Driscoll *Conversions:* Wilkinson (4) *Penalty Goals:* Wilkinson (3)

Referee S J Dickinson (ARU)

19 June, NorthPower Stadium, Gosford
Australia A 28 (1G 7PG)   British and Irish Lions XV 25 (2G 2PG 1T)

Australia A: R Graham; M Bartholomeusz, G Bond, N Grey, S Staniforth; M Edmonds, C Whitaker; C Blades, B Cannon, R Moore, T Bowman, J Harrison, D Lyons, R W Williams, P Waugh (*captain*) *Substitutions:* J Holbeck (ACT) for Graham (25 mins); S Payne (NSW) for Whitaker (59 mins); P Noriega (NSW) for Blades (62 mins); J West (NSW) for Bowman (65 mins); P Ryan (ACT) for Williams (70 mins); T Murphy (ACT) for Cannon (74 mins)

Scorers *Try:* Staniforth *Conversion:* Edmonds *Penalty Goal:* Edmonds (7)

British and Irish Lions XV: M Perry; B Cohen, W Greenwood, M Catt, J Robinson; N Jenkins, A Healey; J Leonard, R McBryde, D Young (*captain*), S Murray, M O'Kelly, L Dallaglio, S Quinnell, M Williams *Substitutions:* C Charvis for Quinnell (35-43 mins); M Taylor for Catt (45 mins); J Davidson and G Bulloch for O'Kelly and McBryde (53 mins); M Dawson for Jenkins (60 mins); D Morris for Young (63 mins)

Scorers *Tries:* M Taylor, Perry, Robinson *Conversions:* Dawson (2) *Penalty Goals:* Jenkins (2)

Referee P G Honiss (New Zealand)

23 June, Sydney Football Stadium
NSW Waratahs 24 (2G 2T)   British and Irish Lions XV 41 (5G 2PG)

NSW Waratahs: D McRae; F Cullimore, L Inman, S Harris, S Qau Qau; M Edmonds, S Payne; C Blades, B Cannon, R Moore, J West, T Bowman, S Pinkerton, F Finau, P Waugh (*captain*) *Substitutions:* P Besseling for Bowman (40 mins); D Hickey for Finau (62 mins); R Tombs for Inman (66 mins); P Noriega and E Carter for Moore and Pinkerton (69 mins); J Mutton and L Green for Blades and Harris (73 mins); Pinkerton back for West (temp 83-87 mins)

Scorers *Tries:* Pinkerton, Cullimore, Harris, Edmonds *Conversions:* Edmonds (2)

British and Irish Lions XV: I Balshaw; D James, B O'Driscoll, W Greenwood, J Robinson; J Wilkinson, M Dawson; D Morris, K Wood, P Vickery, M Johnson (*captain*), D Grewcock, L Dallaglio, S Quinnell, N Back *Substitutions:* R O'Gara for Greenwood (22 mins); M Perry for O'Gara (57 mins); T Smith for Vickery (66 mins); R Hill for Back (72 mins); A Healey for Wilkinson (74 mins); R McBryde for Wood (77 mins)

Scores *Tries:* Robinson (2), O'Driscoll, Wilkinson, James *Conversions:* Wilkinson (4), Dawson *Penalty Goals:* Wilkinson (2)

Referee S Young (ARU)

26 June, International Stadium, Coffs Harbour
NSW Country Cockatoos 3 (1PG) British and Irish Lions XV 46 (5G 2PG 1T)

NSW Country Cockatoos: N Croft; V Tailasa, R Macdougal, K Shepherd, W Crosby; C Doyle, R Petty; A Baldwin, J McCormack, M Bowman, D Lubans, B Wright, B Dale, B Klasen (*captain*), C Taylor *Substitutions:* D Dimmock for Taylor (58 mins); G Refshauge for Wright (60 mins); D Banovich for Macdougal (64 mins); M Brown and J Vaalotu for Shepherd and McCormack (65 mins); D Thomas for Baldwin (70 mins); M Ellis for Doyle (71 mins)

Scorer *Penalty Goal:* Croft

British and Irish Lions XV: Balshaw; B Cohen, M Taylor, S Gibbs, T Howe; N Jenkins, A Healey; J Leonard, G Bulloch, D Young (*captain*), J Davidson, M O'Kelly, C Charvis, M Corry, M Williams *Substitutions:* R O'Gara for Gibbs (temp 49-59 mins); D Wallace for Corry (57 mins); D Morris for Leonard (58 mins); S Murray for O'Kelly (71 mins)

Scorers *Tries:* Cohen (2), Charvis, Gibbs, Healey, Young *Conversions:* Jenkins (5) *Penalty Goals:* Jenkins (2)

Referee G Hinton (ARU)

First Test 30 June, The Gabba, Brisbane
Australia 13 (1PG 2T) British/Irish Isles 29 (3G 1PG 1T)

So often a match does not live up to expectations. This one did. There was a cracking atmosphere at the Gabba, staging a Lions Test match for the first time in 51 years, as 20,000 British and Irish fans made their presence felt. The team showed its colours too, and in devastating fashion. Within four minutes of the start, Jason Robinson had left Wallaby full-back, Chris Latham, grasping at thin air as he skated to the line. It was the beginning of a triumphant night for the Lions as they took the world champions apart.

They were sharper in thought and slicker in deed. The final margin of victory might have been even greater. Wallaby scrum-half George Gregan was lucky not to be yellow-carded when he kicked the ball out of an advancing Lions scrum in the 15th minute. Andrew Walker got the Wallabies on the scoreboard five minutes later with a penalty goal. Lions wing, Dafydd James, touched down in the 39th minute after a darting blindside break by Brian O'Driscoll had pierced the Australian defence.

Just 55 seconds after the second-half restart, O'Driscoll had no need of any assistance, his break from half-way splitting the Wallabies wide open. A final sidestep left Matt Burke on his backside. It was a sensational try. 11 minutes later a sharp burst from Rob Henderson did the initial damage from where Scott Quinnell was able to pick up and drive over. Wilkinson's conversion made it 29-3. The Lions lost concentration in the closing stages as first Martin Corry then Phil Vickery were sin-binned. The Wallabies took advantage of Corry's absence to score two tries through Walker and Nathan Grey. The tries were scant consolation for a real hiding.

Australia: C E Latham; A M Walker, D J Herbert, N P Grey, J W C Roff; S J Larkham, G M Gregan; N B Stiles, J A Paul, G M Panoho, D T Giffin, J A Eales (*captain*), O D A Finegan, R S T Kefu, G B Smith *Substitutions:* M C Burke for Latham (40 mins); M A Foley and E J Flatley for Paul and Larkham (52 mins); B J Darwin for Panoho (61 mins); M J Cockbain for Eales (65 mins); D J Lyons for Finegan (72 mins)

Scorers *Tries:* Walker, Grey *Penalty Goal:* Walker

British/Irish Isles: M B Perry; D R James, B G O'Driscoll, R A J Henderson, J Robinson; J P Wilkinson, R Howley; T J Smith, K G M Wood, P J Vickery, M O Johnson (*captain*), D J Grewcock, M E Corry, L S Quinnell, R A Hill *Substitutions:* I Balshaw for Perry (40 mins); C Charvis for Quinnell (61 mins); G Bulloch for Wood (temp 65 to 72 mins); J Leonard for Smith (72 mins)

Scorers *Tries:* Robinson, James, O'Driscoll, Quinnell *Conversions:* Wilkinson (3) *Penalty Goal:* Wilkinson

Referee A Watson (South Africa)

3 July, Bruce Stadium, Canberra
ACT Brumbies 28 (2G 3PG 1T)   British & Irish Lions 30 (3G 3PG)

ACT Brumbies: M Bartholomeusz; D McInally, G Bond, J Holbeck, W Gordon; P Howard, T Hall; A Scott, A Freier, M Weaver, J Harrison, D Vickerman, D Tuavii, R W Williams (*captain*), P Ryan *Substitutions:* D Pusey for Vickerman (47 mins); R Samo for Williams (52 mins); C Pither for Gordon (71 mins); J Huxley for Holbeck (79 mins)

Scorers *Tries:* Bartholomeusz, Gordon, Tuavii *Conversions:* Hall (2) *Penalty Goals:* Hall (3)

British and Irish Lions XV: I Balshaw; B Cohen, M Taylor, S Gibbs, A Healey; R O'Gara, M Dawson; D Morris, D West, D Young (*captain*), S Murray, J Davidson, D Wallace, M Corry, M Williams *Substitutions:* D James for Taylor (temp 17 to 23 mins); J Leonard for Young (71 mins)

Scorers *Tries:* Healey (2), Wallace *Conversions:* Dawson (3) *Penalty Goals:* Dawson (3)

Referee P L Marshall (ARU)

Second Test 7 July, Colonial Stadium, Melbourne
Australia 35 (1G 6PG 2T)   British/Irish Isles 14 (3PG 1T)

The roof was closed at the Colonial Stadium in Melbourne and a record crowd of 56,605 (some achievement when capacity is supposed to be 55,000) gave full vent to their feelings throughout another absorbing match. Quite how the Lions let slip their position of relative dominance at half-time will haunt them for years to come. But slip it did and in extraordinary fashion.

The Lions led 11-6 at the interval and might have been even further ahead had they managed to put away a couple of gilt-edged openings. Wing Dafydd James spurned one in just the fourth minute when he failed to spot the support runners to his right after making terrific yardage up through the middle of the field. The Lions did not let that early lapse put them off their stride. In the 27th minute they got their reward for a sustained period of pressure. Brian O'Driscoll retrieved his chip ahead with a flying take. From there the Lions worked themselves to the other side of the field, won a lineout and drove hard for the line, Neil Back (restored after missing the first Test through injury) getting the touchdown. Earlier Jonny Wilkinson had kicked two penalties to one from Matt Burke.

The Lions' sense of well-being was completely shattered within nine minutes of the restart. Joe Roff had intercepted a rushed pass from Wilkinson to score within 32 seconds. Eight minutes later the initial damage was done by the Wallaby forward pack who caught the Lions off-balance and turned over their scrum ball. John Eales drove forward for Roff to yet again finish it off. The Lions were holed beneath the plumb line. Wilkinson got a penalty back in the 59th minute but a 65th minute try from Burke and three subsequent penalties saw the Wallabies to a record score.

Australia: M C Burke; A M Walker, D J Herbert, N P Grey, J W C Roff; S J Larkham, G M Gregan; N B Stiles, M A Foley, R S Moore, D T Giffin, J A Eales (*captain*), O D A Finegan, R S T Kefu, G B Smith *Substitutions:* M J Cockbain for Giffin (tcmp 38 to 40 mins and 72 mins); C E Latham for Walker (47 mins); E J Flatley for Larkham (82 mins); B J Cannon for Foley (88 mins)

Scorers *Tries:* Roff (2), Burke *Conversion:* Burke *Penalty Goals:* Burke (6)

British/Irish Isles: M B Perry; D R James, B G O'Driscoll, R A J Henderson, J Robinson; J P Wilkinson, R Howley; T J Smith, K G M Wood, P J Vickery, M O Johnson (*captain*), D J Grewcock, R A Hill, L S Quinnell, N A Back *Substitutions:* M E Corry for Hill (temp 38-40 mins and from 40 mins); I R Balshaw for Perry (53 mins); J Leonard for Vickery (63 mins); N R Jenkins for Wilkinson (73 mins); M J S Dawson for Howley (85 mins)

Scorers *Try:* Back *Penalty Goals:* Wilkinson (3)

Referee J I Kaplan (South Africa)

Third Test 14 July, Stadium Australia, Sydney
Australia 29 (2G 5PG)   British/Irish Isles 23 (2G 3PG)

The Lions tottered to the finishing line, deservedly beaten at the dip by a sharper, more composed side. Their tour finished as it began with the management shuffling personnel to cover for injury. Austin Healey, chosen at wing, was forced to pull out with a bulging disc on the morning of the game. He was replaced by Dafydd James with the Lions having to bump Mark Taylor from the bench to accommodate an emergency call-up, Scotland scrum-half Andy Nicol.

The Wallabies also had injury problems, Elton Flatley replacing fly-half Stephen Larkham and Brumbies lock, Justin Harrison, coming in for his first cap for David Giffin. The Wallabies had the better of the enforced changes. Harrison capped a splendid debut by claiming a decisive lineout ball from the Lions just minutes from the end. A try then and the Lions might well have been claiming an historic victory.

The mood as much as the scoreline of the match ebbed and flowed. Just as it seemed that the Wallabies were laying solid foundations with three Burke penalties, the Lions hit back with the opening try in the 20th minute, Jason Robinson touching down in the corner after a good scrum position. The Wallabies came back into it with the first of two tries from Daniel Herbert in the 40th minute, Harrison triggering the move with a well-judged take at a 22 restart. Wilkinson's second penalty of the evening brought the scores to 16-13 in favour of the Wallabies at half-time.

The Lions were back in the driving seat within three minutes, Wilkinson skipping past Toutai Kefu. Back came Australia, Herbert landing his second try in the 50th minute after good work by Nathan Grey and Kefu. He was then yellow-carded for a high tackle on Brian O'Driscoll. Wilkinson kicked the penalty to tie the scores at 23-23 with 52 minutes gone. But that was as good as it got for the Lions. Burke landed two more goals. One last-gasp attack for the Lions just foundered when the pass to Iain Balshaw did not go to hand.

Australia: M C Burke; A M Walker, D J Herbert, N P Grey, J W C Roff; E J Flatley, G M Gregan; N B Stiles, M A Foley, R S Moore, J B G Harrison, J A Eales (*captain*), O D A Finegan, R S T Kefu, G B Smith *Substitutions:* M J Cockbain for Finegan (74 mins); J C Holbeck for Grey (79 mins)

Scorers *Tries:* Herbert (2) *Conversions:* Burke (2) *Penalty Goals:* Burke (5)

British/Irish Isles: M B Perry; D R James, B G O'Driscoll, R A J Henderson, J Robinson; J P Wilkinson, M J S Dawson; T J Smith, K G M Wood, P J Vickery, M O Johnson (*captain*), D J Grewcock, M E Corry, L S Quinnell, N A Back *Substitutions:* C L Charvis for Quinnell (40 mins); I R Balshaw and D R Morris for James and Smith (74 mins)

Scorers *Tries:* Robinson, Wilkinson *Conversions:* Wilkinson (2) *Penalty Goals:* Wilkinson (3)

Referee P D O'Brien (New Zealand)

BRITISH/IRISH ISLES INTERNATIONAL PLAYERS

(up to 20 October 2001)

From 1891 onwards. (*Uncapped when first selected to play in a Test match for the British Isles.)

Aarvold, C D (Cambridge U, Blackheath and England) 1930 NZ 1,2,3,4, A
Ackerman, R A (London Welsh and Wales) 1983 NZ 1,4 (R)
Ackford, P J (Harlequins and England) 1989 A 1,2,3
Adamson, C Y (Durham) 1899 A 1,2,3,4
Alexander, R (NIFC and Ireland) 1938 SA 1,2,3
Andrew, C R (Wasps and England) 1989 A 2,3, 1993 NZ 1,2,3
Arneil, R J (Edinburgh Acads and Scotland) 1968 SA 1,2,3,4
Archer, H A (Guy's H and *England) 1908 NZ 1,2,3
Ashcroft, A (Waterloo and England) 1959 A 1, NZ 2
Aston, R L (Cambridge U and England) 1891 SA 1,2,3
Ayre – Smith, A (Guy's H) 1899 A 1,2,3,4

Back, N A (Leicester and England) 1997 SA 2(R),3, 2001 A 2,3
Bainbridge, S J (Gosforth and England) 1983 NZ 3,4
Baird, G R T (Kelso and Scotland) 1983 NZ 1,2,3,4
Baker, A M (Newport and Wales) 1910 SA 3
Baker, D G S (Old Merchant Taylors' and England) 1955 SA 3,4
Balshaw, I R (Bath and England) 2001 A 1(R),2(R),3(R)
Bassett, J (Penarth and Wales) 1930 NZ 1,2,3,4, A
Bateman, A G (Richmond and Wales) 1997 SA 3(R)
Bayfield, M C (Northampton and England) 1993 NZ 1,2,3
Beamish, G R (Leicester, RAF and Ireland) 1930 NZ 1,2,3,4, A
Beattie, J R (Glasgow Acads and Scotland) 1983 NZ 2(R)
Beaumont, W B (Fylde and England) 1977 NZ 2,3,4, 1980 SA 1,2,3,4
Bebb, D I E (Swansea and Wales) 1962 SA 2,3, 1966 A 1,2, NZ 1,2,3,4
Bedell-Sivright, D R (Cambridge U and Scotland) 1904 A 1
Bell, S P (Cambridge U) 1896 SA 2,3,4
Belson, F C (Bath) 1899 A 1
Bennett, P (Llanelli and Wales) 1974 SA 1,2,3,4, 1977 NZ 1,2,3,4
Bentley, J (Newcastle and England) 1997 SA 2,3
Bevan, J C (Cardiff Coll of Ed, Cardiff and Wales) 1971 NZ 1
Bevan, T S (Swansea and Wales) 1904 A 1,2,3, NZ
Black, A W (Edinburgh U and Scotland) 1950 NZ 1,2
Black, B H (Oxford U, Blackheath and England) 1930 NZ 1,2,3,4, A
Blakiston, A F (Northampton and England) 1924 SA 1,2,3,4
Bowcott, H M (Cambridge U, Cardiff and Wales) 1930 NZ 1,2,3,4, A
Boyd, C A (Dublin U and *Ireland) 1896 SA 1
Boyle, C V (Dublin U and Ireland) 1938 SA 2,3
Brand, T N (NIFC and *Ireland) 1924 SA 1,2
Bresnihan, F P K (UC Dublin and Ireland) 1968 SA 1,2,4
Bromet, E (Cambridge U) 1891 SA 2,3
Bromet, W E (Oxford U and England) 1891 SA 1,2,3
Brophy, N H (UC Dublin and Ireland) 1962 SA 1,4
Brown, G L (W of Scotland and Scotland) 1971 NZ 3,4, 1974 SA 1,2,3, 1977 NZ 2,3,4
Bucher, A M (Edinburgh A and Scotland) 1899 A 1,3,4
Budge, G M (Edinburgh Wands and Scotland) 1950 NZ 4
Bulger, L Q (Lansdowne and Ireland) 1896 SA 1,2,3,4
Bulloch, G C (Glasgow and Scotland) 2001 A 1(t)
Burcher, D H (Newport and Wales) 1977 NZ 3
Burnell, A P (London Scottish and Scotland) 1993 NZ 1
Bush, P F (Cardiff and *Wales) 1904 A 1,2,3, NZ
Butterfield, J (Northampton and England) 1955 SA 1,2,3,4
Byrne, J F (Moseley and England) 1896 SA 1,2,3,4

Calder, F (Stewart's-Melville FP and Scotland) 1989 A 1,2,3
Calder, J H (Stewart's-Melville FP and Scotland) 1983 NZ 3
Cameron, A (Glasgow HSFP and Scotland) 1955 SA 1,2
Campbell, S O (Old Belvedere and Ireland) 1980 SA 2(R),3,4, 1983 NZ 1,2,3,4

Campbell-Lamerton, M J (Halifax, Army and Scotland) 1962 SA 1,2,3,4, 1966 A 1,2, NZ 1,3
Carey, W J (Oxford U) 1896 SA 1,2,3,4
Carleton, J (Orrell and England) 1980 SA 1,2,4, 1983 NZ 2,3,4
Carling, W D C (Harlequins and England) 1993 NZ 1
Catt, M J (Bath and England) 1997 SA 3
Cave, W T C (Cambridge U and *England) 1903 SA 1,2,3
Chalmers, C M (Melrose and Scotland) 1989 A 1
Chapman, F E (Westoe, W Hartlepool and *England) 1908 NZ 3
Charvis, C L (Swansea and Wales) 2001 A 1(R),3(R)
Clarke, B B (Bath and England) 1993 NZ 1,2,3
Clauss, P R A (Oxford U and Scotland) 1891 SA 1,2,3
Cleaver, W B (Cardiff and Wales) 1950 NZ 1,2,3
Clifford, T (Young Munster and Ireland) 1950 NZ 1,2,3, A 1,2
Clinch, A D (Dublin U and Ireland) 1896 SA 1,2,3,4
Cobner, T J (Pontypool and Wales) 1977 NZ 1,2,3
Colclough, M J (Angoulême and England) 1980 SA 1,2,3,4, 1983 NZ 1,2,3,4
Collett, G F (Cheltenham) 1903 SA 1,2,3
Connell, G C (Trinity Acads and Scotland) 1968 SA 4
Cookson, G (Manchester) 1899 A 1,2,3,4
Corry, M E (Leicester and England) 2001 A 1,2(t+R),3
Cotton, F E (Loughborough Colls, Coventry and England) 1974 SA 1,2,3,4, 1977 NZ 2,3,4
Coulman, M J (Moseley and England) 1968 SA 3
Cove-Smith, R (Old Merchant Taylors' and England) 1924 SA 1,2,3,4
Cowan, R C (Selkirk and Scotland) 1962 SA 4
Crean, T J (Wanderers and Ireland) 1896 SA 1,2,3,4
Cromey, G E (Queen's U, Belfast and Ireland) 1938 SA 3
Crowther, S N (Lennox) 1904 A 1,2,3, NZ
Cunningham, W A (Lansdowne and Ireland) 1924 SA 3

Dallaglio, L B N (Wasps and England) 1997 SA 1,2,3
Dancer, G T (Bedford) 1938 SA 1,2,3
Davey, J (Redruth and England) 1908 NZ 1
Davidson, I G (NIFC and Ireland) 1903 SA 1
Davidson, J W (London Irish and Ireland) 1997 SA 1,2,3
Davies, C (Cardiff and Wales) 1950 NZ 4
Davies, D M (Somerset Police and Wales) 1950 NZ 3,4, A 1
Davies, D S (Hawick and Scotland) 1924 SA 1,2,3,4
Davies, H J (Newport and Wales) 1924 SA 2
Davies, T G R (Cardiff, London Welsh and Wales) 1968 SA 3, 1971 NZ 1,2,3,4
Davies, T J (Llanelli and Wales) 1959 NZ 2,4
Davies, T M (London Welsh, Swansea and Wales) 1971 NZ 1,2,3,4, 1974 SA 1,2,3,4
Davies, W G (Cardiff and Wales) 1980 SA 2
Davies, W P C (Harlequins and England) 1955 SA 1,2,3
Dawes, S J (London Welsh and Wales) 1971 NZ 1,2,3,4
Dawson, A R (Wanderers and Ireland) 1959 A 1,2, NZ 1,2,3,4
Dawson, M J S (Northampton and England) 1997 SA 1,2,3, 2001 A 2(R),3
Dibble, R (Bridgwater A and England) 1908 NZ 1,2,3
Dixon, P J (Harlequins and England) 1971 NZ 1,2,4
Dobson, D D (Oxford U and England) 1904 A 1,2,3, NZ
Dodge, P W (Leicester and England) 1980 SA 3,4
Dooley, W A (Preston Grasshoppers and England) 1989 A 2,3
Doran, G P (Lansdowne and Ireland) 1899 A 1,2
Down, P J (Bristol and *England) 1908 NZ 1,2,3
Doyle, M G (Blackrock Coll and Ireland) 1968 SA 1
Drysdale, D (Heriot's FP and Scotland) 1924 SA 1,2,3,4
Duckham, D J (Coventry and England) 1971 NZ 2,3,4
Duggan, W P (Blackrock Coll and Ireland) 1977 NZ 1,2,3,4
Duff, P L (Glasgow Acads and Scotland) 1938 SA 2,3

Edwards, G O (Cardiff and Wales) 1968 *SA* 1,2, 1971 *NZ* 1,2,3,4, 1974 *SA* 1,2,3,4
Edwards, R W (Malone and Ireland) 1904 *A* 2,3, *NZ*
Evans, G (Maesteg and Wales) 1983 *NZ* 3,4
Evans, G L (Newport and Wales) 1977 *NZ* 2,3,4
Evans, I C (Llanelli and Wales) 1989 *A* 1,2,3, 1993 *NZ* 1,2,3, 1997 *SA* 1
Evans, R T (Newport and Wales) 1950 *NZ* 1,2,3,4, *A* 1,2
Evans, T P (Swansea and Wales) 1977 *NZ* 1
Evans, W R (Cardiff and Wales) 1959 *A* 2, *NZ* 1,2,3
Evers, G V (Moseley) 1899 *A* 2,3,4

Farrell, J L (Bective Rangers and Ireland) 1930 *NZ* 1,2,3,4, *A*
Faull, J (Swansea and Wales) 1959 *A* 1, *NZ* 1,3,4
Fenwick, S P (Bridgend and Wales) 1977 *NZ* 1,2,3,4
Fitzgerald, C F (St Mary's Coll and Ireland) 1983 *NZ* 1,2,3,4
Foster, A R (Queen's U, Belfast and Ireland) 1910 *SA* 1,2
Francombe, J S (Manchester) 1899 *A* 1

Gabe, R T (Cardiff and Wales) 1904 *A* 1,2,3, *NZ*
Gibbs, I S (Swansea and Wales) 1993 *NZ* 2,3, 1997 *SA* 1,2,3
Gibbs, R A (Cardiff and Wales) 1908 *NZ* 1,2
Gibson, C M H (Cambridge U, NIFC and Ireland) 1966 *NZ* 1,2,3,4, 1968 *SA* 1(R),2,3,4, 1971 *NZ* 1,2,3,4
Gibson, G R (Northern and England) 1899 *A* 1,2,3,4
Gibson, T A (Cambridge U and *England) 1903 *SA* 1,2,3
Giles, J L (Coventry and England) 1938 *SA* 1,3
Gillespie, J I (Edinburgh A and Scotland) 1903 *SA* 1,2,3
Gould, J H (Old Leysians) 1891 *SA* 1,2
Gravell, R W R (Llanelli and Wales) 1980 *SA* 1(R),2,3,4
Graves, C R A (Wanderers and Ireland) 1938 *SA* 1,3
Gray, H G S (Scottish Trials) 1899 *A* 1,2
Greenwood, J T (Dunfermline and Scotland) 1955 *SA* 1,2,3,4
Greig, L L (US and *Scotland) 1903 *SA* 1,2,3
Grewcock, D J (Bath and England) 2001 *A* 1,2,3
Grieve, C F (Oxford U and Scotland) 1938 *SA* 2,3
Griffiths, G M (Cardiff and Wales) 1955 *SA* 2,3,4
Griffiths, V M (Newport and Wales) 1924 *SA* 3,4
Guscott, J C (Bath and England) 1989 *A* 2,3, 1993 *NZ* 1,2,3, 1997 *SA* 1,2,3

Hall, M R (Bridgend and Wales) 1989 *A* 1
Hammond, J (Cambridge U, Blackheath) 1891 *SA* 1,2,3, 1896 *SA* 2,4
Hancock, P F (Blackheath and England) 1891 *SA* 1,2,3, 1896 *SA* 1,2,3,4
Hancock, P S (Richmond and *England) 1903 *SA* 1,2,3
Handford, F G (Manchester and England) 1910 *SA* 1,2,3
Harding, A F (London Welsh and Wales) 1904 *A* 1,2,3, *NZ*, 1908 *NZ* 1,2,3
Harding, W R (Cambridge U, Swansea and Wales) 1924 *SA* 2,3,4
Harris, S W (Blackheath and England) 1924 *SA* 3,4
Harrison, E M (Guy's H) 1903 *SA* 1
Hastings, A G (London Scottish, Watsonians and Scotland) 1989 *A* 1,2,3, 1993 *NZ* 1,2,3
Hastings, S (Watsonians and Scotland) 1989 *A* 2,3
Hay, B H (Boroughmuir and Scotland) 1980 *SA* 2,3,4
Hayward, D J (Newbridge and Wales) 1950 *NZ* 1,2,3
Healey, A S (Leicester and England) 1997 *SA* 2(R),3(R)
Henderson, N J (Queen's U, Belfast, NIFC and Ireland) 1950 *NZ* 3
Henderson, R A J (Wasps and Ireland) 2001 *A* 1,2,3
Henderson, R G (Northern and Scotland) 1924 *SA* 3,4
Hendrie, K G P (Heriot's FP and Scotland) 1924 *SA* 2
Hewitt, D (Queen's U, Belfast, Instonians and Ireland) 1959 *A* 1,2, *NZ* 1,3,4, 1962 *SA* 4
Higgins, R (Liverpool and England) 1955 *SA* 1
Hill, R A (Saracens and England) 1997 *SA* 1,2, 2001 *A* 1,2
Hind, G R (Guy's H and *England) 1908 *NZ* 2,3
Hinshelwood, A J W (London Scottish and Scotland) 1966 *NZ* 2,4, 1968 *SA* 2
Hodgson, J McD (Northern and *England) 1930 *NZ* 1,3
Holmes, T D (Cardiff and Wales) 1983 *NZ* 1
Hopkins, R (Maesteg and Wales) 1971 *NZ* 1(R)
Horrocks-Taylor, J P (Leicester and England) 1959 *NZ* 3
Horton, A L (Blackheath and England) 1968 *SA* 2,3,4
Howard, W G (Old Birkonians) 1938 *SA* 1
Howie, R A (Kirkcaldy and Scotland) 1924 *SA* 1,2,3,4
Howley, R (Cardiff and Wales) 2001 *A* 1,2
Hulme, F C (Birkenhead Park and England) 1904 *A* 1

Irvine, A R (Heriot's FP and Scotland) 1974 *SA* 3,4, 1977 *NZ* 1,2,3,4, 1980 *SA* 2,3,4
Irwin, D G (Instonians and Ireland) 1983 *NZ* 1,2,4
Isherwood, G A M (Old Alleynians, Sale) 1910 *SA* 1,2,3

Jackett, E J (Falmouth, Leicester and England) 1908 *NZ* 1,2,3
Jackson, F S (Leicester) 1908 *NZ* 1
Jackson, P B (Coventry and England) 1959 *A* 1,2, *NZ* 1,3,4
James, D R (Llanelli and Wales) 2001 *A* 1,2,3
Jarman, H (Newport and Wales) 1910 *SA* 1,2,3
Jarman, J W (Bristol and *England) 1899 *A* 1,2,3,4
Jeeps, R E G (Northampton and *England) 1955 *SA* 1,2,3,4, 1959 *A* 1,2, *NZ* 1,2,3, 1962 *SA* 1,2,3,4
Jenkins, N R (Pontypridd, Cardiff and Wales) 1997 *SA* 1,2,3, 2001 *A* 2(R)
Jenkins, V G J (Oxford U, London Welsh and Wales) 1938 *SA* 1
John, B (Cardiff and Wales) 1968 *SA* 1, 1971 *NZ* 1,2,3,4
John, E R (Neath and Wales) 1950 *NZ* 1,2,3,4, *A* 1,2
Johnson, M O (Leicester and England) 1993 *NZ* 2,3, 1997 *SA* 1,2,3, 2001 *A* 1,2,3
Johnston, R (Wanderers and Ireland) 1896 *SA* 1,2,3
Jones, B L (Devonport Services, Llanelli and Wales) 1950 *NZ* 4, *A* 1,2
Jones, D K (Llanelli, Cardiff and Wales) 1962 *SA* 1,2,3, 1966 *A* 1,2, *NZ* 1
Jones, E L (Llanelli and *Wales) 1938 *SA* 1,3
Jones, Ivor (Llanelli and Wales) 1930 *NZ* 1,2,3,4, *A*
Jones, J P (Newport and Wales) 1908 *NZ* 1,2,3, 1910 *SA* 1,2,3
Jones, J P "Tuan" (Guy's H and *Wales) 1908 *NZ* 2,3
Jones, K D (Cardiff and Wales) 1962 *SA* 1,2,3,4
Jones, K J (Newport and Wales) 1950 *NZ* 1,2,4
Jones, R N (Swansea and Wales) 1989 *A* 1,2,3
Jones, S T (Pontypool and Wales) 1983 *NZ* 2,3,4
Judkins, W (Coventry) 1899 *A* 2,3,4

Keane, M I (Lansdowne and Ireland) 1977 *NZ* 1
Kennedy, K W (CIYMS, London Irish and Ireland) 1966 *A* 1,2, *NZ* 1,4
Kiernan, M J (Dolphin and Ireland) 1983 *NZ* 2,3,4
Kiernan, T J (Cork Const and Ireland) 1962 *SA* 3, 1968 *SA*, 1,2,3,4
Kininmonth, P W (Oxford U, Richmond and Scotland) 1950 *NZ* 1,2,4
Kinnear, R M (Heriot's FP and *Scotland) 1924 *SA* 1,2,3,4
Kyle, J W (Queen's U, Belfast, NIFC and Ireland) 1950 *NZ* 1,2,3,4, *A* 1,2
Kyrke, G V (Marlborough N) 1908 *NZ* 1

Laidlaw, F A L (Melrose and Scotland) 1966 *NZ* 2,3
Laidlaw, R J (Jedforest and Scotland) 1983 *NZ* 1(R),2,3,4
Lamont, R A (Instonians and Ireland) 1966 *NZ* 1,2,3,4
Lane, M F (UC Cork and Ireland) 1950 *NZ* 4, *A* 2
Larter, P J (Northampton, RAF and England) 1968 *SA* 2
Laxon, H (Cambredge U) 1908 *NZ* 1
Leonard, J (Harlequins and England) 1993 *NZ* 2,3, 1997 *SA* 1(R), 2001 *A* 1(R),2(R)
Lewis, A R (Abertillery and Wales) 1966 *NZ* 2,3,4
Llewellyn, W (Llwynypia, Newport and Wales) 1904 *A* 1,2,3, *NZ*
Lynch, J F (St Mary's Coll and Ireland) 1971 *NZ* 1,2,3,4

McBride, W J (Ballymena and Ireland) 1962 *SA* 3,4, 1966 *NZ* 2,3,4, 1968 *SA* 1,2,3,4, 1971 *NZ* 1,2,3,4, 1974 *SA* 1,2,3,4
Macdonald, R (Edinburgh U and Scotland) 1950 *NZ* 1, *A* 2
McEvedy, P F (Guy's H) 1904 *A* 2,3, *NZ*, 1908 *NZ* 2,3
McFadyean, C W (Moseley and England) 1966 *NZ* 1,2,3,4
McGeechan, I R (Headingley and Scotland) 1974 *SA* 1,2,3,4, 1977 *NZ* 1,2,3(R),4
McGown, T M W (NIFC and Ireland) 1899 *A* 1,2,3,4
McKay, J W (Queen's U, Belfast and Ireland) 1950 *NZ* 1,2,3,4, *A* 1,2
McKibbin, H R (Queen's U, Belfast and Ireland) 1938 *SA* 1,2,3
Mackie, O G (Wakefield T and *England) 1896 *SA* 1,2,3,4
Maclagan, W E (London Scottish and Scotland) 1891 *SA* 1,2,3
McLauchlan, J (Jordanhill and Scotland) 1971 *NZ* 1,2,3,4, 1974 *SA* 1,2,3,4
McLeod, H F (Hawick and Scotland) 1959 *A* 1,2, *NZ* 1,2,3,4

Smith, T W (Leicester) 1908 *NZ* 2,3
Smyth, R S (Dublin U and Ireland) 1903 *SA* 1,2,3
Smyth, T (Malone, Newport and Ireland) 1910 *SA* 2,3
Sole, D M B (Edinburgh Acads and Scotland) 1989 *A* 1,2,3
Spong, R S (Old Millhillians and England) 1930 *NZ* 1,2,3,4, *A*
Spoors, J A (Bristol) 1910 *SA* 1,2,3
Squire, J (Newport, Pontypool and Wales) 1977 *NZ* 4, 1980 *SA* 1,2,3,4, 1983 *NZ* 1
Squires, P J (Harrogate and England) 1977 *NZ* 1
Stagg, P K (Oxford U, Sale and Scotland) 1968 *SA* 1,3,4
Stanger-Leathes, C F (Northern and *England) 1904 *A* 1
Steele, W C C (Bedford, RAF and Scotland) 1974 *SA* 1,2
Stephens, I (Bridgend and Wales) 1983 *NZ* 1
Stephens, J R G (Neath and Wales) 1950 *A* 1,2
Stevenson, R C (St Andrew's U and Scotland) 1910 *SA* 1,2,3
Stimpson, T R G (Newcastle and England) 1997 *SA* 3(R)
Stout, F M (Gloucester and England) 1899 *A* 1,2,3,4, 1903 *SA* 1,2,3
Surtees, A A (Cambridge U) 1891 *SA* 1,2,3
Swannell, B I (Northampton and *Australia) 1899 *A* 2,3,4, 1904 *A* 1,2,3, *NZ*

Tait, A V (Newcastle and Scotland) 1997 *SA* 1,2
Tanner, H (Swansea and Wales) 1938 *SA* 2
Taylor, A R (Cross Keys and Wales) 1938 *SA* 1,2
Taylor, J (London Welsh and Wales) 1971 *NZ* 1,2,3,4
Taylor, R B (Northampton and England) 1968 *SA* 1,2,3,4
Teague, M C (Gloucester, Moseley and England) 1989 *A* 2,3, 1993 *NZ* 2(t)
Tedford, A (Malone and Ireland) 1903 *SA* 1,2,3
Telfer, J W (Melrose and Scotland) 1966 *A* 1,2, *NZ* 1,2,4, 1968 *SA* 2,3,4
Thomas, M C (Devonport Services, Newport and Wales) 1950 *NZ* 2,3, *A* 1, 1959 *NZ* 2
Thomas, R C C (Swansea and Wales) 1955 *SA* 3,4
Thomas, W D (Llanelli and *Wales) 1966 *NZ* 2,3, 1968 *SA* 3(R),4, 1971 *NZ* 1,2,4 (R)
Thompson, C E K (Lancashire) 1899 *A* 2,3,4
Thompson, R (Cambridge U) 1891 *SA* 1,2,3
Thompson, R H (Instonians, London Irish and Ireland) 1955 *SA* 1,2,4
Timms, A B (Edinburgh U and Scotland) 1899 *A* 2,3,4
Todd, A F (Blackheath and *England) 1896 *SA* 1,2,3,4
Townsend, G P J (Northampton and Scotland) 1997 *SA* 1,2
Trail, D H (Guy's H) 1904 *A* 1,2,3, *NZ*
Travers, W H (Newport and Wales) 1938 *SA* 2,3
Tucker, C C (Shannon and Ireland) 1980 *SA* 3,4
Turner, J W C (Gala and Scotland) 1968 *SA* 1,2,3,4

Underwood, R (RAF, Leicester and England) 1989 *A* 1,2,3, 1993 *NZ* 1,2,3
Underwood, T (Newcastle and England) 1997 *SA* 3
Unwin, E J (Rosslyn Park, Army and England) 1938 *SA* 1,2
Uttley, R M (Gosforth and England) 1974 *SA* 1,2,3,4

Vassall, H H (Blackheath and England) 1908 *NZ* 1,2,3
Vickery, P J (Gloucester and England) 2001 *A* 1,2,3
Vile, T H (Newport and *Wales) 1904 *A* 2,3, *NZ*
Voyce, A T (Gloucester and England) 1924 *SA* 3,4

Waddell, G H (Cambridge U, London Scottish and Scotland) 1962 *SA* 1,2
Waddell, H (Glasgow Acads and Scotland) 1924 *SA* 1,2,4
Wainwright, R I (Watsonians and Scotland) 1997 *SA* 3
Walker, E F (Lennox) 1903 *SA* 2,3
Walker, S (Instonians and Ireland) 1938 *SA* 1,2,3
Wallace, Jos (Wanderers and Ireland) 1903 *SA* 1,2,3
Wallace, P S (Saracens and Ireland) 1997 *SA* 1,2,3
Wallace, W (Percy Park) 1924 *SA* 1
Waller, P D (Newport and Wales) 1910 *SA* 1,2,3
Ward, A J P (Garryowen and Ireland) 1980 *SA* 1
Waters, J A (Selkirk and Scotland) 1938 *SA* 3
Watkins, D (Newport and Wales) 1966 *A* 1,2, *NZ* 1,2,3,4
Watkins, S J (Newport and Wales) 1966 *A* 1,2, *NZ* 3
Webb, J (Abertillery and Wales) 1910 *SA* 1,2,3
Welsh, W B (Hawick and Scotland) 1930 *NZ* 4
Weston, M P (Richmond, Durham City and England) 1962 *SA* 1,2,3,4, 1966 *A* 1,2
Wheeler, P J (Leicester and England) 1977 *NZ* 2,3,4, 1980 *SA* 1,2,3,4
White, D B (London Scottish and Scotland) 1989 *A* 1
Whitley, H (Northern and *England) 1924 *SA* 1,3,4
Whittaker, T S (Lancashire) 1891 *SA* 1,2,3
Wilkinson, J P (Newcastle and England) 2001 *A* 1,2,3
Willcox, J G (Oxford U, Harlequins and England) 1962 *SA* 1,2,4
Williams, B L (Cardiff and Wales) 1950 *NZ* 2,3,4, *A* 1,2
Williams, C (Swansea and Wales) 1980 *SA* 1,2,3,4
Williams, D (Ebbw Vale and Wales) 1966 *A* 1,2, *NZ* 1,2,4
Williams, D B (Cardiff and *Wales) 1977 *NZ* 1,2,3
Williams, J F (London Welsh and Wales) 1908 *NZ* 3
Williams, J J (Llanelli and Wales) 1974 *SA* 1,2,3,4, 1977 *NZ* 1,2,3
Williams, J L (Cardiff and Wales) 1908 *NZ* 1,2
Williams, J P R (London Welsh and Wales) 1971 *NZ* 1,2,3,4, 1974 *SA* 1,2,3,4
Williams, R H (Llanelli and Wales) 1955 *SA* 1,2,3,4, 1959 *A* 1,2, *NZ* 1,2,3,4
Williams, S H (Newport and *England) 1910 *SA* 1,2,3
Williams, W O G (Swansea and Wales) 1955 *SA* 1,2,3,4
Willis, W R (Cardiff and Wales) 1950 *NZ* 4, *A* 1,2
Wilson, S (London Scottish and Scotland) 1966 *A* 2, *NZ* 1,2,3,4
Windsor, R W (Pontypool and Wales) 1974 *SA* 1,2,3,4, 1977 *NZ* 1
Winterbottom, P J (Headingley, Harlequins and England) 1983 *NZ* 1,2,3,4, 1993 *NZ*, 1,2,3
Wood, B G M (Garryowen and Ireland) 1959 *NZ* 1,3
Wood, K B (Leicester) 1910 *SA* 1,3
Wood, K G M (Harlequins and Ireland) 1997 *SA* 1,2, 2001 *A* 1,2,3
Woodward, C R (Leicester and England) 1980 *SA* 2,3
Wotherspoon, W (Cambridge U and Scotland) 1891 *SA* 1
Young, A T (Cambridge U, Blackheath and England) 1924 *SA* 2
Young, D (Cardiff and Wales) 1989 *A* 1,2,3
Young, J (Harrogate, RAF and Wales) 1968 *SA* 1
Young, J R C (Oxford U, Harlequins and England) 1959 *NZ* 2
Young, R M (Queen's U, Belfast, Collegians and Ireland) 1966 *A* 1,2, *NZ* 1, 1968 *SA* 3

BRITISH/IRISH ISLES INTERNATIONAL STATISTICS

(up to 20 October 2001)

Match Records

Most Consecutive Test Wins

6 1891 *SA* 1,2,3, 1896 *SA* 1,2,3
3 1899 *A* 2,3,4
3 1904 *A* 1,2,3
3 1950 *A* 1,2, 1955 *SA* 1
3 1974 *SA* 1,2,3

Most Consecutive Tests Without Defeat

Matches	Wins	Draws	Period
6	6	0	1891 to 1896
6	4	2	1971 to 1974

Most Points in a Match
by the team

Pts	Opponents	Venue	Year
31	Australia	Brisbane	1966
29	Australia	Brisbane	2001
28	S Africa	Pretoria	1974
26	S Africa	Port Elizabeth	1974
25	S Africa	Cape Town	1997
24	Australia	Sydney	1950
24	Australia	Sydney	1959

by a player

Pts	Player	Opponents	Venue	Year
18	A J P Ward	S Africa	Cape Town	1980
18	A G Hastings	N Zealand	Christchurch	1993
18	J P Wilkinson	Australia	Sydney	2001
17	T J Kiernan	S Africa	Pretoria	1968
16	B L Jones	Australia	Brisbane	1950

Most Tries in a Match
by the team

Tries	Opponents	Venue	Year
5	Australia	Sydney	1950
5	S Africa	Johannesburg	1955
5	Australia	Sydney	1959
5	Australia	Brisbane	1966
5	S Africa	Pretoria	1974

by a player

Tries	Player	Opponents	Venue	Year
2	A M Bucher	Australia	Sydney	1899
2	W Llewellyn	Australia	Sydney	1904
2	C D Aarvold	N Zealand	Christchurch	1930
2	J E Nelson	Australia	Sydney	1950
2	M J Price	Australia	Sydney	1959
2	M J Price	N Zealand	Dunedin	1959
2	D K Jones	Australia	Brisbane	1966
2	T G R Davies	N Zealand	Christchurch	1971
2	J J Williams	S Africa	Pretoria	1974
2	J J Williams	S Africa	Port Elizabeth	1974

Most Conversions in a Match
by the team

Cons	Opponents	Venue	Year
5	Australia	Brisbane	1966
4	S Africa	Johannesburg	1955
3	Australia	Sydney	1950
3	Australia	Sydney	1959
3	Australia	Brisbane	2001

by a player

Cons	Player	Opponents	Venue	Year
5	S Wilson	Australia	Brisbane	1966
4	A Cameron	S Africa	Johannesburg	1955
3	J P Wilkinson	Australia	Brisbane	2001

Most Penalties in a Match
by the team

Penalties	Opponents	Venue	Year
6	N Zealand	Christchurch	1993
5	S Africa	Pretoria	1968
5	S Africa	Cape Town	1980
5	Australia	Sydney	1989
5	S Africa	Cape Town	1997
5	S Africa	Durban	1997

by a player

Penalties	Player	Opponents	Venue	Year
6	A G Hastings	N Zealand	Christchurch	1993
5	T J Kiernan	S Africa	Pretoria	1968
5	A J P Ward	S Africa	Cape Town	1980
5	A G Hastings	Australia	Sydney	1989
5	N R Jenkins	S Africa	Cape Town	1997
5	N R Jenkins	S Africa	Durban	1997

Most Dropped Goals in a Match
by the team

Drops	Opponents	Venue	Year
2	S Africa	Port Elizabeth	1974

by a player

Drops	Player	Opponents	Venue	Year
2	P Bennett	S Africa	Port Elizabeth	1974

Career Records
Most Capped Players

Caps	Player	Career Span
17	W J McBride	1962 to 1974
13	R E G Jeeps	1955 to 1962
12	C M H Gibson	1966 to 1971
12	G Price	1977 to 1983
10	A J F O'Reilly	1955 to 1959
10	R H Williams	1955 to 1959
10	G O Edwards	1968 to 1974

Most Consecutive Tests

Tests	Player	Span
15	W J McBride	1966 to 1974
12	C M H Gibson	1966 to 1971
12	G Price	1977 to 1983

Most Tests as Captain

Tests	Captain	Span
6	A R Dawson	1959
6	M O Johnson	1997 to 2001

Most Tests in Individual Positions

Position	Player	Tests	Span
Full-back	J P R Williams	8	1971 to 1974
Wing	A J F O'Reilly	9	1955 to 1959
Centre	C M H Gibson	8	1966 to 1971
	J C Guscott	8	1989 to 1997
Fly-half	P Bennett	8	1974 to 1977
Scrum-half	R E G Jeeps	13	1955 to 1962
Prop	G Price	12	1977 to 1983
Hooker	B V Meredith	8	1955 to 1962
Lock	W J McBride	17	1962 to 1974
Flanker	N A A Murphy	8	1959 to 1966
No 8	T M Davies	8	1971 to 1974

Most Points in Tests

Points	Player	Tests	Career
66	A G Hastings	6	1989 to 1993
44	P Bennett	8	1974 to 1977
41	N R Jenkins	4	1997 to 2001
36	J P Wilkinson	3	2001
35	T J Kiernan	5	1962 to 1968
30	S Wilson	5	1966
30	B John	5	1968 to 1971

Most Tries in Tests

Tries	Player	Tests	Career
6	A J F O'Reilly	10	1955 to 1959
5	J J Williams	7	1974 to 1977
4	W Llewellyn	4	1904
4	M J Price	5	1959

Most Conversions in Tests

Cons	Player	Tests	Career
6	S Wilson	5	1966
5	J P Wilkinson	3	2001
4	J F Byrne	4	1896
4	C Y Adamson	4	1899
4	B L Jones	3	1950
4	A Cameron	2	1955

Most Penalty Goals in Tests

Penalties	Player	Tests	Career
20	A G Hastings	6	1989 to 1993
13	N R Jenkins	4	1997 to 2001
11	T J Kiernan	5	1962 to 1968
10	P Bennett	8	1974 to 1977
7	S O Campbell	7	1980 to 1983
7	J P Wilkinson	3	2001

Most Dropped Goals in Tests

Drops	Player	Tests	Career
2	P F Bush	4	1904
2	D Watkins	6	1966
2	B John	5	1968 to 1971
2	P Bennett	8	1974 to 1977
2	C R Andrew	5	1989 to 1993

Series Records

Record	Holder	Detail
Most team points		79 in S Africa 1974
Most team tries		10 in S Africa 1955 & 1974
Most points by player	N R Jenkins	41 in S Africa 1997
Most tries by player	W Llewellyn	4 in Australia 1904
	J J Williams	4 in S Africa 1974

Major Tour Records

Record	Detail	Year	Place
Most team points	842	1959	Australia, NZ & Canada
Most team tries	165	1959	Australia, NZ & Canada
Highest score & biggest win	116–10	2001	v W Australia President's XV
Most individual points	188 by B John	1971	Australia & N Zealand
Most individual tries	22 by A J F O'Reilly	1959	Australia, NZ & Canada
Most points in match	37 by A G B Old	1974 v SW Districts	Mossel Bay, S Africa
Most tries in match	6 by D J Duckham	1971 v W Coast/Buller	Greymouth, N Zealand
	6 by J J Williams	1974 v SW Districts	Mossel Bay, S Africa

Miscellaneous Records

Record	Holder	Detail
Longest Test Career	W J McBride	13 seasons, 1962-1974
Youngest Test Cap	A J F O'Reilly	19 yrs 91 days in 1955
Oldest Test Cap	W J McBride	34 yrs 51 days in 1974

MAJOR TEST TOURS 2000-01

Argentina to England 2000

Tour party

Full-backs: F Contepomi (Bristol), B Stortoni (CASI)

Threequarters: I Corleto (Narbonne), J-N Piossek (Huirapuca, Tucuman), F Soler (Tala, Cordoba), D Giannantonio (La Rochelle), O Bartolucci (Atletico del Rosario), J Orengo (Atletico del Rosario), E Simone (Bristol), D Albanese (Grenoble)

Half-backs: L Arbizu (*captain*) (Begles-Bordeaux), G Quesada (Narbonne), J Fernandez Miranda (Hindu), N Fernandez Miranda (Hindu), A Pichot (Bristol)

Forwards: J Garcia (Cordoba), O Hasan (Agen), M Ledesma (Narbonne), F Mendez (Begles-Bordeaux), M Reggiardo (Castres), R Grau (Dax), L Roldan (BACRC), A Allub (Jockey Club Cordoba), I Fernandez Lobbe (Begles-Bordeaux), R Alvarez (Pucara), G Longo (SIC), R Travaglini (CASI), M Durand (Champagnat), G Ugartemendia (Los Matreros), R Martin (SIC), S Phelan (CASI)

Manager: J-L Rolandi **Assistant:** A Coscia **Coaches:** M Loffreda and D Baetti

Tour Record P 2 W 1 L 1 For 44 Against 26

21 November Won 44-7 v Combined Services (Portsmouth)
25 November Lost 0-19 v ENGLAND (Twickenham)

Details

21 November, United Services Club, Portsmouth
Combined Services 7 (1G)   Argentinian XV 44 (4G 2PG 2T)

Combined Services scorers *Try:* Soper *Conversion:* Cohen

Argentinian XV scorers *Tries:* Ledesma 2, Stortoni 2, Piossek, Alvarez *Conversions:* Giannantonio 3, J Fernandez Miranda *Penalty Goals:* Giannantonio 2

Test Match 25 November, Twickenham
England 19 (1G 3PG 1DG)   Argentina 0

England: I R Balshaw; B C Cohen, M J Tindall, M J Catt, D D Luger; J P Wilkinson, M J S Dawson; J Leonard, M P Regan, J M White, M O Johnson (*captain*), D J Grewcock, R A Hill, L B N Dallaglio, N A Back *Substitutions:* P J Vickery for White (40 mins); D L Flatman for Vickery (temp 50-57 mins); W J H Greenwood for Tindall (57 mins); Flatman for Leonard (69 mins); M E Corry for Hill (74 mins); D E West for Regan (77 mins)

Scorers *Try:* Cohen *Conversion:* Wilkinson Penalty Goals: Wilkinson (3) *Dropped Goal:* Wilkinson

Argentina: F Contepomi; O Bartolucci, J Orengo, L Arbizu (*captain*), I Corleto; G Quesada, A Pichot; R Grau, F Mendez, O Hasan, C I Fernandez Lobbe, A Allub, S Phelan, G Longo, R Martin *Substitution:* G Ugartemendia for Allub (64 mins)

Referee A Lewis (Ireland)

United States to Scotland and Wales 2000

Tour party

Full-backs: A Blom (Denver Barbarians), K Shuman (New York Athletic Club)

Threequarters: C Curtis (Life College, Georgia), M Delai (OMBAC, San Diego), D Fernandez (St Louis Bombers), J Naivalu (San Mateo), M Dunning (Kansas City), P Eloff (Chicago Lions), J Grobler (Denver Barbarians), J Keyter (Roma, Italy)

Half-backs: G Wells (Golden Gate, San Fransisco), L Wilfley (Denver Barbarians), K Dalzell (Montferrand, France), M Timoteo (Hayward Griffins)

Forwards: J Clayton (Old Blues), T Kluempers (Kansas City Blues), P Still (Golden Gate, San Fransisco), J Wood (OMBAC, San Diego), R Flynn (Golden Gate, San Fransisco), R Lehner (Oxford University), K Khasigian (Sydney University, Australia), P Farner (Roma, Italy), L Gross (Roma, Italy), M Kane (Watsonians, Scotland), T Kelleher (Boston), D Hodges (*captain*) (OMBAC, San Diego), D Care (Dallas Harlequins), O Fifita (Hayward Griffins), A Magleby (Gentlemen of Aspen), D Younger (Indianapolis), J Burke (Chicago Lions), D Lyle (Bath, England)

Manager: C Lippert **Coach:** D Hall **Assistant coaches:** T Billups, R Cornbill

Tour record P 5 W 1 L 4 For 76 Against 197

4 November Lost 6-53 v SCOTLAND (Murrayfield)

8 November Lost 17-49 v Scotland Development XV (Aberdeen)

11 November Won 22-7 v Cross Keys

14 November Lost 20-46 v Wales Development XV (Neath)

18 November Lost 11-42 v WALES (Cardiff)

Details

Test Match 4 November, Murrayfield
Scotland 53 (4G 5PG 2T)   United States 6 (2PG)

Scotland: C D Paterson; C A Murray, A J Bulloch, J A Leslie, J F Steel; G P J Townsend, B W Redpath; T J Smith, S J Brotherstone, G Graham, S Murray, S B Grimes, J M Petrie, S M Taylor, A C Pountney (*captain*) *Substitutions:* S Scott for Brotherstone (temp 37 to 40 mins and 64 mins); G R McIlwham for Graham (57 mins); J P R White for Petrie (64 mins); C A Joiner for C Murray (68 mins); R Metcalfe for S Murray (71 mins); G Beveridge for Redpath (79 mins); D W Hodge for Townsend (79 mins)

Scorers *Tries:* Townsend (2), J Leslie (2), Pountney, Paterson *Conversions:* Townsend (4) *Penalty Goals:* Townsend (5)

United States: K Shuman; J Naivalu, P Eloff, J Grobler, M Delai; G Wells, K Dalzell; J Clayton, K Khasigian, P Still, L Gross, P Farner, D Hodges (*captain*), D Lyle, O Fifita *Substitutions:* none.

Scorer *Penalty Goals:* Wells (2)

Referee P C Deluca (Argentina)

8 November, King's College, Aberdeen University
Scotland Development XV 49 (7G)   **United States XV 17** (2G 1PG)

Scotland Development XV scorers *Tries:* Craig (2), Utterson, Reid, Campbell, G Dall, Davidson *Conversions:* McKenzie (5), Irving (2)

United States XV scorers *Tries:* Flynn, Magleby *Conversions:* Wilfley (2) *Penalty Goal:* Wilfley

11 November, Waunfawr Park, Cross Keys
Cross Keys 7 (1G)   **United States XV 22** (2G 1PG 1T)

Cross Keys scorers *Try:* Adebayo *Conversion:* Bushell

United States XV scorers *Tries:* Dalzell, Clayton, Naivalu *Conversions:* Wells (2) *Penalty Goal:* Wells

14 November, The Gnoll, Neath
Wales Development XV 46 (5G 2PG 1T)   **United States XV 20** (1G 1PG 2T)

Wales Development XV scorers *Tries:* C Quinnell (2), Davey, Owen, Watkins, S Williams *Conversions:* Davey (5) *Penalty Goals:* Davey (2)

United States XV scorers *Tries:* Naivulu, Flynn, Care *Conversion:* Wilfley *Penalty Goal:* Wilfley

Test Match 18 November, Millennium Stadium, Cardiff Arms Park
Wales 42 (3G 2PG 3T)   **United States 11** (2PG 1T)

Wales: G R Williams; A G Bateman, M Taylor (*captain*), I S Gibbs, D R James; A C Thomas, R Howley; D R Morris, G R Jenkins, B R Evans, I M Gough, C P Wyatt, N J Budgett, L S Quinnell, C L Charvis *Substitutions:* I D Thomas for Evans (55 mins); G Thomas for Taylor (61 mins); G Lewis for Quinnell (65 mins); A L P Lewis for G Jenkins (65 mins); N R Jenkins for A Thomas (67 mins); A P Moore for Gough (74 mins); R H StJ B Moon for Howley (80 mins)

Scorers *Tries:* James (2), Taylor, A Thomas, Williams, N Jenkins *Conversions:* A Thomas (2) N Jenkins *Penalty Goals:* A Thomas (2)

United States: K Shuman; J Naivalu, P Eloff, J Grobler, M Delai; G Wells, K Dalzell; J Clayton, K Khasigian, P Still, L Gross, P Farner, D Hodges (*captain*), D Lyle, O Fifita *Substitutions:* T Kluempers for Still (temp 18 to 24 mins and 47 mins); A Magleby for Fifita (47 mins); R Flynn for Khasigian (47 mins); J Keyter for Grobler (60 mins); P Still for Clayton (70 mins)

Scorers *Try:* Delai *Penalty Goals:* Wells (2)

Referee D I Ramage (Scotland)

South Africa to Argentina and Britain 2000

Tour party
Full-backs: P C Montgomery (Western Province), G S du Toit (Natal), G M Delport (Lions)

Threequarters: B J Paulse (Western Province), R F Fleck (Western Province), J C Mulder (Lions), G Esterhuizen (Lions), C M Williams (Lions), C S Terblanche (Natal), R Loubscher (Eastern Province), P W G Rossouw (Western Province), D J Kayser (Natal), G Passens (Mpumalanga), *D W Barry (Western Province), *M C Joubert (Boland)

Half-backs: A J J van Straaten (Western Province), C Rossouw (Western Province), J H van der Westhuizen (Blue Bulls), D J van Zyl (Western Province), C Davidson (Natal)

Forwards: R B Kempson (Western Province), W Meyer (Lions), A-H le Roux (Natal), C van der Merwe (Boland), L Sephaka (Falcons), A van der Linde (Western Province), J W Smit (Natal), C F Marais (Western Province), D du Preez (Lions), P A van den Berg (Natal), M G Andrews (Natal), F Louw (Western Province), Q Davids (Western Province), V Matfield (Griqualand West), C P J Krige (Western Province), A G Venter (Free State), A J Venter (Natal), W G Brosnihan (Natal), A N Vos (*captain*) (Lions), H Gerber (Western Province), T Manana (Griqualand West), J Wasserman (South West Districts), *E E Fynn (Natal), *A Badenhorst (Western Province), *P Dixon (Western Province)

*Replacement on tour

Managers: D Sam & T Wakefield **Senior Coach:** H Viljeon **Coaches:** A Coetzee, A Markgraaf, F Ludeke, I McIntosh

Tour record P 9 W 6 L 3 For 253 Against 219

8 November Won 32-21 v Argentina A (Tucuman)

11 November Won 37-33 v ARGENTINA (Buenos Aires)

15 November Lost 11-28 v Ireland A (Limerick)

19 November Won 28-18 v IRELAND (Dublin)

22 November Won 34-15 v Wales A (Cardiff)

26 November Won 23-13 v WALES (Cardiff)

28 November Lost 30-35 v English National Divisions (Worcester)

2 December Lost 17-25 v ENGLAND (Twickenham)

10 December Won 41-31 v Barbarians (Cardiff)

Details

8 November, Tucuman
Argentina A 21 (1G 2PG 1DG 1T)   **South Africa XV 32** (3G 2PG 1T)

Argentina A scorers *Tries:* Grau, Durand *Conversion:* F Contepomi *Penalty Goals:* F Contepomi (2) *Dropped Goal:* J-F Miranda

South Africa XV scorers *Tries:* Terblanche (3), Kayser *Conversions:* Van Straaten (3) *Penalty Goals:* Van Straaten (2)

Test Match 12 November, River Plate Stadium, Buenos Aires
Argentina 33 (3G 4PG)   **South Africa 37** (3G 2PG 2T)

Argentina: I Corleto; O Bartolucci, J Orengo, L Arbizu (*captain*), D Albanese; G Quesada, A Pichot; M Reggiardo, F Mendez, O Hasan, C I Fernandez Lobbe, A Allub, S Phelan, G Longo, R Martin *Substitutions:* F Contepomi for Bartolucci

(14 mins); M Durand for Phelan (40 mins); E Simone for Albanese (43 mins); R D Grau for Reggiardo (67 mins); M Ledesma for Hasan (79 mins)

Scorers *Tries:* Orengo, F Contepomi, Simone *Conversions:* Quesada (3) *Penalty Goals:* Quesada (4)

South Africa: G M Delport; B J Paulse, G Esterhuizen, R F Fleck, C M Williams; P C Montgomery, J H van der Westhuizen; R B Kempson, J W Smit, W Meyer, P A van den Berg, M G Andrews, C P J Krige, A N Vos (*captain*), A G Venter *Substitutions:* A J J van Straaten for Esterhuizen (32 mins); P W G Rossouw for Williams (40 mins); C F Marais for Smit (40 mins); A-H le Roux for Kempson (67 mins)

Scorers *Tries:* Paulse (2), Andrews, Fleck, Van Straaten *Conversions:* Montgomery (3) *Penalty Goals:* Van Straaten (2)

Referee S Young (Australia)

15 November, Thomond Park, Limerick
Ireland A 28 (2G 3PG 1T)   South Africa XV 11 (2PG 1T)

Ireland A scorers *Tries:* Bishop, Mullins, Tierney *Conversions:* Staunton (2) *Penalty Goals:* Staunton (3)

South Africa XV scorers *Try:* Du Toit *Penalty goals:* Du Toit (2)

Test Match 19 November, Lansdowne Road, Dublin
Ireland 18 (1G 2PG 1T)   South Africa 28 (2G 3PG 1T)

Ireland: G T Dempsey; D A Hickie, B G O'Driscoll, R A J Henderson, T G Howe; R J R O'Gara, P A Stringer; P M Clohessy, K G M Wood (*captain*), J J Hayes, G W Longwell, M E O'Kelly, E R P Miller, A G Foley, K Dawson *Substitutions:* D G Humphreys for O'Gara (62 mins); A J Ward for Miller (71 mins); J M Fitzpatrick for Miller (temp 36 to 39 mins) and for Hayes (78 mins); S P Horgan (Lansdowne) for Dempsey (80 mins)

Scorers *Tries:* Hickie, Howe *Conversion:* O'Gara *Penalty Goals:* O'Gara (2)

South Africa: G M Delport; C M Williams, G Esterhuizen, R F Fleck, P W G Rossouw; P C Montgomery, J H van der Westhuizen; R B Kempson, J W Smit, W Meyer, P A van den Berg, M G Andrews, C P J Krige, A N Vos (*captain*), A G Venter *Substitutions:* A-H le Roux for Kempson (temp 35 to 40 mins); A J J van Straaten for Fleck (40 mins); Fleck for Esterhuizen (64 mins)

Scorers *Tries:* Van der Westhuizen, Krige, A G Venter *Conversions:* Montgomery, Van Straaten *Penalty Goals:* Montgomery (2) Van Straaten

Referee S J Lander (England)

22 November, Millennium Stadium, Cardiff Arms Park
Wales A 15 (1G 1PG 1T)   South Africa XV 34 (4G 2PG)

Wales A scorers *Tries:* Walne, Cooper *Conversion:* S Jones *Penalty Goal:* S Jones

South Africa XV scorers *Tries:* Terblanche, Wasserman, Brosnihan, Du Toit *Conversions:* Du Toit (4) *Penalty Goals:* Du Toit, Van Zyl

Test Match 26 November, Millennium Stadium, Cardiff Arms Park
Wales 13 (1G 2PG)   **South Africa 23** (2G 3PG)

Wales: G R Williams; G Thomas, A G Bateman, I S Gibbs, D R James; N R Jenkins, R Howley; P J D Rogers, G R Jenkins, D R Morris, I M Gough, C P Wyatt, N J Budgett, L S Quinnell (*captain*), C L Charvis *Substitutions:* S M Williams for G R Williams (19 mins); I D Thomas for Rogers (41 mins); A L P Lewis for G Jenkins (55 mins); A C Thomas for N Jenkins (60 mins); S C John for Morris (62 mins)

Scorers *Try:* Gibbs *Conversion:* N Jenkins *Penalty Goals:* N Jenkins, A Thomas

South Africa: G M Delport; B J Paulse, R F Fleck, A J J van Straaten, P W G Rossouw; P C Montgomery, J H van der Westhuizen; R B Kempson, J W Smit, W Meyer, P A van den Berg, M G Andrews, C P J Krige, A N Vos (*captain*), A G Venter *Substitutions:* C M Williams for Rossouw (22 mins); G Esterhuizen for Delport (43 mins); A J Venter for van den Berg (56 mins); A-H le Roux for Meyer (66 mins); C F Marais for Smit (80 mins)

Scorers *Tries:* Van der Westhuizen, Paulse *Conversions:* Van Straaten (2) *Penalty Goals:* Van Straaten (3)

Referee S R Walsh (New Zealand)

28 November, Sixways. Worcester
English National Divisions 35 (2G 7PG)   **South Africa XV 30** (2G 2PG 2T)

English National Divisions scorers *Tries:* Scarborough, Mooney *Conversions:* Le Bas (2) *Penalty Goals:* Le Bas (6), Harvey

South Africa XV scorers *Tries:* Passens (2), Du Preez, Barry *Conversions:* Van Zyl (2) *Penalty Goals:* Du Toit, Van Zyl

Test Match 2 December, Twickenham
England 25 (1G 6PG)   **South Africa 17** (4PG 1T)

England: M B Perry; B C Cohen, M J Tindall, W J H Greenwood, D D Luger; J P Wilkinson, M J S Dawson; J Leonard, P B T Greening, J M White, M O Johnson (*captain*), D J Grewcock, R A Hill, L B N Dallaglio, N A Back *Substitutions:* M P Regan for Hill (temp 21 to 33 mins) and for Greening (temp 40 to 60 mins); M E Corry for Back (temp 17 to 33 mins); I R Balshaw for Luger (40 mins); P J Vickery for White (40 mins); A S Healey for Greenwood (80 mins)

Scorers *Try:* Greenwood *Conversion:* Wilkinson *Penalty Goals:* Wilkinson (6)

South Africa: P C Montgomery; B J Paulse, R F Fleck, J C Mulder, C S Terblanche; A J J van Straaten, J H van der Westhuizen; R B Kempson, J W Smit, W Meyer, P A van den Berg, M G Andrews, C P J Krige, A N Vos (*captain*), A G Venter *Substitutions:* G Esterhuizen for Mulder (temp 26 to 40 mins); A J Venter for Van den Berg (59 mins); A-H le Roux for Meyer (61 mins); D J van Zyl for van der Westhuizen (73 mins); W Brosnihan for A J Venter (80 mins)

Scorer *Try:* Van Straaten *Penalty Goals:* Van Straaten (4)

Referee D T M McHugh (Ireland)

10 December, Millennium Stadium, Cardiff Arms Park
Barbarians 31 (4G 1PG)   **South Africa XV 41** (4G 1PG 2T)

Barbarians scorers *Tries:* O'Driscoll. Latham, Pichot, Cullen *Conversions:* Burke (4) *Penalty Goal:* Burke

South Africa XV *Tries:* Paulse (3), Williams (2), A-H le Roux *Conversions:* Montgomery (4) *Penalty Goal:* Van Straaten

New Zealand to Europe 2000

Tour party

Full-back: C M Cullen (Wellington)

Threequarters: D C Howlett (Auckland), J T Lomu (Wellington), B T Reihana (Waikato), J F Umaga (Wellington), P F Alatini (Otago), D P E Gibson (Canterbury), J D O'Halloran (Wellington)

Half-backs: A P Mehrtens (Canterbury), C J Spencer (Auckland), B T Kelleher (Otago), J W Marshall (Canterbury)

Forwards: A D Oliver (Otago), M G Hammett (Canterbury), G M Somerville (Canterbury), G L Slater (Taranaki), G E Feek (Canterbury), N M C Maxwell (Canterbury), T V Flavell (North Harbour), T J Blackadder (*captain*) (Canterbury), F I Tiatia (Wellington), R D Thorne (Canterbury), S M Robertson (Canterbury), T C Randell (Otago), R T Cribb (North Harbour)

Tour record P 3 W 2 L 1 For 128 Against 87

11 November Won 39-26 v FRANCE (Paris)

18 November Lost 33-42 v FRANCE (Marseilles)

25 November Won 56-19 v ITALY (Genoa)

Details

First Test 11 November, Stade de France, Paris
France 26 (2G 4PG)   **New Zealand 39** (1G 9PG 1T)

France: X Garbajosa; T Lombard, R Dourthe, F Comba, D Bory; C Lamaison, F Galthié; S Marconnet, F Landreau, C Califano, D Auradou, F Pelous (*captain*), C Moni, C Juillet, O Magne *Substitutions:* P Bernat-Salles for Lombard (51 mins); P de Villiers for Califano (59 mins); S Betsen for Moni (59 mins); O Brouzet for Auradou (74 mins)

Scorers *Tries:* Bernat-Salles, Pelous *Conversions:* Lamaison (2) *Penalty Goals:* Lamaison (4)

New Zealand: C M Cullen; D C Howlett, J F Umaga, D P E Gibson, J T Lomu; A P Mehrtens, J W Marshall; G E Feek, A D Oliver, G M Somerveille, T J Blackadder (*captain*), N M C Maxwell, R D Thorne, R T Cribb, S M Robertson *Substitutions:* T V Flavell for Maxwell (29 mins); C J Spencer for Gibson (temp 29 to 40 mins and 70 mins); G L Slater for Somerville (70 mins)

Scorers *Tries:* Howlett, Cullen *Conversion:* Mehrtens *Penalty Goals:* Mehrtens (9)

Referee W J Erickson (Australia)

Second Test 18 November, Stade Vélodrome, Marseilles
France 42 (3G 5PG 2DG) **New Zealand 33** (3G 4PG)

France: J-L Sadourny; P Bernat-Salles, R Dourthe, F Comba, X Garbajosa; C Lamaison, F Galthié; S Marconnet, F Landreau, P de Villiers, D Auradou, F Pelous *(captain)*, C Moni, C Juillet, O Magne *Substitutions:* M Dourthe for R Dourthe (temp 26 to 33 mins); C Califano for Marconnet (50 mins); O Brouzet for Auradou (50 mins); S Betsen for Moni (65 mins); P Carbonneau for Galthié (74 mins); O Azam for Landreau (76 mins)
Scorers *Tries:* Garbajosa, Magne, Galthié *Conversions:* Lamaison (3) *Penalty Goals:* Lamaison (5) *Dropped Goals:* Lamaison (2)

New Zealand: C M Cullen; D C Howlett, J F Umaga, D P E Gibson, B T Reihana; A P Mehrtens, J W Marshall; G E Feek, A D Oliver, G M Somerville, T J Blackadder *(captain)*, N M C Maxwell, R D Thorne, R T Cribb, S M Robertson *Substitutions:* G L Slater for Somerville (36 mins); T C Randell for Thorne (48 mins); M G Hammett for Oliver (72 mins); T V Flavell for Maxwell (76 mins)
Scorers *Tries:* Marshall, Howlett, Slater *Conversions:* Mehrtens (3) *Penalty Goals:* Mehrtens (4)
Referee J I Kaplan (South Africa)

Test Match 25 November, Stade Luigi Ferraris, Genoa
Italy 19 (3PG 2T) **New Zealand 56** (5G 2PG 3T)

Italy: A Stoica; M Perziano, L Martin, G Raineri, D Dallan; R Pez, A Troncon; A Lo Cicero, A Moscardi *(captain)*, A Muraro, A Gritti, W Visser, M Zaffiri, R Piovan, C Caione *Substitutions:* F Frati for Troncon (2 mins); A de Rossi for Zaffiri (37 mins); G Preo for Pez (54 mins); L Mastrodomenico for Visser (60 mins); S Saviozzi for Caione (70 mins); C Paoletti for Lo Cicero (71 mins)
Scorers *Tries:* Lo Cicero, Saviozzi *Penalty Goals:* Pez (3)

New Zealand: C M Cullen; D C Howlett, J F Umaga, P F Alatini, B T Reihana; C J Spencer, J W Marshall; G E Feek, A D Oliver, G M Somerville, T J Blackadder *(captain)*, T V Flavell, F I Tiatia, R T Cribb, S M Robertson *Substitutions:* N M C Maxwell for Tiatia (45 mins); G L Slater for Somerville (54 mins); J D O'Halloran for Alatini (69 mins); M G Hammett for Oliver (72 mins); T C Randell for Robertson (70 mins); B T Kelleher for Marshall (75 mins); A P Mehrtens for Cullen (75 mins)
Scorers *Tries:* Reihana (2), Cribb (2), Howlett, Spencer, Marshall, Tiatia *Conversions:* Spencer (5) *Penalty Goals:* Spencer (2)
Referee R Davies (Wales)

Japan to Europe 2000

Tour party
Full-backs: G Tachikawa (Toshiba Fuchu), B Neilson (NEC)
Threequarters: M Oda (World), H Yoshida (Kubota), D Ohata (NEC), P Tuidraki (Toyota Motors), R Kawai (NEC), H Namba (Toyota Motors)

Half-backs: S Fuchigami (Coca Cola, West Japan), K Hirose (Toyota Motors), M Ito (Toshiba Fuchu), K Ohara (Toyota Motors) (*captain*)

Forwards: N Yasuda (Ricoh), M Amino (NEC), T Fumihara (IBM), N Nakamura (Suntory), K Takayanagi (Toyota Motors), M Toyoyama (Toyota Motors), T Akatsuka (Kubota), H Tanuma (Ricoh), K Todd (IBM), A Komura (Kobe Steel), K Kubo (Yamaha Motors), H Sugawara (Toyota Motors), Y Watanabe (Toshiba Fuchu), T Ito (Kobe Steel)

Coach: S Hirao **Assistant coaches:** M Kunda, S Onishi

Tour record P 3 L 3 For 45 Against 201

4 November Lost 23-40 v France A (Lille)
6 November Lost 13-83 v Ireland U25 XV (Belfast)
11 November Lost 9-78 v IRELAND (Dublin)

Details

4 November, Stade du Nord, Lille
France A 40 (4G 4PG)   Japan XV 23 (2G 3PG)

France A scorers *Tries:* penalty try, Bru, Milhères, Larguet *Conversions:* Merceron (4) *Penalty Goals:* Merceron (4)

Japan XV scorers *Tries:* Ohata, Toyoyama *Conversions:* Fuchigami (2) *Penalty Goals:* Hirose (3)

6 November, Ravenhill, Belfast
Ireland U25 XV 83 (9G 4T)   Japan XV 13 (1G 2PG)

Ireland U25 XV scorers *Tries:* D'Arcy (2), Kelly (2), Horan, McMahon, Smyth, Stewart, O'Connor, Cunningham, Cahill, McHugh, Keogh *Conversions:* Staunton (5), Cunningham (4)

Japan XV scorers *Try:* Ohata *Conversion:* Fuchigami *Penalty Goals:* Fuchigami (2)

Test Match 11 November, Lansdowne Road, Dublin
Ireland 78 (10G 1PG 1T)   Japan 9 (3PG)

Ireland: G E A Murphy; D A Hickie, B G O'Driscoll, S P Horgan, T G Howe; R J R O'Gara, P A Stringer; P M Clohessy, K G M Wood (*captain*), J J Hayes, P S Johns, M E O'Kelly, A J Ward, A G Foley, K Dawson *Substitutions:* G W Longwell for Johns (56 mins); R A J Henderson for Horgan (60 mins); D G Humphreys for Murphy (64 mins)

Scorers *Tries:* Hickie (3), Howe (2), O'Driscoll (2), Murphy, Stringer, Clohessy, Henderson *Conversions:* O'Gara (10) *Penalty Goal:* O'Gara

Japan: D Ohata; M Oda, R Kawai, H Namba, P Tuidraki; K Hirose, K Ohara (*captain*); T Fumihara, N Yasuda, N Nakamura, K Todd, H Tanuma, H Sugawara, T Ito, K Kubo *Substitutions:* Y Watanabe for Kubo (temp 38 to 40 mins); S Fuchigami for Hirose (54 mins); M Ito for Ohara (54 mins)

Scorer *Penalty Goals:* Hirose (3)

Referee N Whitehouse (Wales)

Australia to Japan and Europe 2000

Tour party

Full-backs: M C Burke (NSW), C E Latham (Queensland)

Threquarters: J W C Roff (ACT), S A Mortlock (ACT), D J Herbert (Queensland), N P Grey (NSW), A M Walker (ACT)

Half backs: R B Kafer (ACT), E J Flatley (Queensland), C J Whitaker (NSW), S J Cordingley (Queensland)

Forwards: J A Paul (ACT), M A Foley (Queensland), W K Young (ACT), G M Panoho (Queensland), F J Dyson (Queensland), N B Stiles (Queensland), J A Eales *(captain)* (Queensland), D T Giffin (ACT), M J Cockbain (Queensland), M R Connors (Queensland), R S T Kefu (Queensland), R W Williams (ACT), D J Lyons (NSW), G B Smith (ACT), P R Waugh (NSW)

Manager: J McKay **Coach:** R McQueen **Assistant coaches:** G Ella, E McKenzie, J Muggleton

Tour record P 4 W 3 L 1 For 131 Against 57

28 October Won 64-13 v Japan President's XV (Tokyo)

4 November Won 18-13 v FRANCE (Paris)

11 November Won 30-9 v SCOTLAND (Murrayfield)

18 November Lost 19-22 v ENGLAND (Twickenham)

Details

28 October, Prince Chichibu Stadium, Tokyo
Japan Presidents XV 13 (1G 2PG)   Australian XV 64 (7G 3T)

Japan Presidents XV scorers *Try:* Plastow *Conversion:* Milne *Penalty Goals:* Milne (2)

Australian XV scorers *Tries:* Latham (3), Paul (2), Burke (2), Cordingley, Mortlock, Walker *Conversions:* Burke (7)

Test Match 4 November, Stade de France, Paris
France 13 (1G 2PG)   Australia 18 (6PG)

France: X Garbajosa; T Lombard, R Dourthe, F Comba, D Bory; C Lamaison, F Galthié; S Marconnet, F Landreau, C Califano, O Brouzet, F Pelous *(captain)*, C Moni, C Juillet, O Magne *Substitutions:* D Auradou for Brouzet (57 mins); F Tournaire for Marconnet (60 mins); S Betsen for Moni (67 mins); O Azam for Juillet (80 mins)

Scorers *Try:* Galthié *Conversion:* Lamaison *Penalty Goals:* Lamaison (2)

Australia: C E Latham; M C Burke, D J Herbert, S A Mortlock, J W C Roff; R B Kafer, S J Cordingley; W K Young, M A Foley, F J Dyson, D T Giffin, J A Eales *(captain)*, M J Cockbain, R S T Kefu, G B Smith *Substitutions:* J A Paul for Foley (25 mins); M R Connors for Cockbain (49 mins); G M Panoho for Dyson (54 mins); R W Williams for Kefu (64 mins)

Scorer *Penalty Goals:* Burke (6)

Referee P G Honiss (New Zealand)

Test Match 11 November, Murrayfield
Scotland 9 (3PG)   **Australia 30** (3G 3PG)

Scotland: C D Paterson; C A Murray, A J Bulloch, J A Leslie, J F Steel; G P J Townsend, B W Redpath; T J Smith, S J Brotherstone, G Graham, S Murray, S B Grimes, J M Petrie, S M Taylor, A C Pountney (*captain*) *Substitutions:* G C Bulloch for Brotherstone (51 mins); G R McIlwham for Graham (53 mins); R Metcalfe for Grimes (64 mins); J P R White for Petrie (64 mins); G Graham for White (79 mins)

Scorer *Penalty Goals:* Townsend (3)

Australia: C E Latham; M C Burke, D J Herbert, S A Mortlock, J W C Roff; R B Kafer, S J Cordingley; W KYoung, M A Foley, F J Dyson, D T Giffin, J A Eales (*captain*), M J Cockbain, R S T Kefu, G B Smith *Substitutions:* J A Paul for Foley (40 mins); R W Williams for Cockbain (40 mins); G M Panoho for Dyson (47 mins); E J Flatley for Kafer (55 mins); M R Connors for Kefu (68 mins); N P Grey for Mortlock (73 mins); C J Whitaker for Cordingley (76 mins)

Scorers *Tries:* Latham, Roff, Burke *Conversions:* Burke (3) *Penalty Goals:* Burke (3)

Referee C White (England)

Test Match 18 November, Twickenham
England 22 (1G 4PG 1DG)   **Australia 19** (1G 4PG)

England: M B Perry; A S Healey, M J Tindall, M J Catt, D D Luger; J P Wilkinson, K P P Bracken; J Leonard, P B T Greening, P J Vickery, M O Johnson (*captain*), D J Grewcock, R A Hill, L B N Dallaglio, N A Back *Substitutions:* D L Flatman for Vickery (temp 22 to 24 mins); I R Balshaw for Healey (55 mins); M J S Dawson for Bracken (61 mins); M P Regan for Greening (85 mins)

Scorers *Try:* Luger *Conversion:* Wilkinson *Penalty Goals:* Wilkinson (4) *Dropped Goal:* Wilkinson

Australia: C E Latham; M C Burke, D J Herbert, S A Mortlock, J W C Roff; R B Kafer, S J Cordingley; W K Young, M A Foley, F J Dyson, D T Giffin, J A Eales (*captain*), R W Williams, R S T Kefu, G B Smith *Substitutions:* G M Panoho for Dyson (30 mins); N P Grey for Kafer (39 mins); J A Paul for Foley (40 mins); M R Connors for Williams (45 mins); R W Williams for Kefu (58 mins); P R Waugh for Smith (76 mins); M J Cockbain for Giffin (77 mins); F J Dyson for Panoho (82 mins)

Scorer *Try:* Burke *Conversion:* Burke *Penalty Goals:* Burke (4)

Referee A Watson (South Africa)

Samoa to Wales and Scotland 2000

Tour party

Full-backs: M Schuster (Marist St Josephs), H V Patu (Vaiala)

Threequarters: P Misa (Apia), F Toala (La Rochelle, France), S Fa'asua (Otahuhu, NZ), G Elisara (Moataa), F So'olefai (Taranaki, NZ), A Toleafoa (Parma, Italy), F Tuilagi (Leicester, England), *T Suemai (Apia)

Half-backs: C Burnes (East Coast Bays, NZ), Q Sanft (Ponsonby, NZ), I Evalu (Marist), S So'oialo (Western Suburbs, NZ),

Forwards: O Matauiau (*captain*) (Hawkes Bay, NZ), M Schwalger (Taradale, NZ), L Nu'usila (Maagiagi), P Asi (Moataa), H Williams (Marist St Josephs), D Tafeamalii (Vaiala), T Veiru (West Harbour, Australia), S Tone (Manurewa, NZ), O Palepoi (Norths, NZ), S Poching (Otahuhu, NZ), J Mamea (Apia Maroons), F Taua (Maagiagi), P Mavaega (Marist St Jospehs), F Matagitau (Nofoalii), A Vaeluaga (Otahuhu, NZ), J Maligi (Marist St Josephs), L Mealamu (Otahuhu, NZ), *A Mika (Apia) *Replacement on tour

Manager: L K Tuuau **Coach:** F S Patu **Assistant coach:** P P Fatialofa
Tour record P 3 L 3 For 38 Against 118
11 November Lost 6-50 v WALES (Cardiff)
14 November Lost 24-37 v Scotland A (Perth)
18 November Lost 8-31 v SCOTLAND (Murrayfield)

Details

Test Match 11 November, Millennium Stadium, Cardiff Arms Park
Wales 50 (4G 4PG 2T)   Samoa 6 (2PG)

Wales: G R Williams; A G Bateman, M Taylor (*captain*), I S Gibbs, S M Willimas; A C Thomas, R Howley; I D Thomas, G R Jenkins, B R Evans, I M Gough, D L Jones, G Lewis, L S Quinnell, C L Charvis *Substitutions:* S C John for Evans (50 mins); A L P Lewis for G Jenkins (50 mins); J Griffiths for Jones (52 mins); N J Budgett for Quinnell (66 mins); N R Jenkins for A Thomas (69 mins); R H St J B Moon for Howley (69 mins); D R James for Gibbs (72 mins)

Scorers *Tries:* Williams (2), Taylor, Gough, Bateman, penalty try *Conversions:* A Thomas (4) *Penalty Goals:* A Thomas (4)

Samoa: H V Patu; S Fa'asua, F So'olefai, F Tuilagi, F Toala; Q Sanft, S So'oialo; T Veiru, O Matauiau (*captain*), P Asi, O Palepoi, S Poching, A Vaeluaga, J Maligi, L Mealamu *Substitutions:* A Toleafoa for Matauiau (30 mins); S Tone for Palepoi (50 mins); J Mamea for Mealamu (62 mins); D Tafaemali'i for Veiru (69 mins); P Misa for Vaeluaga (80 mins)

Scorers *Penalty Goals:* Patu, Sanft

Referee S J Dickinson (Australia)

14 November, McDiarmid Park, Perth
Scotland A 37 (3G 2PG 2T)   Samoan XV 24 (1G 3PG 1DG 1T)

Scotland A scorers *Tries:* Utterson (2), Craig, Joiner, penalty try *Conversions:* McKenzie (3) *Penalty Goals:* McKenzie (2)

Samoan XV *Tries:* Fa'asua, Tone *Conversion:* Sanft *Penalty Goals:* Burnes, Toleafua, Sanft *Dropped Goal:* Burnes

Test Match 18 November, Murrayfield
Scotland 31 (1G 3PG 3T) Samoa 8 (1PG 1T)

Scotland: C D Paterson; C A Murray, A J Bulloch, J A Leslie, K M Logan; G P J Townsend, B W Redpath; T J Smith, S J Brotherstone, G Graham, S Murray, R Metcalfe, J P R White, J M Petrie, A C Pountney (*captain*) *Substitutions:* R S Beattie for White (temp 23 to 25 mins and 75 mins); G R McIlwham for Graham (51 mins); S B Grimes for Metcalfe (56 mins); G C Bulloch for Brotherstone (68 mins); G Beveridge for Redpath (75 mins); D W Hodge for A Bulloch (75 mins)

Scorers *Tries:* Petrie, Logan, Smith, A Bulloch *Conversion:* Townsend *Penalty Goals:* Townsend (3)

Samoa: H V Patu; M Schuster, F So'olefai, F Tuilagi, F Toala; Q Sanft, S So'oialo; D Tafeamali'i, O Matauiau (*captain*), P Asi, S Poching, S Tone, A Vaeluaga, J Maligi, L Mealamu *Substitutions:* P Misa for Schuster (27 mins); A Toleafoa for Sanft (55 mins); M Schwalger for Tafeamali'i (63 mins); J Mamea for Maligi (66 mins); T Veiru for Vaeluaga (75 mins); A Mika for Mealamu (78 mins)

Scorers *Try:* Patu *Penalty Goal:* Sanft

Referee I Hyde-Lay (Canada)

France to South Africa and New Zealand 2001

Tour party

Full-backs: N Jeanjean (Toulouse), P Elhorga (Agen)

Threequarters: C Dominici (Stade Francais), D Bory (Montferrand), O Sarramea (Castres), S Bonetti (Biarritz), Y Jauzion (Colomiers), S Glas (Bourgoin)

Half-backs: G Merceron (Montferrand), D Skrela (Colomiers), P Mignoni (Dax), F Galthié (*captain*) (Colomiers)

Forwards: O Azam (Gloucester), R Ibanez (Castres), C Califano (Toulouse), P de Villiers (Stade Francais), O Milloud (Bourgoin), J-J Crenca (Agen), O Brouzet (Northampton), L Nallet (Bourgoin), D Auradou (Stade Francais), P Tabacco (Stade Francais), S Chabal (Bourgoin), O Magne (Montferrand), J Bouilhou (Toulouse), E Vermeulen (Brive)

Manager: J Maso **Assistant manager:** J Dunyach Coach B Laporte **Assistant coaches:** Y Ajac, J Brunel, D Ellis
Tour record P 3 W 1 L 2 For 59 Against 80
16 June Won 32-23 v SOUTH AFRICA (Johannesburg)
23 June Lost 15-20 v SOUTH AFRICA (Durban)
30 June Lost 12-37 v NEW ZEALAND (Wellington)

Details

First Test 16 June, Ellis Park Johannesburg
South Africa 23 (6PG 1T)   France 32 (2G 6PG)

South Africa: P C Montgomery; B J Paulse, D W Barry, J C Mulder, D B Hall; A D James, J H van der Westhuizen; R B Kempson, J W Smit, E E Fynn, A G Venter, M G Andrews, J Erasmus, A N Vos (*captain*), C P J Krige *Substitutions:* W Meyer for Fynn (40 mins); P A van den Berg for Andrews (53 mins); A-H le Roux for Kempson (53 mins); R B Skinstad for Krige (62 mins); R F Fleck for Barry (75 mins)

Scorers *Try:* Paulse *Penalty Goals:* Montgomery (6)

France: N Jeanjean; C Dominici, Y Jauzion, S Glas, D Bory; G Merceron, F Galthié (*captain*); J-J Crenca, R Ibanez, P de Villiers, D Auradou, O Brouzet, S Chabal, P Tabacco, O Magne *Substitutions:* E Vermeulen for Chabal (55 mins); L Nallet for Brouzet (77 mins); C Califano for de Villiers (77 mins)

Scorers *Tries:* Dominici, Merceron *Conversions:* Merceron (2) *Penalty Goals:* Merceron (6)

Referee P Deluca (Argentina)

Second Test 23 June, Absa Stadium, King's Park, Durban
South Africa 20 (5PG 1T)   France 15 (4PG 1DG)

South Africa: G M Delport; B J Paulse, R F Fleck, D W Barry, D B Hall; A D James, J H van der Westhuizen; A-H le Roux, J W Smit, W Meyer, P A van den Berg, M G Andrews, J Erasmus, A N Vos (*captain*), C P J Krige *Substitutions:* P C Montgomery (Western Province) for Fleck (temp 37 to 40 mins); R B Skinstad for Krige (47 mins); R B Kempson for Le Roux (69 mins); J N Ackermann for Andrews (83 mins); M G Andrews for van den Berg (86 mins)

Scorers *Try:* Krige *Penalty Goals:* James (5)

France: N Jeanjean; C Dominici, Y Jauzion, S Glas, D Bory; G Merceron, F Galthié (*captain*); J-J Crenca, R Ibanez, P de Villiers, D Auradou, O Brouzet, S Chabal, P Tabacco, O Magne *Substitutions:* O Azam for Ibanez (64 mins); C Califano for Crenca (64 mins); E Vermeulen for Chabal (71 mins); L Nallet for Auradou (74 mins)

Scorer *Penalty Goals:* Merceron (4) *Dropped Goal:* Merceron

Referee C White (England)

Test Match 30 June, Westpac Stadium, Wellington
New Zealand 37 (4G 3PG)   France 12 (4PG)

New Zealand: L R MacDonald; J W Wilson, J F Umaga, P F Alatini, J T Lomu; T E Brown, J W Marshall; C H Hoeft, A D Oliver (*captain*), G M Somerville, N M C Maxwell, T V Flavell, R D Thorne, R T Cribb, T C Randell *Substitutions:* C J Hayman for Somerville (50 mins); M R Holah for Randell (65 mins); B T Kelleher for Marshall (73 mins); D C Howlett for MacDonald (75 mins)

Scorers *Tries:* Wilson, Thorne, Lomu, Howlett *Conversions:* Brown (4) *Penalty Goals:* Brown (3)

France: P Elhorga; N Jeanjean, Y Jauzion, S Glas, C Dominici; D Skrela, F Galthié (*captain*); O Milloud, O Azam, C Califano, L Nallet, O Brouzet, J Bouilhou, P Tabacco, O Magne *Substitutions:* D Auradou for Nallet (37 mins); S Chabal for Bouilhou (45 mins); R Ibanez for Azam (50 mins); J-J Crenca for Milloud (50 mins); P de Villiers for Califano (63 mins); G Merceron for Skrela (70 mins); S Bonetti for Elhorga (75 mins)

Scorer *Penalty Goals:* Skrela (4)

Referee A Lewis (Ireland)

Italy to Southern Hemisphere 2001

Tour party

Full-backs: J M Antoni (Alghero), N Mazzucato (Treviso)

Threequarters: J S Francesio (Viadana), L Martin (Northampton, England), S Pace (Parma), R Pedrazzi (Viadana), M Perziano (Treviso), W Pozzebon (Treviso), G Raineri (Roma), C Stoica (Narbonne, Fra), *F Faggiotto (Viadana)

Half-backs: A Cavalleri (Rovato), F Mazzariol (Treviso), R Pez (Roma), J-M Queirolo (Viadana), A Troncon (Montferrand, France), F Frati (Parma)

Forwards: A Moscardi (Treviso) (*captain*), S Perugini (L'Aquila), C Paoletti (La Rochelle, France), G P de Carli (Roma), C Beltramini (Treviso), M Bortolami (Padova), A Muraro (Padova), C Checchinato (Treviso), M Giacheri (Parma), L Mastrodomenico (Calvisano), O Arancio (Bologna), A de Rossi (Calvisano), S Garozzo (Treviso), F Ongaro (Treviso), A Persico (Viadana), J Ricciardo (Calvisano), W Visser (Treviso) *Replacement on tour

Manager: F Gaetaniello **Assistant manager:** C Peruzza **Coach:** B Johnstone **Assistant coach:** M Vaea

Tour record P 8 W 4 D 0 L 4 For 208 Against 275

20 June Won 58-16 v Namibian President's XV (Windhoek)

23 June Won 49-24 v NAMIBIA (Windhoek)

26 June Lost 11-42 v South African Barbarians (East London)

30 June Lost 14-60 v SOUTH AFRICA (Port Elizabeth)

3 July Won 33-30 v Uruguay A (Punta del Este)

7 July Won 14-3 v URUGUAY (Montevideo)

10 July Lost 12-62 v Argentina A (Salta)

14 July Lost 17-38 v ARGENTINA (Buenos Aires)

Details

20 June, National Stadium, Windhoek
Namibian President's XV 16 (1G 3PG)   Italian XV 58 (6G 2PG 2T)

Namibian President's XV scorers *Try:* Grobler *Conversion:* Du Plessis *Penalty Goals:* Du Plessis (3)

Italian XV scorers *Tries:* Mazzariol (2), Ongaro, Perziano, Mazzucato, Bortolami, Francesio, Troncon *Conversions:* Mazzariol (4), Raineri (2) *Penalty Goals:* Mazzariol (2)

Test Match 23 June, National Stadium, Windhoek
Namibia 24 (3G 1PG)   Italy 49 (7G)

Namibia: G van Wyk; J Kotze, D Gouws, C J Powell, J L Kruger; L Plaath, R R Pedro; S O Lambert, H Horn, A J K Blaauw, A Graham, E Isaacs, J H Duvenhage (*captain*), S Furter, H D Lintvelt *Substitutions:* R Gentz for Isaacs (temp 6 to 10mins); G F Janse van Rensberg, P Kotze and J Redlinghaus for Van Wyk, Furter and Blaauw (65 mins); M Kapitako for Lambert (75 mins)

Scorers *Tries:* Powell, Furter, Blaauw *Conversions:* J Kotze (3) *Penalty Goal:* J Kotze

Italy: J M Antoni; N Mazzucato, W Pozzebon, G Raineri, M Perziano; F Mazzariol, A Troncon; S Perugini, A Moscardi (*captain*), A Muraro, W Visser, L Mastrodomenico, M Bortolami, C Checchinato, A Persico *Substitutions:* F Ongaro for Mastrodomenico (47 mins); R Pedrazzi for Raineri (65 mins); C Paoletti for Muraro (68 mins); M Giacheri for Checchinato (75 mins)

Scorers *Tries:* Checchinato (2), Pozzebon (2), Perziano, Mazzucato, Troncon *Conversions:* Mazzariol (7)

Referee S M Lawrence (South Africa)

26 June, ABSA Stadium, East London
South African Barbarians 42 (3G 2PG 3T)   Italian XV 11 (2PG 1T)

South African Barbarians scorers *Tries:* Kayser (2), J van der Westhuyzen, Van Rensberg, Welsh, Julies *Conversions:* J van der Westhuyzen (3) *Penalty Goals:* J van der Westhuyzen (2)

Italian XV scorers *Try:* De Rossi *Penalty Goals:* Pez (2)

Test Match 30 June, Telkom Park, Port Elizabeth
South Africa 60 (4G 4PG 4T)   Italy 14 (3PG 1T)

South Africa: C A Jantjes; B J Paulse, R F Fleck, J C Mulder, G M Delport; P C Montgomery, N A de Kock; A-H le Roux, J W Smit, W Meyer, J N Ackermann, M G Andrews, A N Vos, R B Skinstad (*captain*), A G Venter *Substitutions:* L van Biljon for Smit (28 mins); D J Kayser, J H van der Westhuyzen and V Matfield for Mulder, de Kock and Ackermann (69 mins); C P J Krige for Vos (76 mins); E E Fynn for Meyer (76 mins); J N B van der Westhuyzen for Montgomery (80 mins)

Scorers *Tries:* J H van der Westhuyzen (2), Paulse (2), Montgomery, Andrews, Venter, Delport *Conversions:* Montgomery (3), Jantjes *Penalty Goals:* Montgomery (4)

Italy: J M Antoni; M Perziano, L Martin, W Pozzebon, N Mazzucato; F Mazzariol, A Troncon; S Perugini, A Moscardi (*captain*), A Muraro, W Visser, M Giacheri, F Ongaro, C Checchinato, A Persico *Substitutions:* G P De Carli for Muraro (49 mins); M Bortolami for Ongaro (56 mins); A De Rossi for Persico (71 mins); G Raineri for Martin (80 mins)

Scorers *Try:* Troncon *Penalty Goals:* Mazzariol (3)

Referee J Dumé (France)

3 July, Campus de Maldonado, Punta del Este
Uruguay A 30 (2G 2PG 2T)   Italian XV 33 (2G 3PG 2T)

Uruguay A scorers *Tries:* Ibarra, Bono, Lapetina, penalty try *Conversions:* Sierra (2) *Penalty Goals:* Sierra, Zeballos

Italian XV scorers *Tries:* Garozzo (2), De Carli, Faggiotto *Conversions:* Pez (2) *Penalty Goals:* Pez (2), Raineri

Test Match 7 July, Club Nacional de Futbol, Parque Central, Montevideo
Uruguay 3 (1PG)   Italy 14 (3PG 1T)

Uruguay: J Menchaca; P Costabile, D Aguirre, P Vecino, E Ibarra; S Aguirre, E Caffera; R Sanchez, F de los Santos, P Lemoine (*captain*), J Alzueta, M Lame, N Brignoni, J C Bado, N Grille *Substitutions:* D Besio for Brignoni (41 mins); M Gutiérrez for Lame (72 mins); H Canessa for S Aguirre (72 mins); A Urrestara for Caffera (75 mins)

Scorer *Penalty Goal:* D Aguirre

Italy: N Mazzucato; M Perziano, W Pozzebon, G Raineri, J S Francesio; F Mazzariol, A Troncon; G P De Carli, A Moscardi (*captain*), S Perugini, W Visser, M Giacheri, S Garozzo, C Checchinato, A Persico *Substitutions:* F Ongaro for Giacheri (temp 5 to 7 mins) and for Garozzo 41 mins); A Muraro for Perugini (46 mins); A De Rossi for Giacheri (80 mins); C Paoletti for Persico (87 mins)

Scorers *Try:* Perziano *Penalty Goals:* Mazzariol (2), Raineri

Referee P C Deluca (Argentina)

10 July, Salta
Argentina A 62 (5G 4PG 3T)   Italian XV 12 (4PG)

Argentina A scorers *Tries:* Soler (3), Nanini (3), Travaglini, penalty try *Conversions:* Quesada (5) *Penalty Goals:* Quesada (4)

Italian XV scorer *Penalty Goals:* Pez (4)

Test Match 14 July, Stadio Ferrocarril Oeste, Buenos Aires
Argentina 38 (3G 3PG 1DG 1T)   Italy 17 (4PG 1T)

Argentina: B Stortoni; G Camardon, E Simone, L Arbizu (*captain*), D Albanese; F Contepomi, A Pichot; M Reggiardo, F E Mendez, O J Hasan, C I Fernandez-Lobbe, G Longo, S Phelan, L Ostiglia, R Martin *Substitutions:* G Quesada for Simone (temp 37 to 40 mins) and for Stortoni (40 mins); M Ledesma for Mendez (71 mins); M Durand for Martin (temp 38 to 40 mins) and for Phelan (73 mins)

Scorers *Tries:* Albanese (2), Quesada, Simone *Conversions:* Quesada (2), Contepomi *Penalty Goals:* Contepomi (2), Quesada *Dropped Goal:* Quesada

Italy: N Mazzucato; M Perziano, W Pozzebon, G Raineri, L Martin; F Mazzariol, A Troncon; S Perugini, A Moscardi (*captain*), A Muraro, W Visser, M Giacheri, S Garozzo, C Checchinato, A Persico *Substitutions:* F Ongaro and L Mastrodomenico for Garozzo and Visser (40 mins); R Pedrazzi for Martin (59

mins); C Paoletti for Muraro (68 mins); A De Rossi for Giacheri (80 mins)
Scorers *Try:* Raineri *Penalty Goals:* Mazzariol (4)
Referee N Whitehouse (Wales)

Wales to Japan 2001

Tour party

Full-backs: G R Williams (Cardiff), K A Morgan (Swansea)

Threequarters: Gareth Thomas (Cardiff), C Morgan (Cardiff), M A Jones (Llanelli), S M Williams (Neath), A G Bateman (Northampton), J Robinson (Cardiff), T Shanklin (Saracens), S M Jones (Llanelli), A Durston (Bridgend), *G Wyatt (Pontypridd)

Half-backs: G Henson (Swansea), L Jarvis (Pontypridd), G J Cooper (Bath), R Powell (Cardiff), D Peel (Llanelli)

Forwards: A L P Lewis (Cardiff), S Nelson (Bristol), Steve Jones (Neath), I D Thomas (Ebbw Vale), D Jones (Neath), P Booth (Llanelli), C T Anthony (Swansea), C Jones (Newport), B R Evans (Swansea), D Jones (Ebbw Vale), J C Quinnell (Cardiff), C Stephens (Bridgend), A P Moore (Swansea) (*captain*), A Lloyd (Bath), *A Jones (Harlequins), A Popham (Newport), N J Budgett (Ebbw Vale), R Sowden-Taylor (Cardiff), Gavin Thomas (Bath), M Owen (Pontypridd), G Lewis (Swansea), J Ringer (Bridgend) *Replacement on tour

Manager: S Simon **Coach:** L Howells

Tour record P 5 W 3 L 2 For 207 Against 143

3 June Lost 41-45 v Suntory (Tokyo)
6 June Won 33-22 v Japan XV (Osaka)
10 June Won 64-10 v JAPAN (Osaka)
13 June Lost 16-36 v Pacific Barbarians (Tokyo)
17 June Won 53-30 v JAPAN (Tokyo)

Details

3 June, Prince Chichibu Stadium, Tokyo
Suntory 45 (6G 1PG)   Wales XV 41 (5G 2PG)

Suntory scorers *Tries:* Sawaki (2), Onozawa, Uluinayau, Kurihara, Hojo *Conversions:* Kurihara (6) *Penalty Goal:* Kurihara

Wales XV scorers *Tries:* S M Jones (2), Robinson (2), A Jones *Conversions:* S M Jones (5) *Penalty Goals:* S M Jones (2)

6 June, Nagai Stadium, Osaka
Japan A 22 (2G 1PG 1T)   Wales XV 33 (3G 4PG)

Japan A scorers *Tries:* Yamaguchi (2), Akune *Conversions:* Tachikawa, Tanaka *Penalty Goal:* Tanaka

Wales XV scorers *Tries:* S M Williams (2), Durston *Conversions:* Jarvis (3) *Penalty Goals:* Jarvis (4)

First Test 10 June, Hanazono Stadium, Osaka
Japan 10 (2T)   Wales 64 (7G 3T)

Japan: T Matsuda; T Kurihara, Y Motoki, N Oto, P Tuidraki; S Onishi, W Murata; S Hasegawa, M Sakata (*captain*), M Toyoyama, L Vatuvei, H Tanuma, T Ito, Y Saito, H Sugawara *Substitutions:* K Iwabuchi for Matsuda (19 mins); K Kubo for Sugarwara (64 mins); H Namba for Onishi (68 mins); Y Sonoda for Murata (68 mins); E Yamamoto for Ito (81 mins)

Scorers *Tries:* Vaturei, Ito

Wales: K A Morgan; M A Jones, Gareth Thomas, A Durston, S M Williams; S M Jones, G J Cooper; I D Thomas, A L P Lewis, C T Anthony, J C Quinnell, A P Moore (*captain*), A Lloyd, G Lewis, Gavin Thomas *Substitutions:* N J Budgett for Moore (38 mins), J Ringer for Lloyd (40 mins); Steve Jones and G Henson for A L P Lewis and Morgan (57 mins); B R Evans for Anthony (68 mins); J Robinson for Gareth Thomas (75 mins); Lloyd for Quinnell (75 mins)

Scorers *Tries:* S M Williams (4), Morgan (2), Gareth Thomas, M A Jones, Lloyd, Durston *Conversions:* S M Jones (7)

Referee R Dickson (Scotland)

13 June, Tokyo Stadium
Pacific Barbarians 36 (2G 4PG 2T)   Wales XV 16 (1G 3PG)

Pacific Barbarians scorers Mafileo, Washington, W Little, Byers *Conversions:* Cashmore (2) *Penalty Goals:* Cashmore (4)

Wales XV scorers *Try:* M A Jones *Conversion:* Jarvis *Penalty Goals:* Jarvis (3)

Second Test 17 June, Prince Chichibu Stadium, Tokyo
Japan 30 (3G 3PG)   Wales 53 (4G 5T)

Japan: H Onozawa; T Kurihara, H Namba, Y Motoki, T Masuho; K Iwabuchi, W Murata; S Hasegawa, M Sakata (*captain*), M Toyoyama, L Vatuvei, H Tanuma, K Kubo, Y Saito, K Koizumi *Substitutions:* T Ito and P Tuidraki for Saito and Masuho (61 mins); R Yamamura for Toyoyama (temp 62 to 69 mins); J Akune for Tanuma (79 mins)

Scorers *Tries:* Kubo, Masuho, Onozawa *Conversions:* Kurihara (3) *Penalty Goals:* Kurihara (3)

Wales: K A Morgan; T Shanklin, Gareth Thomas, A Durston, S M Williams; S M Jones, G J Cooper; I D Thomas, A L P Lewis, C T Anthony, J C Quinnell, A P Moore (*captain*), N J Budgett, G Lewis, Gavin Thomas *Substitutions:* J Ringer for Budgett (64 mins); J Robinson for Shanklin (70 mins); D Peel and C Stephens for Cooper and Quinnell (73 mins)

Scorers *Tries:* Gareth Thomas (3), Gavin Thomas (2), Shanklin (2), S M Williams, Robinson *Conversions:* S M Jones (4)

Referee K M Deaker (New Zealand)

England to North America 2001

Tour party
Full-backs: T R G Stimpson (Leicester), M Stephenson (Newcastle)

Threequarters: D L Rees (Bristol), P C Sampson (Wasps), P Sackey (London Irish), T Voyce (Bath), L D Lloyd (Leicester), O J Lewsey (Wasps), B Johnston (Saracens), J A Ewens (Gloucester), F H H Waters (Wasps), J Noon (Newcastle)

Half-backs: A D King (Wasps), O Barkley (Bath), D J H Walder (Newcastle), K P P Bracken (*captain*) (Saracens), M B Wood (Wasps), S Benton (Leeds), *P J Grayson (Northampton)

Forwards: D E West (Leicester), M P Regan (Bath), A E Long (Bath), C P Fortey (Gloucester), S Thompson (Northampton), D L Flatman (Saracens), J M White (Saracens), T J Woodman (Gloucester), R Nebbett (Leicester), G C Rowntree (Leicester), S D Shaw (Wasps), S W Borthwick (Bath), B J Kay (Leicester), T Palmer (Leeds), A Brown (Bristol), M E Corry (Leicester), A R Hazell (Gloucester), J P R Worsley (Wasps), S White-Cooper (Harlequins), A Sanderson (Sale), P H Sanderson (Harlequins), L W Moody (Leicester), *R J Fidler (Gloucester)

*Replacement on tour

Manager: C R Woodward **Coach:** W B Ashton **Assistant coaches:** J Wells, E Hanley, P J Grayson, D Reddin

Tour record P 5 W 5 For 253 Against 89

2 June Won 22-10 CANADA (Toronto)

5 June Won 41-19 v British Columbia (Vancouver)

9 June Won 59-20 v CANADA (Vancouver)

12 June Won 83-21 v USA A (UCLA)

16 June Won 48-19 v USA (San Fransisco)

Details

First Test 2 June, Fletcher's Field, Markham, Toronto
Canada 10 (1G 1PG)   England 22 (1G 3T)

Canada: W U Stanley; N Witkowski, J Cannon, R P Ross, S Fauth; D S Stewart, M Williams; R G A Snow, P Dunkley, J D Thiel, E R P Knaggs, J N Tait, G A Dixon, A J Charron (*captain*), D R Baugh *Substitutions:* D Burleigh for Dunkley (18 mins); M R Schmid for Knaggs (69 mins); D Major for Baugh (69 mins)

Scorers *Try:* Fauth *Conversion:* Ross *Penalty Goal:* Ross

England: O J Lewsey; P C Sampson, L D Lloyd, J Noon, M Stephenson; D J H Walder, K P P Bracken (*captain*); G C Rowntree, D E West, J M White, S W Borthwick, B J Kay, M E Corry, J P R Worsley, L W Moody *Substitutions:* T R G Stimpson for Stephenson (temp 5 to 40 mins); S D Shaw for Borthwick (64 mins); P H Sanderson for Worsley (64 mins)

Scorers *Tries:* Lewsey (2), West, Bracken *Conversion:* Walder

Referee N Whitehouse (Wales)

5 June, Thunderbird Stadium, Vancouver
British Columbia 19 (1G 4PG)   England XV 41 (4G 1PG 2T)

British Columbia scorers *Try:* Robertson *Conversion:* Graf *Penalty Goals:* Graf (4)

England XV scorers *Tries:* Waters (2), Hazell, Rees, Woodman, Palmer *Conversions:* Barkley (2), Stimpson (2) *Penalty Goal:* Barkley

Second Test 9 June, Swangard Stadium, Burnaby, Vancouver
Canada 20 (2G 2PG)   England 59 (5G 3PG 3T)

Canada: W U Stanley; N Witkowski, J Cannon, R P Ross, S Fauth; D S Stewart, M Williams; R G A Snow, D Burleigh, J D Thiel, A J Charron (*captain*), J N Tait, G A Dixon, R Banks, D R Baugh *Substitutions:* K Nichols for Witkowski (temp 6 to 16 mins) and for Stanley (70 mins); D Major for Thiel (65 mins); M R Schmid for Baugh (65 mins); E R P Knaggs for Tait (68 mins); K Wirachowski for Banks (73 mins)

Scorers *Tries:* Baugh, Fauth *Conversions:* Ross (2) *Penalty Goals:* Ross (2)

England: O J Lewsey; P C Sampson, L D Lloyd, J Noon, M Stephenson; D J H Walder, K P P Bracken (*captain*); G C Rowntree, D E West, J M White, S D Shaw, B J Kay, S White-Cooper, J P R Worsley, L W Moody *Substitutions:* M B Wood for Bracken (36 mins); T R G Stimpson for Sampson (39 mins); S W Borthwick for Kay (42 mins); D L Flatman for White-Cooper (temp 37 to 40 mins) and for Rowntree (61 mins); P H Sanderson for Worsley (62 mins); A D King for Noon (70 mins); M P Regan for West (62 mins)

Scorers *Tries:* Shaw (2), Walder (2), penalty try, Worsley, Wood, Noon *Conversions:* Walder (5) *Penalty Goals:* Walder (3)

Referee J Jutge (France)

12 June, University College, Los Angeles
United States A 21 (1G 3PG 1T)   England XV 83 (9G 4T)

United States A scorers *Tries:* Naqica, Naivalu *Conversion:* Wilfley *Penalty Goals:* Wilfley (3)

England XV scorers *Tries:* Voyce (3), Sackey (2), Rees (2), King (2), A Sanderson, Flatman, Walshe, Waters *Conversions:* Barkley (9)

Test Match 16 June, Balboa Park, San Fransisco
United States 19 (2G 1T)   England 48 (4G 4T)

United States: K Shuman; J Naivalu, P Eloff, J Grobler, J Naqica; G Wells, K Dalzell; M MacDonald, K Khasigian, P Still, L Gross, E Reed, D Hodges (*captain*), D Lyle, K Schubert *Substitutions:* O Fifita for Schubert (40 mins); A Magelby for Reed (68 mins)

Scorers *Tries:* Naqica (2), Grobler *Conversions:* Wells (2)

England: O J Lewsey; L D Lloyd, F H H Waters, J Noon, M Stephenson; D J H Walder, K P P Bracken (*captain*); G C Rowntree, D E West, J M White, S D Shaw, S W Borthwick, S White-Cooper, J P R Worsley, L W Moody *Substitutions:* P H Sanderson for Moody (temp 9 to 12 mins) and for Worsley (62 mins); O Barkley for Noon (48 mins); A E Long for West (68 mins); D L Flatman for White-Cooper (temp 29 to 38 mins) and for Rowntree (68 mins); T Palmer for Borthwick (73 mins); T Voyce for Walder (73 mins); M B Wood for Bracken (79 mins); Noon for Waters (79 mins)

Scorers *Tries:* Lewsey (2), Lloyd (2), West, Sanderson, Worsley, Moody *Conversions:* Walder (4)

Referee A Turner (South Africa)

Argentina to New Zealand 2001

Tour party

Full-backs: B Stortoni (CASI), F Serra (SIC)

Threequarters: F Soler (Tala), D Albanese (Grenoble, Fra), J-N Piossek (Huirapuca), G Camardon (Roma, Ita), E Simone (Bristol, Eng), J Orengo (Atletico de Rosario), L Arbizu (Begles-Bordeaux, Fra) *(captain)*

Half-backs: G Quesada (Narbonne, Fra), J de la C Fernandez-Miranda (Hindu), F Contepomi (Bristol, Eng), N Fernandez-Miranda (Hindu), A Pichot (Bristol, Eng)

Forwards: F E Mendez (Begles-Bordeaux, Fra), M Ledesma (Narbonne, Fra), O J Hasan (Agen, Fra), M Reggiardo (Castres, Fra), R D Grau (Dax, Fra), L de Chazal (Universitario Tucuman), S G Bonorino (Brive, Fra), A Allub (Perpignan, Fra), C I Fernandez-Lobbe (Narbonne, Fra), M Sambucetti (Buenos Aires CRC), L Roldan (Atletico de Rosario), R Alvarez (Pucara), M Durand (Champagnat), R Martin (SIC), L Ostiglia (Hindu), S Phelan (CASI), G Longo (SIC), H Dande (Huirapuca), A Amuchastegui (Jockey Club Rosario), *P Cardinali (Los Tilos)

*Replacement on tour

Manager: J-L Rolandi **Assistant manager:** A Coscia **Coach:** M Loffreda

Tour record P 4 W 2 L 2 For 139 Against 148

17 June Won 70-26 v Counties Manukau (Pukekohe)

19 June Won 26-12 v Thames Valley (Paeroa)

23 June Lost 19-67 v NEW ZEALAND (Christchurch)

26 June Lost 24-43 v New Zealand Maori (Rotorua)

Details

17 June, Lion Red Stadium, Pukekohe
Counties-Manukau 26 (3G 1T)   Argentine XV 70 (6G 1PG 5T)

Counties-Manukau scorers *Tries:* Petelo, Feeney, Lee, Mealamu *Conversions:* Crichton (3)

Argentine XV scorers *Tries:* Stortoni (3), Mendez (2), Martin, Camardon, Fernandez-Lobbe, Contepomi, Albanese, Orengo *Conversions:* Contepomi (6) *Penalty Goal:* Contepomi

19 June, Paeroa Domain
Thames Valley 12 (4PG)   Argentine XV 26 (2G 4PG)

Thames Valley scorer *Penalty Goals:* Steel (4)

Argentine XV scorers *Tries:* Serra, Piossek *Conversions:* Quesada (2) *Penalty Goals:* Quesada (4)

Test Match 23 June, Jade Stadium, Lancaster Park, Christchurch
New Zealand 67 (7G 1PG 3T)   Argentina 19 (3PG 2T)

New Zealand: LR MacDonald; J W Wilson, J F Umaga, P F Alatini, J T Lomu; A P Mehrtens, J W Marshall; C H Hoeft, A D Oliver (*captain*), C J Hayman, N M C Maxwell, T Flavell, R D Thorne, J Collins, T C Randell *Substitutions:* T E Brown for Mehrtens (34 mins); M R Holah for Collins (temp 34 to 36 mins and 39 mins); D C Howlett for MacDonald (40 mins); M G Hammett for Holah (temp 47 to 54 mins); C R Jack for Flavell (54 mins); G M Somerville for Hoeft (62 mins)

Scorers *Tries:* Alatini (2), Wilson (2), Umaga, Randell, MacDonald, Jack, Howlett, Holah *Conversions:* Mehrtens (3), Brown (4) *Penalty Goal:* Mehrtens

Argentina: B Stortoni; G Camardon, J Orengo, L Arbizu (*captain*), D Albanese; F Contepomi, A Pichot; R D Grau, F E Mendez, O Hasan, C I Fernandez-Lobbe, A Allub, S Phelan, G Longo, R Martin *Substitutions:* J-N Piossek for Albanese (54 mins); G Quesada for Contepomi (57 mins); M Reggiardo for Phelan (temp 57 to 60 mins) and for Hasan (66 mins); L Ostiglia for Phelan (66 mins)

Scorers *Tries:* Arbizu, Camardon *Penalty Goals:* Contepomi (3)

Referee A J Cole (Australia)

26 June, Rotorua International Stadium
New Zealand Maori 43 (5G 1PG 1T)   Argentine XV 24 (1G 4PG 1T)

NZ Maori scorers *Tries:* Randle (2), Reihana (2), Hewitt, Duggan *Conversions:* Spencer (5) *Penalty Goal:* Spencer

Argentine XV scorers *Tries:* Piossek, Fernandez-Lobbe *Conversion:* Quesada *Penalty Goals:* Quesada (4)

Ireland to Romania 2001

Tour record P 1 W 1 L 0 For 37 Against 3

Test Match 2 June, Bucharest
Romania 3 (1PG)   Ireland 37 (4G 3PG)

Romania: G Brezoianu; I Teodorescu, V Maftei, N Oprea, V Ghioc; I Tofan, L Sirbu; M Sociaciu, P Balan, S Florea, V Nedelcu, O Tonita, M Bejan, F Corodeanu (*captain*), C Mersiou *Substitutions:* S Soare and S Guranescu for Florea and Maftei (49 mins); S Demci for Bejan (65 mins); M Dragomir for Nedelcu (73 mins); D Tudosa for Sociaciu (74 mins)

Scorer *Penalty Goal:* Tofan

Ireland: G E A Murphy; D A Hickie, M J Mullins, K M Maggs, T G Howe; D G Humphreys, P A Stringer; P M Clohessy, F J Sheahan, J J Hayes, M J Galwey (*captain*), G W Longwell, E R P Miller, A G Foley, K Dawson *Substitutions:* G Easterby for Stringer (56 mins); S J Byrne and J M Fitzpatrick for Sheahan and Clohessy (66 mins); P A Burke for Humphreys (71 mins); J C Bell for Mullins (76 mins), M R Driscoll and D P Wallace for Galwey and Foley (77 mins)

Scorers *Tries:* Foley, Maggs, Galwey, Bell *Conversions:* Humphreys (3), Burke
Penalty Goals: Humphreys (3)
Referee D I Ramage (Scotland)

Samoa to New Zealand 2001

Tour record P 1 W 0 L 1 For 6 Against 50

Test Match 16 June, North Harbour Stadium, Albany
New Zealand 50 (3G 3PG 4T)   Samoa 6 (2PG)

New Zealand: L R MacDonald; D C Howlett, J F Umaga, P F Alatini,
J W Wilson; T E Brown, B T Kelleher; C H Hoeft, A D Oliver *(captain)*,
G M Somerville, N M C Maxwell, T V Flavell, R D Thorne, R T Cribb,
M R Holah *Substitutions:* C J Hayman and R M Ranby for Somerville and Alatini
(58 mins)

Scorers *Tries:* Brown (3), Maxwell, Howlett, Flavell, Wilson *Conversions:* Brown (3)
Penalty Goals: Brown (3)

Samoa: S Leaega; F So'olefai, T Fanolua, F Tuilagi, A So'oalo; E Va'a,
S So'oailo; M Luafaiealo, T Leota, P Asi, O Palepoi, S F Lafaiali'i, S Sititi
(captain), P J Paramore, C Glendinning *Substitutions:* L Tone for Palepoi (50 mins);
P Segi for Glendinning (55 mins), A Tialia, K Lealamanua and E Seveali'i for
Leota, Luafalealo and Tuilagi (69 mins)

Scorer *Penalty Goals:* Leaega (2)
Referee P L Marshall (Australia)

Romania to Wales 2001

Tour record P 1 W 0 L 1 For 9 Against 81

Test Match 19 September, Millennium Stadium, Cardiff Arms Park
Wales 81 (10G 2PG 1T)   Romania 9 (3PG)

Wales: K A Morgan; G Thomas, A G Bateman, S M Jones, D R James;
G L Henson, R Howley; I D Thomas, R C McBryde, D Young *(captain)*,
C P Wyatt, A P Moore, C L Charvis, G Lewis, Gavin Thomas *Substitutions:*
G R Williams for Henson (22 mins); B D Sinkinson for Lewis (50 mins);
B H Williams for McBryde (58 mins); D Peel for Howley (69 mins); J C Quinnell
for Moore (70 mins)

Scorers *Tries:* Charvis (3), James (3), B Williams (2), Wyatt, Bateman, Quinnell
Conversions: Jones (10) *Penalty Goals:* Jones (2)

Romania: G Brezoianu; I Teodorescu, N Oprea, C Lupu, V Ghioc; I Tofan,
L Sirbu; D Dima, S Demci, M Socaciu, M Dragomir, V Nedelcu, M Bejan,
A Petrache *(captain)*, D Iacob *Substitutions:* M Ciolacu for Tofan (temp 6 to 10 mins
and 42 mins); L Dumitrescu for Bejan (temp 34 to 37 mins and 50 mins);
P Toderasc for Socaciu (63 mins); S Soare for Dima (72 mins)

Scorer *Penalty Goals:* Tofan (3)
Referee A C Rolland (Ireland)

THE EUROPEAN NATIONS TOURNAMENTS 2000-01

Georgia Take Romania's Title

Chris Thau

The European scene has become more structured and indeed competitive since the IRB stepped in to help the European governing body FIRA-AER finance its main senior competitions. Since last year, there is a European Nations Cup (ENC), a European Nations Plate (ENP) and a European Nations Bowl (ENB) – three divisions operating on a promotion-relegation basis and involving 30 of the 40-odd FIRA-AER membership.

The elite ENC section – modelled on the Six Nations competition format and calendar – involves the next best six Continental teams after France and Italy, with the Plate accommodating the next six. Romania narrowly won the Cup 23-20 against a bruising Georgian challenge in Tbilisi in 2000, while Russia won the Plate to earn promotion to the elite group. Morocco and Tunisia were granted "temporary guest" status in the first and second division respectively to help the two North African nations undergo the transition from FIRA-AER competitions to the Confederation of African Rugby (CAR) Championship.

The European Nations Cup 2000-01

Interestingly enough, this year's ENC competition, a Six Nations second division in everything but name, confirmed the overwhelming domination of the Eastern Europeans with Georgia, Romania and Russia, in this order, finishing top of the table, undefeated in their encounters with their three Western counterparts Spain, Portugal and Netherlands. In fairness, Russia's reasonably successful campaign could have turned sour had the cliff-hanger against Spain gone the other way. With the Spanish leading by two points in the closing stages, Vladimir Simonov's successful penalty in injury time secured Russia a valuable and somehow unexpected 30-29 win against a young and enterprising opposition.

However, Russia's joy was short-lived, as Georgia stole the show and three valuable Championship points following a similar scenario in Krasnodar, in Southern Russia. The "Lelos" as they are called upset their hosts to win 25-23 in a bad-tempered match full of drama and poetic justice.

Only a win against arch-rivals Romania could have restored Russia's battered Championship fortunes. Buoyed by the arrival of their new South African coach James Stoffberg – assisted by VVA's Nekulai Nerush – the

Russians arrived in the old city of Iasi, the capital of the Principality of Moldova in North East Romania, hoping to emulate the feat of the Georgians.

Unfortunately, they clashed with a Romanian side keen to re-establish its credentials after the autumn mauling at the hands of the visiting New Zealand A side. After the disaster against the New Zealanders, the coaching staff was re-shuffled with former Canterbury coach John Phillips being replaced by former Romanian captain and coach Mircea Paraschiv. He invited some of the professionals playing in France, including Brive's Sorin Socol and Alexandru Manta of Aurillac – who previously had refused to play for the national team – to join in and the Romanians ran riot.

Twelve thousand spectators – arguably the largest crowd at an Eastern European rugby international match during the last decade – turned up to support Romania's quest for rugby credibility at the Emil Alexandrescu Stadium. Their five-try 42-13 demolition job of Russia, coupled with Georgia's 43-10 equally impressive win over Spain in Tbilisi, set the scene for the grand finale between the two nations in Bucharest on 7 April.

The comfortable win against Russia made the newcomers in the Romanian team complacent, while their discipline in the training camp left a lot to be desired. Not for the first time a combination of complacency and ill-discipline, on and off the field, brought about Romania's downfall. Georgia, however, Romania's woes apart, played their cards right, concentrated on the basics, out-muscled and out-thought the Romanians and deserved to win the match and the Cup – a remarkable achievement signalling the coming of age of the Lelos as a power to be reckoned with.

Results and scorers

2 February Netherlands 3 (*PG:* G Viguurs) Georgia 32 (*T:* V Didebulidze 2, L Tsabadze, B Khekhelashvili *C:* P Jimsheladze 3 *PG:* P Jimsheladze 2) (Amsterdam)

2 February Spain 29 (*T:* F Velazco *PG:* J Alonso-Lasheras 5, A Kovalenco 3) Russia 30 (*T:* V Gratchev 2, I Nikolaichuk, A Zakarliouk *C:* Simonov 2 *PG:* V Simonov 2) (Madrid)

2 February Portugal 0, Romania 47 (*T:* A Manta 3, N Oprea, P Mitu *C:* P Mitu 2 *PG:* P Mitu 6) (Lisbon)

17 February Georgia 36 (*T:* I Zedguenidze 2, T Zibzivadze 2, D Bolghashvili, I Abusseridze *C:* P Jimsheladze 3) Portugal 12 (*PG:* G Malheiro 3 *DG:* G Malheiro) (Tbilisi)

18 February Netherlands 20 (*T:* R Lips, K Staats *C:* G Viguurs 2 *PG:* G Viguurs 2) Russia 41 (*T:* K Ratchkov, A Zakarliouk, Y Chelepkov, A Kuzine, S Sergheiev, M Uambaev, R Bibkov *C:* K Ratchkov 3) (Amsterdam)

18 February Spain 12 (*PG:* A Kovalenco 4) Romania 27 (*T:* P Balan, G Brezoianu, V Ghioc *C:* P Mitu 3 *PG:* P Mitu 2) (Seville)

4 March Russia 23 (*T:* S Klimenko, V Gratchev, S Kascheev *C:* K Ratchkov *PG:* V Simonov 2) Georgia 25 (*T:* penalty try, I Zedguenidze, L Labadze *C:* P Jimsheladze 2 *PG:* P Jimsheladze 2) (Krasnodar)

4 March Romania 52 (*T:* M Ciolacu 2, P Mitu, F Corodeanu, D Iacob, O Tonita, V Maftei, P Balan *C:* P Mitu 6) Netherlands 15 (*T:* T Schumacher 2 *C:* G Viguurs *PG:* G Viguurs) (Constanta)

4 March Spain 31 (*T:* C Souto, A León, A Enciso *C:* A Kovalenco 2 *PG:* A Kovalenco 4) Portugal 15 (*PG:* F Carter 4 *DG:* F Carter) (Valladolid)

17 March Georgia 43 (*T:* M Urjukashvili 2, V Katsadze, G Shvelidze, A Guirgadze, penalty try *C:* P Jimsheladze 5 *PG:* P Jimsheladze) Spain 10 (*T:* C Souto *C:* J Alonso-Lasheras *PG:* A Kovalenco) (Rustavi)

18 March Romania 42 (*T:* P Mitu, F Corodeanu, G Solomie, S Socol, P Balan *C:* P Mitu 4 *PG:* P Mitu 3) Russia 13 (*T:* D Diatlov *C:* V Yakovlev *PG:* V Yakovlev 2) (Iasi)

18 March Portugal 23 (*T:* T King, D Coutinho *C:* F Carter 2 *PG:* F Carter 3) Netherlands 6 (*PG:* K de Schutter 2) (Lisbon)

7 April Romania 20 (*T:* F Corodeanu 2, V Ghioc *C:* M. Ciolacu *DG:* R Gontineac) Georgia 31 (*T:* I Abusseridze, D Bolgashvili, L Tsabadze *C:* P Jimsheladze 2 *PG:* P Jimsheladze 3, M Urjukashvili) (Bucharest)

8 April Russia 45 (*T:* M Uambaev 2, V Simonov, I Nikolaichuk, Y Krasnobaev, A Chupin *C:* V Yakovlev 2, V Simonov *PG:* V Yakovlev 2, V Simonov) Portugal 27 (*T:* N Garvao, M Barbosa, F Grenho *C:* F Grenho 3 *PG:* F Grenho, F Carter) (Krasnodar)

8 April Netherlands 13 (*T:* G van der Pol, A Kuipers *PG:* K de Schutter) Spain 36 (*T:* A Kovalenco 2, J Salazar, J-M Bohórquez, O Ripol *C:* A. Kovalenco *PG:* A Kovalenco 3) (Amsterdam)

Final European Nations Cup Table 2000-01

	P	W	D	L	For	Against	Pts
Georgia	5	5	0	0	167	68	15
Romania	5	4	0	1	188	71	13
Russia	5	3	0	2	152	143	11
Spain	5	2	0	3	118	128	9
Portugal	5	1	0	4	77	165	7
Netherlands	5	0	0	5	57	184	5

Three points for a win, two for a draw and one for a defeat.

Previous European Nations Cup Winners: 1999-2000 Romania; 2000-01 Georgia

The European Nations Plate 2000-01

Owing to the scheduling for round two of the 2003 Rugby World Cup qualifiers this autumn, there was no promotion or relegation between the Cup and Plate sections at the end of the 2000-2001 season. The status-quo has been preserved in order to secure the 10 team draw (the six Plate contenders and the four sides promoted from the Bowl section playing in two pools of five) for the second round of the forthcoming European qualifying zone matches. Poland and Ukraine dominated the proceedings in the Plate, with the Germans finishing strongly after a poor showing during the early part of the season. The Czechs took the scalp of Ukraine in the first round, while Croatia seemed unable to match the feats of the 1999 generation when they featured among the leading contenders of the Rugby World Cup European zone.

Results

14 October 2000 Czech Republic 35, Ukraine 3 (Prague); **21 October** Ukraine 16, Denmark 6 (Kiev); Germany 13, Poland 26 (Berlin); **28 October** Denmark 15, Croatia 16 (Copenhagen); **4 November** Poland 34, Czech Republic 16 (Gdynia); **11 November** Croatia 3, Poland 8 (Zapresic); **12 November** Germany 12, Ukraine 19 (Heustenstamm); **8 April 2001** Germany 30, Czech Republic 17 (Constance); **28 April** Denmark 10, Germany 21 (Aalborg); Croatia 32, Czech Republic 22 (Makarska); **5 May** Poland 34, Denmark 12 (Gdynia); **19 May** Ukraine 9, Poland 3 (Odessa); Czech Republic 42, Denmark 10 (Prague); **20 May** Croatia 14, Germany 14 (Split); **26 May** Ukraine 18, Croatia 5 (Kiev).

Final European Nations Plate Table 2000-01

	P	W	D	L	For	Against	Pts
Poland	5	4	0	1	105	53	13
Ukraine	5	4	0	1	65	71	13
Germany	5	2	1	2	90	86	10
Croatia	5	2	1	2	70	67	10
Czech Republic	5	2	0	3	132	109	9
Denmark	5	0	0	5	53	129	5

Three points for a win, two for a draw and one for a defeat.
Previous European Nations Plate Winners: 1999-2000 Russia; 2000-01 Poland

The European Nations Bowl 2000-01

The Bowl section, containing 18 teams divided into three pools of six, doubled as the first round of the 2003 Rugby World Cup qualifying process. The pool winners, Sweden, Switzerland and Belgium, and the best runner-up, Latvia, gained promotion to the Plate Section.

Results
See Rugby World Cup section.

OTHER TOURNAMENTS 2000-01

Wins for Argentina, Japan and Fiji
John Griffiths

Pan American Championship 2001

Argentina retained their unbeaten record in a Championship that dates back to 1994. The Pumas, who are the only major rugby-playing nation who do not compete in an annual tournament, were clear winners of the 2001 event staged in Ontario in May.

The toughest match for coach Marcelo Loffreda's charges was their opening encounter with Uruguay. The favourites led 22-6 at the interval, but a thrilling second half rally by the Uruguayan Teros, who scored two tries and landed three penalties, nearly caused an upset. The Pumas held out by 32-27 before comfortably disposing of the United States 44-16 in the second round of matches.

Canada defeated the Eagles by 19-10 in a match that stood as the annual Can-Am encounter and overcame Uruguay in mid-week. The two unbeaten sides thus came face to face in the final round of matches in front of 2,400 at Fletcher's Fields in Markham. The Pumas quickly opened an 11-0 lead that they never looked likely to relinquish. In an uncompromising match, there were three yellow cards dished out by American referee Al Klemp and Canada's Ryan Banks was sent off five minutes from time for elbowing Agustin Pichot. Three dropped goals by Juan Fernandez Miranda helped Argentina to its fourth straight Pan American Rugby Championship title.

Results

19 May Richardson Stadium, Kingston
Argentina 32 (3G 2PG 1T)   **Uruguay 27** (1G 5PG 1T)

Argentina Scorers *Tries:* H Dande, J-M Nunez Piossek, J Orengo, F Soler *Conversions:* F Contepomi (3) *Penalty Goals:* F Contepomi (2)
Uruguay Scorers *Try:* M Mendaro, E Ibarra *Conversion:* J Menchaca *Penalty Goals:* J Menchaca (5)
Referee I Hyde-Lay (Canada)

19 May Richardson Stadium, Kingston
Canada 19 (1G 4PG)   **United States 10** (1G 1PG)

Canada Scorers *Try:* J Thiel *Conversion:* D S Stewart *Penalty Goals:* D S Stewart (4)
United States Scorers *Try:* K Dalzell *Conversion:* G Wells *Penalty Goal:* G Wells
Referee S Borsani (Argentina)

23 May Hamilton
United States 16 (1G 3PG)   **Argentina 44** (3G 1PG 4T)

United States Scorers *Try:* M Timoteo *Conversion:* G Wells *Penalty Goals:* G Wells (3)
Argentina Scorers *Tries:* R Martin (2), G Longo, F Contepomi, B Stortoni, J Orengo, F Soler *Conversions:* F Contepomi (3) *Penalty Goal:* F Contepomi
Referee E Blengio (Uruguay)

23 May Hamilton
Canada 14 (3PG 1T)   **Uruguay 8** (1PG 1T)

Canada Scorers *Try:* D Burleigh *Penalty Goals:* R Ross (3)
Uruguay Scorers *Try:* N Brignoni *Penalty Goal:* J Menchaca
Referee S Borsani (Argentina)

26 May Fletcher's Field, Markham
United States 31 (2G 4PG 1T)   **Uruguay 28** (2G 3PG 1T)

United States Scorers *Tries:* J Naivalu (2), P Eloff *Conversions:* G Wells (2) *Penalty Goals:* G Wells (4)
Uruguay Scorers *Tries:* N Brignoni, B Amarillo, penalty try *Conversions:* J Menchaca (2) *Penalty Goals:* J Menchaca (3)
Referee I Hyde-Lay (Canada)

26 May Fletcher's Field, Markham
Canada 6 (2PG)   **Argentina 20** (2PG 3DG 1T)

Canada Scorers *Penalty Goals:* S Stewart (2)
Argentina Scorers *Try:* L Roldan *Penalty Goals:* F Contepomi (2) *Drop Goals:* J Fernandez Miranda (3)
Referee A Klemp (United States)
Previous Pan American Champions: 1994 Argentina; 1996 Argentina; 1998 Argentina; 2001 Argentina

IRB/Asian Triangular Series 2001

The biennial Asian Championship has given rugby in the Far East a wonderful shot in the arm since its inception in the late 1960s. In April and May, as part of their drive to develop regional international tournaments, the IRB launched the new Asian Triangular Series.

There were four tiers of competition. The Cup involved Japan, Chinese Taipei and Korea, the leading three nations on the Asian continent. The subsidiary Shield, Plate and Bowl Tri Nations tournaments staged simultaneously meant that a dozen Asian nations were involved in meaningful competition.

The Japanese, under a new management team comprising head coach Shogo Mukai assisted by Kiwi Ross Cooper and Australian Gary Wallace, made good use of the tournament to identify new talent and prepare for its Test series with Wales a month later. As expected, they took the inaugural Cup title, beating Korea in Tokyo before overcoming Chinese Taipei in Taiwan a fortnight later.

The tightness of the Japan-Korea match suggested that the intention of the new competition – closing the gap between the nations at the elite end of the Asian game – had been adequately met. Japan fielded six new caps (with several more newcomers on the bench) but did not make certain of victory until four minutes from time when prop Masahiko Toyoyama scored a try to add to the 17 points contributed by the boot of winger Toru Kurihara.

Japan's 50-point victory over Taipei in Taiwan two Sundays later was a personal triumph for Takafumi Hirao. He ran in four of Japan's eleven tries after winning selection ahead of Kurihara on the wing.

Results

Asia Cup: 13 May Japan 27, Korea 19 (Tokyo); 20 May Korea 74, Chinese Taipei 22 (Seoul); 27 May Chinese Taipei 15, Japan 65 (Taiwan) **Winners:** Japan.

Asia Shield: 5 May Singapore 8, Hong Kong 26 (Singapore); 12 May Hong Kong 25, China 25 (Guangzhou); 19 May China 33, Singapore 6 (Guangzhou) **Winners:** Hong Kong.

Asia Plate: 13 May Malaysia 7, Sri Lanka 18 (Kuala Lumpur); 20 May Sri Lanka 46, Thailand 17 (Colombo); 16 June Thailand 29, Malaysia 13 (Bangkok) **Winners:** Sri Lanka.

Asia Bowl: 26 April Arabian Gulf 66, Kazakhstan 22 (Bahrain); 27 April Kazakhstan 51, India 9 (Bahrain); 28 April India 3, Arabian Gulf 97 (Bahrain) **Winners:** Arabian Gulf.

World Games 2001

International rugby in the form of the seven-a-side game was invited to participate in the World Games held in Akita, Japan in August 2001. All told, more than 3,000 competitors representing over 80 different countries in 32 sports took part in the Games.

IRB Chairman, Vernon Pugh QC, was delighted to accept the invitation. 'The tournament is a continuation of the increasing recognition of Rugby's worth as a truly international sport within a multi-games environment,' he said.

Eight countries divided into two pools of four were involved in a rugby tournament that was spread over two days. The surprise of day one was Fiji's resurgence as a sevens force. Waisale Serevi, arguably the greatest exponent of sevens rugby, spearheaded the Islanders to a surprise 33-14 win in Pool A over New Zealand, who earlier in the year had been crowned winners of both the IRB World Sevens Series and the RWC Sevens Trophy. Australia emerged as the favourites from Pool B to reach the final after disposing of a strong South African challenge with a win by 21-19 in the tightest match of the opening day.

Australia and Fiji duly triumphed in their quarter and semi finals to meet in the grand final. Fero Lasagavibau opened the scoring for Fiji inside the first 90 seconds, lancing the Australian defence with a dummy pass to grab a try. He then sped 50 metres along the touch line a minute later to send Serevi in for a second Fijian try, and with the captain converting both tries, Fiji were 14-0 ahead as the game entered its second quarter. Patrick Phibbs's attack from a scrum created a try for Australia just before the interval so that at the break Fiji led 14 – 5.

Australia's Tui Junior Talaia scored a try on the restart and Julian Huxley's conversion brought Australia to within two points of the Fijians. Midway through the second half, however, came the decisive score of the match. Vilimoni Delasau ran in a try for Fiji and scores by Jope Tuikaba and Serevi, who didn't miss a conversion, took the Fijians out of sight at 35-12. Robert McDonald's consolation try, converted by Huxley, added a touch of Australian respectability to the final 35-19 scoreline.

'This will give the people of Fiji something to celebrate and bring them together,' said Serevi after his side had won their first major sevens title for twelve months. Serevi was the tournament's leading scorer with 98 points from eight tries and 29 conversions. Richard Graham, Australia's captain, spoke for all when he said after the final: 'Serevi was outstanding. We have had a wonderful time and received a very warm welcome from the Akita people. It was a very well organised tournament.'

These were sentiments echoed by Vernon Pugh. 'I am delighted that Rugby participated in a multi-sport environment. It was very clear that the supporters who watched the rugby over the two days enjoyed the fast continuous play, fabulous athletes and the high scoring games. It has been a fantastic boost for us and for our bid for the Olympics.'

Pool Results (25th August 2001)

Pool A: New Zealand 21, Canada 7; Fiji 33, France 12; New Zealand 12, France 21; Fiji 54, Canada 0; Canada 5, France 36; New Zealand 14, Fiji 33.

Pool B: Australia 31, Great Britain 0; South Africa 33, Japan 7; Australia 31, Japan 0; South Africa 43, Great Britain 5; Great Britain 7, Japan 38; Australia 21, South Africa 19.

Results from finals day (26th August 2001)

Quarter Finals: Fiji 35, Great Britain 0; South Africa 12, New Zealand 15; Australia 49, Canada 0; France 40, Japan 0.

Losers' Semi Finals: South Africa 22, Great Britain 19; Canada 21, Japan 19.

Winners' Semi Finals: Fiji 45, New Zealand 0; Australia 35, France 5.

Final (7th/8th place): Great Britain 21, Japan 19.

Final (5th/6th place): South Africa 34, Canada 5.

Final (3rd/4th place): New Zealand 19, France 10.

FINAL (1st/2nd place): Fiji 35, Australia 19.

RUGBY WORLD CUP SEVENS 2001

Lomu puts New Zealand in Sevens Heaven

Rob Wildman

Jonah Lomu dominated the Rugby World Cup Sevens. It was one of the best bets of 2001 that he would play a leading role in delivering a world title to New Zealand for the first time since the inaugural 15-a-side event in 1987. The aura of Lomu is such that he attracts crowds wherever he goes. In Mar del Plata, the vibrant beach resort on the Atlantic coast of Argentina, it was no different. Spectators and stewards packed media conferences in an effort to grab a word or picture with him. It made for some chaotic scenes which helped to fulfil the tournament's billing that it would provide a heady mix of sport and fun as a late evening attraction following a day of sun and sea on the resort's famous beaches.

Overall, Mar del Plata delivered the action. The first Rugby World Cup event outside the senior countries of the International Board was a success in that it demonstrated the growing strength of the so-called minor nations. The memory of Spain toppling England in the group stages, the Plate successes of Kenya against France (yes, Kenya) and Georgia overcoming Wales will be cherished by many. It must be said, however, that Mar del Plata could, and should, have been better. Ignoring the inevitable fact that only a sprinkling of top players made the journey, information for spectators was poor and the lack of a high-quality big screen, like the one used in Hong Kong and elsewhere, to give the stadium a festive atmosphere was a major negative. An alcohol ban – prompted by recent violence at football games – was another drawback for visiting fans.

Other factors also hindered the event. The biggest was the proximity of tournaments in the new sevens world series which made the distinction difficult for a reluctant media. Few leading news organisations from around the world sent representatives and no print journalist made the trip from New Zealand, despite the presence of Lomu.

The tournament came alive on the finals evening after two long days of qualifying where 24 teams had played 60 games to sort out eight quarter-finalists. The schedule was hard on players and officials, especially the small band of referees. Stadia Mundialista rocked for the first time during an exhilarating quarter-final between Argentina and South Africa. Inspired by Agustin Pichot, the Pumas were driven on in front of 30,000 raucous supporters. Somehow, after conceding two early tries, the scrum-half, helped by Felipe Contepomi, took the Pumas into a 14-12 lead which they held until the end. Pichot, after Lomu the tournament's biggest star, explained his presence by stating that it was important for the future of his country's rugby. His breath-taking nerve and bravery won him many fans through 14 minutes of action.

The only downside was that come the semi-finals Argentina were short on gas to stop New Zealand, who had comfortably accounted for Samoa in the quarters, 45-7. Up until the Samoa match Lomu had been rarely spotted in group wins over Spain, Japan and England. That last game brought the most unfortunate incident of the weekend when Eric Rush, a pillar of the sevens world, broke a leg. He was carried off and immediately returned home for an operation.

Rush was still en-route for Auckland when Lomu inspired his depleted group the following day in the knock-out stages. He reserved his best for the final when he contributed three tries in a 31-12 victory. Afterwards, in between the usual soundbites on these triumphal occasions, there appeared some genuine sympathy for Rush. Lomu also praised the 36-year-old for helping to establish his own career. It was a dignified celebration by New Zealand that was a credit to the guiding influence of coach Gordon Tietjens. Lomu said: 'I couldn't have done it if it weren't for the boys and Rushie. If it weren't for Rushie and all the knowledge he's given us, we wouldn't have done it. We did it heart and soul for him and for the whole of New Zealand.' Tietjens admitted that he kept Lomu in the background during the early games. 'We didn't want to show our cards too early,' he said. If Lomu took most of the plaudits, then praise also went to Karl Te Nana, the stand-in captain for Rush.

Afterwards Julian Gardner, the manager of Australia, added to the list of tributes to Lomu by describing him as a freak. 'We were Lomu-ised three times,' he said, almost in awe. Glen Ella, the manager, commented: 'The best tackler in the team, Richard Graham, could not stop him and he used Brendan Williams as a speed bump.'

While Lomu accepted a further honour, the career of another sevens star, Waisale Serevi, took a downturn. Holders Fiji fell at the semi-final stage where Williams, the wing from New South Wales, demonstrated he had many of the dazzling skills that had made Serevi such a feared player. Against Fiji, Williams contributed the first try after Australia had fallen 14-0 behind. That score turned the contest and was part of 22 points without reply. A game earlier, in the quarter-final, the brilliance of Williams helped him to four tries against England in a 33-5 victory. Though Lomu took most of the headlines, Williams would undoubtedly have been the player-of-the-tournament had there been such a prize.

The performance of England, the inaugural champions in 1993, was harmed by the dispute between club and country. For the Six Nations countries, the hectic calendar meant that the January weekend clashed with the Heineken Cup quarter-finals. At least England made the knock-out stages, despite that embarrassing loss to Spain in the group games. They were only saved, however, by a late match-winning try from Japan's Daisuke Ohata that deprived Spain a place in the last eight. Ireland, Wales and

France all failed to make the last 16 prompting Vernon Pugh, the Chairman of the International Board, to comment that it was about time the leading European nations took sevens more seriously. To emphasize the point, Scotland and Italy had failed to qualify for the trip.

In contrast to the embarrassment of the Six Nations, the tournament was an outstanding success for lesser lights like Chile, Portugal, Russia, Georgia, Spain and Kenya. Chile captured the Bowl, defeating Portugal, 21-19, giving scrum-half Nicolas Arancibia the perfect stage to show his talent. Russia also had a natural leader in Gratchev Viatcheslav, whose eight tries in the tournament included one in the 26-12 victory over Georgia in the final of the Plate. Arguably the most startling result was that win of Kenya's over France. No wonder Bernard Lapasset, the President of the French Union, shook his head in despair, though he was the first to admit that the sight of the supple, spring-heeled Kenyans highlighted the potential of the developing nations.

Somehow, in a cluttered calendar there has to be a place for this shortened version of the sport, though if the rugby authorities cannot get the top players to a World Cup then it surely cannot have that title. The many International Board representatives who journeyed to Mar del Plata must have left with mixed feelings. Uplifted, yes, by the development of some countries, but concerned that the tournament has yet to establish itself in the hectic schedule of modern rugby.

Pool Results (26th/27th January 2001)

Pool A: Argentina 49, Russia 7; Korea 33, Kenya 17; Fiji 41, Ireland 5; Kenya 10, Ireland 31; Korea 14, Argentina 27; Fiji 14, Russia 5; Fiji 19, Argentina 12; Russia 14, Kenya 7; Korea 19, Ireland 19; Argentina 33, Ireland 12; Korea 33, Russia 5; Fiji 52, Kenya 7; Russia 28, Ireland 5; Argentina 36, Kenya 7; Fiji 33, Korea 7.

Pool B: Cook Islands 5, Canada 24; France 14, Georgia 10; South Africa 47, Taipei 7; Georgia 24, Taipei 0; France 7, Cook Islands 19; South Africa 24, Canada 0; South Africa 29, Cook Islands 0; Canada 20, Georgia 7; France 35, Taipei 0; Cook Islands 26, Taipei 7; France 17, Canada 12; South Africa 24, Georgia 12; Canada 55, Taipei 7; Cook Islands 19, Georgia 0; South Africa 19, France 0.

Pool C: Zimbabwe 12, Japan 17; England 21, Chile 7; New Zealand 26, Spain 7; Chile 5, Spain 10; England 28, Zimbabwe 7; New Zealand 52, Japan 0; England 12, Spain 14; New Zealand 47, Zimbabwe 0; Japan 7, Chile 5; Zimbabwe 52, Spain 7; England 24, Japan 7; New Zealand 33, Chile 0; Japan 12, Spain 7; Zimbabwe 12, Chile 19; New Zealand 17, England 7.

Pool D: Wales 19, Portugal 19; Australia 29, Hong Kong 5; Samoa 49, United States 19; Hong Kong 0, United States 19; Australia 24, Wales 5; Samoa 33, Portugal 19; Australia 47, United States 0; Samoa 24, Wales 17; Portugal 26, Hong Kong 0; Wales 19, United States 10; Australia 38, Portugal 0; Samoa 21, Hong Kong 12; Portugal 15, United States 20; Wales 26, Hong Kong 12; Samoa 12, Australia 34.

Finals Day (28th January 2001)

Bowl Quarter-Finals: Ireland 24, Chinese Taipei 19; Portugal 19, Zimbabwe 14; France 7, Kenya 12; Chile 19, Hong Kong 14. **Semi-Finals:** Ireland 12, Portugal 33; Kenya 12, Chile 35. **FINAL:** Portugal 19, Chile 21.

Plate Quarter-Finals: Korea 19, Georgia 24; Wales 21, Japan 7; Cook Islands 10, Russia 26; Spain 26, United States 5. **Semi-Finals:** Georgia 17, Wales 10; Russia 26, Spain 7. **FINAL:** Georgia 12, Russia 24.

Melrose Cup Quarter-Finals: Fiji 21, Canada 5; Australia 33, England 5; South Africa 12, Argentina 14; New Zealand 45, Samoa 7. **Semi-Finals:** Fiji 14, Australia 22; Argentina 7, New Zealand 31.

Final: 28 January 2001, Stadia Mundialista, Mar del Plata

Australia 12 (1G 1T) **New Zealand 31** (3G 2T)

Australia: B Williams, C Pither; S Payne, R McDonald; J Huxley, R Graham (captain), A McDonald *Substitutions:* E Carter for R McDonald (16 mins); T Donnelly for A McDonald (17 mins)

Scorers *Tries:* Williams, Donnelly *Conversion:* Huxley

New Zealand: K Te Nana (captain), B Fleming; M Muliaina, A Valence; C Newby, R So'oialo, J Lomu *Substitutions:* R Randle for B Fleming (18 mins), J Going for Valence (19 mins)

Scorers *Tries:* Lomu (3), Muliaina, Valence *Conversions:* Valence (2), Te Nana

Previous Rugby World Cup Sevens Finals: 1993 England 21, Australia 17 (Murrayfield); 1997 Fiji 24, South Africa 21 (Hong Kong); 2001 New Zealand 31, Australia 12 (Mar del Plata).

IRB WORLD SEVENS SERIES 2001

Second Title To New Zealand

Chris Thau

During the early rounds of the nine-tournament IRB World Sevens Series – a tenth round scheduled for Brisbane was cancelled after the Australian Government denied the Fijian team entry visas – it looked as if the event would be a repeat of the inaugural Grand Prix: a two-horse race between the masters of sevens, Fiji, and their New Zealand challengers. Indeed, until the conclusion of the Hong Kong tournament, New Zealand and Fiji were almost neck and neck, New Zealand leading Fiji by the slender margin of two competition points (74-72).

Australia had also given a good account of themselves and, after two lost Cup semi-finals in Durban and Dubai, finally claimed their first-ever Grand Prix title by winning in Wellington. On the other hand New Zealand, probably still day-dreaming after winning the World Cup Sevens title in Mar del Plata in January, had a dismal round (by their standards), failing for the first time in the short history of the Series to reach the last four in the Cup.

Wellington, where the sevens circus had a particularly warm reception, witnessed arguably the most remarkable sequence of upsets in the short history of the IRB World Sevens Series. With the hosts, New Zealand, succumbing to both Fiji and Samoa, the US Eagles, coached by New Zealander John McKittrick, surprised the world and themselves by disposing of Fiji, England and China in succession. Finally the part-timers from the Cook Islands upset the odds to reach the Cup semi-finals at the expense of Samoa and South Africa, surely the biggest upsets of the 2001 Series, if not of the short game's relatively brief international history?

After Hong Kong, however, where New Zealand managed to win 30 tournament points (compared to Fiji's 24 and Australia's 18), the pattern suddenly changed. Fiji, affected by the ban of their new coach Tomasi Cama – suspended for bringing the game into disrepute – somewhat lost their composure. By contrast, the young Wallabies coached by Julian Gardner turned in a series of scintillating performances in Shanghai and Kuala Lumpur to take the lead in the overall World Series team table.

As the 2001 Series moved to Europe, a title decider between New Zealand and Australia in the final match of the Series, at Cardiff's Millennium Stadium in the climax of the Grand Prix events, appeared a distinct possibility. Yet by June 3rd 2001, New Zealand, having made it into the main Cardiff Sevens final and with both the Tokyo and London titles under their belt, had already retained the Series Trophy. Even so, credit was due to coach Gordon Tietjens and his remarkable team for ensuring that the final was far from an anticlimax.

Skipper Karl Te Nana and his talented and ambitious team mates Craig De Goldi, Hayden Reid, Damian Karauna, Amasio Valence Raoma, Malili Muliaina, Jared Going, Jason Tiatia, Chris Masoe (two tries in the final) and Johnny Leo'o produced ten minutes of breathtaking rugby rewarded with four superb tries and a 26-0 half-time lead to stun the Wallabies into submission. The final score was 31-5, leaving New Zealand to retain the World Series title with twelve more competition points than the Aussies.

The quality of rugby and the number of outstanding players to emerge during the eight-month series vindicated the vision of the IRB to launch the Grand Prix in 1999-2000. The status of sevens, regarded for more than a century as no more than an enjoyable pastime, is steadily rising. The established nations use the circuit as an excellent launching pad for their aspiring talent, while the developing Unions including Canada, Georgia, Morocco, Russia and the United States, to mention just a few, have been effectively employing the newly launched series to further develop their ambitions and, of course, establish their rugby credentials.

IRB World Sevens Series Results from the 2000–01 Tournaments

Team	1	2	3	4	5	6	7	8	9	Points
New Zealand	20 (W)	20 (W)	4	30 (W)	12	16 (R)	20 (W)	20 (W)	20 (W)	162
Australia	12	12	20 (W)	18	20 (W)	20 (W)	16 (R)	16 (R)	16 (R)	150
Fiji	16 (R)	16 (R)	16 (R)	24 (R)	8	12	12	12	8	124
Samoa	6	12	8	18	4	8	12	12	12	92
South Africa	8	8	2	8	16 (R)	12	8	8	12	82
Argentina	12	6	6	8	4	4	2	4	4	50
England	0	4	0	8	6	0	6	6	2	32
Canada	4	0	4	8	2	0	4	4	0	26
Wales	0	0	0	3	0	4	4	2	6	19
United States	0	0	12	4	0	0	0	0	0	16
Korea	0	0	0	0	12	2	0	0	0	14
France	4	0	0	2	0	6	0	0	0	12
Cook Islands	0	0	12	0	0	0	0	0	0	12
Portugal	2	0	0	2	0	0	0	0	0	4
Georgia	0	0	0	0	0	0	0	0	4	4
Zimbabwe	0	4	0	0	0	0	0	0	0	4
Ireland	2	0	0	0	0	0	0	0	0	2
Hong Kong	0	0	0	1	0	0	0	0	0	1

Key to the tournaments in the table above: 1 Durban; 2 Dubai; 3 Wellington; 4 Hong Kong; 5 Shanghai; 6 Kuala Lumpur; 7 Tokyo; 8 London; 9 Cardiff. (W) winners; (R) runners-up.

Previous IRB-World Sevens Series Winners: 1999-2000 New Zealand; 2000-01 New Zealand.

IRB/FIRA–AER WORLD JUNIOR CHAMPIONSHIP 2001

New Zealand Rule the Roosters

Frankie Deges

It is hard to imagine what rugby must have been like for under-19 players before the creation of the Junior World Championship. This annual tournament, played every Easter Weekend since 1969, gives budding international players a sense of purpose and belonging.

It all began over three decades ago when the Federation Internationale de Rugby Amateur, otherwise known as FIRA-AER, pushed for the establishment of this unique and now indispensable event. It steadily evolved with competition becoming more intense every year and, although it was the domain of France for many seasons, it opened a few eyes beyond the initial frontiers of FIRA-AER. Once the Argentine Pumitas joined the fray in 1987, it became a major tournament in the international rugby calendar and when the IRB assumed responsibility for organising the tournament and making a significant contribution to participants' travel and accommodation costs, the international flavour extended to embrace the senior major rugby nations.

With 32 nations spread between two divisions, the format of the Junior World Championship makes it the biggest final of any rugby world tournament. Once they arrive at this smorgasbord of oval delicacies the players believe that they are on top of the world. They are right to feel that way. Either this is the start of a long road that will take a few to the very top by representing their nations at full international level or this is the highest they will go and represents their sporting peak.

The 2001 event was truly international with every major playing nation acknowledging the tournament and some of the developing countries undergoing a qualifying process. It was staged in beautiful Santiago de Chile, in the foothills of the enormous Andes Mountains, and was the second time that the tournament had come to South America.

From the outset it was clear that the candidates for the A division would be Australia and New Zealand from the Southern Hemisphere and France and Wales from the Northern Hemisphere. Each was in sharp form and aiming for honours. Meanwhile, in the B division the likely candidates for promotion were those from Eastern Europe.

The nature of the tournament gives no second chances because the teams are reorganised after every round. The first round brought the tournament's surprise when Uruguay upset the odds to beat Ireland 10-9. For the South Americans, coached by the experienced Washington Amarillo (in his eleventh tournament), it was their most important win at this level. That was the closest scoreline of the round, no other losing side coming within 21 points of the winner. Wales took care of Uruguay's 'Teritos' 30-3 in the quarter-finals while New Zealand overcame a spirited South African side 34-20. France and Australia were too strong for England and Argentina respectively. In the quarter-finals for the first-round's losers there were two close games, Italy drawing with Romania but advancing on try-count and Japan pipping Samoa by a solitary point. Scotland and Ireland were too good for Korea and Chile.

No one disagreed with the claims of the four semi-finalists. The talented Gavin Henson spearheaded a Welsh XV that eventually fell to a very good French side whose forwards were outstanding. Australia, who were coached by the former New Zealand wing, Grant Batty, lost its composure under pressure leaving New Zealand deserved finalists after displaying patience and quick thinking in a 35-18 victory in which Luke McAllister contributed five of the winners' goals. At the other end of the ladder, Chile and Romania avoided relegation to the B Division by defeating Korea and Samoa respectively.

The sun shone on finals day. The Universidad Católica Stadium, 'up' (as they say in Santiago) in the mountains, was attended by possibly the biggest turnout for rugby in Chile's history and staged two cracking games. Australia, whose full-back Mark Gerrard revealed the form that would promote him to the NSW Waratahs' Super Twelves team on his return, played with flair to take control of the 3rd/4th place play-off against the Welsh. Later, many asked themselves if the final was in fact being played by two U19 teams. The standard was extremely high and when France reached 20-0, scoring three tries in the first 20 minutes, few reckoned that the young Blacks could come back. Yet the sound leadership of fullback Sam Tuitupou and excellent team work enabled them to come back into the game and finally take the tournament with a 36-23 win over the young French roosters. McAllister, with five goals from seven attempts, made another important contribution with his boot. 'The boys worked extremely hard to achieve this,' said New Zealand coach Dennis Brown after the final. 'They will enjoy their success and I'm very proud of them.'

They celebrated as much as Georgia had done a day earlier after winning the B Division final. They had been pushed to the limit by Spain in their semi-finals (finally winning 11-8), but were clearly stronger than Russia in the final. Their 37-8 win promises a bright future for the Georgians. Russia, too, booked a place among the top 16 for 2002.

Spain failed to realise their dream of promotion and fell heavily 38-0 against a Canadian side that was a 16-13 loser to Russia in the semi-finals stage. At the other end of the B Division scale, new boys Sri Lanka were unlucky to lose to the Czech Republic by a single point, but gained some consolation with a 22-15 win against Belgium to avoid the wooden spoon. They were among the minnow nations who enjoyed basking in the reflected glory of playing international rugby in the company of rugby's future stars.

Division B Results (5th/14th April 2001)

Round One: Spain 34, Tunisia 14; Czech Rep 3, Poland 41; Sri Lanka 5, United States 30; Georgia 29, Germany 0; Russia 49, Morocco 16; Paraguay 6, Lithuania 11; Portugal 3, Ukraine 10; Canada 22, Belgium 7

Quarter-finals: Spain 11, Poland 8; United States 7, Georgia 24; Russia 58, Lithuania 3; Ukraine 0, Canada 30

Semi-finals: Spain 8, Georgia 11; Russia 16, Canada 13

Final: Georgia 37, Russia 8

Division B Final Rankings: 1st Georgia; 2nd Russia; 3rd Canada; 4th Spain; 5th Poland; 6th Ukraine; 7th United States; 8th Lithuania; 9th Morocco; 10th Germany; 11th Portugal; 12th Tunisia; 13th Czech Republic; 14th Paraguay; 15th Sri Lanka; 16th Belgium.

Division A Results (6th/15th April 2001)

Round One: France 94, Korea 11; Scotland 5, England 37; Wales 56, Chile 10; Ireland 9, Uruguay 10; New Zealand 85, Romania 12; South Africa 53, Italy 0; Argentina 60, Italy 15; Australia 31, Samoa 10

Quarter-finals: France 34, England 17; Wales 30, Uruguay 3; New Zealand 34, South Africa 20; Argentina 17, Australia 51

Semi-finals: France 28, Wales 13; New Zealand 35, Australia 18

Final: New Zealand 36 (4G 1PG 1T) **France 23** (1G 2PG 2T)

New Zealand: S Tuitupou (*captain*); W Lafaele, C Laulala, B Milne, J Rokococo; L McAllister, J Cowan; S Tonga'uiha, T Paulo, T Fairbrother, J Ryan, K Thompson, A Thomson, T Waldrom, T Harding *Substitutions*: J Kennedy for Milne; M Williams for McAllister; C Smylie for Cowan; R Kennedy for Ryan; W Rowley for Waldrom

Scorers *Tries*: Waldrom, Harding, Thomson, Cowan, penalty try *Conversions*: McAllister (4) *Penalty Goal*: McAllister

Division A Final Rankings: 1st New Zealand; 2nd France; 3rd Australia; 4th Wales; 5th South Africa; 6th England; 7th Argentina; 8th Uruguay; 9th Scotland; 10th Japan; 11th Ireland 12th Italy; 13th Romania; 14th Chile; 15th Samoa; 16th Korea.

Previous IRB/FIRA-AER World Junior Championship Winners: 1969 France (Barcelona); 1970 France (Vichy), 1971 France (Casablanca); 1972 Romania (Rome); 1973 Romania (Bucharest); 1974 France (Heidelberg); 1975 France (Madrid); 1976 France (Albi); 1977 France (Hilversum); 1978 France (Parma); 1979 France (Lisbon); 1980 France (Tunis); 1981 France (Madrid); 1982 France (Geneva); 1983 France (Casablanca); 1984 Italy (Warsaw); 1985 France (Brussels); 1986 France (Bucharest); 1987 Argentina (Berlin); 1988 France (Makarska); 1989 Argentina (Lisbon); 1990 Argentina (Brescia); 1991 France (Toulouse); 1992 France (Madrid); 1993 Argentina (Lille); 1994 South Africa (Lyon); 1995 France (Bucharest); 1996 Argentina (Brescia); 1997 Argentina (Buenos Aires); 1998 Ireland (Toulouse); 1999 New Zealand (Llanelli); 2000 France (Burgundy); 2001 New Zealand (Santiago de Chile)

ENGLAND TEST SEASON REVIEW 2000-01

Woodward's Record England Run

David Llewellyn

It will probably become known as Woodward's Run – 11 victories on the trot, unprecedented in English rugby history. It might have been 12 but for Ireland. Keith Wood and his warrior band completed an unwelcome hat-trick for England, an inverted Triple Crown of defeats in successive seasons. After Wales in 1999 and Scotland in 2000, it was Ireland's turn to snuff out the chance of a Grand Slam. At least the Irish could not take away the previous 11 results.

It all began in Bloemfontein the summer before last with the historic victory over South Africa, when England recorded a tight victory over the Springboks. That was the start to what was to become a gruelling test of Clive Woodward's men. Because, as hard as the Springboks match had been, the autumn contained nothing easier, with the World Cup holders Australia, Argentina and South Africa again lining up to have a shot at downing the English on their own turf.

The Wallabies were first up, and they were hot having lifted the 2000 Tri Nations championship by virtue of a thrilling one-point victory over South Africa. Sadly the Wallabies, finding England a tougher nut to crack up front than had perhaps been expected, soon turned it into a grim old battle, which degenerated into a succession of time-wasting tactics as they and the game lumbered into injury time.

Their efforts to create a stop-start game were eventually halted by referee André Watson who quipped: 'It's a game of rugby, not chess.' But there was one stop that England and their fans could have done without. That came in the eighth minute of injury time when TV official Brian Stirling studied footage of Dan Luger's well-taken try. A green light for the touchdown gave England their first victory over the Wallabies since the 1995 World Cup.

Argentina were next, although this Test nearly did not take place, or at least, not with the usual suspects in England shirts. This was because captain Martin Johnson and his men went on strike after lengthy discussions with the England management and some serious soul-searching in the luxurious surroundings of their training camp, Pennyhill Park Hotel, near Bagshot in Surrey.

Clive Woodward, the England manager, on learning of their intent, promptly sent them packing to reflect on a payment system that was based primarily on performance with most of their cash coming in win bonuses. The players had wanted the proportions inverted, so that the bulk of their match fee was guaranteed with a smaller percentage, approximately 30 per cent, on offer for victory. While they cogitated and ruminated, Woodward let it be known that he would send a team out to take on the Pumas come what may, prompting the publication of a list of likely stand-ins from National League One. Thankfully 24 hours later they were restored to the England fold having got much of their way over the folding stuff and the Pumas match went ahead.

It was not the prettiest of victories, and it finished with the England players once more immersed in mire as accusations were made of involvement by player or players unknown in the black market for match tickets. That particular scandal drifted away with no one substantiating any of the charges and England were able to contemplate a minor achievement – a hat-trick over Southern Hemisphere opposition.

Then it was noses back to the grindstone with South Africa lining up for a return. And they admitted afterwards that they found England 'far more physical' than any side south of the Equator, which is quite some admission coming from the country which has boasted Ollie Le Roux and Uli Schmidt among other heavyweights. Jonny Wilkinson was foot-perfect with seven kicks from seven attempts and there was a satisfying return to international action for Will Greenwood, whose 33rd-minute try crowned a fine all-round performance.

With the Springboks safely out of the way there was a mid-winter break from Tests. As a sopping wet autumn sloshed into a cold and soaking winter the country's best began preparations for the defence of their Six Nations title. The start of the championship coincided with the outbreak of foot-and-mouth, a disease that was eventually to disrupt the tournament and cause it to spill over into the following season for the first time since 1962.

Chief problem was in Ireland, where the outbreak only gained a finger-hold because of the stringent restrictions placed on the movement of livestock. The Irish government decided to discourage the influx of tourists into the country and racing and rugby were the chief casualties, it being argued that farmers and livestock-holders inside the Republic were in danger of being contaminated by rural folk from over St George's Channel and thus the locals would spread the disease throughout their own regions. So Ireland played it safe and called off their match against England at Lansdowne Road.

There was still plenty to occupy England fans in the interim. The opening against Wales reaffirmed – if reaffirmation were needed – that the Cardiff hoodoo has been well and truly exorcised. Will Greenwood's three tries – the first hat-trick by an Englishman in the Principality since Howard Marshall's treble in the late nineteenth century – a couple from Matt Dawson and a sixth from Ben Cohen as well as 14 points from the prolific boot of Jonny Wilkinson ensured England recorded their highest score and biggest winning margin in Cardiff. Their Six Nations campaign was up and running.

More history awaited England a fortnight later when Italy arrived at Twickenham. The Italians had made it clear that they had not arrived in

South West London just to roll over. Indeed there were moments when they played the steam-roller to England's tarmac. But that was in the first half, when they got to within 10 points of England. Italy's two tries both came over on Ben Cohen's wing, where the Northampton man had an unhappy time. After the interval it was a different story, and a little bit of history was made with the appearance as a substitute for Cohen of Jason Robinson, the convert from Rugby League. Woodward had wanted to fast-track the Sale player into the Test side, but this represented more of a sprint.

Unfortunately he was unable to mark his debut with a try because the ball did not seem to find its way to him. Not that it mattered. England's 43 unopposed second half points took them to the highest score and biggest winning margin by any side in the history of the Championship (as Four, Five or Six Nations). Wilkinson finished with 35 points – another championship best, surpassing Ronan O'Gara's 30 against the same opponents the previous season.

More records awaited them a fortnight later when Scotland made the trip down to Twickenham. England's try count was literally six of the best for this fixture, never before had either side managed to touchdown so many times in the history of the Calcutta Cup. Naturally it was England's highest score and biggest winning margin against Scotland. It was not merely the size of the victory which impressed, it was the manner. England demonstrated power in the pack, electrifying pace out wide, but above all they were disciplined, to the extent that Scotland were awarded just one penalty within range, which Duncan Hodge turned into three points. Individually and collectively England were just too much for the Scots, as bravely as Ian McGeechan's men struggled to compete.

Woodward's bucks, young and old, had to stop there. Foot-and-mouth saw their date in Dublin postponed and there came the first hiatus in their record quest. But it was only temporary. The Dublin date passed and then it was the turn of the French, at Twickenham.

Wing Philippe Bernat-Salles crossed the England line in the 15th minute to launch a French fightback which saw them first draw level, then, just before half-time, ease in front. But their joy was short-lived. England emerged with renewed hunger and put their flabby first half performance behind them. Richard Hill, Iain Balshaw, Phil Greening, the masterful Mike Catt and finally Matt Perry all ran in tries and helped England to their highest score against France.

Even before the delayed Grand Slam match against Ireland they had smashed the record for the total of tries (28, compared with Wales's 21 in 1910) and broken the championship record for most points (215, as opposed to the 183 mustered by England in 2000). There was another notable landmark, this one an individual one. Their prolific goal-kicker, Jonny Wilkinson, had contributed 80 points to that team total and in so doing cruised past Rob Andrew as England's leading points scorer with 407.

The tour to Canada and the United States presented opportunities for a raft of young players thanks to the Lions tour. They had a big responsibility, because England's unbeaten run was now eight matches and it was widely recognized that none of the three Tests was going to be a pushover, not against seasoned internationals who would be looking forward to ripping into the rookies from across the Big Pond.

But under the astute captaincy of Saracens' scrum-half Kyran Bracken their wobbly start in the first Test against Canada in Toronto was transformed into a glorious, high-scoring victory in Vancouver and the good work was continued when they crossed the 49th parallel to take on the United States in San Francisco.

The Eagles were overwhelmed, and England had found another sound goal-kicker in David Walder, a team-mate of Wilkinson at Newcastle, while Wasps' Josh Lewsey was top try scorer in the Tests with four. That triumphant tour took the winning run to 11, and all they had to do to reach the round dozen and complete the Grand Slam was to overcome Ireland.

Sadly it was not to be. Wood, winning his 46th cap, hit England with a sucker punch in the 17th minute with his 12th try for his country and although England did hit back, there was too much passion in Irish bellies. Not even Austin Healey's touchdown could begin to douse the home fires. England did walk away with the Six Nations trophy, but they were not exactly shouting about that piece of silverware after missing out on a Grand Slam for the third successive year, victims once again of the Celtic Curse.

England's Test Record in 2000-2001: Played 11, won 10, lost 1.

Opponents	Date	Venue	Result
Ireland	20th October 2001	A	Lost 14-20
United States	16th June 2001	A	Won 48-19
Canada	9th June 2001	A	Won 59-20
Canada	2nd June 2001	A	Won 22-10
France	7th April 2001	H	Won 48-19
Scotland	3rd March 2001	H	Won 43-3
Italy	17th February 2001	H	Won 80-23
Wales	3rd February 2001	A	Won 44-15
South Africa	2nd December 2000	H	Won 25-17
Argentina	25th November 2000	H	Won 19-0
Australia	18th November 2000	H	Won 22-19

ENGLISH INTERNATIONAL PLAYERS
(up to 20 October 2001)

Note: Years given for International CXhampionship matches are for second half of season; eg 1972 means season 1971-72. Years for all other matches refer to the actual year of the match. When a series has taken place, figures have been used to denote the particular matches in which players have featured. Thus 1984 *SA* 2 indicates that a player appeared in the second Test of the series.

Aarvold, C D (Cambridge U, W Hartlepool, Headingley, Blackheath) 1928 *A, W, I, F, S*, 1929 *W, I, F*, 1931 *W, S, F*, 1932 *SA, W, I, S*, 1933 *W*
Ackford, P J (Harlequins) 1988 *A*, 1989 *S, I, F, W, R, Fj*, 1990 *I, F, W, S, Arg* 3, 1991 *W, S, I, F, A, [NZ, It, F, S, A]*
Adams, A A (London Hospital) 1910 *F*
Adams, F R (Richmond) 1875 *I, S*, 1876 *S*, 1877 *I*, 1878 *S*, 1879 *S, I*
Adebayo, A A (Bath) 1996, *It*, 1997 *Arg* 1,2, *A* 2, *NZ* 1, 1998 *S*
Adey, G J (Leicester) 1976 *I, F*
Adkins, S J (Coventry) 1950 *I, F, S*, 1953 *W, I, F, S*
Agar, A E (Harlequins) 1952 *SA, W, S, I, F*, 1953 *W, I*
Alcock, A (Guy's Hospital) 1906 *SA*
Alderson, F H R (Hartlepool R) 1891 *W, I, S*, 1892 *W, S*, 1893 *W*
Alexander, H (Richmond) 1900 *I, S*, 1901 *W, I, S*, 1902 *W, I*
Alexander, W (Northern) 1927 *F*
Allison, D F (Coventry) 1956 *W, I, S, F*, 1957 *W*, 1958 *W, S*
Allport, A (Blackheath) 1892 *W*, 1893 *I*, 1894 *W, I, S*
Anderson, S (Rockcliff) 1899 *I*
Anderson, W F (Orrell) 1973 *NZ* 1
Anderton, C (Manchester FW) 1889 *M*
Andrew, C R (Cambridge U, Nottingham, Wasps, Toulouse, Newcastle) 1985 *R, F, S, I, W*, 1986 *W, S, I, F*, 1987 *I, F, W, [J (R), US]*, 1988 *S, I* 1,2, *A* 1,2, *Fj, A*, 1989 *S, I, F, W, R, Fj*, 1990 *I, F, W, S, Arg* 3, 1991 *W, S, I, F, Fj, A, [NZ, It, US, F, S, A]*, 1992 *S, I, F, W, C, SA*, 1993 *F, W, NZ*, 1994 *S, I, F, W, SA* 1,2, *R, C*, 1995 *I, F, W, S, [Arg, It, A, NZ, F]*, 1997 *W* (R)
Archer, G S (Bristol, Army, Newcastle) 1996 *S, I*, 1997 *A* 2, *NZ* 1, *SA, NZ* 2, 1998 *F, W, S, I, A* 1, *NZ* 1, *H, It*, 1999 *Tg, Fj*, 2000 *I, F, W, It, S*
Archer, H (Bridgwater A) 1909 *W, F, I*
Armstrong, R (Northern) 1925 *W*
Arthur, T G (Wasps) 1966 *W, I*
Ashby, R C (Wasps) 1966 *I, F*, 1967 *A*
Ashcroft, A (Waterloo) 1956 *W, I, S, F*, 1957 *W, I, F, S*, 1958 *W, A, I, F, S*, 1959 *I, F, S*
Ashcroft, A H (Birkenhead Park) 1909 *A*
Ashford, W (Richmond) 1897 *W, I*, 1898 *S, W*
Ashworth, A (Oldham) 1892 *I*
Askew, J G (Cambridge U) 1930 *W, I, F*
Aslett, A R (Richmond) 1926 *W, I, F, S*, 1929 *S, F*
Assinder, E W (O Edwardians) 1909 *A, W*
Aston, R L (Blackheath) 1890 *S, I*
Auty, J R (Headingley) 1935 *S*

Back, N A (Leicester) 1994 *S, I*, 1995 *[Arg* (t), *It, WS]*, 1997 *NZ* 1(R), *SA, NZ* 2, 1998 *F, W, S, I, H, It, A* 2, *SA* 2, 1999 *S, I, F, W, A, US, C, [It, NZ, Fj, SA]*, 2000 *I, F, W, It, S, SA* 1,2, *A, Arg, SA* 3, 2001 *W, It, S, F, I*
Bailey, M D (Cambridge U, Wasps) 1984 *SA* 1,2, 1987 *[US]*, 1989 *Fj*, 1990 *I, F, S* (R)
Bainbridge, S (Gosforth, Fylde) 1982 *F, W*, 1983 *F, W, S, I, NZ*, 1984 *S, I, F, W*, 1985 *NZ* 1,2, 1987 *F, W, S, [J, US]*
Baker, D G S (OMTs) 1955 *W, I, F, S*
Baker, E M (Moseley) 1895 *W, I, S*, 1896 *W, I, S*, 1897 *W*
Baker, H C (Clifton) 1887 *W*
Balshaw, I R (Bath) 2000 *I* (R), *F* (R), *It* (R), *S* (R), *A* (R), *Arg, SA* 3(R), 2001 *W, It, S, F, I*
Bance, J F (Bedford) 1954 *S*
Barkley, O (Bath) 2001 *US* (R)
Barley, B (Wakefield) 1984 *I, F, W, A*, 1988 *A* 1,2, *Fj*
Barnes, S (Bristol, Bath) 1984 *A*, 1985 *R* (R), *NZ* 1,2, 1986 *S* (R), *F*, 1987 *I* (R), 1988 *Fj*, 1993 *S, I*
Barr, R J (Leicester) 1932 *SA, W, I*
Barrett, E I M (Lennox) 1903 *S*
Barrington, T J M (Bristol) 1931 *W, I*
Barrington-Ward, L E (Edinburgh U) 1910 *W, I, F, S*
Barron, J H (Bingley) 1896 *S*, 1897 *W, I*
Bartlett, J T (Waterloo) 1951 *W*

Bartlett, R M (Harlequins) 1957 *W, I, F, S*, 1958 *I, F, S*
Barton, J (Coventry) 1967 *I, F, W*, 1972 *F*
Batchelor, T B (Oxford U) 1907 *F*
Bates, S M (Wasps) 1989 *R*
Bateson, A H (Otley) 1930 *W, I, F, S*
Bateson, H D (Liverpool) 1879 *I*
Batson, T (Blackheath) 1872 *S*, 1874 *S*, 1875 *I*
Batten, J M (Cambridge U) 1874 *S*
Baume, J L (Northern) 1950 *S*
Baxendell, J J N (Sale) 1998 *NZ* 2, *SA* 1
Baxter, J (Birkenhead Park) 1900 *W, I, S*
Bayfield, M C (Northampton) 1991 *Fj, A*, 1992 *S, I, F, W, C, SA*, 1993 *F, W, S, I*, 1994 *S, I, SA* 1,2, *R, C*, 1995 *I, F, W, S, [Arg, It, A, NZ, F]*, *SA, WS*, 1996 *F, W*
Bazley, R C (Waterloo) 1952 *I, F*, 1953 *W, I, F, S*, 1955 *W, I, F, S*
Beal, N D (Northampton) 1996 *Arg*, 1997 *A* 1, 1998 *NZ* 1,2, *SA* 1, *H* (R), *SA* 2, 1999 *S, F* (R), *A* (t), *C* (R), *[It* (R), *Tg* (R), *Fj, SA]*
Beaumont, W B (Fylde) 1975 *I, A* 1(R),2, 1976 *A, W, S, I, F*, 1977 *S, I, F, W*, 1978 *F, W, S, I, NZ*, 1979 *S, I, F, W, NZ*, 1980 *I, F, W, S*, 1981 *W, S, I, F, Arg* 1,2, 1982 *A, S*
Bedford, H (Morley) 1889 *M*, 1890 *S, I*
Bedford, L L (Headingley) 1931 *W, I*
Beer, I D S (Harlequins) 1955 *F, S*
Beese, M C (Liverpool) 1972 *W, I, F*
Beim, T D (Sale) 1998 *NZ* 1(R),2
Bell, F J (Northern) 1900 *W*
Bell, H (New Brighton) 1884 *I*
Bell, J L (Darlington) 1878 *I*
Bell, P J (Blackheath) 1968 *W, I, F, S*
Bell, R W (Northern) 1900 *W, I, S*
Bendon, G J (Wasps) 1959 *W, I, F, S*
Bennett, N O (St Mary's Hospital, Waterloo) 1947 *W, S, F*, 1948 *A, W, I, S*
Bennett, W N (Bedford, London Welsh) 1975 *S, A*1, 1976 *S* (R), 1979 *S, I, F, W*
Bennetts, B B (Penzance) 1909 *A, W*
Bentley, J (Sale, Newcastle) 1988 *I* 2, *A* 1, 1997 *A* 1, *SA*
Bentley, J E (Gipsies) 1871 *S*, 1872 *S*
Benton, S (Gloucester) 1998 *A* 1
Berridge, M J (Northampton) 1949 *W, I*
Berry, H (Gloucester) 1910 *W, I, F, S*
Berry, J (Tyldesley) 1891 *W, I, S*
Berry, J T W (Leicester) 1939 *W, I, S*
Beswick, E (Swinton) 1882 *I, S*
Biggs, J M (UCH) 1878 *S*, 1879 *I*
Birkett, J G G (Harlequins) 1906 *S, F, SA*, 1907 *F, W, S*, 1908 *F, W,I , S*, 1910 *W, I, S*, 1911 *W, F, I , S*, 1912 *W, I, S, F*
Birkett L (Clapham R) 1875 *S*, 1877 *I, S*
Birkett, R H (Clapham R) 1871 *S*, 1875 *S*, 1876 *S*, 1877 *I*
Bishop, C C (Blackheath) 1927 *F*
Black, B H (Blackheath) 1930 *W, I, F, S*, 1931 *W, I, S, F*, 1932 *S*, 1933 *W*
Blacklock, J H (Aspatria) 1898 *I*, 1899 *I*
Blakeway, P J (Gloucester) 1980 *I, F, W, S*, 1981 *W, S, I, F*, 1982 *I, F, W*, 1984 *I, F, W, SA* 1, 1985 *R, F, S, I*
Blakiston, A F (Northampton) 1920 *S*, 1921 *W, I, S, F*, 1922 *W*, 1923 *S, F*, 1924 *W, I, F, S*, 1925 *NZ, W, I, S, F*
Blatherwick, T (Manchester) 1878 *I*
Body, J A (Gipsies) 1872 *S*, 1873 *S*
Bolton, C A (United Services) 1909 *F*
Bolton, R (Harlequins) 1933 *W*, 1936 *S*, 1937 *S*, 1938 *W, I*
Bolton, W N (Blackheath) 1882 *I, S*, 1883 *W, I, S*, 1884 *W, I, S*, 1885 *I*, 1887 *I, S*
Bonaventura, M S (Blackheath) 1931 *W*
Bond, A M (Sale) 1978 *NZ*, 1979 *S, I, NZ*, 1980 *I*, 1982 *I*
Bonham-Carter, E (Oxford U) 1891 *S*
Bonsor, F (Bradford) 1886 *W, I, S*, 1887 *W, S*, 1889 *M*
Boobbyer, B (Rosslyn Park) 1950 *W, I, F, S*, 1951 *W, F*, 1952 *S, I, F*

Booth, L A (Headingley) 1933 *W, I, S*, 1934 *S*, 1935 *W, I, S*
Borthwick, S W (Bath) 2001 *F, C* 1,2(R), *US*
Botting, I J (Oxford U) 1950 *W, I*
Boughton, H J (Gloucester) 1935 *W, I, S*
Boyle, C W (Oxford U) 1873 *S*
Boyle, S B (Gloucester) 1983 *W, S, I*
Boylen, F (Hartlepool R) 1908 *F, W, I, S*
Bracken, K P P (Bristol, Saracens) 1993 *NZ*, 1994 *S, I, C*, 1995 *I, F, W, S, [It, WS* (t)], *SA*, 1996 *It* (R), 1997 *Arg* 1,2, *A* 2, *NZ* 1,2, 1998 *F, W*, 1999 *S*(R), *I, F, A*, 2000 *SA* 1,2, *A*, 2001 *It* (R), *S* (R), *F* (R), *C* 1,2, *US, I* (R)
Bradby, M S (United Services) 1922 *I, F*
Bradley, R (W Hartlepool) 1903 *W*
Bradshaw, H (Bramley) 1892 *S*, 1893 *W, I, S*, 1894 *W, I, S*
Brain, S E (Coventry) 1984 *SA* 2, *A* (R), 1985 *R, F, S, I, W, NZ* 1,2, 1986 *W, S, I, F*
Braithwaite, J (Leicester) 1905 *NZ*
Braithwaite-Exley, B (Headingley) 1949 *W*
Brettargh, A T (Liverpool OB) 1900 *W*, 1903 *I, S*, 1904 *W, I, S*, 1905 *I, S*
Brewer, J (Gipsies) 1876 *I*
Briggs, A (Bradford) 1892 *W, I, S*
Brinn, A (Gloucester) 1972 *W, I, S*
Broadley, T (Bingley) 1893 *W, S*, 1894 *W, I, S*, 1896 *S*
Bromet, W E (Richmond) 1891 *W, I*, 1892 *W, I, S*, 1893 *W, I, S*, 1895 *W, I, S*, 1896 *I*
Brook, P W P (Harlequins) 1930 *S*, 1931 *F*, 1936 *S*
Brooke, T J (Richmond) 1968 *F, S*
Brooks, F G (Bedford) 1906 *SA*
Brooks, M J (Oxford U) 1874 *S*
Brophy, T J (Liverpool) 1964 *I, F, S*, 1965 *W, I*, 1966 *W, I, F*
Brough, J W (Silloth) 1925 *NZ, W*
Brougham, H (Harlequins) 1912 *W, I, S, F*
Brown, A A (Exeter) 1938 *S*
Brown, L G (Oxford U, Blackheath) 1911 *W, F, I, S*, 1913 *SA, W, F, I, S*, 1914 *W, I, S, F*, 1921 *W, I, S, F*, 1922 *W*
Brown S P (Richmond) 1998 *A* 1, *SA* 1
Brown, T W (Bristol) 1928 *S*, 1929 *W, I, S, F*, 1932 *S*, 1933 *W, I, S*
Brunton, J (N Durham) 1914 *W, I, S*
Brutton, E B (Cambridge U) 1886 *S*
Bryden, C C (Clapham R) 1876 *I*, 1877 *S*
Bryden, H A (Clapham R) 1874 *S*
Buckingham, R A (Leicester) 1927 *F*
Bucknall, A L (Richmond) 1969 *SA*, 1970 *I, W, S, F*, 1971 *W, I, F, S* (2[1C])
Buckton, J R D (Saracens) 1988 *A* (R), 1990 *Arg* 1,2
Budd, A (Blackheath) 1878 *I*, 1879 *S, I*, 1881 *W, S*
Budworth, R T D (Blackheath) 1890 *W*, 1891 *W, S*
Bull, A G (Northampton) 1914 *W*
Bullough, E (Wigan) 1892 *W, I, S*
Bulpitt, M P (Blackheath) 1970 *S*
Bulteel, A J (Manchester) 1876 *I*
Bunting, W L (Moseley) 1897 *I, S*, 1898 *I, S, W*, 1899 *S*, 1900 *S*, 1901 *I, S*
Burland, D W (Bristol) 1931 *W, I, F*, 1932 *I, S*, 1933 *W, I, S*
Burns, B H (Blackheath) 1871 *S*
Burton, G W (Blackheath) 1879 *S, I*, 1880 *S*, 1881 *I, W, S*
Burton, H C (Richmond) 1926 *W*
Burton, M A (Gloucester) 1972 *W, I, F, S, SA*, 1974 *F, W*, 1975 *S, A* 1,2, 1976 *A, W, S, I, F*, 1978 *F, W*
Bush, J A (Clifton) 1872 *S*, 1873 *S*, 1875 *S*, 1876 *I, S*
Butcher, C J S (Harlequins) 1984 *SA* 1,2, *A*
Butcher, W V (Streatham) 1903 *S*, 1904 *W, I, S*, 1905 *W, I, S*
Butler, A G (Harlequins) 1937 *W, I*
Butler, P E (Gloucester) 1975 *A* 1, 1976 *F*
Butterfield, J (Northampton) 1953 *F, S*, 1954 *W, NZ, I, S, F*, 1955 *W, I, F, S*, 1956 *W, I, S, F*, 1957 *W, I, F, S*, 1958 *W, A, I, F, S*, 1959 *W, I, F, S*
Byrne, F A (Moseley) 1897 *W*
Byrne, J F (Moseley) 1894 *W, I, S*, 1895 *I, S*, 1896 *I*, 1897 *W, I, S*, 1898 *I, S, W*, 1899 *I*

Cain, J J (Waterloo) 1950 *W*
Callard, J E B (Bath) 1993 *NZ*, 1994 *S, I*, 1995 *[WS]*, *SA*
Campbell, D A (Cambridge U) 1937 *W, I*
Candler, P L (St Bart's Hospital) 1935 *W*, 1936 *NZ, W, I, S*, 1937 *W, I, S*, 1938 *W, S*
Cannell, L B (Oxford U, St Mary's Hospital) 1948 *F*, 1949 *W, I, F, S*, 1950 *W, I, F, S*, 1952 *SA, W*, 1953 *W, I, F*, 1956 *I, S, F*, 1957 *W, I*
Caplan, D W N (Headingley) 1978 *S, I*
Cardus, R M (Roundhay) 1979 *F, W*

Carey, G M (Blackheath) 1895 *W, I, S*, 1896 *W, I*
Carleton, J (Orrell) 1979 *NZ*, 1980 *I, F, W, S*, 1981 *W, S, I, F, Arg* 1,2, 1982 *A, S, I, F, W*, 1983 *F, W, S, I, NZ*, 1984 *S, I, F, W, A*
Carling, W D C (Durham U, Harlequins) 1988 *F, W, S, I* 1,2, *A2, Fj, A*, 1989 *S, I, F, W, Fj*, 1990 *I, F, W, S, Arg* 1,2,3, 1991 *W, S, I, F, Fj, A, [NZ, It, US, F, S, A]*, 1992 *S, I, F, W, C, SA*, 1993 *F, W, S, I, NZ*, 1994 *S, I, F, W, SA* 1,2, *R, C*, 1995 *I, F, W, S, [Arg, WS, A, NZ, F]*, *SA, WS*, 1996 *F, W, S, I, It, Arg*, 1997 *S, I, F, W*
Carpenter, A D (Gloucester) 1932 *SA*
Carr, R S L (Manchester) 1939 *W, I, S*
Cartwright, V H (Nottingham) 1903 *W, I, S*, 1904 *W, S*, 1905 *W, I, S, NZ*, 1906 *W, I, S, F, SA*
Catcheside, H C (Percy Park) 1924 *W, I, F, S*, 1926 *W, I*, 1927 *I, S*
Catt, M J (Bath) 1994 *W* (R), *C* (R), 1995 *I, F, W, S, [Arg, It, WS, A, NZ, F]*, *SA, WS*, 1996 *F, W, S, I, It, Arg*, 1997 *W, Arg* 1, *A* 1,2, *NZ* 1, *SA*, 1998 *F, W* (R), *I, A* 2(R), *SA* 2, 1999 *S, F, W, A, C* (R), *[Tg* (R), *Fj, SA* (R)], 2000 *I, F, W, It, S, SA* 1,2, *A, Arg*, 2001 *W, It, S, F, I*
Cattell, R H B (Blackheath) 1895 *W, I, S*, 1896 *W, I, S*, 1900 *W*
Cave, J W (Richmond) 1889 *M*
Cave, W T C (Blackheath) 1905 *W*
Challis, R (Bristol) 1957 *I, F, S*
Chambers, E L (Bedford) 1908 *F*, 1910 *W, I*
Chantrill, B S (Bristol) 1924 *W, I, F, S*
Chapman, C E (Cambridge U) 1884 *W*
Chapman, D E (Richmond) 1998 *A* 1(R)
Chapman, F E (Hartlepool) 1910 *W, I, F, S*, 1912 *W*, 1914 *W, I*
Cheesman, W I (OMTs) 1913 *SA, W, F, I*
Cheston, E C (Richmond) 1873 *S*, 1874 *S*, 1875 *I, S*, 1876 *S*
Chilcott, G J (Bath) 1984 *A*, 1986 *I, F*, 1987 *F*(R), *W, [J, US, W* (R)], 1988 *I* 2(R), *Fj*, 1989 *I* (R), *F, W, R*
Christopherson, P (Blackheath) 1891 *W, F, W, R*
Clark, C W H (Liverpool) 1876 *I*
Clarke, A J (Coventry) 1935 *W, I, S*, 1936 *NZ, W, I*
Clarke, B B (Bath, Richmond) 1992 *SA*, 1993 *F, W, S, I, NZ*, 1994 *S, F, W, SA* 1,2, *R, C*, 1995 *I, F, W, S, [Arg, It, A, NZ, F]*, *SA, WS*, 1996 *F, W, S, I, Arg* (R), 1997 *W, Arg* 1,2, *A* 1(R), 1998 *A* 1(t), *NZ* 1,2, *SA* 1, *H, It*, 1999 *A* (R)
Clarke, S J S (Cambridge U, Blackheath) 1963 *W, I, F, S, NZ* 1,2, *A*, 1964 *NZ, W, I*, 1965 *I, F, S*
Clayton, J H (Liverpool) 1871 *S*
Clements, J W (O Cranleighans) 1959 *I, F, S*
Cleveland, C R (Blackheath) 1887 *W, S*
Clibborn, W G (Richmond) 1886 *W, I, S*, 1887 *W, I, S*
Clough, F J (Cambridge U, Orrell) 1986 *I, F*, 1987 *[J* (R), *US]*
Coates, C H (Yorkshire W) 1880 *S*, 1881 *S*, 1882 *S*
Coates, V H M (Bath) 1913 *SA, W, F, I, S*
Cobby, W (Hull) 1900 *W*
Cockerham, A (Bradford Olicana) 1900 *W*
Cockerill, R (Leicester) 1997 *Arg* 1(R),2, *A* 2(t+R), *NZ* 1, *SA, NZ* 2, 1998 *W, S, I, A* 1, *NZ* 1,2, *SA* 1, *H, It, A* 2, *SA* 2, 1999 *S, I, F, W, A, C* (R), *[It, NZ, Tg* (R), *Fj* (R)]
Cohen, B C (Northampton) 2000 *I, F, W, It, S, SA* 2, *Arg, SA* 3, 2001 *W, It, S, F*
Colclough, M J (Angoulême, Wasps, Swansea) 1978 *S, I*, 1979 *NZ*, 1980 *F, W, S*, 1981 *W, S, I, F*, 1982 *A, S, I, F, W*, 1983 *F, NZ*, 1984 *S, I, F, W*, 1986 *W, S, I, F*
Coley, E (Northampton) 1929 *F*, 1932 *W*
Collins, P J (Camborne) 1952 *S, I, F*
Collins, W E (O Cheltonians) 1874 *S*, 1875 *I, S*, 1876 *I, S*
Considine, S G U (Bath) 1925 *F*
Conway, G S (Cambridge U, Rugby, Manchester) 1920 *F, I, S*, 1921 *F, I, S*, 1922 *W, I, F, S*, 1923 *W, I, S, F*, 1924 *W, I, F, S*, 1925 *NZ*, 1927 *W*
Cook, J G (Bedford) 1937 *S*
Cook, P W (Richmond) 1965 *I, F*
Cooke, D A (Harlequins) 1976 *W, S, I, F*
Cooke, D H (Harlequins) 1981 *W, S, I, F*, 1984 *I*, 1985 *R, F, S, I, W, NZ* 1,2
Cooke, P (Richmond) 1939 *W, I*
Coop, T (Leigh) 1892 *S*
Cooper, J G (Moseley) 1909 *A, W*
Cooper, M J (Moseley) 1973 *F, S, NZ* 2(R), 1975 *F, W*, 1976 *A, W*, 1977 *S, I, F, W*
Coopper, S F (Blackheath) 1900 *W*, 1902 *W, I*, 1905 *W, I, S*, 1907 *W*

Corbett, L J (Bristol) 1921 *F*, 1923 *W, I*, 1924 *W, I, F, S*, 1925 *NZ, W, I, S, F*, 1927 *W, I, S, F*
Corless, B J (Coventry, Moseley) 1976 *A, I* (R), 1977 *S, I, F, W*, 1978 *F, W, S, I*
Corry, M E (Bristol, Leicester) 1997 *Arg* 1,2, 1998 *H, It, SA* 2(t), 1999 *F*(R), *A, C* (t), [*It* (R), *NZ* (t+R), *SA* (R)], 2000 *I* (R), *F* (R), *W* (R), *It* (R), *S (R), Arg* (R), *SA* 3(t), 2001 *W* (R), *It* (R), *F* (t), *C 1, I*
Cotton, F E (Loughborough Colls, Coventry, Sale) 1971 *S* (2[1C]), *P*, 1973 *W, I, F, S, NZ* 2, *A*, 1974 *S, I*, 1975 *I, F, W*, 1976 *A, W, S, I, F*, 1977 *S, I, F, W*, 1978 *S, I*, 1979 *NZ*, 1980 *I, F, W, S*, 1981 *W*
Coulman, M J (Moseley) 1967 *A, I, F, S, W*, 1968 *W, I, F, S*
Coulson, T J (Coventry) 1927 *W*, 1928 *A, W*
Court, E D (Blackheath) 1885 *W*
Coverdale, H (Blackheath) 1910 *F*, 1912 *I, F*, 1920 *W*
Cove-Smith, R (OMTs) 1921 *S, F*, 1922 *I, F, S*, 1923 *W, I, S, F*, 1924 *W, I, S, F*, 1925 *NZ, W, I, S, F*, 1927 *W, I, S, F*, 1928 *A, W, I, F, S*, 1929 *W, I*
Cowling, R J (Leicester) 1977 *S, I, F, W*, 1978 *F, NZ*, 1979 *S, I*
Cowman, A R (Loughborough Colls, Coventry) 1971 *S* (2[1C]), *P*, 1973 *W, I*
Cox, N S (Sunderland) 1901 *S*
Cranmer, P (Richmond, Moseley) 1934 *W, I, S*, 1935 *W, I, S*, 1936 *NZ, W, I, S*, 1937 *W, I, S*, 1938 *W, I, S*
Creed, R N (Coventry) 1971 *P*
Cridlan, A G (Blackheath) 1935 *W, I, S*
Crompton, C A (Blackheath) 1871 *S*
Crosse, C W (Oxford U) 1874 *S*, 1875 *I*
Cumberlege, B S (Blackheath) 1920 *W, I, S*, 1921 *W, I, S, F*, 1922 *W*
Cumming, D C (Blackheath) 1925 *S, F*
Cunliffe, F L (RMA) 1874 *S*
Currey, F I (Marlborough N) 1872 *S*
Currie, J D (Oxford U, Harlequins, Bristol) 1956 *W, I, S, F*, 1957 *W, I, F, S*, 1958 *W, A, I, F, S*, 1959 *W, I, F, S*, 1960 *W, I, F, S*, 1961 *SA*, 1962 *W, I, F*
Cusani, D A (Orrell) 1987 *I*
Cusworth, L (Leicester) 1979 *NZ*, 1982 *F, W*, 1983 *F, W, NZ*, 1984 *S, I, F, W*, 1988 *F, W*

D'Aguilar, F B G (Royal Engineers) 1872 *S*
Dallaglio, L B N (Wasps) 1995 *SA* (R), *WS*, 1996 *F, W, S, I, It, Arg*, 1997 *S, I, F*, 1997 *A* 1,2, *NZ* 1, *SA*, 1998 *W, S, I, A* 2, *SA* 2, 1999 *S, I, F, W, US, C*, [*It, NZ, Tg, Fj, SA*], 2000 *I, F, W, It, S, A, Arg, SA* 1,2, 2001 *W, It, S, F*
Dalton, T J (Coventry) 1969 *S*(R)
Danby, T (Harlequins) 1949 *W*
Daniell, J (Richmond) 1899 *W*, 1900 *I, S*, 1902 *I, S*, 1904 *I, S*
Darby, A J L (Birkenhead Park) 1899 *I*
Davenport, A (Ravenscourt Park) 1871 *S*
Davey, J (Redruth) 1908 *S*, 1909 *W*
Davey, R F (Teignmouth) 1931 *W*
Davidson, Jas (Aspatria) 1897 *S*, 1898 *S, W*, 1899 *I, S*
Davidson, Jos (Aspatria) 1899 *W, S*
Davies, G H (Cambridge U, Coventry, Wasps) 1981 *S, I, F, Arg* 1,2, 1982 *A, S, I*, 1983 *F, W, S*, 1984 *S, SA* 1,2, 1985 *R* (R), *NZ* 1,2, 1986 *W, S, I, F*
Davies, P H (Sale) 1927 *I*
Davies, V G (Harlequins) 1922 *W*, 1925 *NZ*
Davies, W J A (United Services, RN) 1913 *SA, W, F, I, S*, 1914 *I, S, F*, 1920 *F, I, S*, 1921 *W, I, S, F*, 1922 *I, F, S*, 1923 *W, I, S, F*
Davies, W P C (Harlequins) 1953 *S*, 1954 *NZ, I*, 1955 *W, I, F, S*, 1956 *W*, 1957 *F, S*, 1958 *W*
Davis, A M (Torquay Ath, Harlequins) 1963 *W, I, S, NZ* 1,2, 1964 *NZ, W, I, F, S*, 1966 *W*, 1967 *A*, 1969 *SA*, 1970 *I, W, S*
Dawe, R G R (Bath) 1987 *I, F, W*, [*US*], 1995 [*WS*]
Dawson, E F (RIEC) 1878 *I*
Dawson, M J S (Northampton) 1995 *WS*, 1996 *F, W, S, I*, 1997 *A* 1, *SA, NZ* 2(R), 1998 *W* (R), *S, I, F, A* 1,2, *SA* 1, *H, It, A* 2, *SA* 2, 1999 *S, F*(R), *W, A*(R), *US, C*, [*It, NZ, Tg, Fj* (R), *SA*], 2000 *I, F, W, It, S, A* (R), *Arg, SA* 3, 2001 *W, It, S, F, I*
Day, H L V (Leicester) 1920 *W*, 1922 *W, F*, 1926 *S*
Dean, G J (Harlequins) 1931 *I*
Dee, J M (Hartlepool R) 1962 *S*, 1963 *NZ* 1
Devitt, Sir T G (Blackheath) 1926 *I, F*, 1928 *A, W*
Dewhurst, J H (Richmond) 1887 *W, I, S*, 1890 *W*
De Glanville, P R (Bath) 1992 *SA* (R), 1993 *W* (R), *NZ*, 1994 *S, I, F, W, SA* 1,2, *C* (R), 1995 [*Arg* (R), *It, WS*], *SA* (R), 1996

W (R), *I* (R), *It*, 1997 *S, I, F, W, Arg* 1,2, *A* 1,2, *NZ* 1,2, 1998 *W* (R), *S* (R), *I* (R), *A* 2, *SA* 2, 1999 *A* (R), *US*, [*It, NZ, Fj* (R), *SA*]
De Winton, R F C (Marlborough N) 1893 *W*
Dibble, R (Bridgwater A) 1906 *S, F, SA*, 1908 *F, W, I, S*, 1909 *A, W, F, I, S*, 1910 *S*, 1911 *W, F, S*, 1912 *W, I, S*
Dicks, J (Northampton) 1934 *W, I, S*, 1935 *W, I, S*, 1936 *S*, 1937 *I*
Dillon, E W (Blackheath) 1904 *W, I, S*, 1905 *W*
Dingle, A J (Hartlepool R) 1913 *I*, 1914 *S, F*
Diprose, A J (Saracens) 1997 *Arg* 1,2, *A* 2, *NZ* 1, 1998 *W* (R), *S* (R), *I, A* 1, *NZ* 2, *SA* 1
Dixon, P J (Harlequins, Gosforth) 1971 *P*, 1972 *W, I, F, S*, 1973 *I, F, S*, 1974 *S, I, F, W*, 1975 *I*, 1976 *F*, 1977 *S, I, F, W*, 1978 *F, S, I, NZ*
Dobbs, G E B (Devonport A) 1906 *W, I*
Doble, S A (Moseley) 1972 *SA*, 1973 *NZ* 1, *W*
Dobson, D D (Newton Abbot) 1902 *W, I, S*, 1903 *W, I, S*
Dobson, T H (Bradford) 1895 *S*
Dodge, P W (Leicester) 1978 *W, S, I, NZ*, 1979 *S, I, F, W*, 1980 *W, S*, 1981 *W, S, I, F, Arg* 1,2, 1982 *A, S, F, W*, 1983 *F, W, S, I, NZ*, 1985 *R, F, S, I, W, NZ* 1,2
Donnelly, M P (Oxford U) 1947 *I*
Dooley, W A (Preston Grasshoppers, Fylde) 1985 *R, F, S, I, W, NZ* 2(R), 1986 *W, S, I, F*, 1987 *F, W*, [*A, US, W*], 1988 *F, W, S, I* 1,2, *A* 1,2, *Fj, A*, 1989 *S, I, F, W, R, Fj*, 1990 *I, F, W, S, Arg* 1,2,3, 1991 *W, S, I, F*, [*NZ, US, F, S, A*], 1992 *S, I, F, W, C, SA*, 1993 *W, S, I*
Dovey, B A (Rosslyn Park) 1963 *W, I*
Down, P J (Bristol) 1909 *A*
Dowson, A O (Moseley) 1899 *S*
Drake-Lee, N J (Cambridge U, Leicester) 1963 *W, I, F, S*, 1964 *NZ, W, I*, 1965 *W*
Duckett, H (Bradford) 1893 *I, S*
Duckham, D J (Coventry) 1969 *I, F, S, W, SA*, 1970 *I, W, S, F*, 1971 *W, I, S* (2[1C]), *P*, 1972 *W, I, F, S*, 1973 *NZ* 1, *W, I, F, S, NZ* 2, *A*, 1974 *S, I, F, W*, 1975 *I, F, W*, 1976 *A, W, S*
Dudgeon, H W (Richmond) 1897 *S*, 1898 *I, S, W*, 1899 *W, I, S*
Dugdale, J M (Ravenscourt Park) 1871 *S*
Dun, A F (Wasps) 1984 *W*
Duncan, R F H (Guy's Hospital) 1922 *I, F, S*
Dunkley, P E (Harlequins) 1931 *I, S*, 1936 *NZ, W, I, S*
Duthie, J (W Hartlepool) 1903 *W*
Dyson, J W (Huddersfield) 1890 *S*, 1892 *S*, 1893 *I, S*

Ebdon, P J (Wellington) 1897 *W, I*
Eddison, J H (Headingley) 1912 *W, I, S, F*
Edgar, C S (Birkenhead Park) 1901 *S*
Edwards, R (Newport) 1921 *W, I, S, F*, 1922 *W, F*, 1923 *W*, 1924 *W, F, S*, 1925 *NZ*
Egerton, D W (Bath) 1988 *I* 2, *A* 1, *Fj* (R), *A*, 1989 *Fj*, 1990 *I, Arg* 2(R)
Elliot, C H (Sunderland) 1886 *W*
Elliot, E W (Sunderland) 1901 *W, I, S*, 1904 *W*
Elliot, W (United Services, RN) 1932 *I, S*, 1933 *W, I, S*, 1934 *W, I*
Elliott, A E (St Thomas's Hospital) 1894 *S*
Ellis, J (Wakefield) 1939 *S*
Ellis, S S (Queen's House) 1880 *I*
Emmott, C (Bradford) 1892 *W*
Enthoven, H J (Richmond) 1878 *I*
Estcourt, N S D (Blackheath) 1955 *S*
Evans, B J (Leicester) 1988 *A* 2, *Fj*
Evans, E (Sale) 1948 *A*, 1950 *W*, 1951 *I, F, S*, 1952 *SA, W, S, I, F*, 1953 *I, F, S*, 1954 *W, NZ, I, F*, 1956 *W, I, S, F*, 1957 *W, I, F, S*, 1958 *W, A, I, F, S*
Evans, G W (Coventry) 1972 *S*, 1973 *W (R), F, S, NZ* 2, 1974 *S, I, F, W*
Evans, N L (RNEC) 1932 *W, I, S*, 1933 *W, I*
Evanson, A M (Richmond) 1883 *W, I, S*, 1884 *S*
Evanson, W A D (Richmond) 1875 *S*, 1877 *S*, 1878 *S*, 1879 *S, I*
Evershed, F (Blackheath) 1889 *M*, 1890 *W, S, I*, 1892 *W, I, S*, 1893 *W, I, S*
Eyres, W C T (Richmond) 1927 *I*

Fagan, A R St L (Richmond) 1887 *I*
Fairbrother, K E (Coventry) 1969 *I, F, S, W, SA*, 1970 *I, W, S, F*, 1971 *W, I, F*
Faithfull, C K T (Harlequins) 1924 *I*, 1926 *F, S*
Fallas, H (Wakefield T) 1884 *I*
Fegan, J H C (Blackheath) 1895 *W, I, S*

Fernandes, C W L (Leeds) 1881 *I, W, S*
Fidler, J H (Gloucester) 1981 *Arg* 1,2, 1984 *SA* 1,2
Fidler, R J (Gloucester) 1998 *NZ* 2, *SA* 1
Field, E (Middlesex W) 1893 *W, I*
Fielding, K J (Moseley, Loughborough Colls) 1969 *I, F, S, SA*, 1970 *I, F,* 1972 *W, I, F, S*
Finch, R T (Cambridge U) 1880 *S*
Finlan, J F (Moseley) 1967 *I, F, S, W, NZ*, 1968 *W, I,* 1969 *I, F, S, W,* 1970 *F,* 1973 *NZ* 1
Finlinson, H W (Blackheath) 1895 *W, I, S*
Finney, S (RIE Coll) 1872 *S,* 1873 *S*
Firth, F (Halifax) 1894 *W, I, S*
Flatman, D L (Saracens) 2000 *SA* 1(t),2(t+R), *A* (t), *Arg* (t+R), 2001 *F* (t), *C* 2(t+R), *US* (t+R)
Fletcher, N C (OMTs) 1901 *W, I, S,* 1903 *S*
Fletcher, T (Seaton) 1897 *W*
Fletcher, W R B (Marlborough N) 1873 *S,* 1875 *S*
Fookes, E F (Sowerby Bridge) 1896 *W, I, S,* 1897 *W, I, S,* 1898 *I, W,* 1899 *I, S*
Ford, P J (Gloucester) 1964 *W, I, F, S*
Forrest, J W (United Services, RN) 1930 *W, I, F, S,* 1931 *W, I, S, F,* 1934 *I, S*
Forrest, R (Wellington) 1899 *W,* 1900 *S,* 1902 *I, S,* 1903 *I, S*
Foulds, R T (Waterloo) 1929 *W, I*
Fowler, F D (Manchester) 1878 *S,* 1879 *S*
Fowler, H (Oxford U) 1878 *S,* 1881 *W, S*
Fowler, R H (Leeds) 1877 *I*
Fox, F H (Wellington) 1890 *W, S*
Francis, T E S (Cambridge U) 1926 *W, I, F, S*
Frankcom, G P (Cambridge U, Bedford) 1965 *W, I, F, S*
Fraser, E C (Blackheath) 1875 *I*
Fraser, G (Richmond) 1902 *W, I, S,* 1903 *W, I*
Freakes, H D (Oxford U) 1938 *W,* 1939 *W, I*
Freeman, H (Marlborough N) 1872 *S,* 1873 *S,* 1874 *S*
French, R J (St Helens) 1961 *W, I, F, S*
Fry, H A (Liverpool) 1934 *W, I, S*
Fry, T W (Queen's House) 1880 *I, S,* 1881 *W*
Fuller, H G (Cambridge U) 1882 *I, S,* 1883 *W, I, S,* 1884 *W*

Gadney, B C (Leicester, Headingley) 1932 *I, S,* 1933 *I, S,* 1934 *W, I, S,* 1935 *S,* 1936 *NZ, W, I, S,* 1937 *S,* 1938 *W*
Gamlin, H T (Blackheath) 1899 *W, S,* 1900 *W, I, S,* 1901 *S,* 1902 *W, I, S,* 1903 *W, I, S,* 1904 *W, I, S*
Gardner, E R (Devonport Services) 1921 *W, I, S,* 1922 *W, I, F,* 1923 *W, I, S, F*
Gardner, H P (Richmond) 1878 *I*
Garforth, D J (Leicester) 1997 *W* (R), *Arg* 1,2, *A* 1, *NZ* 1, *SA, NZ* 2, 1998 *F, W* (R), *S, I, H, It, A* 2, *SA* 2, 1999 *S, I, F, W, A, C* (R), [*It* (R), *NZ* (R), *Fj*], 2000 *It*
Garnett, H W T (Bradford) 1877 *S*
Gavins, M N (Leicester) 1961 *W*
Gay, D J (Bath) 1968 *W, I, F, S*
Gent, D R (Gloucester) 1905 *NZ,* 1906 *W, I,* 1910 *W, I*
Genth, J S M (Manchester) 1874 *S,* 1875 *S*
George, J T (Falmouth) 1947 *S, F,* 1949 *I*
Gerrard, R A (Bath) 1932 *SA, W, I, S,* 1933 *W, I, S,* 1934 *W, I, S,* 1936 *NZ, W, I, S*
Gibbs, G A (Bristol) 1947 *F,* 1948 *I*
Gibbs, J C (Harlequins) 1925 *NZ, W,* 1926 *F,* 1927 *W, I, S, F*
Gibbs, N (Harlequins) 1954 *S, F*
Giblin, L F (Blackheath) 1896 *W, I,* 1897 *S*
Gibson, A S (Manchester) 1871 *S*
Gibson, C O P (Northern) 1901 *W*
Gibson, G R (Northern) 1899 *W,* 1901 *S*
Gibson, T A (Northern) 1905 *W, S*
Gilbert, F G (Devonport Services) 1923 *W, I*
Gilbert, R (Devonport A) 1908 *W, I, S*
Giles, J L (Coventry) 1935 *W, I,* 1937 *W, I,* 1938 *I, S*
Gittings, W J (Coventry) 1967 *NZ*
Glover, P B (Bath) 1967 *A,* 1971 *F, P*
Godfray, R E (Richmond) 1905 *NZ*
Godwin, H O (Coventry) 1959 *F, S,* 1963 *S, NZ* 1,2, *A,* 1964 *NZ, I, F, S,* 1967 *NZ*
Gomarsall, A C T (Wasps, Bedford) 1996 *It, Arg,* 1997 *S, I, F, Arg* 2(R) 2000 *It* (R)
Gordon-Smith, G W (Blackheath) 1900 *W, I, S*
Gotley, A L H (Oxford U) 1910 *F, S,* 1911 *W, F, I, S*
Graham, D (Aspatria) 1901 *W*
Graham, H J (Wimbledon H) 1875 *I, S,* 1876 *I, S*
Graham, J D G (Wimbledon H) 1876 *I*
Gray, A (Otley) 1947 *W, I, S*

Grayson, P J (Northampton) 1995 *WS,* 1996 *F, W, S, I,* 1997 *S, I, F, A* 2(t), *SA* (R), *NZ* 2, 1998 *F, W, S, I, H, It, A* 2, 1999 *I,* [*NZ* (R), *Tg, Fj* (R), *SA*]
Green, J (Skipton) 1905 *I,* 1906 *S, F, SA,* 1907 *F, W, I, S*
Green, J F (West Kent) 1871 *S*
Green, W R (Wasps) 1997 *A* 2, 1998 *NZ* 1(t+R), 1999 *US* (R)
Greening, P B T (Gloucester, Wasps) 1996 *It* (R), 1997 *W* (R), *Arg* 1 1998 *NZ* 1(R),2(R), 1999 *A* (R), *US, C,* [*It* (R), *NZ* (R), *Tg, Fj, SA*], 2000 *I, S, SA* 1,2, *A, SA* 3, 2001 *F, I*
Greenstock, N J J (Wasps) 1997 *Arg* 1,2, *A* 1, *SA*
Greenwell, J H (Rockcliff) 1893 *W, I*
Greenwood, J E (Cambridge U, Leicester) 1912 *F,* 1913 *SA, W, F, I, S,* 1914 *W, S, F,* 1920 *W, F, I, S*
Greenwood, J R H (Waterloo) 1966 *I, F, S,* 1967 *A,* 1969 *I*
Greenwood, W J H (Leicester, Harlequins) 1997 *A* 2, *NZ* 1, *SA, NZ* 2, 1998 *F, W, S, I, H, It,* 1999 *C,* [*It, Tg, Fj, SA*], 2000 *Arg* (R), *SA* 3, 2001 *W, It, S, F, I*
Greg, W (Manchester) 1876 *I, S*
Gregory, G (Bristol) 1931 *I, S, F,* 1932 *SA, W, I, S,* 1933 *W, I, S,* 1934 *W, I, S*
Gregory, J A (Blackheath) 1949 *W*
Grewcock, D J (Coventry, Saracens, Bath) 1997 *Arg* 2, *SA,* 1998 *W* (R), *S* (R), *I* (R), *A* 1, *NZ* 1, *SA* 2(R), 1999 *S* (R), *A* (R), *US, C,* [*It, NZ, Tg* (R), *SA*], 2000 *SA* 1,2, *A, Arg, SA* 3, 2001 *W, It, S, I*
Grylls, W M (Redruth) 1905 *I*
Guest, R H (Waterloo) 1939 *W, I, S,* 1947 *W, I, S, F,* 1948 *A, W, I, S,* 1949 *F, S*
Guillemard, A G (West Kent) 1871 *S,* 1872 *S*
Gummer, C H A (Plymouth A) 1929 *F*
Gunner, C R (Marlborough N) 1876 *I*
Gurdon, C (Richmond) 1880 *I, S,* 1881 *I, W, S,* 1882 *I, S,* 1883 *S,* 1884 *W, S,* 1885 *I,* 1886 *W, I, S*
Gurdon, E T (Richmond) 1878 *S,* 1879 *I,* 1880 *S,* 1881 *I, W, S,* 1882 *S,* 1883 *W, I, S,* 1884 *W, I, S,* 1885 *W, I,* 1886 *W, I, S*
Guscott, J C (Bath) 1989 *R, Fj,* 1990 *I, F, S, Arg* 3, 1991 *W, S, I, F, Fj, A,* [*NZ, It, F, S, A*], 1992 *S, I, F, W, C, SA,* 1993 *F, W, S, I,* 1994 *R, C,* 1995 *I, F, W, S,* [*Arg, It, A, NZ, F*], *SA, WS,* 1996 *F, W, S, I, Arg,* 1997 *I* (R), *W* (R), 1998 *F, W, S, I, H, It, A* 2, *SA* 2, 1999 *S, I, F, A, US, C,* [*It* (R), *NZ, Tg*]

Haag, M (Bath) 1997 *Arg* 1,2
Haigh, L (Manchester) 1910 *W, I, S,* 1911 *W, F, I, S*
Hale, P M (Moseley) 1969 *SA,* 1970 *I, W*
Hall, C (Gloucester) 1901 *I, S*
Hall, J (N Durham) 1894 *W, I, S*
Hall, J P (Bath) 1984 *S* (R), *I, F, SA* 1,2, *A,* 1985 *R, F, S, I, W, NZ* 1,2, 1986 *W, S,* 1987 *I, F, W, S,* 1990 *Arg* 3, 1994 *S*
Hall, N M (Richmond) 1947 *W, I, S, F,* 1949 *W, I,* 1952 *SA, W, S, I, F,* 1953 *W, I, F, S,* 1955 *W, I*
Halliday, S J (Bath, Harlequins) 1986 *W, S,* 1987 *S,* 1988 *S, I* 1,2, *A* 1, *A,* 1989 *S, I, F, W, R, Fj* (R), 1990 *W, S,* 1991 [*US, S, A*], 1992 *S, I, F, W*
Hamersley, A St G (Marlborough N) 1871 *S,* 1872 *S,* 1873 *S,* 1874 *S*
Hamilton-Hill, E A (Harlequins) 1936 *NZ, W, I*
Hamilton-Wickes, R H (Cambridge U) 1924 *I,* 1925 *NZ, W, I, S, F,* 1926 *W, I, S,* 1927 *W*
Hammett, E D G (Newport) 1920 *W, F, S,* 1921 *W, I, S, F,* 1922 *W*
Hammond, C E L (Harlequins) 1905 *S, NZ,* 1906 *W, I, S, F,* 1908 *W, I*
Hancock, A W (Northampton) 1965 *F, S,* 1966 *F*
Hancock, G E (Birkenhead Park) 1939 *W, I, S*
Hancock, J H (Newport) 1955 *W, I*
Hancock, P F (Blackheath) 1886 *W, I,* 1890 *W*
Hancock, P S (Richmond) 1904 *W, I, S*
Handford, F G (Manchester) 1909 *W, F, I, S*
Hands, R H M (Blackheath) 1910 *F, S*
Hanley, J (Plymouth A) 1927 *W, S, F,* 1928 *W, I, F, S*
Hanley, S M (Sale) 1999 *W*
Hannaford, R C (Bristol) 1971 *W, I, F*
Hanvey, R J (Aspatria) 1926 *W, I, F, S*
Harding, E H (Devonport Services) 1931 *I*
Harding, R M (Bristol) 1985 *R, F, S,* 1987 *S,* [*A, J, W*], 1988 *I* 1(R),2, *A* 1,2, *Fj*
Harding, V S J (Saracens) 1961 *F, S,* 1962 *W, I, F, S*
Hardwick, P F (Percy Park) 1902 *I, S,* 1903 *W, I, S,* 1904 *W, I, S*
Hardwick, R J K (Coventry) 1996 *It* (R)
Hardy, E M P (Blackheath) 1951 *I, F, S*

Hare, W H (Nottingham, Leicester) 1974 *W*, 1978 *F, NZ*, 1979 *NZ*, 1980 *I, F, W, S*, 1981 *W, S, Arg* 1,2, 1982 *F, W*, 1983 *F, W, S, I, NZ*, 1984 *S, I, F, W, SA* 1,2
Harper, C H (Exeter) 1899 *W*
Harriman, A T (Harlequins) 1988 *A*
Harris, S W (Blackheath) 1920 *I, S*
Harris, T W (Northampton) 1929 *S*, 1932 *I*
Harrison, A C (Hartlepool R) 1931 *I, S*
Harrison, A L (United Services, RN) 1914 *I, F*
Harrison, G (Hull) 1877 *I, S*, 1879 *S, I*, 1880 *S*, 1885 *W, I*
Harrison, H C (United Services, RN) 1909 *S*, 1914 *I, S, F*
Harrison, M E (Wakefield) 1985 *NZ* 1,2, 1986 *S, I, F*, 1987 *I, F, W, S, [A, J, US, W]*, 1988 *F, W*
Hartley, B C (Blackheath) 1901 *S*, 1902 *S*
Haslett, L W (Birkenhead Park) 1926 *I, F*
Hastings, G W D (Gloucester) 1955 *W, I, F, S*, 1957 *W, I, F, S*, 1958 *W, A, I, F, S*
Havelock, H (Hartlepool R) 1908 *F, W, I*
Hawcridge, J J (Bradford) 1885 *W, I*
Hayward, L W (Cheltenham) 1910 *I*
Hazell, D St G (Leicester) 1955 *W, I, F, S*
Healey, A S (Leicester) 1997 *I* (R), *W, A* 1(R),2(R), *NZ* 1(R), *SA* (R), *NZ* 2, 1998 *F, W, S, I, A* 1, *NZ* 1,2, *H, It, A* 2, *SA* 2(R), 1999 *US, C, [It, NZ, Tg, Fj, SA* (R)], 2000 *I, F, W, It, S, SA* 1,2, *A, SA* 3(R), 2001 *W* (R), *It, S, F, I* (R)
Hearn, R D (Bedford) 1966 *F, S*, 1967 *I, F, S, W*
Heath, A H (Oxford U) 1876 *S*
Heaton, J (Waterloo) 1935 *W, I, S*, 1939 *W, I, S*, 1947 *I, S, F*
Henderson, A P (Edinburgh Wands) 1947 *W, I, S, F*, 1948 *I, S, F*, 1949 *W, I*
Henderson, R S F (Blackheath) 1883 *W, S*, 1884 *W, S*, 1885 *W*
Heppell, W G (Devonport A) 1903 *I*
Herbert, A J (Wasps) 1958 *F, S*, 1959 *W, I, F, S*
Hesford, R (Bristol) 1981 *S* (R), 1982 *A, S, F* (R), 1983 *F* (R), 1985 *R, F, S, I, W*
Heslop, N J (Orrell) 1990 *Arg* 1,2,3, 1991 *W, S, I, F, [US, F]*, 1992 *W* (R)
Hetherington, J G G (Northampton) 1958 *A, I*, 1959 *W, I, F, S*
Hewitt, E N (Coventry) 1951 *W, I, F*
Hewitt, W W (Queen's House) 1881 *I, W, S*, 1882 *I*
Hickson, J L (Bradford) 1887 *W, I, S*, 1890 *W, S, F*
Higgins, R (Liverpool) 1954 *W, NZ, I, S*, 1955 *W, I, F, S*, 1957 *W, I, F, S*, 1959 *W*
Hignell, A J (Cambridge U, Bristol) 1975 *A* 2, 1976 *A, W, S, I*, 1977 *S, I, F, W*, 1978 *W*, 1979 *S, I, F, W*
Hill, B A (Blackheath) 1903 *I, S*, 1904 *W, I*, 1905 *W, NZ*, 1906 *SA*, 1907 *F, W*
Hill, R A (Saracens) 1997 *S, I, F, W, A* 1,2, *NZ* 1, *SA, NZ* 2, 1998 *F, W, H*(R), *It* (R), *A* 2, *SA* 2, 1999 *S, I, F, W, A, US, C, [It, NZ, Tg, Fj* (R), *SA]*, 2000 *I, F, W, It, S, SA* 1,2, *A, Arg, SA* 3, 2001 *W, It, S, F, I*
Hill, R J (Bath) 1984 *SA* 1,2, 1985 *I* (R), *NZ* 2(R), 1986 *F* (R), 1987 *I, F, W, [US]*, 1989 *Fj*, 1990 *I, F, W, S, Arg* 1,2,3, 1991 *W, S, I, F, Fj, A, [NZ, It, US, F, S, A]*
Hillard, R J (Oxford U) 1925 *NZ*
Hiller, R (Harlequins) 1968 *W, I, F, S*, 1969 *I, F, S, W, SA*, 1970 *I, W, S*, 1971 *I, F, S* (2[1C]), *P*, 1972 *W, I*
Hind, A E (Leicester) 1905 *NZ*, 1906 *W*
Hind, G R (Blackheath) 1910 *S*, 1911 *I*
Hobbs, R F A (Blackheath) 1899 *S*, 1903 *W*
Hobbs, R G S (Richmond) 1932 *SA, W, I, S*
Hodges, H A (Nottingham) 1906 *W, I*
Hodgkinson, S D (Nottingham) 1989 *R, Fj*, 1990 *I, F, W, S, Arg* 1,2,3, 1991 *W, S, I, F, [US]*
Hodgson, J McD (Northern) 1932 *SA, W, I, S*, 1934 *W, I*, 1936 *I*
Hodgson, S A M (Durham City) 1960 *W, I, F, S*, 1961 *SA, W*, 1962 *W, I, F, S*, 1964 *W*
Hofmeyr, M B (Oxford U) 1950 *W, F, S*
Hogarth, T B (Hartlepool R) 1906 *F*
Holford, G (Gloucester) 1920 *W, F*
Holland, D (Devonport A) 1912 *W, I, S*
Holliday, T E (Aspatria) 1923 *S, F*, 1925 *I, S, F*, 1926 *F, S*
Holmes, C B (Manchester) 1947 *S*, 1948 *I, F*
Holmes, E (Manningham) 1890 *S, I*
Holmes, W A (Nuneaton) 1950 *W, I, F, S*, 1951 *W, I, F, S*, 1952 *SA, S, I, F*, 1953 *W, I, F, S*
Holmes, W B (Cambridge U) 1949 *W, I, F, S*
Hook, W G (Gloucester) 1951 *S*, 1952 *SA, W*
Hooper, C A (Middlesex W) 1894 *W, I, S*
Hopley, D P (Wasps) 1995 *[WS* (R)], *SA, WS*

Hopley, F J V (Blackheath) 1907 *F, W*, 1908 *I*
Hordern, P C (Gloucester) 1931 *I, S, F*, 1934 *W*
Horley, C H (Swinton) 1885 *I*
Hornby, A N (Manchester) 1877 *I, S*, 1878 *S, I*, 1880 *I*, 1881 *I, S*, 1882 *I, S*
Horrocks-Taylor, J P (Cambridge U, Leicester, Middlesbrough) 1958 *W, A*, 1961 *S*, 1962 *S*, 1963 *NZ* 1,2, *A*, 1964 *NZ, W*
Horsfall, E L (Harlequins) 1949 *W*
Horton, A L (Blackheath) 1965 *W, I, F, S*, 1966 *F, S*, 1967 *NZ*
Horton, J P (Bath) 1978 *W, S, I, NZ*, 1980 *I, F, W, S*, 1981 *W*, 1983 *S, I*, 1984 *SA* 1,2
Horton, N E (Moseley, Toulouse) 1969 *I, F, S, W*, 1971 *I, F, S*, 1974 *S, W*, 1977 *S, I, F, W*, 1978 *F, W*, 1979 *S, I, F, W*, 1980 *I*
Hosen, R W (Bristol, Northampton) 1963 *NZ* 1,2, *A*, 1964 *F, S*, 1967 *A, I, F, S, W*
Hosking, G R d'A (Devonport Services) 1949 *W, I, F, S*, 1950 *W*
Houghton, S (Runcorn) 1892 *I*, 1896 *W*
Howard, P D (O Millhillians) 1930 *W, I, F, S*, 1931 *W, I, S, F*
Hubbard, G C (Blackheath) 1892 *W, I*
Hubbard, J C (Harlequins) 1930 *S*
Hudson, A (Gloucester) 1906 *W, I, F*, 1908 *F, W, I, S*, 1910 *F*
Hughes, G E (Barrow) 1896 *S*
Hull, P A (Bristol, RAF) 1994 *SA* 1,2, *R, C*
Hulme, F C (Birkenhead Park) 1903 *W, I*, 1905 *W, I*
Hunt, J T (Manchester) 1882 *I, S*, 1884 *W*
Hunt, R (Manchester) 1880 *I*, 1881 *W, S*, 1882 *I*
Hunt, W H (Manchester) 1876 *S*, 1877 *I, S*, 1878 *I*
Hunter, I (Northampton) 1992 *C*, 1993 *F, W*, 1994 *F, W*, 1995 *[WS, F]*
Huntsman, R P (Headingley) 1985 *NZ* 1,2
Hurst, A C B (Wasps) 1962 *S*
Huskisson, T F (OMTs) 1937 *W, I, S*, 1938 *W, I*, 1939 *W, I, S*
Hutchinson, F (Headingley) 1909 *F, I, S*
Hutchinson, J E (Durham City) 1906 *I*
Hutchinson, W C (RIE Coll) 1876 *S*, 1877 *I*
Hutchinson, W H H (Hull) 1875 *I*, 1876 *I*
Huth, H (Huddersfield) 1879 *S*
Hyde, J P (Northampton) 1950 *F, S*
Hynes, W B (United Services, RN) 1912 *F*

Ibbitson, E D (Headingley) 1909 *W, F, I, S*
Imrie, H M (Durham City) 1906 *NZ*, 1907 *I*
Inglis, R E (Blackheath) 1886 *W, I, S*
Irvin, S H (Devonport A) 1905 *W*
Isherwood, F W (Ravenscourt Park) 1872 *S*

Jackett, E J (Leicester, Falmouth) 1905 *NZ*, 1906 *W, I, S, F, SA*, 1907 *W, I, S*, 1909 *W, F, I, S*
Jackson, A H (Blackheath) 1878 *I*, 1880 *I*
Jackson, B S (Broughton Park) 1970 *S* (R), *F*
Jackson, P B (Coventry) 1956 *W, I, F*, 1957 *W, I, F, S*, 1958 *W, A, F, S*, 1959 *W, I, F, S*, 1961 *S*, 1963 *W, I, F, S*
Jackson, W J (Halifax) 1894 *S*
Jacob, F (Cambridge U) 1897 *W, I, S*, 1898 *I, S, W*, 1899 *W, I*
Jacob, H P (Blackheath) 1924 *W, I, F, S*, 1930 *F*
Jacob, P G (Blackheath) 1898 *I*
Jacobs, C R (Northampton) 1956 *W, I, S, F*, 1957 *W, I, F, S*, 1958 *W, A, I, F, S*, 1960 *W, I, F, S*, 1961 *SA, W, I, F, S*, 1963 *NZ* 1,2, *A*, 1964 *W, I, F, S*
Jago, R A (Devonport A) 1906 *W, I, S*, 1907 *W, I, F*
Janion, J P A G (Bedford) 1971 *W, I, F, S* (2[1C]), *P*, 1972 *W, S, SA*, 1973 *A*, 1975 *A* 1,2
Jarman, J W (Bristol) 1900 *W*
Jeavons, N C (Moseley) 1981 *S, I, F, Arg* 1,2, 1982 *A, S, I, F, W*, 1983 *F, W, S, I*
Jeeps, R E G (Northampton) 1956 *W*, 1957 *W, I, F, S*, 1958 *W, A, I, F, S*, 1959 *I*, 1960 *W, I, F, S*, 1961 *SA, W, I, F, S*, 1962 *W, I, F, S*
Jeffery, G L (Blackheath) 1886 *W, I, S*, 1887 *W, I, S*
Jennins, C R (Waterloo) 1967 *A, I, F*
Jewitt, J (Hartlepool R) 1902 *W*
Johns, W A (Gloucester) 1909 *W, F, I, S*, 1910 *W, I, F*
Johnson, M O (Leicester) 1993 *F, NZ*, 1994 *S, I, F, W, R, C*, 1995 *I, F, W, S, [Arg, It, WS, A, NZ, F], SA, WS*, 1996 *F, W, S, I, It, Arg*, 1997 *S, I, F, W, A* 2, *NZ* 1,2, 1998 *F, W, S, I, H, It, A* 2, *SA* 2, 1999 *S, I, F, W, A, US, C, [It, NZ, Tg, Fj, SA]*, 2000 *SA* 1,2, *A, Arg, SA* 3, 2001 *W, It, S, F*
Johnston, W R (Bristol) 1910 *W, I, S*, 1912 *W, I, S, F*, 1913 *SA, W, F, I, S*, 1914 *W, I, S, F*
Jones, F P (New Brighton) 1893 *S*

Jones, H A (Barnstaple) 1950 *W, I, F*
Jorden, A M (Cambridge U, Blackheath, Bedford) 1970 *F,* 1973 *I, F, S,* 1974 *F,* 1975 *W, S*
Jowett, D (Heckmondwike) 1889 *M,* 1890 *S, I,* 1891 *W, I, S*
Judd, P E (Coventry) 1962 *W, I, F, S,* 1963 *S, NZ* 1,2, *A,* 1964 *NZ,* 1965 *I, F, S,* 1966 *W, I, F, S,* 1967 *A, I, F, S, W, NZ*

Kay, B J (Leicester) 2001 *C* 1,2
Kayll, H E (Sunderland) 1878 *S*
Keeling, J H (Guy's Hospital) 1948 *A, W*
Keen, B W (Newcastle U) 1968 *W, I, F, S*
Keeton, G H (Leicester) 1904 *W, I, S*
Kelly, G A (Bedford) 1947 *W, I, S,* 1948 *W*
Kelly, T S (London Devonians) 1906 *W, I, S, F, SA,* 1907 *F, W, I, S,* 1908 *F, I, S*
Kemble, A T (Liverpool) 1885 *W, I,* 1887 *I*
Kemp, D T (Blackheath) 1935 *W*
Kemp, T A (Richmond) 1937 *W, I,* 1939 *S,* 1948 *A, W*
Kendall, P D (Birkenhead Park) 1901 *S,* 1902 *W,* 1903 *S*
Kendall-Carpenter, J MacG K (Oxford U, Bath) 1949 *I, F, S,* 1950 *W, I, F, S,* 1951 *I, F, S,* 1952 *SA, W, S, I, F,* 1953 *W, I, F, S,* 1954 *W, NZ, I, F*
Kendrew, D A (Leicester) 1930 *W, I,* 1933 *I, S,* 1934 *S,* 1935 *W, I,* 1936 *NZ, W, I*
Kennedy, R D (Camborne S of M) 1949 *I, F, S*
Kent, C P (Rosslyn Park) 1977 *S, I, F, W,* 1978 *F* (R)
Kent, T (Salford) 1891 *W, I, S,* 1892 *W, I, S*
Kershaw, C A (United Services, RN) 1920 *W, F, I, S,* 1921 *W, I, S, F,* 1922 *W, I, F, S,* 1923 *W, I, S, F*
Kewley, E (Liverpool) 1874 *S,* 1875 *S,* 1876 *I, S,* 1877 *I, S,* 1878 *S*
Kewney, A L (Leicester) 1906 *W, I, S, F,* 1909 *A, W, F, I, S,* 1911 *W, F, I, S,* 1912 *I, S,* 1913 *SA*
Key, A (O Cranleighans) 1930 *I,* 1933 *W*
yworth, M (Swansea) 1976 *A, W, S, I*
Kilner, B (Wakefield T) 1880 *I*
Kindersley, R S (Exeter) 1883 *W,* 1884 *S,* 1885 *W*
King, A D (Wasps) 1997 *Arg* 2(R), 1998 *SA* 2(R), 2000 *It* (R), 2001 *C* 2(R)
King, I (Harrogate) 1954 *W, NZ, I*
King, J A (Headingley) 1911 *W, F, I, S,* 1912 *W, I, S,* 1913 *SA, W, F, I, S*
King, Q E M A (Army) 1921 *S*
Kingston, P (Gloucester) 1975 *A* 1,2, 1979 *I, F, W*
Kitching, A E (Blackheath) 1913 *I*
Kittermaster, H J (Harlequins) 1925 *NZ, W, I,* 1926 *W, I, F, S*
Knight, F (Plymouth) 1909 *A*
Knight, P M (Bristol) 1972 *F, S, SA*
Knowles, E (Millom) 1896 *S,* 1897 *S*
Knowles, T C (Birkenhead Park) 1931 *S*
Krige, J A (Guy's Hospital) 1920 *W*

Labuschagne, N A (Harlequins, Guy's Hospital) 1953 *W,* 1955 *W, I, F, S*
Lagden, R O (Richmond) 1911 *S*
Laird, H C C (Harlequins) 1927 *W, I, S,* 1928 *A, W, I, F, S,* 1929 *W, I*
Lambert, D (Harlequins) 1907 *F,* 1908 *F, W, S,* 1911 *W, F, I*
Lampkowski, M S (Headingley) 1976 *A, W, S, I*
Lapage, W N (United Services, RN) 1908 *F, W, I, S*
Larter, P J (Northampton, RAF) 1967 *A, NZ,* 1968 *W, I, F, S,* 1969 *I, F, S, W, SA,* 1970 *I, W, F, S,* 1971 *W, I, F, S* (2[1C]), *P,* 1972 *SA,* 1973 *NZ* 1, *W*
Law, A F (Richmond) 1877 *S*
Law, D E (Birkenhead Park) 1927 *I*
Lawrence, Hon H A (Richmond) 1873 *S,* 1874 *S,* 1875 *I, S*
Lawrie, P W (Leicester) 1910 *S,* 1911 *S*
Lawson, R G (Workington) 1925 *I*
Lawson, T M (Workington) 1928 *A, W*
Leadbetter, M M (Broughton Park) 1970 *F*
Leadbetter, V H (Edinburgh Wands) 1954 *S, F*
Leake, W R M (Harlequins) 1891 *W, I, S*
Leather, G (Liverpool) 1907 *I*
Lee, F H (Marlborough N) 1876 *S,* 1877 *I*
Lee, H (Blackheath) 1907 *F*
Le Fleming, J (Blackheath) 1887 *W*
Leonard, J (Saracens, Harlequins) 1990 *Arg* 1,2,3, 1991 *W, S, I, F, Fj, A,* [*NZ, It, US, F, S, A*], 1992 *S, I, F, W, C, SA,* 1993 *F, W, S, I, NZ,* 1994 *S, I, F, W, SA* 1,2, *R, C,* 1995 *I, F, W, S,* [*Arg, It, A, NZ, F*], *SA, WS,* 1996 *F, W, S, I, It, Arg,* 1997 *S, I, F, W, A* 2, *NZ* 1, *SA, NZ* 2, 1998 *F, W, S, I, H, It, A* 2 *SA* 2, 1999 *S, I, F, W, A, C* (R), [*It, NZ, Fj, SA*], 2000 *I, F, W, It, S, SA* 1,2, *A, Arg, SA* 3, 2001 *W, It, S, F, I*

Leslie-Jones, F A (Richmond) 1895 *W, I*
Lewis, A O (Bath) 1952 *SA, W, S, I, F,* 1953 *W, I, F, S,* 1954 *F*
Lewsey, O J (Wasps) 1998 *NZ* 1,2, *SA* 1, 2001 *C* 1,2, *US*
Leyland, R (Waterloo) 1935 *W, I, S*
Linnett, M S (Moseley) 1989 *Fj*
Livesay, R O'H (Blackheath) 1898 *W,* 1899 *W*
Lloyd, L D (Leicester) 2000 *SA* 1(R),2(R), 2001 *C* 1,2, *US*
Lloyd, R H (Harlequins) 1967 *NZ,* 1968 *W, I, F, S*
Locke, H M (Birkenhead Park) 1923 *S, F,* 1924 *W, F, S,* 1925 *W, I, S, F,* 1927 *W, I, S*
Lockwood, R E (Heckmondwike) 1887 *W, I, S,* 1889 *M,* 1891 *W, I, S,* 1892 *W, I, S,* 1893 *W, I,* 1894 *W, I*
Login, S H M (RN Coll) 1876 *I*
Lohden, F C (Blackheath) 1893 *W*
Long, A E (Bath) 1997 *A* 2, 2001 *US* (R)
Longland, R J (Northampton) 1932 *S,* 1933 *W, S,* 1934 *W, I, S,* 1935 *W, I, S,* 1936 *NZ, W, I, S,* 1937 *W, I, S,* 1938 *W, I, S*
Lowe, C N (Cambridge U, Blackheath) 1913 *SA, W, F, I, S,* 1914 *W, I, S, F,* 1920 *W, F, I, S,* 1921 *W, I, S, F,* 1922 *W, I, F, S,* 1923 *W, I, S, F*
Lowrie, F (Wakefield T) 1889 *M,* 1890 *W*
Lowry, W M (Birkenhead Park) 1920 *F*
Lozowski, R A P (Wasps) 1984 *A*
Luddington, W G E (Devonport Services) 1923 *W, I, S, F,* 1924 *W, I, F, S,* 1925 *W, I, S, F,* 1926 *W*
Luger, D D (Harlequins, Saracens) 1998 *H, It, SA* 2, 1999 *S, I, F, W, A, US, C,* [*It, NZ, Tg, Fj, SA*], 2000 *SA* 1, *A, Arg, SA* 3, 2001 *W, I*
Luscombe, F (Gipsies) 1872 *S,* 1873 *S,* 1875 *I, S,* 1876 *I, S*
Luscombe, J H (Gipsies) 1871 *S*
Luxmoore, A F C C (Richmond) 1900 *S,* 1901 *W*
Luya, H F (Waterloo, Headingley) 1948 *W, I, S, F,* 1949 *W*
Lyon, A (Liverpool) 1871 *S*
Lyon, G H d'O (United Services, RN) 1908 *S,* 1909 *A*

McCanlis, M A (Gloucester) 1931 *W, I*
McCarthy, N (Gloucester) 1999 *I* (t), *US* (R), 2000 *It* (R)
McFadyean, C W (Moseley) 1966 *I, F, S,* 1967 *A, I, F, S, W, NZ,* 1968 *W, I*
MacIlwaine, A H (United Services, Hull & E Riding) 1912 *W, I, S, F,* 1920 *I*
Mackie, O G (Wakefield T, Cambridge U) 1897 *S,* 1898 *I*
Mackinlay, J E H (St George's Hospital) 1872 *S,* 1873 *S,* 1875 *I*
MacLaren, W (Manchester) 1871 *S*
MacLennan, R R F (OMTs) 1925 *I, S, F*
McLeod, N F (RIE Coll) 1879 *S, I*
Madge, R J P (Exeter) 1948 *A, W, I, S*
Malir, F W S (Otley) 1930 *W, I, S*
Mallett, J A (Bath) 1995 [*WS* (R)]
Mallinder, J (Sale) 1997 *Arg* 1,2
Mangles, R H (Richmond) 1897 *W, I*
Manley, D C (Exeter) 1963 *W, I, F, S*
Mann, W E (United Services, Army) 1911 *W, F, I*
Mantell, N D (Rosslyn Park) 1975 *A* 1
Mapletoft, M S (Gloucester) 1997 *Arg* 2
Markendale, E T (Manchester R) 1880 *I*
Marques, R W D (Cambridge U, Harlequins) 1956 *W, I, S, F,* 1957 *W, I, F, S,* 1958 *W, A, I, F, S,* 1959 *W, I, F, S,* 1960 *W, I, F, S,* 1961 *SA, W*
Marquis, J C (Birkenhead Park) 1900 *I, S*
Marriott, C J B (Blackheath) 1884 *W, I, S,* 1886 *W, I, S,* 1887 *I*
Marriott, E E (Manchester) 1876 *I*
Marriott, V R (Harlequins) 1963 *NZ* 1,2, *A,* 1964 *NZ*
Marsden, G H (Morley) 1900 *W, I, S*
Marsh, H (RIE Coll) 1873 *S*
Marsh, J (Swinton) 1892 *I*
Marshall, H (Blackheath) 1893 *W*
Marshall, M W (Blackheath) 1873 *S,* 1874 *S,* 1875 *I, S,* 1876 *I, S,* 1877 *I, S,* 1878 *S, I*
Marshall, R M (Oxford U) 1938 *I, S,* 1939 *W, I, S*
Martin, C R (Bath) 1985 *F, S, I, W*
Martin, N O (Harlequins) 1972 *F* (R)
Martindale, S A (Kendal) 1929 *F*
Massey, E J (Leicester) 1925 *W, I, S*
Mather, B-J (Sale) 1999 *W*
Mathias, J L (Bristol) 1905 *W, I, S, NZ*
Matters, J C (RNE Coll) 1899 *S*
Matthews, J R C (Harlequins) 1949 *F, S,* 1950 *I, F, S,* 1952 *SA, W, S, I, F*
Maud, P (Blackheath) 1893 *W, I*

Maxwell, A W (New Brighton, Headingley) 1975 *A* 1, 1976 *A, W, S, I, F,* 1978 *F*
Maxwell-Hyslop, J E (Oxford U) 1922 *I, F, S*
Maynard, A F (Cambridge U) 1914 *W, I, S*
Meikle, G W C (Waterloo) 1934 *W, I, S*
Meikle, S S C (Waterloo) 1929 *S*
Mellish, F W (Blackheath) 1920 *W, F, I, S,* 1921 *W, I*
Melville, N D (Wasps) 1984 *A,* 1985 *I, W, NZ* 1,2, 1986 *W, S, I, F,* 1988 *F, W, S, I* 1
Merriam, L P B (Blackheath) 1920 *W, F*
Michell, A T (Oxford U) 1875 *I, S,* 1876 *I*
Middleton, B B (Birkenhead Park) 1882 *I,* 1883 *I*
Middleton, J A (Richmond) 1922 *S*
Miles, J H (Leicester) 1903 *W*
Millett, H (Richmond) 1920 *F*
Mills, F W (Marlborough N) 1872 *S,* 1873 *S*
Mills, S G F (Gloucester) 1981 *Arg* 1,2, 1983 *W,* 1984 *SA* 1, *A*
Mills, W A (Devonport A) 1906 *W, I, S, F, SA,* 1907 *F, W, I, S,* 1908 *F, W*
Milman, D L K (Bedford) 1937 *W,* 1938 *W, I, S*
Milton, C H (Camborne S of M) 1906 *I*
Milton, J G (Camborne S of M) 1904 *W, I, S,* 1905 *S,* 1907 *I*
Milton, W H (Marlborough N) 1874 *S,* 1875 *I*
Mitchell, F (Blackheath) 1895 *W, I, S,* 1896 *W, I, S*
Mitchell, W G (Richmond) 1890 *W, S, I,* 1891 *W, I, S,* 1893 *S*
Mobbs, E R (Northampton) 1909 *A, W, F, I, S,* 1910 *I, F*
Moberley, W O (Ravenscourt Park) 1872 *S*
Moody, L W (Leicester) 2001 *C* 1,2, *US, I* (R)
Moore, B C (Nottingham, Harlequins) 1987 *S, [A, J, W],* 1988 *F, W, S, I* 1,2, *A* 1, 2, *Fj, A,* 1989 *S, I, F, W, R, Fj,* 1990 *I, F, W, S, Arg* 1,2, 1991 *W, S, I, F, Fj, A, [NZ, It, F, S, A],* 1992 *S, I, F, W, SA,* 1993 *F, W, S, I, NZ,* 1994 *S, I, F, W, SA* 1,2, *R, C,* 1995 *I, F, W, S, [Arg, It, WS* (R), *A, NZ, F]*
Moore, E J (Blackheath) 1883 *I, S*
Moore, N J N H (Bristol) 1904 *W, I, S*
Moore, P B C (Blackheath) 1951 *W*
Moore, W K T (Leicester) 1947 *W, I,* 1949 *F, S,* 1950 *I, F, S*
Mordell, R J (Rosslyn Park) 1978 *W*
Morfitt, S (W Hartlepool) 1894 *W, I, S,* 1896 *W, I, S*
Morgan, J R (Hawick) 1920 *W*
Morgan, W G D (Medicals, Newcastle) 1960 *W, I, F, S,* 1961 *SA, W, I, F, S*
Morley, A J (Bristol) 1972 *SA,* 1973 *NZ* 1, *W, I,* 1975 *S, A* 1,2
Morris, A D W (United Services, RN) 1909 *A, W, F*
Morris, C D (Liverpool St Helens, Orrell) 1988 *A,* 1989 *S, I, F, W,* 1992 *S, I, F, W, C, SA,* 1993 *F, W, S, I,* 1994 *F, W, SA* 1,2, *R,* 1995 *S* (t), *[Arg, WS, A, NZ, F]*
Morrison, P H (Cambridge U) 1890 *W, S, I,* 1891 *I*
Morse, S (Marlborough N) 1873 *S,* 1874 *S,* 1875 *S*
Mortimer, W (Marlborough N) 1899 *W*
Morton, H J S (Blackheath) 1909 *I, S,* 1910 *W, I*
Moss, F (Broughton) 1885 *W, I,* 1886 *W*
Mullins, A R (Harlequins) 1989 *Fj*
Mycock, J (Sale) 1947 *W, I, S, F,* 1948 *A*
Myers, E (Bradford) 1920 *I, S,* 1921 *W, I,* 1922 *W, I, F, S,* 1923 *W, I, S, F,* 1924 *W, I, F, S,* 1925 *S, F*
Myers, H (Keighley) 1898 *I*

Nanson, W M B (Carlisle) 1907 *F, W*
Nash, E H (Richmond) 1875 *I*
Neale, B A (Rosslyn Park) 1951 *I, F, S*
Neale, M E (Blackheath) 1912 *F*
Neame, S (O Cheltonians) 1879 *S, I,* 1880 *I, S*
Neary, A (Broughton Park) 1971 *W, I, F, S* (2[1C]), *P,* 1972 *W, I, F, S, SA,* 1973 *NZ* 1, *W, I, F, S, NZ* 2, *A,* 1974 *S, I, F, W,* 1975 *I, F, W, S, A* 1, 1976 *A, W, S, I, F,* 1977 *I,* 1978 *F* (R), 1979 *S, I, F, W, NZ,* 1980 *I, F, W, S*
Nelmes, B G (Cardiff) 1975 *A* 1,2, 1978 *W, S, I, NZ*
Newbold, C J (Blackheath) 1904 *W, I, S,* 1905 *W, I, S*
Newman, S C (Oxford U) 1947 *F,* 1948 *A, W*
Newton, A W (Blackheath) 1907 *S*
Newton, P A (Blackheath) 1882 *S*
Newton-Thompson, J O (Oxford U) 1947 *S, F*
Nichol, W (Brighouse R) 1892 *W, S*
Nicholas, P L (Exeter) 1902 *W*
Nicholson, B E (Harlequins) 1938 *W, I*
Nicholson, E S (Leicester) 1935 *W, I, S,* 1936 *NZ, W*
Nicholson, E T (Birkenhead Park) 1900 *W, I*
Nicholson, T (Rockcliff) 1893 *I*
Ninnes, B F (Coventry) 1971 *W*
Noon, J (Newcastle) 2001 *C* 1,2, *US*
Norman, D J (Leicester) 1932 *SA, W*

North, E H G (Blackheath) 1891 *W, I, S*
Northmore, S (Millom) 1897 *I*
Novak, M J (Harlequins) 1970 *W, S, F*
Novis, A L (Blackheath) 1929 *S, F,* 1930 *W, I, F,* 1933 *I, S*

Oakeley, F E (United Services, RN) 1913 *S,* 1914 *I, S, F*
Oakes, R F (Hartlepool R) 1897 *W, I, S,* 1898 *I, S, W,* 1899 *W, S*
Oakley, L F L (Bedford) 1951 *W*
Obolensky, A (Oxford U) 1936 *NZ, W, I, S*
Ojomoh, S O (Bath, Gloucester) 1994 *I, F, SA* 1(R),2, *R,* 1995 *S* (R), *[Arg, WS, A* (t), *F],* 1996 *F,* 1998 *NZ* 1
Old, A G B (Middlesbrough, Leicester, Sheffield) 1972 *W, I, F, S, SA,* 1973 *NZ* 2, *A,* 1974 *S, I, F, W,* 1975 *I, A* 2, 1976 *S, I,* 1978 *F*
Oldham, W L (Coventry) 1908 *S,* 1909 *A*
Olver, C J (Northampton) 1990 *Arg* 3, 1991 *[US],* 1992 *C*
O'Neill, A (Teignmouth, Torquay A) 1901 *W, I, S*
Openshaw, W E (Manchester) 1879 *I*
Orwin, J (Gloucester, RAF, Bedford) 1985 *R, F, S, I, W, NZ* 1,2, 1988 *F, W, S, I* 1,2, *A* 1,2
Osborne, R R (Manchester) 1871 *S*
Osborne, S H (Oxford U) 1905 *S*
Oti, C (Cambridge U, Nottingham, Wasps) 1988 *S, I* 1, 1989 *S, I, F, W, R,* 1990 *Arg* 1,2, 1991 *Fj, A, [NZ, It]*
Oughtred, B (Hartlepool R) 1901 *S,* 1902 *W, I, S,* 1903 *W, I*
Owen, J E (Coventry) 1963 *W, I, F, S, A,* 1964 *NZ,* 1965 *W, I, F, S,* 1966 *I, F, S,* 1967 *NZ*
Owen-Smith, H G O (St Mary's Hospital) 1934 *W, I, S,* 1936 *NZ, W, I, S,* 1937 *W, I, S*

Page, J J (Bedford, Northampton) 1971 *W, I, F, S,* 1975 *S*
Pallant, J N (Notts) 1967 *I, F, S*
Palmer, A C (London Hospital) 1909 *I, S*
Palmer, F H (Richmond) 1905 *W*
Palmer, G V (Richmond) 1928 *I, F, S*
Palmer, J A (Bath) 1984 *SA* 1,2, 1986 *I* (R)
Palmer, T (Leeds) 2001 *US* (R)
Pargetter, T A (Coventry) 1962 *S,* 1963 *F, NZ* 1
Parker, G W (Gloucester) 1938 *I, S*
Parker, Hon S (Liverpool) 1874 *S,* 1875 *S*
Parsons, E I (RAF) 1939 *S*
Parsons, M J (Northampton) 1968 *W, I, F, S*
Patterson, W M (Sale) 1961 *SA, S*
Pattisson, R M (Blackheath) 1883 *I, S*
Paul, J E (RIE Coll) 1875 *S*
Payne, A T (Bristol) 1935 *I, S*
Payne, C M (Harlequins) 1964 *I, F, S,* 1965 *I, F, S,* 1966 *W, I, F, S*
Payne, J H (Broughton) 1882 *S,* 1883 *W, I, S,* 1884 *I,* 1885 *W, I*
Pearce, G S (Northampton) 1979 *S, I, F, W,* 1981 *Arg* 1,2, 1982 *A, S,* 1983 *F, W, S, I, NZ,* 1984 *S, SA* 2, *A,* 1985 *R, F, S, I, W, NZ* 1,2, 1986 *W, S, I, F,* 1987 *I, F, W, S, [A, US, W],* 1988 *Fj,* 1991 *[US]*
Pears, D (Harlequins) 1990 *Arg* 1,2, 1992 *F* (R), 1994 *F*
Pearson, A W (Blackheath) 1875 *I, S,* 1876 *I, S,* 1877 *S,* 1878 *S, I*
Peart, T G A H (Hartlepool R) 1964 *F, S*
Pease, F E (Hartlepool R) 1887 *I*
Penny, S H (Leicester) 1909 *A*
Penny, W J (United Hospitals) 1878 *I,* 1879 *S, I*
Percival, L J (Rugby) 1891 *I,* 1892 *I,* 1893 *S*
Periton, H G (Waterloo) 1925 *W,* 1926 *W, I, F, S,* 1927 *W, I, S, F,* 1928 *A, I, F, S,* 1929 *W, I, S, F,* 1930 *W, I, F, S*
Perrott, E S (O Cheltonians) 1875 *I*
Perry, D G (Bedford) 1963 *F, S, NZ* 1,2, *A,* 1964 *NZ, W, I,* 1965 *W, I, F, S,* 1966 *W, I, F*
Perry, M B (Bath) 1997 *A* 2, *NZ* 1, *SA, NZ* 2, 1998 *W, S, I, A* 1, *NZ* 1,2, *SA* 1, *H, It, A* 2, 1999 *I, F, W, A US, C, [It, NZ, Tg, Fj, SA],* 2000 *I, F, W, It, S, SA* 1,2, *A, SA* 3, 2001 *W* (R), *F* (R)
Perry, S V (Cambridge U, Waterloo) 1947 *W, I,* 1948 *A, W, I, S, F*
Peters, J (Plymouth) 1906 *S, F,* 1907 *I, S,* 1908 *W*
Phillips, C (Birkenhead Park) 1880 *S,* 1881 *I, S*
Phillips, M S (Fylde) 1958 *A, I, F, S,* 1959 *W, I, F, S,* 1960 *W, I, F, S,* 1961 *W,* 1963 *W, I, F, S, NZ* 1,2, *A,* 1964 *NZ, W, I, F, S*
Pickering, A S (Harrogate) 1907 *I*
Pickering, R D A (Bradford) 1967 *I, F, S, W,* 1968 *F, S*
Pickles, R C W (Bristol) 1922 *I, F*
Pierce, R (Liverpool) 1898 *I,* 1903 *S*
Pilkington, W N (Cambridge U) 1898 *S*

Pillman, C H (Blackheath) 1910 *W, I, F, S,* 1911 *W, F, I, S,* 1912 *W, F,* 1913 *SA, W, F, I, S,* 1914 *W, I, S*
Pillman, R L (Blackheath) 1914 *F*
Pinch, J (Lancaster) 1896 *W, I,* 1897 *S*
Pinching, W W (Guy's Hospital) 1872 *S*
Pitman, I J (Oxford U) 1922 *S*
Plummer, K C (Bristol) 1969 *W,* 1976 *S, I, F*
Pool-Jones, R J (Stade Francais) 1998 *A* 1
Poole, F O (Oxford U) 1895 *W, I, S*
Poole, R W (Hartlepool R) 1896 *S*
Pope, E B (Blackheath) 1931 *W, S, F*
Portus, G V (Blackheath) 1908 *F, I*
Potter, S (Leicester) 1998 *A* 1(t)
Poulton, R W (later Poulton Palmer) (Oxford U, Harlequins, Liverpool) 1909 *F, I, S,* 1910 *W,* 1911 *S,* 1912 *W, I, S,* 1913 *SA, W, F, I, S,* 1914 *W, I, S, F*
Powell, D L (Northampton) 1966 *W, I,* 1969 *I, F, S, W,* 1971 *W, I, F, S* (2[1C])
Pratten, W E (Blackheath) 1927 *S, F*
Preece, I (Coventry) 1948 *I, F,* 1949 *F, S,* 1950 *W, I, F, S,* 1951 *W, I, F, S*
Preece, P S (Coventry) 1972 *SA,* 1973 *NZ* 1, *W, I, F, S, NZ* 2, 1975 *I, F, W, A* 2, 1976 *W* (R)
Preedy, M (Gloucester) 1984 *SA* 1
Prentice, F D (Leicester) 1928 *I, F, S*
Prescott, R E (Harlequins) 1937 *W, I,* 1938 *I,* 1939 *W, I, S*
Preston, N J (Richmond) 1979 *NZ,* 1980 *I, F*
Price, H L (Harlequins) 1922 *I, S,* 1923 *W, I*
Price, J (Coventry) 1961 *I*
Price, P L A (RIE Coll) 1877 *I, S,* 1878 *S*
Price, T W (Cheltenham) 1948 *S, F,* 1949 *W, I, F, S*
Probyn, J A (Wasps, Askeans) 1988 *F, W, S, I* 1,2, *A* 1, 2, *A,* 1989 *S, I, R* (R), 1990 *I, F, W, S, Arg* 1,2,3, 1991 *W, S, I, F, Fj, A,* [*NZ, It, F, S, A*], 1992 *S, I, F, W,* 1993 *F, W, S, I*
Prout, D H (Northampton) 1968 *W, I*
Pullin, J V (Bristol) 1966 *W,* 1968 *W, I, F, S,* 1969 *I, F, S, W, SA,* 1970 *I, W, S, F,* 1971 *W, I, F, S* (2[1C]), *P,* 1972 *W, I, F, S, SA,* 1973 *NZ* 1, *W, I, F, S, NZ* 2, *A,* 1974 *S, I, F, W,* 1975 *I, W* (R), *A* 1,2, 1976 *F*
Purdy, S J (Rugby) 1962 *S*
Pyke, J (St Helens Recreation) 1892 *W*
Pym, J A (Blackheath) 1912 *W, I, S, F*

Quinn, J P (New Brighton) 1954 *W, NZ, I, S, F*

Rafter, M (Bristol) 1977 *S, F, W,* 1978 *F, W, S, I, NZ,* 1979 *S, I, F, W, NZ,* 1980 *W*(R), 1981 *W, Arg* 1,2
Ralston, C W (Richmond) 1971 *S* (C), *P,* 1972 *W, I, F, S, SA,* 1973 *NZ* 1, *W, I, F, S, NZ* 2, *A,* 1974 *S, I, F, W,* 1975 *I, F, W, S*
Ramsden, H E (Bingley) 1898 *W, S*
Ranson, J M (Rosslyn Park) 1963 *NZ* 1,2, *A,* 1964 *W, I, F, S*
Raphael, J E (OMTs) 1902 *W, I, S,* 1905 *W, S, NZ,* 1906 *W, S, F*
Ravenscroft, J (Birkenhead Park) 1881 *I*
Ravenscroft, S C W (Saracens) 1998 *A* 1, *NZ* 2(R)
Rawlinson, W C W (Blackheath) 1876 *S*
Redfern, S (Leicester) 1984 *I* (R)
Redman, N C (Bath) 1984 *A,* 1986 *S* (R), 1987 *I, S,* [*A, J, W*], 1988 *Fj,* 1990 *Arg* 1,2, 1991 *Fj,* [*It, US*], 1993 *NZ,* 1994 *F, W, SA* 1,2, 1997 *Arg* 1, *A* 1
Redmond, G F (Cambridge U) 1970 *F*
Redwood, B W (Bristol) 1968 *W, I*
Rees, D L (Sale) 1997 *A* 2, *NZ* 1, *SA, NZ* 2, 1998 *F, W, SA* 2(R), 1999 *S, I, F, A*
Rees, G W (Nottingham) 1984 *SA* 2(R), *A,* 1986 *I, F,* 1987 *F, W, S,* [*A, J, US, W*], 1988 *S* (R), *I* 1,2, *A* 1,2, *Fj,* 1989 *W* (R), *R* (R), *Fj* (R), 1990 *Arg* 3(R), 1991 *Fj,* [*US*]
Reeve, J S R (Harlequins) 1929 *F,* 1930 *W, I, F, S,* 1931 *W, I, S*
Regan, M (Liverpool) 1953 *W, I, F, S,* 1954 *W, NZ, I, S, F,* 1956 *I, S, F*
Regan, M P (Bristol, Bath) 1995 *SA, WS,* 1996 *F, W, S, I, It, Arg,* 1997 *S, I, F, W, A* 1, *NZ* 2(R), 1998 *F,* 2000 *SA* 1(t), *A* (R), *Arg, SA* 3(t), 2001 *It* (R), *S* (R), *C* 2(R)
Rendall, P A G (Wasps, Askeans) 1984 *W, SA* 2, 1986 *W, S,* 1987 *I, F, S,* [*A, J, W*], 1988 *F, W, S, I* 1,2, *A* 1,2, *A,* 1989 *S, I, F, W, R,* 1990 *I, F, W, S,* 1991 [*It* (R)]
Rew, H (Blackheath) 1929 *S, F,* 1930 *F, S,* 1931 *W, S, F,* 1934 *W, I, S*
Reynolds, F J (O Cranleighans) 1937 *S,* 1938 *I, S*
Reynolds, S (Richmond) 1900 *W, I, S,* 1901 *I*
Rhodes, J (Castleford) 1896 *W, I, S*

Richards, D (Leicester) 1986 *I, F,* 1987 *S,* [*A, J, US, W*], 1988 *F, W, S, I* 1, *A* 1,2, *Fj, A,* 1989 *S, I, F, W, R,* 1990 *Arg* 3, 1991 *W, S, I, F, Fj, A,* [*NZ, It, US*], 1992 *S* (R), *F, W, C,* 1993 *NZ,* 1994 *W, SA* 1, *C,* 1995 *I, F, W, S,* [*WS, A, NZ*], 1996 *F* (t), *S, I*
Richards, E E (Plymouth A) 1929 *S, F*
Richards, J (Bradford) 1891 *W, I, S*
Richards, S B (Richmond) 1965 *W, I, F, S,* 1967 *A, I, F, S, W*
Richardson, J V (Birkenhead Park) 1928 *A, W, I, F, S*
Richardson, W R (Manchester) 1881 *I*
Rickards, C H (Gipsies) 1873 *S*
Rimmer, G (Waterloo) 1949 *W, I,* 1950 *W,* 1951 *W, I, F,* 1952 *SA, W,* 1954 *W, NZ, I, S*
Rimmer, L I (Bath) 1961 *SA, W, I, F, S*
Ripley, A G (Rosslyn Park) 1972 *W, I, F, S, SA,* 1973 *NZ* 1, *W, I, F, S, NZ* 2, *A,* 1974 *S, I, F, W,* 1975 *I, F, S, A* 1,2, 1976 *A, W, S*
Risman, A B W (Loughborough Coll) 1959 *W, I, F, S,* 1961 *SA, W, I, F*
Ritson, J A S (Northern) 1910 *F, S,* 1912 *F,* 1913 *SA, W, F, I, S*
Rittson-Thomas, G C (Oxford U) 1951 *W, I, F*
Robbins, G L (Coventry) 1986 *W, S*
Robbins, P G D (Oxford U, Moseley, Coventry) 1956 *W, I, S, F,* 1957 *W, I, F, S,* 1958 *W, A, I, S,* 1960 *W, I, F, S,* 1961 *SA, W,* 1962 *S*
Roberts, A D (Northern) 1911 *W, F, I, S,* 1912 *I, S, F,* 1914 *I*
Roberts, E W (RNE Coll) 1901 *W, I,* 1905 *NZ,* 1906 *W, I,* 1907 *S*
Roberts, G D (Harlequins) 1907 *S,* 1908 *F, W*
Roberts, J (Sale) 1960 *W, I, F, S,* 1961 *SA, W, I, F, S,* 1962 *W, I, F, S,* 1963 *W, I, F, S,* 1964 *NZ*
Roberts, R S (Coventry) 1932 *I*
Roberts, S (Swinton) 1887 *W, I*
Roberts, V G (Penryn, Harlequins) 1947 *F,* 1949 *W, I, F, S,* 1950 *I, F, S,* 1951 *W, I, F, S,* 1956 *W, I, S, F*
Robertshaw, A R (Bradford) 1886 *W, I, S,* 1887 *W, S*
Robinson, A (Blackheath) 1889 *M,* 1890 *W, S, I*
Robinson, E T (Coventry) 1954 *S,* 1961 *I, F, S*
Robinson, G C (Percy Park) 1897 *I, S,* 1898 *I,* 1899 *W,* 1900 *I, S,* 1901 *I, S*
Robinson, J (Sale) 2001 *It* (R), *S* (R), *F* (R), *I*
Robinson, J J (Headingley) 1893 *S,* 1902 *W, I, S*
Robinson, R A (Bath) 1988 *A* 2, *Fj, A,* 1989 *S, I, F, W,* 1995 *SA*
Robson, A (Northern) 1924 *W, I, F, S,* 1926 *W*
Robson, M (Oxford U) 1930 *W, I, F, S*
Rodber, T A K (Army, Northampton) 1992 *S, I,* 1993 *NZ,* 1994 *I, F, W, SA* 1,2, *R, C,* 1995 *I, F, W, S,* [*Arg, It, WS* (R), *A, NZ, F*], *SA, WS,* 1996 *W, S* (R), *I* (t), *It, Arg,* 1997 *S, I, F, W, A* 1, 1998 *H* (R), *It* (R), *A* 2, *SA* 2, 1999 *S, I, F, W, A, US* (R), [*NZ* (R), *Fj* (R)]
Rogers, D P (Bedford) 1961 *I, F, S,* 1962 *W, I, F,* 1963 *W, I, F, S, NZ* 1,2, *A,* 1964 *NZ, W, I, F, S,* 1965 *W, I, F, S,* 1966 *W, I, F, S,* 1967 *A, S, W, NZ,* 1969 *I, F, S, W*
Rogers, J H (Moseley) 1890 *W, S, I,* 1891 *S*
Rogers, W L Y (Blackheath) 1905 *W, I*
Rollitt, D M (Bristol) 1967 *I, F, S, W,* 1969 *I, F, S, W,* 1975 *S, A* 1,2
Roncoroni, A D S (West Herts, Richmond) 1933 *W, I, S*
Rose, W M H (Cambridge U, Coventry, Harlequins) 1981 *I, F,* 1982 *A, S, I,* 1987 *I, F, W, S,* [*A*]
Rossborough, P A (Coventry) 1971 *W,* 1973 *NZ* 2, *A,* 1974 *S, I,* 1975 *I, F*
Rosser, D W A (Wasps) 1965 *W, I, F, S,* 1966 *W*
Rotherham, Alan (Richmond) 1883 *W, S,* 1884 *W, S,* 1885 *W, I,* 1886 *W, I, S,* 1887 *W, I, S*
Rotherham, Arthur (Richmond) 1898 *S, W,* 1899 *W, I, S*
Roughley, D (Liverpool) 1973 *A,* 1974 *S, I*
Rowell, R E (Leicester) 1964 *W,* 1965 *W*
Rowley, A J (Coventry) 1932 *SA*
Rowley, H C (Manchester) 1879 *S, I,* 1880 *I, S,* 1881 *I, W, S,* 1882 *I, S*
Rowntree, G C (Leicester) 1995 *S* (t), [*It, WS*], *WS,* 1996 *F, W, S, I, It, Arg,* 1997 *S, I, F, W, A* 1, 1998 *A* 1, *NZ* 1, 2, *SA* 1, *H* (R), *It* (R), 1999 *US, C,* [*It* (R), *Tg, Fj* (R)], 2001 *C* 1,2, *US, I* (R)
Royds, P M R (Blackheath) 1898 *S, W,* 1899 *W*
Royle, A V (Broughton R) 1889 *M*
Rudd, E L (Liverpool) 1965 *W, I, S,* 1966 *W, I, S*
Russell, R F (Leicester) 1905 *NZ*
Rutherford, D (Percy Park, Gloucester) 1960 *W, I, F, S,* 1961 *SA,* 1965 *W, I, F, S,* 1966 *W, I, F, S,* 1967 *NZ*
Ryalls, H J (New Brighton) 1885 *W, I*

Ryan, D (Wasps, Newcastle) 1990 *Arg* 1,2, 1992 *C*, 1998 *S*
Ryan, P H (Richmond) 1955 *W, I*

Sadler, E H (Army) 1933 *I, S*
Sagar, J W (Cambridge U) 1901 *W, I*
Salmon, J L B (Harlequins) 1985 *NZ* 1,2, 1986 *W, S*, 1987 *I, F, W, S*, [*A, J, US, W*]
Sample, C H (Cambridge U) 1884 *I*, 1885 *I*, 1886 *S*
Sampson, P C (Wasps) 1998 *SA* 1, 2001 *C* 1,2
Sanders, D L (Harlequins) 1954 *W, NZ, I, S, F*, 1956 *W, I, S, F*
Sanders, F W (Plymouth A) 1923 *I, S, F*
Sanderson, P H (Sale, Harlequins) 1998 *NZ* 1,2, *SA* 1, 2001 *C* 1(R),2(R), *US* (t+R)
Sandford, J R P (Marlborough N) 1906 *I*
Sangwin, R D (Hull and E Riding) 1964 *NZ, W*
Sargent, G A F (Gloucester) 1981 *I* (R)
Savage, K F (Northampton) 1966 *W, I, F, S*, 1967 *A, I, F, S, W, NZ*, 1968 *W, F, S*
Sawyer, C M (Broughton) 1880 *S*, 1881 *I*
Saxby, L E (Gloucester) 1932 *SA, W*
Schofield, J W (Manchester) 1880 *I*
Scholfield, J A (Preston Grasshoppers) 1911 *W*
Schwarz, R O (Richmond) 1899 *S*, 1901 *W, I*
Scorfield, E S (Percy Park) 1910 *F*
Scott, C T (Blackheath) 1900 *W, I*, 1901 *W, I*
Scott, E K (St Mary's Hospital, Redruth) 1947 *W*, 1948 *A, W, I, S*
Scott, F S (Bristol) 1907 *W*
Scott, H (Manchester) 1955 *F*
Scott, J P (Rosslyn Park, Cardiff) 1978 *F, W, S, I, NZ*, 1979 *S* (R), *I, F, W, NZ*, 1980 *I, F, W, S*, 1981 *W, S, I, F, Arg* 1,2, 1982 *I, F, W*, 1983 *F, W, S, I, NZ*, 1984 *S, I, F, W, SA* 1,2
Scott, J S M (Oxford U) 1958 *F*
Scott, M T (Cambridge U) 1887 *I*, 1890 *S, I*
Scott, W M (Cambridge U) 1889 *M*
Seddon, R L (Broughton R) 1887 *W, I, S*
Sellar, K A (United Services, RN) 1927 *W, I, S*, 1928 *A, W, I, F*
Sever, H S (Sale) 1936 *NZ, W, I, S*, 1937 *W, I, S*, 1938 *W, I, S*
Shackleton, I R (Cambridge U) 1969 *SA*, 1970 *I, W, S*
Sharp, R A W (Oxford U, Wasps, Redruth) 1960 *W, I, F, S*, 1961 *I, F*, 1962 *W, I, F*, 1963 *W, I, F, S*, 1967 *A*
Shaw, C H (Moseley) 1906 *S, SA*, 1907 *F, W, I, S*
Shaw, F (Cleckheaton) 1898 *I*
Shaw, J F (RNE Coll) 1898 *S, W*
Shaw, S D (Bristol, Wasps) 1996 *It, Arg*, 1997 *S, I, F, W, A* 1, *SA* (R), 2000 *I, F, W, It, S, SA* 1(R),2(R), 2001 *C* 1(R), 2, *US, I*
Sheasby, C M A (Wasps) 1996 *It, Arg*, 1997 *W* (R), *Arg* 1(R),2(R), *SA* (R), *NZ* 2(t)
Sheppard, A (Bristol) 1981 *W* (R), 1985 *W*
Sherrard, C W (Blackheath) 1871 *S*, 1872 *S*
Sherriff, G A (Saracens) 1966 *S*, 1967 *A, NZ*
Shewring, H E (Bristol) 1905 *I, NZ*, 1906 *W, S, F, SA*, 1907 *F, W, I, S*
Shooter, J H (Morley) 1899 *I, S*, 1900 *I, S*
Shuttleworth, D W (Headingley) 1951 *S*, 1953 *S*
Sibree, H J H (Harlequins) 1908 *F*, 1909 *I, S*
Silk, N (Harlequins) 1965 *W, I, F, S*
Simms, K G (Cambridge U, Liverpool, Wasps) 1985 *R, F, S, I, W*, 1986 *I, F*, 1987 *I, F, W*, [*A, J, W*], 1988 *F, W*
Simpson, C P (Harlequins) 1965 *W*
Simpson, P D (Bath) 1983 *NZ*, 1984 *S*, 1987 *I*
Simpson, T (Rockcliff) 1902 *S*, 1903 *W, I, S*, 1904 *I, S*, 1905 *I, S*, 1906 *S, SA*, 1909 *F*
Sims, D (Gloucester) 1998 *NZ* 1(R),2, *SA* 1
Skinner, M G (Harlequins) 1988 *F, W, S* 1,2, 1989 *Fj*, 1990 *I, F, W, S, Arg* 1,2, 1991 *Fj* (R), [*US, F, S, A*], 1992 *S, I, F, W*
Sladen, G M (United Services, RN) 1929 *W, I, S*
Sleightholme, J M (Bath) 1996 *F, W, S, I, It, Arg*, 1997 *S, I, F, W, Arg* 1,2
Slemen, M A C (Liverpool) 1976 *I, F*, 1977 *S, I, F, W*, 1978 *F, W, S, I, NZ*, 1979 *S, I, F, W, NZ*, 1980 *I, F, W, S, I, F*, 1982 *A, S, I, F, W*, 1983 *NZ*, 1984 *I*
Slocock, L A N (Liverpool) 1907 *F, W, I, S*, 1908 *F, W, I, S*
Slow, C F (Leicester) 1934 *S*
Small, H D (Oxford U) 1950 *W, I, F, S*
Smallwood, A M (Leicester) 1920 *F, I*, 1921 *W, I, S, F*, 1922 *I, S*, 1923 *W, I, S, F*, 1925 *I, S*
Smart, C E (Newport) 1979 *F, W, NZ*, 1981 *S, I, F, Arg* 1,2, 1982 *A, S, I, F, W*, 1983 *F, W, S, I*

Smart, S E J (Gloucester) 1913 *SA, W, F, I, S*, 1914 *W, I, S, F*, 1920 *W, I, S*
Smeddle, R W (Cambridge U) 1929 *W, I, S*, 1931 *F*
Smith, C C (Gloucester) 1901 *W*
Smith, D F (Richmond) 1910 *W, I*
Smith, J V (Cambridge U, Rosslyn Park) 1950 *W, I, F, S*
Smith, K (Roundhay) 1974 *F, W*, 1975 *W, S*
Smith, M J K (Oxford U) 1956 *W*
Smith, S J (Sale) 1973 *I, F, S, A*, 1974 *I, F*, 1975 *W* (R), 1976 *F*, 1977 *F* (R), 1979 *NZ*, 1980 *I, F, W, S*, 1981 *W, S, I, F, Arg* 1,2, 1982 *A, S, I, F, W*, 1983 *F, W, S*
Smith, S R (Richmond) 1959 *W, F, S*, 1964 *F, S*
Smith, S T (Wasps) 1985 *R, F, S, I, W, NZ* 1,2, 1986 *W, S*
Smith, T H (Northampton) 1951 *W*
Soane, F (Bath) 1893 *S*, 1894 *W, I, S*
Sobey, W H (O Millhillians) 1930 *W, F, S*, 1932 *SA, W*
Solomon, B (Redruth) 1910 *W*
Sparks, R H W (Plymouth A) 1928 *I, F, S*, 1929 *W, I, S*, 1931 *I, S, F*
Speed, H (Castleford) 1894 *W, I, S*, 1896 *S*
Spence, F W (Birkenhead Park) 1890 *I*
Spencer, J (Harlequins) 1966 *W*
Spencer, J S (Cambridge U, Headingley) 1969 *I, F, S, W, SA*, 1970 *I, W, S, F*, 1971 *W, I, S* (2[1C]), *P*
Spong, R S (O Millhillians) 1929 *F*, 1930 *W, I, F, S*, 1931 *F*, 1932 *SA, W*
Spooner, R H (Liverpool) 1903 *W*
Springman, H H (Liverpool) 1879 *S*, 1887 *S*
Spurling, A (Blackheath) 1882 *I*
Spurling, N (Blackheath) 1886 *I, S*, 1887 *W*
Squires, P J (Harrogate) 1973 *F, S, NZ* 2, *A*, 1974 *S, I, F, W*, 1975 *I, F, W, S, A* 1,2, 1976 *A, W*, 1977 *S, I, F, W*, 1978 *F, W, S, I, NZ*, 1979 *S, I, F, W*
Stafford, R C (Bedford) 1912 *W, I, S, F*
Stafford, W F H (RE) 1874 *S*
Stanbury, E (Plymouth A) 1926 *W, I, S*, 1927 *W, I, S, F*, 1928 *A, W, I, F, S*, 1929 *W, I, S, F*
Standing, G (Blackheath) 1883 *W, I*
Stanger-Leathes, C F (Northern) 1905 *I*
Stark, K J (O Alleynians) 1927 *W, I, S, F*, 1928 *A, W, I, F, S*
Starks, A (Castleford) 1896 *W, I*
Starmer-Smith, N C (Harlequins) 1969 *SA*, 1970 *I, W, S, F*, 1971 *S* (C), *P*
Start, S P (United Services, RN) 1907 *S*
Steeds, J H (Saracens) 1949 *F, S*, 1950 *I, F, S*
Steele-Bodger, M R (Cambridge U) 1947 *W, I, S, F*, 1948 *A, W, I, S, F*
Steinthal, F E (Ilkley) 1913 *W, F*
Stephenson, M (Newcastle) 2001 *C* 1,2, *US*
Stevens, C B (Penzance-Newlyn, Harlequins) 1969 *SA*, 1970 *I, W, S*, 1971 *P*, 1972 *W, I, F, S, SA*, 1973 *NZ* 1, *W, I, F, S, NZ* 2, *A*, 1974 *S, I, F, W*, 1975 *I, F, W, S*
Still, E R (Oxford U, Ravenscourt P) 1873 *S*
Stimpson, T R G (Newcastle, Leicester) 1996 *It*, 1997 *S, I, F, W, A* 1, *NZ* 2(t+R), 1998 *A* 1, *NZ* 1,2(R), *SA* 1(R), 1999 *US* (R), *C* (R), 2000 *SA* 1, 2001 *C* 1(t),2(R)
Stirling, R V (Leicester, RAF, Wasps) 1951 *W, I, F, S*, 1952 *SA, W, S, I, F*, 1953 *W, I, F, S*, 1954 *W, NZ, I, S, F*
Stoddart, A E (Blackheath) 1885 *W, I*, 1886 *W, I, S*, 1889 *M*, 1890 *W, I*, 1893 *W, S*
Stoddart, W B (Liverpool) 1897 *W, I, S*
Stokes, F (Blackheath) 1871 *S*, 1872 *S*, 1873 *S*
Stokes, L (Blackheath) 1875 *I*, 1876 *S*, 1877 *I, S*, 1878 *S*, 1879 *S, I*, 1880 *I, S*, 1881 *I, W, S*
Stone, F le S (Blackheath) 1914 *F*
Stoop, A D (Harlequins) 1905 *S*, 1906 *S, F, SA*, 1907 *F, W*, 1910 *W, I, S*, 1911 *W, F, I*, 1912 *W, S*
Stoop, F M (Harlequins) 1910 *S*, 1911 *F, I*, 1913 *SA*
Stout, F M (Richmond) 1897 *W, I*, 1898 *I, S, W*, 1899 *I, S*, 1903 *S*, 1904 *W, I, S*, 1905 *W, I, S*
Stout, P W (Richmond) 1898 *S, W*, 1899 *W, I, S*
Stringer, N C (Wasps) 1982 *A* (R), 1983 *NZ* (R), 1984 *SA* 1(R), *A*, 1985 *R*
Strong, E L (Oxford U) 1884 *W, I, S*
Sturnham B (Saracens) 1998 *A* 1, *NZ* 1(t),2(t)
Summerscales, G E (Durham City) 1905 *NZ*
Sutcliffe, J W (Heckmondwike) 1889 *M*
Swarbrick, D W (Oxford U) 1947 *W, I, F*, 1948 *A, W*, 1949 *I*
Swayne, D H (Oxford U) 1931 *W*
Swayne, J W R (Bridgwater) 1929 *W*
Swift, A H (Swansea) 1981 *Arg* 1,2, 1983 *F, W, S*, 1984 *SA* 2
Syddall, J P (Waterloo) 1982 *I*, 1984 *A*
Sykes, A R V (Blackheath) 1914 *F*

Sykes, F D (Northampton) 1955 *F, S*, 1963 *NZ* 2, *A*
Sykes, P W (Wasps) 1948 *F*, 1952 *S, I, F*, 1953 *W, I, F*
Syrett, R E (Wasps) 1958 *W, A, I, F*, 1960 *W, I, F, S*, 1962 *W, I, F*

Tallent, J A (Cambridge U, Blackheath) 1931 *S, F*, 1932 *SA, W*, 1935 *I*
Tanner, C C (Cambridge U, Gloucester) 1930 *S*, 1932 *SA, W, I, S*
Tarr, F N (Leicester) 1909 *A, W, F*, 1913 *S*
Tatham, W M (Oxford U) 1882 *S*, 1883 *W, I, S*, 1884 *W, I, S*
Taylor, A S (Blackheath) 1883 *W, I*, 1886 *W, I*
Taylor, E W (Rockcliff) 1892 *I*, 1893 *I*, 1894 *W, I, S*, 1895 *W, I, S*, 1896 *W, I*, 1897 *W, I, S*, 1899 *I*
Taylor, F (Leicester) 1920 *F, I*
Taylor, F M (Leicester) 1914 *W*
Taylor, H H (Blackheath) 1879 *S*, 1880 *S*, 1881 *I, W*, 1882 *S*
Taylor, J T (W Hartlepool) 1897 *I*, 1899 *I*, 1900 *I*, 1901 *W, I*, 1902 *W, I, S*, 1903 *W, I*, 1905 *S*
Taylor, P J (Northampton) 1955 *W, I*, 1962 *W, I, F, S*
Taylor, R B (Northampton) 1966 *W*, 1967 *I, F, S, W, NZ*, 1969 *F, S, W, SA*, 1970 *I, W, S, F*, 1971 *S* (2[1C])
Taylor, W J (Blackheath) 1928 *A, W, I, F, S*
Teague, M C (Gloucester, Moseley) 1985 *F* (R), *NZ* 1, 2, 1989 *S, I, F, W, R*, 1990 *F, W, S*, 1991 *W, S, I, F, Fj, A*, [*NZ, It, F, S, A*], 1992 *SA*, 1993 *F, W, S, I*
Teden, D E (Richmond) 1939 *W, I, S*
Teggin, A (Broughton R) 1884 *I*, 1885 *W*, 1886 *I, S*, 1887 *I, S*
Tetley, T S (Bradford) 1876 *S*
Thomas, C (Barnstaple) 1895 *W, I, S*, 1899 *I*
Thompson, P H (Headingley, Waterloo) 1956 *W, I, S, F*, 1957 *W, I, F, S*, 1958 *W, A, I, F, S*, 1959 *W, I, F, S*
Thomson, G T (Halifax) 1878 *S*, 1882 *S, I*, 1883 *W, I, S*, 1884 *I, S*, 1885 *I*
Thomson, W B (Blackheath) 1892 *W*, 1895 *W, I, S*
Thorne, J D (Bristol) 1963 *W, I, F*
Tindall, M J (Bath) 2000 *I, F, W, It, S, SA* 1,2, *A Arg, SA* 3, 2001 *W* (R)
Tindall, V R (Liverpool U) 1951 *W, I, F, S*
Tobin, F (Liverpool) 1871 *S*
Todd, A F (Blackheath) 1900 *I, S*
Todd, R (Manchester) 1877 *S*
Toft, H B (Waterloo) 1936 *S*, 1937 *W, I, S*, 1938 *W, I, S*, 1939 *W, I, S*
Toothill, J T (Bradford) 1890 *S, I*, 1891 *W, I*, 1892 *W, I, S*, 1893 *W, I, S*, 1894 *W, I*
Tosswill, L R (Exeter) 1902 *W, I, S*
Touzel, C J C (Liverpool) 1877 *I, S*
Towell, A C (Bedford) 1948 *F*, 1951 *S*
Travers, B H (Harlequins) 1947 *W, I*, 1948 *A, W*, 1949 *F, S*
Treadwell, W T (Wasps) 1966 *I, F, S*
Trick, D M (Bath) 1983 *I*, 1984 *SA* 1
Tristram, H B (Oxford U) 1883 *S*, 1884 *W, S*, 1885 *W*, 1887 *S*
Troop, C L (Aldershot S) 1933 *I, S*
Tucker, J S (Bristol) 1922 *W*, 1925 *NZ, W, I, S, F*, 1926 *W, I, F, S*, 1927 *W, I, S, F*, 1928 *A, W, I, F, S*, 1929 *W, I, F*, 1930 *W, I, F, S*, 1931 *W*
Tucker, W E (Blackheath) 1894 *W, I*, 1895 *W, I, S*
Tucker, W E (Blackheath) 1926 *I*, 1930 *W, I*
Turner, D P (Richmond) 1871 *S*, 1872 *S*, 1873 *S*, 1874 *S*, 1875 *I, S*
Turner, E B (St George's Hospital) 1876 *I*, 1877 *I*, 1878 *I*
Turner, G R (St George's Hospital) 1876 *S*
Turner, H J C (Manchester) 1871 *S*
Turner, M F (Blackheath) 1948 *S, F*
Turquand-Young, D (Richmond) 1928 *A, W*, 1929 *I, S, F*
Twynam, H T (Richmond) 1879 *I*, 1880 *I*, 1881 *W*, 1882 *I*, 1883 *I*, 1884 *W, I, S*

Ubogu, V E (Bath) 1992 *C, SA*, 1993 *NZ*, 1994 *S, I, F, W, SA* 1,2, *R, C*, 1995 *I, F, W, S*, [*Arg, WS, A, NZ, F*], *SA*, 1999 *F* (R), *W* (R), *A* (R)
Underwood, A M (Exeter) 1962 *W, I, F, S*, 1964 *I*
Underwood, R (Leicester, RAF) 1984 *I, F, W, A*, 1985 *R, F, S, I, W*, 1986 *W, I, F*, 1987 *I, F, W, S*, [*A, J, W*], 1988 *F, W, S, I* 1,2, *A* 1,2, *Fj, A*, 1989 *S, I, F, W, R, Fj*, 1990 *I, F, W, S, Arg* 3, 1991 *W, S, I, F, Fj, A*, [*NZ, It, US, F, S, A*], 1992 *S, I, F, W, SA*, 1993 *F, W, S, I, NZ*, 1994 *S, I, F, W, SA* 1,2, *R, C*, 1995 *I, F, W, S*, [*Arg, It, WS, A, NZ, F*], *SA, WS*, 1996 *F, W, S, I*
Underwood, T (Leicester, Newcastle) 1992 *C, SA*, 1993 *S, I, NZ*, 1994 *S, I, W, SA* 1,2, *R, C*, 1995 *I, F, W, S*, [*Arg, It, A, NZ*], 1996 *Arg*, 1997 *S, I, F, W*, 1998 *A* 2, *SA* 2

Unwin, E J (Rosslyn Park, Army) 1937 *S*, 1938 *W, I, S*
Unwin, G T (Blackheath) 1898 *S*
Uren, R (Waterloo) 1948 *I, S, F*, 1950 *I*
Uttley, R M (Gosforth) 1973 *I, F, S, NZ* 2, *A*, 1974 *I, F, W*, 1975 *F, W, S, A* 1,2, 1977 *S, I, F, W*, 1978 *NZ* 1979 *S*, 1980 *I, F, W, S*

Valentine J (Swinton) 1890 *W*, 1896 *W, I, S*
Vanderspar, C H R (Richmond) 1873 *S*
Van Ryneveld, C B (Oxford U) 1949 *W, I, F, S*
Varley, H (Liversedge) 1892 *S*
Vassall, H (Blackheath) 1881 *W, S*, 1882 *I, S*, 1883 *W*
Vassall, H H (Blackheath) 1908 *I*
Vaughan, D B (Headingley) 1948 *A, W, I, S*, 1949 *I, F, S*, 1950 *W*
Vaughan-Jones, A (Army) 1932 *I, S*, 1933 *W*
Verelst, C L (Liverpool) 1876 I, 1878 *I*
Vernon, G F (Blackheath) 1878 *S, I*, 1880 *I, S*, 1881 *I*
Vickery, G (Aberavon) 1905 *I*
Vickery, P J (Gloucester) 1998 *W, A* 1, *NZ* 1,2, *SA* 1, 1999 *US, C,* [*It, NZ, Tg, SA*], 2000 *I, F, W, S, A, Arg* (R), *SA* 3(R), 2001 *W, It, S*
Vivyan, E J (Devonport A) 1901 *W*, 1904 *W, I, S*
Voyce, A T (Gloucester) 1920 *I, S*, 1921 *W, I, S, F*, 1922 *W, I, F, S*, 1923 *W, I, S, F*, 1924 *W, I, F, S*, 1925 *NZ, W, I, S, F*, 1926 *W, I, F, S*
Voyce, T (Bath) 2001 *US* (R)

Wackett, J A S (Rosslyn Park) 1959 *W, I*
Wade, C G (Richmond) 1883 *W, I, S*, 1884 *W, S*, 1885 *W*, 1886 *W, I*
Wade, M R (Cambridge U) 1962 *W, I, F*
Wakefield, W W (Harlequins) 1920 *W, F, I, S*, 1921 *W, I, S, F*, 1922 *W, I, F, S*, 1923 *W, I, S, F*, 1924 *W, I, F, S*, 1925 *NZ, W, I, S, F*, 1926 *W, I, F, S*, 1927 *S, F*
Walder, D J H (Newcastle) 2001 *C* 1,2, *US*
Walker, G A (Blackheath) 1939 *W, I*
Walker, H W (Coventry) 1947 *W, I, S, F*, 1948 *A, W, I, S, F*
Walker, R (Manchester) 1874 *S*, 1875 *I*, 1876 *S*, 1879 *S*, 1880 *S*
Wallens, J N S (Waterloo) 1927 *F*
Walton, E J (Castleford) 1901 *W, I*, 1902 *I, S*
Walton, W (Castleford) 1894 *S*
Ward, G (Leicester) 1913 *W, F, S*, 1914 *W, I, S*
Ward, H (Bradford) 1895 *W*
Ward, J I (Richmond) 1881 *I*, 1882 *I*
Ward, J W (Castleford) 1896 *W, I, S*
Wardlow, C S (Northampton) 1969 *SA* (R), 1971 *W, I, F, S* (2[1C])
Warfield, P J (Rosslyn Park, Durham U) 1973 *NZ* 1, *W, I*, 1975 *I, F, S*
Warr, A L (Oxford U) 1934 *W, I*
Waters, F H H (Wasps) 2001 *US*
Watkins, J A (Gloucester) 1972 *SA*, 1973 *NZ* 1, *W, NZ* 2, *A*, 1975 *F, W*
Watkins, J K (United Services, RN) 1939 *W, I, S*
Watson, F B (United Services, RN) 1908 *S*, 1909 *S*
Watson, J H D (Blackheath) 1914 *W, S, F*
Watt, D E J (Bristol) 1967 *I, F, S, W*
Webb, C S H (Devonport Services, RN) 1932 *SA, W, I, S*, 1933 *W, I, S*, 1935 *S*, 1936 *NZ, W, I, S*
Webb, J M (Bristol, Bath) 1987 [*A* (R), *J, US, W*], 1988 *F, W, S, I* 1,2, *A* 1,2, *A*, 1989 *S, I, F, W*, 1991 *Fj, A*, [*NZ, It, F, S, A*], 1992 *S, I, F, W, C, SA*, 1993 *F, W, S, I*
Webb, J W G (Northampton) 1926 *F, S*, 1929 *S*
Webb, R E (Coventry) 1967 *S, W, NZ*, 1968 *I, F, S*, 1969 *I, F, S, W*, 1972 *I, F*
Webb, St L H (Bedford) 1959 *W, I, F, S*
Webster, J G (Moseley) 1972 *W, I, SA*, 1973 *NZ* 1, *W, NZ* 2, 1974 *S, W*, 1975 *I, F, W*
Wedge, T G (St Ives) 1907 *F*, 1909 *W*
Weighill, R H G (RAF, Harlequins) 1947 *S, F*, 1948 *S, F*
Wells, C M (Cambridge U, Harlequins) 1893 *S*, 1894 *W, S*, 1896 *S*, 1897 *W, S*
West, B R (Loughborough Colls, Northampton) 1968 *W, I, F, S*, 1969 *SA*, 1970 *I, W, S*
West, D E (Leicester) 1998 *F* (R), *S* (R), 2000 *Arg* (R), 2001 *W, It, S, F* (t), *C* 1,2, *US, I* (R)
West, R (Gloucester) 1995 [*WS*]
Weston, H T F (Northampton) 1901 *S*
Weston, L E (W of Scotland) 1972 *F, S*

Weston, M P (Richmond, Durham City) 1960 *W, I, F, S,* 1961 *SA, W, I, F, S,* 1962 *W, I, F,* 1963 *W, I, F, S, NZ* 1,2, *A,* 1964 *NZ, W, I, F, S,* 1965 *F, S,* 1966 *S,* 1968 *F, S*

Weston, W H (Northampton) 1933 *I, S,* 1934 *I, S,* 1935 *W, I, S,* 1936 *NZ, W, S,* 1937 *W, I, S,* 1938 *W, I, S*

Wheatley, A A (Coventry) 1937 *W, I, S,* 1938 *W, S*

Wheatley, H F (Coventry) 1936 *I,* 1937 *S,* 1938 *W, S,* 1939 *W, I, S*

Wheeler, P J (Leicester) 1975 *F, W,* 1976 *A, W, S, I,* 1977 *S, I, F, W,* 1978 *F, W, S, I, NZ,* 1979 *S, I, F, W, NZ,* 1980 *I, F, W, S,* 1981 *W, S, I, F,* 1982 *A, S, I, F, W,* 1983 *F, S, I, NZ,* 1984 *S, I, F, W*

White, C (Gosforth) 1983 *NZ,* 1984 *S, I, F*

White, D F (Northampton) 1947 *W, I, S,* 1948 *I, F,* 1951 *S,* 1952 *SA, W, S, I, F,* 1953 *W, I, S*

White, J (Saracens, Bristol) 2000 *SA* 1,2, *Arg, SA* 3, 2001 *F, C* 1,2, *US, I*

White-Cooper, S (Harlequins) 2001 *C* 2, *US*

Whiteley, E C P (O Alleynians) 1931 *S, F*

Whiteley, W (Bramley) 1896 *W*

Whitely, H (Northern) 1929 *W*

Wightman, B J (Moseley, Coventry) 1959 *W,* 1963 *W, I, NZ* 2, *A*

Wigglesworth, H J (Thornes) 1884 *I*

Wilkins, D T (United Services, RN, Roundhay) 1951 *W, I, F, S,* 1952 *SA, W, S, I, F,* 1953 *W, I, F, S*

Wilkinson, E (Bradford) 1886 *W, I, S,* 1887 *W, S*

Wilkinson, H (Halifax) 1929 *W, I, S,* 1930 *F*

Wilkinson, H J (Halifax) 1889 *M*

Wilkinson, J P (Newcastle) 1998 *I* (R), *A* 1, *NZ* 1, 1999 *S, I, F, W, A, US, C, [It, NZ, Fj, SA* (R)], 2000 *I, F, W, It, S, SA* 2 *A, Arg, SA* 3, 2001 *W, It, S, F, I*

Wilkinson, P (Law Club) 1872 *S*

Wilkinson, R M (Bedford) 1975 *A* 2, 1976 *A, W, S, I, F*

Willcocks, T J (Plymouth) 1902 *W*

Willcox, J G (Oxford U, Harlequins) 1961 *I, F, S,* 1962 *W, I, F, S,* 1963 *W, I, F, S,* 1964 *NZ, W, I, F, S*

William-Powlett, P B R W (United Services, RN) 1922 *S*

Williams, C G (Gloucester, RAF) 1976 *F*

Williams, C S (Manchester) 1910 *F*

Williams, J E (O Millhillians, Sale) 1954 *F,* 1955 *W, I, F, S,* 1956 *I, S, F,* 1965 *W*

Williams, J M (Penzance-Newlyn) 1951 *I, S*

Williams, P N (Orrell) 1987 *S, [A, J, W]*

Williams, S G (Devonport A) 1902 *W, I, S,* 1903 *I, S,* 1907 *I, S*

Williams, S H (Newport) 1911 *W, F, I, S*

Williamson, R H (Oxford U) 1908 *W, I, S,* 1909 *A, F*

Wilson, A J (Camborne S of M) 1909 *I*

Wilson, C E (Blackheath) 1898 *I*

Wilson, C P (Cambridge U, Marlborough N) 1881 *W*

Wilson, D S (Met Police, Harlequins) 1953 *F,* 1954 *W, NZ, I, S, F,* 1955 *F, S*

Wilson, G S (Tyldesley) 1929 *W, I*

Wilson, K J (Gloucester) 1963 *F*

Wilson, R P (Liverpool OB) 1891 *W, I, S*

Wilson, W C (Richmond) 1907 *I, S*

Winn, C E (Rosslyn Park) 1952 *SA, W, S, I, F,* 1954 *W, S, F*

Winterbottom, P J (Headingley, Harlequins) 1982 *A, S, I, F, W,* 1983 *F, W, S, I, NZ,* 1984 *S, F, W, SA* 1,2, 1986 *W, S, I, F,* 1987 *I, F, W, [A, J, US, W],* 1988 *F, W, S,* 1989 *R, Fj,* 1990 *I, F, W, S, Arg* 1,2,3, 1991 *W, S, I, F, A, [NZ, It, F, S, A],* 1992 *S, I, F, W, C, SA,* 1993 *F, W, S, I*

Wintle, T C (Northampton) 1966 *S,* 1969 *I, F, S, W*

Wodehouse, N A (United Services, RN) 1910 *F,* 1911 *W, F, I, S,* 1912 *W, I, S, F,* 1913 *SA, W, F, I, S*

Wood, A (Halifax) 1884 *I*

Wood, A E (Gloucester, Cheltenham) 1908 *F, W, I*

Wood, G W (Leicester) 1914 *W*

Wood, M B (Wasps) 2000 *C* 2(R), *US* (R)

Wood, R (Liversedge) 1894 *I*

Wood, R D (Liverpool OB) 1901 *I,* 1903 *W, I*

Woodgate, E E (Paignton) 1952 *W*

Woodhead, E (Huddersfield) 1880 *I*

Woodman, T J (Gloucester) 1999 *US* (R), 2000 *I* (R), *It* (R), 2001 *W* (R), *It* (R)

Woodruff, C G (Harlequins) 1951 *W, I, F, S*

Woods, S M J (Cambridge U, Wellington) 1890 *W, S, I,* 1891 *W, I, S,* 1892 *I, S,* 1893 *W, I,* 1895 *W, I, S*

Woods, T (Bridgwater) 1908 *S*

Woods, T (United Services, RN) 1920 *S,* 1921 *W, I, S, F*

Woodward, C R (Leicester) 1980 *I* (R), *F, W, S,* 1981 *W, S, I, F, Arg* 1,2, 1982 *A, S, I, F, W,* 1983 *I, NZ,* 1984 *S, I, F, W*

Woodward, J E (Wasps) 1952 *SA, W, S,* 1953 *W, I, F, S,* 1954 *W, NZ, I, S, F,* 1955 *W, I,* 1956 *S*

Wooldridge, C S (Oxford U, Blackheath) 1883 *W, I, S,* 1884 *W, I, S,* 1885 *I*

Wordsworth, A J (Cambridge U) 1975 *A* 1(R)

Worsley, J P R (Wasps) 1999 *[Tg, Fj],* 2000 *It* (R), *S* (R), *SA* 1(R),2(R), 2001 *It* (R), *S* (R), *F* (R), *C* 1,2, *US*

Worton, J R B (Harlequins, Army) 1926 *W,* 1927 *W*

Wrench, D F B (Harlequins) 1964 *F, S*

Wright, C C G (Cambridge U, Blackheath) 1909 *I, S*

Wright, F T (Edinburgh Acady, Manchester) 1881 *S*

Wright, I D (Northampton) 1971 *W, I, F, S* (R)

Wright. J C (Met Police) 1934 *W*

Wright, J F (Bradford) 1890 *W*

Wright, T P (Blackheath) 1960 *W, I, F, S,* 1961 *SA, W, I, F, S,* 1962 *W, I, F, S*

Wright, W H G (Plymouth) 1920 *W, F*

Wyatt, D M (Bedford) 1976 *S* (R)

Yarranton, P G (RAF, Wasps) 1954 *W, NZ, I,* 1955 *F, S*

Yates, K P (Bath) 1997 *Arg* 1,2

Yiend, W (Hartlepool R, Gloucester) 1889 *M,* 1892 *W, I, S,* 1893 *I, S*

Young, A T (Cambridge U, Blackheath, Army) 1924 *W, I, F, S,* 1925 *NZ, F,* 1926 *I, F, S,* 1927 *I, S, F,* 1928 *A, W, I, F, S,* 1929 *I*

Young, J R C (Oxford U, Harlequins) 1958 *I,* 1960 *W, I, F, S,* 1961 *SA, W, I, F*

Young, M (Gosforth) 1977 *S, I, F, W,* 1978 *F, W, S, I, NZ,* 1979 *S*

Young, P D (Dublin Wands) 1954 *W, NZ, I, S, F,* 1955 *W, I, F, S*

Youngs, N G (Leicester) 1983 *I, NZ,* 1984 *S, I, F, W*

ENGLAND INTERNATIONAL STATISTICS

(to 20 October 2001)

Match Records

Most Consecutive Test Wins

11 2000 *SA* 2, *A, Arg, SA* 3, 2001 *W, It, S, F, C*
1,2, *US*
10 1882 *W,* 1883 *I, S,* 1884 *W, I, S,* 1885 *W, I,*
1886 *W, I*
10 1994 *R, C,* 1995 *I, F, W, S, Arg, It, WS, A*

Most Consecutive Tests Without Defeat

Matches	Wins	Draws	Period
12	10	2	1882 to 1887
11	10	1	1922 to 1924
11	11	0	2000 to 2001

Most Points in a Match
by the team

Pts	Opponents	Venue	Year
110	Netherlands	Huddersfield	1998
106	United States	Twickenham	1999
101	Tonga	Twickenham	1999
80	Italy	Twickenham	2001
67	Italy	Twickenham	1999
60	Japan	Sydney	1987
60	Canada	Twickenham	1994
60	Wales	Twickenham	1998

by a player

Pts	Player	Opponents	Venue	Year
36	P J Grayson	Tonga	Twickenham	1999
35	J P Wilkinson	Italy	Twickenham	2001
32	J P Wilkinson	Italy	Twickenham	1999
30	C R Andrew	Canada	Twickenham	1994
30	P J Grayson	Netherlands	Huddersfield	1998
29	D J H Walder	Canada	Burnaby	2001
27	C R Andrew	South Africa	Pretoria	1994
27	J P Wilkinson	South Africa	Bloemfontein	2000
26	J P Wilkinson	United States	Twickenham	1999

Most Tries in a Match
by the team

Tries	Opponents	Venue	Year
16	Netherlands	Huddersfield	1998
16	United States	Twickenham	1999
13	Wales	Blackheath	1881
13	Tonga	Twickenham	1999

10	Japan	Sydney	1987
10	Fiji	Twickenham	1989
10	Italy	Twickenham	2001
9	France	Paris	1906
9	France	Richmond	1907
9	France	Paris	1914
9	Romania	Bucharest	1989

by a player

Tries	Player	Opponents	Venue	Year
5	D Lambert	France	Richmond	1907
5	R Underwood	Fiji	Twickenham	1989
4	G W Burton	Wales	Blackheath	1881
4	A Hudson	France	Paris	1906
4	R W Poulton	France	Paris	1914
4	C Oti	Romania	Bucharest	1989
4	J C Guscott	Netherlands	Huddersfield	1998
4	N A Back	Netherlands	Huddersfield	1998
4	J C Guscott	United States	Twickenham	1999

Most Conversions in a Match
by the team

Cons	Opponents	Venue	Year
15	Netherlands	Huddersfield	1998
13	United States	Twickenham	1999
12	Tonga	Twickenham	1999
9	Italy	Twickenham	2001
8	Romania	Bucharest	1989
7	Wales	Blackheath	1881
7	Japan	Sydney	1987
7	Argentina	Twickenham	1990
7	Wales	Twickenham	1998

by a player

Cons	Player	Opponents	Venue	Year
15	P J Grayson	Netherlands	Huddersfield	1998
13	J P Wilkinson	United States	Twickenham	1999
12	P J Grayson	Tonga	Twickenham	1999
9	J P Wilkinson	Italy	Twickenham	2001
8	S D Hodgkinson	Romania	Bucharest	1989
7	J M Webb	Japan	Sydney	1987
7	S D Hodgkinson	Argentina	Twickenham	1990
7	P J Grayson	Wales	Twickenham	1998

Most Penalties in a Match
by the team

Penalties	Opponents	Venue	Year
8	South Africa	Bloemfontein	2000

7	Wales	Cardiff	1991
7	Scotland	Twickenham	1995
7	France	Twickenham	1999
7	Fiji	Twickenham	1999
7	South Africa	Paris	1999
6	Wales	Twickenham	1986
6	Canada	Twickenham	1994
6	Argentina	Durban	1995
6	Scotland	Murrayfield	1996
6	Ireland	Twickenham	1996
6	South Africa	Twickenham	2000

by a player

Penalties	Player	Opponents	Venue	Year
8	J P Wilkinson	South Africa	Bloemfontein	2000
7	S D Hodgkinson	Wales	Cardiff	1991
7	C R Andrew	Scotland	Twickenham	1995
7	J P Wilkinson	France	Twickenham	1999
7	J P Wilkinson	Fiji	Twickenham	1999
6	C R Andrew	Wales	Twickenham	1986
6	C R Andrew	Canada	Twickenham	1994
6	C R Andrew	Argentina	Durban	1995
6	P J Grayson	Scotland	Murrayfield	1996
6	P J Grayson	Ireland	Twickenham	1996
6	P J Grayson	South Africa	Paris	1999
6	J P Wilkinson	South Africa	Twickenham	2000

Most Dropped Goals in a Match
by the team

Drops	Opponents	Venue	Year
2	Ireland	Twickenham	1970
2	France	Paris	1978
2	France	Paris	1980
2	Romania	Twickenham	1985
2	Fiji	Suva	1991
2	Argentina	Durban	1995
2	France	Paris	1996

by a player

Drops	Player	Opponents	Venue	Year
2	R Hiller	Ireland	Twickenham	1970
2	A G B Old	France	Paris	1978
2	J P Horton	France	Paris	1980
2	C R Andrew	Romania	Twickenham	1985
2	C R Andrew	Fiji	Suva	1991
2	C R Andrew	Argentina	Durban	1995
2	P J Grayson	France	Paris	1996

Career Records
Most Capped Players

Caps	Player	Career Span
92	J Leonard	1990 to 2001
85	R Underwood	1984 to 1996
72	W D C Carling	1988 to 1997
71	C R Andrew	1985 to 1997
65	J C Guscott	1989 to 1999
64	B C Moore	1987 to 1995
62	M O Johnson	1993 to 2001
58	P J Winterbottom	1982 to 1993
55	W A Dooley	1985 to 1993
53	M J Catt	1994 to 2001
48	D Richards	1986 to 1996
47	L B N Dallaglio	1995 to 2001

Most Consecutive Tests

Tests	Player	Span
44	W D C Carling	1989 to 1995
40	J Leonard	1990 to 1995
36	J V Pullin	1968 to 1975
33	W B Beaumont	1975 to 1982
30	R Underwood	1992 to 1996

Most Tests as Captain

Tests	Captain	Span
59	W D C Carling	1988 to 1996
21	W B Beaumont	1978 to 1982
19	M O Johnson	1998 to 2001
14	L B N Dallaglio	1997 to 1999
13	W W Wakefield	1924 to 1926
13	N M Hall	1949 to 1955
13	R E G Jeeps	1960 to 1962
13	J V Pullin	1972 to 1975

Most Tests in Individual Positions

Position	Player	Tests	Span
Full-back	M B Perry	35	1997 to 2001
Wing	R Underwood	85	1984 to 1996
Centre	W D C Carling	72	1988 to 1997
Fly-half	C R Andrew	70	1985 to 1997
Scrum-half	M J S Dawson	42	1995 to 2001
Prop	J Leonard	92	1990 to 2001
Hooker	B C Moore	63*	1987 to 1995
Lock	M O Johnson	62	1993 to 2001
Flanker	P J Winterbottom	58	1982 to 1993
No 8	D Richards	47*	1986 to 1996

excludes an appearance as a temporary replacement

Most Points in Tests

Points	Player	Tests	Career
416	J P Wilkinson	28	1998 to 2001
396	C R Andrew	71	1985 to 1997
310	P J Grayson	23	1995 to 1999
296	J M Webb	33	1987 to 1993
240	W H Hare	25	1974 to 1984
210	R Underwood	85	1984 to 1996

Most Tries in Tests

Tries	Player	Tests	Career
49	R Underwood	85	1984 to 1996
30	J C Guscott	65	1989 to 1999
18	C N Lowe	25	1913 to 1923
14	W J H Greenwood	22	1997 to 2001
13	T Underwood	27	1992 to 1998
13	N A Back	42	1994 to 2001
13	D D Luger	21	1998 to 2001
13	M J S Dawson	42	1995 to 2001
13	A S Healey	39	1997 to 2001
12	W D C Carling	72	1988 to 1997

Most Conversions in Tests

Cons	Player	Tests	Career
71	J P Wilkinson	28	1998 to 2001
52	P J Grayson	23	1995 to 1999
41	J M Webb	33	1987 to 1993
35	S D Hodgkinson	14	1989 to 1991
33	C R Andrew	71	1985 to 1997
17	L Stokes	12	1875 to 1881

Most Penalty Goals in Tests

Penalties	Player	Tests	Career
86	C R Andrew	71	1985 to 1997
85	J P Wilkinson	28	1998 to 2001
67	W H Hare	25	1974 to 1984
66	J M Webb	33	1987 to 1993
61	P J Grayson	23	1995 to 1999
43	S D Hodgkinson	14	1989 to 1991

Most Dropped Goals in Tests

Drops	Player	Tests	Career
21	C R Andrew	71	1985 to 1997
6	P J Grayson	23	1995 to 1999
4	J P Horton	13	1978 to 1984

International Championship Records

Record	Detail		Set
Most points in season	229	in five matches	2001
Most tries in season	29	in five matches	2001
Highest Score	80	80-23 v Italy	2001
Biggest win	57	80-23 v Italy	2001
Highest score conceded	37	12-37 v France	1972
Biggest defeat	27	6-33 v Scotland	1986
Most appearances	50	R Underwood	1984 – 1996
Most points in matches	227	J P Wilkinson	1998-2001
Most points in season	89	J P Wilkinson	2001
Most points in match	35	J P Wilkinson	v Italy, 2001
Most tries in matches	18	C N Lowe	1913 – 1923
	18	R Underwood	1984 – 1996
Most tries in season	8	C N Lowe	1914
Most tries in match	4	R W Poulton	v France, 1914
Most cons in matches	42	J P Wilkinson	1998 – 2001
Most cons in season	24	J P Wilkinson	2001
Most cons in match	9	J P Wilkinson	v Italy, 2001
Most pens in matches	50	W H Hare	1974 – 1984
Most pens in season	18	S D Hodgkinson	1991
	18	J P Wilkinson	2000
Most pens in match	7	S D Hodgkinson	v Wales, 1991
	7	C R Andrew	v Scotland, 1995
	7	J P Wilkinson	v France, 1999
Most drops in matches	9	C R Andrew	1985 – 1997
Most drops in season	3	P J Grayson	1996

Most drops in match	2	R Hiller	v Ireland, 1970
	2	A G B Old	v France, 1978
	2	J P Horton	v France, 1980
	2	P J Grayson	v France, 1996

Miscellaneous Records

Record	Holder	Detail
Longest Test Career	G S Pearce	14 seasons, 1978–79 to 1991–92
Youngest Test Cap	H C C Laird	18 yrs 134 days in 1927
Oldest Test Cap	F Gilbert	38 yrs in 1923

Career Records of England International Players
(up to 20 October 2001)

Player	Debut	Caps	T	C	P	D	Pts
Backs:							
I R Balshaw	2000 v I	12	5	0	0	0	25
O Barkley	2001 v US	1	0	0	0	0	0
N D Beal	1996 v Arg	15	3	0	0	0	15
T D Beim	1998 v NZ	2	1	0	0	0	5
S Benton	1998 v A	1	0	0	0	0	0
K P P Bracken	1993 v NZ	33	3	0	0	0	15
S P Brown	1998 v A	2	0	0	0	0	0
M J Catt	1994 v W	53	5	14	22	2	125
B C Cohen	2000 v I	12	8	0	0	0	40
M J S Dawson	1995 v WS	42	13	3	3	0	80
W J H Greenwood	1997 v A	22	14	0	0	0	70
A C T Gomarsall	1996 v It	7	4	0	0	0	20
S M Hanley	1999 v W	1	1	0	0	0	5
A S Healey	1997 v I	39	13	0	0	0	65
A D King	1997 v Arg	4	1	1	0	0	7
O J Lewsey	1998 v NZ	6	4	0	0	0	20
L D Lloyd	2000 v SA	5	2	0	0	0	10
D D Luger	1998 v H	21	13	0	0	0	65
B-J Mather	1999 v W	1	0	0	0	0	0
J Noon	2001 v C	3	1	0	0	0	5
M B Perry	1997 v A	36	10	0	0	0	50
D L Rees	1997 v A	11	3	0	0	0	15
J Robinson	2001 v It	4	0	0	0	0	0
P C Sampson	1998 v SA	3	0	0	0	0	0
M Stephenson	2001 v C	3	0	0	0	0	0
T R G Stimpson	1996 v It	16	1	3	4	0	23
M J Tindall	2000 v I	11	1	0	0	0	5
T Voyce	2001 v US	1	0	0	0	0	0
D J H Walder	2001 v C	3	2	10	3	0	39
F H H Waters	2001 v US	1	0	0	0	0	0
J P Wilkinson	1998 v I	28	2	71	85	3	416
M B Wood	2001 v C	2	1	0	0	0	5
Forwards:							
G S Archer	1996 v S	21	0	0	0	0	0
N A Back	1994 v S	42	13	0	0	1	68

S W Borthwick	2001 v F	4	0	0	0	0	0
B B Clarke	1992 v SA	40	3	0	0	0	15
R Cockerill	1997 v Arg	27	3	0	0	0	15
M E Corry	1997 v Arg	23	2	0	0	0	10
L B N Dallaglio	1995 v SA	47	10	0	0	0	50
D L Flatman	2000 v SA	7	0	0	0	0	0
D J Garforth	1997 v W	25	0	0	0	0	0
W R Green	1997 v A	3	0	0	0	0	0
P B T Greening	1996 v It	24	6	0	0	0	30
D J Grewcock	1997 v Arg	25	1	0	0	0	5
R A Hill	1997 v S	42	10	0	0	0	50
M O Johnson	1993 v F	62	2	0	0	0	10
B J Kay	2001 v C	2	0	0	0	0	0
J Leonard	1990 v Arg	92	1	0	0	0	5
A E Long	1997 v A	2	0	0	0	0	0
N McCarthy	1999 v I	3	0	0	0	0	0
L W Moody	2001 v C	4	1	0	0	0	5
T Palmer	2001 v US	1	0	0	0	0	0
M P Regan	1995 v SA	22	1	0	0	0	5
T A K Rodber	1992 v S	44	5	0	0	0	25
G C Rowntree	1995 v S	30	0	0	0	0	0
P H Sanderson	1998 v NZ	6	1	0	0	0	5
S D Shaw	1996 v It	19	2	0	0	0	10
P J Vickery	1998 v W	21	0	0	0	0	0
D E West	1998 v F	11	2	0	0	0	10
J M White	2000 v SA	9	0	0	0	0	0
S White-Cooper	2001 v C	2	0	0	0	0	0
T J Woodman	1999 v US	5	0	0	0	0	0
J P R Worsley	1999 v Tg	12	3	0	0	0	15

SCOTLAND TEST SEASON REVIEW 2000-01

Scotland Keep Their Best Till Last

Bill McMurtrie

Scotland began their season by attracting bigger crowds to Murrayfield for the autumn internationals and with a new captain in Budge Pountney. The Northampton open-side led them to convincing 53-6 and 31-8 wins against the United States and Samoa respectively in November, though in between Scotland succumbed (9-30) to their tenth successive defeat by Australia.

Gregor Townsend returned at stand-off to spark a six-try romp against the Eagles, his 33-point haul setting a new record for a Scot in a Murrayfield Test. A week later, Scotland conceded 21 second-half points without reply against the Wallabies after managing to live with the world champions in the first half when Townsend's three penalties took them into the half-time talk all square at 9-all. Even so, the side did not cave in after the break and the sense of purpose which Ian McGeechan and Pountney succeeded in pumping into the side was again evident when the Scots completed their pre-Christmas schedule with a convincing win and a 4-1 try count against the Samoans.

In the Six Nations, Scotland's endgame was far better than the opening moves. Defeat in Paris in February and the Murrayfield victory against Ireland in September were as far apart in the merit ladder as they were in their timings in the calendar year. The performances were from different seasons, though the results counted in one Six Nations Championship.

Against the Irish, it was as if Scotland (their Lions apart) had discovered a new game after their summer away from rugby. The Scots had tightened their defensive resources as a secure foundation off which to launch their wealth of pace.

By beating Ireland in their final 2000-2001 international, a match postponed for more than five months because of the foot-and-mouth epidemic on mainland Britain, Scotland broke even in the championship. Wins against Italy and Ireland, both at Murrayfield, offset away defeats by France and England. In fact, Scotland were unbeaten in their Murrayfield matches in the championship, though they had to come back from a 6-25 deficit to salvage a 28-all draw with Wales.

The 32-10 victory against Ireland was less than eight months after the 16-6 defeat in Paris. After the belated finale, however, that loss to France seemed in a far distant era. It had a faded tag that read as "a game that ought to have been won."

Scotland had enough pressure in that Stade de France match, especially before the interval. Indeed, twice in the first half they led by three points, through Kenny Logan's penalty goals. Each time, Christophe Lamaison responded in kind to leave the scores tied at 6-all at the interval.

Only three minutes into the match, Scotland's cause was upset by Gregor Townsend's knee injury. However, the loss of the stand-off play-maker was not the root of defeat. The Scottish forwards simply could not establish a set-piece platform. Yet it was a Scottish mistake rather than French flair that led to the decisive score. Logan's missed tackle, an isolated blemish on an otherwise secure performance, allowed Philippe Bernat-Salles just enough space to score in the right corner immediately after the interval. Thereafter Scotland could find no way back.

A fortnight later, versus Wales at Murrayfield, the Scots seemed about to fall even more heavily than they had done in Paris. Neil Jenkins was raining blow after blow on the Scots with his accurate boot, and when Mark Taylor raced away for an interception try – converted, of course, by Jenkins – the Welsh led 25-6 only three minutes into the second half. In all, Jenkins kicked three drop goals and four penalty goals as well as that conversion. Once more it seemed he would be the hammer of the Scots. But only two minutes later Scotland dug deep into their reserves to mine a rich vein of resilience. Logan's run down the left touchline released Chris Paterson for a heartening try that lifted the Scottish team and their support.

Logan converted, and on the hour he added his third penalty goal. The margin was down to 16-25, and Wales were no longer on a distant horizon. Even when Jenkins kicked his fourth penalty goal, the Scottish resolve was undiminished as they struck twice in just three minutes. Duncan Hodge unleashed James McLaren's destructive running, the centre bursting Taylor's tackle for a try beside the posts. Logan, incredibly, failed to convert, Rhys Williams charging down the kick. It was a crucial miss, though the Scots were not deflated. Almost immediately Tom Smith, the prop sprinting like a wing, ran in the try that allowed Hodge to convert to tie the match.

Scotland had had a promising first half against France and a better second half against Wales. But they had no such consolations at Twickenham. The English were in championship form in winning 43-3, running in six tries. The Scots acknowledged the rugby lesson with dignity.

A fortnight after the Twickenham defeat, Scotland notched their first championship victory of the season – 23-19 against Italy at Murrayfield. Yet it was by no means a notable Scottish performance nor a memorable match. It almost seemed as though the Scots were still haunted by their defeat in Rome a year earlier. They saw ghosts beside every Italian. Scotland controlled the first-half play, though their only scores were Hodge's first-minute drop goal and his later penalty goal. For the Scots, pressure did not equal points. Indeed, Italy led 10-6 at the interval after Mauro Bergamasco had run in from halfway.

An exchange of penalty goals in the first nine minutes of the second half – two by Hodge sandwiching one by Diego Dominguez – left Italy still leading, though by only 13-12. Suddenly, Smith took a hand. The prop's try had salvaged a draw against Wales – here he had the crucial score, forcing his way over from a close-range lineout. Dominguez regained the lead for Italy with two more penalty goals, but Hodge responded with a final brace of his own.

Who knows how the Scotland v Ireland international would have gone if it had been played on its due date? Certainly, Ireland were the form team – they had won in Rome and beaten France in Dublin. Scotland had had only the draw with Wales and the uneasy victory against Italy. Five months later, however, all that counted for little, even though the talk in the press and on the airwaves was of Ireland as Grand Slam contenders. Nor did the Scots heed the baggage of history. Traditionally they have not been at their best in the autumn. Yet here was a Scottish performance of true quality once they had settled from a nervous start.

A final score of 32-10 was no less than Scotland deserved, though they would have been happier with a try count of 4-0. The Scots' sterling, solid defensive play was punctured only in the dying seconds by Girvan Dempsey. That, though, was only one element of a game of all-round quality. Scott Murray, unconcerned by his disappointments of the Lions' tour, was the master of the line-out, and the pack as a whole won a wealth of second-phase possession.

The match had the odd blemish, but the mind's database recorded four excellent Scottish tries that brought back memories of Paris 1999. John Leslie's break down the left touchline and Chris Paterson's slicing run infield provided the scoring pass for Budge Pountney, Scotland's captain. Gregor Townsend then sent Smith in for the prop's third try of the championship, and Scotland led 17-0 at half-time. Townsend converted the first try, but his kicking – from hand as well as off the ground – had been wayward. So Pountney called on Paterson, who kicked two conversions and two penalty goals.

Though relieved as goal-kicker, Townsend still posed a threat with ball in hand, and it was his break that put Leslie in for the Scots' third try midway through the second half. Then Leslie's replacement, Andy Henderson, the 21 year-old Glasgow centre, supported Glenn Metcalfe's chip and chase for a debut try.

What might the 2000-2001 championship have been if Scotland had played all their games as they did in their first of the following season?

Scotland's Test Record in 2000-2001: Played 8, won 4, drawn 1, lost 3.

Opponents	Date	Venue	Result
Ireland	22nd September 2001	H	Won 32-10
Italy	17th March 2001	H	Won 23-19
England	3rd March 2001	A	Lost 3-43
Wales	17th February 2001	H	Drawn 28-28
France	4th February 2001	A	Lost 6-16
Samoa	18th November 2000	H	Won 31-8
Australia	11th November 2000	H	Lost 9-30
United States	4th November 2000	H	Won 53-6

SCOTTISH INTERNATIONAL PLAYERS
(up to 20 October 2001)

Note: Years given for International Championship matches are for second half of season; eg 1972 means season 1971-72. Years for all other matches refer to the actual year of the match. When a series has taken place, figures have been used to denote the particular matches in which players have featured. Thus 1981 *NZ* 1,2 indicates that a player appeared in the first and second Tests of the series.

Abercrombie, C H (United Services) 1910 *I, E*, 1911 *F, W,* 1913 *F, W*
Abercrombie, J G (Edinburgh U) 1949 *F, W, I*, 1950 *F, W, I, E*
Agnew, W C C (Stewart's Coll FP) 1930 *W, I*
Ainslie, R (Edinburgh Inst FP) 1879 *I, E*, 1880 *I, E*, 1881 *E*, 1882 *I, E*
Ainslie, T (Edinburgh Inst FP) 1881 *E*, 1882 *I, E*, 1883 *W, I, E*, 1884 *W, I, E*, 1885 *W, I* 1,2
Aitchison, G R (Edinburgh Wands) 1883 *I*
Aitchison, T G (Gala) 1929 *W, I, E*
Aitken, A I (Edinburgh Inst FP) 1889 *I*
Aitken, G G (Oxford U) 1924 *W, I, E*, 1925 *F, W, I, E*, 1929 *F*
Aitken, J (Gala) 1977 *E, I, F*, 1981 *F, W, E, I, NZ* 1,2, *R, A*, 1982 *E, I, F, W*, 1983 *F, W, E, NZ*, 1984 *W, E, I, F, R*
Aitken, R (London Scottish) 1947 *W*
Allan, B (Glasgow Acads) 1881 *I*
Allan, J (Edinburgh Acads) 1990 *NZ* 1, 1991, *W, I, R*, [*J, I, WS, E, NZ*]
Allan, J L (Melrose) 1952 *F, W, I*, 1953 *W*
Allan, J L F (Cambridge U) 1957 *I, E*
Allan, J W (Melrose) 1927 *F*, 1928 *I*, 1929 *F, W, I, E*, 1930 *F, E*, 1931 *F, W, I, E*, 1932 *SA, W, I*, 1934 *I, E*
Allan, R C (Hutchesons' GSFP) 1969 *I*
Allardice, W D (Aberdeen GSFP) 1947 *A*, 1948 *F, W, I*, 1949 *F, W, I, E*
Allen, H W (Glasgow Acads) 1873 *E*
Anderson, A H (Glasgow Acads) 1894 *I*
Anderson, D G (London Scottish) 1889 *I*, 1890 *W, I, E*, 1891 *W, E*, 1892 *W, E*
Anderson, E (Stewart's Coll FP) 1947 *I, E*
Anderson, J W (W of Scotland) 1872 *E*
Anderson, T (Merchiston) 1882 *I*
Angus, A W (Watsonians) 1909 *W*, 1910 *F, W, E*, 1911 *W, I*, 1912 *F, W, I, E, SA*, 1913 *F, W*, 1914 *W, I*, 1920 *F, W, I, E*
Anton, P A (St Andrew's U) 1873 *E*
Armstrong, G (Jedforest, Newcastle) 1988 *A*, 1989 *W, E, I, F, Fj, R*, 1990 *I, F, W, E, NZ* 1,2, *Arg*, 1991 *F, W, E, I, R,* [*J, I, WS, E, NZ*], 1993 *I, F, W, E*, 1994 *E, I*, 1996 *NZ,* 1,2, *A*, 1997 *W, SA* (R), 1998 *It, I, F, W, E, SA* (R), 1999 *W, E, I, F, Arg, R,* [*SA, U, Sm, NZ*]
Arneil, R J (Edinburgh Acads, Leicester and Northampton) 1968 *I, E, A*, 1969 *F, W, I, E, SA*, 1970 *F, W, I, E, A*, 1971 *F, W, I, E* (2[1C]), 1972 *F, W, E, NZ*
Arthur, A (Glasgow Acads) 1875 *E*, 1876 *E*
Arthur, J W (Glasgow Acads) 1871 *E*, 1872 *E*
Asher, A G G (Oxford U) 1882 *I*, 1884 *W, I, E*, 1885 *W*, 1886 *I, E*
Auld, W (W of Scotland) 1889 *W*, 1890 *W*
Auldjo, L J (Abertay) 1878 *E*

Bain, D McL (Oxford U) 1911 *E*, 1912 *F, W, E, SA*, 1913 *F, W, I, E*, 1914 *W, I*
Baird, G R T (Kelso) 1981 *A*, 1982 *E, I, F, W, A* 1,2, 1983 *I, F, W, E, NZ*, 1984 *W, E, I, F, A*, 1985 *I, W, E*, 1986 *F, W, E, I, R*, 1987 *E*, 1988 *I*
Balfour, A (Watsonians) 1896 *W, I, E*, 1897 *E*
Balfour, L M (Edinburgh Acads) 1872 *E*
Bannerman, E M (Edinburgh Acads) 1872 *E*, 1873 *E*
Bannerman, J M (Glasgow HSFP) 1921 *F, W, I, E*, 1922 *F, W, I, E*, 1923 *F, W, I, E*, 1924 *F, W, I, E*, 1925 *F, W, I, E*, 1926 *F, W, I, E*, 1927 *F, W, I, E, A*, 1928 *F, W, I, E*, 1929 *F, W, I, E*
Barnes, I A (Hawick) 1972 *W*, 1974 *F* (R), 1975 *E* (R), *NZ*, 1977 *I, F, W*
Barrie, R W (Hawick) 1936 *E*
Bearne, K R F (Cambridge U, London Scottish) 1960 *F, W*
Beattie, J A (Hawick) 1929 *F, W*, 1930 *W*, 1931 *F, W, I, E*, 1932 *SA, W, I, E*, 1933 *W, E, I*, 1934 *I, E*, 1935 *W, I, E, NZ*, 1936 *W, I, E*

Beattie, J R (Glasgow Acads) 1980 *I, F, W, E*, 1981 *F, W, E, I*, 1983 *F, W, E, NZ*, 1984 *E* (R), *R, A*, 1985 *I*, 1986 *F, W, E, I, R*, 1987 *I, F, W, E*
Beattie, R S (Newcastle) 2000 *NZ* 1,2(R), *Sm* (R)
Bedell-Sivright, D R (Cambridge U, Edinburgh U) 1900 *W*, 1901 *W, I, E*, 1902 *W, I, E*, 1903 *W, I*, 1904 *W, I, E*, 1905 *NZ*, 1906 *W, I, E, SA*, 1907 *W, I, E*, 1908 *W, I*
Bedell-Sivright, J V (Cambridge U) 1902 *W*
Begbie, T A (Edinburgh Wands) 1881 *I, E*
Bell, D L (Watsonians) 1975 *I, F, W, E*
Bell, J A (Clydesdale) 1901 *W, I, E*, 1902 *W, I, E*
Bell, L H I (Edinburgh Acads) 1900 *E*, 1904 *W, I*
Berkeley, W V (Oxford U) 1926 *F*, 1929 *F, W, I*
Berry, C W (Fettesian-Lorettonians) 1884 *I, E*, 1885 *W, I* 1, 1887 *I, W, E*, 1888 *W, I*
Bertram, D M (Watsonians) 1922 *F, W, I, E*, 1923 *F, W, I, E*, 1924 *W, I, E*
Beveridge, G (Glasgow) 2000 *NZ* 2(R), *US* (R), *Sm* (R)
Biggar, A G (London Scottish) 1969 *SA*, 1970 *F, I, E, A*, 1971 *F, W, I, E* (2[1C]), 1972 *F, W*
Biggar, M A (London Scottish) 1975 *I, F, W, E*, 1976 *W, E, I*, 1977 *I, F, W*, 1978 *I, F, W, E, NZ*, 1979 *W, E, I, F, NZ*, 1980 *I, F, W, E*
Birkett, G A (Harlequins, London Scottish) 1975 *NZ*
Bishop, J M (Glasgow Acads) 1893 *I*
Bisset, A A (RIE Coll) 1904 *W*
Black, A W (Edinburgh U) 1947 *F, W*, 1948 *E*, 1950 *W, I, E*
Black, W P (Glasgow HSFP) 1948 *F, W, I, E*, 1951 *E*
Blackadder, W F (W of Scotland) 1938 *E*
Blaikie, C F (Heriot's FP) 1963 *I, E*, 1966 *E*, 1968 *A*, 1969 *F, W, I, E*
Blair, P C B (Cambridge U) 1912 *SA*, 1913 *F, W, I, E*
Bolton, W H (W of Scotland) 1876 *E*
Borthwick, J B (Stewart's Coll FP) 1938 *W, I*
Bos, F H ten (Oxford U, London Scottish) 1959 *E*, 1960 *F, W, SA*, 1961 *F, SA, W, I, E*, 1962 *F, W, I, E*, 1963 *F, W, I, E*
Boswell, J D (W of Scotland) 1889 *W, I*, 1890 *W, I, E*, 1891 *W, I, E*, 1892 *W, I, E*, 1893 *I, E*, 1894 *I, E*
Bowie, T C (Watsonians) 1913 *I, E*, 1914 *I, E*
Boyd, G M (Glasgow HSFP) 1926 *E*
Boyd, J L (United Services) 1912 *E, SA*
Boyle, A C W (London Scottish) 1963 *F, W, I*
Boyle, A H W (St Thomas's Hospital, London Scottish) 1966 *A*, 1967 *F, NZ*, 1968 *F, W, I*
Brash, J C (Cambridge U) 1961 *E*
Breakey, R W (Gosforth) 1978 *E*
Brewis, N T (Edinburgh Inst FP) 1876 *E*, 1878 *E*, 1879 *I, E*, 1880 *I, E*
Brewster, A K (Stewart's-Melville FP) 1977 *E*, 1980 *I, F*, 1986 *E, I, R*
Brotherstone, S J (Melrose, Brive) 1999 *I* (R), 2000 *F, W, E, US, A, Sm*
Brown, A H (Heriot's FP) 1928 *E*, 1929 *F, W*
Brown, A R (Gala) 1971 *E* (2[1C]), 1972 *F, W, E*
Brown, C H C (Dunfermline) 1929 *E*
Brown, D I (Cambridge U) 1933 *W, E, I*
Brown, G L (W of Scotland) 1969 *SA*, 1970 *F, W* (R), *I, E, A*, 1971 *F, W, I, E* (2[1C]), 1972 *F, W, E, NZ*, 1973 *E* (R), *P*, 1974 *W, E, I, F*, 1975 *I, F, W, E, A*, 1976 *F, W, E, I*
Brown, J A (Glasgow Acads) 1908 *W, I*
Brown, J B (Glasgow Acads) 1879 *I, E*, 1880 *I, E*, 1881 *I, E*, 1882 *I, E*, 1883 *W, I, E*, 1884 *W, I, E*, 1885 *I* 1,2, 1886 *W, I, E*
Brown, P C (W of Scotland, Gala) 1964 *F, NZ, W, I, E*, 1965 *I, E, SA*, 1966 *A*, 1969 *F, W, E, NZ*, 1971 *F, W, I, E* (2[1C]), 1972 *F, W, E, NZ*, 1973 *F, W, I, E, P*
Brown, T G (Heriot's FP) 1929 *W*
Brown, W D (Glasgow Acads) 1871 *E*, 1872 *E*, 1873 *E*, 1874 *E*, 1875 *E*
Brown, W S (Edinburgh Inst FP) 1880 *I, E*, 1882 *I, E*, 1883 *W, E*

Browning, A (Glasgow HSFP) 1920 *I*, 1922 *F, W, I*, 1923 *W, I, E*

Bruce, C R (Glasgow Acads) 1947 *F, W, I, E*, 1949 *F, W, I, E*

Bruce, N S (Blackheath, Army and London Scottish) 1958 *F, A, I, E*, 1959 *F, W, I, E*, 1960 *F, W, I, E, SA*, 1961 *F, SA, W, I, E*, 1962 *F, W, I, E*, 1963 *F, W, I, E*, 1964 *F, NZ, W, I, E*

Bruce, R M (Gordonians) 1947 *A*, 1948 *F, W, I*

Bruce-Lockhart, J H (London Scottish) 1913 *W*, 1920 *E*

Bruce-Lockhart, L (London Scottish) 1948 *E*, 1950 *F, W*, 1953 *I, E*

Bruce-Lockhart, R B (Cambridge U and London Scottish) 1937 *I*, 1939 *I, E*

Bryce, C C (Glasgow Acads) 1873 *E*, 1874 *E*

Bryce, R D H (W of Scotland) 1973 *I* (R)

Bryce, W E (Selkirk) 1922 *W, I, E*, 1923 *F, W, I, E*, 1924 *F, W, I, E*

Brydon, W R C (Heriot's FP) 1939 *W*

Buchanan, A (Royal HSFP) 1871 *E*

Buchanan, F G (Kelvinside Acads and Oxford U) 1910 *F*, 1911 *F, W*

Buchanan, J C R (Stewart's Coll FP) 1921 *W, I, E*, 1922 *W, I, E*, 1923 *F, W, I, E*, 1924 *F, W, I, E*, 1925 *F, I*

Buchanan-Smith, G A E (London Scottish, Heriot's FP) 1989 *Fj* (R), 1990 *Arg*

Bucher, A M (Edinburgh Acads) 1897 *E*

Budge, G M (Edinburgh Wands) 1950 *F, W, I, E*

Bullmore, H H (Edinburgh U) 1902 *I*

Bulloch, A J (Glasgow) 2000 *US, A, Sm*, 2001 *F* (t+R), *E*

Bulloch, G C (West of Scotland, Glasgow) 1997 *SA*, 1998 *It, I, F, W, E, Fj, A* 1, *SA*, 1999 *W, E, It, I, F, Arg*, [*SA, U, Sm, NZ*], 2000 *It, I, W* (R), *NZ* 1,2, *A* (R), *Sm* (R), 2001 *F, W, E, It, I*

Burnell, A P (London Scottish, Montferrand) 1989 *E, I, F, Fj, R*, 1990 *I, F, W, E, Arg*, 1991 *F, W, E, I, R*, [*J, Z, I, WS, E, NZ*], 1992 *E, I, F, W*, 1993 *I, F, W, E, NZ*, 1994 *W, E, I, F, Arg* 1,2, *SA*, 1995 [*Iv, Tg* (R), *F* (R)], *WS*, 1998 *E, SA*, 1999 *W, E, It, I, F, Arg*, [*Sp, Sm* (R), *NZ*]

Burnet, P J (London Scottish and Edinburgh Acads) 1960 *SA*

Burnet, W (Hawick) 1912 *E*

Burnet, W A (W of Scotland) 1934 *W*, 1935 *W, I, E, NZ*, 1936 *W, I, E*

Burnett, J N (Heriot's FP) 1980 *I, F, W, E*

Burns, G G (Watsonians) 1999 *It* (R)

Burrell, G (Gala) 1950 *F, W, I*, 1951 *SA*

Cairns, A G (Watsonians) 1903 *W, I, E*, 1904 *W, I, E*, 1905 *W, I, E*, 1906 *W, I, E*

Calder, F (Stewart's-Melville FP) 1986 *F, W, E, I, R*, 1987 *I, F, W, E*, [*F, Z, R, NZ*], 1988 *I, F, W, E*, 1989 *W, E, I, F, R*, 1990 *I, F, W, E, NZ* 1,2, 1991 *R*, [*J, I, WS, E, NZ*]

Calder, J H (Stewart's-Melville FP) 1981 *F, W, E, I, NZ* 1,2, *R, A*, 1982 *E, I, F, W, A* 1,2, 1983 *I, F, W, E, NZ*, 1984 *W, E, I, F, A*, 1985 *I, F, W*

Callander, G J (Kelso) 1984 *R*, 1988 *I, F, W, E, A*

Cameron, A (Glasgow HSFP) 1948 *W*, 1950 *I, E*, 1951 *F, W, I, E, SA*, 1953 *I, E*, 1955 *F, W, I, E*

Cameron, A D (Hillhead HSFP) 1951 *F*, 1954 *F, W*

Cameron, A W (Watsonians) 1887 *W*, 1893 *W*, 1894 *I*

Cameron, D (Glasgow HSFP) 1953 *I, E*, 1954 *F, NZ, I, E*

Cameron, N W (Glasgow U) 1952 *E*, 1953 *F, W*

Campbell, A J (Hawick) 1984 *I, F, R*, 1985 *I, F, W, E*, 1986 *F, W, E, I, R*, 1988 *F, W, A*

Campbell, G T (London Scottish) 1892 *W, I, E*, 1893 *I, E*, 1894 *W, I, E*, 1895 *W, I, E*, 1896 *W, I, E*, 1897 *I*, 1899 *I*, 1900 *E*

Campbell, H H (Cambridge U, London Scottish) 1947 *I, E*, 1948 *I, E*

Campbell, J A (W of Scotland) 1878 *E*, 1879 *I, E*, 1881 *I, E*

Campbell, J A (Cambridge U) 1900 *I*

Campbell, N M (London Scottish) 1956 *F, W*

Campbell, S J (Dundee HSFP) 1995 *C, I, F, W, E, R*, [*Iv, NZ* (R)], *WS* (t), 1996 *I, F, W, E*, 1997 *A, SA*, 1998 *Fj* (R), *A* 2(R) [*Z, R*(R)]

Campbell-Lamerton, J R E (London Scottish) 1986 *F*, 1987 [*Z, R*(R)]

Campbell-Lamerton, M J (Halifax, Army, London Scottish) 1961 *F, SA, W, I*, 1962 *F, W, I, E*, 1963 *F, W, I, E*, 1964 *I, E*, 1965 *F, W, I, E, SA*, 1966 *F, W, I, E*

Carmichael, A B (W of Scotland) 1967 *I, NZ*, 1968 *F, W, I, E, A*, 1969 *F, W, I, E, SA*, 1970 *F, W, I, E, A*, 1971 *F, W, I, E* (2[1C]), 1972 *F, W, E, NZ*, 1973 *F, W, I, E, P*, 1974 *W, E, I, F*, 1975 *I, F, W, E, NZ, A*, 1976 *F, W, E, I*, 1977 *E, I* (R), *F, W*, 1978 *I*

Carmichael, J H (Watsonians) 1921 *F, W, I*

Carrick, J S (Glasgow Acads) 1876 *E*, 1877 *E*

Cassels, D Y (W of Scotland) 1880 *E*, 1881 *I*, 1882 *I, E*, 1883 *W, I, E*

Cathcart, C W (Edinburgh U) 1872 *E*, 1873 *E*, 1876 *E*

Cawkwell, G L (Oxford U) 1947 *F*

Chalmers, C M (Melrose) 1989 *W, E, I, F, Fj*, 1990 *I, F, W, E, NZ* 1,2, *Arg*, 1991 *F, W, E, I, R*, [*J, Z* (R), *I, WS, E, NZ*], 1992 *E, I, F, W, A* 1,2, 1993 *I, F, W, E, NZ*, 1994 *W, SA*, 1995 *C, I, F, W, E, R*, [*Iv, Tg, F, NZ*], *WS*, 1996 *A, It*, 1997 *W, I, F, A* (R), *SA*, 1998 *It, I, F, W, E*, 1999 *Arg* (R)

Chalmers, T (Glasgow Acads) 1871 *E*, 1872 *E*, 1873 *E*, 1874 *E*, 1875 *E*, 1876 *E*

Chambers, H F T (Edinburgh U) 1888 *W, I*, 1889 *W, I*

Charters, R G (Hawick) 1955 *W, I, E*

Chisholm, D H (Melrose) 1964 *I, E*, 1965 *E, SA*, 1966 *F, I, E, A*, 1967 *F, W, NZ*, 1968 *F, W, I*

Chisholm, R W T (Melrose) 1955 *I, E*, 1956 *F, W, I, E*, 1958 *F, W, A, I*, 1960 *SA*

Church, W C (Glasgow Acads) 1906 *W*

Clark, R L (Edinburgh Wands, Royal Navy) 1972 *F, W, E, NZ*, 1973 *F, W, I, E, P*

Clauss, P R A (Oxford U) 1891 *W, I, E*, 1892 *W, E*, 1895 *I*

Clay, A T (Edinburgh Acads) 1886 *W, I, E*, 1887 *I, W, E*, 1888 *W*

Clunies-Ross, A (St Andrew's U) 1871 *E*

Coltman, S (Hawick) 1948 *I*, 1949 *F, W, I, E*

Colville, A G (Merchistonians, Blackheath) 1871 *E*, 1872 *E*

Connell, G C (Trinity Acads and London Scottish) 1968 *E, A*, 1969 *F, E*, 1970 *F*

Cooper, M McG (Oxford U) 1936 *W, I*

Corcoran, I (Gala) 1992 *A* 1(R)

Cordial, I F (Edinburgh Wands) 1952 *F, W, I, E*

Cotter, J L (Hillhead HSFP) 1934 *I, E*

Cottington, G S (Kelso) 1934 *I, E*, 1935 *W, I*, 1936 *E*

Coughtrie, S (Edinburgh Acads) 1959 *F, W, I, E*, 1962 *W, I, E*, 1963 *F, W, I, E*

Couper, J H (W of Scotland) 1896 *W, I*, 1899 *I*

Coutts, F H (Melrose, Army) 1947 *W, I, E*

Coutts, I D F (Old Alleynians) 1951 *F*, 1952 *E*

Cowan, R C (Selkirk) 1961 *F*, 1962 *F, W, I, E*

Cowie, W L K (Edinburgh Wands) 1953 *E*

Cownie, W B (Watsonians) 1893 *W, I, E*, 1894 *W, I, E*, 1895 *W, I, E*

Crabbie, G E (Edinburgh Acads) 1904 *W*

Crabbie, J E (Edinburgh Acads, Oxford U) 1900 *W*, 1902 *I*, 1903 *W, I*, 1904 *E*, 1905 *W*

Craig, J B (Heriot's FP) 1939 *W*

Craig, J M (West of Scotland, Glasgow) 1997 *A*, 2001 *W* (R), *E* (R), *It*

Cramb, R I (Harlequins) 1987 [*R*(R)], 1988 *I, F, A*

Cranston, A G (Hawick) 1976 *W, E, I*, 1977 *E, W*, 1978 *F* (R), *W, E, NZ*, 1981 *NZ* 1,2

Crawford, J A (Army, London Scottish) 1934 *I*

Crawford, W H (United Services, RN) 1938 *W, I, E*, 1939 *W, E*

Crichton-Miller, D (Gloucester) 1931 *W, I, E*

Crole, G B (Oxford U) 1920 *F, W, I, E*

Cronin, D F (Bath, London Scottish, Bourges, Wasps) 1988 *I, F, W, E, A*, 1989 *W, E, I, F, Fj, R*, 1990 *I, F, W, E, NZ* 1,2, 1991 *F, W, E, I, R*, [*Z*], 1992 *A* 2, 1993 *I, F, W, E, NZ*, 1995 *C, I, F, [Tg, F, NZ], WS*, 1996 *NZ* 1,2, *A, It*, 1997 *F* (R), 1998 *I, F, W, E*

Cross, M (Merchistonians) 1875 *E*, 1876 *E*, 1877 *I, E*, 1878 *E*, 1879 *I, E*, 1880 *I, E*

Cross, W (Merchistonians) 1871 *E*, 1872 *E*

Cumming, R S (Aberdeen U) 1921 *F, W*

Cunningham, G (Oxford U) 1908 *W, I*, 1909 *W, E*, 1910 *F, I, E*, 1911 *E*

Cunningham, R F (Gala) 1978 *NZ*, 1979 *W, E*

Currie, L R (Dunfermline) 1947 *A*, 1948 *F, W, I*, 1949 *F, W, I, E*

Cuthbertson, W (Kilmarnock, Harlequins) 1980 *I*, 1981 *W, E, I, NZ* 1,2, *R, A*, 1982 *E, I, F, W, A* 1,2, 1983 *I, F, W, NZ*, 1984 *W, E, A*

Dalgleish, A (Gala) 1890 *W, E*, 1891 *W, I*, 1892 *W*, 1893 *W*, 1894 *W, I*

Dalgleish, K J (Edinburgh Wands, Cambridge U) 1951 *I, E*, 1953 *F, W*

Dallas, J D (Watsonians) 1903 *E*

Davidson, J A (London Scottish, Edinburgh Wands) 1959 *E*, 1960 *I, E*

Davidson, J N G (Edinburgh U) 1952 *F, W, I, E*, 1953 *F, W*, 1954 *F*
Davidson, J P (RIE Coll) 1873 *E*, 1874 *E*
Davidson, R S (Royal HSFP) 1893 *E*
Davies, D S (Hawick) 1922 *F, W, I, E*, 1923 *F, W, I, E*, 1924 *F, E*, 1925 *W, I, E*, 1926 *F, W, I, E*, 1927 *F, W, I*
Dawson, J C (Glasgow Acads) 1947 *A*, 1948 *F, W*, 1949 *F, W, I*, 1950 *F, W, I, E*, 1951 *F, W, I, E, SA*, 1952 *F, W, I, E*, 1953 *E*
Deans, C T (Hawick) 1978 *F, W, E, NZ*, 1979 *W, E, I, F, NZ*, 1980 *I, F*, 1981 *F, W, E, I, NZ* 1,2, *R, A*, 1982 *E, I, F, W, A* 1,2, 1983 *I, F, W, E, NZ*, 1984 *W, E, I, F, A*, 1985 *I, F, W, E*, 1986 *F, W, E, I, R*, 1987 *I, F, W, E, [F, Z, R, NZ]*
Deans, D T (Hawick) 1968 *E*
Deas, D W (Heriot's FP) 1947 *F, W*
Dick, L G (Loughborough Colls, Jordanhill, Swansea) 1972 *W* (R), *E*, 1974 *W, E, I, F*, 1975 *I, F, W, E, NZ, A*, 1976 *F*, 1977 *E*
Dick, R C S (Cambridge U, Guy's Hospital) 1934 *W, I, E*, 1935 *W, I, E, NZ*, 1936 *W, I, E*, 1937 *W, I, E*, 1938 *W, I, E*
Dickson, G (Gala) 1978 *NZ*, 1979 *W, E, I, F, NZ*, 1980 *W*, 1981 *F*, 1982 *W* (R)
Dickson, M R (Edinburgh U) 1905 *I*
Dickson, W M (Blackheath, Oxford U) 1912 *F, W, E, SA*, 1913 *F, W, I*
Dobson, J (Glasgow Acads) 1911 *E*, 1912 *F, W, I, E, SA*
Dobson, J D (Glasgow Acads) 1910 *I*
Dobson, W G (Heriot's FP) 1922 *W, I, E*
Docherty, J T (Glasgow HSFP) 1955 *F, W*, 1956 *E*, 1958 *F, W, A, I, E*
Dods, F P (Edinburgh Acads) 1901 *I*
Dods, J H (Edinburgh Acads) 1895 *W, I, E*, 1896 *W, I, E*, 1897 *I, E*
Dods, M (Gala, Northampton) 1994 *I* (t), *Arg* 1,2, 1995 *WS*, 1996 *I, F, W, E*
Dods, P W (Gala) 1983 *I, F, W, E, NZ*, 1984 *W, E, I, F, R, A*, 1985 *I, F, W, E*, 1989 *W, E, I, F*, 1991 *I* (R), *R, [Z, NZ* (R)]
Donald, D G (Oxford U) 1914 *W, I*
Donald, R L H (Glasgow HSFP) 1921 *W, I, E*
Donaldson, W P (Oxford U, W of Scotland) 1893 *I*, 1894 *I*, 1895 *I*, 1896 *I, E*, 1899 *I*
Don-Wauchope, A R (Fettesian-Lorettonians) 1881 *E*, 1882 *E*, 1883 *W*, 1884 *W, I, E*, 1885 *W, I* 1,2, 1886 *W, I, E*, 1888 *I*, 1886 *W*, 1887 *I, W, E*
Don-Wauchope, P H (Fettesian-Lorettonians) 1885 *I* 1,2, 1886 *W*, 1887 *I, W, E*
Dorward, A F (Cambridge U, Gala) 1950 *F*, 1951 *SA*, 1952 *W, I, E*, 1953 *F, W, E*, 1955 *F*, 1956 *I, E*, 1957 *F, W, I, E*
Dorward, T F (Gala) 1938 *W, I, E*, 1939 *I, E*
Douglas, G (Jedforest) 1921 *W*
Douglas, J (Stewart's Coll FP) 1961 *F, SA, W, I, E*, 1962 *F, W, I, E*, 1963 *F, W, I*
Douty, P S (London Scottish) 1927 *A*, 1928 *F, W*
Drew, D (Glasgow Acads) 1871 *E*, 1876 *E*
Druitt, W A H (London Scottish) 1936 *W, I, E*
Drummond, A H (Kelvinside Acads) 1938 *W, I*
Drummond, C W (Melrose) 1947 *F, W, I, E*, 1948 *F, I, E*, 1950 *F, W, I, E*
Drybrough, A S (Edinburgh Wands, Merchistonians) 1902 *I*, 1903 *I*
Dryden, R H (Watsonians) 1937 *E*
Drysdale, D (Heriot's FP) 1923 *F, W, I, E*, 1924 *F, W, I, E*, 1925 *F, W, I, E*, 1926 *F, W, I, E*, 1927 *F, W, I, E, A*, 1928 *F, W, I, E*, 1929 *F*
Duff, P L (Glasgow Acads) 1936 *W, I*, 1938 *W, I, E*, 1939 *W*
Duffy, H (Jedforest) 1955 *F*
Duke, A (Royal HSFP) 1888 *W, I*, 1889 *W, I*, 1890 *W, I*
Duncan, A W (Edinburgh U) 1901 *W, I, E*, 1902 *W, I, E*
Duncan, D D (Oxford U) 1920 *F, W, I, E*
Duncan, M D F (W of Scotland) 1986 *F, W, E, R*, 1987 *I, F, W, E, [F, Z, R, NZ]*, 1988 *I, F, W, E, A*, 1989 *W*
Duncan, M M (Fettesian-Lorettonians) 1888 *W*
Dunlop, J W (W of Scotland) 1875 *E*
Dunlop, Q (W of Scotland) 1971 *E* (2[1C])
Dykes, A S (Glasgow Acads) 1932 *E*
Dykes, J C (Glasgow Acads) 1922 *F, E*, 1924 *I*, 1925 *F, W, I*, 1926 *F, W, I, E*, 1927 *F, W, I, E, A*, 1928 *F, I*, 1929 *F, W, I*
Dykes, J M (Clydesdale, Glasgow HSFP) 1898 *I, E*, 1899 *W, E*, 1900 *W, I*, 1901 *W, I, E*, 1902 *E*

Edwards, D B (Heriot's FP) 1960 *I, E, SA*
Edwards, N G B (Harlequins, Northampton) 1992 *E, I, F, W, A* 1, 1994 *W*

Elgie, M K (London Scottish) 1954 *NZ, I, E, W*, 1955 *F, W, I, E*
Elliot, C (Langholm) 1958 *E*, 1959 *F*, 1960 *F*, 1963 *E*, 1964 *F, NZ, W, I, E*, 1965 *F, W, I*
Elliot, M (Hawick) 1895 *W*, 1896 *E*, 1897 *I, E*, 1898 *I, E*
Elliot, T (Gala) 1905 *E*
Elliot, T (Gala) 1955 *W, I, E*, 1956 *F, W, I, E*, 1957 *F, W, I, E*, 1958 *W, A, I*
Elliot, T G (Langholm) 1968 *W, A*, 1969 *F, W*, 1970 *E*
Elliot, W I D (Edinburgh Acads) 1947 *F, W, E, A*, 1948 *F, W, I, E*, 1949 *F, W, I, E*, 1950 *F, W, I, E*, 1951 *F, W, I, E, SA*, 1952 *F, W, I, E*, 1954 *NZ, I, E, W*
Ellis, D G (Currie) 1997 *W, E, I, F*
Emslie, W D (Royal HSFP) 1930 *F*, 1932 *I*
Eriksson, B R S (London Scottish) 1996 *NZ* 1, *A*, 1997 *E*
Evans, H L (Edinburgh U) 1885 *I* 1,2
Ewart, E N (Glasgow Acads) 1879 *E*, 1880 *I, E*

Fahmy, Dr E C (Abertillery) 1920 *F, W, I, E*
Fairley, I T (Kelso, Edinburgh) 1999 *It, I* (R), *[Sp* (R)]
Fasson, F H (London Scottish, Edinburgh Wands) 1900 *W*, 1901 *W, I*, 1902 *W, E*
Fell, A N (Edinburgh U) 1901 *W, I, E*, 1902 *W, I*, 1903 *W, E*
Ferguson, J H (Gala) 1928 *W*
Ferguson, W G (Royal HSFP) 1927 *A*, 1928 *F, W, I, E*
Fergusson, E A J (Oxford U) 1954 *F, NZ, I, E, W*
Finlay, A B (Edinburgh Acads) 1875 *E*
Finlay, J F (Edinburgh Acads) 1871 *E*, 1872 *E*, 1874 *E*, 1875 *E*
Finlay, N J (Edinburgh Acads) 1875 *E*, 1876 *E*, 1878 *E*, 1879 *I, E*, 1880 *I, E*, 1881 *I, E*
Finlay, R (Watsonians) 1948 *E*
Fisher, A T (Waterloo, Watsonians) 1947 *I, E*
Fisher, C D (Waterloo) 1975 *NZ, A*, 1976 *W, E, I*
Fisher, D (W of Scotland) 1893 *I*
Fisher, J P (Royal HSFP, London Scottish) 1963 *E*, 1964 *F, NZ, W, I, E*, 1965 *F, W, I, E, SA*, 1966 *F, W, I, E, A*, 1967 *F, W, I, E, NZ*, 1968 *F, W, I, E*
Fleming, C J N (Edinburgh Wands) 1896 *I, E*, 1897 *I*
Fleming, G R (Glasgow Acads) 1875 *E*, 1876 *E*
Fletcher, H N (Edinburgh U) 1904 *E*, 1905 *W*
Flett, A B (Edinburgh U) 1901 *W, I, E*, 1902 *W, I*
Forbes, J L (Watsonians) 1905 *W*, 1906 *I, E*
Ford, D St C (United Services, RN) 1930 *I, E*, 1931 *E*, 1932 *W, I*
Ford, J R (Gala) 1893 *I*
Forrest, J E (Glasgow Acads) 1932 *SA*, 1935 *E, NZ*
Forrest, J G S (Cambridge U) 1938 *W, I, E*
Forrest, W T (Hawick) 1903 *W, I, E*, 1904 *W, I, E*, 1905 *W, I*
Forsayth, H H (Oxford U) 1921 *F, W, I, E*, 1922 *W, I, E*
Forsyth, I W (Stewart's Coll FP) 1972 *NZ*, 1973 *F, W, I, E, P*
Forsyth, J (Edinburgh U) 1871 *E*
Foster, R A (Hawick) 1930 *W*, 1932 *SA, I, E*
Fox, J (Gala) 1952 *F, W, I, E*
Frame, J N M (Edinburgh U, Gala) 1967 *NZ*, 1968 *F, W, I, E*, 1969 *W, I, E, SA*, 1970 *F, W, I, E, A*, 1971 *F, W, I, E* (2[1C]), 1972 *F, W, E*, 1973 *P* (R)
France, C (Kelvinside Acads) 1903 *I*
Fraser, C F P (Glasgow U) 1888 *W*, 1889 *W*
Fraser, J W (Edinburgh Inst FP) 1881 *E*
Fraser, R (Cambridge U) 1911 *F, W, I, E*
French, J (Glasgow Acads) 1886 *W*, 1887 *I, W, E*
Frew, A (Edinburgh U) 1901 *W, I, E*
Frew, G M (Glasgow HSFP) 1906 *SA*, 1907 *W, I, E*, 1908 *W, I, E*, 1909 *W, I, E*, 1910 *F, W, I*, 1911 *I, E*
Friebe, J P (Glasgow HSFP) 1952 *E*
Fullarton, I A (Edinburgh) 2000 *NZ* 1(R),2
Fulton, A K (Edinburgh U, Dollar Acads) 1952 *F*, 1954 *F*
Fyfe, K C (Cambridge U, Sale, London Scottish) 1933 *W, E*, 1934 *E*, 1935 *W, I, E, NZ*, 1936 *W, E*, 1939 *I*

Gallie, G H (Edinburgh Acads) 1939 *W*
Gallie, R A (Glasgow Acads) 1920 *F, W, I, E*, 1921 *F, W, I, E*
Gammell, W B B (Edinburgh Wands) 1977 *I, F, W*, 1978 *W, E*
Geddes, I C (London Scottish) 1906 *SA*, 1907 *W, I, E*, 1908 *W, E*
Geddes, K I (London Scottish) 1947 *F, W, I, E*
Gedge, H T S (Oxford U, London Scottish, Edinburgh Wands) 1894 *W, I, E*, 1896 *E*, 1899 *W, E*
Gedge, P M S (Edinburgh Wands) 1933 *I*
Gemmill, R (Glasgow HSFP) 1950 *F, W, I, E*, 1951 *F, W, I*

Gibson, W R (Royal HSFP) 1891 *I, E*, 1892 *W, I, E*, 1893 *W, I, E*, 1894 *W, I, E*, 1895 *W, I, E*
Gilbert-Smith, D S (London Scottish) 1952 *E*
Gilchrist, J (Glasgow Acads) 1925 *F*
Gill, A D (Gala) 1973 *P*, 1974 *W, E, I, F*
Gillespie, J I (Edinburgh Acads) 1899 *E*, 1900 *W, E*, 1901 *W, I, E*, 1902 *W, I*, 1904 *I, E*
Gillies, A C (Watsonians) 1924 *W, I, E*, 1925 *F, W, E*, 1926 *F, W*, 1927 *F, W, I, E*
Gilmour, H R (Heriot's FP) 1998 *Fj*
Gilray, C M (Oxford U, London Scottish) 1908 *E*, 1909 *W, E*, 1912 *I*
Glasgow, I C (Heriot's FP) 1997 *F* (R)
Glasgow, R J C (Dunfermline) 1962 *F, W, I, E*, 1963 *I, E*, 1964 *I, E*, 1965 *W, I*
Glen, W S (Edinburgh Wands) 1955 *W*
Gloag, L G (Cambridge U) 1949 *F, W, I, E*
Goodfellow, J (Langholm) 1928 *W, I, E*
Goodhue, F W J (London Scottish) 1890 *W, I, E*, 1891 *W, I, E*, 1892 *W, I, E*
Gordon, R (Edinburgh Wands) 1951 *W*, 1952 *F, W, I, E*, 1953 *W*
Gordon, R E (Royal Artillery) 1913 *F, W, I*
Gordon, R J (London Scottish) 1982 *A* 1,2
Gore, A C (London Scottish) 1882 *I*
Gossman, B M (W of Scotland) 1980 *W*, 1983 *F, W*
Gossman, J S (W of Scotland) 1980 *E* (R)
Gowans, J J (Cambridge U, London Scottish) 1893 *W*, 1894 *W, E*, 1895 *W, I, E*, 1896 *I, E*
Gowland, G C (London Scottish) 1908 *W*, 1909 *W, E*, 1910 *F, W, I, E*
Gracie, A L (Harlequins) 1921 *F, W, I, E*, 1922 *F, W, I, E*, 1923 *F, W, I, E*, 1924 *F*
Graham, G (Newcastle) 1997 *A* (R), *SA* (R), 1998 *I, F* (R), *W* (R), 1999 *F* (R), *Arg* (R), *R*, [*SA, U, Sm, NZ* (R)], 2000 *I* (R), *US, A, Sm*, 2001 *I* (R)
Graham, I N (Edinburgh Acads) 1939 *I, E*
Graham, J (Kelso) 1926 *I, E*, 1927 *F, W, I, E, A*, 1928 *F, W, I, E*, 1930 *I, E*, 1932 *SA, W*
Graham, J H S (Edinburgh Acads) 1876 *E*, 1877 *I, E*, 1878 *E*, 1879 *I, E*, 1880 *I, E*, 1881 *I, E*
Grant, D (Hawick) 1965 *F, E, SA*, 1966 *F, W, I, E, A*, 1967 *F, W, I, E, NZ*, 1968 *F*
Grant, D M (East Midlands) 1911 *W, I*
Grant, M L (Harlequins) 1955 *F*, 1956 *F, W*, 1957 *F*
Grant, T O (Hawick) 1960 *I, E, SA*, 1964 *F, NZ, W*
Grant, W St C (Craigmount) 1873 *E*, 1874 *E*
Gray, C A (Nottingham) 1989 *W, E, I, F, Fj, R*, 1990 *I, F, W, E, NZ* 1,2, *Arg*, 1991 *F, W, E, [J, I, WS, E, NZ]*
Gray, D (W of Scotland) 1978 *E*, 1979 *I, F, NZ*, 1980 *I, F, W, E*, 1981 *F*
Gray, G L (Gala) 1935 *NZ*, 1937 *W, I, E*
Gray, T (Northampton, Heriot's FP) 1950 *E*, 1951 *F, E*
Greenlees, H D (Leicester) 1927 *A*, 1928 *F, W*, 1929 *I, E*, 1930 *E*
Greenlees, J R C (Cambridge U, Kelvinside Acads) 1900 *I*, 1902 *W, I, E*, 1903 *W, I, E*
Greenwood, J T (Dunfermline and Perthshire Acads) 1952 *F*, 1955 *F, W, I, E*, 1956 *F, W, I, E*, 1957 *F, W, E*, 1958 *F, W, A, I, E*, 1959 *F, W, I*
Greig, A (Glasgow HSFP) 1911 *I*
Greig, L L (Glasgow Acads, United Services) 1905 *NZ*, 1906 *SA*, 1907 *W*, 1908 *W, I*
Greig, R C (Glasgow Acads) 1893 *W*, 1897 *I*
Grieve, C F (Oxford U) 1935 *W*, 1936 *E*
Grieve, R M (Kelso) 1935 *W, I, E, NZ*, 1936 *W, I, E*
Grimes, S B (Watsonians, Newcastle) 1997 *A* (t+R), 1998 *I* (R), *F* (R), *W* (R), *E* (R), *Fj, A* 1, 2, 1999 *W, E, It, I, F, Arg, R*, [*SA, U, Sm* (R), *NZ* (R)], 2000 *I, F* (R), *W, US, A, Sm* (R), 2001 *F* (R), *W* (R), *E* (R), *It, I* (R)
Gunn, A W (Royal HSFP) 1912 *F, W, I, SA*, 1913 *F*

Hamilton, A S (Headingley) 1914 *W*, 1920 *F*
Hamilton, H M (W of Scotland) 1874 *E*, 1875 *E*
Hannah, R S M (W of Scotland) 1971 *I*
Harrower, P R (London Scottish) 1885 *W*
Hart, J G M (London Scottish) 1951 *SA*
Hart, T M (Glasgow U) 1930 *W, I*
Hart, W (Melrose) 1960 *SA*
Harvey, L (Greenock Wands) 1899 *I*
Hastie, A J (Melrose) 1961 *W, I, E*, 1964 *I, E*, 1965 *E, SA*, 1966 *F, W, I, E, A*, 1967 *F, W, I, NZ*, 1968 *F, W*
Hastie, I R (Kelso) 1955 *F*, 1958 *F, E*, 1959 *F, W, I*

Hastie, J D H (Melrose) 1938 *W, I, E*
Hastings, A G (Cambridge U, Watsonians, London Scottish) 1986 *F, W, E, I, R*, 1987 *I, F, W, E*, [*F, Z, R, NZ*], 1988 *I, F, W, E, A*, 1989 *Fj, R*, 1990 *I, F, W, E, NZ* 1,2, *Arg*, 1991 *F, W, E, I*, [*J, I, WS, E, NZ*], 1992 *E, I, F, W, A* 1, 1993 *I, F, W, E, NZ*, 1994 *W, E, I, F, SA*, 1995 *C, I, F, W, E*, [*Iv, Tg, F, NZ*]
Hastings, S (Watsonians) 1986 *F, W, E, I, R*, 1987 *I, F, W*, [*R*], 1988 *I, F, W, A*, 1989 *W, E, I, F, Fj, R*, 1990 *I, F, W, E, NZ* 1,2, *Arg*, 1991 *F, W, E, I*, [*J, Z, I, WS, E, NZ*], 1992 *E, I, F, W, A* 1,2, 1993 *I, F, W, E, NZ*, 1994 *I, F, SA*, 1995 *W, E, R* (R), [*Tg, F, NZ*], 1996 *I, F, W, E, NZ* 2, *It*, 1997 *W, E* (R)
Hay, B H (Boroughmuir) 1975 *NZ, A*, 1976 *F*, 1978 *I, F, W, E, NZ*, 1979 *W, E, I, F, NZ*, 1980 *I, F, W, E*, 1981 *F, W, E, I, NZ* 1,2
Hay, J A (Hawick) 1995 *WS*
Hay-Gordon, J R (Edinburgh Acads) 1875 *E*, 1877 *I, E*
Hegarty, C B (Hawick) 1978 *I, F, W, E*
Hegarty, J J (Hawick) 1951 *F*, 1953 *F, W, I, E*, 1955 *F*
Henderson, A (Glasgow) 2001 *I* (R)
Henderson, B C (Edinburgh Wands) 1963 *E*, 1964 *F, I, E*, 1965 *F, W, I, E*, 1966 *F, W, I, E*
Henderson, F W (London Scottish) 1900 *W, I*
Henderson, I C (Edinburgh Acads) 1939 *I, E*, 1947 *F, W, E, A*, 1948 *I, E*
Henderson, J H (Oxford U, Richmond) 1953 *F, W, I, E*, 1954 *F, NZ, I, E, W*
Henderson, J M (Edinburgh Acads) 1933 *W, E, I*
Henderson, J Y M (Watsonians) 1911 *E*
Henderson, M M (Dunfermline) 1937 *W, I, E*
Henderson, N F (London Scottish) 1892 *I*
Henderson, R G (Newcastle Northern) 1924 *I, E*
Hendric, K G P (Heriot's FP) 1924 *F, W, I*
Hendry, T L (Clydesdale) 1893 *W, I, E*, 1895 *I*
Henriksen, E H (Royal HSFP) 1953 *I*
Hepburn, D P (Woodford) 1947 *A*, 1948 *F, W, I, E*, 1949 *F, W, I, E*
Heron, G (Glasgow Acads) 1874 *E*, 1875 *E*
Hill, C C P (St Andrew's U) 1912 *F, I*
Hilton, D I W (Bath, Glasgow) 1995 *C, I, F, W, E, R*, [*Tg, F, NZ*], *WS*, 1996 *I, F, W, E, NZ* 1,2, *A, It*, 1997 *W, A, SA*, 1998 *It, I* (R), *F, W, E, A* 1,2, *Sa* (R), 1999 *E* (R), *It* (R), *I* (R), *F, R* (R), [*SA* (R), *U* (R), *Sp*], 2000 *It* (R), *F* (R), *W* (R)
Hines, N J (Edinburgh) 2000 *NZ* 2(R)
Hinshelwood, A J W (London Scottish) 1966 *F, W, I, E, A*, 1967 *F, W, I, E, NZ*, 1968 *F, W, I, E, A*, 1969 *F, W, I, SA*, 1970 *F, W*
Hodge D W (Watsonians, Edinburgh) 1997 *F* (R), *A, SA* (t+R), 1998 *A* 2(R), *SA*, 1999 *W, Arg, R*, [*Sp, Sm* (R)], 2000 *F* (R), *W, E, NZ* 1,2, *US* (R), *Sm* (R), 2001 *F* (R), *W, E, It, I* (R)
Hodgson, C G (London Scottish) 1968 *I, E*
Hogg, C D (Melrose) 1992 *A* 1,2, 1993 *NZ* (R), 1994 *Arg* 1,2
Hogg, C G (Boroughmuir) 1978 *F* (R), *W* (R)
Holmes, S D (London Scottish) 1998 *It, I, F*
Holms, W F (RIE Coll) 1886 *W, E*, 1887 *I, E*, 1889 *W, I*
Horsburgh, G B (London Scottish) 1937 *W, I, E*, 1938 *W, I, E*, 1939 *W, I, E*
Howie, D D (Kirkcaldy) 1912 *F, W, I, E, SA*, 1913 *F, W*
Howie, R A (Kirkcaldy) 1924 *F, W, I, E*, 1925 *W, I, E*
Hoyer-Millar, G C (Oxford U) 1953 *I*
Huggan, J L (London Scottish) 1914 *E*
Hume, J (Royal HSFP) 1912 *F*, 1920 *F*, 1921 *F, W, I, E*, 1922 *F*
Hume, J W G (Oxford U, Edinburgh Wands) 1928 *I*, 1930 *F*
Hunter, F (Edinburgh U) 1882 *I*
Hunter, I G (Selkirk) 1984 *I* (R), 1985 *F* (R), *W, E*
Hunter, J M (Cambridge U) 1947 *F*
Hunter, M D (Glasgow High) 1974 *F*
Hunter, W J (Hawick) 1964 *F, NZ, W*, 1967 *F, W, I, E*
Hutchison, W R (Glasgow HSFP) 1911 *E*
Hutton, A H M (Dunfermline) 1932 *I*
Hutton, J E (Harlequins) 1930 *E*, 1931 *F*

Inglis, H M (Edinburgh Acads) 1951 *F, W, I, E, SA*, 1952 *W, I*
Inglis, J M (Selkirk) 1952 *E*
Inglis, W M (Cambridge U, Royal Engineers) 1937 *W, I, E*, 1938 *W, I, E*
Innes, J R S (Aberdeen GSFP) 1939 *W, I, E*, 1947 *A*, 1948 *F, W, I, E*
Ireland, J C H (Glasgow HSFP) 1925 *W, I, E*, 1926 *F, W, I, E*, 1927 *F, W, I, E*
Irvine, A R (Heriot's FP) 1972 *NZ*, 1973 *F, W, I, E, P*, 1974 *W, E, I, F*, 1975 *I, F, W, E, NZ, A*, 1976 *F, W, E, I*, 1977 *E, I, F*,

W, 1978 *I, F, E, NZ*, 1979 *W, E, I, F, NZ*, 1980 *I, F, W, E*, 1981 *F, W, E, I, NZ* 1,2, *R, A*, 1982 *E, I, F, W, A* 1,2
Irvine, D R (Edinburgh Acads) 1878 *E*, 1879 *I, E*
Irvine, R W (Edinburgh Acads) 1871 *E*, 1872 *E*, 1873 *E*, 1874 *E*, 1875 *E*, 1876 *E*, 1877 *I, E*, 1878 *E*, 1879 *I, E*, 1880 *I, E*
Irvine T W (Edinburgh Acads) 1885 *I* 1,2, 1886 *W, I, E*, 1887 *I, W, E*, 1888 *W, I*, 1889 *I*

Jackson, K L T (Oxford U) 1933 *W, E, I*, 1934 *W*
Jackson, T G H (Army) 1947 *F, W, E, A*, 1948 *F, W, I, E*, 1949 *F, W, I, E*
Jackson, W D (Hawick) 1964 *I*, 1965 *E, SA*, 1968 *A*, 1969 *F, W, I, E*
Jamieson, J (W of Scotland) 1883 *W, I, E*, 1884 *W, I, E*, 1885 *W, I* 1,2
Jardine, I C (Stirling County) 1993 *NZ*, 1994 *W, E* (R), *Arg* 1,2, 1995 *C, I, F*, [*Tg, F* (t & R), *NZ* (R)], 1996 *I, F, W, E, NZ* 1,2, 1998 *Fj*
Jeffrey, J (Kelso) 1984 *A*, 1985 *I, E*, 1986 *F, W, E, I, R*, 1987 *I, F, W, E*, [*F, Z, R*], 1988 *I, W, A*, 1989 *W, E, I, F, Fj, R*, 1990 *I, F, W, E, NZ* 1,2, *Arg*, 1991 *F, W, E, I*, [*J, I, WS, E, NZ*]
Johnston, D I (Watsonians) 1979 *NZ*, 1980 *I, F, W, E*, 1981 *R, A*, 1982 *E, I, F, W, A* 1,2, 1983 *I, F, W, NZ*, 1984 *W, E, I, F, R*, 1986 *F, W, E, I, R*
Johnston, H H (Edinburgh Collegian FP) 1877 *I, E*
Johnston, J (Melrose) 1951 *SA*, 1952 *F, W, I, E*
Johnston, W C (Glasgow HSFP) 1922 *F*
Johnston, W G S (Cambridge U) 1935 *W, I*, 1937 *W, I, E*
Joiner, C A (Melrose, Leicester) 1994 *Arg* 1,2, 1995 *C, I, F, W, E, R*, [*Iv, Tg, F, NZ*], 1996 *I, F, W, E, NZ* 1, 1997 *SA*, 1998 *It, I, A* 2(R), 2000 *NZ* 1(R),2, *US* (R)
Jones, P M (Gloucester) 1992 *W* (R)
Junor, J E (Glasgow Acads) 1876 *E*, 1877 *I, E*, 1878 *E*, 1879 *E*, 1881 *I*

Keddie, R R (Watsonians) 1967 *NZ*
Keith, G J (Wasps) 1968 *F, W*
Keller, D H (London Scottish) 1949 *F, W, I, E*, 1950 *F, W, I*
Kelly, R F (Watsonians) 1927 *A*, 1928 *F, W, E*
Kemp, J W Y (Glasgow HSFP) 1954 *W*, 1955 *F, W, I, E*, 1956 *F, W, I, E*, 1957 *F, W, I, E*, 1958 *F, W, A, I, E*, 1959 *F, W, I, E*, 1960 *F, W, I, E, SA*
Kennedy, A E (Watsonians) 1983 *NZ*, 1984 *W, E, A*
Kennedy, F (Stewart's Coll FP) 1920 *F, W, I, E*, 1921 *E*
Kennedy, N (W of Scotland) 1903 *W, I, E*
Ker, A B M (Kelso) 1988 *W, E*
Ker, H T (Glasgow Acads) 1887 *I, W, E*, 1888 *I*, 1889 *W*, 1890 *I, E*
Kerr, D S (Heriot's FP) 1923 *F, W*, 1924 *F*, 1926 *I, E*, 1927 *W, I, E*, 1928 *I, E*
Kerr, G C (Old Dunelmians, Edinburgh Wands) 1898 *I, E*, 1899 *I, W, E*, 1900 *W, I, E*
Kerr, J M (Heriot's FP) 1935 *NZ*, 1936 *I, E*, 1937 *W, I*
Kerr, W (London Scottish) 1953 *E*
Kidston, D W (Glasgow Acads) 1883 *W, E*
Kidston, W H (W of Scotland) 1874 *E*
Kilgour, I J (RMC Sandhurst) 1921 *F*
King, J H F (Selkirk) 1953 *F, W, E*, 1954 *E*
Kininmonth, P W (Oxford U, Richmond) 1949 *F, W, I, E*, 1950 *F, W, I, E*, 1951 *F, W, I, E, SA*, 1952 *F, W, I*, 1954 *F, NZ, I, E, W*
Kinnear, R M (Heriot's FP) 1926 *F, W, I*
Knox, J (Kelvinside Acads) 1903 *W, I, E*
Kyle, W E (Hawick) 1902 *W, I, E*, 1903 *W, I, E*, 1904 *W, I, E*, 1905 *W, I, E, NZ*, 1906 *W, I, E*, 1908 *E*, 1909 *W, I, E*, 1910 *W*

Laidlaw, A S (Hawick) 1897 *I*
Laidlaw, F A L (Melrose) 1965 *F, W, I, E, SA*, 1966 *F, W, I, E, A*, 1967 *F, W, I, E, NZ*, 1968 *F, W, I, A*, 1969 *F, W, I, E, SA*, 1970 *F, W, I, E, A*, 1971 *F, W, I*
Laidlaw, R J (Jedforest) 1980 *I, F, W, E*, 1981 *F, W, E, I, NZ* 1,2, *R, A*, 1982 *E, I, F, W, A* 1,2, 1983 *I, F, W, E, NZ*, 1984 *W, E, I, F, R, A*, 1985 *I, F*, 1986 *F, W, E, I, R*, 1987 *I, F, W, E*, [*F, R, NZ*], 1988 *I, F, W, E*
Laing, A D (Royal HSFP) 1914 *W, I, E*, 1920 *F, W, I*, 1921 *F*
Lambie, I K (Watsonians) 1978 *NZ* (R), 1979 *W, E, NZ*
Lambie, L B (Glasgow HSFP) 1934 *W, I, E*, 1935 *W, I, E, NZ*
Lamond, G A W (Kelvinside Acads) 1899 *W, E*, 1905 *E*
Lang, D (Paisley) 1876 *E*, 1877 *I*
Langrish, R W (London Scottish) 1930 *F*, 1931 *F, W, I*
Lauder, W (Neath) 1969 *I, E, SA*, 1970 *F, W, I, A*, 1973 *F*, 1974 *W, E, I, F*, 1975 *I, F, NZ, A*, 1976 *F*, 1977 *E*

Laughland, I H P (London Scottish) 1959 *F*, 1960 *F, W, I, E*, 1961 *SA, W, I, E*, 1962 *F, W, I, E*, 1963 *F, W, I*, 1964 *F, NZ, W, I, E*, 1965 *F, W, I, E, SA*, 1966 *F, W, I, E*, 1967 *E*
Lawrie, J R (Melrose) 1922 *F, W, I, E*, 1923 *F, W, I, E*, 1924 *W, I, E*
Lawrie, K G (Gala) 1980 *F* (R), *W, E*
Lawson, A J M (Edinburgh Wands, London Scottish) 1972 *F* (R), *E*, 1973 *F*, 1974 *W, E*, 1976 *E, I*, 1977 *E*, 1978 *NZ*, 1979 *W, E, I, F, NZ*, 1980 *W* (R)
Lawther, T H B (Old Millhillians) 1932 *SA, W*
Ledingham, G A (Aberdeen GSFP) 1913 *F*
Lee, D J (London Scottish) 1998 *I* (R), *F, W, E, Fj, A* 1,2, *SA*
Lees, J B (Gala) 1947 *I, A*, 1948 *F, W, E*
Leggatt, H T O (Watsonians) 1891 *W, I, E*, 1892 *W, I*, 1893 *W, E*, 1894 *I, E*
Lely, W G (Cambridge U, London Scottish) 1909 *I*
Leslie, D G (Dundee HSFP, W of Scotland, Gala) 1975 *I, F, W, E, NZ, A*, 1976 *W, E, I*, 1978 *NZ*, 1980 *E*, 1981 *W, E, I, NZ* 1,2, *R, A*, 1982 *E*, 1983 *I, F, W, E*, 1984 *W, E, I, F, R*, 1985 *F, W, E*
Leslie, J A (Glasgow, Northampton) 1998 *SA*, 1999 *W, E, It, I, F*, [*SA*], 2000 *It, F, W, US, A, Sm*, 2001 *F, W, E, It, I*
Leslie, M D (Glasgow) 1998 *SA* (R), 1999 *W, E, It, I, F, R*, [*SA, U, Sm, NZ*], 2000 *It, I, F, W, E, NZ* 1,2, 2001 *F, W, E, It*
Liddell, E H (Edinburgh U) 1922 *F, W, I*, 1923 *F, W, I, E*
Lind, H (Dunfermline) 1928 *I*, 1931 *F, W, I, E*, 1932 *SA, W, E*, 1933 *W, E, I*, 1934 *W, I, E*, 1935 *I*, 1936 *E*
Lindsay, A B (London Hospital) 1910 *I*, 1911 *I*
Lindsay, G C (London Scottish) 1884 *W*, 1885 *I* 1, 1887 *W, E*
Lindsay-Watson, R H (Hawick) 1909 *I*
Lineen, S R P (Boroughmuir) 1989 *W, E, I, F, Fj, R*, 1990 *I, F, W, E, NZ* 1,2, *Arg*, 1991 *F, W, E, I, R*, [*J, Z, I, E, NZ*], 1992 *E, I, F, W, A* 1,2
Little, A W (Hawick) 1905 *W*
Logan, K M (Stirling County, Wasps) 1992 *A* 2, 1993 *E* (R), *NZ* (t), 1994 *W, E, I, F, Arg* 1,2, *SA*, 1995 *C, I, F, W, E, R*, [*Iv, Tg, F, NZ*], *WS*, 1996 *W* (R), *NZ* 1,2, *A, It*, 1997 *W, E, I, F, A*, 1998 *I, F, SA* (R), 1999 *W, E, It, I, F, Arg, R*, [*SA, U, Sm, NZ*], 2000 *It, I, F, Sm*, 2001 *F, W, E, It*
Logan, W R (Edinburgh U, Edinburgh Wands) 1931 *E*, 1932 *SA, W, I*, 1933 *W, E, I*, 1934 *W, I, E*, 1935 *W, I, E, NZ*, 1936 *W, I, E*, 1937 *W, I, E*
Longstaff, S L (Dundee HSFP, Glasgow) 1998 *F* (R), *W, E, Fj, A* 1,2 1999 *It* (R), *I* (R), *Arg* (R), *R*, [*U* (R), *Sp*], 2000 *It, I, NZ* 1
Lorraine, H D B (Oxford U) 1933 *W, E, I*
Loudoun-Shand, E G (Oxford U) 1913 *E*
Lowe, J D (Heriot's FP) 1934 *W*
Lumsden, I J M (Bath, Watsonians) 1947 *F, W, A*, 1949 *F, W, I, E*
Lyall, G G (Gala) 1947 *A*, 1948 *F, W, I, E*
Lyall, W J C (Edinburgh Acads) 1871 *E*

Mabon, J T (Jedforest) 1898 *I, E*, 1899 *I*, 1900 *I*
Macarthur, J P (Waterloo) 1932 *E*
MacCallum, J C (Watsonians) 1905 *E, NZ*, 1906 *W, I, E, SA*, 1907 *W, I, E*, 1908 *W, I, E*, 1909 *W, I, E*, 1910 *F, W, I, E*, 1911 *F, I, E*, 1912 *F, W, I, E*
McClung, T (Edinburgh Acads) 1956 *I, E*, 1957 *W, I, E*, 1959 *F, W, I*, 1960 *W*
McClure, G B (W of Scotland) 1873 *E*
McClure, J H (W of Scotland) 1872 *E*
McCowan, D (W of Scotland) 1880 *I, E*, 1881 *I, E*, 1882 *I, E*, 1883 *I, E*, 1884 *I, E*
McCowat, R H (Glasgow Acads) 1905 *I*
McCrae, I G (Gordonians) 1967 *E*, 1968 *I*, 1969 *F* (R), *W*, 1972 *F, NZ*
McCrow, J W S (Edinburgh Acads) 1921 *I*
Macdonald, A E D (Heriot's FP) 1993 *NZ*
McDonald, C (Jedforest) 1947 *A*
Macdonald, D C (Edinburgh U) 1953 *F, W*, 1958 *I, E*
Macdonald, D S M (Oxford U, London Scottish, W of Scotland) 1977 *E, I, F, W*, 1978 *I, W, E*
Macdonald, J D (London Scottish, Army) 1966 *F, W, I, E*, 1967 *F, W, I, E*
Macdonald, J M (Edinburgh Wands) 1911 *W*
Macdonald, J S (Edinburgh U) 1903 *E*, 1904 *W, I, E*, 1905 *W*
Macdonald, K R (Stewart's Coll FP) 1956 *F, W, I*, 1957 *W, I, E*
Macdonald, R (Edinburgh U) 1950 *F, W, I, E*
McDonald, W A (Glasgow U) 1889 *W*, 1892 *I, E*
Macdonald, W G (London Scottish) 1969 *I* (R)

Macdougall, J B (Greenock Wands, Wakefield) 1913 *F*, 1914 *I*, 1921 *F, I, E*
McEwan, M C (Edinburgh Acads) 1886 *E*, 1887 *I, W, E*, 1888 *W, I*, 1889 *W, I*, 1890 *W, I, E*, 1891 *W, I, E*, 1892 *E*
MacEwan, N A (Gala, Highland) 1971 *F, W, I, E* (2[1C]), 1972 *F, W, E, NZ*, 1973 *F, W, I, E, P*, 1974 *W, E, I, F*, 1975 *W, E*
McEwan, W M C (Edinburgh Acads) 1894 *W, E*, 1895 *W, E*, 1896 *W, I, E*, 1897 *I, E*, 1898 *I, E*, 1899 *I, W, E*, 1900 *W, E*
MacEwen, R K G (Cambridge U, London Scottish) 1954 *F, NZ, I, W*, 1956 *F, W, I, E*, 1957 *F, W, I, E*, 1958 *W*
Macfarlan, D J (London Scottish) 1883 *W*, 1884 *W, I, E*, 1886 *W, I*, 1887 *I*, 1888 *I*
McFarlane, J L H (Edinburgh U) 1871 *E*, 1872 *E*, 1873 *E*
McGaughey, S K (Hawick) 1984 *R*
McGeechan, I R (Headingley) 1972 *NZ*, 1973 *F, W, I, E, P*, 1974 *W, E, I, F*, 1975 *I, F, W, E, NZ, A*, 1976 *F, W, E, I*, 1977 *E, I, F, W*, 1978 *I, F, W, NZ*, 1979 *W, E, I, F*
McGlashan, T P L (Royal HSFP) 1947 *F, I, E*, 1954 *F, NZ, I, E, W*
MacGregor, D G (Watsonians, Pontypridd) 1907 *W, I, E*
MacGregor, G (Cambridge U) 1890 *W, I, E*, 1891 *W, I, E*, 1893 *W, I, E*, 1894 *W, I, E*, 1896 *E*
MacGregor, I A A (Hillhead HSFP, Llanelli) 1955 *I, E*, 1956 *F, W, I, E*, 1957 *F, W, I*
MacGregor, J R (Edinburgh U) 1909 *I*
McGuinness, G M (W of Scotland) 1982 *A* 1,2, 1983 *I*, 1985 *I, F, W, E*
McHarg, A F (W of Scotland, London Scottish) 1968 *I, E, A*, 1969 *F, W, I, E*, 1971 *F, W, I, E* (2[1C]), 1972 *F, E, NZ*, 1973 *F, W, I, E, P*, 1974 *W, E, I, F*, 1975 *I, F, W, E, NZ, A*, 1976 *F, W, E, I*, 1977 *E, I, F, W*, 1978 *I, F, W, NZ*, 1979 *W, E*
McIlwham, G R (Glasgow Hawks, Glasgow) 1998 *Fj, A* 2(R), 2000 *E* (R), *NZ* 2(R), *US* (R), *A* (R), *Sm* (R), 2001 *F* (R), *W* (R), *E* (R), *It* (R)
McIndoe, F (Glasgow Acads) 1886 *W, I*
MacIntyre, I (Edinburgh Wands) 1890 *W, I, E*, 1891 *W, I, E*
McIvor, D J (Edinburgh Acads) 1992 *E, I, F, W*, 1993 *NZ*, 1994 *SA*
Mackay, E B (Glasgow Acads) 1920 *W*, 1922 *E*
McKeating, E (Heriot's FP) 1957 *F, W*, 1961 *SA, W, I, E*
McKelvey, G (Watsonians) 1997 *A*
McKendrick, J G (W of Scotland) 1889 *I*
Mackenzie, A D G (Selkirk) 1984 *A*
Mackenzie, C J G (United Services) 1921 *E*
Mackenzie, D D (Edinburgh U) 1947 *W, I, E*, 1948 *F, W, I*
Mackenzie, D K A (Edinburgh Wands) 1939 *I, E*
Mackenzie, J M (Edinburgh U) 1905 *NZ*, 1909 *W, I, E*, 1910 *W, I, E*, 1911 *W, I*
McKenzie, K D (Stirling County) 1994 *Arg* 1,2, 1995 *R*, [*Iv*], 1996 *I, F, W, E, NZ* 1,2, *A, It*, 1998 *A* 1(R), 2
Mackenzie, R C (Glasgow Acads) 1877 *I, E*, 1881 *I, E*
Mackie, G Y (Highland) 1975 *A*, 1976 *F, W*, 1978 *F*
MacKinnon, A (London Scottish) 1898 *I, E*, 1899 *I, W, E*, 1900 *E*
Mackintosh, C E W C (London Scottish) 1924 *F*
Mackintosh, H S (Glasgow U, W of Scotland) 1929 *F, W, I, E*, 1930 *F, W, I, E*, 1931 *F, W, I, E*, 1932 *SA, W, I, E*
MacLachlan, L P (Oxford U, London Scottish) 1954 *NZ, I, E, W*
Maclagan, W E (Edinburgh Acads) 1878 *E*, 1879 *I, E*, 1880 *I, E*, 1881 *I, E*, 1882 *I, E*, 1883 *W, I, E*, 1884 *W, I, E*, 1885 *W, I* 1,2, 1887 *I, W, E*, 1888 *W, I*, 1890 *W, I, E*
McLaren, A (Durham County) 1931 *F*
McLaren, E (London Scottish, Royal HSFP) 1923 *F, W, I, E*, 1924 *F*
McLaren, J G (Bourgoin, Glasgow) 1999 *Arg, R*, [*Sp, Sm*], 2000 *It* (R), *F, E, NZ* 1, 2001 *F, W, E* (R), *I*
McLauchlan, J (Jordanhill) 1969 *E, SA*, 1970 *F, W*, 1971 *F, W, I, E* (2[1C]), 1972 *F, W, E, NZ*, 1973 *F, W, I, E, P*, 1974 *W, E, I, F*, 1975 *I, F, W, E, NZ, A*, 1976 *F, W, E, I*, 1977 *W, I, F, W, E, NZ*, 1979 *W, E, I, F, NZ*
McLean, D I (Royal HSFP) 1947 *I, E*
Maclennan, W D (Watsonians) 1947 *F, I*
MacLeod, D A (Glasgow U) 1886 *I, E*
MacLeod, G (Edinburgh Acads) 1878 *E*, 1882 *I*
McLeod, H F (Hawick) 1954 *F, NZ, I, E, W*, 1955 *F, W, I, E*, 1956 *F, W, I, E*, 1957 *F, W, I, E*, 1958 *F, W, A, I, E*, 1959 *F, W, I, E*, 1960 *F, W, I, E, SA*, 1961 *F, SA, W, I, E*, 1962 *F, W, I, E*
MacLeod, K G (Cambridge U) 1905 *NZ*, 1906 *W, I, E, SA*, 1907 *W, I, E*, 1908 *I, E*
MacLeod, L M (Cambridge U) 1904 *W, I, E*, 1905 *W, I, NZ*

Macleod, W M (Fettesian-Lorettonians, Edinburgh Wands) 1886 *W, I*
McMillan, K H D (Sale) 1953 *F, W, I, E*
MacMillan, R G (London Scottish) 1887 *W, I, E*, 1890 *W, I, E*, 1891 *W, E*, 1892 *W, I, E*, 1893 *W, E*, 1894 *W, I, E*, 1895 *W, I, E*, 1897 *I, E*
MacMyn, D J (Cambridge U, London Scottish) 1925 *F, W, I, E*, 1926 *F, W, I, E*, 1927 *E, A*, 1928 *F*
McNeil, A S B (Watsonians) 1935 *I*
McPartlin, J J (Harlequins, Oxford U) 1960 *F, W*, 1962 *F, W, I, E*
Macphail, J A R (Edinburgh Acads) 1949 *E*, 1951 *SA*
Macpherson, D G (London Hospital) 1910 *I, E*
Macpherson, G P S (Oxford U, Edinburgh Acads) 1922 *F, W, I, E*, 1924 *W, E*, 1925 *F, W, E*, 1927 *F, W, I, E*, 1928 *F, W, E*, 1929 *I, E*, 1930 *F, W, I, E*, 1931 *W, E*, 1932 *SA, E*
Macpherson, N C (Newport) 1920 *W, I, E*, 1921 *F, E*, 1923 *I, E*
McQueen, S B (Waterloo) 1923 *F, W, I, E*
Macrae, D J (St Andrew's U) 1937 *W, I, E*, 1938 *W, I, E*, 1939 *W, I, E*
Madsen, D F (Gosforth) 1974 *W, E, I, F*, 1975 *I, F, W, E*, 1976 *F*, 1977 *E, I, F, W*, 1978 *I*
Mair, N G R (Edinburgh U) 1951 *F, W, I, E*
Maitland, G (Edinburgh Inst FP) 1885 *W, I* 2
Maitland, R (Edinburgh Inst FP) 1881 *E*, 1882 *I, E*, 1884 *W*, 1885 *W*
Maitland, R P (Royal Artillery) 1872 *E*
Malcolm, A G (Glasgow U) 1888 *I*
Manson, J J (Dundee HSFP) 1995 *E* (R)
Marsh, J (Edinburgh Inst FP) 1889 *W, I*
Marshall, A (Edinburgh Acads) 1875 *E*
Marshall, G R (Selkirk) 1988 *A* (R), 1989 *Fj*, 1990 *Arg*, 1991 [*Z*]
Marshall, J C (London Scottish) 1954 *F, NZ, I, E, W*
Marshall, K W (Edinburgh Acads) 1934 *W, I, E*, 1935 *W, I, E*, 1936 *W, I*, 1937 *E*
Marshall, T R (Edinburgh Acads) 1871 *E*, 1872 *E*, 1873 *E*, 1874 *E*
Marshall, W (Edinburgh Acads) 1872 *E*
Martin, H (Edinburgh Acads, Oxford U) 1908 *W, I, E*, 1909 *W, E*
Masters, W H (Edinburgh Inst FP) 1879 *I*, 1880 *I, E*
Mather, C G (Edinburgh) 1999 *R* (R), [*Sp, Sm* (R)], 2000 *F* (t)
Maxwell, F T (Royal Engineers) 1872 *E*
Maxwell, G H H P (Edinburgh Acads, RAF, London Scottish) 1913 *I, E*, 1914 *W, I, E*, 1920 *W, E*, 1921 *F, W, I, E*, 1922 *F, E*
Maxwell, J M (Langholm) 1957 *I*
Mayer, M J M (Watsonians, Edinburgh) 1998 *SA*, 1999 [*SA* (R), *U, Sp, Sm, NZ*], 2000 *It, I*
Mein, J (Edinburgh Acads) 1871 *E*, 1872 *E*, 1873 *E*, 1874 *E*, 1875 *E*
Melville, C L (Army) 1937 *W, I, E*
Menzies, H F (W of Scotland) 1893 *W, I*, 1894 *W, E*
Metcalfe, G H (Glasgow Hawks, Glasgow) 1998 *A* 1,2, 1999 *W, E, It, I, F, Arg, R*, [*SA, U, Sm, NZ*], 2000 *It, I, F, W, E*, 2001 *I*
Metcalfe, R (Northampton, Edinburgh) 2000 *E, NZ* 1,2, *US* (R), *A* (R), *Sm*, 2001 *F, W, E*
Methuen, A (London Scottish) 1889 *W, I*
Michie, E J S (Aberdeen U, Aberdeen GSFP) 1954 *F, NZ, I, E*, 1955 *W, I, E*, 1956 *F, W, I, E*, 1957 *F, W, I, E*
Millar, J N (W of Scotland) 1892 *W, I, E*, 1893 *W*, 1895 *I, E*
Millar, R K (London Scottish) 1924 *I*
Millican, J G (Edinburgh U) 1973 *W, I, E*
Milne, C J B (Fettesian-Lorettonians, W of Scotland) 1886 *W, I, E*
Milne, D F (Heriot's FP) 1991 [*J*(R)]
Milne, I G (Heriot's FP, Harlequins) 1979 *I, F, NZ*, 1980 *I, F*, 1981 *NZ* 1,2, *R, A*, 1982 *E, I, F, W, A* 1,2, 1983 *I, F, W, E, NZ*, 1984 *W, E, I, F, A*, 1985 *F, W, E*, 1986 *F, W, E, I, R*, 1987 *I, F, W, E*, [*F, Z, NZ*], 1988 *A*, 1989 *W, I*, 1990 *NZ* 1,2
Milne, K S (Heriot's FP) 1989 *W, E, I, F, Fj, R*, 1990 *I, F, W, E, NZ* 2, *Arg*, 1991 *W* (R), *E*, [*Z*], 1992 *E, I, F, W, A* 1, 1993 *I, F, W, E, NZ*, 1994 *W, E, I, F, SA*, 1995 *C, I, F, W, E*, [*Tg, F, NZ*]
Milne, W M (Glasgow Acads) 1904 *I, E*, 1905 *W, I*
Milroy, E (Watsonians) 1910 *W, I*, 1911 *E, I*, 1912 *W, I, E, SA*, 1913 *F, W, I, E*, 1914 *I, E*
Mitchell, G W E (Edinburgh Wands) 1967 *NZ*, 1968 *F, W*
Mitchell, J G (W of Scotland) 1885 *W, I* 1,2

Moir, C C (Northampton) 2000 *W, E, NZ* 1
Moncreiff, F J (Edinburgh Acads) 1871 *E*, 1872 *E*, 1873 *E*
Monteith, H G (Cambridge U, London Scottish) 1905 *E*, 1906 *W, I, E, SA*, 1907 *W, I*, 1908 *E*
Monypenny, D B (London Scottish) 1899 *I, W, E*
Moodie, A R (St Andrew's U) 1909 *E*, 1910 *F*, 1911 *F*
Moore, A (Edinburgh Acads) 1990 *NZ* 2, *Arg*, 1991 *F, W, E*
Morgan, D W (Stewart's-Melville FP) 1973 *W, I, E, P*, 1974 *I, F*, 1975 *I, F, W, E, NZ, A*, 1976 *F, W*, 1977 *I, F, W*, 1978 *I, F, W, E*
Morrison, I R (London Scottish) 1993 *I, F, W, E*, 1994 *W, SA*, 1995 *C, I, F, W, E, R*, [*Tg, F, NZ*]
Morrison, M C (Royal HSFP) 1896 *W, I, E*, 1897 *I, E*, 1898 *I, E*, 1899 *I, W, E*, 1900 *W, E*, 1901 *W, I, E*, 1902 *W, I, E*, 1903 *W, I*, 1904 *W, I, E*
Morrison, R H (Edinburgh U) 1886 *W, I, E*
Morrison, W H (Edinburgh Acads) 1900 *W*
Morton, D S (W of Scotland) 1887 *I, W, E*, 1888 *W, I*, 1889 *W, I*, 1890 *I, E*
Mowat, J G (Glasgow Acads) 1883 *W, E*
Muir, D E (Heriot's FP) 1950 *F, W, I, E*, 1952 *W, I, E*
Munnoch, N M (Watsonians) 1952 *F, W, I*
Munro, D S (Glasgow High Kelvinside) 1994 *W, E, I, F, Arg* 1,2, 1997 *W* (R)
Munro, P (Oxford U, London Scottish) 1905 *W, I, E, NZ*, 1906 *W, I, E, SA*, 1907 *I, E*, 1911 *F, W, I*
Munro, R (St Andrew's U) 1871 *E*
Munro, S (Ayr, W of Scotland) 1980 *I, F*, 1981 *F, W, E, I, NZ* 1,2, *R*, 1984 *W*
Munro, W H (Glasgow HSFP) 1947 *I, E*
Murdoch, W C W (Hillhead HSFP) 1935 *E, NZ*, 1936 *W, I*, 1939 *E*, 1948 *F, W, I, E*
Murray, C A (Hawick, Edinburgh) 1998 *E* (R), *Fj, A* 1,2, *SA*, 1999 *W, E, It, I, F, Arg*, [*SA, U, Sm, NZ*], 2000 *NZ* 2, *US, A, Sm*, 2001 *F, W, E, It* (R)
Murray, G M (Glasgow Acads) 1921 *I*, 1926 *W*
Murray, H M (Glasgow U) 1936 *W, I*
Murray, K T (Hawick) 1985 *I, F, W*
Murray, R O (Cambridge U) 1935 *W, E*
Murray, S (Bedford, Saracens) 1997 *A, SA*, 1998 *It, Fj, A* 1,2, *SA*, 1999 *W, E, It, I, F, Arg, R*, [*SA, U, Sm, NZ*], 2000 *It, I, F, W, E, NZ* 1, *US, A, Sm*, 2001 *F, W, E, It, I*
Murray, W A K (London Scottish) 1920 *F, I*, 1921 *F*

Napier, H M (W of Scotland) 1877 *I, E*, 1878 *E*, 1879 *I, E*
Neill, J B (Edinburgh Acads) 1963 *E*, 1964 *F, NZ, W, I, E*, 1965 *F*
Neill, R M (Edinburgh Acads) 1901 *E*, 1902 *I*
Neilson, G T (W of Scotland) 1891 *W, I, E*, 1892 *W, E*, 1893 *W*, 1894 *W, I*, 1895 *W, I, E*, 1896 *W, I, E*
Neilson, J A (Glasgow Acads) 1878 *E*, 1879 *E*
Neilson, R T (W of Scotland) 1898 *I, E*, 1899 *I, W*, 1900 *I, E*
Neilson, T (W of Scotland) 1874 *E*
Neilson, W (Merchiston, Cambridge U, London Scottish) 1891 *W, E*, 1892 *W, I, E*, 1893 *I, E*, 1894 *E*, 1895 *W, I, E*, 1896 *I*, 1897 *I, E*
Neilson, W G (Merchistonians) 1894 *E*
Nelson, J B (Glasgow Acads) 1925 *F, W, I, E*, 1926 *F, W, I, E*, 1927 *F, W, I, E*, 1928 *I, E*, 1929 *F, W, I, E*, 1930 *F, W, I, E*, 1931 *F, W, I*
Nelson, T A (Oxford U) 1898 *E*
Nichol, J A (Royal HSFP) 1955 *W, I, E*
Nichol, S A (Selkirk) 1994 *Arg* 2(R)
Nicol, A D (Dundee HSFP, Bath, Glasgow) 1992 *E, I, F, W, A* 1,2, 1993 *NZ*, 1994 *W*, 1997 *A, SA*, 2000 *I* (R), *F, W, E, NZ* 1,2, 2001 *F, W, E, I* (R)
Nimmo, C S (Watsonians) 1920 *E*

Ogilvy, C (Hawick) 1911 *I, E*, 1912 *I*
Oliver, G H (Hawick) 1987 [*Z*], 1990 *NZ* 2(R), 1991 [*Z*]
Oliver, G K (Gala) 1970 *A*
Orr, C E (W of Scotland) 1887 *I, E, W*, 1888 *W, I*, 1889 *W, I*, 1890 *W, I, E*, 1891 *W, I, E*, 1892 *W, I, E*
Orr, H J (London Scottish) 1903 *W, I, E*, 1904 *W, I*
Orr, J E (W of Scotland) 1889 *I*, 1890 *W, I, E*, 1891 *W, I, E*, 1892 *W, I, E*, 1893 *I, E*
Orr, J H (Edinburgh City Police) 1947 *F, W*
Osler, F L (Edinburgh U) 1911 *F, W*

Park, J (Royal HSFP) 1934 *W*
Paterson, C D (Edinburgh) 1999 [*Sp*], 2000 *F, W, E, NZ* 1,2, *US, A, Sm*, 2001 *F, W, E, It, I*

Paterson, D S (Gala) 1969 *SA*, 1970 *I, E, A*, 1971 *F, W, I, E* (2[1C]), 1972 *W*
Paterson, G Q (Edinburgh Acads) 1876 *E*
Paterson, J R (Birkenhead Park) 1925 *F, W, I, E*, 1926 *F, W, I, E*, 1927 *F, W, I, E, A*, 1928 *F, W, I, E*, 1929 *F, W, I, E*
Paterson, D (Hawick) 1896 *W*
Patterson, D W (West Hartlepool) 1994 *SA*, 1995 [*Tg*]
Pattullo, G L (Panmure) 1920 *F, W, I, E*
Paxton, I A M (Selkirk) 1981 *NZ* 1,2, *R, A*, 1982 *E, I, F, W, A* 1,2, 1983 *I, E, NZ*, 1984 *W, E, I, F*, 1985 *I* (R), *F, W, E*, 1986 *W, E, I, R*, 1987 *I, F, W, E*, [*F, Z, R, NZ*], 1988 *I, E, A*
Paxton, R E (Kelso) 1982 *I, A* 2(R)
Pearson, J (Watsonians) 1909 *I, E*, 1910 *F, W, I, E*, 1911 *F*, 1912 *F, W, SA*, 1913 *I, E*
Pender, I M (London Scottish) 1914 *E*
Pender, N E K (Hawick) 1977 *I*, 1978 *F, W, E*
Penman, W M (RAF) 1939 *I*
Peterkin, W A (Edinburgh U) 1881 *E*, 1883 *I*, 1884 *W, I, E*, 1885 *W, I* 1,2
Peters, E W (Bath) 1995 *C, I, F, W, E, R*, [*Tg, F, NZ*], 1996 *I, F, W, E, NZ* 1,2, *A, It*, 1997 *A, SA*, 1998 *W, E, Fj, A* 1,2, *SA*, 1999 *W, E, It, I*
Petrie, A G (Royal HSFP) 1873 *E*, 1874 *E*, 1875 *E*, 1876 *E*, 1877 *I, E*, 1878 *E*, 1879 *I, E*, 1880 *I, E*
Petrie, J M (Glasgow) 2000 *NZ* 2, *US, A, Sm*, 2001 *F, W, It* (R), *I* (R)
Philp, A (Edinburgh Inst FP) 1882 *E*
Pocock, E I (Edinburgh Wands) 1877 *I, E*
Pollock, J A (Gosforth) 1982 *W*, 1983 *E, NZ*, 1984 *E* (R), *I, F, R*, 1985 *F*
Polson, A H (Gala) 1930 *E*
Pountney, A C (Northhampton) 1998 *SA*, 1999 *W* (t+R), *E* (R), *It* (t+R), *I* (R), *F, Arg*, [*SA, U, Sm, NZ*], 2000 *It, I, F, W, E, US,A, Sm*, 2001 *F, W, E, It, I*
Proudfoot, M C (Melrose) 1998 *Fj, A* 1,2
Purdie, W (Jedforest) 1939 *W, I, E*
Purves, A B H L (London Scottish) 1906 *W, I, E, SA*, 1907 *W, I, E*, 1908 *W, I, E*
Purves, W D C L (London Scottish) 1912 *F, W, I, SA*, 1913 *I, E*

Rea, C W W (W of Scotland, Headingley) 1968 *A*, 1969 *F, W, I, SA*, 1970 *F, W, I, A*, 1971 *F, W, E* (2[1C])
Redpath, B W (Melrose, Narbonne, Sale) 1993 *NZ* (t), 1994 *E* (t), *F, Arg* 1,2, 1995 *C, I, F, W, E, R*, [*Iv, F, NZ*], *WS*, 1996 *I, F, W, E, A* (R), *It*, 1997 *E, I, F*, 1998 *Fj, A* 1,2, *SA*, 1999 *R* (R), [*U* (R), *Sp*], 2000 *It, I, US, A, Sm*, 2001 *F* (R), *E* (R), *It, I*
Reed, A I (Bath, Wasps) 1993 *I, F, W, E*, 1994 *E, I, F, Arg* 1,2, *SA*, 1996 *It*, 1997 *W, E, I, F*, 1999 *It* (R), *F, NZ*, [*Sp*]
Reid, C (Edinburgh Acads) 1881 *I, E*, 1882 *I, E*, 1883 *W, I, E*, 1884 *W, I, E*, 1885 *W, I* 1,2, 1886 *W, I, E*, 1887 *I, W, E*, 1888 *W, I*
Reid, J (Edinburgh Wands) 1874 *E*, 1875 *E*, 1876 *E*, 1877 *I, E*
Reid, J M (Edinburgh Acads) 1898 *I, E*, 1899 *I*
Reid, M F (Loretto) 1883 *I, E*
Reid, S J (Boroughmuir, Leeds, Narbonne) 1995 *WS*, 1999 *F, Arg*, [*Sp*], 2000 *It* (t), *F, W, E* (t)
Reid-Kerr, J (Greenock Wand) 1909 *E*
Relph, W K L (Stewart's Coll FP) 1955 *F, W, I, E*
Renny-Tailyour, H W (Royal Engineers) 1872 *E*
Renwick, J M (Hawick) 1972 *F, W, E, NZ*, 1973 *F*, 1974 *W, E, I, F*, 1975 *I, F, W, E, NZ, A*, 1976 *F, W, E* (R), 1977 *I, F, W*, 1978 *I, F, W, E, NZ*, 1979 *W, E, I, F, NZ*, 1980 *I, F, W, E*, 1981 *F, W, E, I, NZ* 1,2, *R, A*, 1982 *E, I, F, W*, 1983 *I, F, W, E*, 1984 *R*
Renwick, W L (London Scottish) 1989 *R*
Renwick, W N (London Scottish, Edinburgh Wands) 1938 *E*, 1939 *W*
Richardson, J F (Edinburgh Acads) 1994 *SA*
Ritchie, G (Merchistonians) 1871 *E*
Ritchie, G F (Dundee HSFP) 1932 *E*
Ritchie, J M (Watsonians) 1933 *W, E, I*, 1934 *W, I, E*
Ritchie, W T (Cambridge U) 1905 *I, E*
Robb, G H (Glasgow U) 1881 *I*, 1885 *W*
Roberts, G (Watsonians) 1938 *W, I, E*, 1939 *W, E*
Robertson, A H (W of Scotland) 1871 *E*
Robertson, A W (Edinburgh Acads) 1897 *E*
Robertson, D (Edinburgh Acads) 1875 *E*
Robertson, D D (Cambridge U) 1893 *W*
Robertson, I (London Scottish, Watsonians) 1968 *E*, 1969 *E, SA*, 1970 *F, W, I, E, A*
Robertson, I P M (Watsonians) 1910 *F*

Robertson, J (Clydesdale) 1908 *E*
Robertson, K W (Melrose) 1978 *NZ*, 1979 *W, E, I, F, NZ*, 1980 *W, E*, 1981 *F, W, E, I, R, A*, 1982 *E, I, F, A* 1,2, 1983 *I, F, W, E*, 1984 *E, I, F, R, A*, 1985 *I, F, W, E*, 1986 *I*, 1987 *F* (R), *W, E*, [*F, Z, NZ*], 1988 *E, A*, 1989 *E, I, F*
Robertson, L (London Scottish United Services) 1908 *E*, 1911 *W*, 1912 *W, I, E, SA*, 1913 *W, I, E*
Robertson, M A (Gala) 1958 *F*
Robertson, R D (London Scottish) 1912 *F*
Robson, A (Hawick) 1954 *F*, 1955 *F, W, I, E*, 1956 *F, W, I, E*, 1957 *F, W, I, E*, 1958 *W, A, I, E*, 1959 *F, W, I, E*, 1960 *F*
Rodd, J A T (United Services, RN, London Scottish) 1958 *F, W, A, I, E*, 1960 *F, W*, 1962 *F*, 1964 *F, NZ, W*, 1965 *F, W, I*
Rogerson, J (Kelvinside Acads) 1894 *W*
Roland, E T (Edinburgh Acads) 1884 *I, E*
Rollo, D M D (Howe of Fife) 1959 *E*, 1960 *F, W, I, E, SA*, 1961 *F, SA, W, I, E*, 1962 *F, W, E*, 1963 *F, W, I, E*, 1964 *F, NZ, W, I, E*, 1965 *F, W, I, E, SA*, 1966 *F, W, I, E, A*, 1967 *F, W, E, NZ*, 1968 *F, W, I*
Rose, D M (Jedforest) 1951 *F, W, I, E, SA*, 1953 *F, W*
Ross, A (Kilmarnock) 1924 *F, W*
Ross, A (Royal HSFP) 1905 *W, I, E*, 1909 *W, I*
Ross, A R (Edinburgh U) 1911 *W*, 1914 *W, I, E*
Ross, E J (London Scottish) 1904 *W*
Ross, G T (Watsonians) 1954 *NZ, I, E, W*
Ross, I A (Hillhead HSFP) 1951 *F, W, I, E*
Ross, J (London Scottish) 1901 *W, I, E*, 1902 *W*, 1903 *E*
Ross, K I (Boroughmuir FP) 1961 *SA, W, I, E*, 1962 *F, W, I, E*, 1963 *F, W, E*
Ross, W A (Hillhead HSFP) 1937 *W, E*
Rottenburg, H (Cambridge U, London Scottish) 1899 *W, E*, 1900 *W, I, E*
Roughead, W N (Edinburgh Acads, London Scottish) 1927 *A*, 1928 *F, W, I, E*, 1930 *I, E*, 1931 *E, W, I, E*, 1932 *W*
Rowan, N A (Boroughmuir) 1980 *W, E*, 1981 *F, W, E, I*, 1984 *R*, 1985 *I*, 1987 [*R*], 1988 *I, F, W, E*
Rowand, R (Glasgow HSFP) 1930 *F, W*, 1932 *E*, 1933 *W, E, I*, 1934 *W*
Roxburgh, A J (Kelso) 1997 *A*, 1998 *It, F* (R), *W, E, Fj, A* 1(R),2(R)
Roy, A (Waterloo) 1938 *W, I, E*, 1939 *W, I, E*
Russell, R R (Saracens) 1999 *R*, [*U* (R), *Sp, Sm* (R), *NZ* (R)], 2000 *I* (R), 2001 *F* (R)
Russell, W L (Glasgow Acads) 1905 *NZ*, 1906 *W, I, E*
Rutherford, J Y (Selkirk) 1979 *W, E, I, F, NZ*, 1980 *I, F, E*, 1981 *F, W, E, I, NZ* 1,2, *A*, 1982 *E, I, F, W, A* 1,2, 1983 *E, NZ*, 1984 *W, E, I, F, R*, 1985 *I, F, W, E*, 1986 *F, W, E, I, R*, 1987 *I, F, W, E*, [*F*]

Sampson, R W F (London Scottish) 1939 *W*, 1947 *W*
Sanderson, G A (Royal HSFP) 1907 *W, I, E*, 1908 *I*
Sanderson, J L P (Edinburgh Acads) 1873 *E*
Schulze, D G (London Scottish) 1905 *E*, 1907 *I, E*, 1908 *W, I, E*, 1909 *W, I, E*, 1910 *W, I, E*, 1911 *W*
Scobie, R M (Royal Military Coll) 1914 *W, I, E*
Scotland, K J F (Heriot's FP, Cambridge U, Leicester) 1957 *F, W, I, E*, 1958 *E*, 1959 *F, W, I, E*, 1960 *F, W, I, E*, 1961 *F, SA, W, I, E*, 1962 *F, W, I, E*, 1963 *F, W, I, E*, 1965 *F*
Scott, D M (Langholm, Watsonians) 1950 *I, E*, 1951 *W, I, E, SA*, 1952 *F, W, I*, 1953 *F*
Scott, J M B (Edinburgh Acads) 1907 *E*, 1908 *W, I, E*, 1909 *W, I, E*, 1910 *F, W, I, E*, 1911 *F, W, I*, 1912 *W, I, E, SA*, 1913 *W, I, E*
Scott, J S (St Andrew's U) 1950 *E*
Scott, J W (Stewart's Coll FP) 1925 *F, W, I, E*, 1926 *F, W, I, E*, 1927 *F, W, I, E, A*, 1928 *F, W, I, E*, 1929 *E*, 1930 *F*
Scott, M (Dunfermline) 1992 *A* 2
Scott, R (Hawick) 1898 *I*, 1900 *I, E*
Scott, S (Edinburgh) 2000 *NZ* 2 (R), *US* (t+R), 2001 *It* (R), *I* (R)
Scott, T (Langholm, Hawick) 1896 *W*, 1897 *I, E*, 1898 *I, E*, 1899 *I, W, E*, 1900 *W, I, E*
Scott, T M (Hawick) 1893 *E*, 1895 *W, I, E*, 1896 *W, E*, 1897 *I, E*, 1898 *I, E*, 1900 *W, I*
Scott, W P (W of Scotland) 1900 *I, E*, 1902 *I, E*, 1903 *W, I, E*, 1904 *W, I, E*, 1905 *W, I, E, NZ*, 1906 *W, I, E, SA*, 1907 *W, I, E*
Scoular, J G (Cambridge U) 1905 *NZ*, 1906 *W, I, E, SA*
Selby, J A R (Watsonians) 1920 *W, I*
Shackleton, J A P (London Scottish) 1959 *E*, 1963 *F, W*, 1964 *NZ, W*, 1965 *I, SA*
Sharp, A V (Bristol) 1994 *E, I, F, Arg* 1,2 *SA*
Sharp, G (Stewart's FP, Army) 1960 *F*, 1964 *F, NZ, W*

Shaw, G D (Sale) 1935 *NZ*, 1936 *W*, 1937 *W, I, E*, 1939 *I*
Shaw, I (Glasgow HSFP) 1937 *I*
Shaw, J N (Edinburgh Acads) 1921 *W, I*
Shaw, R W (Glasgow HSFP) 1934 *W, I, E*, 1935 *W, I, E, NZ*, 1936 *W, I, E*, 1937 *W, I, E*, 1938 *W, I, E*, 1939 *W, I, E*
Shedden, D (W of Scotland) 1972 *NZ*, 1973 *F, W, I, E, P*, 1976 *W, E, I*, 1977 *I, F, W*, 1978 *I, F, W*
Shepherd, R J S (Melrose) 1995 *WS*, 1996 *I, F, W, E, NZ* 1,2, *A, It*, 1997 *W, E, I, F, SA*, 1998 *It, I, W* (R), *Fj* (t), *A* 1,2
Shiel, A G (Melrose, Edinburgh) 1991 [*I* (R), *WS*], 1993 *I, F, W, E, NZ*, 1994 *Arg* 1,2, *SA*, 1995 *R*, [*Iv, F, NZ*], *WS*, 2000 *I, NZ* 1(R),2
Shillinglaw, R B (Gala, Army) 1960 *I, E, SA*, 1961 *F, SA*
Simmers, B M (Glasgow Acads) 1965 *F, W*, 1966 *A*, 1967 *F, W, I*, 1971 *F* (R)
Simmers, W M (Glasgow Acads) 1926 *W, I, E*, 1927 *F, W, I, E, A*, 1928 *F, W, I, E*, 1929 *F, W, I, E*, 1930 *F, W, I, E*, 1931 *F, W, I, E*, 1932 *SA, W, I, E*
Simpson, G L (Kirkcaldy, Glasgow) 1998 *A* 1,2, 1999 *Arg* (R), *R*, [*SA, U, Sm, NZ*], 2000 *It, I, NZ* 1(R), 2001 *I*
Simpson, J W (Royal HSFP) 1893 *I, E*, 1894 *W, I, E*, 1895 *W, I, E*, 1896 *W, I*, 1897 *E*, 1899 *W, E*
Simpson, R S (Glasgow Acads) 1923 *I*
Simson, E D (Edinburgh U, London Scottish) 1902 *E*, 1903 *W, I, E*, 1904 *W, I, E*, 1905 *W, I, E, NZ*, 1906 *W, I, E*, 1907 *W, I, E*
Simson, J T (Watsonians) 1905 *NZ*, 1909 *W, I, E*, 1910 *F, W*, 1911 *I*
Simson, R F (London Scottish) 1911 *E*
Sloan, A T (Edinburgh Acads) 1914 *W*, 1920 *F, W, I, E*, 1921 *F, W, I, E*
Sloan, D A (Edinburgh Acads, London Scottish) 1950 *F, W, E*, 1951 *W, I, E*, 1953 *F*
Sloan, T (Glasgow Acads, Oxford U) 1905 *NZ*, 1906 *W, SA*, 1907 *W, E*, 1908 *W*, 1909 *I*
Smeaton, P W (Edinburgh Acads) 1881 *I*, 1883 *I, E*
Smith, A R (Oxford U) 1895 *W, I, E*, 1896 *W, I*, 1897 *I, E*, 1898 *I, E*, 1900 *I, E*
Smith, A R (Cambridge U, Gosforth, Ebbw Vale, Edinburgh Wands) 1955 *W, I, E*, 1956 *F, W, I, E*, 1957 *F, W, I, E*, 1958 *F, W, A, I*, 1959 *F, W, I, E*, 1960 *F, W, I, E, SA*, 1961 *F, SA, W, I, E*, 1962 *F, W, I, E*
Smith, D W C (London Scottish) 1949 *F, W, I, E*, 1950 *F, W, I*, 1953 *I*
Smith, E R (Edinburgh Acads) 1879 *I*
Smith, G K (Kelso) 1957 *I, E*, 1958 *F, W, A*, 1959 *F, W, I, E*, 1960 *F, W, I, E*, 1961 *F, SA, W, I, E*
Smith, H O (Watsonians) 1895 *W*, 1896 *W, I, E*, 1898 *I, E*, 1899 *W, I, E*, 1900 *I, E*, 1902 *E*
Smith, I R (Gloucester, Moseley) 1992 *E, I, W, A* 1,2, 1994 *E* (R), *I, F, Arg* 1,2, 1995 [*Iv*], *WS*, 1996 *I, F, W, E, NZ* 1,2, *A, It*, 1997 *E, I, F, A, SA*
Smith, I S (Oxford U, Edinburgh U) 1924 *W, I, E*, 1925 *F, W, I, E*, 1926 *F, W, I, E*, 1927 *F, I, E*, 1929 *F, W, I, E*, 1930 *F, W, I*, 1931 *F, W, I, E*, 1932 *SA, W, I, E*, 1933 *W, E, I*
Smith, I S G (London Scottish) 1969 *SA*, 1970 *F, W, I, E*, 1971 *F, W, I*
Smith, M A (London Scottish) 1970 *W, I, E, A*
Smith, R T (Kelso) 1929 *F, W, I, E*, 1930 *F, W, I*
Smith, S H (Glasgow Acads) 1877 *I*, 1878 *E*
Smith, T J (Gala) 1983 *E, NZ*, 1985 *I, F*
Smith, T J (Watsonians, Dundee HSFP, Glasgow, Brive, Northampton) 1997 *E, I, F*, 1998 *SA*, 1999 *W, E, It, I, Arg, R*, [*SA, U, Sm, NZ*], 2000 *It, I, F, W, E, NZ* 1,2, *US, A, Sm*, 2001 *F, W, E, It, I*
Sole, D M B (Bath, Edinburgh Acads) 1986 *F, W*, 1987 *I, F, W, E*, [*F, Z, R, NZ*], 1988 *I, F, W, E, A*, 1989 *W, E, I, F, Fj, R*, 1990 *I, F, W, E, NZ* 1,2, *Arg*, 1991 *F, W, E, I, R*, [*J, I, WS, E, NZ*], 1992 *E, I, F, W, A* 1,2
Somerville, D (Edinburgh Inst FP) 1879 *I*, 1882 *I*, 1883 *W, I, E*, 1884 *W*
Speirs, L M (Watsonians) 1906 *SA*, 1907 *W, I, E*, 1908 *W, I, E*, 1910 *F, W, E*
Spence, K M (Oxford U) 1953 *I*
Spencer, E (Clydesdale) 1898 *I*
Stagg, P K (Sale) 1965 *F, W, E, SA*, 1966 *F, W, I, E, A*, 1967 *F, W, I, E, NZ*, 1968 *F, W, I, E, A*, 1969 *F, W, I* (R), *SA*, 1970 *F, W, I, E, A*
Stanger, A G (Hawick) 1989 *Fj, R*, 1990 *I, F, W, E, NZ* 1,2, *Arg*, 1991 *F, W, E, I, R*, [*J, Z, I, WS, E, NZ*], 1992 *E, I, F, W, A* 1,2, 1993 *I, F, W, E, NZ*, 1994 *W, E, I, F, SA*, 1995 *R*, [*Iv*], 1996 *NZ* 2, *A, It*, 1997 *W, E, I, F, A, SA*, 1998 *It, I* (R), *F, W, E*

Stark, D A (Boroughmuir, Melrose, Glasgow Hawks) 1993 *I, F, W, E,* 1996 *NZ* 2(R), *It* (R), 1997 *W* (R), *E, SA*
Steel, J F (Glasgow) 2000 *US, A,* 2001 *I*
Steele, W C C (Langholm, Bedford, RAF, London Scottish) 1969 *E,* 1971 *F, W, I, E* (2[1C]), 1972 *F, W, E, NZ,* 1973 *F, W, I, E,* 1975 *I, F, W, E, NZ* (R), 1976 *W, E, I,* 1977 *E*
Stephen, A E (W of Scotland) 1885 *W,* 1886 *I*
Steven, P D (Heriot's FP) 1984 *A,* 1985 *F, W, E*
Steven, R (Edinburgh Wands) 1962 *I*
Stevenson, A K (Glasgow Acads) 1922 *F,* 1923 *F, W, E*
Stevenson, A M (Glasgow U) 1911 *F*
Stevenson, G D (Hawick) 1956 *E,* 1957 *F,* 1958 *F, W, A, I, E,* 1959 *W, I, E,* 1960 *W, I, E, SA,* 1961 *F, SA, W, I, E,* 1963 *F, W, I,* 1964 *E,* 1965 *F*
Stevenson, H J (Edinburgh Acads) 1888 *W, I,* 1889 *W, I,* 1890 *W, I, E,* 1891 *W, I, E,* 1892 *W, I, E,* 1893 *I, E*
Stevenson, L E (Edinburgh U) 1888 *W*
Stevenson, R C (London Scottish) 1897 *I, E,* 1898 *E,* 1899 *I, W, E*
Stevenson, R C (St Andrew's U) 1910 *F, I, E,* 1911 *F, W, I*
Stevenson, W H (Glasgow Acads) 1925 *F*
Stewart, A K (Edinburgh U) 1874 *E,* 1876 *E*
Stewart, A M (Edinburgh Acads) 1914 *W*
Stewart, B D (Edinburgh Acads, Edinburgh) 1996 *NZ* 2, *A,* 2000 *NZ* 1,2
Stewart, C A R (W of Scotland) 1880 *I, E*
Stewart, C E B (Kelso) 1960 *W,* 1961 *F, E*
Stewart, J (Glasgow HSFP) 1930 *F*
Stewart, J L (Edinburgh Acads) 1921 *I*
Stewart M J (Northampton) 1996 *It,* 1997 *W, E, I, F, A, SA,* 1998 *It, I, F, W, Fj* (R), 2000 *It, I, F, W, E, NZ* 1(R), 2001 *F, W, E, It, I*
Stewart, M S (Stewart's Coll FP) 1932 *SA, W, I,* 1933 *W, E, I,* 1934 *W, I, E*
Stewart, W A (London Hospital) 1913 *F, W, I,* 1914 *W*
Steyn, S S L (Oxford U) 1911 *E,* 1912 *I*
Strachan, G M (Jordanhill) 1971 *E* (C) (R), 1973 *W, I, E, P*
Stronach, R S (Glasgow Acads) 1901 *W, E,* 1905 *W, I, E*
Stuart, C D (W of Scotland) 1909 *I,* 1910 *F, W, I, E,* 1911 *I, E*
Stuart, L M (Glasgow HSFP) 1923 *F, W, I, E,* 1924 *F,* 1928 *E,* 1930 *I, E*
Suddon, N (Hawick) 1965 *W, I, E, SA,* 1966 *A,* 1968 *E, A,* 1969 *F, W, I,* 1970 *I, E, A*
Sutherland, W R (Hawick) 1910 *W, E,* 1911 *F, E,* 1912 *F, W, E, SA,* 1913 *F, W, I, E,* 1914 *W*
Swan, J S (Army, London Scottish, Leicester) 1953 *E,* 1954 *F, NZ, I, E, W,* 1955 *F, W, I, E,* 1956 *F, W, I, E,* 1957 *F, W,* 1958 *F*
Swan, M W (Oxford U, London Scottish) 1958 *F, W, A, I, E,* 1959 *F, W, I*
Sweet, J B (Glasgow HSFP) 1913 *E,* 1914 *I*
Symington, A W (Cambridge U) 1914 *W, E*

Tait, A V (Kelso, Newcastle, Edinburgh) 1987 [*F*(R), *Z, R, NZ*], 1988 *I, F, W, E,* 1997 *I, F, A,* 1998 *It, I, F, W, E, SA,* 1999 *W* (R), *E, It, I, F, Arg, R,* [*A, U, NZ*]
Tait, J G (Edinburgh Acads) 1880 *I,* 1885 *I* 2
Tait, P W (Royal HSFP) 1935 *E*
Taylor, E G (Oxford U) 1927 *W, A*
Taylor, R C (Kelvinside-West) 1951 *W, I, E, SA*
Taylor, S M (Edinburgh) 2000 *US, A,* 2001 *E, It, I*
Telfer, C M (Hawick) 1968 *A,* 1969 *F, W, I, E,* 1972 *F, W, E,* 1973 *W, I, E, P,* 1974 *W, E, I,* 1975 *A,* 1976 *F*
Telfer, J W (Melrose) 1964 *F, NZ, W, I, E,* 1965 *F, W, I,* 1966 *F, W, I, E,* 1967 *W, I, E,* 1968 *E, A,* 1969 *F, W, I, E, SA,* 1970 *F, W, I*
Tennent, J M (W of Scotland) 1909 *W, I, E,* 1910 *F, W, E*
Thom, D A (London Scottish) 1934 *W,* 1935 *W, I, E, NZ*
Thom, G (Kirkcaldy) 1920 *F, W, I, E*
Thom, J R (Watsonians) 1933 *W, E, I*
Thomson, A E (United Services) 1921 *F, W, E*
Thomson, A M (St Andrew's U) 1949 *F*
Thomson, B E (Oxford U) 1953 *F, W, I*
Thomson, I H M (Heriot's FP, Army) 1951 *W, I,* 1952 *F, W, I,* 1953 *I, E*
Thomson, J S (Glasgow Acads) 1871 *E*
Thomson, R H (London Scottish, PUC) 1960 *I, E, SA,* 1961 *F, SA, W, I, E,* 1963 *F, W, I, E,* 1964 *F, NZ, W*
Thomson, W H (W of Scotland) 1906 *SA*
Thomson, W J (W of Scotland) 1899 *W, E,* 1900 *W*

Timms, A B (Edinburgh U, Edinburgh Wands) 1896 *W,* 1900 *W, I,* 1901 *W, I, E,* 1902 *W, E,* 1903 *W, E,* 1904 *I, E,* 1905 *I, E*
Tod, H B (Gala) 1911 *F*
Tod, J (Watsonians) 1884 *W, I, E,* 1885 *W, I* 1,2, 1886 *W, I, E*
Todd, J K (Glasgow Acads) 1874 *E,* 1875 *E*
Tolmie, J M (Glasgow HSFP) 1922 *E*
Tomes, A J (Hawick) 1976 *E, I,* 1977 *E,* 1978 *I, F, W, E, NZ,* 1979 *W, E, I, F, NZ,* 1980 *F, W, E,* 1981 *F, W, E, I, NZ* 1,2, *R, A,* 1982 *E, I, F, W, A* 1,2, 1983 *I, F, W,* 1984 *W, E, I, F, R, A,* 1985 *W, E,* 1987 *I, F, E* (R), [*F, Z, R, NZ*]
Torrie, T J (Edinburgh Acads) 1877 *E*
Townsend, G P J (Gala, Northampton, Brive, Castres) 1993 *E* (R), 1994 *W, E, I, F, Arg* 1,2, 1995 *C, I, F, W, E, WS,* 1996 *I, F, W, E, NZ* 1,2, *A, It,* 1997 *W, E, I, F, A, SA,* 1998 *It, I, F, W, E, Fj, A* 1,2, *SA* (R), 1999 *W, E, It, I, F,* [*SA, U, Sp* (R), *Sm, NZ*], 2000 *It, I, F, W, E, NZ* 1,2, *US, A, Sm,* 2001 *F, It, I*
Tukalo, I (Selkirk) 1985 *I,* 1987 *I, F, W, E,* [*F, Z, R, NZ*], 1988 *F, W, E, A,* 1989 *W, E, I, F, Fj,* 1990 *I, F, W, E, NZ* 1, 1991 *I, R,* [*J, Z, I, WS, E, NZ*], 1992 *E, I, F, W, A* 1,2
Turk, A S (Langholm) 1971 *E* (R)
Turnbull, D J (Hawick) 1987 [*NZ*], 1988 *F, E,* 1990 *E* (R), 1991 *F, W, E, I, R,* [*Z*], 1993 *I, F, W, E,* 1994 *W*
Turnbull, F O (Kelso) 1951 *F, SA*
Turnbull, G O (W of Scotland) 1896 *I, E,* 1897 *I, E,* 1904 *W*
Turnbull, P (Edinburgh Acads) 1901 *W, I, E,* 1902 *W, I, E*
Turner, F H (Oxford U, Liverpool) 1911 *F, W, I, E,* 1912 *F, W, I, E, SA,* 1913 *F, W, I, E,* 1914 *I, E*
Turner, J W C (Gala) 1966 *W, A,* 1967 *F, W, I, E, NZ,* 1968 *F, W, I, E, A,* 1969 *F,* 1970 *E, A,* 1971 *F, W, I, E* (2[1C])

Usher, C M (United Services, Edinburgh Wands) 1912 *E,* 1913 *F, W, I, E,* 1914 *E,* 1920 *F, W, I, E,* 1921 *W, E,* 1922 *F, W, I, E*

Valentine, A R (RNAS, Anthorn) 1953 *F, W, I*
Valentine, D D (Hawick) 1947 *I, E*
Veitch, J P (Royal HSFP) 1882 *E,* 1883 *I,* 1884 *W, I, E,* 1885 *I* 1,2, 1886 *E*
Villar, C (Edinburgh Wands) 1876 *E,* 1877 *I, E*

Waddell, G H (London Scottish, Cambridge U) 1957 *E,* 1958 *F, W, A, I, E,* 1959 *F, W, I, E,* 1960 *I, E, SA,* 1961 *F,* 1962 *F, W, I, E*
Waddell, H (Glasgow Acads) 1924 *F, W, I, E,* 1925 *I, E,* 1926 *F, W, I, E,* 1927 *F, W, I, E,* 1930 *W*
Wade, A L (London Scottish) 1908 *E*
Wainwright, R I (Edinburgh Acads, West Hartlepool, Watsonians, Army, Dundee HSFP) 1992 *I* (R), *F, A* 1,2, 1993 *NZ,* 1994 *W, E,* 1995 *C, I, F, W, E, It,* [*Iv, Tg, F, NZ*], *WS,* 1996 *I, F, W, E, NZ* 1,2, 1997 *W, E, I, F, SA,* 1998 *It, I, F, W, E, Fj, A* 1,2
Walker, A (W of Scotland) 1881 *I,* 1882 *E,* 1883 *W, I, E,* 1932 *I*
Walker, A W (Cambridge U, Birkenhead Park) 1931 *F, W, I, E,* 1932 *I*
Walker, J G (W of Scotland) 1882 *E,* 1883 *W*
Walker, M (Oxford U) 1952 *F*
Wallace, A C (Oxford U) 1923 *F,* 1924 *F, W, E,* 1925 *F, W, I, E,* 1926 *F*
Wallace, W M (Cambridge U) 1913 *E,* 1914 *W, I, E*
Wallace, M J (Glasgow High Kelvinside) 1996 *A, It,* 1997 *W*
Walls, W A (Glasgow Acads) 1882 *E,* 1883 *W, I, E,* 1884 *W, I, E,* 1886 *W, I, E*
Walter, M W (London Scottish) 1906 *I, E, SA,* 1907 *W, I,* 1908 *W, I,* 1910 *I*
Walton, P (Northampton, Newcastle) 1994 *E, I, F, Arg* 1,2, 1995 [*Iv*], 1997 *W, E, I, F, SA* (R), 1998 *I, F, SA,* 1999 *W, E, It, I, F* (R), *Arg, R,* [*SA* (R), *U* (R), *Sp*]
Warren, J R (Glasgow Acads) 1914 *I*
Warren, R C (Glasgow Acads) 1922 *W, I,* 1930 *W, I, E*
Waters, F H (Cambridge U, London Scottish) 1930 *F, W, I, E,* 1932 *SA, W, I*
Waters, J A (Selkirk) 1933 *W, E, I,* 1934 *W, I, E,* 1935 *W, I, E, NZ,* 1936 *W, I, E,* 1937 *W, I, E*
Waters, J B (Cambridge U) 1904 *I, E*
Watherston, J G (Edinburgh Wands) 1934 *I, E*
Watherston, W R A (London Scottish) 1963 *F, W, I*
Watson, D H (Glasgow Acads) 1876 *E,* 1877 *I, E*
Watson, W S (Boroughmuir) 1974 *W, E, I, F,* 1975 *NZ,* 1977 *I, F, W,* 1979 *I, F*
Watt, A G J (Glasgow High Kelvinside) 1991 [*Z*], 1993 *I, NZ,* 1994 *Arg* 2(t & R)
Watt, A G M (Edinburgh Acads) 1947 *F, W, I, A,* 1948 *F, W*

Weatherstone, T G (Stewart's Coll FP) 1952 *E*, 1953 *I, E*, 1954 *F, NZ, I, E, W*, 1955 *F*, 1958 *W, A, I, E*, 1959 *W, I, E*
Weir, G W (Melrose, Newcastle) 1990 *Arg*, 1991 *R, [J, Z, I, WS, E, NZ]*, 1992 *E, I, F, W, A* 1,2, 1993 *I, F, W, E, NZ*, 1994 *W* (R), *E, I, F, SA*, 1995 *F* (R), *W, E, R, [Iv, Tg, F, NZ], WS,* 1996 *I, F, W, E, NZ* 1,2, *A, It* (R), 1997 *W, E, I, F*, 1998 *It, I, F, W, E, SA*, 1999 *W, Arg* (R), *R* (R), *[SA* (R), *Sp, Sm, NZ]*, 2000 *It* (R), *I* (R), *F*
Welsh, R (Watsonians) 1895 *W, I, E*, 1896 *W*
Welsh, R B (Hawick) 1967 *I, E*
Welsh, W B (Hawick) 1927 *A*, 1928 *F, W, I*, 1929 *I, E*, 1930 *F, W, I, E*, 1931 *F, W, I, E*, 1932 *SA, W, I, E*, 1933 *W, E, I*
Welsh, W H (Edinburgh U) 1900 *I, E*, 1901 *W, I, E*, 1902 *W, I, E*
Wemyss, A (Gala, Edinburgh Wands) 1914 *W, I*, 1920 *F, E*, 1922 *F, W, I*
West, L (Edinburgh U, West Hartlepool) 1903 *W, I, E*, 1905 *I, E, NZ*, 1906 *W, I, E*
Weston, V G (Kelvinside Acads) 1936 *I, E*
White, D B (Gala, London Scottish) 1982 *F, W, A* 1,2, 1987 *W, E, [F, R, NZ]*, 1988 *I, F, W, E, A*, 1989 *W, E, I, F, Fj, R*, 1990 *I, F, W, E, NZ* 1,2, 1991 *F, W, E, I, R, [J, Z, I, WS, E, NZ]*, 1992 *E, I, F, W*
White, D M (Kelvinside Acads) 1963 *F, W, I, E*
White, J P R (Glasgow) 2000 *E, NZ* 1,2, *US* (R), *A* (R), *Sm*, 2001 *F* (R), *I*
White, T B (Edinburgh Acads) 1888 *W, I*, 1889 *W*
Whittington, T P (Merchistonians) 1873 *E*
Whitworth, R J E (London Scottish) 1936 *I*
Whyte, D J (Edinburgh Wands) 1965 *W, I, E, SA*, 1966 *F, W, I, E, A*, 1967 *F, W, I, E*
Will, J G (Cambridge U) 1912 *F, W, I, E*, 1914 *W, I, E*
Wilson, A W (Dunfermline) 1931 *F, I, E*
Wilson, G A (Oxford U) 1949 *F, W, E*
Wilson, G R (Royal HSFP) 1886 *E*, 1890 *W, I, E*, 1891 *I*

Wilson, J H (Watsonians) 1953 *I*
Wilson, J S (St Andrew's U) 1931 *F, W, I, E*, 1932 *E*
Wilson, J S (United Services, London Scottish) 1908 *I*, 1909 *W*
Wilson, R (London Scottish) 1976 *E, I*, 1977 *E, I, F*, 1978 *I, F*, 1981 *R*, 1983 *I*
Wilson, R L (Gala) 1951 *F, W, I, E, SA*, 1953 *F, W, E*
Wilson, R W (W of Scotland) 1873 *E*, 1874 *E*
Wilson, S (Oxford U, London Scottish) 1964 *F, NZ, W, I, E*, 1965 *W, I, E, SA*, 1966 *F, W, I, A*, 1967 *F, W, I, E, NZ*, 1968 *F, W, I, E*
Wood, A (Royal HSFP) 1873 *E*, 1874 *E*, 1875 *E*
Wood, G (Gala) 1931 *W, I*, 1932 *W, I, E*
Woodburn, J C (Kelvinside Acads) 1892 *I*
Woodrow, A N (Glasgow Acads) 1887 *I, W, E*
Wotherspoon, W (W of Scotland) 1891 *I*, 1892 *I*, 1893 *W, E*, 1894 *W, I, E*
Wright, F A (Edinburgh Acads) 1932 *E*
Wright, H B (Watsonians) 1894 *W*
Wright, K M (London Scottish) 1929 *F, W, I, E*
Wright, P H (Boroughmuir) 1992 *A* 1,2, 1993 *F, W, E*, 1994 *W*, 1995 *C, I, F, W, E, R, [Iv, Tg, F, NZ]*, 1996 *W, E, NZ* 1
Wright, R W J (Edinburgh Wands) 1973 *F*
Wright, S T H (Stewart's Coll FP) 1949 *E*
Wright, T (Hawick) 1947 *A*
Wyllie, D S (Stewart's-Melville FP) 1984 *A*, 1985 *W* (R), *E*, 1987 *I, F, [F, Z, R, NZ]*, 1989 *R*, 1991 *R*, *[J* (R), *Z]*, 1993 *NZ* (R), 1994 *W* (R), *E, I, F*

Young, A H (Edinburgh Acads) 1874 *E*
Young, E T (Glasgow Acads) 1914 *E*
Young, R G (Watsonians) 1970 *W*
Young, T E B (Durham) 1911 *F*
Young, W B (Cambridge U, London Scottish) 1937 *W, I, E*, 1938 *W, I, E*, 1939 *W, I, E*, 1948 *E*

SCOTLAND INTERNATIONAL STATISTICS
(to 20 October 2001)

Match Records

Most Consecutive Test Wins
6 1925 *F,W,I,E*, 1926 *F,W*
6 1989 *Fj ,R*, 1990 *I,F,W,E*

Most Consecutive Tests Without Defeat

Matches	Wins	Draws	Period
9	6*	3	1885 to 1887
6	6	0	1925 to 1926
6	6	0	1989 to 1990
6	4	2	1877 to 1880
6	5	1	1983 to 1984

* includes an abandoned match

Most Points in a Match
by the team

Pts	Opponents	Venue	Year
89	Ivory Coast	Rustenburg	1995
60	Zimbabwe	Wellington	1987
60	Romania	Hampden Park	1999
55	Romania	Dunedin	1987
53	United States	Murrayfield	2000
51	Zimbabwe	Murrayfield	1991
49	Argentina	Murrayfield	1990
49	Romania	Murrayfield	1995

by a player

Pts	Player	Opponents	Venue	Year
44	A G Hastings	Ivory Coast	Rustenburg	1995
33	G P J Townsend	United States	Murrayfield	2000
31	A G Hastings	Tonga	Pretoria	1995
27	A G Hastings	Romania	Dunedin	1987
26	K M Logan	Romania	Hampden Park	1999
21	A G Hastings	England	Murrayfield	1986
21	A G Hastings	Romania	Bucharest	1986

Most Tries in a Match
by the team

Tries	Opponents	Venue	Year
13	Ivory Coast	Rustenburg	1995
12	Wales	Raeburn Place	1887
11	Zimbabwe	Wellington	1987
9	Romania	Dunedin	1987
9	Argentina	Murrayfield	1990

by a player

Tries	Player	Opponents	Venue	Year
5	G C Lindsay	Wales	Raeburn Place	1887
4	W A Stewart	Ireland	Inverleith	1913
4	I S Smith	France	Inverleith	1925
4	I S Smith	Wales	Swansea	1925
4	A G Hastings	Ivory Coast	Rustenburg	1995

Most Conversions in a Match
by the team

Cons	Opponents	Venue	Year
9	Ivory Coast	Rustenburg	1995
8	Zimbabwe	Wellington	1987
8	Romania	Dunedin	1987

by a player

Cons	Player	Opponents	Venue	Year
9	A G Hastings	Ivory Coast	Rustenburg	1995
8	A G Hastings	Zimbabwe	Wellington	1987
8	A G Hastings	Romania	Dunedin	1987

Most Penalties in a Match
by the team

Penalties	Opponents	Venue	Year
8	Tonga	Pretoria	1995
6	France	Murrayfield	1986

by a player

Penalties	Player	Opponents	Venue	Year
8	A G Hastings	Tonga	Pretoria	1995
6	A G Hastings	France	Murrayfield	1986

Most Dropped Goals in a Match
by the team

Drops	Opponents	Venue	Year
3	Ireland	Murrayfield	1973
2	on several	occasions	

by a player

Drops	Player	Opponents	Venue	Year
2	R C MacKenzie	Ireland	Belfast	1877
2	N J Finlay	Ireland	Glasgow	1880
2	B M Simmers	Wales	Murrayfield	1965
2	D W Morgan	Ireland	Murrayfield	1973
2	B M Gossman	France	Parc des Princes	1983
2	J Y Rutherford	New Zealand	Murrayfield	1983
2	J Y Rutherford	Wales	Murrayfield	1985
2	J Y Rutherford	Ireland	Murrayfield	1987
2	C M Chalmers	England	Twickenham	1995

Most Tests in Individual Positions

Position	Player	Tests	Span
Full-back	A G Hastings	61	1986 to 1995
Wing	K M Logan	51	1992 to 2001
Centre	S Hastings	63	1986 to 1997
Fly-half	C M Chalmers	55	1989 to 1999
Scrum-half	G Armstrong	51	1988 to 1999
Prop	A P Burnell	52	1989 to 1999
Hooker	C T Deans	52	1978 to 1987
Lock	G W Weir	50	1990 to 2000
Flanker	J Jeffrey	40	1984 to 1991
No 8	D B White	29	1982 to 1992
	E W Peters	29	1995 to 1999

Career Records

Most Capped Players

Caps	Player	Career Span
65	S Hastings	1986 to 1997
61	A G Hastings	1986 to 1995
61	G W Weir	1990 to 2000
60	C M Chalmers	1989 to 1999
59	G P J Townsend	1993 to 2001
53	K M Logan	1992 to 2001
52	J M Renwick	1972 to 1984
52	C T Deans	1978 to 1987
52	A G Stanger	1989 to 1998
52	A P Burnell	1989 to 1999
51	A R Irvine	1972 to 1982
51	G Armstrong	1988 to 1999
50	A B Carmichael	1967 to 1978
48	A J Tomes	1976 to 1987

Most Points in Tests

Points	Player	Tests	Career
667	A G Hastings	61	1986 to 1995
273	A R Irvine	51	1972 to 1982
215	K M Logan	53	1992 to 2001
210	P W Dods	23	1983 to 1991
166	C M Chalmers	60	1989 to 1999
141	G P J Townsend	59	1993 to 2001
107	D W Hodge	22	1997 to 2001
106	A G Stanger	52	1989 to 1998

Most Tries in Tests

Tries	Player	Tests	Career
24	I S Smith	32	1924 to 1933
24	A G Stanger	52	1989 to 1998
17	A G Hastings	61	1986 to 1995
17	A V Tait	27	1987 to 1999
15	I Tukalo	37	1985 to 1992
14	G P J Townsend	59	1993 to 2001
12	A R Smith	33	1955 to 1962
12	K M Logan	53	1992 to 2001

Most Consecutive Tests

Tests	Player	Span
49	A B Carmichael	1967 to 1978
40	H F McLeod	1954 to 1962
37	J M Bannerman	1921 to 1929
35	A G Stanger	1989 to 1994

Most Tests as Captain

Tests	Captain	Span
25	D M B Sole	1989 to 1992
20	A G Hastings	1993 to 1995
19	J McLauchlan	1973 to 1979
16	R I Wainwright	1995 to 1998
15	M C Morrison	1899 to 1904
15	A R Smith	1957 to 1962
15	A R Irvine	1980 to 1982

Most Conversions in Tests

Cons	Player	Tests	Career
86	A G Hastings	61	1986 to 1995
34	K M Logan	53	1992 to 2001
26	P W Dods	23	1983 to 1991
25	A R Irvine	51	1972 to 1982
19	D Drysdale	26	1923 to 1929
15	D W Hodge	22	1997 to 2001
14	F H Turner	15	1911 to 1914
14	R J S Shepherd	20	1995 to 1998

Most Penalty Goals in Tests

Penalties	Player	Tests	Career
140	A G Hastings	61	1986 to 1995
61	A R Irvine	51	1972 to 1982
50	P W Dods	23	1983 to 1991
32	C M Chalmers	60	1989 to 1999
29	K M Logan	53	1992 to 2001
21	M Dods	8	1994 to 1996
21	R J S Shepherd	20	1995 to 1998

Most Dropped Goals in Tests

Drops	Player	Tests	Career
12	J Y Rutherford	42	1979 to 1987
9	C M Chalmers	60	1989 to 1999
7	I R McGeechan	32	1972 to 1979
6	D W Morgan	21	1973 to 1978
5	H Waddell	15	1924 to 1930

International Championship Records

Record	Detail	Holder	Set
Most points in season	120	in four matches	1999
Most tries in season	17	in four matches	1925
Highest Score	38	38–10 v Ireland	1997
Biggest win	28	31–3 v France	1912
	28	38–10 v Ireland	1997
Highest score conceded	51	16–51 v France	1998
Biggest defeat	40	3–43 v England	2001
Most appearances	42	J M Renwick	1972–1983
Most points in matches	288	A G Hastings	1986–1995
Most points in season	56	A G Hastings	1995
Most points in match	21	A G Hastings	v England, 1986
Most tries in matches	24	I S Smith	1924–1933
Most tries in season	8	I S Smith	1925
Most tries in match	5	G C Lindsay	v Wales, 1887
Most cons in matches	20	A G Hastings	1986–1995
Most cons in season	11	K M Logan	1999
Most cons in match	5	F H Turner	v France, 1912
	5	J W Allan	v England, 1931
	5	R J S Shepherd	v Ireland, 1997
Most pens in matches	77	A G Hastings	1986–1995
Most pens in season	14	A G Hastings	1986
Most pens in match	6	A G Hastings	v France, 1986
Most drops in matches	8	J Y Rutherford	1979–1987
	8	C M Chalmers	1989–1998
Most drops in season	3	J Y Rutherford	1987
Most drops in match	2	on several occasions	

Miscellaneous Records

Record	Holder	Detail
Longest Test Career	W C W Murdoch	14 seasons, 1934–35 to 1947–48
Youngest Test Cap	N J Finlay	17 yrs 36 days in 1875*
Oldest Test Cap	J McLauchlan	37 yrs 210 days in 1979

* C Reid, also 17 yrs 36 days on debut in 1881, was a day *older* than Finlay, having lived through an extra leap-year day.

Career Records of Scotland International Players
(up to 20 October 2001)

Player	Debut	Caps	T	C	P	D	Pts
Backs:							
G Armstrong	1988 v A	51	5	0	0	0	21
G Beveridge	2000 v NZ	3	0	0	0	0	0
A J Bulloch	2000 v US	5	1	0	0	0	5
G G Burns	1999 v It	1	0	0	0	0	0
C M Chalmers	1989 v W	60	5	11	32	9	166
J M Craig	1997 v A	4	0	0	0	0	0
I T Fairley	1999 v It	3	0	0	0	0	0
H R Gilmour	1998 v Fj	1	1	0	0	0	5
A Henderson	2001 v I	1	1	0	0	0	5
D W Hodge	1997 v F	22	4	15	18	1	107
I C Jardine	1993 v NZ	18	0	0	0	0	0
C A Joiner	1994 v Arg	24	3	0	0	0	15
D J Lee	1998 v I	8	0	4	7	0	29
J A Leslie	1998 v SA	18	4	0	0	0	20
K M Logan	1992 v A	53	12	34	29	0	215
S L Longstaff	1998 v F	15	2	0	0	0	10
J G McLaren	1999 v Arg	12	3	0	0	0	15
M J M Mayer	1998 v SA	8	0	0	0	0	0
G H Metcalfe	1998 v A	19	3	0	0	0	15
C C Moir	2000 v W	3	0	0	0	0	0
C A Murray	1998 v E	24	7	0	0	0	35
A D Nicol	1992 v E	20	2	0	0	0	9
C D Paterson	1999 v Sp	14	3	3	4	0	33
B W Redpath	1993 v NZ	40	0	0	0	0	0
R J S Shepherd	1995 v WS	20	2	14	21	1	104
A G Shiel	1991 v I	18	3	0	2	0	20
J F Steel	2000 v US	3	0	0	0	0	0
A V Tait	1987 v F	27	17	0	0	0	81
G P J Townsend	1993 v E	59	14	7	12	7	141
Forwards:							
R S Beattie	2000 v NZ	3	0	0	0	0	0
S J Brotherstone	1999 v I	7	0	0	0	0	0
G C Bulloch	1997 v SA	31	2	0	0	0	10
S J Campbell	1995 v C	17	0	0	0	0	0
I A Fullarton	2000 v NZ	2	0	0	0	0	0
G Graham	1997 v A	17	1	0	0	0	5
S B Grimes	1997 v A	31	2	0	0	0	10
N Hines	2000 v NZ	1	0	0	0	0	0
M D Leslie	1998 v SA	22	8	0	0	0	40
G R McIlwham	1998 v Fj	11	0	0	0	0	0
K D McKenzie	1994 v Arg	14	1	0	0	0	5
C G Mather	1999 v R	4	2	0	0	0	10
R Metcalfe	2000 v E	9	1	0	0	0	5
S Murray	1997 v A	32	2	0	0	0	10
J M Petrie	2000 v NZ	8	1	0	0	0	5
A C Pountney	1998 v SA	24	3	0	0	0	15
M C Proudfoot	1998 v Fj	3	0	0	0	0	0
S J Reid	1995 v WS	8	0	0	0	0	0

A J Roxburgh	1997 v A	8	0	0	0	0	0
R R Russell	1999 v R	7	1	0	0	0	5
S Scott	2000 v NZ	4	0	0	0	0	0
G L Simpson	1998 v A	12	2	0	0	0	10
T J Smith	1997 v E	29	5	0	0	0	25
B D Stewart	1996 v NZ	4	0	0	0	0	0
M J Stewart	1996 v It	23	0	0	0	0	0
S M Taylor	2000 v US	5	0	0	0	0	0
G W Weir	1990 v Arg	61	4	0	0	0	19
J P R White	2000 v E	8	0	0	0	0	0

IRELAND TEST SEASON REVIEW 2000-01

A Delicious, Delirious End

Peter O'Reilly

Ireland's protracted season finally came to an end on a delicious and delirious afternoon at Lansdowne Road in late October. The end was over six months late but not too many folks in the old stadium were complaining at the time. As Keith Wood led his men on a raucous lap of honour after the 20-14 victory over England, the hiatus caused by foot-and-mouth seemed wholly immaterial.

The statisticians will record this as Ireland's best finish to the championship in 16 years, the first time they have won four games in a season since the 1948 Grand Slam. But the post-match scenes were more instructive than any cold stat. As the bedraggled England players trooped up to receive the Lloyds TSB Six Nations Trophy, their opponents were dancing a merry jig just metres away. To the visitors the trophy, to Ireland the spoils of victory.

Amid the riotous celebration, it was easiest to ignore the fact that, were it not for the soulless performance in Murrayfield four weeks previously, Ireland would have been playing for their own Grand Slam. That dream had been wrecked by a rejuvenated Scotland that had blown Warren Gatland's team aside by 32-10. That defeat prompted some fearful flak for both the coach and his players. But a month later, any talk of Gatland's job security became pointless. Along with assistant coach Eddie O'Sullivan and, at short notice, Leinster's Matt Williams, he had masterminded an heroic win, establishing Ireland as the principal challengers to England's pre-eminence in Europe.

In many ways, it was a case of mission accomplished. For this season had always been about building upon the advances of the previous year, when Ireland had scaled the dizzy heights of three championship wins in a row. After a few false dawns during the 90's, Irish rugby was apparently about to rise and shine.

South Africa provided a useful yardstick to begin with. Gatland's team had played the Springboks on three occasions in the previous 24 months and had struggled to provide a meaningful contest, relying mainly on muscle and mayhem. Now, there was enough talent and pace in the three-quarters to pose a more sophisticated test. And that is largely the way this November match panned out. The backs had accounted for 10 of the 11 tries scored against a hapless Japanese side in the previous week's warm-up Test (Ireland won 78-9). Once again, they were the principal threat to Harry Viljoen's team, which was rather flattered by a final scoreline of 28-18.

In fact, Ireland had blown a marvellous opportunity to beat the Springboks for the first time since 1965. While there were excellent tries by wings Denis Hickie and Tyrone Howe to celebrate, it was a basic lack of composure that saw Ireland fade from a situation where the teams were tied at 18-18 with 15 minutes remaining. The Springboks had played dull, robotic rugby by comparison but were street-wise enough to shut the game out, with André Venter's try settling the issue three minutes into injury time.

Still, a fine launching pad for the Six Nations. Gatland's only problem was he failed to secure very much time with his players in the intervening months. It is one of the ironies of his situation. Having been instrumental in encouraging players home from abroad, he has helped in the strengthening of the Irish provinces; at the same time, the provinces often seem to have first call on those players.

It thus transpired that Gatland's preparation for the first championship game in Rome was severely limited – either the provinces were busy in Europe or sessions were cancelled because of weather conditions. When, on the Tuesday before the game itself, another session was lost because someone had arranged an audience with The Pope, the coach's frustration was thinly disguised.

Thankfully, the trip to The Vatican had the desired effect, as Ireland opened their account by beating Italy 41-22. The win was not quite as easy as the scoreline might suggest. A half-time Ireland lead by 19-15 gives an indication of how much they struggled to contain an Italian side cruelly deprived of Diego Dominguez, their talisman and chief points harvester. Dominguez's replacement, Ramiro Pez, had a wretched afternoon, while the Italian place-kickers managed just three successful kicks between them. In contrast, Ronan O'Gara finished with 21 points, while Rob Henderson laid down an early Lions marker by scoring a hat-trick of tries.

An imperfect start, perhaps, but it was worth remembering that Ireland hadn't opened their championship account with a win in 13 seasons. Relief then turned to rejoicing two weeks later as France came to Lansdowne Road and were sent packing for the second year in succession. After his hat-trick in the Stade de France the previous year, it was improbable that Brian O'Driscoll would again stand centre-stage. But so it proved. He and Henderson tormented the French midfield all day, and the difference between the sides was O'Driscoll's 'try' during the second half.

No one, least of all O'Driscoll himself, believed he had managed to ground the ball properly through Xavier Garbajosa's tackle in the left-hand corner under the East Stand. No one, except video referee Brian Campsall, that is, who instructed Scott Young that the try was good. O'Gara kicked an excellent conversion and Ireland won by seven points, 22-17.

And there the momentum ended. As the foot-and-mouth crisis developed, there was much talk of alternative venues, of re-scheduling Ireland's three remaining games to May. But it came to nothing. Ireland did win a meaningless match against Romania in Bucharest in June (37-3), but we can only imagine the frustration felt by Gatland and his players, especially those challenging for Lions plaes. The likes of Denis Hickie, John Hayes, Peter Clohessy and Anthony Foley were particularly unfortunate to be idle for so long.

And gradually Gatland became a little itchy himself. Because of a directive by the IRFU's fitness director, Liam Hennessy, he had been denied the opportunity to tour his native New Zealand during the summer, settling instead for a three-week training camp in Poland. Then he made the near-fatal error of agitating through the media for a contract extension up until the 2003 World Cup.

The IRFU committee men were not best pleased at being pressurised in this way, and Gatland's situation suddenly became critical when his team failed utterly in the first of the rescheduled championship games, in Edinburgh. For all their fitness, his players looked tired and under-motivated, while tactically, Gatland had been thoroughly out-thought by the old fox, Ian McGeechan.

It meant that a win in Cardiff three weeks later was practically essential in order for the coach to hold his position after three and a half years in the job. He called in old reliables like Mick Galwey, Kevin Maggs and David Humphreys and they duly did the trick, with Humphreys kicking 19 points and running the show. An under-strength Welsh team were undeniably woeful and Ireland only sealed the win with tries by Hickie, O'Driscoll and Shane Horgan in the final ten minutes. But there wasn't much arguing with a 36-6 final score-line, Ireland's highest score and their biggest win against Wales.

But everything paled in comparison to the wonderful win in Dublin seven days later. England may have been missing key players, Ireland may have had the advantage of two warm-up games. But nothing can detract from the heroism of the players, perhaps best illustrated by Peter Stringer's dramatic tap-tackle on Dan Luger midway through the second half. The end had been a long time coming but it was worth every minute of the wait.

Ireland's Test Record in 2000-2001:
Played 8, won 6, lost 2.

Opponents	Date	Venue	Result
England	20th October 2001	H	Won 20-14
Wales	13th October 2001	A	Won 36-6
Scotland	22nd September 2001	A	Lost 10-32
Romania	2nd June 2001	A	Won 37-3
France	17th February 2001	H	Won 22-15
Italy	3rd February 2001	A	Won 41-22
South Africa	19th November 2000	H	Lost 18-28
Japan	11th November 2000	H	Won 78-9

IRISH INTERNATIONAL PLAYERS
(up to 20 October 2001)

Note: Years given for International Championship matches are for second half of season; eg 1972 means season 1971-72. Years for all other matches refer to the actual year of the match. When a series has taken place, figures have been used to denote the particular matches in which players have featured. Thus 1981 *SA* 2 indicates that a player appeared in the second Test of the series.

Abraham, M (Bective Rangers) 1912 *E, S, W, SA*, 1914 *W*
Adams, C (Old Wesley), 1908 *E*, 1909 *E, F*, 1910 *F*, 1911 *E, S, W, F*, 1912 *S, W, SA*, 1913 *W, F*, 1914 *F, E, S*
Agar, R D (Malone) 1947 *F, E, S, W*, 1948 *F*, 1949 *S, W*, 1950 *F, E, W*
Agnew, P J (CIYMS) 1974 *F* (R), 1976 *A*
Ahearne, T (Queen's Coll, Cork) 1899 *E*
Aherne, L F P (Dolphin, Lansdowne) 1988 *E* 2, *WS, It*, 1989 *F, W, E, S, NZ*, 1990 *E, S, F, W* (R), 1992 *E, S, F, A*
Alexander, R (NIFC, Police Union) 1936 *E, S, W*, 1937 *E, S, W*, 1938 *E, S*, 1939 *E, S, W*
Allen, C E (Derry, Liverpool) 1900 *E, S, W*, 1901 *E, S, W*, 1903 *S, W*, 1904 *E, S, W*, 1905 *E, S, W, NZ*, 1906 *E, S, W, SA*, 1907 *S, W*
Allen, G G (Derry, Liverpool) 1896 *E, S, W*, 1897 *E, S*, 1898 *E, S*, 1899 *E, W*
Allen, T C (NIFC) 1885 *E, S* 1
Allen, W S (Wanderers) 1875 *E*
Allison, J B (Edinburgh U) 1899 *E, S*, 1900 *E, S, W*, 1901 *E, S, W*, 1902 *E, S, W*, 1903 *S*
Anderson, F E (Queen's U, Belfast, NIFC) 1953 *F, E, S, W*, 1954 *NZ, F, E, S, W*, 1955 *F, E, S, W*
Anderson, H J (Old Wesley) 1903 *E, S*, 1906 *E, S*
Anderson, W A (Dungannon) 1984 *A*, 1985 *S, F, W, E*, 1986 *F, S, R*, 1987 *E, S, F, W*, [*W, C, Tg, A*], 1988 *S, F, W, E* 1,2, 1989 *F, W, E, NZ*, 1990 *E, S*
Andrews, G (NIFC) 1875 *E*, 1876 *E*
Andrews, H W (NIFC) 1888 *M*, 1889 *S, W*
Archer, A M (Dublin U, NIFC) 1879 *S*
Arigho, J E (Lansdowne) 1928 *F, E, W*, 1929 *F, E, S, W*, 1930 *F, E, S, W*, 1931 *F, E, S, W, SA*
Armstrong, W K (NIFC) 1960 *SA*, 1961 *E*
Arnott, D T (Lansdowne) 1876 *E*
Ash, W H (NIFC) 1875 *E*, 1876 *E*, 1877 *S*
Aston, H R (Dublin U) 1908 *E, W*
Atkins, A P (Bective Rangers) 1924 *F*
Atkinson, J M (NIFC) 1927 *F, A*
Atkinson, J R (Dublin U) 1882 *W, S*

Bagot, J C (Dublin U, Lansdowne) 1879 *S, E*, 1880 *E, S*, 1881 *S*
Bailey, A H (UC Dublin, Lansdowne) 1934 *W*, 1935 *E, S, W, NZ*, 1936 *E, S, W*, 1937 *E, S, W*, 1938 *E, S*
Bailey, N (Northampton) 1952 *E*
Bardon, M E (Bohemians) 1934 *E*
Barlow, M (Wanderers) 1875 *E*
Barnes, R J (Dublin U, Armagh) 1933 *W*
Barr, A (Methodist Coll, Belfast) 1898 *W*, 1899 *S*, 1901 *E, S*
Barry, N J (Garryowen) 1991 *Nm* 2(R)
Beamish, C E St J (RAF, Leicester) 1933 *W, S*, 1934 *S, W*, 1935 *E, S, W, NZ*, 1936 *E, S, W*, 1938 *W*
Beamish, G R (RAF, Leicester) 1925 *E, S, W*, 1928 *F, E, S, W*, 1929 *F, E, S, W*, 1930 *F, S, W*, 1931 *F, E, S, W, SA*, 1932 *E, S, W*, 1933 *E, W, S*
Beatty, W J (NIFC, Richmond) 1910 *F*, 1912 *F, W*
Becker, V A (Lansdowne) 1974 *F, W*
Beckett, G G P (Dublin U) 1908 *E, S, W*
Bell, J C (Ballymena, Northampton, Dungannon) 1994 *A* 1,2, *US*, 1995 *S, It*, [*NZ, W, F*], *Fj*, 1996 *US, S, F, W, E, WS, A*, 1997 *It* 1, *F, W, E, S*, 1998 *Gg, R, SA* 3, 1999 *F, W, S It* (R), [*US* (R), *A* 3(R), *R*], 2001 *R* (R)
Bell, R J (NIFC) 1875 *E*, 1876 *E*
Bell, W E (Belfast Collegians) 1953 *F, E, S, W*
Bennett, F (Belfast Collegians) 1913 *S*
Bent, G C (Dublin U) 1882 *W, E*
Berkery, P J (Lansdowne) 1954 *W*, 1955 *W*, 1956 *S, W*, 1957 *F, E, S, W*, 1958 *A, E, S*
Bermingham, J J C (Blackrock Coll) 1921 *E, S, W, F*
Bishop, J P (London Irish) 1998 *SA*, 1,2, *Gg, R, SA* 3, 1999 *F, W, E, S, It, A* 1,2, *Arg* 1, [*US, A* 3, *Arg* 2], 2000 *E, Arg, C*

Blackham, J C (Queen's Coll, Cork) 1909 *S, W, F*, 1910 *E, S, W*
Blake-Knox, S E F (NIFC) 1976 *E, S*, 1977 *F* (R)
Blayney, J J (Wanderers) 1950 *S*
Bond, A T W (Derry) 1894 *S, W*
Bornemann, W W (Wanderers) 1960 *E, S, W, SA*
Bowen, D St J (Cork Const) 1977 *W, E, S*
Boyd, C A (Dublin U) 1900 *S*, 1901 *S, W*
Boyle, C V (Dublin U) 1935 *NZ*, 1936 *E, S, W*, 1937 *E, S, W*, 1938 *W*, 1939 *W*
Brabazon, H M (Dublin U) 1884 *E*, 1885 *S* 1, 1886 *E*
Bradley, M J (Dolphin) 1920 *W, F*, 1922 *E, S, W, F*, 1923 *E, S, W, F*, 1925 *F, S, W*, 1926 *F, E, S, W*, 1927 *F, W*
Bradley, M T (Cork Constitution) 1984 *A*, 1985 *S, F, W, E*, 1986 *F, W, E, S, R*, 1987 *E, S, F, W*, [*W, C, Tg, A*], 1988 *S, F, W, E* 1, 1990 *W*, 1992 *NZ* 1,2, 1993 *S, F, W, E, R*, 1994 *F, W, E, S, A* 1,2, *US*, 1995 *S, F*, [*NZ*]
Bradshaw, G (Belfast Collegians) 1903 *W*
Bradshaw, R M (Wanderers) 1885 *E, S* 1,2
Brady, A M (UC Dublin, Malone) 1966 *S*, 1968 *E, S, W*
Brady, J A (Wanderers) 1976 *E, S*
Brady, J R (CIYMS) 1951 *S, W*, 1953 *F, E, S, W*, 1954 *W*, 1956 *W*, 1957 *F, E, S, W*
Bramwell, T (NIFC) 1928 *F*
Brand, T N (NIFC) 1924 *NZ*
Brennan, J I (CIYMS) 1957 *S, W*
Brennan, T (St Mary's Coll) 1998 *SA* 1(R),2(R), 1999 *F* (R), *S* (R), *It, A* 2, *Arg* 1, [*US, A* 3], 2000 *E* (R), 2001 *W* (R), *E* (R)
Bresnihan, F P K (UC Dublin, Lansdowne, London Irish) 1966 *E, W*, 1967 *A* 1, *E, S, W, F*, 1968 *F, E, S, W, A*, 1969 *F, E, S, W*, 1970 *SA, F, E, S, W*, 1971 *F, E, S, W*
Brett, J T (Monkstown) 1914 *W*
Bristow, J R (NIFC) 1879 *E*
Brophy, N H (Blackrock Coll, UC Dublin, London Irish) 1957 *F, E*, 1959 *E, S, W, F*, 1960 *F, SA*, 1961 *S, W*, 1962 *E, S, W*, 1963 *E, W*, 1967 *E, S, W, F, A* 2
Brown, E L (Instonians) 1958 *F*
Brown, G S (Monkstown, United Services) 1912 *S, W, SA*
Brown, H (Windsor) 1877 *E*
Brown, T (Windsor) 1877 *E, S*
Brown, W H (Dublin U) 1899 *E*
Brown, W J (Malone) 1970 *SA, F, S, W*
Brown, W S (Dublin U) 1893 *S, W*, 1894 *E, S, W*
Browne, A W (Dublin U) 1951 *SA*
Browne, D (Blackrock Coll) 1920 *F*
Browne, H C (United Services and RN) 1929 *E, S, W*
Browne, W F (United Services and Army) 1925 *E, S, W*, 1926 *S, W*, 1927 *F, E, S, W, A*, 1928 *E, S*
Browning, D R (Wanderers) 1881 *E, S*
Bruce, S A M (NIFC) 1883 *E, S*, 1884 *E*
Brunker, A A (Lansdowne) 1895 *E, W*
Bryant, C H (Cardiff) 1920 *E, S*
Buchanan, A McM (Dublin U) 1926 *E, S, W*, 1927 *S, W, A*
Buchanan, J W B (Dublin U) 1882 *S*, 1884 *E, S*
Buckley, J H (Sunday's Well) 1973 *E, S*
Bulger, L Q (Lansdowne) 1896 *E, S, W*, 1897 *E, S*, 1898 *E, S, W*
Bulger, M J (Dublin U) 1888 *M*
Burges, J H (Rosslyn Park) 1950 *F, E*
Burgess, R B (Dublin U) 1912 *SA*
Burke, P A (Cork Constitution, Bristol, Harlequins) 1995 *E, S, W* (R), *It*, [*J*], *Fj*, 1996 *US* (R), *A*, 1997 *It* 1, *S* (R), 2001 *R* (R)
Burkitt, J C S (Queen's Coll, Cork) 1881 *E*
Burns, I J (Wanderers) 1980 *E* (R)
Butler, L G (Blackrock Coll) 1960 *W*
Butler, N (Bective Rangers) 1920 *E*
Byers, R M (NIFC) 1928 *S, W*, 1929 *E, S, W*
Byrne, E (St Mary's Coll) 2001 *It* (R), *F* (R), *S* (R), *W* (R), *E* (R)
Byrne, E M J (Blackrock Coll) 1977 *S, F*, 1978 *F, W, E, NZ*

Byrne, N F (UC Dublin) 1962 *F*
Byrne, S J (UC Dublin, Lansdowne) 1953 *S, W*, 1955 *F*
Byrne, S J (Blackrock Coll) 2001 *R* (R)
Byron, W G (NIFC) 1896 *E, S, W*, 1897 *E, S*, 1898 *E, S, W*, 1899 *E, S, W*

Caddell, E D (Dublin U, Wanderers) 1904 *S*, 1905 *E, S, W, NZ*, 1906 *E, S, W, SA*, 1907 *E, S*, 1908 *S, W*
Cagney, S J (London Irish) 1925 *W*, 1926 *F, E, S, W*, 1927 *F*, 1928 *E, S, W*, 1929 *F, E, S, W*
Callan, C P (Lansdowne) 1947 *F, E, S, W*, 1948 *F, E, S, W*, 1949 *F, E*
Cameron, E D (Bective Rangers) 1891 *S, W*
Campbell, C E (Old Wesley) 1970 *SA*
Campbell, E F (Monkstown) 1899 *S, W*, 1900 *E, W*
Campbell, S B B (Derry) 1911 *E, S, W, F*, 1912 *F, E, S, W, SA*, 1913 *E, S, W*
Campbell, S O (Old Belvedere) 1976 *A*, 1979 *A* 1,2, 1980 *E, S, F, W*, 1981 *F, W, E, S, SA* 1, 1982 *W, E, S, F*, 1983 *S, F, W, E*, 1984 *F, W*
Canniffe, D M (Lansdowne) 1976 *W, E*
Cantrell, J L (UC Dublin, Blackrock Coll) 1976 *A, F, W, E, S*, 1981 *S, SA* 1,2, *A*
Carey, R W (Dungannon) 1992 *NZ* 1,2
Carpendale, M J (Monkstown) 1886 *S*, 1887 *W*, 1888 *W, S*
Carr, N J (Ards) 1985 *S, F, W, E*, 1986 *W, E, S, R*, 1987 *E, S, W*
Carroll, C (Bective Rangers) 1930 *F*
Carroll, R (Lansdowne) 1947 *F*, 1950 *S, W*
Casement, B N (Dublin U) 1875 *E*, 1876 *E*, 1879 *E*
Casement, F (Dublin U) 1906 *E, S, W*
Casey, J C (Young Munster) 1930 *S*, 1932 *E*
Casey, P J (UC Dublin, Lansdowne) 1963 *F, E, S, W, NZ*, 1964 *E, S, W, F*, 1965 *F, E, S*
Casey, R E (Blackrock Coll) 1999 [*A* 3(t), *Arg* 2(R)], 2000 *E, US* (R), *C* (R)
Chambers, J (Dublin U) 1886 *E, S*, 1887 *E, S, W*
Chambers, R R (Instonians) 1951 *E, S, W*, 1952 *F, W*
Clancy, T P J (Lansdowne) 1988 *W, E* 1,2, *WS, It*, 1989 *F, W, E, S*
Clarke, A T H (Northampton, Dungannon) 1995 *Fj* (R), 1996 *W, E, WS*, 1997 *F* (R), *It* 2(R), 1998 *Gg* (R), *R*
Clarke, C P (Terenure Coll) 1993 *F, W, E*, 1998 *W, E*
Clarke, D J (Dolphin) 1991 *W, Nm* 1,2, [*J, A*], 1992 *NZ* 2(R)
Clarke, J A B (Bective Rangers) 1922 *S, W, F*, 1923 *F*, 1924 *E, S, W*
Clegg, R J (Bangor) 1973 *F*, 1975 *E, S, F, W*
Clifford, J T (Young Munster) 1949 *F, E, S, W*, 1950 *F, E, S, W*, 1951 *F, E, SA*, 1952 *F, S*
Clinch, A D (Dublin U, Wanderers) 1892 *S*, 1893 *W*, 1895 *E, S, W*, 1896 *E, S, W*, 1897 *E, S*
Clinch, J D (Wanderers, Dublin U) 1923 *W*, 1924 *F, E, S, W, NZ*, 1925 *F, E, S*, 1926 *E, S, W*, 1927 *F*, 1928 *F, E, S, W*, 1929 *F, E, S, W*, 1930 *F, E, S, W*, 1931 *F, E, S, W, SA*
Clohessy, P M (Young Munster) 1993 *F, W, E*, 1994 *F, W, E, S, A* 1,2, 1995 *E, S, F, W*, 1996 *S, F*, 1997 *It* 2, 1998 *F* (R), *W* (R), *SA* 2(R), *Gg, R, SA* 3, 1999 *F, W, E, S, It, A* 1,2 *Arg* 1, [*US, A* 3(R)], 2000 *E, S, It, F, W, Arg, J, SA*, 2001 *It, F, R, S, W, E*
Clune, J J (Blackrock Coll) 1912 *SA*, 1913 *W, F*, 1914 *F, E, W*
Coffey, J J (Lansdowne) 1900 *E*, 1901 *W*, 1902 *E, S, W*, 1903 *E, S, W*, 1905 *E, S, W, NZ*, 1906 *E, S, W, SA*, 1907 *E*, 1908 *W*, 1910 *F*
Cogan, W St J (Queen's Coll, Cork) 1907 *E, S*
Collier, S R (Queen's Coll, Belfast) 1883 *S*
Collins, P C (Lansdowne, London Irish) 1987 [*C*], 1990 *S* (R)
Collis, W R F (KCH, Harlequins) 1924 *F, W, NZ*, 1925 *F, E, S*, 1926 *F*
Collis, W S (Wanderers) 1884 *W*
Collopy, G (Bective Rangers) 1891 *S*, 1892 *S*
Collopy, R (Bective Rangers) 1923 *E, S, W, F*, 1924 *F, E, S, W, NZ*, 1925 *F, E, S, W*
Collopy, W P (Bective Rangers) 1914 *F, E, S, W*, 1921 *E, S, W, F*, 1922 *E, S, W, F*, 1923 *S, W, F*, 1924 *F, E, S, W*
Combe, A (NIFC) 1875 *E*
Condon, H C (London Irish) 1984 *S* (R)
Cook, H G (Lansdowne) 1884 *W*
Coote, P B (RAF, Leicester) 1933 *S*
Corcoran, J C (London Irish) 1947 *A*, 1948 *F*
Corken, T S (Belfast Collegians) 1937 *E, S, W*

Corkery, D S (Cork Constitution, Bristol) 1994 *A* 1,2, *US*, 1995 *E*, [*NZ, J, W, F*], *Fj*, 1996 *US, S, F, W, E, WS, A*, 1997 *It* 1, *F, W, E, S*, 1998 *S, F, W, E*, 1999 *A* 1(R),2(R)
Corley, H H (Dublin U, Wanderers) 1902 *E, S, W*, 1903 *E, S, W*, 1904 *E, S*
Cormac, H S T (Clontarf) 1921 *E, S, W*
Corrigan, R (Greystones, Lansdowne) 1997 *C* (R), *It* 2, 1998 *S, F, W, E, SA* 3(R), 1999 *A* 1(R),2(R), [*Arg* 2]
Costello, P (Bective Rangers) 1960 *F*
Costello, R A (Garryowen) 1993 *S*
Costello, V C P (St Mary's Coll, London Irish) 1996 *US, F, W, E. WS* (R), 1997 *C, It* 2(R), 1998 *S* (R), *F, W, E, SA* 1,2, *Gg, R, SA* 3, 1999 *F, W* (R), *E, S* (R), *It, A* 1
Cotton, J (Wanderers) 1889 *W*
Coulter, H H (Queen's U, Belfast) 1920 *E, S, W*
Courtney, A W (UC Dublin) 1920 *S, W, F*, 1921 *E, S, W, F*
Cox, H L (Dublin U) 1875 *E*, 1876 *E*, 1877 *E, S*
Craig, R G (Queen's U, Belfast) 1938 *S, W*
Crawford, E C (Dublin U) 1885 *E, S* 1
Crawford, W E (Lansdowne) 1920 *E, S, W, F*, 1921 *E, S, W, F*, 1922 *E, S*, 1923 *E, S, W, F*, 1924 *F, E, W, NZ*, 1925 *F, E, S, W*, 1926 *F, E, S, W*, 1927 *F, E, S, W*
Crean, T J (Wanderers) 1894 *E, S, W*, 1895 *E, S, W*, 1896 *E, S, W*
Crichton, R Y (Dublin U) 1920 *E, S, W, F*, 1921 *F*, 1922 *E*, 1923 *W, F*, 1924 *F, E, S, W, NZ*, 1925 *E, S*
Croker, E W D (Limerick) 1878 *E*
Cromey, G E (Queen's U, Belfast) 1937 *E, S, W*, 1938 *E, S, W*, 1939 *E, S, W*
Cronin, B M (Garryowen) 1995 *S*, 1997 *S*
Cronyn, A P (Dublin U, Lansdowne) 1875 *E*, 1876 *E*, 1880 *S*
Crossan, K D (Instonians) 1982 *S*, 1984 *F, W, E, S*, 1985 *S, F, W, E*, 1986 *E, S, R*, 1987 *E, S, F, W*, [*W, C, Tg, A*], 1988 *S, F, W, E* 1, *WS, It*, 1989 *W, S, NZ*, 1990 *E, S, F, W, Arg*, 1991 *E, S, Nm* 2 [*Z, J, S*], 1992 *W*
Crotty, D J (Garryowen) 1996 *A*, 1997 *It* 1, *F, W*, 2000 *C*
Crowe, J F (UC Dublin) 1974 *NZ*
Crowe, L (Old Belvedere) 1950 *E, S, W*
Crowe, M P (Lansdowne) 1929 *W*, 1930 *E, S, W*, 1931 *F, E, W, SA*, 1932 *S, W*, 1933 *W, S*, 1934 *E*
Crowe, P M (Blackrock Coll) 1935 *E*, 1938 *E*
Cullen, T J (UC Dublin) 1949 *F*
Cullen, W J (Monkstown and Manchester) 1920 *E*
Culliton, M G (Wanderers) 1959 *E, S, W, F*, 1960 *E, S, W, F, SA*, 1961 *E, S, W, F*, 1962 *S, F*, 1964 *E, S, W, F*
Cummins, W E A (Queen's Coll, Cork) 1879 *S*, 1881 *E*, 1882 *E*
Cunningham, D McC (NIFC) 1923 *E, S, W*, 1925 *F, E, W*
Cunningham, M J (UC Cork) 1955 *F, E, S, W*, 1956 *F, S, W*
Cunningham, V J G (St Mary's Coll) 1988 *E* 2, *It*, 1990 *Arg* (R), 1991 *Nm* 1,2, [*Z, J*(R)], 1992 *NZ* 1,2, *A*, 1993 *S, F, W, E, R*, 1994 *F*
Cunningham, W A (Lansdowne) 1920 *W*, 1921 *E, S, W, F*, 1922 *E*, 1923 *S, W*
Cuppaidge, J L (Dublin U) 1879 *E*, 1880 *E, S*
Currell, J (NIFC) 1877 *S*
Curtis, A B (Oxford U) 1950 *F, E, S*
Curtis, D M (London Irish) 1991 *W, E, S, Nm* 1,2, [*Z, J, A*], 1992 *W, E, S* (R), *F*
Cuscaden, W A (Dublin U, Bray) 1876 *E*
Cussen, D J (Dublin U) 1921 *E, S, W, F*, 1922 *E*, 1923 *E, S, W, F*, 1926 *F, E, S, W*, 1927 *F, E*

Daly, J C (London Irish) 1947 *F, E, S, W*, 1948 *E, S, W*
Daly, M J (Harlequins) 1938 *E*
Danaher, P P A (Lansdowne, Garryowen) 1988 *S, F, W, WS, It*, 1989 *F, NZ* (R), 1990 *F*, 1992 *S, F, NZ* 1, *A*, 1993 *S, F, W, E, R*, 1994 *F, W, E, S, A* 1,2, *US*, 1995 *E, S, F, W*
D'Arcy, G M (Lansdowne) 1999 [*R* (R)]
Dargan, M J (Old Belvedere) 1952 *S, W*
Davidson, C T (NIFC) 1921 *F*
Davidson, I G (NIFC) 1899 *E*, 1900 *S, W*, 1901 *E, S, W*, 1902 *E, S, W*
Davidson, J C (Dungannon) 1969 *F, E, S, W*, 1973 *NZ*, 1976 *NZ*
Davidson, J W (Dungannon, London Irish, Castres) 1995 *Fj*, 1996 *S, F, W, E, WS, A*, 1997 *It* 1, *F, W, E, S*, 1998 *Gg* (R), *R* (R), *SA* 3(R), 1999 *F, W, E, S, It, A* 1,2(R), *Arg* 1, [*US,R* (R), *Arg* 2], 2000 *S* (R), *W* (R), *US, C*, 2001 *It* (R), *S*
Davies, F E (Lansdowne) 1892 *S, W*, 1893 *E, S, W*
Davis, J L (Monkstown) 1898 *E, S*
Davis, W J N (Edinburgh U, Bessbrook) 1890 *S, W, E*, 1891 *E, S, W*, 1892 *E, S*, 1895 *S*

Davison, W (Belfast Academy) 1887 *W*
Davy, E O'D (UC Dublin, Lansdowne) 1925 *W*, 1926 *F, E, S, W*, 1927 *F, E, S, W, A*, 1928 *F, E, S, W*, 1929 *F, E, S, W*, 1930 *F, E, S, W*, 1931 *F, E, S, W, SA*, 1932 *E, S, W*, 1933 *E, W, S*, 1934 *E*
Dawson, A R (Wanderers) 1958 *A, E, S, W, F*, 1959 *E, S, W, F*, 1960 *F, SA*, 1961 *E, S, W, F, SA*, 1962 *S, F, W*, 1963 *F, E, S, W, NZ*, 1964 *E, S, F*
Dawson, K (London Irish) 1997 *NZ, C*, 1998 *S*, 1999 *[R, Arg 2]*, 2000 *E, S, It, F, W, J, SA*, 2001 *R, S, W* (R), *E* (R)
Dean, P M (St Mary's Coll) 1981 *SA* 1,2, *A*, 1982 *W, E, S, F*, 1984 *A*, 1985 *S, F, W, E*, 1986 *F, W, R*, 1987 *E, S, F, W*, *[W, A]*, 1988 *S, F, W, E* 1,2, *WS, It*, 1989 *F, W, E, S*
Deane, E C (Monkstown) 1909 *E*
Deering, M J (Bective Rangers) 1929 *W*
Deering, S J (Bective Rangers) 1935 *E, S, W, NZ*, 1936 *E, S, W*, 1937 *E, S*
Deering, S M (Garryowen, St Mary's Coll) 1974 *W*, 1976 *F, W, E, S*, 1977 *W, E*, 1978 *NZ*
de Lacy, H (Harlequins) 1948 *E, S*
Delany, M G (Bective Rangers) 1895 *W*
Dempsey, G (Terenure Coll) 1998 *Gg* (R). *SA* 3, 1999 *F, E, S, It, A* 2, 2000 *E* (R), *S, It, F, W, SA*, 2001 *It, F, S, W, E*
Dennison, S P (Garryowen) 1973 *F*, 1975 *E, S*
Dick, C J (Ballymena) 1961 *W, F, SA*, 1962 *W*, 1963 *F, E, S, W*
Dick, J S (Queen's U, Belfast) 1962 *E*
Dick, J S (Queen's U, Cork) 1887 *E, S, W*
Dickson, J A N (Dublin U) 1920 *W, F*
Doherty, A E (Old Wesley) 1974 *P* (R)
Doherty, W D (Guy's Hospital) 1920 *E, S, W*, 1921 *E, S, W, F*
Donaldson, J A (Belfast Collegians) 1958 *A, E, S, W*
Donovan, T M (Queen's Coll, Cork) 1889 *S*
Dooley, J F (Galwegians) 1959 *E, S, W*
Doran, B R W (Lansdowne) 1900 *S, W*, 1901 *E, S, W*, 1902 *E, S, W*
Doran, E F (Lansdowne) 1890 *S, W*
Doran, G P (Lansdowne) 1899 *S, W*, 1900 *E, S*, 1902 *S, W*, 1903 *W*, 1904 *E*
Douglas, A C (Instonians) 1923 *F*, 1924 *E, S*, 1927 *A*, 1928 *S*
Downing, A J (Dublin U) 1882 *W*
Dowse, J C A (Monkstown) 1914 *F, S, W*
Doyle, J A P (Greystones) 1984 *E, S*
Doyle, J T (Bective Rangers) 1935 *W*
Doyle, M G (Blackrock Coll, UC Dublin, Cambridge U, Edinburgh Wands) 1965 *F, E, S, W, SA*, 1966 *F, E, S, W*, 1967 *A* 1, *E, S, W, F, A* 2, 1968 *F, E, S, W, A*
Doyle, T J (Wanderers) 1968 *E, S, W*
Duggan, A T A (Lansdowne) 1963 *NZ*, 1964 *F*, 1966 *W*, 1967 *A* 1, *S, W, A* 2, 1968 *F, E, S, W*, 1969 *F, E, S, W*, 1970 *SA, F, E, S, W*, 1971 *F, E, S, W*, 1972 *F* 2
Duggan, W (UC Cork) 1920 *S, W*
Duggan, W P (Blackrock Coll) 1975 *E, S, F, W*, 1976 *A, F, W, S, NZ*, 1977 *W, E, S, F*, 1978 *S, F, W, E, NZ*, 1979 *E, S, A* 1,2, 1980 *E*, 1981 *F, W, E, S, SA* 1,2, *A*, 1982 *W, E, S*, 1983 *S, F, W, E*, 1984 *F, W, E, S*
Duignan, P (Galwegians) 1998 *Gg, R*
Duncan, W R (Malone) 1984 *W, E*
Dunlea, F J (Lansdowne) 1989 *W, E, S*
Dunlop, R (Dublin U) 1889 *W*, 1890 *S, W, E*, 1891 *E, S, W*, 1892 *E, S*, 1893 *W*, 1894 *W*
Dunn, P E F (Bective Rangers) 1923 *S*
Dunn, T B (NIFC) 1935 *NZ*
Dunne, M J (Lansdowne) 1929 *F, E, S*, 1930 *F, E, S, W*, 1932 *E, S, W*, 1933 *E, W, S*, 1934 *E, S, W*
Dwyer, P J (UC Dublin) 1962 *W*, 1963 *F, NZ*, 1964 *S, W*

Easterby, G (Ebbw Vale, Ballynahinch, Llanelli) 2000 *US, C* (R), 2001 *R* (R), *S, W* (R)
Easterby, S H (Llanelli) 2000 *S, It, F, W, Arg, US, C*, 2001 *S*
Edwards, H G (Dublin U) 1877 *E*, 1878 *E*
Edwards, R W (Malone) 1904 *W*
Edwards, T (Lansdowne) 1888 *M*, 1890 *S, W, E*, 1892 *W*, 1893 *E*
Edwards, W V (Malone) 1912 *F, E*
Egan, J D (Bective Rangers) 1922 *S*
Egan, J T (Cork Constitution) 1931 *F, E, SA*
Egan, M S (Garryowen) 1893 *E*, 1895 *S*
Ekin, W (Queen's Coll, Belfast) 1888 *W, S*
Elliott, W R J (Bangor) 1979 *S*
Elwood, E P (Lansdowne, Galwegians) 1993 *W, E, R*, 1994 *F, W, E, S, A* 1,2, 1995 *F, W*, *[NZ, W, F]*, 1996 *US, S*, 1997 *F,*

W, E, NZ, C, It 2(R), 1998 *F, W, E, SA* 1,2, *Gg, R, SA* 3, 1999 *It, Arg* 1(R), *[US* (R), *A* 3(R), *R]*
English, M A F (Lansdowne, Limerick Bohemians) 1958 *W, F*, 1959 *E, S, F*, 1960 *E, S*, 1961 *S, W, F*, 1962 *F, W*, 1963 *E, S, W, NZ*
Ennis, F N G (Wanderers) 1979 *A* 1(R)
Ensor, A H (Wanderers) 1973 *W, F*, 1974 *F, W, E, S, P, NZ*, 1975 *E, S, F, W*, 1976 *A, F, W, E, NZ*, 1977 *E*, 1978 *S, F, W, E*
Entrican, J C (Queen's U, Belfast) 1931 *S*
Erskine, D J (Sale) 1997 *NZ* (R), *C, It* 2

Fagan, G L (Kingstown School) 1878 *E*
Fagan, W B C (Wanderers) 1956 *F, E, S*
Farrell, J L (Bective Rangers) 1926 *F, E, S, W*, 1927 *F, E, S, W, A*, 1928 *F, E, S, W*, 1929 *F, E, S, W*, 1930 *F, E, S, W*, 1931 *F, E, S, W, SA*, 1932 *E, S, W*
Feddis, N (Lansdowne) 1956 *E*
Feighery, C F P (Lansdowne) 1972 *F* 1, *E, F* 2
Feighery, T A O (St Mary's Coll) 1977 *W, E*
Ferris, H H (Queen's Coll, Belfast) 1901 *W*
Ferris, J H (Queen's Coll, Belfast) 1900 *E, S, W*
Field, M J (Malone) 1994 *E, S, A* 1(R), 1995 *F* (R), *W* (t), *It* (R), *[NZ(t + R), J]*, *Fj*, 1996 *F* (R), *W, E, A* (R), 1997 *F, W, E, S*
Finlay, J E (Queen's Coll, Belfast) 1913 *E, S, W*, 1920 *E, S, W*
Finlay, W (NIFC) 1876 *E*, 1877 *E, S*, 1878 *E*, 1879 *S, E*, 1880 *S*, 1882 *S*
Finn, M C (UC Cork, Cork Constitution) 1979 *E*, 1982 *W, E, S, F*, 1983 *S, F, W, E*, 1984 *E, S, A*, 1986 *F, W*
Finn, R G A (UC Dublin) 1977 *F*
Fitzgerald, C C (Glasgow U, Dungannon) 1902 *E*, 1903 *E, S*
Fitzgerald, C F (St Mary's Coll) 1979 *A* 1,2, 1980 *E, S, F, W*, 1982 *W, E, S, F*, 1983 *S, F, W, E*, 1984 *F, W, A*, 1985 *S, F, W, E*, 1986 *F, W, E, S*
Fitzgerald, D C (Lansdowne, De La Salle Palmerston) 1984 *E, S*, 1986 *W, E, S, R*, 1987 *E, S, F, W*, *[W, C, A]*, 1988 *S, F, W, E* 1, 1989 *NZ* (R), 1990 *E, S, F, W, Arg*, 1991 *F, W, E, S, Nm* 1,2, *[Z, S, A]*, 1992 *W, S* (R)
Fitzgerald, J (Wanderers) 1884 *W*
Fitzgerald, J J (Young Munster) 1988 *S, F*, 1990 *S, F, W*, 1991 *F, W, E, S*, *[J]*, 1994 *A* 1,2
Fitzgibbon, M J J (Shannon) 1992 *W, E, S, F, NZ* 1,2
Fitzpatrick, J M (Dungannon) 1998 *SA* 1,2 *Gg* (R), *R* (R), *SA* 3, 1999 *F* (R), *W* (R), *E* (R), *It, Arg* 1(R), *[US* (R), *A* 3, *R, Arg* 2(t&R)], 2000 *S* (R), *It* (R), *Arg* (R), *US, C, SA* (t&R), 2001 *R* (R)
Fitzpatrick, M P (Wanderers) 1978 *S*, 1980 *S, F, W*, 1981 *F, W, E, S, A*, 1985 *F* (R)
Flavin, P (Blackrock Coll) 1997 *F* (R), *S*
Fletcher, W W (Kingstown) 1882 *W, S*, 1883 *E*
Flood, R S (Dublin U) 1925 *W*
Flynn, M K (Wanderers) 1959 *F*, 1960 *F*, 1962 *E, S, F, W*, 1964 *E, S, W, F*, 1965 *F, E, S, W, SA*, 1966 *F, E, S*, 1972 *F* 1, *E, F* 2, 1973 *NZ*
Fogarty, T (Garryowen) 1891 *W*
Foley, A G (Shannon) 1995 *E, S, F, W, It*, *[J(t + R)]*, 1996 *A*, 1997 *It* 1, *E* (R), 2000 *E, S, It, F, W, Arg, C, J, SA*, 2001 *It, F, R, S, W, E*
Foley, B O (Shannon) 1976 *F, E*, 1977 *W* (R), 1980 *F, W*, 1981 *F, E, S, SA* 1,2, *A*
Forbes, R E (Malone) 1907 *E*
Forrest, A J (Wanderers) 1880 *E, S*, 1881 *E, S*, 1882 *W, E*, 1883 *E*, 1885 *S* 2
Forrest, E G (Wanderers) 1888 *M*, 1889 *S, W*, 1890 *S, E*, 1891 *E*, 1893 *S*, 1894 *E, S, W*, 1895 *W*, 1897 *E, S*
Forrest, H (Wanderers) 1893 *S, W*
Fortune, J J (Clontarf) 1963 *NZ*, 1964 *E*
Foster, A R (Derry) 1910 *E, S, F*, 1911 *E, S, W, F*, 1912 *F, E, S, W*, 1914 *E, S, W*, 1921 *E, S, W*
Francis, N P J (Blackrock Coll, London Irish, Old Belvedere) 1987 *[Tg, A]*, 1988 *WS, It*, 1989 *S*, 1990 *E, F, W*, 1991 *E, S, Nm* 1,2, *[Z, J, S, A]*, 1992 *W, E, S*, 1993 *F, R*, 1994 *F, W, E, S, A* 1,2, *US*, 1995 *E*, *[NZ, J, W, F]*, *Fj*, 1996 *US, S*
Franks, J G (Dublin U) 1898 *E, S, W*
Frazer, E F (Bective Rangers) 1891 *S*, 1892 *S*
Freer, A E (Lansdowne) 1901 *E, S, W*
Fulcher, G M (Cork Constitution, London Irish) 1994 *A* 2, *US*, 1995 *E* (R), *S, F, W, It*, *[NZ, W, F]*, *Fj*, 1996 *US, S, F, W, E, A*, 1997 *It* 1, *W* (R), 1998 *SA* 1(R)
Fulton, J (NIFC) 1895 *S, W*, 1896 *E*, 1897 *E*, 1898 *W*, 1899 *E*, 1900 *W*, 1901 *E*, 1902 *E, S, W*, 1903 *E, S, W*, 1904 *E, S*
Furlong, J N (UC Galway) 1992 *NZ* 1,2

Gaffikin, W (Windsor) 1875 *E*
Gage, J H (Queen's U, Belfast) 1926 *S, W,* 1927 *S, W*
Galbraith, E (Dublin U) 1875 *E*
Galbraith, H T (Belfast Acad) 1890 *W*
Galbraith, R (Dublin U) 1875 *E,* 1876 *E,* 1877 *E*
Galwey, M J (Shannon) 1991 *F, W, Nm* 2(R), [*J*], 1992 *E, S, F, NZ* 1,2, *A,* 1993 *F, W, E, R,* 1994 *F, W, E, S, A* 1, *US* (R), 1995 *E,* 1996 *WS,* 1998 *F* (R), 1999 *W* (R), 2000 *E* (R), *S, It, F, W, Arg, C,* 2001 *It, F, R, W, E*
Ganly, J B (Monkstown) 1927 *F, E, S, W, A,* 1928 *F, E, S, W,* 1929 *F, S,* 1930 *F*
Gardiner, F (NIFC) 1900 *E, S,* 1901 *E, W,* 1902 *E, S, W,* 1903 *E, W,* 1904 *E, S, W,* 1906 *E, S, W,* 1907 *S, W,* 1908 *S, W,* 1909 *E, S, F*
Gardiner, J B (NIFC) 1923 *E, S, W, F,* 1924 *F, E, S, W, NZ,* 1925 *F, E, S, W*
Gardiner, S (Belfast Albion) 1893 *E, S*
Gardiner, W (NIFC) 1892 *E, S,* 1893 *E, S, W,* 1894 *E, S, W,* 1895 *E, S, W,* 1896 *E, S, W,* 1897 *E, S,* 1898 *W*
Garry, M G (Bective Rangers) 1909 *E, S, W, F,* 1911 *E, S, W*
Gaston, J T (Dublin U) 1954 *NZ, F, E, S,* 1955 *W* 1956 *F, E*
Gavin, T J (Moseley, London Irish) 1949 *F, E*
Geoghegan, S P (London Irish, Bath) 1991 *F, W, E, S, Nm* 1, [*Z, S, A*], 1992 *E, S, F, A,* 1993 *F, W, E, R,* 1994 *F, W, E, S, A* 1,2, *US,* 1995 *E, S, F, W,* [*NZ, J, W, F*], *Fj,* 1996 *US, S, W, E*
Gibson, C M H (Cambridge U, NIFC) 1964 *E, S, W, F,* 1965 *F, E, S, W, SA,* 1966 *F, E, S, W,* 1967 *A* 1, *E, S, W, F, A* 2, 1968 *E, S, W, A,* 1969 *E, S, W,* 1970 *SA, F, E, S, W,* 1971 *F, E, S, W,* 1972 *F* 1, *E, F* 2, 1973 *NZ, E, S, W, F,* 1974 *F, W, E, S, P,* 1975 *E, S, F, W,* 1976 *A, F, W, E, S, NZ,* 1977 *W, E, S, F,* 1978 *F, W, E, NZ,* 1979 *S, A* 1,2
Gibson, M E (Lansdowne, London Irish) 1979 *F, W, E, S,* 1981 *W* (R), 1986 *R,* 1988 *S, F, W, E* 2
Gifford, H P (Wanderers) 1890 *S*
Gillespie, J C (Dublin U) 1922 *W, F*
Gilpin, F G (Queen's U, Belfast) 1962 *E, S, F*
Glass, D C (Belfast Collegians) 1958 *F,* 1960 *W,* 1961 *W, SA*
Glennon, B T (Lansdowne) 1993 *F* (R)
Glennon, J J (Skerries) 1980 *E, S,* 1987 *E, S, F,* [*W* (R)]
Godfrey, R P (UC Dublin) 1954 *S, W*
Goodall, K G (City of Derry, Newcastle U) 1967 *A* 1, *E, S, W, F, A* 2, 1968 *F, E, S, W, A,* 1969 *F, E, S,* 1970 *SA, F, E, S, W*
Gordon, A (Dublin U) 1884 *S*
Gordon, T G (NIFC) 1877 *E, S,* 1878 *E*
Gotto, R P C (NIFC) 1906 *SA*
Goulding, W J (Cork) 1879 *S*
Grace, T O (UC Dublin, St Mary's Coll) 1972 *F* 1, *E,* 1973 *NZ, E, S, W,* 1974 *E, S, P, NZ,* 1975 *S, F, W,* 1976 *A, F, W, E, S, NZ,* 1977 *W, E, S, F,* 1978 *S*
Graham, R I (Dublin U) 1911 *F*
Grant, E L (CIYMS) 1971 *F, E, S, W*
Grant, P J (Bective Rangers) 1894 *S, W*
Graves, C R A (Wanderers) 1934 *E, S, W,* 1935 *E, S, W, NZ,* 1936 *E, S, W,* 1937 *E, S,* 1938 *E, S, W*
Gray, R D (Old Wesley) 1923 *E, S,* 1925 *F,* 1926 *F*
Greene, E H (Dublin U, Kingstown) 1882 *W,* 1884 *W,* 1885 *E, S* 2, 1886 *E*
Greer, R (Kingstown) 1876 *E*
Greeves, T J (NIFC) 1907 *E, S, W,* 1909 *W, F*
Gregg, R J (Queen's U, Belfast) 1953 *F, E, S, W,* 1954 *F, E, S*
Griffin, C S (London Irish) 1951 *F, E*
Griffin, J L (Wanderers) 1949 *S, W*
Griffiths, W (Limerick) 1878 *E*
Grimshaw, C (Queen's U, Belfast) 1969 *E* (R)
Guerin, B N (Galwegians) 1956 *S*
Gwynn, A P (Dublin U) 1895 *W*
Gwynn, L H (Dublin U) 1893 *S,* 1894 *E, S, W,* 1897 *S,* 1898 *E, S*

Hakin, R F (CIYMS) 1976 *W, S, NZ,* 1977 *W, E, F*
Hall, R O N (Dublin U) 1884 *W*
Hall, W H (Instonians) 1923 *E, S, W, F,* 1924 *F, S*
Hallaran, C F G T (Royal Navy) 1921 *E, S, W,* 1922 *E, S, W,* 1923 *E, F,* 1924 *F, E, S, W,* 1925 *F,* 1926 *F, E*
Halpin, G F (Wanderers, London Irish) 1990 *E,* 1991 [*J*], 1992 *E, S, F,* 1993 *A,* 1994 *F* (R), 1995 *It,* [*NZ, W, F*]
Halpin, T (Garryowen) 1909 *S, W, F,* 1910 *E, S, W,* 1911 *E, S, W, F,* 1912 *F, E, S*
Halvey, E O (Shannon) 1995 *F, W, It,* [*J, W* (t), *F* (R)], 1997 *NZ, C* (R)
Hamilton, A J (Lansdowne) 1884 *W*

Hamilton, G F (NIFC) 1991 *F, W, E, S, Nm* 2, [*Z, J, S, A*], 1992 *A*
Hamilton, R L (NIFC) 1926 *F*
Hamilton, R W (Wanderers) 1893 *W*
Hamilton, W J (Dublin U) 1877 *E*
Hamlet, G T (Old Wesley) 1902 *E, S, W,* 1903 *E, S, W,* 1904 *S, W,* 1905 *E, S, W, NZ,* 1906 *SA,* 1907 *E, S, W,* 1908 *E, S, W,* 1909 *E, S, W, F,* 1910 *E, S, F,* 1911 *E, S, W, F*
Hanrahan, C J (Dolphin) 1926 *S, W,* 1927 *E, S, W, A,* 1928 *F, E, S,* 1929 *F, E, S, W,* 1930 *F, E, S, W,* 1931 *F,* 1932 *S, W*
Harbison, H T (Bective Rangers) 1984 *W* (R), *E, S,* 1986 *R,* 1987 *E, S, F, W*
Hardy, G G (Bective Rangers) 1962 *S*
Harman, G R A (Dublin U) 1899 *E, W*
Harper, J (Instonians) 1947 *F, E, S*
Harpur, T G (Dublin U) 1908 *E, S, W*
Harrison, T (Cork) 1879 *S,* 1880 *S,* 1881 *E*
Harvey, F M W (Wanderers) 1907 *W,* 1911 *F*
Harvey, G A D (Wanderers) 1903 *E, S,* 1904 *W,* 1905 *E, S*
Harvey, T A (Dublin U) 1900 *W,* 1901 *S, W,* 1902 *E, S, W,* 1903 *E, W*
Haycock, P P (Terenure Coll) 1989 *E*
Hayes, J J (Shannon) 2000 *S, It, F, W, Arg, C, J, SA,* 2001 *It, F, R, S, W, E*
Headon, T A (UC Dublin) 1939 *S, W*
Healey, P (Limerick) 1901 *E, S, W,* 1902 *E, S, W,* 1903 *E, S, W,* 1904 *S*
Heffernan, M R (Cork Constitution) 1911 *E, S, W, F*
Hemphill, R (Dublin U) 1912 *F, E, S, W*
Henderson, N J (Queen's U, Belfast, NIFC) 1949 *S, W,* 1950 *F,* 1951 *F, E, S, W, SA,* 1952 *F, S, W, E,* 1953 *F, E, S, W,* 1954 *NZ, F, E, S, W,* 1955 *F, E, S, W,* 1956 *S, W,* 1957 *F, E, S, W,* 1958 *A, E, S, W, F,* 1959 *E, S, W, F*
Henderson R A J (London Irish, Wasps) 1996 *WS,* 1997 *NZ, C,* 1998 *F, W, SA* 1(R),2(R), 1999 *F* (R), *E, S* (R), *It,* 2000 *S* (R), *It* (R), *F, W, Arg, US, J* (R), *SA,* 2001 *It, F*
Henebrey, G J (Garryowen) 1906 *E, S, W, SA,* 1909 *W, F*
Heron, A G (Queen's Coll, Belfast) 1901 *E*
Heron, J (NIFC) 1877 *S,* 1879 *E*
Heron, W T (NIFC) 1880 *E, S*
Herrick, R W (Dublin U) 1886 *S*
Heuston, F S (Kingstown) 1882 *W,* 1883 *E, S*
Hewitt, D (Queen's U, Belfast, Instonians) 1958 *A, E, S, F,* 1959 *S, W,* 1960 *E, S, W, F,* 1961 *E, S, W, F,* 1962 *S, F,* 1965 *W*
Hewitt, F S (Instonians) 1924 *W, NZ,* 1925 *F, E, S,* 1926 *E,* 1927 *E, S, W*
Hewitt, J A (NIFC) 1981 *SA* 1(R),2(R)
Hewitt, T R (Queen's U, Belfast) 1924 *W, NZ,* 1925 *F, E, S,* 1926 *F, E, S, W*
Hewitt, V A (Instonians) 1935 *S, W, NZ,* 1936 *E, S, W*
Hewitt, W J (Instonians) 1954 *E,* 1956 *S,* 1959 *W,* 1961 *SA*
Hewson, F T (Wanderers) 1875 *E*
Hickie, D A (St Mary's Coll) 1997 *W, E, S, NZ, C, It* 2, 1998 *S, F, W, E, SA* 1,2, 2000 *S, It, F, W, J, SA,* 2001 *F, R, S, W, E*
Hickie, D J (St Mary's Coll) 1971 *F, E, S, W,* 1972 *F* 1, *E*
Higgins, J A D (Civil Service) 1947 *S, W, A,* 1948 *F, S, W*
Higgins, W W (NIFC) 1884 *E, S*
Hillary, M F (UC Dublin) 1952 *E*
Hingerty, D J (UC Dublin) 1947 *F, E, S, W*
Hinton, W P (Old Wesley) 1907 *W,* 1908 *E, S, W,* 1909 *E, S,* 1910 *E, S, W, F,* 1911 *E, S, W, F,* 1912 *F, E, W*
Hipwell, M L (Terenure Coll) 1962 *E, S,* 1968 *F, A,* 1969 *F* (R), *S* (R), *W,* 1971 *F, E, S, W,* 1972 *F* 2
Hobbs, T H M (Dublin U) 1884 *S,* 1885 *E*
Hobson, E W (Dublin U) 1876 *E*
Hogan, N A (Terenure Coll, London Irish) 1995 *E, W,* [*J, W, F*], 1996 *F, W, E, WS,* 1997 *F, W, E, It* 2
Hogan, P (Garryowen) 1992 *F*
Hogg, W (Dublin U) 1885 *S* 2
Holland, J J (Wanderers) 1981 *SA* 1,2, 1986 *W*
Holmes, G W (Dublin U) 1912 *SA,* 1913 *E, S*
Holmes, L J (Lisburn) 1889 *S, W*
Hooks, K J (Queen's U, Belfast, Ards, Bangor) 1981 *S,* 1989 *NZ,* 1990 *F, W, Arg,* 1991 *F*
Horan, A K (Blackheath) 1920 *E, W*
Horan, M (Shannon) 2000 *US* (R)
Horgan, S P (Lansdowne) 2000 *S, It, W, Arg, C, J, SA* (R), 2001 *It, S, W, E*
Houston, K J (Oxford U, London Irish) 1961 *SA,* 1964 *S, W,* 1965 *F, E, SA*
Howe, T G (Dungannon, Ballymena) 2000 *US, J, SA,* 2001 *It, F, R*

Hughes, R W (NIFC) 1878 *E*, 1880 *E*, *S*, 1881 *S*, 1882 *E*, *S*, 1883 *E*, *S*, 1884 *E*, *S*, 1885 *E*, 1886 *E*

Humphreys, D G (London Irish, Dungannon) 1996 *F*, *W*, *E*, *WS*, 1997 *E* (R), *S*, *It* 2, 1998 *S*, *E* (R), *SA* 2(t + R), *R* (R), 1999 *F*, *W*, *E*, *S*, *A* 1,2, *Arg* 1, [*US*, *A* 3, *Arg* 2], 2000 *E*, *S* (R), *F* (t&R), *W* (R), *Arg*, *US* (R), *C*, *J* (R), *SA* (R), 2001 *It* (R), *R*, *S* (R), *W*, *E*

Hunt, E W F de Vere (Army, Rosslyn Park) 1930 *F*, 1932 *E*, *S*, *W*, 1933 *E*

Hunter, D V (Dublin U) 1885 *S* 2

Hunter, L (Civil Service) 1968 *W*, *A*

Hunter, W R (CIYMS) 1962 *E*, *S*, *W*, *F*, 1963 *F*, *E*, *S*, 1966 *F*, *E*, *S*

Hurley, H D (Old Wesley, Moseley) 1995 *Fj* (t), 1996 *WS*

Hutton, S A (Malone) 1967 *S*, *W*, *F*, *A* 2

Ireland J (Windsor) 1876 *E*, 1877 *E*

Irvine, H A S (Collegians) 1901 *S*

Irwin, D G (Queen's U, Belfast, Instonians) 1980 *F*, *W*, 1981 *F*, *W*, *E*, *S*, *SA* 1,2, *A*, 1982 *W*, 1983 *S*, *F*, *W*, *E*, 1984 *F*, *W*, 1987 [*Tg*, *A* (R)], 1989 *F*, *W*, *E*, *S*, *NZ*, 1990 *E*, *S*

Irwin, J W S (NIFC) 1938 *E*, *S*, 1939 *E*, *S*, *W*

Irwin, S T (Queen's Coll, Belfast) 1900 *E*, *S*, *W*, 1901 *E*, *W*, 1902 *E*, *S*, *W*, 1903 *S*

Jack, H W (UC Cork) 1914 *S*, *W*, 1921 *W*

Jackson, A R V (Wanderers) 1911 *E*, *S*, *W*, *F*, 1913 *W*, *F*, 1914 *F*, *E*, *S*, *W*

Jackson, F (NIFC) 1923 *E*

Jackson, H W (Dublin U) 1877 *E*

Jameson, J S (Lansdowne) 1888 *M*, 1889 *S*, *W*, 1891 *W*, 1892 *E*, *W*, 1893 *S*

Jeffares, E W (Wanderers) 1913 *E*, *S*

Johns, P S (Dublin U, Dungannon, Saracens) 1990 *Arg*, 1992 *NZ* 1,2, *A*, 1993 *S*, *F*, *W*, *E*, *R*, 1994 *F*, *W*, *E*, *S*, *A* 1,2, *US*, 1995 *E*, *S*, *W*, *It*, [*NZ*, *J*, *W*, *F*], *Fj*, 1996 *US*, *S*, *F*, *W*, *E*, *S*, *NZ*, *C*, *It* 2, 1998 *S*, *F*, *W*, *E*, *SA* 1,2, *Gg*, *R*, *SA* 3, 1999 *F*, *W*, *E*, *S*, *It*, *A* 1,2, *Arg* 1, [*US*, *A* 3, *R*], 2000 *F* (R), *J*

Johnston, J (Belfast Acad) 1881 *S*, 1882 *S*, 1884 *S*, 1885 *S* 1,2, 1886 *E*, 1887 *E*, *S*, *W*

Johnston, M (Dublin U) 1880 *E*, *S*, 1881 *E*, *S*, 1882 *E*, 1884 *E*, *S*, 1886 *E*

Johnston, R (Wanderers) 1893 *E*, *W*

Johnston, R W (Dublin U) 1890 *S*, *W*, *E*

Johnston, T J (Queen's Coll, Belfast) 1892 *E*, *S*, *W*, 1893 *E*, *S*, 1895 *E*

Johnstone, W E (Dublin U) 1884 *W*

Johnstone-Smyth, T R (Lansdowne) 1882 *E*

Kavanagh, J R (UC Dublin, Wanderers) 1953 *F*, *E*, *S*, *W*, 1954 *NZ*, *S*, *W*, 1955 *F*, *E*, 1956 *E*, *S*, *W*, 1957 *F*, *E*, *S*, *W*, 1958 *A*, *E*, *S*, *W*, 1959 *E*, *S*, *W*, *F*, 1960 *E*, *S*, *W*, *F*, *SA*, 1961 *E*, *S*, *W*, *F*, *SA*, 1962 *F*

Kavanagh, P J (UC Dublin, Wanderers) 1952 *E*, 1955 *W*

Keane, K P (Garryowen) 1998 *E* (R)

Keane, M I (Lansdowne) 1974 *F*, *W*, *E*, *S*, *P*, *NZ*, 1975 *E*, *S*, *F*, *W*, 1976 *A*, *F*, *W*, *E*, *S*, *NZ*, 1977 *W*, *E*, *S*, *F*, 1978 *S*, *F*, *W*, *E*, *NZ*, 1979 *F*, *W*, *E*, *S*, *A* 1,2, 1980 *E*, *S*, *F*, *W*, 1981 *F*, *W*, *E*, *S*, 1982 *W*, *E*, *S*, *F*, 1983 *S*, *F*, *W*, *E*, 1984 *F*, *W*, *E*, *S*

Kearney, R K (Wanderers) 1982 *F*, 1984 *A*, 1986 *F*, *W*

Keeffe, E (Sunday's Well) 1947 *F*, *E*, *S*, *W*, *A*, 1948 *F*

Kelly, H (NIFC) 1877 *E*, *S*, 1878 *E*, 1879 *S*, 1880 *E*, *S*

Kelly, J C (UC Dublin) 1962 *F*, *W*, 1963 *F*, *E*, *S*, *W*, *NZ*, 1964 *E*, *S*, *W*, *F*

Kelly, S (Lansdowne) 1954 *S*, *W*, 1955 *S*, 1960 *W*, *F*

Kelly, W (Wanderers) 1884 *S*

Kennedy, A G (Belfast Collegians) 1956 *F*

Kennedy, A P (London Irish) 1986 *W*, *E*

Kennedy, F (Wanderers) 1880 *E*, 1881 *E*, 1882 *W*

Kennedy, F A (Wanderers) 1904 *E*, *W*

Kennedy, H (Bradford) 1938 *S*, *W*

Kennedy, J M (Wanderers) 1882 *W*, 1884 *W*

Kennedy, K W (Queen's U, Belfast, London Irish) 1965 *F*, *E*, *S*, *W*, *SA*, 1966 *F*, *E*, *W*, 1967 *A* 1, *E*, *S*, *W*, *F*, *A* 2, 1968 *F*, *A*, 1969 *F*, *E*, *S*, *W*, 1970 *SA*, *F*, *E*, *S*, *W*, 1971 *F*, *E*, *F* 2, 1973 *NZ*, *E*, *S*, *W*, *F*, 1974 *F*, *W*, *E*, *S*, *P*, *NZ*, 1975 *F*, *W*

Kennedy, T J (St Mary's Coll) 1978 *NZ*, 1979 *F*, *W*, *E* (R), *A* 1,2, 1980 *E*, *S*, *F*, *W*, 1981 *SA* 1,2, *A*

Kenny, P (Wanderers) 1992 *NZ* 2(R)

Keogh, F S (Bective Rangers) 1964 *W*, *F*

Keon, J J (Limerick) 1879 *E*

Keyes, R P (Cork Constitution) 1986 *E*, 1991 [*Z*, *J*, *S*, *A*], 1992 *W*, *E*, *S*

Kidd, F W (Dublin U, Lansdowne) 1877 *E*, *S*, 1878 *E*

Kiely, M D (Lansdowne) 1962 *W*, 1963 *F*, *E*, *S*, *W*

Kiernan, M J (Dolphin, Lansdowne) 1982 *W* (R), *E*, *S*, *F*, 1983 *S*, *F*, *W*, *E*, 1984 *E*, *S*, *A*, 1985 *S*, *F*, *W*, *E*, 1986 *F*, *W*, *E*, *S*, *R*, 1987 *E*, *S*, *F*, *W*, [*W*, *C*, *A*], 1988 *S*, *F*, *W*, *E* 1,2, *WS*, 1989 *F*, *W*, *E*, *S*, 1990 *E*, *S*, *F*, *W*, *Arg*, 1991 *F*

Kiernan, T J (UC Cork, Cork Const) 1960 *E*, *S*, *W*, *F*, *SA*, 1961 *E*, *S*, *W*, *F*, *SA*, 1962 *E*, *W*, 1963 *F*, *S*, *W*, *NZ*, 1964 *E*, *S*, 1965 *F*, *E*, *S*, *W*, *SA*, 1966 *F*, *E*, *S*, *W*, 1967 *A* 1, *E*, *S*, *W*, *F*, *A* 2, 1968 *F*, *E*, *S*, *W*, *A*, 1969 *F*, *E*, *S*, *W*, 1970 *SA*, *F*, *E*, *S*, *W*, 1971 *F*, 1972 *F* 1, *E*, *F* 2, 1973 *NZ*, *E*, *S*

Killeen, G V (Garryowen) 1912 *E*, *S*, *W*, 1913 *E*, *S*, *W*, *F*, 1914 *E*, *S*, *W*

King, H (Dublin U) 1883 *E*, *S*

Kingston, T J (Dolphin) 1987 [*W*, *Tg*, *A*], 1988 *S*, *F*, *W*, *E* 1, 1990 *F*, *W*, 1991 [*J*], 1993 *F*, *W*, *E*, *R*, 1994 *F*, *W*, *E*, *S*, 1995 *F*, *W*, *It*, [*NZ*, *J* (R), *W*, *F*], *Fj*, 1996 *US*, *S*, *F*

Knox, J H (Dublin U, Lansdowne) 1904 *W*, 1905 *E*, *S*, *W*, *NZ*, 1906 *E*, *S*, *W*, 1907 *W*, 1908 *S*

Kyle, J W (Queen's U, Belfast, NIFC) 1947 *F*, *E*, *S*, *W*, *A*, 1948 *F*, *E*, *S*, *W*, 1949 *F*, *E*, *S*, *W*, 1950 *F*, *E*, *S*, *W*, 1951 *F*, *E*, *S*, *W*, *SA*, 1952 *F*, *S*, *W*, *E*, 1953 *F*, *E*, *S*, *W*, 1954 *NZ*, *F*, 1955 *F*, *E*, *W*, 1956 *F*, *E*, *S*, *W*, 1957 *F*, *E*, *S*, *W*, 1958 *A*, *E*, *S*

Lambert, N H (Lansdowne) 1934 *S*, *W*

Lamont, R A (Instonians) 1965 *F*, *E*, *SA*, 1966 *F*, *E*, *S*, *W*, 1970 *SA*, *F*, *E*, *S*, *W*

Landers, M F (Cork Const) 1904 *W*, 1905 *E*, *S*, *W*, *NZ*

Lane, D (UC Cork) 1934 *S*, *W*, 1935 *E*, *S*

Lane, M F (UC Cork) 1947 *W*, 1949 *F*, *E*, *S*, *W*, 1950 *F*, *E*, *S*, *W*, 1951 *F*, *S*, *W*, *SA*, 1952 *F*, *S*, 1953 *F*, *E*

Lane, P (Old Crescent) 1964 *W*

Langan, D J (Clontarf) 1934 *W*

Langbroek, J A (Blackrock Coll) 1987 [*Tg*]

Lavery, P (London Irish) 1974 *W*, 1976 *W*

Lawlor, P J (Clontarf) 1951 *S*, *SA*, 1952 *F*, *S*, *W*, *E*, 1953 *F*, 1954 *NZ*, *E*, *S*, 1956 *F*, *E*

Lawlor, P J (Bective Rangers) 1935 *E*, *S*, *W*, 1937 *E*, *S*, *W*

Lawlor, P J (Bective Rangers) 1990 *Arg*, 1992 *A*, 1993 *S*

Leahy, K T (Wanderers) 1992 *NZ* 1

Leahy, M W (UC Cork) 1964 *W*

Lee, S (NIFC) 1891 *E*, *S*, *W*, 1892 *E*, *S*, *W*, 1893 *E*, *S*, *W*, 1894 *E*, *S*, *W*, 1895 *E*, *W*, 1896 *E*, *S*, *W*, 1897 *E*, 1898 *E*, *W*, 1888 *S*, 1889 *W*, 1890 *E*, 1891 *E*, 1892 *E*, *S*, *W*

Le Fanu, V C (Cambridge U, Lansdowne) 1886 *E*, *S*, 1887 *E*, *W*, 1888 *S*, 1889 *W*, 1890 *E*, 1891 *E*, 1892 *E*, *S*, *W*

Lenihan, D G (UC Cork, Cork Const) 1981 *A*, 1982 *W*, *E*, *S*, *F*, 1983 *S*, *F*, *W*, *E*, 1984 *F*, *W*, *E*, *S*, *A*, 1985 *S*, *F*, *W*, *E*, 1986 *F*, *W*, *E*, *S*, *R*, 1987 *E*, *S*, *F*, *W*, [*W*, *C*, *Tg*, *A*], 1988 *S*, *F*, *W*, *E* 1,2, *WS*, *It*, 1989 *F*, *W*, *E*, *S*, *NZ*, 1990 *S*, *F*, *W*, *Arg*, 1991 *Nm* 2, [*Z*, *S*, *A*], 1992 *W*

L'Estrange, L P F (Dublin U) 1962 *E*

Levis, F H (Wanderers) 1884 *E*

Lightfoot, E J (Lansdowne) 1931 *F*, *E*, *S*, *W*, *SA*, 1932 *E*, *S*, *W*, 1933 *E*, *W*, *S*

Lindsay, H (Dublin U, Armagh) 1893 *E*, *S*, *W*, 1894 *E*, *S*, *W*, 1895 *E*, 1896 *E*, *S*, *W*, 1898 *E*, *S*, *W*

Little, T J (Bective Rangers) 1898 *W*, 1899 *S*, *W*, 1900 *S*, *W*, 1901 *E*, *S*

Lloyd, R A (Dublin U, Liverpool) 1910 *E*, *S*, 1911 *E*, *S*, *W*, *F*, 1912 *F*, *E*, *S*, *W*, *SA*, 1913 *E*, *S*, *W*, *F*, 1914 *F*, *E*, 1920 *E*, *F*

Longwell, G W (Ballymena) 2000 *J* (R), *SA*, 2001 *F* (R), *R*, *S* (R)

Lydon, C T J (Galwegians) 1956 *S*

Lyle, R K (Dublin U) 1910 *W*, *F*

Lyle, T R (Dublin U) 1885 *E*, *S* 1,2, 1886 *E*, 1887 *E*, *S*

Lynch, J F (St Mary's Coll) 1971 *F*, *E*, *S*, *W*, 1972 *F* 1, *E*, *F* 2, 1973 *NZ*, *E*, *S*, *W*, 1974 *F*, *W*, *E*, *S*, *P*, *NZ*

Lynch, L (Lansdowne) 1956 *S*

Lytle, J H (NIFC) 1894 *E*, *S*, *W*, 1895 *W*, 1896 *E*, *S*, *W*, 1897 *E*, *S*, 1898 *E*, *S*, 1899 *S*

Lytle, J N (NIFC) 1888 *M*, 1889 *W*, 1890 *E*, 1891 *E*, *S*, 1894 *E*, *S*, *W*

Lyttle, V J (Collegians, Bedford) 1938 *E*, 1939 *E*, *S*

McAleese, D R (Ballymena) 1992 *F*

McAllan, G H (Dungannon) 1896 *S*, *W*

Macauley, A (Limerick) 1887 *E*, *S*

McBride, W D (Malone) 1988 *W*, *E* 1, *WS*, *It*, 1989 *S*, 1990 *F*, *W*, *Arg*, 1993 *S*, *F*, *W*, *E*, *R*, 1994 *W*, *E*, *S*, *A* 1(R), 1995 *S*, *F*, [*NZ*, *W*, *F*], *Fj* (R), 1996 *W*, *E*, *WS*, *A*, 1997 *It* 1(R), *F*, *W*, *E*, *S*

McBride, W J (Ballymena) 1962 *E, S, F, W*, 1963 *F, E, S, W, NZ*, 1964 *E, S, F*, 1965 *F, E, S, W, SA*, 1966 *F, E, S, W*, 1967 *A 1, E, S, W, F, A 2*, 1968 *F, E, S, W, A*, 1969 *F, E, S, W*, 1970 *SA, F, E, S, W*, 1971 *F, E, S, W*, 1972 *F 1, E, F 2*, 1973 *NZ, E, S, W, F*, 1974 *F, W, E, S, P, NZ*, 1975 *E, S, F, W*
McCahill, S A (Sunday's Well) 1995 *Fj* (t)
McCall, B W (London Irish) 1985 *F* (R), 1986 *E, S*
McCall, M C (Bangor, Dungannon, London Irish) 1992 *NZ* 1(R),2, 1994 *W*, 1996 *E* (R), *A*, 1997 *It* 1, *NZ, C, It* 2, 1998 *S, E, SA* 1,2
McCallan, B (Ballymena) 1960 *E, S*
McCarten, R J (London Irish) 1961 *E, W, F*
McCarthy, E A (Kingstown) 1882 *W*
McCarthy, J S (Dolphin) 1948 *F, E, S, W*, 1949 *F, E, S, W*, 1950 *W*, 1951 *F, E, S, W, SA*, 1952 *F, S, W, E*, 1953 *F, E, S*, 1954 *NZ, F, E, S, W*, 1955 *F, E*
McCarthy, P D (Cork Const) 1992 *NZ* 1,2, *A*, 1993 *S, R* (R)
MacCarthy, St G (Dublin U) 1882 *W*
McCarthy, T (Cork) 1898 *W*
McClelland, T A (Queen's U, Belfast) 1921 *E, S, W, F*, 1922 *E, W, F*, 1923 *E, S, W, F*, 1924 *F, E, S, W, NZ*
McClenahan, R O (Instonians) 1923 *E, S, W*
McClinton, A N (NIFC) 1910 *W, F*
McCombe, W McM (Dublin U, Bangor) 1968 *F*, 1975 *E, S, F, W*
McConnell, A A (Collegians) 1947 *A*, 1948 *F, E, S, W*, 1949 *F, E*
McConnell, G (Derry, Edinburgh U) 1912 *F, E*, 1913 *W, F*
McConnell, J W (Lansdowne) 1913 *S*
McCormac, F M (Wanderers) 1909 *W*, 1910 *W, F*
McCormick, W J (Wanderers) 1930 *E*
McCoull, H C (Belfast Albion) 1895 *E, S, W*, 1899 *E*
McCourt, D (Queen's U, Belfast) 1947 *A*
McCoy, J J (Dungannon, Bangor, Ballymena) 1984 *W, A*, 1985 *S, F, W, E*, 1986 *F*, 1987 *[Tg]*, 1988 *E 2, W 3, It*, 1989 *F, W, E, S, NZ*
McCracken, H (NIFC) 1954 *W*
McDermott, S J (London Irish) 1955 *S, W*
Macdonald, J A (Methodist Coll, Belfast) 1875 *E*, 1876 *E*, 1877 *S*, 1878 *E*, 1879 *S*, 1880 *E*, 1881 *S*, 1882 *E, S*, 1883 *E, S*, 1884 *E, S*
McDonald, J P (Malone) 1987 *[C]*, 1990 *E* (R), *S, Arg*
McDonnell, A C (Dublin U) 1889 *W*, 1890 *S, W*, 1891 *E*
McDowell, J C (Instonians) 1924 *F, NZ*
McFarland, B A T (Derry) 1920 *S, W, F*, 1922 *W*
McGann, B J (Lansdowne) 1969 *F, E, S, W*, 1970 *SA, F, E, S, W*, 1971 *F, E, S, W*, 1972 *F 1, E, F 2*, 1973 *NZ, E, S, W*, 1976 *F, W, E, S, NZ*
McGowan, A N (Blackrock Coll) 1994 *US*
McGown, T M W (NIFC) 1899 *E, S*, 1901 *S*
McGrath, D G (UC Dublin, Cork Const) 1984 *S*, 1987 *[W, C, Tg, A]*
McGrath, N F (Oxford U, London Irish) 1934 *W*
McGrath, P J (UC Cork) 1965 *E, S, W, SA*, 1966 *F, E, S, W*, 1967 *A 1, A 2*
McGrath, R J M (Wanderers) 1977 *W, E, F* (R), 1981 *SA* 1,2, *A*, 1982 *W, E, S, F*, 1983 *S, F, W, E*, 1984 *F, W*
McGrath, T (Garryowen) 1956 *W*, 1958 *F*, 1960 *E, S, W, F*, 1961 *SA*
McGuinness, C D (St Mary's Coll) 1997 *NZ, C*, 1998 *F, W, E, SA* 1,2, *Gg, R* (R), *SA* 3, 1999 *F, W, E, S*
McGuire, E P (UC Galway) 1963 *E, S, W, NZ*, 1964 *E, S, W, F*
MacHale, S (Lansdowne) 1965 *F, E, S, W, SA*, 1966 *F, E, S, W*, 1967 *S, W, F*
McIldowie, G (Malone) 1906 *SA*, 1910 *E, S, W*
McIlrath, J A (Ballymena) 1976 *A, F, NZ*, 1977 *W, E*
McIlwaine, E H (NIFC) 1895 *S, W*
McIlwaine, E N (NIFC) 1875 *E*, 1876 *E*
McIlwaine, J E (NIFC) 1897 *E, S*, 1898 *E, S, W*, 1899 *E, W*
McIntosh, L M (Dublin U) 1884 *S*
MacIvor, C V (Dublin U) 1912 *F, E, S, W*, 1913 *E, S, F*
McIvor, S C (Garryowen) 1996 *A*, 1997 *It* 1, *S* (R)
McKay, J W (Queen's U, Belfast) 1947 *F, E, S, W, A*, 1948 *F, E, S, W*, 1949 *F, E, S, W*, 1950 *F, E, S, W*, 1951 *F, E, S, W, SA*, 1952 *F*
McKee, W D (NIFC) 1947 *A*, 1948 *F, E, S, W*, 1949 *F, E, S, W*, 1950 *F, E*, 1951 *SA*
McKeen, A J W (Lansdowne) 1999 *[R* (R)]
McKelvey, J M (Queen's U, Belfast) 1956 *F, E*
McKenna, P (St Mary's Coll) 2000 *Arg*
McKibbin, A R (Instonians, London Irish) 1977 *W, E, S*, 1978 *S, F, W, E, NZ*, 1979 *F, W, E, S*, 1980 *E, S*

McKibbin, C H (Instonians) 1976 *S* (R)
McKibbin, D (Instonians) 1950 *F, E, S, W*, 1951 *F, E, S, W*
McKibbin, H R (Queen's U, Belfast) 1938 *W*, 1939 *E, S, W*
McKinney, S A (Dungannon) 1972 *F 1, E, F 2*, 1973 *W, F*, 1974 *F, E, S, P, NZ*, 1975 *E, S*, 1976 *A, F, W, E, S, NZ*, 1977 *W, E, S*, 1978 *S* (R), *F, W, E*
McLaughlin, J H (Derry) 1887 *E, S*, 1888 *W, S*
McLean, R E (Dublin U) 1881 *S*, 1882 *W, E, S*, 1883 *E, S*, 1884 *E, S*, 1885 *E, S* 1
Maclear, B (Cork County, Monkstown) 1905 *E, S, W, NZ*, 1906 *E, S, W, SA*, 1907 *E, S, W*
McLennan, A C (Wanderers) 1977 *F*, 1978 *S, F, W, E, NZ*, 1979 *F, W, E, S*, 1980 *E, F*, 1981 *F, W, E, S, SA* 1,2
McLoughlin, F M (Northern) 1976 *A*
McLoughlin, G A J (Shannon) 1979 *F, W, E, S, A* 1,2, 1980 *F*, 1981 *SA* 1,2, 1982 *W, E, S, F*, 1983 *S, F, W, E*, 1984 *F*
McLoughlin, R J (UC Dublin, Blackrock Coll, Gosforth) 1962 *E, S, F*, 1963 *E, S, W, NZ*, 1964 *E, S*, 1965 *F, E, S, W, SA*, 1966 *F, E, S, W*, 1971 *F, E, S, W*, 1972 *F 1, E, F 2*, 1973 *NZ, E, S, W, F*, 1974 *F, W, E, S, P, NZ*, 1975 *E, S, F, W*
McMahon, L B (Blackrock Coll, UC Dublin) 1931 *E, SA*, 1933 *E*, 1934 *E*, 1936 *E, S, W*, 1937 *E, S, W*, 1938 *E, S*
McMaster, A W (Ballymena) 1972 *F 1, E, F 2*, 1973 *NZ, E, S, W, F*, 1974 *F, E, S, P*, 1975 *F, W*, 1976 *A, F, W, NZ*
McMordie, J (Queen's Coll, Belfast) 1886 *S*
McMorrow, A (Garryowen) 1951 *W*
McMullen, A R (Cork) 1881 *E, S*
McNamara, V (UC Cork) 1914 *E, S, W*
McNaughton, P P (Greystones) 1978 *S, F, W, E*, 1979 *F, W, E, S, A* 1,2, 1980 *E, S, F, W*, 1981 *F*
MacNeill, H P (Dublin U, Oxford U, Blackrock Coll, London Irish) 1981 *F, W, E, S, A*, 1982 *W, E, S, F*, 1983 *S, F, W, E*, 1984 *F, W, A*, 1985 *S, F, W, E*, 1986 *F, W, E, S, R*, 1987 *E, S, F, W, [W, C, Tg, A]*, 1988 *S* (R), *E* 1,2
McQuilkin, K P (Bective Rangers, Lansdowne) 1996 *US, S, F*, 1997 *F* (t & R), *S*
MacSweeney, D A (Blackrock Coll) 1955 *S*
McVicker, H (Army, Richmond) 1927 *E, S, W, A*, 1928 *F*
McVicker, J (Collegians) 1924 *F, E, S, W, NZ*, 1925 *F, E, S, W*, 1926 *F, E, S, W*, 1927 *F, E, S, W, A*, 1928 *W*, 1930 *F*
McVicker, S (Queen's U, Belfast) 1922 *E, S, W, F*
McWeeney, J P J (St Mary's Coll) 1997 *NZ*
Madden, M N (Sunday's Well) 1955 *E, S, W*
Magee, J T (Bective Rangers) 1895 *E, S*
Magee, A M (Louis) (Bective Rangers, London Irish) 1895 *E, S, W*, 1896 *E, S, W*, 1897 *E, S*, 1898 *E, S, W*, 1899 *E, S, W*, 1900 *E, S, W*, 1901 *E, S, W*, 1902 *E, S, W*, 1903 *E, S, W*, 1904 *W*
Maggs, K M (Bristol, Bath) 1997 *NZ* (R), *C, It* 2, 1998 *S, F, W, E, SA* 1,2, *Gg, R* (R), *SA* 3, 1999 *F, W, E, S, It, A* 1,2, *Arg* 1, *[US, A* 3, *Arg* 2], 2000 *E, F, Arg, US* (R), *C*, 2001 *It* (R), *F* (R), *R, S* (R), *W, E*
Maginiss, R M (Dublin U) 1875 *E*, 1876 *E*
Magrath, R M (Cork Constitution) 1909 *S*
Maguire, J F (Cork) 1884 *S*
Mahoney, J (Dolphin) 1923 *F*
Malcolmson, G L (RAF, NIFC) 1935 *NZ*, 1936 *E, S, W*, 1937 *E, S, W*
Malone, N G (Oxford U, Leicester) 1993 *S, F*, 1994 *US* (R)
Mannion, N P (Corinthians, Lansdowne, Wanderers) 1988 *WS, It*, 1989 *F, W, E, S, NZ*, 1990 *E, S, F, W, Arg*, 1991 *Nm* 1(R),2, *[J]*, 1993 *S*
Marshall, B D E (Queen's U, Belfast) 1963 *E*
Mason, S J P (Orrell, Richmond) 1996 *W, E, WS*
Massey-Westropp, R H (Limerick, Monkstown) 1886 *E*
Matier, R N (NIFC) 1878 *E*, 1879 *S*
Matthews, P M (Ards, Wanderers) 1984 *A*, 1985 *S, F, W, E*, 1986 *R*, 1987 *E, S, F, W, [W, Tg, A]*, 1988 *S, F, W, E* 1,2, *WS, It*, 1989 *F, W, E, S, NZ*, 1990 *E, S*, 1991 *F, W, E, S, Nm* 1 [*Z, S, A*], 1992 *W, E, S*
Mattsson, J (Wanderers) 1948 *E*
Mayne, R B (Queen's U, Belfast) 1937 *W*, 1938 *E, W*, 1939 *E, S, W*
Mayne, R H (Belfast Academy) 1888 *W, S*
Mayne, T (NIFC) 1921 *E, S, F*
Mays, K M A (UC Dublin) 1973 *NZ, E, S, W*
Meares, A W D (Dublin U) 1899 *S, W*, 1900 *E, W*
Megaw, J (Richmond, Instonians) 1934 *W*, 1938 *E*
Millar, A (Kingstown) 1880 *E, S*, 1883 *E*
Millar, H J (Monkstown) 1904 *W*, 1905 *E, S, W*
Millar, S (Ballymena) 1958 *F*, 1959 *E, S, W, F*, 1960 *E, S, W, F, SA*, 1961 *E, S, W, F, SA*, 1962 *E, S, F*, 1963 *F, E, S, W*, 1964 *F*, 1968 *F, E, S, W, A*, 1969 *F, E, S, W*, 1970 *SA, F, E, S, W*

Millar, W H J (Queen's U, Belfast) 1951 *E, S, W*, 1952 *S, W*
Miller, E R P (Leicester, Tererure Coll) 1997 *It* 1, *F, W, E, NZ, It* 2, 1998 *S, W* (R), *Gg, R*, 1999 *F, W, E* (R), *S, Arg* 1(R), [*US* (R), *A* 3(t&R), *Arg* 2(R)], 2000 *US, C* (R), *SA*, 2001 *R, W, E*
Miller, F H (Wanderers) 1886 *S*
Milliken, R A (Bangor) 1973 *E, S, W, F*, 1974 *F, W, E, S, P, NZ*, 1975 *E, S, F, W*
Millin, T J (Dublin U) 1925 *W*
Minch, J B (Bective Rangers) 1912 *SA*, 1913 *E, S*, 1914 *E, S*
Moffat, J (Belfast Academy) 1888 *W, S, M*, 1889 *S*, 1890 *S, W*, 1891 *S*
Moffatt, J E (Old Wesley) 1904 *S*, 1905 *E, S, W*
Moffett, J W (Ballymena) 1961 *E, S*
Molloy, M G (UC Galway, London Irish) 1966 *F, E*, 1967 *A* 1, *E, S, W, F, A* 2, 1968 *F, E, S, W, A*, 1969 *F, E, S, W*, 1970 *F, E, S, W*, 1971 *F, E, S, W*, 1973 *F, W*, 1976 *A*
Moloney, J J (St Mary's Coll) 1972 *F* 1, *E, F* 2, 1973 *NZ, E, S, W, F*, 1974 *F, W, E, S, P, NZ*, 1975 *E, S, F, W*, 1976 *S*, 1978 *S, F, W, E*, 1979 *A* 1,2, 1980 *S, W*
Moloney, L A (Garryowen) 1976 *W* (R), *S*, 1978 *S* (R), *NZ*
Molony, J U (UC Dublin) 1950 *S*
Monteith, J D E (Queen's U, Belfast) 1947 *E, S, W*
Montgomery, A (NIFC) 1895 *S*
Montgomery, F P (Queen's U, Belfast) 1914 *E, S, W*
Montgomery, R (Cambridge U) 1887 *E, S, W*, 1891 *E*, 1892 *W*
Moore, C M (Dublin U) 1887 *S*, 1888 *W, S*
Moore, D F (Wanderers) 1883 *E, S*, 1884 *E, W*
Moore, F W (Wanderers) 1884 *W*, 1885 *E, S* 2, 1886 *S*
Moore, H (Windsor) 1876 *E*, 1877 *S*
Moore, H (Queen's U, Belfast) 1910 *S*, 1911 *W, F*, 1912 *F, E, S, W, SA*
Moore, T A P (Highfield) 1967 *A* 2, 1973 *NZ, E, S, W, F*, 1974 *F, W, E, S, P, NZ*
Moore, W D (Queen's Coll, Belfast) 1878 *E*
Moran, F G (Clontarf) 1936 *E*, 1937 *E, S, W*, 1938 *S, W*, 1939 *E, S, W*
Morell, H B (Dublin U) 1881 *E, S*, 1882 *W, E*
Morgan, G J (Clontarf) 1934 *E, S, W*, 1935 *E, S, W, NZ*, 1936 *E, S, W*, 1937 *E, S, W*, 1938 *E, S, W*, 1939 *E, S, W*
Moriarty, C C H (Monkstown) 1899 *W*
Moroney, J C M (Garryowen) 1968 *W, A*, 1969 *F, E, S, W*
Moroney, R J M (Lansdowne) 1984 *F, W*, 1985 *F*
Moroney, T A (UC Dublin) 1964 *W*, 1967 *A* 1, *E*
Morphy, E McG (Dublin U) 1908 *E*
Morris, D P (Bective Rangers) 1931 *W*, 1932 *E*, 1935 *E, S, W, NZ*
Morrow, J W R (Queen's Coll, Belfast) 1882 *S*, 1883 *E, S*, 1884 *E, W*, 1885 *S* 1,2, 1886 *E, S*, 1888 *S*
Morrow, R D (Bangor) 1986 *F, E, S*
Mortell, M (Bective Rangers, Dolphin) 1953 *F, E, S, W*, 1954 *NZ, F, E, S, W*
Morton, W A (Dublin U) 1888 *S*
Mostyn, M R (Galwegians) 1999 *A* 1, *Arg* 1, [*US, A* 3, *R, Arg* 2]
Moyers, L W (Dublin U) 1884 *W*
Moylett, M M F (Shannon) 1988 *E* 1
Mulcahy, W A (UC Dublin, Bective Rangers, Bohemians) 1958 *A, E, S, W, F*, 1959 *E, S, W, F*, 1960 *E, S, W, SA*, 1961 *E, S, W, SA*, 1962 *E, S, F, W*, 1963 *E, S, W, NZ*, 1964 *E, S, W, F*, 1965 *F, E, S, W, SA*
Mullan, B (Clontarf) 1947 *F, E, S, W*, 1948 *F, E, S, W*
Mullane, J P (Limerick Bohemians) 1928 *W*, 1929 *F*
Mullen, K D (Old Belvedere) 1947 *F, E, S, W, A*, 1948 *F, E, S, W*, 1949 *F, E, S, W*, 1950 *F, E, S, W*, 1951 *F, E, S, W, SA*, 1952 *F, S, W*
Mulligan, A A (Wanderers) 1956 *F, E*, 1957 *F, E, S, W*, 1958 *A, E, S, F*, 1959 *E, S, W, F*, 1960 *E, S, W, F, SA*, 1961 *W, F, SA*
Mullin, B J (Dublin U, Oxford U, Blackrock Coll, London Irish) 1984 *A*, 1985 *S, W, E*, 1986 *F, W, E, S, R*, 1987 *E, S, F, W*, [*W, C, Tg, A*], 1988 *S, F, W, E* 1,2, *WS, It*, 1989 *F, W, E, S, NZ*, 1990 *E, S, W, Arg*, 1991 *F, W, E, S, Nm* 1,2, [*J, S, A*], 1992 *W, E, S*, 1994 *US*, 1995 *E, S, F, W, It*, [*NZ, J, W, F*]
Mullins, M J (Young Munster) 1999 *Arg* 1(R), [*R*], 2000 *E, S, It, Arg* (t&R), *US, C*, 2001 *It, R, W, F* (R), *E* (R)
Murphy, C J (Lansdowne) 1939 *E, S, W*, 1947 *F, E*
Murphy, G E A (Leicester) 2000 *US, C* (R), *J*, 2001 *R, S*
Murphy, J G M W (London Irish) 1951 *SA*, 1952 *S, W, E*, 1954 *NZ*, 1958 *W*
Murphy, J J (Greystones) 1981 *SA* 1, 1982 *W* (R), 1984 *S*
Murphy, J N (Greystones) 1992 *A*

Murphy, K J (Cork Constitution) 1990 *E, S, F, W, Arg*, 1991 *F, W* (R), *S* (R), 1992 *S, F, NZ* 2(R)
Murphy, N A A (Cork Constitution) 1958 *A, E, S, W, F*, 1959 *E, S, W, F*, 1960 *E, S, W, F, SA*, 1961 *E, S, W*, 1962 *E*, 1963 *NZ*, 1964 *E, S, W, F*, 1965 *F, E, S, W, SA*, 1966 *F, E, S, W*, 1967 *A* 1, *E, S, W, F*, 1969 *F, E, S, W*
Murphy, N F (Cork Constitution) 1930 *E, W*, 1931 *F, E, S, W, SA*, 1932 *E, S, W*, 1933 *E*
Murphy-O'Connor, J (Bective Rangers) 1954 *E*
Murray, H W (Dublin U) 1877 *S*, 1878 *E*, 1879 *E*
Murray, J B (UC Dublin) 1963 *F*
Murray, P F (Wanderers) 1927 *F*, 1929 *F, E, S*, 1930 *F, E, S, W*, 1931 *F, E, S, W, SA*, 1932 *E, S, W*, 1933 *E, W, S*
Murtagh, C W (Portadown) 1977 *S*
Myles, J (Dublin U) 1875 *E*

Nash, L C (Queen's Coll, Cork) 1889 *S*, 1890 *W, E*, 1891 *E, S, W*
Neely, M R (Collegians) 1947 *F, E, S, W*
Neill, H J (NIFC) 1885 *E, S* 1,2, 1886 *S*, 1887 *E, S, W*, 1888 *W, S*
Neill, J McF (Instonians) 1926 *F*
Nelson, J E (Malone) 1947 *A*, 1948 *E, S, W*, 1949 *F, E, S, W*, 1950 *F, E, S, W*, 1951 *F, E, W*, 1954 *F*
Nelson, R (Queen's Coll, Belfast) 1882 *E, S*, 1883 *S*, 1886 *S*
Nesdale, R P (Newcastle) 1997 *W, E, S, NZ* (R), *C*, 1998 *F* (R), *W* (R), *Gg, SA* 3(R), 1999 *It, A* 2(R), [*US* (R), *R*]
Nesdale, T J (Garryowen) 1961 *F*
Neville, W C (Dublin U) 1879 *S, E*
Nicholson, P C (Dublin U) 1900 *E, S, W*
Norton, G W (Bective Rangers) 1949 *F, E, S, W*, 1950 *F, E, S, W*, 1951 *F, E, S*
Notley, J R (Wanderers) 1952 *F, S*
Nowlan, K W (St Mary's Coll) 1997 *NZ, C, It* 2

O'Brien, B (Derry) 1893 *S, W*
O'Brien, B A P (Shannon) 1968 *F, E, S*
O'Brien, D J (London Irish, Cardiff, Old Belvedere) 1948 *E, S, W*, 1949 *F, E, S, W*, 1950 *F, E, S, W*, 1951 *F, E, S, W, SA*, 1952 *F, S, W, E*
O'Brien, K A (Broughton Park) 1980 *E*, 1981 *SA* 1(R),2
O'Brien-Butler, P E (Monkstown) 1897 *S*, 1898 *E, S*, 1899 *S, W*, 1900 *E*
O'Callaghan, C T (Carlow) 1910 *W, F*, 1911 *E, S, W, F*, 1912 *F*
O'Callaghan, M P (Sunday's Well) 1962 *W*, 1964 *E, F*
O'Callaghan, P (Dolphin) 1967 *A* 1, *E, A* 2, 1968 *F, E, S, W*, 1969 *F, E, S, W*, 1970 *SA, F, E, S, W*, 1976 *F, W, E, S, NZ*
O'Connell, K D (Sunday's Well) 1994 *F, E* (t)
O'Connell, P (Bective Rangers) 1913 *W, F*, 1914 *F, E, S, W*
O'Connell, W J (Lansdowne) 1955 *F*
O'Connor, H S (Dublin U) 1957 *F, E, S, W*
O'Connor, J (Garryowen) 1895 *S*
O'Connor, J H (Bective Rangers) 1888 *M*, 1890 *S, W, E*, 1891 *E, S*, 1892 *E, W*, 1893 *E, S*, 1894 *E, S, W*, 1895 *E*, 1896 *E, S, W*
O'Connor, J J (Garryowen) 1909 *F*
O'Connor, J J (UC Cork) 1933 *S*, 1934 *E, S, W*, 1935 *E, S, W, NZ*, 1936 *S, W*, 1938 *S*
O'Connor, P J (Lansdowne) 1887 *W*
O'Cuinneagain, D (Sale, Ballymena) 1998 *SA* 1,2, *Gg* (R), *R* (R), *SA* 3, 1999 *F, W, E, S, It, A* 1,2, *Arg* 1, [*US, A* 3, *R, Arg* 2], 2000 *E, It* (R)
Odbert, R V M (RAF) 1928 *F*
O'Donnell, R C (St Mary's Coll) 1979 *A* 1,2, 1980 *S, F, W*
O'Donoghue, P J (Bective Rangers) 1955 *F, E, S, W*, 1956 *W*, 1957 *F, E, S, W*
O'Driscoll, B G (Blackrock Coll) 1999 *A* 1,2, *Arg* 1, [*US, A* 3, *R* (R), *Arg* 2], 2000 *E, S, It, F, W, J, SA*, 2001 *F, S, W, E*
O'Driscoll, B J (Manchester) 1971 *F* (R), *E, S, W*
O'Driscoll, J B (London Irish, Manchester) 1978 *S*, 1979 *A* 1,2, 1980 *E, S, F, W*, 1981 *F, W, E, S, SA* 1,2, *A*, 1982 *W, E, S, F*, 1983 *F, W, E*, 1984 *F, W, E, S*
O'Driscoll, M (Cork Const) 2001 *R* (R)
O'Flanagan, K P (London Irish) 1947 *A*
O'Flanagan, M (Lansdowne) 1948 *S*
O'Gara, R J R (Cork Const) 2000 *S, It, F, W, Arg* (R), *US, C* (R), *J, SA*, 2001 *It, F, S, W* (R), *E* (R)
O'Grady, D (Sale) 1997 *It* 2
O'Hanlon, B (Dolphin) 1947 *E, S, W*, 1948 *F, E, S, W*, 1949 *F, E, S, W*, 1950 *F*

Brian O'Driscoll evades Daisuke Ohata to score one of Ireland's 11 tries in their record 78-9 defeat of Japan at Lansdowne Road in November.

O'Hara, P T J (Sunday's Well, Cork Const) 1988 *WS* (R), 1989 *F, W, E, NZ*, 1990 *E, S, F, W*, 1991 *Nm* 1, [*J*], 1993 *F, W, E*, 1994 *US*

O'Kelly, M E (London Irish, St Mary's Coll) 1997 *NZ, C, It* 2, 1998 *S, F, W, E, SA* 1,2, *Gg, R, SA* 3, 1999 *A* 1(R),2, *Arg* 1(R), [*US* (R), *A* 3, *R, Arg* 2], 2000 *E, S, It, F, W, Arg, US, J, SA*, 2001 *It, F, S, W, E*

O'Leary, A (Cork Constitution) 1952 *S, W, E*

O'Loughlin, D B (UC Cork) 1938 *E, S, W*, 1939 *E, S, W*

O'Mahony, D W (UC Dublin, Moseley, Bedford) 1995 *It*, [*F*], 1997 *It* 2, 1998 *R*

O'Mahony, David (Cork Constitution) 1995 *It*

O'Meara, B T (Cork Constitution) 1997 *E* (R), *S, NZ* (R), 1998 *S*, 1999 [*US* (R), *R* (R)], 2001 *It* (R)

O'Meara, J A (UC Cork, Dolphin) 1951 *F, E, S, W, SA*, 1952 *F, S, W, E*, 1953 *F, E, S, W*, 1954 *NZ, F, E, S*, 1955 *F, E*, 1956 *S, W*, 1958 *W*

O'Neill, H O'H (Queen's U, Belfast, UC Cork) 1930 *E, S, W*, 1933 *E, S, W*

O'Neill, J B (Queen's U, Belfast) 1920 *S*

O'Neill, W A (UC Dublin, Wanderers) 1952 *E*, 1953 *F, E, S, W*, 1954 *NZ*

O'Reilly, A J F (Old Belvedere, Leicester) 1955 *F, E, S, W*, 1956 *F, E, S, W*, 1957 *F, E, S, W*, 1958 *A, E, S, W, F*, 1959 *E, S, W, F*, 1960 *E*, 1961 *E, F, SA*, 1963 *F, S, W*, 1970 *E*

Orr, P A (Old Wesley) 1976 *F, W, E, S, NZ*, 1977 *W, E, S, F*, 1978 *S, F, W, E, NZ*, 1979 *F, W, E, S, A* 1,2, 1980 *E, S, F, W*, 1981 *F, W, E, S, SA* 1,2, *A*, 1982 *W, E, S, F*, 1983 *S, F, W, E*, 1984 *F, W, E, S, A*, 1985 *S, F, W, E*, 1986 *F, S, R*, 1987 *E, S, F, W*, [*W, C, A*]

O'Shea, C M P (Lansdowne, London Irish) 1993 *R*, 1994 *F, W, E, S, A* 1,2, *US*, 1995 *E, S*, [*J, W, F*], 1997 *It* 1, *F, S* (R), 1998 *S, F, SA* 1,2, *Gg, R, SA* 3, 1999 *F, W, E, S, It, A* 1, *Arg* 1, [*US, A* 3, *R, Arg* 2], 2000 *E*

O'Sullivan, A C (Dublin U) 1882 *S*

O'Sullivan, J M (Limerick) 1884 *S*, 1887 *S*

O'Sullivan, P J A (Galwegians) 1957 *F, E, S, W*, 1959 *E, S, W, F*, 1960 *SA*, 1961 *E, S*, 1962 *F, W*, 1963 *F, NZ*

O'Sullivan, W (Queen's Coll, Cork) 1895 *S*

Owens, R H (Dublin U) 1922 *E, S*

Parfrey, P (UC Cork) 1974 *NZ*

Parke, J C (Monkstown) 1903 *W*, 1904 *E, S, W*, 1905 *W, NZ*, 1906 *E, S, W, SA*, 1907 *E, S, W*, 1908 *E, S, W*, 1909 *E, S, W, F*

Parr, J S (Wanderers) 1914 *F, E, S, W*

Patterson, C S (Instonians) 1978 *NZ*, 1979 *F, W, E, S, A* 1,2, 1980 *E, S, F, W*

Patterson, R d'A (Wanderers) 1912 *F, S, W, SA*, 1913 *E, S, W, F*

Payne, C T (NIFC) 1926 *E*, 1927 *F, E, S, A*, 1928 *F, E, S, W*, 1929 *F, E, W*, 1930 *F, E, S, W*

Pedlow, A C (CIYMS) 1953 *W*, 1954 *NZ, F, E*, 1955 *F, E, S, W*, 1956 *F, E, S, W*, 1957 *F, E, S, W*, 1958 *A, E, S, W, F*, 1959 *E*, 1960 *E, S, W, F, SA*, 1961 *S, W*, 1962 *W*, 1963 *F*

Pedlow, J (Bessbrook) 1882 *S*, 1884 *W*

Pedlow, R (Bessbrook) 1891 *W*

Pedlow, T B (Queen's Coll, Belfast) 1889 *S, W*

Peel, T (Limerick) 1892 *E, S, W*

Peirce, W (Cork) 1881 *E*

Phipps, G C (Army) 1950 *E, W*, 1952 *F, W, E*

Pike, T O (Lansdowne) 1927 *E, S, W, A*, 1928 *F, E, S, W*

Pike, V J (Lansdowne) 1931 *E, S, W, SA*, 1932 *E, S, W*, 1933 *E, W, S*, 1934 *E, S, W*

Pike, W W (Kingstown) 1879 *E*, 1881 *E, S*, 1882 *E*, 1883 *S*

Pinion, G (Belfast Collegians) 1909 *E, S, W, F*

Piper, O J S (Cork Constitution) 1909 *E, S, W, F*, 1910 *E, S, W, F*

Polden, S E (Clontarf) 1913 *W, F*, 1914 *F*, 1920 *F*

Popham, I (Cork Constitution) 1922 *S, W, F*, 1923 *F*

Popplewell, N J (Greystones, Wasps, Newcastle) 1989 *NZ*, 1990 *Arg*, 1991 *Nm* 1,2, [*Z, S, A*], 1992 *W, E, S, F, NZ* 1,2, *A*, 1993 *S, F, W, E, R*, 1994 *F, W, E, S, US*, 1995 *E, S, F, W, It*, [*NZ, J, W, F*], *Fj*, 1996 *US, S, F, W, E, A*, 1997 *It* 1, *F, W, E, NZ, C*, 1998 *S* (t), *F* (R)

Potterton, H N (Wanderers) 1920 *W*

Pratt, R H (Dublin U) 1933 *E, W, S*, 1934 *E, S*

Price, A H (Dublin U) 1920 *S, F*

Pringle, J C (NIFC) 1902 *S, W*

Purcell, N M (Lansdowne) 1921 *E, S, W, F*

Purdon, H (NIFC) 1879 *S, E*, 1880 *E*, 1881 *E, S*

Purdon, W B (Queen's Coll, Belfast) 1906 *E, S, W*

Purser, F C (Dublin U) 1898 *E, S, W*

Quinlan, A (Shannon) 1999 [*R* (R)], 2001 *It, F*

Quinlan, S V J (Blackrock Coll) 1956 *F, E, W*, 1958 *W*

Quinn, B T (Old Belvedere) 1947 *F*

Quinn, F P (Old Belvedere) 1981 *F, W, E*

Quinn, J P (Dublin U) 1910 *E, S*, 1911 *E, S, W, F*, 1912 *E, S, W*, 1913 *E, W, F*, 1914 *F, E, S*

Quinn, K (Old Belvedere) 1947 *F, A*, 1953 *F, E, S*

Quinn, M A M (Lansdowne) 1973 *F*, 1974 *F, W, E, S, P, NZ*, 1977 *S, F*, 1981 *SA* 2

Quirke, J M T (Blackrock Coll) 1962 *E, S*, 1968 *S*

Rainey, P I (Ballymena) 1989 *NZ*

Rambaut, D F (Dublin U) 1887 *E, S, W*, 1888 *W*

Rea, H H (Edinburgh U) 1967 *A* 1, 1969 *F*

Read, H M (Dublin U) 1910 *E, S*, 1911 *E, S, W, F*, 1912 *F, E, S, W, SA*, 1913 *E, S*

Reardon, J V (Cork Constitution) 1934 *E, S*

Reid, C (NIFC) 1899 *S, W*, 1900 *E*, 1903 *W*

Reid, J L (Richmond) 1934 *S, W*

Reid, P J (Garryowen) 1947 *A*, 1948 *F, E, W*

Reid, T E (Garryowen) 1953 *E, S, W*, 1954 *NZ, F*, 1955 *E, S*, 1956 *F, E*, 1957 *F, E, S*

Reidy, C J (London Irish) 1937 *W*

Reidy, G F (Dolphin, Lansdowne) 1953 *W*, 1954 *F, E, S, W*

Richey, H A (Dublin U) 1889 *W*, 1890 *S*

Ridgeway, E C (Wanderers) 1932 *S, W*, 1935 *E, S, W*

Rigney, B J (Greystones) 1991 *F, W, E, S, Nm* 1, 1992 *F, NZ* 1(R),2

Ringland, T M (Queen's U, Belfast, Ballymena) 1981 *A*, 1982 *W, E, F*, 1983 *S, F, W, E*, 1984 *F, W, E, S, A*, 1985 *S, F, W, E*, 1986 *F, W, E, S, R*, 1987 *E, S, F, W*, [*W, C, Tg, A*], 1988 *S, F, W, E* 1

Riordan, W F (Cork Constitution) 1910 *E*

Ritchie, J S (London Irish) 1956 *F, E*

Robb, C G (Queen's Coll, Belfast) 1904 *E, S, W*, 1905 *NZ*, 1906 *S*

Robbie, J C (Dublin U, Greystones) 1976 *A, F, NZ*, 1977 *S, F*, 1981 *F, W, E, S*

Robinson, B F (Ballymena, London Irish) 1991 *F, W, E, S, Nm* 1,2, [*Z, S, A*], 1992 *W, E, S, F, NZ* 1,2, *A*, 1993 *W, E, R*, 1994 *F, W, E, S, A* 1,2

Robinson, T T H (Wanderers) 1904 *E, S*, 1905 *E, S, W, NZ*, 1906 *SA*, 1907 *E, S, W*

Roche, J (Wanderers) 1890 *S, W, E*, 1891 *E, S, W*, 1892 *W*

Roche, R E (UC Galway) 1955 *E, S*, 1957 *S, W*

Roche, W J (UC Cork) 1920 *E, S, F*

Roddy, P J (Bective Rangers) 1920 *S, F*

Roe, R (Lansdowne) 1952 *E*, 1953 *F, E, S, W*, 1954 *F, E, S, W*, 1955 *F, E, S, W*, 1956 *F, E, S, W*, 1957 *F, E, S, W*

Rolland, A C (Blackrock Coll) 1990 *Arg*, 1994 *US* (R), 1995 *It* (R)

Rooke, C V (Dublin U) 1891 *E, W*, 1892 *E, S, W*, 1893 *E, S, W*, 1894 *E, S, W*, 1895 *E, S, W*, 1896 *E, S, W*, 1897 *E, S*

Ross, D J (Belfast Academy) 1884 *E*, 1885 *S* 1,2, 1886 *E, S*

Ross, G R P (CIYMS) 1955 *W*

Ross, J F (NIFC) 1886 *S*

Ross, J P (Lansdowne) 1885 *E, S* 1,2, 1886 *E, S*

Ross, N G (Malone) 1927 *F, E*

Ross, W McC (Queen's U, Belfast) 1932 *E, S, W*, 1933 *E, W, S*, 1934 *E, S*, 1935 *NZ*

Russell, J (UC Cork) 1931 *F, E, S, W, SA*, 1933 *E, W, S*, 1934 *E, S, W*, 1935 *E, S, W*, 1936 *E, S, W*, 1937 *E, S*

Russell, P (Instonians) 1990 *E*, 1992 *NZ* 1,2, *A*

Rutherford, W G (Tipperary) 1884 *E, S*, 1885 *E, S* 1, 1886 *E*, 1888 *W*

Ryan, E (Dolphin) 1937 *W*, 1938 *E, S*

Ryan, J (Rockwell Coll) 1897 *E*, 1898 *E, S, W*, 1899 *E, S, W*, 1900 *S, W*, 1901 *E, S, W*, 1902 *E*, 1904 *E*

Ryan, J G (UC Dublin) 1939 *E, S, W*

Ryan, M (Rockwell Coll) 1897 *E, S*, 1898 *E, S, W*, 1899 *E, S, W*, 1900 *E, S, W*, 1901 *E, S, W*, 1903 *E, S, W*, 1904 *E, S*

Saunders, R (London Irish) 1991 *F, W, E, S, Nm* 1,2, [*Z, J, S, A*], 1992 *W*, 1994 *F* (t)

Saverimutto, C (Sale) 1995 *Fj*, 1996 *US, S*

Sayers, H J M (Lansdowne) 1935 *E, S, W*, 1936 *E, S, W*, 1938 *W*, 1939 *E, S, W*

Scally, C J (U C Dublin) 1998 *Gg* (R), *R*, 1999 *S* (R), *It*

Schute, F (Wanderers) 1878 *E*, 1879 *E*

Schute, F G (Dublin U) 1912 *SA*, 1913 *E, S*

Scott, D (Malone) 1961 *F, SA*, 1962 *S*

Scott, R D (Queen's U, Belfast) 1967 *E, F*, 1968 *F, E, S*

Scovell, R H (Kingstown) 1883 *E*, 1884 *E*

Scriven, G (Dublin U) 1879 *S, E*, 1880 *E, S*, 1881 *E*, 1882 *S*, 1883 *E, S*

Sealy, J (Dublin U) 1896 *E, S, W*, 1897 *S*, 1899 *E, S, W*, 1900 *E, S*

Sexton, J F (Dublin U, Lansdowne) 1988 *E* 2, *WS, It*, 1989 *F*

Sexton, W J (Garryowen) 1984 *A*, 1988 *S, E* 2

Shanahan, T (Lansdowne) 1885 *E, S* 1,2, 1886 *E*, 1888 *S, W*

Shaw, G M (Windsor) 1877 *S*

Sheahan, F J (Cork Const) 2000 *US* (R), 2001 *It* (R), *R, W* (R)

Sheehan, M D (London Irish) 1932 *E*

Sherry, B F (Terenure Coll) 1967 *A* 1, *E, S, A* 2, 1968 *F, E*

Sherry, M J A (Lansdowne) 1975 *F, W*

Siggins, J A E (Belfast Collegians) 1931 *F, E, S, W, SA*, 1932 *E, S, W*, 1933 *E, W, S*, 1934 *E, S, W*, 1935 *E, S, W, NZ*, 1936 *E, S, W*, 1937 *S, W*

Slattery, J F (UC Dublin, Blackrock Coll) 1970 *SA, F, E, S, W*, 1971 *F, E, S, W*, 1972 *F* 1, *E, F* 2, 1973 *NZ, E, S, W, F*, 1974 *F, W, E, S, P, NZ*, 1975 *E, S, F, W*, 1976 *A*, 1977 *S, F*, 1978 *S, F, W, E, NZ*, 1979 *F, W, E, S, A* 1,2, 1980 *E, S, F, W*, 1981 *F, W, E, SA* 1,2, *A*, 1982 *W, E, S, F*, 1983 *F, W, E*, 1984 *F*

Smartt, F N B (Dublin U) 1908 *E, S*, 1909 *E*

Smith, B A (Oxford U, Leicester) 1989 *NZ*, 1990 *S, F, W, Arg*, 1991 *F, W, E, S*

Smith, J H (London Irish) 1951 *F, E, S, W, SA*, 1952 *F, S, W, E*, 1954 *NZ, W, F*

Smith, R E (Lansdowne) 1892 *E*

Smith, S J (Ballymena) 1988 *E* 2, *WS, It*, 1989 *F, W, E, S, NZ*, 1990 *E*, 1991 *F, W, E, S, Nm* 1,2, [*Z, S, A*], 1992 *W, E, S, F, NZ* 1,2, 1993 *S*

Smithwick, F F S (Monkstown) 1898 *S, W*

Smyth, J T (Queen's U, Belfast) 1920 *F*

Smyth, P J (Belfast Collegians) 1911 *E, S, F*

Smyth, R S (Dublin U) 1903 *E, S*, 1904 *E*

Smyth, T (Malone, Newport) 1908 *E, S, W*, 1909 *E, S, W*, 1910 *E, S, W, F*, 1911 *E, S, W*, 1912 *E*

Smyth, W S (Belfast Collegians) 1910 *W, F*, 1920 *E*

Solomons, B A H (Dublin U) 1908 *E, S, W*, 1909 *E, S, W, F*, 1910 *E, S, W*

Spain, A W (UC Dublin) 1924 *NZ*

Sparrow, W (Dublin U) 1893 *W*, 1894 *E*

Spillane, B J (Bohemians) 1985 *S, F, W, E*, 1986 *F, W, E*, 1987 *F, W*, [*W, C, A* (R)], 1989 *E* (R)

Spring, D E (Dublin U) 1978 *S, NZ*, 1979 *S*, 1980 *S, F, W*, 1981 *W*

Spring, R M (Lansdowne) 1979 *F, W, E*

Spunner, H F (Wanderers) 1881 *E, S*, 1884 *W*

Stack, C R R (Dublin U) 1889 *S*

Stack, G H (Dublin U) 1875 *E*

Staples, J E (London Irish, Harlequins) 1991 *W, E, S, Nm* 1,2, [*Z, J, S, A*], 1992 *W, E, NZ* 1,2, *A*, 1995 *F, W, It*, [*NZ*], *Fj*, 1996 *US, S, F, A*, 1997 *W, E, S*

Steele, H W (Ballymena) 1976 *E*, 1977 *F*, 1978 *F, W, E*, 1979 *F, W, E, A* 1,2

Stephenson, G V (Queen's U, Belfast, London Hosp) 1920 *F*, 1921 *E, S, W, F*, 1922 *E, S, W, F*, 1923 *E, S, W, F*, 1924 *F, E, S, W, NZ*, 1925 *F, E, S, W*, 1926 *F, E, S, W*, 1927 *F, E, S, W, A*, 1928 *F, E, S, W*, 1929 *F, E, W*, 1930 *F, E, S, W*

Stephenson, H W V (United Services) 1922 *S, W, F*, 1924 *F, E, S, W, NZ*, 1925 *F, E, S, W*, 1927 *A*, 1928 *E*

Stevenson, J (Dungannon) 1888 *M*, 1889 *S*

Stevenson, J B (Instonians) 1958 *A, E, S, W, F*

Stevenson, R (Dungannon) 1887 *E, S, W*, 1888 *M*, 1889 *S, W*, 1890 *S, W, E*, 1891 *W*, 1892 *W*, 1893 *E, S, W*

Stevenson, T H (Belfast Acad) 1895 *E, W*, 1896 *E, S, W*, 1897 *E, S*

Stewart, A L (NIFC) 1913 *W, F*, 1914 *F*

Stewart, W J (Queen's U, Belfast, NIFC) 1922 *F*, 1924 *S*, 1928 *F, E, S, W*, 1929 *F, E, S, W*

Stoker, E W (Wanderers) 1888 *W, S*

Stoker, F O (Wanderers) 1886 *S*, 1888 *W, M*, 1889 *S*, 1891 *W*

Stokes, O S (Cork Bankers) 1882 *E*, 1884 *S*

Stokes, P (Garryowen) 1913 *E, S*, 1914 *F*, 1920 *E, S, W, F*, 1921 *E, S, F*, 1922 *W, F*

Stokes, R D (Queen's Coll, Cork) 1891 *S, W*

Strathdee, E (Queen's U, Belfast) 1947 *E, S, W, A*, 1948 *W, F*, 1949 *E, S, W*

Stringer, P A (Shannon) 2000 *S, It, F, W, Arg, C, J, SA*, 2001 *It, F, R, S* (R), *W, E*

Stuart, C P (Clontarf) 1912 *SA*

Stuart, I M B (Dublin U) 1924 *E, S*

Sugars, H S (Dublin U) 1905 *NZ*, 1906 *SA*, 1907 *S*

Sugden, M (Wanderers) 1925 *F, E, S, W*, 1926 *F, E, S, W*, 1927 *E, S, W, A*, 1928 *F, E, S, W*, 1929 *F, E, S, W*, 1930 *F, E, S, W*, 1931 *F, E, S, W*

Sullivan, D B (UC Dublin) 1922 *E, S, W, F*

Sweeney, J A (Blackrock Coll) 1907 *E, S, W*

Symes, G R (Monkstown) 1895 *E*

Synge, J S (Lansdowne) 1929 *S*

Taggart, T (Dublin U) 1887 *W*

Taylor, A S (Queen's Coll, Belfast) 1910 *E, S, W*, 1912 *F*

Taylor, D R (Queen's Coll, Belfast) 1903 *E*

Taylor, J (Belfast Collegians) 1914 *E, S, W*

Taylor, J W (NIFC) 1879 *S*, 1880 *E, S*, 1881 *S*, 1882 *E, S*, 1883 *E, S*

Tector, W R (Wanderers) 1955 *F, E, S*

Tedford, A (Malone) 1902 *E, S, W*, 1903 *E, S, W*, 1904 *E, S, W*, 1905 *E, S, W, NZ*, 1906 *E, S, W, SA*, 1907 *E, S, W*, 1908 *E, S, W*

Teehan, C (UC Cork) 1939 *E, S, W*

Thompson, C (Belfast Collegians) 1907 *E, S*, 1908 *E, S, W*, 1909 *E, S, W, F*, 1910 *E, S, W, F*

Thompson, J A (Queen's Coll, Belfast) 1885 *S* 1,2

Thompson, J K S (Dublin U) 1921 *W*, 1922 *E, S, F*, 1923 *E, S, W, F*

Thompson, R G (Lansdowne) 1882 *W*

Thompson, R H (Instonians) 1951 *SA*, 1952 *F*, 1954 *NZ, F, E, S, W*, 1955 *F, S, W*, 1956 *W*

Thornhill, T (Wanderers) 1892 *E, S, W*, 1893 *E*

Thrift, H (Dublin U) 1904 *W*, 1905 *E, S, W, NZ*, 1906 *E, W, SA*, 1907 *E, S, W*, 1908 *E, S, W*, 1909 *E, S, W, F*

Tierney, D (UC Cork) 1938 *S, W*, 1939 *E*

Tierney, T A (Garryowen) 1999 *A* 1,2, *Arg* 1, [*US, A* 3, *R, Arg* 2], 2000 *E*

Tillie, C R (Dublin U) 1887 *E, S*, 1888 *W, S*

Todd, A W P (Dublin U) 1913 *W, F*, 1914 *F*

Topping, J A (Ballymena) 1996 *WS, A*, 1997 *It* 1, *F, E*, 1999 [*R*], 2000 *US*

Torrens, J D (Bohemians) 1938 *W*, 1939 *E, S, W*

Tucker, C C (Shannon) 1979 *F, W*, 1980 *F* (R)

Tuke, B B (Bective Rangers) 1890 *E*, 1891 *E, S*, 1892 *E*, 1894 *E, S, W*, 1895 *E, S*

Turley, N (Blackrock Coll) 1962 *E*

Tweed, D A (Ballymena) 1995 *F, W, It*, [*J*]

Tydings, J J (Young Munster) 1968 *A*

Tyrrell, W (Queen's U, Belfast) 1910 *F*, 1913 *E, S, W, F*, 1914 *F, E, S, W*

Uprichard, R J H (Harlequins, RAF) 1950 *S, W*

Waide, S L (Oxford U, NIFC) 1932 *E, S, W*, 1933 *E, W*

Waites, J (Bective Rangers) 1886 *S*, 1888 *M*, 1889 *W*, 1890 *S, W, E*, 1891 *E*

Waldron, O C (Oxford U, London Irish) 1966 *S, W*, 1968 *A*

Walker, S (Instonians) 1934 *E, S*, 1935 *E, S, W, NZ*, 1936 *E, S, W*, 1937 *E, S, W*, 1938 *E, S, W*

Walkington, D B (NIFC) 1887 *E, W*, 1888 *W*, 1890 *W, E*, 1891 *E, S, W*

Walkington, R B (NIFC) 1875 *E*, 1876 *E*, 1877 *E, S*, 1878 *E*, 1879 *S*, 1880 *E, S*, 1882 *E, S*

Wall, H (Dolphin) 1965 *S, W*

Wallace, D P (Garryowen) 2000 *Arg, US*, 2001 *It, F, R* (R), *S* (R), *W, E*

Wallace, Jas (Wanderers) 1904 *E, S*

Wallace, Jos (Wanderers) 1903 *S, W*, 1904 *E, S, W*, 1905 *E, S, W, NZ*, 1906 *W*

Wallace, P S (Blackrock Coll, Saracens) 1995 [*J*], *Fj*, 1996 *US, W, E, WS, A*, 1997 *It* 1, *F, W, E, S, NZ, C*, 1998 *S, F, W, E, SA* 1,2, *Gg, R*, 1999 *F, W, E, S, It* (R), 1999 *A* 1,2, *Arg* 1, [*US, A* 3, *R, Arg* 2], 2000 *E, US, C* (R)

Wallace, R M (Garryowen, Saracens) 1991 *Nm* 1(R), 1992 *W, E, S, F, A*, 1993 *S, F, W, E, R*, 1994 *F, W, E, S*, 1995 *W, It*, [*NZ, J, W*], *Fj*, 1996 *US, S, F, WS*, 1998 *S, F, W, E*

Wallace, T H (Cardiff) 1920 *E, S, W*

Wallis, A K (Wanderers) 1892 *E, S, W*, 1893 *E, W*

Wallis, C O'N (Old Cranleighans, Wanderers) 1935 *NZ*

Wallis, T G (Wanderers) 1921 *F*, 1922 *E, S, W, F*

Wallis, W A (Wanderers) 1880 *S*, 1881 *E, S*, 1882 *W*, 1883 *S*

Walmsley, G (Bective Rangers) 1894 *E*

Walpole, A (Dublin U) 1888 *S, M*

Walsh, E J (Lansdowne) 1887 *E, S, W*, 1892 *E, S, W*, 1893 *E*

Walsh, H D (Dublin U) 1875 *E*, 1876 *E*

Walsh, J C (UC Cork, Sunday's Well) 1960 *S, SA*, 1961 *E, S, F, SA*, 1963 *E, S, W, NZ*, 1964 *E, S, W, F*, 1965 *F, S, W, SA*, 1966 *F, S, W*, 1967 *E, S, W, F, A* 2

Ward, A J (Ballynahinch) 1998 *F, W, E, SA* 1,2, *Gg, R, SA* 3, 1999 *W, E, S, It* (R), *A* 1,2, *Arg* 1, [*US, A* 3, *R, Arg* 2], 2000 *F* (R), *W* (t&R), *Arg* (R), *US* (R), *C, J, SA* (R), 2001 *It* (R), *F* (R)

Ward, A J P (Garryowen, St Mary's Coll, Greystones) 1978 *S, F, W, E, NZ*, 1979 *F, W, E, S*, 1981 *W, E, S, A*, 1983 *E* (R), 1984 *E, S*, 1986 *S*, 1987 [*C, Tg*]

Warren, J P (Kingstown) 1883 *E*

Warren, R G (Lansdowne) 1884 *W*, 1885 *E, S* 1,2, 1886 *E*, 1887 *E, S, W*, 1888 *W, S, M*, 1889 *S, W*, 1890 *S, W, E*

Watson, R (Wanderers) 1912 *SA*

Wells, H G (Bective Rangers) 1891 *S, W*, 1894 *E, S*

Westby, A J (Dublin U) 1876 *E*

Wheeler, G H (Queen's Coll, Belfast) 1884 *S*, 1885 *E*

Wheeler, J R (Queen's U, Belfast) 1922 *E, S, W, F*, 1924 *E*

Whelan, P C (Garryowen) 1975 *E, S*, 1976 *NZ*, 1977 *W, E, S, F*, 1978 *S, F, W, E, NZ*, 1979 *F, W, E, S*, 1981 *F, W, E*

White, M (Queen's Coll, Cork) 1906 *E, S, W, SA*, 1907 *E, W*

Whitestone, A M (Dublin U) 1877 *E*, 1879 *S, E*, 1880 *E*, 1883 *S*

Whittle, D (Bangor) 1988 *F*

Wilkinson, C R (Malone) 1993 *S*

Wilkinson, R W (Wanderers) 1947 *A*

Williamson, F W (Dolphin) 1930 *E, S, W*

Willis, W J (Lansdowne) 1879 *E*

Wilson, F (CIYMS) 1977 *W, E, S*

Wilson, H G (Glasgow U, Malone) 1905 *E, S, W, NZ*, 1906 *E, S, W, SA*, 1907 *E, S, W*, 1908 *E, S, W*, 1909 *E, S, W*, 1910 *W*

Wilson, W H (Bray) 1877 *E, S*

Withers, H H C (Army, Blackheath) 1931 *F, E, S, W, SA*

Wolfe, E J (Armagh) 1882 *E*

Wood, G H (Dublin U) 1913 *W*, 1914 *F*

Wood, B G M (Garryowen) 1954 *E, S*, 1956 *F, E, S, W*, 1957 *F, E, S, W*, 1958 *A, E, S, W, F*, 1959 *E, S, W, F*, 1960 *E, S, W, F, SA*, 1961 *E, S, W, F, SA*

Wood, K G M (Garryowen, Harlequins) 1994 *A* 1,2, *US*, 1995 *E, S*, [*J*], 1996 *A*, 1997 *It* 1, *F*, 1997 *NZ, It* 2, 1998 *S, F, W, E, SA* 1,2, *R* (R), *SA* 3, 1999 *F, W, E, S, It* (R), *A* 1,2, *Arg* 1, [*US, A* 3, *R* (R), *Arg* 2], 2000 *E, S, It, F, W, Arg, US, C, J, SA*, 2001 *It, F, S, W, E*

Woods, D C (Bessbrook) 1888 *M*, 1889 *S*

Woods, N K P J (Blackrock Coll, London Irish) 1994 *A* 1,2, 1995 *E, F*, 1996 *F, W, E*, 1999 *W*

Wright, R A (Monkstown) 1912 *S*

Yeates, R A (Dublin U) 1889 *S, W*

Young, G (UC Cork) 1913 *E*

Young, R M (Collegians) 1965 *F, E, S, W, SA*, 1966 *F, E, S, W*, 1967 *W, F*, 1968 *W, A*, 1969 *F, E, S, W*, 1970 *SA, F, E, S, W*, 1971 *F, E, S, W*

IRELAND INTERNATIONAL STATISTICS

(up to 20 October 2001)

Match Records

Most Consecutive Test Wins

6 1968 *S,W,A*, 1969 *F,E,S*

Most Consecutive Tests Without Defeat

Matches	Wins	Draws	Period
7	6	1	1968 to 1969
5	4	1	1972 to 1973

Most Points in a Match
by the team

Pts	Opponents	Venue	Year
83	United States	Manchester (NH)	2000
78	Japan	Dublin	2000
70	Georgia	Dublin	1998
60	Romania	Dublin	1986
60	Italy	Dublin	2000
55	Zimbabwe	Dublin	1991
53	Romania	Dublin	1998
53	United States	Dublin	1999
50	Japan	Bloemfontein	1995

by a player

Pts	Player	Opponents	Venue	Year
30	R J R O'Gara	Italy	Dublin	2000
24	P A Burke	Italy	Dublin	1997
24	D G Humphreys	Argentina	Lens	1999
23	R P Keyes	Zimbabwe	Dublin	1991
23	R J R O'Gara	Japan	Dublin	2000
21	S O Campbell	Scotland	Dublin	1982
21	S O Campbell	England	Dublin	1983
21	R J R O'Gara	Italy	Rome	2001
20	M J Kiernan	Romania	Dublin	1986
20	E P Elwood	Romania	Dublin	1993
20	S J P Mason	Samoa	Dublin	1996
20	E P Elwood	Georgia	Dublin	1998
20	K G M Wood	United States	Dublin	1999

Most Tries in a Match
by the team

Tries	Opponents	Venue	Year
13	United States	Manchester (NH)	2000
11	Japan	Dublin	2000
10	Romania	Dublin	1986
10	Georgia	Dublin	1998
8	Western Samoa	Dublin	1988
8	Zimbabwe	Dublin	1991
7	Japan	Bloemfontein	1995
7	Romania	Dublin	1998
7	United States	Dublin	1999

by a player

Tries	Player	Opponents	Venue	Year
4	B F Robinson	Zimbabwe	Dublin	1991
4	K G M Wood	United States	Dublin	1999
3	R Montgomery	Wales	Birkenhead	1887
3	J P Quinn	France	Cork	1913
3	E O'D Davy	Scotland	Murrayfield	1930
3	S J Byrne	Scotland	Murrayfield	1953
3	K D Crossan	Romania	Dublin	1986
3	B J Mullin	Tonga	Brisbane	1987
3	M R Mostyn	Argentina	Dublin	1999
3	B G O'Driscoll	France	Paris	2000
3	M J Mullins	United States	Manchester (NH)	2000
3	D A Hickie	Japan	Dublin	2000
3	R A J Henderson	Italy	Rome	2001

Most Conversions in a Match
by the team

Cons	Opponents	Venue	Year
10	Georgia	Dublin	1998
10	Japan	Dublin	2000
9	United States	Manchester (NH)	2000
7	Romania	Dublin	1986
6	Japan	Bloemfontein	1995
6	Romania	Dublin	1998
6	United States	Dublin	1999
6	Italy	Dublin	2000

by a player

Cons	Player	Opponents	Venue	Year
10	E P Elwood	Georgia	Dublin	1998
10	R J R O'Gara	Japan	Dublin	2000
8	R J R O'Gara	United States	Manchester (NH)	2000
7	M J Kiernan	Romania	Dublin	1986
6	P A Burke	Japan	Bloemfontein	1995
6	R J R O'Gara	Italy	Dublin	2000
5	M J Kiernan	Canada	Dunedin	1987
5	E P Elwood	Romania	Dublin	1999

Most Penalties in a Match
by the team

Penalties	Opponents	Venue	Year
8	Italy	Dublin	1997
7	Argentina	Lens	1999
6	Scotland	Dublin	1982
6	Romania	Dublin	1993
6	United States	Atlanta	1996
6	Western Samoa	Dublin	1996
6	Italy	Dublin	2000

by a player

Penalties	Player	Opponents	Venue	Year
8	P A Burke	Italy	Dublin	1997
7	D G Humphreys	Argentina	Lens	1999
6	S O Campbell	Scotland	Dublin	1982
6	E P Elwood	Romania	Dublin	1993
6	S J P Mason	Western Samoa	Dublin	1996
6	R J R O'Gara	Italy	Dublin	2000

Most Dropped Goals in a Match
by the team

Drops	Opponents	Venue	Year
2	Australia	Dublin	1967
2	France	Dublin	1975
2	Australia	Sydney	1979
2	England	Dublin	1981
2	Canada	Dunedin	1987
2	England	Dublin	1993
2	Wales	Wembley	1999

by a player

Drops	Player	Opponents	Venue	Year
2	C M H Gibson	Australia	Dublin	1967
2	W M McCombe	France	Dublin	1975
2	S O Campbell	Australia	Sydney	1979
2	E P Elwood	England	Dublin	1993
2	D G Humphreys	Wales	Wembley	1999

52	D G Lenihan	1981 to 1992
51	M I Keane	1974 to 1984
48	N J Popplewell	1989 to 1998

Most Consecutive Tests

Tests	Player	Span
52	W J McBride	1964 to 1975
49	P A Orr	1976 to 1986
43	D G Lenihan	1981 to 1989
39	M I Keane	1974 to 1981
37	G V Stephenson	1920 to 1929

Most Tests as Captain

Tests	Captain	Span
24	T J Kiernan	1963 to 1973
24	K G M Wood	1996 to 2001
19	C F Fitzgerald	1982 to 1986
17	J F Slattery	1979 to 1981
17	D G Lenihan	1986 to 1990

Most Tests in Individual Positions

Position	Player	Tests	Span
Full-back	T J Kiernan	54	1960 to 1973
Wing	K D Crossan	41	1982 to 1992
Centre	B J Mullin	55	1984 to 1995
Fly-half	J W Kyle	46	1947 to 1958
Scrum-half	M T Bradley	40	1984 to 1995
Prop	P A Orr	58	1976 to 1987
Hooker	K W Kennedy	45	1965 to 1975
	K G M Wood	45	1994 to 2001
Lock	W J McBride	63	1962 to 1975
Flanker	J F Slattery	61	1970 to 1984
No 8	W P Duggan	39	1975 to 1984

Career Records

Most Capped Players

Caps	Player	Career Span
69	C M H Gibson	1964 to 1979
63	W J McBride	1962 to 1975
61	J F Slattery	1970 to 1984
59	P S Johns	1990 to 2000
58	P A Orr	1976 to 1987
55	B J Mullin	1984 to 1995
54	T J Kiernan	1960 to 1973

Most Points in Tests

Points	Player	Tests	Career
308	M J Kiernan	43	1982 to 1991
296	E P Elwood	35	1993 to 1999
255	D G Humphreys	35	1996 to 2001
217	S O Campbell	22	1976 to 1984
163	R J R O'Gara	14	2000 to 2001
158	T J Kiernan	54	1960 to 1973
113	A J P Ward	19	1978 to 1987

Most Tries in Tests

Tries	Player	Tests	Career
17	B J Mullin	55	1984 to 1995
14	G V Stephenson	42	1920 to 1930
12	K D Crossan	41	1982 to 1992
12	K G M Wood	46	1994 to 2001
11	A T A Duggan	25	1963 to 1972
11	S P Geoghegan	37	1991 to 1996

Most Conversions in Tests

Cons	Player	Tests	Career
43	E P Elwood	35	1993 to 1999
40	M J Kiernan	43	1982 to 1991
34	R J R O'Gara	14	2000 to 2001
27	D G Humphreys	35	1996 to 2001
26	T J Kiernan	54	1960 to 1973
16	R A Lloyd	19	1910 to 1920
15	S O Campbell	22	1976 to 1984

Most Penalty Goals in Tests

Penalties	Player	Tests	Career
68	E P Elwood	35	1993 to 1999
62	M J Kiernan	43	1982 to 1991
57	D G Humphreys	35	1996 to 2001
54	S O Campbell	22	1976 to 1984
31	T J Kiernan	54	1960 to 1973
30	R J R O'Gara	14	2000 to 2001
29	A J P Ward	19	1978 to 1987

Most Dropped Goals in Tests

Drops	Player	Tests	Career
7	R A Lloyd	19	1910 to 1920
7	S O Campbell	22	1976 to 1984
6	C M H Gibson	69	1964 to 1979
6	B J McGann	25	1969 to 1976
6	M J Kiernan	43	1982 to 1991

International Championship Records

Record	Detail		Set
Most points in season	168	in five matches	2000
Most tries in season	17	in five matches	2000
Highest Score	60	60-13 v Italy	2000
Biggest win	47	60-13 v Italy	2000
Highest score conceded	50	18-50 v England	2000
Biggest defeat	40	6-46 v England	1997
Most appearances	56	C M H Gibson	1964 – 1979
Most points in matches	207	M J Kiernan	1982 – 1991
Most points in season	58	R J R O'Gara	2000
Most points in match	30	R J R O'Gara	v Italy, 2000
Most tries in matches	14	G V Stephenson	1920 – 1930
Most tries in season	5	J E Arigho	1928
	5	B G O'Driscoll	2000
Most tries in match	3	R Montgomery	v Wales, 1887
	3	J P Quinn	v France, 1913
	3	E O'D Davy	v Scotland, 1930
	3	S J Byrne	v Scotland, 1953
	3	B G O'Driscoll	v France, 2000
	3	R A J Henderson	v Italy, 2001
Most cons in matches	21	M J Kiernan	1982 – 1991
Most cons in season	11	R J R O'Gara	2000
Most cons in match	6	R J R O'Gara	v Italy, 2000
Most pens in matches	48	S O Campbell	1980 – 1984
Most pens in season	14	S O Campbell	1983
	14	E P Elwood	1994
Most pens in match	6	S O Campbell	v Scotland, 1982
	6	R J R O'Gara	v Italy, 2000
Most drops in matches	7	R A Lloyd	1910 – 1920
Most drops in season	2	on several occasions	
Most drops in match	2	W M McCombe	v France, 1975
	2	E P Elwood	v England, 1993
	2	D G Humphreys	v Wales, 1999

Miscellaneous Records

Record	Holder	Detail
Longest Test Career	A J F O'Reilly	16 seasons, 1954–55 to 1969–70
	C M H Gibson	16 seasons, 1963–64 to 1979
Youngest Test Cap	F S Hewitt	17 yrs 157 days in 1924
Oldest Test Cap	C M H Gibson	36 yrs 195 days in 1979

Career Records of Ireland International Players
(up to 20 October 2001)

Player	Debut	Caps	T	C	P	D	Pts
Backs:							
J C Bell	1994 v A	33	7	0	0	0	35
J P Bishop	1998 v SA	19	7	0	0	0	35
P A Burke	1995 v E	11	0	12	26	1	105
D J Crotty	1996 v A	5	0	0	0	0	0
G M D'Arcy	1999 v R	1	0	0	0	0	0
G T Dempsey	1998 v Gg	18	5	0	0	0	25
G Easterby	2000 v US	5	2	0	0	0	10
E P Elwood	1993 v W	35	0	43	68	2	296
R A J Henderson	1996 v WS	21	5	0	0	0	25
D A Hickie	1997 v W	23	10	0	0	0	50
S P Horgan	2000 v S	11	7	0	0	0	35
T G Howe	2000 v US	6	3	0	0	0	15
D G Humphreys	1996 v F	35	3	27	57	5	255
P McKenna	2000 v Arg	1	0	0	0	0	0
J P J McWeeney	1997 v NZ	1	0	0	0	0	0
K M Maggs	1997 v NZ	34	7	0	0	0	35
S J P Mason	1996 v W	3	0	3	12	0	42
M R Mostyn	1999 v A	6	3	0	0	0	15
M J Mullins	1999 v Arg	12	3	0	0	0	15
G E A Murphy	2000 v US	5	3	0	0	0	15
B G O'Driscoll	1999 v A	18	10	0	0	1	53
R J R O'Gara	2000 v S	14	1	34	30	0	163
B T O'Meara	1997 v E	7	0	0	0	0	0
C M P O'Shea	1993 v R	35	6	1	3	1	44
P A Stringer	2000 v S	14	1	0	0	0	5
T A Tierney	1999 v A	8	1	0	0	0	5
J A Topping	1996 v WS	7	1	0	0	0	5
Forwards:							
T Brennan	1998 v SA	11	0	0	0	0	0
E Byrne	2001 v It	5	0	0	0	0	0
S J Byrne	2001 v R	1	0	0	0	0	0
R E Casey	1999 v A	5	0	0	0	0	0
P M Clohessy	1993 v F	47	4	0	0	0	20
D S Corkery	1994 v A	27	3	0	0	0	15
R Corrigan	1997 v C	10	0	0	0	0	0
V C P Costello	1996 v US	22	3	0	0	0	15
J W Davidson	1995 v Fj	32	0	0	0	0	0
K Dawson	1997 v NZ	16	1	0	0	0	5
S H Easterby	2000 v S	8	2	0	0	0	10
J M Fitzpatrick	1998 v SA	21	0	0	0	0	0

A G Foley	1995 v E	24	2	0	0	0	10
G M Fulcher	1994 v A	20	1	0	0	0	5
M J Galwey	1991 v F	36	3	0	0	0	15
J J Hayes	2000 v S	14	0	0	0	0	0
M Horan	2000 v US	1	0	0	0	0	0
P S Johns	1990 v Arg	59	4	0	0	0	20
G W Longwell	2000 v J	5	0	0	0	0	0
A J W McKeen	1999 v R	1	0	0	0	0	0
E R P Miller	1997 v It	24	1	0	0	0	5
R P Nesdale	1997 v W	13	0	0	0	0	0
D O'Cuinneagain	1998 v SA	19	1	0	0	0	5
M R O'Driscoll	2001 v R	1	0	0	0	0	0
M E O'Kelly	1997 v NZ	33	3	0	0	0	15
A Quinlan	1999 v R	3	0	0	0	0	0
F J Sheahan	2000 v US	4	0	0	0	0	0
D P Wallace	2000 v Arg	8	0	0	0	0	0
P S Wallace	1995 v J	37	5	0	0	0	25
A J Ward	1998 v F	28	3	0	0	0	15
K G M Wood	1994 v A	46	12	0	0	0	60

NB Humphreys's figures include a penalty try awarded against Scotland in 1999

WALES TEST SEASON REVIEW 2000-01

Tackle Must be the Battlecry

John Billot

Not a Welsh try in sight. Minimal creativity. Patchy periods of passion. That was the gruesome reality of a record 36-6 October defeat by Ireland, who have not lost at Cardiff since 1983. Coach Graham Henry and his squad of advisers and players must look to the defiant words of Virgil, Roman history's distinguished poet, to fortify them: 'Yield you not to ill-fortune, but go against it with more daring.'

Ireland, in this match held over from the previous season because of the foot-and-mouth epidemic in the United Kingdom, dismantled a defence that needs to hit the tackle bags in sustained practice sessions before the 2002 Six Nations occupies attention. Never had the Green Gladiators raised such a grand total against the Welsh. Indeed, it could have been considerably more, but David Humphreys's sky-scraping drop-shot was beyond the ken of referee Jonathan Kaplan and three more points were denied to the game's outstanding tactical controller.

There were those who warned of a backlash after Ireland's shambles at Murrayfield and it was not as if Wales were unprepared. Alas, there were too many key men on the injury list. David Young, who led his side out for his 50th cap accompanied by his three young sons as mascots, was deprived of the services of such as Neil Jenkins, Gareth Thomas, Mark Taylor, Scott Quinnell, Darren Morris, Martyn Williams and Ian Gough. It was not an excuse; merely an observation.

The Irish forwards fell ravenously on their victims and with the home pack in bondage there was never going to be enough quality possession for a back division pinned like butterflies to the collector's card by tacklers who showed how it should be done. So Wales were undone: a bedraggled flock, raked by a volley of second half tries. Kevin Morgan was a hero at full-back for the lacklustre losers and Wales will need many more like him in the coming months.

A warm-up fixture with what amounted to Romania's second fifteen (six first choice men were refused release by their French clubs, three were left behind because of misconduct, and one was in custody on suspicion of murdering his wife) predictably resulted in a record home victory by 81-9. Colin Charvis, always a man for the main chance, made history as the first Wales forward to score three tries in a match; but there only 20,400 to witness his feat and perhaps this sent a message to the WRU that the public are unimpressed by such contrived matches. Scott Gibbs was omitted after 53 appearances for his country and announced his retirement from the international scene.

The autumn 2000 international match programme settled the controversial Neil Jenkins/Arwel Thomas debate. The Swansea outside-half had his loyal lobby. To them he was all daring scurry and flurry when there was a gap to be explored and a cool, calculating opportunist who dropped cheeky goals. Jenkins enjoyed the reputation as a proven master-tactician and supreme goal kicker, well on his way to 1,000 points for Wales. But after Arwel did duty in the less than hazardous games against Samoa and the United States, it was Neil Jenkins who donned the No 10 jersey to oppose South Africa.

Back in 1949 and 1950, Wales had been vociferously divided over the Glyn Davies/Billy Cleaver wrangle. Cleaver, the orthodox, superb tactical kicker, covered across the field with clear perception of every need. Glyn Davies, classical, side-stepping, dummying breaker of defences was a guileful maker of tries. Cardiff's Cleaver won the selectors' favour. Now Cardiff's Jenkins triumphed as Henry's chosen man.

In another twist to the tale, Henry pulled Jenkins off with 20 minutes left for play against the Springboks and Wales trailing 13-10. Arwel was sent out. 'On his day, Arwel can win matches,' insisted the coach, defending his decision. 'We thought Arwel might produce some magic.' Instead, after finding the target with a 40-metre penalty shot, he missed a comparatively easy second attempt, failed with two drop-goal attempts, gave away a penalty goal for handling in a ruck with the score 13-all, and bungled a quick drop-out to allow the Springboks to score again and win 23-13. His talent was undeniable; his luck was simply wretched.

Rhys Williams, the highly promising Cardiff full-back who had figured in the victories over Samoa (by 50-6) and the United States (by 42-11) before the South African defeat, lost his place for the England match. It was that old compulsion for solidity above all else that urged Henry to invest his faith in Llanelli outside-half Stephen Jones as the new full-back. The Scarlets' star had not filled that role for his club for three years, but it was certainly not his fault that England, dynamic attackers from all quarters behind a scourging pack, snapped up six tries as Wales were blown away by 44-15. This was England's first visit to the Millennium Stadium and they took merciless vengeance for Wembley 1999.

Scotland found themselves in a pitiful plight at Murrayfield, trailing by 25-6 and Wales well placed to continue the pillage. Alas, two missed tackles cost tries and it was to Neil Jenkins in desperation that Wales looked to salvage a 28-all draw. The only Welsh try had been a gifted interception to Mark Taylor for a long run in. Coach Henry, who had called for the WRU to increase the number of professional coaches to groom the national side, now demanded that fitness levels be improved with some urgency. He was not a happy Henry.

Under siege after Murrayfield, the coach deflected criticism. 'I don't think we have a lot of choice in selection,' he protested. 'I don't think we should panic. The club structure is our Achilles' heel. I'm so frustrated because there is real potential waiting to be released in the Welsh game. When I came here, rugby was in a mess. I'll ensure it is in a far better state when I leave. I'm not going to let a few setbacks deter me. I am not advocating a system where we have more coaches than players. But I do feel we should have more coaches employed on a full time basis which would allow them to liaise with the top clubs, one of the strengths of the English system.' Former England and Cardiff captain John Scott remarked: 'Not to put too fine a point on it, Henry is surrounded by second-raters and nodding dogs.'

Paris saved the season for harassed Henry and his team. Neil Jenkins, with a masterly display of control, scored 28 points and reached a world record 1,000 in international rugby; Wales completed a second successive victory in Paris for the first time since 1957; and Rob Howley's audacious 70-metres solo try was considered the most hypnotic Wales had ever scored in Paris in more than 90 years. It was 43-35 to David Young's side and heady stuff indeed. Delighted coach Henry praised it as the best performance since he took over. Victory in Rome followed, Lynn Howells coached the side to a 2-0 Test series win in Japan in June while Henry was on Lions duty, and then came the long wait for Romania in September and Ireland in October – and one of the most doleful displays of the Henry era.

Wales's Test Record in 2000–2001: Played 11, won 7, drawn 1, lost 3.

Opponents	Date	Venue	Result
Ireland	13th October 2001	H	Lost 6-36
Romania	22nd September 2001	H	Won 81-9
Japan	17th June 2001	A	Won 53-30
Japan	10th June 2001	A	Won 64-10
Italy	8th April 2001	A	Won 33-23
France	17th March 2001	A	Won 43-35
Scotland	17th February 2001	A	Drawn 28-28
England	3rd February 2001	H	Lost 15-44
South Africa	26th November 2000	H	Lost 13-23
United States	18th November 2000	H	Won 42-11
Samoa	11th November 2000	H	Won 50-6

WELSH INTERNATIONAL PLAYERS

(up to 20 October 2001)

Note: Years given for International Championship matches are for second half of season; eg 1972 means season 1971-72. Years for all other matches refer to the actual year of the match. When a series has taken place, figures have been used to denote the particular matches in which players have featured. Thus 1969 *NZ* 2 indicates that a player appeared in the second Test of the series.

Ackerman, R A (Newport, London Welsh) 1980 *NZ*, 1981 *E, S, A*, 1982 *I, F, E, S*, 1983 *S, I, F, R*, 1984 *S, I, F, E, A*, 1985 *S, I, F, E, Fj*
Alexander, E P (Llandovery Coll, Cambridge U) 1885 *S*, 1886 *E, S*, 1887 *E, I*
Alexander, W H (Llwynypia) 1898 *I, E*, 1899 *E, S, I*, 1901 *S, I*
Allen, A G (Newbridge) 1990 *F, E, I*
Allen, C P (Oxford U, Beaumaris) 1884 *E, S*
Andrews, F (Pontypool) 1912 *SA*, 1913 *E, S, I*
Andrews, F G (Swansea) 1884 *E, S*
Andrews, G E (Newport) 1926 *E, S*, 1927 *E, F, I*
Anthony, C T (Swansea, Newport) 1997 *US* 1(R),2(R), *C* (R), *Tg* (R), 1998 *SA* 2, *Arg*, 1999 *S, I* (R), 2001 *J* 1,2, *I* (R)
Anthony, L (Neath) 1948 *E, S, F*
Appleyard, R C (Swansea) 1997 *C, R, Tg, NZ*, 1998 *It, E* (R), *S, I, F*
Arnold, P (Swansea) 1990 *Nm* 1, 2, *Bb*, 1991 *E, S, I, F* 1, *A*, [*Arg, A*], 1993 *F* (R), *Z* 2, 1994 *Sp, Fj*, 1995 *SA*, 1996 *Bb* (R)
Arnold, W R (Swansea) 1903 *S*
Arthur, C S (Cardiff) 1888 *I, M*, 1891 *E*
Arthur, T (Neath) 1927 *S, F, I*, 1929 *E, S, F, I*, 1930 *E, S, I, F*, 1931 *E, S, F, I, SA*, 1933 *E, S*
Ashton, C (Aberavon) 1959 *E, S, I*, 1960 *E, S, I*, 1962 *I*
Attewell, S L (Newport) 1921 *E, S, F*

Back, M J (Bridgend) 1995 *F* (R), *E* (R), *S, I*
Badger, O (Llanelli) 1895 *E, S, I*, 1896 *E*
Baker, A (Neath) 1921 *I*, 1923 *E, S, F, I*
Baker, A M (Newport) 1909 *S, F*, 1910 *S*
Bancroft, J (Swansea) 1909 *E, S, F, I*, 1910 *F, E, S, I*, 1911 *E, F, I*, 1912 *E, S, I*, 1913 *I*, 1914 *E, S, F*
Bancroft, W J (Swansea) 1890 *S, E, I*, 1891 *E, S, I*, 1892 *E, S, I*, 1893 *E, S, I*, 1894 *E, S, I*, 1895 *E, S, I*, 1896 *E, S, I*, 1897 *E*, 1898 *I, E*, 1899 *E, S, I*, 1900 *E, S, I*, 1901 *E, S, I*
Barlow, T M (Cardiff) 1884 *I*
Barrell, R J (Cardiff) 1929 *S, F, I*, 1933 *I*
Bartlett, J D (Llanelli) 1927 *S*, 1928 *E, S*
Bassett, A (Cardiff) 1934 *I*, 1935 *E, S, I*, 1938 *E, S*
Bassett, J A (Penarth) 1929 *E, S, F, I*, 1930 *E, S, I*, 1931 *E, S, F, I, SA*, 1932 *E, S, I*
Bateman, A G (Neath, Richmond, Northampton) 1990 *S, I, Nm* 1,2, 1996 *SA*, 1997 *US, S, F, E, R, NZ*, 1998 *It, E, S, I*, 1999 *S, Arg* 1,2, *SA, C*, [*J, A* (R)], 2000 *It, E, S, I, Sm, US, SA*, 2001 *E* (R), *It* (t), *R, I*
Bayliss, G (Pontypool) 1933 *S*
Bebb, D I E (Carmarthen TC, Swansea) 1959 *E, S, I, F*, 1960 *E, S, I, F, SA*, 1961 *E, S, I, F*, 1962 *E, S, F, I*, 1963 *E, F, NZ*, 1964 *E, S, F, SA*, 1965 *E, S, I, F*, 1966 *F, A*, 1967 *S, I, F, E*
Beckingham, G (Cardiff) 1953 *E, S*, 1958 *F*
Bennett, A M (Cardiff) 1995 [*NZ*] *SA, Fj*
Bennett, I (Aberavon) 1937 *I*
Bennett, P (Cardiff Harlequins) 1891 *E, S*, 1892 *S, I*
Bennett, P (Llanelli) 1969 *F* (R), 1970 *SA, S, F*, 1972 *S* (R), *NZ*, 1973 *E, S, I, F, A*, 1974 *S, I, F, E*, 1975 *S* (R), *I*, 1976 *E, S, I, F*, 1977 *I, F, E, S*, 1978 *E, S, I, F*
Bergiers, R T E (Cardiff Coll of Ed, Llanelli) 1972 *E, S, F, NZ*, 1973 *E, S, I, F, A*, 1974 *E*, 1975 *I*
Bevan, G W (Llanelli) 1947 *E*
Bevan, J A (Cambridge U) 1881 *E*
Bevan, J C (Cardiff, Cardiff Coll of Ed) 1971 *E, S, I, F*, 1972 *E, S, F, NZ*, 1973 *E, S*
Bevan, J D (Aberavon) 1975 *F, E, S, A*
Bevan, S (Swansea) 1904 *I*
Beynon, B (Swansea) 1920 *E, S*
Beynon, G E (Swansea) 1925 *F, I*
Bidgood, R A (Newport) 1992 *S*, 1993 *Z* 1,2, *Nm, J* (R)
Biggs, N W (Cardiff) 1888 *M*, 1889 *I*, 1892 *I*, 1893 *E, S, I*, 1894 *E, I*
Biggs, S H (Cardiff) 1895 *E, S*, 1896 *S*, 1897 *E*, 1898 *I, E*, 1899 *S, I*, 1900 *I*

Birch, J (Neath) 1911 *S, F*
Birt, F W (Newport) 1911 *E, S*, 1912 *E, S, I, SA*, 1913 *E*
Bishop, D J (Pontypool) 1984 *A*
Bishop, E H (Swansea) 1889 *S*
Blackmore, J H (Abertillery) 1909 *E*
Blackmore, S W (Cardiff) 1987 *I*, [*Tg* (R), *C, A*]
Blake, J (Cardiff) 1899 *E, S, I*, 1900 *E, S, I*, 1901 *E, S, I*
Blakemore, R E (Newport) 1947 *E*
Bland, A F (Cardiff) 1887 *E, S, I*, 1888 *S, I, M*, 1890 *S, E, I*
Blyth, L (Swansea) 1951 *SA*, 1952 *E, S*
Blyth, W R (Swansea) 1974 *E*, 1975 *S* (R), 1980 *F, E, S, I*
Boobyer, N (Llanelli) 1993 *Z* 1(R),2, *Nm*, 1994 *Fj, Tg*, 1998 *It* (R)
Boon, R W (Cardiff) 1930 *S, F*, 1931 *E, S, F, I, SA*, 1932 *E, S, I*, 1933 *E, I*
Booth, J (Pontymister) 1898 *I*
Boots, J G (Newport) 1898 *I, E*, 1899 *I*, 1900 *E, S, I*, 1901 *E, S, I*, 1902 *E, S, I*, 1903 *E, S, I*, 1904 *E*
Boucher, A W (Newport) 1892 *E, S, I*, 1893 *E, S, I*, 1894 *E, S, I*, 1895 *E, S, I*, 1896 *E, I*, 1897 *E*
Bowcott, H M (Cardiff, Cambridge U) 1929 *S, F, I*, 1930 *E*, 1931 *E, S*, 1933 *E, I*
Bowdler, F A (Cross Keys) 1927 *A*, 1928 *E, S, I, F*, 1929 *E, S, F, I*, 1930 *E, S, I, SA*, 1932 *E, S, I*, 1933 *I*
Bowen, B (S Wales Police, Swansea) 1983 *R*, 1984 *S, I, F, E*, 1985 *Fj*, 1986 *E, S, I, F, Fj, Tg, WS*, 1987 [*C, E, NZ*], *US*, 1988 *E, S, I, F, WS*, 1989 *S, I*
Bowen, C A (Llanelli) 1896 *E, S, I*, 1897 *E*
Bowen, D H (Llanelli) 1883 *E*, 1886 *E, S*, 1887 *E*
Bowen, G E (Swansea) 1887 *S, I*, 1888 *S, I*
Bowen, W (Swansea) 1921 *S, F*, 1922 *E, S, I, F*
Bowen, Wm A (Swansea) 1886 *E, S*, 1887 *E, S, I*, 1888 *M*, 1889 *S, I*, 1890 *E, S, I*, 1891 *E, S*
Brace, D O (Llanelli, Oxford U) 1956 *E, S, I, F*, 1957 *E*, 1960 *S, I, F*, 1961 *I*
Braddock, K J (Newbridge) 1966 *A*, 1967 *S, I*
Bradshaw, K (Bridgend) 1964 *E, S, I, F, SA*, 1966 *E, S, I, F*
Brewer, T J (Newport) 1950 *E*, 1955 *E, S*
Brice, A B (Aberavon) 1899 *E, S, I*, 1900 *E, S, I*, 1901 *E, S, I*, 1902 *E, S, I*, 1903 *E, S, I*, 1904 *E, S, I*
Bridges, C J (Neath) 1990 *Nm* 1,2, *Bb*, 1991 *E* (R), *I, F* 1, *A*
Bridie, R H (Newport) 1882 *I*
Britton, G R (Newport) 1961 *S*
Broughton, A S (Treorchy) 1927 *A*, 1929 *S*
Brown, A (Newport) 1921 *I*
Brown, J (Cardiff) 1925 *I*
Brown, J A (Cardiff) 1907 *E, S, I*, 1908 *E, S, F*, 1909 *E*
Brown, M (Pontypool) 1983 *R*, 1986 *E, S, Fj* (R), *Tg, WS*
Bryant, D J (Bridgend) 1988 *NZ* 1,2, *WS, R*, 1989 *S, I, F, E*
Buchanan, A (Llanelli) 1987 [*Tg, E, NZ, A*], 1988 *I*
Buckett, I M (Swansea) 1994 *Tg*, 1997 *US* 2, *C*
Budgett, N J (Ebbw Vale, Bridgend) 2000 *S, I, Sm* (R), *US, SA*, 2001 *J* 1(R),2
Burcher, D H (Newport) 1977 *I, F, E, S*
Burgess, R C (Ebbw Vale) 1977 *I, F, E, S*, 1981 *I, F*, 1982 *F, E, S*
Burnett, R (Newport) 1953 *E*
Burns, J (Cardiff) 1927 *F, I*
Bush, P F (Cardiff) 1905 *NZ*, 1906 *E, SA*, 1907 *I*, 1908 *E, S*, 1910 *S, I*
Butler, E T (Pontypool) 1980 *F, E, S, I, NZ* (R), 1982 *S*, 1983 *E, S, I, F, R*, 1984 *S, I, F, E, A*

Cale, W R (Newbridge, Pontypool) 1949 *E, S, I*, 1950 *E, S, I, F*
Cardey, M D (Llanelli) 2000 *S*
Carter, A J (Newport) 1991 *E, S*
Cattell, A (Llanelli) 1883 *E, S*
Challinor, C (Neath) 1939 *E*

Charvis, C L (Swansea) 1996 *A* 3(R), *SA*, 1997 *US, S, I, F*, 1998 *It*(R), *E, S, I, F, Z*(R), *SA* 1,2, *Arg*, 1999 *S, I, F* 1, *It, E, Arg* 1, *SA, F* 2, [*Arg* 3, *A*], 2000 *F, It*(R), *E, S, I, Sm, US, SA*, 2001 *E, S, F, It, R, I*
Clapp, T J S (Newport) 1882 *I*, 1883 *E, S*, 1884 *E, S, I*, 1885 *E, S*, 1886 *S*, 1887 *E, S, I*, 1888 *S, I*
Clare, J (Cardiff) 1883 *E*
Clark, S S (Neath) 1882 *I*, 1887 *I*
Cleaver, W B (Cardiff) 1947 *E, S, F, I, A*, 1948 *E, S, F, I*, 1949 *I*, 1950 *E, S, I, F*
Clegg, B G (Swansea) 1979 *F*
Clement, A (Swansea) 1987 *US* (R), 1988 *E, NZ* 1, *WS* (R), *R*, 1989 *NZ*, 1990 *S* (R), *I* (R), *Nm* 1,2, 1991 *S* (R), *A* (R), *F* 2, [*WS, A*], 1992 *I, F, E, S*, 1993 *I* (R), *F, J, C*, 1994 *S, I, F, Sp, C* (R), *Tg, WS, It, SA*, 1995 *F, E, S, I*
Clement, W H (Llanelli) 1937 *E, S, I*, 1938 *E, S, I*
Cobner, T J (Pontypool) 1974 *S, I, F, E*, 1975 *F, E, S, I, A*, 1976 *E, S*, 1977 *F, E, S*, 1978 *E, S, I, F, A* 1
Coldrick, A P (Newport) 1911 *E, S, I*, 1912 *E, S, F*
Coleman, E (Newport) 1949 *E, S, I*
Coles, F C (Pontypool) 1960 *S, I, F*
Collins, J (Aberavon) 1958 *A, E, S, F*, 1959 *E, S, I, F*, 1960 *E*, 1961 *F*
Collins, R G (S Wales Police, Cardiff, Pontypridd) 1987 *E* (R), *I*, [*I, E, NZ*], *US*, 1988 *E, S, I, F, R*, 1990 *E, S, I*, 1991 *A, F* 2, [*WS*], 1994 *C, Fj, Tg, WS, R, It, SA*, 1995 *F, E, S, I*
Collins, T (Mountain Ash) 1923 *I*
Conway-Rees, J (Llanelli) 1892 *S*, 1893 *E*, 1894 *E*
Cook, T (Cardiff) 1949 *S, I*
Cooper, G J (Bath) 2001 *F, J* 1,2
Cope, W (Cardiff, Blackheath) 1896 *S*
Copsey, A H (Llanelli) 1992 *I, F, E, S, A*, 1993 *E, S, I, J, C*, 1994 *E* (R), *Pt, Sp* (R), *Fj, Tg, WS* (R)
Cornish, A H (Cardiff) 1897 *E*, 1898 *I, E*, 1899 *I*
Cornish, R A (Cardiff) 1923 *E, S*, 1924 *E*, 1925 *E, S, F*, 1926 *E, S, I, F*
Coslett, K (Aberavon) 1962 *E, S, F*
Cowey, B T V (Welch Regt, Newport) 1934 *E, S, I*, 1935 *E*
Cresswell, B (Newport) 1960 *E, S, I, F*
Cummins, W (Treorchy) 1922 *E, S, I, F*
Cunningham, L J (Aberavon) 1960 *E, S, I, F*, 1962 *E, S, F, I*, 1963 *NZ*, 1964 *E, S, I, F, SA*

Dacey, M (Swansea) 1983 *E, S, I, F, R*, 1984 *S, I, F, E, A*, 1986 *Fj, Tg, WS*, 1987 *F* (R), [*Tg*]
Daniel, D J (Llanelli) 1891 *S*, 1894 *E, S, I*, 1898 *I, E*, 1899 *E, I*
Daniel, L T D (Newport) 1970 *S*
Daniels, P C T (Cardiff) 1981 *A*, 1982 *I*
Darbishire, G (Bangor) 1881 *E*
Dauncey, F H (Newport) 1896 *E, S, I*
Davey, C (Swansea) 1930 *F*, 1931 *E, S, F, I, SA*, 1932 *E, S, I*, 1933 *E, S*, 1934 *E, S, I*, 1935 *E, S, I, NZ*, 1936 *S*, 1937 *E, I*, 1938 *E, I*
David, R J (Cardiff) 1907 *I*
David, T P (Llanelli, Pontypridd) 1973 *F, A*, 1976 *I, F*
Davidge, G D (Newport) 1959 *F*, 1960 *S, I, F, SA*, 1961 *E, S, I*, 1962 *F*
Davies, A (Cambridge U, Neath, Cardiff) 1990 *Bb* (R), 1991 *A*, 1993 *Z* 1,2, *J, C*, 1994 *Fj*, 1995 [*J, I*]
Davies, A C (London Welsh) 1889 *I*
Davies, A E (Llanelli) 1984 *A*
Davies, B (Llanelli) 1895 *E*, 1896 *E*
Davies, C (Cardiff) 1947 *S, F, I, A*, 1948 *E, S, F, I*, 1949 *F*, 1950 *E, S, I, F*, 1951 *E, S, I*
Davies, C (Llanelli) 1988 *WS*, 1989 *S, I* (R), *F*
Davies, C H A (Llanelli, Cardiff) 1957 *I*, 1958 *A, E, S, I*, 1960 *SA*, 1961 *E*
Davies, C L (Cardiff) 1956 *E, S, I*
Davies, C R (Bedford, RAF) 1934 *E*
Davies, D (Bridgend) 1921 *I*, 1925 *I*
Davies, D B (Llanelli) 1907 *E*
Davies, D B (Llanelli) 1962 *I*, 1963 *E, S*
Davies, D G (Cardiff) 1923 *E, S*
Davies, D H (Neath) 1904 *S*
Davies, D H (Aberavon) 1924 *E*
Davies, D I (Swansea) 1939 *E*
Davies, D J (Neath) 1962 *I*
Davies, D M (Somerset Police) 1950 *E, S, I, F*, 1951 *E, S, I, F*, *SA*, 1952 *E, S, I, F*, 1953 *I, F, NZ*, 1954 *E*
Davies, E (Aberavon) 1947 *A*, 1948 *I*
Davies, E (Maesteg) 1919 *NZA*
Davies, E G (Cardiff) 1912 *E, F*

Davies, E G (Cardiff) 1928 *F*, 1929 *E*, 1930 *S*
Davies, G (Swansea) 1900 *E, S, I*, 1901 *E, S, I*, 1905 *E, S, I*
Davies, G (Cambridge U, Pontypridd) 1947 *S, A*, 1948 *E, S, F, I*, 1949 *E, S, F*, 1951 *E, S*
Davies, G (Llanelli) 1921 *F, I*, 1925 *F*
Davies, H (Swansea) 1898 *I, E*, 1901 *S, I*
Davies, H (Swansea, Llanelli) 1939 *S, I*, 1947 *E, S, F, I*
Davies, H (Neath) 1912 *E, S*
Davies, H (Bridgend) 1984 *S, I, F, E*
Davies, H J (Cambridge U, Aberavon) 1959 *E, S*
Davies, H J (Newport) 1924 *S*
Davies, I T (Llanelli) 1914 *S, F, I*
Davies, J (Neath, Llanelli, Cardiff) 1985 *E, Fj*, 1986 *E, S, I, F, Fj, Tg, WS*, 1987 *F, E, S, I,* [*I, Tg* (R), *C, E, NZ, A*], 1988 *E, S, I, F, NZ* 1,2, *WS, R*, 1996 *A* 3, 1997 *US* (t), *S* (R), *F* (R), *E*
Davies, Rev J A (Swansea) 1913 *S, F, I*, 1914 *E, S, F, I*
Davies, J D (Neath, Richmond) 1991 *I, F* 1, 1993 *F* (R), *Z* 2, *J, C*, 1994 *S, I, F, E, Pt, Sp, C, WS, R, It, SA*, 1995 *F, E,* [*J, NZ, I*] *SA*, 1996 *It, E, S, I, F* 1, *A* 1, *Bb, F* 2, *It*, 1998 *Z, SA* 1
Davies, J H (Aberavon) 1923 *I*
Davies, L (Swansea) 1939 *S, I*
Davies, L (Bridgend) 1966 *E, S, I*
Davies, L B (Neath, Cardiff, Llanelli) 1996 *It, E, S, I, F* 1, *A* 1, *Bb, F* 2, *It* (R), 1997 *US* 1,2, *C, R, Tg, NZ* (R), 1998 *E* (R), *I, F*, 1999 *C*, 2001 *I*
Davies, L M (Llanelli) 1954 *F, S*, 1955 *I*
Davies, M (Swansea) 1981 *A*, 1982 *I*, 1985 *Fj*
Davies, M J (Blackheath) 1939 *S, I*
Davies, N G (London Welsh) 1955 *E*
Davies, N G (Llanelli) 1988 *NZ* 2, *WS*, 1989 *S, I*, 1993 *F*, 1994 *S, I, E, Pt, Sp, C, Fj, Tg* (R), *WS, R, It*, 1995 *E, S, I, Fj*, 1996 *E, S, I, F* 1, *A* 1,2, *Bb, F* 2, 1997 *E*
Davies, P T (Llanelli) 1985 *E, Fj*, 1986 *E, S, I, F, Fj, Tg, WS*, 1987 *F, E, I,* [*Tg, C, NZ*], 1988 *WS, R*, 1989 *S, I, F, E, NZ*, 1990 *F, E, S*, 1991 *I, F* 1, *A, F* 2, [*WS, Arg, A*], 1993 *F, Z* 1, *Nm*, 1994 *S, I, F, E, C, Fj* (R), *WS, R, It*, 1995 *F, I*
Davies, R H (Oxford U, London Welsh) 1957 *S, I, F*, 1958 *A*, 1962 *E, S*
Davies, S (Treherbert) 1923 *I*
Davies, S (Swansea) 1992 *I, F, E, S, A*, 1993 *E, S, I, Z* 1(R),2, *Nm, J*, 1995 *F,* [*J, I*], 1998 *I* (R), *F*
Davies, T G R (Cardiff, London Welsh) 1966 *A*, 1967 *S, I, F, E*, 1968 *E, S*, 1969 *S, I, F, NZ* 1,2, *A*, 1971 *E, S, I, F*, 1972 *E, S, F, NZ*, 1973 *E, S, I, F, A*, 1974 *S, F, E*, 1975 *F, E, S, I*, 1976 *E, S, I, F*, 1977 *I, F, E, S*, 1978 *E, S, I, A* 1,2
Davies, T J (Devonport Services, Swansea, Llanelli) 1953 *E, S, I, F*, 1957 *E, S, I, F*, 1958 *A, E, S, F*, 1959 *E, S, I, F*, 1960 *E, SA*, 1961 *E, S, F*
Davies, T M (London Welsh, Swansea) 1969 *S, I, F, E, NZ* 1,2, *A*, 1970 *SA, S, E, I, F*, 1971 *E, S, I, F*, 1972 *E, S, F, NZ*, 1973 *E, S, I, F, A*, 1974 *S, I, F, E*, 1975 *F, E, S, I, A*, 1976 *E, S, I, F*
Davies, W (Cardiff) 1896 *S*
Davies, W (Swansea) 1931 *SA*, 1932 *E, S, I*
Davies, W A (Aberavon) 1912 *S, I*
Davies, W G (Cardiff) 1978 *A* 1,2, *NZ*, 1979 *S, I, F, E*, 1980 *F, E, S, NZ*, 1981 *E, S, A*, 1982 *I, F, E, S*, 1985 *S, I, F*
Davies, W T H (Swansea) 1936 *I*, 1937 *E, I*, 1939 *E, S, I*
Davis, C E (Newbridge) 1978 *A* 2, 1981 *E, S*
Davis, M (Newport) 1991 *A*
Davis, W E N (Cardiff) 1939 *E, S, I*
Dawes, S J (London Welsh) 1964 *I, F, SA*, 1965 *E, S, I, F*, 1966 *A*, 1968 *I, F*, 1969 *E, NZ* 2, *A*, 1970 *SA, S, E, I, F*, 1971 *E, S, I, F*
Day, H C (Newport) 1930 *S, I, F*, 1931 *E, S*
Day, H T (Newport) 1892 *I*, 1893 *E, S*, 1894 *S, I*
Day, T B (Swansea) 1931 *E, S, F, I, SA*, 1932 *E, S, I*, 1934 *S, I*, 1935 *E, S, I*
Deacon, J T (Swansea) 1891 *I*, 1892 *E, S, I*
Delahay, W J (Bridgend) 1922 *E, S, I, F*, 1923 *E, S, F, I*, 1924 *NZ*, 1925 *E, S, F, I*, 1926 *E, S, I, F*, 1927 *S*
Delaney, L (Llanelli) 1989 *I, F, E*, 1990 *E*, 1991 *F* 2, [*WS, Arg, A*], 1992 *I, F, E*
Devereux, D (Neath) 1958 *A, E, S*
Devereux, J A (S Glamorgan Inst, Bridgend) 1986 *E, S, I, F, Fj, Tg, WS*, 1987 *F, E, S, I,* [*I, C, E, NZ, A*], 1988 *NZ* 1,2, *R*, 1989 *S, I*
Diplock, R (Bridgend) 1988 *R*
Dobson, G (Cardiff) 1900 *S*
Dobson, T (Cardiff) 1898 *I, E*, 1899 *E, S*
Donovan, A J (Swansea) 1978 *A* 2, 1981 *I* (R), *A*, 1982 *E, S*
Donovan, R (S Wales Police) 1983 *F* (R)
Douglas, M H J (Llanelli) 1984 *S, I, F*

Douglas, W M (Cardiff) 1886 *E, S,* 1887 *E, S*
Dowell, W H (Newport) 1907 *E, S, I,* 1908 *E, S, F, I*
Durston, A (Bridgend) 2001 *J* 1,2
Dyke, J C M (Penarth) 1906 *SA*
Dyke, L M (Penarth, Cardiff) 1910 *I,* 1911 *S, F, I*

Edmunds, D A (Neath) 1990 *I* (R), *Bb*
Edwards, A B (London Welsh, Army) 1955 *E, S*
Edwards, B O (Newport) 1951 *I*
Edwards, D (Glynneath) 1921 *E*
Edwards, G O (Cardiff, Cardiff Coll of Ed) 1967 *F, E, NZ,*
1968 *E, S, I, F,* 1969 *S, I, F, E, NZ* 1,2, *A,* 1970 *SA, S, E, I, F,*
1971 *E, S, I, F,* 1972 *E, S, F, NZ,* 1973 *E, S, I, F, A,* 1974 *S, I,*
F, E, 1975 *F, E, S, I, A,* 1976 *E, S, I, F,* 1977 *I, F, E, S,* 1978 *E,*
S, I, F
Eidman, I H (Cardiff) 1983 *S, R,* 1984 *I, F, E, A,* 1985 *S, I, Fj,*
1986 *E, S, I, F*
Elliott, J E (Cardiff) 1894 *I,* 1898 *I, E*
Elsey, W J (Cardiff) 1895 *E*
Emyr, Arthur (Swansea) 1989 *E, NZ,* 1990 *F, E, S, I, Nm* 1,2,
1991 *F* 1,2, [*WS, Arg, A*]
Evans, A (Pontypool) 1924 *E, I, F*
Evans, B (Swansea) 1933 *S*
Evans, B (Llanelli) 1933 *E, S,* 1936 *E, S, I,* 1937 *E*
Evans, B R (Swansea) 1998 *SA* 2(R), 1999 *F* 1, *It, E, Arg* 1,2,
C, [*J* (R), *Sm* (R), *A* (R)], 2000 *Sm, US,* 2001 *J* 1(R)
Evans, B S (Llanelli) 1920 *E,* 1922 *E, S, I, F*
Evans, C (Pontypool) 1960 *E*
Evans, D (Penygraig) 1896 *S, I,* 1897 *E,* 1898 *E*
Evans, D B (Swansea) 1926 *E*
Evans, D D (Cheshire, Cardiff U) 1934 *E*
Evans, D P (Llanelli) 1960 *SA*
Evans, D W (Cardiff) 1889 *S, I,* 1890 *E, I,* 1891 *E*
Evans, D W (Oxford U, Cardiff, Treorchy) 1989 *F, E, NZ,*
1990 *F, E, S, I, Bb,* 1991 *A* (R), *F* 2(R), [*A* (R)], 1995 [*J* (R)]
Evans, E (Llanelli) 1937 *E,* 1939 *S, I*
Evans, F (Llanelli) 1921 *S*
Evans, G (Cardiff) 1947 *E, S, F, I, A,* 1948 *E, S, F, I,* 1949 *E,*
S, I
Evans, G (Maesteg) 1981 *S* (R), *I, F, A,* 1982 *I, F, E, S,* 1983
F, R
Evans, G L (Newport) 1977 *F* (R), 1978 *F, A* 2(R)
Evans, G R (Llanelli) 1998 *SA* 1
Evans, I (London Welsh) 1934 *S, I*
Evans, I (Swansea) 1922 *E, S, I, F*
Evans, I C (Llanelli, Bath) 1987 *F, E, S, I,* [*I, C, E, NZ, A*],
1988 *E, S, I, F, NZ* 1,2, 1989 *I, F, E,* 1991 *E, S, I, F* 1, *A,* 1992 *I,*
[*WS, Arg, A*], 1992 *I, F, E, S, A,* 1993 *S, I, F, J, C,* 1994 *S, I,*
E, Pt, Sp, C, Fj, Tg, WS, R, 1995 *E, S, I,* [*J, NZ, I*], *SA, Fj,* 1996
It, E, S, I, F 1, *A* 1,2, *SA, A* 3, *SA,* 1997 *US, S, I, F,* 1998
It
Evans, I L (Llanelli) 1991 *F* 2(R)
Evans, J (Llanelli) 1896 *S, I,* 1897 *E*
Evans, J (Blaina) 1904 *E*
Evans, J (Pontypool) 1907 *E, S, I*
Evans, J D (Cardiff) 1958 *I, F*
Evans, J E (Llanelli) 1924 *S*
Evans, J R (Newport) 1934 *E*
Evans, O J (Cardiff) 1887 *E, S,* 1888 *S, I*
Evans, P D (Llanelli) 1951 *E, F*
Evans, R (Cardiff) 1889 *S*
Evans, R (Bridgend) 1963 *S, I, F*
Evans, R L (Llanelli) 1993 *E, S, I, F,* 1994 *S, I, F, E, Pt, Sp, C,*
Fj, WS, R, It, SA, 1995 *F,* [*NZ, I* (R)]
Evans, R T (Newport) 1947 *F, I,* 1950 *E, S, I, F,* 1951 *E, S, I,*
F
Evans, S (Swansea, Neath) 1985 *F, E,* 1986 *Fj, Tg, WS,* 1987
F, E, [*I, Tg*]
Evans, T (Swansea) 1924 *I*
Evans, T G (London Welsh) 1970 *SA, S, E, I,* 1972 *E, S, F*
Evans, T H (Llanelli) 1906 *I,* 1907 *E, S, I,* 1908 *I, A,* 1909 *E,*
S, F, I, 1910 *F, E, S, I,* 1911 *S, F, I*
Evans, T P (Swansea) 1975 *F, E, S, I, A,* 1976 *E, S, I, F,* 1977
I
Evans, V (Neath) 1954 *I, F, S*
Evans, W (Llanelli) 1958 *A*
Evans, W F (Rhymney) 1882 *I,* 1883 *S*
Evans, W G (Brynmawr) 1911 *I*
Evans, W H (Llwynypia) 1914 *E, S, F, I*
Evans, W J (Pontypool) 1947 *S*
Evans, W R (Bridgend) 1958 *A, E, S, I, F,* 1960 *SA,* 1961 *E,*
S, I, F, 1962 *E, S, I*
Everson, W A (Newport) 1926 *S*

Faulkner, A G (Pontypool) 1975 *F, E, S, I, A,* 1976 *E, S, I, F,*
1978 *E, S, I, F, A* 1,2, *NZ,* 1979 *S, I, F*
Faull, J (Swansea) 1957 *I, F,* 1958 *A, E, S, I, F,* 1959 *E, S, I,*
1960 *E, F*
Fauvel, T J (Aberavon) 1988 *NZ* 1(R)
Fear, A G (Newport) 1934 *S, I,* 1935 *S, I*
Fender, N H (Cardiff) 1930 *I, F,* 1931 *E, S, F, I*
Fenwick, S P (Bridgend) 1975 *F, E, S, A,* 1976 *E, S, I, F,* 1977
I, F, E, S, 1978 *E, S, I, F, A* 1,2, *NZ,* 1979 *S, I, F, E,* 1980 *F, E,*
S, I, NZ, 1981 *E, S*
Finch, E (Llanelli) 1924 *F, NZ,* 1925 *F, I,* 1926 *F,* 1927 *A,*
1928 *I*
Finlayson, A A J (Cardiff) 1974 *I, F, E*
Fitzgerald, D (Cardiff) 1894 *S, I*
Ford, F J V (Welch Regt, Newport) 1939 *E*
Ford, I (Newport) 1959 *E, S*
Ford, S P (Cardiff) 1990 *I, Nm* 1,2, *Bb,* 1991 *E, S, I, A*
Forward, A (Pontypool, Mon Police) 1951 *S, SA,* 1952 *E, S,*
I, F
Fowler, I J (Llanelli) 1919 *NZA*
Francis, D G (Llanelli) 1919 *NZA,* 1924 *S*
Francis, P (Maesteg) 1987 *S*
Funnell, J S (Ebbw Vale) 1998 *Z* (R), *SA* 1

Gabe, R T (Cardiff, Llanelli) 1901 *I,* 1902 *E, S, I,* 1903 *E, S,*
I, 1904 *E, S, I,* 1905 *E, S, I, NZ,* 1906 *E, I, SA,* 1907 *E, S, I,*
1908 *E, S, F, I*
Gale, N R (Swansea, Llanelli) 1960 *I,* 1963 *E, S, I, NZ,* 1964
E, S, I, F, SA, 1965 *E, S, I, F,* 1966 *E, S, I, F, A,* 1967 *E, NZ,*
1968 *E,* 1969 *NZ* 1(R),2, *A*
Gallacher, I S (Llanelli) 1970 *F*
Garrett, R M (Penarth) 1888 *M,* 1889 *S,* 1890 *S, E, I,* 1891 *S,*
I, 1892 *E*
Geen, W P (Oxford U, Newport) 1912 *SA,* 1913 *E, I*
George, E E (Pontypridd, Cardiff) 1895 *S, I,* 1896 *F*
George, G M (Newport) 1991 *E, S*
Gething, G I (Neath) 1913 *F*
Gibbs, A (Newbridge) 1995 *I, SA,* 1996 *A* 2, 1997 *US* 1,2, *C*
Gibbs, I S (Neath, Swansea) 1991 *E, S, I, F* 1, *A, F* 2, [*WS,*
Arg, A], 1992 *I, F, E, S, A,* 1993 *E, S, I, F, C,* 1996 *It, A* 3,
SA, 1997 *US, S, I, F, Tg, NZ,* 1998 *It, E, S, SA* 2, *Arg,* 1999 *S,*
I, F 1, *It, E, C, F* 2, [*Arg* 3, *J, Sm, A*], 2000 *I, Sm, US, SA,* 2001
E, S, F, It
Gibbs, R A (Cardiff) 1906 *S, I,* 1907 *E, S,* 1908 *E, S, F, I,*
1910 *F, E, S, I,* 1911 *E, S, F, I*
Giles, R (Aberavon) 1983 *R,* 1985 *Fj* (R), 1987 [*C*]
Girling, B E (Cardiff) 1881 *E*
Goldsworthy, S J (Swansea) 1884 *I,* 1885 *E, S*
Gore, J H (Blaina) 1924 *I, F, NZ,* 1925 *E*
Gore, W (Newbridge) 1947 *S, F, I*
Gough, I M (Newport, Pontypridd) 1998 *SA* 1, 1999 *S,* 2000
F, It (R), *E* (R), *S, I, Sm, US, SA,* 2001 *E, S, F, It*
Gould, A J (Newport) 1885 *E, S,* 1886 *E, S,* 1887 *E, S, I,*
1888 *S,* 1889 *I,* 1890 *S, E, I,* 1892 *F, S, I,* 1893 *E, S, I,* 1894 *E,*
S, 1895 *E, S, I,* 1896 *E, S, I,* 1897 *E*
Gould, G H (Newport) 1892 *I,* 1893 *S, I*
Gould, R (Newport) 1882 *I,* 1883 *E, S,* 1884 *E, S, I,* 1885 *E,*
S, 1886 *E,* 1887 *E, S*
Graham, T C (Newport) 1890 *I,* 1891 *S, I,* 1892 *E, S,* 1893 *E,*
S, I, 1894 *E, S,* 1895 *E, S*
Gravell, R W R (Llanelli) 1975 *F, E, S, I, A,* 1976 *E, S, I, F,*
1978 *E, S, I, F, A* 1,2, *NZ,* 1979 *S, I,* 1981 *I, F,* 1982 *F, E, S*
Gray, A J (London Welsh) 1968 *E, S*
Greenslade, D (Newport) 1962 *S*
Greville, H G (Llanelli) 1947 *A*
Griffin, Dr J (Edinburgh U) 1883 *S*
Griffiths, C (Llanelli) 1979 *E* (R)
Griffiths, D (Llanelli) 1888 *M,* 1889 *I*
Griffiths, G (Llanelli) 1889 *I*
Griffiths, G M (Cardiff) 1953 *E, S, I, F, NZ,* 1954 *I, F, S,*
1955 *I, F,* 1957 *E, S*
Griffiths, J (Swansea) 2000 *Sm* (R)
Griffiths, J L (Llanelli) 1988 *NZ* 2, 1989 *S*
Griffiths, M (Bridgend, Cardiff, Pontypridd) 1988 *WS, R,*
1989 *S, I, F, E, NZ,* 1990 *F, E, Nm* 1,2, *Bb,* 1991 *I, F* 1,2, [*WS,*
Arg, A], 1992 *I, F, E, S, A,* 1993 *Z* 1,2, *Nm, J, C,* 1995 *F* (R), *E,*
S, I, [*J, I*], 1998 *SA* 1
Griffiths, W (Newport) 1924 *S, I, F*
Gronow, B (Bridgend) 1910 *F, E, S, I*
Gwilliam, J A (Cambridge U, Newport) 1947 *A,* 1948 *I,*
1949 *E, S, I, F,* 1950 *E, S, I, F,* 1951 *E, S, I, SA,* 1952 *E, S, I, F,*
1953 *E, I, F, NZ,* 1954 *E*
Gwynn, D (Swansea) 1883 *E,* 1887 *S,* 1890 *E, I,* 1891 *E, S*

Gwynn, W H (Swansea) 1884 *E, S, I*, 1885 *E, S*

Hadley, A M (Cardiff) 1983 *R*, 1984 *S, I, F, E*, 1985 *F, E, Fj*, 1986 *E, S, I, F, Fj, Tg*, 1987 *S* (R), *I*, [*I, Tg, C, E, NZ, A*], *US*, 1988 *E, S, I, F*
Hall, I (Aberavon) 1967 *NZ*, 1970 *SA, S, E*, 1971 *S*, 1974 *S, I, F*
Hall, M R (Cambridge U, Bridgend, Cardiff) 1988 *NZ* 1(R),2, *WS, R*, 1989 *S, I, F, E, NZ*, 1990 *F, E, S*, 1991 *A, F* 2, [*WS, Arg, A*], 1992 *I, F, E, S, A*, 1993 *E, S, I*, 1994 *S, I, F, E, Pt, Sp, C, Tg, R, It, SA*, 1995 *F, S, I*, [*J, NZ, I*]
Hall, W H (Bridgend) 1988 *WS*
Hancock, F E (Cardiff) 1884 *I*, 1885 *E, S*, 1886 *S*
Hannan, J (Newport) 1888 *M*, 1889 *S, I*, 1890 *S, E, I*, 1891 *E*, 1892 *E, S, I*, 1893 *E, S, I*, 1894 *E, S, I*, 1895 *E, S, I*
Harding, A F (London Welsh) 1902 *E, S, I*, 1903 *E, S, I*, 1904 *E, S, I*, 1905 *E, S, I, NZ*, 1906 *E, S, I, SA*, 1907 *I*, 1908 *E, S*
Harding, G F (Newport) 1881 *E*, 1882 *I*, 1883 *E, S*
Harding, R (Swansea, Cambridge U) 1923 *E, S, F, I*, 1924 *I, F, NZ*, 1925 *F, I*, 1926 *E, I, F*, 1927 *E, S, F, I*, 1928 *E*
Harding, T (Newport) 1888 *M*, 1889 *S, I*
Harris, D J E (Pontypridd, Cardiff) 1959 *I, F*, 1960 *S, I, F, SA*, 1961 *E, S*
Harris, T (Aberavon) 1927 *A*
Hathway, G F (Newport) 1924 *I, F*
Havard, Rev W T (Llanelli) 1919 *NZA*
Hawkins, F (Pontypridd) 1912 *I, F*
Hayward, B I (Ebbw Vale) 1998 *Z* (R), *SA* 1
Hayward, D (Newbridge) 1949 *E, F*, 1950 *E, S, I, F*, 1951 *E, S, I, F, SA*, 1952 *E, S, I, F*
Hayward, D J (Cardiff) 1963 *E, NZ*, 1964 *S, I, F, SA*
Hayward, G (Swansea) 1908 *S, F, I, A*, 1909 *E*
Hellings, R S (Llwynypia) 1897 *E*, 1898 *I, E*, 1899 *S, I*, 1900 *E, I*, 1901 *E, S*
Henson, G L (Swansea) 2001 *J* 1(R), *R*
Herrerá, R C (Cross Keys) 1925 *S, F, I*, 1926 *E, S, I, F*, 1927 *E*
Hiams, H (Swansea) 1912 *I, F*
Hickman, A (Neath) 1930 *E*, 1933 *S*
Hiddlestone, D D (Neath) 1922 *E, S, I, F*, 1924 *NZ*
Hill, A F (Cardiff) 1885 *S*, 1886 *E, S*, 1888 *S, I, M*, 1889 *S*, 1890 *S, I*, 1893 *E, S, I*, 1894 *E, S, I*
Hill, S D (Cardiff) 1993 *Z* 1,2, *Nm*, 1994 *I* (R), *F, SA*, 1995 *F, SA*, 1996 *A* 2, *F* 2(R), *It*, 1997 *E*
Hinam, S (Cardiff) 1925 *I*, 1926 *E, S, I, F*
Hinton, J T (Cardiff) 1884 *I*
Hirst, G L (Newport) 1912 *S*, 1913 *S*, 1914 *E, S, F, I*
Hodder, W (Pontypool) 1921 *E, S, F*
Hodges, J J (Newport) 1899 *E, S, I*, 1900 *E, S, I*, 1901 *E, S*, 1902 *E, S, I*, 1903 *E, S, I*, 1904 *E, S, I*, 1905 *E, S, I, NZ*, 1906 *E, S, I*
Hodgson, G T R (Neath) 1962 *I*, 1963 *E, S, I, F, NZ*, 1964 *E, S, I, F, SA*, 1966 *S, I, F*, 1967 *I*
Hollingdale, H (Swansea) 1912 *SA*, 1913 *E*
Hollingdale, T H (Neath) 1927 *A*, 1928 *E, S, I, F*, 1930 *E*
Holmes, T D (Cardiff) 1978 *A* 2, *NZ*, 1979 *S, I, F, E*, 1980 *F, E, S, I, NZ*, 1981 *A*, 1982 *I, F, E*, 1983 *E, S, I, F*, 1984 *E*, 1985 *S, I, F, E, Fj*
Hopkin, W H (Newport) 1937 *S*
Hopkins, K (Cardiff, Swansea) 1985 *E*, 1987 *F, E, S*, [*Tg, C* (R)], *US*
Hopkins, P L (Swansea) 1908 *A*, 1909 *E, I*, 1910 *E*
Hopkins, R (Maesteg) 1970 *E* (R)
Hopkins, T (Swansea) 1926 *E, S, I, F*
Hopkins, W J (Aberavon) 1925 *E, S*
Howarth, S P (Sale, Newport) 1998 *SA* 2, *Arg*, 1999 *S, I, F* 1, *It, E, Arg* 1,2, *SA, C, F* 2, [*Arg* 3, *J, Sm, A*], 2000 *F, It, E*
Howells, B (Llanelli) 1934 *E*
Howells, W G (Llanelli) 1957 *E, S, I, F*
Howells, W H (Swansea) 1888 *S, I*
Howley, R (Bridgend, Cardiff) 1996 *E, S, I, F* 1, *A* 1,2, *Bb, F* 2, *It, A* 3, *SA*, 1997 *US, S, I, F, E, Tg* (R), *NZ*, 1998 *It, E, S, I, F, Z, SA* 2, *Arg*, 1999 *S, I, F* 1, *It, E, Arg* 1,2, *SA, C, F* 2, [*Arg* 3, *J, Sm, A*], 2000 *F, It, E, Sm, US, SA*, 2001 *E, S, F, R, I*
Hughes, D (Newbridge) 1967 *NZ*, 1969 *NZ* 2, 1970 *SA, S, E, I*
Hughes, G (Penarth) 1934 *E, S, I*
Hughes, H (Cardiff) 1887 *S*, 1889 *S*
Hughes, K (Cambridge U, London Welsh) 1970 *I*, 1973 *A*, 1974 *S*
Hullin, W (Cardiff) 1967 *S*

Humphreys, J M (Cardiff) 1995 [*NZ, I*], *SA, Fj*, 1996 *It, E, S, I, F* 1, *A* 1,2, *Bb, It, A* 3, *SA*, 1997 *S, I, F, E, Tg* (R), *NZ* (R), 1998 *It* (R), *E* (R), *S* (R), *I* (R), *F* (R), *SA* 2, *Arg*, 1999 *S, Arg* 2(R), *SA* (R), *C*, [*J* (R)]
Hurrell, J (Newport) 1959 *F*
Hutchinson, F (Neath) 1894 *I*, 1896 *S, I*
Huxtable, R (Swansea) 1920 *F, I*
Huzzey, H V P (Cardiff) 1898 *I, E*, 1899 *E, S, I*
Hybart, A J (Cardiff) 1887 *E*

Ingledew, H M (Cardiff) 1890 *I*, 1891 *E, S*
Isaacs, I (Cardiff) 1933 *E, S*

Jackson, T H (Swansea) 1895 *E*
James, B (Bridgend) 1968 *E*
James, C R (Llanelli) 1958 *A, F*
James, D (Swansea) 1891 *I*, 1892 *S, I*, 1899 *E*
James, D R (Treorchy) 1931 *F, I*
James, D R (Bridgend, Pontypridd, Llanelli) 1996 *A* 2(R), *It, A* 3, *SA*, 1997 *I, Tg* (R), 1998 *F* (R), *Z, SA* 1,2, *Arg*, 1999 *S, I, F* 1, *It, E, Arg* 1,2, *SA, F* 2, [*Arg* 3, *Sm, A*], 2000 *F, It* (R), *I* (R), *Sm* (R), *US, SA*, 2001 *E, S, F, It, R, I*
James, E (Swansea) 1890 *S*, 1891 *I*, 1892 *S, I*, 1899 *E*
James, M (Cardiff) 1947 *A*, 1948 *E, S, F, I*
James, T O (Aberavon) 1935 *I*, 1937 *S*
James, W J (Aberavon) 1983 *E, S, I, F, R*, 1984 *S*, 1985 *S, I, F, E, Fj*, 1986 *E, S, I, F, Fj, Tg, WS*, 1987 *E, S, I*
James, W P (Aberavon) 1925 *E, S*
Jarman, H (Newport) 1910 *E, S, I*, 1911 *E*
Jarrett, K S (Newport) 1967 *E*, 1968 *E, S*, 1969 *S, I, F, E, NZ* 1,2, *A*
Jarvis, L (Cardiff) 1997 *R* (R)
Jeffery, J J (Cardiff Coll of Ed, Newport) 1967 *NZ*
Jenkin, A M (Swansea) 1895 *I*, 1896 *E*
Jenkins, A (Llanelli) 1920 *E, S, F, I*, 1921 *S, F*, 1922 *F*, 1923 *E, S, F, I*, 1924 *NZ*, 1928 *S, I*
Jenkins, D M (Treorchy) 1926 *E, S, I, F*
Jenkins, D R (Swansea) 1927 *A*, 1929 *E*
Jenkins, E (Newport) 1910 *S, I*
Jenkins, E M (Aberavon) 1927 *S, F, I, A*, 1928 *E, S, I, F*, 1929 *F*, 1930 *E, S, I, F*, 1931 *E, S, F, I, SA*, 1932 *E, S, I*
Jenkins, G R (Pontypool, Swansea) 1991 *F* 2, [*WS* (R), *Arg, A*], 1992 *I, F, E, S, A*, 1993 *C*, 1994 *S, I, F, E, Pt, Sp, C, Tg, WS, R, It, SA*, 1995 *F, E, S, I*, [*J*], *SA* (R), *Fj* (t), 1996 *E* (R), 1997 *US, US* 1, *C*, 1998 *S, I, F, Z, SA* 1(R), 1999 *I* (R), *F* 1, *It, E, Arg* 1,2, *SA, F* 2, [*Arg* 3, *J, Sm, A*], 2000 *F, It, E, S, I, Sm, US, SA*
Jenkins, J C (London Welsh) 1906 *SA*
Jenkins, J L (Aberavon) 1923 *S, F*
Jenkins, L H (Mon TC, Newport) 1954 *I*, 1956 *E, S, I, F*
Jenkins, N R (Pontypridd, Cardiff) 1991 *E, S, I, F* 1, 1992 *I, F, E, S*, 1993 *E, S, I, F, Z* 1,2, *Nm, J, C*, 1994 *S, I, F, E, Pt, Sp, C, Tg, WS, R, It, SA*, 1995 *F, E, S, I*, [*J, NZ, I*], *SA, Fj*, 1996 *F* 1, *A* 1,2, *Bb, F* 2, *It, A* 3(R), *SA*, 1997 *S, I, F, E, Tg, NZ*, 1998 *It, E, S, I, F, SA* 2, *Arg*, 1999 *S, I, F* 1, *It, E, Arg* 1,2, *SA, C, F* 2, [*Arg* 3, *J, Sm, A*], 2000 *F, It, E, I* (R), *Sm* (R), *US* (R), *SA*, 2001 *E, S, F, It*
Jenkins, V G J (Oxford U, Bridgend, London Welsh) 1933 *E, I*, 1934 *S, I*, 1935 *E, S, NZ*, 1936 *E, S, I*, 1937 *E*, 1938 *E, S*, 1939 *E*
Jenkins, W (Cardiff) 1912 *I, F*, 1913 *S, I*
John, B (Llanelli, Cardiff) 1966 *A*, 1967 *S, NZ*, 1968 *E, S, I, F*, 1969 *S, I, F, E, NZ* 1,2, *A*, 1970 *SA, S, E, I*, 1971 *E, S, I, F*, 1972 *E, S, F*
John, D A (Llanelli) 1925 *I*, 1928 *E, S, I*
John, D E (Llanelli) 1923 *F, I*, 1928 *E, S, I*
John, E R (Neath) 1950 *E, S, I, F*, 1951 *E, S, I, F, SA*, 1952 *E, S, I, F*, 1953 *E, S, I, F, NZ*, 1954 *E*
John G (St Luke's Coll, Exeter) 1954 *E, F*
John, J H (Swansea) 1926 *E, S, I, F*, 1927 *E, S, F, I*
John, P (Pontypridd) 1994 *Tg*, 1996 *Bb* (t), 1997 *US* (R), *US* 1,2, *C, R, Tg*, 1998 *Z* (R), *SA* 1
John, S C (Llanelli, Cardiff) 1995 *S, I*, 1997 *E* (R), *Tg, NZ* (R), 2000 *F* (R), *It* (R), *E* (R), *Sm* (R), *SA* (R), 2001 *E* (R), *S* (R)
Johnson, T A (Cardiff) 1921 *E, F, I*, 1923 *E, S, F*, 1924 *E, S, NZ*, 1925 *E, S, F*
Johnson, W D (Swansea) 1953 *E*
Jones, A H (Cardiff) 1933 *E, S*
Jones, B (Abertillery) 1914 *E, S, F, I*
Jones, Bert (Llanelli) 1934 *S, I*
Jones, Bob (Llwynypia) 1901 *I*
Jones, B J (Newport) 1960 *I, F*

Jones, B Lewis (Devonport Services, Llanelli) 1950 *E, S, I, F,* 1951 *E, S, SA,* 1952 *E, I, F*
Jones, C W (Cambridge U, Cardiff) 1934 *E, S, I,* 1935 *E, S, I, NZ,* 1936 *E, S, I,* 1938 *E, S, I*
Jones, C W (Bridgend) 1920 *E, S, F*
Jones, D (Neath) 1927 *A*
Jones, D (Aberavon) 1897 *E*
Jones, D (Swansea) 1947 *E, F, I,* 1949 *E, S, I, F*
Jones, D (Treherbert) 1902 *E, S, I,* 1903 *E, S, I,* 1905 *E, S, I, NZ,* 1906 *E, S, SA*
Jones, D (Newport) 1926 *E, S, I, F,* 1927 *E*
Jones, D (Llanelli) 1948 *E*
Jones, D (Cardiff) 1994 *SA,* 1995 *F, E, S,* [*J, NZ, I*], *SA, Fj,* 1996 *It, E, S, I, F* 1, *A* 1,2, *Bb, It, A* 3
Jones, D K (Llanelli, Cardiff) 1962 *E, S, F, I,* 1963 *E, F, NZ,* 1964 *E, S, SA,* 1966 *E, S, I, F*
Jones, D L (Ebbw Vale) 2000 *Sm*
Jones, D P (Pontypool) 1907 *I*
Jones, E H (Neath) 1929 *E, S*
Jones, E L (Llanelli) 1930 *F,* 1933 *E, S, I,* 1935 *E*
Jones, Elvet L (Llanelli) 1939 *S*
Jones, G (Ebbw Vale) 1963 *S, I, F*
Jones, G (Llanelli) 1988 *NZ* 2, 1989 *F, E, NZ,* 1990 *F*
Jones, G G (Cardiff) 1930 *S,* 1933 *I*
Jones, G H (Bridgend) 1995 *SA*
Jones, H (Penygraig) 1902 *S, I*
Jones, H (Neath) 1904 *I*
Jones, H (Swansea) 1930 *I, F*
Jones, Iorwerth (Llanelli) 1927 *A,* 1928 *E, S, I, F*
Jones, I C (London Welsh) 1968 *I*
Jones, Ivor E (Llanelli) 1924 *E, S,* 1927 *S, F, I, A,* 1928 *E, S, I, F,* 1929 *E, S, F, I,* 1930 *E, S*
Jones, J (Aberavon) 1901 *E*
Jones, J (Swansea) 1924 *F*
Jones, Jim (Aberavon) 1919 *NZA,* 1920 *E, S,* 1921 *S, F, I*
Jones, J A (Cardiff) 1883 *S*
Jones, J P (Tuan) (Pontypool) 1913 *S*
Jones, J P (Pontypool) 1908 *A,* 1909 *E, S, F, I,* 1910 *F, E,* 1912 *E, F,* 1913 *E, I,* 1920 *F, I,* 1921 *E*
Jones, K D (Cardiff) 1960 *SA,* 1961 *E, S, I,* 1962 *E, F,* 1963 *E, S, I, NZ*
Jones, K J (Newport) 1947 *E, S, F, I, A,* 1948 *E, S, F, I,* 1949 *E, S, I, F,* 1950 *E, S, I, F,* 1951 *E, S, I, F, SA,* 1952 *E, S, I, F,* 1953 *E, S, I, F, NZ,* 1954 *E, I, F, S,* 1955 *E, S, I, F,* 1956 *E, S, I, F,* 1957 *S*
Jones, K P (Ebbw Vale) 1996 *Bb, F* 2, *It, A* 3, 1997 *I* (R), *E,* 1998 *S, I, F*(R), *SA* 1
Jones, K W J (Oxford U, London Welsh) 1934 *E*
Jones, M A (Neath, Ebbw Vale) 1987 *S,* 1988 *NZ* 2(R), 1989 *S, I, F, E, NZ,* 1990 *F, E, S, I, Nm* 1,2, *Bb,* 1998 *Z*
Jones, M A (Llanelli) 2001 *E* (R), *S, J* 1
Jones, P (Newport) 1912 *SA,* 1913 *E, S, F,* 1914 *E, S, F, I*
Jones, P B (Newport) 1921 *S*
Jones, R (Swansea) 1901 *I,* 1902 *E,* 1904 *E, S, I,* 1905 *E,* 1908 *F, I, A,* 1909 *E, S, F, I,* 1910 *F, E*
Jones, R (London Welsh) 1929 *E*
Jones, R (Northampton) 1926 *E, S, F*
Jones, R (Swansea) 1927 *A,* 1928 *F*
Jones, R B (Cambridge U) 1933 *E, S*
Jones, R E (Coventry) 1967 *F, E,* 1968 *S, I, F*
Jones, R G (Llanelli, Cardiff) 1996 *It, E, S, I, F* 1, *A* 1, 1997 *US* (R), *S* (R), *US* 1,2, *R, Tg, NZ*
Jones, R L (Llanelli) 1993 *Z* 1,2, *Nm, J, C*
Jones, R N (Swansea) 1986 *E, S, I, F, Fj, Tg, WS,* 1987 *F, E, S, I,* [*I, Tg, E, NZ, A*], *US,* 1988 *E, S, I, F, NZ* 1, *WS, R,* 1989 *I, F, E, NZ,* 1990 *F, E, S, I,* 1991 *E, S, F* 2, [*WS, Arg, A*], 1992 *I, F, E, S, A,* 1993 *E, S, I,* 1994 *I* (R), *Pt,* 1995 *F, E, S, I,* [*NZ, I*]
Jones, S (Neath) 2001 *J* 1(R)
Jones, S M (Llanelli) 1998 *SA* 1(R), 1999 *C* (R), [*J* (R)], 2000 *It* (R), *S, I,* 2001 *E, F* (R), *J* 1,2, *R, I*
Jones, S T (Pontypool) 1983 *S, I, F, R,* 1984 *S,* 1988 *E, S, F, NZ* 1,2
Jones, Tom (Newport) 1922 *E, S, I, F,* 1924 *E, S*
Jones, T B (Newport) 1882 *I,* 1883 *E, S,* 1884 *S,* 1885 *E, S*
Jones, W (Cardiff) 1898 *I, E*
Jones, W (Mountain Ash) 1905 *I*
Jones, W I (Llanelli, Cambridge U) 1925 *E, S, F, I*
Jones, W J (Llanelli) 1924 *I*
Jones, W K (Cardiff) 1967 *NZ,* 1968 *E, S, I, F*
Jones-Davies, T E (London Welsh) 1930 *E, I,* 1931 *E, S*
Jones-Hughes, J (Newport) 1999 [*Arg* 3(R), *I*], 2000 *F*
Jordan, H M (Newport) 1885 *E, S,* 1889 *S*

Joseph, W (Swansea) 1902 *E, S, I,* 1903 *E, S, I,* 1904 *E, S,* 1905 *E, S, I, NZ,* 1906 *E, S, I, SA*
Jowett, W F (Swansea) 1903 *E*
Judd, S (Cardiff) 1953 *E, S, I, F, NZ,* 1954 *E, F, S,* 1955 *E, S*
Judson, J H (Llanelli) 1883 *E, S*

Kedzlie, Q D (Cardiff) 1888 *S, I*
Keen, L (Aberavon) 1980 *F, E, S, I*
Knight, P (Pontypridd) 1990 *Nm* 1,2, *Bb* (R), 1991 *E, S*
Knill, F M D (Cardiff) 1976 *F* (R)

Lamerton, A E H (Llanelli) 1993 *F, Z* 1,2, *Nm, J*
Lane, S M (Cardiff) 1978 *A* 1(R),2, 1979 *I* (R), 1980 *S, I*
Lang, J (Llanelli) 1931 *F, I,* 1934 *S, I,* 1935 *E, S, I, NZ,* 1936 *E, S, I,* 1937 *E*
Lawrence, S (Bridgend) 1925 *S, I,* 1926 *S, I, F,* 1927 *E*
Law, V J (Newport) 1939 *I*
Legge, W S G (Newport) 1937 *I,* 1938 *I*
Leleu, J (London Welsh, Swansea) 1959 *E, S,* 1960 *F, SA*
Lemon, A (Neath) 1929 *I,* 1930 *S, I, F,* 1931 *E, S, F, I, SA,* 1932 *E, S, I,* 1933 *I*
Lewis, A J L (Ebbw Vale) 1970 *F,* 1971 *E, I, F,* 1972 *E, S, F,* 1973 *E, S, I, F*
Lewis, A L P (Cardiff) 1996 *It, E, S, I, A* 2(t), 1998 *It, E, S, I, F, SA* 2, *Arg,* 1999 *F* 1(R), *E* (R), *Arg* 1(R),2(R), *SA* (R), *C* (R), [*J* (R), *Sm* (R), *A* (R)], 2000 *Sm* (R), *US* (R), SA (R), 2001 *F* (R), *J* 1,2
Lewis, A R (Abertillery) 1966 *E, S, I, F, A,* 1967 *I*
Lewis, B R (Swansea, Cambridge U) 1912 *I,* 1913 *I*
Lewis, C P (Llandovery Coll) 1882 *I,* 1883 *E, S,* 1884 *E, S*
Lewis, D H (Cardiff) 1886 *E, S*
Lewis, E J (Llandovery) 1881 *E*
Lewis, E W (Llanelli, Cardiff) 1991 *I, F* 1, *A, F* 2, [*WS, Arg, A*], 1992 *I, F, S, A,* 1993 *E, S, I, F, Z* 1,2, *Nm, J, C,* 1994 *S, I, F, E, Pt, Sp, Fj, WS, R, It, SA,* 1995 *E, S, I,* [*J, I*], 1996 *It, E, S, I, F* 1
Lewis, G (Pontypridd, Swansea) 1998 *SA* 1(R), 1999 *It* (R), *Arg* 2, *C,* [*J*], 2000 *F* (R), *It, S, I, Sm, US* (t+R), 2001 *F* (R), *J* 1,2, *R, I*
Lewis, G W (Richmond) 1960 *E, S*
Lewis, H (Swansea) 1913 *S, F, I,* 1914 *E*
Lewis, J G (Llanelli) 1887 *I*
Lewis, J M C (Cardiff, Cambridge U) 1912 *E,* 1913 *S, F, I,* 1914 *E, S, F, I,* 1921 *I,* 1923 *E, S*
Lewis, J R (S Glam Inst, Cardiff) 1981 *E, S, I, F,* 1982 *F, E, S*
Lewis, M (Treorchy) 1913 *F*
Lewis, P I (Llanelli) 1984 *A,* 1985 *S, I, F, E,* 1986 *E, S, I*
Lewis, T W (Cardiff) 1926 *E,* 1927 *E, S*
Lewis, W (Llanelli) 1925 *F*
Lewis, W H (London Welsh, Cambridge U) 1926 *I,* 1927 *E, F, I, A,* 1928 *F*
Llewellyn, D B (Newport, Llanelli) 1970 *SA, S, E, I, F,* 1971 *E, S, I, F,* 1972 *E, S, F, NZ*
Llewellyn, D S (Ebbw Vale, Newport) 1998 *SA* 1(R), 1999 *F* 1(R), *It* (R), [*J* (R)]
Llewellyn, G (Neath) 1990 *Nm* 1,2, *Bb,* 1991 *E, S, I, F* 1, *A, F* 2
Llewellyn, G O (Neath, Harlequins) 1989 *NZ,* 1990 *E, S, I,* 1991 *E, S, A* (R), 1992 *I, F, E, S, A,* 1993 *E, S, I, F, Z* 1,2, *Nm, J, C,* 1994 *S, I, F, E, Pt, Sp, C, Tg, WS, R, It, SA,* 1995 *F, E, S, I,* [*J, NZ, I*], 1996 *It, E, S, I, F* 1, *A* 1,2, *Bb, F* 2, *It, A* 3, *SA,* 1997 *US, S, I, F, E, US* 1,2, *NZ,* 1998 *It, E,* 1999 *C* (R), [*Sm*]
Llewellyn, P D (Swansea) 1973 *I, F, A,* 1974 *S, E*
Llewellyn, W (Llwynypia) 1899 *E, S, I,* 1900 *E, S, I,* 1901 *E, S, I,* 1902 *E, S, I,* 1903 *I,* 1904 *E, S, I,* 1905 *E, S, I, NZ*
Lloyd, A (Bath) 2001 *J* 1
Lloyd, D J (Bridgend) 1966 *E, S, I, F, A,* 1967 *S, I, F, E,* 1968 *S, I, F,* 1969 *S, I, F, E, NZ* 1, *A,* 1970 *F,* 1972 *E, S, F,* 1973 *E, S, I*
Lloyd, E (Llanelli) 1895 *S*
Lloyd, G L (Newport) 1896 *I,* 1899 *S, I,* 1900 *E, S,* 1901 *E, S,* 1902 *S, I,* 1903 *E, S, I*
Lloyd, P (Llanelli) 1890 *S, E,* 1891 *E, I*
Lloyd, R A (Pontypool) 1913 *S, F, I,* 1914 *E, S, F, I*
Lloyd, T (Maesteg) 1953 *I, F*
Lloyd, T C (Neath) 1909 *F,* 1913 *F, I,* 1914 *E, S, F, I*
Loader, C D (Swansea) 1995 *SA, Fj,* 1996 *F* 1, *A* 1,2, *Bb, F* 2, *It, A* 3, *SA,* 1997 *US, S, I, F, E, US* 1, *R, Tg, NZ*
Lockwood, T W (Newport) 1887 *E, S, I*
Long, E C (Swansea) 1936 *E, S, I,* 1937 *E, S,* 1939 *S, I*
Lyne, H S (Newport) 1883 *S,* 1884 *E, S, I,* 1885 *E*

Payne, H (Swansea) 1935 *NZ*
Peacock, H (Newport) 1929 *S, F, I*, 1930 *S, I, F*
Peake, E (Chepstow) 1881 *E*
Pearce, G P (Bridgend) 1981 *I, F*, 1982 *I* (R)
Pearson, T W (Cardiff, Newport) 1891 *E, I*, 1892 *E, S*, 1894 *S, I*, 1895 *E, S, I*, 1897 *E*, 1898 *I, E*, 1903 *E*
Peel, D (Llanelli) 2001 *J* 2(R), *R* (R)
Pegge, E V (Neath) 1891 *E*
Perego, M A (Llanelli) 1990 *S*, 1993 *F, Z* 1, *Nm* (R), 1994 *S, I, F, E, Sp*
Perkins, S J (Pontypool) 1983 *S, I, F, R*, 1984 *S, I, F, E, A*, 1985 *S, I, F, E, Fj*, 1986 *E, S, I, F*
Perrett, F L (Neath) 1912 *SA*, 1913 *E, S, F, I*
Perrins, V C (Newport) 1970 *SA, S*
Perry, W (Neath) 1911 *E*
Phillips, A J (Cardiff) 1979 *E*, 1980 *F, E, S, I, NZ*, 1981 *I, F, A*, 1982 *I, F, E, S*, 1987 *[C, E, A]*
Phillips, B (Aberavon) 1925 *E, S, F, I*, 1926 *E*
Phillips, D H (Swansea) 1952 *F*
Phillips, H P (Newport) 1892 *E*, 1893 *E, S, I*, 1894 *E, S*
Phillips, H T (Newport) 1927 *E, S, F, I, A*, 1928 *E, S, I, F*
Phillips, K H (Neath) 1987 *F*, *[I, Tg, NZ]*, *US*, 1988 *E, NZ* 1, 1989 *NZ*, 1990 *F, E, S, I, Nm* 1,2, *Bb*, 1991 *E, S, I, F* 1, *A*
Phillips, L A (Newport) 1900 *E, S, I*, 1901 *S*
Phillips, R (Neath) 1987 *US*, 1988 *E, S, I, F, NZ* 1,2, *WS*, 1989 *S, I*
Phillips, W D (Cardiff) 1881 *E*, 1882 *I*, 1884 *E, S, I*
Pickering, D F (Llanelli) 1983 *E, S, I, F, R*, 1984 *S, I, F, E, A*, 1985 *S, I, F, E, Fj*, 1986 *E, S, I, F, Fj*, 1987 *F, E, S*
Plummer, R C S (Newport) 1912 *S, I, F, SA*, 1913 *E*
Pook, T (Newport) 1895 *S*
Powell, G (Ebbw Vale) 1957 *I, F*
Powell, J (Cardiff) 1906 *I*
Powell, J (Cardiff) 1923 *I*
Powell, R W (Newport) 1888 *S, I*
Powell, W C (London Welsh) 1926 *S, I, F*, 1927 *F, I*, 1928 *S, I, F*, 1929 *E, S, F, I*, 1930 *S, I, F*, 1931 *E, S, F, I, SA*, 1932 *E, S, I*, 1935 *E, S, I*
Powell, W J (Cardiff) 1920 *E, S, F, I*
Price, B (Newport) 1961 *I, F*, 1962 *E, S*, 1963 *E, S, F, NZ*, 1964 *E, S, I, F, SA*, 1965 *E, S, I, F*, 1966 *E, S, I, F, A*, 1967 *S, I, F, E*, 1969 *S, I, F, NZ* 1,2, *A*
Price, G (Pontypool) 1975 *F, E, S, I, A*, 1976 *E, S, I, F*, 1977 *I, F, E, S*, 1978 *E, S, I, F, A* 1,2, *NZ*, 1979 *S, I, F, E*, 1980 *F, E, S, I, NZ*, 1981 *E, S, I, F, A*, 1982 *I, F, E, S*, 1983 *E, I, F*
Price, M J (Pontypool, RAF) 1959 *E, S, I, F*, 1960 *E, S, I, F*, 1962 *F*
Price, R E (Weston-s-Mare) 1939 *S, I*
Price, T G (Llanelli) 1965 *E, S, I, F*, 1966 *E, A*, 1967 *S, F*
Priday, A J (Cardiff) 1958 *I*, 1961 *I*
Pritchard, C (Pontypool) 1928 *E, S, I, F*, 1929 *E, S, F, I*
Pritchard, C C (Newport, Pontypool) 1904 *S, I*, 1905 *NZ*, 1906 *E, S*
Pritchard, C M (Newport) 1904 *I*, 1905 *E, S, NZ*, 1906 *E, S, I, SA*, 1907 *E, S, I*, 1908 *E*, 1910 *F, E, A* 1,2, *Bb, F* 2, *It, A* 3, 1997 *E* (R)
Proctor, W T (Llanelli) 1992 *A*, 1993 *E, S, Z* 1,2, *Nm, C*, 1994 *I, C, Fj, WS, R, It, SA*, 1995 *S, I, [NZ], Fj*, 1996 *It, E, S, I, A* 1,2, *Bb, F* 2, *It, A* 3, 1997 *E*(R), *US* 1,2, *C, R*, 1998 *E* (R), *S, I, F, Z*
Prosser, D R (Neath) 1934 *S, I*
Prosser, G (Neath) 1934 *E, S, I*, 1935 *NZ*
Prosser, G (Pontypridd) 1995 *[NZ]*
Prosser, J (Cardiff) 1921 *I*
Prosser, T R (Pontypool) 1956 *S, F*, 1957 *E, S, I, F*, 1958 *A, E, S, I, F*, 1959 *E, S, I, F*, 1960 *E, S, I, F, SA*, 1961 *I, F*
Prothero, G J (Bridgend) 1964 *S, I, F*, 1965 *E, S, I, F*, 1966 *E, S, I, F*
Pryce-Jenkins, T J (London Welsh) 1888 *S, I*
Pugh, C (Maesteg) 1924 *E, S, I, F, NZ*, 1925 *E, S*
Pugh, J D (Neath) 1987 *US*, 1988 *S* (R), 1990 *S*
Pugh, P (Neath) 1989 *NZ*
Pugsley, J (Cardiff) 1910 *E, S, I*, 1911 *E, S, F, I*
Pullman, J J (Neath) 1910 *F*
Purdon, F T (Newport) 1881 *E*, 1882 *I*, 1883 *E, S*

Quinnell, D L (Llanelli) 1972 *F* (R), *NZ*, 1973 *E, S, A*, 1974 *S, F*, 1975 *E* (R), 1977 *I* (R), *F, E, S*, 1978 *E, S, I, F, A* 1, *NZ*, 1979 *S, I, F, E*, 1980 *NZ*
Quinnell, J C (Llanelli, Richmond, Cardiff) 1995 *Fj*, 1996 *A* 3(R), 1997 *US* (R), *S* (R), *I* (R), *E* (R), 1998 *SA* 2, *Arg*, 1999 *I, F* 1, *It, E, Arg* 1,2, *SA, C, F* 2, *[Arg* 3, *J, A]*, 2000 *It, E*, 2001 *S* (R), *F* (R), *It* (R), *J* 1,2, *R* (R), *I* (R)

Quinnell, L S (Llanelli, Richmond) 1993 *C*, 1994 *S, I, F, E, Pt, Sp, C, WS*, 1997 *US, S, I, F, E*, 1998 *It, E, S* (R), *Z, SA* 2, *Arg*, 1999 *S, I, F* 1, *It, E, Arg* 1,2, *SA, C, F* 2, *[Arg* 3, *Sm, A]*, 2000 *F, It, E, Sm, US, SA*, 2001 *E, S, F, It*

Radford, W J (Newport) 1923 *I*
Ralph, A R (Newport) 1931 *F, I, SA*, 1932 *E, S, I*
Ramsey, S H (Treorchy) 1896 *E*, 1904 *E*
Randell, R (Aberavon) 1924 *I, F*
Raybould, W H (London Welsh, Cambridge U, Newport) 1967 *S, I, F, E, NZ*, 1968 *I, F*, 1970 *SA, E, I, F* (R)
Rayer, M A (Cardiff) 1991 *[WS* (R), *Arg, A* (R)], 1992 *E* (R), *A*, 1993 *E, S, I, Z* 1, *Nm, J* (R), 1994 *S* (R), *I* (R), *F, E, Pt, C, Fj, WS, R, It*
Rees, Aaron (Maesteg) 1919 *NZA*
Rees, Alan (Maesteg) 1962 *E, S, F*
Rees, A M (London Welsh) 1934 *E*, 1935 *E, S, I, NZ*, 1936 *E, S, I*, 1937 *E, S, I*, 1938 *E, S*
Rees, B I (London Welsh) 1967 *S, I, F*
Rees, C F W (London Welsh) 1974 *I*, 1975 *A*, 1978 *NZ*, 1981 *F, A*, 1982 *I, F, E, S*, 1983 *E, S, I, F*
Rees, D (Swansea) 1968 *S, I, F*
Rees, Dan (Swansea) 1900 *E*, 1903 *E, S*, 1905 *E, S*
Rees, E B (Swansea) 1919 *NZA*
Rees, H (Cardiff) 1937 *S, I*, 1938 *E, S, I*
Rees, H E (Neath) 1979 *S, I, F, E*, 1980 *F, E, S, I, NZ*, 1983 *E, S, I, F*
Rees, J (Swansea) 1920 *E, S, F, I*, 1921 *E, S, I*, 1922 *E*, 1923 *E, F, I*, 1924 *E*
Rees, J I (Swansea) 1934 *E, S, I*, 1935 *S, NZ*, 1936 *E, S, I*, 1937 *E, S, I*, 1938 *E, S*
Rees, L M (Cardiff) 1933 *I*
Rees, P (Llanelli) 1947 *F, I*
Rees, P M (Newport) 1961 *E, S, I*, 1964 *I*
Rees, R (Swansea) 1998 *Z*
Rees, T (Newport) 1935 *S, I, NZ*, 1936 *E, S, I*, 1937 *E, S*
Rees, T A (Llandovery) 1881 *E*
Rees, T E (London Welsh) 1926 *I, F*, 1927 *A*, 1928 *E*
Rees-Jones, G R (Oxford U, London Welsh) 1934 *E, S*, 1935 *I, NZ*, 1936 *E*
Reeves, F (Cross Keys) 1920 *F, I*, 1921 *E*
Reynolds, A (Swansea) 1990 *Nm* 1,2(R), 1992 *A* (R)
Rhapps, J (Penygraig) 1897 *E*
Rice-Evans, W (Swansea) 1890 *S*, 1891 *E, S*
Richards, B (Swansea) 1960 *F*
Richards, C (Pontypool) 1922 *E, S, I, F*, 1924 *I*
Richards, D S (Swansea) 1979 *F, E*, 1980 *F, E, S, I, NZ*, 1981 *E, S, I, F*, 1982 *I, F*, 1983 *E, S, I, R* (R)
Richards, E G (Cardiff) 1927 *S*
Richards, E S (Swansea) 1885 *E*, 1887 *S*
Richards, H D (Neath) 1986 *Tg* (R), 1987 *[Tg, E* (R), *NZ]*
Richards, I (Cardiff) 1925 *E, S, F*
Richards, K H L (Bridgend) 1960 *SA*, 1961 *E, S, I, F*
Richards, M C R (Cardiff) 1968 *I, F*, 1969 *S, I, F, E, NZ* 1,2, *A*
Richards, R (Aberavon) 1913 *S, F, I*
Richards, R (Cross Keys) 1956 *F*
Richards, T L (Maesteg) 1923 *I*
Richardson, S J (Aberavon) 1978 *A* 2(R), 1979 *E*
Rickards, A R (Cardiff) 1924 *F*
Ring, J (Aberavon) 1921 *E*
Ring, M G (Cardiff, Pontypool) 1983 *E*, 1984 *A*, 1985 *S, I, F*, 1987 *I, [I, Tg, A]*, *US*, 1988 *E, S, I, F, NZ* 1,2, 1989 *NZ*, 1990 *F, E, S, I, Nm* 1,2, *Bb*, 1991 *E, S, I, F* 1,2, *[WS, Arg, A]*
Ringer, J (Bridgend) 2001 *J* 1(R),2(R)
Ringer, P (Ebbw Vale, Llanelli) 1978 *NZ*, 1979 *S, I, F, E*, 1980 *F, E, NZ*
Roberts, C (Neath) 1958 *I, F*
Roberts, D E A (London Welsh) 1930 *E*
Roberts, E (Llanelli) 1886 *E*, 1887 *I*
Roberts, E J (Llanelli) 1888 *S, I*, 1889 *I*
Roberts, G J (Cardiff) 1985 *F* (R), *E*, 1987 *[I, Tg, C, E, A]*
Roberts, H M (Cardiff) 1960 *SA*, 1961 *E, S, I, F*, 1962 *S, F*, 1963 *I*
Roberts, J (Cardiff) 1927 *E, S, F, I, A*, 1928 *E, S, I, F*, 1929 *E, S, F, I*
Roberts, M G (London Welsh) 1971 *E, S, I, F*, 1973 *I, F*, 1975 *S*, 1979 *E*
Roberts, T (Newport, Risca) 1921 *S, F, I*, 1922 *E, S, I, F*, 1923 *E, S*
Roberts, W (Cardiff) 1929 *E*
Robins, J D (Birkenhead Park) 1950 *E, S, I, F*, 1951 *E, S, I, F*, 1953 *E, I, F*

Robins, R J (Pontypridd) 1953 *S*, 1954 *F*, *S*, 1955 *E*, *S*, *I*, *F*, 1956 *E*, *F*, 1957 *E*, *S*, *I*, *F*
Robinson, I R (Cardiff) 1974 *F*, *E*
Robinson, J (Cardiff) 2001 *J* 1(R),2(R)
Robinson, M F D (Swansea) 1999 *S*, *I*, *F* 1, *Arg* 1
Rocyn-Jones, D N (Cambridge U) 1925 *I*
Roderick, W B (Llanelli) 1884 *I*
Rogers, P J D (London Irish, Newport, Cardiff) 1999 *F* 1, *It*, *E*, *Arg* 1,2, *SA*, *C*, *F* 2, [*Arg* 3, *J*, *Sm*, *A*], 2000 *F*, *It*, *E*, *S*, *I*, *SA*
Rosser, M A (Penarth) 1924 *S*, *F*
Rowland, E M (Lampeter) 1885 *E*
Rowlands, C F (Aberavon) 1926 *I*
Rowlands, D C T (Pontypool) 1963 *E*, *S*, *I*, *F*, *NZ*, 1964 *E*, *S*, *I*, *F*, *SA*, 1965 *E*, *S*, *I*, *F*
Rowlands, G (RAF, Cardiff) 1953 *NZ*, 1954 *E*, *F*, 1956 *F*
Rowlands, K A (Cardiff) 1962 *F*, *I*, 1963 *I*, 1965 *I*, *F*
Rowles, G R (Penarth) 1892 *E*
Rowley, M (Pontypridd) 1996 *SA*, 1997 *US*, *S*, *I*, *F*, *R*
Roy, W S (Cardiff) 1995 [*J* (R)]
Russell, S (London Welsh) 1987 *US*

Samuel, D (Swansea) 1891 *I*, 1893 *I*
Samuel, F (Mountain Ash) 1922 *S*, *I*, *F*
Samuel, J (Swansea) 1891 *I*
Scourfield, T (Torquay) 1930 *F*
Scrine, G F (Swansea) 1899 *E*, *S*, 1901 *I*
Shanklin, J L (London Welsh) 1970 *F*, 1972 *NZ*, 1973 *I*, *F*
Shanklin, T (Saracens) 2001 *J* 2
Shaw, G (Neath) 1972 *NZ*, 1973 *E*, *S*, *I*, *F*, *A*, 1974 *S*, *I*, *F*, *E*, 1977 *I*, *F*
Shaw, T W (Newbridge) 1983 *R*
Shea, J (Newport) 1919 *NZA*, 1920 *E*, *S*, 1921 *E*
Shell, R C (Aberavon) 1973 *A* (R)
Simpson, H J (Cardiff) 1884 *E*, *S*, *I*
Sinkinson, B D (Neath) 1999 *F* 1, *It*, *E*, *Arg* 1,2, *SA*, *F* 2, [*Arg* 3, *J*, *Sm*, *A*], 2000 *F*, *It*, *E*, 2001 *R* (R), *I*
Skrimshire, R T (Newport) 1899 *E*, *S*, *I*
Skym, A (Llanelli) 1928 *E*, *S*, *I*, *F*, 1930 *E*, *S*, *I*, *F*, 1931 *E*, *S*, *F*, *I*, *SA*, 1932 *E*, *S*, *I*, 1933 *E*, *S*, *I*, 1935 *E*
Smith, J S (Cardiff) 1884 *E*, *I*, 1885 *E*
Smith, N (Ebbw Vale) 2000 *F* (R)
Sparks, B (Neath) 1954 *I*, 1955 *E*, *F*, 1956 *E*, *S*, *I*, 1957 *S*
Spiller, W J (Cardiff) 1910 *S*, *I*, 1911 *E*, *S*, *F*, *I*, 1912 *E*, *F*, *SA*, 1913 *E*
Squire, J (Newport, Pontypool) 1977 *I*, *F*, 1978 *E*, *S*, *I*, *F*, *A* 1, *NZ*, 1979 *S*, *I*, *F*, *E*, 1980 *F*, *E*, *S*, *I*, *NZ*, 1981 *E*, *S*, *I*, *F*, *A*, 1982 *I*, *F*, *E*, 1983 *E*, *S*, *I*, *F*
Stadden, W J W (Cardiff) 1884 *I*, 1886 *E*, *S*, 1887 *I*, 1888 *S*, *M*, 1890 *S*, *E*
Stephens, C (Bridgend) 1998 *E* (R), 2001 *J* 2(R)
Stephens, C J (Llanelli) 1992 *I*, *F*, *E*, *A*
Stephens, G (Neath) 1912 *E*, *S*, *I*, *F*, *SA*, 1913 *E*, *S*, *F*, *I*, 1919 *NZA*
Stephens, I (Bridgend) 1981 *E*, *S*, *I*, *F*, *A*, 1982 *I*, *F*, *E*, *S*, 1984 *I*, *F*, *E*, *A*
Stephens, Rev J G (Llanelli) 1922 *E*, *S*, *I*, *F*
Stephens, J R G (Neath) 1947 *E*, *S*, *F*, *I*, 1948 *I*, 1949 *S*, *I*, *F*, 1951 *F*, *SA*, 1952 *E*, *S*, *I*, *F*, 1953 *E*, *S*, *I*, *F*, *NZ*, 1954 *E*, *I*, 1955 *E*, *S*, *I*, *F*, 1956 *S*, *I*, *F*, 1957 *E*, *S*, *I*, *F*
Stock, A (Newport) 1924 *F*, *NZ*, 1926 *E*, *S*
Stone, P (Llanelli) 1949 *F*
Strand-Jones, J (Llanelli) 1902 *E*, *S*, *I*, 1903 *E*, *S*
Summers, R H B (Haverfordwest) 1881 *E*
Sutton, S (Pontypool, S Wales Police) 1982 *F*, *E*, 1987 *F*, *E*, *S*, *I*, [*C*, *NZ* (R), *A*]
Sweet-Escott, R B (Cardiff) 1891 *S*, 1894 *I*, 1895 *I*

Tamplin, W E (Cardiff) 1947 *S*, *F*, *I*, *A*, 1948 *E*, *S*, *F*
Tanner, H (Swansea, Cardiff) 1935 *NZ*, 1936 *E*, *S*, *I*, 1937 *E*, *S*, *I*, 1938 *E*, *S*, *I*, 1939 *E*, *S*, *I*, 1947 *E*, *S*, *F*, *I*, 1948 *E*, *S*, *F*, *I*, 1949 *E*, *S*, *I*, *F*
Tarr, D J (Swansea, Royal Navy) 1935 *NZ*
Taylor, A R (Cross Keys) 1937 *I*, 1938 *I*, 1939 *E*
Taylor, C G (Ruabon) 1884 *E*, *S*, *I*, 1885 *E*, *S*, 1886 *E*, *S*, 1887 *E*, *I*
Taylor, H T (Cardiff) 1994 *Pt*, *C*, *Fj*, *Tg*, *WS* (R), *R*, *It*, *SA*, 1995 *E*, *S*, [*J*, *NZ*, *I*], *SA*, *Fj*, 1996 *It*, *E*, *S*, *I*, *F* 1, *A* 1,2, *It*, *A* 3
Taylor, J (London Welsh) 1967 *S*, *I*, *F*, *E*, *NZ*, 1968 *I*, *F*, 1969 *S*, *I*, *F*, *E*, *NZ* 1, *A*, 1970 *F*, 1971 *E*, *S*, *I*, *F*, 1972 *E*, *S*, *F*, *NZ*, 1973 *E*, *S*, *I*, *F*
Taylor, M (Pontypool, Swansea) 1994 *SA*, 1995 *F*, *E*, *SA* (R), 1998 *Z*, *SA* 1,2, *Arg*, 1999 *I*, *F* 1, *It*, *E*, *Arg* 1,2, *SA*, *F* 2, [*Arg* 3, *J*, *Sm*, *A*], 2000 *F*, *It*, *E*, *S*, *Sm*, *US*, 2001 *E*, *S*, *F*, *It*

Thomas, A (Newport) 1963 *NZ*, 1964 *E*
Thomas, A C (Bristol, Swansea) 1996 *It*, *E*, *S*, *I*, *F* 2(R), *SA*, 1997 *US*, *S*, *I*, *F*, *US* 1,2, *C*, *R*, *NZ* (t), 1998 *It*, *E*, *S* (R), *Z*, *SA* 1, 2000 *Sm*, *US*, *SA* (R)
Thomas, A G (Swansea, Cardiff) 1952 *E*, *S*, *I*, *F*, 1953 *S*, *I*, *F*, 1954 *E*, *I*, *F*, 1955 *S*, *I*, *F*
Thomas, Bob (Swansea) 1900 *E*, *S*, *I*, 1901 *E*
Thomas, Brian (Neath, Cambridge U) 1963 *E*, *S*, *I*, *F*, *NZ*, 1964 *E*, *S*, *I*, *F*, *SA*, 1965 *E*, 1966 *E*, *S*, *I*, 1967 *NZ*, 1969 *S*, *I*, *F*, *E*, *NZ* 1,2
Thomas, C (Bridgend) 1925 *E*, *S*
Thomas, C J (Newport) 1888 *I*, *M*, 1889 *S*, *I*, 1890 *S*, *E*, *I*, 1891 *E*, *I*
Thomas, D (Aberavon) 1961 *I*
Thomas, D (Llanelli) 1954 *I*
Thomas, Dick (Mountain Ash) 1906 *SA*, 1908 *F*, *I*, 1909 *S*
Thomas, D J (Swansea) 1904 *E*, 1908 *A*, 1910 *E*, *S*, *I*, 1911 *E*, *S*, *F*, *I*, 1912 *E*
Thomas, D J (Swansea) 1930 *S*, *I*, 1932 *E*, *S*, *I*, 1933 *E*, *S*, 1934 *E*, 1935 *E*, *S*, *I*
Thomas, D L (Neath) 1937 *E*
Thomas, E (Newport) 1904 *S*, *I*, 1909 *S*, *F*, *I*, 1910 *F*
Thomas, G (Llanelli) 1923 *E*, *S*, *F*, *I*
Thomas, G (Newport) 1888 *M*, 1890 *I*, 1891 *S*
Thomas, G (Bridgend, Cardiff) 1995 [*J*, *NZ*, *I*], *SA*, *Fj*, 1996 *F* 1, *A* 1,2, *Bb*, *F* 2, *It*, *A* 3, 1997 *US*, *S*, *I*, *F*, *E*, *US* 1,2, *C*, *R*, *Tg*, *NZ*, 1998 *It*, *E*, *S*, *I*, *F*, *SA* 2, *Arg*, 1999 *F* 1(R), *It*, *E*, *Arg* 2, *SA*, *F* 2, [*Arg* 3, *J* (R), *Sm*, *A*], 2000 *F*, *It*, *E*, *S*, *I*, *US* (R), *SA*, 2001 *E*, *F*, *It*, *J* 1,2, *R*
Thomas, G (Bath) 2001 *J* 1,2, *R*, *I* (R)
Thomas, H (Llanelli) 1912 *F*
Thomas, H (Neath) 1936 *E*, *S*, *I*, 1937 *E*, *S*, *I*
Thomas, H W (Swansea) 1912 *SA*, 1913 *E*
Thomas, I (Bryncethin) 1924 *E*
Thomas, I D (Ebbw Vale) 2000 *Sm*, *US* (R), *SA* (R), 2001 *J* 1,2, *R*, *I*
Thomas, L C (Cardiff) 1885 *E*, *S*
Thomas, M C (Newport, Devonport Services) 1949 *F*, 1950 *E*, *S*, *I*, *F*, 1951 *E*, *S*, *I*, *F*, *SA*, 1952 *E*, *S*, *I*, *F*, 1953 *E*, 1956 *E*, *S*, *I*, *F*, 1957 *E*, *S*, 1958 *E*, *S*, *I*, *F*, 1959 *I*, *F*
Thomas, M G (St Bart's Hospital) 1919 *NZA*, 1921 *S*, *F*, *I*, 1923 *F*, 1924 *E*
Thomas, N (Bath) 1996 *SA* (R), 1997 *US* 1(R),2, *C* (R), *R*, *Tg*, *NZ*, 1998 *Z*, *SA* 1
Thomas, R (Pontypool) 1909 *F*, *I*, 1911 *S*, *F*, 1912 *E*, *S*, *SA*, 1913 *E*
Thomas, R C C (Swansea) 1949 *F*, 1952 *I*, *F*, 1953 *S*, *I*, *F*, *NZ*, 1954 *E*, *I*, *F*, *S*, 1955 *S*, *I*, 1956 *E*, *S*, *I*, 1957 *E*, 1958 *A*, *E*, *S*, *I*, *F*, 1959 *E*, *S*, *I*, *F*
Thomas, R L (London Welsh) 1889 *S*, *I*, 1890 *I*, 1891 *E*, *S*, *I*, 1892 *E*
Thomas, S (Llanelli) 1890 *S*, *E*, 1891 *I*
Thomas, W D (Llanelli) 1966 *A*, 1968 *S*, *I*, *F*, 1969 *E*, *NZ* 2, *A*, 1970 *SA*, *S*, *E*, *I*, *F*, 1971 *E*, *S*, *I*, *F*, 1972 *E*, *S*, *F*, *NZ*, 1973 *E*, *S*, *I*, *F*, 1974 *E*
Thomas, W G (Llanelli, Waterloo, Swansea) 1927 *E*, *S*, *F*, *I*, 1929 *E*, 1931 *E*, *S*, *SA*, 1932 *E*, *S*, *I*, 1933 *E*, *S*, *I*
Thomas, W H (Llandovery Coll, Cambridge U) 1885 *S*, 1886 *E*, *S*, 1887 *E*, *S*, 1888 *S*, *I*, 1890 *E*, *I*, 1891 *S*, *I*
Thomas, W J (Cardiff) 1961 *F*, 1963 *F*
Thomas, W J L (Llanelli, Cardiff) 1995 *SA*, *Fj*, 1996 *It*, *E*, *S*, *I*, *F* 1, 1996 *Bb* (R), 1997 *US*
Thomas, W L (Newport) 1894 *S*, 1895 *E*, *I*
Thomas, W T (Abertillery) 1930 *E*
Thompson, J F (Cross Keys) 1923 *E*
Thorburn, P H (Neath) 1985 *F*, *E*, *Fj*, 1986 *E*, *S*, *I*, *F*, 1987 *F*, [*I*, *Tg*, *C*, *E*, *NZ*, *A*], *US*, 1988 *S*, *I*, *F*, *WS*, *R* (R), 1989 *S*, *I*, *F*, *E*, *NZ*, 1990 *F*, *E*, *S*, *I*, *Nm* 1,2, *Bb*, 1991 *E*, *S*, *I*, *F* 1, *A*
Titley, M H (Bridgend, Swansea) 1983 *R*, 1984 *S*, *I*, *F*, *E*, *A*, 1985 *S*, *I*, *Fj*, 1986 *F*, *Fj*, *Tg*, *WS*, 1990 *F*, *E*
Towers, W H (Swansea) 1887 *I*, 1888 *M*
Travers, G (Pill Harriers) 1903 *E*, *S*, *I*, 1905 *E*, *S*, *I*, *NZ*, 1906 *E*, *S*, *I*, *SA*, 1907 *E*, *S*, *I*, 1908 *E*, *S*, *F*, *I*, *A*, 1909 *E*, *S*, *I*, 1911 *S*, *F*, *I*
Travers, W H (Newport) 1937 *S*, *I*, 1938 *E*, *S*, *I*, 1939 *E*, *S*, *I*, 1949 *E*, *S*, *I*, *F*
Treharne, E (Pontypridd) 1881 *E*, 1883 *E*
Trew, W J (Swansea) 1900 *E*, *S*, *I*, 1901 *E*, *S*, 1903 *S*, 1905 *S*, 1906 *S*, 1907 *E*, *S*, 1908 *E*, *S*, *F*, *I*, *A*, 1909 *E*, *S*, *F*, *I*, 1910 *F*, *E*, *S*, 1911 *E*, *S*, *F*, *I*, 1912 *S*, 1913 *S*, *F*
Trott, R F (Cardiff) 1948 *E*, *S*, *F*, *I*, 1949 *E*, *S*, *I*, *F*
Truman, W H (Llanelli) 1934 *E*, 1935 *E*
Trump, L C (Newport) 1912 *E*, *S*, *I*, *F*

Turnbull, B R (Cardiff) 1925 *I*, 1927 *E, S*, 1928 *E, F*, 1930 *S*
Turnbull, M J L (Cardiff) 1933 *E, I*
Turner, P (Newbridge) 1989 *I* (R), *F, E*

Uzzell, H (Newport) 1912 *E, S, I, F*, 1913 *S, F, I*, 1914 *E, S, F, I*, 1920 *E, S, F, I*
Uzzell, J R (Newport) 1963 *NZ*, 1965 *E, S, I, F*

Vickery, W E (Aberavon) 1938 *E, S, I*, 1939 *E*
Vile, T H (Newport) 1908 *E, S*, 1910 *I*, 1912 *I, F, SA*, 1913 *E*, 1921 *S*
Vincent, H C (Bangor) 1882 *I*
Voyle, M J (Newport, Llanelli, Cardiff) 1996 *A* 1(t), *F* 2, 1997 *E, US* 1,2, *C, Tg, NZ*, 1998 *It, E, S, I, F, Arg* (R), 1999 *S* (R), *I* (t), *It* (R), *SA* (R), *F* 2(R), [*J, A* (R)], 2000 *F* (R)

Wakeford, J D M (S Wales Police) 1988 *WS, R*
Waldron, R (Neath) 1965 *E, S, I, F*
Walker, N (Cardiff) 1993 *I, F, J*, 1994 *S, F, E, Pt, Sp*, 1995 *F, E*, 1997 *US* 1,2, *C, R* (R), *Tg, NZ*, 1998 *E*
Waller, P D (Newport) 1908 *A*, 1909 *E, S, F, I*, 1910 *F*
Walne, N J (Richmond, Cardiff) 1999 *It* (R), *E* (R), *C*
Walters, N (Llanelli) 1902 *E*
Wanbon, R (Aberavon) 1968 *E*
Ward, W S (Cross Keys) 1934 *S, I*
Warlow, J (Llanelli) 1962 *I*
Waters, D R (Newport) 1986 *E, S, I, F*
Waters, K (Newbridge) 1991 [*WS*]
Watkins, D (Newport) 1963 *E, S, I, F, NZ*, 1964 *E, S, I, F, SA*, 1965 *E, S, I, F*, 1966 *E, S, I, F*, 1967 *I, F, E*
Watkins, E (Neath) 1924 *E, S, I, F*
Watkins, E (Blaina) 1926 *S, I, F*
Watkins, E (Cardiff) 1935 *NZ*, 1937 *S, I*, 1938 *E, S, I*, 1939 *E, S*
Watkins, H (Llanelli) 1904 *S, I*, 1905 *E, S, I*, 1906 *E*
Watkins, I J (Ebbw Vale) 1988 *E* (R), *S, I, F, NZ* 2, *R*, 1989 *S, I, F, E*
Watkins, L (Oxford U, Llandaff) 1881 *E*
Watkins, M J (Newport) 1984 *I, F, E, A*
Watkins, S J (Newport, Cardiff) 1964 *S, I, F*, 1965 *E, S, I, F*, 1966 *E, S, I, F, A*, 1967 *S, I, F, E, NZ*, 1968 *E, S*, 1969 *S, I, F, E, NZ* 1, 1970 *E, I*
Watkins, W R (Newport) 1959 *F*
Watts, D (Maesteg) 1914 *E, S, F, I*
Watts, J (Llanelli) 1907 *E, S, I*, 1908 *E, S, F, I, A*, 1909 *S, F, I*
Watts, W (Llanelli) 1914 *E*
Watts, W H (Newport) 1892 *E, S, I*, 1893 *E, S, I*, 1894 *E, S, I*, 1895 *E, I*, 1896 *E*
Weatherley, D J (Swansea) 1998 *Z*
Weaver, D (Swansea) 1964 *E*
Webb, J (Abertillery) 1907 *S*, 1908 *E, S, F, I, A*, 1909 *E, S, F, I*, 1910 *F, E, S, I*, 1911 *E, S, F, I*, 1912 *E, S*
Webb, J E (Newport) 1888 *M*, 1889 *S*
Webbe, G M C (Bridgend) 1986 *Tg* (R), *WS*, 1987 *F, E, S*, [*Tg*], *US*, 1988 *F* (R), *NZ* 1, *R*
Webster, R E (Swansea) 1987 [*A*], 1990 *Bb*, 1991 [*Arg, A*], 1992 *I, F, E, S, A*, 1993 *E, S, I, F*
Wells, G T (Cardiff) 1955 *E, S*, 1957 *I, F*, 1958 *A, E, S*
Westacott, D (Cardiff) 1906 *I*
Wetter, H (Newport) 1912 *SA*, 1913 *E*
Wetter, J J (Newport) 1914 *S, F, I*, 1920 *E, S, F, I*, 1921 *E*, 1924 *I, NZ*
Wheel, G A D (Swansea) 1974 *I, E* (R), 1975 *F, E, I, A*, 1976 *E, S, I, F*, 1977 *I, E, S*, 1978 *E, S, I, F, A* 1,2, *NZ*, 1979 *S, I*, 1980 *F, E, S, I*, 1981 *E, S, I, F, A*, 1982 *I*
Wheeler, P J (Aberavon) 1967 *NZ*, 1968 *E*
Whitefoot, J (Cardiff) 1984 *A* (R), 1985 *S, I, F, E, Fj*, 1986 *E, S, I, F, Fj, Tg, WS*, 1987 *F, E, S, I*, [*I, C*]
Whitfield, J (Newport) 1919 *NZA*, 1920 *E, S, F, I*, 1921 *E*, 1922 *E, S, I, F*, 1924 *S, I*
Whitson, G K (Newport) 1956 *F*, 1960 *S, I*
Wilkins, G (Bridgend) 1994 *Tg*
Williams, A (Bridgend, Swansea) 1990 *Nm* 2(R), 1995 *Fj* (R)
Williams, B (Llanelli) 1920 *S, F, I*
Williams, B H (Neath, Richmond, Bristol) 1996 *F* 2, 1997 *R, Tg, NZ*, 1998 *It, E, Z* (R), *SA* 1, *Arg* (R), 1999 *S* (R), *I, It* (R), 2000 *F* (R), *It* (R), *E* (t+R), *R* (R), *I* (R)
Williams, B L (Cardiff) 1947 *E, S, F, I, A*, 1948 *E, S, F, I*, 1949 *E, S, I*, 1951 *I, SA*, 1952 *S*, 1953 *E, S, I, F, NZ*, 1954 *S*, 1955 *E*
Williams, B R (Neath) 1990 *S, I, Bb*, 1991 *E, S*
Williams, C (Llanelli) 1924 *NZ*, 1925 *E*

Williams, C (Aberavon, Swansea) 1977 *E, S*, 1980 *F, E, S, I, NZ*, 1983 *E*
Williams, C D (Cardiff, Neath) 1955 *F*, 1956 *F*
Williams, D (Llanelli) 1998 *SA* 1(R)
Williams, D (Ebbw Vale) 1963 *E, S, I, F*, 1964 *E, S, I, F, SA*, 1965 *E, S, I, F*, 1966 *E, S, I, A*, 1967 *F, E, NZ*, 1968 *E*, 1969 *S, I, F, E, NZ* 1,2, *A*, 1970 *SA, S, E, I*, 1971 *E, S, I, F*
Williams, D B (Newport, Swansea) 1978 *A* 1, 1981 *E, S*
Williams, E (Neath) 1924 *NZ*, 1925 *F*
Williams, E (Aberavon) 1925 *E, S*
Williams, F L (Cardiff) 1929 *S, F, I*, 1930 *E, S, I, F*, 1931 *F, I, SA*, 1932 *E, S, I*, 1933 *I*
Williams, G (Aberavon) 1936 *E, S, I*
Williams, G (London Welsh) 1950 *I, F*, 1951 *E, S, I, F, SA*, 1952 *E, S, I, F*, 1953 *NZ*, 1954 *E*
Williams, G (Bridgend) 1981 *I, F*, 1982 *E* (R), *S*
Williams, G P (Bridgend) 1980 *NZ*, 1981 *E, S, A*, 1982 *I*
Williams, G (Cardiff) 2000 *I, Sm, US, SA*, 2001 *S, F, It, R* (R), *I* (R)
Williams, J (Blaina) 1920 *E, S, F, I*, 1921 *S, F, I*
Williams, J F (London Welsh) 1905 *I, NZ*, 1906 *S, SA*
Williams, J J (Llanelli) 1973 *F* (R), *A*, 1974 *S, I, F, E*, 1975 *F, E, S, I, A*, 1976 *E, S, I, F*, 1977 *I, F, E, S*, 1978 *E, S, I, F, A* 1,2, *NZ*, 1979 *S, I, F, E*
Williams, J L (Cardiff) 1906 *SA*, 1907 *E, S, I*, 1908 *E, S, I, A*, 1909 *E, S, F, I*, 1910 *I*, 1911 *E, S, F, I*
Williams, J P R (London Welsh, Bridgend) 1969 *S, I, F, E, NZ* 1,2, *A*, 1970 *SA, S, E, I, F*, 1971 *E, S, I, F*, 1972 *E, S, F*, 1973 *E, S, I, F, A*, 1974 *S, I, F*, 1975 *F, E, S, I, A*, 1976 *E, S, I, F*, 1977 *I, F, E, S*, 1978 *E, S, I, F, A* 1,2, *NZ*, 1979 *S, I, F, E*, 1980 *NZ*, 1981 *E, S*
Williams, L (Llanelli, Cardiff) 1947 *E, S, F, I, A*, 1948 *I*, 1949 *E*
Williams, L H (Cardiff) 1957 *S, I, F*, 1958 *E, S, I, F*, 1959 *E, S, I*, 1961 *F, I*, 1962 *E, S*
Williams, M (Newport) 1923 *F*
Williams, M E (Pontypridd, Cardiff) 1996 *Bb*, *F* 2, *It* (t), 1998 *It, E, Z, SA* 2, *Arg*, 1999 *S, I, C, J*, [*Sm*], 2000 *E* (R), 2001 *E, S, F, It*
Williams, O (Bridgend) 1990 *Nm* 2
Williams, O (Llanelli) 1947 *E, S, A*, 1948 *E, S, F, I*
Williams, R (Llanelli) 1954 *S*, 1957 *F*, 1958 *A*
Williams, R D G (Newport) 1881 *E*
Williams, R F (Cardiff) 1912 *SA*, 1913 *E, S*, 1914 *I*
Williams, R H (Llanelli) 1954 *I, F, S*, 1955 *S, I, F*, 1956 *E, S, I*, 1957 *E, S, I, F*, 1958 *A, E, S, I, F*, 1959 *E, S, I, F*, 1960 *E*
Williams, S (Llanelli) 1947 *E, S, F, I*, 1948 *S, F*
Williams, S A (Aberavon) 1939 *E, S, I*
Williams, S M (Neath, Cardiff) 1994 *Tg*, 1996 *E* (t), *A* 1,2, *Bb, F* 2, *It, A* 3, *SA*, 1997 *US, S, I, F, E, US* 1,2(R), *C, R* (R), *Tg* (R), *NZ* (t+R)
Williams, S M (Neath) 2000 *F* (R), *It, E, S, I, Sm, SA* (R), 2001 *J* 1,2, *I*
Williams, T (Pontypridd) 1882 *I*
Williams, T (Swansea) 1888 *S, I*
Williams, T (Swansea) 1912 *I*, 1913 *F*, 1914 *E, S, F, I*
Williams, Tudor (Swansea) 1921 *F*
Williams, T G (Cross Keys) 1935 *S, I, NZ*, 1936 *E, S, I*, 1937 *S, I*
Williams, W A (Crumlin) 1927 *E, S, F, I*
Williams, W A (Newport) 1952 *I, F*, 1953 *E*
Williams, W E O (Cardiff) 1887 *S, I*, 1889 *S*, 1890 *S, E*
Williams, W H (Pontymister) 1900 *E, S, I*, 1901 *E*
Williams, W O G (Swansea, Devonport Services) 1951 *F, SA*, 1952 *E, S, I, F*, 1953 *E, S, I, F, NZ*, 1954 *I, F, S*, 1955 *E, S, I, F*, 1956 *E, S, I*
Williams, W P J (Neath) 1974 *I, F*
Williams-Jones, H (S Wales Police, Llanelli) 1989 *S* (R), 1990 *F* (R), *I*, 1991 *A*, 1992 *S, A*, 1993 *E, S, I, F, Z* 1, *Nm*, 1994 *Fj, Tg, WS* (R), *It* (t), 1995 *E* (R)
Willis, W R (Cardiff) 1950 *E, S, I, F*, 1951 *E, S, I, F, SA*, 1952 *E, S*, 1953 *S, NZ*, 1954 *E, S, I, F*, 1955 *E, S, I, F*
Wiltshire, M L (Aberavon) 1967 *NZ*, 1968 *E, S, F*
Windsor, R W (Pontypool) 1973 *A*, 1974 *S, I, F, E*, 1975 *F, E, S, I, A*, 1976 *E, S, I, F*, 1977 *I, F, E, S*, 1978 *E, S, I, F, A* 1,2, *NZ*, 1979 *S, I, F*
Winfield, H B (Cardiff) 1903 *I*, 1904 *E, S, I*, 1905 *NZ*, 1906 *E, S, I*, 1907 *S, I*, 1908 *E, S, F, I, A*
Winmill, S (Cross Keys) 1921 *E, S, F, I*
Wintle, M E (Llanelli) 1996 *It*
Wintle, R V (London Welsh) 1988 *WS* (R)
Wooller, W (Sale, Cambridge U, Cardiff) 1933 *E, S, I*, 1935 *E, S, I, NZ*, 1936 *E, S, I*, 1937 *E, S, I*, 1938 *S, I*, 1939 *E, S, I*

Wyatt, C P (Llanelli) 1998 *Z* (R), *SA* 1(R),2, *Arg,* 1999 *S, I, F* 1, *It, E, Arg* 1,2, *SA, C* (R), *F* 2, [*Arg* 3, *J* (R), *Sm, A*], 2000 *F, It, E, US, SA,* 2001 *E, R, I*
Wyatt, G (Pontypridd) 1997 *Tg*
Wyatt, M A (Swansea) 1983 *E, S, I, F,* 1984 *A,* 1985 *S, I,* 1987 *E, S, I*

Young, D (Swansea, Cardiff) 1987 [*E, NZ*], *US,* 1988 *E, S, I, F, NZ* 1,2, *WS, R,* 1989 *S, NZ,* 1990 *F,* 1996 *A* 3, *SA,* 1997 *US, S, I, F, E, R, NZ,* 1998 *It, E, S, I, F,* 1999 *I, E* (R), *Arg* 1(R),2(R), *SA, C* (R), *F* 2, [*Arg* 3, *J, Sm, A*], 2000 *F, It, E, S, I,* 2001 *E, S, F, It, R, I*
Young, G A (Cardiff) 1886 *E, S*

Young, J (Harrogate, RAF, London Welsh) 1968 *S, I, F,* 1969 *S, I, F, E, NZ* 1, 1970 *E, I, F,* 1971 *E, S, I, F,* 1972 *E, S, F, NZ,* 1973 *E, S, I, F*

WALES INTERNATIONAL STATISTICS

(up to 20 October 2001)

Match Records

Most Consecutive Test Wins

11 1907 *I*, 1908 *E, S, F, I, A*, 1909 *E, S, F, I,* 1910 *F*
10 1999 *F* 1, *It, E, Arg* 1,2, *SA, C, F* 2, *Arg* 3, *J*
8 1970 *F,* 1971 *E, S, I, F,* 1972 *E, S, F*

Most Consecutive Tests Without Defeat

Matches	Wins	Draws	Period
11	11	0	1907 to 1910
10	10	0	1999 to 1999
8	8	0	1970 to 1972

Most Points in a Match
by the team

Pts	Opponents	Venue	Year
102	Portugal	Lisbon	1994
81	Romania	Cardiff	2001
70	Romania	Wrexham	1997
64	Japan	Cardiff	1999
64	Japan	Osaka	2001
60	Italy	Treviso	1999
57	Japan	Bloemfontein	1995
55	Japan	Cardiff	1993

by a player

Pts	Player	Opponents	Venue	Year
30	N R Jenkins	Italy	Treviso	1999
29	N R Jenkins	France	Cardiff	1999
28	N R Jenkins	Canada	Cardiff	1999
28	N R Jenkins	France	Paris	2001
27	N R Jenkins	Italy	Cardiff	2000
26	S M Jones	Romania	Cardiff	2001
24	N R Jenkins	Canada	Cardiff	1993
24	N R Jenkins	Italy	Cardiff	1994
23	A C Thomas	Romania	Wrexham	1997
23	N R Jenkins	Argentina	Llanelli	1998
23	N R Jenkins	Scotland	Murrayfield	2001
22	N R Jenkins	Portugal	Lisbon	1994
22	N R Jenkins	Japan	Bloemfontein	1995
22	N R Jenkins	England	Wembley	1999

Most Tries in a Match
by the team

Tries	Opponents	Venue	Year
16	Portugal	Lisbon	1994
11	France	Paris	1909
11	Romania	Wrexham	1997
11	Romania	Cardiff	2001
10	France	Swansea	1910
10	Japan	Osaka	2001
9	France	Cardiff	1908
9	Japan	Cardiff	1993
9	Japan	Cardiff	1999
9	Japan	Tokyo	2001

by a player

Tries	Player	Opponents	Venue	Year
4	W Llewellyn	England	Swansea	1899
4	R A Gibbs	France	Cardiff	1908
4	M C R Richards	England	Cardiff	1969
4	I C Evans	Canada	Invercargill	1987
4	N Walker	Portugal	Lisbon	1994
4	G Thomas	Italy	Treviso	1999
4	S M Williams	Japan	Osaka	2001

Most Conversions in a Match
by the team

Cons	Opponents	Venue	Year
11	Portugal	Lisbon	1994
10	Romania	Cardiff	2001
8	France	Swansea	1910
8	Japan	Cardiff	1999
7	France	Paris	1909
7	Japan	Osaka	2001

by a player

Cons	Player	Opponents	Venue	Year
11	N R Jenkins	Portugal	Lisbon	1994
10	S M Jones	Romania	Cardiff	2001
8	J Bancroft	France	Swansea	1910
8	N R Jenkins	Japan	Cardiff	1999
7	S M Jones	Japan	Osaka	2001
6	J Bancroft	France	Paris	1909

Most Penalties in a Match
by the team

Penalties	Opponents	Venue	Year
9	France	Cardiff	1999
8	Canada	Cardiff	1993
7	Italy	Cardiff	1994
7	Canada	Cardiff	1999
7	Italy	Cardiff	2000
6	France	Cardiff	1982
6	Tonga	Nuku'alofa	1994
6	England	Wembley	1999

by a player

Penalties	Player	Opponents	Venue	Year
9	N R Jenkins	France	Cardiff	1999
8	N R Jenkins	Canada	Cardiff	1993
7	N R Jenkins	Italy	Cardiff	1994
7	N R Jenkins	Canada	Cardiff	1999
7	N R Jenkins	Italy	Cardiff	2000
6	G Evans	France	Cardiff	1982
6	N R Jenkins	Tonga	Nuku'alofa	1994
6	N R Jenkins	England	Wembley	1999

Most Dropped Goals in a Match
by the team

Drops	Opponents	Venue	Year
3	Scotland	Murrayfield	2001
2	Scotland	Swansea	1912
2	Scotland	Cardiff	1914
2	England	Swansea	1920
2	Scotland	Swansea	1921
2	France	Paris	1930
2	England	Cardiff	1971
2	France	Cardiff	1978
2	England	Twickenham	1984
2	Ireland	Wellington	1987
2	Scotland	Cardiff	1988
2	France	Paris	2001

by a player

Drops	Player	Opponents	Venue	Year
3	N R Jenkins	Scotland	Murrayfield	2001
2	J Shea	England	Swansea	1920
2	A Jenkins	Scotland	Swansea	1921
2	B John	England	Cardiff	1971
2	M Dacey	England	Twickenham	1984
2	J Davies	Ireland	Wellington	1987
2	J Davies	Scotland	Cardiff	1988
2	N R Jenkins	France	Paris	2001

Career Records
Most Capped Players

Caps	Player	Career Span
84	N R Jenkins	1991 to 2001
72	I C Evans	1987 to 1998
64	G O Llewellyn	1989 to 1999
58	G R Jenkins	1991 to 2000
55	J P R Williams	1969 to 1981
54	R N Jones	1986 to 1995
53	G O Edwards	1967 to 1978
53	I S Gibbs	1991 to 2001
53	G Thomas	1995 to 2001
51	R Howley	1996 to 2001
50	D Young	1987 to 2001
46	T G R Davies	1966 to 1978
46	P T Davies	1985 to 1995
44	K J Jones	1947 to 1957
43	L S Quinnell	1993 to 2001
42	M R Hall	1988 to 1995

Most Consecutive Tests

Tests	Player	Span
53	G O Edwards	1967 to 1978
43	K J Jones	1947 to 1956
39	G Price	1975 to 1983
38	T M Davies	1969 to 1976
33	W J Bancroft	1890 to 1901

Most Tests as Captain

Tests	Captain	Span
28	I C Evans	1991 to 1995
22	R Howley	1998 to 1999
18	A J Gould	1889 to 1897
17	J M Humphreys	1995 to 1997
14	D C T Rowlands	1963 to 1965
14	W J Trew	1907 to 1913

Most Tests in Individual Positions

Position	Player	Tests	Span
Full-back	J P R Williams	54	1969 to 1981
Wing	I C Evans	72	1987 to 1998
Centre	I S Gibbs	53	1991 to 2001
Fly-half	N R Jenkins	67	1991 to 2001
Scrum-half	G O Edwards	53	1967 to 1978
	R N Jones	53	1986 to 1995
Prop	D Young	50	1987 to 2001
Hooker	G R Jenkins	57	1991 to 2000
Lock	G O Llewellyn	63	1989 to 1999
Flanker	C L Charvis	36	1996 to 2001
No 8	L S Quinnell	42	1993 to 2001

Most Points in Tests

Points	Player	Tests	Career
1029	N R Jenkins	84	1991 to 2001
304	P H Thorburn	37	1985 to 1991
211	A C Thomas	23	1996 to 2000
166	P Bennett	29	1969 to 1978
157	I C Evans	72	1987 to 1998

Most Tries in Tests

Tries	Player	Tests	Career
33	I C Evans	72	1987 to 1998
25	G Thomas	53	1995 to 2001
20	G O Edwards	53	1967 to 1978
20	T G R Davies	46	1966 to 1978
17	R A Gibbs	16	1906 to 1911
17	J L Williams	17	1906 to 1911
17	K J Jones	44	1947 to 1957

Most Conversions in Tests

Cons	Player	Tests	Career
126	N R Jenkins	84	1991 to 2001
43	P H Thorburn	37	1985 to 1991
38	J Bancroft	18	1909 to 1914
30	A C Thomas	23	1996 to 2000
25	S M Jones	12	1998 to 2001
20	W J Bancroft	33	1890 to 1901

Most Penalty Goals in Tests

Penalties	Player	Tests	Career
231	N R Jenkins	84	1991 to 2001
70	P H Thorburn	37	1985 to 1991
36	P Bennett	29	1969 to 1978
35	S P Fenwick	30	1975 to 1981
32	A C Thomas	23	1996 to 2000
22	G Evans	10	1981 to 1983

Most Dropped Goals in Tests

Drops	Player	Tests	Career
13	J Davies	32	1985 to 1997
10	N R Jenkins	84	1991 to 2001
8	B John	25	1966 to 1972
7	W G Davies	21	1978 to 1985

International Championship Records

Record	Detail		Set
Most points in season	125	in five matches	2001
Most tries in season	21	in four matches	1910
Highest Score	49	49-14 v France	1910
Biggest win	35	49-14 v France	1910
Highest score conceded	60	26-60 v England	1998
Biggest defeat	51	0-51 v France	1998
Most appearances	45	G O Edwards	1967 – 1978
Most points in matches	406	N R Jenkins	1991 – 2001
Most points in season	74	N R Jenkins	2001
Most points in match	28	N R Jenkins	v France, 2001
Most tries in matches	18	G O Edwards	1967 – 1978
Most tries in season	6	M C R Richards	1969
Most tries in match	4	W Llewellyn	v England, 1899
	4	M C R Richards	v England, 1969
Most cons in matches	41	N R Jenkins	1991 – 2001
Most cons in season	9	J Bancroft	1910
	9	J A Bassett	1931
	9	N R Jenkins	2001
Most cons in match	8	J Bancroft	v France, 1910
Most pens in matches	93	N R Jenkins	1991 – 2001
Most pens in season	16	P H Thorburn	1986
	16	N R Jenkins	1999

Most pens in match	7	N R Jenkins	v Italy, 2000
Most drops in matches	8	J Davies	1985 – 1997
Most drops in season	5	N R Jenkins	2001
Most drops in match	3	N R Jenkins	v Scotland, 2001

Miscellaneous Records

Record	Holder	Detail
Longest Test Career	D Young	15 seasons, 1987 to 2001
Youngest Test Cap	N Biggs	18 yrs 49 days in 1888
Oldest Test Cap	T H Vile	38 yrs 152 days in 1921

Career Records of Wales International Players
(up to 20 October 2001)

PLAYER	Debut	Caps	T	C	P	D	Pts
Backs:							
A G Bateman	1990 v S	33	10	0	0	0	50
N Boobyer	1993 v Z	7	0	0	0	0	0
M.D.Cardey	2000 v S	1	0	0	0	0	0
G J Cooper	2001 v F	3	1	0	0	0	5
L B Davies	1996 v It	20	4	0	0	0	20
A P R Durston	2001 v J	2	1	0	0	0	5
G R Evans	1998 v SA	1	0	0	0	0	0
J Funnell	1998 v Z	2	0	0	0	0	0
I S Gibbs	1991 v E	53	10	0	0	0	50
B I Hayward	1998 v Z	2	3	0	0	0	15
G L Henson	2001 v J	2	0	0	0	0	0
R Howley	1996 v E	51	9	0	0	0	45
D R James	1996 v A	35	12	0	0	0	60
L Jarvis	1997 v R	1	0	1	0	0	2
N R Jenkins	1991 v E	84	11	126	231	10	1029
Paul John	1994 v Tg	10	1	0	0	0	5
M A Jones	2001 v E	3	1	0	0	0	5
S M Jones	1998 v SA	12	1	25	9	0	82
J Jones-Hughes	1999 v Arg	3	0	0	0	0	0
D S Llewellyn	1998 v SA	4	1	0	0	0	5
R H StJ B Moon	1993 v F	24	3	0	0	0	15
K A Morgan	1997 v US	12	4	0	0	0	20
D Peel	2001 v J	2	0	0	0	0	0
J Robinson	2001 v J	2	1	0	0	0	5
M F D Robinson	1999 v S	4	0	0	0	0	0
T Shanklin	2001 v J	1	2	0	0	0	10
R Smith	2000 v F	1	0	0	0	0	0
M Taylor	1994 v SA	30	8	0	0	0	40
A C Thomas	1996 v It	23	11	30	32	0	211
Gareth Thomas	1995 v J	53	25	0	0	0	125
D Williams	1998 v SA	1	0	0	0	0	0
G R Williams	2000 v I	9	1	0	0	0	5
S M Williams	2000 v F	10	10	0	0	0	50
Forwards:							
C T Anthony	1997 v US	11	1	0	0	0	5

N J Budgett	2000 v S	7	1	0	0	0	5
C L Charvis	1996 v A	39	7	0	0	0	35
B R Evans	1998 v SA	13	0	0	0	0	0
I M Gough	1998 v SA	14	1	0	0	0	5
J Griffiths	2000 v Sm	1	0	0	0	0	0
J M Humphreys	1995 v NZ	33	2	0	0	0	10
G R Jenkins	1991 v F	58	2	0	0	0	10
S C John	1995 v S	12	0	0	0	0	0
D L Jones	2000 v Sm	1	0	0	0	0	0
Steve Jones	2001 v J	1	0	0	0	0	0
A L P Lewis	1996 v It	27	0	0	0	0	0
G Lewis	1998 v SA	16	0	0	0	0	0
A Lloyd	2001 v J	1	1	0	0	0	5
R C McBryde	1994 v Fj	10	0	0	0	0	0
A P Moore	1995 v SA	19	0	0	0	0	0
S J Moore	1997 v C	3	0	0	0	0	0
D R Morris	1998 v Z	12	0	0	0	0	0
J C Quinnell	1995 v Fj	29	4	0	0	0	20
L S Quinnell	1993 v C	43	8	0	0	0	40
J Ringer	2001 v J	2	0	0	0	0	0
P J D Rogers	1999 v F	18	0	0	0	0	0
B D Sinkinson	1999 v F	16	1	0	0	0	5
C Stephens	1998 v E	2	0	0	0	0	0
Gavin Thomas	2001 v J	4	2	0	0	0	10
I D Thomas	2000 v Sm	7	0	0	0	0	0
N Thomas	1996 v SA	9	0	0	0	0	0
M J Voyle	1996 v A	22	0	0	0	0	0
B H Williams	1996 v F	17	4	0	0	0	20
M E Williams	1996 v Bb	18	0	0	0	0	0
C P Wyatt	1998 v Z	26	2	0	0	0	10
D Young	1987 v E	50	1	0	0	0	4

FRANCE TEST SEASON REVIEW 2000-01

Transition or Revolution?

Ian Borthwick

This was yet another year of doubt and self-questioning for French rugby as the *Tricolores*, their management and those who govern them in the FFR, limped from one identity crisis to another. With only four wins from eleven games, the results on paper could hardly be called positive for coach Bernard Laporte. But despite a number of mediocre performances, including three losses from the four internationals at Stade de France and conceding their heaviest score ever against England (48-19) in the six-try rout at Twickenham, the enigmatic French ended their season on a positive note.

At times, as in the games against Scotland, Ireland and Italy, they were lethargic and desperately short of inspiration. It was if they were so obsessed with the latest fad of 15-man defence that they had forgotten the very thing that made their game great: 15-man attack. On the rare occasions things clicked for France, however, they looked like world-beaters, and the lasting irony of the season is that their best performances were recorded against Southern Hemisphere opposition.

In the first two games of the season against Australia and New Zealand in Paris, the French looked ponderous and uninspired. The New Zealanders, desperate to avenge their shock defeat in the Rugby World Cup semi-final, shut them down with a display of controlled clinical rugby to win 39-26. But a week later, in the steaming cauldron of the Stade Vélodrome in Marseilles, the French once again rocked the rugby world. In a devastating display of speed, skill and pure passion, with early tries to Xavier Garbajosa and Olivier Magne and 27 points from Christophe Lamaison, they turned the tables on the All Blacks to win 42-33.

Unfortunately, the resulting wave of optimism was short-lived and, after the intoxicating high of Marseilles, France came crashing back down to earth in the Six Nations championship. Even the return of the revitalised former captain Raphaël Ibanez at hooker failed to light the spark as they struggled to beat Scotland 16-6 in a dour encounter in Paris before losing in Dublin for the first time since 1983.

Down 22-3 after 54 minutes, the French were cut to pieces by the brilliance of Brian O'Driscoll, Rob Henderson and Ronan O'Gara and although finishing with a more respectable score at 22-15, nothing could hide the difference in freshness and enthusiasm between the two teams. 'It is time for new blood,' announced Bernard Laporte who, although picking the young Biarritz centre Sébastien Bonetti, proceeded to call the evergreen

Jean-Luc Sadourny out of retirement for the game against Italy. Sadourny as it happens was one of the best players on the park, but despite winning 30-19, the *Tricolores* were largely unconvincing.

Scoring 15 points from three penalties and three conversions against Italy, Christophe Lamaison became the highest scorer in the history of French international rugby, his 369 points putting him two ahead of Thierry Lacroix's old mark of 367. The new record did him little good however, as Lamaison was dropped for the next game against Wales in favour of the nuggety fly-half from Montferrand, Gérald Merceron.

Graham Henry's Welshmen had won an historic victory in Paris in 1999, their first since 1975, and in 2001 they did it again, running out handsome winners by 43-35. Failing to take at least five try-scoring opportunities, the French were booed off the pitch by their own crowd, while FFR President Bernard Lapasset took no prisoners in his after-match comments. 'These players are mediocre, how can we like them?' he declared. ' Tonight French rugby has been humiliated, wounded and offended by their display.'

More than a defeat, this was to be a turning point for the season, setting off yet another crisis in the French Federation. A number of new players were brought into the squad in the build up to the final game against England, but in the end the changes were only cosmetic, with Stéphane Glas and Xavier Garbajosa returning in the centres, Fabien Pelous moving to No 8 and Christophe Milhères and Lionel Nallet picked at flanker and lock respectively. Predictably enough, against the polished English side the French lacked cohesion and despite only trailing by one point (20-19) after 60 minutes of play, the final quarter was all one-way traffic with England running in 28 unanswered points.

It was hardly surprising then that France's end of year tour to South Africa and New Zealand was widely expected to be a disaster, especially after Stade Français had failed to salvage any French pride on the club scene by losing to Leicester in the European Cup final. Once again, however, the French rose to the occasion, trouncing the Springboks 32-23 in the first Test and maintaining their astonishing unbeaten record at Ellis Park. The 20 year-old Nicolas Jeanjean, a new cap at full-back, played with maturity beyond his years, Patrick Tabacco in his first Test at No 8 looked world-class as did prop Jean-Jacques Crenca, while Merceron came of age as an international fly-half.

Out-muscled in Durban a week later, the French lost the vicious second Test 20-15. But they achieved a major victory over themselves by maintaining their discipline in the face of continuous provocation from the Springboks.

Finally, what started as a year of transition for French rugby ended up looking more like a full-blooded revolution and, of the 15 who started the first international of the season against Australia on November 4th, only three (Christian Califano, Olivier Brouzet and the new captain Fabien Galthié) were left when France took the field against the All Blacks in Wellington on June 30th. Gone were seasoned internationals like Sadourny,

Lamaison, Richard Dourthe, Franck Comba, Christophe Juillet, Abdelatif Benazzi, Philippe Bernat-Salles and Philippe Carbonneau as coach Laporte took the bold option of blooding some of France's new generation of multi-talented young players.

Their bodies mashed by the full-blooded Springbok attack and the horrendous itinerary which saw them leave Durban on Sunday and fly to Wellington via Johannesburg, Mauritius, Singapore and Auckland, the French were overwhelmed 37-12 by the power of the All Blacks. Even so, the final Test of the season was still cause for optimism despite the loss.

Once again the French held their discipline, they remained competitive in all sectors for sixty minutes of the match, and a number of new players proved their ability to make the vital step up to the top international level. Thanks to the injection of new talents like Tabacco, Crenca and Jeanjean, flankers Sébastien Chabal and Jean Bouilhou, No 8 Elvis Vermeulen, full-back Pepito Elhorga, centre Yannick Jauzion and prop Olivier Milloud, France's future looks bright.

France's Test Record in 2000-2001:
Played 11, won 4, lost 7.

Opponents	Date	Venue	Result
New Zealand	30th June 2001	A	Lost 12-37
South Africa	23rd June 2001	A	Lost 15-20
South Africa	16th June 2001	A	Won 32-23
England	7th April 2001	A	Lost 19-48
Wales	17th March 2001	H	Lost 35-43
Italy	3rd March 2001	A	Won 30-19
Ireland	17th February 2001	A	Lost 15-22
Scotland	4th February 2001	H	Won 16-6
New Zealand	18th November 2000	H	Won 42-33
New Zealand	11th November 2000	H	Lost 26-39
Australia	4th November 2000	H	Lost 13-18

FRENCH INTERNATIONAL PLAYERS
(up to 20 October 2001)

Note: Years given for International Championship matches are for second half of season, eg 1972 refers to season 1971-72. Years for all other matches refer to the actual year of the match. When a series has taken place, or more than one match has been played against a country in the same year, figures have been used to denote the particular matches in which players have featured. Thus 1967 *SA* 2,4 indicates that a player appeared in the second and fourth Tests of the 1967 series against South Africa. This list includes only those players who have appeared in FFR International Matches '*donnant droit au titre d'international*'.

Abadie, A (Pau) 1964 *I*
Abadie, A (Graulhet) 1965 *R*, 1967 *SA* 1,3,4, *NZ*, 1968 *S, I*
Abadie, L (Tarbes) 1963 *R*
Accoceberry, G (Bègles) 1994 *NZ* 1,2, *C* 2, 1995 *W, E, S, I, R* 1, [*Iv, S*], *It*, 1996 *I, W* 1, *R, Arg* 1, *W* 2(R), *SA* 2, 1997 *S, It* 1
Aguerre, R (Biarritz O) 1979 *S*
Aguilar, D (Pau) 1937 *G*
Aguirre, J-M (Bagnères) 1971 *A* 2, 1972 *S*, 1973 *W, I, J, R*, 1974 *I, W, Arg* 2, *R, SA* 1, 1976 *W* (R), *E, US, A* 2, *R*, 1977 *W, E, S, I, Arg* 1,2, *NZ* 1,2, *R*, 1978 *E, S, I, W, R*, 1979 *I, W, E, S, NZ* 1,2, *R*, 1980 *W, I*
Ainciart, E (Bayonne) 1933 *G*, 1934 *G*, 1935 *G*, 1937 *G, It*, 1938 *G* 1
Albaladejo, P (Dax) 1954 *E, It*, 1960 *W, I, It, R*, 1961 *S, SA, E, W, I, NZ* 1,2, *A*, 1962 *S, E, W, I*, 1963 *S, I, E, W, It*, 1964 *S, NZ, W, It, I, SA, Fj*
Alvarez, A-J (Tyrosse) 1945 *B*2, 1946 *B, I, K, W*, 1947 *S, I, W, E*, 1948 *I, A, S, W, E*, 1949 *I, E, W*, 1951 *S, E, W*
Amand, H (SF) 1906 *NZ*
Ambert, A (Toulouse) 1930 *S, I, F, G, W*
Amestoy, J-B (Mont-de-Marsan) 1964 *NZ, E*
André, G (RCF) 1913 *SA, E, W, I*, 1914 *I, W, E*
Andrieu, M (Nîmes) 1986 *Arg* 2, *NZ* 1, *R* 2, *NZ* 2, 1987 [*R, Z*], *R*, 1988 *E, S, I, W, Arg* 1,2,3,4, *R*, 1989 *I, W, E, S, NZ* 2, *B, A* 2, 1990 *W, E, I* (R)
Anduran, J (SCUF) 1910 *W*
Aqua, J-L (Toulon) 1999 *R, Tg, NZ* 1(R)
Araou, R (Narbonne) 1924 *R*
Arcalis, R (Brive) 1950 *S, I*, 1951 *I, E, W*
Arino, M (Agen) 1962 *R*
Aristouy, P (Pau) 1948 *S*, 1949 *Arg* 2, 1950 *S, I, E, W*
Arlettaz, P (Perpignan) 1995 *R* 2
Armary, L (Lourdes) 1987 [*R*], *R*, 1988 *S, I, W, Arg* 3,4, *R*, 1989 *W, S, A* 1,2, 1990 *W, E, S, I, A* 1,2,3, *NZ* 1, 1991 *W* 2, 1992 *S, I, R, Arg* 1,2, *SA* 1,2, *Arg*, 1993 *E, S, I, W, SA* 1,2, *R* 2, *A* 1,2, 1994 *I, W, NZ* 1(t),2(t), 1995 *I, R* 1 [*Tg, I, SA*]
Arnal, J-M (RCF) 1914 *I, W*
Arnaudet, M (Lourdes) 1964 *I*, 1967 *It, W*
Arotca, R (Bayonne) 1938 *R*
Arrieta, J (SF) 1953 *F, W*
Arthapignet, P (see Harislur-Arthapignet)
Artiguste, E (Castres) 1999 *WS*
Astre, R (Béziers) 1971 *R*, 1972 *I* 1, 1973 *E* (R), 1975 *E, S, I, SA* 1,2, *Arg* 2, 1976 *A* 2, *R*
Aucagne, D (Pau) 1997 *W* (R), *S, It* 1, *R* 1(R), *A* 1, *R* 2(R), *SA* 2(R), 1998 *S* (R), *W* (R), *Arg* 2(R), *Fj* (R), *Arg* 3, *A*, 1999 *W* 1(R), *S* (R)
Audebert, A (Montferrand) 2000 *R*
Aué, J-M (Castres) 1998 *W* (R)
Augé, J (Dax) 1929 *S, W*
Augras-Fabre, L (Agen) 1931 *I, S, W*
Auradou, D (SF) 1999 *E* (R), *S* (R), *WS* (R), *Tg, NZ* 1, *W* 2(R), [*Arg* (R)], 2000 *A* (R), *NZ* 1,2, 2001 *S, I, It, W, E* (R), *SA* 1,2, *NZ* (R)
Averous, J-L (La Voulte) 1975 *S, I, SA* 1,2, 1976 *I, W, E, US, A* 1,2, *R*, 1977 *W, E, S, I, Arg* 1, *R*, 1978 *E, S, I*, 1979 *NZ* 1,2, 1980 *E, S*, 1981 *A* 2
Azam, O (Montferrand, Gloucester) 1995 *R* 2, *Arg* (R), 2000 *A* (R), *NZ* 2(R), 2001 *SA* 2(R), *NZ*
Azarete, J-L (Dax, St Jean-de-Luz) 1969 *W, R*, 1970 *S, I, W, R*, 1971 *S, I, A* 1, 1972 *E, W, I* 2, *A* 1, *R*, 1973 *NZ, W, I, R*, 1974 *I, R, SA* 1,2, 1975 *W*

Bacqué, N (Pau) 1997 *R* 2
Bader, E (Primevères) 1926 *M*, 1927 *I, S*
Badin, C (Chalon) 1973 *W, I*, 1975 *Arg* 1
Baillette, M (Perpignan) 1925 *I, NZ, S*, 1926 *W, M*, 1927 *I, W, G* 2, 1929 *G*, 1930 *S, I, E, G*, 1931 *I, S, E*, 1932 *G*
Baladie, G (Agen) 1945 *B* 1,2, *W*, 1946 *B, I, K*

Ballarin, J (Tarbes) 1924 *E*, 1925 *NZ, S*
Baquey, J (Toulouse) 1921 *I*
Barbazanges, A (Roanne) 1932 *G*, 1933 *G*
Barrau, M (Beaumont, Toulouse) 1971 *S, E, W*, 1972 *E, W, A* 1,2, 1973 *S, NZ, E, I, J, R*, 1974 *I, S*
Barrère, P (Toulon) 1929 *G*, 1931 *W*
Barrière, R (Béziers) 1960 *R*
Barthe, E (SBUC) 1925 *W, E*
Barthe, J (Lourdes) 1954 *Arg* 1,2, 1955 *S*, 1956 *I, W, It, E, Cz*, 1957 *S, I, E, W, R* 1,2, 1958 *S, E, A, W, It, I, SA* 1,2, 1959 *S, E, It, W*
Basauri, R (Albi) 1954 *Arg* 1
Bascou, P (Bayonne) 1914 *E*
Basquet, G (Agen) 1945 *W*, 1946 *B, I, K, W*, 1947 *S, I, W, E*, 1948 *I, A, S, W, E*, 1949 *S, I, E, W, Arg* 1, 1950 *S, I, E, W*, 1951 *S, I, E, W*, 1952 *S, I, SA, W, E, It*
Bastiat, J-P (Dax) 1969 *R*, 1970 *S, I, W*, 1971 *S, I, SA* 2, 1972 *S, A* 1, 1973 *E*, 1974 *Arg* 1,2, *SA* 2, 1975 *W, Arg* 1,2, *R*, 1976 *S, I, W, E, A* 1,2, *R*, 1977 *W, E, S, I*, 1978 *E, S, I, W*
Baudry, N (Montferrand) 1949 *S, I, W, Arg* 1,2
Baulon, R (Vienne, Bayonne) 1954 *S, NZ, W, E, It*, 1955 *I, E, W, It*, 1956 *S, I, W, It, E, Cz*, 1957 *S, I, It*
Baux, J-P (Lannemezan) 1968 *NZ* 1,2, *SA* 1,2
Bavozet, J (Lyon) 1911 *S, E, W*
Bayard, J (Toulouse) 1923 *S, W, E*, 1924 *W, R, US*
Bayardon, J (Chalon) 1964 *S, NZ, E*
Beaurin-Gressier, C (SF) 1907 *E*, 1908 *E*
Bégu, J (Dax) 1982 *Arg* 2(R), 1984 *E, S*
Béguerie, C (Agen) 1979 *NZ* 1
Beguet, L (RCF) 1922 *I*, 1923 *S, W, E, I*, 1924 *S, I, E, R, US*
Behoteguy, A (Bayonne, Cognac) 1923 *E*, 1924 *S, I, E, W, R, US*, 1926 *E, I, W, G* 2, 1928 *A, I, E, G, W*, 1929 *S, W, E*
Behoteguy, H (RCF, Cognac) 1923 *W*, 1928 *A, I, E, G, W*
Belascain, C (Bayonne) 1977 *R*, 1978 *E, S, I, W, R*, 1979 *I, W, E, S*, 1982 *W, E, S, I*, 1983 *E, S, I, W*
Belletante, G (Nantes) 1951 *I, E, W*
Belot, F (Toulouse) 2000 *I* (R)
Benazzi, A (Agen) 1990 *A* 1,2,3, *NZ* 1,2, 1991 *E, US* 1(R),2, [*R, Fj, C*], 1992 *SA* 1(R),2, *Arg*, 1993 *E, S, I, W, A* 1,2, 1994 *I, W, E, S, C* 1, *NZ* 1,2, *C* 2, 1995 *W, E, S, I*, [*Tg, Iv, S, I, SA, E*], *NZ* 1,2, 1996 *E, S, I, W* 1, *Arg* 1,2, *W* 2, *SA* 1,2, 1997 *I, W, E, S, R* 1, *A* 1,2, *It* 2, *R* 2(R), *Arg, SA* 1,2, 1999 *R, WS, W* 2, [*C, Nm* (R), *Fj, Arg, NZ* 2, *A*], 2000 *W, E, I, It* (R), *R*, 2001 *S* (R), *I* (t&R), *E*
Bénésis, R (Narbonne) 1969 *W, R*, 1970 *S, I, W, E, R*, 1971 *S, I, E, W, A* 2, *R*, 1972 *S, I* 1, *E, W, I* 2, *A* 1, *R*, 1973 *NZ, E, W, I, J, R*, 1974 *I, W, E, S*
Benetière, J (Roanne) 1954 *It, Arg* 1
Benetton, P (Agen) 1989 *B*, 1990 *NZ* 2, 1991 *US* 2, 1992 *Arg* 1,2(R), *SA* 1(R),2, *Arg*, 1993 *E, S, I, W, SA* 1,2, *R* 2, *A* 1,2, 1994 *I, W, E, S, C* 1, *NZ* 1,2, 1995 *W, E, S, I*, [*Tg, Iv* (R), *S*], *It, R* 2(R), *Arg, NZ* 1,2, 1996 *Arg* 1,2, *W* 2, *SA* 1,2, 1997 *I, It* 1,2(R), *R* 2, *Arg, SA* 1,2 1998 *E, S* (R), *I* (R), *W* (R), *Arg* 1(R),2(R), *Fj* (R), 1999 *I, W* 1, *S* (R)
Benezech, L (RCF) 1994 *E, S, C* 1, *NZ* 1,2, *C* 2, 1995 *W, E*, [*Iv, S, E*], *R* 2, *Arg, NZ* 1,2
Berbizier, P (Lourdes, Agen) 1981 *S, I, W, E, NZ* 1,2, 1982 *I, R*, 1983 *S, I*, 1984 *NZ* 1,2, 1985 *Arg* 1,2, 1986 *S, I, W, E, R* 1, *Arg* 1, *A, NZ* 1, *R* 2, *NZ* 2,3, 1987 *W, E, S, I*, [*S, R, Fj, A, NZ*], *R*, 1988 *E, S, I, W, Arg* 1,2, 1989 *I, W, E, S, NZ* 1,2, *B, A* 1, 1990 *W, E*, 1991 *S, I, W* 1, *E*
Berejnoi, J-C (Tulle) 1963 *R*, 1964 *S, W, It, I, SA, Fj, R*, 1965 *S, I, E, W, It, R*, 1966 *S, I, E, W, It, R*, 1967 *S, A, E, It, W, I, R*
Berges, B (Toulouse) 1926 *I*
Berges-Cau, R (Lourdes) 1976 *E* (R)
Bergese, F (Bayonne) 1936 *G* 2, 1937 *G, It*, 1938 *G* 1, *R, G* 2
Bergougnan, Y (Toulouse) 1945 *B* 1, *W*, 1946 *B, I, K, W*, 1947 *S, I, W, E*, 1948 *S, W, E*, 1949 *S, E, Arg* 1,2
Bernard, R (Bergerac) 1951 *S, I, E, W*

225

Bernat-Salles, P (Pau, Bègles-Bordeaux, Biarritz) 1992 *Arg*, 1993 *R* 1, *SA* 1,2, *R* 2, *A* 1,2, 1994 *I*, 1995 *E*, *S*, 1996 *E* (R), 1997 *R* 1, *A* 1,2, 1998 *E*, *S*, *I*, *W*, *Arg* 1,2, *Fj*, *Arg* 3(R), *A* 1999 *I*, *W* 1, *R*, *Tg*, [*Nm*, *Fj*, *Arg*, *NZ* 2, *A*], 2000 *I*, *It*, *NZ* 1(R),2, 2001 *S*, *I*, *It*, *W*, *E*
Bernon, J (Lourdes) 1922 *I*, 1923 *S*
Bérot, J-L (Toulouse) 1968 *NZ* 3, *A*, 1969 *S*, *I*, 1970 *E*, *R*, 1971 *S*, *I*, *E*, *W*, *SA* 1,2, *A* 1,2, *R*, 1972 *S*, *I* 1, *E*, *W*, *A* 1, 1974 *I*
Bérot, P (Agen) 1986 *R* 2, *NZ* 2,3, 1987 *W*, *E*, *S*, *I*, *R*, 1988 *E*, *S*, *I*, *Arg* 1,2,3,4, *R*, 1989 *S*, *NZ* 1,2
Bertrand, P (Bourg) 1951 *I*, *E*, *W*, 1953 *S*, *I*, *E*, *W*, *It*
Bertranne, R (Bagnères) 1971 *E*, *W*, *SA* 2, *A* 1,2, 1972 *S*, *I* 1, 1973 *NZ*, *E*, *J*, *R*, 1974 *I*, *W*, *E*, *S*, *Arg* 1,2, *R*, *SA* 1,2, 1975 *W*, *E*, *S*, *I*, *SA* 1,2, *Arg* 1,2, *R*, 1976 *S*, *I*, *W*, *E*, *US*, *A* 1,2, *R*, 1977 *W*, *E*, *S*, *I*, *Arg* 1,2, *NZ* 1,2, *R*, 1978 *E*, *S*, *I*, *W*, *R*, 1979 *I*, *W*, *E*, *S*, *R*, 1980 *W*, *E*, *S*, *I*, *SA*, *R*, 1981 *S*, *I*, *W*, *E*, *R*, *NZ* 1,2
Berty, D (Toulouse) 1990 *NZ* 2, 1992 *R* (R), 1993 *R* 2, 1995 *NZ* 1(R), 1996 *W* 2(R), *SA* 1
Besset, E (Grenoble) 1924 *S*
Besset, L (SCUF) 1914 *W*, *E*
Besson, M (CASG) 1924 *I*, 1925 *I*, *E*, 1926 *S*, *W*, 1927 *I*
Besson, P (Brive) 1963 *S*, *I*, *E*, 1965 *R*, 1968 *SA* 1
Betsen, S (Biarritz) 1997 *It* 1(R), 2000 *W* (R), *E* (R), *A* (R), *NZ* 1(R),2(R), 2001 *S* (R), *I* (R), *It* (R), *W* (R)
Bianchi, J (Toulon) 1986 *Arg* 1
Bichindaritz, J (Biarritz O) 1954 *It*, *Arg* 1,2
Bidart, L (La Rochelle) 1953 *W*
Biemouret, P (Agen) 1969 *E*, *W*, 1970 *I*, *W*, *E*, 1971 *W*, *SA* 1,2, *A* 1, 1972 *E*, *W*, *I* 2, *A* 2, *R*, 1973 *S*, *NZ*, *E*, *W*, *I*
Biénès, R (Cognac) 1950 *S*, *I*, *E*, *W*, 1951 *S*, *I*, *E*, *W*, 1952 *S*, *I*, *SA*, *W*, *E*, *It*, 1953 *S*, *I*, *E*, 1954 *S*, *I*, *NZ*, *W*, *E*, *Arg* 1,2, 1956 *S*, *I*, *W*, *It*, *E*
Bigot, C (Quillan) 1930 *S*, *E*, 1931 *I*, *S*
Bilbao, L (St Jean-de-Luz) 1978 *I*, 1979 *I*
Billac, E (Bayonne) 1920 *S*, *E*, *W*, *I*, *US*, 1921 *S*, *W*, 1922 *W*, 1923 *E*
Billière, M (Toulouse) 1968 *NZ* 3
Bioussa, A (Toulouse) 1924 *W*, *US*, 1925 *I*, *NZ*, *S*, *E*, 1926 *S*, *I*, *E*, 1928 *E*, *G*, *W*, 1929 *I*, *S*, *W*, *E*, 1930 *S*, *I*, *E*, *G*, *W*
Bioussa, C (Toulouse) 1913 *W*, *I*, 1914 *I*
Biraben, M (Dax) 1920 *W*, *I*, *US*, 1921 *S*, *W*, *E*, *I*, 1922 *S*, *E*, *I*, *W*, *E*, 1949 *S*, *I*, *E*, *W*, *Arg* 1,2
Blain, A (Carcassonne) 1934 *G*
Blanco, S (Biarritz O) 1980 *SA*, *R*, 1981 *S*, *W*, *E*, *A* 1,2, *R*, *NZ* 1,2, 1982 *W*, *E*, *S*, *I*, *R*, *Arg* 1,2, 1983 *E*, *S*, *I*, *W*, 1984 *I*, *W*, *E*, *S*, *NZ* 1,2, *R*, 1985 *E*, *S*, *I*, *W*, *Arg* 1,2, 1986 *S*, *I*, *W*, *E*, *R* 1, *Arg* 2, *A*, *NZ* 1, *R* 2, *NZ* 2,3, 1987 *W*, *E*, *S*, *I*, [*S*, *R*, *Fj*, *A*, *NZ*], 1988 *E*, *S*, *I*, *W*, *Arg* 1,2,3,4, *R*, 1989 *I*, *W*, *E*, *S*, *NZ* 1,2, *B*, *A* 1, 1990 *E*, *W*, *I*, *R*, *A* 1,2,3, *NZ* 1,2, 1991 *S*, *I*, *W* 1, *R*, *US* 1,2, *W* 2, [*R*, *Fj*, *C*, *E*]
Blond, J (SF) 1935 *G*, 1936 *G* 2, 1937 *G*, 1938 *G* 1, *R*, *G* 2
Blond, X (RCF) 1990 *A* 3, 1991 *S*, *I*, *W* 1, *E*, 1994 *NZ* 2(R)
Boffelli, V (Aurillac) 1971 *A* 2, *R*, 1972 *S*, *I* 1, 1973 *J*, *R*, 1974 *I*, *W*, *E*, *S*, *Arg* 1,2, *R*, *SA* 1,2, 1975 *W*, *S*, *I*
Bonal, J-M (Toulouse) 1968 *E*, *W*, *Cz*, *NZ* 2,3, *SA* 1,2, *R*, 1969 *S*, *I*, *E*, *R*, 1970 *W*, *E*
Bonamy, R (SB) 1928 *A*, *I*
Bondouy, P (Narbonne, Toulouse) 1997 *S* (R), *It* 1, *A* 2(R), *R* 2, 2000 *R* (R)
Bonetti, S (Biarritz) 2001 *It*, *W*, *NZ* (R)
Boniface, A (Mont-de-Marsan) 1954 *I*, *NZ*, *W*, *E*, *It*, *Arg* 1,2, 1955 *S*, *I*, 1956 *S*, *I*, *W*, *It*, *Cz*, 1957 *S*, *I*, *W*, *R* 2, 1958 *S*, *E*, 1959 *E*, 1961 *NZ* 1,3, *A*, *R*, 1962 *E*, *W*, *I*, *It*, *R*, 1963 *S*, *I*, *E*, *W*, *It*, *R*, 1964 *S*, *NZ*, *E*, *W*, *It*, 1965 *W*, *It*, *R*, 1966 *S*, *I*, *E*, *W*
Boniface, G (Mont-de-Marsan) 1960 *W*, *I*, *It*, *R*, *Arg* 1,2,3, 1961 *S*, *SA*, *E*, *W*, *It*, *I*, *NZ* 1,2,3, *R*, 1962 *R*, 1963 *S*, *I*, *E*, *W*, *It*, *R*, 1964 *S*, 1965 *S*, *I*, *E*, *W*, *It*, 1966 *S*, *I*, *E*, *W*
Bonnes, E (Narbonne) 1924 *W*, *R*, *US*
Bonneval, E (Toulouse) 1984 *NZ* 2(R), 1985 *W*, *Arg* 1, 1986 *W*, *E*, *R* 1, *Arg* 1,2, *A*, *R* 2, *NZ* 2,3, 1987 *W*, *E*, *S*, *I*, [*Z*], 1988 *E*
Bonnus, F (Toulon) 1950 *S*, *I*, *E*, *W*
Bonnus, M (Toulon) 1937 *It*, 1938 *G* 1, *R*, *G* 2, 1940 *B*
Bontemps, D (La Rochelle) 1968 *SA* 2
Borchard, G (RCF) 1908 *E*, 1909 *E*, *W*, *I*, 1911 *I*
Borde, F (RCF) 1920 *I*, *US*, 1921 *S*, *W*, *E*, 1922 *S*, *W*, 1923 *S*, *I*, 1924 *I*, 1925 *I*, 1926 *E*
Bordenave, L (Toulon) 1948 *A*, *S*, *W*, *E*, 1949 *S*
Bory, D (Montferrand) 2000 *I*, *It*, *A*, *NZ* 1, 2001 *S*, *I*, *SA* 1,2
Boubée, J (Tarbes) 1921 *S*, *E*, *I*, 1922 *E*, *W*, 1923 *E*, *I*, 1925 *NZ*, *S*
Boudreaux, R (SCUF) 1910 *W*, *S*
Bouet, D (Dax) 1989 *NZ* 1,2, *B*, *A* 2, 1990 *A* 3
Bouguyon, G (Grenoble) 1961 *SA*, *E*, *W*, *It*, *I*, *NZ* 1,2,3, *A*

Bouic, G (Agen) 1996 *SA* 1
Bouilhou, J (Toulouse) 2001 *NZ*
Boujet, C (Grenoble) 1968 *NZ* 2, *A* (R), *SA* 1
Bouquet, J (Bourgoin, Vienne) 1954 *S*, 1955 *E*, 1956 *S*, *I*, *W*, *It*, *E*, *Cz*, 1957 *S*, *E*, *W*, *R* 2, 1958 *S*, *E*, 1959 *S*, *It*, *W*, *I*, 1960 *S*, *E*, *W*, *I*, *R*, 1961 *S*, *SA*, *E*, *W*, *It*, *I*, *R*, 1962 *S*, *E*, *W*, *I*
Bourdeu, J R (Lourdes) 1952 *S*, *I*, *SA*, *W*, *E*, *It*, 1953 *S*, *I*, *E*
Bourgarel, R (Toulouse) 1969 *R*, 1970 *S*, *I*, *E*, *R*, 1971 *W*, *SA* 1,2, 1973 *S*
Bourguignon, G (Narbonne) 1988 *Arg* 3, 1989 *I*, *E*, *B*, *A* 1, 1990 *R*
Bousquet, A (Béziers) 1921 *E*, *I*, 1924 *R*
Bousquet, R (Albi) 1926 *M*, 1927 *I*, *S*, *W*, *E*, *G* 1, 1929 *W*, *E*, 1930 *W*
Boyau, M (SBUC) 1912 *I*, *S*, *W*, *E*, 1913 *W*, *I*
Boyer, P (Toulon) 1935 *G*
Branca, G (SF) 1928 *S*, 1929 *I*, *S*
Branlat, A (RCF) 1906 *NZ*, *E*, 1908 *W*
Brejassou, R (Tarbes) 1952 *S*, *I*, *SA*, *W*, *E*, 1953 *W*, *E*, 1954 *S*, *I*, *NZ*, 1955 *S*, *I*, *E*, *W*, *It*
Brethes, R (St Sever) 1960 *Arg* 2
Bringeon, A (Biarritz O) 1925 *W*
Brouzet, O (Grenoble, Bègles, Northampton) 1994 *S*, *NZ* 2(R), 1995 *E*, *S*, *I*, *R* 1, [*Tg*, *Iv*, *E* (t)], *It*, *Arg* (R), 1996 *W* 1(R), 1997 *R* 1, *A* 1,2, *It* 2, *Arg*, *SA* 1,2, 1998 *E*, *S*, *I*, *W*, *Arg* 1,2, *Fj*, *Arg* 3, *A*, 1999 *I*, *W* 1, *E*, *S*, *R*, [*C* (R), *Nm*, *Fj* (R), *Arg*, *NZ* 2(R), *A* (R)], 2000 *W*, *E*, *S*, *I*, *It*, *A*, *NZ* 1(R),2(R), 2001 *SA* 1,2, *NZ*
Brun, G (Vienne) 1950 *E*, *W*, 1951 *S*, *E*, *W*, 1952 *S*, *I*, *SA*, *W*, *E*, *It*, 1953 *E*, *W*, *It*
Bruneau, M (SBUC) 1910 *W*, *E*, 1913 *SA*, *E*
Brunet, Y (Perpignan) 1975 *SA* 1, 1977 *Arg* 1
Brusque, N (Pau) 1997 *R* 2(R)
Buchet, E (Nice) 1980 *R*, 1982 *E*, *R* (R), *Arg* 1,2
Buisson, H (see Empereur-Buisson)
Buonomo, Y (Béziers) 1971 *A* 2, *R*, 1972 *I* 1
Burgun, M (RCF) 1909 *I*, 1910 *W*, *S*, *I*, 1911 *S*, *E*, 1912 *I*, *S*, 1913 *S*, *E*, 1914 *E*
Bustaffa, D (Carcassonne) 1977 *Arg* 1,2, *NZ* 1,2, 1978 *W*, *R*, 1980 *W*, *E*, *S*, *SA*, *R*
Buzy, C-E (Lourdes) 1946 *K*, *W*, 1947 *S*, *I*, *W*, *E*, 1948 *I*, *A*, *S*, *W*, *E*, 1949 *S*, *I*, *E*, *W*, *Arg* 1,2

Cabanier, J-M (Montauban) 1963 *R*, 1964 *S*, *Fj*, 1965 *S*, *I*, *W*, *It*, *R*, 1966 *S*, *I*, *E*, *W*, *It*, *R*, 1967 *S*, *A*, *E*, *It*, *W*, *I*, *SA* 1,3, *NZ*, *R*, 1968 *S*, *I*
Cabannes, L (RCF, Harlequins) 1990 *NZ* 2(R), 1991 *S*, *I*, *W* 1, *US* 2, *W* 2, [*R*, *Fj*, *C*, *E*], 1992 *W*, *E*, *S*, *I*, *R*, *Arg* 2, *SA* 1,2, 1993 *E*, *S*, *I*, *W*, *A* 1,2, 1994 *E*, *S*, *C* 1, *NZ* 1,2, 1995 *W*, *E*, *S*, *R* 1, [*Tg* (R), *Iv*, *S*, *I*, *SA*, *E*], 1996 *E*, *S*, *I*, *W* 1, 1997 *It* 2, *Arg*, *SA* 1,2
Cabrol, H (Béziers) 1972 *A* 1(R),2, 1973 *J*, 1974 *SA* 2
Cadenat, J (SCUF) 1910 *S*, *E*, 1911 *W*, *I*, 1912 *W*, *E*, 1913 *I*
Cadieu, J-M (Toulouse) 1991 *R*, *US* 1, [*R*, *Fj*, *C*, *E*], 1992 *W*, *I*, *R*, *Arg* 1,2, *SA* 1
Cahuc, F (St Girons) 1922 *S*
Califano, C (Toulouse) 1994 *NZ* 1,2, *C* 2, 1995 *W*, *E*, *S*, *I*, [*Iv*, *S*, *I*, *SA*, *E*], *It*, *Arg*, *NZ* 1,2, 1996 *E*, *S*, *I*, *W* 1, *R*, *Arg* 1,2, *SA* 1,2, 1997 *I*, *W*, *E*, *A* 1,2, *It* 2, *R* 2(R), *Arg*, *SA* 1,2, 1998 *E*, *S*, *I*, *W*, 1999 *I*, *W* 1, *E* (R), *S*, *WS*, *Tg* (R), *NZ* 1, *W* 2, [*C*, *Nm*, *Fj*], 2000 *W*, *E*, *S*, *I*, *It*, *R*, *A*, *NZ* 1,2(R), 2001 *S* (R), *I* (R), *It*, *W*, *SA* 1(R),2(R), *NZ*
Cals, R (RCF) 1938 *G* 1
Calvo, G (Lourdes) 1961 *NZ* 1,3
Camberabero, D (La Voulte, Béziers) 1982 *R*, *Arg* 1,2, 1983 *E*, *W*, 1987 [*R* (R), *Z*, *Fj* (R), *A*, *NZ*], 1988 *I*, 1989 *B*, *A* 1, 1990 *W*, *S*, *I*, *R*, *A* 1,2,3, *NZ* 1,2, 1991 *S*, *I*, *W* 1, *E*, *R*, *US* 1,2, *W* 2, [*R*, *Fj*, *C*], 1993 *E*, *S*, *I*
Camberabero, G (La Voulte) 1961 *NZ* 3, 1962 *R*, 1964 *R*, 1967 *A*, *E*, *It*, *W*, *I*, *SA* 1,3,4, 1968 *S*, *E*, *W*
Camberabero, L (La Voulte) 1964 *W*, 1965 *S*, *I*, 1966 *E*, *W*, 1967 *A*, *E*, *It*, *W*, *I*, 1968 *S*, *E*, *W*
Cambré, T (Oloron) 1920 *E*, *W*, *I*, *US*
Camel, A (Toulouse) 1928 *S*, *A*, *I*, *E*, *G*, *W*, 1929 *W*, *E*, *G*, 1930 *S*, *I*, *E*, *G*, *W*, 1935 *G*
Camel, M (Toulouse) 1929 *S*, *W*, *E*
Camicas, F (Tarbes) 1927 *G* 2, 1928 *S*, *I*, *E*, *G*, *W*, 1929 *I*, *S*, *W*, *E*
Camo, E (Villeneuve) 1931 *I*, *S*, *W*, *E*, *G*, 1932 *G*
Campaes, A (Lourdes) 1965 *W*, 1967 *NZ*, 1968 *S*, *I*, *E*, *W*, *Cz*, *NZ* 1,2, *A*, 1969 *S*, *W*, 1972 *R*, 1973 *NZ*
Campan, O (Agen) 1993 *SA* 1(R),2(R), *R* 2(R), 1996 *I*, *W* 1, *R*

Cantoni, J (Béziers) 1970 *W, R*, 1971 *S, I, E, W, SA* 1,2, *A* 1, *R*, 1972 *S, I* 1, 1973 *S, NZ, W, I*, 1975 *W* (R)
Capdouze, J (Pau) 1964 *SA, Fj, R*, 1965 *S, I, E*
Capendeguy, J-M (Bègles) 1967 *NZ, R*
Capitani, P (Toulon) 1954 *Arg* 1,2
Capmau, J-L (Toulouse) 1914 *E*
Carabignac, G (Agen) 1951 *S, I*, 1952 *SA, W, E*, 1953 *S, I*
Carbonne, J (Perpignan) 1927 *W*
Carbonneau, P (Toulouse, Brive, Pau) 1995 *R* 2, *Arg, NZ* 1,2, 1996 *E, S, R* (R), *Arg* 2, *W* 2, *SA* 1, 1997 *I* (R), *W, E, S* (R), *R* 1(R), *A* 1,2, 1998 *E, S, I, W, Arg* 1,2, *Fj, Arg* 3, *A*, 1999 *I, W* 1, *E, S*, 2000 *NZ* 2(R), 2001 *I*
Carminati, A (Béziers, Brive) 1986 *R* 2, *NZ* 2, 1987 [*R, Z*], 1988 *I, W, Arg* 1,2, 1989 *I, W, S, NZ* 1(R),2, *A* 2, 1990 *S*, 1995 *It, R* 2, *Arg, NZ* 1,2
Caron, L (Lyon O, Castres) 1947 *E*, 1948 *I, A, W, E*, 1949 *S, I, E, W, Arg* 1
Carpentier, M (Lourdes) 1980 *E, SA, R*, 1981 *S, I, A* 1, 1982 *E, S*
Carrère, C (Toulon) 1966 *R*, 1967 *S, A, E, W, I, SA* 1,3,4, *NZ, R*, 1968 *S, I, E, W, Cz, NZ* 3, *A, R*, 1969 *S, I*, 1970 *S, I, W, E*, 1971 *E, W*
Carrère, J (Vichy, Toulon) 1956 *S*, 1957 *E, W, R* 2, 1958 *S, SA* 1,2, 1959 *I*
Carrère, R (Mont-de-Marsan) 1953 *E, It*
Casadei, D (Brive) 1997 *S, R* 1, *SA* 2(R)
Casaux, L (Tarbes) 1959 *I, It*, 1962 *S*
Cassagne, P (Pau) 1957 *It*
Cassayet-Armagnac, A (Tarbes, Narbonne) 1920 *S, E, W, US*, 1921 *W, E, I*, 1922 *S, E, W*, 1923 *S, W, E, I*, 1924 *S, E, W, R, US*, 1925 *I, NZ, S, W*, 1926 *S, I, E, W, M*, 1927 *I, S, W*
Cassiède, M (Dax) 1961 *NZ* 3, *A, R*
Castaignède, S (Mont-de-Marsan) 1999 *W* 2, [*C* (R), *Nm* (R), *Fj, Arg* (R), *NZ* 2(R), *A* (R)]
Castaignède, T (Toulouse, Castres) 1995 *R* 2, *Arg, NZ* 1,2, 1996 *E, S, I, W* 1, *Arg* 1,2, 1997 *I, A* 1,2, *It* 2, 1998 *E, S, I, W, Arg* 1,2, *Fj*, 1999 *I, W* 1, *E, S, R, WS, Tg* (R), *NZ* 1, *W* 2, [*C*], 2000 *W, E, S, It*
Castel, R (Toulouse, Béziers) 1996 *I, W* 1, *W* 2, *SA* 1(R),2, 1997 *I* (R), *W, E* (R), *S* (R), *A* 1(R), 1998 *Arg* 3(R), *A* (R), 1999 *W* 1(R), *E, S*
Castets, J (Toulon) 1923 *W, E, I*
Caujolle, J (Tarbes) 1909 *E*, 1913 *SA, E*, 1914 *W, E*
Caunègre, R (SB) 1938 *R, G* 2
Caussade, A (Lourdes) 1978 *R*, 1979 *I, W, E, NZ* 1,2, *R*, 1980 *W, E, S*, 1981 *W, I*
Caussarieu, G (Pau) 1929 *I*
Cayrefourcq, E (Tarbes) 1921 *E*
Cazalbou, J (Toulouse) 1997 *It* 2(R), *R* 2, *Arg, SA* 2(R)
Cazals, M (Mont-de-Marsan) 1961 *NZ* 1, *A, R*
Cazenave, A (Pau) 1927 *E, G* 1, 1928 *S, A, G*
Cazenave, F (RCF) 1950 *E*, 1952 *S*, 1954 *I, NZ, W, E*
Cecillon, M (Bourgoin) 1988 *I, W, Arg* 2,3,4, *R*, 1989 *I, E, NZ* 1,2, *A* 1, 1991 *S, I, E* (R), *R, US* 1, *W* 2, [*E*], 1992 *W, E, S, I, R, Arg* 1,2, *SA* 1,2, 1993 *E, S, I, W, SA* 1,2, *A* 1,2, 1994 *I, W, NZ* 1(R), 1995 *I, R* 1, [*Tg, S* (R), *I, SA*]
Celaya, M (Biarritz O, SBUC) 1953 *E, W, It*, 1954 *I, E, It, Arg* 1,2, 1955 *S, I, E, W, It*, 1956 *S, I, W, It, E, Cz* 1957 *S, I, E, W, R* 2, 1958 *S, E, A, W, It*, 1959 *S, E, It, I, NZ* 1,2,3, *A, R*
Celhay, M (Bayonne) 1935 *G*, 1936 *G* 1, 1937 *G, It*, 1938 *G* 1, 1940 *B*
Cermeno, F (Perpignan) 2000 *R*
Cessieux, N (Lyon) 1906 *NZ*
Cester, E (TOEC, Valence) 1966 *S, I, E*, 1967 *W*, 1968 *S, I, E, W, Cz, NZ* 1,3, *A, SA* 1,2, *R*, 1969 *S, I, E, W*, 1970 *S, I, W, E*, 1971 *A* 1, 1972 *R*, 1973 *S, NZ, W, I, J, R*, 1974 *I, W, E, S*
Chabal, S (Bourgoin) 2000 *S*, 2001 *SA* 1,2, *NZ* (R)
Chaban-Delmas, J (CASG) 1945 *B* 2
Chabowski, H (Nice, Bourgoin) 1985 *Arg* 2, 1986 *R* 2, *NZ* 2, 1989 *B* (R)
Chadebech, P (Brive) 1982 *R, Arg* 1,2, 1986 *S, I*
Champ, E (Toulon) 1985 *Arg* 1,2, 1986 *I, W, E, R* 1, *Arg* 1,2, *A, NZ* 1, *R* 2, *NZ* 2,3, 1987 *W, E, S, I*, [*S, R, Fj, A, NZ*], *R*, 1988 *E, S, Arg* 1,3,4, *R*, 1989 *W, S, A* 1,2, 1990 *W, E, NZ* 1, 1991 *R, US* 1, [*R, Fj, C, E*]
Chapuy, L (SF) 1926 *S*
Charpentier, G (SF) 1911 *E*, 1912 *W, E*
Charton, P (Montferrand) 1940 *B*
Charvet, D (Toulouse) 1986 *W, E, R* 1, *Arg* 1, *A, NZ* 1,3, 1987 *W, E, S, I*, [*S, R, Z, Fj, A, NZ*], *R*, 1989 *E* (R), 1990 *W, E*, 1991 *S, I*
Chassagne, J (Montferrand) 1938 *G* 1

Chatau, A (Bayonne) 1913 *SA*
Chaud, E (Toulon) 1932 *G*, 1934 *G*, 1935 *G*
Chazalet, A (Bourgoin) 1999 *Tg*
Chenevay, C (Grenoble) 1968 *SA* 1
Chevallier, B (Montferrand) 1952 *S, I, SA, W, E, It*, 1953 *E, W, It*, 1954 *S, I, NZ, W, Arg* 1, 1955 *S, I, E, W, It*, 1956 *S, I, W, It, E, Cz*, 1957 *S*
Chiberry, J (Chambéry) 1955 *It*
Chilo, A (RCF) 1920 *S, W*, 1925 *I, NZ*
Cholley, G (Castres) 1975 *E, S, I, SA* 1,2, *Arg* 1,2, *R*, 1976 *S, I, W, E, A* 1,2, *R*, 1977 *W, E, S, I, Arg* 1,2, *NZ* 1,2, *R*, 1978 *E, S, I, W, R*, 1979 *I, S*
Choy, J (Narbonne) 1930 *S, I, E, G, W*, 1931 *I*, 1933 *G*, 1934 *G*, 1935 *G*, 1936 *G* 2
Cigagna, A (Toulouse) 1995 [*E*]
Cimarosti, J (Castres) 1976 *US* (R)
Cistacq, J-C (Agen) 2000 *R* (R)
Clady, A (Lezignan) 1929 *G*, 1931 *I, S, E, G*
Clarac, H (St Girons) 1938 *G* 1
Claudel, R (Lyon) 1932 *G*, 1934 *G*
Clauzel, F (Béziers) 1924 *E, W*, 1925 *W*
Clavé, J (Agen) 1936 *G* 2, 1938 *R, G* 2
Claverie, H (Lourdes) 1954 *NZ, W*
Cléda, T (Pau) 1998 *E* (R), *S* (R), *I* (R), *W* (R), *Arg* 1(R), *Fj* (R), *Arg* 3(R), 1999 *I* (R), *S*
Clément, G (RCF) 1931 *W*
Clément, J (RCF) 1921 *S, W, E*, 1922 *S, E, W, I*, 1923 *S, W, I*
Clemente, M (Oloron) 1978 *R*, 1980 *S, I*
Cluchague, L (Biarritz O) 1924 *S*, 1925 *E*
Coderc, J (Chalon) 1932 *G*, 1933 *G*, 1934 *G*, 1935 *G*, 1936 *G* 1
Codorniou, D (Narbonne) 1979 *NZ* 1,2, *R*, 1980 *W, E, S, I*, 1981 *S, W, E, A* 2, 1983 *E, S, I, W, A* 1,2, *R*, 1984 *I, W, E, S, NZ* 1,2, *R*, 1985 *E, S, I, W, Arg* 1,2
Coeurveille, C (Agen) 1992 *Arg* 1(R),2
Cognet, L (Montferrand) 1932 *G*, 1936 *G* 1,2, 1937 *G, It*
Collazo, P (Bègles) 2000 *R*
Colombier, J (St Junien) 1952 *SA, W, E*
Colomine, G (Narbonne) 1979 *NZ* 1
Comba, F (SF) 1998 *Arg* 1,2, *Fj, Arg* 3, 1999 *I, W* 1, *E, S*, 2000 *A, NZ* 1,2, 2001 *S, I*
Combe, J (SF) 1910 *S, E, I*, 1911 *S*
Combes, G (Fumel) 1945 *B* 2
Communeau, M (SF) 1906 *NZ, E*, 1907 *E*, 1908 *E, W*, 1909 *E, W, I*, 1910 *S, E, I*, 1911 *S, E, I*, 1912 *I, S, W, E*, 1913 *SA, E, W*
Condom, J (Boucau, Biarritz O) 1982 *R*, 1983 *E, S, I, W, A* 1,2, *R*, 1984 *I, W, E, S, NZ* 1,2, *R*, 1985 *E, S, I, W, Arg* 1,2, 1986 *S, I, W, E, R* 1, *Arg* 1,2, *NZ* 1, *R* 2, *NZ* 2,3, 1987 *W, E, S, I*, [*S, R, Z, A, NZ*], *R*, 1988 *E, S, W, Arg* 1,2,3,4, *R*, 1989 *I, W, E, S, NZ* 1,2, *A* 1, 1990 *I, R, A* 2,3(R)
Conilh de Beyssac, J-J (SBUC) 1912 *I, S*, 1914 *I, W, E*
Constant, G (Perpignan) 1920 *W*
Coscolla, G (Béziers) 1921 *S, W*
Costantino, J (Montferrand) 1973 *R*
Costes, A (Montferrand) 1994 *C* 2, 1995 *R* 1, [*Iv*], 1997 *It* 1, 1999 *WS, Tg* (R), *NZ* 1, [*Nm* (R), *Fj* (R), *Arg* (R), *NZ* 2(R), *A* (t&R)], 2000 *S* (R), *I*
Costes, F (Montferrand) 1979 *E, S, NZ* 1,2, *R*, 1980 *W, I*
Couffignal, H (Colomiers) 1993 *R* 1
Coulon, E (Grenoble) 1928 *S*
Courtiols, M (Bègles) 1991 *R, US* 1, *W* 2
Crabos, R (RCF) 1920 *S, E, W, I, US*, 1921 *S, W, E, I*, 1922 *S, E, W, I*, 1923 *S, I*, 1924 *S, I*
Crampagne, J (Bègles) 1967 *SA* 4
Crancee, R (Lourdes) 1960 *Arg* 3, 1961 *S*
Crauste, M (RCF, Lourdes) 1957 *R* 1,2, 1958 *S, E, A, W, It, I*, 1959 *E, It, W, I*, 1960 *S, E, W, I, It, R, Arg* 1,3, 1961 *S, SA, E, W, It, I, NZ* 1,2,3, *A, R*, 1962 *S, E, W, I, It, R*, 1963 *S, I, E, W, It, R*, 1964 *S, NZ, E, W, It, I, SA, Fj, R*, 1965 *S, I, E, W, It, R*, 1966 *S, I, E, W, It*
Cremaschi, M (Lourdes) 1980 *R*, 1981 *R, NZ* 1,2, 1982 *W, S*, 1983 *A* 1,2, *R*, 1984 *I, W*
Crenca, J-J (Agen) 1996 *SA* 2(R), 1999 *R, Tg, WS* (R), *NZ* 1(R), 2001 *SA* 1,2, *NZ* (R)
Crichton, W H (Le Havre) 1906 *NZ, E*
Cristina, J (Montferrand) 1979 *R*
Cussac, P (Biarritz O) 1934 *G*
Cutzach, A (Quillan) 1929 *G*

Daguerre, F (Biarritz O) 1936 *G* 1
Daguerre, J (CASG) 1933 *G*

Dal Maso, M (Mont-de-Marsan, Agen, Colomiers) 1988 *R*
(R), 1990 *NZ* 2, 1996 *SA* 1(R),2, 1997 *I, W, E, S, It* 1, *R* 1(R),
A 1,2, *It* 2, *Arg, SA* 1,2, 1998 *W* (R), *Arg* 1(t), *Fj* (R), 1999 *R*
(R), *WS* (R), *Tg, NZ* 1(R), *W* 2(R), [*Nm* (R), *Fj* (R), *Arg* (R),
A (R)], 2000 *W, E, S, I, It*
Danion, J (Toulon) 1924 *I*
Danos, P (Toulon, Béziers) 1954 *Arg* 1,2, 1957 *R* 2, 1958 *S,
E, W, It, I, SA* 1,2, 1959 *S, E, It, W, I*, 1960 *S, E*
Dantiacq, D (Pau) 1997 *R* 1
Darbos, P (Dax) 1969 *R*
Darracq, R (Dax) 1957 *It*
Darrieussecq, A (Biarritz O) 1973 *E*
Darrieussecq, J (Mont-de-Marsan) 1953 *It*
Darrouy, C (Mont-de-Marsan) 1957 *I, E, W, It, R* 1, 1959 *E*,
1961 *R*, 1963 *S, I, E, W, It*, 1964 *NZ, E, W, It, I, SA, Fj, R*,
1965 *S, I, E, It, R*, 1966 *S, I, E, W, It, R*, 1967 *S, A, E, It, W, I,
SA* 1,2,4
Daudé, J (Bourgoin) 2000 *S*
Daudignon, G (SF) 1928 *S*
Dauga, B (Mont-de-Marsan) 1964 *S, NZ, E, W, It, I, SA, Fj,
R*, 1965 *S, I, E, W, It, R*, 1966 *S, I, E, W, It, R*, 1967 *S, A, E, It,
W, I, SA* 1,2,3,4, *NZ, R*, 1968 *S, I, NZ* 1,2,3, *A, SA* 1,2,
1969 *S, I, E, R*, 1970 *S, I, W, E, R*, 1971 *S, I, E, W, SA* 1,2, *A*
1,2, *R*, 1972 *S, I* 1, *W*
Dauger, J (Bayonne) 1945 *B* 1,2, 1953 *S*
Daulouede, P (Tyrosse) 1937 *G, It*, 1938 *G* 1, 1940 *B*
De Besombes, S (Perpignan) 1998 *Arg* 1(R), *Fj* (R)
Decamps, P (RCF) 1911 *S*
Dedet, J (SF) 1910 *S, E, I*, 1911 *W, I*, 1912 *S*, 1913 *E, I*
Dedeyn, P (RCF) 1906 *NZ*
Dedieu, P (Béziers) 1963 *E, It*, 1964 *W, It, I, SA, Fj, R*, 1965
S, I, E, W
De Gregorio, J (Grenoble) 1960 *S, E, W, I, It, R, Arg* 1,2,
1961 *S, SA, E, W, It, I*, 1962 *S, E, W*, 1963 *S, W, It*, 1964 *NZ,
E*
Dehez, J-L (Agen) 1967 *SA* 2, 1969 *R*
De Jouvencel, E (SF) 1909 *W, I*
De Laborderie, M (RCF) 1921 *I*, 1922 *I*, 1925 *W, E*
Delage, C (Agen) 1983 *S, I*
De Malherbe, H (CASG) 1932 *G*, 1933 *G*
De Malmann, R (RCF) 1908 *E, W*, 1909 *E, W, I*, 1910 *E, I*
De Muizon, J J (SF) 1910 *I*
Delaigue, G (Toulon) 1973 *J, R*
Delaigue, Y (Toulon) 1994 *S, NZ* 2(R), *C* 2, 1995 *I, R* 1, [*Tg,
Iv*], *It* 2(R), 1997 *It* 1
Delmotte, G (Toulon) 1999 *R, Tg*
Delque, A (Toulouse) 1937 *It*, 1938 *G* 1, *R, G* 2
De Rougemont, M (Toulon) 1995 *E* (t), *R* 1(t), [*Iv*], *NZ* 1,2,
1996 *I* (R), *Arg* 1,2, *W* 2, *SA* 1, 1997 *S* (R), *It* 1
Desbrosse, C (Toulouse) 1999 [*Nm* (R)], 2000 *I*
Descamps, P (SB) 1927 *G* 2
Desclaux, F (RCF) 1949 *Arg* 1,2, 1953 *It*
Desclaux, J (Perpignan) 1934 *G*, 1935 *G*, 1936 *G* 1,2, 1937
G, It, 1938 *G* 1, *R, G* 2, 1945 *B* 1
Deslandes, C (RCF) 1990 *A* 1, *NZ* 2, 1991 *W* 1, 1992 *R, Arg*
1,2
Desnoyer, L (Brive) 1974 *R*
Destarac, L (Tarbes) 1926 *S, I, E, W, M*, 1927 *W, E, G* 1,2
Desvouges, R (SF) 1914 *W*
Detrez, P-E (Nîmes) 1983 *A* 2(R), 1986 *Arg* 1(R),2, *A* (R),
*NZ*1
Devergie, T (Nîmes) 1988 *R*, 1989 *NZ* 1,2, *B, A* 2, 1990 *W, E,
S, I, R, A* 1,2,3, 1991 *US* 2, *W* 2, 1992 *R* (R), *Arg* 2(R)
De Villiers, P (SF) 1999 *W* 2, [*Arg* (R), *NZ* 2(R), *A* (R)], 2000
W (R), *E* (R), *S* (R), *I* (R), *It* (R), *NZ* 1(R),2, 2001 *S, I, It, W,
E, SA* 1,2, *NZ* (R)
Deygas, M (Vienne) 1937 *It*
Deylaud, C (Toulouse) 1992 *R, Arg* 1,2, *SA* 1, 1994 *C* 1, *NZ*
1,2, 1995 *W, E, S*, [*Iv* (R), *SA*], *It, Arg*
Dintrans, P (Tarbes) 1979 *NZ* 1,2, *R*, 1980 *E, S, I, SA, R*,
1981 *S, I, W, E, A* 1,2, *R, NZ* 1,2, 1982 *W, E, S, I, R, Arg* 1,2,
1983 *E, W, A* 1,2, *R*, 1984 *I, W, E, S, NZ* 1,2, *R*, 1985 *E, S, I,
W, Arg* 1,2, 1987 [*R*], 1988 *Arg* 1,2,3, 1989 *W, E, S*, 1990 *R*
Dispagne, S (Toulouse) 1996 *I* (R), *W* 1
Dizabo, P (Tyrosse) 1948 *A, S, E*, 1949 *S, I, E, W, Arg* 2, 1950
S, I, 1960 *Arg* 1,2,3
Domec, A (Carcassonne) 1929 *W*
Domec, H (Lourdes) 1953 *W, It*, 1954 *S, I, NZ, W, E, It*, 1955
S, I, E, W, 1956 *I, W, It*, 1958 *E, A, W, It, I*
Domenech, A (Vichy, Brive) 1954 *W, E, It*, 1955 *S, I, E, W*,
1956 *S, I, W, It, E, Cz*, 1957 *S, I, E, W, It, R* 1,2, 1958 *S, E, It*,
1959 *It*, 1960 *S, E, W, I, It, R, Arg* 1,2,3, 1961 *S, SA, E, W, It, I,
NZ* 1,2,3, *A, R*, 1962 *S, E, W, I, It, R*, 1963 *W, It*

Domercq, J (Bayonne) 1912 *I, S*
Dominici, C (SF) 1998 *E, S, Arg* 1,2, 1999 *E, S, WS, NZ* 1, *W*
2, [*C, Fj, Arg, NZ* 2, *A*], 2000 *W, E, S, R*, 2001 *I* (R), *It, W, E,
SA* 1,2, *NZ*
Dorot, J (RCF) 1935 *G*
Dospital, P (Bayonne) 1977 *R*, 1980 *I*, 1981 *S, I, W, E*, 1982
I, R, Arg 1,2, 1983 *E, S, I, W*, 1984 *E, S, NZ* 1,2, *R*, 1985 *E, S,
I, W, Arg* 1
Dourthe, C (Dax) 1966 *R*, 1967 *S, A, E, W, I, SA* 1,2,3, *NZ*,
1968 *W, NZ* 3, *SA* 1,2, 1969 *W*, 1971 *SA* 2(R), *R*, 1972 *I* 1,2,
A 1,2, *R*, 1973 *S, NZ, E*, 1974 *I, Arg* 1,2, *SA* 1,2, 1975 *W, E, S*
Dourthe, M (Dax) 2000 *NZ* 2(t)
Dourthe, R (Dax, SF, Béziers) 1995 *R* 2, *Arg, NZ* 1,2, 1996 *E,
R*, 1996 *Arg* 1,2, *W* 2, *SA* 1,2, 1997 *W, A* 1, 1999 *I, W* 1,2, [*C,
Nm, Fj, Arg, NZ* 2, *A*], 2000 *W, E, It, R, A, NZ* 1,2, 2001 *S, I*
Doussau, E (Angoulême) 1938 *R*
Droitecourt, M (Montferrand) 1972 *R*, 1973 *NZ* (R), *E*, 1974
E, S, Arg 1, *SA* 2, 1975 *SA* 1,2, *Arg* 1,2, *R*, 1976 *S, I, W, A* 1,
1977 *Arg* 2
Dubertrand, A (Montferrand) 1971 *A* 2, *R*, 1972 *I* 2, 1974 *I,
W, E, SA* 2, 1975 *Arg* 1,2, *R*, 1976 *S, US*
Dubois, D (Bègles) 1971 *S*
Dubroca, D (Agen) 1979 *NZ* 2, 1981 *NZ* 2(R), 1982 *E, S,
1984 W, E, S, 1985 Arg* 2, 1986 *S, I, W, E, R* 1, *Arg* 2, *A, NZ* 1,
R 2, *NZ* 2,3, 1987 *W, E, S, I,* [*S, Z, Fj, A, NZ*], *R*, 1988 *E, S, I,
W*
Duché, A (Limoges) 1929 *G*
Duclos, A (Lourdes) 1931 *S*
Ducousso, J (Tarbes) 1925 *S, W, E*
Dufau, G (RCF) 1948 *I, A*, 1949 *I, W*, 1950 *S, E, W*, 1951 *S,
I, E, W*, 1952 *SA, W*, 1953 *S, I, E, W*, 1954 *S, I, NZ, W, E, It*,
1955 *S, I, E, W, It*, 1956 *S, I, W, It*, 1957 *S, I, E, W, It, R* 1
Dufau, J (Biarritz) 1912 *I, S, W, E*
Duffaut, Y (Agen) 1954 *Arg* 1,2
Duffour, R (Tarbes) 1911 *W*
Dufourcq, J (SBUC) 1906 *NZ, E*, 1907 *E*, 1908 *W*
Duhard, Y (Bagnères) 1980 *E*
Duhau, J (SF) 1928 *I*,1930 *I, G*, 1931 *I, S, W*, 1933 *G*
Dulaurens, C (Toulouse) 1926 *I*, 1928 *S*, 1929 *W*
Duluc, A (Béziers) 1934 *G*
Du Manoir, Y le P (RCF) 1925 *I, NZ, S, W, E*, 1926 *S*, 1927
I, S
Dupont, C (Lourdes) 1923 *S, W, I*, 1924 *S, I, W, R, US*, 1925
S, 1927 E, G 1,2, 1928 *A, G, W*, 1929 *I*
Dupont, J-L (Agen) 1983 *S*
Dupont, L (RCF) 1934 *G*, 1935 *G*, 1936 *G* 1,2, 1938 *R, G* 2
Dupouy, A (SB) 1924 *W, R*
Duprat, B (Bayonne) 1966 *E, W, It, R*, 1967 *S, A, E, SA* 2,3,
1968 *S, I*, 1972 *E, W, I* 2, *A* 1
Dupré, P (RCF) 1909 *W*
Dupuy, J (Tarbes) 1956 *S, I, W, It, E, Cz*, 1957 *S, I, E, W, It, R*
2, 1958 *S, E, SA* 1,2, 1959 *S, E, It, W, I*, 1960 *W, I, It, Arg* 1,3,
1961 *S, SA, E, NZ* 2, *R*, 1962 *S, E, W, I*, 1963 *W, It, R*, 1964
S
Du Souich, C J (see Judas du Souich)
Dutin, B (Mont-de-Marsan) 1968 *NZ* 2, *A, SA* 2, *R*
Dutour, F X (Toulouse) 1911 *E, I*, 1912 *S, W, E*, 1913 *S*
Dutrain, H (Toulouse) 1945 *W*, 1946 *B, I*, 1947 *E*, 1949 *I, E,
W, Arg* 1
Dutrey, J (Lourdes) 1940 *B*
Duval, R (SF) 1908 *E, W*, 1909 *E*, 1911 *E, W, I*

Echavé, L (Agen) 1961 *S*
Elhorga, P (Agen) 2001 *NZ*
Elissalde, E (Bayonne) 1936 *G* 2, 1940 *B*
Elissalde, J-B (La Rochelle) 2000 *S* (R), *R* (R)
Elissalde, J-P (La Rochelle) 1980 *SA, R*, 1981 *A* 1,2, *R*
Empereur-Buisson, H (Béziers) 1931 *E, G*
Erbani, D (Agen) 1981 *A* 1,2, *NZ* 1,2, 1982 *Arg* 1,2, 1983 *S*
(R), *I, W, A* 1,2, *R*, 1984 *W, E, R*, 1985 *E, W* (R), *Arg* 2, 1986
S, I, W, E, R 1, *Arg* 2, *NZ* 1,2(R),3, 1987 *W, E, S, I*, [*S, R, Fj, A,
NZ*], 1988 *E, S*, 1989 *I* (R), *W, E, S, NZ* 1, *A* 2, 1990 *W, E*
Escaffre, P (Narbonne) 1933 *G*, 1934 *G*
Escommier, M (Montelimar) 1955 *It*
Esponda, J-M (RCF) 1967 *SA* 1,2, *R*, 1968 *NZ* 1,2, *SA* 2, *R*,
1969 *S, I* (R), *E*
Estève, A (Béziers) 1971 *SA* 1, 1972 *I* 1, *E, W, I* 2, *A* 2, *R*,
1973 *S, NZ, E, I*, 1974 *I, W, E, S, R, SA* 1,2, 1975 *W, E*
Estève, P (Narbonne, Lavelanet) 1982 *R, Arg* 1,2, 1983 *E, S,
I, W, A* 1,2, *R*, 1984 *I, W, E, S, NZ* 1,2, *R*, 1985 *E, S, I, W*,
1986 *S, I*, 1987 [*S, Z*]
Etcheberry, J (Rochefort, Cognac) 1923 *W, I*, 1924 *S, I, E, W,
R, US*, 1926 *S, I, E, M*, 1927 *I, S, W, G* 2

Etchenique, J-M (Biarritz O) 1974 *R, SA* 1, 1975 *E, Arg* 2
Etchepare, A (Bayonne) 1922 *I*
Etcheverry, M (Pau) 1971 *S, I*
Eutrope, A (SCUF) 1913 *I*

Fabre, E (Toulouse) 1937 *It*, 1938 *G* 1,2
Fabre, J (Toulouse) 1963 *S, I, E, W, It*, 1964 *S, NZ, E*
Fabre, L (Lezignan) 1930 *G*
Fabre, M (Béziers) 1981 *A* 1, *R, NZ* 1,2, 1982 *I, R*
Failliot, P (RCF) 1911 *S, W, I*, 1912 *I, S, E*, 1913 *E, W*
Fargues, G (Dax) 1923 *I*
Fauré, F (Tarbes) 1914 *I, W, E*
Fauvel, J-P (Tulle) 1980 *R*
Favre, M (Lyon) 1913 *E, W*
Ferrand, L (Chalon) 1940 *B*
Ferrien, R (Tarbes) 1950 *S, I, E, W*
Finat, R (CASG) 1932 *G*, 1933 *G*
Fite, R (Brive) 1963 *W, It*
Forestier, J (SCUF) 1912 *W*
Forgues, F (Bayonne) 1911 *S, E, W*, 1912 *I, W, E*, 1913 *S, SA, W*, 1914 *I, E*
Fort, J (Agen) 1967 *It, W, I, SA* 1,2,3,4
Fourcade, G (BEC) 1909 *E, W*
Foures, H (Toulouse) 1951 *S, I, E, W*
Fournet, F (Montferrand) 1950 *W*
Fouroux, J (La Voulte) 1972 *I* 2, 1974 *W, E, Arg* 1,2, *R, SA* 1,2, 1975 *W, Arg* 1, *R*, 1976 *S, I, W, E, US, A* 1, 1977 *W, E, S, I, Arg* 1,2, *NZ* 1,2, *R*
Francquenelle, A (Vaugirard) 1911 *S*, 1913 *W, I*
Furcade, R (Perpignan) 1952 *S*

Gabernet, S (Toulouse) 1980 *E, S*, 1981 *S, I, W, E, A* 1,2, *R, NZ* 1,2, 1982 *I*, 1983 *A* 2, *R*
Gachassin, J (Lourdes) 1961 *S, I*, 1963 *R*, 1964 *S, NZ, E, W, It, I, SA, Fj, R*, 1965 *S, I, E, W, It, R*, 1966 *S, I, E, W*, 1967 *S, A, It, W, I, NZ*, 1968 *I, E*, 1969 *S, I*
Galasso, A (Toulon, Montferrand) 2000 *R* (R), 2001 *E* (R)
Galau, H (Toulouse) 1924 *S, I, E, W, US*
Galia, J (Quillan) 1927 *E, G* 1,2, 1928 *S, A, I, E, W*, 1929 *I, E, G*, 1930 *S, I, E, G, W*, 1931 *S, W, E, G*
Gallart, P (Béziers) 1990 *R, A* 1,2(R),3, 1992 *S, I, R, Arg* 1,2, *SA* 1,2, *Arg*, 1994 *I, W, E*, 1995 *I* (t), *R* 1, [*Tg*]
Gallion, J (Toulon) 1978 *E, S, I, W*, 1979 *I, W, E, S, NZ* 2, *R*, 1980 *W, E, S, I*, 1983 *A* 1,2, *R*, 1984 *I, W, E, S, R*, 1985 *E, S, I, W*, 1986 *Arg* 2
Galthié, P (Colomiers) 1991 *R, US* 1, [*R, Fj, C, E*], 1992 *W, E, S, R, Arg*, 1994 *I, W, E*, 1995 [*SA, E*], 1996 *W* 1(R), 1997 *I, It* 2, *SA* 1,2, 1998 *W* (R), *Fj* (R), 1999 *R, WS* (R), *Tg, NZ* 1(R), [*Fj* (R), *Arg, NZ* 2, *A*], 2000 *W, E, A, NZ* 1,2, 2001 *S, It, W, E, SA* 1,2, *NZ*
Galy, J (Perpignan) 1953 *W*
Garbajosa, X (Toulouse) 1998 *I, W, Arg* 2(R), *Fj*, 1999 *W* 1(R), *E, S, WS, NZ* 1, *W* 2, [*C, Nm* (R), *Fj* (R), *Arg, NZ* 2, *A*], 2000 *A, NZ* 1,2, 2001 *S, I, E*
Garuet-Lempirou, J-P (Lourdes) 1983 *A* 1,2, *R*, 1984 *I, NZ* 1,2, *R*, 1985 *E, S, I, W, Arg* 1, 1986 *S, I, W, E, R* 1, *Arg* 1, *NZ* 1, *R* 2, *NZ* 2,3, 1987 *W, E, S, I*, [*S, R, Fj, A, NZ*], 1988 *E, S, Arg* 1,2, *R*, 1989 *E* (R), *S, NZ* 1,2, 1990 *W, F*
Gasc, J (Graulhet) 1977 *NZ* 2
Gasparotto, G (Montferrand) 1976 *A* 2, *R*
Gauby, G (Perpignan) 1956 *Cz*
Gaudermen, P (RCF) 1906 *E*
Gayraud, W (Toulouse) 1920 *I*
Geneste, R (BEC) 1945 *B* 1, 1949 *Arg* 2
Genet, J-P (RCF) 1992 *S, I, R*
Gensane, R (Béziers) 1962 *S, E, W, I, It, R*, 1963 *S*
Gerald, G (RCF) 1927 *E, G* 2, 1928 *S*, 1929 *I, S, W, E, G*, 1930 *S, I, E, G, W*, 1931 *I, S, E, G*
Gérard, D (Bègles) 1999 *Tg*
Gerintes, G (CASG) 1924 *R*, 1925 *I*, 1926 *W*
Geschwind, P (RCF) 1936 *G* 1,2
Giacardy, M (SBUC) 1907 *E*
Gimbert, P (Bègles) 1991 *R, US* 1, 1992 *W, E*
Giordani, P (Dax) 1999 *E, S*
Glas, S (Bourgoin) 1996 *S* (t), *I* (R), *W* 1, *R, Arg* 2(R), *W* 2, *SA* 1,2, 1997 *I, W, E, S, It* 2(R), *R* 2, *Arg, SA* 1,2, 1998 *E, S, I, W, Arg* 1,2, *Fj, Arg* 3, *A*, 1999 *W* 2, [*C,Nm, Arg* (R), *NZ* 2(R), *A* (t&R)], 2000 *I*, 2001 *E, SA* 1,2, *NZ*
Gomès, A (SF) 1998 *Arg* 1,2, *Fj, Arg* 3, *A*, 1999 *I* (R)
Gommes, J (RCF) 1909 *I*
Gonnet, C-A (Albi) 1921 *E, I*, 1922 *E, W*, 1924 *S, E*, 1926 *S, I, E, W, M*, 1927 *I, S, W, E, G* 1

Gonzalez, J-M (Bayonne) 1992 *Arg* 1,2, *SA* 1,2, *Arg*, 1993 *R* 1, *SA* 1,2, *R* 2, *A* 1,2, 1994 *I, W, E, S, C* 1, *NZ* 1,2, *C* 2, 1995 *W, E, S, I, R* 1, [*Tg, S, I, SA, E*], *It, Arg*, 1996 *E, S, I, W* 1
Got, R (Perpignan) 1920 *I, US*, 1921 *S, W*, 1922 *S, E, W, I*, 1924 *I, E, W, R, US*
Gourdon, J-F (RCF, Bagnères) 1974 *S, Arg* 1,2, *R, SA* 1,2, 1975 *W, E, S, I, R*, 1976 *S, I, W, E*, 1978 *E, S*, 1979 *W, E, S, R*, 1980 *I*
Gourragne, J-F (Béziers) 1990 *NZ* 2, 1991 *W* 1
Goyard, A (Lyon U) 1936 *G* 1,2, 1937 *G, It*, 1938 *G* 1, *R, G* 2
Graciet, R (SBUC) 1926 *I, W*, 1927 *S, G* 1, 1929 *E*, 1930 *W*
Graou, S (Auch, Colomiers) 1992 *Arg* (R), 1993 *SA* 1,2, *R* 2, *A* 2(R), 1995 *R* 2, *Arg* (t), *NZ* 2(R)
Gratton, J (Agen) 1984 *NZ* 2, *R*, 1985 *E, S, I, W, Arg* 1,2, 1986 *S, NZ* 1
Graule, V (Arl Perpignan) 1926 *I, E, W*, 1927 *S, W*, 1931 *G*
Greffe, M (Grenoble) 1968 *W, Cz, NZ* 1,2, *SA* 1
Griffard, J (Lyon U) 1932 *G*, 1933 *G*, 1934 *G*
Gruarin, A (Toulon) 1964 *W, It, I, SA, Fj, R*, 1965 *S, I, E, W, It*, 1966 *S, I, E, W, It, R*, 1967 *S, A, E, It, W, I, NZ*, 1968 *S, I*
Guelorget, P (RCF) 1931 *E, G*
Guichemerre, A (Dax) 1920 *E*, 1921 *E, I*, 1923 *S*
Guilbert, A (Toulon) 1975 *E, S, I, SA* 1,2, 1976 *A* 1, 1977 *Arg* 1,2, *NZ* 1,2, *R*, 1979 *I, W, E*
Guillemin, P (RCF) 1908 *E, W*, 1909 *E, I*, 1910 *W, S, E, I*, 1911 *S, E, W*
Guilleux, P (Agen) 1952 *SA, It*
Guiral, M (Agen) 1931 *G*, 1932 *G*, 1933 *G*
Guiraud, H (Nîmes) 1996 *R*

Haget, A (PUC) 1953 *E*, 1954 *I, NZ, E, Arg* 2, 1955 *E, W, It*, 1957 *I, E, It, R* 1, 1958 *It, SA* 2
Haget, F (Agen, Biarritz O) 1974 *Arg* 1,2, 1975 *SA* 2, *Arg* 1,2, *R*, 1976 *S*, 1978 *S, I, W, R*, 1979 *I, W, E, S, NZ* 1,2, *R*, 1980 *W, S, I*, 1984 *S, NZ* 1,2, *R*, 1985 *E, S, I*, 1986 *S, I, W, E, R* 1, *Arg* 1, *A, NZ* 1, 1987 *S, I*, [*R, Fj*]
Haget, H (CASG) 1928 *S*, 1930 *G*
Harislur-Arthapignet, P (Tarbes) 1988 *Arg* 4(R)
Harize, D (Cahors, Toulouse) 1975 *SA* 1,2, 1976 *A* 1,2, *R*, 1977 *W, E, S, I*
Hauc, A (Toulon) 1928 *E, G*, 1929 *I, S, G*
Hauser, M (Lourdes) 1969 *E*
Hedembaigt, M (Bayonne) 1913 *S, SA*, 1914 *W*
Hericé, D (Bègles) 1950 *I*
Herrero, A (Toulon) 1963 *R*, 1964 *NZ, E, W, It, I, SA, Fj, R*, 1965 *S, I, E, W*, 1966 *W, It, R*, 1967 *S, A, E, It, I, R*
Herrero, B (Nice) 1983 *I*, 1986 *Arg* 1
Heyer, F (Montferrand) 1990 *A* 2
Heymans, C (Agen) 2000 *It* (R) *R*
Hiquet, J-C (Agen) 1964 *E*
Hoche, M (PUC) 1957 *I, E, W, It, R* 1
Hondagné-Monge, M (Tarbes) 1988 *Arg* 2(R)
Hontas, P (Biarritz) 1990 *S, I, R*, 1991 *R*, 1992 *Arg*, 1993 *E, S, I, W*
Hortoland, J-P (Béziers) 1971 *A* 2
Houblain, H (SCUF) 1909 *E*, 1910 *W*
Houdet, R (SF) 1927 *S, W, G* 1, 1928 *G, W*, 1929 *I, S, E*, 1930 *S, E*
Hourdebaigt, A (SBUC) 1909 *I*, 1910 *W, S, E, I*
Hubert, A (ASF) 1906 *E*, 1907 *E*, 1908 *E, W*, 1909 *E, W, I*
Hueber, A (Lourdes, Toulon) 1990 *A* 3, *NZ* 1, 1991 *US* 2, 1992 *I, Arg* 1,2, *SA* 1,2, 1993 *E, S, I, W, R* 1, *SA* 1,2, *R* 2, *A* 1,2, 1995 [*Tg, S* (R), *I*], 2000 *It, R*
Hutin, R (CASG) 1927 *I, S, W*
Hyardet, A (Castres) 1995 *It, Arg* (R)

Ibanez, R (Dax, Perpignan, Castres) 1996 *W* 1(R), 1997 *It* 1(R), *R* 1, *It* 2(R), *R* 2, *SA* 2(R), 1998 *E, S, I, W, Arg* 1,2, *Fj, Arg* 3, *A*, 1999 *I, W* 1, *E, S, R, WS, Tg* (R), *NZ* 1, *W* 2, [*C, Nm, Fj, Arg, NZ* 2, *A*], 2000 *W* (R), *E* (R), *S* (R), *I* (R), *It* (R), *R*, 2001 *S, I, It, W, E, SA* 1,2, *NZ* (R)
Icard, J (SF) 1909 *E, W*
Iguiniz, E (Bayonne) 1914 *E*
Ihingoué, D (BEC) 1912 *I, S*
Imbernon, J-F (Perpignan) 1976 *I, W, E, US, A* 1, 1977 *W, E, S, I, Arg* 1,2, *NZ* 1,2, 1978 *E, R*, 1979 *I*, 1981 *S, I, W, E*, 1982 *I*, 1983 *I, W*
Iracabal, J (Bayonne) 1968 *NZ* 1,2, *SA* 1, 1969 *S, I, W, R*, 1970 *S, I, W, E*, 1971 *W, SA* 1,2, *A* 1, 1972 *E, W, I* 2, *A* 2, *R*, 1973 *S, NZ, E, W, I, J*, 1974 *I, W, E, S, Arg* 1,2, *SA* 2(R)
Isaac, H (RCF) 1907 *E*, 1908 *E*
Ithurra, E (Biarritz O) 1936 *G* 1,2, 1937 *G*

Janeczek, T (Tarbes) 1982 *Arg* 1,2, 1990 *R*
Janik, K (Toulouse) 1987 *R*
Jarasse, A (Brive) 1945 *B* 1
Jardel, J (SB) 1928 *I, E*
Jaureguy, A (RCF, Toulouse, SF) 1920 *S, E, W, I, US*, 1922 *S, W*, 1923 *S, W, E, I*, 1924 *S, W, R, US*, 1925 *I, NZ*, 1926 *S, E, W, M*, 1927 *I, E*, 1928 *S, A, E, G, W*, 1929 *I, S, E*
Jaureguy, P (Toulouse) 1913 *S, SA, W, I*
Jauzion, Y (Colomiers) 2001 *SA* 1,2, *NZ*
Jeangrand, M-H (Tarbes) 1921 *I*
Jeanjean, N (Toulouse) 2001 *SA* 1,2, *NZ*
Jeanjean, P (Toulon) 1948 *I*
Jérôme, G (SF) 1906 *NZ, E*
Joinel, J-L (Brive) 1977 *NZ* 1, 1978 *R*, 1979 *I, W, E, S, NZ* 1,2, *R*, 1980 *W, E, S, I, SA*, 1981 *S, I, W, E, R, NZ* 1,2, 1982 *E, S, I, R*, 1983 *E, S, I, W, A* 1,2, *R*, 1984 *I, W, E, S, NZ* 1,2, 1985 *S, I, W, Arg* 1, 1986 *S, I, W, E, R* 1, *Arg* 1,2, *A*, 1987 [*Z*]
Jol, M (Biarritz O) 1947 *S, I, W, E*, 1949 *S, I, E, W, Arg* 1,2
Jordana, J-L (Pau, Toulouse) 1996 *R* (R), *Arg* 1(t),2, *W* 2, 1997 *I* (t), *W, S* (R)
Judas du Souich, C (SCUF) 1911 *W, I*
Juillet, C (Montferrand, SF) 1995 *R* 2, *Arg*, 1999 *E, S, WS, NZ* 1, [*C, Fj, Arg, NZ* 2, *A*], 2000 *A, NZ* 1,2, 2001 *S, I, It, W*
Junquas, L (Tyrosse) 1945 *B* 1,2, *W*, 1946 *B, I, K, W*, 1947 *S, I, W, E*, 1948 *S, W*

Kaczorowski, D (Le Creusot) 1974 *I* (R)
Kaempf, A (St Jean-de-Luz) 1946 *B*

Labadie, P (Bayonne) 1952 *S, I, SA, W, E, It*, 1953 *S, I, It*, 1954 *S, I, NZ, W, E, Arg* 2, 1955 *S, I, E, W*, 1956 *I*, 1957 *I*
Labarthete, R (Pau) 1952 *S*
Labazuy, A (Lourdes) 1952 *I*, 1954 *S, W*, 1956 *E*, 1958 *A, W, I*, 1959 *S, E, It, W*
Labit, C (Toulouse) 1999 *S, R* (R), *WS* (R), *Tg*, 2000 *R* (R)
Laborde, C (RCF) 1962 *It, R*, 1963 *R*, 1964 *SA*, 1965 *R*
Labrousse, T (Brive) 1996 *R, SA* 1
Lacans, P (Béziers) 1980 *SA*, 1981 *W, E, A* 2, *R*, 1982 *W*
Lacassagne, H (SBUC) 1906 *NZ*, 1907 *E*
Lacaussade, R (Bègles) 1948 *A, S*
Lacaze, C (Lourdes, Angoulême) 1961 *NZ* 2,3, *A, R*, 1962 *E, W, I, It*, 1963 *W, R*, 1964 *S, NZ, E*, 1965 *S, I, W, E, It, R*, 1967 *S, E, SA* 1,3,4, 1968 *S, E, W, Cz, NZ* 1, 1969 *E*
Lacaze, H (Périgueux) 1928 *I, G, W*, 1929 *I, W*
Lacaze, P (Lourdes) 1958 *SA* 1,2, 1959 *S, E, It, W, I*
Lacazedieu, C (Dax) 1923 *W, I*, 1928 *A, I*, 1929 *S*
Lacombe, B (Agen) 1989 *B*, 1990 *A* 2
Lacome, M (Pau) 1960 *Arg* 2
Lacoste, R (Tarbes) 1914 *I, W, E*
Lacrampe, F (Béziers) 1949 *Arg* 2
Lacroix, P (Mont-de-Marsan, Agen) 1958 *A*, 1960 *W, I, It, R, Arg* 1,2,3, 1961 *S, SA, E, W, I, NZ* 1,2,3, *A, R*, 1962 *S, E, W, I, R*, 1963 *S, I, E, W*
Lacroix, T (Dax, Harlequins) 1989 *A* 1(R),2, 1991 *W* 1(R),2(R), [*R, C* (R), *E*], 1992 *SA* 2, 1993 *E, S, I, W, SA* 1,2, *R* 2, *A* 1,2, 1994 *I, W, E, S, C* 1, *NZ* 1,2, *C* 2, 1995 *W, E, S, R* 1, [*Tg, Iv, S, I, SA, E*], 1996 *E, S, I*, 1997 *It* 2, *R* 2, *Arg, SA* 1,2
Lafarge, Y (Montferrand) 1978 *R*, 1979 *NZ* 1, 1981 *I* (R)
Laffitte, R (SCUF) 1910 *W, S*
Laffont, H (Narbonne) 1926 *W*
Lafond, A (Bayonne) 1922 *E*
Lafond, J-B (RCF) 1983 *A* 1, 1985 *Arg* 1,2 1986 *S, I, W, E, R* 1, 1987 *I* (R), 1988 *W*, 1989 *I, W, E*, 1990 *W, A* 3(R), *NZ* 2, 1991 *S, I, W* 1, *E, R, US* 1, *W* 2, [*R* (R), *Fj, C, E*], 1992 *W, E, S, I* (R), *SA* 2, 1993 *E, S, I, W*
Lagisquet, P (Bayonne) 1983 *A* 1,2, *R*, 1984 *I, W, NZ* 1,2, 1986 *R* 1(R), *Arg* 1,2, *A, NZ* 1, 1987 [*S, R, Fj, A, NZ*], *R*, 1988 *S, I, W, Arg* 1,2,3,4, 1989 *I, W, E, S, NZ* 1,2, *B, A* 1,2, 1990 *W, E, S, I, A* 1,2,3, 1991 *S, I, US* 2, [*R*]
Lagrange, J-C (RCF) 1966 *It*
Lalande, M (RCF) 1923 *S, W, I*
Lalanne, F (Mont-de-Marsan) 2000 *R*
Lamaison, C (Brive, Agen) 1996 *SA* 1(R),2, 1997 *W, E, S, R* 1, *A* 2, *It* 2, *R* 2, *Arg, SA* 1,2, 1998 *E, S, I, W, Arg* 3(R), *A*, 1999 *R, WS* (R), *Tg, NZ* 1(R), *W* 2(R), [*C* (R), *Nm, Fj, Arg, NZ* 2, *A*], 2000 *W, A, NZ* 1,2, 2001 *S, I, It, W* (R)
Landreau, F (SF) 2000 *A, NZ* 1,2, 2001 *E* (R)
Lane, G (RCF) 1906 *NZ, E*, 1907 *E*, 1908 *E, W*, 1909 *E, W, I*, 1910 *W, E*, 1911 *S, W*, 1912 *I, W, E*, 1913 *S*
Langlade, J-C (Hyères) 1990 *R, A* 1, *NZ* 1
Laperne, D (Dax) 1997 *R* 1(R)
Laporte, G (Graulhet) 1981 *I, W, E, R, NZ* 1,2, 1986 *S, I, W, E, R* 1, *Arg* 1, *A* (R), 1987 [*R, Z* (R), *Fj*]

Larreguy, P (Bayonne) 1954 *It*
Larribau, J (Périgueux) 1912 *I, S, W, E*, 1913 *S*, 1914 *I, E*
Larrieu, J (Tarbes) 1920 *I, US*, 1921 *W*, 1923 *S, W, E, I*
Larrieux, M (SBUC) 1927 *G* 2
Larrue, H (Carmaux) 1960 *W, I, It, R, Arg* 1,2,3
Lasaosa, P (Dax) 1950 *I*, 1952 *S, I, E, It*, 1955 *It*
Lascubé, G (Agen) 1991 *S, I, W* 1, *E, US* 2, *W* 2, [*R, Fj, C, E*], 1992 *W, E*
Lassegue, J-B (Toulouse) 1946 *W*, 1947 *S, I, W*, 1948 *W*, 1949 *I, E, W, Arg* 1
Lasserre, F (René) (Bayonne, Cognac, Grenoble) 1914 *I*, 1920 *S*, 1921 *S, W, I*, 1922 *S, E, W, I*, 1923 *W, E*, 1924 *S, I, R, US*
Lasserre, J-C (Dax) 1963 *It*, 1964 *S, NZ, E, W, It, I, Fj*, 1965 *W, It, R*, 1966 *R*, 1967 *S*
Lasserre, M (Agen) 1967 *SA* 2,3, 1968 *E, W, Cz, NZ* 3, *A, SA* 1,2, 1969 *S, I, E*, 1970 *E*, 1971 *E, W*
Laterrade, G (Tarbes) 1910 *E, I*, 1911 *S, E, I*
Laudouar, J (Soustons, SBUC) 1961 *NZ* 1,2, *R*, 1962 *I, R*
Lauga, P (Vichy) 1950 *S, I, E, W*
Laurent, A (Biarritz O) 1925 *NZ, S, W, E*, 1926 *W*
Laurent, J (Bayonne) 1920 *S, E, W*
Laurent, M (Auch) 1932 *G*, 1933 *G*, 1934 *G*, 1935 *G*, 1936 *G* 1
Lassucq, C (SF) 1999 *S* (R), 2000 *W* (R), *S, I*
Lavail, G (Perpignan) 1937 *G*, 1940 *B*
Lavaud, R (Carcassonne) 1914 *I, W*
Lavergne, P (Limoges) 1950 *S*
Lavigne, B (Agen) 1984 *R*, 1985 *E*
Lavigne, J (Dax) 1920 *E, W*
Lazies, H (Auch) 1954 *Arg* 2, 1955 *It*, 1956 *E*, 1957 *S*
Le Bourhis, R (La Rochelle) 1961 *R*
Lecointre, M (Nantes) 1952 *It*
Le Droff, J (Auch) 1963 *It, R*, 1964 *S, NZ, E*, 1970 *E, R*, 1971 *S, I*
Lefevre, R (Brive) 1961 *NZ* 2
Leflamand, L (Bourgoin) 1996 *SA* 2, 1997 *W, E, S, It* 2, *Arg, SA* 1,2(R)
Lefort, J-B (Biarritz O) 1938 *G* 1
Le Goff, R (Métro) 1938 *R, G* 2
Legrain, M (SF) 1909 *I*, 1910 *I*, 1911 *S, E, W, I*, 1913 *S, SA, E, I*, 1914 *I, W*
Lemeur, Y (RCF) 1993 *R* 1
Lenient, J-J (Vichy) 1967 *R*
Lepatey, J (Mazamet) 1954 *It*, 1955 *S, I, E, W*
Lepatey, L (Mazamet) 1924 *S, I, E*
Lescarboura, J-P (Dax) 1982 *W, E, S, I*, 1983 *A* 1,2, *R*, 1984 *I, W, E, S, NZ* 1,2, *R*, 1985 *E, S, I, W, Arg* 1,2, 1986 *Arg* 2, *A, NZ* 1, *R* 2, *NZ* 2, 1988 *S, W*, 1990 *R*
Lesieur, E (SF) 1906 *E*, 1908 *E, W*, 1909 *E, W, I*, 1910 *S, E, I*, 1911 *E, I*, 1912 *W*
Leuvielle, M (SBUC) 1908 *W*, 1913 *S, SA, E, W*, 1914 *W, E*
Levasseur, R (SF) 1925 *W, E*
Levée, H (RCF) 1906 *NZ*
Lewis, E W (Le Havre) 1906 *E*
Lhermet, J-M (Montferrand) 1990 *S, I*, 1993 *R* 1
Libaros, G (Tarbes) 1936 *G* 1, 1940 *B*
Lievremont, M (Perpignan, SF) 1995 *It, R* 2, *Arg* (R), *NZ* 2(R), 1996 *R, Arg* 1(R), *SA* 2(R), 1997 *R* 1, *A* 2(R), 1998 *E* (R), *S, I, W, Arg* 1,2, *Fj, Arg* 3, *A*, 1999 *W* 2, [*C, Nm, Fj, Arg, NZ* 2, *A*]
Lievremont, T (Perpignan, SF, Biarritz) 1996 *W* 2(R), 1998 *E, S, I, W, Arg* 1,2, *Fj, Arg* 3, *A*, 1999 *I, W* 1, *E, W* 2, [*Nm*], 2000 *W* (R), *E* (R), *S* (R), *I, It*, 2001 *E* (R)
Lira, M (La Voulte) 1962 *R*, 1963 *I, E, W, It, R*, 1964 *W, It, I, SA*, 1965 *S, I, R*
Llari, R (Carcassonne) 1926 *S*
Lobies, J (RCF) 1921 *S, W, E*
Lombard, F (Narbonne) 1934 *G*, 1937 *It*
Lombard, T (SF) 1998 *Arg* 3, *A*, 1999 *I, W* 1, *S* (R), 2000 *W, E, S, A, NZ* 1, 2001 *It, W*
Lombarteix, R (Montferrand) 1938 *R, G* 2
Londios, J (Montauban) 1967 *SA* 3
Loppy, L (Toulon) 1993 *R* 2
Lorieux, A (Grenoble, Aix) 1981 *A* 1, *R, NZ* 1,2, 1982 *W*, 1983 *A* 2, *R*, 1984 *I, W, E*, 1985 *Arg* 1,2(R), 1986 *R* 2, *NZ* 2,3, 1987 *W, E*, [*S, Z, Fj, A, NZ*], 1988 *S, I, W, Arg* 1,2,4, 1989 *W, A* 2
Loury, J (RCF) 1927 *E, G* 1,2, 1928 *S, A, I*
Loustau, M (Dax) 1923 *E*
Lubin-Lebrère, M-F (Toulouse) 1914 *I, W, E*, 1920 *S, E, W, I, US*, 1921 *S*, 1922 *S, E, W*, 1924 *W, US*, 1925 *I*
Lubrano, A (Béziers) 1972 *A* 2, 1973 *S*

Lux, J-P (Tyrosse, Dax) 1967 *E, It, W, I, SA* 1,2,4, *R*, 1968 *I, E, Cz, NZ* 3, *A, SA* 1,2, 1969 *S, I, E,* 1970 *S, I, W, E, R*, 1971 *S, I, E, W, A* 1,2, 1972 *S, I* 1, *E, W, I* 2, *A* 1,2, *R*, 1973 *S, NZ, E*, 1974 *I, W, E, S, Arg* 1,2, 1975 *W*

Macabiau, A (Perpignan) 1994 *S, C* 1
Maclos, P (SF) 1906 *E*, 1907 *E*
Magne, O (Dax, Brive, Montferrand) 1997 *W* (R), *E, S, R* 1(R), *A* 1,2, *It* 2(R), *R* 2, *Arg* (R), 1998 *E, S, I, W, Arg* 1,2, *Fj, Arg* 3, *A*, 1999 *I, R, WS, NZ* 1, *W* 2, [*C, Nm, Fj, Arg, NZ* 2, *A*], 2000 *W, E, S, It, R, A, NZ* 1,2, 2001 *S, I, It, W, E, SA* 1,2, *NZ*
Magnanou, C (RCF) 1923 *E*, 1925 *W, E*, 1926 *S*, 1929 *S, W*, 1930 *S, I, E, W*
Magnol, L (Toulouse) 1928 *S*, 1929 *S, W, E*
Magois, H (La Rochelle) 1968 *SA* 1,2, *R*
Majerus, R (SF) 1928 *W*, 1929 *I, S*, 1930 *S, I, E, G, W*
Malbet, J-C (Agen) 1967 *SA* 2,4
Maleig, A (Oloron) 1979 *W, E, NZ* 2, 1980 *W, E, SA, R*
Mallier, L (Brive) 1999 *R, W* 2(R), [*C* (R)], 2000 *I* (R), *It*
Malquier, Y (Narbonne) 1979 *S*
Manterola, T (Lourdes) 1955 *It*, 1957 *R* 1
Mantoulan, C (Pau) 1959 *I*
Marcet, J (Albi) 1925 *I, NZ, S, W, E*, 1926 *I, E*
Marchal, J-F (Lourdes) 1979 *S, R*, 1980 *W, S, I*
Marconnet, S (SF) 1998 *Arg* 3, *A*, 1999 *I* (R), *W* 1(R), *E, S* (R), *R, Tg*, 2000 *A, NZ* 1,2, 2001 *S, I, It* (R), *W* (R), *E*
Marchand, R (Poitiers) 1920 *S, W*
Marfaing, M (Toulouse) 1992 *R, Arg* 1
Marlu, J (Montferrand) 1998 *Fj* (R)
Marocco, P (Montferrand) 1968 *S, I, W, E, R* 1, *Arg* 1,2, *A*, 1988 *Arg* 4, 1989 *I*, 1990 *E* (R), *NZ* 1(R), 1991 *S, I, W* 1, *E, US* 2, [*R, Fj, C, E*]
Marot, A (Brive) 1969 *R*, 1970 *S, I, W*, 1971 *SA* 1, 1972 *I* 2, 1976 *A* 1
Marquesuzaa, A (RCF) 1958 *It, SA* 1,2, 1959 *S, E, It, W*, 1960 *S, E, Arg* 1
Marracq, H (Pau) 1961 *R*
Martin, C (Lyon) 1909 *I*, 1910 *W, S*
Martin, H (SBUC) 1907 *E*, 1908 *W*
Martin, J-L (Béziers) 1971 *A* 2, *R*, 1972 *S, I* 1
Martin, L (Pau) 1948 *I, A, S, W, E*, 1950 *S*
Martine, R (Lourdes) 1952 *S, I, It*, 1953 *It*, 1954 *S, I, NZ, W, E, It, Arg* 2, 1955 *S, I, W*, 1958 *A, W, It, I, SA* 1,2, 1960 *S, E, Arg* 3, 1961 *S, It*
Martinez, G (Toulouse) 1982 *W, E, S, Arg* 1,2, 1983 *E, W*
Mas, F (Béziers) 1962 *R*, 1963 *S, I, E, W*
Maso, J (Perpignan, Narbonne) 1966 *It, R*, 1967 *S, R*, 1968 *S, W, Cz, NZ* 1,2,3, *A, R*, 1969 *S, I, W*, 1971 *SA* 1,2, *R*, 1972 *E, W, A* 2, 1973 *W, I, J, R*
Massare, J (PUC) 1945 *B* 1,2, *W*, 1946 *B, I, W*
Massé, A (SBUC) 1908 *W*, 1909 *E, W*, 1910 *W, S, E, I*
Masse, H (Grenoble) 1937 *G*
Matheu-Cambas, J (Agen) 1945 *W*, 1946 *B, I, K, W*, 1947 *S, I, W, E*, 1948 *I, A, S, W, E*, 1949 *S, I, E, W, Arg* 1,2, 1950 *F, W*, 1951 *S, I*
Matiu, L (Biarritz) 2000 *W, E*
Mauduy, G (Périgueux) 1957 *It, R* 1,2, 1958 *S, E*, 1961 *W, It*
Mauran, J (Castres) 1952 *SA, W, E, It*, 1953 *I, E*
Mauriat, P (Lyon) 1907 *E*, 1908 *E, W*, 1909 *W, I*, 1910 *W, S, E, I*, 1911 *S, E, W, I*, 1912 *I, S*, 1913 *S, SA, W, I*
Maurin, G (ASF) 1906 *E*
Maury, A (Toulouse) 1925 *I, NZ, S, W, E*, 1926 *S, I, E*
Mayssonnié, A (Toulouse) 1908 *E, W*, 1910 *W*
Mazas, L (Colomiers, Biarritz) 1992 *Arg*, 1996 *SA* 1
Melville, E (Toulon) 1990 *I* (R), *A* 1,2,3, *NZ* 1, 1991 *US* 2
Menrath, R (SCUF) 1910 *W*
Menthiller, Y (Romans) 1964 *W, It, SA, R*, 1965 *E*
Merceron, G (Montferrand) 1999 *R* (R), *Tg*, 2000 *S, I, R*, 2001 *S* (R), *W, E, SA* 1,2, *NZ* (R)
Meret, F (Tarbes) 1940 *B*
Mericq, S (Agen) 1959 *I*, 1960 *S, E, W*, 1961 *I*
Merle, O (Grenoble, Montferrand) 1993 *SA* 1,2, *R* 2, *A* 1,2, 1994 *I, W, E, S, C* 1, *NZ* 1,2, *C* 2, 1995 *W, I, R* 1, [*Tg, S, I, SA, E*], *It, R* 2, *Arg, NZ* 1,2, 1996 *E, S, R, Arg* 1,2, *W* 2, *SA* 2, 1997 *I, W, E, S, It* 1, *R* 1, *A* 1,2, *It* 2, *R* 2, *SA* 1(R),2
Merquey, J (Toulon)1950 *S, I, E, W*
Mesnel, F (RCF) 1986 *NZ* 2(R),3, 1987 *W, E, S, I*, [*S, Z, Fj, A, NZ*], *R*, 1988 *E, Arg* 1,2,3,4, *R*, 1989 *I, W, E, S, NZ* 1, *A* 1,2, 1990 *E, S, I, A* 2,3, *NZ* 1,2, 1991 *S, I, W* 1, *E, R, US* 1,2, *W* 2, [*R, Fj, C, E*], 1992 *W, E, S, I, SA* 1,2, 1993 *E* (R), *W*, 1995 *I, R* 1, [*Iv, E*]
Mesny, P (RCF, Grenoble) 1979 *NZ* 1,2, 1980 *SA, R*, 1981 *I, W* (R), *A* 1,2, *R, NZ* 1,2, 1982 *I, Arg* 1,2

Meyer, G-S (Périgueux) 1960 *S, E, It, R, Arg* 2
Meynard, J (Cognac) 1954 *Arg* 1, 1956 *Cz*
Mias, L (Mazamet) 1951 *S, I, E, W*, 1952 *I, SA, W, E, It*, 1953 *S, I, W, It*, 1954 *S, I, NZ, W*, 1957 *R* 2, 1958 *S, E, A, W, I, SA* 1,2, 1959 *S, It, W, I*
Mignoni, P (Béziers) 1997 *R* 2(R), *Arg* (t), 1999 *R* (R), *WS, NZ* 1, *W* 2(R), [*C, Nm*]
Milhères, C (Biarritz) 2001 *E*
Milliand, P (Grenoble) 1936 *G* 2, 1937 *G, It*
Milloud, O (Bourgoin) 2000 *R* (R), 2001 *NZ*
Minjat, R (Lyon) 1945 *B* 1
Miorin, H (Toulouse) 1996 *R, SA* 1, 1997 *I, W, E, S, It* 1, 2000 *It* (R), *R* (R)
Mir, J-H (Lourdes) 1967 *R*, 1968 *I*
Mir, J-P (Lourdes) 1967 *A*
Modin, R (Brive) 1987 [*Z*]
Moga, A-M-A (Bègles) 1945 *B* 1,2, *W*, 1946 *B, I, K, W*, 1947 *S, I, W, E*, 1948 *I, A, S, W, E*, 1949 *S, I, E, W, Arg* 1,2
Mola, U (Dax, Castres) 1997 *S* (R), 1999 *R* (R), *WS, Tg* (R), *NZ* 1, *W* 2, [*C, Nm, Fj, Arg* (R), *NZ* 2, *A* (R)]
Mommejat, B (Cahors, Albi) 1958 *It, I, SA* 1,2, 1959 *S, E, It, W, I*, 1960 *S, E, I, R*, 1962 *S, E, W, I, It, R*, 1963 *S, I, W*
Moncla, F (RCF, Pau) 1956 *Cz*, 1957 *I, E, W, It, R* 1, 1958 *SA* 1,2, 1959 *S, E, It, W, I*, 1960 *S, E, W, I, It, R, Arg* 1,2,3, 1961 *S, SA, E, W, It, I, NZ* 1,2,3
Moni, C (Nice, SF) 1996 *R*, 2000 *A, NZ* 1,2, 2001 *S, I, It, W*
Monié, R (Perpignan) 1956 *Cz*, 1957 *E*
Monier, R (SBUC) 1911 *I*, 1912 *S*
Monniot, M (RCF) 1912 *W, E*
Montade, A (Perpignan) 1925 *I, NZ, S, W*, 1926 *W*
Montlaur, P (Agen) 1992 *E* (R), 1994 *S* (R)
Moraitis, B (Toulon) 1969 *E, W*
Morel, A (Grenoble) 1954 *Arg* 2
Morere, J (Toulouse) 1927 *E, G* 1, 1928 *S, A*
Moscato, V (Bègles) 1991 *R, US* 1, 1992 *W, E*
Mougeot, C (Bègles) 1992 *W, E, Arg*
Mouniq, P (Toulouse) 1911 *S, E, W, I*,1912 *I, E*, 1913 *S, SA, E*
Moure, H (SCUF) 1908 *E*
Moureu, P (Béziers) 1920 *I, US*, 1921 *W, E, I*, 1922 *S, W, I*, 1923 *S, W, E, I*, 1924 *S, I, E, W*
Mournet, A (Bagnères) 1981 *A* 1(R)
Mouronval, F (SF) 1909 *I*
Muhr, A H (RCF) 1906 *NZ, E*, 1907 *E*
Murillo, G (Dijon) 1954 *It, Arg* 1

Nallet, L (Bourgoin) 2000 *R*, 2001 *E, SA* 1(R),2(R), *NZ*
Namur, H (Toulon) 1931 *E, G*
Noble, J-C (La Voulte) 1968 *E, W, Cz, NZ* 3, *A, R*
Normand, A (Toulouse) 1957 *R* 1
Novès, G (Toulouse) 1977 *NZ* 1,2, *R*, 1978 *W, R*, 1979 *I, W*
Ntamack, E (Toulouse) 1994 *W, C* 1, *NZ* 1,2, *C* 2, 1995 *W, I, R* 1, [*Tg, S, I, SA, E*], *It, R* 2, *Arg, NZ* 1,2, 1996 *E, S, I, W* 1, *R* (R), *Arg* 1,2, *W* 2, 1997 *I*, 1998 *Arg* 3, 1999 *I, W* 1, *E, S, WS, NZ* 1, *W* 2(R), [*C* (R), *Nm, Fj, Arg, NZ* 2, *A*], 2000 *W, E, S, I, It*

Olive, D (Montferrand) 1951 *I*, 1952 *I*
Ondarts, P (Biarritz O) 1986 *NZ* 3, 1987 *W, E, S, I*, [*S, Z, Fj, A, NZ*], *R*, 1988 *E, I, W, Arg* 1,2,3,4, *R*, 1989 *I, W, E, NZ* 1,2, *A* 2, 1990 *W, E, S, I, R* (R), *NZ* 1,2, 1991 *S, I, W* 1, *E, US* 2, *W* 2, [*R, Fj, C, E*]
Orso, J-C (Nice, Toulon) 1982 *Arg* 1,2, 1983 *E, S, A* 1, 1984 *E* (R), *S, NZ* 1, 1985 *I* (R), *W*, 1988 *I*
Othats, J (Dax) 1960 *Arg* 2,3
Ougier, S (Toulouse) 1992 *R, Arg* 1, 1993 *E* (R), 1997 *It* 1

Paco, A (Béziers) 1974 *Arg* 1,2, *R, SA* 1,2, 1975 *W, E, Arg* 1,2, *R*, 1976 *S, I, W, E, US, A* 1,2, *R*, 1977 *W, E, S, I, NZ* 1,2, *R*, 1978 *E, S, I, W, R*, 1979 *I, W, E, S*, 1980 *W*
Palat, J (Perpignan) 1938 *G* 2
Palmié, M (Béziers) 1975 *SA* 1,2, *Arg* 1,2, 1976 *S, I, W, E, US*, 1977 *W, E, S, I, Arg* 1,2, *NZ* 1,2, *R*, 1978 *E, S, I, W*
Paoli, R (see Simonpaoli)
Paparemborde, R (Pau) 1975 *SA* 1,2, *Arg* 1,2, *R*, 1976 *S, I, W, E, US, A* 1,2, *R*, 1977 *W, E, S, I, Arg* 1, *NZ* 1,2, 1978 *E, S, I, W, R*, 1979 *I, W, E, S, NZ* 1,2, *R*, 1980 *W, E, S, SA, R*, 1981 *S, I, W, E, A* 1,2, *R, NZ* 1,2, 1982 *W, I, R, Arg* 1,2 1983 *E, S, I, W*
Pardo, L (Hendaye) 1924 *I, E*
Pardo, L (Bayonne) 1980 *SA, R*, 1981 *S, I, W, E, A* 1, 1982 *W, E, S*, 1983 *A* 1(R), 1985 *S, I, Arg* 2
Pargade, J-H (Lyon U) 1953 *It*

Paries, L (Biarritz O) 1968 *SA* 2, *R*, 1970 *S, I, W*, 1975 *E, S, I*

Pascalin, P (Mont-de-Marsan) 1950 *I, E, W*, 1951 *S, I, E, W*

Pascarel, J-R (TOEC) 1912 *W, E*, 1913 *S, SA, E, I*

Pascot, J (Perpignan) 1922 *S, E, I*, 1923 *S*, 1926 *I*, 1927 *G* 2

Paul, R (Montferrand) 1940 *B*

Pauthe, G (Graulhet) 1956 *E*

Pebeyre, E-J (Fumel, Brive) 1945 *W*, 1946 *I, K, W*, 1947 *S, I, W, E*

Pebeyre, M (Vichy, Montferrand) 1970 *E, R*, 1971 *I, SA* 1,2, *A* 1, 1973 *W*

Pecune, J (Tarbes) 1974 *W, E, S*, 1975 *Arg* 1,2, *R*, 1976 *I, W, E, US*

Pedeutour, P (Begles) 1980 *I*

Pellissier, L (RCF) 1928 *A, I, E, G, W*

Pelous, F (Dax, Toulouse) 1995 *R* 2, *Arg, NZ* 1,2, 1996 *E, S, I, R* (R), *Arg* 1,2, *W* 2, *SA* 1,2, 1997 *I, W, E, S, It* 1, *R* 1, *A* 1,2, *It* 2, *R* 2, *Arg, SA* 1,2(R), 1998 *E, S, I, W, Arg* 1,2, *Fj, Arg* 3, *A*, 1999 *I, W* 1, *E, R* (R), *WS, Tg* (R), *NZ* 1, *W* 2, [*C, Nm, Fj, NZ* 2, *A*], 2000 *W, E, S, I, It, A, NZ* 1,2, 2001 *S, I, It, W, E*

Penaud, A (Brive, Toulouse) 1992 *W, E, S, I, R, Arg* 1,2, *SA* 1,2, *Arg*, 1993 *R* 1, *SA* 1,2, *R* 2, *A* 1,2, 1994 *I, W, E*, 1995 *NZ* 1,2, 1996 *S, R, Arg* 1,2, *W* 2, 1997 *I, E, R* 1, *A* 2, 2000 *W* (R), *It*

Périé, M (Toulon) 1996 *E, S, I* (R)

Peron, P (RCF) 1975 *SA* 1,2

Perrier, P (Bayonne) 1982 *W, E, S, I* (R)

Pesteil, J-P (Béziers) 1975 *SA* 1, 1976 *A* 2, *R*

Petit, C (Lorrain) 1931 *W*

Peyrelade, H (Tarbes) 1940 *B*

Peyroutou, G (Périgueux) 1911 *S, E*

Phliponeau, J-F (Montferrand) 1973 *W, I*

Piazza, A (Montauban) 1968 *NZ* 1, *A*

Picard, T (Montferrand) 1985 *Arg* 2, 1986 *R* 1(R), *Arg* 2

Pierrot, G (Pau) 1914 *I, W, E*

Pilon, J (Périgueux) 1949 *E*, 1950 *E*

Piqué, J (Pau) 1961 *NZ* 2,3, *A*, 1962 *S, It*, 1964 *NZ, E, W, It, I, SA, Fj, R*, 1965 *S, I, E, W, It*

Piquemal, M (Tarbes) 1927 *I, S*, 1929 *I, G*, 1930 *S, I, E, G, W*

Piquiral, E (RCF) 1924 *S, I, E, W, R, US*, 1925 *E*, 1926 *S, I, E, W, M*, 1927 *I, S, W, E, G* 1,2, 1928 *E*

Piteu, R (Pau) 1921 *S, W, E, I*, 1922 *S, E, W, I*, 1923 *E*, 1924 *E*, 1925 *I, NZ, W, E*, 1926 *E*

Plantefol, A (RCF) 1967 *SA* 2,3,4, *NZ, R*, 1968 *E, W, Cz, NZ* 2, 1969 *E, W*

Plantey, S (RCF) 1961 *A*, 1962 *It*

Podevin, G (SF) 1913 *W, I*

Poeydebasque, F (Bayonne) 1914 *I, W*

Poirier, A (SCUF) 1907 *E*

Pomathios, M (Agen, Lyon U, Bourg) 1948 *I, A, S, W, E*, 1949 *I, E, W, Arg* 1,2, 1950 *S, I, W*, 1951 *S, I, E, W*, 1952 *W, E*, 1953 *S, I, W*, 1954 *S*

Pons, P (Toulouse) 1920 *S, E, W*, 1921 *S, W*, 1922 *S*

Porra, M (Lyon) 1931 *I*

Porthault, A (RCF) 1951 *S, E, W*, 1952 *I*, 1953 *S, I, It*

Portolan, C (Toulouse) 1986 *A*, 1989 *I, E*

Potel, A (Begles) 1932 *G*

Prat, J (Lourdes) 1945 *B* 1,2, *W*, 1946 *B, I, K, W*, 1947 *S, I, W, E*, 1948 *I, A, S, W, E*, 1949 *S, I, E, W, Arg* 1,2, 1950 *S, I, E, W*, 1951 *S, E, W*, 1952 *S, I, SA, W, E, It*, 1953 *S, I, E, W, It*, 1954 *S, I, NZ, W, E, It*, 1955 *S, I, E, W, It*

Prat, M (Lourdes) 1951 *I*, 1952 *S, I, SA, W, E*, 1953 *S, I, E*, 1954 *I, NZ, W, E, It*, 1955 *S, I, E, W, It*, 1956 *I, W, It, Cz*, 1957 *S, I, W, It, E*, 1958 *A, W, I*

Prevost, A (Albi) 1926 *M*, 1927 *I, S, W*

Prin-Clary, J (Cavaillon, Brive) 1945 *B* 1,2, *W*, 1946 *B, I, K, W*, 1947 *S, I, W*

Puech, L (Toulouse) 1920 *S, E, I*, 1921 *E, I*

Puget, M (Toulouse) 1961 *It*, 1966 *S, I, It*, 1967 *SA* 1,3,4, *NZ*, 1968 *Cz, NZ* 1,2, *SA* 1,2, *R*, 1969 *E, R*, 1970 *W*

Puig, A (Perpignan) 1926 *S, E*

Pujol, A (SOE Toulouse) 1906 *NZ*

Pujolle, M (Nice) 1989 *B, A* 1, 1990 *S, I, R, A* 1,2, *NZ* 2

Quaglio, A (Mazamet) 1957 *R* 2, 1958 *S, E, A, W, I, SA* 1,2, 1959 *S, E, It, W, I*

Quilis, A (Narbonne) 1967 *SA* 1,4, *NZ*, 1970 *R*, 1971 *I*

Ramis, R (Perpignan) 1922 *E, I*, 1923 *W*

Rancoule, H (Lourdes, Toulon, Tarbes) 1955 *E, W, It*, 1958 *A, W, It, I, SA* 1, 1959 *S, It, W*, 1960 *I, It, R, Arg* 1,2, 1961 *SA, E, W, It, NZ* 1,2, 1962 *S, E, W, I, It*

Rapin, A (SBUC) 1938 *R*

Raymond, F (Toulouse) 1925 *S*, 1927 *W*, 1928 *I*

Raynal, F (Perpignan) 1935 *G*, 1936 *G* 1,2, 1937 *G, It*

Raynaud, F (Carcassonne) 1933 *G*

Raynaud, M (Narbonne) 1999 *W* 1, *E* (R)

Razat, J-P (Agen) 1962 *R*, 1963 *S, I, R*

Rebujent, R (RCF) 1963 *E*

Revailler, D (Graulhet) 1981 *S, I, W, E, A* 1,2, *R, NZ* 1,2, 1982 *W, S, I, R, Arg* 1

Revillon, J (RCF) 1926 *I, E*, 1927 *S*

Ribère, E (Perpignan, Quillan) 1924 *I*, 1925, *I, NZ, S*, 1926 *S, I, W, M*, 1927 *I, S, W, E, G* 1,2, 1928 *S, A, I, E, G, W*, 1929 *I, E, G*, 1930 *S, I, E, W*, 1931 *I, S, W, E, G*, 1932 *G*, 1933 *G*

Rives, J-P (Toulouse, RCF) 1975 *E, S, I, Arg* 1,2, *R*, 1976 *S, I, W, E, US, A* 1,2, *R*, 1977 *W, E, S, I, Arg* 1,2, *R*, 1978 *E, S, I, W, R*, 1979 *I, W, E, S, NZ* 1,2, *R*, 1980 *W, E, S, I, SA*, 1981 *S, I, W, E, A* 2, 1982 *W, E, S, I, R*, 1983 *E, S, I, W, A* 1,2, *R*, 1984 *I, W, E, S*

Rochon, A (Montferrand) 1936 *G* 1

Rodrigo, M (Mauléon) 1931 *I, W*

Rodriguez, L (Mont-de-Marsan, Montferrand, Dax) 1981 *A* 1,2, *R, NZ* 1,2, 1982 *W, E, S, I, R*, 1983 *E, S*, 1984 *I, NZ* 1,2, *R*, 1985 *E, S, I, W*, 1986 *Arg* 1, *A, R* 2, *NZ* 2,3, 1987 *W, E, S, I, [S, Z, Fj, A, NZ], R*, 1988 *E, S, I, W, Arg* 1,2,3,4, *R*, 1989 *I, E, S, NZ* 1,2, *B, A* 1, 1990 *W, E, S, I, NZ* 1

Rogé, L (Béziers) 1952 *It*, 1953 *E, W, It*, 1954 *S, Arg* 1,2, 1955 *S, I*, 1956 *W, It, E*, 1957 *S*, 1960 *S, E*

Rollet, J (Bayonne) 1960 *Arg* 3, 1961 *NZ* 3, *A*, 1962 *It*, 1963 *I*

Romero, H (Montauban) 1962 *S, E, W, I, It, R*, 1963 *E*

Romeu, J-P (Montferrand) 1972 *R*, 1973 *S, NZ, E, W, I, R*, 1974 *W, E, S, Arg* 1,2, *R, SA* 1,2(R), 1975 *W, SA* 2, *Arg* 1,2, *R*, 1976 *S, I, W, E, US*, 1977 *W, E, S, I, Arg* 1,2, *NZ* 1,2, *R*

Roques, A (Cahors) 1958 *A, W, It, I, SA* 1,2, 1959 *S, E, W, I*, 1960 *S, E, W, I, It, Arg* 1,2,3, 1961 *S, SA, E, W, It, I*, 1962 *S, E, W, I, It*, 1963 *S*

Roques, J-C (Brive) 1966 *S, I, It, R*

Rossignol, J-C (Brive) 1972 *A* 2

Rouan, J (Narbonne) 1953 *S, I*

Roucaries, G (Perpignan) 1956 *S*

Rouffia, L (Narbonne) 1945 *B* 2, *W*, 1946 *W*, 1948 *I*

Rougerie, J (Montferrand) 1973 *J*

Rougé-Thomas, P (Toulouse) 1989 *NZ* 1,2

Roujas, F (Tarbes) 1910 *I*

Roumat, O (Dax) 1989 *NZ* 2(R), *B*, 1990 *W, E, S, I, R, A* 1,2,3, *NZ* 1,2, 1991 *S, I, W* 1, *E, R, US* 1, *W* 2, [*R, Fj, C, E*], 1992 *W* (R), *E* (R), *S, I, SA* 1,2, *Arg*, 1993 *E, S, I, W, R* 1, *SA* 1,2, *R* 2, *A* 1,2, 1994 *I, W, E, C* 1, *NZ* 1,2, *C* 2, 1995 *W, E, S, [Iv, S, I, SA, E]*, 1996 *E, S, I, W* 1, *R, Arg* 1,2, *W* 2

Rousie, M (Villeneuve) 1931 *S, G*, 1932 *G*, 1933 *G*

Rousset, G (Béziers) 1975 *SA* 1, 1976 *US*

Ruiz, A (Tarbes) 1968 *SA* 2, *R*

Rupert, J-J (Tyrosse) 1963 *R*, 1964 *S, Fj*, 1965 *E, W, It*, 1966 *S, I, E, W, It*, 1967 *It, R*, 1968 *S*

Sadourny, J-L (Colomiers) 1991 *W* 2(R), [*C* (R)], 1992 *E* (R), *S, I, Arg* 1(R),2, *SA* 1,2, 1993 *R* 1, *SA* 1,2, *R* 2, 1994 *I, W, E, S, C* 1, *NZ* 1,2, *C* 2, 1995 *W, E, S, I, R* 1, [*Tg, S, I, SA, E*], *It, R* 2, *Arg, NZ* 1,2, 1996 *E, S, I, W* 1, *Arg* 1,2, *W* 2, *SA* 1,2, 1997 *I, W, E, S, It* 1, *R* 1, *A* 1,2, *It* 2, *R* 2, *Arg, SA* 1,2, 1998 *E, S, I, W*, 1999 *R, Tg, NZ* 1(R), 2000 *NZ* 2, 2001 *It, W, E*

Sagot, P (SF) 1906 *NZ*, 1908 *E*, 1909 *W*

Sahuc, A (Métro) 1945 *B* 1,2

Sahuc, F (Toulouse) 1936 *G* 2

Saint-André, P (Montferrand, Gloucester) 1990 *R, A* 3, *NZ* 1,2, 1991 *I* (R), *W* 1, *E, US* 1,2, *W* 2, [*R, Fj, C, E*], 1992 *W, E, S, I, R, Arg* 1,2, *SA* 1,2, 1993 *E, S, I, W, R* 1, *SA* 1,2, *A* 1,2, 1994 *I, W, E, S, C* 1, *NZ* 1,2, *C* 2, 1995 *W, E, S, I, R* 1, [*Tg, Iv, S, I, SA, E*], *It, R* 2, *Arg, S, I, W* 1, *R, Arg* 1,2, *W* 2, 1997 *It* 1,2, *R* 2, *Arg, SA* 1,2

Saisset, O (Béziers) 1971 *R*, 1972 *S, I* 1, *A* 1,2, 1973 *S, NZ, E, W, I, J, R*, 1974 *I, Arg* 2, *SA* 1,2, 1975 *W*

Salas, P (Narbonne) 1979 *NZ* 1,2, *R*, 1980 *W, E*, 1981 *A* 1, 1982 *Arg* 2

Salinié, R (Perpignan) 1923 *E*

Sallefranque, M (Dax) 1981 *A* 2, 1982 *W, E, S*

Salut, J (TOEC) 1966 *R*, 1967 *S*, 1968 *I, E, Cz, NZ* 1, 1969 *I*

Samatan, R (Agen) 1930 *S, I, E, G, W*, 1931 *I, S, W, E, G*

Sanac, A (Perpignan) 1952 *It*, 1953 *S, I*, 1954 *E*, 1956 *Cz*, 1957 *S, I, E, W, It*

Sangalli, F (Narbonne) 1975 *I, SA* 1,2, 1976 *S, A* 1,2, *R*, 1977 *W, E, S, I, Arg* 1,2, *NZ* 1,2

Sanz, H (Narbonne) 1988 *Arg* 3,4, *R*, 1989 *A* 2, 1990 *S, I, R, A* 1,2, *NZ* 2, 1991 *W* 2

Sappa, M (Nice) 1973 *J, R*, 1977 *R*
Sarrade, R (Pau) 1929 *I*
Sarraméa, O (Castres) 1999 *R, WS* (R), *Tg, NZ* 1
Saux, J-P (Pau) 1960 *W, It, Arg* 1,2, 1961 *SA, E, W, It, I, NZ* 1,2,3, *A*, 1962 *S, E, W, I, It*, 1963 *S, I, E, It*
Savitsky, M (La Voulte) 1969 *R*
Savy, M (Montferrand) 1931 *I, S, W, E*, 1936 *G* 1
Sayrou, J (Perpignan) 1926 *W, M*, 1928 *E, G, W*, 1929 *S, W, E, G*
Scohy, R (BEC) 1931 *S, W, E, G*
Sébedio, J (Tarbes) 1913 *S, E*, 1914 *I*, 1920 *S, I, US*, 1922 *S, E*, 1923 *S*
Seguier, N (Béziers) 1973 *J, R*
Seigne, L (Agen, Merignac) 1989 *B, A* 1, 1990 *NZ* 1, 1993 *E, S, I, W, R* 1, *A* 1,2, 1994 *S, C* 1, 1995 *E* (R), *S*
Sella, P (Agen) 1982 *R, Arg* 1,2, 1983 *E, S, I, W, A* 1,2, *R*, 1984 *I, W, F, S, NZ* 1,2, *R*, 1985 *E, S, I, W, Arg* 1,2, 1986 *S, I, W, E, R* 1, *Arg* 1,2, *A, NZ* 1, *R* 2, *NZ* 2,3, 1987 *W, E, S, I, [S, R, Z* (R), *Fj, A, NZ*], 1988 *E, S, I, W, Arg* 1,2,3,4, *R*, 1989 *I, W, E, S, NZ* 1,2, *B, A* 1,2, 1990 *W, E, S, I, A* 1,2,3, 1991 *W* 1, *E, R, US* 1,2, *W* 2, *[Fj, C, E]*, 1992 *W, E, S, I, Arg*, 1993 *E, S, I, W, R* 1, *SA* 1,2, *R* 2, *A* 1,2, 1994 *I, W, E, S, C* 1, *NZ* 1,2, *C* 2, 1995 *W, E, S, I, [Tg, S, I, SA, E]*
Semmartin, J (SCUF) 1913 *W, I*
Senal, G (Béziers) 1974 *Arg* 1,2, *R, SA* 1,2, 1975 *W*
Sentilles, J (Tarbes) 1912 *W, E*, 1913 *S, SA*
Serin, L (Béziers) 1928 *E*, 1929 *W, E, G*, 1930 *S, I, E, G, W*, 1931 *I, W, E*
Serre, P (Perpignan) 1920 *S, E*
Serrière, P (RCF) 1986 *A*, 1987 *R*, 1988 *E*
Servole, L (Toulon) 1931 *I, S, W, E, G*, 1934 *G*, 1935 *G*
Sicart, N (Perpignan) 1922 *I*
Sillières, J (Tarbes) 1968 *R*, 1970 *S, I*, 1971 *S, I, E*, 1972 *E, W*
Siman, M (Montferrand) 1948 *E*, 1949 *S*, 1950 *S, I, E, W*
Simon, S (Bègles) 1991 *R, US* 1
Simonpaoli, R (SF) 1911 *I*, 1912 *I, S*
Sitjar, M (Agen) 1964 *W, It, I, R*, 1965 *It, R*, 1967 *A, E, It, W, I, SA* 1,2
Skrela, D (Colomiers) 2001 *NZ*
Skrela, J-C (Toulouse) 1971 *SA* 2, *A* 1,2, 1972 *I* 1(R), *E, W, I* 2, *A* 1, 1973 *W, J, R*, 1974 *W, E, S, Arg* 1, *R*, 1975 *W* (R), *E, S, I, SA* 1,2, *Arg* 1,2, *R*, 1976 *S, I, W, E, US, A* 1,2, *R*, 1977 *W, E, S, I, Arg* 1,2, *NZ* 1,2, *R*, 1978 *E, S, I, W*
Soler, M (Quillan) 1929 *G*
Soro, R (Lourdes, Romans) 1945 *B* 1,2, *W*, 1946 *B, I, K*, 1947 *S, I, W, E*, 1948 *I, A, S, W, E*, 1949 *S, I, E, W, Arg* 1,2
Sorondo, L-M (Montauban) 1946 *K*, 1947 *S, I, W, E*, 1948 *I, W* (R), *Arg* 1,2, *Fj*, 1999 *W* 2(R), *[C* (R), *Nm* (R), *Arg, NZ* 2, *A]*
Soulette, C (Béziers, Toulouse) 1997 *R* 2, 1998 *S* (R), *I* (R), *W* (R), *Arg* 1,2, *Fj*, 1999 *W* 2(R), *[C* (R), *Nm* (R), *Arg, NZ* 2, *A]*
Soulié, E (CASG) 1920 *E, I, US*, 1921 *S, E, I*, 1922 *E, W, I*
Sourgens, J (Bègles) 1926 *M*
Souverbie, J-M (Bègles) 2000 *R*
Spanghero, C (Narbonne) 1971 *E, W, SA* 1,2, *A* 1,2, *R*, 1972 *S, E, W, I* 2, *A* 1,2, 1974 *I, W, E, S, R, SA* 1, 1975 *E, S, I*
Spanghero, W (Narbonne) 1964 *SA, Fj, R*, 1965 *S, I, E, W, It, R*, 1966 *S, I, E, W, It, R*, 1967 *S, A, E, SA* 1,2,3,4, *NZ*, 1968 *S, I, E, W, NZ* 1,2,3, *A, SA* 1,2, *R*, 1969 *S, I, W*, 1970 *R*, 1971 *E, W, SA* 1, 1972 *E, I* 2, *A* 1,2, *R*, 1973 *S, NZ, E, W, I*
Stener, G (PUC) 1956 *S, I, E*, 1958 *SA* 1,2
Struxiano, P (Toulouse) 1913 *W, I*, 1920 *S, E, W, I, US*
Sutra, G (Narbonne) 1967 *SA* 2, 1969 *W*, 1970 *S, I*
Swierczinski, C (Bègles) 1969 *E*, 1977 *Arg* 2

Tabacco, P (SF) 2001 *SA* 1,2, *NZ*
Tachdjian, M (RCF) 1991 *S, I, E*
Taffary, M (RCF) 1975 *W, E, S, I*
Taillantou, J (Pau) 1930 *I, G, W*
Tarricq, P (Lourdes) 1958 *A, W, It, I*
Tavernier, H (Toulouse) 1913 *I*
Techoueyres, W (SBUC) 1994 *E, S*, 1995 *[Iv]*
Terreau, M-M (Bourg) 1945 *W*, 1946 *B, I, K, W*, 1947 *S, I, W, E*, 1948 *I, A, W, E*, 1949 *S, Arg* 1,2, 1951 *S*

Theuriet, A (SCUF) 1909 *E, W*, 1910 *S*, 1911 *W*, 1913 *E*
Thevenot, M (SCUF) 1910 *W, E, I*
Thierry, R (RCF) 1920 *S, E, W, US*
Thiers, P (Montferrand) 1936 *G* 1,2, 1937 *G, It*, 1938 *G* 1,2, 1940 *R*, 1945 *B*, 1,2
Tignol, P (Toulouse) 1953 *S, I*
Tilh, H (Nantes) 1912 *W, E*, 1913 *S, SA, E, W*
Tolot, J-L (Agen) 1987 *[Z]*
Tordo, J-F (Nice) 1991 *US* 1(R), 1992 *W, E, S, I, R, Arg* 1,2, *SA* 1, *Arg*, 1993 *E, S, I, W, R* 1
Torossian, F (Pau) 1997 *R* 1
Torreilles, S (Perpignan) 1956 *S*
Tournaire, F (Narbonne, Toulouse) 1995 *It*, 1996 *I, W* 1, *R, Arg* 1,2(R), *W* 2, *SA* 1,2, 1997 *I, E, S, It* 1, *R* 1, *A* 1,2, *It* 2, *R* 2, *Arg, SA* 1,2, 1998 *E, S, I, W, Arg* 1,2, *Fj, Arg* 3, *A*, 1999 *I, W* 1, *E, S, R* (R), *WS, NZ* 1, *[C, Nm, Fj, Arg, NZ* 2, *A]*, 2000 *W, E, S, I, It, A* (R)
Tourte, R (St Girons) 1940 *B*
Trillo, J (Bègles) 1967 *SA* 3,4, *NZ, R*, 1968 *S, I, NZ* 1,2,3, *A*, 1969 *I, E, W, R*, 1970 *E, R*, 1971 *S, I, SA* 1,2, *A* 1,2, 1972 *S, A* 1,2, *R*, 1973 *S, E*
Triviaux, R (Cognac) 1931 *E, G*
Tucco-Chala, M (PUC) 1940 *B*

Ugartemendia, J-L (St Jean-de-Luz) 1975 *S, I*

Vaills, G (Perpignan) 1928 *A*, 1929 *G*
Vallot, C (SCUF) 1912 *S*
Van Heerden, A (Tarbes) 1992 *E, S*
Vannier, M (RCF, Chalon) 1953 *W*, 1954 *S, I, Arg* 1,2, 1955 *S, I, E, W, It*, 1956 *S, I, W, It, E*, 1957 *S, I, E, W, It, R* 1,2, 1958 *S, E, A, W, It, I*, 1960 *S, E, W, I, It, R, Arg* 1,3, 1961 *SA, E, W, It, I, NZ* 1, *A*
Vaquer, F (Perpignan) 1921 *S, W*, 1922 *W*
Vaquerin, A (Béziers) 1971 *R*, 1972 *S, I* 1, *A* 1, 1973 *S*, 1974 *W, E, S, Arg* 1,2, *R, SA* 1,2, 1975 *W, E, S, I*, 1976 *US, A* 1(R),2, *R*, 1977 *Arg* 2, 1979 *W, E*, 1980 *S, I*
Vareilles, C (SF) 1907 *E*, 1908 *E, W*, 1910 *S, E*
Varenne, F (RCF) 1952 *S*
Varvier, T (RCF) 1906 *E*, 1909 *E, W*, 1911 *E, W*, 1912 *I*
Vassal, G (Carcassonne) 1938 *R, G* 2
Vaysse, J (Albi) 1924 *US*, 1926 *M*
Vellat, E (Grenoble) 1927 *I, E, G* 1,2, 1928 *A*
Venditti, D (Bourgoin, Brive) 1996 *R, SA* 1(R),2, 1997 *I, W, E, S, R* 1, *A* 1,2, 2000 *W* (R), *E, S, It* (R)
Vergé, L (Bègles) 1993 *R* 1(R)
Verger, A (SF) 1927 *W, E, G* 1, 1928 *I, E, G, W*
Verges, S-A (SF) 1906 *NZ, E*, 1907 *E*
Vermeulen, E (Brive) 2001 *SA* 1(R),2(R)
Viard, G (Narbonne) 1969 *W*, 1970 *S, R*, 1971 *S, I*
Viars, S (Brive) 1992 *W, E, I, R, Arg* 1,2, *SA* 1,2(R), *Arg*, 1993 *R* 1, 1994 *C* 1(R), *NZ* 1(t), 1995 *E* (R), *[Iv]*, 1997 *R* 1(R), *A* 1(R),2
Vigerie, M (Agen) 1931 *W*
Vigier, R (Montferrand) 1956 *S, W, It, E, Cz*, 1957 *S, E, W, It, R* 1,2, 1958 *S, E, A, W, It, I, SA* 1,2, 1959 *S, E, It, W, I*
Vigneau, A (Bayonne) 1935 *G*
Vignes, C (RCF) 1957 *R* 1,2, 1958 *S, E*
Vila, E (Tarbes) 1926 *M*
Vilagra, J (Vienne) 1945 *B* 2
Villepreux, P (Toulouse) 1967 *It, I, SA* 2, 1968 *I, Cz, NZ* 1,2,3, *A*, 1969 *S, I, E, W, R*, 1970 *S, I, W, E, R*, 1971 *S, I, E, W, A* 1,2, *R*, 1972 *S, I* 1, *E, W, I* 2, *A* 1,2
Viviès, B (Agen) 1978 *E, S, I, W*, 1980 *SA, R*, 1981 *S, A* 1, 1983 *A* 1(R)
Volot, M (SF) 1945 *W*, 1946 *B, I, K, W*

Weller, S (Grenoble) 1989 *A* 1,2, 1990 *A* 1, *NZ* 1
Wolf, J-P (Béziers) 1980 *SA, R*, 1981 *A* 2, 1982 *E*

Yachvili, M (Tulle, Brive) 1968 *E, W, Cz, NZ* 3, *A, R*, 1969 *S, I, R*, 1971 *E, SA* 1,2 *A* 1, 1972 *E, W*, 1975 *SA* 2

Zago, F (Montauban) 1963 *I, E*

FRANCE INTERNATIONAL STATISTICS
(up to 20th October 2001)

Match Records

Most Consecutive Test Wins
10 1931 *E, G,* 1932 *G,* 1933 *G,* 1934 *G,* 1935 *G,* 1936 *G* 1,2, 1937 *G, It*
8 1998 *E, S, I, W, Arg* 1,2, *Fj, Arg* 3

Most Consecutive Tests Without Defeat

Matches	Wins	Draws	Period
10	10	0	1931 to 1938
10	8	2	1958 to 1959
10	9	1	1986 to 1987

Most Points in a Match
by the team

Pts	Opponents	Venue	Year
70	Zimbabwe	Auckland	1987
67	Romania	Bucharest	2000
64	Romania	Aurillac	1996
62	Romania	Castres	1999
60	Italy	Toulon	1967
59	Romania	Paris	1924
55	Romania	Wellington	1987

by a player

Pts	Player	Opponents	Venue	Year
30	D Camberabero	Zimbabwe	Auckland	1987
28	C Lamaison	New Zealand	Twickenham	1999
27	G Camberabero	Italy	Toulon	1967
27	C Lamaison	New Zealand	Marseilles	2000
27	G Merceron	South Africa	Johannesburg	2001
26	T Lacroix	Ireland	Durban	1995
25	J-P Romeu	United States	Chicago	1976
25	P Berot	Romania	Agen	1987
25	T Lacroix	Tonga	Pretoria	1995

Most Tries in a Match
by the team

Tries	Opponents	Venue	Year
13	Romania	Paris	1924
13	Zimbabwe	Auckland	1987
11	Italy	Toulon	1967
10	Romania	Aurillac	1996
10	Romania	Bucharest	2000

by a player

Tries	Player	Opponents	Venue	Year
4	A Jauréguy	Romania	Paris	1924
4	M Celhay	Italy	Paris	1937

Most Conversions in a Match
by the team

Cons	Opponents	Venue	Year
9	Italy	Toulon	1967
9	Zimbabwe	Auckland	1987
8	Romania	Wellington	1987

by a player

Cons	Player	Opponents	Venue	Year
9	G Camberabero	Italy	Toulon	1967
9	D Camberabero	Zimbabwe	Auckland	1987
8	G Laporte	Romania	Wellington	1987

Most Penalties in a Match
by the team

Penalties	Opponents	Venue	Year
8	Ireland	Durban	1995
7	Wales	Paris	2001
6	Argentina	Buenos Aires	1977
6	Scotland	Paris	1997
6	Italy	Auch	1997
6	Ireland	Paris	2000
6	South Africa	Johannesburg	2001

by a player

Penalties	Player	Opponents	Venue	Year
8	T Lacroix	Ireland	Durban	1995
6	J-M Aguirre	Argentina	Buenos Aires	1977
6	C Lamaison	Scotland	Paris	1997
6	C Lamaison	Italy	Auch	1997
6	G Merceron	Ireland	Paris	2000
6	G Merceron	South Africa	Johannesburg	2001

Most Dropped Goals in a Match
by the team

Drops	Opponents	Venue	Year
3	Ireland	Paris	1960
3	England	Twickenham	1985
3	New Zealand	Christchurch	1986

3	Australia	Sydney	1990
3	Scotland	Paris	1991
3	New Zealand	Christchurch	1994

by a player

Drops	Player	Opponents	Venue	Year
3	P Albaladejo	Ireland	Paris	1960
3	J-P Lescarboura	England	Twickenham	1985
3	J-P Lescarboura	New Zealand	Christchurch	1986
3	D Camberabero	Australia	Sydney	1990

Career Records

Most Capped Players

Caps	Player	Career Span
111	P Sella	1982 to 1995
93	S Blanco	1980 to 1991
78	A Benazzi	1990 to 2001
71	J-L Sadourny	1991 to 2001
69	R Bertranne	1971 to 1981
69	P Saint-André	1990 to 1997
66	C Califano	1994 to 2001
63	M Crauste	1957 to 1966
63	B Dauga	1964 to 1972
61	J Condom	1982 to 1990
61	O Roumat	1989 to 1996
61	F Pelous	1995 to 2001

Most Consecutive Tests

Tests	Player	Span
46	R Bertranne	1973 to 1979
45	P Sella	1982 to 1987
44	M Crauste	1960 to 1966
35	B Dauga	1964 to 1968

Most Tests as Captain

Tests	Captain	Span
34	J-P Rives	1978 to 1984
34	P Saint-André	1994 to 1997
25	D Dubroca	1986 to 1988
24	G Basquet	1948 to 1952
23	R Ibanez	1998 to 1999
22	M Crauste	1961 to 1966

Most Tests in Individual Positions

Position	Player	Tests	Span
Full-back	S Blanco	81	1980 to 1991
Wing	P Saint-André	67	1990 to 1997
Centre	P Sella	104	1982 to 1995
Fly-half	J-P Romeu	33	1972 to 1977
Scrum-half	P Berbizier	56	1981 to 1991

Prop	C Califano	66	1994 to 2001
Hooker	P Dintrans	50	1979 to 1990
Lock	J Condom	61	1982 to 1990
Flanker	J-P Rives	59	1975 to 1984
No 8	G Basquet	33	1945 to 1952

Most Points in Tests

Points	Player	Tests	Career
380	C Lamaison	37	1996 to 2001
367	T Lacroix	43	1989 to 1997
354	D Camberabero	36	1982 to 1993
265	J-P Romeu	34	1972 to 1977
233	S Blanco	93	1980 to 1991
222	T Castaignède	35	1995 to 2000
200	J-P Lescarboura	28	1982 to 1990

Most Tries in Tests

Tries	Player	Tests	Career
38	S Blanco	93	1980 to 1991
33	P Saint-André	69	1990 to 1997
30	P Sella	111	1982 to 1995
26	E Ntamack	46	1994 to 2000
26	P Bernat Salles	41	1992 to 2001
23	C Darrouy	40	1957 to 1967

Most Conversions in Tests

Cons	Player	Tests	Career
59	C Lamaison	37	1996 to 2001
48	D Camberabero	36	1982 to 1993
45	M Vannier	43	1953 to 1961
41	T Castaignède	35	1995 to 2000
36	R Dourthe	31	1995 to 2001
32	T Lacroix	43	1989 to 1997
29	P Villepreux	34	1967 to 1972

Most Penalty Goals in Tests

Penalties	Player	Tests	Career
89	T Lacroix	43	1989 to 1997
78	C Lamaison	37	1996 to 2001
59	D Camberabero	36	1982 to 1993
56	J-P Romeu	34	1972 to 1977
33	P Villepreux	34	1967 to 1972
33	P Bérot	19	1986 to 1989

Most Dropped Goals in Tests

Drops	Player	Tests	Career
15	J-P Lescarboura	28	1982 to 1990
12	P Albaladejo	30	1954 to 1964
11	G Camberabero	14	1961 to 1968
11	D Camberabero	36	1982 to 1993
9	J-P Romeu	34	1972 to 1977

International Championship Records

Record	Detail		Set
Most team points in season	144	in four matches	1998
Most team tries in season	18	in four matches	1998
Highest Score	51	51–16 v Scotland	1998
	51	51–0 v Wales	1998
Biggest win	51	51–0 v Wales	1998
Highest score conceded	49	14–49 v Wales	1910
Biggest defeat	37	0–37 v England	1911
Most appearances	50	P Sella	1983–1995
Most points in matches	144	C Lamaison	1997–2001
Most points in season	54	J-P Lescarboura	1984
Most points in match	24	S Viars	v Ireland, 1992
	24	C Lamaison	v Scotland, 1997
Most tries in matches	14	S Blanco	1981–1991
	14	P Sella	1983–1995
Most tries in season	5	P Estève	1983
	5	E Bonneval	1987
	5	E Ntamack	1999
	5	P Bernat Salles	2001
Most tries in match	3	M Crauste	v England, 1962
	3	C Darrouy	v Ireland, 1963
	3	E Bonneval	v Scotland, 1987
	3	D Venditti	v Ireland, 1997
	3	E Ntamack	v Wales, 1999
Most cons in matches	23	C Lamaison	1997–2001
Most cons in season	9	C Lamaison	1998
Most cons in match	5	P Villepreux	v England, 1972
	5	S Viars	v Ireland, 1992
	5	T Castaignède	v Ireland, 1996
	5	C Lamaison	v Wales, 1998
Most pens in matches	29	C Lamaison	1997–2001
Most pens in season	10	J-P Lescarboura	1984
	10	C Lamaison	2001
Most pens in match	6	C Lamaison	v Scotland, 1997
	6	G Merceron	v Ireland, 2000
Most drops in matches	9	J-P Lescarboura	1982–1988
Most drops in season	5	G Camberabero	1967
Most drops in match	3	P Albaladejo	v Ireland, 1960
	3	J-P Lescarboura	v England, 1985

Miscellaneous Records

Record	Holder	Detail
Longest Test Career	F Haget	14 seasons, 1974 to 1987
Youngest Test Cap	C Dourthe	18 yrs 7 days in 1966
Oldest Test Cap	A Roques	37 yrs 329 days in 1963

Career Records of France International Players
(up to 20 October 2001)

Player	Debut	Caps	T	C	P	D	Pts
Backs:							
P Bernat-Salles	1992 v Arg	41	26	0	0	0	130
P Bondouy	1997 v S	5	2	0	0	0	10
S Bonetti	2001 v It	3	2	0	0	0	10
D Bory	2000 v I	8	0	0	0	0	0
P Carbonneau	1995 v R	32	5	0	0	0	25
T Castaignède	1995 v R	35	13	41	21	4	222
F Cermeno	2000 v R	1	0	0	0	0	0
J-C Cistacq	2000 v R	1	0	0	0	0	0
F Comba	1998 v Arg	13	2	0	0	0	10
G Delmotte	1999 v R	2	2	0	0	0	10
C Desbrosse	1999 v Nm	2	0	0	0	0	0
C Dominici	1998 v E	25	10	0	0	0	50
M Dourthe	2000 v NZ	1	0	0	0	0	0
R Dourthe	1995 v R	31	3	36	32	0	183
P Elhorga	2001 v NZ	1	0	0	0	0	0
J-B Elissalde	2000 v S	2	1	0	0	0	5
F Galthié	1991 v R	43	7	0	0	0	34
X Garbajosa	1998 v I	22	7	0	0	0	35
S Glas	1996 v S	37	9	0	0	0	45
C Heymans	2000 v It	2	0	0	0	0	0
A Hueber	1990 v A	23	3	0	0	2	21
Y Jauzion	2001 v SA	3	0	0	0	0	0
N Jeanjean	2001 v SA	3	0	0	0	0	0
C Lamaison	1996 v SA	37	2	59	78	6	380
C Laussucq	1999 v S	4	1	0	0	0	5
T Lombard	1998 v Arg	12	1	0	0	0	5
G Merceron	1999 v R	11	2	7	26	2	108
P Mignoni	1997 v R	8	3	0	0	0	15
U Mola	1997 v S	12	6	0	0	0	30
E Ntamack	1994 v W	46	26	1	1	0	135
A Penaud	1992 v W	32	10	0	0	5	62
J-L Sadourny	1991 v W	71	15	0	0	4	86
O Sarraméa	1999 v R	4	2	0	0	0	10
D Skrela	2001 v NZ	1	0	0	4	0	12
J-M Souverbie	2000 v R	1	1	0	0	0	5
D Venditti	1996 v R	14	6	0	0	0	30
Forwards:							
J-L Aqua	1999 v R	3	0	0	0	0	0
A Audebert	2000 v R	1	0	0	0	0	0
D Auradou	1999 v E	18	0	0	0	0	0
O Azam	1995 v R	6	0	0	0	0	0
F Belot	2000 v I	1	0	0	0	0	0
A Benazzi	1990 v A	78	9	0	0	0	45
S Betsen	1997 v It	10	0	0	0	0	0
J Bouilhou	2001 v NZ	1	0	0	0	0	0
O Brouzet	1994 v S	50	2	0	0	0	10
C Califano	1994 v NZ	66	6	0	0	0	30
S Chabal	2000 v S	4	0	0	0	0	0

A Chazalet	1999 v Tg	1	0	0	0	0	0
P Collazo	2000 v R	1	0	0	0	0	0
A Costes	1994 v C	14	1	0	0	0	5
J-J Crenca	1996 v SA	8	1	0	0	0	5
J Daudé	2000 v S	1	0	0	0	0	0
P de Villiers	1999 v W	19	0	0	0	0	0
A Galasso	2000 v R	2	0	0	0	0	0
D Gérard	1999 v Tg	1	0	0	0	0	0
R Ibañez	1996 v W	44	4	0	0	0	20
C Juillet	1995 v R	18	2	0	0	0	10
C Labit	1999 v S	5	0	0	0	0	0
F Lalanne	2000 v R	1	0	0	0	0	0
F Landreau	2000 v A	4	0	0	0	0	0
T Lièvremont	1996 v W	21	2	0	0	0	10
M Lièvremont	1995 v It	25	5	0	0	0	25
O Magne	1997 v W	45	7	0	0	0	35
L Mallier	1999 v R	5	1	0	0	0	5
S Marconnet	1998 v Arg	16	0	0	0	0	0
L Matiu	2000 v W	2	0	0	0	0	0
C Milhères	2001 v E	1	0	0	0	0	0
O Milloud	2000 v R	2	0	0	0	0	0
C Moni	1996 v R	8	1	0	0	0	5
L Nallet	2000 v R	5	1	0	0	0	5
F Pelous	1995 v R	61	5	0	0	0	25
C Soulette	1997 v R	13	2	0	0	0	10
P Tabacco	2001 v SA	3	0	0	0	0	0
F Tournaire	1995 v It	49	2	0	0	0	10
E Vermeulen	2001 v SA	2	0	0	0	0	0

ITALY TEST SEASON REVIEW 2000-01

Where is the Next Dominguez?

Paolo Pacitti

The lasting memory of Italy's season was without doubt the try Mauro Bergamasco scored at Murrayfield in the Six Nations match against Scotland. It was a marvellous effort that threatened to give Scotland a recurring nightmare after Diego Dominguez's wonderful day at the Flaminio Stadium in the opening match of the 2000 campaign. Yet for all that, the Championship season was nothing more than one of disillusion for coach Brad Johnstone, who had predicted victories in the home games against Ireland, France and Wales.

That was always going to be a far too optimistic view to take, given that he had at his disposal a squad that had begun the season in a state of transition. Diego Dominguez, Italy's key player, had decided to retire from the international stage after his first Six Nations and Johnstone's troop had discovered how acutely they would miss the little Argentinian on a summer tour that finished with Test defeats against both Samoa and Fiji.

The negative record continued in the first autumn Test, played against Canada in Rovigo, where Italy suffered intense pressure, particularly on the fringes of the scrum, and were well beaten despite the apparent closeness of a 17-22 scoreline. The crisis was temporarily arrested in Benevento where Italy defeated Romania 37-17. For this match, the Union had restored Alessandro Troncon at the base of the scrum after he had refused to tour with the squad in the summer, preferring instead to see the Championship season out with his French club, Montferrand.

Troncon injected new life into the Italian side just in time for the Genoa clash against the All Blacks. For the event, the Luigi Ferraris Stadium was sold out and the Italian side responded by giving a huge first half display. Prop Andrea Lo Cicero asserted himself admirably in the scrums and rucks, but the big difference in skills between an ordinary All Black side and Italy was too great for the *azzurri* to overcome. It was 19-56 at the end, but the cumulative disappointment felt at an eighth successive defeat in nine Tests led to criticism of the management of the side.

The FIR general meeting and elections for the President saved Johnstone's position as coach for the Six Nations Championship while the appointment of former captain, Massimo Giovanelli, as assistant manager of the squad proved an enlightened move. He was the perfect link between the players and hierarchy and persuaded Diego Dominguez to re-join the national squad. Unfortunately the sparkling Argentinian fly-half had to miss the first two games with injury and Italy went to sleep in the opening game

Diego Dominguez, an automatic Test choice for Italy for the past decade, demonstrates perfect technique in clearing the ball against Scotland at Murrayfield as Budge Pountney attempts to charge down the kick.

against Ireland after a good first half display. In the second part of the match, Rob Henderson tore the Italian defence to shreds three times for a final result of 22-41.

No-one carried any misconceptions about the size of the task facing Italy at Twickenham. Johnstone, with nothing to lose, built a wall with fly-half Nanni Raineri and Andrea Scanavacca in the full-back position. Raineri directed a dream start as the *azzurri* played with courage, passion and purpose against the unbeaten English for 40 minutes. Order in defence and huge tackles created many problems for the attacking tactics of Clive Woodward and Andy Robinson's men and by half-time England had conceded 23 points, including two tries. The second half was another story. England found new lines of attack and, taking a firm grip of the game, ran out easy winners.

Two under-achieving sides were on display when France came to Rome. In arguably the worst game of the series, Italy let the French off the hook when there were only four points between the sides with ten minutes to play. Italy's lack of ideas, despite the return of Diego Dominguez, meant France were able to control the game.

Then came the visit to Murrayfield and the Bergamasco try Johnstone began with Filippo Frati in the scrum-half position, but then replaced him after only half an hour with Matteo Mazzantini. The Treviso half-back gave Dominguez quicker ball enabling Italy to transform their game. The upshot was their best 50 minutes of the entire tournament. Quality possession was skilfully used and only desperate Scottish defence prevented Italy from adding to Bergamasco's 70-metre first half effort.

All the good ground made at Murrayfield was lost in a lacklustre display in the final match of the season back in Rome against Graham Henry's Welsh side. The Italians were anonymous in a physical game that demonstrated that, above all, a tougher mentality is required if the *azzurri* are to make a lasting impact on future Six Nations tournaments.

Then in June and July came a 35-day, eight-match tour that included four Tests, embraced two continents and started in Namibia and closed, via Port Elizabeth and Montevideo, in Argentina. The target ? To build a team for the next Rugby World Cup. The reality ? Very different. Johnstone named his squad, but the stars declined to go. Injuries, university examinations (as in Bergamasco's case) and other excuses such as procedural problems obtaining from the Government the Italian passport the Federation had promised Cristian Stoica, meant that the objective was unrealised.

During the Six Nations, Massimo Giovanelli had given the players the confidence to build relations with the Union. But in the first week of the preparation camp in Tabiano (near Parma) there was concern that the building's foundations were subsiding. There was a new manager in Fabrizio Gaetaniello, 24 players declined the invitation to tour, and rumours persisted after the tour that Johnstone could be removed from his position as coach.

Even so, Italy undertook the tour with courage. They won easily against Namibia (49-24), lost against South Africa (14-60) after a constructive first half, and defeated Uruguay (14-3) in a mud bath in Montevideo. On the last leg of the tour, there was a heavy defeat in a midweek game against Argentina A before the Test with the Pumas was lost (17-38), despite the margin having been only one point in Argentina's favour early in the second half. It was not a poor tour, for it showed that Italy still possesses the players to raise its Test ranking. Players like Francesco Mazzariol, who impressed in the match at Port Elizabeth, and youngsters such as Walter Pozzebon have the ability to restore Italian rugby to its past glories. But they also still need the talent of a Cordoba guy like Diego Dominguez.

Italy's Test Record in 2000-2001: Played 12, won 3, lost 9.

Opponents	Date	Venue	Result
Argentina	14th July 2001	A	Lost 17-38
Uruguay	7th July 2001	A	Won 14-3
South Africa	30th June 2001	A	Lost 14-60
Namibia	23rd June 2001	A	Won 49-24
Wales	8th April 2001	H	Lost 23-33
Scotland	17th March 2001	A	Lost 19-23
France	3rd March 2001	H	Lost 19-30
England	17th February 2001	A	Lost 23-80
Ireland	3rd February 2001	H	Lost 22-41
New Zealand	25th November 2000	H	Lost 19-56
Romania	18th November 2000	H	Won 37-17
Canada	11th November 2000	H	Lost 17-22

ITALY INTERNATIONAL STATISTICS

(to 20 October 2001)

Match Records

Most Consecutive Test Wins

6 1968 *Pt, G, Y*, 1969 *Bu, Sp, Be*

Most Consecutive Tests Without Defeat

Matches	Wins	Draws	Period
6	6	0	1968–69
5	4	1	1982–83

Most Points in a Match
by the team

Pts	Opponents	Venue	Year
104	Czech Republic	Viadana	1994
78	Croatia	Perpignan	1993
70	Morocco	Carcassonne	1993
67	Netherlands	Huddersfield	1998
64	Portugal	Lisbon	1996

by a player

Pts	Player	Opponents	Venue	Year
29	S Bettarello	Canada	Toronto	1983
29	D Dominguez	Scotland	Rome	2000
28	D Dominguez	Netherlands	Calvisano	1994
27	D Dominguez	Ireland	Bologna	1997
25	D Dominguez	Romania	Tarbes	1997
24	L Troiani	Spain	Parma	1994

Most Tries in a Match
by the team

Tries	Opponents	Venue	Year
16	Czech Republic	Viadana	1994
11	Croatia	Perpignan	1993
11	Netherlands	Huddersfield	1998
10	Belgium	Paris	1937
10	Morocco	Carcassonne	1993
10	Portugal	Lisbon	1996

by a player

Tries	Player	Opponents	Venue	Year
4	R Cova	Belgium	Paris	1937
4	I Francescato	Morocco	Carcassonne	1993

Most Conversions in a Match
by the team

Cons	Opponents	Venue	Year
12	Czech Republic	Viadana	1994
10	Croatia	Perpignan	1993
10	Morocco	Carcassonne	1993
8	Spain	Parma	1994

by a player

Cons	Player	Opponents	Venue	Year
12	L Troiani	Czech Reuplic	Viadana	1994
10	L Troiani	Croazia	Perpignan	1993
10	G Filizzola	Morocco	Carcassonne	1993
8	L Troiani	Spain	Parma	1994

Most Penalties in a Match
by the team

Penalties	Opponents	Venue	Year
8	Romania	Catania	1994
6	Scotland	Rovigo	1993
6	Argentina	Lourdes	1997
6	Ireland	Bologna	1997
6	Scotland	Treviso	1998
6	Tonga	Leicester	1999
6	Scotland	Rome	2000

by a player

Penalties	Player	Opponents	Venue	Year
8	D Dominguez	Romania	Catania	1994
6	D Dominguez	Scotland	Rovigo	1993
6	D Dominguez	Argentina	Lourdes	1997
6	D Dominguez	Ireland	Bologna	1997
6	D Dominguez	Scotland	Treviso	1998
6	D Dominguez	Tonga	Leicester	1999
6	D Dominguez	Scotland	Rome	2000

Most Dropped Goals in a Match
by the team

Drops	Opponents	Venue	Year
3	Transvaal	Johannesburg	1973
3	Scotland	Rome	2000

by a player

Drops	Player	Opponents	Venue	Year
3	R Caligiuri	Tranvaal	Johannesburg	1973
3	D Dominguez	Scotland	Rome	2000

Career Records

Most Capped Players

Caps	Player	Career Span
69	Massimo Cuttitta	1990–2000
67	C Checchinato	1990–2001
64	D Dominguez	1991–2001
60	S Ghizzoni	1977–87
60	M Giovanelli	1989–2000
59	A Troncon	1994–2001
55	S Bettarello	1979–88
54	M Mascioletti	1977–90
54	Marcello Cuttitta	1987–99
54	P Vaccari	1991–99
54	F Properzi-Curti	1990–2001
53	G Pivetta	1979–93

Most Consecutive Tests

Tests	Player	Span
29	M Bollesan	1968–72
27	Massimo Cuttitta	1991–94
25	C Orlandi	1995–98
24	D Dominguez	1995–99
23	A Sgorlon	1995–98
23	C Stoica	1999–2001
23	A Moscardi	1999–2001

Most Tests as Captain

Tests	Captain	Span
34	M Bollesan	1969–75
30	M Giovanelli	1992–99
22	Massimo Cuttitta	1993–99
20	M Innocenti	1985–88

Most Tests in Individual Positions

Position	Player	Tests	Span
Full-back	L Troiani	41	1985–95
Wing	Marcello Cuttitta	54	1987–99
Centre	N Francescato	39	1972–82
Fly-half	D Dominguez	58	1991–2001
Scrum-half	A Troncon	59	1994–2001

Prop	M Cuttitta	69	1990–2000
Hooker	C Orlandi	41*	1992–2000
Lock	R Favaro	42	1988–96
Flanker	M Giovanelli	60	1989–2000
No 8	C Checchinato	39	1991–2001

excludes an appearance as a temporary replacement

Most Points in Tests

Points	Player	Tests	Career
865	D Dominguez	64	1991–2001
483	S Bettarello	55	1979–88
296	L Troiani	47	1985–95
133	E Ponzi	20	1973–77
110	Marc Cuttitta	54	1987–99

Most Tries in Tests

Tries	Player	Tests	Career
25	Marc Cuttitta	54	1987–99
21	M Marchetto	43	1972–81
21	P Vaccari	54	1991–99
18	C Checchinato	67	1990–2001
17	S Ghizzoni	60	1977–87
17	M Mascioletti	54	1977–90

Most Conversions in Tests

Cons	Player	Tests	Career
117	D Dominguez	64	1991–2001
58	L Troiani	47	1985–95
46	S Bettarello	55	1979–88
17	E Ponzi	20	1973–77
16	G Filizzola	12	1993–95

Most Penalty Goals in Tests

Penalties	Player	Tests	Career
181	D Dominguez	64	1991–2001
104	S Bettarello	55	1979–88
57	L Troiani	47	1985–95
31	E Ponzi	20	1973–77

Most Dropped Goals in Tests

Drops	Player	Tests	Career
17	S Bettarello	55	1979–88
16	D Dominguez	64	1991–2001
5	M Bonomi	34	1988–96
5	O Collodo	15	1977–87

International Championship Records

Record	Detail		Set
Most team points in season	106	in five matches	2000
	106	in five matches	2001
Most team tries in season	9	in five matches	2000
Highest Score	34	34–20 v Scotland	2000
Biggest win	14	34–20 v Scotland	2000
Highest score conceded	80	23–80 v England	2001
Biggest defeat	57	23–80 v England	2001
Most appearances	10	C Stoica	2000–2001
	10	A Moscardi	2000–2001
	10	M Bergamasco	2000–2001
	10	C Checchinato	2000–2001
Most points in matches	107	D Dominguez	2000–2001
Most points in season	61	D Dominguez	2000
Most points in match	29	D Dominguez	v Scotland, 2000
Most tries in matches	3	C Checchinato	2000–2001
Most tries in season	3	C Checchinato	2001
Most tries in match	2	A Troncon	v France, 2000
Most cons in matches	10	D Dominguez	2000–2001
Most cons in season	8	D Dominguez	2000
Most cons in match	4	D Dominguez	v France, 2000
Most pens in matches	23	D Dominguez	2000–2001
Most pens in season	13	D Dominguez	2001
Most pens in match	6	D Dominguez	v Scotland, 2000
Most drops in matches	6	D Dominguez	2000–2001
Most drops in season	5	D Dominguez	2000
Most drops in match	3	D Dominguez	v Scotland, 2000

Miscellaneous Records

Record	Holder	Detail
Longest Test Career	S Lanfranchi	16 seasons, 1949 to 1964

Career Records of Italy International Players
(up to 20 October 2001)

PLAYER	Debut	Caps	T	C	P	D	Pts
Backs:							
J A Antoni	2001 v Nm	2	0	0	0	0	0
M Baroni	1999 v F	6	1	0	0	0	5
A Ceppolino	1999 v U	5	1	0	0	0	5
D Dallan	1999 v F	15	1	0	0	0	5
M Dallan	1997 v Arg	13	3	0	0	0	15
D Dominguez	1991 v F	64	8	117	181	16	865
J S Francesio	2000 v W	4	0	0	0	0	0
F Frati	2000 v C	4	0	0	0	0	0
E Galon	2001 v I	1	0	0	0	0	0
L Martin	1997 v F	33	8	0	0	0	40
M Mazzantini	2000 v S	3	0	0	0	0	0
F Mazzariol	1995 v F	22	1	10	14	0	67
G Mazzi	1998 v H	5	1	0	0	0	5
N Mazzucato	1995 v SA	16	3	0	0	0	15
R Pedrazzi	2001 v Nm	2	0	0	0	0	0

J A Pertile	1994 v R	15	1	0	0	0	5
M Perziano	2000 v NZ	8	3	0	0	0	15
R Pez	2000 v Sm	6	1	5	6	1	36
C Pilat	1997 v I	7	2	0	1	0	13
M J Pini	1998 v H	12	2	0	0	0	10
W Pozzebon	2001 v I	9	2	0	0	0	10
G Preo	1999 v I	7	0	1	0	0	2
J-M Queirolo	2000 v Sm	4	0	0	2	0	6
G Raineri	1998 v H	12	2	0	1	0	13
M Rivaro	2000 v S	4	0	0	0	0	0
A Scanavacca	1999 v U	2	0	2	3	0	13
C Stoica	1997 v I	35	8	0	0	0	40
A Troncon	1994 v Sp	59	13	0	0	0	65
L Villagra	2000 v Sm	2	0	0	0	0	0
N Zisti	1999 v E	4	0	0	0	0	0
Forwards:							
M Bergamasco	1998 v H	15	4	0	0	0	20
M Birtig	1998 v H	2	0	0	0	0	0
M Bortolami	2001 v Nm	2	0	0	0	0	0
C Caione	1995 v R	24	3	0	0	0	15
A Castellani	1994 v Cz	20	1	0	0	0	5
C Checchinato	1990 v Sp	67	18	0	0	0	90
W Cristofoletto	1992 v R	31	1	0	0	0	5
G Croci	1990 v Sp	24	3	0	0	0	13
D Dal Maso	2000 v Sm	4	0	0	0	0	0
G P De Carli	1996 v W	21	3	0	0	0	15
A De Rossi	1999 v U	13	1	0	0	0	5
G Faliva	1999 v SA	1	0	0	0	0	0
J M Gardner	1992 v R	20	4	0	0	0	20
S Garozzo	2001 v U	2	0	0	0	0	0
M Giacheri	1992 v R	36	0	0	0	0	0
A Gritti	1996 v Pt	15	0	0	0	0	0
G Lanzi	1998 v Arg	8	0	0	0	0	0
A Lo Cicero	2000 v E	12	2	0	0	0	10
L Mastrodomenico	2000 v Sm	5	0	0	0	0	0
A Moreno	1999 v Tg	2	0	0	0	0	0
A Moretti	1997 v R	6	0	0	0	0	0
A Moscardi	1993 v Pt	36	5	0	0	0	25
A Muraro	2000 v C	9	0	0	0	0	0
F Ongaro	2000 v C	5	0	0	0	0	0
C Orlandi	1992 v S	42	4	0	0	0	20
C Paoletti	2000 v S	13	0	0	0	0	0
A Persico	2000 v S	13	0	0	0	0	0
S Perugini	2000 v I	10	0	0	0	0	0
R Piovan	1996 v Pt	4	0	0	0	0	0
F Properzi-Curti	1990 v Po	54	3	0	0	0	15
F Pucciariello	1999 v Sp	3	1	0	0	0	5
S Saviozzi	1998 v Ru	12	2	0	0	0	10
S Stocco	1998 v H	4	1	0	0	0	5
L Travini	1999 v SA	5	0	0	0	0	0
W Visser	1999 v I	19	1	0	0	0	5
M Zaffiri	2000 v Fj	4	0	0	0	0	0

SOUTH AFRICA TEST SEASON REVIEW 2000-01

100th Test in Nine Years Since Isolation

Dan Retief

As an indication of just how seriously South Africa takes its rugby look no further than the saga of Nick Mallett. In spite of compiling a win rate of 71% in the 38 internationals he was in charge, the forthright former Springbok No 8 was forced to relinquish the post of Springbok coach. It was called a resignation, but everyone knew Mallett had "taken a package" when it became apparent that he no longer had the support of the South African Rugby Football Union's (SARFU) executive. Mallett had been summoned to appear before a SARFU disciplinary tribunal for having publicly criticised the union – an act that allegedly put him in breach of his contract. Mallett had been quoted by a female reporter in Durban – ahead of the final Tri Nations match of 2000 – as saying that tickets for Test matches, at R300 apiece (some 30 pounds), were too expensive.

The former Oxford Blue had been in charge since November 1997 and among his achievements counted a run of 17 straight victories, winning the Tri Nations in 1998 and taking the Boks to third place in the 1999 Rugby World Cup. His record was even more impressive when you consider that well over half of his matches in charge, 22, or 57%, were against the like of Australia, New Zealand, England and France.

Mallett's sudden departure brought to the helm Harry Viljoen – South Africa's eighth coach in the eight seasons since re-admission in 1992. A successful businessman who had amassed a fortune in the financial planning industry, Viljoen is a former Transvaal scrum-half who turned his hand to coaching at a relatively young age. Having made his provincial debut as a player by the age of 19, he became Transvaal's coach at the age of 30 and guided them to two Currie Cup Finals, moved to Natal and steered them to a final, took a three-year sabbatical and then returned as coach of the Western Province team that broke a dry spell of 11 years to win the Currie Cup in 1997.

Poor performances by the Stormers in the following year's Super 12 precipitated Viljoen's resignation and it was something of a surprise when, at the age of 40, he was appointed as the Springbok coach. A keen disciple of the Australian way, Viljoen had spent vast quantities of his own money to travel the world and exchange ideas with coaching experts such as Rod Macqueen and Bob Dwyer and made an immediate impact with his radical innovations.

Mark Andrews, South Africa's most-capped lock, holds off Neil Jenkins and Chris Wyatt of Wales to slip a pass to his scrum-half in the Test at the Millennium Stadium in Cardiff. South Africa won 23-13.

He was literally a stranger to all but a few of the team when he took over just a week ahead of the end-of-year tour to Argentina, Ireland, Wales and England and his first Test in charge was against Argentina in Buenos Aires on November 12. Determined that the Springboks would transform themselves into exponents of the expansive game, Viljoen raised a few eyebrows when he picked Percy Montgomery at fly-half and sent the Boks out with instructions not to kick the ball at all.

With André Markgraaff, one of his predecessors as Springbok coach, as his assistant and additional input from another former Bok coach in Ian McIntosh, the Springboks turned in a hair-raising performance at the River Plate Stadium that was far removed from their traditional pattern. In the end they won, but not before the Pumas had come strongly back into the picture after the Boks had literally run themselves off their feet. It was an apt beginning to the Viljoen era, because the young coach would continue to ring the changes in his efforts to modernise Springbok rugby.

Springbok teams have to win, though, and soon reality eroded Viljoen's idealism as the Springboks gradually reverted to a more conservative approach to beat Ireland and Wales before they were forced to resort to Braam van Straaten, a brilliant goal-kicker but cumbersome fly-half, in an effort to beat England at Twickenham. The experiment failed, England winning 25-17, but a free-wheeling 41-31 victory over the Barbarians in Cardiff seemed to add to Viljoen's conviction that Springbok rugby was in need of a dramatic overhaul.

In 2001 Viljoen had to sit back while the Super 12 was completed, with the excellent augury of South Africa providing two semi-finalists in the Sharks and the Cats, before he announced his plans to mate the Springbok with the Wallaby. Former Wallaby Tim Lane, who had helped to coach Australia's World Cup winners in 1999, was named as Viljoen's assistant, while he also introduced two other Aussies – Les Kiss, a defensive coach with a background in rugby league, and kicking expert Michael Byrne.

Hopes of a bright new beginning were derailed, though, when the Boks underestimated a French team, who had seemingly come on a suicide mission, and there was further controversy when Viljoen decided to make Bob Skinstad – the player who under Mallett had been the catalyst in Gary Teichmann's axing – the team's captain instead of André Vos.

Hit by injuries, especially in midfield, the Tri Nations turned into a roller-coaster ride with a fine win over the Australians at Loftus Versfeld being juxtaposed with a shocker against the All Blacks at Eden Park. In spite of all Viljoen's innovations the Springboks' renaissance had floundered on an ancient reality – the absence of a reliable goal-kicker who earned his position in the team on merit.

Along the way an amazing anniversary took place. The Test against the Wallabies in Perth was South Africa's 100th since re-admission – almost nine years to the day that they had marked the end of isolation by playing the All Blacks at Ellis Park on August 15, 1992. An indication of the intensity of the modern game was that their previous 174 Tests had taken 97 years.

South Africa's Test Record in 2000–2001: Played 11, won 6, drawn 1 lost 4.

Opponents	Date	Venue	Result
New Zealand	25th August 2001	A	Lost 15-26
Australia	18th August 2001	A	Drawn 14-14
Australia	28th July 2001	H	Won 20-15
New Zealand	21st July 2001	H	Lost 3-12
Italy	30th June 2001	H	Won 60-14
France	23rd June 2001	H	Won 20-15
France	16th June 2001	H	Lost 23-32
England	2nd December 2000	A	Lost 17-25
Wales	26th November 2000	A	Won 23-13
Ireland	19th November 2000	A	Won 28-18
Argentina	12th November 2000	A	Won 37-33

SOUTH AFRICAN INTERNATIONAL PLAYERS

(up to 20 October 2001)

Ackermann, D S P (WP) 1955 *BI* 2,3,4, 1956 *A* 1,2, *NZ* 1,3, 1958 *F* 2
Ackermann, J N (NT, BB) 1996 *Fj*, *A* 1, *NZ* 1, *A* 2, 2001 *F* 2(R), *It*, *NZ* 1(R), *A* 1
Aitken, A D (WP) 1997 *F* 2(R), *E*, 1998 *I* 2(R), *W* 1(R), *NZ* 1,2(R), *A* 2(R)
Albertyn, P K (SWD) 1924 *BI* 1,2,3,4
Alexander, F A (GW) 1891 *BI* 1,2
Allan, J (N) 1993 *A* 1(R), *Arg* 1,2(R), 1994 *E* 1,2, *NZ* 1,2,3, 1996 *Fj*, *A* 1, *NZ* 1, *A* 2, *NZ* 2
Allen, P B (EP) 1960 *S*
Allport, P H (WP) 1910 *BI* 2,3
Anderson, J W (WP) 1903 *BI* 3
Anderson, J H (WP) 1896 *BI* 1,3,4
Andrew, J B (Tvl) 1896 *BI* 2
Andrews, K S (WP) 1992 *E*, 1993 *F* 1,2, *A* 1(R), 2,3, *Arg* 1(R), 2, 1994 *NZ* 3
Andrews, M G (N) 1994 *E* 2, *NZ* 1,2,3, *Arg* 1,2, *S, W*, 1995 *WS*, [*A, WS, F, NZ*], *W, It, E*, 1996 *Fj, A* 1, *NZ* 1, *A* 2, *NZ* 2,3,4,5, *Arg* 1,2, *F* 1,2, *W*, 1997 *Tg* (R), *BI* 1,2, *NZ* 1, *A* 1, *NZ* 2, *A* 2, *It, F* 1,2, *E, S*, 1998 *I* 1,2, *W* 1, *E* 1, *A* 1, *NZ* 1,2, *A* 2, *W* 2, *S, I* 3, *E* 2, 1999 *NZ* 1,2(R), *A* 2(R), [*S, U, E, A* 3, *NZ* 3], 2000 *A* 2, *NZ* 2, *A* 3, *Arg, I, W, E* 3, 2001 *F* 1,2, *It, NZ* 1, *A* 1,2, *NZ* 2
Antelme, M J G (Tvl) 1960 *NZ* 1,2,3,4, 1961 *F*
Apsey, J T (WP) 1933 *A* 4,5, 1938 *BI* 2
Ashley, S (WP) 1903 *BI* 2
Aston, F T D (Tvl) 1896 *BI* 1,2,3,4
Atherton, S (N) 1993 *Arg* 1,2, 1994 *E* 1,2, *NZ* 1,2,3, 1996 *NZ* 2
Aucamp, J (WT) 1924 *BI* 1,2

Baard, A P (WP) 1960 *I*
Babrow, L (WP) 1937 *A* 1,2, *NZ* 1,2,3
Badenhorst, C (OFS) 1994 *Arg* 2, 1995 *WS* (R)
Barnard, A S (EP) 1984 *S Am* 1,2, 1986 *Cv* 1,2
Barnard, J H (Tvl) 1965 *S, A* 1,2, *NZ* 3,4
Barnard, R W (Tvl) 1970 *NZ* 2(R)
Barnard, W H M (NT) 1949 *NZ* 4, 1951 *W*
Barry, D W (WP) 2000 *C, E* 1,2, *A* 1(R), *NZ* 1, *A* 2, 2001 *F* 1,2
Barry, J (WP) 1903 *BI* 1,2,3
Bartmann, W J (Tvl, N) 1986 *Cv* 1,2,3,4, 1992 *NZ, A, F*, 1,2
Bastard, W E (N) 1937 *A* 1, *NZ* 1,2,3, 1938 *BI* 1,3
Bates, A J (WT) 1969 *E*, 1970 *NZ* 1,2, 1972 *E*
Bayvel, P C R (Tvl) 1974 *BI* 2,4, *F* 1,2, 1975 *F* 1,2, 1976 *NZ* 1,2,3,4
Beck, J J (WP) 1981 *NZ* 2(R), 3(R), *US*
Bedford, T P (N) 1963 *A* 1,2,3,4, 1964 *W, F*, 1965 *I, A* 1,2, 1968 *BI* 1,2,3,4, *F* 1,2, 1969 *A* 1,2,3,4, *S, E*, 1970 *I, W*, 1971 *F* 1,2
Bekker, H J (WP) 1981 *NZ* 1,3
Bekker, H P J (NT) 1952 *E, F*, 1953 *A* 1,2,3,4, 1955 *BI* 2,3,4, 1956 *A* 1,2, *NZ* 1,2,3,4
Bekker, M J (NT) 1960 *S*
Bekker, R P (NT) 1953 *A* 3,4
Bekker, S (NT) 1997 *A* 2(t)
Bennett, R G (Border) 1997 *Tg* (R), *BI* 1(R), 3, *NZ* 1, *A* 1, *NZ* 2
Bergh, W F (SWD) 1931 *W, I*, 1932 *E, S*, 1933 *A* 1,2,3,4,5, 1937 *A* 1,2, *NZ* 1,2,3, 1938 *BI* 1,2,3
Bestbier, A (OFS) 1974 *F* 2(R)
Bester, J J N (WP) 1924 *BI* 2,4
Bester, J L A (WP) 1938 *BI* 2,3
Beswick, A M (Bor) 1896 *BI* 2,3,4
Bezuidenhoudt, C E (NT) 1962 *BI* 2,3,4
Bezuidenhoudt, N S E (NT) 1972 *E*, 1974 *BI* 2,3,4, *F* 1,2, 1975 *F* 1,2, 1977 *Wld*
Bierman, J N (Tvl) 1931 *I*
Bisset, W M (WP) 1891 *BI* 1,3
Blair, R (WP) 1977 *Wld*
Boome, C S (WP) 1999 *It* 1,2, *W, NZ* 1(R), *A* 1, *NZ* 2, *A* 2, 2000 *C, E* 1,2
Bosch, G R (Tvl) 1974 *BI* 2, *F* 1,2, 1975 *F* 1,2, 1976 *NZ* 1,2,3,4
Bosman, N J S (Tvl) 1924 *BI* 2,3,4
Botha, D S (NT) 1981 *NZ* 1

Botha, H E (NT) 1980 *S Am* 1,2, *BI* 1,2,3,4, *S Am* 3,4, *F*, 1981 *I* 1,2, *NZ* 1,2,3, *US*, 1982 *S Am* 1,2, 1986 *Cv* 1,2,3,4, 1989 *Wld* 1,2, 1992 *NZ, A, F* 1,2, *E*
Botha, J A (Tvl) 1903 *BI* 3
Botha, J P F (NT) 1962 *BI* 2,3,4
Botha, P H (Tvl) 1965 *A* 1,2
Boyes, H C (GW) 1891 *BI* 1,2
Brand, G H (WP) 1928 *NZ* 2,3, 1931 *W, I*, 1932 *E, S*, 1933 *A* 1,2,3,4,5, 1937 *A* 1,2, *NZ* 2,3, 1938 *BI* 1
Bredenkamp, M J (GW) 1896 *BI* 1,3
Breedt, J C (Tvl) 1986 *Cv* 1,2,3,4, 1989 *Wld* 1,2, 1992 *NZ, A*
Brewis, J D (NT) 1949 *NZ* 1,2,3,4, 1951 *S, I, W*, 1952 *E, F*, 1953 *A* 1
Briers, T P D (WP) 1955 *BI* 1,2,3,4, 1956 *NZ* 2,3,4
Brink, D J (WP) 1906 *S, W, E*
Brink, R (WP) 1995 [*R, C*]
Brooks, D (Bor) 1906 *S*
Brosnihan, W (GL, N) 1997 *A* 2, 2000 *NZ* 1(t+R), *A* 2(t+R), *NZ* 2(R), *A* 3(R), *E* 3(R)
Brown, C B (WP) 1903 *BI* 1,2,3
Brynard, G S (WP) 1965 *A* 1, *NZ* 1,2,3,4, 1968 *BI* 3,4
Buchler, J U (Tvl) 1951 *S, I, W*, 1952 *E, F*, 1953 *A* 1,2,3,4, 1956 *A* 2
Burdett, A F (WP) 1906 *S, I*
Burger, J M (WP) 1989 *Wld* 1,2
Burger, M B (NT) 1980 *BI* 2(R), *S Am* 3, 1981 *US* (R)
Burger, S W P (WP) 1984 *E* 1,2, 1986 *Cv* 1,2,3,4
Burger, W A G (Bor) 1906 *S, I, W*, 1910 *BI* 2

Carelse, G (EP) 1964 *W, F*, 1965 *I, S*, 1967 *F* 1,2,3, 1968 *F* 1,2, 1969 *A* 1,2,3,4, *S*
Carlson, R A (WP) 1972 *E*
Carolin, H W (WP) 1903 *BI* 3, 1906 *S, I*
Castens, H H (WP) 1891 *BI* 1
Chignell, T W (WP) 1891 *BI* 3
Cilliers, G D (OFS) 1963 *A* 1,3,4
Cilliers, N V (WP) 1996 *NZ* 3(t)
Claassen, J T (WT) 1955 *BI* 1,2,3,4, 1956 *A* 1,2, *NZ* 1,2,3,4, 1958 *F* 1,2, 1960 *S, NZ* 1,2,3, *W, I*, 1961 *E, S, F, I, A* 1,2, 1962 *BI* 1,2,3,4
Claassen, W (N) 1981 *I* 1,2, *NZ* 2,3, *US*, 1982 *S Am* 1,2
Clark, W H G (Tvl) 1933 *A* 3
Clarkson, W A (N) 1921 *NZ* 1,2, 1924 *BI* 1
Cloete, H A (WP) 1896 *BI* 4
Cockrell, C H (WP) 1969 *S*, 1970 *I, W*
Cockrell, R J (WP) 1974 *F* 1,2, 1975 *F* 1,2, 1976 *NZ* 1,2, 1977 *Wld*, 1981 *NZ* 1,2(R), 3, *US*
Coetzee, J H H (WP) 1974 *BI* 1, 1975 *F* 2(R), 1976 *NZ* 1,2,3,4
Cope, D K (Tvl) 1896 *BI* 2
Cotty, W (GW) 1896 *BI* 3
Crampton, G (GW) 1903 *BI* 2
Craven, D H (WP) 1931 *W, I*, 1932 *S*, 1933 *A* 1,2,3,4,5, 1937 *A* 1,2, *NZ* 1,2,3, 1938 *BI* 1,2,3
Cronje, P A (Tvl) 1971 *F* 1,2, *A* 1,2,3, 1974 *BI* 3,4
Crosby, J H (Tvl) 1896 *BI* 2
Crosby, N J (Tvl) 1910 *BI* 1,3
Currie, C (GW) 1903 *BI* 2

D'Alton, G (WP) 1933 *A* 1
Dalton, J (Tvl, GL) 1994 *Arg* 1(R), 1995 [*A, C*], *W, It, E*, 1996 *NZ* 4(R),5, *Arg* 1,2, *F* 1,2, *W*, 1997 *Tg* (R), *BI* 3, *NZ* 2, *A* 2, *It, F* 1,2, *E, S*, 1998 *I* 1,2, *W* 1, *E* 1, *A* 1, *NZ* 1,2, *A* 2, *W* 2, *S, I* 3, *E* 2
Daneel, G M (WP) 1928 *NZ* 1,2,3,4, 1931 *W, I*, 1932 *E, S*
Daneel, H J (WP) 1906 *S, I, W, E*
Davison, P M (EP) 1910 *BI* 1
De Beer, J H (OFS) 1997 *BI* 3, *NZ* 1, *A* 1, *NZ* 2, *A* 2, *F* 2(R), *S*, 1999 *A* 2, [*S, Sp, U, E, A* 3]
De Bruyn, J (OFS) 1974 *BI* 3
De Jongh, H P K (WP) 1928 *NZ* 3
De Klerk, I J (Tvl) 1969 *E*, 1970 *I, W*
De Klerk, K B H (Tvl) 1974 *BI* 1,2,3(R), 1975 *F* 1,2, 1976 *NZ* 2(R), 1980 *S Am* 1,2, *BI* 2, 1981 *I* 1,2
De Kock, A N (GW) 1891 *BI* 2
De Kock, J S (WP) 1921 *NZ* 3, 1924 *BI* 3
De Kock, N A (WP) 2001 *It*

251

Delport, G M (GL) 2000 *C* (R), *E* 1(t+R), *A* 1, *NZ* 1, *A* 2, *NZ* 2, *A* 3, *Arg, I, W*, 2001 *F* 2, *It*
Delport, W H (EP) 1951 *S, I, W*, 1952 *E, F*, 1953 *A* 1,2,3,4
De Melker, S C (GW) 1903 *BI* 2, 1906 *E*
Devenish, C E (GW) 1896 *BI* 2
Devenish, G St L (Tvl) 1896 *BI* 2
Devenish, G E (Tvl) 1891 *BI* 1
De Villiers, D I (Tvl) 1910 *BI* 1,2,3
De Villiers, D J (WP, Bol) 1962 *BI* 2,3, 1965 *I, NZ* 1,3,4, 1967 *F* 1,2,3,4, 1968 *BI* 1,2,3,4, *F* 1,2, 1969 *A* 1,4, *E*, 1970 *I, W, NZ* 1,2,3,4
De Villiers, H A (WP) 1906 *S, W, E*
De Villiers, H O (WP) 1967 *F* 1,2,3,4, 1968 *F* 1,2, 1969 *A* 1,2,3,4, *S, E*, 1970 *I, W*
De Villiers, P du P (WP) 1928 *NZ* 1,3,4, 1932 *E*, 1933 *A* 4, 1937 *A* 1,2, *NZ* 1
Devine, D (Tvl) 1924 *BI* 3, 1928 *NZ* 2
De Vos, D J J (WP) 1965 *S*, 1969 *A* 3, *S*
De Waal, A N (WP) 1967 *F* 1,2,3,4
De Waal, P J (WP) 1896 *BI* 4
De Wet, A E (WP) 1969 *A* 3,4, *E*
De Wet, P J (WP) 1938 *BI* 1,2,3
Dinkelmann, E E (NT) 1951 *S, I*, 1952 *E, F*, 1953 *A* 1,2
Dirksen, C W (NT) 1963 *A* 4, 1964 *W*, 1965 *I, S*, 1967 *F* 1,2,3,4, 1968 *BI* 1,2
Dobbin, F J (GW) 1903 *BI* 1,2, 1906 *S, W, E*, 1910 *BI* 1, 1912 *S, I, W*
Dobie, J A R (Tvl) 1928 *NZ* 2
Dormehl, P J (WP) 1896 *BI* 3,4
Douglass, F W (EP) 1896 *BI* 1
Drotské, A E (OFS) 1993 *Arg* 2, 1995 [*WS* (R)], 1996 *A* 1(R), 1997 *Tg, BI* 1,2,3(R), *NZ* 1, *A* 1, *NZ* 2(R), 1998 *I* 2(R), *W* 1(R), *I* 3(R), 1999 *It* 1,2, *W, NZ* 1, *A* 1, *NZ* 2, *A* 2, [*S, Sp* (R), *U, E, A* 3, *NZ* 3]
Dryburgh, R G (WP) 1955 *BI* 2,3,4, 1956 *A* 2, *NZ* 1,4, 1960 *NZ* 1,2
Duff, B R (WP) 1891 *BI* 1,2,3
Duffy, B A (Bor) 1928 *NZ* 1
Du Plessis, C J (WP) 1982 *S Am* 1,2, 1984 *E* 1,2, *S Am* 1,2, 1986 *Cv* 1,2,3,4, 1989 *Wld* 1,2
Du Plessis, D C (NT) 1977 *Wld*, 1980 *S Am* 2
Du Plessis, F (Tvl) 1949 *NZ* 1,2,3
Du Plessis, M (WP) 1971 *A* 1,2,3, 1974 *BI* 1,2, *F* 1,2, 1975 *F* 1,2, 1976 *NZ* 1,2,3,4, 1977 *Wld*, 1980 *S Am* 1,2, *BI* 1,2,3,4, *S Am* 4, *F*
Du Plessis, M J (WP) 1984 *S Am* 1,2, 1986 *Cv* 1,2,3,4, 1989 *Wld* 1,2
Du Plessis, N J (WT) 1921 *NZ* 2,3, 1924 *BI* 1,2,3
Du Plessis, P G (NT) 1972 *E*
Du Plessis, T D (NT) 1980 *S Am* 1,2
Du Plessis, W (WP) 1980 *S Am* 1,2, *BI* 1,2,3,4, *S Am* 3,4, *F*, 1981 *NZ* 1,2,3, 1982 *S Am* 1,2
Du Plooy, A J J (EP) 1955 *BI* 1
Du Preez, F C H (NT) 1961 *E, S, A* 1,2, 1962 *BI* 1,2,3,4, 1963 *A* 1, 1964 *W, F*, 1965 *A* 1,2, *NZ* 1,2,3,4, 1967 *F* 4, 1968 *BI* 1,2,3,4, *F* 1,2, 1969 *A* 1,2, *S*, 1970 *I, W, NZ* 1,2,3,4, 1971 *F* 1,2, *A* 1,2,3
Du Preez, J G H (WP) 1956 *NZ* 1
Du Preez, R J (N) 1992 *NZ, A*, 1993 *F* 1,2, *A* 1,2,3
Du Rand, J A (R, NT) 1949 *NZ* 2,3, 1951 *S, I, W*, 1952 *E, F*, 1953 *A* 1,2,3,4, 1955 *BI* 1,2,3,4, 1956 *A* 1,2, *NZ* 1,2,3,4
Du Randt, J P (OFS) 1994 *Arg* 1,2, *S, W*, 1995 *WS*, [*A, WS, F, NZ*], 1996 *Fj, A* 1, *NZ* 1, *A* 2, *NZ* 2,3,4, 1997 *Tg, BI* 1,2,3, *NZ* 1, *A* 1, *NZ* 2, *A* 2, *It, F* 1,2, *E, S*, 1999 *NZ* 1, *A* 1, *NZ* 2, *A* 2, [*S, Sp* (R), *U, E, A* 3, *NZ* 3]
Du Toit, A F (WP) 1928 *NZ* 3,4
Du Toit, B A (Tvl) 1938 *BI* 1,2,3
Du Toit, G S (GW) 1998 *I* 1, 1999 *It* 1,2, *W* (R), *NZ* 1,2
Du Toit, P A (NT) 1949 *NZ* 2,3,4, 1951 *S, I, W*, 1952 *E, F*
Du Toit, P G (WP) 1981 *NZ* 1, 1982 *S Am* 1,2, 1984 *E* 1,2
Du Toit, P S (WP) 1958 *F* 1,2, 1960 *NZ* 1,2,3,4, *W, I*, 1961 *E, S, F, I, A* 1,2
Duvenhage, F P (GW) 1949 *NZ* 1,3

Edwards, P (NT) 1980 *S Am* 1,2
Ellis, J H (SWA) 1965 *NZ* 1,2,3,4, 1967 *F* 1,2,3,4, 1968 *BI* 1,2,3,4, *F* 1,2, 1969 *A* 1,2,3,4, *S*, 1970 *I, W, NZ* 1,2,3,4, 1971 *F* 1,2, *A* 1,2,3, 1972 *E*, 1974 *BI* 1,2,3,4, *F* 1,2, 1976 *NZ* 1
Ellis, M C (Tvl) 1921 *NZ* 2,3, 1924 *BI* 1,2,3,4
Els, W W (OFS) 1997 *A* 2(R)
Engelbrecht, J P (WP) 1960 *S, W, I*, 1961 *E, S, F, A* 1,2, 1962 *BI* 2,3,4, 1963 *A* 2,3, 1964 *W, F*, 1965 *I, S, A* 1,2, *NZ* 1,2,3,4, 1967 *F* 1,2,3,4, 1968 *BI* 1,2, *F* 1,2, 1969 *A* 1,2

Erasmus, F S (NT, EP) 1986 *Cv* 3,4, 1989 *Wld* 2
Erasmus, J C (OFS, GL) 1997 *BI* 3, *A* 2, *It, F* 1,2, *S*, 1998 *I* 1,2, *W* 1, *E* 1, *A* 1, *NZ* 2, *A* 2, *S, W* 2, *I* 3, *E* 2, 1999 *It* 1,2, *W, A* 1, *NZ* 2, *A* 2, [*S, U, E, A* 3, *NZ* 3], 2000 *C, E* 1, *A* 1, *NZ* 1,2, *A* 3, 2001 *F* 1,2
Esterhuizen, G (GL) 2000 *NZ* 1(R),2, *A* 3, *Arg, I, W* (R), *E* 3(t)
Etlinger, T E (WP) 1896 *BI* 4

Ferreira, C (OFS) 1986 *Cv* 1,2
Ferreira, P S (WP) 1984 *S Am* 1,2
Ferris, H H (Tvl) 1903 *BI* 3
Fleck R F (WP) 1999 *It* 1,2, *NZ* 1(R), *A* 1, *NZ* 2(R), *A* 2, [*S, U, E, A* 3, *NZ* 3], 2000 *C, E* 1,2, *A* 1, *NZ* 1, *A* 2, *NZ* 2, *A* 3, *Arg, I, W, E* 3, 2001 *F* 1(R),2, *It, NZ* 1, *A* 1,2
Forbes, H H (Tvl) 1896 *BI* 2
Fourie, C (EP) 1974 *F* 1,2, 1975 *F* 1,2
Fourie, T T (SET) 1974 *BI* 3
Fourie, W L (SWA) 1958 *F* 1,2
Francis, J A J (Tvl) 1912 *S, I, W*, 1913 *E, F*
Frederickson, C A (Tvl) 1974 *BI* 2, 1980 *S Am* 1,2
Frew, A (Tvl) 1903 *BI* 1
Froneman, D C (OFS) 1977 *Wld*
Froneman, I L (Bor) 1933 *A* 1
Fuls, H T (Tvl, EP) 1992 *NZ* (R), 1993 *F* 1,2, *A* 1,2,3, *Arg* 1,2
Fry, S P (WP) 1951 *S, I, W*, 1952 *E, F*, 1953 *A* 1,2,3,4, 1955 *BI* 1,2,3,4
Fynn, E E (N) 2001 *F* 1, *It* (R)
Fyvie, W (N) 1996 *NZ* 4(t & R), 5(R), *Arg* 2(R)

Gage, J H (OFS) 1933 *A* 1
Gainsford, J L (WP) 1960 *S, NZ* 1,2,3,4, *W, I*, 1961 *E, S, F, A* 1,2, 1962 *BI* 1,2,3,4, 1963 *A* 1,2,3,4, 1964 *W, F*, 1965 *I, S, A* 1,2, *NZ* 1,2,3,4, 1967 *F* 1,2,3
Garvey, A C (N) 1996 *Arg* 1,2, *F* 1,2, *W*, 1997 *Tg, BI* 1,2,3(R), *A* 1(t), *It, F* 1,2, *E, S*, 1998 *I* 1,2, *W* 1, *E* 1, *A* 1, *NZ* 1,2, *A* 2, *W* 2, *S, I* 3, *E* 2, 1999 [*Sp*]
Geel, P J (OFS) 1949 *NZ* 3
Geere, V (Tvl) 1933 *A* 1,2,3,4,5
Geffin, A O (Tvl) 1949 *NZ* 1,2,3,4, 1951 *S, I, W*
Geldenhuys, A (EP) 1992 *NZ, A, F* 1,2
Geldenhuys, S B (NT) 1981 *NZ* 2,3, *US*, 1982 *S Am* 1,2, 1989 *Wld* 1,2
Gentles, T A (WP) 1955 *BI* 1,2,4, 1956 *NZ* 2,3, 1958 *F* 2
Geraghty, E M (Bor) 1949 *NZ* 4
Gerber, D M (EP, WP) 1980 *S Am* 3,4, *F*, 1981 *I* 1,2, *NZ* 1,2,3, *US*, 1982 *S Am* 1,2, 1984 *E* 1,2, *S Am* 1,2, 1986 *Cv* 1,2,3,4, 1992 *NZ, A, F* 1,2, *E*
Gerber, M C (EP) 1958 *F* 1,2, 1960 *S*
Gericke, F W (Tvl) 1960 *S*
Germishuys, J S (OFS, Tvl) 1974 *BI* 2, 1976 *NZ* 1,2,3,4, 1977 *Wld*, 1980 *S Am* 1,2, *BI* 1,2,3,4, *S Am* 3,4, *F*, 1981 *I* 1,2, *NZ* 2,3, *US*
Gibbs, B (GW) 1903 *BI* 2
Goosen, C P (OFS) 1965 *NZ* 2
Gorton, H C (Tvl) 1896 *BI* 1
Gould, R L (N) 1968 *BI* 1,2,3,4
Gray, B G (WP) 1931 *W*, 1932 *E, S*, 1933 *A* 5
Greenwood, C M (WP) 1961 *I*
Greyling, P J F (OFS) 1967 *F* 1,2,3,4, 1968 *BI* 1, *F* 1,2, 1969 *A* 1,2,3,4, *S, E*, 1970 *I, W, NZ* 1,2,3,4, 1971 *F* 1,2, *A* 1,2,3, 1972 *E*
Grobler, C J (OFS) 1974 *BI* 4, 1975 *F* 1,2
Guthrie, F H (WP) 1891 *BI* 1,3, 1896 *BI* 1

Hahn, C H L (Tvl) 1910 *BI* 1,2,3
Hall, D B (GL) 2001 *F* 1,2, *NZ* 1, *A* 1,2, *NZ* 2
Hamilton, F (EP) 1891 *BI* 1
Harris, T A (Tvl) 1937 *NZ* 2,3, 1938 *BI* 1,2,3
Hartley, A J (WP) 1891 *BI* 3
Hattingh, H (NT) 1992 *A* (R), *F* 2(R), *E*, 1994 *Arg* 1,2
Hattingh, L B (OFS) 1933 *A* 2
Heatlie, B H (WP) 1891 *BI* 2,3, 1896 *BI* 1,4, 1903 *BI* 1,3
Hendricks, M (Bol) 1998 *I* 2(R), *W* 1(R)
Hendriks, P (Tvl) 1992 *NZ, A*, 1994 *S, W*, 1995 [*A, R, C*], 1996 *A* 1, *NZ* 1, *A* 2, *NZ* 2,3,4,5
Hepburn, T B (WP) 1896 *BI* 4
Heunis, J W (NT) 1981 *NZ* 3(R), *US*, 1982 *S Am* 1,2, 1984 *E* 1,2, *S Am* 1,2, 1986 *Cv* 1,2,3,4, 1989 *Wld* 1,2
Hill, R A (N, WP) 1960 *W, I*, 1961 *A* 1,2, 1962 *BI* 4, 1963 *A* 3
Hills, W G (NT) 1992 *F* 1,2, *E*, 1993 *F* 1,2, *A* 1
Hirsch, J G (EP) 1906 *I*, 1910 *BI* 1
Hobson, T E C (WP) 1903 *BI* 3

Hoffman, R S (Bol) 1953 *A* 3
Holton, D N (EP) 1960 *S*
Honiball, H W (N) 1993 *A* 3(R), *Arg* 2, 1995 *WS* (R), 1996 *Fj*, *A* 1, *NZ* 5, *Arg* 1,2, *F* 1,2, *W*, 1997 *Tg*, *BI* 1,2,3(R), *NZ* 1(R), *A* 1(R), *NZ* 2, *A* 2, *It*, *F* 1,2, *E*, 1998 *W* 1(R), *E* 1, *A* 1, *NZ* 1,2, *A* 2, *W* 2, *S*, *I* 3, *E* 2, 1999 [*A* 3(R), *NZ* 3]
Hopwood, D J (WP) 1960 *S*, *NZ* 3,4, *W*, 1961 *E*, *S*, *F*, *I*, *A* 1,2, 1962 *BI* 1,2,3,4, 1963 *A* 1,2,4, 1964 *W*, *F*, 1965 *S*, *NZ* 3,4
Howe, B F (Bor) 1956 *NZ* 1,4
Howe-Browne, N R F G (WP) 1910 *BI* 1,2,3
Hugo, D P (WP) 1989 *Wld* 1,2
Hurter, M H (NT) 1995 [*R*, *C*], *W*, 1996 *Fj*, *A* 1, *NZ* 1,2,3,4,5, 1997 *NZ* 1,2, *A* 2

Immelman, J H (WP) 1913 *F*

Jackson, D C (WP) 1906 *I*, *W*, *E*
Jackson, J S (WP) 1903 *BI* 2
James, A D (N) 2001 *F* 1,2, *NZ* 1, *A* 1,2, *NZ* 2
Jansen, E (OFS) 1981 *NZ* 1
Jansen, J S (OFS) 1970 *NZ* 1,2,3,4, 1971 *F* 1,2, *A* 1,2,3, 1972 *E*
Jantjes, C A (GL) 2001 *It*, *A* 1,2, *NZ* 2
Jennings, C B (Bor) 1937 *NZ* 1
Johnson, G K (Tvl) 1993 *Arg* 2, 1994 *NZ* 3, *Arg* 1, 1995 *WS*, [*R*, *C*, *WS*]
Johnstone, P G A (WP) 1951 *S*, *I*, *W*, 1952 *E*, *F*, 1956 *A* 1, *NZ* 1,2,4
Jones, C H (Tvl) 1903 *BI* 1,2
Jones, P S T (WP) 1896 *BI* 1,3,4
Jordaan, R P (NT) 1949 *NZ* 1,2,3,4
Joubert, A J (OFS, N) 1989 *Wld* 1(R), 1993 *A* 3, *Arg* 1, 1994 *E* 1,2, *NZ* 1,2(R), 3, *Arg* 2, *S*, *W*, 1995 [*A*, *C*, *WS*, *F*, *NZ*], *W*, *It*, *E*, 1996 *Fj*, *A* 1, *NZ* 1,3,4,5, *Arg* 1,2, *F* 1,2, *W*, 1997 *Tg*, *BI* 1,2, *A* 2
Joubert, M C (Bol) 2001 *NZ* 1
Joubert, S J (WP) 1906 *I*, *W*, *E*
Julies, W (Bol) 1999 [*Sp*]

Kahts, W J H (NT) 1980 *BI* 1,2,3, *S Am* 3,4, *F*, 1981 *I* 1,2, *NZ* 2, 1982 *S Am* 1,2
Kaminer, J (Tvl) 1958 *F* 2
Kayser, D J (EP, N) 1999 *It* 2(R), *A* 1(R), *NZ* 2, *A* 2, [*S*, *Sp* (R), *U*, *E*, *A* 3], 2001 *It* (R), *NZ* 1(R), *A* 2, *NZ* 2(R)
Kebble, G R (N) 1993 *Arg* 1,2, 1994 *NZ* 1(R), 2
Kelly, E W (GW) 1896 *BI* 3
Kempson, R (N, WP) 1998 *I* 2(R), *W* 1, *E* 1, *A* 1, *NZ* 1,2 *A* 2, *W* 2, *S*, *I* 3, *E* 2, 1999 *It* 1,2, *W*, 2000 *C*, *E* 1,2, *A* 1, *NZ* 1, *A* 2,3, *Arg*, *I*, *W*, *E* 3, 2001 *F* 1,2(R), *NZ* 1, *A* 1,2, *NZ* 2
Kenyon, B J (Bor) 1949 *NZ* 4
Kipling, H G (GW) 1931 *W*, *I*, 1932 *E*, *S*, 1933 *A* 1,2,3,4,5
Kirkpatrick, A I (GW) 1953 *A* 2, 1956 *NZ* 2, 1958 *F* 1, 1960 *S*, *NZ* 1,2,3,4, *W*, *I*, 1961 *E*, *S*, *F*
Knight, A S (Tvl) 1912 *S*, *I*, *W*, 1913 *E*, *F*
Knoetze, F (WP) 1989 *Wld* 1,2
Koch, A C (Bol) 1949 *NZ* 2,3,4, 1951 *S*, *I*, *W*, 1952 *E*, *F*, 1953 *A* 1,2,4, 1955 *BI* 1,2,3,4, 1956 *A* 1, *NZ* 2,3, 1958 *F* 1,2, 1960 *NZ* 1,2
Koch, H V (WP) 1949 *NZ* 1,2,3,4
Koen, L J (GL) 2000 *A* 1
Kotze, G J M (WP) 1967 *F* 1,2,3,4
Krantz, E F W (OFS) 1976 *NZ* 1, 1981 *I* 1,
Krige, C P J (WP) 1999 *It* 2, *W*, *NZ* 1, 2000 *C* (R), *E* 1(R),2, *A* 1(R), *NZ* 1, *A* 2, *NZ* 2, *A* 3, *Arg*, *I*, *W*, *E* 3, 2001 *F* 1,2, *It* (R), *A* 1(t+R)
Krige, J D (WP) 1903 *BI* 1,3, 1906 *S*, *I*, *W*
Kritzinger, J L (Tvl) 1974 *BI* 3,4, *F* 1,2, 1975 *F* 1,2, 1976 *NZ* 4
Kroon, C M (EP) 1955 *BI* 1
Kruger, P E (Tvl) 1986 *Cv* 3,4
Kruger, R J (NT, BB) 1993 *Arg* 1,2, 1994 *S*, *W*, 1995 *WS*, [*A*, *R*, *WS*, *F*, *NZ*], *W*, *It*, *E*, 1996 *Fj*, *A* 1, *NZ* 1,2, *A* 2, *NZ* 2,3,4,5, *Arg* 1,2, *F* 1,2, *W*, 1997 *Tg*, *BI* 1,2, *NZ* 1, *A* 1, *NZ* 2, 1999 *NZ* 2, *A* 2(R), [*Sp*, *NZ* 3(R)]
Kruger, T L (Tvl) 1921 *NZ* 1,2, 1924 *BI* 1,2,3,4, 1928 *NZ* 1,2
Kuhn, S P (Tvl) 1960 *NZ* 3,4, *W*, *I*, 1961 *E*, *S*, *F*, *I*, *A* 1,2, 1962 *BI* 1,2,3,4, 1963 *A* 1,2,3, 1965 *I*, *S*

Labuschagne, J J (GL) 2000 *NZ* 1(R)
La Grange, J B (WP) 1924 *BI* 3,4
Larard, A (Tvl) 1896 *BI* 2,4
Lategan, M T (WP) 1949 *NZ* 1,2,3,4, 1951 *S*, *I*, *W*, 1952 *E*, *F*, 1953 *A* 1,2

Laubscher, T G (WP) 1994 *Arg* 1,2, *S*, *W*, 1995 *It*, *E*
Lawless, M J (WP) 1964 *F*, 1969 *E* (R), 1970 *I*, *W*
Ledger, S H (GW) 1912 *S*, *I*, 1913 *E*, *F*
Leonard, A (WP, SWD) 1999 *A* 1, [*Sp*]
Le Roux, A H (OFS, N) 1994 *E* 1, 1998 *I* 1,2, *W* 1(R), *E* 1(R), *A* 1(R), *NZ* 1(R),2(R), *A* 2(R), *W* 2(R), *S* (R), *I* 3(R), *E* 2(t+R), 1999 *It* 1(R),2(R), *W* (R), *NZ* 1(R), *A* 1(R), *NZ* 2(R), *A* 2(R), [*S*(R), *Sp*, *U* (R), *E* (R), *A* 3(R), *NZ* 3(R)], 2000 *E* 1(t+R),2(R), *A* 1(R),2(R), *NZ* 2, *A* 3(R), *Arg* (R), *I* (t), *W* (R), *E* 3(R), 2001 *F* 1(R),2, *It*, *NZ* 1(R), *A* 1(R),2(R), *NZ* 2(R)
Le Roux, H P (Tvl) 1993 *F* 1,2, 1994 *E* 1,2, *NZ* 1,2,3, *Arg* 2, *S*, *W*, 1995 *WS* [*A*, *R*, *C* (R), *WS*, *F*, *NZ*], *W*, *It*, *E*, 1996 *Fj*, *NZ* 2, *Arg* 1,2, *F* 1,2, *W*
Le Roux, J H S (Tvl) 1994 *E* 2, *NZ* 1,2
Le Roux, M (OFS) 1980 *BI* 1,2,3,4, *S Am* 3,4, *F*, 1981 *I* 1
Le Roux, P A (WP) 1906 *I*, *W*, *E*
Little, E M (GW) 1891 *BI* 1,3
Lochner, G P (WP) 1955 *BI* 3, 1956 *A* 1,2, *NZ* 1,2,3,4, 1958 *F* 1,2
Lochner, G P (EP) 1937 *NZ* 3, 1938 *BI* 1,2
Lockyear, R J (GW) 1960 *NZ* 1,2,3,4, 1960 *I*, 1961 *F*
Lombard, A C (EP) 1910 *BI* 2
Lötter, D (Tvl) 1993 *F* 2, *A* 1,2
Lotz, J W (Tvl) 1937 *A* 1,2, *NZ* 1,2,3, 1938 *BI* 1,2,3
Loubser, J A (WP) 1903 *BI* 3, 1906 *S*, *I*, *W*, *E*, 1910 *BI* 1,3
Lourens, M J (NT) 1968 *BI* 2,3,4
Louw, J S (Tvl) 1891 *BI* 1,2,3
Louw, M J (Tvl) 1971 *A* 2,3
Louw, M M (WP) 1928 *NZ* 3,4, 1931 *W*, *I*, 1932 *E*, *S*, 1933 *A* 1,2,3,4,5, 1937 *A* 1,2, *NZ* 2,3, 1938 *BI* 1,2,3
Louw, R J (WP) 1980 *S Am* 1,2, *BI* 1,2,3,4 *S Am* 3,4, *F*, 1981 *I* 1,2, *NZ* 1,3, 1982 *S Am* 1,2, 1984 *E* 1,2, *S Am* 1,2
Louw, S C (WP) 1933 *A* 1,2,3,4,5, 1937 *A* 1, *NZ* 1,2,3, 1938 *BI* 1,2,3
Lubbe, E (CW) 1997 *Tg*, *BI* 1
Luyt, F P (WP) 1910 *BI* 1,2,3, 1912 *S*, *I*, *W*, 1913 *E*
Luyt, J D (EP) 1912 *S*, *W*, 1913 *E*, *F*
Luyt, R R (W P) 1910 *BI* 2,3, 1912 *S*, *I*, *W*, 1913 *E*, *F*
Lyons, D J (EP) 1896 *BI* 1
Lyster, P J (N) 1933 *A* 2,5, 1937 *NZ* 1

McCallum, I D (WP) 1970 *NZ* 1,2,3,4, 1971 *F* 1,2, *A* 1,2,3, 1974 *BI* 1,2
McCallum, R J (WP) 1974 *BI* 1
McCulloch, J D (GW) 1913 *E*, *F*
MacDonald, A W (R) 1965 *A* 1, *NZ* 1,2,3,4
Macdonald, D A (WP) 1974 *BI* 2
Macdonald, I (Tvl) 1992 *NZ*, *A*, 1993 *F* 1, *A* 3, 1994 *E* 2, 1995 *WS* (R)
McDonald, J A J (WP) 1931 *W*, *I*, 1932 *E*, *S*
McEwan, W M C (Tvl) 1903 *BI* 1,3
McHardy, E E (OFS) 1912 *S*, *I*, *W*, 1913 *E*, *F*
McKendrick, J A (WP) 1891 *BI* 3
Malan, A S (Tvl) 1960 *NZ* 1,2,3,4, *W*, *I*, 1961 *E*, *S*, *F*, 1962 *BI* 1, 1963 *A* 1,2,3, 1964 *W*, 1965 *I*, *S*
Malan, A W (NT) 1989 *Wld* 1,2, 1992 *NZ*, *A*, *F* 1,2, *E*
Malan, E (NT) 1980 *BI* 3(R), 4
Malan, G F (WP) 1958 *F* 2, 1960 *NZ* 1,3,4, 1961 *E*, *S*, *F*, 1962 *BI* 1,2,3, 1963 *A* 1,2,4, 1964 *W*, 1965 *A* 1,2, *NZ* 1,2
Malan, P (Tvl) 1949 *NZ* 4
Mallett, N V H (WP) 1984 *S Am* 1,2
Malotana K (Bor) 1999 [*Sp*]
Mans, W J (WP) 1965 *I*, *S*
Marais, C F (WP) 1999 *It* 1(R),2(R), 2000 *C*, *E* 1,2, *A* 1, *NZ* 1, *A* 2, *NZ* 2, *A* 3, *Arg* (R), *W* (R)
Marais, F P (Bol) 1949 *NZ* 1,2, 1951 *S*, 1953 *A* 1,2
Marais, J F K (WP) 1963 *A* 3, 1964 *W*, *F*, 1965 *I*, *S*, *A* 2, 1968 *BI*, 1,2,3,4, *F* 1,2, 1969 *A* 1,2,3,4, *S*, *E*, 1970 *I*, *W*, *NZ* 1,2,3,4, 1971 *F* 1,2, *A* 1,2,3, 1974 *BI* 1,2,3,4, *F* 1,2
Maré, D S (Tvl) 1906 *S*
Marsberg, A F W (GW) 1906 *S*, *W*, *E*
Marsberg, P A (GW) 1910 *BI* 1
Martheze, W C (GW) 1903 *BI* 2, 1906 *I*, *W*
Martin, H J (Tvl) 1937 *A* 2
Matfield, V (BB) 2001 *It* (R), *NZ* 1, *A* 2, *NZ* 2
Mellet, T B (GW) 1896 *BI* 2
Mellish, F W (WP) 1921 *NZ* 1,3, 1924 *BI* 1,2,3,4
Merry, J (EP) 1891 *BI* 1
Metcalf, H D (Bor) 1903 *BI* 2
Meyer, C du P (WP) 1921 *NZ* 1,2,3
Meyer, P J (GW) 1896 *BI* 1

Meyer, W (OFS, GL) 1997 *S* (R), 1999 *It* 2, *NZ* 1(R), *A* 1(R), 2000 *C* (R), *E* 1, *NZ* 1(R),2(R), *Arg, I, W, E* 3, 2001 *F* 1(R),2, *It*
Michau, J M (Tvl) 1921 *NZ* 1
Michau, J P (WP) 1921 *NZ* 1,2,3
Millar, W A (WP) 1906 *E*, 1910 *BI* 2,3, 1912 *I, W*, 1913 *F*
Mills, W J (WP) 1910 *BI* 2
Moll, T (Tvl) 1910 *BI* 2
Montini, P E (WP) 1956 *A* 1,2
Montgomery, P C (WP) 1997 *BI* 2,3, *NZ* 1, *A* 1, *NZ* 2, *A* 2, *F* 1,2, *E, S*, 1998 *I* 1,2, *W* 1, *E* 1, *A* 1, *NZ* 1,2, *A* 2, *W* 2, *S, I* 3, *E* 2, 1999 *It* 1,2, *W, NZ* 1, *A* 1, *NZ* 2, *A* 2, [*S, U, E, A* 3, *NZ* 3], 2000 *C, E* 1,2, *A* 1, *NZ* 1, *A* 2(R), *Arg, I, W, E* 3, 2001 *F* 1, 2(t), *It, NZ* 1
Moolman, L C (NT) 1977 *Wld*, 1980 *S Am* 1,2, *BI* 1,2,3,4, *S Am* 3,4, *F*, 1981 *I* 1,2, *NZ* 1,2,3, *US*, 1982 *S Am* 1,2, 1984 *S Am* 1,2, 1986 *Cv* 1,2,3,4
Mordt, R H (Z-R, NT) 1980 *S Am* 1,2, *BI* 1,2,3,4, *S Am* 3,4, *F*, 1981 *I* 1,2, *NZ* 1,2,3, *US*, 1982 *S Am* 1,2, 1984 *S Am* 1,2
Morkel, D A (Tvl) 1903 *BI* 1
Morkel, D F T (Tvl) 1906 *I, E*, 1910 *BI* 1,3, 1912 *S, I, W*, 1913 *E, F*
Morkel, H J (WP) 1921 *NZ* 1
Morkel, H W (WP) 1921 *NZ* 1,2
Morkel, J A (WP) 1921 *NZ* 2,3
Morkel, J W H (WP) 1912 *S, I, W*, 1913 *E, F*
Morkel, P G (WP) 1912 *S, I, W*, 1913 *E, F*, 1921 *NZ* 1,2,3
Morkel, P K (WP) 1928 *NZ* 4
Morkel, W H (WP) 1910 *BI* 3, 1912 *S, I, W*, 1913 *E, F*, 1921 *NZ* 1,2,3
Morkel, W S (Tvl) 1906 *S, I, W, E*
Moss, C (N) 1949 *NZ* 1,2,3,4
Mostert, P J (WP) 1921 *NZ* 1,2,3, 1924 *BI* 1,2,4, 1928 *NZ* 1,2,3,4, 1931 *W, I*, 1932 *E, S*
Mulder, J C (Tvl, GL) 1994 *NZ* 2,3, *S, W*, 1995 *WS*, [*A, WS, F, NZ*], *W, It, E*, 1996 *Fj, A* 1, *NZ* 1, *A* 2, *NZ* 2,5, *Arg* 1,2, *F* 1,2, *W*, 1997 *Tg, BI* 1, 1999 *It* 1(R),2, *W, NZ* 1, 2000 *C*(R), *A* 1, *E* 3, 2001 *F* 1, *It*
Muller, G H (WP) 1969 *A* 3,4, *S*, 1970 *W, NZ* 1,2,3,4, 1971 *F* 1,2, 1972 *E*, 1974 *BI* 1,3,4
Muller, H L (OFS) 1986 *Cv* 4(R), 1989 *Wld* 1(R)
Muller, H S V (Tvl) 1949 *NZ* 1,2,3,4, 1951 *S, I, W*, 1952 *E, F*, 1953 *A* 1,2,3,4
Muller, L J J (N) 1992 *NZ, A*
Muller, P G (N) 1992 *NZ, A, F* 1,2, *E*, 1993 *F* 1,2, *A* 1,2,3, *Arg* 1,2, 1994 *E* 1,2, *NZ* 1, *S, W*, 1998 *I* 1,2, *W* 1, *E* 1, *A* 1, *NZ* 1,2, *A* 2, 1999 *It* 1, *W, NZ* 1, *A* 1, [*Sp, E, A* 3, *NZ* 3]
Muir, D J (WP) 1997 *It, F* 1,2, *E, S*
Myburgh, F R (EP) 1896 *BI* 1
Myburgh, J L (NT) 1962 *BI* 1, 1963 *A* 4, 1964 *W, F*, 1968 *BI* 1,2,3, *F* 1,2, 1969 *A* 1,2,3,4, *E*, 1970 *I, W, NZ* 3,4
Myburgh, W H (WT) 1924 *BI* 1

Naude, J P (WP) 1963 *A* 4, 1965 *A* 1,2, *NZ* 1,3,4, 1967 *F* 1,2,3,4, 1968 *BI* 1,2,3,4
Neethling, J B (WP) 1967 *F* 1,2,3,4, 1968 *BI* 4, 1969 *S*, 1970 *NZ* 1,2
Nel, J A (Tvl) 1960 *NZ* 1,2, 1963 *A* 1,2, 1965 *A* 2, *NZ* 1,2,3,4, 1970 *NZ* 3,4
Nel, J J (WP) 1956 *A* 1,2, *NZ* 1,2,3,4, 1958 *F* 1,2
Nel, P A R O (WP) 1903 *BI* 1,2,3
Nel, P J (N) 1928 *NZ* 1,2,3,4, 1931 *W, I*, 1932 *E, S*, 1933 *A* 1,3,4,5, 1937 *A* 1,2, *NZ* 2,3
Nimb, C F (WP) 1961 *I*
Nomis, S H (Tvl) 1967 *F* 4, 1968 *BI* 1,2,3,4, *F* 1,2, 1969 *A* 1,2,3,4, *S, E*, 1970 *I, W, NZ* 1,2,3,4, 1971 *F* 1,2, *A* 1,2,3, 1972 *E*
Nykamp, J L (Tvl) 1933 *A* 2

Ochse, J K (WP) 1951 *I, W*, 1952 *E, F*, 1953 *A* 1,2,4
Oelofse, J S A (Tvl) 1953 *A* 1,2,3,4
Oliver, J F (Tvl) 1928 *NZ* 3,4
Olivier, E (WP) 1967 *F* 1,2,3,4, 1968 *BI* 1,2,3,4, *F* 1,2, 1969 *A* 1,2,3,4, *S, E*
Olivier, J (NT) 1992 *F* 1,2, *E*, 1993 *F* 1,2 *A* 1,2,3, *Arg* 1, 1995 *W, It* (R), *E*, 1996 *Arg* 1,2, *F* 1,2, *W*
Olver, E (EP) 1896 *BI* 1
Oosthuizen, J J (WP) 1974 *BI* 1, *F* 1,2, 1975 *F* 1,2, 1976 *NZ* 1,2,3,4
Oosthuizen, O W (NT, Tvl) 1981 *I* 1(R), 2, *NZ* 2,3, *US*, 1982 *S Am* 1,2, 1984 *E* 1,2
Osler, B L (WP) 1924 *BI* 1,2,3,4, 1928 *NZ* 1,2,3,4, 1931 *W, I*, 1932 *E, S*, 1933 *A* 1,2,3,4,5

Osler, S G (WP) 1928 *NZ* 1
Otto, K (NT, BB) 1995 [*R, C* (R), *WS* (R)], 1997 *BI* 3, *A* 1, *NZ* 2, *A* 2, *It, F* 1,2, *E, S*, 1998 *I* 1,2, *W* 1, *E* 1, *A* 1, *NZ* 1,2, *A* 2, *W* 2, *S, I* 3, *E* 2, 1999 *It* 1, *W, NZ* 1, *A* 1, [*S* (R), *Sp, U, E, A* 3, *NZ* 3], 2000 *C, E* 1,2, *A* 1
Oxlee, K (N) 1960 *NZ* 1,2,3,4, *W, I*, 1961 *S, A* 1,2, 1962 *BI* 1,2,3,4, 1963 *A* 1,2,4, 1964 *W*, 1965 *NZ* 1,2

Pagel, G L (WP) 1995 [*A* (R), *R, C, NZ* (R)], 1996 *NZ* 5(R)
Parker, W H (EP) 1965 *A* 1,2
Partridge, J E C (Tvl) 1903 *BI* 1
Paulse, B J (WP) 1999 *It* 1,2, *NZ* 1, *A* 1,2(R), [*S* (R), *Sp, NZ* 3], 2000 *C, E* 1,2, *A* 1, *NZ* 1, *A* 2, *NZ* 2, *A* 3, *Arg, W, E* 3, 2001 *F* 1,2, *It, NZ* 1, *A* 1,2, *NZ* 2
Payn, C (N) 1924 *BI* 1,2
Pelser, H J M (Tvl) 1958 *F* 1, 1960 *NZ* 1,2,3,4, *W, I*, 1961 *F, I, A* 1,2
Pfaff, B D (WP) 1956 *A* 1
Pickard, J A J (WP) 1953 *A* 3,4, 1956 *NZ* 2, 1958 *F* 2
Pienaar, J F (Tvl) 1993 *F* 1,2, *A* 1,2,3, *Arg* 1,2, 1994 *E* 1,2, *NZ* 2,3, *Arg* 1,2, *S, W*, 1995 *WS*, [*A, C, WS, F, NZ*], *W, It, E*, 1996 *Fj, A* 1, *NZ* 1, *A* 2, *NZ* 2
Pienaar, Z M J (OFS) 1980 *S Am* 2(R), *BI* 1,2,3,4, *S Am* 3,4, *F*, 1981 *I* 1,2, *NZ* 1,2,3
Pitzer, G (NT) 1967 *F* 1,2,3,4, 1968 *BI* 1,2,3,4, *F* 1,2, 1969 *A* 3,4
Pope, C F (WP) 1974 *BI* 1,2,3,4, 1975 *F* 1,2, 1976 *NZ* 2,3,4
Potgieter, H J (OFS) 1928 *NZ* 1,2
Potgieter, H L (OFS) 1977 *Wld*
Powell, A W (GW) 1896 *BI* 3
Powell, J M (GW) 1891 *BI* 2, 1896 *BI* 3, 1903 *BI* 1,2
Prentis, R F (Tvl) 1980 *S Am* 1,2, *BI* 1,2,3,4, *S Am* 3,4, *F*, 1981 *I* 1,2
Pretorius, N F (Tvl) 1928 *NZ* 1,2,3,4
Prinsloo, J (Tvl) 1958 *F* 1,2
Prinsloo, J (NT) 1963 *A* 3
Prinsloo, J P (Tvl) 1928 *NZ* 1
Putter, D J (WT) 1963 *A* 1,2,4

Raaff, J W E (GW) 1903 *BI* 1,2, 1906 *S, W, E*, 1910 *BI* 1
Ras, W J de Wet (OFS) 1976 *NZ* 1(R), 1980 *S Am* 2(R)
Reece-Edwards, H (N) 1992 *F* 1,2, 1993 *A* 2
Reid, A (WP) 1903 *BI* 3
Reid, B (Bor) 1933 *A* 4
Reinach, J (OFS) 1986 *Cv* 1,2,3,4
Rens, I J (Tvl) 1953 *A* 3,4
Retief, D F (NT) 1955 *BI* 1,2,4, 1956 *A* 1,2, *NZ* 1,2,3,4
Reyneke, H J (WP) 1910 *BI* 3
Richards, A R (WP) 1891 *BI* 1,2,3
Richter, A (NT) 1992 *F* 1,2, *E*, 1994 *E* 2, *NZ* 1,2,3, 1995 [*R, C, WS* (R)]
Riley, N M (ET) 1963 *A* 3
Riordan, C A (Tvl) 1910 *BI* 1,2
Robertson, I W (R) 1974 *F* 1,2, 1976 *NZ* 1,2,4
Rodgers, P H (NT, Tvl) 1989 *Wld* 1,2, 1992 *NZ, F* 1,2
Rogers, C D (Tvl) 1984 *E* 1,2, *S Am* 1,2
Roos, G D (WP) 1910 *BI* 2,3
Roos, P J (WP) 1903 *BI* 3, 1906 *I, W, E*
Rosenberg, W (Tvl) 1955 *BI* 2,3,4, 1956 *NZ* 3, 1958 *F* 1
Rossouw, C L C (Tvl, N) 1995 *WS*, [*R, WS, F, NZ*], 1999 *NZ* 2(R), *A* 2(t), [*Sp, NZ* 3(R)]
Rossouw, D H (WP) 1953 *A* 3, 4
Rossouw, P W G (WP) 1997 *BI* 2,3, *NZ* 1, *A* 1, *NZ* 2(R), *A* 2(R), *It, F* 1,2, *E, S*, 1998 *I* 1,2, *W* 1, *E* 1, *A* 1, *NZ* 1,2, *A* 2, *W* 2, *S, I* 3, *E* 2, 1999 *It* 1, *W, NZ* 1, *A* 1(R), *NZ* 2, *A* 2, [*S, U, E, A* 3], 2000 *C, E* 1,2, *A* 2, *Arg* (R), *I, W*
Rousseau, W P (WP) 1928 *NZ* 3,4
Roux, F du T (WP) 1960 *W*, 1961 *F, A* 1,2, 1962 *BI* 1,2,3,4, 1963 *A* 2, 1965 *A* 1,2, *NZ* 1,2,3,4, 1968 *BI* 3,4, *F* 1,2 1969 *A* 1,2,3,4, 1970 *I, NZ* 1,2,3,4
Roux, J P (Tvl) 1994 *E* 2, *NZ* 1,2,3, *Arg* 1, 1995 [*R, C, F* (R)], 1996 *A* 1(R), *NZ* 1, *A* 2, *NZ* 3
Roux, O A (NT) 1969 *S, E*, 1970 *I, W*, 1972 *E*, 1974 *BI* 3,4

Samuels, T A (GW) 1896 *BI* 2,3,4
Sauermann, J T (Tvl) 1971 *F* 1,2, *A* 1, 1972 *E*, 1974 *BI* 1
Schlebusch, J J J (OFS) 1974 *BI* 3,4, 1975 *F* 2
Schmidt, L U (NT) 1958 *F* 2, 1962 *BI* 2
Schmidt, U L (NT, Tvl) 1986 *Cv* 1,2,3,4, 1989 *Wld* 1,2, 1992 *NZ, A*, 1993 *F* 1,2, *A* 1,2,3, 1994 *Arg* 1,2, *S, W*
Schoeman, J (WP) 1963 *A* 3,4, 1965 *I, S, A* 1, *NZ* 1,2
Scholtz, C P (WP, Tvl) 1994 *Arg* 1, 1995 [*R, C, WS*]
Scholtz, H H (WP) 1921 *NZ* 1,2

Schutte, P J W (Tvl) 1994 *S, W*
Scott, P A (Tvl) 1896 *BI* 1,2,3,4
Sendin, W D (GW) 1921 *NZ* 2
Serfontein, D J (WP) 1980 *BI* 1,2,3,4, *S Am* 3,4, *F*, 1981 *I* 1,2, *NZ* 1,2,3, *US*, 1982 *S Am* 1,2, 1984 *E* 1,2, *S Am* 1,2
Shand, R (GW) 1891 *BI* 2,3
Sheriff, A R (Tvl) 1938 *BI* 1,2,3
Shum, E H (Tvl) 1913 *E*
Sinclair, D J (Tvl) 1955 *BI* 1,2,3,4
Sinclair, J H (Tvl) 1903 *BI* 1
Skene, A L (WP) 1958 *F* 2
Skinstad, R B (WP) 1997 *E* (t), 1998 *W* 1(R), *E* 1(t), *NZ* 1(R),2(R), *A* 2(R), *W* 2(R), *S, I* 3, *E* 2, 1999 [*S, Sp* (R), *U, E, A* 3], 2001 *F* 1(R),2(R), *It, NZ* 1, *A* 1,2, *NZ* 2
Slater, J T (EP) 1924 *BI* 3,4, 1928 *NZ* 1
Smal, G P (WP) 1986 *Cv* 1,2,3,4, 1989 *Wld* 1,2
Small, J T (Tvl, N, WP) 1992 *NZ, A, F* 1,2, *E*, 1993 *F* 1,2, *A* 1,2,3, *Arg* 1,2, 1994 *E* 1,2, *NZ* 1,2,3(t), *Arg* 1, 1995 *WS*, [*A, R, F, NZ*], *W, It, E* (R), 1996 *Fj, A* 1, *NZ* 1, *A* 2, *NZ* 2, *Arg* 1,2, *F* 1,2, *W*, 1997 *Tg, BI* 1, *NZ* 1(R), *A* 1(R), *NZ* 2, *A* 2, *It, F* 1,2, *E, S*
Smit, F C (WP) 1992 *E*
Smit, J W (N) 2000 *C* (t), *A* 1(R), *NZ* 1(t+R), *A* 2(R), *NZ* 2(R), *A* 3(R), *Arg, I, W, E* 3, 2001 *F* 1,2, *It, NZ* 1(R), *A* 1(R),2(R), *NZ* 2(R)
Smith, C M (OFS) 1963 *A* 3,4, 1964 *W, F*, 1965 *A* 1,2, *NZ* 2
Smith, C W (GW) 1891 *BI* 2, 1896 *BI* 2,3
Smith, D (GW) 1891 *BI* 2
Smith D J (Z-R) 1980 *BI* 1,2,3,4
Smith, G A C (EP) 1938 *BI* 3
Smith, P F (GW) 1997 *S* (R), 1998 *I* 1(t),2, *W* 1, *NZ* 1(R),2(R), *A* 2(R), *W* 2, 1999 *NZ* 2
Smollan, F C (Tvl) 1933 *A* 3,4,5
Snedden, R C D (GW) 1891 *BI* 2
Snyman, A H (NT, BB) 1996 *NZ* 3,4, *Arg* 2(R), *W* (R), 1997 *Tg, BI* 1,2,3, *NZ* 1, *A* 1, *NZ* 2, *A* 2, *It, F* 1,2, *E, S*, 1998 *F* 1,2, *W* 1, *E* 1, *A* 1, *NZ* 1,2, *A* 2, *W* 2, *S, I* 3, *E* 2, 1999 *NZ* 2, 2001 *NZ* 2
Snyman, D S L (WP) 1972 *E*, 1974 *BI* 1,2(R), *F* 1,2, 1975 *F* 1,2, 1976 *NZ* 2,3, 1977 *Wld*
Snyman, J C P (OFS) 1974 *BI* 2,3,4
Sonnekus, G H H (OFS) 1974 *BI* 3, 1984 *E* 1,2
Spies, J J (NT) 1970 *NZ* 1,2,3,4
Stander, J C J (OFS) 1974 *BI* 4(R), 1976 *NZ* 1,2,3,4
Stapelberg, W P (NT) 1974 *F* 1,2
Starke, J J (WP) 1956 *NZ* 4
Starke, K T (WP) 1924 *BI* 1,2,3,4
Steenekamp, J G A (Tvl) 1958 *F* 1
Stegmann, A C (WP) 1906 *S, I*
Stegmann, J A (Tvl) 1912 *S, I, W*, 1913 *E, F*
Stewart, C (WP) 1998 *S, I* 3, *E* 2
Stewart, D A (WP) 1960 *S*, 1961 *E, S, F, I*, 1963 *A* 1,3,4, 1964 *W, F*, 1965 *I*
Stofberg, M T S (OFS, NT, WP) 1976 *NZ* 2,3, 1977 *Wld*, 1980 *S Am* 1,2, *BI* 1,2,3,4, *S Am* 3,4, *F*, 1981 *I* 1,2, *NZ* 1,2, *US*, 1982 *S Am* 1,2, 1984 *E* 1,2
Strachan, L C (Tvl) 1932 *E, S*, 1937 *A* 1,2, *NZ* 1,2,3, 1938 *BI* 1,2,3
Stransky, J (N, WP) 1993 *A* 1,2,3, *Arg* 1, 1994 *Arg* 1,2, 1995 *WS*, [*A, R* (t), *C, F, NZ*], *W, It, E*, 1996 *Fj* (R), *NZ* 1, *A* 2, *NZ* 2,3,4,5(R)
Straeuli, R A W (Tvl) 1994 *NZ* 1, *Arg* 1,2, *S, W*, 1995 *WS*, [*A, WS, NZ* (R)], *E* (R)
Strauss, C P (WP) 1992 *F* 1,2, *E*, 1993 *F* 1,2, *A* 1,2,3, *Arg* 1,2, 1994 *E* 1, *NZ* 1,2, *Arg* 1,2
Strauss, J A (WP) 1984 *S Am* 1,2
Strauss, J H P (Tvl) 1976 *NZ* 3,4, 1980 *S Am* 1
Strauss, S S F (GW) 1921 *NZ* 3
Strydom, C F (OFS) 1955 *BI* 3, 1956 *A* 1,2, *NZ* 1,4, 1958 *F* 1,
Strydom, J J (Tvl, GL) 1993 *F* 2, *A* 1,2,3, *Arg* 1,2, 1994 *E* 1, 1995 [*A, C, F, NZ*], 1996 *A* 2(R), *NZ* 2(R), 3,4, *W* (R), 1997 *Tg, BI* 1,2,3, *A* 2
Strydom, L J (NT) 1949 *NZ* 1,2
Styger, J J (OFS) 1992 *NZ* (R), *A, F* 1,2, *E*, 1993 *F* 2(R), *A* 3(R)
Suter, M R (N) 1965 *I, S*
Swanepoel, W (OFS, GL) 1997 *BI* 3(R), *A* 2(R), *F* 1(R), 2, *E, S*, 1998 *I* 2(R), *W* 1(R), *E* 2(R), 1999 *It* 1,2(R), *W, A* 1, [*Sp, NZ* 3(t)], 2000 *A* 1, *NZ* 1, *A* 2, *NZ* 2, *A* 3
Swart, J J N (SWA) 1955 *BI* 1
Swart, J (WP) 1996 *Fj, NZ* 1(R), *A* 2, *NZ* 2,3,4,5, 1997 *BI* 3(R), *It, S* (R)

Swart, I S (Tvl) 1993 *A* 1,2,3, *Arg* 1, 1994 *E* 1,2, *NZ* 1,3, *Arg* 2(R), 1995 *WS*, [*A, WS, F, NZ*], *W*, 1996 *A* 2

Taberer, W S (GW) 1896 *BI* 2
Taylor, O B (N) 1962 *BI* 1
Terblanche, C S (Bol, N) 1998 *I* 1,2, *W* 1, *E* 1, *A* 1, *NZ* 1,2, *A* 2, *W* 2, *S, I* 3, *E* 2, 1999 *It* 1(R),2, *W, A* 1, *NZ* 2(R), [*Sp, E* (R), *A* 3(R), *NZ* 3], 2000 *E* 3
Teichmann, G H (N) 1995 *W*, 1996 *Fj, A* 1, *NZ* 1, *A* 2, *NZ* 2,3,4,5, *Arg* 1,2, *F* 1,2, *W*, 1997 *Tg, BI* 1,2,3, *NZ* 1, *A* 1, *NZ* 2, *A* 2, *It, F* 1,2 *E, S*, 1998 *I* 1,2, *W* 1, *E* 1, *A* 1, *NZ* 1,2, *A* 2, *W* 2, *S, I* 3, *E* 2, 1999 *It* 1, *W, NZ* 1
Theron, D F (GW) 1996 *A* 2(R), *NZ* 2(R), 5, *Arg* 1,2, *F* 1,2, *W*, 1997 *BI* 2(R), 3, *NZ* 2(R), *A* 1, *NZ* 2(R)
Theunissen, D J (GW) 1896 *BI* 3
Thompson, G (WP) 1912 *S, I, W*
Tindall, J C (WP) 1924 *BI* 1, 1928 *NZ* 1,2,3,4
Tobias, E G (SARF, Bol) 1981 *I* 1,2, 1984 *E* 1,2, *S Am* 1,2
Tod, N S (N) 1928 *NZ* 2
Townsend, W H (N) 1921 *NZ* 1
Trenery, W E (GW) 1891 *BI* 2
Tromp, H (NT) 1996 *NZ* 3,4, *Arg* 2(R), *F* 1(R)
Truter, D R (WP) 1924 *BI* 2,4
Truter, J T (N) 1963 *A* 1, 1964 *F*, 1965 *A* 2
Turner, F G (EP) 1933 *A* 1,2,3, 1937 *A* 1,2, *NZ* 1,2,3, 1938 *BI* 1,2,3
Twigge, R J (NT) 1960 *S*

Ulyate, C A (Tvl) 1955 *BI* 1,2,3,4, 1956 *NZ* 1,2,3
Uys, P de W (NT) 1960 *W*, 1961 *E, S, I, A* 1,2, 1962 *BI* 1,4, 1963 *A* 1,2, 1969 *A* 1(R), 2

Van Aswegen, H J (WP) 1981 *NZ* 1, 1982 *S Am* 2(R)
Van Biljon, L (N) 2001 *It* (R), *NZ* 1, *A* 1,2, *NZ* 2
Van Broekhuizen, H D (WP) 1896 *BI* 4
Van Buuren, M C (Tvl) 1891 *BI* 1
Van de Vyver, D F (WP) 1937 *A* 2
Van den Berg, D S (N) 1975 *F* 1,2, 1976 *NZ* 1,2
Van den Berg, M A (WP) 1937 *A* 1, *NZ* 1,2,3
Van den Berg, P A (WP, GW, N) 1999 *It* 1(R),2, *NZ* 2, *A* 2, [*S, U* (t+R), *E* (R), *A* 3(R), *NZ* 3(R)], 2000 *E* 1(R), *A* 1, *NZ* 1, *A* 2, *NZ* 2(R), *A* 3(t+R), *Arg, I, W, E* 3, 2001 *F* 1(R),2, *A* 2(R), *NZ* 2(R)
Van den Bergh, E (EP) 1994 *Arg* 2(t & R)
Van der Linde, A (WP) 1995 *It, E*, 1996 *Arg* 1(R), 2(R), *F* 1(R), *W* (R)
Van der Merwe, A J (Bol) 1955 *BI* 2,3,4, 1956 *A* 1,2, *NZ* 1,2,3,4, 1958 *F* 1, 1960 *S, NZ* 2
Van der Merwe, A V (WP) 1931 *W*
Van der Merwe, B S (NT) 1949 *NZ* 1
Van der Merwe, H S (NT) 1960 *NZ* 4, 1963 *A* 2,3,4, 1964 *F*
Van der Merwe, J P (WP) 1970 *W*
Van der Merwe, P R (SWD, WT, GW) 1981 *NZ* 2,3, *US*, 1986 *Cv* 1,2, 1989 *Wld* 1
Vanderplank, B E (N) 1924 *BI* 3,4
Van der Schyff, J H (GW) 1949 *NZ* 1,2,3,4, 1955 *BI* 1
Van der Watt, A E (WP) 1969 *S* (R), *E*, 1970 *I*
Van der Westhuizen, J C (WP) 1928 *NZ* 2,3,4, 1931 *I*
Van der Westhuizen, J H (WP) 1931 *I*, 1932 *E, S*
Van der Westhuizen, J H (NT, BB) 1993 *Arg* 1,2, 1994 *E* 1,2(R), *Arg* 2, *S, W*, 1995 *WS*, [*A, C* (R), *WS, F, NZ*], *W, It, E*, 1996 *Fj, A* 1,2(R), *NZ* 2,3(R), 4,5, *Arg* 1,2, *F* 1,2, *W*, 1997 *Tg, BI* 1,2,3, *NZ* 1, *A* 1, *NZ* 2, *A* 2, *It, F* 1, 1998 *I* 1,2, *W* 1, *E* 1, *A* 1, *NZ* 1,2, *A* 2, *W* 2, *S, I* 3, *E* 2, 1999 *NZ* 2, *A* 2, [*S, Sp* (R), *U, E, A* 3, *NZ* 3], 2000 *C, E* 1,2, *A* 1(R), *NZ* 1(R), *A* 2(R), *Arg, I, W, E* 3, 2001 *F* 1,2, *It* (R), *NZ* 1, *A* 1,2, *NZ* 2
Van der Westhuyzen, J N B (Mp) 2000 *NZ* 2(R), 2001 *It* (R)
Van Druten, N J V (Tvl) 1924 *BI* 1,2,3,4, 1928 *NZ* 1,2,3,4
Van Heerden, A J (Tvl) 1921 *NZ* 1,3
Van Heerden, F J (WP) 1994 *E* 1,2(R), *NZ* 3, 1995 *It, E*, 1996 *NZ* 5(R), *Arg* 1(R),2(R), 1997 *Tg, BI* 2(t+R),3(R), *NZ* 1(R),2(R), 1999 [*Sp*]
Van Heerden, J L (NT, Tvl) 1974 *BI* 3,4, *F* 1,2, 1975 *F* 1,2, 1976 *NZ* 1,2,3,4, 1977 *Wld*, 1980 *BI* 1,3,4, *S Am* 3,4, *F*
Van Jaarsveld, C J (Tvl) 1949 *NZ* 1
Van Jaarsveldt, D C (R) 1960 *S*
Van Niekerk, J A (WP) 1928 *NZ* 4
Van Kiekerk, J C (GL) 2001 *NZ* 1(R), *A* 1(R), *NZ* 2(t+R)
Van Reenen, G L (WP) 1937 *A* 2, *NZ* 1
Van Renen, C G (WP) 1891 *BI* 3, 1896 *BI* 1,4
Van Renen, W (WP) 1903 *BI* 1,3
Van Rensburg, J T J (Tvl) 1992 *NZ, A, E*, 1993 *F* 1,2, *A* 1, 1994 *NZ* 2

Van Rooyen, G W (Tvl) 1921 *NZ* 2,3
Van Ryneveld, R C B (WP) 1910 *BI* 2,3
Van Schalkwyk, D (NT) 1996 *Fj* (R), *NZ* 3,4,5, 1997 *BI* 2,3, *NZ* 1, *A* 1
Van Schoor, R A M (R) 1949 *NZ* 2,3,4, 1951 *S, I, W,* 1952 *E, F,* 1953 *A* 1,2,3,4
Van Straaten, A J J (WP) 1999 *It* 2(R), *W, NZ* 1(R), *A* 1, 2000 *C, E* 1,2, *NZ* 1, *A* 2, *NZ* 2, *A* 3, *Arg* (R), *I* (R), *W, E* 3, 2001 *A* 1,2, *NZ* 2
Van Vollenhoven, K T (NT) 1955 *BI* 1,2,3,4, 1956 *A* 1,2, *NZ* 3
Van Vuuren, T F (EP) 1912 *S, I, W,* 1913 *E, F*
Van Wyk, C J (Tvl) 1951 *S, I, W,* 1952 *E, F,* 1953 *A* 1,2,3,4, 1955 *BI* 1
Van Wyk, J F B (NT) 1970 *NZ* 1,2,3,4, 1971 *F* 1,2, *A* 1,2,3, 1972 *E,* 1974 *BI* 1,3,4, 1976 *NZ* 3,4
Van Wyk, S P (WP) 1928 *NZ* 1,2
Van Zyl, B P (WP) 1961 *I*
Van Zyl, C G P (OFS) 1965 *NZ* 1,2,3,4
Van Zyl, D J (WP) 2000 *E* 3(R)
Van Zyl, G H (WP) 1958 *F* 1, 1960 *S, NZ* 1,2,3,4, *W, I,* 1961 *E, S, F, I, A* 1,2, 1962 *BI* 1,3,4
Van Zyl, H J (Tvl) 1960 *NZ* 1,2,3,4, *I,* 1961 *E, S, I, A* 1,2
Van Zyl, P J (Bol) 1961 *I*
Veldsman, P E (WP) 1977 *Wld*
Venter, A G (OFS) 1996 *NZ* 3,4,5, *Arg* 1,2, *F* 1,2, *W,* 1997 *Tg, BI* 1,2,3, *NZ* 1, *A* 1, *NZ* 2, *It, F* 1,2, *E, S,* 1998 *I* 1,2, *W* 1, *E* 1, *A* 1, *NZ* 1,2, *A* 2, *W* 2, *S* (R), *I* 3(R), *E* 2(R), 1999 *It* 1,2(R), *W* (R), *NZ* 1, *A* 1, *NZ* 2, *A* 2, [*S, U, E, A* 3, *NZ* 3], 2000 *C, E* 1,2, *A* 1, *NZ* 1, *A* 2, *NZ* 2, *A* 3, *Arg, I, W, E* 3, 2001 *F* 1, *It, NZ* 1, *A* 1,2, *NZ* 2
Venter, A J (N) 2000 *W* (R), *E* 3(R)
Venter, B (OFS) 1994 *E* 1,2, *NZ* 1,2,3, *Arg* 1,2, 1995 [*R, C, WS* (R), *NZ* (R)], 1996 *A* 1, *NZ* 1, *A* 2, 1999 *A* 2, [*S, U*]
Venter, F D (Tvl) 1931 *W,* 1932 *S,* 1933 *A* 3
Versfeld, C (WP) 1891 *BI* 3
Versfeld, M (WP) 1891 *BI* 1,2,3
Vigne, J T (Tvl) 1891 *BI* 1,2,3
Viljoen, J F (GW) 1971 *F* 1,2, *A* 1,2,3, 1972 *E*
Viljoen, J T (N) 1971 *A* 1,2,3
Villet, J V (WP) 1984 *E* 1,2
Visagie, I J (WP) 1999 *It* 1, *W, NZ* 1, *A* 1, *NZ* 2, *A* 2, [*S, U, E, A* 3, *NZ* 3], 2000 *C, E* 2, *A* 1, *NZ* 1, *A* 2, *NZ* 2, *A* 3, 2001 *NZ* 1, *A* 1,2, *NZ* 2

Visagie, P J (GW) 1967 *F* 1,2,3,4, 1968 *BI* 1,2,3,4, *F* 1,2, 1969 *A* 1,2,3,4, *S, E,* 1970 *NZ* 1,2,3,4, 1971 *F* 1,2, *A* 1,2,3
Visagie, R G (OFS, N) 1984 *E* 1,2, *S Am* 1,2, 1993 *F* 1
Visser, J de V (WP) 1981 *NZ* 2, *US*
Visser, M (WP) 1995 *WS* (R)
Visser, P J (Tvl) 1933 *A* 2
Viviers, S S (OFS) 1956 *A* 1,2, *NZ* 2,3,4
Vogel, M L (OFS) 1974 *BI* 2(R)
Von Hoesslin, D J B (GW) 1999 *It* 1(R),2, *W* (R), *NZ* 1, *A* 1(R)
Vos, A N (GL) 1999 *It* 1(t+R),2, *NZ* 1(R),2(R), *A* 2, [*S* (R), *Sp, E* (R), *A* 3(R), *NZ* 3], 2000 *C, E* 1,2, *A* 1, *NZ* 1, *A* 2, *NZ* 2, *A* 3, *Arg, I, W, E* 3, 2001 *F* 1,2, *It, NZ* 1, *A* 1,2, *NZ* 2

Wagenaar, C (NT) 1977 *Wld*
Wahl, J J (WP) 1949 *NZ* 1
Walker, A P (N) 1921 *NZ* 1,3, 1924 *BI* 1,2,3,4
Walker, H N (OFS) 1953 *A* 3, 1956 *A* 2, *NZ* 1,4
Walker, H W (Tvl) 1910 *BI* 1,2,3
Walton, D C (N) 1964 *F,* 1965 *I, S, NZ* 3,4, 1969 *A* 1,2, *E*
Waring, F W (WP) 1931 *I,* 1932 *E,* 1933 *A* 1,2,3,4,5
Wegner, N (WP) 1993 *F* 2, *A* 1,2,3
Wessels, J J (WP) 1896 *BI* 1,2,3
Whipp, P J M (WP) 1974 *BI* 1,2, 1975 *F* 1, 1976 *NZ* 1,3,4, 1980 *S Am* 1,2
White, J (Bor) 1931 *W,* 1933 *A* 1,2,3,4,5, 1937 *A* 1,2, *NZ* 1,2
Wiese, J J (Tvl) 1993 *F* 1, 1995 *WS,* [*R, C, WS, F, NZ*], *W, It, E,* 1996 *NZ* 3(R), 4(R), 5, *Arg* 1,2, *F* 1,2, *W*
Williams, A E (GW) 1910 *BI* 1
Williams, A P (WP) 1984 *E* 1,2
Williams, C M (WP, GL) 1993 *Arg* 2, 1994 *E* 1,2, *NZ* 1,2,3, *Arg* 1,2, *S, W,* 1995 *WS,* [*WS, F, NZ*], *It, E,* 1998 *A* 1(t), *NZ* 1(t), 2000 *C* (R), *E* 1(t),2(R), *A* 1(R), *NZ* 2, *A* 3, *Arg, I, W* (R)
Williams, D O (WP) 1937 *A* 1,2, *NZ* 1,2,3, 1938 *BI* 1,2,3
Williams, J G (NT) 1971 *F* 1,2, *A* 1,2,3, 1972 *E,* 1974 *BI* 1,2,4, *F* 1,2, 1976 *NZ* 1,2
Wilson, L G (WP) 1960 *NZ* 3,4, *W, I,* 1961 *E, F, I, A* 1,2, 1962 *BI* 1,2,3,4, 1963 *A* 1,2,3,4, 1964 *W, F,* 1965 *I, S, A* 1,2, *NZ* 1,2,3,4
Wolmarans, B J (OFS) 1977 *Wld*
Wright, G D (EP, Tvl) 1986 *Cv* 3,4, 1989 *Wld* 1,2, 1992 *F* 1,2, *E*
Wyness, M R K (WP) 1962 *BI* 1,2,3,4, 1963 *A* 2

Zeller, W C (N) 1921 *NZ* 2,3
Zimerman, M (WP) 1931 *W, I,* 1932 *E, S*

SOUTH AFRICA INTERNATIONAL STATISTICS
(up to 20 October 2001)

Match Records

Most Consecutive Test Wins

17 1997 *A* 2, *It, F* 1,2, *E, S,* 1998 *I* 1,2, *W* 1, *E* 1, *A* 1, NZ 1,2, *A* 2, *W* 2, *S, I* 3
15 1994 *Arg* 1,2, *S, W* 1995 *WS, A, R, C, WS, F, NZ, W, It, E,* 1996 *Fj*

Most Consecutive Tests without Defeat

Matches	Wins	Draws	Period
17	17	0	1997 to 1998
16	15	1	1994 to 1996
15	12	3	1960 to 1963

Most Points in a Match
by the team

Pts	Opponents	Venue	Year
101	Italy	Durban	1999
96	Wales	Pretoria	1998
74	Tonga	Cape Town	1997
74	Italy	Port Elizabeth	1999
68	Scotland	Murrayfield	1997
62	Italy	Bologna	1997
61	Australia	Pretoria	1997

by a player

Pts	Player	Opponents	Venue	Year
34	J H de Beer	England	Paris	1999
31	P C Montgomery	Wales	Pretoria	1998
29	G S du Toit	Italy	Port Elizabeth	1999
28	G K Johnson	W Samoa	Johannesburg	1995
26	J H de Beer	Australia	Pretoria	1997
26	P C Montgomery	Scotland	Murrayfield	1997
25	J T Stransky	Australia	Bloemfontein	1996
25	C S Terblanche	Italy	Durban	1999

Most Tries in a Match
by the team

Tries	Opponents	Venue	Year
15	Wales	Pretoria	1998
15	Italy	Durban	1999
12	Tonga	Cape Town	1997
11	Italy	Port Elizabeth	1999
10	Ireland	Dublin	1912
10	Scotland	Murrayfield	1997

by a player

Tries	Player	Opponents	Venue	Year
5	C S Terblanche	Italy	Durban	1999
4	C M Williams	W Samoa	Johannesburg	1995
4	P W G Rossouw	France	Parc des Princes	1997
4	C S Terblanche	Ireland	Bloemfontein	1998

Most Conversions in a Match
by the team

Cons	Opponents	Venue	Year
13	Italy	Durban	1999
9	Scotland	Murrayfield	1997
9	Wales	Pretoria	1998
8	Italy	Port Elizabeth	1999
7	Scotland	Murrayfield	1951
7	Tonga	Cape Town	1997
7	Italy	Bologna	1997
7	France	Parc des Princes	1997

by a player

Cons	Player	Opponents	Venue	Year
9	P C Montgomery	Wales	Pretoria	1998
8	P C Montgomery	Scotland	Murrayfield	1997
8	G S du Toit	Italy	Port Elizabeth	1999
8	G S du Toit	Italy	Durban	1999
7	A Geffin	Scotland	Murrayfield	1951
7	E Lubbe	Tonga	Cape Town	1997
7	H W Honiball	Italy	Bologna	1997
7	H W Honiball	France	Parc des Princes	1997

Most Penalties in a Match
by the team

Penalties	Opponents	Venue	Year
7	France	Pretoria	1975
6	Australia	Bloemfontein	1996
6	Australia	Twickenham	1999
6	England	Pretoria	2000
6	Australia	Durban	2000
6	France	Johannesburg	2001

by a player

Penalties	Player	Opponents	Venue	Year
6	G R Bosch	France	Pretoria	1975
6	J T Stransky	Australia	Bloemfontein	1996
6	J H de Beer	Australia	Twickenham	1999
6	A J J van Straaten	England	Pretoria	2000
6	A J J van Straaten	Australia	Durban	2000
6	P C Montgomery	France	Johannesburg	2001
5	A Geffin	N Zealand	Cape Town	1949
5	R Blair	World XV	Pretoria	1977
5	H E Botha	N Zealand	Wellington	1981
5	J W Heunis	England	Port Elizabeth	1984
5	H E Botha	NZ Cavaliers	Johannesburg	1986
5	J T J van Rensburg	France	Durban	1993
5	A J Joubert	England	Pretoria	1994
5	P C Montgomery	Australia	Johannesburg	1998
5	J H de Beer	England	Paris	1999
5	A D James	France	Durban	2001
5	A J J van Straaten	Australia	Pretoria	2001
5	A J J van Straaten	New Zealand	Auckland	2001

Most Dropped Goals in a Match
by the team

Drops	Opponents	Venue	Year
5	England	Paris	1999
3	S America	Durban	1980
3	Ireland	Durban	1981

by a player

Drops	Player	Opponents	Venue	Year
5	J H de Beer	England	Paris	1999
3	H E Botha	S America	Durban	1980
3	H E Botha	Ireland	Durban	1981
2	B L Osler	N Zealand	Durban	1928
2	H E Botha	NZ Cavaliers	Cape Town	1986
2	J T Stransky	N Zealand	Johannesburg	1995

Career Records

Most Capped Players

Caps	Player	Career Span
75	M G Andrews	1994 to 2001
75	J H van der Westhuizen	1993 to 2001
62	A G Venter	1996 to 2001
48	P C Montgomery	1997 to 2001
47	J T Small	1992 to 1997
43	A-H le Roux	1994 to 2001
42	G H Teichmann	1995 to 1999
40	P W G Rossouw	1997 to 2000
39	J P du Randt	1994 to 1999
38	F C H du Preez	1961 to 1971

38	J H Ellis	1965 to 1976
38	K Otto	1995 to 2000

Most Consecutive Tests

Tests	Player	Span
39	G H Teichmann	1996 to 1999
25	S H Nomis	1967 to 1972
25	A G Venter	1997 to 1999
24	P C Montgomery	1997 to 1999
24	P W G Rossouw	1997 to 1999

Most Tests as Captain

Tests	Captain	Span
36	G H Teichmann	1996 to 1999
29	J F Pienaar	1993 to 1996
22	D J de Villiers	1965 to 1970
15	M du Plessis	1975 to 1980
15	A N Vos	1999 to 2001
11	J F K Marais	1971 to 1974

Most Tests in Individual Positions

Position	Player	Tests	Span
Full-back	P C Montgomery	36	1997 to 2001
Wing	J T Small	43*	1992 to 1997
Centre	J C Mulder	34	1994 to 2001
Fly-half	H E Botha	28	1980 to 1992
Scrum-half	J H van der Westhuizen	73	1993 to 2001
Prop	A-H Le Roux	43	1994 to 2001
Hooker	J Dalton	34	1994 to 1998
Lock	M G Andrews	73	1994 to 2001
Flanker	A G Venter	54	1996 to 2001
No 8	G H Teichmann	42	1995 to 1999

* excludes an appearance as a temporary replacement

Most Points in Tests

Points	Player	Tests	Career
312	H E Botha	28	1980 to 1992
261	P C Montgomery	48	1997 to 2001
240	J T Stransky	22	1993 to 1996
197	A J J van Straaten	18	1999 to 2001
181	J H de Beer	13	1997 to 1999
170	J H van der Westhuizen	75	1993 to 2001
154	H W Honiball	35	1993 to 1999
130	P J Visagie	25	1967 to 1971

Most Tries in Tests

Tries	Player	Tests	Career
34	J H van der Westhuizen	75	1993 to 2001
20	J T Small	47	1992 to 1997
19	D M Gerber	24	1980 to 1992
19	P W G Rossouw	40	1997 to 2000
15	P C Montgomery	48	1997 to 2001
15	C S Terblanche	22	1998 to 2000
14	B J Paulse	26	1999 to 2001
14	C M Williams	27	1993 to 2000

Most Penalty Goals in Tests

Penalties	Player	Tests	Career
51	A J J van Straaten	18	1999 to 2001
50	H E Botha	28	1980 to 1992
47	J T Stransky	22	1993 to 1996
31	P C Montgomery	48	1997 to 2001
27	J H de Beer	13	1997 to 1999
25	H W Honiball	35	1993 to 1999
23	G R Bosch	9	1974 to 1976
19	P J Visagie	25	1967 to 1971

Most Conversions in Tests

Cons	Player	Tests	Career
50	H E Botha	28	1980 to 1992
42	P C Montgomery	48	1997 to 2001
37	H W Honiball	35	1993 to 1999
33	J H de Beer	13	1997 to 1999
30	J T Stransky	22	1993 to 1996

Most Dropped Goals in Tests

Drops	Player	Tests	Career
18	H E Botha	28	1980 to 1992
8	J H de Beer	13	1997 to 1999
5	J D Brewis	10	1949 to 1953
5	P J Visagie	25	1967 to 1971
4	B L Osler	17	1924 to 1933

Tri Nations Records

Record	Detail		Set
Most team points in season	148	in four matches	1997
Most team tries in season	18	in four matches	1997
Highest Score	61	61-22 v Australia (h)	1997
Biggest win	39	61-22 v Australia (h)	1997
Highest score conceded	55	35-55 v N Zealand (a)	1997
Biggest defeat	28	0-28 v N Zealand (a)	1999
Most points in matches	94	A J J van Straaten	1999 to 2001
Most points in season	64	J H de Beer	1997
Most points in match	26	J H de Beer	v Australia (h),1997
Most tries in matches	4	J H vd Westhuizen	1996 to 2001
Most tries in season	3	P C Montgomery	1997
Most tries in match	3	P C Montgomery	v Australia (h),1997
Most cons in matches	13	J H de Beer	1997 to 1999
Most cons in season	12	J H de Beer	1997
Most cons in match	6	J H de Beer	v Australia (h),1997
Most pens in matches	28	A J J van Straaten	1999 to 2001
Most pens in season	13	A J J van Straaten	2000
	13	A J J van Straaten	2001
Most pens in match	6	J T Stransky	v Australia (h),1996
	6	A J J van Straaten	v Australia (h),2000

Series Records

Record	Holder	Detail
Most tries	P W G Rossouw	8 in Europe, 1997
Most points	H E Botha	69 v NZ Cavaliers, 1986

Miscellaneous Records

Record	Holder	Detail
Longest Test Career	J M Powell/B H Heatlie/D M Gerber/ H E Botha	13 seasons, 1891-1903/1891-1903/1980-1992/1980-1992
Youngest Test Cap	A J Hartley	17 yrs 18 days in 1891
Oldest Test Cap	W H Morkel	36 yrs 258 days in 1921

Career Records of South Africa International Players
(up to 20 October 2001)

Player	Debut	Caps	T	C	P	D	Pts
Backs:							
D W Barry	2000 v C	8	1	0	0	0	5
J H de Beer	1997 v BI	13	2	33	27	8	181
N A de Kock	2001 v It	1	0	0	0	0	0
G M Delport	2000 v C	12	2	0	0	0	10
G S du Toit	1998 v I	6	2	20	6	0	68
G Esterhuizen	2000 v NZ	7	0	0	0	0	0
R F Fleck	1999 v It	29	10	0	0	0	50
D B Hall	2001 v F	6	0	0	0	0	0
A D James	2001 v F	6	0	0	5	0	15
C A Jantjes	2001 v It	4	0	1	0	0	2
M C Joubert	2001 v NZ	1	0	0	0	0	0
D J Kayser	1999 v It	13	5	0	0	0	25
L J Koen	2000 v A	1	0	1	2	0	8
P C Montgomery	1997 v BI	48	15	42	31	3	261
J C Mulder	1994 v NZ	34	6	0	0	0	30
P G Muller	1992 v NZ	33	3	0	0	0	15
B J Paulse	1999 v It	26	14	0	0	0	70
P W G Rossouw	1997 v BI	40	19	0	0	0	95
A H Snyman	1996 v NZ	31	9	0	0	0	45
W Swanepoel	1997 v BI	20	6	0	0	0	30
C S Terblanche	1998 v I	22	15	0	0	0	75
J H van der Westhuizen	1993 v Arg	75	34	0	0	0	170
J N B van der Westhuyzen	2000 v NZ	2	0	0	0	0	0
A J J van Straaten	1999 v It	18	2	17	51	0	197
D J van Zyl	2000 v E	1	0	0	0	0	0
B D Venter	1994 v E	17	1	0	0	0	5
D J B von Hoesslin	1999 v It	5	2	0	0	0	10
C M Williams	1993 vArg	27	14	0	0	0	70
Forwards:							
J N Ackermann	1996 v Fj	8	0	0	0	0	0
M G Andrews	1994 v E	75	12	0	0	0	60
C S Boome	1999 v It	10	1	0	0	0	5
W G Brosnihan	1997 v A	6	1	0	0	0	5
J Erasmus	1997 v BI	36	7	0	0	0	35
E E Fynn	2001 v F	2	0	0	0	0	0
R B Kempson	1998 v I	31	1	0	0	0	5
C P J Krige	1999 v It	19	2	0	0	0	10
J J Labuschagne	2000 v NZ	1	0	0	0	0	0
A-H le Roux	1994 v E	43	1	0	0	0	5
C F Marais	1999 v It	12	1	0	0	0	5
V Matfield	2001 v It	4	0	0	0	0	0
W Meyer	1997 v S	15	0	0	0	0	0
R B Skinstad	1997 v E	22	7	0	0	0	35
J W Smit	2000 v C	17	0	0	0	0	0
L van Biljon	2001 v It	5	0	0	0	0	0
P A van den Berg	1999 v It	23	2	0	0	0	10
J C van Niekerk	2001 v NZ	3	0	0	0	0	0
A G Venter	1996 v NZ	62	9	0	0	0	45
A J Venter	2000 v W	2	0	0	0	0	0
I J Visagie	1999 v It	22	0	0	0	0	0
A N Vos	1999 v It	29	4	0	0	0	20

NEW ZEALAND TEST SEASON REVIEW 2000-01

All Blacks in Mourning

Don Cameron

At first glance the All Blacks' statistics from the ten Test matches between 11th November 2000 and 1st September 2001 would suggest a satisfactory 12 months. There were seven wins from the ten, 361 points to 194, and an impressive 40 tries against 13. Yet in the early days of September the hyper-critical New Zealand public were in morbid mourning. The coaches, selectors and the big All Black management staff were either seeking answers, or wondering whether they still had long-range employment toward their stated goal of the 2003 World Cup. For all New Zealand the state of All Black rugby was definitely NOT satisfactory.

The All Blacks had on 1st September lost 26-29 to an Australian team which scored a converted try in the last minute of John Eales's last Test, confirming his elevation to Australian rugby sainthood. This was the second loss to Australia in 2001. So marked has been the Wallabies' superiority over the All Blacks that in the last four years the Wallabies have won seven matches to two. The fact that most of the matches were close-fought is shown by the statistics that Australia had only a 212-197 points-scoring advantage, and scored 21 tries to 16.

The All Blacks' losing wounds of 2001 will take a long time to heal. The deepest cuts came in the first Tri Nations and Bledisloe Cup game at Carisbrook in August when the Wallabies' winning score of 23-15 did not measure the gap between an Australian side so much smarter and tactically aware, and a New Zealand side with no apparent attacking plan and a defensive pattern which too often conceded easy points through madcap and sometimes illegal manoeuvres.

But the September loss at Sydney made even more damage to the New Zealand belief that the All Blacks' tradition will bring forth shining victories when the hour seems darkest. At Sydney the Wallabies reached half-time 19-6, with the All Blacks having no real impact. In 15 or so minutes after half-time the All Blacks had scored two dazzling backline tries, kicked the goals and worked their way to the 26-19 lead – their feet firmly back again on the golden road of success.

Yet in the last quarter of the game the All Black pattern, especially their line-out, was shattered by the unflustered, well-drilled Australian side. The Wallabies picked up a penalty goal. Aided by their line-out monopoly, whomever had the throw-in, the Wallabies parked inside the All Black 22, turned down three penalty-goal kicking chances, and kept belting away at the All Black line until Toutai Kefu barrelled through by an upright in the last minute. The conversion was superfluous and the grey-faced All Black leaders, Anton Oliver, the captain, hooker and commander of a sinking line-out, and Wayne Smith, the coach, could barely raise a strangled, shell-shocked comment on their side's most humbling defeat.

The road to what might become a rugby Calvary started smoothly enough the previous November when the All Blacks out-played an erratic French side 39-26 in Paris, but then found the French inspired at Marseilles as they marched away to a second-half victory 42-33. Italy, coached by the former All Black prop Brad Johnstone, offered stouter resistance than the 56-19 score might indicate.

This sweet after-taste of 2000 was followed by the June 2001 start to the home season. Once again the All Blacks were offered soft opposition, Samoa again first course on the menu, and a new-look All Black backline built round the Otago halves, Byron Kelleher and Tony Brown, contributed much to the 50-6 *entrée*. Argentina, with several new or unknown Puma cubs, suggested another easy romp. Instead they helped develop among the All Blacks a tough-minded defensive spirit which was to remain their main asset for the rest of the season. After reaching half-time 14-31 because their backline defence was full of holes, the Pumas reverted to their traditional forward methods. For 20 minutes or so they fought the hand-to-hand forward battles which are part of their manly tradition. The All Blacks reeled back, but then re-gathered and their young and greenish pack planted their battle standard and refused to be intimidated or forced to retreat. The battle over, the All Blacks nevertheless scored five more tries in the last quarter to triumph 67-19.

A fleeting visit from a French side, minus many of the heroes of their epic World Cup semi-final win over the All Blacks, did not offer much of a threat as the All Blacks worked to a 37-12 win. With Brown remaining at fly-half and Andrew Mehrtens somewhere in the outer darkness, the All Blacks took their solid defensive game to South Africa and simply shut-down a tactically-challenged Springbok side 12-3, four penalty goals to one. Any victory, and especially one as clear-cut as this one, over South Africa is a rich All Black prize, and the All Blacks faced the sharp end of their home season – Australia-South Africa-Australia – with confidence in an apparently strong tactical approach.

After the 15-23 loss (and with it the Bledisloe Cup), the All Blacks were in crisis, as once again they were out-pointed, out-played and out-thought by a Wallaby team playing at about 75 per cent efficiency. Desperate times. Brown was discarded, Mehrtens returned as the goal-kicking master-tactician, and Troy Flavell moved from lock to blind-side flanker to bring in a tall new line-out lock, Chris Jack. At Auckland the All Blacks were rejuvenated, the Springboks as cumbersome and tactically-unaware as before, and the All Blacks had the rare freedom of a 26-15 win, two tries to none, over their famous rivals.

New Zealand opened their home Test season with a 50-6 defeat of Samoa under the Albany floodlights in June. All Black captain Anton Oliver and Carl Hoeft prepare for another scrum. Polo Asi is the Samoan tight-head prop with his back to the camera.

So it was full-steam ahead for Sydney and the prospect of squaring the trans-Tasman tussle. Instead, the All Blacks faltered, for they looked like a team unsure how it could win, whereas the Wallabies looked a composed side confident they had the men and the tactics to win. Wayne Smith afterward wondered whether he should resign. He had, he maintained, the best players in the country. They did not play to lose. But were they well-directed? Even over-coached?

Various marketing ploys had hammered the players with the traditions of their country and its black jersey and its haka. Famous old All Blacks joined the All Black camps, trying to mix their amateur pride with the highly-paid professional armour that Test players take on these days. The All Black management became heavily involved with technology, video replays and the like, and for too long overlooked what looked like faulty selections among the half-backs and the back-row trio. Compared with the cool, confident and competent Wallabies, the All Blacks looked over-promoted, over-coached, over-wrought when things did not go well, and eventually over-powered.

New Zealand's Test Record in 2000-2001: Played 10, won 7, lost 3.

Opponents	Date	Venue	Result
Australia	1st September 2001	A	Lost 26-29
South Africa	25th August 2001	H	Won 26-15
Australia	11th August 2001	H	Lost 15-23
South Africa	21st July 2001	A	Won 12-3
France	30th June 2001	H	Won 37-12
Argentina	23rd June 2001	H	Won 67-19
Samoa	16th June 2001	H	Won 50-6
Italy	25th November 2000	A	Won 56-19
France	18th November 2000	A	Lost 33-42
France	11th November 2000	A	Won 39-26

NEW ZEALAND INTERNATIONAL PLAYERS
(up to 20 October 2001)

Abbott, H L (Taranaki) 1906 *F*
Aitken, G G (Wellington) 1921 *SA* 1,2
Aitken, G G (Wellington) 1921 *SA* 1,2
Alatini, P P F (Otago) 1999 *F* 1(R), [*It*, *SA* 3(R)], 2000 *Tg, S* 1, *A* 1, *SA* 1, *A* 2, *SA* 2, *It*, 2001 *Sm, Arg, F, SA* 1, *A* 1, *SA* 2, *A* 2
Allen, M R (Taranaki, Manawatu) 1993 *WS* (t), 1996 *S* 2 (t), 1997 *Arg* 1(R),2(R), *SA* 2(R), *A* 3(R), *E* 2, *W* (R)
Allen, N H (Counties) 1980 *A* 3, *W*
Alley, G T (Canterbury) 1928 *SA* 1,2,3
Anderson, A (Canterbury) 1983 *S, E*, 1984 *A* 1,2,3, 1987 [*Fj*]
Anderson, B L (Wairarapa-Bush) 1986 *A* 1
Archer, W R (Otago, Southland) 1955 *A* 1,2, 1956 *SA* 1,3
Argus, W G (Canterbury) 1946 *A* 1,2, 1947 *A* 1,2
Arnold, D A (Canterbury) 1963 *I, W*, 1964 *E, F*
Arnold, K D (Waikato) 1947 *A* 1,2
Ashby, D L (Southland) 1958 *A* 2
Asher, A A (Auckland) 1903 *A*
Ashworth, B G (Auckland) 1978 *A* 1,2
Ashworth, J C (Canterbury, Hawke's Bay) 1978 *A* 1,2,3, 1980 *A* 1,2,3, 1981 *SA* 1,2,3, 1982 *A* 1,2, 1983 *BI* 1,2,3,4, *A*, 1984 *F* 1,2, *A* 1,2,3, 1985 *E* 1,2, *A*
Atkinson, H (West Coast) 1913 *A* 1
Avery, H E (Wellington) 1910 *A* 1,2,3

Bachop, G T M (Canterbury) 1989 *W, I*, 1990 *S* 1,2, *A* 1,2,3, *F* 1,2, 1991 *Arg* 1,2, *A* 1,2, [*E, US, C, A, S*], 1992 *Wld* 1, 1994 *SA* 1,2,3, *A*, 1995 *C*, [*I, W, S, E, SA*], *A* 1,2
Bachop, S J (Otago) 1994 *F* 2, *SA* 1,2,3, *A*
Badeley, C E O (Auckland) 1921 *SA* 1,2
Baird, J A S (Otago) 1913 *A* 2
Ball, N (Wellington) 1931 *A*, 1932 *A* 2,3, 1935 *W*, 1936 *E*
Barrett, J (Auckland) 1913 *A* 2,3
Barry, E F (Wellington) 1934 *A* 2
Barry, L J (North Harbour) 1995 *F* 2
Batty, G B (Wellington, Bay of Plenty) 1972 *W, S*, 1973 *E* 1, *I, F, E* 2, 1974 *A* 1,3, *I*, 1975 *S*, 1976 *SA* 1,2,3,4, 1977 *BI* 1
Batty, W (Auckland) 1930 *BI* 1,3,4, 1931 *A*
Beatty, G E (Taranaki) 1950 *BI* 1
Bell, R H (Otago) 1951 *A* 3, 1952 *A* 1,2
Bellis, E A (Wanganui) 1921 *SA* 1,2,3
Bennet, R (Otago) 1905 *A*
Berghan, T (Otago) 1938 *A* 1,2,3
Berry, M J (Wairarapa-Bush) 1986 *A* 3(R)
Berryman, N R (Northland) 1998 *SA* 2(R)
Bevan, V D (Wellington) 1949 *A* 1,2, 1950 *BI* 1,2,3,4
Birtwistle, W M (Canterbury) 1965 *SA* 1,2,3,4, 1967 *E, W, S*
Black, J E (Canterbury) 1977 *F* 1, 1979 *A*, 1980 *A* 3
Black, N W (Auckland) 1949 *SA* 3
Black, R S (Otago) 1914 *A* 1
Blackadder, T J (Canterbury) 1998 *E* 1(R),2, 2000 *Tg, S* 1,2, *A* 1, *SA* 1, *A* 2, *SA* 2, *F* 1,2, *It*
Blake, A W (Wairarapa) 1949 *A* 1
Blowers, A F (Auckland) 1996 *SA* 2(R),4(R), 1997 *I, E* 1(R), *W* (R), 1999 *F* 1(R), *SA* 1, *A* 1(R), *SA* 2, *A* 2(R), [*It*]
Boggs, E G (Auckland) 1946 *A* 2, 1949 *SA* 1
Bond, J G (Canterbury) 1949 *A* 2
Booth, E E (Otago) 1906 *F*, 1907 *A* 1,3
Boroevich, K G (Wellington) 1986 *F* 1, *A* 1, *F* 3(R)
Botica, F M (North Harbour) 1986 *F* 1, *A* 1,2,3, *F* 2,3, 1989 *Arg* 1(R)
Bowden, N J G (Taranaki) 1952 *A* 2
Bowers, R G (Wellington) 1954 *I, F*
Bowman, A W (Hawke's Bay) 1938 *A* 1,2,3
Braid, G J (Bay of Plenty) 1983 *S, E*
Bremner, S G (Auckland, Canterbury) 1952 *A* 2, 1956 *SA* 2
Brewer, M R (Otago, Canterbury) 1986 *F* 1, *A* 1,2,3, *F* 2,3, 1988 *A* 1, 1989 *A, W, I*, 1990 *S* 1,2, *A* 1,2,3, *F* 1,2, 1992 *I* 2, *A* 1, 1994 *F* 1,2, *SA* 1,2,3, *A*, 1995 *C*, [*I, W, E, SA*], *A* 1,2
Briscoe, K C (Taranaki) 1959 *BI* 2, 1960 *SA* 1,2,3,4, 1963 *I, W*, 1964 *E, S*
Brooke, R M (Auckland) 1992 *I* 2, *A* 1,2,3, *SA*, 1993 *BI* 1,2,3, *A, WS*, 1994 *SA* 2,3, 1995 *C*, [*J, S, E, SA*], *A* 1,2, *It, F* 1,2, 1996 *WS, S* 1,2, *A* 1, *SA* 1, *A* 2, *SA* 2, *A* 3, *I, E* 1, *W, E* 2, 1998 *E* 1,2, *A* 1, *SA* 1, *A* 2, *SA* 2
Brooke, Z V (Auckland) 1987 [*Arg*], 1989 *Arg* 2(R), 1990 *A* 1,2,3, *F* 1(R), 1991 *Arg* 2, *A* 1,2, [*E, It, C, A, S*], 1992 *A* 2,3, *SA*, 1993 *BI* 1,2,3(R), *WS* (R), *S, E*, 1994 *F* 2, *SA* 1,2,3, *A*, 1995 [*J, S, E, SA*], *A* 1,2, *It, F* 1,2, 1996 *WS, S* 1,2, *A* 1, *SA* 1, *A* 2, *SA* 2,3,4,5, 1997 *Arg* 1,2, *A* 1, *SA* 1, *A* 2, *SA* 2, *A* 3, *I, E* 1, *W, E* 2
Brooke-Cowden, M (Auckland) 1986 *F* 1, *A* 1, 1987 [*W*]
Brown, C (Taranaki) 1913 *A* 2,3
Brown, O M (Auckland) 1992 *I* 2, *A* 1,2,3, *SA*, 1993 *BI* 1,2,3, *A, S, E*, 1994 *F* 1,2, *SA* 1,2,3, *A*, 1995 *C*, [*I, W, S, E, SA*], *A* 1,2, *It, F* 1,2, 1996 *WS, S* 1,2, *A* 1, *SA* 1, *A* 2, *SA* 2,3,4,5, 1997 *Fj, Arg* 1,2, *A* 1, *SA* 2, *A* 3, *I, E* 1, *W, E* 2, 1998 *E* 1,2, *A* 1, *SA* 1, *A* 2, *SA* 2
Brown, R H (Taranaki) 1955 *A* 3, 1956 *SA* 1,2,3,4, 1957 *A* 1,2, 1958 *A* 1,2,3, 1959 *BI* 1,3, 1961 *F* 1,2,3, 1962 *A* 1
Brown, T E (Otago) 1999 *WS, F* 1(R), *SA* 1(R), *A* 1(R),2(R), [*E* (R), *It, S* (R)], 2000 *Tg, S* 2(R), *A* 1(R), *SA* 1(R), *A* 2(R), 2001 *Sm, Arg* (R), *F, SA* 1, *A* 1
Brownlie, C J (Hawke's Bay) 1924 *W*, 1925 *E, F*
Brownlie, M J (Hawke's Bay) 1924 *I, W*, 1925 *E, F*, 1928 *SA* 1,2,3,4
Bruce, J A (Auckland) 1914 *A* 1,2
Bruce, O D (Canterbury) 1976 *SA* 1,2,4, 1977 *BI* 2,3,4, *F* 1,2, 1978 *A* 1,2, *I, W, E, S*
Bryers, R F (King Country) 1949 *A* 1
Budd, T A (Southland) 1946 *A* 2, 1949 *A* 2
Bullock-Douglas, G A H (Wanganui) 1932 *A* 1,2,3, 1934 *A* 1,2,3,4
Bunce, F E (North Harbour) 1992 *Wld* 1,2,3, *I* 1,2, *A* 1,2,3, *SA*, 1993 *BI* 1,2,3, *A, WS, S, E*, 1994 *F* 1,2, *SA* 1,2,3, *A*, 1995 *C*, [*I, W, S, E, SA*], *A* 1,2, *It, F* 1,2, 1996 *WS, S* 1,2, *A*1, *SA* 1, *A* 2, *SA* 2,3,4,5, 1997 *Fj, Arg* 1,2, *A* 1, *SA* 1, *A* 2, *SA* 2, *A* 3, *I, E* 1, *W, E* 2
Burgess, G A J (Auckland) 1981 *SA* 2
Burgess, G F (Southland) 1905 *A*
Burgess, R E (Manawatu) 1971 *BI* 1,2,3, 1972 *A* 3, *W*, 1973 *I, F*
Burke, P S (Taranaki) 1955 *A* 1, 1957 *A* 1,2
Burns, P J (Canterbury) 1908 *AW* 2, 1910 *A* 1,2,3, 1913 *A* 3
Bush, R G (Otago) 1931 *A*
Bush, W K (Canterbury) 1974 *A* 1,2, 1975 *S*, 1976 *I, SA*, 2,4, 1977 *BI* 2,3,4(R), 1978 *I, W*, 1979 *A*
Buxton, J B (Canterbury) 1955 *A* 3, 1956 *SA* 1

Cain, M J (Taranaki) 1913 *US*, 1914 *A* 1,2,3
Callesen, J A (Manawatu) 1974 *A* 1,2,3, 1975 *S*
Cameron, D (Taranaki) 1908 *AW* 1,2,3
Cameron, L M (Manawatu) 1980 *A* 3, 1981 *SA* 1(R),2,3, *R*
Carleton, S R (Canterbury) 1928 *SA* 1,2,3, 1929 *A* 1,2,3
Carrington, K R (Auckland) 1971 *BI* 1,3,4
Carter, M P (Auckland) 1991 *A* 2, [*It, A*], 1997 *Fj* (R), *A* 1(R), 1998 *E* 2(R), *A* 2
Casey, S T (Otago) 1905 *S, I, E, W*, 1907 *A* 1,2,3, 1908 *AW* 1
Cashmore, A R (Auckland) 1996 *S* 2(R), 1997 *A* 2(R)
Catley, E H (Waikato) 1946 *A* 1, 1947 *A* 1,2, 1949 *SA* 1,2,3,4
Caughey, T H C (Auckland) 1932 *A* 1,3, 1934 *A* 1,2, 1935 *S, I*, 1936 *E, A* 1, 1937 *SA* 3
Caulton, R W (Wellington) 1959 *BI* 2,3,4, 1960 *SA* 1,4, 1961 *F* 2, 1963 *E* 1,2, *I, W*, 1964 *E, S, F, A* 1,2,3
Cherrington, N P (North Auckland) 1950 *BI* 1
Christian, D L (Auckland) 1949 *SA* 4
Clamp, M (Wellington) 1984 *A* 2,3
Clark, D W (Otago) 1964 *A* 1,2
Clark, W H (Wellington) 1953 *W*, 1954 *I, E, S*, 1955 *A* 1,2, 1956 *SA* 2,3,4
Clarke, A H (Auckland) 1958 *A* 3, 1959 *BI* 4, 1960 *SA* 1
Clarke, D B (Waikato) 1956 *SA* 3,4, 1957 *A* 1,2, 1958 *A* 1,3, 1959 *BI* 1,2,3,4, 1960 *SA* 1,2,3,4, 1961 *F* 1,2,3, 1962 *A* 1,2,3,4,5, 1963 *E* 1,2, *I, W*, 1964 *E, S, F, A* 2
Clarke, E (Auckland) 1992 *Wld* 2,3, *I* 1,2, 1993 *BI* 1,2, *S* (R), *E*, 1998 *SA* 2, *A* 3
Clarke, I J (Waikato) 1953 *W*, 1955 *A* 1,2,3, 1956 *SA* 1,2,3,4, 1957 *A* 1,2, 1958 *A* 1,3, 1959 *BI* 1,2, 1960 *SA* 2,4, 1961 *F* 1,2,3, 1962 *A* 1,2,3, 1963 *E* 1,2
Clarke, R L (Taranaki) 1932 *A* 2,3
Cobden, D G (Canterbury) 1937 *SA* 1
Cockerill, M S (Taranaki) 1951 *A* 1,2,3

265

Cockroft, E A P (South Canterbury) 1913 *A* 3, 1914 *A* 2,3
Codlin, B W (Counties) 1980 *A* 1,2,3
Collins, A H (Taranaki) 1932 *A* 2,3, 1934 *A* 1
Collins, J (Wellington) 2001 *Arg*
Collins, J L (Poverty Bay) 1964 *A* 1, 1965 *SA* 1,4
Colman, J T H (Taranaki) 1907 *A* 1,2, 1908 *AW* 1,3
Connor, D M (Auckland) 1961 *F* 1,2,3, 1962 *A* 1,2,3,4,5, 1963 *E* 1,2, 1964 *A* 2,3
Conway, R J (Otago, Bay of Plenty) 1959 *BI* 2,3,4, 1960 *SA* 1,3,4, 1965 *SA* 1,2,3,4
Cooke, A E (Auckland, Wellington) 1924 *I, W,* 1925 *E, F,* 1930 *BI* 1,2,3,4
Cooke, R J (Canterbury) 1903 *A*
Cooksley, M S B (Counties, Waikato) 1992 *Wld* 1, 1993 *BI* 2,3(R), *A,* 1994 *F* 1,2, *SA* 1,2, *A,* 2001 *A* 1(R), *SA* 2(t&R)
Cooper, G J L (Auckland, Otago) 1986 *F* 1, *A* 1,2, 1992 *Wld* 1,2,3, *I* 1
Cooper, M J A (Waikato) 1992 *I* 2, *SA* (R), 1993 *BI* 1(R),3(t), *WS* (t), *S,* 1994 *F* 1,2
Corner, M M N (Auckland) 1930 *BI* 2,3,4, 1931 *A,* 1934 *A* 1, 1936 *E*
Cossey, R R (Counties) 1958 *A* 1
Cottrell, A I (Canterbury) 1929 *A* 1,2,3, 1930 *BI* 1,2,3,4, 1931 *A,* 1932 *A* 1,2,3
Cottrell, W D (Canterbury) 1968 *A* 1,2, *F* 2,3, 1970 *SA* 1, 1971 *BI* 1,2,3,4
Couch, M B R (Wairarapa) 1947 *A* 1, 1949 *A* 1,2
Coughlan, T D (South Canterbury) 1958 *A* 1
Creighton, J N (Canterbury) 1962 *A* 4
Cribb, R T (North Harbour) 2000 *S* 1,2, *A* 1, *SA* 1, *A* 2, *SA* 2, *F* 1,2, *It,* 2001 *Sm, F, SA* 1, *A* 1, *SA* 2, *A* 2
Crichton, S (Wellington) 1983 *S, E*
Cross, T (Canterbury) 1904 *BI,* 1905 *A*
Crowley, K J (Taranaki) 1985 *E* 1,2, *A, Arg* 1,2, 1986 *A* 3, *F* 2,3, 1987 *[Arg],* 1990 *S* 1,2, *A* 1,2,3, *F* 1,2, 1991 *Arg* 1,2, *[A]*
Crowley, P J B (Auckland) 1949 *SA* 3,4, 1950 *BI* 1,2,3,4
Culhane, S D (Southland) 1995 *[J], It, F* 1,2, 1996 *SA* 3,4
Cullen C M (Manawatu, Central Vikings, Wellington) 1996 *WS, S* 1,2, *A* 1, *SA* 1, *A* 2, *SA* 2,3,4,5, 1997 *Fj, Arg* 1,2, *A* 1, *SA* 1, *A* 2, *SA* 2, *A* 3, *I, E* 1, *W, E* 2, 1998 *E* 1,2, *A* 1, *SA* 1, *A* 2, *SA* 2, *A* 3, 1999 *WS, F* 1, *SA* 1, *A* 2, *SA* 2, *A* 2, *[Tg, E, It* (R), *S, F* 2, *SA* 3], 2000 *Tg, S* 1,2, *A* 1, *SA* 1, *A* 2, *SA* 2, *F* 1,2, *It,* 2001 *A* 2(R)
Cummings, W (Canterbury) 1913 *A* 2,3
Cundy, R T (Wairarapa) 1929 *A* 2(R)
Cunningham, G R (Auckland) 1979 *A, S, E,* 1980 *A* 1,2
Cunningham, W (Auckland) 1905 *S, I,* 1906 *F,* 1907 *A* 1,2,3, 1908 *AW* 1,2,3
Cupples, L F (Bay of Plenty) 1924 *I, W*
Currie, C J (Canterbury) 1978 *I, W*
Cuthill, J E (Otago) 1913 *A* 1, *US*

Dalley, W C (Canterbury) 1924 *I,* 1928 *SA* 1,2,3,4
Dalton, A G (Counties) 1977 *F* 2, 1978 *A* 1,2,3, *I, W, E, S,* 1979 *F* 1,2, *S,* 1981 *S* 1,2, *SA* 1,2,3, *R, F* 1,2, 1982 *A* 1,2,3, 1983 *BI* 1,2,3,4, *A,* 1984 *F* 1,2, *A* 1,2,3, 1985 *E* 1,2, *A*
Dalton, D (Hawke's Bay) 1935 *I, W,* 1936 *A* 1,2, 1937 *SA* 1,2,3, 1938 *A* 1,2
Dalton, R A (Wellington) 1947 *A* 1,2
Dalzell, G N (Canterbury) 1953 *W,* 1954 *I, E, S, F*
Davie, M G (Canterbury) 1983 *E* (R)
Davies, W A (Auckland, Otago) 1960 *SA* 4, 1962 *A* 4,5
Davis, K (Auckland) 1952 *A* 2, 1953 *W,* 1954 *I, E, S, F,* 1955 *A* 2, 1958 *A* 1,2,3
Davis, L J (Canterbury) 1976 *I,* 1977 *BI* 3,4
Davis, W L (Hawke's Bay) 1967 *A, E, W, F, S,* 1968 *A* 1,2, *F* 1, 1969 *W* 1,2, 1970 *SA* 2
Deans, I B (Canterbury) 1988 *W* 1,2, *A* 1,2,3, 1989 *F* 1,2, *Arg* 1,2, *A*
Deans, R G (Canterbury) 1905 *S, I, E, W,* 1908 *AW* 3
Deans, R M (Canterbury) 1983 *S, E,* 1984 *A* 1(R),2,3
Delamore, G W (Wellington) 1949 *SA* 4
Dewar, H (Taranaki) 1913 *A* 1, *US*
Diack, E S (Otago) 1959 *BI* 2
Dick, J (Auckland) 1937 *SA* 1,2, 1938 *A* 3
Dick, M J (Auckland) 1963 *I, W,* 1964 *E, S, F,* 1965 *SA* 3, 1966 *BI* 4, 1967 *A, E, W, F,* 1969 *W* 1,2, 1970 *SA* 1,4
Dixon, M J (Canterbury) 1954 *I, E, S, F,* 1956 *SA* 1,2,3,4, 1957 *A* 1,2
Dobson, R L (Auckland) 1949 *A* 1
Dodd, E H (Wellington) 1905 *A*
Donald, A J (Wanganui) 1983 *S, E,* 1984 *F* 1,2, *A* 1,2,3
Donald, J G (Wairarapa) 1921 *SA* 1,2

Donald, Q (Wairarapa) 1924 *I, W,* 1925 *E, F*
Donaldson, M W (Manawatu) 1977 *F* 1,2, 1978 *A* 1,2,3, *I, E, S,* 1979 *F* 1,2, *A, S* (R), 1981 *SA* 3(R)
Dougan, J P (Wellington) 1972 *A* 1, 1973 *E* 2
Dowd, C W (Auckland) 1993 *BI* 1,2,3, *A, WS, S, E,* 1994 *SA* 1(R), 1995 *C, [I, W, J, E, SA], A* 1,2, *It, F* 1,2, 1996 *WS, S* 1,2, *A* 1, *SA* 1, *A* 2, *SA* 2,3,4,5, 1997 *Fj, Arg* 1,2, *A* 1, *SA* 1, *A* 2, *SA* 2, *A* 3, *I, E* 1, *W,* 1998 *E* 1,2, *A* 1, *SA* 1, *A* 2, *SA* 2, *A* 3, *I, E* 1, *W,* 1998 *E* 1,2, *A* 1, *SA* 1, *A* 2, *SA* 2, *A* 3, *I, E* 1, *W,* 1999 *SA* 2(R), *A* 2(R), *[Tg* (R), *E, It, S, F* 2, *SA* 3], 2000 *Tg, S* 1(R),2(R), *A* 1(R), *SA* 1(R), *A* 2(R)
Dowd, G W (North Harbour) 1992 *I* 1(R)
Downing, A J (Auckland) 1913 *A* 1, *US,* 1914 *A* 1,2,3
Drake, J A (Auckland) 1986 *F* 2,3, 1987 *[Fj, Arg, S, W, F], A* 2,3, 1956 *SA* 1,2,3,4
Duff, R H (Canterbury) 1951 *A* 1,2,3, 1952 *A* 1,2, 1955 *A* 2,3, 1956 *SA* 1,2,3,4
Duggan, R J L (Waikato) 1999 *[It* (R)]
Duncan, J (Otago) 1903 *A*
Duncan, M G (Hawke's Bay) 1971 *BI* 3(R),4
Duncan, W D (Otago) 1921 *SA* 1,2,3
Dunn, E J (North Auckland) 1979 *S,* 1981 *S* 1
Dunn, I T W (North Auckland) 1983 *BI* 1,4, *A*
Dunn, J M (Auckland) 1946 *A* 1

Earl, A T (Canterbury) 1986 *F* 1, *A* 1, *F* 3(R), 1987 *[Arg],* 1989 *W, I,* 1991 *Arg* 1(R),2, *A* 1, *[E* (R), *US, S],* 1992 *A* 2,3(R)
Eastgate, B P (Canterbury) 1952 *A* 1,2, 1954 *S*
Elliott, K G (Wellington) 1946 *A* 1,2
Ellis, M C G (Otago) 1993 *S, E,* 1995 *C, [I* (R), *W, J, S, SA* (R)]
Elsom, A E G (Canterbury) 1952 *A* 1,2, 1953 *W,* 1955 *A* 1,2,3
Elvidge, R R (Otago) 1946 *A* 1,2, 1949 *SA* 1,2,3,4, 1950 *BI* 1,2,3
Erceg, C P (Auckland) 1951 *A* 1,2,3, 1952 *A* 1
Evans, D A (Hawke's Bay) 1910 *A* 2
Eveleigh, K A (Manawatu) 1976 *SA* 2,4, 1977 *BI* 1,2

Fanning, A H N (Canterbury) 1913 *A* 3
Fanning, B J (Canterbury) 1903 *A,* 1904 *BI*
Farrell, C P (Auckland) 1977 *BI* 1,2
Fawcett, C L (Auckland) 1976 *SA* 2,3
Fea, W R (Otago) 1921 *SA* 3
Feek, G E (Canterbury) 1999 *WS* (R), *A* 1(R), *SA* 2, *[E* (t), *It],* 2000 *F* 1,2, *It*
Finlay, B E L (Manawatu) 1959 *BI* 1
Finlay, J (Manawatu) 1946 *A* 1
Finlayson, I (North Auckland) 1928 *SA* 1,2,3,4, 1930 *BI* 1,2
Fitzgerald, J T (Wellington) 1952 *A* 1
Fitzpatrick, B B J (Wellington) 1953 *W,* 1954 *I, F*
Fitzpatrick, S B T (Auckland) 1986 *F* 1, *A* 1, *F* 2,3, 1987 *[It, Fj, Arg, S, W, F], A,* 1988 *W* 1,2, *A* 1,2,3, 1989 *F* 1,2, *Arg* 1,2, *A, W, I,* 1990 *S* 1,2, *A* 1,2,3, *F* 1,2, 1991 *Arg* 1,2, *A* 1,2, *[E, US, It, C, A, S],* 1992 *Wld* 1,2,3, *I* 1,2, *A* 1,2,3, *SA,* 1993 *BI* 1,2,3, *A, WS, S, E,* 1994 *F* 1,2, *SA* 1,2,3, *A,* 1995 *C, [I, W, S, E, SA], A* 1,2, *It, F* 1,2, 1996 *WS, S* 1,2, *A* 1, *SA* 1, *A* 2, *SA* 2,3,4,5, 1997 *Fj, Arg* 1,2, *A* 1, *SA* 1, *A* 2, *SA* 2, *A* 3, *W* (R)
Flavell, T V (North Harbour) 2000 *Tg, S* 1(R), *A* 1(R), *SA* 1,2(t), *F* 1(R),2(R), *It,* 2001 *Sm, Arg, F, SA* 1, *A* 1, *SA* 2, *A* 2
Fleming, J K (Wellington) 1979 *S, E,* 1980 *A* 1,2,3
Fletcher, C J C (North Auckland) 1921 *SA* 3
Fogarty, R (Taranaki) 1921 *SA* 1,3
Ford, B R (Marlborough) 1977 *BI* 3,4, 1978 *I,* 1979 *E*
Forster, S T (Otago) 1993 *S, E,* 1994 *F* 1,2, 1995 *It, F* 1
Fox, G J (Auckland) 1985 *Arg* 1, 1987 *[It, Fj, Arg, S, W, F], A,* 1988 *W* 1,2, *A* 1,2,3, 1989 *F* 1,2, *Arg* 1,2, *A* 1,2,3, *F* 1,2, 1991 *Arg* 1,2, *A* 1,2, *[E, It, C, A],* 1992 *Wld* 1,2(R), *A* 1,2,3, *SA,* 1993 *BI* 1,2,3, *A, WS*
Francis, A R H (Auckland) 1905 *A,* 1907 *A* 1,2,3, 1908 *AW* 1,2,3, 1910 *A* 1,2,3
Francis, W C (Wellington) 1913 *A* 2,3, 1914 *A* 1,2,3
Fraser, B G (Wellington) 1979 *S, E,* 1980 *A* 3, *W,* 1981 *S* 1,2, *SA* 1,2,3, *R, F* 1,2, 1982 *A* 1,2,3, 1983 *BI* 1,2,3,4, *A, S, E,* 1984 *A* 1
Frazer, H F (Hawke's Bay) 1946 *A* 1,2, 1947 *A* 1,2, 1949 *SA* 2
Fryer, F C (Canterbury) 1907 *A* 1,2,3, 1908 *AW* 2
Fuller, W B (Canterbury) 1910 *A* 1,2
Furlong, B D M (Hawke's Bay) 1970 *SA* 4

Gallagher, J A (Wellington) 1987 *[It, Fj, S, W, F], A,* 1988 *W* 1,2, *A* 1,2,3, 1989 *F* 1,2, *Arg* 1,2, *A, W, I*
Gallaher, D (Auckland) 1903 *A,* 1904 *BI,* 1905 *S, E, W,* 1906 *F*

Joseph, J W (Otago) 1992 *Wld* 2,3(R), *I* 1, *A* 1(R),3, *SA*, 1993 *BI* 1,2,3, *A, WS, S, E*, 1994 *SA* 2(t), 1995 *C*, [*I, W, J* (R), *S, SA* (R)]

Karam, J F (Wellington, Horowhenua) 1972 *W, S*, 1973 *E* 1, *I, F*, 1974 *A* 1,2,3, *I*, 1975 *S*
Katene, T (Wellington) 1955 *A* 2
Kearney, J C (Otago) 1947 *A* 2, 1949 *SA* 1,2,3
Kelleher, B T (Otago) 1999 *WS* (R), *SA* 1(R), *A* 2(R), [*Tg* (R), *E* (R), *It, F* 2], 2000 *S* 1, *A* 1(R),2(R), *It* (R), 2001 *Sm, F* (R), *A* 1(R), *SA* 2, *A* 2
Kelly, J W (Auckland) 1949 *A* 1,2
Kember, G F (Wellington) 1970 *SA* 4
Ketels, R C (Counties) 1980 *W*, 1981 *S* 1,2, *R, F* 1
Kiernan, H A D (Auckland) 1903 *A*
Kilby, F D (Wellington) 1932 *A* 1,2,3, 1934 *A* 2
Killeen, B A (Auckland) 1936 *A* 1
King, R R (West Coast) 1934 *A* 2, 1935 *S, I, W*, 1936 *E, A* 1,2, 1937 *SA* 1,2,3, 1938 *A* 1,2,3
Kingstone, C N (Taranaki) 1921 *SA* 1,2,3
Kirk, D E (Auckland) 1985 *E* 1,2, *A, Arg* 1, 1986 *F* 1, *A* 1,2,3, *F* 2,3, 1987 [*It, Fj, Arg, S, W, F*], *A*
Kirkpatrick, I A (Canterbury, Poverty Bay) 1967 *F*, 1968 *A* 1(R),2, *F* 1,2,3, 1969 *W* 1,2, 1970 *SA* 1,2,3,4, 1971 *BI* 1,2,3,4, 1972 *A* 1,2,3, *W, S*, 1973 *E* 1, *I, F, E* 2, 1974 *A* 1,2,3, *I* 1975 *S*, 1976 *I, SA* 1,2,3,4, 1977 *BI* 1,2,3,4
Kirton, E W (Otago) 1967 *E, W, F, S*, 1968 *A* 1,2, *F* 1,2,3, 1969 *W* 1,2, 1970 *SA* 2,3
Kirwan, J J (Auckland) 1984 *F* 1,2, 1985 *E* 1,2, *A, Arg* 1,2, 1986 *F* 1, *A* 1,2,3, *F* 2,3, 1987 [*It, Fj, Arg, S, W, F*], *A*, 1988 *W* 1,2, *A* 1,2,3, 1989 *F* 1,2, *Arg* 1,2, *A*, 1990 *S* 1,2, *A* 1,2,3, *F* 1,2, 1991 *Arg* 2, *A* 1,2, [*E, It, C, A, S*], 1992 *Wld* 1,2(R),3, *I* 1,2, *A* 1,2,3, *SA*, 1993 *BI* 2,3, *A, WS*, 1994 *F* 1,2, *SA* 1,2,3
Kivell, A L (Taranaki) 1929 *A* 2,3
Knight, A (Auckland) 1934 *A* 1
Knight, G A (Manawatu) 1977 *F* 1,2, 1978 *A* 1,2,3, *E, S*, 1979 *F* 1,2, *A*, 1980 *A* 1,2,3, *W*, 1981 *S* 1,2, *SA* 1,3, 1982 *A* 1,2,3, 1983 *BI* 1,2,3,4, *A*, 1984 *F* 1,2, *A* 1,2,3, 1985 *E* 1,2, *A*, 1986 *A* 2,3
Knight, L G (Poverty Bay) 1977 *BI* 1,2,3,4, *F* 1,2
Koteka, T T (Waikato) 1981 *F* 2, 1982 *A* 3
Kreft, A J (Otago) 1968 *A* 2
Kronfeld, J A (Otago) 1995 *C*, [*I, W, S, E, SA*], *A* 1,2(R) 1996 *WS, S* 1,2, *A* 1, *SA* 1, *A* 2, *SA* 2,3,4,5, 1997 *Fj, Arg* 1,2, *A* 1, *SA* 1, *A* 2, *SA* 2, *A* 3, *I* (R), *E* 1, *W, E* 2, 1998 *E* 1,2, *A* 1, *SA* 1,2 *A* 3, 1999 *WS, F* 1, *SA* 1, *A* 1, *SA* 2, *A* 2, [*Tg, E, S, F* 2, *SA* 3], 2000 *Tg, S* 1(R),2, *A* 1(R), *SA* 1, *A* 2, *SA* 2

Laidlaw, C R (Otago, Canterbury) 1964 *F, A* 1, 1965 *SA* 1,2,3,4, 1966 *BI* 1,2,3,4, 1967 *E, W, S*, 1968 *A* 1,2, *F* 1,2, 1970 *SA* 1,2,3
Laidlaw, K F (Southland) 1960 *SA* 2,3,4
Lambert, K K (Manawatu) 1972 *S* (R), 1973 *E* 1, *I, F, E* 2, 1974 *I*, 1976 *SA* 1,3,4, 1977 *BI* 1,4
Lambourn, A (Wellington) 1934 *A* 1,2, 1935 *S, I, W*, 1936 *E*, 1937 *SA* 1,2,3, 1938 *A* 3
Larsen, B P (North Harbour) 1992 *Wld* 2,3, *I* 1, 1994 *F* 1,2, *SA* 1,2,3, *A* (t), 1995 [*I, W, J, E*(R)], *It, F* 1, 1996 *S* 2(t), *SA* 4(R)
Le Lievre, J M (Canterbury) 1962 *A* 4
Lendrum, R N (Counties) 1973 *E* 2
Leslie, A R (Wellington) 1974 *A* 1,2,3, *I*, 1975 *S*, 1976 *I, SA* 1,2,3,4
Leys, E T (Wellington) 1929 *A* 3
Lilburne, H T (Canterbury, Wellington) 1928 *SA* 3,4, 1929 *A* 1,2,3, 1930 *BI* 1,4, 1931 *A*, 1932 *A* 1, 1934 *A* 2
Lindsay, D F (Otago) 1928 *SA* 1,2,3
Lineen, T R (Auckland) 1957 *A* 1,2, 1958 *A* 1,2,3, 1959 *BI* 1,2,3,4, 1960 *SA* 1,2,3
Lister, T N (South Canterbury) 1968 *A* 1,2, *F* 1, 1969 *W* 1,2, 1970 *SA* 1,4, 1971 *BI* 4
Little, P F (Auckland) 1961 *F* 2,3, 1962 *A* 2,3,5, 1963 *I, W*, 1964 *E, S, F*
Little, W K (North Harbour) 1990 *S* 1,2, *A* 1,2,3, *F* 1,2, 1991 *Arg* 1,2, *A* 1, [*It, S*], 1992 *Wld* 1,2,3, *I* 1,2, *A* 1,2,3, *SA*, 1993 *BI* 1, *WS* (R), 1994 *SA* 2(R), *A*, 1995 *C*, [*I, W, S, E, SA*], *A* 1,2, *It*, *F* 1,2, 1996 *S* 2, *A* 1, *SA* 1, *A* 2, *SA* 2,3,4,5, 1997 *W, E* 2, 1998 *E* 1, *A* 1, *SA* 1, *A* 2
Loader, C J (Wellington) 1954 *I, E, S, F*
Lochore, B J (Wairarapa) 1964 *E, S*, 1965 *SA* 1,2,3,4, 1966 *BI* 1,2,3,4, 1967 *A, E, W, F, S*, 1968 *A* 1, *F* 2,3, 1969 *W* 1,2, 1970 *SA* 1,2,3,4, 1971 *BI* 3

Loe, R W (Waikato, Canterbury) 1987 [*It, Arg*], 1988 *W* 1,2, *A* 1,2,3, 1989 *F* 1,2, *Arg* 1,2, *A, W, I*, 1990 *S* 1,2, *A* 1,2,3, *F* 1,2, 1991 *Arg* 1,2, *A* 1,2, [*E, It, C, A, S*], 1992 *Wld* 1,2,3, *I* 1, *A* 1,2,3, *SA*, 1994 *F* 1,2, *SA* 1,2,3, *A*, 1995 [*J, S, SA* (R)], *A* 2(t), *F* 2(R)
Lomu, J T (Counties Manukau, Wellington) 1994 *F* 1,2, 1995 [*I, W, S, E, SA*], *A* 1,2, *It, F* 1,2, 1996 *WS, S* 1, *A* 1, *SA* 1, *A* 2, 1997 *E* 1, *W, E* 2, 1998 *E* 1,2, *A* 1(R), *SA* 1, *A* 2, *SA* 2, *A* 3, 1999 *WS* (R), *SA* 1(R), *A* 1(R), *SA* 2(R), *A* 2(R), [*Tg, E, It, S, F* 2, *SA* 3], 2000 *Tg, S* 1,2, *A* 1, *SA* 1, *A* 2, *SA* 2, *F* 1, 2001 *Arg, F, SA* 1, *A* 1, *SA* 2, *A* 2
Long, A J (Auckland) 1903 *A*
Loveridge, D S (Taranaki) 1978 *W*, 1979 *S, E*, 1980 *A* 1,2,3, *W*, 1981 *S* 1,2, *SA* 1,2,3, *R, F* 1,2, 1982 *A* 1,2,3, 1983 *BI* 1,2,3,4, *A*, 1985 *Arg* 2
Lucas, F W (Auckland) 1924 *I*, 1925 *F*, 1928 *SA* 4, 1930 *BI* 1,2,3,4
Lunn, W A (Otago) 1949 *A* 1,2
Lynch, T W (South Canterbury) 1913 *A* 1, 1914 *A* 1,2,3
Lynch, T W (Canterbury) 1951 *A* 1,2,3

McAtamney, F S (Otago) 1956 *SA* 2
McCahill, B J (Auckland) 1987 [*Arg, S* (R), *W* (R)], 1989 *Arg* 1(R),2(R), 1991 *A* 2, [*E, US, C, A*]
McCaw, W A (Southland) 1951 *A* 1,2,3, 1953 *W*, 1954 *F*
McCool, M J (Wairarapa-Bush) 1979 *A*
McCormick, W F (Canterbury) 1965 *SA* 4, 1967 *E, W, F, S*, 1968 *A* 1,2, *F* 1,2,3, 1969 *W* 1,2, 1970 *SA* 1,2,3, 1971 *BI* 1
McCullough, J F (Taranaki) 1959 *BI* 2,3,4
McDonald, A (Otago) 1905 *S, I, E, W*, 1907 *A* 1, 1908 *AW* 1, 1913 *A* 1, *US*
Macdonald, H H (Canterbury, North Auckland) 1972 *W, S*, 1973 *E* 1, *I, F, E* 2, 1974 *I*, 1975 *S*, 1976 *I, SA* 1,2,3
MacDonald, L R (Canterbury) 2000 *S* 1(R),2(R), *SA* 1(t),2(R), 2001 *Sm, Arg, F, SA* 1(R), *A* 2, *SA* 2, *A* 2
McDowell, S C (Auckland, Bay of Plenty) 1985 *Arg* 1,2, 1986 *A* 2,3, *F* 2,3, 1987 [*It, Fj, S, W, F*], *A*, 1988 *W* 1,2, *A* 1,2,3, 1989 *F* 1,2, *Arg* 1,2, *A, W, I*, 1990 *S* 1,2, *A* 1,2,3, *F* 1,2, 1991 *Arg* 1,2, *A* 1,2, [*E, US, It, C, A, S*], 1992 *Wld* 1,2,3, *I* 1,2
McEldowney, J T (Taranaki) 1977 *BI* 3,4
MacEwan, I N (Wellington) 1956 *SA* 2, 1957 *A* 1,2, 1958 *A* 1,2,3, 1959 *BI* 1,2,3, 1960 *SA* 1,2,3,4, 1961 *F* 1,2,3, 1962 *A* 1,2,3,4
McGrattan, B (Wellington) 1983 *S, E*, 1985 *Arg* 1,2, 1986 *F* 1, *A* 1
McGregor, A J (Auckland) 1913 *A* 1, *US*
McGregor, D (Canterbury, Southland) 1903 *A*, 1904 *BI*, 1905 *E, W*
McGregor, N P (Canterbury) 1924 *W*, 1925 *E*
McGregor, R W (Auckland) 1903 *A*, 1904 *BI*
McHugh, M J (Auckland) 1946 *A* 1,2, 1949 *SA* 3
McIntosh, D N (Wellington) 1956 *SA* 1,2, 1957 *A* 1,2
McKay, D W (Auckland) 1961 *F* 1,2,3, 1963 *E* 1,2
McKechnie, B J (Southland) 1977 *F* 1,2, 1978 *A* 2(R),3, *W* (R), *E, S*, 1979 *A*, 1981 *SA* 1(R), *F* 1
McKellar, G F (Wellington) 1910 *A* 1,2,3
McKenzie, R J (Wellington) 1913 *A* 1, *US*, 1914 *A* 2,3
McKenzie, R McC (Manawatu) 1934 *A* 1, 1935 *S*, 1936 *A* 1, 1937 *SA* 1,2,3, 1938 *A* 1,2,3
McLachlan, J S (Auckland) 1974 *A* 2
McLaren, H C (Waikato) 1952 *A* 1
McLean, A L (Bay of Plenty) 1921 *SA* 2,3
McLean, H F (Wellington, Auckland) 1930 *BI* 3,4, 1932 *A* 1,2,3, 1934 *A* 1, 1935 *I, W*, 1936 *E*
McLean, J K (King Country, Auckland) 1947 *A* 1, 1949 *A* 2
McLeod, B E (Counties) 1964 *A* 1,2,3, 1965 *SA* 1,2,3,4, 1966 *BI* 1,2,3,4, 1967 *E, W, F, S*, 1968 *A* 1,2, *F* 1,2,3, 1969 *W* 1,2, 1970 *SA* 1,2,3
McLeod, S J (Waikato) 1996 *WS, S* 1, 1997 *Fj* (R), *Arg* 2(t + R), *I* (R), *E* 1(R), *W* (t), *E* 2(R), 1998 *A* 1, *SA* 1(R)
McMinn, A F (Wairarapa, Manawatu) 1903 *A*, 1905 *A*
McMinn, F A (Manawatu) 1904 *BI*
McMullen, R F (Auckland) 1957 *A* 1,2, 1958 *A* 1,2,3, 1959 *BI* 1,2,3, 1960 *SA* 2,3,4
McNab, J R (Otago) 1949 *SA* 1,2,3, 1950 *BI* 1,2,3
McNaughton, A M (Bay of Plenty) 1971 *BI* 1,2,3
McNeece, J (Southland) 1913 *A* 2,3, 1914 *A* 1,2,3
McPhail, B E (Canterbury) 1959 *BI* 1,4
Macpherson, D G (Otago) 1905 *A*
MacPherson, G L (Otago) 1986 *F* 1
MacRae, I R (Hawke's Bay) 1966 *BI* 1,2,3,4, 1967 *A, E, W, F, S*, 1968 *F* 1,2, 1969 *W* 1,2, 1970 *SA* 1,2,3,4
McRae, J A (Southland) 1946 *A* 1(R),2

McWilliams, R G (Auckland) 1928 *SA* 2,3,4, 1929 *A* 1,2,3, 1930 *BI* 1,2,3,4
Mackrell, W H C (Auckland) 1906 *F*
Macky, J V (Auckland) 1913 *A* 2
Maguire, J R (Auckland) 1910 *A* 1,2,3
Mahoney, A (Bush) 1935 *S, I, W,* 1936 *E*
Mains, L W (Otago) 1971 *BI* 2,3,4, 1976 *I*
Major, J (Taranaki) 1967 *A*
Maka, I (Otago) 1998 *E* 2(R), *A* 1(R), *SA* 1(R),2
Manchester, J E (Canterbury) 1932 *A* 1,2,3, 1934 *A* 1,2, 1935 *S, I, W,* 1936 *E*
Mannix, S J (Wellington) 1994 *F* 1
Marshall, J W (Southland, Canterbury) 1995 *F* 2, 1996 *WS, S* 1,2, *A* 1, *SA* 1, *A* 2, *SA* 2,3,4,5, 1997 *Fj, Arg* 1,2, *A* 1, *SA* 1, *A* 2, *SA* 2, *A* 3, *I, E* 1, *W, E* 2, 1998 *A* 1, *SA* 1, *A* 2, *SA* 2, *A* 3, 1999 *WS, F* 1, *SA* 1, *A* 1, *SA* 2, *A* 2, [*Tg, E, S, F* 2(R), *SA* 3], 2000 *Tg, S* 2, *A* 1, *SA* 1, *A* 2, *SA* 2, *F* 1,2, *It,* 2001 *Arg, F, SA* 1, *A* 1,2(R)
Mason, D F (Wellington) 1947 *A* 2(R)
Masters, R R (Canterbury) 1924 *I, W,* 1925 *E, F*
Mataira, H K (Hawke's Bay) 1934 *A* 2
Matheson, J D (Otago) 1972 *A* 1,2,3, *W, S*
Max, D S (Nelson) 1931 *A,* 1934 *A* 1,2
Maxwell, N M C (Canterbury) 1999 *WS, F* 1, *SA* 1, *A* 1, *SA* 2, *A* 2, [*Tg, E, S, F* 2, *SA* 3], 2000 *S* 1,2, *A* 1, *SA* 1(R), *A* 2, *SA* 2, *F* 1,2, *It* (R), 2001 *Sm, Arg, F, SA* 1, *A* 1, *SA* 2, A2
Mayerhofler, M A (Canterbury) 1998 *E* 1,2, *SA* 1, *A* 2, *SA* 2, *A* 3
Meads, C E (King Country) 1957 *A* 1,2, 1958 *A* 1,2,3, 1959 *BI* 2,3,4, 1960 *SA* 1,2,3,4, 1961 *F* 1,2,3, 1962 *A* 1,2,3,5, 1963 *E* 1,2, *I, W,* 1964 *E, S, F, A* 1,2,3, 1965 *SA* 1,2,3,4, 1966 *BI* 1,2,3,4, 1967 *A, E, W, F, S,* 1968 *A* 1,2, *F* 1,2,3, 1969 *W* 1,2, 1970 *SA* 3,4, 1971 *BI* 1,2,3,4
Meads, S T (King Country) 1961 *F* 1, 1962 *A* 4,5, 1963 *I,* 1964 *A* 1,2,3, 1965 *SA* 1,2,3,4, 1966 *BI* 1,2,3,4
Meates, K F (Canterbury) 1952 *A* 1,2
Meates, W A (Otago) 1949 *SA* 2,3,4, 1950 *BI* 1,2,3,4
Meeuws, K J (Otago) 1998 *A* 3, 1999 *WS, F* 1, *SA* 1, *A* 1, *SA* 2, *A* 2, [*Tg, It* (R), *S* (R), *F* 2(R), *SA* 3], 2000 *Tg* (R), *S* 2, *A* 1, *SA* 1, *A* 2, *SA* 2
Mehrtens, A P (Canterbury) 1995 *C,* [*I, W, S, E, SA*], *A* 1,2, 1996 *WS, S* 1,2, *A* 1, *SA* 1, *A* 2, *SA* 2,5, 1997 *Fj, SA* 2(R), *I, E* 1, *W, E* 2, 1998 *E* 1,2, *A* 1, *SA* 1, *A* 2, *SA* 2, *A* 3, 1999 *F* 1, *SA* 1, *A* 1, *SA* 2, *A* 2, [*Tg, E, S, F* 2, *SA* 3], 2000 *S* 1,2, *A* 1, *SA* 1, *A* 2, *SA* 2, *F* 1,2, *It* (R), 2001 *Arg, A* 1(R), *SA* 2, A2
Metcalfe, T C (Southland) 1931 *A,* 1932 *A* 1
Mexted, G G (Wellington) 1950 *BI* 4
Mexted, M G (Wellington) 1979 *S, E,* 1980 *A* 1,2,3, *W,* 1981 *S* 1,2, *SA* 1,2,3, *R, F* 1,2, 1982 *A* 1,2,3, 1983 *BI* 1,2,3,4, *A, S, E,* 1984 *F* 1,2, *A* 1,2,3, 1985 *E* 1,2, *A, Arg* 1,2
Mika, D G (Auckland) 1999 *WS, F* 1, *SA* 1(R), *A* 1,2, [*It, SA* 3(R)]
Mill, J J (Hawke's Bay, Wairarapa) 1924 *W,* 1925 *E, F,* 1930 *BI* 1
Milliken, H M (Canterbury) 1938 *A* 1,2,3
Milner, H P (Wanganui) 1970 *SA* 3
Mitchell, N A (Southland, Otago) 1935 *S, I, W,* 1936 *E, A* 2, 1937 *SA* 3, 1938 *A* 1,2
Mitchell, T W (Canterbury) 1976 *SA* 4(R)
Mitchell, W J (Canterbury) 1910 *A* 2,3
Mitchinson, F E (Wellington) 1907 *A* 1,2,3, 1908 *AW* 1,2,3, 1910 *A* 1,2,3, 1913 *A* 1(R), *US*
Moffitt, J E (Wellington) 1921 *SA* 1,2,3
Moore, G J T (Otago) 1949 *A* 1
Moreton, R C (Canterbury) 1962 *A* 3,4, 1964 *A* 1,2,3, 1965 *SA* 2,3
Morgan, J E (North Auckland) 1974 *A* 3, *I,* 1976 *SA* 2,3,4
Morris, T J (Nelson Bays) 1972 *A* 1,2,3
Morrison, T C (South Canterbury) 1938 *A* 1,2,3
Morrison, T G (Otago) 1973 *E* 2(R)
Morrissey, P J (Canterbury) 1962 *A* 3,4,5
Mourie, G N K (Taranaki) 1977 *BI* 3,4, *F* 1,2, 1978 *I, W, E, S,* 1979 *F* 1,2, *A, S, E,* 1980 *W,* 1981 *S* 1,2, *F* 1,2, 1982 *A* 1,2,3
Muller, B L (Taranaki) 1967 *A, E, W, F,* 1968 *A* 1, *F* 1, 1969 *W* 1, 1970 *SA* 1,2,4, 1971 *BI* 1,2,3,4
Mumm, W J (Buller) 1949 *A* 1
Murdoch, K (Otago) 1970 *SA* 4, 1972 *A* 3, *W*
Murdoch, P H (Auckland) 1964 *A* 2,3, 1965 *SA* 1,2,3
Murray, H V (Canterbury) 1913 *A* 1, *US,* 1914 *A* 2,3
Murray, P C (Wanganui) 1908 *AW* 2
Myers, R G (Waikato) 1978 *A* 3

Mynott, H J (Taranaki) 1905 *I, W,* 1906 *F,* 1907 *A* 1,2,3, 1910 *A* 1,3

Nathan, W J (Auckland) 1962 *A* 1,2,3,4,5, 1963 *E* 1,2, *W,* 1964 *F,* 1966 *BI* 1,2,3,4, 1967 *A*
Nelson, K A (Otago) 1962 *A* 4,5
Nepia, G (Hawke's Bay, East Coast) 1924 *I, W,* 1925 *E, F,* 1929 *A* 1, 1930 *BI* 1,2,3,4
Nesbit, S R (Auckland) 1960 *SA* 2,3
Newton, F (Canterbury) 1905 *E, W,* 1906 *F*
Nicholls, H E (Wellington) 1921 *SA* 1
Nicholls, M F (Wellington) 1921 *SA* 1,2,3, 1924 *I, W,* 1925 *E, F,* 1928 *SA* 4, 1930 *BI* 2,3
Nicholson, G W (Auckland) 1903 *A,* 1904 *BI,* 1907 *A* 2,3
Norton, R W (Canterbury) 1971 *BI* 1,2,3,4, 1972 *A* 1,2,3, *W, S,* 1973 *E* 1, *I, F, E* 2, 1974 *A* 1,2,3, *I,* 1975 *S,* 1976 *I, SA* 1,2,3,4, 1977 *BI* 1,2,3,4

O'Brien, J G (Auckland) 1914 *A* 1
O'Callaghan, M W (Manawatu) 1968 *F* 1,2,3
O'Callaghan, T R (Wellington) 1949 *A* 2
O'Donnell, D H (Wellington) 1949 *A* 2
O'Halloran, J D (Wellington) 2000 *It* (R)
Old, G H (Manawatu) 1981 *SA* 3, *R* (R), 1982 *A* 1(R)
O'Leary, M J (Auckland) 1910 *A* 1,3, 1913 *A* 2,3
Oliver, A D (Otago) 1997 *Fj* (t), 1998 *E* 1,2, *A* 1, *SA* 1, *A* 2, *SA* 2, *A* 3, 1999 *WS, F* 1, *SA* 1, *A* 1, *SA* 2, *A* 2, [*Tg, E, S, F* 2, *SA* 3(R)], 2000 *Tg, S* 1,2, *A* 1, *SA* 1, *A* 2, *SA* 2, *F* 1,2, *It,* 2001 *Sm, Arg, F, SA* 1, *A* 1, *SA* 2, *A* 2
Oliver, C J (Canterbury) 1929 *A* 1,2, 1934 *A* 1, 1935 *S, I, W,* 1936 *E*
Oliver, D J (Wellington) 1930 *BI* 1,2
Oliver, D O (Otago) 1954 *I, F*
Oliver, F J (Southland, Otago, Manawatu) 1976 *SA* 4, 1977 *BI* 1,2,3,4, *F* 1,2, 1978 *A* 1,2,3, *I, W, E, S,* 1979 *F* 1,2, 1981 *SA* 2
Orr, R W (Otago) 1949 *A* 1
Osborne, G M (North Harbour) 1995 *C,* [*I, W, J, E, SA*], *A* 1,2, *F* 1(R),2, 1996 *SA* 2,3,4,5, 1997 *Arg* 1(R), *A* 2,3, *I,* 1999 [*It*]
Osborne, W M (Wanganui) 1975 *S,* 1976 *SA* 2(R),4(R), 1977 *BI* 1,2,3,4, *F* 1(R),2, 1978 *I, W, E, S,* 1980 *W,* 1982 *A* 1,3
O'Sullivan, J M (Taranaki) 1905 *S, I, E, W,* 1907 *A* 3
O'Sullivan, T P A (Taranaki) 1960 *SA* 1, 1961 *F* 1, 1962 *A* 1,2

Page, J R (Wellington) 1931 *A,* 1932 *A* 1,2,3, 1934 *A* 1,2
Palmer, B P (Auckland) 1929 *A* 2, 1932 *A* 2,3
Parker, J H (Canterbury) 1924 *I, W,* 1925 *E*
Parkhill, A A (Otago) 1937 *SA* 1,2,3, 1938 *A* 1,2,3
Parkinson, R M (Poverty Bay) 1972 *A* 1,2,3, *W, S,* 1973 *E* 1,2
Paterson, A M (Otago) 1908 *AW* 2,3, 1910 *A* 1,2,3
Paton, H (Otago) 1910 *A* 1,3
Pene, A R B (Otago) 1992 *Wld* 1(R),2,3, *I* 1,2, *A* 1,2(R), 1993 *BI* 3, *A, WS, S, E,* 1994 *F* 1,2(R), *SA* 1(R)
Phillips, W J (King Country) 1937 *SA* 2, 1938 *A* 1,2
Philpott, S (Canterbury) 1991 [*It* (R), *S* (R)]
Pickering, E A R (Waikato) 1958 *A* 2, 1959 *BI* 1,4
Pierce, M J (Wellington) 1985 *E* 1,2, *A, Arg* 1, 1986 *A* 2,3, *F* 2,3, 1987 [*It, Arg, S, W, F*], *A,* 1988 *W* 1,2, *A* 1,2,3, 1989 *F* 1,2, *Arg* 1,2, *A* 1
Pokere, S T (Southland, Auckland) 1981 *SA* 3, 1982 *A* 1,2,3, 1983 *BI* 1,2,3,4, *A, S, E,* 1984 *F* 1,2, *A* 2,3, 1985 *E* 1,2, *A*
Pollock, H R (Wellington) 1932 *A* 1,2,3, 1936 *A* 1,2
Porter, C G (Wellington) 1925 *F,* 1929 *A* 2,3, 1930 *BI* 1,2,3,4
Preston, J P (Canterbury, Wellington) 1991 [*US, S*], 1992 *SA* (R), 1993 *BI* 2,3, *A, WS,* 1996 *SA* 4(R), 1997 *I* (R), *E* 1(R)
Procter, A C (Otago) 1932 *A* 1
Purdue, C A (Southland) 1905 *A*
Purdue, E (Southland) 1905 *A*
Purdue, G B (Southland) 1931 *A,* 1932 *A* 1,2,3
Purvis, G H (Waikato) 1991 [*US*], 1993 *WS*
Purvis, N A (Otago) 1976 *I*

Quaid, C E (Otago) 1938 *A* 1,2

Ralph, C S (Auckland) 1998 *E* 2
Ranby, R M (Waikato) 2001 *Sm* (R)
Randell, T C (Otago) 1997 *Fj, Arg* 1,2, *A* 1, *SA* 1, *A* 2, *SA* 2, *A* 3, *I, E* 1, *W, E* 2, 1998 *E* 1,2, *A* 1, *SA* 1, *A* 2, *SA* 2, *A* 3, 1999

WS, F 1, *SA* 1, *A* 1, *SA* 2, *A* 2, [*Tg, E, It, S, F* 2, *SA* 3], 2000 *Tg, S* 1,2(R), *A* 1, *SA* 1, *A* 2, *SA* 2, *F* 2(R), *It* (R), 2001 *Arg, F, SA* 1, *A* 1, *SA* 2, *A* 2
Rangi, R E (Auckland) 1964 *A* 2,3, 1965 *SA* 1,2,3,4, 1966 *BI* 1,2,3,4
Rankin, J G (Canterbury) 1936 *A* 1,2, 1937 *SA* 2
Reedy, W J (Wellington) 1908 *AW* 2,3
Reid, A R (Waikato) 1952 *A* 1, 1956 *SA* 3,4, 1957 *A* 1,2
Reid, H R (Bay of Plenty) 1980 *A* 1,2, *W,* 1983 *S, E,* 1985 *Arg* 1,2, 1986 *A* 2,3
Reid, K H (Wairarapa) 1929 *A* 1,3
Reid, S T (Hawke's Bay) 1935 *S, I, W,* 1936 *E, A* 1,2, 1937 *SA* 1,2,3
Reihana, B T (Waikato) 2000 *F* 2, *It*
Reside, W B (Wairarapa) 1929 *A* 1
Rhind, P K (Canterbury) 1946 *A* 1,2
Richardson, J (Otago, Southland) 1921 *SA* 1,2,3, 1924 *I, W,* 1925 *E, F*
Rickit, H (Waikato) 1981 *S* 1,2
Riechelmann, C C (Auckland) 1997 *Fj* (R), *Arg* 1(R), *A* 1(R), *SA* 2(t), *I* (R), *E* 2(t)
Ridland, A J (Southland) 1910 *A* 1,2,3
Roberts, E J (Wellington) 1914 *A* 1,2,3, 1921 *SA* 2,3
Roberts, F (Wellington) 1905 *S, I, E, W,* 1907 *A* 1,2,3, 1908 *AW* 1,3, 1910 *A* 1,2,3
Roberts, R W (Taranaki) 1913 *A* 1, *US,* 1914 *A* 1,2,3
Robertson, B J (Counties) 1972 *A* 1,3, *S,* 1973 *E* 1, *I, F,* 1974 *A* 1,2,3, *I,* 1976 *I, SA* 1,2,3,4, 1977 *BI* 1,3,4, *F* 1,2, 1978 *A* 1,2,3, *W, E, S,* 1979 *F* 1,2, *A,* 1980 *A* 2,3, *W,* 1981 *S* 1,2
Robertson, D J (Otago) 1974 *A* 1,2,3, *I,* 1975 *S,* 1976 *I, SA* 1,3,4, 1977 *BI* 1
Robertson, S M (Canterbury) 1998 *A* 2(R), *SA* 2(R), *A* 3(R), 1999 [*It* (R)], 2000 *Tg* (R), *S* 1,2(R), *A* 1, *SA* 1(R),2(R), *F* 1,2, *It*
Robilliard, A C C (Canterbury) 1928 *SA* 1,2,3,4
Robinson, C E (Southland) 1951 *A* 1,2,3, 1952 *A* 1,2
Robinson, M D (North Harbour) 1998 *E* 1(R)
Robinson, M P (Canterbury) 2000 *S* 2, *SA* 1
Rollerson, D L (Manawatu) 1980 *W,* 1981 *S* 2, *SA* 1,2,3, *R, F* 1(R),2
Roper, R A (Taranaki) 1949 *A* 2, 1950 *BI* 1,2,3,4
Rowley, H C B (Wanganui) 1949 *A* 2
Rush, E J (North Harbour) 1995 [*W* (R), *J*], *It, F* 1,2, 1996 *S* 1(R),2, *A* 1(t), *SA* 1(R)
Rush, S J (Auckland) 1998 *A* 3
Rutledge, L M (Southland) 1978 *A* 1,2,3, *I, W, E, S,* 1979 *F* 1,2, *A,* 1980 *A* 1,2,3
Ryan, J (Wellington) 1910 *A* 2, 1914 *A* 1,2,3

Sadler, B S (Wellington) 1935 *S, I, W,* 1936 *A* 1,2
Salmon, J L B (Wellington) 1981 *R, F* 1,2(R)
Savage, L T (Canterbury) 1949 *SA* 1,2,4
Saxton, C K (South Canterbury) 1938 *A* 1,2,3
Schuler, K J (Manawatu, North Harbour) 1990 *A* 2(R), 1992 *A* 2, 1995 [*I* (R), *J*]
Schuster, N J (Wellington) 1988 *A* 1,2,3, 1989 *F* 1,2, *Arg* 1,2, *A, W, I*
Scott, R W H (Auckland) 1946 *A* 1,2, 1947 *A* 1,2, 1949 *SA* 1,2,3,4, 1950 *BI* 1,2,3,4, 1953 *W,* 1954 *I, E, S, F*
Scown, A I (Taranaki) 1972 *A* 1,2,3, *W* (R), *S*
Scrimshaw, G (Canterbury) 1928 *SA* 1
Seear, G A (Otago) 1977 *F* 1,2, 1978 *A* 1,2,3, *I, W, E, S,* 1979 *F* 1,2, *A*
Seeling, C E (Auckland) 1904 *BI,* 1905 *S, I, E, W,* 1906 *F,* 1907 *A* 1,2, 1908 *AW* 1,2,3
Sellars, G M V (Auckland) 1913 *A* 1, *US*
Shaw, M W (Manawatu, Hawke's Bay) 1980 *A* 1,2,3(R), *W,* 1981 *S* 1,2, *SA* 1,2, *R, F* 1,2, 1982 *A* 1,2,3, 1983 *BI* 1,2,3,4, *A, S, E,* 1984 *F* 1,2, *A* 1, 1985 *E* 1,2, *A, Arg* 1,2, 1986 *A* 3
Shelford, F N K (Bay of Plenty) 1981 *SA* 3, *R,* 1984 *A* 2,3
Shelford, W T (North Harbour) 1986 *F* 2,3, 1987 [*It, Fj, S, W, F*], *A,* 1988 *W* 1,2, *A* 1,2,3, 1989 *F* 1,2, *Arg* 1,2, *A, W, I,* 1990 *S* 1,2
Siddells, S K (Wellington) 1921 *SA* 3
Simon, H J (Otago) 1937 *SA* 1,2,3
Simpson, J G (Auckland) 1947 *A* 1,2, 1949 *SA* 1,2,3,4, 1950 *BI* 1,2,3
Simpson, V L J (Canterbury) 1985 *Arg* 1,2
Sims, G S (Otago) 1972 *A* 2
Skeen, J R (Auckland) 1952 *A* 2
Skinner, K L (Otago, Counties) 1949 *SA* 1,2,3,4, 1950 *BI* 1,2,3,4, 1951 *A* 1,2,3, 1952 *A* 1,2, 1953 *W,* 1954 *I, E, S, F,* 1956 *SA* 3,4

Skudder, G R (Waikato) 1969 *W* 2
Slater, G L (Taranaki) 2000 *F* 1(R),2(R), *It* (R)
Sloane, P H (North Auckland) 1979 *E*
Smith, A E (Taranaki) 1969 *W* 1,2, 1970 *SA* 1
Smith, B W (Waikato) 1984 *F* 1,2, *A* 1
Smith, G W (Auckland) 1905 *S, I*
Smith, I S T (Otago, North Otago) 1964 *A* 1,2,3, 1965 *SA* 1,2,4, 1966 *BI* 1,2,3
Smith, J B (North Auckland) 1946 *A* 1, 1947 *A* 2, 1949 *A* 1,2
Smith, R M (Canterbury) 1955 *A* 1
Smith, W E (Nelson) 1905 *A*
Smith, W R (Canterbury) 1980 *A* 1, 1982 *A* 1,2,3, 1983 *BI* 2,3, *S, E,* 1984 *F* 1,2, *A* 1,2,3, 1985 *E* 1,2, *A, Arg* 2
Snow, E M (Nelson) 1929 *A* 1,2,3
Solomon, F (Auckland) 1931 *A,* 1932 *A* 2,3
Somerville, G M (Canterbury) 2000 *Tg, S* 1, *SA* 2(R), *F* 1,2, *It,* 2001 *Sm, Arg* (R), *F, SA* 1, *A* 1, *SA* 2, *A* 2
Sonntag, W T C (Otago) 1929 *A* 1,2,3
Speight, M W (Waikato) 1986 *A* 1
Spencer, C J (Auckland) 1997 *Arg* 1,2, *A* 1, *SA* 1, *A* 2, *SA* 2, *A* 3, *E* 2(R), 1998 *E* 2(R), *A* 1(R), *SA* 1, *A* 3(R), 2000 *F* 1(t&R), *It*
Spencer, J C (Wellington) 1905 *A,* 1907 *A* 1(R)
Spiers, J E (Counties) 1979 *S, E,* 1981 *R, F* 1,2
Spillane, A P (South Canterbury) 1913 *A* 2,3
Stanley, J T (Auckland) 1986 *F* 1, *A* 1,2,3, *F* 2,3, 1987 [*It, Fj, Arg, S, W, F*], *A,* 1988 *W* 1,2, *A* 1,2,3, 1989 *F* 1,2, *Arg* 1,2, *A, W, I,* 1990 *S* 1,2
Stead, J W (Southland) 1904 *BI,* 1905 *S, I, E,* 1906 *F,* 1908 *AW* 1,3
Steel, A G (Canterbury) 1966 *BI* 1,2,3,4, 1967 *A, F, S,* 1968 *A* 1,2
Steel, J (West Coast) 1921 *SA* 1,2,3, 1924 *W,* 1925 *E, F*
Steele, L B (Wellington) 1951 *A* 1,2,3
Steere, E R G (Hawke's Bay) 1930 *BI* 1,2,3,4, 1931 *A,* 1932 *A* 1
Stensness, L (Auckland) 1993 *BI* 3, *A, WS,* 1997 *Fj, Arg* 1,2, *A* 1, *SA* 1
Stephens, O G (Wellington) 1968 *F* 3
Stevens, I N (Wellington) 1972 *S,* 1973 *E* 1, 1974 *A* 3
Stewart, A J (Canterbury, South Canterbury) 1963 *E* 1,2, *I, W,* 1964 *E, S, F, A* 3
Stewart, J D (Auckland) 1913 *A* 2,3
Stewart, K W (Southland) 1973 *E* 2, 1974 *A* 1,2,3, *I,* 1975 *S,* 1976 *I, SA* 1,3, 1979 *S, E,* 1981 *SA* 1,2
Stewart, R T (South Canterbury, Canterbury) 1928 *SA* 1,2,3,4, 1930 *BI* 2
Stohr, L B (Taranaki) 1910 *A* 1,2,3
Stone, A M (Waikato, Bay of Plenty) 1981 *F* 1,2, 1983 *BI* 3(R), 1984 *A* 3, 1986 *F* 1, *A* 1,3, *F* 2,3
Storey, P W (South Canterbury) 1921 *SA* 1,2
Strachan, A D (Auckland, North Harbour) 1992 *Wld* 2,3, *I* 1,2, *A* 1,2,3, *SA,* 1993 *BI* 1, 1995 [*J, SA* (t)]
Strahan, S C (Manawatu) 1967 *A, E, W, F, S,* 1968 *A* 1,2, *F* 1,2,3, 1970 *SA* 1,2,3, 1972 *A* 1,2,3, 1973 *E* 2
Strang, W A (South Canterbury) 1928 *SA* 1,2, 1930 *BI* 3,4, 1931 *A*
Stringfellow, J C (Wairarapa) 1929 *A* 1(R),3
Stuart, K C (Canterbury) 1955 *A* 1
Stuart, R C (Canterbury) 1949 *A* 1,2, 1953 *W,* 1954 *I, E, S, F*
Stuart, R L (Hawke's Bay) 1977 *F* 1(R)
Sullivan, J L (Taranaki) 1937 *SA* 1,2,3, 1938 *A* 1,2,3
Sutherland, A R (Marlborough) 1970 *SA* 2,4, 1971 *BI* 1, 1972 *A* 1,2,3, *W,* 1973 *E* 1, *I, F*
Svenson, K S (Wellington) 1924 *I, W,* 1925 *E, F*
Swain, J P (Hawke's Bay) 1928 *SA* 1,2,3,4

Tanner, J M (Auckland) 1950 *BI* 4, 1951 *A* 1,2,3, 1953 *W*
Tanner, K J (Canterbury) 1974 *A* 1,2,3, *I,* 1975 *S,* 1976 *I, SA* 1
Taylor, G L (Northland) 1996 *SA* 5(R)
Taylor, H M (Canterbury) 1913 *A* 1, *US,* 1914 *A* 1,2,3
Taylor, J M (Otago) 1937 *SA* 1,2,3, 1938 *A* 1,2,3
Taylor, M B (Waikato) 1979 *F* 1,2, *A, S, E,* 1980 *A* 1,2
Taylor, N M (Bay of Plenty, Hawke's Bay) 1977 *BI* 2,4(R), *F* 1,2, 1978 *A* 1,2,3, *I,* 1982 *A* 2
Taylor, R (Taranaki) 1913 *A* 2,3
Taylor, W T (Canterbury) 1983 *BI* 1,2,3,4, *A, S,* 1984 *F* 1,2, *A* 1,2, 1985 *E* 1,2, *A, Arg* 1,2, 1986 *A* 2, 1987 [*It, Fj, S, W, F*], *A,* 1988 *W* 1,2
Tetzlaff, P L (Auckland) 1947 *A* 1,2
Thimbleby, N W (Hawke's Bay) 1970 *SA* 3
Thomas, B T (Auckland, Wellington) 1962 *A* 5, 1964 *A* 1,2,3

Thomson, H D (Wellington) 1908 *AW* 1
Thorne, G S (Auckland) 1968 *A* 1,2, *F* 1,2,3, 1969 *W* 1, 1970 *SA* 1,2,3,4
Thorne, R D (Canterbury) 1999 *SA* 2(R), [*Tg, E, S, F* 2, *SA* 3], 2000 *Tg, S* 2, *A* 2(R), *F* 1,2, 2001 *Sm, Arg, F, SA* 1, *A* 1
Thornton, N H (Auckland) 1947 *A* 1,2, 1949 *SA* 1
Tiatia, F I (Wellington) 2000 *Tg* (R), *It*
Tilyard, J T (Wellington) 1913 *A* 3
Timu, J K R (Otago) 1991 *Arg* 1, *A* 1,2, [*E, US, C, A*], 1992 *Wld* 2, *I* 2, *A* 1,2,3, *SA*, 1993 *BI* 1,2,3, *A, WS, S, E*, 1994 *F* 1,2, *SA* 1,2,3, *A*
Tindill, E W T (Wellington) 1936 *E*
Tonu'u, O F J (Auckland) 1997 *Fj* (R), *A* 3(R), 1998 *E* 1,2, *SA* 1(R)
Townsend, L J (Otago) 1955 *A* 1,3
Tremain, K R (Canterbury, Hawke's Bay) 1959 *BI* 2,3,4, 1960 *SA* 1,2,3,4, 1961 *F* 2,3 1962 *A* 1,2,3, 1963 *E* 1,2, *I, W*, 1964 *E, S, F, A* 1,2,3, 1965 *SA* 1,2,3,4, 1966 *BI* 1,2,3,4, 1967 *A, E, W, S*, 1968 *A* 1, *F* 1,2,3
Trevathan, D (Otago) 1937 *SA* 1,2,3
Tuck, J M (Waikato) 1929 *A* 1,2,3
Tuigamala, V L (Auckland) 1991 [*US, It, C, S*], 1992 *Wld* 1,2,3, *I* 1, *A* 1,2,3, *SA*, 1993 *BI* 1,2,3, *A, WS, S, E*
Turner, R S (North Harbour) 1992 *Wld* 1,2(R)
Turtill, H S (Canterbury) 1905 *A*
Twigden, T M (Auckland) 1980 *A* 2,3
Tyler, G A (Auckland) 1903 *A*, 1904 *BI*, 1905 *S, I, E, W*, 1906 *F*

Udy, D K (Wairarapa) 1903 *A*
Umaga, J F (Wellington) 1997 *Fj, Arg* 1,2, *A* 1, *SA* 1,2, 1999 *WS, F* 1, *SA* 1, *A* 1, *SA* 2, *A* 2, [*Tg, E, S, F* 2, *SA* 3], 2000 *Tg, S* 1,2, *A* 1, *SA* 1, *A* 2, *SA* 2, *F* 1,2, *It*, 2001 *Sm, Arg, F, SA* 1, *A* 1, *SA* 2, *A* 2
Urbahn, R J (Taranaki) 1959 *BI* 1,3,4
Urlich, R A (Auckland) 1970 *SA* 3,4
Uttley, I N (Wellington) 1963 *E* 1,2

Vidiri, J (Counties Manukau) 1998 *E* 2(R), *A* 1
Vincent, P B (Canterbury) 1956 *SA* 1,2
Vodanovich, I M H (Wellington) 1955 *A* 1,2,3

Wallace, W J (Wellington) 1903 *A*, 1904 *BI*, 1905 *S, I, E, W*, 1906 *F*, 1907 *A* 1,2,3, 1908 *AW* 2
Walsh, P T (Counties) 1955 *A* 1,2,3, 1956 *SA* 1,2,4, 1957 *A* 1,2, 1958 *A* 1,2,3, 1959 *BI* 1, 1963 *E* 2
Ward, R H (Southland) 1936 *A* 2, 1937 *SA* 1,3
Waterman, A C (North Auckland) 1929 *A* 1,2
Watkins, E L (Wellington) 1905 *A*
Watt, B A (Canterbury) 1962 *A* 1,4, 1963 *E* 1,2, *W*, 1964 *E, S, A* 1
Watt, J M (Otago) 1936 *A* 1,2
Watt, J R (Wellington) 1958 *A* 2, 1960 *SA* 1,2,3,4, 1961 *F* 1,3, 1962 *A* 1,2
Watts, M G (Taranaki) 1979 *F* 1,2, 1980 *A* 1,2,3(R)
Webb, D S (North Auckland) 1959 *BI* 2
Wells, J (Wellington) 1936 *A* 1,2
West, A H (Taranaki) 1921 *SA* 2,3
Whetton, A J (Auckland) 1984 *A* 1(R),3(R), 1985 *A* (R), *Arg* 1(R), 1986 *A* 2, 1987 [*It, Fj, Arg, S, W, F*], *A*, 1988 *W* 1,2, *A* 1,2,3, 1989 *F* 1,2, *Arg* 1,2, *A*, 1990 *S* 1,2, *A* 1,2,3, *F* 1,2, 1991 *Arg* 1, [*E, US, It, C, A*]

Whetton, G W (Auckland) 1981 *SA* 3, *R, F* 1,2, 1982 *A* 3, 1983 *BI* 1,2,3,4, 1984 *F* 1,2, *A* 1,2,3, 1985 *E* 1,2, *A, Arg* 2, 1986 *A* 2,3, *F* 2,3, 1987 [*It, Fj, Arg, S, W, F*], *A*, 1988 *W* 1,2, *A* 1,2,3, 1989 *F* 1,2, *Arg* 1,2, *A, W, I*, 1990 *S* 1,2, *A* 1,2,3, *F* 1,2, 1991 *Arg* 1,2, *A* 1,2, [*E, US, It, C, A, S*]
Whineray, W J (Canterbury, Waikato, Auckland) 1957 *A* 1,2, 1958 *A* 1,2,3, 1959 *BI* 1,2,3,4, 1960 *SA* 1,2,3,4, 1961 *F* 1,2,3, 1962 *A* 1,2,3,4,5, 1963 *E* 1,2, *I, W*, 1964 *E, S, F*, 1965 *SA* 1,2,3,4
White, A (Southland) 1921 *SA* 1, 1924 *I*, 1925 *E, F*
White, H L (Auckland) 1954 *I, E, F*, 1955 *A* 3
White, R A (Poverty Bay) 1949 *A* 1,2, 1950 *BI* 1,2,3,4, 1951 *A* 1,2,3, 1952 *A* 1,2, 1953 *W*, 1954 *I, E, S, F*, 1955 *A* 1,2,3, 1956 *SA* 1,2,3,4
White, R M (Wellington) 1946 *A* 1,2, 1947 *A* 1,2
Whiting, G J (King Country) 1972 *A* 1,2, *S*, 1973 *E* 1, *I, F*
Whiting, P J (Auckland) 1971 *BI* 1,2,4, 1972 *A* 1,2,3, *W, S*, 1973 *E* 1, *I, F*, 1974 *A* 1,2,3, *I*, 1976 *I, SA* 1,2,3,4
Williams, B G (Auckland) 1970 *SA* 1,2,3,4, 1971 *BI* 1,2,4, 1972 *A* 1,2,3, *W, S*, 1973 *E* 1, *I, F, E* 2, 1974 *A* 1,2,3, *I* 1975 *S*, 1976 *I, SA* 1,2,3,4, 1977 *BI* 1,2,3,4, *F* 1, 1978 *A* 1,2,3, *I* (R), *W, E, S*
Williams, G C (Wellington) 1967 *E, W, F, S*, 1968 *A* 2
Williams, P (Otago) 1913 *A* 1
Williment, M (Wellington) 1964 *A* 1, 1965 *SA* 1,2,3, 1966 *BI* 1,2,3,4, 1967 *A*
Willis, R K (Waikato) 1998 *SA* 2, *A* 3, 1999 *SA* 1(R), *A* 1(R), *SA* 2(R), *A* 2(R), [*Tg* (R), *E* (R), *It, F* 2(R), *SA* 3]
Willocks, C (Otago) 1946 *A* 1,2, 1949 *SA* 1,3,4
Wilson, B W (Otago) 1977 *BI* 3,4, 1978 *A* 1,2,3, 1979 *F* 1,2, *A*
Wilson, D D (Canterbury) 1954 *E, S*
Wilson, H W (Otago) 1949 *A* 1, 1950 *BI* 4, 1951 *A* 1,2,3
Wilson, J W (Otago) 1993 *S, E*, 1994 *A*, 1995 *C*, [*I, J, S, E, SA*], *A* 1,2, *It, F* 1, 1996 *WS, S* 1,2, *A* 1, *SA* 1, *A* 2, *SA* 2,3,4,5, 1997 *Fj, Arg* 1,2, *A* 1, *SA* 1, *A* 2, *SA* 2, *A* 3, *I, E* 1, *W, E* 2, 1998 *E* 1,2, *A* 1, *SA* 1, *A* 2, *SA* 2, *A* 3, 1999 *WS, F* 1, *SA* 1, *A* 1, *SA* 2, *A* 2, [*Tg, E, It, S, F* 2, *SA* 3], 2001 *Sm, Arg, F, SA* 1, *A* 1, *SA* 2
Wilson, N A (Wellington) 1908 *AW* 1,2, 1910 *A* 1,2,3, 1913 *A* 2,3, 1914 *A* 1,2,3
Wilson, N L (Otago) 1951 *A* 1,2,3
Wilson, R G (Canterbury) 1979 *S, E*
Wilson, S S (Wellington) 1977 *F* 1,2, 1978 *A* 1,2,3, *I, W, E, S*, 1979 *F* 1,2, *A, S, E*, 1980 *A* 1, *W*, 1981 *S* 1,2, *SA* 1,2,3, *R, F* 1,2, 1982 *A* 1,2,3, 1983 *BI* 1,2,3,4, *A, S, E*
Wolfe, T N (Wellington, Taranaki) 1961 *F* 1,2,3, 1962 *A* 2,3, 1963 *E* 1
Wood, M E (Canterbury, Auckland) 1903 *A*, 1904 *BI*
Woodman, F A (North Auckland) 1981 *SA* 1,2, *F* 2
Wrigley, E (Wairarapa) 1905 *A*
Wright, T J (Auckland) 1986 *F* 1, *A* 1, 1987 [*Arg*], 1988 *W* 1,2, *A* 1,2,3, 1989 *F* 1,2, *Arg* 1,2, *A, W, I*, 1990 *S* 1,2, *A* 1,2,3, *F* 1,2, 1991 *Arg* 1,2, *A* 1,2, [*E, US, It, S*]
Wylie, J T (Auckland) 1913 *A* 1, *US*
Wyllie, A J (Canterbury) 1970 *SA* 2,3, 1971 *BI* 2,3,4, 1972 *W, S*, 1973 *E* 1, *I, F, E* 2

Yates, V M (North Auckland) 1961 *F* 1,2,3
Young, D (Canterbury) 1956 *SA* 2, 1958 *A* 1,2,3, 1960 *SA* 1,2,3,4, 1961 *F* 1,2,3, 1962 *A* 1,2,3,5, 1963 *E* 1,2, *I, W*, 1964 *E, S, F*

NEW ZEALAND INTERNATIONAL STATISTICS

(up to 20 October 2001)

Match Records

Most Consecutive Test Wins

17 1965 *SA* 4, 1966 *BI* 1,2,3,4, 1967 *A, E, W, F, S,* 1968 *A* 1,2, *F* 1,2,3, 1969 *W* 1,2
12 1988 *A* 3, 1989 *F* 1,2, *Arg* 1,2, *A, W, I,* 1990 *S* 1,2, *A* 1,2

Most Consecutive Tests Without Defeat

Matches	Wins	Draws	Period
23	22	1	1987 to 1990
17	15	2	1961 to 1964
17	17	0	1965 to 1969

Most Points in a Match
by the team

Pts	Opponents	Venue	Year
145	Japan	Bloemfontein	1995
102	Tonga	Albany	2000
101	Italy	Huddersfield	1999
93	Argentina	Wellington	1997
74	Fiji	Christchurch	1987
73	Canada	Auckland	1995
71	Fiji	Albany	1997
71	Samoa	Albany	1999

by a player

Pts	Player	Opponents	Venue	Year
45	S D Culhane	Japan	Bloemfontein	1995
36	T E Brown	Italy	Huddersfield	1999
33	C J Spencer	Argentina	Wellington	1997
33	A P Mehrtens	Ireland	Dublin	1997
32	T E Brown	Tonga	Albany	2000
30	M C G Ellis	Japan	Bloemfontein	1995
30	T E Brown	Samoa	Albany	2001
29	A P Mehrtens	Australia	Auckland	1999
29	A P Mehrtens	France	Paris	2000
28	A P Mehrtens	Canada	Auckland	1995

Most Tries in a Match
by the team

Tries	Opponents	Venue	Year
21	Japan	Bloemfontein	1995
15	Tonga	Albany	2000
14	Argentina	Wellington	1997
14	Italy	Huddersfield	1999
13	U S A	Berkeley	1913
12	Italy	Auckland	1987
12	Fiji	Christchurch	1987

by a player

Tries	Player	Opponents	Venue	Year
6	M C G Ellis	Japan	Bloemfontein	1995
5	J W Wilson	Fiji	Albany	1997
4	D McGregor	England	Crystal Palace	1905
4	C I Green	Fiji	Christchurch	1987
4	J A Gallagher	Fiji	Christchurch	1987
4	J J Kirwan	Wales	Christchurch	1988
4	J T Lomu	England	Cape Town	1995
4	C M Cullen	Scotland	Dunedin	1996
4	J W Wilson	Samoa	Albany	1999

Most Conversions in a Match
by the team

Cons	Opponents	Venue	Year
20	Japan	Bloemfontein	1995
12	Tonga	Albany	2000
11	Italy	Huddersfield	1999
10	Fiji	Christchurch	1987
10	Argentina	Wellington	1997
8	Italy	Auckland	1987
8	Wales	Auckland	1988
8	Fiji	Albany	1997

by a player

Cons	Player	Opponents	Venue	Year
20	S D Culhane	Japan	Bloemfontein	1995
12	T E Brown	Tonga	Albany	2000
11	T E Brown	Italy	Huddersfield	1999
10	G J Fox	Fiji	Christchurch	1987
10	C J Spencer	Argentina	Wellington	1997
8	G J Fox	Italy	Auckland	1987
8	G J Fox	Wales	Auckland	1988

Most Penalties in a Match
by the team

Penalties	Opponents	Venue	Year
9	Australia	Auckland	1999
9	France	Paris	2000
7	Western Samoa	Auckland	1993
7	South Africa	Pretoria	1999
6	British/Irish Isles	Dunedin	1959
6	England	Christchurch	1985
6	Argentina	Wellington	1987
6	Scotland	Christchurch	1987
6	France	Paris	1990
6	South Africa	Auckland	1994
6	Australia	Brisbane	1996
6	Ireland	Dublin	1997
6	South Africa	Cardiff	1999

by a player

Penalties	Player	Opponents	Venue	Year
9	A P Mehrtens	Australia	Auckland	1999
9	A P Mehrtens	France	Paris	2000
7	G J Fox	Western Samoa	Auckland	1993
7	A P Mehrtens	South Africa	Pretoria	1999
6	D B Clarke	British/Irish Isles	Dunedin	1959
6	K J Crowley	England	Christchurch	1985
6	G J Fox	Argentina	Wellington	1987
6	G J Fox	Scotland	Christchurch	1987
6	G J Fox	France	Paris	1990
6	S P Howarth	South Africa	Auckland	1994
6	A P Mehrtens	Australia	Brisbane	1996
6	A P Mehrtens	Ireland	Dublin	1997
6	A P Mehrtens	South Africa	Cardiff	1999

Most Dropped Goals in a Match
by the team

Drops	Opponents	Venue	Year
3	France	Christchurch	1986

by a player

Drops	Player	Opponents	Venue	Year
2	O D Bruce	Ireland	Dublin	1978
2	F M Botica	France	Christchurch	1986
2	A P Mehrtens	Australia	Auckland	1995

Career Records
Most Capped Players

Caps	Player	Career Span
92	S B T Fitzpatrick	1986 to 1997
79	I D Jones	1990 to 1999
63	J J Kirwan	1984 to 1994
62	R M Brooke	1992 to 1999
60	C W Dowd	1993 to 2001
60	J W Wilson	1993 to 2001
58	G W Whetton	1981 to 1991
58	Z V Brooke	1987 to 1997
56	O M Brown	1992 to 1998
55	C E Meads	1957 to 1971
55	F E Bunce	1992 to 1997
55	M N Jones	1987 to 1998
54	J A Kronfeld	1995 to 2000
53	J W Marshall	1995 to 2001
52	A P Mehrtens	1995 to 2001
52	C M Cullen	1996 to 2001
52	J T Lomu	1994 to 2001

Most Consecutive Tests

Tests	Player	Span
63	S B T Fitzpatrick	1986 to 1995
51	C M Cullen	1996 to 2000
49	R M Brooke	1995 to 1999
41	J W Wilson	1996 to 1999
40	G W Whetton	1986 to 1991

Most Tests as Captain

Tests	Captain	Span
51	S B T Fitzpatrick	1992 to 1997
30	W J Whineray	1958 to 1965
19	G N K Mourie	1977 to 1982
19	T C Randell	1998 to 1999
18	B J Lochore	1966 to 1970
17	A G Dalton	1981 to 1985

Most Tests in Individual Positions

Position	Player	Tests	Span
Full-back	C M Cullen	39	1996 to 2000
Wing	J J Kirwan	63	1984 to 1994
Centre	F E Bunce	55	1992 to 1997
Fly-half	A P Mehrtens	52	1995 to 2001
Scrum-half	J W Marshall	53	1995 to 2001
Prop	C W Dowd	58	1993 to 2000
Hooker	S B T Fitzpatrick	92	1986 to 1997
Lock	I D Jones	79	1990 to 1999
Flanker	J A Kronfeld	54	1995 to 2000
No 8	Z V Brooke	52	1990 to 1997

Most Points in Tests

Points	Player	Tests	Career
763	A P Mehrtens	52	1995 to 2001
645	G J Fox	46	1985 to 1993
234	J W Wilson	60	1993 to 2001
216	C M Cullen	52	1996 to 2001
207	D B Clarke	31	1956 to 1964
201	A R Hewson	19	1981 to 1984
177	C J Spencer	14	1997 to 2000

Most Tries in Tests

Tries	Player	Tests	Career
44	J W Wilson	60	1993 to 2001
42	C M Cullen	52	1996 to 2001
35	J J Kirwan	63	1984 to 1994
31	J T Lomu	52	1994 to 2001
22	J F Umaga	34	1999 to 2001
21	J W Marshall	53	1995 to 2001
20	F E Bunce	55	1992 to 1997
19	S S Wilson	34	1977 to 1983
19	T J Wright	30	1986 to 1991

Most Conversions in Tests

Cons	Player	Tests	Career
130	A P Mehrtens	52	1995 to 2001
118	G J Fox	46	1985 to 1993
43	T E Brown	18	1999 to 2001
39	C J Spencer	14	1997 to 2000
33	D B Clarke	31	1956 to 1964
32	S D Culhane	6	1995 to 1996

Most Penalty Goals in Tests

Penalties	Player	Tests	Career
147	A P Mehrtens	52	1995 to 2001
128	G J Fox	46	1985 to 1993
43	A R Hewson	19	1981 to 1984
38	D B Clarke	31	1956 to 1964
24	W F McCormick	16	1965 to 1971

Most Dropped Goals in Tests

Drops	Player	Tests	Career
9	A P Mehrtens	52	1995 to 2001
7	G J Fox	46	1985 to 1993
5	D B Clarke	31	1956 to 1964
5	M A Herewini	10	1962 to 1967
5	O D Bruce	14	1976 to 1978

Tri Nations Records

Record	Detail	Holder	Set
Most team points in season	159	in four matches	1997
Most team tries in season	17	in four matches	1997
Highest score	55	55-35 v S Africa (h)	1997
Biggest win	37	43-6 v Australia (h)	1996
Highest score conceded	46	40-46 v S Africa (a)	2000
Biggest defeat	21	7-28 v Austraslia (a)	1999
Most points in matches	262	A P Mehrtens	1996 to 2001
Most points in season	84	C J Spencer	1997
Most points in match	29	A P Mehrtens	v Australia (h) 1999
Most tries in matches	16	C M Cullen	1996 to 2001
Most tries in season	7	C M Cullen	2000
Most tries in match	2	F E Bunce	v S Africa (a) 1997
	2	C M Cullen	v S Africa (h) 1997
	2	C M Cullen	v S Africa (a) 1999
	2	C M Cullen	v S Africa (h) 2000
	2	C M Cullen	v Australia (h) 2000
	2	C M Cullen	v S Africa (a) 2000
	2	J F Umaga	v S Africa (a) 2000
Most cons in matches	28	A P Mehrtens	1996 to 2001
Most cons in season	13	C J Spencer	1997
Most cons in match	4	C J Spencer	v S Africa (h) 1997
	4	A P Mehrtens	v Australia (a) 2000
	4	A P Mehrtens	v S Africa (a) 2000
Most pens in matches	65	A P Mehrtens	1996 to 2001

Most pens in season	19	A P Mehrtens	1996
	19	A P Mehrtens	1999
Most pens in match	9	A P Mehrtens	v Australia (h) 1999

Series Records

Record	Holder	Detail
Most tries	C M Cullen	7 v Tri Nations 2000
Most points	C J Spencer	84 v Tri Nations 1997

Miscellaneous Records

Record	Holder	Detail
Longest Test Career	E Hughes/C E Meads	15 seasons, 1907–21/1957–71
Youngest Test Cap	J T Lomu	19 yrs 45 days in 1994
Oldest Test Cap	E Hughes	40 yrs 123 days in 1921

Career Records of New Zealand International Players
(up to 20 October 2001)

Player	Debut	Caps	T	C	P	D	Pts
Backs:							
P P F Alatini	1999 v F	17	6	0	0	0	30
T E Brown	1999 v WS	18	5	43	20	0	171
C M Cullen	1996 v WS	52	42	3	0	0	216
R J L Duggan	1999 v It	1	0	0	0	0	0
D P E Gibson	1999 v WS	13	1	0	0	0	5
D C Howlett	2000 v Tg	10	9	0	0	0	45
B T Kelleher	1999 v WS	16	2	0	0	0	10
J T Lomu	1994 v F	52	31	0	0	0	155
L R MacDonald	2000 v S	11	2	0	0	0	10
J W Marshall	1995 v F	53	21	0	0	0	105
A P Mehrtens	1995 v C	52	7	130	147	9	763
J D O'Halloran	2000 v It	1	0	0	0	0	0
R M Ranby	2001 v Sm	1	0	0	0	0	0
B T Reihana	2000 v F	2	2	0	0	0	10
M P Robinson	2000 v S	2	1	0	0	0	5
C J Spencer	1997 v Arg	14	6	39	23	0	177
J F Umaga	1997 v Fj	34	22	0	0	0	110
J W Wilson	1993 v S	60	44	1	3	1	234
Forwards:							
T J Blackadder	1998 v E	12	1	0	0	0	5
A F Blowers	1996 v SA	11	0	0	0	0	0
J Collins	2001 v Arg	1	0	0	0	0	0
M S B Cooksley	1992 v Wld	11	0	0	0	0	0
R T Cribb	2000 v S	15	4	0	0	0	20
C W Dowd	1993 v BI	60	2	0	0	0	10
G E Feek	1999 v WS	8	0	0	0	0	0
T V Flavell	2000 v Tg	15	5	0	0	0	25
M G Hammett	1999 v F	15	2	0	0	0	10
C J Hayman	2001 v Sm	6	0	0	0	0	0
C H Hoeft	1998 v E	27	0	0	0	0	0

M R Holah	2001 v Sm	7	1	0	0	0	5
C R Jack	2001 v Arg	4	1	0	0	0	5
J A Kronfeld	1995 v C	54	14	0	0	0	70
N M C Maxwell	1999 v WS	27	3	0	0	0	15
K J Meeuws	1998 v A	18	0	0	0	0	0
D G Mika	1999 v WS	7	1	0	0	0	5
A D Oliver	1997 v Fj	36	2	0	0	0	10
T C Randell	1997 v Fj	46	12	0	0	0	60
S M Robertson	1998 v A	13	1	0	0	0	5
G L Slater	2000 v F	3	1	0	0	0	5
G M Somerville	2000 v Tg	13	0	0	0	0	0
R D Thorne	1999 v SA	16	1	0	0	0	5
F I Tiatia	2000 v Tg	2	2	0	0	0	10
R K Willis	1998 v SA	11	0	0	0	0	0

NB MacDonald's figures include a penalty try awarded against South Africa in 2001

AUSTRALIA TEST SEASON REVIEW 2000-01

Not A Season To Rival It

Peter Jenkins

At half-time in the second Test against the Lions in Melbourne the Wallabies were, for all intents and purposes, dead and buried. They had lost the first Test, trailed 11-6 with 40 minutes to play at Colonial Stadium, and were struggling to contain the Lions pack. Given those circumstances, the hopes of a fitting farewell for coach Rod Macqueen appeared as far from reality as Michael Jackson.

Then came the intercept from winger Joe Roff. It turned a Test, and an Australian winter, on its head. Fast forward eight weeks and the Wallabies had won the Lions series and had annexed back to back Tri Nations titles after a miraculous last-minute Toutai Kefu try to beat the All Blacks at Stadium Australia.

There is not a season in Australian rugby, whose international record dates back to 1899, to rival it. Never had a Wallaby side been asked to play the might of the Lions, the All Blacks and the Springboks over such an intensive period. Never had they returned better results. The Test series victory over the Lions was a first. The Tri Nations title repeated the success from the previous season, and the Bledisloe Cup was won for an unprecedented fourth successive occasion.

Yet the enduring memories of the season are the departures of Macqueen, Australia's most successful coach, and John Eales, the most celebrated skipper to lead the national side. It was a staggered departure for the two men most responsible for a Wallaby renaissance, with Macqueen leaving after the emotion and drama of the Lions series, and Eales saying his goodbyes after the win over New Zealand in September.

The season ushered in Eddie Jones as the new Wallaby coach. A man who speaks his mind, he opened his career with a loss to the Springboks in Pretoria. But a shaky beginning was soon turned around, and players speak of him in glowing terms. Kefu, who has been coached by Macqueen and, at the Queensland Reds, by John Connolly, already describes Jones as the best coach he has played under.

If there was any vacuum left by Macqueen's departure, it was soon filled. Eales will not be so replaceable. He dominated at Test level for ten years. But in the 27-year-old Justin Harrison, the eventual hero of the series decider against the Lions, Australia have a player determined to stamp his mark on the game, if not over a similar tenure.

The 2000-01 season saw the Wallabies prove with a series of close results that they have a strength of mind and purpose unsurpassed in the modern

The Wallaby squad celebrates with the substantial Bledisloe Cup and Tri Nations silverware after the last-minute victory, 29-26, against the All Blacks at Stadium Australia in Sydney. Earlier the same season the Wallabies had defeated the Lions in a Test series for the first time.

game. It opened in Europe in November with internationals on consecutive Saturdays against France, Scotland and England. The Wallabies undertook the trip without their leading half-back pairing of George Gregan and Stephen Larkham, and their absence hurt.

On the plus side, it saw the introduction of an open-side flanker, George Smith, who stepped into the boots of the long-serving David Wilson and proved, at age 20, that his career would likely outstrip the veteran he had replaced. Smith was a standout at Stade de France as the Wallabies downed the French 18-13. Matthew Burke, playing on the wing with Chris Latham at full-back, was named man of the match for his six penalty goals. But it was Smith who caught the eye.

Australia defeated a poor Scottish side 30-9 at Murrayfield, but struggled for back-line precision. Sam Cordingley at half-back was disappointing and fly-half Rod Kafer too ponderous to make an impact. Had replacement Elton Flatley not broken his wrist, he would have played the following week against England. The tour finale was a gut-wrenching blow, Australia losing 22-19 to a controversial try in the corner by Dan Luger after referee André Watson went to the video referee.

The annual European jaunt was a mere front-runner to the domestic season that opened the following June. The Lions won the first international 29-13 in Brisbane on a night when there were whispers that perhaps this had been a season too far for Macqueen. But the Australians had done their best to emulate a hapless rabble. They struggled to pass, kick or tackle, as though their memory banks for the basic skills had somehow been erased. Larkham had neither time nor space to go exploring for gaps, numerous balls were spilled in midfield and the passing was wayward.

At Melbourne the Wallabies were in trouble for the first 40 minutes before the Roff intercept and a scrum shunt that provided the possession for another try to the French-bound left wing reversed the momentum of this match. It was one of the Wallabies' greatest comebacks as they outscored the Lions 29-3 in the second half to win 35-14. Kefu and flanker Owen Finegan at last found their game, running the angles and leaving the advantage line behind them. Once that occurred, Gregan went from barking sergeant major to five-star general.

Then to the decider and Australia's 29-23 win after new cap Harrison, in for the injured David Giffin, won a late lineout against the throw inside his own quarter. The result gave the Wallabies a Grand Slam, securing for them the last missing trophy since opening their hunt for the Big Four titles in 1998. The World Cup, the Bledisloe Cup and the Tri Nations trophy had now been joined by the Tom Richards crystal. 'My greatest memories of this side will be the composure they have shown under extreme conditions,' said the coach in his farewell speech.

In the Tri Nations, the Wallabies lost 15-20 in Pretoria, continuing their drought at the high veld venue, but did manage to end a near century-long jinx when they beat the All Blacks in Dunedin for the first time, ensuring a successful defence of the Bledisloe Cup. New Zealand expected the Austral-

Stephen Larkham, Australia's influential play-maker at fly-half, sets off on one of his elusive runs against the Springboks in Perth. The match ended in the first draw between the nations since the series began in 1933.

ians to play the way the Brumbies had under Jones for the past four seasons: control the ball through endless phases until the defence runs out of numbers, or until the silken running skills of Larkham prise open the opposition backline. Jones presumed the All Blacks would base their game plan on offensive defence. Larkham, the gifted runner, became Larkham, the chip, grubber and long-punt kicker.

In Perth, the Wallabies played out a draw with the Boks before game seven of the domestic programme: the Tri Nations decider with New Zealand. The impending retirement of Eales dominated the build-up to the game, but he received the farewell present he craved with the Wallabies winning 29-26 courtesy of a late Kefu try. Eales, moreover, stamped his own mark on the Test. With six minutes to play, with the Wallabies trailing and the pressure intense in the cauldron that was Stadium Australia, Eales calmly made the most telling and courageous decision of his time as captain.

The Wallabies were awarded a penalty on the All Black quarter line within easy kicking range. Eales pointed to the sideline. While the Wallabies were struggling to crack the All Blacks defence, the captain was backing his men. 'That decision by Ealesy was courageous,' said hooker Michael Foley. 'He backed us and that was a good thing. It lifted everybody.'

Australia's Test Record in 2000-2001: Played 10, won 6, drawn 1, lost 3.

Opponents	Date	Venue	Result
New Zealand	1st September 2001	H	Won 29-26
South Africa	18th August 2001	H	Drawn 14-14
New Zealand	11th August 2001	A	Won 23-15
South Africa	28th July 2001	A	Lost 15-20
British/Irish Lions	14th July 2001	H	Won 29-23
British/Irish Lions	7th July 2001	H	Won 35-14
British/Irish Lions	30th June 2001	H	Lost 13-29
England	18th November 2000	A	Lost 19-22
Scotland	11th November 2000	A	Won 30-9
France	4th November 2000	A	Won 18-13

AUSTRALIAN INTERNATIONAL PLAYERS
(up to 20 October 2001)

Abrahams, A M F (NSW) 1967 NZ, 1968 NZ 1, 1969 W
Adams, N J (NSW) 1955 NZ 1
Adamson, R W (NSW) 1912 US
Allan, T (NSW) 1946 NZ 1, M, NZ 2, 1947 NZ 2, S, I, W, 1948 E, F, 1949 M 1,2,3, NZ 1,2
Anderson, R P (NSW) 1925 NZ 1
Anlezark, E A (NSW) 1905 NZ
Armstrong, A R (NSW) 1923 NZ 1,2
Austin, L R (NSW) 1963 E

Baker, R L (NSW) 1904 BI 1,2
Baker, W H (NSW) 1914 NZ 1,2,3
Ballesty, J P (NSW) 1968 NZ 1,2, F, I, S, 1969 W, SA 2,3,4,
Bannon, D P (NSW) 1946 M
Bardsley, E J (NSW) 1928 NZ 1,3, M (R)
Barker, H S (NSW) 1952 Fj 1,2, NZ 1,2, 1953 SA 4, 1954 Fj 1,2
Barnett, J T (NSW) 1907 NZ 1,2,3, 1908 W, 1909 E
Barry, M J (Q) 1971 SA 3
Barton, R F D (NSW) 1899 BI 3
Batch, P G (Q) 1975 S, W, 1976 E, Fj 1,2,3, F 1,2, 1978 W 1,2, NZ 1,2,3, 1979 Arg 2
Batterham, R P (NSW) 1967 NZ, 1970 S
Battishall, B R (NSW) 1973 E
Baxter, A J (NSW) 1949 M 1,2,3, NZ 1,2, 1951 NZ 1,2, 1952 NZ 1,2
Baxter, T J (Q) 1958 NZ 3
Beith, B McN (NSW) 1914 NZ 3, 1920 NZ 1,2,3
Bell, K R (Q) 1968 S
Bell, M D NSW) 1996 C
Bennett, W G (Q) 1931 M, 1933 SA 1,2,3,
Bermingham, J V (Q) 1934 NZ 1,2, 1937 SA 1
Berne, J E (NSW) 1975 S
Besomo, K S (NSW) 1979 I 2
Betts, T N (Q) 1951 NZ 2,3, 1954 Fj 2
Biilmann, R R (NSW) 1933 SA 1,2,3,4
Birt, R (Q) 1914 NZ 2
Black, J W (NSW) 1985 C 1,2, NZ, Fj 1
Blackwood, J G (NSW) 1922 M 1, NZ 1,2,3, 1923 M 1, NZ 1,2,3, 1924 NZ 1,2,3, 1925 NZ 1,4, 1926 NZ 1,2,3, 1927 I, W, S, 1928 E, F
Blades, A T (NSW) 1996 S, I, W 3, 1997 NZ 1(R), E 1(R), SA 1(R), NZ 3, SA 2, Arg 1,2, E 2, S, 1998 E 1, S 1,2, NZ 1, SA 1, NZ 2, SA 2, NZ 3, Fj, WS, F, E 2, 1999 I 1(R), SA 2, NZ 2, [R, I 3, W, SA 3, F]
Blades, C D (NSW) 1997 E 1
Blair, M R (NSW) 1928 F, 1931 M, NZ
Bland, G V (NSW) 1928 N 3, M, 1932 NZ 1,2,3, 1933 SA 1,2,4,5
Blomley, J (NSW) 1949 M 1,2,3, NZ 1,2, 1950 BI 1,2
Boland, S B (Q) 1899 BI 3,4, 1903 NZ
Bond, G S G (ACT) 2001 SA 2(R)
Bond, J H (NSW) 1920 NZ 1,2,3, 1921 NZ
Bondfield, C (NSW) 1925 NZ 2
Bonis, E T (Q) 1929 NZ 1,2,3, 1930 BI, 1931 M, NZ, 1932 NZ 1,2,3, 1933 SA 1,2,3,4,5, 1934 NZ 1,2, 1936 NZ 1,2, M, 1937 SA 1, 1938 NZ 1
Bonner, J E (NSW) 1922 NZ 1,2,3, 1923 M 1,2,3, 1924 NZ 1,2
Bosler, J M (NSW) 1953 SA 1
Bouffler, R G (NSW) 1899 BI 3
Bourke, T K (Q) 1947 NZ 2
Bowden, R (NSW) 1926 NZ 4
Bowen, S (NSW) 1993 SA 1,2,3, 1995 [R], NZ 1,2, 1996 C, NZ 1, SA 2
Bowers, A J A (NSW) 1923 M 2(R),3, NZ, 3, 1925 NZ 1,4, 1926 NZ 1, 1927 I
Bowman, T M (NSW) 1998 E 1, S 1,2, NZ 1, SA 1, NZ 2, SA 2, NZ 3, Fj, WS, F, E 2, 1999 I 1,2, SA 2, [US]
Boyce, E S (NSW) 1962 NZ 1,2, 1964 NZ 1,2,3, 1965 SA 1,2, 1966 W, S, 1967 E, I 1, F, I 2
Boyce, J S (NSW) 1962 NZ 3,4,5, 1963 E, SA 1,2,3,4, 1964 NZ 1,3, 1965 SA 1,2
Boyd, A (NSW) 1899 BI 3
Boyd, A F McC (Q) 1958 M 1
Brass, J E (NSW) 1966 BI 2, W, S, 1967 E, I 1, F, I 2, NZ, 1968 NZ 1, F, I, S

Breckenridge, J W (NSW) 1925 NZ 2(R),3, 1927 I, W, S, 1928 E, F, 1929 NZ 1,2,3, 1930 BI
Brial, M C (NSW) 1993 F 1(R), 2, 1996 W 1(R), 2, C, NZ 1, SA 1, NZ 2, SA 2, It, I, W 3, 1997 NZ 2
Bridle, O L (V) 1931 M, 1932 NZ 1,2,3, 1933 SA 3,4,5, 1934 NZ 1,2, 1936 NZ 1,2, M
Broad, E G (Q) 1949 M 1
Brockhoff, J D (NSW) 1949 M 2,3, NZ 1,2, 1950 BI 1,2, 1951 NZ 2,3
Brown, B R (Q) 1972 NZ 1,3
Brown, J V (NSW) 1956 SA 1,2, 1957 NZ 1,2, 1958 W, I, E, S, F
Brown, R C (NSW) 1975 E 1,2
Brown, S W (NSW) 1953 SA 2,3,4
Bryant, H (NSW) 1925 NZ 1,3,4
Buchan, A J (NSW) 1946 NZ 1,2, 1947 NZ 1,2, S, I, W, 1948 E, F, 1949 M 3
Buchanan, P N (NSW) 1923 M 2(R),3
Bull, D (NSW) 1928 M
Buntine, H (NSW) 1923 NZ 1(R), 1924 NZ 2
Burdon, A (NSW) 1903 NZ, 1904 BI 1,2, 1905 NZ
Burge, A B (NSW) 1907 NZ 3, 1908 W
Burge, P H (NSW) 1907 NZ 1,2,3
Burge, R (NSW) 1928 NZ 1,2,3(R), M (R)
Burke, B T (NSW) 1988 S (R)
Burke, C T (NSW) 1946 NZ 2, 1947 NZ 1,2, S, I, W, 1948 E, F, 1949 M 2,3, NZ 1,2, 1950 BI 1,2, 1951 NZ 1,2,3, 1953 SA 2,3,4, 1954 Fj 1, 1955 NZ 1,2,3, 1956 SA 1,2
Burke, M C (NSW) 1993 SA 3(R), F 1, 1994 I 1,2, It 1,2, 1995 [C, R, E], NZ 1,2, 1996 W 1,2, C, NZ 1, SA 1, NZ 2, SA 2, It, S, I, W 3, 1997 E 1, NZ 2 , 1998 E 1, S 1,2, NZ 1, SA 1, NZ 2, SA 2, NZ 3, 1999 I 2(R), E (R), SA 1, NZ 1, SA 2, NZ 2, [R, I 3, US, W, SA 3, F], 2000 F, S, E, 2001 BI 1(R),2,3, SA 1, NZ 1, SA 2, NZ 2
Burke, M P (NSW) 1984 E (R), I, 1985 C 1,2, NZ, Fj 1,2, 1986 It (R), F, Arg 1,2, NZ 1,2,3, 1987 SK, [US, J, I, F, W], NZ, Arg 1,2
Burnet, D R (NSW) 1972 F 1,2, NZ 1,2,3, Fj
Butler, O F (NSW) 1969 SA 1,2, 1970 S, 1971 SA 2,3, F 1,2

Calcraft, W J (NSW) 1985 C 1, 1986 It, Arg 2
Caldwell, B C (NSW) 1928 NZ 3
Cameron, A S (NSW) 1951 NZ 1,2,3, 1952 Fj 1,2, NZ 1,2, 1953 SA 1,2,3,4, 1954 Fj 1,2, 1955 NZ 1,2,3, 1956 SA 1,2, 1957 NZ 1, 1958 I
Campbell, J D (NSW) 1910 NZ 1,2,3
Campbell, W A (Q) 1984 Fj, 1986 It, F, Arg 1,2, NZ 1,2,3, 1987 SK, [E, US, J (R), I, F], NZ, 1988 E, 1989 BI 1,2,3, NZ, 1990 NZ 2,3
Campese, D I (ACT, NSW) 1982 NZ 1,2,3, 1983 US, Arg 1,2, NZ, It, F 1,2, 1984 Fj, NZ 1,2,3, E, I, W, S, 1985 Fj 1,2, 1986 It, F, Arg 1,2, NZ 1,2,3, 1987 [E, US, J, I, F, W], NZ, 1988 E 1,2, NZ 1,2,3, E, S, It, 1989 BI 1,2,3, NZ, F 1,2, 1990 F 2,3, US, NZ 1,2,3, 1991 W, E, NZ 1,2, [Arg, WS, W, I, NZ, E], 1992 S 1,2, NZ 1,2,3, SA, I, W, 1993 Tg, NZ, SA 1,2,3, C, F 1,2, 1994 I 1,2, It 1,2, WS, Arg 1,2, 1995 Arg 1,2, [SA, C, E], NZ 2(R), 1996 W 1,2, C, NZ 1, SA 1, NZ 2, SA 2, It, W3
Canniffe, W D (Q) 1907 NZ 2
Cannon, B J (NSW) 2001 BI 2(R), NZ 1(R)
Caputo, M E (ACT) 1996 W 1,2, 1997 F 1,2, NZ 1
Carberry, C M (NSW, Q) 1973 Tg 2, E, 1976 I, US, Fj 1,2,3, 1981 F 1,2, I, W, S, 1982 E
Cardy, A M (NSW) 1966 BI 1,2, W, S, 1967 E, I 1, F, 1968 NZ 1,2
Carew, P J (Q) 1899 BI 1,2,3,4
Carmichael, P (Q) 1904 BI 2, 1907 NZ 1, 1908 W, 1909 E
Carozza, P V (Q) 1990 F 1,2,3, NZ 2,3, 1992 S 1,2, NZ 1,2,3, SA, I, W, 1993 Tg, NZ
Carpenter, M G (V) 1938 NZ 1,2,
Carr, E T A (NSW) 1913 NZ 1,2,3, 1914 NZ 1,2,3
Carr, E W (NSW) 1921 SA 1,2, NZ (R)
Carroll, D B (NSW) 1908 W, 1912 US
Carroll, J C (NSW) 1953 SA 1
Carroll, J H (NSW) 1958 M 2,3, NZ 1,2,3, 1959 BI 1,2
Carson, J (NSW) 1899 BI 1
Carson, P J (NSW) 1979 NZ, 1980 NZ 3
Carter, D G (NSW) 1988 E 1,2, NZ 1, 1989 F 1,2

Casey, T V (NSW) 1963 *SA* 2,3,4, 1964 *NZ* 1,2,3
Catchpole, K W (NSW) 1961 *Fj* 1,2,3, *SA* 1,2, *F*, 1962 *NZ* 1,2,4, 1963 *SA* 2,3,4, 1964 *NZ* 1,2,3, 1965 *SA* 1,2, 1966 *BI* 1,2, *W, S*, 1967 *E, I* 1, *F, I* 2, *NZ*, 1968 *NZ* 1
Cawsey, R M (NSW) 1949 *M* 1, *NZ* 1,2
Cerutti, W H (NSW) 1928 *NZ* 1,2,3, *M*, 1929 *NZ* 1,2,3, 1930 *BI*, 1931 *M, NZ*, 1932 *NZ* 1,2,3, 1933 *SA* 1,2,3,4,5, 1936 *M*, 1937 *SA* 1,2
Challoner, R L (NSW) 1899 *BI* 2
Chambers, R (NSW) 1920 *NZ* 1,3
Chapman, G A (NSW) 1962 *NZ* 3,4,5
Clark, J G (Q) 1931 *M, NZ*, 1932 *NZ* 1,2, 1933 *SA* 1
Clarken, J C (NSW) 1905 *NZ*, 1910 *NZ* 1,2,3
Cleary, M A (NSW) 1961 *Fj* 1,2,3, *SA* 1,2, *F*
Clements, P (NSW) 1982 *NZ* 3
Clifford, M (NSW) 1938 *NZ* 3
Cobb, W G (NSW) 1899 *BI* 3,4
Cockbain, M J (Q) 1997 *F* 2(R), *NZ* 1, *SA* 1,2, 1998 *E* 1, *S* 1,2, *NZ* 1, *SA* 1, *NZ* 2, *SA* 2, *NZ* 3, *Fj, Tg* (R), *WS, F, E* 2, 1999 *I* 1,2, *E, SA* 1, *NZ* 1, *SA* 2, *NZ* 2, [*US* (t&R), *W, SA* 3, *F*], 2000 *Arg* 1,2, *SA* 2(t&R),3(t&R), *F, S, E* (R), 2001 *BI* 1(R),2(R),3(R), *SA* 1(R), *NZ* 1(R), *SA* 2(R), *NZ* 2(R)
Cocks, M R (NSW, Q) 1972 *F* 1,2, *NZ* 2,3, *Fj*, 1973 *Tg* 1,2, *W, E*, 1975 *J* 1
Codey, D (NSW Country, Q) 1983 *Arg* 1, 1984 *E, W, S*, 1985 *C* 2, *NZ*, 1986 *F, Arg* 1, 1987 [*US, J, F* (R), *W*], *NZ*
Cody, E W (NSW) 1913 *NZ* 1,2,3
Coker, T (Q, ACT) 1987 [*E, US, F, W*], 1991 *NZ* 2, [*Arg, WS, NZ, E*], 1992 *NZ* 1,2,3, *W* (R), 1993 *Tg, NZ*, 1995 *Arg* 2, *NZ* 1(R), 1997 *F* 1(R), 2, *NZ* 1, *E* 1, *NZ* 2(R), *SA* 1(R), *NZ* 3, *SA* 2, *Arg* 1,2
Colbert, R (NSW) 1952 *Fj* 2, *NZ* 1,2, 1953 *SA* 2,3,4
Cole, J W (NSW) 1968 *NZ* 1,2, *F, I, S*, 1969 *W, SA* 1,2,3,4, 1970 *S*, 1971 *SA* 1,2,3, *F* 1,2, 1972 *NZ* 1,2,3, 1973 *Tg* 1,2, 1974 *NZ* 1,2,3
Collins, P K (NSW) 1937 *SA* 2, 1938 *NZ* 2,3
Colton, A J (Q) 1899 *BI* 1,3
Colton, T (Q) 1904 *BI* 1,2
Comrie-Thomson, I R (NSW) 1926 *NZ* 4, 1928 *NZ* 1,2,3 *M*
Connor, D M (Q) 1958 *W, I, E, S, F, M* 2,3, *NZ* 1,2,3, 1959 *BI* 1,2
Connors, M R (Q) 1999 *SA* 1(R), *NZ* 1(R), *SA* 2(R), *NZ* 2, [*R* (R), *I* 3, *US, W* (R), *SA* 3(R), *F*(R)], 2000 *Arg* 1(R),2(R), *SA* 1, *NZ* 1, *SA* 2, *NZ* 2(t&R), *SA* 3, *F* (R), *S* (R), *E* (R)
Constable, R (Q) 1994 *I* 2(t & R)
Cook, M T (Q) 1986 *F*, 1987 *SK*, [*J*], 1988 *E* 1,2, *NZ* 1,2,3, *E, S, It*
Cooke, B P (Q) 1979 *I* 1
Cooke, G M (Q) 1932 *NZ* 1,2,3, 1933 *SA* 1,2,3, 1946 *NZ* 2, 1947 *NZ* 2, *S, I, W*, 1948 *E, F*
Coolican, J E (NSW) 1982 *NZ* 1, 1983 *It, F* 1,2
Cooney, R C (NSW) 1922 *M* 2
Cordingley, S J (Q) 2000 *Arg* 1(R), *SA* 1(R), *F, S, E*
Corfe, A C (Q) 1899 *BI* 2
Cornelsen, G (NSW) 1974 *NZ* 2,3, 1975 *J* 2, *S, W*, 1976 *E, F* 1,2, 1978 *W* 1,2, *NZ* 1,2,3, 1979 *I* 1,2, *NZ, Arg* 1,2, 1980 *NZ* 1,2,3, 1981 *I, W, S*, 1982 *E*
Cornes, J R (Q) 1972 *Fj*
Cornforth, R G W (NSW) 1947 *NZ* 1, 1950 *BI* 2
Cornish, P (ACT) 1990 *F* 2,3, *NZ* 1
Costello, P P S (Q) 1950 *BI* 2
Cottrell, N V (Q) 1949 *M* 1,2,3, *NZ* 1,2, 1950 *BI* 1,2, 1951 *NZ* 1,2,3, 1952 *Fj* 1,2, *NZ* 1,2
Cowper, D L (V) 1931 *NZ*, 1932 *NZ* 1,2,3, 1933 *SA* 1,2,3,4,5
Cox, B P (NSW) 1952 *Fj* 1,2, *NZ* 1,2, 1954 *Fj* 2, 1955 *NZ* 1, 1956 *SA* 2, 1957 *NZ* 1,2
Cox, M H (NSW) 1981 *W, S*
Cox, P A (NSW) 1979 *Arg* 1,2, 1980 *Fj, NZ* 1,2, 1981 *W* (R), *S*, 1982 *S* 1,2, *NZ* 1,2,3, 1984 *Fj, NZ* 1,2,3
Craig, R R (NSW) 1908 *W*
Crakanthorp, J S (NSW) 1923 *NZ* 3
Cremin, J F (NSW) 1946 *NZ* 1,2, 1947 *NZ* 1
Crittle, C P (NSW) 1962 *NZ* 4,5, 1963 *SA* 2,3,4, 1964 *NZ* 1,2,3, 1965 *SA* 1,2, 1966 *BI* 1,2, *S*, 1967 *E, I*
Croft, B H D (NSW) 1928 *M*
Cross, J R (NSW) 1955 *NZ* 1,2,3
Cross, K A (NSW) 1949 *M* 1, *NZ* 1,2, 1950 *BI* 1,2, 1951 *NZ* 2,3, 1952 *NZ* 1, 1953 *SA* 1,2,3,4, 1954 *Fj* 1,2, 1955 *NZ* 3, 1956 *SA* 1,2, 1957 *NZ* 1,2
Crossman, O C (NSW) 1923 *M* 1(R),2,3, 1924, *NZ* 1,2,3, 1925 *NZ* 1,3,4, 1926 *NZ* 1,2,3,4, 1929 *NZ* 2, 1930 *BI*
Crowe, P J (NSW) 1976 *F* 2, 1978 *W* 1,2, 1979 *I* 2, *NZ, Arg* 1

Crowley, D J (Q) 1989 *BI* 1,2,3, 1991 [*WS*], 1992 *I, W*, 1993 *C* (R), 1995 *Arg* 1,2, [*SA, E*], *NZ* 1, 1996 *W* 2(R), *C, NZ* 1, *SA* 1,2, *I, W* 3, 1998 *E* 1(R), *S* 1(R),2(R), *NZ* 1(R), *SA* 1, *NZ* 2, *SA* 2, *NZ* 3, *Tg, WS*, 1999 *I* 1,2(R), *E* (R), *SA* 1, *NZ* 1(R), [*R* (R), *I* 3(t&R), *US, F*(R)]
Curley, T G P (NSW) 1957 *NZ* 1,2, 1958 *W, I, E, S, F, M* 1, *NZ* 1,2,3
Curran, D J (NSW) 1980 *NZ* 3, 1981 *F* 1,2, *W*, 1983 *Arg* 1
Currie, E W (Q) 1899 *BI* 2
Cutler, S A G (NSW) 1982 *NZ* 2(R), 1984 *NZ* 1,2,3, *E, I, W, S*, 1985 *C* 1,2, *NZ, Fj* 1,2, 1986 *It, F, NZ* 1,2,3, 1987 *SK*, [*E, J, I, F, W*], *NZ, Arg* 1,2, 1988 *E* 1,2, *NZ* 1,2,3, *E, S, It*, 1989 *BI* 1,2,3, *NZ*, 1991 [*WS*]

Daly, A J (NSW) 1989 *NZ, F* 1,2, 1990 *F* 1,2,3, *US, NZ* 1,2,3, 1991 *W, E, NZ* 1,2, [*Arg, W, I, NZ, E*], 1992 *S* 1,2, *NZ* 1,2,3, *SA*, 1993 *Tg, NZ, SA* 1,2,3, *C, F* 1,2, 1994 *I* 1,2, *It* 1,2, *WS, NZ*, 1995 [*C, R*]
D'Arcy, A M (Q) 1980 *Fj, NZ* 3, 1981 *F* 1,2, *I, W, S*, 1982 *E, S* 1,2
Darveniza, P (NSW) 1969 *W, SA* 2,3,4
Darwin, B J (ACT) 2001 *BI* 1(R), *SA* 1(R), *NZ* 1(R), *SA* 2(R), *NZ* 2(t&R)
Davidson, R A L (NSW) 1952 *Fj* 1,2, *NZ* 1,2, 1953 *SA* 1, 1957 *NZ* 1,2, 1958 *W, I, E, S, F, M* 1
Davis, C C (NSW) 1949 *NZ* 1, 1951 *NZ* 1,2,3
Davis, E H (V) 1947 *S, W*, 1949 *M* 1,2
Davis, G V (NSW) 1963 *E, SA* 1,2,3,4, 1964 *NZ* 1,2,3, 1965 *SA* 1, 1966 *BI* 1,2, *W, S*, 1967 *E, I* 1, *F, I* 2, *NZ*, 1968 *NZ* 1,2, *F, I, S*, 1969 *W, SA* 1,2,3,4, 1970 *S*, 1971 *SA* 1,2,3, *F* 1,2, 1972 *F* 1,2, *NZ* 1,2,3
Davis, G W G (NSW) 1955 *NZ* 2,3
Davis, R A (NSW) 1974 *NZ* 1,2,3
Davis, T S R (NSW) 1920 *NZ* 1,2,3, 1921 *SA* 1,2,3, *NZ*, 1922 *M* 1,2,3, *NZ* 1,2,3, 1923 *M* 3, *NZ* 1,2,3, 1924 *NZ* 1,2, 1925 *NZ* 1
Davis, W (NSW) 1899 *BI* 1,3,4
Dawson, W L (NSW) 1946 *NZ* 1,2
Diett, L J (NSW) 1959 *BI* 1,2
Dix, W (NSW) 1907 *NZ* 1,2,3, 1909 *E*
Dixon, E J (Q) 1904 *BI* 3
Donald, K J (Q) 1957 *NZ* 1, 1958 *W, I, E, S, M* 2,3, 1959 *BI* 1,2
Dore, E (Q) 1904 *BI* 1
Dore, M J (Q) 1905 *NZ*
Dorr, R W (V) 1936 *M*, 1937 *SA* 1
Douglas, J A (V) 1962 *NZ* 3,4,5
Douglas, W A (NSW) 1922 *NZ* 3(R)
Dowse, J H (NSW) 1961 *Fj* 1,2, *SA* 1,2
Dunbar, A R (NSW) 1910 *NZ* 1,2,3, 1912 *US*
Duncan, J L (NSW) 1926 *NZ* 4
Dunlop, E E (V) 1932 *NZ* 3, 1934 *NZ* 1
Dunn, P K (NSW) 1958 *NZ* 1,2,3, 1959 *BI* 1,2
Dunn, V A (NSW) 1920 *NZ* 1,2,3, 1921 *SA* 1,2,3, *NZ*
Dunworth, D A (Q) 1971 *F* 1,2, 1972 *F* 1,2, 1976 *Fj* 2
Dwyer, L J (NSW) 1910 *NZ* 1,2,3, 1912 *US*, 1913 *NZ* 3, 1914 *NZ* 1,2,3
Dyson, F J (Q) 2000 *Arg* 1,2, *SA* 1, *NZ* 1, *SA* 2, *NZ* 2, *SA* 3, *F, S, E*

Eales, J A (Q) 1991 *W, E, NZ* 1,2, [*Arg, WS, W, I, NZ, E*], 1992 *S* 1,2, *NZ* 1,2,3, *SA, I*, 1994 *I* 1,2, *It* 1,2, *WS, NZ*, 1995 *Arg* 1,2, [*SA, C, R, E*], *NZ* 1,2, 1996 *W* 1,2, *C, NZ* 1, *SA* 1, *NZ* 2, *SA* 2, *It, S, I*, 1997 *F* 1,2, *NZ* 1, *E* 1, *NZ* 2, *SA* 1, *Arg* 1,2, *E* 2, *S*, 1998 *E* 1, *S* 1,2, *NZ* 1, *SA* 1, *NZ* 2, *SA* 2, *Fj, Tg, WS, F, E* 2, 1999 [*R, I* 3, *W, SA* 3, *F*], 2000 *Arg* 1,2, *SA* 1, *NZ* 1, *SA* 2, *NZ* 2, *SA* 3, *F, S, E*, 2001 *BI* 1,2,3, *SA* 1, *NZ* 1, *SA* 2, *NZ* 2
Eastes, C C (NSW) 1946 *NZ* 1,2, 1947 *NZ* 1,2, 1949 *M* 1,2
Edmonds, M H M (NSW) 1998 *Tg*, 2001 *SA* 1(R)
Egerton, R H (NSW) 1991 *W, E, NZ* 1,2, [*Arg, W, I, NZ, E*]
Ella, G A (NSW) 1982 *NZ* 1,2, 1983 *F* 1,2, 1988 *E* 2, *NZ* 1
Ella, G J (NSW) 1982 *S* 1, 1983 *It*, 1985 *C* 2(R), *Fj* 2
Ella, M G (NSW) 1980 *NZ* 1,2,3, 1981 *F* 2, *S*, 1982 *E, S* 1, *NZ* 1,2,3, 1983 *US, Arg* 1,2, *NZ, It, F* 1,2, 1984 *Fj, NZ* 1,2,3, *E, I, W, S*
Ellem, M A (NSW) 1976 *Fj* 3(R)
Elliott, F M (NSW) 1957 *NZ* 1
Elliott, R E (NSW) 1920 *NZ* 1, 1921 *NZ*, 1922 *M* 1,2, *NZ* 1(R),2,3, 1923 *M* 1,2,3, *NZ* 1,2,3
Ellis, C S (NSW) 1899 *BI* 1,2,3,4
Ellis, K J (NSW) 1958 *NZ* 1,2,3, 1959 *BI* 1,2

Ellwood, B J (NSW) 1958 *NZ* 1,2,3, 1961 *Fj* 2,3, *SA* 1, *F*, 1962 *NZ* 1,2,3,4,5, 1963 *SA* 1,2,3,4, 1964 *NZ* 3, 1965 *SA* 1,2, 1966 *BI* 1
Emanuel, D M (NSW) 1957 *NZ* 2, 1958 *W, I, E, S, F, M* 1,2,3
Emery, N A (NSW) 1947 *NZ* 2, *S, I, W*, 1948 *E, F*, 1949 *M* 2,3, *NZ* 1,2
Erasmus, D J (NSW) 1923 *NZ* 1,2
Erby, A B (NSW) 1923 *M* 1,2, *NZ* 2,3, 1925 *NZ* 2
Evans, L J (Q) 1903 *NZ*, 1904 *BI* 1,3
Evans, W T (Q) 1899 *BI* 1,2

Fahey, E J (NSW) 1912 *US*, 1913 *NZ* 1,2, 1914 *NZ* 3
Fairfax, R L (NSW) 1971 *F* 1,2, 1972 *F* 1,2, *NZ* 1, *Fj*, 1973 *W, E*
Farmer, E H (Q) 1910 *NZ* 1
Farquhar, C R (NSW) 1920 *NZ* 2
Farr-Jones, N C (NSW) 1984 *E, I, W, S*, 1985 *C* 1,2, *NZ, Fj* 1,2, 1986 *It, F, Arg* 1,2, *NZ* 1,2,3, 1987 *SK, [E, I, F, W* (R)], *NZ, Arg* 2, 1988 *E* 1,2, *NZ* 1,2,3, *E, S, It*, 1989 *BI* 1,2,3, *NZ, F* 1,2, 1990 *F* 1,2,3, *US, NZ* 1,2,3, 1991 *W, E, NZ* 1,2, [*Arg, WS, I, NZ, E*], 1992 *S* 1,2, *NZ* 1,2,3, *SA*, 1993 *NZ, SA* 1,2,3
Fay, G (NSW) 1971 *SA* 2, 1972 *NZ* 1,2,3, 1973 *Tg* 1,2, *W, E*, 1974 *NZ* 1,2,3, 1975 *E* 1,2, *J* 1, *S, W*, 1976 *I, US*, 1978 *W* 1,2, *NZ* 1,2,3, 1979 *I* 1
Fenwicke, P T (NSW) 1957 *NZ* 1, 1958 *W, I, E*, 1959 *BI* 1,2
Ferguson, R T (NSW) 1922 *M* 3, *NZ* 1, 1923 *M* 3, *NZ* 3
Fihelly, J A (Q) 1907 *NZ* 2
Finau, S F (NSW) 1997 *NZ* 3
Finegan, O D A (ACT) 1996 *W* 1,2, *C, NZ* 1, *SA* 1(t), *S, W* 3, 1997 *SA* 1, *NZ* 3, *SA* 2, *Arg* 1,2, *E* 2, *S*, 1998 *E* 1(R), *S* 1(t + R),2(t + R), *NZ* 1(R), *SA* 1(t),2(R), *NZ* 3(R), *Fj* (R), *Tg, WS* (t + R), *F* (R), *E* 2(R), 1999 *NZ* 2(R), [*R, I* 3(R), *US, W* (R), *SA* 3(R), *F* (R)], 2001 *BI* 1,2,3, *SA* 1, *NZ* 1, *SA* 2, *NZ* 2
Finlay, A N (NSW) 1926 *NZ* 1,2,3, 1927 *I, W, S*, 1928 *E, F*, 1929 *NZ* 1,2,3, 1930 *BI*
Finley, F G (NSW) 1904 *BI* 3
Finnane, S C (NSW) 1975 *E* 1, *J* 1,2, 1976 *E*, 1978 *W* 1,2
FitzSimons, P (NSW) 1989 *F* 1,2, 1990 *F* 1,2,3, *US, NZ* 1
Flanagan, P (Q) 1907 *NZ* 1,2
Flatley, E J (Q) 1997 *E* 2, *S*, 2000 *S* (R), 2001 *BI* 1(R),2(R),3, *SA* 1, *NZ* 1(R),2(R)
Flett, J A (NSW) 1990 *US, NZ* 2,3, 1991 [*WS*]
Flynn, J P (Q) 1914 *NZ* 1,2
Fogarty, J R (Q) 1949 *M* 2,3
Foley, M A (Q) 1995 [*C* (R), *R*], 1996 *W* 2(R), *NZ* 1, *SA* 1, *NZ* 2, *SA* 2, *It, S, I, W* 3, 1997 *NZ* 1(R), *E* 1, *NZ* 2, *SA* 1, *NZ* 3, *SA* 2, *Arg* 1,2, *E* 2, *S*, 1998 *Tg* (R), *F* (R), *E* 2(R), 1999 *NZ* 2(R), [*US, W, SA* 3, *F*], 2000 *Arg* 1,2, *SA* 1, *NZ* 1, *SA* 2, *NZ* 2, *SA* 3, *F, S, E*, 2001 *BI* 1(R),2(R),3, *SA* 1, *NZ* 1, *SA* 2, *NZ* 2
Foote, R H (NSW) 1924 *NZ* 2,3, 1926 *NZ* 2
Forbes, C F (Q) 1953 *SA* 2,3,4, 1954 *Fj* 1, 1956 *SA* 1,2
Ford, B (Q) 1957 *NZ* 2
Ford, E E (NSW) 1927 *I, W, S*, 1928 *E, F*, 1929 *NZ* 1,3
Ford, J A (NSW) 1925 *NZ* 4, 1926 *NZ* 1,2, 1927 *I, W, S*, 1928 *E*, 1929 *NZ* 1,2,3, 1930 *BI*
Forman, T R (NSW) 1968 *I, S*, 1969 *W, SA* 1,2,3,4
Fowles, D G (NSW) 1921 *SA* 1,2,3, 1922 *M* 2,3, 1923 *M* 2,3
Fox, C L (NSW) 1920 *NZ* 1,2,3, 1921 *SA* 1, *NZ*, 1922 *M* 1,2, *NZ* 1, 1924 *NZ* 1,2,3, 1925 *NZ* 1,2,3, 1926 *NZ* 1,3, 1928 *F*
Fox, O G (NSW) 1958 *F*
Francis, E (Q) 1914 *NZ* 1,2
Frawley, D (Q, NSW) 1986 *Arg* 2(R), 1987 *Arg* 1,2, 1988 *E* 1,2, *NZ* 1,2,3, *S, It*
Freedman, J E (NSW) 1962 *NZ* 3,4,5, 1963 *SA* 1
Freeman, E (NSW) 1946 *NZ* 1(R), *M*
Freney, M E (Q) 1972 *NZ* 1,2,3, 1973 *Tg* 1, *W, E* (R)
Friend, W S (NSW) 1920 *NZ* 3, 1921 *SA* 1,2,3, 1922 *NZ* 1,2,3, 1923 *M* 1,2,3
Furness, D C (NSW) 1946 *M*
Futter, F C (NSW) 1904 *BI* 3

Gardner, J M (Q) 1987 *Arg* 2, 1988 *E* 1, *NZ* 1, *E*
Gardner, W C (NSW) 1950 *BI* 1
Garner, R L (NSW) 1949 *NZ* 1,2
Gavin, K A (NSW) 1909 *E*
Gavin, T B (NSW) 1988 *NZ* 2,3, *S, It* (R), 1989 *NZ* (R), *F* 1,2, 1990 *F* 1,2,3, *US, NZ* 1,2,3, 1991 *W, E, NZ* 1, 1992 *S* 1,2, *SA, I, W*, 1993 *Tg, NZ, SA* 1,2,3, *C, F* 1,2, 1994 *I* 1,2, *It* 1,2, *WS, NZ*, 1995 *Arg* 1,2, [*SA, C, R, E*], *NZ* 1,2, 1996 *NZ* 2(R), *SA* 2, *W* 3
Gelling, A M (NSW) 1972 *NZ* 1, *Fj*
George, H W (NSW) 1910 *NZ* 1,2,3, 1912 *US*, 1913 *NZ* 1,3, 1914 *NZ* 1,3

George, W G (NSW) 1923 *M* 1,3, *NZ* 1,2, 1924 *NZ* 3, 1925 *NZ* 2,3, 1926 *NZ* 4, 1928 *NZ* 1,2,3, *M*
Gibbons, E de C (NSW) 1936 *NZ* 1,2, *M*
Gibbs, P R (V) 1966 *S*
Giffin, D T (ACT) 1996 *W* 3, 1997 *F* 1,2, 1999 *I* 1,2, *E, SA* 1, *NZ* 1, *SA* 2, *NZ* 2, [*R, I* 3, *US* (R), *W, SA* 3, *F*], 2000 *Arg* 1,2, *SA* 1, *NZ* 1, *SA* 2, *NZ* 2, *SA* 3, *F, S, E*, 2001 *BI* 1,2, *SA* 1, *NZ* 2
Gilbert, H (NSW) 1910 *NZ* 1,2,3
Girvan, B (ACT) 1988 *E*
Gordon, G C (NSW) 1929 *NZ* 1
Gordon, K M (NSW) 1950 *BI* 1,2
Gould, R G (Q) 1980 *NZ* 1,2,3, 1981 *I, W, S*, 1982 *S* 2, *NZ* 1,2,3, 1983 *US, Arg* 1, *F* 1,2, 1984 *NZ* 1,2,3, *E, I, W, S*, 1985 *NZ*, 1986 *It*, 1987 *SK*, [*E*]
Gourley, S R (NSW) 1988 *S, It*, 1989 *BI* 1,2,3
Graham, C S (Q) 1899 *BI* 2
Graham, R (NSW) 1973 *Tg* 1,2, *W, E*, 1974 *NZ* 2,3, 1975 *E* 2, *J* 1,2, *S, W*, 1976 *I, US, Fj* 1,2,3, *F* 1,2
Gralton, A S I (Q) 1899 *BI* 1,4, 1903 *NZ*
Grant, J C (NSW) 1988 *E* 1, *NZ* 2,3, *E*
Graves, R H (NSW) 1907 *NZ* 1(R)
Greatorex, E N (NSW) 1923 *M* 3, *NZ* 3, 1924 *NZ* 1,2,3, 1925 *NZ* 1, 1928 *E, F*
Gregan, G M (ACT) 1994 *It* 1,2, *WS, NZ*, 1995 *Arg* 1,2, [*SA, C* (R), *R, E*], 1996 *W* 1, *C* (t), *SA* 1, *NZ* 2, *SA* 2, *It, I, W* 3, 1997 *F* 1,2, *NZ* 2, *E* 1, *NZ* 2, *SA* 1, *NZ* 3, *SA* 2, *Arg* 1,2, *E* 2, *S*, 1998 *E* 1, *S* 1,2, *NZ* 1, *SA* 1, *NZ* 2, *SA* 2, *NZ* 3, *Fj, WS, F, E* 2, 1999 *I* 1,2, *E, SA* 1, *NZ* 1, *SA* 2, *NZ* 2, [*R, I* 3, *W, SA* 3, *F*], 2000 *Arg* 1,2, *SA* 1, *NZ* 1, *SA* 2, *NZ* 2, *SA* 3, 2001 *BI* 1,2,3, *SA* 1, *NZ* 1, *SA* 2, *NZ* 2
Gregory, S C (Q) 1968 *NZ* 3, *F, I, S*, 1969 *SA* 1,3, 1971 *SA* 1,3, *F* 1,2, 1972 *F* 1,2, 1973 *Tg* 1,2, *W, E*
Grey, G O (NSW) 1972 *F* 2(R), *NZ* 1,2,3, *Fj* (R)
Grey, N P (NSW) 1998 *S* 2(R), *SA* 2(R), *Fj* (R), *Tg* (R), *F, E* 2, 1999 *I* 1(R),2(R), *E, SA* 1, *NZ* 1, *SA* 2, *NZ* 2(t&R), [*R* (R), *I* 3(R), *US, SA* 3(R), *F* (R)], 2000 *S* (R), *E* (R), 2001 *BI* 1,2,3, *SA* 1, *NZ* 1, *SA* 2, *NZ* 2
Griffin, T S (NSW) 1907 *NZ* 1,3, 1908 *W*, 1910 *NZ* 1,2, 1912 *US*
Grigg, P C (Q) 1980 *NZ* 3, 1982 *S* 2, *NZ* 1,2,3, 1983 *Arg* 2, *NZ*, 1984 *Fj, W, S*, 1985 *C* 1,2, *NZ, Fj* 1,2, 1986 *Arg* 1,2, *NZ* 1,2, 1987 *SK*, [*E, J, I, F, W*]
Grimmond, D N (NSW) 1964 *NZ* 2
Gudsell, K E (NSW) 1951 *NZ* 1,2,3
Guerassimoff, J (Q) 1963 *SA* 2,3,4, 1964 *NZ* 1,2,3, 1965 *SA* 2, 1966 *BI* 1,2, 1967 *E, I, F*
Gunther, W J (NSW) 1957 *NZ* 2

Hall, D (Q) 1980 *Fj, NZ* 1,2,3, 1981 *F* 1,2, 1982 *S* 1,2, *NZ* 1,2, 1983 *US, Arg* 1,2, *NZ, It*
Hamalainen, H A (Q) 1929 *NZ* 1,2,3
Hamilton, B G (NSW) 1946 *M*
Hammand, C A (NSW) 1908 *W*, 1909 *E*
Hammon, J D C (V) 1937 *SA* 2
Handy, C B (Q) 1978 *NZ* 3, 1979 *NZ, Arg* 1,2, 1980 *NZ* 1,2
Hanley, R G (Q) 1983 *US* (R), *It* (R), 1985 *Fj* 2(R)
Hardcastle, P A (NSW) 1946 *NZ* 1, *M, NZ* 2, 1947 *NZ* 1, 1949 *M* 3
Hardcastle, W R (NSW) 1899 *BI* 4, 1903 *NZ*
Harding, M A (NSW) 1983 *It*
Hardy, M D (ACT) 1997 *F* 1(t), 2(R), *NZ* 1(R), 3(R), *Arg* 1(R), 2(R), 1998 *Tg, WS*
Harrison, J B (ACT) 2001 *BI* 3, *NZ* 1, *SA* 2
Harry, R L L (NSW) 1996 *W* 1,2, *NZ* 1, *SA* 1(t), *NZ* 2, *It, S*, 1997 *F* 1,2, *NZ* 1,2, *SA* 1, *NZ* 3, *SA* 2, *Arg* 1,2, *E* 2, *S*, 1998 *E* 1, *S* 1,2, *NZ* 1, *Fj*, 1999 *SA* 2, *NZ* 2, [*R, I* 3, *W, SA* 3, *F*], 2000 *Arg* 1,2, *SA* 1, *NZ* 1, *SA* 2, *NZ* 2, *SA* 3
Hartill, M N (NSW) 1986 *NZ* 1,2,3, 1987 *SK*, [*J*], *Arg* 1, 1988 *NZ* 1,2, *E, It*, 1989 *BI* 1(R), 2,3, *F* 1,2, 1995 *Arg* 1(R), 2(R), [*C*], *NZ* 1,2
Harvey, P B (Q) 1949 *M* 1,2
Harvey, R M (NSW) 1958 *F, M* 3
Hatherell, W I (Q) 1952 *Fj* 1,2
Hauser, R G (Q) 1975 *J* 1(R), 2, *W* (R), 1976 *E, I, US, Fj* 1,2,3, *F* 1,2, 1978 *W* 1,2, 1979 *I* 1,2
Hawker, M J (NSW) 1980 *Fj, NZ* 1,2,3, 1981 *F* 1,2, *I, W*, 1982 *E, S* 1,2, *NZ* 1,2,3, 1983 *US, Arg* 1,2, *NZ, It, F* 1,2, 1984 *NZ* 1,2,3, 1987 *NZ*
Hawthorne, P F (NSW) 1962 *NZ* 3,4,5, 1963 *E, SA* 1,2,3,4, 1964 *NZ* 1,2,3, 1965 *SA* 1,2, 1966 *BI* 1,2, *W*, 1967 *E, I* 1, *F, I* 2, *NZ*
Hayes, E S (Q) 1934 *NZ* 1,2, 1938 *NZ* 1,2,3

Heath, A (NSW) 1996 *C, SA* 1, *NZ* 2, *SA* 2, *It*, 1997 *NZ* 2, *SA* 1, *E* 2(R)
Heinrich, E L (NSW) 1961 *Fj* 1,2,3, *SA* 2, *F*, 1962 *NZ* 1,2,3, 1963 *E, SA* 1
Heinrich, V W (NSW) 1954 *Fj* 1,2
Heming, R J (NSW) 1961 *Fj* 2,3, *SA* 1,2, *F*, 1962 *NZ* 2,3,4,5, 1963 *SA* 2,3,4, 1964 *NZ* 1,2,3, 1965 *SA* 1,2, 1966 *BI* 1,2, *W*, 1967 *F*
Hemingway, W H (NSW) 1928 *NZ* 2,3, 1931 *M, NZ*, 1932 *NZ* 3
Henry, A R (Q) 1899 *BI* 2
Herbert, A G (Q) 1987 *SK* (R), [*F* (R)], 1990 *F* 1(R), *US, NZ* 2,3, 1991 [*WS*], 1992 *NZ* 3(R), 1993 *NZ* (R), *SA* 2(R)
Herbert, D J (Q) 1994 *I* 2, *It* 1,2, *WS* (R), 1995 *Arg* 1,2, [*SA, R*], 1996 *C, SA* 2, *It, S, I*, 1997 *NZ* 1, 1998 *E* 1, *S* 1,2, *NZ* 1, *SA* 1, *NZ* 2, *SA* 2, *Fj, Tg, WS, F, E* 2, 1999 *I* 1,2, *E, SA* 1, *NZ* 1, *SA* 2, *NZ* 2, [*R, I* 3, *W, SA* 3, *F*], 2000 *Arg* 1,2, *SA* 1, *NZ* 1, *SA* 2, *NZ* 2, *SA* 3, *F, S, E*, 2001 *BI* 1,2,3, *SA* 1, *NZ* 1, *SA* 2, *NZ* 2
Herd, H V (NSW) 1931 *M*
Hickey, J (NSW) 1908 *W*, 1909 *E*
Hill, J (NSW) 1925 *NZ* 1
Hillhouse, D W (Q) 1975 *S*, 1976 *E, Fj* 1,2,3, *F* 1,2, 1978 *W* 1,2, 1983 *US, Arg* 1,2, *NZ, It, F* 1,2
Hills, E F (V) 1950 *BI* 1,2
Hindmarsh, J A (Q) 1904 *BI* 1
Hindmarsh, J C (NSW) 1975 *J* 2, *S, W*, 1976 *US, Fj* 1,2,3, *F* 1,2
Hipwell, J N B (NSW) 1968 *NZ* 1(R), 2, *F, I, S*, 1969 *W, SA* 1,2,3,4, 1970 *S*, 1971 *SA* 1,2, *F* 1,2, 1972 *F* 1,2, 1973 *Tg* 1, *W, E*, 1974 *NZ* 1,2,3, 1975 *E* 1,2, *J* 1, *S, W*, 1978 *NZ* 1,2,3, 1981 *F* 1,2, *I, W*, 1982 *E*
Hirschberg, W A (NSW) 1905 *NZ*
Hodgins, C H (NSW) 1910 *NZ* 1,2,3
Hodgson, A J (NSW) 1933 *SA* 2,3,4, 1934 *NZ* 1, 1936 *NZ* 1,2, *M*, 1937 *SA* 2, 1938 *NZ* 1,2,3
Holbeck, J C (ACT) 1997 *NZ* 1(R), *E* 1, *NZ* 2, *SA* 1, *NZ* 3, *SA* 2, 2001 *BI* 3(R)
Holdsworth, J W (NSW) 1921 *SA* 1,2,3, 1922 *M* 2,3, *NZ* 1(R)
Holt, N C (Q) 1984 *Fj*
Honan, B D (Q) 1968 *NZ* 1(R), 2, *F, I, S*, 1969 *SA* 1,2,3,4
Honan, R E (Q) 1964 *NZ* 1,2
Horan, T J (Q) 1989 *NZ, F* 1,2, 1990 *F* 1, *NZ* 1,2,3, 1991 *W, E, NZ* 1,2, [*Arg, WS, W, I, NZ, E*], 1992 *S* 1,2, *NZ* 1,2,3, *SA, I, W*, 1993 *Tg, NZ, SA* 1,2,3, *C, F* 1,2, 1995 [*C, R, E*], *NZ* 1,2, 1996 *W* 1,2, *C, NZ* 1, *SA* 1, *It, S, I, W* 3, 1997 *F* 1,2, *NZ* 1, *E* 1, *NZ* 2, *Arg* 1,2, *E* 2, *S*, 1998 *E* 1, *S* 1,2, *NZ* 1, *SA* 1, *NZ* 2, *SA* 2, *NZ* 3, *Fj, Tg, WS*, 1999 *I* 1,2, *E, SA* 1, *NZ* 1, [*I* 3, *W, SA* 3, *F*], 2000 *Arg* 1
Horodam, D J (Q) 1913 *NZ* 2
Horsley, G R (Q) 1954 *Fj* 2
Horton, P A (NSW) 1974 *NZ* 1,2,3, 1975 *E* 1,2, *J* 1,2, *S, W*, 1976 *E, F* 1,2, 1978 *W* 1,2, *NZ* 1,2,3, 1979 *NZ, Arg* 1
Hoskins, J E (NSW) 1924 *NZ* 1,2,3
How, R A (NSW) 1967 *I* 2
Howard, J (Q) 1938 *NZ* 1,2
Howard, J L (NSW) 1970 *S*, 1971 *SA* 1, 1972 *F* 1(R), *NZ* 2, 1973 *Tg* 1,2, *W*
Howard, P W (Q, ACT) 1993 *NZ*, 1994 *WS, NZ*, 1995 *NZ* 1(R), 2(t), 1996 *W* 1,2, *SA* 1, *NZ* 2, *SA* 2, *It, S, W* 3, 1997 *F* 1,2, *NZ* 1, *Arg* 1,2, *E* 2, *S*
Howell, M L (NSW) 1946 *NZ* 1(R), 1947 *NZ* 1, *S, I, W*
Hughes, B D (NSW) 1913 *NZ* 2,3
Hughes, J C (NSW) 1907 *NZ* 1,3
Hughes, N McL (NSW) 1953 *SA* 1,2,3,4, 1955 *NZ* 1,2,3, 1956 *SA* 1,2, 1958 *W, I, E, S, F*
Humphreys, O W (NSW) 1920 *NZ* 3, 1921 *NZ*, 1922 *M* 1,2,3, 1925 *NZ* 1
Hutchinson, E E (NSW) 1937 *SA* 1,2
Hutchinson, F E (NSW) 1936 *NZ* 1,2, 1938 *NZ* 1,3

Ide, W P J (Q) 1938 *NZ* 2,3
Ives, W N (NSW) 1926 *NZ* 1,2,3,4, 1929 *NZ* 3

James, P M (Q) 1958 *M* 2,3
James, S L (NSW) 1987 *SK* (R), [*E* (R)], *NZ, Arg* 1,2, 1988 *NZ* 2(R)
Jamieson, A E (NSW) 1925 *NZ* 3(R)
Jaques, T (ACT) 2000 *SA* 1(R), *NZ* 1(R)
Jessep, E M (V) 1934 *NZ* 1,2
Johnson, A P (NSW) 1946 *NZ* 1, *M*

Johnson, B B (NSW) 1952 *Fj* 1,2, *NZ* 1,2, 1953 *SA* 2,3,4, 1955 *NZ* 1,2
Johnson, P G (NSW) 1959 *BI* 1,2, 1961 *Fj* 1,2,3, *SA* 1,2, *F*, 1962 *NZ* 1,2,3,4,5, 1963 *E, SA* 1,2,3,4, 1964 *NZ* 1,2,3, 1965 *SA* 1,2, 1966 *BI* 1,2, *W, S*, 1967 *E, I* 1, *F, I* 2, *NZ*, 1968 *NZ* 1,2, *F, I, S*, 1970 *S*, 1971 *SA* 1,2, *F* 1,2
Johnstone, B (Q) 1993 *Tg* (R)
Jones, G G (Q) 1952 *Fj* 1,2, 1953 *SA* 1,2,3,4, 1954 *Fj* 1,2, 1955 *NZ* 1,2,3, 1956 *SA* 1
Jones, H (NSW) 1913 *NZ* 1,2,3
Jones, P A (NSW) 1963 *E, SA* 1
Jorgensen, P (NSW) 1992 *S* 1(R), 2(R)
Joyce, J E (NSW) 1903 *NZ*
Judd, H A (NSW) 1903 *NZ*, 1904 *BI* 1,2,3, 1905 *NZ*
Judd, P B (NSW) 1925 *NZ* 4, 1926 *NZ* 1,2,3,4, 1927 *I, W, S*, 1928 *E*, 1931 *M, NZ*
Junee, D K (NSW) 1989 *F* 1(R), 2(R), 1994 *WS* (R), *NZ* (R)

Kafer, R B (ACT) 1999 *NZ* 2, [*R, US* (R)], 2000 *Arg* 1(R),2, *SA* 1, *NZ* 1(t&R), *SA* 2(R),3(R), *F, S, E*
Kahl, P R (Q) 1992 *W*
Kassulke, N (Q) 1985 *C* 1,2
Kay, A R (V) 1958 *NZ* 2, 1959 *BI* 2
Kay, P (NSW) 1988 *E* 2
Kearney, K H (NSW) 1947 *NZ* 1,2, *S, I, W*, 1948 *E, F*
Kearns, P N (NSW) 1989 *NZ, F* 1,2, 1990 *F* 1,2,3, *US, NZ* 1,2,3, 1991 *W, E, NZ* 1,2, [*Arg, WS, W, I, NZ, E*], 1992 *S* 1,2, *NZ* 1,2,3, *SA, I, W*, 1993 *Tg, NZ, SA* 1,2,3, *C, F* 1,2, 1994 *I* 1,2, *It* 1,2, *WS, NZ*, 1995 *Arg* 1,2, [*SA, C, E*], *NZ* 1,2, 1998 *E* 1, *S* 1,2, *NZ* 1, *SA* 1, *NZ* 2, *SA* 2, *NZ* 3, *Fj, WS, F, E* 2, 1999 *I* 2(R), *SA* 1(R),2, *NZ* 2, [*R, I* 3]
Kefu, R S T (Q) 1997 *SA* 2(R), 1998 *E* 1, *S* 1,2, *NZ* 1, *SA* 1, *NZ* 2, *SA* 2, *NZ* 3, *Fj* (R), *Tg, WS* (R), *F, E* 2, 1999 *I* 1,2, *E, SA* 1, *NZ* 1(R), *SA* 2, *NZ* 2, [*R, I* 3, *SA* 3, *F*], 2000 *SA* 1(t&R), *NZ* 1(R), *SA* 2(R), *NZ* 2, *SA* 3(R), *F, S, E*, 2001 *BI* 1,2,3, *SA* 1, *NZ* 1, *SA* 2, *NZ* 2
Kelaher, J D (NSW) 1933 *SA* 1,2,3,4,5, 1934 *NZ* 1,2, 1936 *NZ* 1,2, *M*, 1937 *SA* 1,2, 1938 *NZ* 3
Kelaher, T P (NSW) 1992 *NZ* 1, *I* (R), 1993 *NZ*
Kelleher, R J (Q) 1969 *SA* 2,3
Keller, D H (NSW) 1947 *NZ* 1, *S, I, W*, 1948 *E, F*
Kelly, A J (NSW) 1899 *BI* 1
Kelly, R L F (NSW) 1936 *NZ* 1,2, *M*, 1937 *SA* 1,2, 1938 *NZ* 1,2
Kent, A (Q) 1912 *US*
Kerr, F R (V) 1938 *NZ* 1
King, S C (NSW) 1926 *NZ* 1,2,3,4(R), 1927 *W, S*, 1928 *E, F*, 1929 *NZ* 1,2,3, 1930 *BI*, 1932 *NZ* 1,2
Knight, M (NSW) 1978 *W* 1,2, *NZ* 1
Knight, S O (NSW) 1969 *SA* 2,4, 1970 *S*, 1971 *SA* 1,2,3
Knox, D J (NSW, ACT) 1985 *Fj* 1,2, 1990 *US* (R), 1994 *WS, NZ*, 1996 *It, S, I*, 1997 *SA* 1, *NZ* 3, *SA* 2, *Arg* 1,2
Kraefft, D F (NSW) 1947 *NZ* 2, *S, I, W*, 1948 *E, F*
Kreutzer, S D (Q) 1914 *NZ* 2

Lamb, J S (NSW) 1928 *NZ* 1,2, *M*
Lambie, J K (NSW) 1974 *NZ* 1,2,3, 1975 *W*
Lane, R E (NSW) 1921 *SA* 1
Lane, T A (Q) 1985 *C* 1,2, *NZ*
Lang, C W P (V) 1938 *NZ* 2,3
Langford, J F (ACT) 1997 *NZ* 3, *SA* 2, *E* 2, *S*
Larkham, S J (ACT) 1996 *W* 2(R), 1997 *F* 1,2, *NZ* 1,2(R), *SA* 1, *NZ* 3, *SA* 2, *Arg* 1,2, *E* 2, *S*, 1998 *E* 1, *S* 1,2, *NZ* 1, *SA* 1, *NZ* 2, *SA* 2, *NZ* 3, *Fj, Tg* (t), *WS, F, E* 2, 1999 [*I* 3, *US, W, SA* 3, *F*], 2000 *Arg* 1,2, *SA* 1, *NZ* 1, *SA* 2, *NZ* 2, *SA* 3, 2001 *BI* 1,2, *NZ* 1, *SA* 2, *NZ* 2
Larkin, E R (NSW) 1903 *NZ*
Larkin, K K (Q) 1958 *M* 2,3
Latham, C E (Q) 1998 *F, E* 2, 1999 *I* 1,2, *E*, [*US*], 2000 *Arg* 1,2, *SA* 1, *NZ* 1, *SA* 2, *NZ* 2, *SA* 3, *F, S, E*, 2001 *BI* 1,2(R), *SA* 1(R), *NZ* 1(R), *SA* 2, *NZ* 2
Latimer, N B (NSW) 1957 *NZ* 2
Lawton, R (Q) 1988 *E* 1, *NZ* 2(R), 3, *S*
Lawton, T (NSW, Q) 1920 *NZ* 1,2, 1925 *NZ* 4, 1927 *I, W, S*, 1928 *E, F*, 1929 *NZ* 1,2,3, 1930 *BI*, 1932 *NZ* 1,2
Lawton, T A (Q) 1983 *F* 1(R), 2, 1984 *Fj, NZ* 1,2,3, *E, I, W, S*, 1985 *C* 1,2, *NZ, Fj* 1, 1986 *It, F, Arg* 1,2, *NZ* 1,2,3, 1987 *SK*, [*E, US, I, F, W*], *NZ, Arg* 1,2, 1988 *E* 1,2, *NZ* 1,2,3, *E, S, It*, 1989 *BI* 1,2,3
Laycock, W M B (NSW) 1925 *NZ* 2,3,4, 1926 *NZ* 2
Leeds, A J (NSW) 1986 *NZ* 3, 1987 [*US, W*], *NZ, Arg* 1,2, 1988 *E* 1,2, *NZ* 1,2,3, *E, S, It*

Lenehan, J K (NSW) 1958 *W, E, S, F, M* 1,2,3, 1959 *BI* 1,2, 1961 *SA* 1,2, *F*, 1962 *NZ* 2,3,4,5, 1965 *SA* 1,2, 1966 *W, S*, 1967 *E, I* 1, *F, I* 2
L'Estrange, R D (Q) 1971 *F* 1,2, 1972 *NZ* 1,2,3, 1973 *Tg* 1,2, *W, E*, 1974 *NZ* 1,2,3, 1975 *S, W*, 1976 *I, US*
Lewis, L S (Q) 1934 *NZ* 1,2, 1936 *NZ* 2, 1938 *NZ* 1
Lidbury, S (NSW) 1987 *Arg* 1, 1988 *E* 2
Lillicrap, C P (Q) 1985 *Fj* 2, 1987 [*US, I, F, W*], 1989 *BI* 1, 1991 [*WS*]
Lindsay, R T G (Q) 1932 *NZ* 3
Lisle, R J (NSW) 1961 *Fj* 1,2,3, *SA* 1
Little, J S (Q, NSW) 1989 *F* 1,2, 1990 *F* 1,2,3, *US*, 1991 *W, E, NZ* 1,2, [*Arg, W, I, NZ, E*], 1992 *NZ* 1,2,3, *SA, I, W*, 1993 *Tg, NZ, SA* 1,2,3, *C, F* 1,2, 1994 *WS, NZ*, 1995 *Arg* 1,2, [*SA, C, E*], *NZ* 1,2, 1996 *It* (R), *I, W* 3, 1997 *F* 1,2, *E* 1, *NZ* 2, *SA* 1, *NZ* 3, *SA* 2, 1998 *E* 1(R), *S* 2(R), *NZ* 2, *SA* 2(R), *NZ* 3, *Fj, Tg, WS, F, E* 2, 1999 *I* 1(R),2, *SA* 2(R), *NZ* 2, [*R, I* 3(t&R), *US, W* (R), *SA* 3(t&R), *F* (R)], 2000 *Arg* 1(R),2(R), *SA* 1(R), *NZ* 1, *SA* 2, *NZ* 2, *SA* 3
Livermore, A E (Q) 1946 *NZ* 1, *M*
Loane, M E (Q) 1973 *Tg* 1,2, 1974 *NZ* 1, 1975 *E* 1,2, *J* 1, 1976 *E, I, Fj* 1,2,3, *F* 1,2, 1978 *NZ* 1,2, 1979 *I* 1,2, *NZ, Arg* 1,2, 1981 *F* 1,2, *I, W, S*, 1982 *E, S* 1,2
Logan, D L (NSW) 1958 *M* 1
Loudon, D B (NSW) 1921 *NZ*, 1922 *M* 1,2,3
Loudon, R B (NSW) 1923 *NZ* 1(R), 2,3, 1928 *NZ* 1,2,3, *M*, 1929 *NZ* 2, 1933 *SA* 2,3,4,5, 1934 *NZ* 2
Love, E W (NSW) 1932 *NZ* 1,2,3
Lowth, D R (NSW) 1958 *NZ* 1
Lucas, B C (Q) 1905 *NZ*
Lucas, P W (NSW) 1982 *NZ* 1,2,3
Lutge, D (NSW) 1903 *NZ*, 1904 *BI* 1,2,3
Lynagh, M P (Q) 1984 *Fj, E, I, W, S*, 1985 *C* 1,2, *NZ*, 1986 *It, F, Arg* 1,2, *NZ* 1,2,3, 1987 [*E, US, J, I, F, W*], *Arg* 1,2, 1988 *E* 1,2, *NZ* 1,3(R), *E, S, It*, 1989 *BI* 1,2,3, *NZ, F* 1,2, 1990 *F* 1,2,3, *US, NZ* 1,2,3, 1991 *W, E, NZ* 1,2, [*Arg, WS, W, I, NZ, E*], 1992 *S* 1,2, *NZ* 1,2,3, *SA, I*, 1993 *Tg, C, F* 1,2, 1994 *I* 1,2, *It* 1, 1995 *Arg* 1,2, [*SA, C, E*]
Lyons, D J (NSW) 2000 *Arg* 1(t&R),2(R), 2001 *BI* 1(R), *SA* 1(R)

McArthur, M (NSW) 1909 *E*
McBain, M I (Q) 1983 *It, F* 1, 1985 *Fj* 2, 1986 *It* (R), 1987 [*J*], 1988 *E* 2(R), 1989 *BI* 1(R)
MacBride, J W T (NSW) 1946 *NZ* 1, *M, NZ* 2, 1947 *NZ* 1,2, *S, I, W*, 1948 *E, F*
McCabe, A J M (NSW) 1909 *E*
McCall, R J (Q) 1989 *F* 1,2, 1990 *F* 1,2,3, *US, NZ* 1,2,3, 1991 *W, E, NZ* 1,2, [*Arg, W, I, NZ, E*], 1992 *S* 1,2, *NZ* 1,2,3, *SA, I, W*, 1993 *Tg, NZ, SA* 1,2,3, *C, F* 1,2, 1994 *It* 2, 1995 *Arg* 1,2, [*SA, R, E*]
McCarthy, F J C (Q) 1950 *BI* 1
McCowan, R H (Q) 1899 *BI* 1,2,4
McCue, P A (NSW) 1907 *NZ* 1,3, 1908 *W*, 1909 *E*
McDermott, L C (Q) 1962 *NZ* 1,2
McDonald, B S (NSW) 1969 *SA* 4, 1970 *S*
McDonald, J C (Q) 1938 *NZ* 2,3
Macdougall, D G (NSW) 1961 *Fj* 1, *SA* 1
Macdougall, S G (NSW, ACT) 1971 *SA* 3, 1973 *E*, 1974 *NZ* 1,2,3, 1975 *E* 1,2, 1976 *E*
McGhie, G H (Q) 1929 *NZ* 2,3, 1930 *BI*
McGill, A N (NSW) 1968 *NZ* 1,2, *F*, 1969 *W, SA* 1,2,3,4, 1970 *S*, 1971 *SA* 1,2,3, *F* 1,2, 1972 *F* 1,2, *NZ* 1,2,3, 1973 *Tg* 1,2
McIntyre, A J (Q) 1982 *NZ* 1,2,3, 1983 *F* 1,2, 1984 *Fj, NZ* 1,2,3, *E, I, W, S*, 1985 *C* 1,2, *NZ, Fj* 1,2, 1986 *It, F, Arg* 1,2, 1987 [*E, US, I, F, W*], *NZ, Arg* 2, 1988 *E* 1,2, *NZ* 1,2,3, *E, S, It*, 1989 *NZ*
McKay, G R (NSW) 1920 *NZ* 2, 1921 *SA* 2,3, 1922 *M* 1,2,3
McKenzie, E J A (NSW, ACT) 1990 *F* 1,2,3, *US, NZ* 1,2,3, 1991 *W, E, NZ* 1,2, [*Arg, W, I, NZ, E*], 1992 *S* 1,2, *NZ* 1,2,3, *SA, I, W*, 1993 *Tg, NZ, SA* 1,2,3, *C, F* 1,2, 1994 *I* 1,2, *It* 1,2, *WS, NZ*, 1995 *Arg* 1,2, [*SA, C* (R), *R, E*], *NZ* 2, 1996 *W* 1,2, 1997 *F* 1,2, *NZ* 1, *E* 1
McKid, W A (NSW) 1976 *E, Fj* 1, 1978 *NZ* 2,3, 1979 *I* 1,2
McKinnon, A (Q) 1904 *BI* 2
McKivat, C H (NSW) 1907 *NZ* 1,3, 1908 *W*, 1909 *E*
McLaren, S D (NSW) 1926 *NZ* 4
McLaughlin, R E M (NSW) 1936 *NZ* 1,2
McLean, A D (Q) 1933 *SA* 1,2,3,4,5, 1934 *NZ* 1,2, 1936 *NZ* 1,2, *M*
McLean, J D (Q) 1904 *BI* 2,3, 1905 *NZ*

McLean, J J (Q) 1971 *SA* 2,3, *F* 1,2, 1972 *F* 1,2, *NZ* 1,2,3, *Fj*, 1973 *W, E*, 1974 *NZ* 1
McLean, P E (Q) 1974 *NZ* 1,2,3, 1975 *J* 1,2, *S, W*, 1976 *E, I, Fj* 1,2,3, *F* 1,2, 1978 *W* 1,2, *NZ* 2, 1979 *I* 1,2, *NZ, Arg* 1,2, 1980 *Fj*, 1981 *F* 1,2, *I, W, S*, 1982 *E, S* 2
McLean, P W (Q) 1978 *NZ* 1,2,3, 1979 *I* 1,2, *NZ, Arg* 1,2, 1980 *Fj* (R), *NZ* 3, 1981 *I, W, S*, 1982 *E, S* 1,2
McLean, R A (NSW) 1971 *SA* 1,2,3, *F* 1,2
McLean, W M (Q) 1946 *NZ* 1, *M, NZ* 2, 1947 *NZ* 1,2
McMahon, M J (Q) 1913 *NZ* 1
McMaster, R E (Q) 1946 *NZ* 1, *M, NZ* 2, 1947 *NZ* 1,2, *I, W*
MacMillan, D I (Q) 1950 *BI* 1,2
McMullen, K V (NSW) 1962 *NZ* 3,5, 1963 *E, SA* 1
McShane, J M S (NSW) 1937 *SA* 1,2
Mackay, G (NSW) 1926 *NZ* 4
Mackney, W A R (NSW) 1933 *SA* 1,5, 1934 *NZ* 1,2
Magrath, E (NSW) 1961 *Fj* 1, *SA* 2, *F*
Maguire, D J (Q) 1989 *BI* 1,2,3
Malcolm, S J (NSW) 1927 *S*, 1928 *E, F, NZ* 1,2, *M*, 1929 *NZ* 1,2,3, 1930 *BI*, 1931 *NZ*, 1932 *NZ* 1,2,3, 1933 *SA* 4,5, 1934 *NZ* 1,2
Malone, J H (NSW) 1936 *NZ* 1,2, *M*, 1937 *SA* 2
Malouf, B P (NSW) 1982 *NZ* 1
Mandible, E F (NSW) 1907 *NZ* 2,3, 1908 *W*
Manning, J (NSW) 1904 *BI* 2
Manning, R C S (Q) 1967 *NZ*
Mansfield, B W (NSW) 1975 *J* 2
Manu, D T (NSW) 1995 [*R* (t)], *NZ* 1,2, 1996 *W* 1,2(R), *SA* 1, *NZ* 2, *It, S, I*, 1997 *F* 1, *NZ* 1(t), *E* 1, *NZ* 2, *SA* 1
Marks, H (NSW) 1899 *BI* 1,2
Marks, R J P (Q) 1962 *NZ* 4,5, 1963 *E, SA* 2,3,4, 1964 *NZ* 1,2,3, 1965 *SA* 1,2, 1966 *W, S*, 1967 *E, I* 1, *F, I* 2
Marrott, R (NSW) 1920 *NZ* 1,3
Marrott, W J (NSW) 1922 *NZ* 2,3, 1923 *M* 1,2,3, *NZ* 1,2
Marshall, J S (NSW) 1949 *M* 1
Martin, G J (Q) 1989 *BI* 1,2,3, *NZ, F* 1,2, 1990 *F* 1,3(R), *NZ* 1
Martin, M C (NSW) 1980 *Fj, NZ* 1,2, 1981 *F* 1,2, *W* (R)
Massey-Westropp, M (NSW) 1914 *NZ* 3
Mathers, M J (NSW) 1980 *Fj, NZ* 2(R)
Maund, J W (NSW) 1903 *NZ*
Mayne, A V (NSW) 1920 *NZ* 1,2,3, 1922 *M* 1
Meadows, J E C (V, Q) 1974 *NZ* 1, 1975 *S, W*, 1976 *I, US, Fj* 1,3, *F* 1,2, 1978 *NZ* 1,2,3, 1979 *I* 1,2, 1981 *I, S*, 1982 *E, NZ* 2,3, 1983 *US, Arg* 2, *NZ*
Meadows, R W (NSW) 1958 *M* 1,2,3, *NZ* 1,2,3
Meagher, F W (NSW) 1923 *NZ* 3, 1924 *NZ* 3, 1925 *NZ* 4, 1926 *NZ* 1,2,3, 1927 *I, W*
Meibusch, J H (Q) 1904 *BI* 3
Meibusch, L S (Q) 1912 *US*
Melrose, T C (NSW) 1978 *NZ* 3, 1979 *I* 1,2, *NZ, Arg* 1,2
Merrick, S (NSW) 1995 *NZ* 1,2
Messenger, H H (NSW) 1907 *NZ* 2,3
Middleton, S A (NSW) 1909 *E*, 1910 *NZ* 1,2,3
Miller, A R (NSW) 1952 *Fj* 1,2, *NZ* 1,2, 1953 *SA* 1,2,3,4, 1954 *Fj* 1,2, 1955 *NZ* 1,2,3, 1956 *SA* 1,2, 1957 *NZ* 1,2, 1958 *W, E, S, F, M* 1,2,3, 1959 *BI* 1,2, 1961 *Fj* 1,2,3, *SA* 2, *F*, 1962 *NZ* 1,2, 1966 *BI* 1,2, *W, S*, 1967 *I* 1, *F, I* 2, *NZ*
Miller, J M (NSW) 1962 *NZ* 1, 1963 *E, SA* 1, 1966 *W, S*, 1967 *E*
Miller, J S (Q) 1986 *NZ* 2,3, 1987 *SK*, [*US, I, F*], *NZ, Arg* 1,2, 1988 *E* 1,2, *NZ* 2,3, *E, S, It*, 1989 *BI* 1,2,3, *NZ*, 1990 *F* 1,3, 1991 *W*, [*WS, W, I*]
Miller, S W J (NSW) 1899 *BI* 3
Mingey, N (NSW) 1920 *NZ* 3, 1921 *SA* 1,2,3, 1923 *M* 1, *NZ* 1,2
Monaghan, L E (NSW) 1973 *E*, 1974 *NZ* 1,2,3, 1975 *E* 1,2, *S, W*, 1976 *E, I, US, F* 1, 1978 *W* 1,2, *NZ* 1, 1979 *I* 1,2
Monti, C I A (Q) 1938 *NZ* 2
Moon, B J (Q) 1978 *NZ* 2,3, 1979 *I* 1,2, *NZ, Arg* 1,2, 1980 *Fj, NZ* 1,2,3, 1981 *F* 1,2, *I, W, S*, 1982 *E, S* 1,2, 1983 *US, Arg* 1,2, *NZ, It, F* 1,2, 1984 *Fj, NZ* 1,2,3, *E*, 1986 *It, F, Arg* 1,2
Mooney, T P (Q) 1954 *Fj* 1,2
Moore, R S (ACT, NSW) 1999 [*US*], 2001 *BI* 2,3, *SA* 1, *NZ* 1, *SA* 2, *NZ* 2
Moran, H M (NSW) 1908 *W*
Morgan, G (Q) 1992 *NZ* 1(R), 3(R), *W*, 1993 *Tg, NZ, SA* 1,2,3, *C, F* 1,2, 1994 *I* 1,2, *It* 1, *WS, NZ*, 1996 *W* 1,2, *C, NZ* 1, *SA* 1, *NZ* 2, 1997 *E* 1, *NZ* 2
Morrissey, C V (NSW) 1925 *NZ* 2,3,4, 1926 *NZ* 2,3
Morrissey, W (Q) 1914 *NZ* 2
Mortlock, S A (ACT) 2000 *Arg* 1,2, *SA* 1, *NZ* 1, *SA* 2, *NZ* 2, *SA* 3, *F, S, E*

Morton, A R (NSW) 1957 *NZ* 1,2, 1958 *F, M* 1,2,3, *NZ* 1,2,3, 1959 *BI* 1,2
Mossop, R P (NSW) 1949 *NZ* 1,2, 1950 *BI* 1,2, 1951 *NZ* 1
Moutray, I E (NSW) 1963 *SA* 2
Mulligan, P J (NSW) 1925 *NZ* 1(R)
Munsie, A (NSW) 1928 *NZ* 2
Murdoch, A R (NSW) 1993 *F* 1, 1996 *W* 1
Murphy, P J (Q) 1910 *NZ* 1,2,3, 1913 *NZ* 1,2,3, 1914 *NZ* 1,2,3
Murphy, W (Q) 1912 *US*

Nasser, B P (Q) 1989 *F* 1,2, 1990 *F* 1,2,3, *US, NZ* 2, 1991 [*WS*]
Newman, E W (NSW) 1922 *NZ* 1
Nicholson, F C (Q) 1904 *BI* 3
Nicholson, F V (Q) 1903 *NZ*, 1904 *BI* 1
Niuqila, A S (NSW) 1988 *S, It*, 1989 *BI* 1
Noriega, E P (ACT) 1998 *F, E* 2, 1999 *I* 1,2, *E, SA* 1, *NZ* 1, *SA* 2(R), *NZ* 2(R)
Nothling, O E (NSW) 1921 *SA* 1,2,3, *NZ*, 1922 *M* 1,2,3, *NZ* 1,2,3, 1923 *M* 1,2,3, *NZ* 1,2,3, 1924 *NZ* 1,2,3
Nucifora, D V (Q) 1991 [*Arg* (R)], 1993 *C* (R)

O'Brien, F W H (NSW) 1937 *SA* 2, 1938 *NZ* 3
O'Connor, J A (NSW) 1928 *NZ* 1,2,3, *M*
O'Connor, M (ACT) 1994 *I* 1
O'Connor, M D (ACT, Q) 1979 *Arg* 1,2, 1980 *Fj, NZ* 1,2,3, 1981 *F* 1,2, *I*, 1982 *E, S* 1,2
O'Donnell, C (NSW) 1913 *NZ* 1,2
O'Donnell, I C (NSW) 1899 *BI* 3,4
O'Donnell, J B (NSW) 1928 *NZ* 1,3, *M*
O'Donnell, J M (NSW) 1899 *BI* 4
O'Gorman, J F (NSW) 1961 *Fj* 1, *SA* 1,2, *F*, 1962 *NZ* 2, 1963 *E, SA* 1,2,3,4, 1965 *SA* 1,2, 1966 *W, S*, 1967 *E, I* 1, *F, I* 2
O'Neill, D J (Q) 1964 *NZ* 1,2
O'Neill, J M (Q) 1952 *NZ* 1,2, 1956 *SA* 1,2
Ofahengaue, V (NSW) 1990 *NZ* 1,2,3, 1991 *W, E, NZ* 1,2, [*Arg, W, I, NZ, E*], 1992 *S* 1,2, *SA, I, W*, 1994 *WS, NZ*, 1995 *Arg* 1,2(R), [*SA, C, E*], *NZ* 1,2, 1997 *Arg* 1(t + R), 2(R), *E* 2, *S*, 1998 *E* 1(R), *S* 1(R),2(R), *NZ* 1(R), *SA* 1(R), *NZ* 2(R), *SA* 2(R), *NZ* 3(R), *Fj, WS, F* (R)
Ormiston, I W L (NSW) 1920 *NZ* 1,2,3
Osborne, D H (V) 1975 *E* 1,2, *J* 1
Outterside, R (NSW) 1959 *BI* 1,2
Oxenham, A McE (Q) 1904 *BI* 2, 1907 *NZ* 2
Oxlade, A M (Q) 1904 *BI* 2,3, 1905 *NZ*, 1907 *NZ* 2
Oxlade, B D (Q) 1938 *NZ* 1,2,3

Palfreyman, J R I. (NSW) 1929 *NZ* 1, 1930 *BI*, 1931 *NZ*, 1932 *NZ* 3
Panoho, G M (Q) 1998 *SA* 2(R), *NZ* 3(R), *Fj* (R), *Tg, WS* (R), 1999 *I* 2, *E, SA* 1(R), *NZ* 1, 2000 *Arg* 1(R),2(R), *SA* 1(R), *NZ* 1, *SA* 2(R),3(R), *F* (R), *S* (R), *E* (R), 2001 *BI* 1
Papworth, B (NSW) 1985 *Fj* 1,2, 1986 *It, Arg* 1,2, *NZ* 1,2,3, 1987 [*E, US, J* (R), *I, F*], *NZ, Arg* 1,2
Parker, A J (Q) 1983 *Arg* 1(R), 2, *NZ*
Parkinson, C E (Q) 1907 *NZ* 2
Paul, J A (ACT) 1998 *S* 1(R), *NZ* 1(R), *SA* 1(t), *Fj* (R), *Tg*, 1999 *I* 1,2, *E, SA* 1, *NZ* 1, [*R* (R), *I* 3(R), *W* (t), *F* (R)], 2000 *Arg* 1(R),2(R), *SA* 1(R), *NZ* 1(R), *SA* 2(R), *NZ* 2(R), *SA* 3(R), *F* (R), *S* (R), *E* (R), 2001 *BI* 1
Pashley, J J (NSW) 1954 *Fj* 1,2, 1958 *M* 1,2,3
Pauling, T P (NSW) 1936 *NZ* 1, 1937 *SA* 1
Payne, S J (NSW) 1996 *W* 2, *C, NZ* 1, *S*, 1997 *F* 1(t), *NZ* 2(R), *Arg* 2(t)
Pearse, G K (NSW) 1975 *W* (R), 1976 *I, US, Fj* 1,2,3, 1978 *NZ* 1,2,3
Penman, A P (NSW) 1905 *NZ*
Perrin, P D (Q) 1962 *NZ* 1
Perrin, T D (NSW) 1931 *M, NZ*
Phelps, R (NSW) 1955 *NZ* 2,3, 1956 *SA* 1,2, 1957 *NZ* 1,2, 1958 *W, I, E, S, F, M* 1, *NZ* 1,2,3, 1961 *Fj* 1,2,3, *SA* 1,2, *F*, 1962 *NZ* 1,2
Phipps, J A (NSW) 1953 *SA* 1,2,3,4, 1954 *Fj* 1,2, 1955 *NZ* 1,2,3, 1956 *SA* 1,2
Phipps, W J (NSW) 1928 *NZ* 2
Piggott, H R (NSW) 1922 *M* 3(R)
Pilecki, S J (Q) 1978 *W* 1,2, *NZ* 1,2, 1979 *I* 1,2, *NZ, Arg* 1,2, 1980 *Fj, NZ* 1,2, 1982 *S* 1,2, 1983 *US, Arg* 1,2, *NZ*
Pini, M (Q) 1994 *I* 1, *It* 2, *WS, NZ*, 1995 *Arg* 1,2, [*SA, R* (t)]
Piper, B J C (NSW) 1946 *NZ* 1, *M, NZ* 2, 1947 *NZ* 1, *S, I, W*, 1948 *E, F*, 1949 *M*, 1,2,3

Poidevin, S P (NSW) 1980 *Fj, NZ* 1,2,3, 1981 *F* 1,2, *I, W, S*, 1982 *E, NZ* 1,2,3, 1983 *US, Arg* 1,2, *NZ, It, F* 1,2, 1984 *Fj, NZ* 1,2,3, *E, I, W, S*, 1985 *C* 1,2, *NZ, Fj* 1,2, 1986 *It, F, Arg* 1,2, *NZ* 1,2,3, 1987 *SK*, [*E, J, I, F, W*], *Arg* 1, 1988 *NZ* 1,2,3, 1989 *NZ*, 1991 *E, NZ* 1,2, [*Arg, W, I, NZ, E*]
Pope, A M (Q) 1968 *NZ* 2(R)
Potter, R T (Q) 1961 *Fj* 2
Potts, J M (NSW) 1957 *NZ* 1,2, 1958 *W, I*, 1959 *BI* 1
Prentice, C W (NSW) 1914 *NZ* 3
Prentice, W S (NSW) 1908 *W*, 1909 *E*, 1910 *NZ* 1,2,3, 1912 *US*
Price, R A (NSW) 1974 *NZ* 1,2,3, 1975 *E* 1,2, *J* 1,2, 1976 *US*
Primmer, C J (Q) 1951 *NZ* 1,3
Proctor, I J (NSW) 1967 *NZ*
Prosser, R B (NSW) 1967 *E, I* 1,2, *NZ*, 1968 *NZ* 1,2, *F, I, S*, 1969 *W, SA* 1,2,3,4, 1971 *SA* 1,2,3, *F* 1,2, 1972 *F* 1,2, *NZ* 1,2,3, *Fj*
Pugh, G H (NSW) 1912 *US*
Purcell, M P (Q) 1966 *W, S*, 1967 *I* 2
Purkis, E M (NSW) 1958 *S, M* 1
Pym, J E (NSW) 1923 *M* 1

Rainbow, A E (NSW) 1925 *NZ* 1
Ramalli, C (NSW) 1938 *NZ* 2,3
Ramsay, K M (NSW) 1936 *M*, 1937 *SA* 1, 1938 *NZ* 1,3
Rankin, R (NSW) 1936 *NZ* 1,2, *M*, 1937 *SA* 1,2, 1938 *NZ* 1,2
Rathie, D S (Q) 1972 *F* 1,2
Raymond, R L (NSW) 1920 *NZ* 1,2, 1921 *SA* 2,3, *NZ*, 1922 *M* 1,2,3, *NZ* 1,2,3, 1923 *M* 1,2
Redwood, C (Q) 1903 *NZ*, 1904 *BI* 1,2,3
Reid, E J (NSW) 1925 *NZ* 2,3,4
Reid, T W (NSW) 1961 *Fj* 1,2,3, *SA* 1, 1962 *NZ* 1
Reilly, N P (Q) 1968 *NZ* 1,2, *F, I, S*, 1969 *W, SA* 1,2,3,4
Reynolds, L J (NSW) 1910 *NZ* 2(R), 3
Reynolds, R J (NSW) 1984 *Fj, NZ* 1,2,3, 1985 *Fj* 1,2, 1986 *Arg* 1,2, *NZ* 1, 1987 [*J*]
Richards, E W (Q) 1904 *BI* 1,3, 1905 *NZ*, 1907 *NZ* 1(R), 2
Richards, G (NSW) 1978 *NZ* 2(R), 3, 1981 *F* 1
Richards, T J (Q) 1908 *W*, 1909 *E*, 1912 *US*
Richards, V S (NSW) 1936 *NZ* 1,2(R), *M*, 1937 *SA* 1, 1938 *NZ* 1
Richardson, G C (Q) 1971 *SA* 1,2,3, 1972 *NZ* 2,3, *Fj*, 1973 *Tg* 1,2, *W*
Rigney, W A (NSW) 1925 *NZ* 2,4, 1926 *NZ* 4
Riley, S A (NSW) 1903 *NZ*
Ritchie, E V (NSW) 1924 *NZ* 1,3, 1925 *NZ* 2,3
Roberts, B T (NSW) 1956 *SA* 2
Roberts, H F (Q) 1961 *Fj* 1,3, *SA* 2, *F*
Robertson, I J (NSW) 1975 *J* 1,2
Robinson, B J (ACT) 1996 *It* (R), *S* (R), *I* (R), 1997 *F* 1,2, *NZ* 1, *E* 1, *NZ* 2, *SA* 1(R), *NZ* 3(R), *SA* 2(R), *Arg* 1,2, *E* 2, *S*, 1998 *Tg*
Roche, C (Q) 1982 *S* 1,2, *NZ* 1,2,3, 1983 *US, Arg* 1,2, *NZ, It, F* 1,2, 1984 *Fj, NZ* 1,2,3, *I*
Rodriguez, E E (NSW) 1984 *Fj, NZ* 1,2,3, *E, I, W, S*, 1985 *C* 1,2, *NZ, Fj* 1, 1986 *It, F, Arg* 1,2, *NZ* 1,2,3, 1987 *SK*, [*E, J, W* (R)], *NZ, Arg* 1,2
Roebuck, M C (NSW) 1991 *W, E, NZ* 1,2, [*Arg, WS, W, I, NZ, E*], 1992 *S* 1,2, *NZ* 2,3, *SA, I, W*, 1993 *Tg, SA* 1,2,3, *C, F* 2
Roff, J W C (ACT) 1995 [*C, R*], *NZ* 1,2, 1996 *W* 1,2, *NZ* 1, *SA* 1, *NZ* 2, *SA* 2(R), *S, I, W* 3, 1997 *F* 1,2, *NZ* 1, *E* 1, *NZ* 2, *NZ* 3, *SA* 2, *Arg* 1,2, *E* 2, *S*, 1998 *E* 1, *S* 1,2, *NZ* 1, *SA* 1, *NZ* 2, *SA* 2, *NZ* 3, *Fj, Tg, WS, F, E* 2, 1999 *I* 1,2, *E, SA* 1, *NZ* 1, *SA* 2, *NZ* 2(R), [*R* (R), *I* 3, *US* (R), *W, SA* 3, *F*], 2000 *Arg* 1,2, *SA* 1, *NZ* 1, *SA* 2, *NZ* 2, *SA* 3, *F, S, E*, 2001 *BI* 1,2,3, *SA* 1, *NZ* 1, *SA* 2, *NZ* 2
Rose, H A (NSW), 1967 *I* 2, *NZ*, 1968 *NZ* 1,2, *F, I, S*, 1969 *W, SA* 1,2,3,4, 1970 *S*
Rosenblum, M E (NSW) 1928 *NZ* 1,2,3, *M*
Rosenblum, R G (NSW) 1969 *SA* 1,3, 1970 *S*
Rosewell, J S H (NSW) 1907 *NZ* 1,3
Ross, A W (NSW) 1925 *NZ* 1,2,3, 1926 *NZ* 1,2,3, 1927 *I, W, S*, 1928 *E, F*, 1929 *NZ* 1, 1930 *BI*, 1931 *M, NZ*, 1932 *NZ* 2,3, 1933 *SA* 5, 1934 *NZ* 1,2
Ross, W S (Q) 1979 *I* 1,2, *Arg* 2, 1980 *Fj, NZ* 1,2,3, 1982 *S* 1,2, 1983 *US, Arg* 1,2, *NZ*
Rothwell, P R (NSW) 1951 *NZ* 1,2,3, 1952 *Fj* 1
Row, F L (NSW) 1899 *BI* 1,3,4
Row, N E (NSW) 1907 *NZ* 1,3, 1909 *E*, 1910 *NZ* 1,2,3
Rowles, P G (NSW) 1972 *Fj*, 1973 *E*

Roxburgh, J R (NSW) 1968 *NZ* 1,2, *F*, 1969 *W, SA* 1,2,3,4, 1970 *S*
Ruebner, G (NSW) 1966 *BI* 1,2
Russell, C J (NSW) 1907 *NZ* 1,2,3, 1908 *W*, 1909 *E*
Ryan, J R (NSW) 1975 *J* 2, 1976 *I, US, Fj* 1,2,3
Ryan, K J (Q) 1958 *E, M* 1, *NZ* 1,2,3
Ryan, P F (NSW) 1963 *E, SA* 1, 1966 *BI* 1,2
Rylance, M H (NSW) 1926 *NZ* 4(R)

Sampson, J H (NSW) 1899 *BI* 4
Sayle, J L (NSW) 1967 *NZ*
Schulte, B G (Q) 1946 *NZ* 1, *M*
Scott, P R I (NSW) 1962 *NZ* 1,2
Scott-Young, S J (Q) 1990 *F* 2,3(R), *US, NZ* 3, 1992 *NZ* 1,2,3
Shambrook, G G (Q) 1976 *Fj* 2,3
Shaw, A A (NSW) 1973 *W, E*, 1975 *E* 1,2, *J* 2, *S, W*, 1976 *E, I, US, Fj* 1,2,3, *F* 1,2, 1978 *W* 1,2, *NZ* 1,2,3, 1979 *I* 1,2, *NZ, Arg* 1,2, 1980 *Fj, NZ* 1,2,3, 1981 *F* 1,2, *I, W, S*, 1982 *S* 1,2
Shaw, C (NSW) 1925 *NZ* 2,3,4(R)
Shaw, G A (NSW) 1969 *W, SA* 1(R), 1970 *S*, 1971 *SA* 1,2,3, *F* 1,2, 1973 *W, E*, 1974 *NZ* 1,2,3, 1975 *E* 1,2, *J* 1,2, *W*, 1976 *E, I, US, Fj* 1,2,3, *F* 1,2, 1979 *NZ*
Sheehan, W B J (NSW) 1921 *SA* 1,2,3, 1922 *NZ* 1,2,3, 1923 *M* 1,2, *NZ* 1,2,3, 1924 *NZ* 1,2, 1926 *NZ* 1,2,3, 1927 *W, S*
Shehadie, N M (NSW) 1947 *NZ* 2, 1948 *E, F*, 1949 *M* 1,2,3, *NZ* 1,2, 1950 *BI* 1,2, 1951 *NZ* 1,2,3, 1952 *Fj* 1,2, *NZ* 2, 1953 *SA* 1,2,3,4, 1954 *Fj* 1,2, 1955 *NZ* 1,2,3, 1956 *SA* 1, 1957 *NZ* 2, 1958 *W, I*
Sheil, A G R (Q) 1956 *SA* 1
Shepherd, D J (V) 1964 *NZ* 3, 1965 *SA* 1,2, 1966 *BI* 1,2
Shute, J L (NSW) 1920 *NZ* 3, 1922 *M* 2,3
Simpson, R J (NSW) 1913 *NZ* 2
Skinner, A J (NSW) 1969 *W, SA* 4, 1970 *S*
Slack, A G (Q) 1978 *W* 1,2, *NZ* 1,2, 1979 *NZ, Arg* 1,2, 1980 *Fj*, 1981 *I, W, S*, 1982 *E, S* 1, *NZ* 3, 1983 *US, Arg* 1,2 *NZ, It*, 1984 *Fj, NZ* 1,2,3, *E, I, W, S*, 1986 *It, F, NZ* 1,2,3, 1987 *SK*, [*E, US, J, I, F, W*]
Slater, S H (NSW) 1910 *NZ* 3
Slattery, P J (Q) 1990 *US* (R), 1991 *W* (R), *E* (R), [*WS* (R), *W, I* (R)], 1992 *I, W* (R), 1993 *Tg, C, F* 1,2, 1994 *I* 1,2, *It* 1(R), 1995 [*C, R* (R)]
Smairl, A M (NSW) 1928 *NZ* 1,2,3
Smith, B A (Q) 1987 *SK*, [*US, J, I* (R), *W*], *Arg* 1
Smith, D P (Q) 1993 *SA* 1,2,3, *C, F* 2, 1994 *I* 1,2, *It* 1,2, *WS, NZ*, 1995 *Arg* 1,2, [*SA, R, E*], *NZ* 1,2, 1998 *SA* 1(R), *NZ* 3(R), *Fj*
Smith, F B (NSW) 1905 *NZ*, 1907 *NZ* 1,2,3
Smith, G B (ACT) 2000 *F, S, E*, 2001 *BI* 1,2,3, *SA* 1, *NZ* 1, *SA* 2, *NZ* 2
Smith, L M (NSW) 1905 *NZ*
Smith, N C (NSW) 1922 *NZ* 2,3, 1923 *NZ* 1, 1924 *NZ* 1,3(R), 1925 *NZ* 2,3
Smith, P V (NSW) 1967 *NZ*, 1968 *NZ* 1,2, *F, I, S*, 1969 *W, SA* 1
Smith, R A (NSW) 1971 *SA* 1,2, 1972 *F* 1,2, *NZ* 1,2(R), 3, *Fj*, 1975 *E* 1,2, *J* 1,2, *S, W*, 1976 *I, US, Fj* 1,2,3, *F* 1,2
Smith, T S (NSW) 1921 *SA* 1,2,3, *NZ*, 1922 *M* 2,3, *NZ* 1,2,3, 1925 *NZ* 1,3,4
Snell, H W (NSW) 1925 *NZ* 2,3, 1928 *NZ* 3
Solomon, H J (NSW) 1949 *M* 3, *NZ* 2, 1950 *BI* 1,2, 1951 *NZ* 1,2, 1952 *Fj* 1,2, *NZ* 1,2, 1953 *SA* 1,2,3, 1955 *NZ* 1
Spooner, N R (Q) 1999 *I* 1,2
Spragg, S A (NSW) 1899 *BI* 1,2,3,4
Staniforth, S N G (NSW) 1999 [*US*]
Stanley, R G (NSW) 1921 *NZ*, 1922 *M* 1,2,3, *NZ* 1,2,3, 1923 *M* 2,3, *NZ* 1,2,3, 1924 *NZ* 1,3
Stapleton, E T (NSW) 1951 *NZ* 1,2,3, 1952 *Fj* 1,2, *NZ* 1,2, 1953 *SA* 1,2,3,4, 1954 *Fj* 1, 1955 *NZ* 1,2,3, 1958 *NZ* 1
Steggall, J C (Q) 1931 *M, NZ*, 1932 *NZ* 1,2,3, 1933 *SA* 1,2,3,4,5
Stegman, T R (NSW) 1973 *Tg* 1,2
Stephens, O G (NSW) 1973 *Tg* 1,2, *W*, 1974 *NZ* 2,3
Stewart, A A (NSW) 1979 *NZ, Arg* 1,2
Stiles, N B (Q) 2001 *BI* 1,2,3, *SA* 1, *NZ* 1, *SA* 2, *NZ* 2
Stone, A H (NSW) 1937 *SA* 2, 1938 *NZ* 2,3
Stone, C G (NSW) 1938 *NZ* 1
Stone, J M (NSW) 1946 *M, NZ* 2
Storey, G P (NSW) 1926 *NZ* 4, 1927 *I, W, S*, 1928 *E, F*, 1929 *NZ* 3(R), 1930 *BI*
Storey, K P (NSW) 1936 *NZ* 2
Storey, N J D (NSW) 1962 *NZ* 1
Strachan, D J (NSW) 1955 *NZ* 2,3

Strauss, C P (NSW) 1999 *I* 1(R),2(R), *E* (R), *SA* 1(R), *NZ* 1, *SA* 2(R), *NZ* 2(R), [*R* (R), *I* 3(R), *US, W*]
Street, N O (NSW) 1899 *BI* 2
Streeter, S F (NSW) 1978 *NZ* 1
Stuart, R (NSW) 1910 *NZ* 2,3
Stumbles, B D (NSW) 1972 *NZ* 1(R), 2,3, *Fj*
Sturtridge, G S (V) 1929 *NZ* 2, 1932 *NZ* 1,2,3, 1933 *SA* 1,2,3,4,5
Sullivan, P D (NSW) 1971 *SA* 1,2,3, *F* 1,2, 1972 *F* 1,2, *NZ* 1,2, *Fj*, 1973 *Tg* 1,2, *W*
Summons, A J (NSW) 1958 *W, I, E, S, M* 2, *NZ* 1,2,3, 1959 *BI* 1,2
Suttor, D C (NSW) 1913 *NZ* 1,2,3
Swannell, B I (NSW) 1905 *NZ*
Sweeney, T L (Q) 1953 *SA* 1

Taafe, B S (NSW) 1969 *SA* 1, 1972 *F* 1,2
Tabua, I (Q) 1993 *SA* 2,3, *C, F* 1, 1994 *I* 1,2, *It* 1,2, 1995 [*C, R*]
Tancred, A J (NSW) 1927 *I, W, S*
Tancred, H E (NSW) 1923 *M* 1,2
Tancred, J L (NSW) 1926 *NZ* 3,4, 1928 *F*
Tanner, W H (Q) 1899 *BI* 1,2
Tarleton, K (NSW) 1925 *NZ* 2,3
Tasker, W G (NSW) 1913 *NZ* 1,2,3, 1914 *NZ* 1,2,3
Tate, M J (NSW) 1951 *NZ* 3, 1952 *Fj* 1,2, *NZ* 1,2, 1953 *SA* 1, 1957 *Fj* 1,2
Taylor, D A (Q) 1968 *NZ* 1,2, *F, I, S*
Taylor, H C (NSW) 1923 *NZ* 1,2,3, 1924 *NZ* 4
Taylor, J I (NSW) 1971 *SA* 1, 1972 *F* 1,2, *Fj*
Taylor, J M (NSW) 1922 *M* 1,2
Teitzel, R G (Q) 1966 *W, S*, 1967 *E, I* 1, *F, I* 2, *NZ*
Telford, D G (NSW) 1926 *NZ* 3(R)
Thompson, C E (NSW) 1922 *M* 1, 1923 *M* 1,2, *NZ* 1, 1924 *NZ* 2,3
Thompson, E G (Q) 1929 *NZ* 1,2,3, 1930 *BI*
Thompson, F (NSW) 1913 *NZ* 1,2,3, 1914 *NZ* 1,2,3
Thompson, J (Q) 1914 *NZ* 1
Thompson, P D (Q) 1950 *BI* 1
Thompson, R J (WA) 1971 *SA* 3, *F* 2(R), 1972 *Fj*
Thorn, A M (NSW) 1921 *SA* 1,2,3, *NZ*, 1922 *M* 1,3
Thorn, E J (NSW) 1922 *NZ* 1,2,3, 1923 *NZ* 1,2,3, 1924 *NZ* 1,2,3, 1925 *NZ* 1,2, 1926 *NZ* 1,2,3,4
Thornett, J E (NSW) 1955 *NZ* 1,2,3, 1956 *SA* 1,2, 1958 *W, I, S, F, M* 2,3, *NZ* 2,3, 1959 *BI* 1,2, 1961 *Fj* 2,3, *SA* 1,2, *F*, 1962 *NZ* 2,3,4,5, 1963 *E, SA* 1,2,3,4, 1964 *NZ* 1,2,3, 1965 *SA* 1,2, 1966 *BI* 1,2, 1967 *F*
Thornett, R N (NSW) 1961 *Fj* 1,2,3, *SA* 1,2, *F*, 1962 *NZ* 1,2,3,4,5
Thorpe, A C (NSW) 1929 *NZ* 1(R)
Timbury, F R V (Q) 1910 *NZ* 1,2,
Tindall, E N (NSW) 1973 *Tg* 2
Toby, A E (NSW) 1925 *NZ* 1,4
Tolhurst, H A (NSW) 1931 *M, NZ*
Tombs, R C (NSW) 1992 *S* 1,2, 1994 *I* 2, *It* 1, 1996 *NZ* 2
Tonkin, A E J (NSW) 1947 *S, I, W*, 1948 *E, F*, 1950 *BI* 2
Tooth, R M (NSW) 1951 *NZ* 1,2,3, 1954 *Fj* 1,2, 1955 *NZ* 1,2,3, 1957 *NZ* 1,2
Towers, C H T (NSW) 1926 *NZ* 1,3(R),4, 1927 *I*, 1928 *E, F, NZ* 1,2,3, *M*, 1929 *NZ* 1,3, 1930 *BI*, 1931 *M, NZ*, 1934 *NZ* 1,2, 1937 *SA* 1,2
Trivett, R K (Q) 1966 *BI* 1,2
Tune, B N (Q) 1996 *W* 2, *C, NZ* 1, *SA* 1, *NZ* 2, *SA* 2, 1997 *F* 1,2, *NZ* 1, *E* 1, *NZ* 2, *SA* 1, *NZ* 3, *SA* 2, *Arg*, 1,2, *E* 2, *S*, 1998 *E* 1, *S* 1,2, *NZ* 1, *SA* 1, 1999 *I* 1, *E, SA* 1, *NZ* 1, *SA* 2, *NZ* 2, [*R, I* 3, *W, SA* 3, *F*], 2000 *SA* 2(R), *NZ* 2(t&R), *SA* 3(R)
Turnbull, A (V) 1961 *Fj* 3
Turnbull, R V (NSW) 1968 *I*
Tuynman, S N (NSW) 1983 *F* 1,2, 1984 *E, I, W, S*, 1985 *C* 1,2, *NZ, Fj* 1,2, 1986 *It, F, Arg* 1,2, *NZ* 1,2,3, 1987 *SK*, [*E, US, J, I, W*], *NZ, Arg* 1(R), 2, 1988 *E, It*, 1989 *BI* 1,2,3, *NZ*, 1990 *NZ* 1
Tweedale, E (NSW) 1946 *NZ* 1,2, 1947 *NZ* 2, *S, I*, 1948 *E, F*, 1949 *M* 1,2,3

Vaughan, D (NSW) 1983 *US, Arg* 1, *It, F* 1,2
Vaughan, G N (V) 1958 *E, S, F, M* 1,2,3
Verge, A (NSW) 1904 *BI* 1,2

Walden, R J (NSW) 1934 *NZ* 2, 1936 *NZ* 1,2, *M*
Walker, A K (NSW) 1947 *NZ* 1, 1948 *E, F*, 1950 *BI* 1,2
Walker, A M (ACT) 2000 *NZ* 1(R), 2001 *BI* 1,2,3, *SA* 1, *NZ* 1,2(R)

Walker, A S B (NSW) 1912 *US*, 1920 *NZ* 1,2, 1921 *SA* 1,2,3, *NZ*, 1922 *M* 1,3, *NZ* 1,2,3, 1923 *M* 2,3, 1924 *NZ* 1,2
Walker, L F (NSW) 1988 *NZ* 2,3, *S, It*, 1989 *BI* 1,2,3, *NZ*
Walker, L R (NSW) 1982 *NZ* 2,3
Wallace, A C (NSW) 1921 *NZ*, 1926 *NZ* 3,4, 1927 *I, W, S*, 1928 *E, F*
Wallace, T M (NSW) 1994 *It* 1(R), 2
Wallach, C (NSW) 1913 *NZ* 1,3, 1914 *NZ* 1,2,3
Walsh, J J (NSW) 1953 *SA* 1,2,3,4
Walsh, P B (NSW) 1904 *BI* 1,2,3
Walsham, K P (NSW) 1962 *NZ* 3, 1963 *E*
Ward, P G (NSW) 1899 *BI* 1,2,3,4
Ward, T (Q) 1899 *BI* 2
Watson, G W (Q) 1907 *NZ* 1
Watson, W T (NSW) 1912 *US*, 1913 *NZ* 1,2,3, 1914 *NZ* 1, 1920 *NZ* 1,2,3
Waugh, P R (NSW) 2000 *E* (R), *NZ* 1(R), *SA* 2(R), *NZ* 2(R)
Waugh, W W (NSW, ACT) 1993 *SA* 1, 1995 [*C*], *NZ* 1,2, 1996 *S, I*, 1997 *Arg* 1,2
Weatherstone, L J (ACT) 1975 *E* 1,2, *J* 1,2, *S* (R), 1976 *E, I*
Webb, W (NSW) 1899 *BI* 3,4
Welborn J P (NSW) 1996 *SA* 2, *It*, 1998 *Tg*, 1999 *E, SA* 1, *NZ* 1
Wells, B G (NSW) 1958 *M* 1
Westfield, R E (NSW) 1928 *NZ* 1,2,3, *M*, 1929 *NZ* 2,3
Whitaker, C J (NSW) 1998 *SA* 2(R), *Fj* (R), *Tg*, 1999 *NZ* 2(R), [*R* (R), *US, F* (R)], 2000 *S* (R)
White, C J B (NSW) 1899 *BI* 1, 1903 *NZ*, 1904 *BI* 1
White, J M (NSW) 1904 *BI* 3
White, J P L (NSW) 1958 *NZ* 1,2,3, 1961 *Fj* 1,2,3, *SA* 1,2, *F*, 1962 *NZ* 1,2,3,4,5, 1963 *E, SA* 1,2,3,4, 1964 *NZ* 1,2,3, 1965 *SA* 1,2
White, M C (Q) 1931 *M, NZ* 1932 *NZ* 1,2, 1933 *SA* 1,2,3,4,5
White, S W (NSW) 1956 *SA* 1,2, 1958 *I, E, S, M* 2,3
White, W G S (Q) 1933 *SA* 1,2,3,4,5, 1934 *NZ* 1,2, 1936 *NZ* 1,2, *M*
White, W J (NSW) 1928 *NZ* 1, *M*, 1932 *NZ* 1
Wickham, S M (NSW) 1903 *NZ*, 1904 *BI* 1,2,3, 1905 *NZ*

Williams, D (Q) 1913 *NZ* 3, 1914 *NZ* 1,2,3
Williams, I M (NSW) 1987 *Arg* 1,2, 1988 *E* 1,2, *NZ* 1,2,3, 1989 *BI* 2,3, *NZ, F* 1,2, 1990 *F* 1,2,3, *US, NZ* 1
Williams, J L (NSW) 1963 *SA* 1,3,4
Williams, R W (ACT) 1999 *I* 1(t&R),2(t&R), *E* (R), [*US*], 2000 *Arg* 1,2, *SA* 1, *NZ* 1, *SA* 2, *NZ* 2, *SA* 3, *F* (R), *S* (R), *E*
Williams, S A (NSW) 1980 *Fj, NZ* 1,2, 1981 *F* 1,2, 1982 *E, NZ* 1,2,3, 1983 *US, Arg* 1(R), 2, *NZ, It, F* 1,2, 1984 *NZ* 1,2,3, *E, I, W, S*, 1985 *C* 1,2, *NZ, Fj* 1,2
Wilson, B J (NSW) 1949 *NZ* 1,2
Wilson, C R (Q) 1957 *NZ* 1, 1958 *NZ* 1,2,3
Wilson, D J (Q) 1992 *S* 1,2, *NZ* 1,2,3, *SA, I, W*, 1993 *Tg, NZ, SA* 1,2,3, *C, F* 1,2, 1994 *I* 1,2, *It* 1,2, *WS, NZ*, 1995 *Arg* 1,2, [*SA, R, E*], 1996 *W* 1,2, *C, NZ* 1, *SA* 1, *NZ* 2, *SA* 2, *It, S, I, W* 3, 1997 *F* 1,2, *NZ* 1, *E* 1(t + R), *NZ* 2(R), *SA* 1, *NZ* 3, *SA* 2, *E* 2(R), *S* (R), 1998 *E* 1, *S* 1,2, *NZ* 1, *SA* 1, *NZ* 2, *SA* 2, *NZ* 3, *Fj, WS, F, E* 2, 1999 *I* 1,2, *E, SA* 1, *NZ* 1, *SA* 2, *NZ* 2, [*R, I* 3, *W, SA* 3, *F*], 2000 *Arg* 1,2, *SA* 1, *NZ* 1, *SA* 2, *NZ* 2, *SA* 3
Wilson, V W (Q) 1937 *SA* 1,2, 1938 *NZ* 1,2,3
Windon, C J (NSW) 1946 *NZ* 1,2, 1947 *NZ* 1, *S, I, W*, 1948 *E, F*, 1949 *M* 1,2,3, *NZ* 1,2, 1951 *NZ* 1,2,3, 1952 *Fj* 1,2, *NZ* 1,2
Windon, K S (NSW) 1937 *SA* 1,2, 1946 *M*
Windsor, J C (Q) 1947 *NZ* 2
Winning, K C (Q) 1951 *NZ* 1
Wogan, L W (NSW) 1913 *NZ* 1,2,3, 1914 *NZ* 1,2,3, 1920 *NZ* 1,2,3, 1921 *SA* 1,2,3, *NZ*, 1922 *M* 3, *NZ* 1,2,3, 1923 *M* 1,2, 1924 *NZ* 1,2,3
Wood, F (NSW) 1907 *NZ* 1,2,3, 1910 *NZ* 1,2,3, 1913 *NZ* 1,2,3, 1914 *NZ* 1,2,3
Wood, R N (Q) 1972 *Fj*
Woods, H F (NSW) 1925 *NZ* 4, 1926 *NZ* 1,2,3, 1927 *I, W, S*, 1928 *E*
Wright, K J (NSW) 1975 *E* 1,2, *J* 1, 1976 *US, F* 1,2, 1978 *NZ* 1,2,3
Wyld, G (NSW) 1920 *NZ* 2

Yanz, K (NSW) 1958 *F*
Young, W K (ACT) 2000 *F, S, E*

AUSTRALIA INTERNATIONAL STATISTICS

(up to 20 October 2001)

Match Records

Most Consecutive Test Wins

10 1991 *Arg, WS, W, I, NZ, E,* 1992 *S* 1,2, *NZ* 1,2
10 1998 *NZ* 3, *Fj, Tg, Sm, F, E* 2, 1999 *I* 1,2, *E, SA* 1
10 1999 *NZ* 2, *R, I* 3, *US, W, SA* 3, *F,* 2000 *Arg* 1,2, *SA* 1

Most Consecutive Tests Without Defeat

Matches	Wins	Draws	Period
10	10	0	1991 to 1992
10	10	0	1998 to 1999
10	10	0	1999 to 2000

Most Points in a Match
by the team

Pts	Opponents	Venue	Year
76	England	Brisbane	1998
74	Canada	Brisbane	1996
74	Tonga	Canberra	1998
73	Western Samoa	Sydney	1994
67	United States	Brisbane	1990

by a player

Pts	Player	Opponents	Venue	Year
39	M C Burke	Canada	Brisbane	1996
29	S A Mortlock	South Africa	Melbourne	2000
28	M P Lynagh	Argentina	Brisbane	1995
25	M C Burke	Scotland	Sydney	1998
25	M C Burke	France	Cardiff	1999
25	M C Burke	British/Irish Lions	Melbourne	2001
24	M P Lynagh	United States	Brisbane	1990
24	M P Lynagh	France	Brisbane	1990
24	M C Burke	New Zealand	Melbourne	1998
24	M C Burke	South Africa	Twickenham	1999

Most Tries in a Match
by the team

Tries	Opponents	Venue	Year
13	South Korea	Brisbane	1987
12	United States	Brisbane	1990
12	Wales	Brisbane	1991
12	Tonga	Canberra	1998
11	Western Samoa	Sydney	1994
11	England	Brisbane	1998

by a player

Tries	Player	Opponents	Venue	Year
4	G Cornelsen	New Zealand	Auckland	1978
4	D I Campese	United States	Sydney	1983
4	J S Little	Tonga	Canberra	1998
4	C E Latham	Argentina	Brisbane	2000
3	A D McLean	NZ Maori	Palmerston N	1936
3	J R Ryan	Japan	Brisbane	1975
3	M P Burke	Canada	Brisbane	1985
3	M P Burke	South Korea	Brisbane	1987
3	D I Campese	Italy	Rome	1988
3	A S Nuiqila	Italy	Rome	1988
3	D I Campese	Canada	Calgary	1993
3	M Burke	Canada	Brisbane	1996
3	S J Larkham	England	Brisbane	1998
3	B N Tune	England	Brisbane	1998
3	C P Strauss	Ireland	Brisbane	1999
3	R S T Kefu	Romania	Belfast	1999

Most Conversions in a Match
by the team

Cons	Opponents	Venue	Year
9	Canada	Brisbane	1996
9	Fiji	Parramatta	1998
8	Italy	Rome	1988
8	United States	Brisbane	1990
7	Canada	Sydney	1985
7	Tonga	Canberra	1998

by a player

Cons	Player	Opponents	Venue	Year
9	M Burke	Canada	Brisbane	1996
9	J A Eales	Fiji	Parramatta	1998
8	M P Lynagh	Italy	Rome	1988
8	M P Lynagh	United States	Brisbane	1990
7	M P Lynagh	Canada	Sydney	1985

Most Penalties in a Match
by the team

Penalties	Opponents	Venue	Year
8	South Africa	Twickenham	1999
7	New Zealand	Sydney	1999
7	France	Cardiff	1999
6	New Zealand	Sydney	1984
6	France	Sydney	1986
6	England	Brisbane	1988
6	Argentina	Buenos Aires	1997
6	Ireland	Perth	1999

| 6 | France | Paris | 2000 |
| 6 | British/Irish Lions | Melbourne | 2001 |

by a player

Penalties	Player	Opponents	Venue	Year
8	M C Burke	South Africa	Twickenham	1999
7	M C Burke	New Zealand	Sydney	1999
7	M C Burke	France	Cardiff	1999
6	M P Lynagh	France	Sydney	1986
6	M P Lynagh	England	Brisbane	1988
6	D J Knox	Argentina	Buenos Aires	1997
6	M C Burke	France	Paris	2000
6	M C Burke	British/Irish Lions	Melbourne	2001

Most Dropped Goals in a Match

by the team

Drops	Opponents	Venue	Year
3	England	Twickenham	1967
3	Ireland	Dublin	1984
3	Fiji	Brisbane	1985

by a player

Drops	Player	Opponents	Venue	Year
3	P FHawthorne	England	Twickenham	1967
2	M G Ella	Ireland	Dublin	1984
2	D J Knox	Fiji	Brisbane	1985

Career Records

Most Capped Players

Caps	Player	Career Span
101	D I Campese	1982 to 1996
86	J A Eales	1991 to 2001
80	T J Horan	1989 to 2000
79	D J Wilson	1992 to 2000
75	J S Little	1989 to 2000
72	M P Lynagh	1984 to 1995
68	J W C Roff	1995 to 2001
68	G M Gregan	1994 to 2001
67	P N Kearns	1989 to 1999
63	N C Farr Jones	1984 to 1993
59	S P Poidevin	1980 to 1991
55	D J Herbert	1994 to 2001
54	M C Burke	1993 to 2001

Most Consecutive Tests

Tests	Player	Span
58	J W C Roff	1996 to 2001
46	P N Kearns	1989 to 1995
42	D I Campese	1990 to 1995
37	P G Johnson	1959 to 1968

Most Tests as Captain

Tests	Captain	Span
55	J A Eales	1996 to 2001
36	N C Farr Jones	1988 to 1992
19	A G Slack	1984 to 1987
16	J E Thornett	1962 to 1967
16	G V Davis	1969 to 1972

Most Tests in Individual Positions

Position	Player	Tests	Span
Full-back	M C Burke	46	1993 to 2001
Wing	D I Campese	85	1982 to 1996
Centre	T J Horan	69	1989 to 2000
Fly-half	M P Lynagh	64	1984 to 1995
Scrum-half	G M Gregan	67*	1994 to 2001
Prop	E J A McKenzie	51	1990 to 1997
Hooker	P N Kearns	66	1989 to 1999
Lock	J A Eales	84	1991 to 2001
Flanker	D J Wilson	78	1992 to 2000
No 8	B T Gavin	43	1988 to 1996

* excludes an additional appearance as a temporary replacement

Most Points in Tests

Points	Player	Tests	Career
911	M P Lynagh	72	1984 to 1995
663	M C Burke	54	1993 to 2001
315	D I Campese	101	1982 to 1996
260	P E McLean	30	1974 to 1982
173	J A Eales	86	1991 to 2001

Most Tries in Tests

Tries	Player	Tests	Career
64	D I Campese	101	1982 to 1996
30	T J Horan	80	1989 to 2000
25	J W C Roff	68	1995 to 2001
23	M C Burke	54	1993 to 2001
22	B N Tune	39	1996 to 2000
21	J S Little	75	1989 to 2000

Most Conversions in Tests

Cons	Player	Tests	Career
140	M P Lynagh	72	1984 to 1995
76	M C Burke	54	1993 to 2001
31	J A Eales	86	1991 to 2001
27	P E McLean	30	1974 to 1982
19	D J Knox	13	1985 to 1997

Most Penalty Goals in Tests

Penalties	Player	Tests	Career
177	M P Lynagh	72	1984 to 1995
132	M C Burke	54	1993 to 2001
62	P E McLean	30	1974 to 1982
34	J A Eales	86	1991 to 2001
23	M C Roebuck	23	1991 to 1993
23	S A Mortlock	10	2000

Most Dropped Goals in Tests

Drops	Player	Tests	Career
9	P F Hawthorne	21	1962 to 1967
9	M P Lynagh	72	1984 to 1995
8	M G Ella	25	1980 to 1984
4	P E McLean	30	1974 to 1982

Tri Nations Records

Record	Detail	Holder	Set
Most points in season	104	in four matches	2000
Most tries in season	13	in four matches	1997
Highest Score	35	35-39 v N Zeealand (h)	2000
Biggest win	26	32-6 v S Africa (h)	1999
Highest score conceded	61	22-61 v S Africa (a)	1997
Biggest defeat	39	22-61 v S Africa (a)	1997
Most points in matches	205	M C Burke	1996 to 2001
Most points in season	71	S A Mortlock	2000
Most points in match	24	M C Burke	v N Zealand (h) 1998
Most tries in matches	8	J W C Roff	1996 to 2001
Most tries in season	4	S A Mortlock	2000
Most tries in match	2	B N Tune	v S Africa (h) 1997
	2	M C Burke	v N Zealand (h) 1998
	2	J W C Roff	v S Africa (h) 1999
	2	S A Mortlock	v N Zealand (h) 2000
Most cons in matches	11	M C Burke	1996 to 2001
Most cons in season	7	D J Knox	1997
Most cons in match	3	D J Knox	v S Africa (h) 1997
	3	M C Burke	v S Africa (h) 1999
Most pens in matches	51	M C Burke	1996 to 2001
Most pens in season	14	M C Burke	2001
Most pens in match	7	M C Burke	v N Zealand (h) 1999

Series Records

Record	Holder	Detail
Most tries	D I Campese	6 in Europe 1988
Most points	M C Burke	74 in Europe 1996

Miscellaneous Records

Record	Holder	Detail
Longest Test Career	G M Cooke/A R Miller	16 seasons, 1932-1947-48/ 1952-67
Youngest Test Cap	B W Ford	18 yrs 90 days in 1957
Oldest Test Cap	A R Miller	38 yrs 113 days in 1967

Career Records of Australia International Players
(up to 20 October 2001)

Player	Debut	Caps	T	C	P	D	Pts
Backs:							
G S G Bond	2001 v SA	1	0	0	0	0	0
M C Burke	1993 v SA	54	23	76	132	0	663
S J Cordingley	2000 v Arg	5	0	0	0	0	0
M H M Edmonds	1998 v Tg	2	2	5	1	0	23
E J Flatley	1997 v E	9	0	1	0	0	2
G M Gregan	1994 v It	68	11	0	0	0	55
N P Grey	1998 v S	27	4	0	0	0	20
D J Herbert	1994 v I	55	9	0	0	0	45
J C Holbeck	1997 v NZ	7	0	0	0	0	0
T J Horan	1989 v NZ	80	30	0	0	0	140
R B Kafer	1999 v NZ	12	0	0	0	0	0
S J Larkham	1996 v W	42	14	2	0	1	77
C E Latham	1998 v F	22	11	0	0	0	55
J S Little	1989 v F	75	21	0	0	0	102
S A Mortlock	2000 v Arg	10	7	9	23	0	122
J W C Roff	1995 v C	68	25	10	6	0	163
N R Spooner	1999 v I	2	0	5	5	0	25
S T G Staniforth	1999 v US	1	2	0	0	0	10
B N Tune	1996 v W	39	22	0	0	0	110
A M Walker	2000 v NZ	7	1	0	2	0	11
C J Whitaker	1998 v SA	8	2	0	0	0	10
Forwards:							
T M Bowman	1998 v E	16	2	0	0	0	10
B J Cannon	2001 v BI	2	0	0	0	0	0
M J Cockbain	1997 v F	42	0	0	0	0	0
M R Connors	1999 v SA	20	2	0	0	0	10
B J Darwin	2001 v BI	5	0	0	0	0	0
F J Dyson	2000 v Arg	10	0	0	0	0	0
J A Eales	1991 v W	86	2	31	34	0	173
O D A Finegan	1996 v W	40	6	0	0	0	30
M A Foley	1995 v C	46	3	0	0	0	15
D T Giffin	1996 v W	30	0	0	0	0	0
J B G Harrison	2001 v BI	3	0	0	0	0	0
T Jaques	2000 v SA	2	0	0	0	0	0
R S T Kefu	1997 v SA	40	7	0	0	0	35
D J Lyons	2000 v Arg	4	0	0	0	0	0
R S Moore	1999 v US	7	0	0	0	0	0
E P Noriega	1998 v F	9	0	0	0	0	0
G M Panoho	1998 v SA	19	0	0	0	0	0
J A Paul	1998 v S	25	5	0	0	0	25
G B Smith	2000 v F	10	0	0	0	0	0
N B Stiles	2001 v BI	7	0	0	0	0	0
P R Waugh	2000 v E	4	0	0	0	0	0
J P Welborn	1996 v SA	6	0	0	0	0	0
R W Williams	1999 v I	14	2	0	0	0	10
D J Wilson	1992 v S	79	13	0	0	0	65
W K Young	2000 v F	3	0	0	0	0	0

NB Roff's figures include a penalty try awarded against New Zealand in 2001

CANADA TEST SEASON REVIEW 2000-01

Strength Required in Depth
Peter McMullan

It's just 10 years since Canada went as far as the quarter-finals of the 1991 Rugby World Cup before losing in the most gallant of circumstances to New Zealand, the defending champions from 1987. This was and remains an historic high point and there was a definite sense that Canada could perhaps go even further in the decade ahead. Unhappily events have proved otherwise, never more so than over the course of the past year.

While the final game of 2000, against Italy in Rovigo on November 11, brought a testy but worthwhile 22-17 victory, with the visitors drawing three of French referee Didier Mené's five yellow cards, the first stanza of the 2001 international programme was beset with problems. Seven more Tests were contested between 19 May and 8 July, all but the final two with home advantage, for a record of two wins, neither of them very convincing, and five successive defeats.

That left Canada to reflect on a three and five record in the period between November and July and, more significantly, to statistics that tell a dismal tale. In terms of tries Canada was outscored 27-8 in the eight matches while the five losses saw the Canadians manage only 66 points and five tries to the combined oppositions' 192 points and 23 tries.

The defeat of Italy included four penalties, a conversion and a drop goal from outside-half Jared Barker but he was subsequently ruled out of contention as the natural successor to Gareth Rees following surgery to repair a knee ligament injury. At No 10 Canada then called on Scott Stewart, a distinguished full-back and sometime wing who announced his retirement after the second Test against England, and Bob Ross, who himself retired in 1999. The hope now is that Barker will be restored to full fitness in time for the 2002 campaign for this is a key position in any team. For the record Stewart, most recently of Bedford, won 64 caps in a career dating back to 1989, a magnificent achievement by a supremely competitive athlete.

Canada has played 15 times since the 1999 Rugby World Cup winning five and drawing one while scoring 382 points to their opponents' 442. The win over Italy and the earlier inspired draw with Ireland were seen as hopeful omens but, based on respective world rankings, successes against Japan, since heavily reversed, Tonga, United States and Uruguay could hardly be claimed as evidence of significant progress. Canada now stands 13th in the world order after the losses to Japan and Fiji in Tokyo.

In early August the Rugby Canada Board of Directors announced it had terminated the contract of Australian-born national coach David Clark. The decision prompted a vigorous reaction on the part of the players with many indicating they would not play again for Canada unless Clark was reinstated. The Board stood its ground and the result of the impasse was that the 27 October Test in Vancouver against world champions Australia and a short Canadian tour to Scotland and Ireland with Tests scheduled for 17 and 24 November were cancelled.

Recent results will be carefully reviewed as Canada prepares for the Americas Qualifying tournament for Rugby World Cup 2003. This event will be staged in the second half of 2002.

The schedule sees Canada embarking on a six-match home and away tournament involving the United States, Uruguay and the winner of three earlier rounds involving eight teams from the Caribbean and six South American countries. The winner and runner-up in the Americas round go through to the 2003 finals with the third placed team getting another chance to qualify by way of the Repechage.

Before then there will be an incoming tour by Scotland, in the Spring of 2002, with Canada also due to travel to Australia and Wales for a possible total of up to 13 Tests for the year compared to eight in 2000 and seven in 2001. Considering the limitations of the available financial, playing and administrative resources, the demands on all aspects of Canadian rugby are simply immense and this at a time when a number of the best players are earning a living as overseas professionals.

Fourteen fell into this category in 2001, John Tait, Dan Baugh and Rod Snow in Wales, Scott Stewart, John Thiel, Winston Stanley and Mike Schmid (England), Duane Major (New Zealand) and Al Charron, Mike James, Morgan Williams, Gregor Dixon, Phil Murphy and Nik Witkowski (France).

Despite IRB Regulation 9, the release of overseas players by their clubs has been problematic from the outset of professionalism in 1995. Twelve were on call when England toured Canada and the United States in the early summer but only three, Snow, Murphy and Williams, then made themselves available for the long journey to Tokyo for the Pacific Rim Championship games against Fiji and Japan. In this context it should be noted that highly regarded team captain Al Charron was a late injury-enforced withdrawal.

Heavy losses were sustained, 52-23 and 39-7, confirming the ongoing problem of a lack in depth at the highest level. While younger and less experienced players are being given an earlier opportunity to represent their country, with 11 new caps introduced this year, they are quite obviously finding the learning curve steep indeed.

This was all too evident when England came calling in June with Canada simply unable to contain the visitors, especially in the second Test when a fragile defence was brutally exposed. All credit to wing Sean Fauth who had a try in each Test and another against Fiji – three of the four scored in Canada in these games.

Keith Wilkinson, Rugby Canada's Director of National teams, stresses Canada has not stood still since the 1999 Rugby World Cup but acknowledges the forward progress has not been as swift as many would have liked. 'As we have marched towards the new professional age, others in the top 12 of world rugby have been sprinting'.

'In 1999, following the Rugby World Cup, Rugby Canada took an enormous step in deciding to appoint a professional coach. The move was not revolutionary in concept, for professional coaches have been in position in most countries for many years; the revolution was in Rugby Canada committing large sums of money to a staff position which had previously been ably handled by volunteers. With limited revenues and many worthwhile programmes to fund, Rugby Canada took a bold step.'

'However, unclear reporting lines and responsibilities, unrealistic expectations and different management styles, all in the context of the changing world of professional rugby at the elite level, have led to frustration, in-fighting and problems. This is probably no different than in many other unions but in a small community like Rugby Canada it is devastating', he adds.

On the positive side there has been excellent and growing support for the national team with crowds of between 7000 and 8000 on hand for the two England games and this despite most welcome live television coverage.

Rugby Canada welcomed Graham Baldwin, a former Board member, as acting CEO during the summer and said farewell to John Billingsley, who retired as Chief Operating Officer after a 20-year career. Billingsley's contribution to the Canadian game was immense, as an international player nine times between 1974 and 1984, as a club referee and as a professional sports administrator who represented his country's interests with distinction during a period of unprecedented change.

Canada's Test Record in 2000-01:
Played 8, won 3, lost 5.

Opponents	Date	Venue	Result
Japan	8th July 2001	A	Lost 7-39
Fiji	4th July 2001	A	Lost 23-52
England	9th June 2001	H	Lost 20-59
England	2nd June 2001	H	Lost 10-22
Argentina	26th May 2001	H	Lost 6-20
Uruguay	23rd May 2001	H	Won 14-8
United States	19th May 2001	H	Won 19-10
Italy	11th November 2000	A	Won 22-17

CANADA INTERNATIONAL STATISTICS

(up to 20 October 2001)

Match Records

Most Consecutive Test Wins

6 1990 *Arg 2*, 1991 *J, S, US, F, R*
6 1998 *US* 1,2, *HK, J, U, US* 3

Most Consecutive Tests Without Defeat

Matches	Wins	Draws	Period
6	6	0	1990 to 1991
6	6	0	1998 to 1998

Most Points in a Match

by the team

Pts	Opponents	Venue	Year
72	Namibia	Toulouse	1999
62	Japan	Markham	2000
57	Hong Kong	Vancouver	1996
53	United States	Vancouver	1997
51	Japan	Vancouver	1996

by a player

Pts	Player	Opponents	Venue	Year
27	G L Rees	Namibia	Toulouse	1999
26	R P Ross	Japan	Vancouver	1996
24	M A Wyatt	Scotland	Saint John	1991
23	G L Rees	Argentina	Buenos Aires	1998
22	R P Ross	Hong Kong	Vancouver	1996
22	G L Rees	Japan	Vancouver	1997
22	G L Rees	United States	Burlington	1998
22	J Barker	Japan	Markham	2000

Most Tries in a Match

by the team

Tries	Opponents	Venue	Year
9	Namibia	Toulouse	1999
8	Tonga	Napier	1987
8	Japan	Vancouver	1991
8	Japan	Markham	2000
7	Hong Kong	Vancouver	1996
7	United States	Vancouver	1997

by a player

Tries	Player	Opponents	Venue	Year
4	K S Nichols	Japan	Markham	2000
3	S D Gray	United States	Vancouver	1987

Most Conversions in a Match

by the team

Cons	Opponents	Venue	Year
9	Namibia	Toulouse	1999
8	Japan	Markham	2000
7	Japan	Vancouver	1991
6	United States	Vancouver	1997
5	Hong Kong	Vancouver	1996

by a player

Cons	Player	Opponents	Venue	Year
9	G L Rees	Namibia	Toulouse	1999
8	J Barker	Japan	Markham	2000
7	M A Wyatt	Japan	Vancouver	1991
6	G L Rees	United States	Vancouver	1997
5	R P Ross	Hong Kong	Vancouver	1996

Most Penalties in a Match

by the team

Penalties	Opponents	Venue	Year
8	Scotland	Saint John	1991
7	Argentina	Buenos Aires	1998
6	United States	Vancouver	1985
6	Ireland	Victoria	1989
6	France	Nepean	1994
6	United States	Burlington	1998

by a player

Penalties	Player	Opponents	Venue	Year
8	M A Wyatt	Scotland	Saint John	1991
7	G L Rees	Argentina	Buenos Aires	1998
6	M A Wyatt	United States	Vancouver	1985
6	M A Wyatt	Ireland	Victoria	1989
6	G L Rees	France	Nepean	1994
6	G L Rees	United States	Burlington	1998

Most Dropped Goals in a match

by the team

Drops	Opponents	Venue	Year
2	United States	Saranac Lake (NY)	1980
2	United States	Tucson	1986
2	Hong Kong	Hong Kong	1997
2	Fiji	Tokyo	2001

by a player

Drops	Player	Opponents	Venue	Year
2	R P Ross	Hong Kong	Hong Kong	1997
2	R P Ross	Fiji	Tokyo	2001

Career Records

Most Capped Players

Caps	Player	Career Span
65	A J Charron	1990 to 2001
64	D S Stewart	1989 to 2001
55	G L Rees	1986 to 1999
54	J D Graf	1989 to 1999
50	J Hutchinson	1993 to 2000
49	E A Evans	1986 to 1998
47	S D Gray	1984 to 1997
47	W U Stanley	1994 to 2001
43	R P Ross	1989 to 2001
38	R G A Snow	1995 to 2001

Most Consecutive Tests

Tests	Player	Span
40	J Hutchinson	1995 to 1999
25	J N Tait	1998 to 2001
21	W U Stanley	1998 to 2000
17	R P Ross	1996 to 1997
15	S D Gray	1991 to 1994

Mosts Tests as Captain

Tests	Captain	Span
25	G L Rees	1994 to 1999
16	J D Graf	1995 to 1999
14	A J Charron	1996 to 2001
9	M A Wyatt	1990 to 1991
8	M Luke	1974 to 1981
8	H de Goede	1984 to 1987

Most Tests in Individual Positions

Position	Player	Tests	Span
Full-back	D S Stewart	46	1989 to 2001
Wing	W U Stanley	35	1994 to 2001
Centre	S D Gray	31	1984 to 1997
Fly-half	G L Rees	49	1986 to 1999
Scrum-half	J D Graf	39	1989 to 1999
Prop	E A Evans	49	1986 to 1998
Hooker	M E Cardinal	34	1986 to 1998
Lock	M B James	36	1994 to 2000
Flanker	J Hutchinson	46	1995 to 1999
No 8	C McKenzie	25	1992 to 1997

Most Points in Tests

Points	Player	Tests	Career
492	G L Rees	55	1986 to 1999
347	R P Ross	43	1989 to 2001
263	M A Wyatt	29	1982 to 1991
103	W U Stanley	47	1994 to 2001
90	J D Graf	54	1989 to 1999

Most Tries in Tests

Tries	Player	Tests	Career
20	W U Stanley	47	1994 to 2001
9	K S Nichols	25	1996 to 2001
9	P Palmer	17	1983 to 1992
9	J D Graf	54	1989 to 1999
9	G L Rees	55	1986 to 1999
9	A J Charron	65	1990 to 2001

Most Conversions in Tests

Cons	Player	Tests	Career
51	G L Rees	55	1986 to 1999
43	R P Ross	43	1989 to 2001
24	M A Wyatt	29	1982 to 1991
9	J Barker	3	2000
9	D S Stewart	64	1989 to 2001

Most Penalty Goals in Tests

Penalties	Player	Tests	Career
110	G L Rees	55	1986 to 1999
68	R P Ross	43	1989 to 2001
64	M A Wyatt	29	1982 to 1991
14	D S Stewart	64	1989 to 2001
9	J D Graf	54	1989 to 1999
8	M D Schiefler	9	1980 to 1984

Most Dropped Goals in Tests

Drops	Player	Tests	Career
9	G L Rees	55	1986 to 1999
9	R P Ross	43	1989 to 2001
5	M A Wyatt	29	1982 to 1991

Career Records of Canada International Players
(up to 20 October 2001)

Player	Debut	Caps	T	C	P	D	Pts
Backs:							
F C Asselin	1999 v Fj	7	0	0	0	0	0
J Barker	2000 v Tg	3	0	9	7	1	42
J Cannon	2001 v US	6	0	0	0	0	0
J A Cordle	1998 v HK	6	1	0	0	0	5
M Danskin	2001 v J	1	0	0	0	0	0
M di Girolamo	2001 v U	2	0	0	0	0	0
E Fairhurst	2001 v Arg	2	0	0	0	0	0
S Fauth	2000 v Tg	14	4	0	0	0	20
M Irvine	2000 v Tg	8	0	0	0	0	0
K S Nichols	1996 v U	25	9	1	3	0	56
C B Robertson	1997 v HK	7	3	0	0	0	15
R P Ross	1989 v I	43	6	43	68	9	347
W U Stanley	1994 v US	47	20	0	0	1	103
D S Stewart	1989 v US	64	5	9	14	0	84
S Thompson	2001 v Fj	2	0	0	0	0	0
J Williams	2001 v US	5	0	0	0	0	0
M Williams	1999 v Tg	17	4	0	0	0	20
N Witkowski	1998 v US	13	2	0	0	0	10
Forwards:							
R Banks	1999 v J	20	2	0	0	0	10
D Baugh	1998 v J	23	4	0	0	0	20
D Burleigh	2001 v U	4	0	0	0	0	0
A J Charron	1990 v Arg	65	9	0	0	0	44
G G Cooke	2000 v Tg	4	0	0	0	0	0
G A Dixon	2000 v US	11	0	0	0	0	0
P Dunkley	1998 v J	26	2	0	0	0	10
M B James	1994 v US	36	2	0	0	0	10
R Johnstone	2001 v U	3	0	0	0	0	0
E R P Knaggs	2000 v Tg	14	0	0	0	0	0
B Major	2001 v Fj	2	0	0	0	0	0
D Major	1999 v E	10	0	0	0	0	0
P Murphy	2000 v Tg	9	4	0	0	0	20
M R Schmid	1996 v U	24	2	0	0	0	10
R G A Snow	1995 v Arg	38	7	0	0	0	35
B Stoikos	2001 v U	1	0	0	0	0	0
J N Tait	1997 v US	31	1	0	0	0	5
J Thiel	1998 v HK	23	1	0	0	0	5
K Tkachuk	2000 v Tg	8	0	0	0	0	0
H Toews	1998 v J	11	1	0	0	0	5
J B Tomlinson	1996 v A	2	0	0	0	0	0
K M Wirachowski	1992 v E	14	3	0	0	0	15
C Yukes	2001 v U	3	0	0	0	0	0

ARGENTINA TEST SEASON REVIEW 2000-01

Pumas Among the Best of the Rest

Frankie Deges

After a much celebrated fifth position at the 1999 Rugby World Cup, Los Pumas were never going to have it easy in 2000 and 2001, especially when the fixture list included games against Ireland, Australia, South Africa, England and New Zealand. But, riding the wave, the team led by Lisandro Arbizu gave a good account of itself. Equally important, moreover, for the standing of Argentine rugby was its successful organisation of the Rugby World Cup Sevens in Mar del Plata in January 2001. In front of their own ecstatic crowds Los Pumas gave a stirring performance to finish third.

That fifth place in Wales in 1999 had generated huge interest in the team in particular and for the game of rugby in general in Argentina. So when Ireland arrived in Buenos Aires for a one-off game, it was billed as the re-match of that famous repechage win in Lens, France. Having been without a coach for five months, common sense thankfully prevailed and former national captain Marcelo Loffreda was installed, bringing with him another former Puma captain in assistant coach Daniel Baetti. Their work ethic, vast knowledge of the game and the respect they commanded as distinguished former Pumas made them ideal choices.

Ireland were beaten 34-23 in a game that saw scrum-half Agustín Pichot lead the side for the first time (Arbizu was injured) and in doing so was involved in the three tries scored by Argentina. Although Ireland scored four, it was the unerring boot of Gonzalo Quesada that once again steered Los Pumas to victory.

With no time to celebrate, the team flew to Australia, where after beating Queensland Reds 35-29 they met the Wallabies who were playing in their first Test since winning the Webb Ellis Trophy. The hype and razzmatazz affected Argentina. They crashed 53-6, failing to show any spark and playing for thirty minutes with only 14 players because of three different sin-bin incidents.

After beating the New South Wales Waratahs 27-26, the team recovered and frightened the world champions in the second Test. With a better defensive organisation, tighter discipline and better cohesion, Los Pumas were deep in attack in the dying seconds and seemed destined for a pushover try, only to be called back for an infringement. It could have been a famous draw; in any case, it was a moral victory. In the process, Los Pumas scored their season's best try through Ignacio Corleto, which began with a deep counterattack.

The four-and-a-half month wait for the next Test enabled Loffreda and Baetti to fly to Bordeaux in mid-October to hold a training camp with the 15 of their Test squad players who were based in France and England. In a move thought to be unique in the annals of international rugby, it clearly demonstrated the problems Argentina faces with its top players having to play professional rugby overseas.

When the Springboks, en route for a tour of Britain and Ireland, arrived to play at the River Plate Stadium (the biggest and most famous of Argentina's sporting arenas), Los Pumas and a vociferous crowd of 55,000 were awaiting them. Again, and understandably, Los Pumas failed to win, but the manner of their loss spoke volumes for their potential at this level. They had a try scoring opportunity near the end that could have turned the game, but their rolling maul was penalised and South Africa escaped with a 37-33 win after Braam van Straaten landed a penalty goal in the third minute of injury time.

On to Twickenham, where the high expectations were brought crashing to earth. Failing to win quality ball and to launch attacks, Los Pumas fell 19-0 in awful conditions to an excellent England side to close their season.

A Development side comprising players not in the international squad won the South American Championship in Uruguay, beating Chile 18-16 and Los Teros 29-19. The close season saw the World Cup Sevens turn players such as Pichot, Felipe Contepomi, Corleto and Pedro Baraldi into household names. True, they failed to conquer the eventual World Champions, New Zealand, in the semi-final, but theirs will be forever remembered as one of the best Argentine sporting performances.

The new 2001 season brought few changes behind the scenes, although Luis Gradín was replaced by Miguel Servera as President of the Unión Argentina de Rugby after his two terms had expired.

Los Pumas travelled to Eastern Canada to play in the fourth Pan American tournament in May and even without most of their European-based players they still managed to maintain their unbeaten record in this competition. They opened with a close win against Uruguay (32-27), a good victory against the United States followed (44-16) and, in what was effectively the grand final, they had to show their resolve in a hard contest against Canada before winning 20-6.

The next stop was not easy. With the strongest available squad, Argentina travelled to New Zealand for a four-match tour, a stopover for a Test against Fiji having to be called off prior to departure. Loffreda and his troops faced the biggest challenge of his tenure. 'Coming to New Zealand is like doing a Masters Degree in Rugby, all in three weeks,' said captain Arbizu, who on tour was to break Hugo Porta's record as the player with the most overall appearances for Argentina. Arbizu has now played in 95 games for the national side.

After wins against Counties-Manukau and Thames Valley, several of the experienced heads in the team were speaking optimistically of Argentina's chances against the All Blacks. These hopes were soon dispelled. Although

Los Pumas dominated the scrums and the forwards had a good game, the general play of the home side was too good and too precise for a surprised Puma team that left with a 19-67 loss. An end of tour loss against the NZ Maoris 24-43 emphasised further the deep differences between Argentine rugby and that of the game's superpowers.

Italy arrived in July at the end of a globe-trotting tour that had previously taken them to Namibia, South Africa and Uruguay. Without a number of their first choice players, the *azzurri* crashed to their biggest ever defeat against Los Pumas, losing 38-17. It was a good end to the first part of the 2001 season for Argentina.

Among the future challenges for the current squad of Test players is one that lies off the field as they try to convince the establishment of the need for a professional squad. If they are successful in persuading some of the more sceptic stalwarts about the advantages of change, it could be argued that Los Pumas might finally break into the top echelon of nations. Then, given regular competition – they are one of the few nations with no annual Test tournament – the sky will be the limit.

As things stand today, they are only among the best of the rest.

Argentina's Test Record in 2000-2001:
Played 7, won 4, lost 3.

Opponents	Date	Venue	Result
Italy	14th July 2001	H	Won 38-17
New Zealand	23rd June 2001	A	Lost 19-67
Canada	26th May 2001	A	Won 20-6
United States	23rd May 2001	A	Won 44-16
Uruguay	19th May 2001	A	Won 32-27
England	19th November 2000	A	Lost 0-19
South Africa	12th November 2000	H	Lost 33-37

ARGENTINA INTERNATIONAL STATISTICS
(up to 20 October 2001)

Match Records

Most Consecutive Test Wins

10 1992 *Sp* 1,2, *R, F,* 1993 *J* 1,2, *Br, Ch, P, U*
7 1972 *Gz* 2, 1973 *Pg, U, Br, Ch, R* 1,2

Most Consecutive Tests Without Defeat

Matches	Wins	Draws	Period
10	10	0	1992 to 1993
7	7	0	1972 to 1973

Most Points in a Match
by the team

Pts	Opponents	Venue	Year
114	Brazil	Sao Paulo	1993
109	Brazil	Santiago	1979
103	Paraguay	Asuncion	1995
103	Brazil	Montevideo	1989
102	Paraguay	Asuncion	1985
98	Paraguay	San Pablo	1973
96	Brazil	San Pablo	1973

by a player

Pts	Player	Opponents	Venue	Year
50	E Morgan	Paraguay	San Pablo	1973
40	G M Jorge	Brazil	Sao Paulo	1993
32	M Sansot	Brazil	Tucuman	1977
31	E Morgan	Uruguay	San Pablo	1973
31	E De Forteza	Paraguay	Asuncion	1975
31	J Luna	Romania	Buenos Aires	1995
30	J Capalbo	Uruguay	Tucuman	1977
29	P Guarrochena	Paraguay	Tucuman	1977
29	S E Meson	Canada	Buenos Aires	1995
29	G Quesada	Canada	Buenos Aires	1998
28	E Morgan	Chile	San Pablo	1973
27	G Quesada	Samoa	Llanelli	1999

Most Tries in a Match
by the team

Tries	Opponents	Venue	Year
19	Brazil	Santiago	1979
19	Paraguay	Asuncion	1985
18	Paraguay	San Pablo	1973
18	Brazil	San Pablo	1973
18	Brazil	Sao Paulo	1993
17	Brazil	Buenos Aires	1991
16	Paraguay	Asuncion	1995
15	Paraguay	Asuncion	1975
14	Paraguay	Montevideo	1989
14	Brazil	Montevideo	1961

by a player

Tries	Player	Opponents	Venue	Year
8	G M Jorge	Brazil	Sao Paulo	1993
6	E Morgan	Paraguay	San Pablo	1973
6	G M Jorge	Brazil	Montevideo	1989
5	H Goti	Brazil	Montevideo	1961
5	M Rodriguez Jurado	Brazil	Montevideo	1971
5	P Grande	Paraguay	Asuncion	1998

Most Conversions in a Match
by the team

Cons	Opponents	Venue	Year
15	Brazil	Santiago	1979
13	Paraguay	San Pablo	1973
13	Paraguay	Asuncion	1985
12	Paraguay	Asuncion	1975
12	Brazil	Buenos Aires	1993
10	Paraguay	Tucuman	1977
10	Brazil	Montevideo	1989

by a player

Cons	Player	Opponents	Venue	Year
13	E Morgan	Paraguay	San Pablo	1973
13	H Porta	Paraguay	Asuncion	1985
11	E De Forteza	Paraguay	Asuncion	1975
10	P Guarrochena	Paraguay	Tucuman	1977
10	S E Meson	Brazil	Montevideo	1989
10	S E Meson	Brazil	Sao Paulo	1993

Most Penalties in a Match
by the team

Penalties	Opponents	Venue	Year
8	Canada	Buenos Aires	1995
8	Samoa	Llanelli	1999
7	France	Buenos Aires	1974
7	France	Nantes	1992
7	Canada	Buenos Aires	1998
7	Japan	Cardiff	1999
7	Ireland	Lens	1999

by a player

Penalties	Player	Opponents	Venue	Year
8	S E Meson	Canada	Buenos Aires	1995
8	G Quesada	Samoa	Llanelli	1999
7	H Porta	France	Buenos Aires	1974
7	S E Meson	France	Nantes	1992
7	G Quesada	Canada	Buenos Aires	1998
7	G Quesada	Japan	Cardiff	1999
7	G Quesada	Ireland	Lens	1999

Most Dropped Goals in a Match
by the team

Drops	Opponents	Venue	Year
3	SA Gazelles	Pretoria	1971
3	Uruguay	Asuncion	1975
3	Australia	Buenos Aires	1979
3	New Zealand	Buenos Aires	1985
3	Canada	Markham	2001
2	SA Gazelles	Buenos Aires	1966
2	Scotland	Buenos Aires	1969
2	Uruguay	Montevideo	1971
2	Chile	Asuncion	1975
2	New Zealand	Dunedin	1979
2	Australia	Buenos Aires	1987
2	Chile	Santiago	1991
2	Australia	Llanelli	1991

by a player

Drops	Player	Opponents	Venue	Year
3	T Harris Smith	SA Gazelles	Pretoria	1971
3	H Porta	Australia	Buenos Aires	1979
3	H Porta	New Zealand	Buenos Aires	1985
3	J Fernadez Miranda	Canada	Markham	2001
2	E Poggi	SA Gazelles	Buenos Aires	1966
2	T Harris Smith	Scotland	Buenos Aires	1969
2	H Porta	Uruguay	Montevideo	1971
2	E De Forteza	Chile	Asuncion	1975
2	H Porta	New Zealand	Dunedin	1979
2	H Porta	Australia	Buenos Aires	1987
2	L Arbizu	Chile	Santiago	1991
2	L Arbizu	Australia	Llanelli	1991

Career Records

Most Capped Players

Caps	Player	Career Span
75	L Arbizu	1990 to 2001
65	P L Sporleder	1990 to 1999
64	R Martin	1994 to 2001
63	D Cuesta Silva	1983 to 1995
58	H Porta	1971 to 1990

51	F E Mendez	1990 to 2001
46	M Loffreda	1978 to 1994
43	G A Llanes	1990 to 2000
40	E Branca	1976 to 1990
39	R Madero	1978 to 1990
39	D M Cash	1985 to 1992
38	D Albanese	1995 to 2001
37	S Salvat	1987 to 1995
36	A Pichot	1995 to 2001

Most Points in Tests

Points	Player	Tests	Career
590	H Porta	58	1971 to 1990
371	G Quesada	27	1996 to 2001
364	S E Meson	34	1987 to 1997
160	L Arbizu	73	1990 to 2001
129	J Luna	8	1995 to 1997
127	E Morgan	12	1972 to 1975
125	D Cuesta Silva	62	1983 to 1995

Most Tries in Tests

Tries	Player	Tests	Career
28	D Cuesta Silva	62	1983 to 1995
23	G M Jorge	22	1989 to 1994
15	R Martin	64	1994 to 2001
13	G Morgan	7	1977 to 1979
13	G Alvarez	9	1975 to 1977

Most Conversions in Tests

Cons	Player	Tests	Career
84	H Porta	58	1971 to 1990
68	S E Meson	34	1987 to 1997
48	G Quesada	27	1996 to 2001
26	E Morgan	12	1972 to 1975
26	J Luna	8	1995 to 1997

Most Penalty Goals in Tests

Penalties	Player	Tests	Career
101	H Porta	58	1971 to 1990
81	G Quesada	27	1996 to 2001
63	S E Meson	34	1987 to 1997
22	F Contepomi	20	1998 to 2001
20	J L Cilley	11	1994 to 1996
19	J Luna	8	1995 to 1997

Most Dropped Goals in Tests

Drops	Player	Tests	Career
26	H Porta	58	1971 to 1990
10	L Arbizu	75	1990 to 2001
6	J Fernandez Miranda	9	1997 to 2001
5	T Harris Smith	5	1969 to 1972
4	G Quesada	27	1996 to 2001

Career Records of Argentina International Players
(up to 20 October 2001)

Player	Debut	Caps	T	C	P	D	Pts
Backs:							
D Albanese	1995 v U	38	8	0	0	0	40
M Albina	2001 v US	1	0	0	0	0	0
L Arbizu	1990 v I	75	12	14	14	10	160
O Bartolucci	1996 v US	17	8	0	0	0	40
G Camardon	1990 v E	33	8	0	0	0	40
F Contepomi	1998 v Ch	20	3	11	24	0	109
I Corleto	1998 v J	6	3	0	0	0	15
J Fernandez Miranda	1997 v U	9	1	14	7	6	72
J M Nunez Piossek	2001 v U	3	1	0	0	0	5
J Orengo	1996 v U	19	6	0	0	0	30
A Pichot	1995 v A	36	10	0	0	0	50
G Quesada	1996 v US	27	4	48	81	4	371
E Simone	1996 v US	34	7	0	0	0	35
F Soler	1996 v U	23	12	0	0	0	60
B Stortoni	1998 v J	7	2	1	0	0	12
Forwards:							
A Allub	1997 v Pg	28	1	0	0	0	5
R Alvarez	1998 v Pg	5	0	0	0	0	0
E Bergamaschi	2001 v US	1	0	0	0	0	0
S Bonorino	2001 v U	3	0	0	0	0	0
A Canalda	1999 v S	4	0	0	0	0	0
H Dande	2001 v U	2	1	0	0	0	5
L de Chazal	2001 v U	2	0	0	0	0	0
M Durand	1998 v Ch	12	2	0	0	0	10
R D Grau	1993 v J	32	2	0	0	0	10
O Hasan	1995 v U	31	1	0	0	0	5
M Ledesma	1996 v U	27	0	0	0	0	0
C I Fernandez Lobbe	1996 v US	28	2	0	0	0	10
G Longo	1999 v W	16	1	0	0	0	5
R Martin	1994 v US	64	15	0	0	0	75
F E Mendez	1990 v I	51	10	0	0	0	50
G Morales Olivier	2001 v U	3	0	0	0	0	0
L Ostiglia	1999 v W	9	0	0	0	0	0
S Phelan	1997 v U	22	0	0	0	0	0
M Reggiardo	1996 v U	33	1	0	0	0	5
L Roldan	2001 v U	2	1	0	0	0	5
M Sambucetti	2001 v U	2	0	0	0	0	0
G Ugartemendia	1991 v U	13	1	0	0	0	5
J J Villar	2001 v U	3	0	0	0	0	0

WOMEN'S TEST SEASON REVIEW 2000-01

England Threaten New Zealand Dominance

Nicola Goodwin

The 2000-01 season saw great gains made in women's rugby across the globe. With the major nations beginning their preparation for the 2002 World Cup, the first full-time professional women's coaches were appointed and the standards of skill and fitness across the game continued to grow.

In September, the United States, England and World Champions New Zealand travelled to Winnipeg for the Canada Cup. With the top three world-ranked countries coming face to face for the first time since the World Cup in Holland in 1998, the tournament was a benchmark for standards in women's international rugby. New Zealand and England both beat Canada and the United States comfortably in the opening rounds before the Black Ferns sealed their reputation as the number one nation in the world with a 32-13 final victory over England. In the 3rd/4th place play off host nation Canada lost 9-15 to the United States but they will be pleased with some major improvements in their standards of play.

The standards of domestic rugby in both Canada and the United States have improved dramatically since the 1998 World Cup. The United States has an enviable calendar packed with domestic sevens, tens and fifteens tournaments and trial matches, and their college rugby set-up is the best in the world. In August, Martin Gallagher, former coach of Emerging England, was appointed Head Coach of the United States on a part-time professional basis with the aim of improving on their World Cup second place finish in 1998.

England and New Zealand marked themselves out as being the forerunners in the women's game with the appointment of full-time professional coaches in 2000. Daryl Suasua was appointed as head of the Black Ferns coaching team whilst former Australian full-back Geoff Richards took over the England squad in September. Born in England, Richards boasts an impressive playing and coaching cv and headed up a team of full and part-time professional coaches and back-room staff.

The impact of Richards was evident during the 2001 Six Nations Championship where England proved their dominance of the Northern Hemisphere. The inaugural women's Six Nations saw Ireland return after a year spent rebuilding their domestic game; but their appearances were frustratingly cut to just two owing to the foot-and-mouth crisis. They were disappointed with heavy losses against Spain and France, but the recently introduced provincial championship has proved to be a good breeding ground for new talent. Spain, as temporary replacements for Ireland, deservedly kept their place

The England Women's squad celebrate winning the Six Nations Championship title after beating France at Northampton in April.

following convincing performances in the 1999-2000 season and proved their strength with three wins and a third-place finish.

Top honours went to England with four wins from four and they seized the crown with a thrilling 50-6 victory over France at Northampton. Despite a shaky 18-0 victory in the opening match against Wales, England's fitness and strength was too much for their opposition and their defence held strong as they conceded just 18 points in the championship. France finished in second place and despite coach Daniel Dupouy's disappointment at the defeat by England, he did well with a mixed squad of experienced internationals and fresh newcomers.

Scotland and Wales were very disappointed at their fourth and fifth placed finishes, though both nations have undergone positive regeneration both on and off the field. Scotland have found life difficult since losing lottery funding in 1999, but meetings with Jim Telfer, the SRU and the men's officials have proved positive and they now have a full time administration officer to boost their back-room staff. A new lottery bid has been successful and the impact of funding on the players for the World Cup season will be a great boost. Wales are experiencing good relations with the WRU and new funding has benefited grass roots rugby in the country, allowing more time and resources to be spent identifying future talent. The changes also gave coach John Williams the chance to meet more frequently with the squad, improving the structure of their game.

The Six Nations all travelled to Lille in May for the European Championships with England taking the bold step of sending a development squad. The move paid off, though, as a team containing just six capped players beat Kazakhstan and holders France to take third place. Top honours went to the triumphant Scotland side who beat Spain in a hard fought final to lift the European Cup for the first time. The win boosted the Scottish players and gave them renewed confidence after a disappointing Six Nations. The accolade of European Champions together with financial assistance from their new lottery grant should make Scotland a side to watch in forthcoming seasons.

The European Championships proved to be a well-organised and popular tournament, giving all countries a chance for valuable international competition. A 17-6 win over Kazakhstan, who again proved themselves to be a team capable of causing major upset, gave Wales a fifth place finish; their highest ever in the tournament. Ireland managed their first victory of the season with a nail-bitingly close 9-8 victory over Italy to gain seventh place and retain a place in the senior pool that is crucial for their development.

In the junior pool the emergence of Sweden brought a smile to everybody's faces as they overcame frost, floods and appalling conditions to win the pool and gain promotion to the senior competition. Coached by New Zealander John Shand, the side had not played in six months owing to severe weather conditions in Sweden, but they managed wins over Germany, Belgium and Holland to gain the chance to meet the major nations. With women's rugby also emerging in Norway and Luxembourg, the European Championships look set to grow in forthcoming seasons.

Nations from across the world met at the Hong Kong Sevens in April which received IRB funding and doubled as the Asian Championships. Emerging countries China, Japan, Arabian Gulf, Singapore, Thailand and Hong Kong got a taste of international rugby and are continuing to develop their domestic games. New Zealand, Samoa, United States and England reached the semi final stages before New Zealand repeated last year's performance with a 22-0 victory over the United States.

The final international matches of the season caused much interest as England toured Australia and New Zealand in May and June. The Six Nations champions secured two Test wins in Australia but were stretched by a vastly improved Australian side who will be a force to watch at the World Cup. Australia's decision to keep their cards to themselves and play no more internationals until May 2002 underlines their confidence. In New Zealand, England faced a sterner challenge, but a narrow 15-10 loss against the Black Ferns in the opening Test was a thrilling encounter. A week later at North Harbour Stadium England upset the world of women's rugby with a 22-17 victory, thus ending New Zealand's unbeaten run of 24 victories. This was the Black Ferns' first defeat since they started playing international matches but it confirmed the considerable advance of England's game.

The 2002 World Cup kicks off in Barcelona in May 2002 and will be a true celebration of the women's game. Enormous gains have been made since the first World Cup in Wales in 1991 and every season a new country emerges on the international scene. Australia and Samoa will be countries to watch and news that women's rugby is now being played in South Africa will cause much interest across the globe. With professional coaches, bigger crowds, improved media interest and lottery funding for players the game is making big strides. The 2001-02 season promises to be the best yet.

International Results: 2000-01

Test Match
6 August United States 10 Canada 17 (New York)

Women's Canada Cup 2000
New Zealand win
23 September England 31, United States 7; Canada 0, New Zealand 41;
27 September Canada 10, England 34; United States 0, New Zealand 45;
30 September New Zealand 32, England 13; Canada 9, United States 15 (all matches staged in Winnipeg, Manitoba)

Six Nations 2001
England win
2 February Spain 42, Ireland 0 (Barcelona); 3 February France 13, Scotland 0 (Paris); 4 February Wales 0, England 18 (Newport); 17 February Ireland 0, France 53 (Clontarf); 18 February Scotland 22, Wales 0 (Boroughmuir); England 28, Spain 12 (Worcester); 3 March Spain 6, France 0 (Madrid); 4 March England 39,

Scotland 0 (Richmond); 16 March France 24, Wales 3 (Nanterre); 18 March Scotland 19, Spain 8 (Melrose); 7 April Wales 0, Spain 5 (Wrexham); 8 April England 50, France 6 (Northampton)

European Women's Championship 2001

Group A – Scotland win

7 May France 45, Ireland 9 (Marquette lez Lille); Spain 34, Italy 3 (Lille UC); England 29, Kazakhstan 15 (Tourcoing); Scotland 13, Wales 3 (Hazebrouk); 9 May France 6, Scotland 9 (Armentieres); Ireland 10, Wales 15 (Tourcoing); Spain 15, England 8 (Roubaix); Italy 0, Kazakhstan 20 (Villeneuve d'Ascq); 12 May Scotland 15, Spain 3 (Stadium Nord); France 23, England 34 (Stadium Nord); Wales 17, Kazakhstan 7 (Villeneuve d'Ascq); Ireland 9, Italy 8 (Lille)

Group B – Sweden win

7 May Holland 66, Belgium 0 (Lille); Germany 13, Sweden 15 (Villeneuve d'Ascq); 9 May Holland 17, Germany 6 (Armentieres); Belgium 0, Sweden 90 (Roubaix); 12 May Holland 12, Sweden 13 (Lille UC); Germany 67, Belgium 0 (Armentieres)

Tour Tests 2001

26 May Australia 19, England 41 (Sydney); 2 June Australia 5, England 15 (Newcastle); 9 June New Zealand 15, England 10 (Rotorua); 16 June New Zealand 17, England 22 (North Harbour)

INTERNATIONAL RECORDS

Results of International Matches
(up to 20 October 2001)

Cap matches involving senior executive council member unions only.
Years for International Championship matches are for the second half of the season: eg 1972 means season 1971-72. Years for matches against touring teams from the Southern Hemisphere refer to the actual year of the match.
Points-scoring was first introduced in 1886, when an International Board was formed by Scotland, Ireland and Wales. Points values varied between countries until 1890, when England agreed to join the Board, and uniform values were adopted.

Northern Hemisphere seasons	Try	Conversion	Penalty goal	Dropped goal	Goal from mark
1890-91	1	2	2	3	3
1891-92 to 1892-93	2	3	3	4	4
1893-94 to 1904-05	3	2	3	4	4
1905-06 to 1947-48	3	2	3	4	3
1948-49 to 1970-71	3	2	3	3	3
1971-72 to 1991-92	4	2	3	3	3*
1992-93 onwards	5	2	3	3	–

*The goal from mark ceased to exist when the free-kick clause was introduced, 1977-78.
WC indicates a fixture played during the Rugby World Cup finals. LC indicates a fixture played in the Latin Cup. TN indicates a fixture played in the Tri Nations.

ENGLAND v SCOTLAND
Played 118   England won 61, Scotland won 40, Drawn 17
Highest scores England 43-3 in 2001, Scotland 33-6 in 1986
Biggest wins England 43-3 in 2001, Scotland 33-6 in 1986

1871 Raeburn Place (Edinburgh) **Scotland** 1G 1T to 1T	1889 No Match
1872 The Oval (London) **England** 1G 1DG 2T to 1DG	1890 Raeburn Place **England** 1G 1T to 0
1873 Glasgow **Drawn** no score	1891 Richmond (London) **Scotland** 9-3
1874 The Oval **England** 1DG to 1T	1892 Raeburn Place **England** 5-0
1875 Raeburn Place **Drawn** no score	1893 Leeds **Scotland** 8-0
1876 The Oval **England** 1G 1T to 0	1894 Raeburn Place **Scotland** 6-0
1877 Raeburn Place **Scotland** 1 DG to 0	1895 Richmond **Scotland** 6-3
1878 The Oval **Drawn** no score	1896 Glasgow **Scotland** 11-0
1879 Raeburn Place **Drawn** Scotland 1DG England 1G	1897 Manchester **England** 12-3
1880 Manchester **England** 2G 3T to 1G	1898 Powderhall (Edinburgh) **Drawn** 3-3
1881 Raeburn Place **Drawn** Scotland 1G 1T England 1DG 1T	1899 Blackheath **Scotland** 5-0
1882 Manchester **Scotland** 2T to 0	1900 Inverleith (Edinburgh) **Drawn** 0-0
1883 Raeburn Place **England** 2T to 1T	1901 Blackheath **Scotland** 18-3
1884 Blackheath (London) **England** 1G to 1T	1902 Inverleith **England** 6-3
1885 No Match	1903 Richmond **Scotland** 10-6
1886 Raeburn Place **Drawn** no score	1904 Inverleith **Scotland** 6-3
1887 Manchester **Drawn** 1T each	1905 Richmond **Scotland** 8-0
1888 No Match	1906 Inverleith **England** 9-3
	1907 Blackheath **Scotland** 8-3
	1908 Inverleith **Scotland** 16-10
	1909 Richmond **Scotland** 18-8
	1910 Inverleith **England** 14-5

1911	Twickenham **England** 13-8		1964	Murrayfield **Scotland** 15-6
1912	Inverleith **Scotland** 8-3		1965	Twickenham **Drawn** 3-3
1913	Twickenham **England** 3-0		1966	Murrayfield **Scotland** 6-3
1914	Inverleith **England** 16-15		1967	Twickenham **England** 27-14
1920	Twickenham **England** 13-4		1968	Murrayfield **England** 8-6
1921	Inverleith **England** 18-0		1969	Twickenham **England** 8-3
1922	Twickenham **England** 11-5		1970	Murrayfield **Scotland** 14-5
1923	Inverleith **England** 8-6		1971	Twickenham **Scotland** 16-15
1924	Twickenham **England** 19-0		1971	Murrayfield **Scotland** 26-6
1925	Murrayfield **Scotland** 14-11			*Special centenary match – non-championship*
1926	Twickenham **Scotland** 17-9		1972	Murrayfield **Scotland** 23-9
1927	Murrayfield **Scotland** 21-13		1973	Twickenham **England** 20-13
1928	Twickenham **England** 6-0		1974	Murrayfield **Scotland** 16-14
1929	Murrayfield **Scotland** 12-6		1975	Twickenham **England** 7-6
1930	Twickenham **Drawn** 0-0		1976	Murrayfield **Scotland** 22-12
1931	Murrayfield **Scotland** 28-19		1977	Twickenham **England** 26-6
1932	Twickenham **England** 16-3		1978	Murrayfield **England** 15-0
1933	Murrayfield **Scotland** 3-0		1979	Twickenham **Drawn** 7-7
1934	Twickenham **England** 6-3		1980	Murrayfield **England** 30-18
1935	Murrayfield **Scotland** 10-7		1981	Twickenham **England** 23-17
1936	Twickenham **England** 9-8		1982	Murrayfield **Drawn** 9-9
1937	Murrayfield **England** 6-3		1983	Twickenham **Scotland** 22-12
1938	Twickenham **Scotland** 21-16		1984	Murrayfield **Scotland** 18-6
1939	Murrayfield **England** 9-6		1985	Twickenham **England** 10-7
1947	Twickenham **England** 24-5		1986	Murrayfield **Scotland** 33-6
1948	Murrayfield **Scotland** 6-3		1987	Twickenham **England** 21-12
1949	Twickenham **England** 19-3		1988	Murrayfield **England** 9-6
1950	Murrayfield **Scotland** 13-11		1989	Twickenham **Drawn** 12-12
1951	Twickenham **England** 5-3		1990	Murrayfield **Scotland** 13-7
1952	Murrayfield **England** 19-3		1991	Twickenham **England** 21-12
1953	Twickenham **England** 26-8		1991	Murrayfield *WC* **England** 9-6
1954	Murrayfield **England** 13-3		1992	Murrayfield **England** 25-7
1955	Twickenham **England** 9-6		1993	Twickenham **England** 26-12
1956	Murrayfield **England** 11-6		1994	Murrayfield **England** 15-14
1957	Twickenham **England** 16-3		1995	Twickenham **England** 24-12
1958	Murrayfield **Drawn** 3-3		1996	Murrayfield **England** 18-9
1959	Twickenham **Drawn** 3-3		1997	Twickenham **England** 41-13
1960	Murrayfield **England** 21-12		1998	Murrayfield **England** 34-20
1961	Twickenham **England** 6-0		1999	Twickenham **England** 24-21
1962	Murrayfield **Drawn** 3-3		2000	Murrayfield **Scotland** 19-13
1963	Twickenham **England** 10-8		2001	Twickenham **England** 43-3

ENGLAND v IRELAND

Played 114   England won 67, Ireland won 39, Drawn 8
Highest scores England 50-18 in 2000, Ireland 26-21 in 1974
Biggest wins England 46-6 in 1997, Ireland 22-0 in 1947

1875	The Oval (London) **England** 1G 1DG 1T to 0		1888	No Match
			1889	No Match
1876	Dublin **England** 1G 1T to 0		1890	Blackheath (London) **England** 3T to 0
1877	The Oval **England** 2G 2T to 0		1891	Dublin **England** 9-0
1878	Dublin **England** 2G 1T to 0		1892	Manchester **England** 7-0
1879	The Oval **England** 2G 1DG 2T to 0		1893	Dublin **England** 4-0
1880	Dublin **England** 1G 1T to 1T		1894	Blackheath **Ireland** 7-5
1881	Manchester **England** 2G 2T to 0		1895	Dublin **England** 6-3
1882	Dublin **Drawn** 2T each		1896	Leeds **Ireland** 10-4
1883	Manchester **England** 1G 3T to 1T		1897	Dublin **Ireland** 13-9
1884	Dublin **England** 1G to 0		1898	Richmond (London) **Ireland** 9-6
1885	Manchester **England** 2T to 1T		1899	Dublin **Ireland** 6-0
1886	Dublin **England** 1T to 0		1900	Richmond **England** 15-4
1887	Dublin **Ireland** 2G to 0		1901	Dublin **Ireland** 10-6

Scotland 14 England 11, Murrayfield, 21 March 1925
The opening match at Murrayfield. A C 'Johnnie' Wallace, the Scotland winger, dives under the attempted tackle by T E Holliday, the English full-back, to score a vital try which was converted by A C Gillies to make the score 10-11. Later, H Waddell dropped a goal to win the match for Scotland and thus secure the Calcutta Cup and Scotland's first-ever Grand Slam.

1902	Leicester	England 6-3	1959	Dublin	England 3-0
1903	Dublin	Ireland 6-0	1960	Twickenham	England 8-5
1904	Blackheath	England 19-0	1961	Dublin	Ireland 11-8
1905	Cork	Ireland 17-3	1962	Twickenham	England 16-0
1906	Leicester	Ireland 16-6	1963	Dublin	Drawn 0-0
1907	Dublin	Ireland 17-9	1964	Twickenham	Ireland 18-5
1908	Richmond	England 13-3	1965	Dublin	Ireland 5-0
1909	Dublin	England 11-5	1966	Twickenham	Drawn 6-6
1910	Twickenham	Drawn 0-0	1967	Dublin	England 8-3
1911	Dublin	Ireland 3-0	1968	Twickenham	Drawn 9-9
1912	Twickenham	England 15-0	1969	Dublin	Ireland 17-15
1913	Dublin	England 15-4	1970	Twickenham	England 9-3
1914	Twickenham	England 17-12	1971	Dublin	England 9-6
1920	Dublin	England 14-11	1972	Twickenham	Ireland 16-12
1921	Twickenham	England 15-0	1973	Dublin	Ireland 18-9
1922	Dublin	England 12-3	1974	Twickenham	Ireland 26-21
1923	Leicester	England 23-5	1975	Dublin	Ireland 12-9
1924	Belfast	England 14-3	1976	Twickenham	Ireland 13-12
1925	Twickenham	Drawn 6-6	1977	Dublin	England 4-0
1926	Dublin	Ireland 19-15	1978	Twickenham	England 15-9
1927	Twickenham	England 8-6	1979	Dublin	Ireland 12-7
1928	Dublin	England 7-6	1980	Twickenham	England 24-9
1929	Twickenham	Ireland 6-5	1981	Dublin	England 10-6
1930	Dublin	Ireland 4-3	1982	Twickenham	Ireland 16-15
1931	Twickenham	Ireland 6-5	1983	Dublin	Ireland 25-15
1932	Dublin	England 11-8	1984	Twickenham	England 12-9
1933	Twickenham	England 17-6	1985	Dublin	Ireland 13-10
1934	Dublin	England 13-3	1986	Twickenham	England 25-20
1935	Twickenham	England 14-3	1987	Dublin	Ireland 17-0
1936	Dublin	Ireland 6-3	1988	Twickenham	England 35-3
1937	Twickenham	England 9-8	1988	Dublin	England 21-10
1938	Dublin	England 36-14			*Non-championship match*
1939	Twickenham	Ireland 5-0	1989	Dublin	England 16-3
1947	Dublin	Ireland 22-0	1990	Twickenham	England 23-0
1948	Twickenham	Ireland 11-10	1991	Dublin	England 16-7
1949	Dublin	Ireland 14-5	1992	Twickenham	England 38-9
1950	Twickenham	England 3-0	1993	Dublin	Ireland 17-3
1951	Dublin	Ireland 3-0	1994	Twickenham	Ireland 13-12
1952	Twickenham	England 3-0	1995	Dublin	England 20-8
1953	Dublin	Drawn 9-9	1996	Twickenham	England 28-15
1954	Twickenham	England 14-3	1997	Dublin	England 46-6
1955	Dublin	Drawn 6-6	1998	Twickenham	England 35-17
1956	Twickenham	England 20-0	1999	Dublin	England 27-15
1957	Dublin	England 6-0	2000	Twickenham	England 50-18
1958	Twickenham	England 6-0	2001	Dublin	Ireland 20-14

ENGLAND v WALES

Played 107   England won 46, Wales won 49, Drawn 12
Highest scores England 60-26 in 1998, Wales 34-21 in 1967
Biggest wins England 60-26 in 1998, 46-12 in 2000, Wales 25-0 in 1905

1881	Blackheath (London)	England 7G 1DG 6T to 0	1890	Dewsbury	Wales 1T to 0
1882		No Match	1891	Newport	England 7-3
1883	Swansea	England 2G 4T to 0	1892	Blackheath	England 17-0
1884	Leeds	England 1G 2T to 1G	1893	Cardiff	Wales 12-11
1885	Swansea	England 1G 4T to 1G 1T	1894	Birkenhead	England 24-3
1886	Blackheath	England 1GM 2T to 1G	1895	Swansea	England 14-6
1887	Llanelli	Drawn no score	1896	Blackheath	England 25-0
1888		No Match	1897	Newport	Wales 11-0
1889		No Match	1898	Blackheath	England 14-7

1899 Swansea **Wales** 26-3
1900 Gloucester **Wales** 13-3
1901 Cardiff **Wales** 13-0
1902 Blackheath **Wales** 9-8
1903 Swansea **Wales** 21-5
1904 Leicester **Drawn** 14-14
1905 Cardiff **Wales** 25-0
1906 Richmond (London) **Wales** 16-3
1907 Swansea **Wales** 22-0
1908 Bristol **Wales** 28-18
1909 Cardiff **Wales** 8-0
1910 Twickenham **England** 11-6
1911 Swansea **Wales** 15-11
1912 Twickenham **England** 8-0
1913 Cardiff **England** 12-0
1914 Twickenham **England** 10-9
1920 Swansea **Wales** 19-5
1921 Twickenham **England** 18-3
1922 Cardiff **Wales** 28-6
1923 Twickenham **England** 7-3
1924 Swansea **England** 17-9
1925 Twickenham **England** 12-6
1926 Cardiff **Drawn** 3-3
1927 Twickenham **England** 11-9
1928 Swansea **England** 10-8
1929 Twickenham **England** 8-3
1930 Cardiff **England** 11-3
1931 Twickenham **Drawn** 11-11
1932 Swansea **Wales** 12-5
1933 Twickenham **Wales** 7-3
1934 Cardiff **England** 9-0
1935 Twickenham **Drawn** 3-3
1936 Swansea **Drawn** 0-0
1937 Twickenham **England** 4-3
1938 Cardiff **Wales** 14-8
1939 Twickenham **England** 3-0
1947 Cardiff **England** 9-6
1948 Twickenham **Drawn** 3-3
1949 Cardiff **Wales** 9-3
1950 Twickenham **Wales** 11-5
1951 Swansea **Wales** 23-5
1952 Twickenham **Wales** 8-6
1953 Cardiff **England** 8-3
1954 Twickenham **England** 9-6
1955 Cardiff **Wales** 3-0
1956 Twickenham **Wales** 8-3

1957 Cardiff **England** 3-0
1958 Twickenham **Drawn** 3-3
1959 Cardiff **Wales** 5-0
1960 Twickenham **England** 14-6
1961 Cardiff **Wales** 6-3
1962 Twickenham **Drawn** 0-0
1963 Cardiff **England** 13-6
1964 Twickenham **Drawn** 6-6
1965 Cardiff **Wales** 14-3
1966 Twickenham **Wales** 11-6
1967 Cardiff **Wales** 34-21
1968 Twickenham **Drawn** 11-11
1969 Cardiff **Wales** 30-9
1970 Twickenham **Wales** 17-13
1971 Cardiff **Wales** 22-6
1972 Twickenham **Wales** 12-3
1973 Cardiff **Wales** 25-9
1974 Twickenham **England** 16-12
1975 Cardiff **Wales** 20-4
1976 Twickenham **Wales** 21-9
1977 Cardiff **Wales** 14-9
1978 Twickenham **Wales** 9-6
1979 Cardiff **Wales** 27-3
1980 Twickenham **England** 9-8
1981 Cardiff **Wales** 21-19
1982 Twickenham **England** 17-7
1983 Cardiff **Drawn** 13-13
1984 Twickenham **Wales** 24-15
1985 Cardiff **Wales** 24-15
1986 Twickenham **England** 21-18
1987 Cardiff **Wales** 19-12
1987 Brisbane *WC* **Wales** 16-3
1988 Twickenham **Wales** 11-3
1989 Cardiff **Wales** 12-9
1990 Twickenham **England** 34-6
1991 Cardiff **England** 25-6
1992 Twickenham **England** 24-0
1993 Cardiff **Wales** 10-9
1994 Twickenham **England** 15-8
1995 Cardiff **England** 23-9
1996 Twickenham **England** 21-15
1997 Cardiff **England** 34-13
1998 Twickenham **England** 60-26
1999 Wembley **Wales** 32-31
2000 Twickenham **England** 46-12
2001 Cardiff **England** 44-15

ENGLAND v FRANCE
Played 78 England won 43, France won 28, Drawn 7
Highest scores England 48-19 in 2001, France 37-12 in 1972
Biggest wins England 37-0 in 1911, France 37-12 in 1972

1906 Paris **England** 35-8
1907 Richmond (London) **England** 41-13
1908 Paris **England** 19-0
1909 Leicester **England** 22-0
1910 Paris **England** 11-3
1911 Twickenham **England** 37-0
1912 Paris **England** 18-8
1913 Twickenham **England** 20-0

1914 Paris **England** 39-13
1920 Twickenham **England** 8-3
1921 Paris **England** 10-6
1922 Twickenham **Drawn** 11-11
1923 Paris **England** 12-3
1924 Twickenham **England** 19-7
1925 Paris **England** 13-11
1926 Twickenham **England** 11-0

1927	Paris **France** 3-0	1973	Twickenham **England** 14-6
1928	Twickenham **England** 18-8	1974	Paris **Drawn** 12-12
1929	Paris **England** 16-6	1975	Twickenham **France** 27-20
1930	Twickenham **England** 11-5	1976	Paris **France** 30-9
1931	Paris **France** 14-13	1977	Twickenham **France** 4-3
1947	Twickenham **England** 6-3	1978	Paris **France** 15-6
1948	Paris **France** 15-0	1979	Twickenham **England** 7-6
1949	Twickenham **England** 8-3	1980	Paris **England** 17-13
1950	Paris **France** 6-3	1981	Twickenham **France** 16-12
1951	Twickenham **France** 11-3	1982	Paris **England** 27-15
1952	Paris **England** 6-3	1983	Twickenham **France** 19-15
1953	Twickenham **England** 11-0	1984	Paris **France** 32-18
1954	Paris **France** 11-3	1985	Twickenham **Drawn** 9-9
1955	Twickenham **France** 16-9	1986	Paris **France** 29-10
1956	Paris **France** 14-9	1987	Twickenham **France** 19-15
1957	Twickenham **England** 9-5	1988	Paris **France** 10-9
1958	Paris **England** 14-0	1989	Twickenham **England** 11-0
1959	Twickenham **Drawn** 3-3	1990	Paris **England** 26-7
1960	Paris **Drawn** 3-3	1991	Twickenham **England** 21-19
1961	Twickenham **Drawn** 5-5	1991	Paris *WC* **England** 19-10
1962	Paris **France** 13-0	1992	Paris **England** 31-13
1963	Twickenham **England** 6-5	1993	Twickenham **England** 16-15
1964	Paris **England** 6-3	1994	Paris **England** 18-14
1965	Twickenham **England** 9-6	1995	Twickenham **England** 31-10
1966	Paris **France** 13-0	1995	Pretoria *WC* **France** 19-9
1967	Twickenham **France** 16-12	1996	Paris **France** 15-12
1968	Paris **France** 14-9	1997	Twickenham **France** 23-20
1969	Twickenham **England** 22-8	1998	Paris **France** 24-17
1970	Paris **France** 35-13	1999	Twickenham **England** 21-10
1971	Twickenham **Drawn** 14-14	2000	Paris **England** 15-9
1972	Paris **France** 37-12	2001	Twickenham **England** 48-19

ENGLAND v NEW ZEALAND

Played 23   England won 4, New Zealand won 18, Drawn 1
Highest scores England 29-45 in 1995, New Zealand 64-22 in 1998
Biggest wins England 13-0 in 1936, New Zealand 64-22 in 1998

1905	Crystal Palace (London) **New Zealand** 15-0	1985	*1* Christchurch **New Zealand** 18-13
1925	Twickenham **New Zealand** 17-11		*2* Wellington **New Zealand** 42-15
1936	Twickenham **England** 13-0		*New Zealand won series 2-0*
1954	Twickenham **New Zealand** 5-0	1991	Twickenham *WC* **New Zealand** 18-12
1963	*1* Auckland **New Zealand** 21-11	1993	Twickenham **England** 15-9
	2 Christchurch **New Zealand** 9-6	1995	Cape Town *WC* **New Zealand** 45-29
	New Zealand won series 2-0	1997	*1* Manchester **New Zealand** 25-8
1964	Twickenham **New Zealand** 14-0		*2* Twickenham **Drawn** 26-26
1967	Twickenham **New Zealand** 23-11		*New Zealand won series 1-0, with 1 draw*
1973	Twickenham **New Zealand** 9-0	1998	*1* Dunedin **New Zealand** 64-22
1973	Auckland **England** 16-10		*2* Auckland **New Zealand** 40-10
1978	Twickenham **New Zealand** 16-6		*New Zealand won series 2-0*
1979	Twickenham **New Zealand** 10-9	1999	Twickenham *WC* **New Zealand** 30-16
1983	Twickenham **England** 15-9		

ENGLAND v SOUTH AFRICA

Played 20   England won 7, South Africa won 12, Drawn 1
Highest scores England 33-16 in 1992, South Africa 44-21 in 1999
Biggest wins England 33-16 in 1992 & 32-15 in 1994, South Africa 35-9 in 1984

1906	Crystal Palace (London) **Drawn** 3-3	1932	Twickenham **South Africa** 7-0
1913	Twickenham **South Africa** 9-3	1952	Twickenham **South Africa** 8-3

1961 Twickenham **South Africa** 5-0	1995 Twickenham **South Africa** 24-14
1969 Twickenham **England** 11-8	1997 Twickenham **South Africa** 29-11
1972 Johannesburg **England** 18-9	1998 Cape Town **South Africa** 18-0
1984 *1* Port Elizabeth **South Africa** 33-15	1998 Twickenham **England** 13-7
2 Johannesburg **South Africa** 35-9	1999 Paris *WC* **South Africa** 44-21
South Africa won series 2-0	2000 *1* Pretoria **South Africa** 18-13
1992 Twickenham **England** 33-16	*2* Bloemfontein **England** 27-22
1994 *1* Pretoria **England** 32-15	*Series drawn 1-1*
2 Cape Town **South Africa** 27-9	2000 Twickenham **England** 25-17
Series drawn 1-1	

ENGLAND v AUSTRALIA

Played 25   England won 8, Australia won 16, Drawn 1
Highest scores England 28-19 in 1988, Australia 76-0 in 1998
Biggest wins England 20-3 in 1973 & 23-6 in 1976, Australia 76-0 in 1998

1909 Blackheath (London) **Australia** 9-3	*2* Sydney **Australia** 28-8
1928 Twickenham **England** 18-11	*Australia won series 2-0*
1948 Twickenham **Australia** 11-0	1988 Twickenham **England** 28-19
1958 Twickenham **England** 9-6	1991 Sydney **Australia** 40-15
1963 Sydney **Australia** 18-9	1991 Twickenham *WC* **Australia** 12-6
1967 Twickenham **Australia** 23-11	1995 Cape Town *WC* **England** 25-22
1973 Twickenham **England** 20-3	1997 *1* Sydney **Australia** 25-6
1975 *1* Sydney **Australia** 16-9	*2* Twickenham **Drawn** 15-15
2 Brisbane **Australia** 30-21	*Australia won series 1-0, with 1 draw*
Australia won series 2-0	1998 *1* Brisbane **Australia** 76-0
1976 Twickenham **England** 23-6	*2* Twickenham **Australia** 12-11
1982 Twickenham **England** 15-11	*Australia won series 2-0*
1984 Twickenham **Australia** 19-3	1999 Sydney **Australia** 22-15
1987 Sydney *WC* **Australia** 19-6	2000 Twickenham **England** 22-19
1988 *1* Brisbane **Australia** 22-16	

ENGLAND v NEW ZEALAND NATIVES

Played 1   England won 1
Highest score England 7-0 in 1889, NZ Natives 0-7 in 1889
Biggest win England 7-0 in 1889, NZ Natives no win

1889 Blackheath **England** 1G 4T to 0

ENGLAND v RFU PRESIDENT'S XV

Played 1   President's XV won 1
Highest score England 11-28 in 1971, RFU President's XV 28-11 in 1971
Biggest win RFU President's XV 28-11 in 1971

1971 Twickenham **President's XV** 28-11

ENGLAND v ARGENTINA

Played 10   England won 7, Argentina won 2, Drawn 1
Highest scores England 51-0 in 1990, Argentina 33-13 in 1997
Biggest wins England 51-0 in 1990, Argentina 33-13 in 1997

1981 *1* Buenos Aires **Drawn** 19-19	*2* Buenos Aires **Argentina** 15-13
2 Buenos Aires **England** 12-6	*Series drawn 1-1*
England won series 1-0 with 1 draw	1990 Twickenham **England** 51-0
1990 *1* Buenos Aires **England** 25-12	1995 Durban *WC* **England** 24-18
	1996 Twickenham **England** 20-18

1997   *1* Buenos Aires **England** 46-20
        2 Buenos Aires **Argentina** 33-13
        Series drawn 1-1

2000   Twickenham **England** 19-0

ENGLAND v ROMANIA
Played 3   England won 3
Highest scores England 58-3 in 1989, Romania 15-22 in 1985
Biggest win England 58-3 in 1989, Romania no win

1985   Twickenham **England** 22-15
1989   Bucharest **England** 58-3

1994   Twickenham **England** 54-3

ENGLAND v JAPAN
Played 1   England won 1
Highest score England 60-7 in 1987, Japan 7-60 in 1987
Biggest win England 60-7 in 1987, Japan no win

1987   Sydney *WC* **England** 60-7

ENGLAND v UNITED STATES
Played 4   England won 4
Highest scores England 106-8 in 1999, United States 19-48 in 2001
Biggest win England 106-8 in 1999, United States no win

1987   Sydney *WC* **England** 34-6
1991   Twickenham *WC* **England** 37-9

1999   Twickenham **England** 106-8
2001   San Francisco **England** 48-19

ENGLAND v FIJI
Played 4 . England won 4
Highest scores England 58-23 in 1989, Fiji 24-45 in 1999
Biggest win England 58-23 in 1989, Fiji no win

1988   Suva **England** 25-12
1989   Twickenham **England** 58-23

1991   Suva **England** 28-12
1999   Twickenham *WC* **England** 45-24

ENGLAND v ITALY
Played 7   England won 7
Highest scores England 80-23 in 2001, Italy 23-80 in 2001
Biggest win England 80-23 in 2001, Italy no win

1991   Twickenham *WC* **England** 36-6
1995   Durban *WC* **England** 27-20
1996   Twickenham **England** 54-21
1998   Huddersfield **England** 23-15

1999   Twickenham *WC* **England** 67-7
2000   Rome **England** 59-12
2001   Twickenham **England** 80-23

ENGLAND v CANADA
Played 5   England won 5
Highest scores England 60-19 in 1994, Canada 20-59 in 2001
Biggest win England 60-19 in 1994, Canada no win

1992   Wembley **England** 26-13
1994   Twickenham **England** 60-19
1999   Twickenham **England** 36-11
2001   *1* Markham **England** 22-10

        2 Burnaby **England** 59-20
        England won series 2-0

318

ENGLAND v SAMOA
Played 2   England won 2
Highest scores England 44-22 in 1995, Samoa 22-44 in 1995
Biggest win England 44-22 in 1995, Samoa no win

1995	Durban *WC* **England** 44-22	1995	Twickenham **England** 27-9

ENGLAND v THE NETHERLANDS
Played 1   England won 1
Highest scores England 110-0 in 1998, The Netherlands 0-110 in 1998
Biggest win England 110-0 in 1998, The Netherlands no win

1998   Huddersfield **England** 110-0

ENGLAND v TONGA
Played 1   England won 1
Highest scores England 101-10 in 1999, Tonga 10-101 in 1999
Biggest win England 101-10 in 1999, Tonga no win

1999   Twickenham *WC* **England** 101-10

SCOTLAND v IRELAND
Played 113   Scotland won 61, Ireland won 46, Drawn 5, Abandoned 1
Highest scores Scotland 38-10 in 1997, Ireland 44-22 in 2000
Biggest wins Scotland 38-10 in 1997, Ireland 44-22 in 2000

1877 Belfast **Scotland** 4G 2DG 2T to 0	1906 Dublin **Scotland** 13-6
1878 No Match	1907 Inverleith **Scotland** 15-3
1879 Belfast **Scotland** 1G 1DG 1T to 0	1908 Dublin **Ireland** 16-11
1880 Glasgow **Scotland** 1G 2DG 2T to 0	1909 Inverleith **Scotland** 9-3
1881 Belfast **Ireland** 1DG to 1T	1910 Belfast **Scotland** 14-0
1882 Glasgow **Scotland** 2T to 0	1911 Inverleith **Ireland** 16-10
1883 Belfast **Scotland** 1G 1T to 0	1912 Dublin **Ireland** 10-8
1884 Raeburn Place (Edinburgh) **Scotland** 2G 2T to 1T	1913 Inverleith **Scotland** 29-14
	1914 Dublin **Ireland** 6-0
1885 Belfast **Abandoned** Ireland 0 Scotland 1T	1920 Inverleith **Scotland** 19-0
1885 Raeburn Place **Scotland** 1G 2T to 0	1921 Dublin **Ireland** 9-8
1886 Raeburn Place **Scotland** 3G 1DG 2T to 0	1922 Inverleith **Scotland** 6-3
	1923 Dublin **Scotland** 13-3
1887 Belfast **Scotland** 1G 1GM 2T to 0	1924 Inverleith **Scotland** 13-8
1888 Raeburn Place **Scotland** 1G to 0	1925 Dublin **Scotland** 14-8
1889 Belfast **Scotland** 1DG to 0	1926 Murrayfield **Ireland** 3-0
1890 Raeburn Place **Scotland** 1DG 1T to 0	1927 Dublin **Ireland** 6-0
1891 Belfast **Scotland** 14-0	1928 Murrayfield **Ireland** 13-5
1892 Raeburn Place **Scotland** 2-0	1929 Dublin **Scotland** 16-7
1893 Belfast **Drawn** 0-0	1930 Murrayfield **Ireland** 14-11
1894 Dublin **Ireland** 5-0	1931 Dublin **Ireland** 8-5
1895 Raeburn Place **Scotland** 6-0	1932 Murrayfield **Ireland** 20-8
1896 Dublin **Drawn** 0-0	1933 Dublin **Scotland** 8-6
1897 Powderhall (Edinburgh) **Scotland** 8-3	1934 Murrayfield **Scotland** 16-9
1898 Belfast **Scotland** 8-0	1935 Dublin **Ireland** 12-5
1899 Inverleith (Edinburgh) **Ireland** 9-3	1936 Murrayfield **Ireland** 10-4
1900 Dublin **Drawn** 0-0	1937 Dublin **Ireland** 11-4
1901 Inverleith **Scotland** 9-5	1938 Murrayfield **Scotland** 23-14
1902 Belfast **Ireland** 5-0	1939 Dublin **Ireland** 12-3
1903 Inverleith **Scotland** 3-0	1947 Murrayfield **Ireland** 3-0
1904 Dublin **Scotland** 19-3	1948 Dublin **Ireland** 6-0
1905 Inverleith **Ireland** 11-5	

1949 Murrayfield **Ireland** 13-3	1976 Dublin **Scotland** 15-6
1950 Dublin **Ireland** 21-0	1977 Murrayfield **Scotland** 21-18
1951 Murrayfield **Ireland** 6-5	1978 Dublin **Ireland** 12-9
1952 Dublin **Ireland** 12-8	1979 Murrayfield **Drawn** 11-11
1953 Murrayfield **Ireland** 26-8	1980 Dublin **Ireland** 22-15
1954 Belfast **Ireland** 6-0	1981 Murrayfield **Scotland** 10-9
1955 Murrayfield **Scotland** 12-3	1982 Dublin **Ireland** 21-12
1956 Dublin **Ireland** 14-10	1983 Murrayfield **Ireland** 15-13
1957 Murrayfield **Ireland** 5-3	1984 Dublin **Scotland** 32-9
1958 Dublin **Ireland** 12-6	1985 Murrayfield **Ireland** 18-15
1959 Murrayfield **Ireland** 8-3	1986 Dublin **Scotland** 10-9
1960 Dublin **Scotland** 6-5	1987 Murrayfield **Scotland** 16-12
1961 Murrayfield **Scotland** 16-8	1988 Dublin **Ireland** 22-18
1962 Dublin **Scotland** 20-6	1989 Murrayfield **Scotland** 37-21
1963 Murrayfield **Scotland** 3-0	1990 Dublin **Scotland** 13-10
1964 Dublin **Scotland** 6-3	1991 Murrayfield **Scotland** 28-25
1965 Murrayfield **Ireland** 16-6	1991 Murrayfield *WC* **Scotland** 24-15
1966 Dublin **Scotland** 11-3	1992 Dublin **Scotland** 18-10
1967 Murrayfield **Ireland** 5-3	1993 Murrayfield **Scotland** 15-3
1968 Dublin **Ireland** 14-6	1994 Dublin **Drawn** 6-6
1969 Murrayfield **Ireland** 16-0	1995 Murrayfield **Scotland** 26-13
1970 Dublin **Ireland** 16-11	1996 Dublin **Scotland** 16-10
1971 Murrayfield **Ireland** 17-5	1997 Murrayfield **Scotland** 38-10
1972 No Match	1998 Dublin **Scotland** 17-16
1973 Murrayfield **Scotland** 19-14	1999 Murrayfield **Scotland** 30-13
1974 Dublin **Ireland** 9-6	2000 Dublin **Ireland** 44-22
1975 Murrayfield **Scotland** 20-13	2001 Murrayfield **Scotland** 32-10

SCOTLAND v WALES

Played 105   Scotland won 45, Wales won 57, Drawn 3
Highest scores Scotland 35-10 in 1924, Wales 35-12 in 1972
Biggest wins Scotland 35-10 in 1924, Wales 35-12 in 1972 & 29-6 in 1994

1883 Raeburn Place (Edinburgh) **Scotland** 3G to 1G	1909 Inverleith **Wales** 5-3
	1910 Cardiff **Wales** 14-0
1884 Newport **Scotland** 1DG 1T to 0	1911 Inverleith **Wales** 32-10
1885 Glasgow **Drawn** no score	1912 Swansea **Wales** 21-6
1886 Cardiff **Scotland** 2G 1T to 0	1913 Inverleith **Wales** 8-0
1887 Raeburn Place **Scotland** 4G 8T to 0	1914 Cardiff **Wales** 24-5
1888 Newport **Wales** 1T to 0	1920 Inverleith **Scotland** 9-5
1889 Raeburn Place **Scotland** 2T to 0	1921 Swansea **Scotland** 14-8
1890 Cardiff **Scotland** 1G 2T to 1T	1922 Inverleith **Drawn** 9-9
1891 Raeburn Place **Scotland** 15-0	1923 Cardiff **Scotland** 11-8
1892 Swansea **Scotland** 7-2	1924 Inverleith **Scotland** 35-10
1893 Raeburn Place **Wales** 9-0	1925 Swansea **Scotland** 24-14
1894 Newport **Wales** 7-0	1926 Murrayfield **Scotland** 8-5
1895 Raeburn Place **Scotland** 5-4	1927 Cardiff **Scotland** 5-0
1896 Cardiff **Wales** 6-0	1928 Murrayfield **Wales** 13-0
1897 No Match	1929 Swansea **Wales** 14-7
1898 No Match	1930 Murrayfield **Scotland** 12-9
1899 Inverleith (Edinburgh) **Scotland** 21-10	1931 Cardiff **Wales** 13-8
1900 Swansea **Wales** 12-3	1932 Murrayfield **Wales** 6-0
1901 Inverleith **Scotland** 18-8	1933 Swansea **Scotland** 11-3
1902 Cardiff **Wales** 14-5	1934 Murrayfield **Wales** 13-6
1903 Inverleith **Scotland** 6-0	1935 Cardiff **Wales** 10-6
1904 Swansea **Wales** 21-3	1936 Murrayfield **Wales** 13-3
1905 Inverleith **Wales** 6-3	1937 Swansea **Scotland** 13-6
1906 Cardiff **Wales** 9-3	1938 Murrayfield **Scotland** 8-6
1907 Inverleith **Scotland** 6-3	1939 Cardiff **Wales** 11-3
1908 Swansea **Wales** 6-5	1947 Murrayfield **Wales** 22-8

1948 Cardiff **Wales** 14-0	1975 Murrayfield **Scotland** 12-10
1949 Murrayfield **Scotland** 6-5	1976 Cardiff **Wales** 28-6
1950 Swansea **Wales** 12-0	1977 Murrayfield **Wales** 18-9
1951 Murrayfield **Scotland** 19-0	1978 Cardiff **Wales** 22-14
1952 Cardiff **Wales** 11-0	1979 Murrayfield **Wales** 19-13
1953 Murrayfield **Wales** 12-0	1980 Cardiff **Wales** 17-6
1954 Swansea **Wales** 15-3	1981 Murrayfield **Scotland** 15-6
1955 Murrayfield **Scotland** 14-8	1982 Cardiff **Scotland** 34-18
1956 Cardiff **Wales** 9-3	1983 Murrayfield **Wales** 19-15
1957 Murrayfield **Scotland** 9-6	1984 Cardiff **Scotland** 15-9
1958 Cardiff **Wales** 8-3	1985 Murrayfield **Wales** 25-21
1959 Murrayfield **Scotland** 6-5	1986 Cardiff **Wales** 22-15
1960 Cardiff **Wales** 8-0	1987 Murrayfield **Scotland** 21-15
1961 Murrayfield **Scotland** 3-0	1988 Cardiff **Wales** 25-20
1962 Cardiff **Scotland** 8-3	1989 Murrayfield **Scotland** 23-7
1963 Murrayfield **Wales** 6-0	1990 Cardiff **Scotland** 13-9
1964 Cardiff **Wales** 11-3	1991 Murrayfield **Scotland** 32-12
1965 Murrayfield **Wales** 14-12	1992 Cardiff **Wales** 15-12
1966 Cardiff **Wales** 8-3	1993 Murrayfield **Scotland** 20-0
1967 Murrayfield **Scotland** 11-5	1994 Cardiff **Wales** 29-6
1968 Cardiff **Wales** 5-0	1995 Murrayfield **Scotland** 26-13
1969 Murrayfield **Wales** 17-3	1996 Cardiff **Scotland** 16-14
1970 Cardiff **Wales** 18-9	1997 Murrayfield **Wales** 34-19
1971 Murrayfield **Wales** 19-18	1998 Wembley **Wales** 19-13
1972 Cardiff **Wales** 35-12	1999 Murrayfield **Scotland** 33-20
1973 Murrayfield **Scotland** 10-9	2000 Cardiff **Wales** 26-18
1974 Cardiff **Wales** 6-0	2001 Murrayfield **Drawn** 28-28

SCOTLAND v FRANCE

Played 73   Scotland won 33, France won 37, Drawn 3
Highest scores Scotland 36-22 in 1999, France 51-16 in 1998
Biggest wins Scotland 31-3 in 1912, France 51-16 in 1998

1910 Inverleith (Edinburgh) **Scotland** 27-0	1957 Paris **Scotland** 6-0
1911 Paris **France** 16-15	1958 Murrayfield **Scotland** 11-9
1912 Inverleith **Scotland** 31-3	1959 Paris **France** 9-0
1913 Paris **Scotland** 21-3	1960 Murrayfield **France** 13-11
1914 No Match	1961 Paris **France** 11-0
1920 Paris **Scotland** 5-0	1962 Murrayfield **France** 11-3
1921 Inverleith **France** 3-0	1963 Paris **Scotland** 11-6
1922 Paris **Drawn** 3-3	1964 Murrayfield **Scotland** 10-0
1923 Inverleith **Scotland** 16-3	1965 Paris **France** 16-8
1924 Paris **France** 12-10	1966 Murrayfield **Drawn** 3-3
1925 Inverleith **Scotland** 25-4	1967 Paris **Scotland** 9-8
1926 Paris **Scotland** 20-6	1968 Murrayfield **France** 8-6
1927 Murrayfield **Scotland** 23-6	1969 Paris **Scotland** 6-3
1928 Paris **Scotland** 15-6	1970 Murrayfield **France** 11-9
1929 Murrayfield **Scotland** 6-3	1971 Paris **France** 13-8
1930 Paris **France** 7-3	1972 Murrayfield **Scotland** 20-9
1931 Murrayfield **Scotland** 6-4	1973 Paris **France** 16-13
1947 Paris **France** 8-3	1974 Murrayfield **Scotland** 19-6
1948 Murrayfield **Scotland** 9-8	1975 Paris **France** 10-9
1949 Paris **Scotland** 8-0	1976 Murrayfield **France** 13-6
1950 Murrayfield **Scotland** 8-5	1977 Paris **France** 23-3
1951 Paris **France** 14-12	1978 Murrayfield **France** 19-16
1952 Murrayfield **France** 13-11	1979 Paris **France** 21-17
1953 Paris **France** 11-5	1980 Murrayfield **Scotland** 22-14
1954 Murrayfield **France** 3-0	1981 Paris **France** 16-9
1955 Paris **France** 15-0	1982 Murrayfield **Scotland** 16-7
1956 Murrayfield **Scotland** 12-0	1983 Paris **France** 19-15

1984	Murrayfield **Scotland** 21-12	1993	Paris **France** 11-3
1985	Paris **France** 11-3	1994	Murrayfield **France** 20-12
1986	Murrayfield **Scotland** 18-17	1995	Paris **Scotland** 23-21
1987	Paris **France** 28-22	1995	Pretoria *WC* **France** 22-19
1987	Christchurch *WC* **Drawn** 20-20	1996	Murrayfield **Scotland** 19-14
1988	Murrayfield **Scotland** 23-12	1997	Paris **France** 47-20
1989	Paris **France** 19-3	1998	Murrayfield **France** 51-16
1990	Murrayfield **Scotland** 21-0	1999	Paris **Scotland** 36-22
1991	Paris **France** 15-9	2000	Murrayfield **France** 28-16
1992	Murrayfield **Scotland** 10-6	2001	Paris **France** 16-6

SCOTLAND v NEW ZEALAND
Played 23   Scotland won 0, New Zealand won 21, Drawn 2
Highest scores Scotland 31-62 in 1996, New Zealand 69-20 in 2000
Biggest wins Scotland no win, New Zealand 69-20 in 2000

1905	Inverleith (Edinburgh) **New Zealand** 12-7	1990	*1* Dunedin **New Zealand** 31-16
1935	Murrayfield **New Zealand** 18-8		*2* Auckland **New Zealand** 21-18
1954	Murrayfield **New Zealand** 3-0		*New Zealand won series 2-0*
1964	Murrayfield **Drawn** 0-0	1991	Cardiff *WC* **New Zealand** 13-6
1967	Murrayfield **New Zealand** 14-3	1993	Murrayfield **New Zealand** 51-15
1972	Murrayfield **New Zealand** 14-9	1995	Pretoria *WC* **New Zealand** 48-30
1975	Auckland **New Zealand** 24-0	1996	*1* Dunedin **New Zealand** 62-31
1978	Murrayfield **New Zealand** 18-9		*2* Auckland **New Zealand** 36-12
1979	Murrayfield **New Zealand** 20-6		*New Zealand won series 2-0*
1981	*1* Dunedin **New Zealand** 11-4	1999	Murrayfield *WC* **New Zealand** 30-18
	2 Auckland **New Zealand** 40-15	2000	*1* Dunedin **New Zealand** 69-20
	New Zealand won series 2-0		*2* Auckland **New Zealand** 48-14
1983	Murrayfield **Drawn** 25-25		*New Zealand won series 2-0*
1987	Christchurch *WC* **New Zealand** 30-3		

SCOTLAND v SOUTH AFRICA
Played 12   Scotland won 3, South Africa won 9, Drawn 0
Highest scores Scotland 29-46 in 1999, South Africa 68-10 in 1997
Biggest wins Scotland 6-0 in 1906, South Africa 68-10 in 1997

1906	Glasgow **Scotland** 6-0	1965	Murrayfield **Scotland** 8-5
1912	Inverleith **South Africa** 16-0	1969	Murrayfield **Scotland** 6-3
1932	Murrayfield **South Africa** 6-3	1994	Murrayfield **South Africa** 34-10
1951	Murrayfield **South Africa** 44-0	1997	Murrayfield **South Africa** 68-10
1960	Port Elizabeth **South Africa** 18-10	1998	Murrayfield **South Africa** 35-10
1961	Murrayfield **South Africa** 12-5	1999	Murrayfield *WC* **South Africa** 46-29

SCOTLAND v AUSTRALIA
Played 19   Scotland won 7, Australia won 12, Drawn 0
Highest scores Scotland 24-15 in 1981, Australia 45-3 in 1998
Biggest wins Scotland 24-15 in 1981, Australia 45-3 in 1998

1927	Murrayfield **Scotland** 10-8		*2* Sydney **Australia** 33-9
1947	Murrayfield **Australia** 16-7		*Series drawn 1-1*
1958	Murrayfield **Scotland** 12-8	1984	Murrayfield **Australia** 37-12
1966	Murrayfield **Scotland** 11-5	1988	Murrayfield **Australia** 32-13
1968	Murrayfield **Scotland** 9-3	1992	*1* Sydney **Australia** 27-12
1970	Sydney **Australia** 23-3		*2* Brisbane **Australia** 37-13
1975	Murrayfield **Scotland** 10-3		*Australia won series 2-0*
1981	Murrayfield **Scotland** 24-15	1996	Murrayfield **Australia** 29-19
1982	*1* Brisbane **Scotland** 12-7	1997	Murrayfield **Australia** 37-8

1998 *1* Sydney **Australia** 45-3
    2 Brisbane **Australia** 33-11
    Australia won series 2-0

2000 Murrayfield **Australia** 30-9

SCOTLAND v SRU PRESIDENT'S XV
Played 1   Scotland won 1
Highest scores Scotland 27-16 in 1972, SRU President's XV 16-27 in 1973
Biggest win Scotland 27-16 in 1973, SRU President's XV no win

1973 Murrayfield **Scotland** 27-16

SCOTLAND v ROMANIA
Played 8   Scotland won 6, Romania won 2, Drawn 0
Highest scores Scotland 60-19 in 1999, Romania 28-55 in 1987 & 28-22 in 1984
Biggest wins Scotland 60-19 in 1999, Romania 28-22 in 1984 & 18-12 in 1991

1981	Murrayfield **Scotland** 12-6	
1984	Bucharest **Romania** 28-22	
1986	Bucharest **Scotland** 33-18	
1987	Dunedin *WC* **Scotland** 55-28	

1989 Murrayfield **Scotland** 32-0
1991 Bucharest **Romania** 18-12
1995 Murrayfield **Scotland** 49-16
1999 Glasgow **Scotland** 60-19

SCOTLAND v ZIMBABWE
Played 2   Scotland won 2
Highest scores Scotland 60-21 in 1987, Zimbabwe 21-60 in 1987
Biggest win Scotland 60-21 in 1987 & 51-12 in 1991, Zimbabwe no win

1987 Wellington *WC* **Scotland** 60-21

1991 Murrayfield *WC* **Scotland** 51-12

SCOTLAND v FIJI
Played 2   Scotland won 1, Fiji won 1
Highest scores Scotland 38-17 in 1989, Fiji 51-26 in 1998
Biggest win Scotland 38-17 in 1989, Fiji 51-26 in 1998

1989 Murrayfield **Scotland** 38-17

1998 Suva **Fiji** 51-26

SCOTLAND v ARGENTINA
Played 4   Scotland won 1, Argentina won 3, Drawn 0
Highest scores Scotland 49-3 in 1990, Argentina 31-22 in 1999
Biggest wins Scotland 49-3 in 1990, Argentina 31-22 in 1999

1990 Murrayfield **Scotland** 49-3
1994 *1* Buenos Aires **Argentina** 16-15
    2 Buenos Aires **Argentina** 19-17
    Argentina won series 2-0

1999 Murrayfield **Argentina** 31-22

SCOTLAND v JAPAN
Played 1   Scotland won 1
Highest scores Scotland 47-9 in 1991, Japan 9-47 in 1991
Biggest win Scotland 47-9 in 1991, Japan no win

1991 Murrayfield *WC* **Scotland** 47-9

SCOTLAND v SAMOA
Played 4 Scotland won 3, Drawn 1
Highest scores Scotland 35-20 in 1999, Samoa 20-35 in 1999
Biggest win Scotland 31-8 in 2000, Samoa no win

1991	Murrayfield *WC* **Scotland** 28-6	1999	Murrayfield *WC* **Scotland** 35-20
1995	Murrayfield **Drawn** 15-15	2000	Murrayfield **Scotland** 31-8

SCOTLAND v CANADA
Played 1 Scotland won 1
Highest scores Scotland 22-6 in 1995, Canada 6-22 in 1995
Biggest win Scotland 22-6 in 1995, Canada no win

1995 Murrayfield **Scotland** 22-6

SCOTLAND v IVORY COAST
Played 1 Scotland won 1
Highest scores Scotland 89-0 in 1995, Ivory Coast 0-89 in 1995
Biggest win Scotland 89-0 in 1995, Ivory Coast no win

1995 Rustenburg *WC* **Scotland** 89-0

SCOTLAND v TONGA
Played 1 Scotland won 1
Highest scores Scotland 41-5 in 1995, Tonga 5-41 in 1995
Biggest win Scotland 41-5 in 1995, Tonga no win

1995 Pretoria *WC* **Scotland** 41-5

SCOTLAND v ITALY
Played 5 Scotland won 3, Italy won 2
Highest scores Scotland 30-12 in 1999, Italy 34-20 in 2000
Biggest wins Scotland 30-12 in 1999, Italy 34-20 in 2000

1996	Murrayfield **Scotland** 29-22	2000	Rome **Italy** 34-20
1998	Treviso **Italy** 25-21	2001	Murrayfield **Scotland** 23-19
1999	Murrayfield **Scotland** 30-12		

SCOTLAND v URUGUAY
Played 1 Scotland won 1
Highest scores Scotland 43-12 in 1999, Uruguay 12-43 in 1999
Biggest win Scotland 43-12 in 1999, Uruguay no win

1999 Murrayfield *WC* **Scotland** 43-12

SCOTLAND v SPAIN
Played 1 Scotland won 1
Highest scores Scotland 48-0 in 1999, Spain 0-48 in 1999
Biggest win Scotland 48-0 in 1999, Spain no win

1999 Murrayfield *WC* **Scotland** 48-0

SCOTLAND v UNITED STATES
Played 1   Scotland won 1
Highest scores Scotland 53-6 in 2000, United States 6-53 in 2000
Biggest win Scotland 53-6 in 2000, United States no win

2000   Murrayfield **Scotland** 53-6

IRELAND v WALES
Played 105   Ireland won 39, Wales won 60, Drawn 6
Highest scores Ireland 36-6 in 2001, Wales 34-9 in 1976
Biggest wins Ireland 36-6 in 2001, Wales 29-0 in 1907

1882 Dublin **Wales** 2G 2T to 0
1883 No Match
1884 Cardiff **Wales** 1DG 2T to 0
1885 No Match
1886 No Match
1887 Birkenhead **Wales** 1DG 1T to 3T
1888 Dublin **Ireland** 1G 1DG 1T to 0
1889 Swansea **Ireland** 2T to 0
1890 Dublin **Drawn** 1G each
1891 Llanelli **Wales** 6-4
1892 Dublin **Ireland** 9-0
1893 Llanelli **Wales** 2-0
1894 Belfast **Ireland** 3-0
1895 Cardiff **Wales** 5-3
1896 Dublin **Ireland** 8-4
1897 No Match
1898 Limerick **Wales** 11-3
1899 Cardiff **Ireland** 3-0
1900 Belfast **Wales** 3-0
1901 Swansea **Wales** 10-9
1902 Dublin **Wales** 15-0
1903 Cardiff **Wales** 18-0
1904 Belfast **Ireland** 14-12
1905 Swansea **Wales** 10-3
1906 Belfast **Ireland** 11-6
1907 Cardiff **Wales** 29-0
1908 Belfast **Wales** 11-5
1909 Swansea **Wales** 18-5
1910 Dublin **Wales** 19-3
1911 Cardiff **Wales** 16-0
1912 Belfast **Ireland** 12-5
1913 Swansea **Wales** 16-13
1914 Belfast **Wales** 11-3
1920 Cardiff **Wales** 28-4
1921 Belfast **Wales** 6-0
1922 Swansea **Wales** 11-5
1923 Dublin **Ireland** 5-4
1924 Cardiff **Ireland** 13-10
1925 Belfast **Ireland** 19-3
1926 Swansea **Wales** 11-8
1927 Dublin **Ireland** 19-9
1928 Cardiff **Ireland** 13-10
1929 Belfast **Drawn** 5-5
1930 Swansea **Wales** 12-7
1931 Belfast **Wales** 15-3
1932 Cardiff **Ireland** 12-10
1933 Belfast **Ireland** 10-5
1934 Swansea **Wales** 13-0
1935 Belfast **Ireland** 9-3

1936 Cardiff **Wales** 3-0
1937 Belfast **Ireland** 5-3
1938 Swansea **Wales** 11-5
1939 Belfast **Wales** 7-0
1947 Swansea **Wales** 6-0
1948 Belfast **Ireland** 6-3
1949 Swansea **Ireland** 5-0
1950 Belfast **Wales** 6-3
1951 Cardiff **Drawn** 3-3
1952 Dublin **Wales** 14-3
1953 Swansea **Wales** 5-3
1954 Dublin **Wales** 12-9
1955 Cardiff **Wales** 21-3
1956 Dublin **Ireland** 11-3
1957 Cardiff **Wales** 6-5
1958 Dublin **Wales** 9-6
1959 Cardiff **Wales** 8-6
1960 Dublin **Wales** 10-9
1961 Cardiff **Wales** 9-0
1962 Dublin **Drawn** 3-3
1963 Cardiff **Ireland** 14-6
1964 Dublin **Wales** 15-6
1965 Cardiff **Wales** 14-8
1966 Dublin **Ireland** 9-6
1967 Cardiff **Ireland** 3-0
1968 Dublin **Ireland** 9-6
1969 Cardiff **Wales** 24-11
1970 Dublin **Ireland** 14-0
1971 Cardiff **Wales** 23-9
1972 No Match
1973 Cardiff **Wales** 16-12
1974 Dublin **Drawn** 9-9
1975 Cardiff **Wales** 32-4
1976 Dublin **Wales** 34-9
1977 Cardiff **Wales** 25-9
1978 Dublin **Wales** 20-16
1979 Cardiff **Wales** 24-21
1980 Dublin **Ireland** 21-7
1981 Cardiff **Wales** 9-8
1982 Dublin **Ireland** 20-12
1983 Cardiff **Wales** 23-9
1984 Dublin **Wales** 18-9
1985 Cardiff **Ireland** 21-9
1986 Dublin **Wales** 19-12
1987 Cardiff **Ireland** 15-11
1987 Wellington *WC* **Wales** 13-6
1988 Dublin **Wales** 12-9
1989 Cardiff **Ireland** 19-13
1990 Dublin **Ireland** 14-8

1991 Cardiff **Drawn** 21-21	1996 Dublin **Ireland** 30-17
1992 Dublin **Wales** 16-15	1997 Cardiff **Ireland** 26-25
1993 Cardiff **Ireland** 19-14	1998 Dublin **Wales** 30-21
1994 Dublin **Wales** 17-15	1999 Wembley **Ireland** 29-23
1995 Cardiff **Ireland** 16-12	2000 Dublin **Wales** 23-19
1995 Johannesburg *WC* **Ireland** 24-23	2001 Cardiff **Ireland** 36-6

IRELAND v FRANCE
Played 75   Ireland won 27, France won 43, Drawn 5
Highest scores Ireland 27-25 in 2000 & 25-6 in 1975, France 45-10 in 1996
Biggest wins Ireland 24-0 in 1913, France 45-10 in 1996

1909 Dublin **Ireland** 19-8	1968 Paris **France** 16-6
1910 Paris **Ireland** 8-3	1969 Dublin **Ireland** 17-9
1911 Cork **Ireland** 25-5	1970 Paris **France** 8-0
1912 Paris **Ireland** 11-6	1971 Dublin **Drawn** 9-9
1913 Cork **Ireland** 24-0	1972 Paris **Ireland** 14-9
1914 Paris **Ireland** 8-6	1972 Dublin **Ireland** 24-14
1920 Dublin **France** 15-7	*Non-championship match*
1921 Paris **France** 20-10	1973 Dublin **Ireland** 6-4
1922 Dublin **Ireland** 8-3	1974 Paris **France** 9-6
1923 Paris **France** 14-8	1975 Dublin **Ireland** 25-6
1924 Dublin **Ireland** 6-0	1976 Paris **France** 26-3
1925 Paris **Ireland** 9-3	1977 Dublin **France** 15-6
1926 Belfast **Ireland** 11-0	1978 Paris **France** 10-9
1927 Paris **Ireland** 8-3	1979 Dublin **Drawn** 9-9
1928 Belfast **Ireland** 12-8	1980 Paris **France** 19-18
1929 Paris **Ireland** 6-0	1981 Dublin **France** 19-13
1930 Belfast **France** 5-0	1982 Paris **France** 22-9
1931 Paris **France** 3-0	1983 Dublin **Ireland** 22-16
1947 Dublin **France** 12-8	1984 Paris **France** 25-12
1948 Paris **Ireland** 13-6	1985 Dublin **Drawn** 15-15
1949 Dublin **France** 16-9	1986 Paris **France** 29-9
1950 Paris **Drawn** 3-3	1987 Dublin **France** 19-13
1951 Dublin **Ireland** 9-8	1988 Paris **France** 25-6
1952 Paris **Ireland** 11-8	1989 Dublin **France** 26-21
1953 Belfast **Ireland** 16-3	1990 Paris **France** 31-12
1954 Paris **France** 8-0	1991 Dublin **France** 21-13
1955 Dublin **France** 5-3	1992 Paris **France** 44-12
1956 Paris **France** 14-8	1993 Dublin **France** 21-6
1957 Dublin **Ireland** 11-6	1994 Paris **France** 35-15
1958 Paris **France** 11-6	1995 Dublin **France** 25-7
1959 Dublin **Ireland** 9-5	1995 Durban *WC* **France** 36-12
1960 Paris **France** 23-6	1996 Paris **France** 45-10
1961 Dublin **France** 15-3	1997 Dublin **France** 32-15
1962 Paris **France** 11-0	1998 Paris **France** 18-16
1963 Dublin **France** 24-5	1999 Dublin **France** 10-9
1964 Paris **France** 27-6	2000 Paris **Ireland** 27-25
1965 Dublin **Drawn** 3-3	2001 Dublin **Ireland** 22-15
1966 Paris **France** 11-6	
1967 Dublin **France** 11-6	

IRELAND v NEW ZEALAND
Played 14   Ireland won 0, New Zealand won 13, Drawn 1
Highest scores Ireland 21-24 in 1992, New Zealand 63-15 in 1997
Biggest win Ireland no win, New Zealand 59-6 in 1992

1905 Dublin **New Zealand** 15-0	1954 Dublin **New Zealand** 14-3
1924 Dublin **New Zealand** 6-0	1963 Dublin **New Zealand** 6-5
1935 Dublin **New Zealand** 17-9	1973 Dublin **Drawn** 10-10

1974	Dublin **New Zealand** 15-6
1976	Wellington **New Zealand** 11-3
1978	Dublin **New Zealand** 10-6
1989	Dublin **New Zealand** 23-6
1992	*1* Dunedin **New Zealand** 24-21

	2 Wellington **New Zealand** 59-6
	New Zealand won series 2-0
1995	Johannesburg *WC* **New Zealand** 43-19
1997	Dublin **New Zealand** 63-15

IRELAND v SOUTH AFRICA

Played 14   Ireland won 1, South Africa won 12, Drawn 1
Highest scores Ireland 18-28 in 2000, South Africa 38-0 in 1912
Biggest wins Ireland 9-6 in 1965, South Africa 38-0 in 1912

1906	Belfast **South Africa** 15-12
1912	Dublin **South Africa** 38-0
1931	Dublin **South Africa** 8-3
1951	Dublin **South Africa** 17-5
1960	Dublin **South Africa** 8-3
1961	Cape Town **South Africa** 24-8
1965	Dublin **Ireland** 9-6
1970	Dublin **Drawn** 8-8

1981	*1* Cape Town **South Africa** 23-15
	2 Durban **South Africa** 12-10
	South Africa won series 2-0
1998	*1* Bloemfontein **South Africa** 37-13
	2 Pretoria **South Africa** 33-0
	South Africa won series 2-0
1998	Dublin **South Africa** 27-13
2000	Dublin **South Africa** 28-18

IRELAND v AUSTRALIA

Played 20   Ireland won 6, Australia won 14, Drawn 0
Highest scores Ireland 27-12 in 1979, Australia 46-10 in 1999
Biggest wins Ireland 27-12 in 1979, Australia 46-10 in 1999

1927	Dublin **Australia** 5-3
1947	Dublin **Australia** 16-3
1958	Dublin **Ireland** 9-6
1967	Dublin **Ireland** 15-8
1967	Sydney **Ireland** 11-5
1968	Dublin **Ireland** 10-3
1976	Dublin **Australia** 20-10
1979	*1* Brisbane **Ireland** 27-12
	2 Sydney **Ireland** 9-3
	Ireland won series 2-0
1981	Dublin **Australia** 16-12
1984	Dublin **Australia** 16-9

1987	Sydney *WC* **Australia** 33-15
1991	Dublin *WC* **Australia** 19-18
1992	Dublin **Australia** 42-17
1994	*1* Brisbane **Australia** 33-13
	2 Sydney **Australia** 32-18
	Australia won series 2-0
1996	Dublin **Australia** 22-12
1999	*1* Brisbane **Australia** 46-10
	2 Perth **Australia** 32-26
	Australia won series 2-0
1999	Dublin *WC* **Australia** 23-3

IRELAND v NEW ZEALAND NATIVES

Played 1   New Zealand Natives won 1
Highest scores Ireland 4-13 in 1888, Zew Zealand Natives 13-4 in 1888
Biggest win Ireland no win, New Zealand Natives 13-4 in 1888

1888 Dublin **New Zealand Natives**
    4G 1T to 1G 1T

IRELAND v IRU PRESIDENT'S XV

Played 1   Drawn 1
Highest scores Ireland 18-18 in 1974, IRFU President's XV 18-18 in 1974

1974   Dublin **Drawn** 18-18

IRELAND v ROMANIA
Played 5   Ireland won 5
Highest scores Ireland 60-0 in 1986, Romania 35-53 in 1998
Biggest win Ireland 60-0 in 1986, Romania no win

1986	Dublin	**Ireland** 60-0	1999	Dublin *WC* **Ireland** 44-14
1993	Dublin	**Ireland** 25-3	2001	Bucharest **Ireland** 37-3
1998	Dublin	**Ireland** 53-35		

IRELAND v CANADA
Played 3   Ireland won 2   Drawn 1
Highest scores Ireland 46-19 in 1987, Canada 27-27 in 2000
Biggest win Ireland 46-19 in 1987, Canada no win

1987	Dunedin *WC* **Ireland** 46-19	2000	Markham **Drawn** 27-27
1997	Dublin **Ireland** 33-11		

IRELAND v TONGA
Played 1   Ireland won 1
Highest scores Ireland 32-9 in 1987, Tonga 9-32 in 1987
Biggest win Ireland 32-9 in 1987, Tonga no win

1987   Brisbane *WC* **Ireland** 32-9

IRELAND v SAMOA
Played 2   Ireland won 1, Samoa won 1, Drawn 0
Highest scores Ireland 49-22 in 1988, Samoa 40-25 in 1996
Biggest wins Ireland 49-22 in 1988, Samoa 40-25 in 1996

1988	Dublin **Ireland** 49-22	1996	Dublin **Samoa** 40-25

IRELAND v ITALY
Played 7   Ireland won 4, Italy won 3, Drawn 0
Highest scores Ireland 60-13 in 2000, Italy 37-29 in 1997 & 37-22 in 1997
Biggest wins Ireland 60-13 in 2000, Italy 37-22 in 1997

1988	Dublin **Ireland** 31-15	1999	Dublin **Ireland** 39-30
1995	Treviso **Italy** 22-12	2000	Dublin **Ireland** 60-13
1997	Dublin **Italy** 37-29	2001	Rome **Ireland** 41-22
1997	Bologna **Italy** 37-22		

IRELAND v ARGENTINA
Played 3   Ireland won 2   Argentina won 1
Highest scores Ireland 32-24 in 1999, Argentina 28-24 in 1999
Biggest win Ireland 32-24 in 1999, Argentina 28-24 in 1999

1990	Dublin **Ireland** 20-18	1999	Lens *WC* **Argentina** 28-24
1999	Dublin **Ireland** 32-24		

IRELAND v NAMIBIA
Played 2   Namibia won 2
Highest scores Ireland 15-26 in 1991, Namibia 26-15 in 1991
Biggest win Ireland no win, Namibia 26-15 in 1991

1991　*1*　Windhoek **Namibia** 15-6
　　　2　Windhoek **Namibia** 26-15
　　　Namibia won series 2-0

IRELAND v ZIMBABWE
Played 1　Ireland won 1
Highest scores Ireland 55-11 in 1991, Zimbabwe 11-55 in 1991
Biggest win Ireland 55-11 in 1991, Zimbabwe no win

1991　Dublin *WC* **Ireland** 55-11

IRELAND v JAPAN
Played 3　Ireland won 3
Highest scores Ireland 78-9 in 2000, Japan 28-50 in 1995
Biggest win Ireland 78-9 in 2000, Japan no win

1991　Dublin *WC* **Ireland** 32-16　　　　2000　Dublin **Ireland** 78-9
1995　Bloemfontein *WC* **Ireland** 50-28

IRELAND v UNITED STATES
Played 4　Ireland won 4
Highest scores Ireland 83-3 in 2000, United States 18-25 in 1996
Biggest win Ireland 83-3 in 2000, United States no win

1994　Dublin **Ireland** 26-15　　　　　1999　Dublin *WC* **Ireland** 53-8
1996　Atlanta **Ireland** 25-18　　　　　2000　Manchester (NH) **Ireland** 83-3

IRELAND v FIJI
Played 1　Ireland won 1
Highest scores Ireland 44-8 in 1995, Fiji 8-44 in 1995
Biggest win Ireland 44-8 in 1995, Fiji no win

1995　Dublin **Ireland** 44-8

IRELAND v GEORGIA
Played 1　Ireland won 1
Highest scores Ireland 70-0 in 1998, Georgia 0-70 in 1998
Biggest win Ireland 70-0 in 1998, Georgia no win

1998　Dublin **Ireland** 70-0

WALES v FRANCE
Played 77　Wales won 41, France won 33, Drawn 3
Highest scores Wales 49-14 in 1910, France 51-0 in 1998
Biggest wins Wales 47-5 in 1909, France 51-0 in 1998

1908	Cardiff **Wales** 36-4		1921	Cardiff **Wales** 12-4
1909	Paris **Wales** 47-5		1922	Paris **Wales** 11-3
1910	Swansea **Wales** 49-14		1923	Swansea **Wales** 16-8
1911	Paris **Wales** 15-0		1924	Paris **Wales** 10-6
1912	Newport **Wales** 14-8		1925	Cardiff **Wales** 11-5
1913	Paris **Wales** 11-8		1926	Paris **Wales** 7-5
1914	Swansea **Wales** 31-0		1927	Swansea **Wales** 25-7
1920	Paris **Wales** 6-5		1928	Paris **France** 8-3

1929	Cardiff **Wales** 8-3		1976	Cardiff **Wales** 19-13
1930	Paris **Wales** 11-0		1977	Paris **France** 16-9
1931	Swansea **Wales** 35-3		1978	Cardiff **Wales** 16-7
1947	Paris **Wales** 3-0		1979	Paris **France** 14-13
1948	Swansea **France** 11-3		1980	Cardiff **Wales** 18-9
1949	Paris **France** 5-3		1981	Paris **France** 19-15
1950	Cardiff **Wales** 21-0		1982	Cardiff **Wales** 22-12
1951	Paris **France** 8-3		1983	Paris **France** 16-9
1952	Swansea **Wales** 9-5		1984	Cardiff **France** 21-16
1953	Paris **Wales** 6-3		1985	Paris **France** 14-3
1954	Cardiff **Wales** 19-13		1986	Cardiff **France** 23-15
1955	Paris **Wales** 16-11		1987	Paris **France** 16-9
1956	Cardiff **Wales** 5-3		1988	Cardiff **France** 10-9
1957	Paris **Wales** 19-13		1989	Paris **France** 31-12
1958	Cardiff **France** 16-6		1990	Cardiff **France** 29-19
1959	Paris **France** 11-3		1991	Paris **France** 36-3
1960	Cardiff **France** 16-8		1991	Cardiff **France** 22-9
1961	Paris **France** 8-6			*Non-championship match*
1962	Cardiff **Wales** 3-0		1992	Cardiff **France** 12-9
1963	Paris **France** 5-3		1993	Paris **France** 26-10
1964	Cardiff **Drawn** 11-11		1994	Cardiff **Wales** 24-15
1965	Paris **France** 22-13		1995	Paris **France** 21-9
1966	Cardiff **Wales** 9-8		1996	Cardiff **Wales** 16-15
1967	Paris **France** 20-14		1996	Cardiff **France** 40-33
1968	Cardiff **France** 14-9			*Non-championship match*
1969	Paris **Drawn** 8-8		1997	Paris **France** 27-22
1970	Cardiff **Wales** 11-6		1998	Wembley **France** 51-0
1971	Paris **Wales** 9-5		1999	Paris **Wales** 34-33
1972	Cardiff **Wales** 20-6		1999	Cardiff **Wales** 34-23
1973	Paris **France** 12-3			*Non-championship match*
1974	Cardiff **Drawn** 16-16		2000	Cardiff **France** 36-3
1975	Paris **Wales** 25-10		2001	Paris **Wales** 43-35

WALES v NEW ZEALAND
Played 17   Wales won 3, New Zealand won 14, Drawn 0
Highest scores Wales 16-19 in 1972, New Zealand 54-9 in 1988
Biggest wins Wales 13-8 in 1953, New Zealand 52-3 in 1988

1905	Cardiff **Wales** 3-0		1978	Cardiff **New Zealand** 13-12
1924	Swansea **New Zealand** 19-0		1980	Cardiff **New Zealand** 23-3
1935	Cardiff **Wales** 13-12		1987	Brisbane *WC* **New Zealand** 49-6
1953	Cardiff **Wales** 13-8		1988	*1* Christchurch **New Zealand** 52-3
1963	Cardiff **New Zealand** 6-0			*2* Auckland **New Zealand** 54-9
1967	Cardiff **New Zealand** 13-6			*New Zealand won series 2-0*
1969	*1* Christchurch **New Zealand** 19-0		1989	Cardiff **New Zealand** 34-9
	2 Auckland **New Zealand** 33-12		1995	Johannesburg *WC* **New Zealand** 34-9
	New Zealand won series 2-0		1997	Wembley **New Zealand** 42-7
1972	Cardiff **New Zealand** 19-16			

WALES v SOUTH AFRICA
Played 14   Wales won 1, South Africa won 12, Drawn 1
Highest scores Wales 29-19 in 1999, South Africa 96-13 in 1998
Biggest win Wales 29-19 in 1999, South Africa 96-13 in 1998

1906	Swansea **South Africa** 11-0		1970	Cardiff **Drawn** 6-6
1912	Cardiff **South Africa** 3-0		1994	Cardiff **South Africa** 20-12
1931	Swansea **South Africa** 8-3		1995	Johannesburg **South Africa** 40-11
1951	Cardiff **South Africa** 6-3		1996	Cardiff **South Africa** 37-20
1960	Cardiff **South Africa** 3-0		1998	Pretoria **South Africa** 96-13
1964	Durban **South Africa** 24-3		1998	Wembley **South Africa** 28-20

Neil Jenkins kicks the penalty goal against France in Paris that took him past 1000 points in Tests for Wales. All told, the Welshman has scored a world record 1070 at Test level. He has collected 1029 for Wales and a further 41 in Tests for the Lions.

1999 Cardiff **Wales** 29-19   2000 Cardiff **South Africa** 23-13

WALES v AUSTRALIA
Played 20   Wales won 8, Australia won 12, Drawn 0
Highest scores Wales 28-3 in 1975, Australia 63-6 in 1991
Biggest wins Wales 28-3 in 1975, Australia 63-6 in 1991

1908 Cardiff **Wales** 9-6	1981 Cardiff **Wales** 18-13
1927 Cardiff **Australia** 18-8	1984 Cardiff **Australia** 28-9
1947 Cardiff **Wales** 6-0	1987 Rotorua *WC* **Wales** 22-21
1958 Cardiff **Wales** 9-3	1991 Brisbane **Australia** 63-6
1966 Cardiff **Australia** 14-11	1991 Cardiff *WC* **Australia** 38-3
1969 Sydney **Wales** 19-16	1992 Cardiff **Australia** 23-6
1973 Cardiff **Wales** 24-0	1996 *1* Brisbane **Australia** 56-25
1975 Cardiff **Wales** 28-3	*2* Sydney **Australia** 42-3
1978 *1* Brisbane **Australia** 18-8	*Australia won series 2-0*
2 Sydney **Australia** 19-17	1996 Cardiff **Australia** 28-19
Australia won series 2-0	1999 Cardiff *WC* **Australia** 24-9

WALES v NEW ZEALAND NATIVES
Played 1   Wales won 1
Highest scores Wales 5-0 in 1888, New Zealand Natives 0-5 in 1888
Biggest win Wales 5-0 in 1888, New Zealand Natives no win

1888 Swansea **Wales** 1G 2T to 0

WALES v NEW ZEALAND ARMY
Played 1   New Zealand Army won 1
Highest scores Wales 3-6 in 1919, New Zealand Army 6-3 in 1919
Biggest win Wales no win, New Zealand Army 6-3 in 1919

1919 Swansea **New Zealand Army** 6-3

WALES v ROMANIA
Played 5   Wales won 3, Romania won 2
Highest scores Wales 81-9 in 2001, Romania 24-6 in 1983
Biggest wins Wales 81-9 in 2001, Romania 24-6 in 1983

1983 Bucharest **Romania** 24-6	1997 Wrexham **Wales** 70-21
1988 Cardiff **Romania** 15-9	2001 Cardiff **Wales** 81-9
1994 Bucharest **Wales** 16-9	

WALES v FIJI
Played 4   Wales won 4
Highest scores Wales 40-3 in 1985, Fiji 15-22 in 1986 & 15-19 in 1995
Biggest win Wales 40-3 in 1985, Fiji no win

1985 Cardiff **Wales** 40-3	1994 Suva **Wales** 23-8
1986 Suva **Wales** 22-15	1995 Cardiff **Wales** 19-15

WALES v TONGA
Played 4   Wales won 4
Highest scores Wales 46-12 in 1997, Tonga 16-29 in 1987
Biggest win Wales 46-12 in 1997, Tonga no win

1986	Nuku'Alofa **Wales** 15-7	1994	Nuku'Alofa **Wales** 18-9
1987	Palmerston North *WC* **Wales** 29-16	1997	Swansea **Wales** 46-12

WALES v SAMOA
Played 6   Wales won 3, Samoa won 3, Drawn 0
Highest scores Wales 50-6 in 2000, Samoa 38-31 in 1999
Biggest wins Wales 50-6 in 2000, Samoa 34-9 in 1994

1986	Apia **Wales** 32-14	1994	Moamoa **Samoa** 34-9
1988	Cardiff **Wales** 28-6	1999	Cardiff *WC* **Samoa** 38-31
1991	Cardiff *WC* **Samoa** 16-13	2000	Cardiff **Wales** 50-6

WALES v CANADA
Played 5   Wales won 4, Canada won 1, Drawn 0
Highest scores Wales 40-9 in 1987, Canada 26-24 in 1993
Biggest wins Wales 40-9 in 1987, Canada 26-24 in 1993

1987	Invercargill *WC* **Wales** 40-9	1997	Toronto **Wales** 28-25
1993	Cardiff **Canada** 26-24	1999	Cardiff **Wales** 33-19
1994	Toronto **Wales** 33-15		

WALES v UNITED STATES
Played 5   Wales won 5
Highest scores Wales 46-0 in 1987, United States 23-28 in 1997
Biggest win Wales 46-0 in 1987, United States no win

1987	Cardiff **Wales** 46-0		*2* San Francisco **Wales** 28-23
1997	Cardiff **Wales** 34-14		*Wales won series 2-0*
1997	*1* Wilmington **Wales** 30-20	2000	Cardiff **Wales** 42-11

WALES v NAMIBIA
Played 3   Wales won 3
Highest scores Wales 38-23 in 1993, Namibia 30-34 in 1990
Biggest win Wales 38-23 in 1993, Namibia no win

1990	*1* Windhoek **Wales** 18-9	1993	Windhoek **Wales** 38-23
	2 Windhoek **Wales** 34-30		
	Wales won series 2-0		

WALES v BARBARIANS
Played 2   Wales won 1, Barbarians won 1
Highest scores Wales 31-10 in 1996, Barbarians 31-24 in 1990
Biggest wins Wales 31-10 in 1996, Barbarians 31-24 in 1990

1990	Cardiff **Barbarians** 31-24	1996	Cardiff **Wales** 31-10

WALES v ARGENTINA
Played 5   Wales won 5
Highest scores Wales 43-30 in 1998, Argentina 30-43 in 1998
Biggest win Wales 43-30 in 1998, Argentina no win

1991 Cardiff *WC* **Wales** 16-7	*2* Buenos Aires **Wales** 23-16
1998 Llanelli **Wales** 43-30	*Wales won series 2-0*
1999 *1* Buenos Aires **Wales** 36-26	1999 Cardiff *WC* **Wales** 23-18

WALES v ZIMBABWE
Played 3   Wales won 3
Highest scores Wales 49-11 in 1998, Zimbabwe 14-35 in 1993
Biggest win Wales 49-11 in 1998, Zimbabwe no win

1993 *1* Bulawayo **Wales** 35-14	1998 Harare **Wales** 49-11
2 Harare **Wales** 42-13	
Wales won series 2-0	

WALES v JAPAN
Played 5   Wales won 5
Highest scores Wales 64-15 in 1999 & 64-10 in 2001, Japan 30-53 in 2001
Biggest win Wales 64-10 in 2001, Japan no win

1993 Cardiff **Wales** 55-5	2001 *1* Osaka **Wales** 64-10
1995 Bloemfontein *WC* **Wales** 57-10	*2* Tokyo **Wales** 53-30
1999 Cardiff *WC* **Wales** 64-15	*Wales won series 2-0*

WALES v PORTUGAL
Played 1   Wales won 1
Highest scores Wales 102-11 in 1994, Portugal 11-102 in 1994
Biggest win Wales 102-11 in 1994, Portugal no win

1994   Lisbon **Wales** 102-11

WALES v SPAIN
Played 1   Wales won 1
Highest scores Wales 54-0 in 1994, Spain 0-54 in 1994
Bigegst win Wales 54-0 in 1994, Spain no win

1994   Madrid **Wales** 54-0

WALES v ITALY
Played 7   Wales won 7
Highest scores Wales 60-21 in 1999, Italy 26-31 in 1996
Biggest win Wales 60-21 in 1999, Italy no win

1994 Cardiff **Wales** 29-19	1999 Treviso **Wales** 60-21
1996 Cardiff **Wales** 31-26	2000 Cardiff **Wales** 47-16
1996 Rome **Wales** 31-22	2001 Rome **Wales** 33-23
1998 Llanelli **Wales** 23-20	

BRITISH/IRISH ISLES v SOUTH AFRICA

Played 43   British/Irish won 16, South Africa won 21, Drawn 6
Highest scores: British/Irish 28–9 in 1974, South Africa 35–16 in 1997
Biggest wins: British/Irish 28–9 in 1974, South Africa 34–14 in 1962

1891 *1* Port Elizabeth **British/Irish** 4-0
        2 Kimberley **British/Irish** 3-0
        3 Cape Town **British/Irish** 4-0
        British/Irish won series 3-0
1896 *1* Port Elizabeth **British/Irish** 8-0
        2 Johannesburg **British/Irish** 17-8
        3 Kimberley **British/Irish** 9-3
        4 Cape Town **South Africa** 5-0
        British/Irish won series 3-1
1903 *1* Johannesburg **Drawn** 10-10
        2 Kimberley **Drawn** 0-0
        3 Cape Town **South Africa** 8-0
        South Africa won series 1-0 with two drawn
1910 *1* Johannesburg **South Africa** 14–10
        2 Port Elizabeth **British/Irish** 8–3
        3 Cape Town **South Africa** 21–5
        South Africa won series 2-1
1924 *1* Durban **South Africa** 7–3
        2 Johannesburg **South Africa** 17–0
        3 Port Elizabeth **Drawn** 3–3
        4 Cape Town **South Africa** 16–9
        South Africa won series 3-0, with 1 draw
1938 *1* Johannesburg **South Africa** 26–12
        2 Port Elizabeth **South Africa** 19–3
        3 Cape Town **British/Irish** 21–16
        South Africa won series 2-1
1955 *1* Johannesburg **British/Irish** 23–22
        2 Cape Town **South Africa** 25–9

        3 Pretoria **British/Irish** 9–6
        4 Port Elizabeth **South Africa** 22–8
        Series drawn 2-2
1962 *1* Johannesburg **Drawn** 3–3
        2 Durban **South Africa** 3–0
        3 Cape Town **South Africa** 8–3
        4 Bloemfontein **South Africa** 34–14
        South Africa won series 3-0, with 1 draw
1968 *1* Pretoria **South Africa** 25–20
        2 Port Elizabeth **Drawn** 6–6
        3 Cape Town **South Africa** 11–6
        4 Johannesburg **South Africa** 19–6
        South Africa won series 3-0, with 1 draw
1974 *1* Cape Town **British/Irish** 12–3
        2 Pretoria **British/Irish** 28–9
        3 Port Elizabeth **British/Irish** 26–9
        4 Johannesburg **Drawn** 13–13
        British/Irish won series 3-0, with 1 draw
1980 *1* Cape Town **South Africa** 26–22
        2 Bloemfontein **South Africa** 26–19
        3 Port Elizabeth **South Africa** 12–10
        4 Pretoria **British/Irish** 17–13
        South Africa won series 3-1
1997 *1* Cape Town **British/Irish** 25-16
        2 Durban **British/Irish** 18-15
        3 Johannesburg **South Africa** 35-16
        British/Irish won series 2-1

BRITISH/IRISH ISLES v NEW ZEALAND

Played 32   British/Irish won 6, New Zealand won 24, Drawn 2
Highest scores: British/Irish 20–7 in 1993, New Zealand 38–6 in 1983
Biggest wins: British/Irish 20–7 in 1993, New Zealand 38–6 in 1983

1904 Wellington **New Zealand** 9-3
1930 *1* Dunedin **British/Irish** 6–3
        2 Christchurch **New Zealand** 13–10
        3 Auckland **New Zealand** 15–10
        4 Wellington **New Zealand** 22–8
        New Zealand won series 3-1
1950 *1* Dunedin **Drawn** 9–9
        2 Christchurch **New Zealand** 8–0
        3 Wellington **New Zealand** 6–3
        4 Auckland **New Zealand** 11–8
        New Zealand won series 3-0, with 1 draw
1959 *1* Dunedin **New Zealand** 18–17
        2 Wellington **New Zealand** 11–8
        3 Christchurch **New Zealand** 22–8
        4 Auckland **British/Irish** 9–6
        New Zealand won series 3-1
1966 *1* Dunedin **New Zealand** 20–3
        2 Wellington **New Zealand** 16–12
        3 Christchurch **New Zealand** 19–6
        4 Auckland **New Zealand** 24–11
        New Zealand won series 4-0

1971 *1* Dunedin **British/Irish** 9–3
        2 Christchurch **New Zealand** 22–12
        3 Wellington **British/Irish** 13–3
        4 Auckland **Drawn** 14–14
        British/Irish won series 2-1, with 1 draw
1977 *1* Wellington **New Zealand** 16–12
        2 Christchurch **British/Irish** 13–9
        3 Dunedin **New Zealand** 19–7
        4 Auckland **New Zealand** 10–9
        New Zealand won series 3-1
1983 *1* Christchurch **New Zealand** 16–12
        2 Wellington **New Zealand** 9–0
        3 Dunedin **New Zealand** 15–8
        4 Auckland **New Zealand** 38–6
        New Zealand won series 4-0
1993 *1* Christchurch **New Zealand** 20–18
        2 Wellington **British/Irish** 20–7
        3 Auckland **New Zealand** 30–13
        New Zealand won series 2-1

ANGLO-WELSH v NEW ZEALAND
Played 3   New Zealand won 2, Drawn 1
Highest scores Anglo Welsh 5-32 in 1908, New Zealand 32-5 in 1908
Biggest win Anglo Welsh no win, New Zealand 29-0 in 1908

1908 *1* Dunedin **New Zealand** 32-5
2 Wellington **Drawn** 3-3

3 Auckland **New Zealand** 29-0
New Zealand won series 2-0 with one drawn

BRITISH/IRISH ISLES v AUSTRALIA
Played 20   British/Irish won 15, Australia won 5, Drawn 0
Highest scores: British/Irish 31–0 in 1966, Australia 35–14 in 2001
Biggest wins: British/Irish 31–0 in 1966, Australia 35–14 in 2001

1899 *1* Sydney **Australia** 13-3
2 Brisbane **British/Irish** 11-0
3 Sydney **British/Irish** 11-10
4 Sydney **British/Irish** 13-0
British/Irish won series 3-1
1904 *1* Sydney **British/Irish** 17-0
2 Brisbane **British/Irish** 17-3
3 Sydney **British/Irish** 16-0
British/Irish won series 3-0
1930 Sydney **Australia** 6–5
1950 *1* Brisbane **British/Irish** 19–6
2 Sydney **British/Irish** 24–3
British/Irish won series 2-0
1959 *1* Brisbane **British/Irish** 17–6

2 Sydney **British/Irish** 24–3
British/Irish won series 2-0
1966 *1* Sydney **British/Irish** 11–8
2 Brisbane **British/Irish** 31–0
British/Irish won series 2-0
1989 *1* Sydney **Australia** 30–12
2 Brisbane **British/Irish** 19–12
3 Sydney **British/Irish** 19–18
British/Irish won series 2-1
2001 *1* Brisbane **British/Irish** 29-13
2 Melbourne **Australia** 35-14
3 Sydney **Australia** 29-23
Australia won series 2-1

FRANCE v NEW ZEALAND
Played 37   France won 10, New Zealand won 27, Drawn 0
Highest scores France 43-31 in 1999, New Zealand 54-7 in 1999
Biggest wins France 22-8 in 1994, New Zealand 54-7 in 1999

1906 Paris **New Zealand** 38-8
1925 Toulouse **New Zealand** 30-6
1954 Paris **France** 3-0
1961 *1* Auckland **New Zealand** 13-6
2 Wellington **New Zealand** 5-3
3 Christchurch **New Zealand** 32-3
New Zealand won series 3-0
1964 Paris **New Zealand** 12-3
1967 Paris **New Zealand** 21-15
1968 *1* Christchurch **New Zealand** 12-9
2 Wellington **New Zealand** 9-3
3 Auckland **New Zealand** 19-12
New Zealand won series 3-0
1973 Paris **France** 13-6
1977 *1* Toulouse **France** 18-13
2 Paris **New Zealand** 15-3
Series drawn 1-1
1979 *1* Christchurch **New Zealand** 23-9
2 Auckland **France** 24-19
Series drawn 1-1
1981 *1* Toulouse **New Zealand** 13-9
2 Paris **New Zealand** 18-6
New Zealand won series 2-0
1984 *1* Christchurch **New Zealand** 10-9

2 Auckland **New Zealand** 31-18
New Zealand won series 2-0
1986 Christchurch **New Zealand** 18-9
1986 *1* Toulouse **New Zealand** 19-7
2 Nantes **France** 16-3
Series drawn 1-1
1987 Auckland *WC* **New Zealand** 29-9
1989 *1* Christchurch **New Zealand** 25-17
2 Auckland **New Zealand** 34-20
New Zealand won series 2-0
1990 *1* Nantes **New Zealand** 24-3
2 Paris **New Zealand** 30-12
New Zealand won series 2-0
1994 *1* Christchurch **France** 22-8
2 Auckland **France** 23-20
France won series 2-0
1995 *1* Toulouse **France** 22-15
2 Paris **New Zealand** 37-12
Series drawn 1-1
1999 Wellington **New Zealand** 54-7
1999 Twickenham *WC* **France** 43-31
2000 *1* Paris **New Zealand** 39-26
2 Marseilles **France** 42-33
Series drawn 1-1
2001 Wellington **New Zealand** 37-12

FRANCE v SOUTH AFRICA

Played 30   France won 6, South Africa won 19, Drawn 5
Highest scores France 32-36 in 1997 & 32-23 in 2001, South Africa 52-10 in 1997
Biggest wins France 29-16 in 1992, South Africa 52-10 in 1997

1913   Bordeaux **South Africa** 38-5
1952   Paris **South Africa** 25-3
1958   *1* Cape Town **Drawn** 3-3
    2 Johannesburg **France** 9-5
    France won series 1-0, with 1 draw
1961   Paris **Drawn** 0-0
1964   Springs (SA) **France** 8-6
1967   *1* Durban **South Africa** 26-3
    2 Bloemfontein **South Africa** 16-3
    3 Johannesburg **France** 19-14
    4 Cape Town **Drawn** 6-6
    South Africa won series 2-1, with 1 draw
1968   *1* Bordeaux **South Africa** 12-9
    2 Paris **South Africa** 16-11
    South Africa won series 2-0
1971   *1* Bloemfontein **South Africa** 22-9
    2 Durban **Drawn** 8-8
    South Africa won series 1-0, with 1 draw
1974   *1* Toulouse **South Africa** 13-4
    2 Paris **South Africa** 10-8
    South Africa won series 2-0

1975   *1* Bloemfontein **South Africa** 38-25
    2 Pretoria **South Africa** 33-18
    South Africa won series 2-0
1980   Pretoria **South Africa** 37-15
1992   *1* Lyons **South Africa** 20-15
    2 Paris **France** 29-16
    Series drawn 1-1
1993   *1* Durban **Drawn** 20-20
    2 Johannesburg **France** 18-17
    France won series 1-0, with 1 draw
1995   Durban *WC* **South Africa** 19-15
1996   *1* Bordeaux **South Africa** 22-12
    2 Paris **South Africa** 13-12
    South Africa won series 2-0
1997   *1* Lyons **South Africa** 36-32
    2 Paris **South Africa** 52-10
    South Africa won series 2-0
2001   *1* Johannesburg **France** 32-23
    2 Durban **South Africa** 20-15
    Series drawn 1-1

FRANCE v AUSTRALIA

Played 30   France won 13, Australia won 15, Drawn 2
Highest scores France 34-6 in 1976, Australia 48-31 in 1990
Biggest wins France 34-6 in 1976, Australia 35-12 in 1999

1928   Paris **Australia** 11-8
1948   Paris **France** 13-6
1958   Paris **France** 19-0
1961   Sydney **France** 15-8
1967   Paris **France** 20-14
1968   Sydney **Australia** 11-10
1971   *1* Toulouse **Australia** 13-11
    2 Paris **France** 18-9
    Series drawn 1-1
1972   *1* Sydney **Drawn** 14-14
    2 Brisbane **France** 16-15
    France won series 1-0, with 1 draw
1976   *1* Bordeaux **France** 18-15
    2 Paris **France** 34-6
    France won series 2-0
1981   *1* Brisbane **Australia** 17-15
    2 Sydney **Australia** 24-14
    Australia won series 2-0
1983   *1* Clermont-Ferrand **Drawn** 15-15
    2 Paris **France** 15-6
    France won series 1-0, with 1 draw

1986   Sydney **Australia** 27-14
1987   Sydney *WC* **France** 30-24
1989   *1* Strasbourg **Australia** 32-15
    2 Lille **France** 25-19
    Series drawn 1-1
1990   *1* Sydney **Australia** 21-9
    2 Brisbane **Australia** 48-31
    3 Sydney **France** 28-19
    Australia won series 2-1
1993   *1* Bordeaux **France** 16-13
    2 Paris **Australia** 24-3
    Series drawn 1-1
1997   *1* Sydney **Australia** 29-15
    2 Brisbane **Australia** 26-19
    Australia won series 2-0
1998   Paris **Australia** 32-21
1999   Cardiff *WC* **Australia** 35-12
2000   Paris **Australia** 18-13

FRANCE v UNITED STATES

Played 5 France won 4, United States won 1, Drawn 0
Highest scores France 41-9 in 1991, United States 17-3 in 1924
Biggest wins France 41-9 in 1991, United States 17-3 in 1924

1920	Paris **France** 14-5	
1924	Paris **United States** 17-3	
1976	Chicago **France** 33-14	
1991	*1* Denver **France** 41-9	

2 Colorado Springs **France** 10-3*
*Abandoned after 43 mins
France won series 2-0

FRANCE v ROMANIA

Played 47 France won 37, Romania won 8, Drawn 2
Highest scores France 67-20 in 2000, Romania 21-33 in 1991
Biggest wins France 59-3 in 1924, Romania 15-0 in 1980

1924	Paris **France** 59-3	1980	Bucharest **Romania** 15-0
1938	Bucharest **France** 11-8	1981	Narbonne **France** 17-9
1957	Bucharest **France** 18-15	1982	Bucharest **Romania** 13-9
1957	Bordeaux **France** 39-0	1983	Toulouse **France** 26-15
1960	Bucharest **Romania** 11-5	1984	Bucharest **France** 18-3
1961	Bayonne **Drawn** 5-5	1986	Lille **France** 25-13
1962	Bucharest **Romania** 3-0	1986	Bucharest **France** 20-3
1963	Toulouse **Drawn** 6-6	1987	Wellington *WC* **France** 55-12
1964	Bucharest **France** 9-6	1987	Agen **France** 49-3
1965	Lyons **France** 8-3	1988	Bucharest **France** 16-12
1966	Bucharest **France** 9-3	1990	Auch **Romania** 12-6
1967	Nantes **France** 11-3	1991	Bucharest **France** 33-21
1968	Bucharest **Romania** 15-14	1991	Béziers *WC* **France** 30-3
1969	Tarbes **France** 14-9	1992	Le Havre **France** 25-6
1970	Bucharest **France** 14-3	1993	Bucharest **France** 37-20
1971	Béziers **France** 31-12	1993	Brive **France** 51-0
1972	Constanza **France** 15-6	1995	Bucharest **France** 24-15
1973	Valence **France** 7-6	1995	Tucumán *LC* **France** 52-8
1974	Bucharest **Romania** 15-10	1996	Aurillac **France** 64-12
1975	Bordeaux **France** 36-12	1997	Bucharest **France** 51-20
1976	Bucharest **Romania** 15-12	1997	Lourdes *LC* **France** 39-3
1977	Clermont-Ferrand **France** 9-6	1999	Castres **France** 62-8
1978	Bucharest **France** 9-6	2000	Bucharest **France** 67-20
1979	Montauban **France** 30-12		

FRANCE v NEW ZEALAND MAORIS

Played 1 New Zealand Maoris won 1
Highest scores France 3-12 in 1926, New Zealand Maoris 12-3 in 1926
Biggest win France no win, New Zealand Maoris 12-3 in 1926

1926 Paris **New Zealand Maoris** 12-3

FRANCE v GERMANY

Played 15 France won 13, Germany won 2, Drawn 0
Highest scores France 38-17 in 1933, Germany 17-16 in 1927 & 17-38 in 1933
Biggest wins France 34-0 in 1931, Germany 3-0 in 1938

1927	Paris **France** 30-5	1931	Paris **France** 34-0
1927	Frankfurt **Germany** 17-16	1932	Frankfurt **France** 20-4
1928	Hanover **France** 14-3	1933	Paris **France** 38-17
1929	Paris **France** 24-0	1934	Hanover **France** 13-9
1930	Berlin **France** 31-0	1935	Paris **France** 18-3

1936 *1* Berlin **France** 19-14
     2 Hanover **France** 6-3
     France won series 2-0

1937 Paris **France** 27-6
1938 Frankfurt **Germany** 3-0
1938 Bucharest **France** 8-5

FRANCE v ITALY

Played 22   France won 21, Italy won 1, Drawn 0
Highest scores France 60-13 in 1967, Italy 40-32 in 1997
Biggest wins France 60-13 in 1967, Italy 40-32 in 1997

1937 Paris **France** 43-5	1962 Brescia **France** 6-3
1952 Milan **France** 17-8	1963 Grenoble **France** 14-12
1953 Lyons **France** 22-8	1964 Parma **France** 12-3
1954 Rome **France** 39-12	1965 Pau **France** 21-0
1955 Grenoble **France** 24-0	1966 Naples **France** 21-0
1956 Padua **France** 16-3	1967 Toulon **France** 60-13
1957 Agen **France** 38-6	1995 Buenos Aires *LC* **France** 34-22
1958 Naples **France** 11-3	1997 Grenoble **Italy** 40-32
1959 Nantes **France** 22-0	1997 Auch *LC* **France** 30-19
1960 Treviso **France** 26-0	2000 Paris **France** 42-31
1961 Chambéry **France** 17-0	2001 Rome **France** 30-19

FRANCE v BRITISH XVs

Played 5   France won 2, British XVs won 3, Drawn 0
Highest scores France 27-29 in 1989, British XV 36-3 in 1940
Biggest wins France 21-9 in 1945, British XV 36-3 in 1940

1940 Paris **British XV** 36-3	1946 Paris **France** 10-0
1945 Paris **France** 21-9	1989 Paris **British XV** 29-27
1945 Richmond **British XV** 27-6	

FRANCE v WALES XVs

Played 2   France won 1, Wales XV won 1
Highest scores France 12-0 in 1946, Wales XV 8-0 in 1945
Biggest win France 12-0 in 1946, Wales XV 8-0 in 1945

1945 Swansea **Wales XV** 8-0	1946 Paris **France** 12-0

FRANCE v IRELAND XVs

Played 1   France won 1
Highest scores France 4-3 in 1946, Ireland XV 3-4 in 1946
Biggest win France 4-3 in 1946, Ireland XV no win

1946 Dublin **France** 4-3

FRANCE v NEW ZEALAND ARMY

Played 1   New Zealand Army won 1
Highest scores France 9-14 in 1946, New Zealand Army 14-9 in 1946
Biggest win France no win, New Zealand Army 14-9 in 1946

1946 Paris **New Zealand Army** 14-9

FRANCE v ARGENTINA

Played 34   France won 29, Argentina won 4, Drawn 1
Highest scores France 47-12 in 1995 & 47-26 in 1999, Argentina 27-31 in 1974 & 27-34 in 1996 & 27-32 in 1997
Biggest wins France 47-12 in 1995, Argentina 18-6 in 1988

1949 *1* Buenos Aires **France** 5-0	1986 *1* Buenos Aires **Argentina** 15-13
2 Buenos Aires **France** 12-3	*2* Buenos Aires **France** 22-9
France won series 2-0	*Series drawn 1-1*
1954 *1* Buenos Aires **France** 22-8	1988 *1* Buenos Aires **France** 18-15
2 Buenos Aires **France** 30-3	*2* Buenos Aires **Argentina** 18-6
France won series 2-0	*Series drawn 1-1*
1960 *1* Buenos Aires **France** 37-3	1988 *1* Nantes **France** 29-9
2 Buenos Aires **France** 12-3	*2* Lille **France** 28-18
3 Buenos Aires **France** 29-6	*France won series 2-0*
France won series 3-0	1992 *1* Buenos Aires **France** 27-12
1974 *1* Buenos Aires **France** 20-15	*2* Buenos Aires **France** 33-9
2 Buenos Aires **France** 31-27	*France won series 2-0*
France won series 2-0	1992 Nantes **Argentina** 24-20
1975 *1* Lyons **France** 29-6	1995 Buenos Aires *LC* **France** 47-12
2 Paris **France** 36-21	1996 *1* Buenos Aires **France** 34-27
France won series 2-0	*2* Buenos Aires **France** 34-15
1977 *1* Buenos Aires **France** 26-3	*France won series 2-0*
2 Buenos Aires **Drawn** 18-18	1997 Tarbes *LC* **France** 32-27
France won series 1-0, with 1 draw	1998 *1* Buenos Aires **France** 35-18
1982 *1* Toulouse **France** 25-12	*2* Buenos Aires **France** 37-12
2 Paris **France** 13-6	*France won series 2-0*
France won series 2-0	1998 Nantes **France** 34-14
1985 *1* Buenos Aires **Argentina** 24-16	1999 Dublin *WC* **France** 47-26
2 Buenos Aires **France** 23-15	
Series drawn 1-1	

FRANCE v CZECHOSLOVAKIA

Played 2   France won 2
Highest scores France 28-3 in 1956, Czechoslovakia 6-19 in 1968
Biggest win France 28-3 in 1956, Czechoslovakia no win

1956 Toulouse **France** 28-3	1968 Prague **France** 19-6

FRANCE v FIJI

Played 5   France won 5
Highest scores France 34-9 in 1998, Fiji 19-28 in 1999
Biggest win France 34-9 in 1998, Fiji no win

1964 Paris **France** 21-3	1998 Suva **France** 34-9
1987 Auckland *WC* **France** 31-16	1999 Toulouse *WC* **France** 28-19
1991 Grenoble *WC* **France** 33-9	

FRANCE v JAPAN

Played 1   France won 1
Highest scores France 30-18 in 1973, Japan 18-30 in 1973
Biggest win France 30-18 in 1973, Japan no win

1973 Bordeaux **France** 30-18

FRANCE v ZIMBABWE
Played 1   France won 1
Highest scores France 70-12 in 1987, Zimbabwe 12-70 in 1987
Biggest win France 70-12 in 1987, Zimbabwe no win

1987   Auckland *WC* **France** 70-12

FRANCE v CANADA
Played 4   France won 3, Canada won 1, Drawn 0
Highest scores France 33-20 in 1999, Canada 20-33 in 1999
Biggest wins France 28-9 in 1994, Canada 18-16 in 1994

1991 Agen *WC* **France** 19-13	1994 Besançon **France** 28-9
1994 Nepean **Canada** 18-16	1999 Béziers *WC* **France** 33-20

FRANCE v TONGA
Played 2   France won 1, Tonga won 1
Highest scores France 38-10 in 1995, Tonga 20-16 in 1999
Biggest win France 38-10 in 1995, Tonga 20-16 in 1999

1995 Pretoria *WC* **France** 38-10	1999 Nuku'alofa **Tonga** 20-16

FRANCE v IVORY COAST
Played 1   France won 1
Highest scores France 54-18 in 1995, Ivory Coast 18-54 in 1995
Biggest win France 54-18 in 1995, Ivory Coast no win

1995   Rustenburg *WC* **France** 54-18

FRANCE v SAMOA
Played 1   France won 1
Highest scores France 39-22 in 1999, Samoa 22-39 in 1999
Biggest win France 39-22 in 1999, Samoa no win

1999   Apia **France** 39-22

FRANCE v NAMIBIA
Played 1   France won 1
Highest scores France 47-13 in 1999, Namibia 13-47 in 1999
Biggest win France 47-13 in 1999, Namibia no win

1999   Bordeaux *WC* **France** 47-13

SOUTH AFRICA v NEW ZEALAND
Played 58   New Zealand won 29, South Africa won 26, Drawn 3
Highest scores New Zealand 55-35 in 1997, South Africa 46-40 in 2000
Biggest wins New Zealand 28-0 in 1999, South Africa 17-0 in 1928

1921 *1* Dunedin **New Zealand** 13-5	1928 *1* Durban **South Africa** 17-0
2 Auckland **South Africa** 9-5	*2* Johannesburg **New Zealand** 7-6
3 Wellington **Drawn** 0-0	*3* Port Elizabeth **South Africa** 11-6
Series drawn 1-1, with 1 draw	*4* Cape Town **New Zealand** 13-5
	Series drawn 2-2

1937　*1* Wellington **New Zealand** 13-7
　　　2 Christchurch **South Africa** 13-6
　　　3 Auckland **South Africa** 17-6
　　　South Africa won series 2-1
1949　*1* Cape Town **South Africa** 15-11
　　　2 Johannesburg **South Africa** 12-6
　　　3 Durban **South Africa** 9-3
　　　4 Port Elizabeth **South Africa** 11-8
　　　South Africa won series 4-0
1956　*1* Dunedin **New Zealand** 10-6
　　　2 Wellington **South Africa** 8-3
　　　3 Christchurch **New Zealand** 17-10
　　　4 Auckland **New Zealand** 11-5
　　　New Zealand won series 3-1
1960　*1* Johannesburg **South Africa** 13-0
　　　2 Cape Town **New Zealand** 11-3
　　　3 Bloemfontein **Drawn** 11-11
　　　4 Port Elizabeth **South Africa** 8-3
　　　South Africa won series 2-1, with 1 draw
1965　*1* Wellington **New Zealand** 6-3
　　　2 Dunedin **New Zealand** 13-0
　　　3 Christchurch **South Africa** 19-16
　　　4 Auckland **New Zealand** 20-3
　　　New Zealand won series 3-1
1970　*1* Pretoria **South Africa** 17-6
　　　2 Cape Town **New Zealand** 9-8
　　　3 Port Elizabeth **South Africa** 14-3
　　　4 Johannesburg **South Africa** 20-17
　　　South Africa won series 3-1
1976　*1* Durban **South Africa** 16-7
　　　2 Bloemfontein **New Zealand** 15-9

　　　3 Cape Town **South Africa** 15-10
　　　4 Johannesburg **South Africa** 15-14
　　　South Africa won series 3-1
1981　*1* Christchurch **New Zealand** 14-9
　　　2 Wellington **South Africa** 24-12
　　　3 Auckland **New Zealand** 25-22
　　　New Zealand won series 2-1
1992　Johannesburg **New Zealand** 27-24
1994　*1* Dunedin **New Zealand** 22-14
　　　2 Wellington **New Zealand** 13-9
　　　3 Auckland **Drawn** 18-18
　　　New Zealand won series 2-0, with 1 draw
1995　Johannesburg *WC* **South Africa** 15-12 (*aet*)
1996　Christchurch *TN* **New Zealand** 15-11
1996　Cape Town *TN* **New Zealand** 29-18
1996　*1* Durban **New Zealand** 23-19
　　　2 Pretoria **New Zealand** 33-26
　　　3 Johannesburg **South Africa** 32-22
　　　New Zealand won series 2-1
1997　Johannesbury *TN* **New Zealand** 35-32
1997　Auckland *TN* **New Zealand** 55-35
1998　Wellington *TN* **South Africa** 13-3
1998　Durban *TN* **South Africa** 24-23
1999　Dunedin *TN* **New Zealand** 28-0
1999　Pretoria *TN* **New Zealand** 34-18
1999　Cardiff *WC* **South Africa** 22-18
2000　Christchurch *TN* **New Zealand** 25-12
2000　Johannesburg *TN* **South Africa** 46-40
2001　Cape Town *TN* **New Zealand** 12-3
2001　Auckland *TN* **New Zealand** 26-15

SOUTH AFRICA v AUSTRALIA

Played 47　South Africa won 29, Australia won 17, Drawn 1
Highest scores South Africa 61-22 in 1997, Australia 44-23 in 2000
Biggest wins South Africa 61-22 in 1997, Australia 32-6 in 1999

1933　*1* Cape Town **South Africa** 17-3
　　　2 Durban **Australia** 21-6
　　　3 Johannesburg **South Africa** 12-3
　　　4 Port Elizabeth **South Africa** 11-0
　　　5 Bloemfontein **Australia** 15-4
　　　South Africa won series 3-2
1937　*1* Sydney **South Africa** 9-5
　　　2 Sydney **South Africa** 26-17
　　　South Africa won series 2-0
1953　*1* Johannesburg **South Africa** 25-3
　　　2 Cape Town **Australia** 18-14
　　　3 Durban **South Africa** 18-8
　　　4 Port Elizabeth **South Africa** 22-9
　　　South Africa won series 3-1
1956　*1* Sydney **South Africa** 9-0
　　　2 Brisbane **South Africa** 9-0
　　　South Africa won series 2-0
1961　*1* Johannesburg **South Africa** 28-3
　　　2 Port Elizabeth **South Africa** 23-11
　　　South Africa won series 2-0
1963　*1* Pretoria **South Africa** 14-3
　　　2 Cape Town **Australia** 9-5
　　　3 Johannesburg **Australia** 11-9

　　　4 Port Elizabeth **South Africa** 22-6
　　　Series drawn 2-2
1965　*1* Sydney **Australia** 18-11
　　　2 Brisbane **Australia** 12-8
　　　Australia won series 2-0
1969　*1* Johannesburg **South Africa** 30-11
　　　2 Durban **South Africa** 16-9
　　　3 Cape Town **South Africa** 11-3
　　　4 Bloemfontein **South Africa** 19-8
　　　South Africa won series 4-0
1971　*1* Sydney **South Africa** 19-11
　　　2 Brisbane **South Africa** 14-6
　　　3 Sydney **South Africa** 18-6
　　　South Africa won series 3-0
1992　Cape Town **Australia** 26-3
1993　*1* Sydney **South Africa** 19-12
　　　2 Brisbane **Australia** 28-20
　　　3 Sydney **Australia** 19-12
　　　Australia won series 2-1
1995　Cape Town *WC* **South Africa** 27-18
1996　Sydney *TN* **Australia** 21-16
1996　Bloemfontein *TN* **South Africa** 25-19
1997　Brisbane *TN* **Australia** 32-20
1997　Pretoria *TN* **South Africa** 61-22

1998	Perth *TN* **South Africa** 14-13	2000	Melbourne **Australia** 44-23
1998	Johannesburg *TN* **South Africa** 29-15	2000	Sydney *TN* **Australia** 26-6
1999	Brisbane *TN* **Australia** 32-6	2000	Durban *TN* **Australia** 19-18
1999	Cape Town *TN* **South Africa** 10-9	2001	Pretoria *TN* **South Africa** 20-15
1999	Twickenham *WC* **Australia** 27-21	2001	Perth *TN* **Drawn** 14-14

SOUTH AFRICA v WORLD XVs

Played 3   South Africa won 3
Highest scores South Africa 45-24 in 1977, World XV 24-45 in 1977
Biggest win South Africa 45-24 in 1977, World XV no win

1977	Pretoria **South Africa** 45-24		*2* Johannesburg **South Africa** 22-16
1989	*1* Cape Town **South Africa** 20-19		*South Africa won series 2-0*

SOUTH AFRICA v SOUTH AMERICA

Played 8   South Africa won 7, South America won 1, Drawn 0
Highest scores South Africa 50-18 in 1982, South America 21-12 in 1982
Biggest wins South Africa 50-18 in 1982, South America 21-12 in 1982

1980	*1* Johannesburg **South Africa** 24-9	1982 *1* Pretoria **South Africa** 50-18
	2 Durban **South Africa** 18-9	*2* Bloemfontein **South America** 21-12
	South Africa won series 2-0	*Series drawn 1-1*
1980	*1* Montevideo **South Africa** 22-13	1984 *1* Pretoria **South Africa** 32-15
	2 Santiago **South Africa** 30-16	*2* Cape Town **South Africa** 22-13
	South Africa won series 2-0	*South Africa won series 2-0*

SOUTH AFRICA v UNITED STATES

Played 1   South Africa won 1
Highest scores South Africa 38-7 in 1981, United States 7-38 in 1981
Biggest win South Africa 38-7 in 1981, United States no win

1981	Glenville **South Africa** 38-7

SOUTH AFRICA v NEW ZEALAND CAVALIERS

Played 4   South Africa won 3, New Zealand Cavaliers won 1, Drawn 0
Highest scores South Africa 33-18 in 1986, New Zealand Cavaliers 19-18 in 1986
Biggest wins South Africa 33-18 in 1986, New Zealand Cavaliers 19-18 in 1986

1986	*1* Cape Town **South Africa** 21-15	*4* Johannesburg **South Africa** 24-10
	2 Durban **New Zealand Cavaliers** 19-18	*South Africa won series 3-1*
	3 Pretoria **South Africa** 33-18	

SOUTH AFRICA v ARGENTINA

Played 7   South Africa won 7
Highest scores South Africa 52-23 in 1993, Argentina 33-37 in 2000
Biggest wins South Africa 46-15 in 1996, Argentina no win

1993	*1* Buenos Aires **South Africa** 29-26	1996 *1* Buenos Aires **South Africa** 46-15
	2 Buenos Aires **South Africa** 52-23	*2* Buenos Aires **South Africa** 44-21
	South Africa won series 2-0	*South Africa win series 2-0*
1994	*1* Port Elizabeth **South Africa** 42-22	2000 Buenos Aires **South Africa** 37-33
	2 Johannesburg **South Africa** 46-26	
	South Africa won series 2-0	

SOUTH AFRICA v SAMOA
Played 2   South Africa won 2
Highest scores South Africa 60-8 in 1995, Samoa 14-42 in 1995
Biggest win South Africa 60-8 in 1995, Samoa no win

1995 Johannesburg **South Africa** 60-8	1995 Johannesburg *WC* **South Africa** 42-14

SOUTH AFRICA v ROMANIA
Played 1   South Africa won 1
Highest score South Africa 21-8 in 1995, Romania 8-21 in 1995
Biggest win South Africa 21-8 in 1995, Romania no win

1995   Cape Town *WC* **South Africa** 21-8

SOUTH AFRICA v CANADA
Played 2   South Africa won 2
Highest scores South Africa 51-18 in 2000, Canada 18-51 in 2000
Biggest win South Africa 51-18 in 2000, Canada no win

1995 Port Elizabeth *WC* **South Africa** 20-0	2000 East London **South Africa** 51-18

SOUTH AFRICA v ITALY
Played 5   South Africa won 5
Highest scores South Africa 101-0 in 1999, Italy 31-62 in 1997
Biggest win South Africa 101-0 in 1999, Italy no win

1995 Rome **South Africa** 40-21	*2* Durban **South Africa** 101-0
1997 Bologna **South Africa** 62-31	*South Africa won series 2-0*
1999 *1* Port Elizabeth **South Africa** 74-3	2001 Port Elizabeth **South Africa** 60-14

SOUTH AFRICA v FIJI
Played 1   South Africa won 1
Highest scores South Africa 43-18 in 1996, Fiji 18-43 in 1996
Biggest win South Africa 43-18 in 1996, Fiji no win

1996   Pretoria **South Africa** 43-18

SOUTH AFRICA v TONGA
Played 1   South Africa won 1
Higest scores South Africa 74-10 in 1997, Tonga 10-74 in 1997
Biggest win South Africa 74-10 in 1997, Tonga no win

1997   Cape Town **South Africa** 74-10

SOUTH AFRICA v SPAIN
Played 1   South Africa won 1
Highest scores South Africa 47-3, Spain 3-47 in 1999
Biggest win South Africa 47-3 in 1999, Spain no win

1999   Murrayfield *WC* **South Africa** 47-3

SOUTH AFRICA v URUGUAY

Played 1   South Africa won 1
Highest scores South Africa 39-3 in 1999, Uruguay 3-39 in 1999
Biggest win South Africa 39-3 in 1999, Uruguay no win

1999   Glasgow *WC* **South Africa** 39-3

NEW ZEALAND v AUSTRALIA

Played 114   New Zealand won 75, Australia won 34, Drawn 5
Highest scores New Zealand 43-6 in 1996, Australia 35-39 in 2000
Biggest wins New Zealand 43-6 in 1996, Australia 28-7 in 1999

1903   Sydney **New Zealand** 22-3
1905   Dunedin **New Zealand** 14-3
1907   *1* Sydney **New Zealand** 26-6
    2 Brisbane **New Zealand** 14-5
    3 Sydney **Drawn** 5-5
    New Zealand won series 2-0, with 1 draw
1910   *1* Sydney **New Zealand** 6-0
    2 Sydney **Australia** 11-0
    3 Sydney **New Zealand** 28-13
    New Zealand won series 2-1
1913   *1* Wellington **New Zealand** 30-5
    2 Dunedin **New Zealand** 25-13
    3 Christchurch **Australia** 16-5
    New Zealand won series 2-1
1914   *1* Sydney **New Zealand** 5-0
    2 Brisbane **New Zealand** 17-0
    3 Sydney **New Zealand** 22-7
    New Zealand won series 3-0
1929   *1* Sydney **Australia** 9-8
    2 Brisbane **Australia** 17-9
    3 Sydney **Australia** 15-13
    Australia won series 3-0
1931   Auckland **New Zealand** 20-13
1932   *1* Sydney **Australia** 22-17
    2 Brisbane **New Zealand** 21-3
    3 Sydney **New Zealand** 21-13
    New Zealand won series 2-1
1934   *1* Sydney **Australia** 25-11
    2 Sydney **Drawn** 3-3
    Australia won series 1-0, with 1 draw
1936   *1* Wellington **New Zealand** 11-6
    2 Dunedin **New Zealand** 38-13
    New Zealand won series 2-0
1938   *1* Sydney **New Zealand** 24-9
    2 Brisbane **New Zealand** 20-14
    3 Sydney **New Zealand** 14-6
    New Zealand won series 3-0
1946   *1* Dunedin **New Zealand** 31-8
    2 Auckland **New Zealand** 14-10
    New Zealand won series 2-0
1947   *1* Brisbane **New Zealand** 13-5
    2 Sydney **New Zealand** 27-14
    New Zealand won series 2-0
1949   *1* Wellington **Australia** 11-6
    2 Auckland **Australia** 16-9
    Australia won series 2-0
1951   *1* Sydney **New Zealand** 8-0
    2 Sydney **New Zealand** 17-11

    3 Brisbane **New Zealand** 16-6
    New Zealand won series 3-0
1952   *1* Christchurch **Australia** 14-9
    2 Wellington **New Zealand** 15-8
    Series drawn 1-1
1955   *1* Wellington **New Zealand** 16-8
    2 Dunedin **New Zealand** 8-0
    3 Auckland **Australia** 8-3
    New Zealand won series 2-1
1957   *1* Sydney **New Zealand** 25-11
    2 Brisbane **New Zealand** 22-9
    New Zealand won series 2-0
1958   *1* Wellington **New Zealand** 25-3
    2 Christchurch **Australia** 6-3
    3 Auckland **New Zealand** 17-8
    New Zealand won series 2-1
1962   *1* Brisbane **New Zealand** 20-6
    2 Sydney **New Zealand** 14-5
    New Zealand won series 2-0
1962   *1* Wellington **Drawn** 9-9
    2 Dunedin **New Zealand** 3-0
    3 Auckland **New Zealand** 16-8
    New Zealand won series 2-0, with1 draw
1964   *1* Dunedin **New Zealand** 14-9
    2 Christchurch **New Zealand** 18-3
    3 Wellington **Australia** 20-5
    New Zealand won series 2-1
1967   Wellington **New Zealand** 29-9
1968   *1* Sydney **New Zealand** 27-11
    2 Brisbane **New Zealand** 19-18
    New Zealand won series 2-0
1972   *1* Wellington **New Zealand** 29-6
    2 Christchurch **New Zealand** 30-17
    3 Auckland **New Zealand** 38-3
    New Zealand won series 3-0
1974   *1* Sydney **New Zealand** 11-6
    2 Brisbane **Drawn** 16-16
    3 Sydney **New Zealand** 16-6
    New Zealand won series 2-0, with 1 draw
1978   *1* Wellington **New Zealand** 13-12
    2 Christchurch **New Zealand** 22-6
    3 Auckland **Australia** 30-16
    New Zealand won series 2-1
1979   Sydney **Australia** 12-6
1980   *1* Sydney **Australia** 13-9
    2 Brisbane **New Zealand** 12-9
    3 Sydney **Australia** 26-10
    Australia won series 2-1
1982   *1* Christchurch **New Zealand** 23-16

2 Wellington **Australia** 19-16
3 Auckland **New Zealand** 33-18
New Zealand won series 2-1

1983 Sydney **New Zealand** 18-8
1984 *1* Sydney **Australia** 16-9
     2 Brisbane **New Zealand** 19-15
     3 Sydney **New Zealand** 25-24
     New Zealand won series 2-1
1985 Auckland **New Zealand** 10-9
1986 *1* Wellington **Australia** 13-12
     2 Dunedin **New Zealand** 13-12
     3 Auckland **Australia** 22-9
     Australia won series 2-1
1987 Sydney **New Zealand** 30-16
1988 *1* Sydney **New Zealand** 32-7
     2 Brisbane **Drawn** 19-19
     3 Sydney **New Zealand** 30-9
     New Zealand won series 2-0, with 1 draw
1989 Auckland **New Zealand** 24-12
1990 *1* Christchurch **New Zealand** 21-6
     2 Auckland **New Zealand** 27-17
     3 Wellington **Australia** 21-9
     New Zealand won series 2-1
1991 *1* Sydney **Australia** 21-12
     2 Auckland **New Zealand** 6-3
1991 Dublin *WC* **Australia** 16-6
1992 *1* Sydney **Australia** 16-15

2 Brisbane **Australia** 19-17
3 Sydney **New Zealand** 26-23
Australia won series 2-1

1993 Dunedin **New Zealand** 25-10
1994 Sydney **Australia** 20-16
1995 Auckland **New Zealand** 28-16
1995 Sydney **New Zealand** 34-23
1996 Wellington *TN* **New Zealand** 43-6
1996 Brisbane *TN* **New Zealand** 32-25
     New Zealand won series 2-0
1997 Christchurch **New Zealand** 30-13
1997 Melbourne *TN* **New Zealand** 33-18
1997 Dunedin *TN* **New Zealand** 36-24
     New Zealand won series 3-0
1998 Melbourne *TN* **Australia** 24-16
1998 Christchurch *TN* **Australia** 27-23
1998 Sydney **Australia** 19-14
     Australia won series 3-0
1999 Auckland *TN* **New Zealand** 34-15
1999 Sydney *TN* **Australia** 28-7
     Series drawn 1-1
2000 Sydney *TN* **New Zealand** 39-35
2000 Wellington *TN* **Australia** 24-23
     Series drawn 1-1
2001 Dunedin *TN* **Australia** 23-15
2001 Sydney *TN* **Australia** 29-26
     Australia won series 2-0

NEW ZEALAND v UNITED STATES
Played 2   New Zealand won 2
Highest scores New Zealand 51-3 in 1913, United States 6-46 in 1991
Biggest win New Zealand 51-3 in 1913, United States no win

1913 Berkeley **New Zealand** 51-3

1991 Gloucester *WC* **New Zealand** 46-6

NEW ZEALAND v ROMANIA
Played 1   New Zealand won 1
Highest score New Zealand 14-6 in 1981, Romania 6-14 in 1981
Biggest win New Zealand 14-6 in 1981, Romania no win

1981 Bucharest **New Zealand** 14-6

NEW ZEALAND v ARGENTINA
Played 10   New Zealand won 9, Drawn 1
Highest scores New Zealand 93-8 in 1997, Argentina 21-21 in 1985
Biggest win New Zealand 93-8 in 1997, Argentina no win

1985 *1* Buenos Aires **New Zealand** 33-20
     2 Buenos Aires **Drawn** 21-21
     New Zealand won series 1-0, with 1 draw
1987 Wellington *WC* **New Zealand** 46-15
1989 *1* Dunedin **New Zealand** 60-9
     2 Wellington **New Zealand** 49-12
     New Zealand won series 2-0

1991 *1* Buenos Aires **New Zealand** 28-14
     2 Buenos Aires **New Zealand** 36-6
     New Zealand won series 2-0
1997 *1* Wellington **New Zealand** 93-8
     2 Hamilton **New Zealand** 62-10
     New Zealand won series 2-0
2001 Christchurch **New Zealand** 67-19

NEW ZEALAND v ITALY

Played 5   New Zealand won 5
Highest scores New Zealand 101-3 in 1999, Italy 21-31 in 1991
Biggest win New Zealand 101-3 in 1999, Italy no win

1987 Auckland *WC* **New Zealand** 70-6	1999 Huddersfield *WC* **New Zealand** 101-3
1991 Leicester *WC* **New Zealand** 31-21	2000 Genoa **New Zealand** 56-19
1995 Bologna **New Zealand** 70-6	

NEW ZEALAND v FIJI

Played 2   New Zealand won 2
Highest scores New Zealand 74-13 in 1987, Fiji 13-74 in 1987
Biggest win New Zealand 71-5 in 1997, Fiji no win

1987 Christchurch *WC* **New Zealand** 74-13	1997 Albany **New Zealand** 71-5

NEW ZEALAND v CANADA

Played 2   New Zealand won 2
Highest scores New Zealand 73-7 in 1995, Canada 13-29 in 1991
Biggest win New Zealand 73-7 in 1995, Canada no win

1991 Lille *WC* **New Zealand** 29-13	1995 Auckland **New Zealand** 73-7

NEW ZEALAND v WORLD XVs

Played 3   New Zealand won 2, World XV won 1, Drawn 0
Highest scores New Zealand 54-26 in 1992, World XV 28-14 in 1992
Biggest wins New Zealand 54-26 in 1992, World XV 28-14 in 1992

1992 *1* Christchurch **World XV** 28-14	*3* Auckland **New Zealand** 26-15
2 Wellington **New Zealand** 54-26	*New Zealand won series 2-1*

NEW ZEALAND v SAMOA

Played 4   New Zealand won 4
Highest scores New Zealand 71-13 in 1999, Samoa 13-35 in 1993 & 13-71 in 1999
Biggest win New Zealand 71-13 in 1999, Samoa no win

1993 Auckland **New Zealand** 35-13	1999 Albany **New Zealand** 71-13
1996 Napier **New Zealand** 51-10	2001 Albany **New Zealand** 50-6

NEW ZEALAND v JAPAN

Played 1   New Zealand won 1
Highest scores New Zealand 145-17 in 1995, Japan 17-145 in 1995
Biggest win New Zealand 145-17 in 1995, Japan no win

1995 Bloemfontein *WC* **New Zealand** 145-17

NEW ZEALAND v TONGA

Played 2   New Zealand won 2
Highest scores New Zealand 102-0 in 2000, Tonga 9-45 in 1999
Biggest win New Zealand 102-0 in 2000, Tonga no win

1999 Bristol *WC* **New Zealand** 45-9	2000 Albany **New Zealand** 102-0

AUSTRALIA v UNITED STATES

Played 6 Australia won 6
Highest scores Australia 67-9 in 1990, United States 19-55 in 1999
Biggest win Australia 67-9 in 1990, United States no win

1912	Berkeley **Australia** 12-8	1987	Brisbane *WC* **Australia** 47-12
1976	Los Angeles **Australia** 24-12	1990	Brisbane **Australia** 67-9
1983	Sydney **Australia** 49-3	1999	Limerick *WC* **Australia** 55-19

AUSTRALIA v NEW ZEALAND XVs

Played 24 Australia won 6, New Zealand XVs won 18, Drawn 0
Highest scores Australia 26-20 in 1926, New Zealand XV 38-11 in 1923 and 38-8 in 1924
Biggest win Australia 17-0 in 1921, New Zealand XV 38-8 in 1924

1920	*1* Sydney **New Zealand XV** 26-15	1925	*1* Sydney **New Zealand XV** 26-3
	2 Sydney **New Zealand XV** 14-6		*2* Sydney **New Zealand XV** 4-0
	3 Sydney **New Zealand XV** 24-13		*3* Sydney **New Zealand XV** 11-3
	New Zealand XV won series 3-0		*New Zealand XV won series 3-0*
1921	Christchurch **Australia** 17-0	1925	Auckland **New Zealand XV** 36-10
1922	*1* Sydney **New Zealand XV** 26-19	1926	*1* Sydney **Australia** 26-20
	2 Sydney **Australia** 14-8		*2* Sydney **New Zealand XV** 11-6
	3 Sydney **Australia** 8-6		*3* Sydney **New Zealand XV** 14-0
	Australia won series 2-1		*4* Sydney **New Zealand XV** 28-21
1923	*1* Dunedin **New Zealand XV** 19-9		*New Zealand XV won series 3-1*
	2 Christchurch **New Zealand XV** 34-6	1928	*1* Wellington **New Zealand XV** 15-12
	3 Wellington **New Zealand XV** 38-11		*2* Dunedin **New Zealand XV** 16-14
	New Zealand XV won series 3-0		*3* Christchurch **Australia** 11-8
1924	*1* Sydney **Australia** 20-16		*New Zealand XV won series 2-1*
	2 Sydney **New Zealand XV** 21-5		
	3 Sydney **New Zealand XV** 38-8		
	New Zealand XV won series 2-1		

AUSTRALIA v SOUTH AFRICA XVs

Played 3 South Africa XVs won 3
Highest scores Australia 11-16 in 1921, South Africa XV 28-9 in 1921
Biggest win Australia no win, South Africa XV 28-9 in 1921

1921	*1* Sydney **South Africa XV** 25-10	*3* Sydney **South Africa XV** 28-9
	2 Sydney **South Africa XV** 16-11	*South Africa XV won series 3-0*

AUSTRALIA v NEW ZEALAND MAORIS

Played 16 Australia won 8, New Zealand Maoris won 6, Drawn 2
Highest scores Australia 31-6 in 1936, New Zealand Maoris 25-22 in 1922
Biggest wins Australia 31-6 in 1936, New Zealand Maoris 20-0 in 1946

1922	*1* Sydney **New Zealand Maoris** 25-22	1936	Palmerston North **Australia** 31-6
	2 Sydney **Australia** 28-13	1946	Hamilton **New Zealand Maoris** 20-0
	3 Sydney **New Zealand Maoris** 23-22	1949	*1* Sydney **New Zealand Maoris** 12-3
	New Zealand Maoris won series 2-1		*2* Brisbane **Drawn** 8-8
1923	*1* Sydney **Australia** 27-23		*3* Sydney **Australia** 18-3
	2 Sydney **Australia** 21-16		*Series drawn 1-1, with 1 draw*
	3 Sydney **Australia** 14-12	1958	*1* Brisbane **Australia** 15-14
	Australia won series 3-0		*2* Sydney **Drawn** 3-3
1928	Wellington **New Zealand Maoris** 9-8		*3* Melbourne **New Zealand Maoris** 13-6
1931	Palmerston North **Australia** 14-3		*Series drawn 1-1, with 1 draw*

AUSTRALIA v FIJI

Played 16   Australia won 13, Fiji won 2, Drawn 1
Highest scores Australia 66-20 in 1998, Fiji 28-52 in 1985
Biggest wins Australia 66-20 in 1998, Fiji 17-15 in 1952 & 18-16 in 1954

1952 *1* Sydney **Australia** 15-9	1976 *1* Sydney **Australia** 22-6
2 Sydney **Fiji** 17-15	*2* Brisbane **Australia** 21-9
Series drawn 1-1	*3* Sydney **Australia** 27-17
1954 *1* Brisbane **Australia** 22-19	*Australia won series 3-0*
2 Sydney **Fiji** 18-16	1980 Suva **Australia** 22-9
Series drawn 1-1	1984 Suva **Australia** 16-3
1961 *1* Brisbane **Australia** 24-6	1985 *1* Brisbane **Australia** 52-28
2 Sydney **Australia** 20-14	*2* Sydney **Australia** 31-9
3 Melbourne **Drawn** 3-3	*Australia won series 2-0*
Australia won series 2-0, with 1 draw	1998 Sydney **Australia** 66-20
1972 Suva **Australia** 21-19	

AUSTRALIA v TONGA

Played 4   Australia won 3, Tonga won 1, Drawn 0
Highest scores Australia 74-0 in 1998, Tonga 16-11 in 1973
Biggest wins Australia 74-0 in 1998, Tonga 16-11 in 1973

1973 *1* Sydney **Australia** 30-12	1993 Brisbane **Australia** 52-14
2 Brisbane **Tonga** 16-11	1998 Canberra **Australia** 74-0
Series drawn 1-1	

AUSTRALIA v JAPAN

Played 3   Australia won 3
Highest scores Australia 50-25 in 1975, Japan 25-50 in 1973
Biggest win Australia 50-25 in 1975, Japan no win

1975 *1* Sydney **Australia** 37-7	1987 Sydney *WC* **Australia** 42-23
2 Brisbane **Australia** 50-25	
Australia won series 2-0	

AUSTRALIA v ARGENTINA

Played 15   Australia won 10, Argentina won 4, Drawn 1
Highest scores Australia 53-7 in 1995 & 53-6 in 2000, Argentina 27-19 in 1987
Biggest wins Australia 53-6 in 2000, Argentina 18-3 in 1983

1979 *1* Buenos Aires **Argentina** 24-13	1991 Llanelli *WC* **Australia** 32-19
2 Buenos Aires **Australia** 17-12	1995 *1* Brisbane **Australia** 53-7
Series drawn 1-1	*2* Sydney **Australia** 30-13
1983 *1* Brisbane **Argentina** 18-3	*Australia won series 2-0*
2 Sydney **Australia** 29-13	1997 *1* Buenos Aires **Australia** 23-15
Series drawn 1-1	*2* Buenos Aires **Argentina** 18-16
1986 *1* Brisbane **Australia** 39-19	*Series drawn 1-1*
2 Sydney **Australia** 26-0	2000 *1* Brisbane **Australia** 53-6
Australia won series 2-0	*2* Canberra **Australia** 32-25
1987 *1* Buenos Aires **Drawn** 19-19	*Australia won series 2-0*
2 Buenos Aires **Argentina** 27-19	
Argentina won series 1-0, with 1 draw	

AUSTRALIA v SAMOA
Played 3   Australia won 3
Highest scores Australia 73-3 in 1994, Samoa 13-25 in 1998
Biggest win Australia 73-3 in 1994, Samoa no win

1991	Pontypool *WC* **Australia** 9-3		1998	Brisbane **Australia** 25-13
1994	Sydney **Australia** 73-3			

AUSTRALIA v ITALY
Played 6   Australia won 6
Highest scores Australia 55-6 in 1988, Italy 20-23 in 1994
Biggest win Australia 55-6 in 1988, Italy no win

1983	Rovigo **Australia** 29-7		*2* Melbourne **Australia** 20-7
1986	Brisbane **Australia** 39-18		*Australia won series 2-0*
1988	Rome **Australia** 55-6	1996	Padua **Australia** 40-18
1994	*1* Brisbane **Australia** 23-20		

AUSTRALIA v CANADA
Played 5   Australia won 5
Highest scores Australia 74-9 in 1996, Canada 16-43 in 1993
Biggest win Australia 74-9 in 1996, Canada no win

1985	*1* Sydney **Australia** 59-3	1993	Calgary **Australia** 43-16
	2 Brisbane **Australia** 43-15	1995	Port Elizabeth *WC* **Australia** 27-11
	Australia won series 2-0	1996	Brisbane **Australia** 74-9

AUSTRALIA v KOREA
Played 1   Australia won 1
Highest scores Australia 65-18 in 1987, Korea 18-65 in 1987
Biggest win Australia 65-18 in 1987, Korea no win

1987   Brisbane **Australia** 65-18

AUSTRALIA v ROMANIA
Played 2   Australia won 2
Highest scores Australia 57-9 in 1999, Romania 9-57 in 1999
Biggest win Australia 57-9 in 1999, Romania no win

1995	Stellenbosch *WC* **Australia** 42-3	1999	Belfast *WC* **Australia** 57-9

WORLD INTERNATIONAL RECORDS

The match and career records cover **official cap matches** *played by the dozen Executive Council Member Unions of the International Board (England, Scotland, Ireland, Wales, France, Italy, South Africa, New Zealand, Australia, Argentina, Canada and Japan) from 1871 up to 20 October 2001. Figures include Test performances for the (British/Irish Isles) Lions and (South American) Jaguars (shown in brackets). Where a world record has been set in a cap match played by another nation in membership of the IRB, this is shown as a footnote to the relevant table.*

Match Records

Most Consecutive Test Wins

17 by N Zealand 1965 *SA* 4, 1966 *BI* 1,2,3,4, 1967 *A, E, W, F, S,* 1968 *A* 1,2, *F* 1,2,3, 1969 *W* 1,2
17 by S Africa 1997 *A* 2, *It, F* 1,2, *E* , *S,* 1998 *I* 1,2, *W* 1, *E* 1, *A* 1, *NZ* 1,2, *A* 2, *W* 2, *S* 3

Most Consecutive Tests Without Defeat

Matches	Wins	Draws	Period
23 by N Zealand	22	1	1987 to 1990
17 by N Zealand	15	2	1961 to 1964
17 by N Zealand	17	0	1965 to 1969
17 by S Africa	17	0	1997 to 1998

Most Points in a Match
by a team

Pts	Opponents	Venue	Year
145 by N Zealand	Japan	Bloemfontein	1995
134 by Japan	Ch Taipei	Singapore	1998
114 by Argentina	Brazil	Sao Paulo	1993
110 by England	Holland	Huddersfield	1998
109 by Argentina	Brazil	Santiago	1979

Hong Kong scored 164 points against Singapore at Kuala Lumpur in 1994

by a player

Pts	Player	Opponents	Venue	Year
50 for Argentina	E Morgan	Paraguay	San Pablo	1973
45 for N Zealand	S D Culhane	Japan	Bloemfontein	1995
44 for Scotland	A G Hastings	Ivory Coast	Rustenburg	1995
40 for Argentina	G M Jorge	Brazil	Sao Paulo	1993
39 for Australia	M C Burke	Canada	Brisbane	1996

50 points were scored for Hong Kong by A Billington against Singapore at Kuala Lumpur in 1994

Most Tries in a Match
by the team

Tries	Opponents	Venue	Year
21 by N Zealand	Japan	Bloemfontein	1995
20 by Japan	Ch Taipei	Singapore	1998
19 by Argentina	Brazil	Santiago	1979
19 by Argentina	Paraguay	Asuncion	1985

Hong Kong scored 26 tries against Singapore at Kuala Lumpur in 1994

by a player

Tries	Player	Opponents	Venue	Year
8 for Argentina	G M Jorge	Brazil	Sao Paulo	1993
6 for Argentina	E Morgan	Paraguay	San Pablo	1973
6 for Argentina	G M Jorge	Brazil	Montevideo	1989
6 for N Zealand	M C G Ellis	Japan	Bloemfontein	1995
5 for Scotland	G C Lindsay	Wales	Racburn Place	1887
5 for England	D Lambert	France	Richmond	1907
5 for Argentina	H Goti	Brazil	Montevideo	1961
5 for Argentina	M R Jurado	Brazil	Montevideo	1971
5 for England	R Underwood	Fiji	Twickenham	1989
5 for N Zealand	J W Wilson	Fiji	Albany	1997
5 for Japan	T Masuho	Ch Taipei	Singapore	1998
5 for Argentina	P Grande	Paraguay	Asuncion	1998
5 for S Africa	C S Terblanche	Italy	Durban	1999

10 tries were scored for Hong Kong by A Billington against Singapore at Kuala Lumpur in 1994

Most Conversions in a Match
by the team

Cons	Opponents	Venue	Year
20 by N Zealand	Japan	Bloemfontein	1995
17 by Japan	Ch Taipei	Singapore	1998
15 by Argentina	Brazil	Santiago	1979
15 by England	Holland	Huddersfield	1998

by a player

Cons	Player	Opponents	Venue	Year
20 for N Zealand	S D Culhane	Japan	Bloemfontein	1995
15 for England	P J Grayson	Holland	Huddersfield	1998

Most Penalties in a Match
by the team

Penalties	Opponents	Venue	Year
9 by Japan	Tonga	Tokyo	1999
9 by N Zealand	Australia	Auckland	1999
9 by Wales	France	Cardiff	1999
9 by N Zealand	France	Paris	2000

Portugal scored nine penalties against Georgia at Lisbon in 2000

by a player

Penalties	Player	Opponents	Venue	Year
9 for Japan	K Hirose	Tonga	Tokyo	1999
9 for N Zealand	A P Mehrtens	Australia	Auckland	1999
9 for Wales	N R Jenkins	France	Cardiff	1999
9 for N Zealand	A P Mehrtens	France	Paris	2000

Nine penalties were scored for Portugal by T Teixeira against Georgia at Lisbon in 2000

Most Dropped Goals in a Match
by the team

Drops	Opponents	Venue	Year
5 by South Africa	England	Paris	1999
3 by several nations			

by a player

Drops	Player	Opponents	Venue	Year
5 for S Africa	J H de Beer	England	Paris	1999
3 for several	nations			

Career Records

Most Capped Players

Caps	Player	Career Span
111	P Sella (France)	1982 to 1995
101	D I Campese (Australia)	1982 to 1996
97 (5)	J Leonard (England/Lions)	1990 to 2001
93	S Blanco (France)	1980 to 1991
92	S B T Fitzpatrick (N Zealand)	1986 to 1997
91 (6)	R Underwood (England/Lions)	1984 to 1996

Most Consecutive Tests

Tests	Player	Span
63	S B T Fitzpatrick (N Zealand)	1986 to 1995
58	J W C Roff (Australia)	1996 to 2001
53	G O Edwards (Wales)	1967 to 1978
52	W J McBride (Ireland)	1964 to 1975
51	C M Cullen (N Zealand)	1996 to 2000

Most Tests as Captain

Tests	Captain	Span
59	W D C Carling (England)	1988 to 1996
55	J A Eales (Australia)	1996 to 2001
51	S B T Fitzpatrick (N Zealand)	1992 to 1997
46 (8)	H Porta (Argentina/Jaguars)	1971 to 1990
36	N C Farr-Jones (Australia)	1988 to 1992
36	G H Teichmann (S Africa)	1996 to 1999

Most Tests in Individual Positions

Position	Player	Tests	Span
Full-back	S Blanco (France)	81	1980 to 1991
Wing	R Underwood (England/Lions)	91 (6)	1984 to 1996
Centre	P Sella (France)	104	1982 to 1995
Fly-half	C R Andrew (England/Lions)	75 (5)	1985 to 1997
Scrum-half	J H van der Westhuizen (S Africa)	73	1993 to 2001
Prop	J Leonard (England/Lions)	97 (5)	1990 to 2001
Hooker	S B T Fitzpatrick (N Zealand)	92	1986 to 1997
Lock	J A Eales (Australia)	84	1991 to 2001
Flanker	D J Wilson (Australia)	78	1992 to 2000
No 8	D Richards (England/Lions)	53* (6)	1986 to 1996

* excludes an appearance as a temporary replacement

Most Points in Tests

Points	Player	Tests	Career
1070 (41)	N R Jenkins (Wales/Lions))	88 (4)	1991 to 2001
911	M P Lynagh (Australia)	72	1984 to 1995
892 (27)	D Dominguez (Italy/Argentina)	66 (2)	1989 to 2001
763	A P Mehrtens (N Zealand)	52	1995 to 2001
733 (66)	A G Hastings (Scotland/Lions)	67 (6)	1986 to 1995
663	M C Burke (Australia)	54	1993 to 2001

Most Tries in Tests

Tries	Player	Tests	Career
64	D I Campese (Australia)	101	1982 to 1996
50 (1)	R Underwood (England/Lions)	91 (6)	1984 to 1996
44	J W Wilson (N Zealand)	60	1993 to 2001
42	C M Cullen (N Zealand)	52	1996 to 2001
38	S Blanco (France)	93	1980 to 1991
35	J J Kirwan (N Zealand)	63	1984 to 1994
34 (1)	I C Evans (Wales/Lions)	79 (7)	1987 to 1998
34	J H van der Westhuizen (S Africa)	75	1993 to 2001

Most Conversions in Tests

Cons	Player	Tests	Career
140	M P Lynagh (Australia)	72	1984 to 1995
130	A P Mehrtens (N Zealand)	52	1995 to 2001
127 (1)	N R Jenkins (Wales/Lions))	88 (4)	1991 to 2001
123 (6)	D Dominguez (Italy/Argentina)	66 (2)	1989 to 2001

118	G J Fox (N Zealand)	46	1985 to 1993

Most Penalty Goals in Tests

Penalties	Player	Tests	Career
244 (13)	N R Jenkins (Wales/Lions)	88 (4)	1991 to 2001
186 (5)	D Dominguez (Italy/Argentina)	66 (2)	1989 to 2001
177	M P Lynagh (Australia)	72	1984 to 1995
160 (20)	A G Hastings (Scotland/Lions)	67 (6)	1986 to 1995
147	A P Mehrtens (N Zealand)	52	1995 to 2001
132	M C Burke (Australia)	54	1993 to 2001

Most Dropped Goals in Tests

Drops	Player	Tests	Career
28 (2)	H Porta (Argentina/Jaguars)	66 (8)	1971 to 1990
23 (2)	C R Andrew (England/Lions)	76 (5)	1985 to 1997
18	H E Botha (S Africa)	28	1980 to 1992
16 (0)	D Dominguez (Italy/Argentina)	66 (2)	1989 to 2001
15	J-P Lescarboura (France)	28	1982 to 1990

Partnership Records

Position	Holders	Detail	Span
Centre threequarters	W D C Carling & J C Guscott	45 (1) for England/Lions	1989 to 1996
Half backs	M P Lynagh & N C Farr-Jones	47 for Australia	1985 to 1992
Front row	A J Daly, P N Kearns & E J A McKenzie	37 for Australia	1990 to 1995
Second row	I D Jones & R M Brooke	49 for N Zealand	1992 to 1999
Back row	R A Hill, L B N Dallaglio & N A Back	31 for England	1997 to 2001

HEINEKEN CUP 2000–01

Leicester at Last

David Llewellyn

So at long last the Tigers managed to get their claws on the Heineken Cup. They had failed at the last hurdle four years ago, but this time around there was to be no mistake, well, not on their part at least, although there were a couple of telling errors as the tournament reached its climax.

Leicester were one of the beneficiaries when the referee in their semi-final against Gloucester failed to award a scrum when no advantage accrued after a Tigers knock-on. Munster, moreover, had a perfectly good try that might well have changed the course of their semi-final against Stade Francais disallowed.

It was all grist to the competition's mill. There was the abject failure of the reigning champions Northampton. Their performance in finishing bottom of Pool One could not, by any stretch of the imagination, be described as a title defence – indeed if it were boxing they would have been hauled before a commission.

The previous season's champions, Ulster, also ended up at the bottom of their particular pile in Pool Three, while, even if they had not been deducted a point for fielding an ineligible player, the New Zealander Norm Berryman in October, Castres would still have held fourth place in Pool Four.

Italy's two representatives, L'Aquila and Roma, lost all six of their matches and to the former went the dubious distinction of conceding most points in the tournament. Roma at least made something of a fight of things, giving Gloucester a fright in their final game.

Glasgow Caledonians did manage one win, at home over Pontypridd, but that came in the penultimate round, far too late for the Scots to emulate their rivals Edinburgh Reivers who pipped Leinster to second place in Pool One by virtue of a victory over the Irish side.

The competition had barely got under way when the question of player eligibility reared up. Clubs had been obliged to register squads of 30 before matters began, although there was another opportunity to register players in time for the quarter-finals. By the start, though, several clubs had been hit by injuries especially in key positions such as front-row, lock and back-row.

It meant Cardiff doing without Peter Rogers for the first phase of pool matches and Saracens being unable to pick Aussie Tim Horan (by the time they could he was injured). In the end eligibility was a mere bagatelle when set alongside the action.

Leicester dominated from the outset when they thrashed Pau at Welford Road, the 46 points leaked by the French side being the most they conceded in the competition. (Not even Stade Francais could better Leicester when they met Pau in the quarter final). In fact Leicester only came unstuck once, against Pontypridd at Sardis Road.

There was a clinical approach to their campaign and their predominance in other competitions was never allowed to distract them from their real purpose in professional life – to provide incontrovertible proof that they were the best club side in Europe, indeed in the Northern Hemisphere, until the next tournament anyway.

When it came to the crucial closing phase of the pool stage of the tournament the Tigers found they had to manage without their inspirational captain Martin Johnson, whose five week ban imposed after he was cited for dropping a knee on Saracens fly-half, Duncan McRae, meant he could not return until after the quarter final round.

Leicester's strength in depth, however, merely saw the hugely talented youngster Ben Kay stepping up and not putting a foot a wrong, just as he had done in the autumn when England calls also deprived Leicester of Johnson's services.

One of their most satisfying results in Pool Six was at Pau, where, in 1998 the Tigers had come off second best in the quarter finals. This time they went to the Pyrenees and climbed their own personal mountain, winning convincingly, to repeat their feat of the 1996-97 tournament, although this time around it was not easy.

Will Johnson, younger brother of Martin, described the scene just before the kick-off, saying: 'They [the Pau team] came flying out of the tunnel like wild men, the crowd went nuts, and their players were at it from the start . . . I got a finger in the eye, but I am pretty sure it was accidental.' Tigers kept their cool, maintained their discipline and thus completed a commendable double for the season over the French club, Pau's only two defeats.

Gloucester turned out to be the dark horses of the tournament getting the better of the much-fancied Colomiers and Llanelli to top Pool Five by a point from the Scarlets.

The composition of the last eight was not decided until a veritable choir of Fat Ladies sang. Swansea snatched one runners-up spot, the remaining one had to be fought over by Llanelli, Bath, Saracens and Pau. In the end Llanelli had a stab at it, but Pau took the laurels with four tries at Pontypridd – the last and most important one which gave them the try-count superiority over their rivals coming in the third minute of injury time at Sardis Road.

There were one or two glitches which rather detracted from the drama of the final weekend of the pool phase. Firstly, ill-advised, television-dictated, staggered kick-off times on the Friday night had left Llanelli at a greater disadvantage than Saracens because the Scarlets' game got under way 25 minutes before the Watford-based club's, thus leaving them knowing precisely what was required and presenting them with that margin of time in which to try to score the necessary number of tries. In the end it was of little import.

The other glitch was more farcical and centred around Bath's Recreation Ground, which had not been covered in time to avoid a freeze-up thus forcing the postponement of the tie against Newport. Initially that was put back 24 hours, but a further inspection the following morning convinced everyone that the tie had to be delayed until the Tuesday. When they got around to playing it, Bath came out needing an unlikely, but not impossible, 11 tries. They could only manage half a dozen, an impressive enough performance on the by then glutinous surface of The Rec after the pitch had thawed out with a vengeance.

While there was no Irish presence in the final for the first time in three years, at least Munster had provided drama and passion on the way through as they reinforced their reputation at fortress Thomond Park and also knocked a few over-confident sides off their perches away from home. Bath were given a shake-up in front of 12,500 fervent fans in Limerick, although they got their own back the following week, albeit by a smaller margin. The moral victory was definitely Munster's, a situation they underlined by finishing top of Pool Four by a clear four points.

Biarritz controlled Pool One, although they still lost a couple of games, including a veritable walloping at Donnybrook against Leinster and later at Northampton as the Saints belatedly began firing. Pool Three was a tight little group with Cardiff finally prevailing over Saracens, thanks to beating Francois Pienaar's charges in both meetings. Stade Francais meanwhile found Pool Two plain sailing, apart from a two-point defeat at Swansea.

Pool Results

Pool One

6 Oct Edinburgh Reivers 29, Leinster 21; 7 Oct Biarritz 37, Northampton 30; 13 Oct Leinster 35, Biarritz 9; 14 Oct Northampton 22, Edinburgh Reivers 23; 21 Oct Biarritz 29, Edinburgh Reivers 18; 21 Oct Northampton 8, Leinster 14; 27 Oct Edinburgh Reivers 27, Biarritz 35; 27 Oct Leinster 40, Northampton 31; 12 Jan Leinster 34, Edinburgh Reivers 34; 13 Jan Northampton 32, Biarritz 24; 19 Jan Edinburgh Reivers 18, Northampton 15; 20 Jan Biarritz 30, Leinster 10.

Pool One Final Table

	P	W	D	L	For	Against	Pts
Biarritz	6	4	0	2	164	152	8
Edinburgh Reivers	6	3	1	2	149	156	7
Leinster	6	3	1	2	154	141	7
Northampton	6	1	0	5	138	156	2

Pool Two

7 Oct Swansea 54, Wasps 28; 7 Oct Stade Français 92, L'Aquila 7; 14 Oct Swansea 18, Stade Français 16; 15 Oct L'Aquila 10, Wasps 39; 21 Oct Stade Français 40, Wasps 10; 22 Oct L'Aquila 6, Swansea 70; 28 Oct Swansea 73, L'Aquila 3; 29 Oct Wasps 28, Stade Français 31; 13 Jan L'Aquila 9, Stade Francais 76; 14 Jan Wasps 28, Swansea 16; 20 Jan Stade Français 42, Swansea 13; 21 Jan Wasps 42, L'Aquila 5.

Pool Two Final Table

	P	W	D	L	For	Against	Pts
Stade Français	6	5	0	1	297	85	10
Swansea	6	4	0	2	244	123	8
Wasps	6	3	0	3	175	156	6
L'Aquila	6	0	0	6	40	392	0

Pool Three

6 Oct Ulster 32, Cardiff 23; 7 Oct Toulouse 22, Saracens 32; 14 Oct Cardiff 26, Toulouse 17; 15 Oct Saracens 55, Ulster 25; 21 Oct Saracens 23, Cardiff 32; 22 Oct Toulouse 35, Ulster 35; 27 Oct Ulster 25, Toulouse 29; 27 Oct Cardiff 24, Saracens 14; 12 Jan Cardiff 42, Ulster 16; 14 Jan Saracens 37, Toulouse 30; 19 Jan Ulster 13, Saracens 21; 20 Jan Toulouse 38, Cardiff 27.

Pool Three Final Table

	P	W	D	L	For	Against	Pts
Cardiff	6	4	0	2	174	140	8
Saracens	6	4	0	2	182	146	8
Toulouse	6	2	1	3	171	182	5
Ulster	6	1	1	4	146	205	3

Pool Four

7 Oct Munster 26, Newport 18; 7 Oct Bath 25, Castres 13; 13 Oct Newport 28, Bath 17; 14 Oct Castres 29, Munster 32; 21 Oct Newport 21, Castres 20; 21 Oct Munster 31, Bath 9; 28 Oct Bath 18, Munster 5; 28 Oct Castres 43, Newport 21; 13 Jan Newport 24, Munster 39; 13 Jan Castres 19, Bath 32; 20 Jan Munster 21, Castres 11; 23 Jan Bath 38, Newport 10.

Pool Four Final Table

	P	W	D	L	For	Against	Pts
Munster	6	5	0	1	154	109	10
Bath	6	4	0	2	139	106	8
Newport	6	2	0	4	122	183	4
Castres	6	1	0	5	135	152	1*

* one point deducted for fielding an ineligible player

Pool Five

6 Oct Llanelli 20, Gloucester 27; 7 Oct Roma 5, Colomiers 14; 14 Oct Colomiers 6, Llanelli 19; 15 Oct Gloucester 52, Roma 12; 21 Oct Gloucester 22, Colomiers 22; 21 Oct Llanelli 46, Roma 0; 28 Oct Colomiers 30, Gloucester 19; 28 Oct Roma 21, Llanelli 41; 13 Jan Colomiers 55, Roma 21; 13 Jan Gloucester 28, Llanelli 27; 19 Jan Llanelli 34, Colomiers 21; 20 Jan Roma 29, Gloucester 38.

Pool Five Final Table

	P	W	D	L	For	Against	Pts
Gloucester	6	4	1	1	186	140	9
Llanelli	6	4	0	2	187	103	8
Colomiers	6	3	1	2	148	120	7
Roma	6	0	0	6	88	246	0

Pool Six

7 Oct Leicester 46, Pau 18; 7 Oct Pontypridd 40, Glasgow Caledonians 25; 14 Oct Pau 12, Pontypridd 9; 15 Oct Glasgow Caledonians 21, Leicester 33; 20 Oct Pontypridd 18, Leicester 11; 22 Oct Glasgow Caledonians 24, Pau 46; 28 Oct Leicester 27, Pontypridd 19; 28 Oct Pau 44, Glasgow Caledonians 16; 13 Jan Pau 3, Leicester 20; 14 Jan Glasgow Caledonians 25, Pontypridd 23; 20 Jan Leicester 41, Glasgow Caledonians 26; 21 Jan Pontypridd 27, Pau 31.

Pool Six Final Table

	P	W	D	L	For	Against	Pts
Leicester	6	5	0	1	178	105	10
Pau	6	4	0	2	154	142	8
Pontypridd	6	2	0	4	136	131	4
Glasgow Caledonians	6	1	0	5	137	227	2

The Quarter-Finals

27 January, Kingsholm, Gloucester
Gloucester 21 (7PG)   Cardiff 15 (1G 1PG 1T)

Given that Simon Mannix landed half a dozen penalty goals, it is remarkable that he still managed to miss a further three and eschewed two other very kickable opportunities as his nerve failed him. Despite all their points coming from the boot, this was a spirited Gloucester performance. Cardiff in the end lacked the passion and the cohesion which their opponents demonstrated throughout. Cardiff came off second best in the scrum, were bettered in the line-out and lost out in the loose. They also had not a glimmer of an opening until very late – too late – in the match to make any difference to the outcome, thanks to Gloucester's uncompromising and stout defence. The late converted try by Gareth Thomas merely served to flatter. Gloucester's cosmopolitan collection of players even persuaded the Kingsholm faithful among the 11,800 present that the wearing of the famous jersey actually meant something to them, so much so that when the final whistle went the players were mobbed by the fans from The Shed in unprecedented scenes.

Gloucester: C Catling; J Ewens, T Fanolua, J Little, T Beim; S Mannix, E Moncrieff; T Woodman, O Azam, P Vickery, R Fidler, I Jones, J Boer, J Paramore, K Jones (*captain*) *Substitutions:* A Gomarsall for Moncrieff (45 mins); B Hayward for Mannix (64 mins); A Hazell for Paramore (69 mins); C Fortey for Azam (75 mins); A Deacon for Vickery (76 mins); C Yates for Boer (78 mins)

Scorers *Penalty Goals:* Mannix (6), Hayward

Cardiff: R Williams; N Walne, J Robinson, P Muller, G Thomas; N Jenkins, R Howley; S John, J Humphreys, D Young (*captain*), C Quinnell, J Tait, O Williams, E Lewis, M Williams *Substitutions:* O Kacala for Williams (58 mins); P Rogers for Young (60 mins)

Scorers *Tries:* Walne, G Thomas *Conversion:* N Jenkins *Penalty Goal:* N Jenkins

Referee J Jutge (France).

27 January, Stade Jean Bouin, Paris
Stade Francais 36 (3G 3PG 2DG)   Pau 19 (1G 3PG 1DG)

Pau coach Jacques Brunel went into this match with the claim that he had never been in charge of a team that had lost to the French champions and indeed the 'Mountain Men' had beaten Stade in a French Championship match some three weeks earlier. Unfortunately that claim was ground underfoot and driven into history by as forceful a forward performance as there could be. Although Pau had the effrontery to take the lead with the first of David Aucagne's three penalties, thereafter they were only ever able to play catch-up. Stade were content to build up slowly and steadily, while taking in along the way some ferocious confrontations, particularly between the two front-rows. There was a clinical feel to Stade's opening try. David Auradou won a 10th minute line-out, the centres scissored sharply and opened up a hole through which Raphael Poulain sped. Later, as matters came down to a kicking duel, there was only ever going to be one winner as once again Diego Dominguez proved too accurate. Attendance: 8,000.

Stade Francais: C Dominici; A Gomes, F Comba, C Mytton, R Poulain; D Dominguez, C Laussucq; S Marconnet, F Landreau, P de Villiers, D Auradou, M James, C Moni, C Juillet (*captain*), R Pool-Jones *Substitutions:* M Blin for Landreau (32 mins); P Tabacco for Moni (57 mins); T Lombard for Mytton (70 mins); P Lemoine for Marconnet (71 mins); H Chaffardon for Auradou (78 mins); D George for James (78 mins)

Scorers *Tries:* Poulain, Laussucq, Comba *Conversions:* Dominguez (3) *Penalty Goals:* Dominguez (3) *Drop Goals:* Dominguez (2)

Pau: D Arrieta; P Bomati, J-C Cistacq, C Paille, L Arbo; D Aucagne, P Carbonneau; P Triep-Capdeville, M Dal Maso, S Bria, A Charron (*captain*), A Lagouarde, G Combes, I Harinordoquy, L Mallier *Substitutions:* G Chasserieau for Lagouarde (40 mins); J Espag for Triep-Capdeville (40 mins); J Rey for Dal Maso (60 mins); D Agueb for Harinordoquy (62 mins); T Cléda for Mallier (62 mins); D Traille for Paille (70 mins)

Scorers *Try:* Paille *Conversion:* Aucagne *Penalty Goals:* Aucagne (3) *Drop Goal:* Aucagne

Referee N Whitehouse (Wales).

28 January, Welford Road, Leicester
Leicester 41 (3G 4PG 1DG 1T)   Swansea 10 (1G 1PG)

There was one moment, towards the end of the first half, which summed up the difference between the two sides. Geordan Murphy, the Tigers brilliant Irish wing, popped up in midfield as the ball went left. With his back to the Swansea posts Murphy executed a stunning overhead bicycle kick and Leon Lloyd was only just beaten to the touchdown by Silelo Martens. Leicester may not have had their inspirational captain Martin Johnson, who was still serving his suspension, but they had the confidence, the wit and the imagination to attempt the improbable. Swansea were mere open-mouthed spectators at the display of prowess, disappointingly out of this tie from the start. Indeed by the time Murphy had scored his first try in the 25th minute the Welsh side was out of it. Murphy scored another try just after the interval and was later joined on the score sheet by Austin Healey and Andy Goode to underline Leicester's superiority.

Leicester: T Stimpson; F Tuilagi, L Lloyd, P Howard, G Murphy; A Goode, A Healey; G Rowntree, D West, D Garforth, L Deacon, B Kay, W Johnson, M Corry, N Back *Substitutions:* G Gelderbloom for Lloyd (45 mins); J Hamilton for Healey (52 mins); P Freshwater for Rowntree (62 mins); L Moody for Back (66 mins); R Cockerill for West (67 mins); R Nebbett for Garforth (73 mins)

Scorers *Tries:* Murphy (2), Healey, Goode *Conversions:* Stimpson (3) *Penalty Goals:* Stimpson (4) *Drop Goal:* A Goode

Swansea: K Morgan; S Payne, M Taylor, S Gibbs (*captain*), M Robinson; A Thomas, S Martens; D Morris, G Jenkins, B Evans, J Griffiths, A Moore, G Lewis, L Jones, C Charvis *Substitutions:* C Anthony for Evans (59 mins); G Smith for L Jones (temp 62 to 71 mins); D Thomas for Charvis (67 mins); P Moriarty for L Jones (71 mins); C Rees for Thomas (70 mins); R Jones for Martens (70 mins)

Scorers *Try:* Moriarty *Conversion:* C Rees *Penalty Goal:* A Thomas

Referee A Lewis (Ireland).

28 January, Thomond Park, Limerick
Munster 38 (1G 7PG 2T)   Biarritz 29 (3G 1PG 1T)

The atmosphere at Thomond Park should be an inspiration to all sporting crowds. There is a daunting, physical quality to the wall of sound created in the Limerick stadium where Munster have never lost a Heineken Cup tie. Biarritz certainly gave it a go, but ultimately they were subdued. Munster, for their part, did not even have to draw on any of their replacements – a rarity in these days of 22-man rugby. The Irish side was blessed with a superlative back row trio – no surprise that No 8 Anthony Foley scored a hat-trick of tries – and a ferocious front three along with a couple of locks who were always up with the game. There were one or two worrying moments for the impassioned 14,000 spectators crammed in the ground, not least Sebastien Bonnet's interception of a Mick Galwey pass that resulted in a try for the scrum-half under the posts which Frano Botica converted. Another try followed through Christophe Milhères to bring the French total to four, but Munster had Ronan O'Gara and his seventh penalty, shortly after Biarritz's final touchdown, made the game safe.

Munster: D Crotty; J Kelly, M Mullins, J Holland, A Horgan; R O'Gara, P Stringer; P Clohessy, F Sheahan, J Hayes, M Galwey (captain), J Langford, A Quinlan, A Foley, D Wallace

Scorers Tries: Foley (3) Conversion: O'Gara Penalty Goals: O'Gara (7)

Biarritz: S Bonetti; P Bernat-Salles, P Bidabe, N Couttet, S Legg; F Botica, S Bonnet; E Menieu, J-M Gonzalez (captain), D Avril, J-P Versailles, O Roumat, S Betsen, O Nauroy, C Milhères Substitutions: T Lièvremont for Roumat (47 mins); M Lefevre for Versailles (53 mins); M Fitzgerald for Milhères (temp 61 to 70 mins) and for Menieu (75 mins); M Lièvremont for Betsen (66 mins)

Scorers Tries: Milhères (2), Legg, Bonnet Conversions: Botica (3) Penalty Goal: Botica

Referee E Morrison (England).

The Semi-Finals

21 April, Vicarage Road, Watford
Leicester 19 (1G 4PG)   Gloucester 15 (5PG)

Perhaps there was a moment of controversy involving the refereeing, but this first all-English semi-final in the brief history of this competition produced worthy winners in the end. It was not pretty, but it was pretty exciting.

The controversy arose when Leicester prop Graham Rowntree spilled a ball in front of him. Gloucester's French hooker Olivier Azam scooped the ball backwards, Fijian style, between his legs. James Simpson-Daniel hoofed the ball upfield, straight into the arms of Tim Stimpson, who countered with a 50-metre break before sending Leon Lloyd over at the posts. Defenders waiting for the whistle to be blown were reduced to helpless onlookers when no sound was heard other than the roar of the Leicester faithful who had come in droves to Vicarage Road.

Gloucester director of rugby Philippe Saint-André felt there should have been a scrum for the original knock-on because no real advantage had accrued to the Cherry and Whites; Joel Dumé of France thought differently. At least injury-ravaged Gloucester put up a brave show, but they just needed more than Simon Mannix's five penalties.

Leicester: G Murphy; W Stanley, L Lloyd, P Howard, T Stimpson; A Goode, A Healey; G Rowntree, D West, D Garforth, M Johnson (*captain*), B Kay, W Johnson, M Corry, N Back *Substitution:* R Cockerill for West (39 mins)

Scorers *Try:* Lloyd *Conversion:* Stimpson *Penalty Goals:* Stimpson (4)

Gloucester: B Hayward; R Greenslade-Jones, T Fanolua, J Little, J Simpson-Daniel; S Mannix, A Gomarsall; A Deacon, O Azam, P Vickery (*captain*), R Fidler, I Jones, J Boer, J Paramore, K Jones *Substitutions:* M Cornwell for Fidler (64 mins); S Ojomoh for Paramore (75 mins)

Scorer *Penalty Goals:* Mannix (5)

Referee J Dumé (France)

21 April, Stade Metropole, Lille
Stade Francais 16 (1G 3PG) Munster 15 (5PG)

This was the match in which the 'stir' went out of Munster. There was little of the spirit which had fired them through so many tense European matches. Instead Munster were dragged into a kicking duel with Stade Francais – a duel which they were fated never to win.

Defeat was all the more unpalatable since, just like the previous year's Heineken Cup final, it was by a single point. But Stade at least scored the only try of the tie, a beautifully executed score by Cliff Mytton, which was sparked by a scorching break by Thomas Lombard.

True, Munster scored a perfectly good try themselves. They were trailing by seven points early in the second half when scrum-half Peter Stringer knocked up a perfectly weighted box kick. The ball bounced obligingly for wing John O'Neill, and although the big man from Shannon was shoulder charged by Christophe Dominici, he was still able to touch down before hitting the corner flag. Well that is what everyone else saw, unfortunately it was not the view of touch judge Steve Lander.

After consultation with referee Chris White the score was disallowed. It was a close call, so was the result.

Stade Francais: C Dominici; T Lombard, C Mytton, F Comba, R Poulain; D Dominguez, M Williams; S Marconnet, F Landreau, P de Villiers, D Auradou, M James, C Moni, C Juillet (*captain*), R Pool-Jones *Substitutions:* D George for Gomes (81 mins); A Gomes for Juillet (73-81 mins)

Scorers *Try:* Mytton *Conversion:* Dominguez *Penalty Goals:* Dominguez (3)

Munster: D Crotty; J O'Neill, M Mullins, J Holland, A Horgan; R O'Gara, P Stringer; P Clohessy, F Sheahan, J Hayes, M Galwey (*captain*), J Langford, D O'Callaghan, A Foley, D Wallace *Substitutions*: D O Cuinneagáin for O'Callaghan (70 mins); M Horan for Clohessy (81 mins)

Scorer *Penalty Goals:* O'Gara (5)

Referee C White (England)

Heineken Cup Final

19 May, Parc des Princes, Paris
Leicester 34 (2G 5PG 1T)   **Stade Francais 30** (9PG 1DG)

This pulsating finale to a great European season did not merely go to the wire, it stretched the wire and the nerves of those watching to breaking point. From first to last this was a battle royal.

Even before they had kicked off the two sides were facing off, advancing on each other with apparent intent. It took an intervention by Irish referee David McHugh to keep the protagonists apart until they could legitimately go at each others' throats. Which they did willingly on a number of occasions, with Martin Johnson a victim at one point.

By the end, after a coruscating moment by the hugely talented footballer Austin Healey had helped settle the matter, neither side had the time or the inclination to scrap off the ball. The French stormed the English ramparts and increased the pressure, but Leicester defended tigerishly to the end before the celebrations broke out.

Healey, who ran on at scrum-half but moved to fly-half for the final 10 minutes or so, left it late. With three minutes of normal time remaining, the Leicester Lip for once let his prodigious talents do the talking. The Tigers won an attacking scrum and Healey tore away across field, he straightened, drew the cover and, having committed them, sent out a perfect pass to Leon Lloyd. The centre latched on to it, pumped his knees ever higher and finally launched himself in a despairing dive for the corner with Christophe Dominici clinging to him like a burr on wool.

Lloyd, to his credit, managed to touch the ball down over the line a fraction of a second before taking out the corner flag. That try secured the lead for the third time in the match, but what was then called for was a conversion from Tim Stimpson to ensure that the French team had to score a try of their own in order to win.

Anything less would have let in Diego Dominguez for yet another kick at goal, because the score was 32-30 at that point, and since the Italian fly-half had scored all 30 of Stade's points, with nine penalties and a drop goal, the chances of him conjuring up victory for the French by a point were extremely high.

So Stimpson's long range conversion from the right-hand touchline was paramount. The full-back behaved as if he were in a sound-proof booth. If he was aware of the cacophony he gave no sign. He went through his meticulous preparations, a routine he adopts wherever he is playing. Once satisfied with everything, he made his usual approach and boot met ball. It sailed unerringly, unwaveringly, between the uprights and the Tigers settled down for a couple more minutes of Gallic assaults on their line before the final whistle sounded.

The moral victory was also Leicester's. This was as close as it could get to a home game for the French, with their Stade Jean Bouin ground sitting as it does under the shadow of the monolith that is the Parc des Princes.

Dominguez had kicked the first five of his penalties by half time to give the 'home' side the lead. But thanks to Stimpson's three successful first half kicks, Leicester were able to drag themselves back within touching distance within 60 seconds of the start of the second half when Lloyd nipped ahead of Dominici to score from Geordan Murphy's delicate grubber. Sadly Johnson then found himself in the sin-bin for throwing a punch at Christophe Juillet and Dominguez landed the resulting penalty, followed by his seventh shortly afterwards, just as Johnson was returning to the frontline.

Back came Leicester. They surged upfield and Neil Back slipped over after a tap penalty. Stimpson's conversion levelled matters at 21-21. Two more penalties were exchanged, then Dominguez kicked his ninth and sent over a drop goal to set up that outstanding climax.

Leicester: T Stimpson; G Murphy, L Lloyd, P Howard, W Stanley; A Goode, A Healey; G Rowntree, D West, D Garforth, M Johnson (*captain*), B Kay, M Corry, W Johnson, N Back *Substitutions:* P Gustard for W Johnson (37 mins); J Hamilton for Goode (73 mins); G Gelderbloom for Murphy (76 mins)

Scorers *Tries:* Lloyd (2), Back *Conversions:* Stimpson (2) *Penalty Goals:* Stimpson (5)

Stade Francais: C Dominici; T Lombard, C Mytton, F Comba, A Gomes; D Dominguez, M Williams; S Marconnet, F Landreau, P de Villiers, D Auradou, M James, C Moni, C Juillet (*captain*), R Pool-Jones *Substitutions:* M Blin for Juillet (temp 8 mins to 16 mins); P Tabacco for Moni (66 mins); D Venditti for Mytton (75 mins)

Scorer *Penalty Goals:* Dominguez (9) *Drop Goal:* Dominguez

Referee D McHugh (Ireland)

Previous Heineken Cup Finals: 1996 Toulouse 21, Cardiff 18 (Cardiff); 1997 Brive 28, Leicester 9 (Cardiff); 1998 Bath 19, Brive 18 (Bordeaux); 1999 Ulster 21, Colomiers 6 (Dublin); 2000 Northampton 9, Munster 8 (Twickenham); 2001 Leicester 34, Stade Francais 30 (Paris)

HEINEKEN CUP RECORDS 1995-2001

Record	Detail		Set
Most team points in season	379 by Stade Francais	in 9 matches	2000-01
Highest team score	108 by Toulouse	108-16 v Ebbw Vale	1998-99
Biggest team win	92 by Toulouse	108-16 v Ebbw Vale	1998-99
Most team tries in match	92 by Toulouse	v Ebbw Vale	1998-99
Most appearances	39 for Toulouse	S Ougier	1995-2001
Most points in matches	476 for Pontypridd/Cardiff	N R Jenkins	1995-2001
Most points in season	188 for Stade Francais	D Dominguez	2000-2001
Most points in match	35 for Leicester	J Stransky v Glasgow	1997-98
Most tries in matches	20 for Toulouse	M Marfaing	1996-2001
Most tries in season	9 for Swansea	M F D Robinson	2000-2001
Most tries in match	5 for Gloucester	T D Beim v Roma	2000-2001
Most cons in match	12 for Stade Francais	D Dominguez v L'Aquila	2000-2001
Most pens in match	9 for Stade Francais	D Dominguez v Leicester	2000-2001

THE EUROPEAN SHIELD 2000-01

French Monopoly Broken

David Llewellyn

It may not have attracted a sponsor, but the European Shield certainly attracted a lot of interest, especially with the French monopoly finally being broken.

A spirited and transformed Harlequins side that had reinvented itself over the season under the skilful manipulations of Mark Evans off the field and the indubitable leadership qualities of David Wilson, their captain, on it, took the Shield and won a place in the 2001-2002 Heineken Cup for their grand efforts.

They stamped their mark indelibly on the game and reasserted English values. Moreover, they were not alone. Newcastle made it two English clubs among half a dozen of France in the last eight, while Rotherham, who even led their Pool Three for the bulk of the season, only falling away at the very last when they were turned over at home by Perpignan, also put up a creditable show.

London Irish were another club who went close, but not close enough, in a strong group (Pool Six) that contained a powerful Brive side. Irish were second by a point – the very point they were deducted for playing back rower Richard Bates against Aurillac in the Pool's opening match.

Treviso put up a good show and ran Newcastle close for the top spot in Pool One, losing out on try count. In the same group Welsh representatives Cross Keys failed to gain a single point, a feat matched elsewhere only by Italian sides, Piacenza and Viadana. Caerphilly's solitary point at the foot of Pool Four came courtesy of a draw with Auch, and Connacht only picked up their two points in the final round of matches when they beat Neath narrowly.

Harlequins' vastly superior try count ensured that, having finished level on points with Dax, they would go through to the knock-out phase where they pulled off an unbelievably good victory away at Brive. That was a match which tested their very core but in which they were not found wanting. After that wonderful quarter-final and Newcastle's dazzling defeat of Mont de Marsan, it was a shame that the semi-finals drew French against French and English against English. Narbonne disposed of Agen and Harlequins eased through against Rob Andrew's men to reach the final.

Tables

Pool One Final Table

	P	W	D	L	For	Against	Pts
Newcastle	6	5	0	1	234	99	10
Treviso	6	5	0	1	157	97	10
Bègles-Bordeaux	6	2	0	4	136	152	4
Cross Keys	6	0	0	6	60	239	0

Pool Two Final Table

	P	W	D	L	For	Against	Pts
Béziers	6	5	0	1	151	112	10
Montferrand	6	4	0	2	201	107	8
Neath	6	2	0	4	151	192	4
Connacht	6	1	0	5	60	152	2

Pool Three Final Table

	P	W	D	L	For	Against	Pts
Perpignan	6	4	0	2	187	105	8
Rotherham	6	4	0	2	122	136	8
Bridgend	6	2	0	4	144	166	4
Grenoble	6	2	0	4	120	166	4

Pool Four Final Table

	P	W	D	L	For	Against	Pts
Agen	6	5	0	1	261	91	10
Sale	6	4	0	2	178	155	8
Auch	6	2	1	3	134	187	5
Caerphilly	6	0	1	5	128	268	1

Pool Five Final Table

	P	W	D	L	For	Against	Pts
Harlequins	6	5	0	1	188	80	10
Dax	6	5	0	1	152	103	10
Ebbw Vale	6	1	0	5	120	151	2
Perpignan	6	1	0	5	94	220	2

Pool Six Final Table

	P	W	D	L	For	Against	Pts
Brive	6	5	0	1	184	143	10
London Irish	6	5	0	1	254	106	9*
Aurillac	6	2	0	4	155	179	4
Piacenza	6	0	0	6	90	255	0

* one point deducted for fielding an ineligible player

Pool Seven Final Table

	P	W	D	L	For	Against	Pts
Mont de Marsan	6	5	0	1	175	113	10
La Rochelle	6	3	1	2	167	113	7
Bristol	6	3	1	2	199	147	7
Parma	6	0	0	6	92	260	0

Pool Eight Final Table

	P	W	D	L	For	Against	Pts
Narbonne	4	3	1	0	124	76	7
Bourgoin	4	2	1	1	104	83	5
Viadana	4	0	0	4	78	147	0

Quarter-Finals:

Narbonne 34 (*T:* penalty try *C:* Rosalen *PG:* Rosalen 9) **Perpignan 24** (*PG:* Lacroix 8)

Agen 31 (*T:* Manas, Benazzi, Benetton *C:* Lamaison 2 P: Lamaison 4) **Béziers 0**

Newcastle 61 (*T:* Walder 2, Noon, Botham, Hurter, Armstrong, May, McLure *C:* Wilkinson 3 *PG:* Wilkinson 3, Walder 2) **Mont de Marsan 23** (*T:* Loubsens, Bonnan, Ducamp *C:* Prosper *PG:* Prosper 2)

Brive 13 (*T:* Christophers *C:* Burton *PG:* Burton 2) **Harlequins 20** (*T:* White-Cooper, Greenwood *C:* Burke 2 *PG:* Burke 2)

Semi-Finals:

Narbonne 22 (*T:* Raynaud, Ledesma *PG:* Quesada 2 *DG:* Quesada 2) **Agen 15** (*PG:* Gelez 5)

Newcastle 12 (*PG:* Wilkinson 4) **Harlequins 17** (*T:* Chalmers *PG:* Chalmers 3 *DG:* Chalmers)

European Shield Final

20 May, The Madejski Stadium, Reading
Harlequins 42 (3G 6PG 1DG)   **Narbonne 33** (3G 3PG 1DG) (aet: 26-26 after 80 minutes)

There was a singularly satisfactory twist to Harlequins' magnificent tale of European Shield triumph. Their stunning victory over Narbonne – historic since it was the first Shield final that was not an all-French affair – also carried a special spin-off for Quins' chief executive Mark Evans. The win meant they qualified for the following season's Heineken Cup – at the expense of Saracens, the club at which Evans once held the post of coach.

There was no gloating, however, because with the fizz from the glasses of celebratory bubbly still hitting their noses they also discovered the downside to their success – the loss of their inspirational captain David Wilson with cruciate ligament damage in his right knee that ruled him out of action for the next nine months.

Harlequins owed their victory to qualities previously alien to the game's commonly-perceived fancy-dans of rugby. Those qualities included tenacity, determination, heart, guts, character and all of them in spades, because this final at the Madejski Stadium in Reading went into extra time and was only settled deep into that when Paul Burke finally booted them clear.

Quins were tested just seven minutes into extra time when Wilson was carried off after attempting to change direction in open field but instead dropping like a pole-axed ox. Later Evans said: 'I have to admit it has taken some of the gloss off the day.'

It was the former Ireland fly-half Paul Burke's first match for five weeks after his recovery from a broken finger. He justified his presence in the side with a total of 27 points including a penalty and drop goal which eventually settled the match as extra time was coming to an end.

Pat Sanderson put in a tremendous performance in the Harlequins' back row, one which clinched his selection on England's tour of Canada and the United States in the summer – he was called into the squad 24 hours after the final. There was also a more than useful display from Will Greenwood, whose off-load in a tackle put Daren O'Leary in under the posts for Quins' third try. Earlier the England centre had sent in Ben Gollings for the opening score and then combined with Burke to get Sanderson on to the score sheet for the second. For the rest of the time he tested, teased and tormented the entire Narbonne midfield.

The French scrum was awesome throughout normal time, heaving and squeezing the breath and stamina from their opponents. They too scored three tries, one of them from Stuart Reid, the former Scotland lock who was playing his last professional game in an exemplary career. The other touchdowns came from Ignacio Corleto and their excellent hooker Mario Ledesma. But they had a couple of penalty decisions reversed, which betrayed their own lack of self-discipline, lost scrum-half Gregory Sudre to the sin-bin and were on the wrong end of a couple of difficult refereeing decisions. All those seemingly minor things when taken together, ultimately, cost them dear.

Harlequins: J Williams; B Gollings, W Greenwood, N Greenstock, D O'Leary; P Burke, M Powell; J Leonard, K Wood, J Dawson, G Morgan, S White-Cooper, P Sanderson, R Winters, D Wilson (*captain*) *Substitutions:* E Jennings for Gollings (32 mins); A Codling for Morgan (72 mins); R Jenkins for Winters (72 mins); B Starr for Dawson (79 mins); T Fuga for Wilson (88 mins)

Scorers *Tries:* Gollings, Sanderson, O'Leary *Conversions:* Burke (3) *Penalty Goals:* Burke (6) *Drop Goal:* Burke

Narbonne: I Corleto; A Joubert, D Douy, C Stoica, S Rouch; G Quesada, G Sudre; A Martinez, M Ledesma, F Pucciariello, C Gaston, O Merle, P Furet, S Reid (*captain*), M Raynaud *Substitutions:* F Azéma for Corleto (78 mins); J-B Poux for Martinez (78 mins); C Mathieu for Furet (95 mins)

Scorers *Tries:* Corleto, Ledesma, Reid *Conversions:* Quesada (3) *Penalty Goals:* Quesada (3) *Drop Goal:* Quesada

Referee N Whitehouse (Wales)

Previous European Shield Finals: 1997 Bourgoin 18, Castres 9 (Béziers); 1998 Colomiers 43, Agen 5 (Toulouse); 1999 Montferrand 35, Bourgoin 16 (Lyons); 2000 Pau 34, Castres 21 (Toulouse); 2001 Harlequins 42, Narbonne 33 (Reading)

EUROPEAN SHIELD RECORDS 1996-2001

Record	Detail		Set
Most team points in season	431 by Montferrand	in 9 matches	1998-99
Highest team score	99 by Newcastle	99-8 v Cross Keys	2000-01
Biggest team win	91 by Newcastle	99-8 v Cross Keys	2000-01
Most team tries in match	15 by Newcastle	99-8 v Cross Keys	2000-01
	15 by Montferrand	97-13 v Aberavon	1998-99
Most points in matches	289 for Montferrand	G Merceron	1996-2001
Most points in match	34 for Gloucester	M Mapletoft v Ebbw Vale	1996-97
Most tries in matches	14	P Escalle/D Bory/P Arlettaz	1996-2001
Most tries in match	5 for Northampton	M J S Dawson v Nice	1998-99
Most cons in match	12 for Newcastle	D J H Walder v Cross Keys	2000-2001
Most pens in match	9 for Ebbw Vale	J Strange v Toulon	1999-2000
	9 for Bristol	S Vile v Mont-de-Marsan	2000-01
	9 for Narbonne	C Rosalen v Perpignan	2000-01

SUPER TWELVE SERIES 2001

Brumbies Break New Zealand's Dominance

Paul Dobson

The tension to see who would reach the semi-finals in the Super Twelve series of 2001 stretched throughout the round-robin phase. It was not until the very last round of matches that the four survivors were decided, but after that the tournament ran a predictable course with both semi-finals and the final turning out to be anticlimaxes.

From the outset the Brumbies were expected to win, and they reinforced their position as favourites by thrashing the Crusaders, three-time champions, in the opening round. Like all other teams, the Brumbies stumbled in this long race of many hazards. Unlike the Crusaders, the Hurricanes and the Blues, who were the year's big disappointments, the Brumbies managed to raise their game to race on to become the first side to wrest the Super Twelve title from New Zealand, who had provided the winners of all five previous series of the professional era.

The Crusaders failed to perform their Lazarus act by rising again to glory. Their place as resurrectionists belonged to the Reds who lost their first four matches, suffered internal problems yet trudged into the semi-finals. The Hurricanes and the Blues, festooned with stars, showed only brief glimmers of glory.

Those who performed better than expected were the Sharks, who sank to the very bottom in 2000 but surged this year, and the Chiefs, who for the first time in Super Twelve showed their potential and earned respect. The baby Waratahs started out as if bolting for the final, but they came unstuck at one away hurdle after another. The Stormers and the Highlanders lacked consistency, while the Bulls remained consistently at the bottom of the table despite showing greater competitiveness this year in all but their match with the Waratahs.

For the first time since the inauguration of the Super Twelve series, there was no New Zealand team in the semi-finals. That is the stage of the competition where it is of paramount importance to secure home advantage. One semi-final was an all-Australian affair, the other an all-South African matter. The Brumbies and the Sharks had played in semi-finals before – the Brumbies twice, the Sharks three times – and their experience of this stage of the competition proved useful. The Brumbies won comfortably 30-6 against the Reds in Canberra while the Sharks beat the Cats 30-12 in Durban.

2001 Round Robin Results

23 Feb: ACT Brumbies 51-16 Canterbury Crusaders (Canberra); Otago Highlanders 23-8 Auckland Blues (Dunedin); Coastal Sharks 30-17 Northern Bulls (Durban).

24 Feb: Queensland Reds 27-18 Wellington Hurricanes (Brisbane); NSW Waratahs 42-23 Waikato Chiefs (Sydney); Western Stormers 24-29 Golden Cats (Cape Town).

2 Mar: Auckland Blues 17-12 Canterbury Crusaders (Auckland).

3 Mar: Waikato Chiefs 32-29 Queensland Reds (Rotorua); Wellington Hurricanes 26-20 Northern Bulls (Wellington); Coastal Sharks 17-16 ACT Brumbies (Durban); Golden Cats 56-21 Otago Highlanders (Johannesburg).

4 Mar: NSW Waratahs 35-7 Western Stormers (Sydney).

9 Mar: Wellington Hurricanes 15-27 Western Stormers (Wellington).

10 Mar: NSW Waratahs 53-7 Northern Bulls (Sydney); Canterbury Crusaders 40-11 Waikato Chiefs (Christchurch); Coastal Sharks 30-29 Otago Highlanders (Durban); Golden Cats 17-19 ACT Brumbies (Johannesburg).

11 Mar: Auckland Blues 39-35 Queensland Reds (Albany).

16 Mar: Waikato Chiefs 34-16 Auckland Blues (Rotorua).

17 Mar: ACT Brumbies 39-30 Northern Bulls (Canberra); Coastal Sharks 39-21 Wellington Hurricanes (Durban); Golden Cats 28-21 NSW Waratahs (Bloemfontein).

18 Mar: Otago Highlanders 24-23 Western Stormers (Dunedin).

23 Mar: Golden Cats 18-15 Wellington Hurricanes (Bloemfontein); Canterbury Crusaders 32-26 Queensland Reds (Christchurch).

24 Mar: Otago Highlanders 32-10 Northern Bulls (Dunedin); ACT Brumbies 40-25 Western Stormers (Canberra); Coastal Sharks 42-17 NSW Waratahs (Durban).

30 Mar: Queensland Reds 15-23 ACT Brumbies (Brisbane); Waikato Chiefs 50-19 Otago Highlanders (Rotorua); Golden Cats 26-25 Coastal Sharks (Bloemfontein).

31 Mar: NSW Waratahs 35-19 Auckland Blues (Sydney); Canterbury Crusaders 29-41 Wellington Hurricanes (Christchurch).

6 Apr: Wellington Hurricanes 34-19 ACT Brumbies (Wellington).

7 Apr: Auckland Blues 27-41 Coastal Sharks (Auckland); Otago Highlanders 39-20 NSW Waratahs (Dunedin); Western Stormers 29-27 Queensland Reds (George).

8 Apr: Waikato Chiefs 22-18 Golden Cats (Tauranga); Northern Bulls 29-42 Canterbury Crusaders (Pretoria).

13 Apr: Auckland Blues 23-26 Golden Cats (Whangarei); ACT Brumbies 48-21 NSW Waratahs (Canberra).

14 Apr: Wellington Hurricanes 35-33 Otago Highlanders (Napier); Waikato Chiefs 8-24 Coastal Sharks (Taupo); Northern Bulls 19-29 Queensland Reds (Pretoria); Western Stormers 49-28 Canterbury Crusaders (Cape Town).

20 Apr: Otago Highlanders 16-9 ACT Brumbies (Dunedin).

21 Apr: Northern Bulls 37-49 Waikato Chiefs (Pretoria); Western Stormers 12-26 Auckland Blues (Cape Town).

22 Apr: Canterbury Crusaders 31-32 Golden Cats (Nelson); Queensland Reds 32-27 Coastal Sharks (Brisbane).

27 Apr: Wellington Hurricanes 42-17 NSW Waratahs (New Plymouth); Western Stormers 29-15 Waikato Chiefs (Cape Town).

28 Apr: Canterbury Crusaders 34-24 Coastal Sharks (Christchurch); Northern Bulls 28-25 Auckland Blues (Pretoria).

29 Apr: Queensland Reds 22-16 Golden Cats (Brisbane).

4 May: Wellington Hurricanes 27-51 Waikato Chiefs (Wellington).

5 May: Auckland Blues 7-35 ACT Brumbies (Auckland); NSW Waratahs 25-22 Canterbury Crusaders (Sydney); Northern Bulls 23-34 Western Stormers (Pretoria).

6 May: Queensland Reds 33-22 Otago Highlanders (Brisbane).

11 May: Auckland Blues 36-17 Wellington Hurricanes (Auckland); ACT Brumbies 49-6 Waikato Chiefs (Canberra); Golden Cats 19-21 Northern Bulls (Johannesburg).

12 May: Otago Highlanders 26-21 Canterbury Crusaders (Dunedin); NSW Waratahs 20-25 Queensland Reds (Sydney); Western Stormers 19-23 Coastal Sharks (Wellington, SA).

Super Twelve 2001: Round Robin Table

	P	W	L	Bonus Points	Pts
ACT Brumbies	11	8	3	8	40
Coastal Sharks	11	8	3	6	38
Golden Cats	11	7	4	6	34
Queensland Reds	11	6	5	8	32
Otago Highlanders	11	6	5	5	29
Waikato Chiefs	11	6	5	4	28
Western Stormers	11	5	6	6	26
NSW Waratahs	11	5	6	5	25
Wellington Hurricanes	11	5	6	5	25
Canterbury Crusaders	11	4	7	7	23
Auckland Blues	11	4	7	5	21
Northern Bulls	11	2	9	3	11

Points: win 4; draw 2; four or more tries, or defeat by seven or fewer points 1

First semi-final 19 May Bruce Stadium, Canberra
ACT Brumbies 30 (3G 2PG 1DG)   **Queensland Reds 6** (2PG)

ACT Brumbies: A M Walker; G S G Bond, S A Mortlock, R B Kafer, J W C Roff; S J Larkham, G M Gregan (*captain*); W K Young, J A Paul, B J Darwin, J B G Harrison, D T Giffin, O D A Finegan, R W Williams, G B Smith *Substitutions:* P J Ryan for Williams (blood 27-31 mins); J C Holbeck for Mortlock (39 mins); M Weaver for Darwin (73mins); M A Bartholomeusz for Holbeck (73mins); D Pusey for Giffin (76mins); T D Murphy for Paul (77 mins); T S Hall for Gregan (78mins)

Scorers *Tries:* Mortlock, Finegan, Paul *Conversions:* Walker (3) *Penalty Goals:* Walker (2) *Drop Goal:* Larkham

Queensland Reds: C E Latham; J Pelesasa, D J Herbert, S Kefu, F H Nalatu; E J Flatley, J S Rauluni; N B Stiles, M A Foley, G M Panoho, J A Eales *(captain)*, N C Sharpe, M J Cockbain, T S Kefu, D Croft *Substitutes:* S J Drahm for Flatley (31mins); M R Connors for Cockbain (blood 36-42mins); F J Dyson for Panoho (40mins); N G Williams for Nalatu (40mins); Connors for Sharpe (60mins); S P Hardman for Foley (60mins); J W C Roff for Cockbain (69mins); S J Cordingley for Rauluni (69mins); Rauluni for Cordingley (blood 71mins)

Scorers *Penalty Goals:* Flatley, Drahm

Referee J I Kaplan (Natal)

Second semi-final 19 May ABSA Stadium, King's Park, Durban
Coastal Sharks 30 (1G 1PG 4T)   Golden Cats 12 (4PG)

Coastal Sharks: R Loubscher; C S Terblanche, D J Kayser, T M Halstead, J Swart; A D James, C D Davidson; A H le Roux, J W Smit, E E Fynn, P A van den Berg, M G Andrews *(captain)*, C Van Rensburg, A J Venter, W K Britz *Substitutions:* B S Moyle for Fynn (56mins); B M MacLeod-Henderson for Venter (65mins); A H Snyman for Kayser (69mins); G S du Toit for James (74mins); R S Sowerby for van den Berg (74mins); H J Martens for Davidson (78mins); L van Biljon for le Roux (78mins)

Scorers *Tries:* van Rensburg (2), Halstead, Terblanche, Britz *Conversion:* James *Penalty Goal:* James

Golden Cats: G M Delport; W Human, G Esterhuizen, E Meyer, D B Hall; L J Koen, W Swanepoel; M Mostert, L Boshoff, M F Nell, J N Ackermann, J J Labuschagne, J C Erasmus *(captain)*, A N Vos, A G Venter *Substitutions:* P J Krause for Vos (blood 12-18mins); C van Rensburg for Meyer (38mins); A van Niekerk for Labuschagne (temp 39-48mins); C A Jantjes for Human (56mins); P van Niekerk for Mostert (65mins); K Tromp for Ackermann (71mins); C D Alcock for Swanepoel (71mins)

Scorers *Penalty Goals:* Koen (4).

Referee S J Dickinson (Australia).

Final

26 May Bruce Stadium, Canberra
ACT Brumbies 36 (3G 5PG)   Coastal Sharks 6 (2PG)

The Sharks blew their chance of a home final with two surprise defeats – against the Reds in Brisbane when they decided to rest several top players, and against the Crusaders in Christchurch. That meant that after their semi-final victory, the Sharks had to make the long journey to cold Canberra instead of waiting by the warm waters of Durban to welcome the Brumbies.

The Sharks had lost a final in 1996. The Brumbies had lost two finals – in 1997 and, icily, in 2000 when a penalty goal by Andrew Mehrtens froze the hearts of the partisan Bruce Stadium crowd. In 2001 they stayed warm in Bruce Stadium, set alight above all by Joe Roff who was in the greatest form and reduced the Sharks' hope to ashes. Even so, the Sharks did make a brave fight of it. They battered and bashed at the Brumbies early on and at half-time the score was 6-all. They could in fact have led had Butch James, newly and controversially a personality in Super Twelve, not missed four kicks at goal.

Then came the second half and glittering Joe Roff, living off ball won by George Smith and scattered into diamonds by George Gregan. Roff's stroll for a try off a pass by Jeremy Paul broke the deadlock and signalled the end of the travellers' hopes. Five minutes later, Roff came off a George Gregan pass to rocket clean through for a 40-metre burst at the line. Their third try came when David Giffin, athleticism personified at lock, charged down a Butch James clearance to drop onto the ball for a try.

Complementing the Brumbies' attacking power was their watertight defence. The Sharks, for all their earnest endeavour, could simply not get through. When Paddy O'Brien of New Zealand blew the final whistle, there was raucous joy in Bruce Stadium and it grew even louder when George Gregan became the first non-Kiwi to hoist the Super 12 trophy. How they deserved their joy!

ACT Brumbies: A M Walker; G S G Bond, J C Holbeck, R B Kafer, J W C Roff; S J Larkham, G M Gregan (*captain*); W K Young, J A Paul, B J Darwin, J B G Harrison, D T Giffin, P J Ryan, R W Williams, G B Smith *Substitutions:* M Weaver for Young (26mins); M A Bartholomeusz for Holbeck (70mins)

Scorers *Tries:* Roff (2), Giffin *Conversions:* Walker (3) *Penalty Goals:* Walker (5)

Coastal Sharks: R Loubscher; C S Terblanche, D J Kayser, T M Halstead, J Swart; A D James, C D Davidson; A H le Roux, J W Smit, E E Fynn, P A van den Berg, M G Andrews (*captain*), C van Rensburg, A J Venter, W K Britz *Substitutes:* B M MacLeod-Henderson for van Rensburg (56mins); L van Biljon for Fynn (60mins); R S Sowerby for Venter (64mins); H J Martens for Davidson (68mins); G S du Toit for Loubscher (70 mins); B S Moyle for le Roux (72mins)

Scorers *Penalty Goals:* James (2)

Referee P D O'Brien (New Zealand)

Previous Super Twelve Finals: 1996 Auckland Blues 45, Coastal Sharks 21 (Auckland); 1997 Auckland Blues 23, Australian Capital Territory Brumbies 7 (Auckland); 1998 Canterbury Crusaders 20, Auckland Blues 13 (Auckland); 1999 Canterbury Crusaders 24, Otago Highlanders 19 (Dunedin); 2000 Canterbury Crusaders 20, Australian Capital Territory Brumbies 19 (Canberra); 2001 Australian Capital Territory Brumbies 36, Coastal Sharks 6 (Canberra)

SUPER TWELVE RECORDS 1996–2001

Record	Detail		Set
Most team points in season	513 by Auckland Blues	in 13 matches	1997
Most team tries in season	70 by Auckland Blues	in 13 matches	1996
Highest team score	75 by Coastal Sharks	75-43 v Otago Highlanders	1997
	75 by Canterbury Crusaders	75-27 v Northern Bulls	2000
Biggest team win	64 by ACT Brumbies	73-9 v Northern Bulls	1999
	64 by ACT Brumbies	64-0 v Golden Cats	2000
Most team tries in match	11 by Auckland Blues	v Western Stormers	1998
	11 by Canterbury Crusaders	v Northern Bulls	2000
Most appearances	71 for Canterbury Crusaders	T J Blackadder	1996-2001
Most points in matches	701 for Canterbury Crusaders	A P Mehrtens	1997-2001
Most points in season	206 for Canterbury Crusaders	A P Mehrtens	1998
Most points in match	50 for Coastal Sharks	G Lawless v Otago Highlanders	1997
Most tries in matches	44 for Wellington Hurricanes	C M Cullen	1996-2001
	44 for ACT Brumbies	J W C Roff	1996-2001
Most tries in season	15 for ACT Brumbies	J W C Roff	1997
Most tries in match	4 for ACT Brumbies	J W C Roff v Coastal Sharks	1997
	4 for Coastal Sharks	G Lawless v Otago Highlanders	1997
	4 for Coastal Sharks	C S Terblanche v Waikato Chiefs	1998
	4 for Auckland Blues	J Vidiri v Northern Bulls	2000
Most cons in matches	106 for Auckland Blues	A R Cashmore	1996-2000
Most cons in season	39 for ACT Brumbies	S A Mortlock	2000
Most cons in match	9 for Coastal Sharks	G Lawless v Otago Highlanders	1997
Most pens in matches	151 for Canterbury Crusaders	A P Mehrtens	1997-2001
Most pens in season	43 for Canterbury Crusaders	A P Mehrtens	2000
Most pens in match	8 for Northern Bulls	J Kruger v Otago Highlanders	1997
Most drops in matches	9 for Canterbury Crusaders	A P Mehrtens	1997-2001
Most drops in season	4 for Canterbury Crusaders	A P Mehrtens	1998
	4 for Northern Bulls	J H de Beer	2000
Most drops in match	3 for Canterbury Crusaders	A P Mehrtens v Otago Highlanders	1998

DOMESTIC RUGBY IN ENGLAND 2000-01

Tigers Burn Brightly: The Zurich Premiership & Championship

David Llewellyn

It was quite some feat by Leicester to get their claws on the Premiership title for the third year running. That they did so on St Patrick's Day with something of a flourish was even more impressive, and capped off a season in which the English language was given a variation on a well-known saying, thanks to the eagerness of the new sponsors to make an even bigger impact on the club game.

Rather than being 'one over the eight' as used to happen in the good old amateur days, the object now was to avoid being 'one under the eight' as clubs strove for a place in the play-offs, hereafter known as the Zurich Championship, which carried a fair amount of kudos, an automatic qualifying place in Europe and a sizeable trophy.

It was also quite some feat that the competition reached a conclusion, given the off-field talks and politicking that went on throughout a fraught season, not to mention the foot-and-mouth outbreak (which disrupted numerous fixtures further down the league) and of course the weather, which occasioned postponements and raised the prospect of a whole new ball game – sub aqua rugby.

The clubs in National League Division One (formerly the Second Division) insisted for much of the season that they would not accept a play-off to gain access to the elite: they wanted automatic promotion and relegation. There were threats of legal action and howls of outrage at claim and counter-claim. Thankfully sanity was restored, although both sides left it almost to the final whistle.

Agreement was finally reached late in April, a month before the so-called end of the season and just 24 hours before an SGM of the RFU. Even then the agreement of one-up, one-down for the next three years between Premiership and National League One clubs was challenged by the Reform Group.

At least with that out of the way the clubs were able to get on with what they were paid to do – play. A mere half a dozen years ago the dawn of the professional era had suggested an end to the old order and a takeover of all that had been deemed to be good about the game by the more ambitious, new-age clubs. Certainly the usual suspects did appear to be under threat from the wealthier pretenders.

The Tigers, though, are made of sterner stuff. Not for them lashings of lolly and inflated wages for inflated egos. Instead they made discreet forays into the market-place where they signed wisely and well. A common denominator throughout those three successful years was one of those astute signings, Australian centre Pat Howard, a vastly talented player (and coach by all accounts), possibly the best import to date and certainly not the costliest. In fact, compared with Jason Little, who was expected to do so much for Gloucester, and his Wallaby centre partner Tim Horan, in whom Saracens invested a great deal of cash, Howard was easily the bargain of the season.

Leicester's title, however, was still earned the hard way. England's autumn internationals ensured the loss of key personnel, yet the Premiership – in this rough, tough professional world – carried on regardless. So too did Leicester. When their England squad members returned for action they found that the understudies had won all three Zurich matches and had lifted Leicester into first place, where they remained for the rest of the season.

They had to squeeze past Harlequins to get to the summit, but thereafter burned brightly to remain unbeaten until the end of March, by which time they had done all they needed to take the title. At one stage the gap between first and second place had opened up to a remarkable 18 points before Wasps reeled them back to a more acceptable eight. It was still a runaway triumph for the East Midlands club and testament to the talent of Tigers' coaching team of John Wells and Howard, as well as to the management and motivational skill of their living legend Dean Richards.

So much had been expected of Saracens who had got their campaign off to a flier by putting a half century on Gloucester on a hot August afternoon. They tripped a couple of times after that though, losing at London Irish and, more shockingly, at home to Wasps. Although they then inflicted a defeat on Leicester – one of just three suffered by the Tigers in the season – and another on Bath (at the Recreation Ground), another short, sharp trot of three defeats effectively ended their challenge. They finally missed out on a place in the European Cup by finishing in fifth place in the Premiership and proving unable to make a showing in any other competition which was offering qualification for the Heineken Cup. Saracens also had the dubious distinction of losing to Rotherham in the New Year – one of only two clubs to lose at Clifton Lane last season, the other being London Irish.

Wasps left their charge for the runners-up spot a mite late but they finally managed to pip Bath for it in the run-in. The West Country side ended the season with the most bonus points, chiefly picked up through their try-scoring feats. Although outdone by Wasps in the Premiership by 75 tries to 72, Bath then picked up in the Zurich Championship, adding a further nine to Wasps' five.

Lest anyone think that Leicester did not get in the frame in the try-scoring stakes, they can think again. The Tigers managed 50 in the Premiership, as did Saracens, and touched down a further seven times in the Championship for a grand total of 67.

The play-offs, where the top four clubs were drawn at home in the quarter-finals of the Zurich Championship went with the home ties, Saracens subsiding alarmingly at Northampton. In the semi-finals, Bath won a thriller at Wasps and a tired Leicester just scraped past Northampton at Welford Road. The final too was something of an anti-climax as a drained Bath slipped meekly to defeat against Leicester in front of only 33,500 at Twickenham in the final.

The first club to experience the automatic 'one-down' sensation was Rotherham. They were a brave side, but unable to get to grips with the wealthier and more seasoned teams in the Premiership. They had wanted to take a step back and see what was necessary to maintain a place in the top flight. The answer was a lot more than they managed.

In their two solitary victories over Saracens and Irish they scored 19 points each time, whereas when they lost it was generally to far bigger scores. They conceded more than 50 points on no fewer than four occasions and leaked 68 to Bath. Seven times they let in 30 plus and in three other games more than 40 were stuck on them. They did, however, seem to have the measure of Leicester, who were contained in the mid-20s on both occasions. Ultimately, though, as good as they were, Rotherham were just lacking that extra edge to stay up, but at least they know what they must do next time around – as does every other club, including Leeds Tykes, promoted from National League One.

The mission, if they accept it, is to try to stop Leicester Tigers from getting their claws on a fourth successive Premiership title. It will not be easy. Indeed, it looks impossible.

Final Zurich Premiership Table 2000–01

Team	P	W	D	L	For	Against	Bonus	Pts
Leicester	22	18	1	3	571	346	8	82
Wasps	22	16	0	6	663	428	10	74
Bath	22	14	0	8	680	430	14	70
Northampton	22	13	0	9	518	463	7	59
Saracens	22	12	0	10	589	501	10	58
Newcastle	22	11	0	11	554	568	13	57
Gloucester	22	10	0	12	473	526	8	48
London Irish	22	10	1	11	476	576	3	45
Bristol	22	9	1	12	443	492	6	44
Sale	22	8	1	13	561	622	9	43
Harlequins	22	7	0	15	440	538	10	38
Rotherham	22	2	0	20	335	813	4	12

Four points awarded for a win; two for a draw and none for a defeat.

Previous English Club League Winners: 1987-88 Leicester; 1988-89 Bath; 1989-90 Wasps; 1990-91 Bath; 1991-92 Bath; 1992-93 Bath; 1993-94 Bath; 1994-95 Leicester; 1995-96 Bath; 1996-97 Wasps; 1997-98 Newcastle; 1998-99 Leicester; 1999-2000 Leicester; 2000-01 Leicester

The Zurich Championship Final

13 May 2001, Twickenham
Leicester 22 (2G 1PG 1T)   **Bath 10** (1G 1PG)

It filled the slot vacated by the RFU Cup Final, but not even the prospect of a Leicester-Bath showdown could fill Twickenham for this inaugural Zurich Championship final. Only 33,500 turned up to see Leicester add the Championship to the League title they had wrapped up earlier in the season.

The story of this second triumph in Leicester's 2001 Triple Crown – League, Championship and Heineken Cup – is easily told. The Tigers held too many aces up front for Bath to trump them in a humdrum match. Martin Johnson inspired from the front and it was his 27th-minute try, converted by Tim Stimpson, that put his side 7-3 ahead at the interval, Matt Perry having earlier landed a Bath penalty.

Leicester's pack out-manoeuvred Bath in the tight and loose throughout the first 70 minutes and their backs were far more inventive in attack. Austin Healey scored the second try from a tap penalty nine minutes into the second half and Winston Stanley added a third nearly 20 minutes later. Thereafter the Tigers eased up, conserving their energy, perhaps, for the European final the week later. Bath managed a consolation try when Rob Thirlby skated down the wing to score two minutes from time, but it was too little, too late.

'We were totally outgunned,' said Bath director of rugby Jon Callard afterwards. Everyone agreed.

Leicester: T Stimpson; G Murphy, L Lloyd, P Howard, W Stanley; A Goode, A Healey; G Rowntree, D West, D Garforth, M Johnson (*captain*), B Kay, M Corry, W Johnson, N Back *Substitutions:* P Freshwater for Rowntree (48 mins); J Hamilton for A Healey (50 mins); A Healey for Goode (60 mins); P Gustard for Corry (69 mins); L Moody for Back (69 mins); G Gelderbloom for Lloyd (70 mins); R Cockerill for West (70 mins); R Nebbett for Garforth (70 mins)

Scorers *Tries:* M Johnson, Healey, Stanley *Conversions:* Stimpson (2) *Penalty goal:* Stimpson

Bath: M Perry; I Balshaw, K Maggs, S Berne, T Voyce; M Catt, G Cooper; S Emms, A Long, J Mallett, M Gabey, S Borthwick, A Gardiner, D Lyle, B Clarke *Substitutions:* S Cox for Berne (19 mins); R Thirlby for Perry (temp 28 mins to 38 mins) and for Balshaw (64 mins); D Barnes for Emms (40 mins); M Regan for Long (40 mins); G Thomas for Gardiner (50 mins); A Lloyd for Clarke (64 mins)

Scorers *Try:* Thirlby *Conversion:* Perry *Penalty Goal:* Perry

Referee S Lander (RFU)

Previous English Championship Finals: 2001 Leicester 22, Bath 10 (Twickenham)

ZURICH PREMIERSHIP CLUB DIRECTORY

Bath

Year of formation 1865
Ground Recreation Ground, London Road, Bath BA2 6PW
Contacts Web: www.bathrugby.co.uk Tel: Bath (01225) 460588
Colours Blue, white and black shirts; royal blue shorts
Captain 2000-01 Ben Clarke
Zurich Premiership League 2000-01 3rd
Zurich Championship Record 2000-01 Lost 10-22 to Leicester in final
Tetley's Bitter Cup 2000-01 Lost 18-24 to Gloucester (4th round)

Zurich League Record 2000-01

Date	Venue	Opponents	Result	Scorers
19 Aug	A	Sale	32-33	*T:* Thirlby, Perry *C:* Preston 2 *PG:* Preston 6
27 Aug	A	Wasps	36-12	*T:* Clarke, G. Thomas, Maggs, Tindall *C:* Preston 2 *PG:* Preston 4
2 Sep	H	Harlequins	38-22	*T:* Thirlby, Clarke, Adebayo, N. Thomas *C:* Preston 3 *PG:* Preston 4
9 Sep	A	Gloucester	22-21	*T:* Thirlby, Balshaw *PG:* Preston 4
16 Sep	H	Newcastle	19-12	*T:* Tindall *C:* Preston *PG:* Preston 4
23 Sep	A	Northampton	13-24	*T:* G. Thomas *C:* Thirlby *PG:* Preston 2
30 Sep	H	Saracens	21-33	*T:* A. Adebayo 2 *C:* Perry *PG:* Perry 3
19 Nov	H	Sale	34-32	*T:* Mallett, Clarke, Berne *C:* Preston 2 *PG:* Preston 5
26 Nov	H	Rotherham	42-19	*T:* Lyle 2, Thirlby, Gabey, Berne, Maggs *C:* Berne 3 *PG:* Berne 2
2 Dec	A	Bristol	9-16	*PG:* Preston, Berne 2
16 Dec	A	Leicester	19-27	*T:* Cooper *C:* Perry *PG:* Perry 4
23 Dec	H	London Irish	56-20	*T:* Cooper 2, Balshaw, Tindall, Catt, Maggs, Berne *C:* Perry 5, Preston *PG:* Perry 3
26 Dec	H	Leicester	16-17	*T:* Balshaw *C:* Perry *PG:* Perry 3
30 Dec	A	Saracens	31-11	*T:* Tindall 2, Balshaw, Long *C:* Perry 4 *PG:* Perry
6 Jan	H	Northampton	36-13	*T:* Voyce 2, Balshaw, Cooper, Tindall *C:* Perry 4 *PG:* Perry
11 Feb	A	Newcastle	23-24	*T:* Voyce 2, Tindall *C:* Preston *PG:* Preston 2
24 Feb	H	Gloucester	50-16	*T:* Catt 2, Balshaw, Berne, Clarke, Perry *C:* Preston 3, Perry *PG:* Preston 4
10 Mar	A	Harlequins	22-24	*T:* Voyce *C:* Perry *PG:* Perry 5
14 Mar	A	London Irish	58-13	*T:* Catt 3, Berne, Haag, N. Thomas, Thirlby *C:* Preston 6, Perry *PG:* Preston 3
17 Mar	H	Wasps	16-13	*T:* Catt *C:* Preston *PG:* Preston 3
31 Mar	H	Bristol	19-16	*T:* Voyce *C:* Perry *PG:* Perry 4
14 Apr	A	Rotherham	68-12	*T:* Thirlby 3, Voyce 3, Berne 2, Cox, Cooper *C:* Perry 6 *PG:* Perry 2

Zurich Championship Record 2000-01

Date	Venue	Opponents	Result	Scorers
28 Apr	H	Newcastle (¼-finals)	18-9	*T:* Gardiner, Berne *C:* Perry *PG:* Perry 2
6 May	A	Wasps (½-final)	36-31	*T:* Voyce 2, pen try, Barnes, Lyle, Balshaw *C:* Perry 3
13 May	-	Leicester (FINAL)	10-22	*T:* Thirlby *C:* Perry *PG:* Perry

Bristol

Year of formation 1888
Ground Memorial Ground, Filton Avenue, Horfield, Bristol, BS7 0AQ

Contacts Web: www.bristolrugby.co.uk Tel: Bristol (0117) 3111461
Colours Navy blue and white stripes
Captain 2000-01 Agustin Pichot
Zurich Premiership League 2000-01 9th
Zurich Championship Record 2000-01 Did not qualify
Tetley's Bitter Cup 2000-01 Lost 16-32 to Newcastle (5th round)

League Record 2000-01

Date	Venue	Opponents	Result	Scorers
20 Aug	A	Rotherham	23-20	T: Dewdney PG: Bowen 6
26 Aug	H	Saracens	23-34	T: Dewdney, Vander C: Bowen, Vile PG: Bowen 3
3 Sep	A	Wasps	17-23	T: Best, Brownrigg C: Bowen 2 PG: Bowen
6 Sep	H	Sale	13-36	T: Mayer C: Bowen PG: Bowen 2
10 Sep	H	London Irish	26-30	T: S. Brown, Johnstone C: Vile 2 PG: Vile 4
16 Sep	A	Harlequins	25-31	T: Dewdney, Davies, Vile C: Vile 2 PG: Vile 2
23 Sep	H	Leicester	24-20	T: Pichot, S Brown C: Vile PG: Vile 4
30 Sep	A	Gloucester	16-38	T: Williams C: Vile PG: Vile 3
18 Nov	H	Rotherham	32-21	T: Sturnham, Baber C: Vile 2 PG: Vile 6
25 Nov	A	Northampton	6-24	PG: Vile 2
2 Dec	H	Bath	16-9	T: Pichot C: Contepomi PG: Contepomi 3
17 Dec	H	Newcastle	27-14	T: Baber, Contepomi, Rees C: Contepomi 3 PG: Contepomi 2
23 Dec	A	Sale	26-25	T: Rees, Johnstone C: Contepomi 2 PG: Contepomi 4
27 Dec	A	Newcastle	16-32	T: Mabuse 2 C: Contepomi PG: Contepomi
6 Jan	H	Gloucester	18-9	PG: Contepomi 6
6 Feb	A	Leicester	10-17	T: Contepomi C: Contepomi PG: Contepomi
11 Feb	H	Harlequins	13-9	T: Johnstone C: Contepomi PG: Contepomi 2
24 Feb	A	London Irish	26-26	T: Rees, Mayer C: Contepomi 2 PG: Contepomi 4
11 Mar	H	Wasps	12-24	PG: Contepomi 4
18 Mar	A	Saracens	13-24	T: Mayer C: Contepomi PG: Contepomi 2
31 Mar	A	Bath	16-19	T: Contepomi C: Contepomi PG: Contepomi 3
16 Apr	H	Northampton	46-16	T: Mayer 2, Contepomi, Simone C: Contepomi 4 PG: Contepomi 6

Gloucester

Year of formation 1873
Ground Kingsholm, Kingsholm Road, Gloucester, GL1 3AX
Contacts Web: www.gloucesterrugby club.com Tel: Gloucester (01452) 422422
Colours Cherry and white stripes; black shorts
Captain 2000-01 Ian Jones
Zurich Premiership League 2000-01 7th
Zurich Championship Record 2000-01 Lost 6-18 to Wasps (quarter-final)
Tetley's Bitter Cup 2000-01 Lost 13-25 to Leicester (5th round)

League Record 2000-01

Date	Venue	Opponents	Result	Scorers
20 Aug	A	Saracens	20-50	T: Simon, Yates C: Hayward 2 PG: Hayward 2
26 Aug	H	Sale	18-19	T: Boer, Schisano C: Hayward PG: Hayward 2
2 Sep	A	Rotherham	29-23	T: Schisano 3, Jewell C: Hayward 3 PG: Hayward
6 Sep	A	Newcastle	19-18	T: Hazell, Ewens PG: Hayward 3
9 Sep	H	Bath	21-22	T: Gomarsall, Hayward C: Gomarsall PG: Gomarsall 2, Hayward
17 Sep	A	Wasps	23-43	T: Beim, Yates C: Mannix 2 PG: Mannix 3
23 Sep	H	Harlequins	27-23	PG: Mannix 9
30 Sep	H	Bristol	38-16	T: Little 2, Azam, Vickery C: Mannix 3 PG: Mannix 4
18 Nov	H	Saracens	16-15	T: Beim C: Hayward PG: Hayward 3

25 Nov	H	London Irish	26-6	*T:* K Jones, Beim *C:* Mannix 2 *PG:* Mannix 4
2 Dec	A	Leicester	28-31	*T:* Deacon, Yates, Paramore *C:* Hayward 2 *PG:* Hayward 3
16 Dec	A	Northamprton	15-34	*PG:* Mannix 4 *DG:* Moncrieff
23 Dec	H	Newcastle	28-13	*T:* Beim, Little, Cornwell *C:* Mannix 2 *PG:* Mannix 3
27 Dec	H	Northampton	12-15	*T:* Fanolua, Mannix *C:* Fanolua
6 Jan	A	Bristol	9-18	PG: Mannix 3
6 Feb	A	Harlequins	19-21	*T:* Greenslade-Jones *C:* Hayward *PG:* Hayward 2, Mannix 2
10 Feb	H	Wasps	3-28	*PG:* Mannix
24 Feb	A	Bath	16-50	*T:* Catling *C:* Mannix *PG:* Mannix 3
10 Mar	H	Rotherham	50-17	*T:* Beim, Catling, Cornwell, Simpson-Daniel, pen try, Little, Todd *C:* Mannix 5, Hayward *PG:* Mannix
17 Mar	A	Sale	24-16	*T:* Little 2 *C:* Mannix. *PG:* Mannix 4
31 Mar	H	Leicester	22-13	*T:* I Jones, Gomarsall *PG:* Gomarsall 4
16 Apr	A	London Irish	10-35	*T:* Forrester *C:* Hayward *PG:* Hayward

Zurich Championship Record 2000-01

Date	Venue	Opponents	Result	Scorers
29 Apr	A	Wasps (¼-finals)	6-18	*PG:* Mannix 2

Harlequins

Year of formation 1866
Ground Stoop Memorial Ground, Langhorn Drive, Twickenham, Middlesex, TW2 7SX
Contacts Web: www.quins.co.uk Tel: 0208 410 6000
Colours Light blue, magenta, chocolate, French grey, black and light green; white shorts
Captain 2000-01 David Wilson
Zurich Premiership League 2000-01 11th
Zurich Championship Record 2000-01 Did not qualify
Tetley's Bitter Cup 2000-01 Lost 27-30 to Newcastle (FINAL)

League Record 2000-01

Date	Venue	Opponents	Result	Scorers
19 Aug	H	London Irish	16-22	*T:* Greenwood *C:* Burke *PG:* Burke 2 *DG:* Burke
26 Aug	H	Rotherham	26-13	*T:* White-Cooper, O'Leary, Greenwood, Greenstock *C:* Burke 3
2 Sep	A	Bath	22-38	*T:* Greenwood 2 *PG:* Burke 4
6 Sep	A	Northampton	20-27	*T:* Gollings, Richards *C:* Burke 2 *PG:* Burke 2
9 Sep	H	Wasps	18-31	*T:* Gollings 2, Greenwood *PG:* Gollings
16 Sep	H	Bristol	31-25	*T:* Morgan, Wood, Daniel *C:* Gollings 2 *PG:* Gollings 4
23 Sep	A	Gloucester	23-27	*T:* Greenwood, Burrows *C:* Burke 2 *PG:* Burke 3
30 Sep	A	Newcastle	18-20	*T:* White-Cooper, O'Neill *C:* Burke *PG:* Burke 2
19 Nov	A	London Irish	16-21	*T:* Greenstock *C:* Woods *PG:* Woods 3
24 Nov	H	Leicester	13-16	*T:* Wilson *C:* Woods *PG:* Woods 2
2 Dec	A	Sale	10-35	*T:* J. Powell *C:* Woods *PG:* Woods
17 Dec	A	Saracens	18-26	*PG:* Woods 6
23 Dec	H	Northampton	25-34	*T:* Jennings, Daniel, Gollings *C:* Woods, Chalmers *PG:* Woods 2
27 Dec	H	Saracens	14-30	*T:* Daniel *PG:* Woods 3
6 Feb	H	Gloucester	21-19	*T:* Sanderson, Gollings *C:* Burke *PG:* Burke 2 *DG:* Burke
11 Feb	A	Bristol	9-13	*PG:* Burke 2 *DG:* Greenwood
6 Mar	A	Newcastle	24-22	*T:* O'Neill, Wilson *C:* Burke *PG:* Burke 4
10 Mar	H	Bath	24-22	*T:* O'Leary, Greenwood *C:* Burke *PG:* Burke 4
17 Mar	A	Rotherham	32-12	*T:* O'Leary, Wood, Jewell, Wilson *C:* Burke 2, Chalmers *PG:* Burke *DG:* Burke

31 Mar	H	Sale	36-10	T: O'Leary 2, Morgan, Wilson C: Burke 2 PG: Burke 4
10 Apr	A	Wasps	19-38	T: Morgan, Oliver, Gollings C: Burke 2
14 Apr	A	Leicester	5-37	T: Jewell

Leicester

Year of formation 1880
Ground Welford Road, Aylestone Road, Leicester, LE2 7LF
Contacts Web: www.tigers.co.uk Tel: Leicester (0116) 254 0505
Colours Scarlet, green and white shirts; white shorts
Captain 2000-01 Martin Johnson
Zurich Premiership League 2000-01 Winners
Zurich Championship Record 2000-01 Winners Won 22-10 against Bath (FINAL)
Tetley's Bitter Cup 2000-01 Lost 18-22 to Harlequins (semi-final)

League Record 2000-01

Date	Venue	Opponents	Result	Scorers
19 Aug	A	Wasps	24-22	T: Healey 2, Stanley C: Stimpson 3 PG: Stimpson
27 Aug	A	Newcastle	25-22	T: Murphy, Lloyd, West, Stanley C: Murphy PG: Stimpson
2 Sep	H	Northampton	33-19	T: Lloyd, Corry, Healey C: Murphy 3 PG: Murphy 4
6 Sep	H	Rotherham	20-18	T: Back 2, Healey, Booth C: Healey 2, Murphy
10 Sep	A	Saracens	9-17	PG: Stimpson 3
16 Sep	H	London Irish	33-20	T: Back, Howard, Stanley, Newmarch C: Stimpson 2 PG: Stimpson 3
23 Sep	A	Bristol	20-24	T: Goode, Howard, Gustard C: Goode PG: Stimpson
30 Sep	A	Sale	17-17	T: Murphy PG: Stimpson 4.
18 Nov	H	Wasps	28-13	T: Hamilton. C: Stimpson PG: Stimpson 7
24 Nov	A	Harlequins	16-13	T: Stimpson C: Stimpson PG: Stimpson 3
2 Dec	H	Gloucester	31-28	T: Tuilagi C: Stimpson PG: Stimpson 8
16 Dec	H	Bath	27-19	T: Rowntree, Howard C: Stimpson PG: Stimpson 5
23 Dec	A	Rotherham	27-9	T: Smith, Booth, W. Johnson C: Booth 3 PG: Booth 2
26 Dec	A	Bath	17-16	T: Back PG: Stimpson 3 DG: Goode
6 Feb	H	Bristol	17-10	T: Stanley PG: Stimpson 4
10 Feb	A	London Irish	28-9	T: Stimpson 2, Back, Murphy C: Stimpson 4
24 Feb	H	Saracens	56-15	T: Murphy 4, Stimpson 2, Garforth C: Stimpson 6 PG: Stimpson 3
6 Mar	H	Sale	24-12	T: M. Johnson, Balding C: Stimpson PG: Stimpson 4
10 Mar	A	Northampton	12-9	PG: Stimpson 4
17 Mar	H	Newcastle	51-7	T: Back 2, Stimpson 2, Stanley, Goode, Lloyd, Booth C: Stimpson 4 PG: Stimpson
31 Mar	A	Gloucester	13-22	T: Cockerill, Stanley PG: Booth
14 Apr	H	Harlequins	37-5	T: Healey, Murphy, Howard, Back, Lloyd C: Stimpson 3 PG: Stimpson 2

Zurich Championship Record 2000-01

Date	Venue	Opponents	Result	Scorers
28 Apr	H	London Irish (¼-finals)	24-11	T: Stanley, Healey C: Stimpson PG: Stimpson 4
5 May	H	Northampton (½-final)	17-13	T: Howard, Booth C: Stimpson 2 PG: Stimpson
13 May	-	Bath (FINAL)	22-10	T: M Johnson, Healey, Stanley C: Stimpson 2 PG: Stimpson

London Irish

Year of formation 1898
Ground Madejski Stadium, Reading
Contacts Web: www.london-irish-rugby.com Tel: Reading (0118) 968 1000
Colours Green and white shirts
Captain 2000-01 Conor O'Shea
Zurich Premiership League 2000-01 8th
Zurich Championship Record 2000-01 Lost 11-24 to Leicester (quarter-final)
Tetley's Bitter Cup 2000-01 Lost 20-33 to Newcastle (quarter-final)

League Record 2000-01

Date	Venue	Opponents	Result	Scorers
19 Aug	A	Harlequins	22-16	T: Kirke C: Cunningham PG: Cunningham 5
26 Aug	A	Northampton	10-27	T: O'Shea C: Cunningham PG: Cunningham
2 Sep	H	Saracens	27-22	T: Sackey, Dawson C: Cunningham PG: Cunningham 5
10 Sep	A	Bristol	30-26	PG: Cunningham 8, O'Shea DG: Cunningham
16 Sep	A	Leicester	20-33	T: Sackey, Halvey C: Cunningham 2 PG: Cunningham, O'Shea
24 Sep	H	Sale	28-13	T: Halvey, Bishop, O'Shea C: Cunningham 2 PG: Cunningham 3
30 Sep	A	Rotherham	18-19	T: Sackey, Ellis C: Cunningham PG: Cunningham 2
19 Nov	H	Harlequins	21-16	PG: Everitt 7
25 Nov	A	Gloucester	6-26	PG: Cunningham 2
5 Dec	H	Newcastle	19-17	T: pen try C: Everitt PG: Everitt 4
16 Dec	H	Wasps	14-13	T: Tonu'u PG: Everitt 3.
23 Dec	A	Bath	20-56	T: Oliver, Worsley C: Cunningham, Ashforth PG: Cunningham 2
27 Dec	A	Wasps	16-29	T: Sackey C: Everitt PG: Everitt 3
10 Feb	H	Leicester	9-28	PG: Everitt 3
20 Feb	H	Rotherham	54-11	T: Ezulike, Appleford, Strudwick, Hatley, Sackey, Alexopoulous C: Everitt 6 PG: Everitt 4
24 Feb	H	Bristol	26-26	T: Wright PG: Everitt 7
11 Mar	A	Saracens	22-35	T: Everitt, pen try, Appleford C: Everitt 2 PG: Everitt
14 Mar	H	Bath	13-58	T: Oliver C: Everitt PG: Everitt 2
17 Mar	H	Northampton	13-10	T: Sackey C: Everitt PG: Everitt 2
1 Apr	A	Newcastle	35-42	T: Kirke, Tonu'u, Sackey C:Everitt PG: Everitt 6
10 Apr	A	Sale	18-43	T; Ezulike, Halvey C: Cunningham PG: Everitt 2
16 Apr	H	Gloucester	35-10	T: Campbell, Ezulike, Sackey C: Everitt PG: Everitt 5, Cunningham

Zurich Championship Record 2000-01

Date	Venue	Opponents	Result	Scorers
28 Apr	A	Leicester (¼-finals)	11-24	T: Ezulike PG: Everitt 2

Newcastle

Year of formation 1877, reformed in 1995
Ground Kingston Park, Brunton Road, Kenton Bank Foot, Newcastle upon Tyne NE13 8AF
Contacts Web: www.newcastle-falcons.co.uk Tel: Newcastle (0191) 214 2800
Colours Black and white shirts; black shorts
Captain 2000-01 Doddie Weir
Zurich Premiership League 2000-01 6th
Zurich Championship Record 2000-01 Lost 9-18 to Bath (quarter-final)
Tetley's Bitter Cup 2000-01 Winners Won 30-27 against Harlequins (FINAL)

League Record 2000-01

Date	Venue	Opponents	Result	Scorers
20 Aug	H	Northampton	27-21	T: Mower, Tuigamala, Beattie C: Wilkinson 3 PG: Wilkinson 2
27 Aug	H	Leicester	22-25	T: Grimes C: Wilkinson PG: Wilkinson 5
2 Sep	A	Sale	27-13	T: Leslie 2, Vyvyan C: Wilkinson 3 PG: Wilkinson 2
6 Sep	H	Gloucester	18-19	PG: Wilkinson 6
10 Sep	H	Rotherham	34-19	T: Leslie, Mower, Botham, Jenner C: Wilkinson 4 PG: Wilkinson 2
16 Sep	A	Bath	12-19	PG: Wilkinson 3 DG: Wilkinson
23 Sep	H	Wasps	59-21	T: Botham 2, Armstrong 2, Leslie, Noon C: Wilkinson 4 PG: Wilkinson 6 DG: Wilkinson
30 Sep	A	Harlequins	20-18	T: Stephenson 2 C: Wilkinson 2 PG: Wilkinson 2
18 Nov	A	Northampton	18-26	T: Tuigamala, May C: Walder PG: Walder 2
26 Nov	H	Saracens	32-27	T: Walder 2 C: Walder 2 PG: Walder 6
5 Dec	A	London Irish	17-19	T: Maclure PG: Walder 4
17 Dec	A	Bristol	14-27	T: May PG: Wilkinson 2 DG: Wilkinson
23 Dec	A	Gloucester	13-28	T: Wilkinson C: Wilkinson PG: Wilkinson 2
27 Dec	H	Bristol	23-15	T: Armstrong, Ward C: Wilkinson 2 PG: Wilkinson 3
11 Feb	H	Bath	24-23	T: Wilkinson, Walder, Stephenson, Armstrong C: Wilkinson 2
6 Mar	H	Harlequins	22-24	T: Maclure C: Walder PG: Walder 5
11 Mar	H	Sale	48-24	T: Stephenson 2, Weir, Walder, May, Grimes, Armstrong C: Wilkinson 5 PG: Wilkinson
17 Mar	A	Leicester	7-51	T: Maclure C: Walder
28 Mar	A	Wasps	7-44	T: Massey C: Walder
1 Apr	H	London Irish	42-35	T: Stephenson, Wilkinson, Vyvyan, Walder, Nesdale, Armstrong C: Wilkinson 6
10 Apr	A	Rotherham	39-36	T: Graham 2, Jenner, Stephenson, Armstrong C: Armstrong 4 PG: Armstrong 2
15 Apr	A	Saracens	29-34	T: Vyvyan, Weir, Graham, Grimes C: Walder 2, Wilkinson PG: Wilkinson

Zurich Championship Record 2000-01

Date	Venue	Opponents	Result	Scorers
28 Apr	A	Bath (¼-finals)	9-18	PG: Walder 3

Northampton

Year of formation 1880
Ground Franklins Gardens, Weedon Road, St James', Northampton, NN5 5BG
Contacts Web: www.northamptonsaints.co.uk Tel: Northampton (01604) 581000
Colours Black, green and gold shirts; black shorts
Captain 2000-01 Pat Lam
Zurich Premiership League 2000-01 4th
Zurich Championship Record 2000-01 Lost 13-17 to Leicester (semi-final)
Tetley's Bitter Cup 2000-01 Lost 6-11 to Harlequins (quarter-final)

League Record 2000-01

Date	Venue	Opponents	Result	Scorers
20 Aug	A	Newcastle	21-27	T: Martin, Pagel C: Grayson PG: Grayson 3
26 Aug	H	London Irish	27-10	T: Cohen 2 C: Grayson PG: Grayson 5
2 Sep	A	Leicester	19-33	T: Thompson C: Grayson PG: Grayson 4
6 Sep	H	Harlequins	27-20	T: Pountney, Moir C: Grayson PG: Grayson 5
9 Sep	A	Sale	23-34	T: Grayson, pen try C: Grayson 2 PG: Grayson 3
16 Sep	A	Rotherham	32-19	T: Cohen, Pountney, Webster, Phillips C: Grayson 3 PG: Grayson 2

23 Sep	H	Bath	24-13	T: Cohen, Tucker, Pountney C: Tucker 2, Grayson PG: Tucker
1 Oct	A	Wasps	17-53	T: pen try, Martin C: Tucker 2 PG: Tucker
18 Nov	H	Newcastle	26-18	T: Hepher, Newman C: Grayson 2 PG: Grayson 4
25 Nov	H	Bristol	24-6	T: Pountney, Allen C: Grayson PG: Grayson 4
3 Dec	A	Saracens	30-10	T: Lam, Shaw C: Grayson PG: Grayson 5 DG: Hepher
16 Dec	H	Gloucester	34-15	T: Allen, Cohen, Thorneycroft C: Dawson 2 PG: Dawson 5
23 Dec	A	Harlequins	34-25	T: Hepher 2, Cohen, Martin C: Dawson 4 PG: Dawson 2
27 Dec	A	Gloucester	15-12	PG: Grayson 5
30 Dec	H	Wasps	18-21	PG: Grayson 6
6 Jan	A	Bath	13-36	T: Brooks C: Grayson PG: Grayson 2
10 Feb	H	Rotherham	42-0	T: Cohen 2, Shaw, Leslie, Blowers C: Hepher 2, Grayson 2 PG: Hepher 3
24 Feb	H	Sale	32-26	T: Rodber, Pountney, Cohen C: Grayson PG: Grayson 5
10 Mar	H	Leicester	9-12	PG: Dawson 3
17 Mar	A	London Irish	10-13	T: Tucker C: Hepher PG: Hepher
31 Mar	H	Saracens	25-14	T: Leslie, Bateman, Dawson C: Dawson, Grayson PG: Grayson 2
16 Apr	A	Bristol	16-46	T: Thompson C: Grayson PG: Grayson 3

Zurich Championship Record 2000-01

Date	Venue	Opponents	Result	Scorers
28 Apr	H	Saracens (¼-finals)	45-17	T: Dawson 2, Martin, Rodber, Cohen, Thompson, Blowers C: Grayson 5
5 May	A	Leicester (½-final)	13-17	T: Martin C: Grayson PG: Grayson 2

Rotherham

Year of formation 1923
Ground Clifton Lane Sports Ground, Badsley Moor Lane, Rotherham, South Yorkshire S65 2PH
Contacts Web: www.rotherhamrufc.co.uk Tel: Rotherham (01709) 370763
Colours Maroon, white and navy blue shirts; black shorts
Captain 2000-01 Mike Schmid
Zurich Premiership League 2000-01 12th Relegated
Zurich Championship Record 2000-01 Did not qualify
Tetley's Bitter Cup 2000-01 Lost 12-20 to Sale (5th round)

League Record 2000-01

Date	Venue	Opponents	Result	Scorers
20 Aug	H	Bristol	20-23	T: Fea'unati PG: Umaga 5
26 Aug	A	Harlequins	13-26	T: Thorp C: Umaga PG: Umaga 2
2 Sep	H	Gloucester	23-29	T: Scully, Thorp C: Umaga 2 PG: Umaga 3
6 Sep	A	Leicester	18-26	T: Naylor, pen try C: Umaga PG: Umaga 2
10 Sep	A	Newcastle	19-34	T: Naylor, Umaga, Garnett C: Umaga 2
16 Sep	H	Northampton	19-32	T: Naylor C: Umaga PG: Umaga 4
24 Sep	A	Saracens	5-59	T: Umaga
30 Sep	H	London Irish	19-18	T: Simpson C: Umaga PG: Umaga 4
18 Nov	A	Bristol	21-32	T: Umaga, Murphy C: Smith PG: Smith 3
26 Nov	A	Bath	19-42	T: Turner C: Smith PG: Smith 4
2 Dec	H	Wasps	15-30	PG: Smith 4 DG: Smith
16 Dec	A	Sale	12-45	PG: Smith 4
23 Dec	H	Leicester	9-27	PG: Smith 3
6 Jan	H	Saracens	19-8	T: Binns, Massey PG: Umaga 3
10 Feb	A	Northampton	0-42	

20 Feb	A	London Irish	11-54	*T:* Fea'unati *PG:* Umaga *DG:* Binns
10 Mar	A	Gloucester	17-50	*T:* Wood, Binns *C:* Umaga 2 *PG:* Umaga
17 Mar	H	Harlequins	12-32	*PG:* Umaga 4
24 Mar	H	Sale	13-39	*T:* Wade, Greaves *PG:* Umaga
1 Apr	A	Wasps	3-58	*PG:* Umaga
10 Apr	H	Newcastle	36-39	*T:* Dixon 2, Dawson, Johnson, Schmid *C:* Umaga 3, Scully *PG:* Umaga
14 Apr	H	Bath	12-68	*T:* Wade, Wood *C:* Umaga

Sale

Year of formation 1861
Ground Heywood Road, Brooklands, Sale, Cheshire, M33 3WB
Contacts Web: www.salesharks.com Tel: 0161 283 1861
Colours Royal blue and white shirts; blue shorts
Captain 2000-01 Alex Sanderson
Zurich Premiership League 2000-01 10th
Zurich Championship Record 2000-01 Did not qualify
Tetley's Bitter Cup 2000-01 Lost 25-37 to Newcastle (semi-final)

League Record 2000-01

Date	Venue	Opponents	Result	Scorers
19 Aug	H	Bath	33-32	*T:* Redpath, Hanley *C:* Little *PG:* Little 7
26 Aug	A	Gloucester	19-18	*T:* Going *C:* Little *PG:* Little 4
2 Sep	H	Newcastle	13-27	*T:* Black *C:* Little *PG:* Little 2
6 Sep	A	Bristol	36-13	*T:* Little, Hanley, Davidson *C:* Little 3 *PG:* Little 5
9 Sep	H	Northampton	34-23	*T:* Hanley 2, Manson-Bishop, Sanderson *C:* Little 4 *PG:* Little 2
16 Sep	H	Saracens	6-51	*PG:* Little 2
24 Sep	A	London Irish	13-28	*T:* Deane, Sanderson *PG:* Little
30 Sep	H	Leicester	17-17	*T:* Going *PG:* Little 3 *DG:* Little
19 Nov	A	Bath	32-34	*T:* Going 2, Moore, Manson-Bishop *C:* Little 2, Davidson *PG:* Little 2
26 Nov	A	Wasps	24-33	*T:* Redpath, Deane *C:* Little *PG:* Little 4
2 Dec	H	Harlequins	35-10	*T:* Hanley 3, Robinson 2 *C:* Hodgson, Little *PG:* Hodgson 2
16 Dec	H	Rotherham	45-12	*T:* Hodgson 2, Bell, Redpath, Hanley, Harris *C:* Hodgson 2, Little *PG:* Hodgson 3
23 Dec	H	Bristol	25-26	*T:* Going *C:* Hodgson *PG:* Hodgson 4, Little 2
11 Feb	A	Saracens	30-44	*T:* Hodgson 2, Going *C:* Hodgson 3 *PG:* Hodgson 3
24 Feb	A	Northampton	26-32	*T:* Baxendell, Robinson *C:* Hodgson 2 *PG:* Hodgson 4
6 Mar	A	Leicester	12-24	*PG:* Little 4
11 Mar	A	Newcastle	24-48	*T:* Manson-Bishop, Bell, Moore *C:* Little 2, Hodgson *PG:* Hodgson
17 Mar	H	Gloucester	16-24	*T:* Robinson *C:* Hodgson *PG:* Hodgson 3
24 Mar	A	Rotherham	39-13	*T:* Elliott 2, Baxendell, Robinson, Lines *C:* Hodgson 4 *PG:* Hodgson 2
31 Mar	A	Harlequins	10-36	*T:* Baldwin *C:* Little *PG:* Hodgson
10 Apr	H	London Irish	43-18	*T:* Davidson 2, Anglesea, Titterrell, Robinson, Hanley *C:* Hodgson 2 *PG:* Hodgson 2, Little
14 Apr	H	Wasps	29-59	*T:* Robinson, Hanley, Davidson *C:* Little *PG:* Hodgson 4

Saracens

Year of formation 1876
Ground Vicarage Road Stadium, Watford, Hertfordshire, WD17 8ER
Contacts Web: www.saracens.com Tel: Watford (01923) 475222
Colours Black, red and white shirts
Captain 2000-01 Kyran Bracken
Zurich Premiership League 2000-01 5th
Zurich Championship Record 2000-01 Lost 17-45 to Northampton (quarter-final)
Tetley's Bitter Cup 2000-01 Lost 24-41 to Leicester (quarter-final)

League Record 2000-01

Date	Venue	Opponents	Result	Scorers
20 Aug	H	Gloucester	50-20	T: Bracken, Davison, Sorrell, Murray, Luger, Johnston C: Castaignede 4 PG: Castaignede 4
26 Aug	A	Bristol	34-23	T: Chesney, McRae, O'Mahony C: McRae 2 PG: McRae 5
2 Sep	A	London Irish	22-27	T: Castaignede C: Castaignede PG: Castaignede 4 DG: Castaignede
6 Sep	H	Wasps	24-30	T: Johnson, Diprose C: McRae PG: Castaignede 3, McRae
10 Sep	H	Leicester	17-9	T: McRae PG: Castaignede 4
16 Sep	A	Sale	51-6	T: Castaignede 2, Sparg, Murray, McRae, Davison, Wallace, Arasa C: Castaignede 3, Sparg PG: Castaignede
24 Sep	H	Rotherham	59-5	T: Luger 3, Castaignede 2, Hill, Bracken, Wallace C: Castaignede 5 PG: Castaignede 3
30 Sep	A	Bath	33-21	T: O'Mahony, Sorrell C: Castaignede PG: Castaignede 7
18 Nov	A	Gloucester	15-16	T: Wallace, Russell C: McRae PG: McRae
26 Nov	A	Newcastle	27-32	T: Arasa 2, Murray C: McRae 3 PG: McRae 2
3 Dec	H	Northampton	10-30	T: Haughton C: McRae PG: McRae
17 Dec	H	Harlequins	26-18	T: Luger PG: Sorrell 7
23 Dec	A	Wasps	6-25	PG: Sorrell 2
27 Dec	A	Harlequins	30-14	T: Sorrell, Horan, Diprose, Luger C: Sorrell 2 PG: Sorrell 2
30 Dec	H	Bath	11-31	T: Hill PG: Sorrell 2
6 Jan	A	Rotherham	8-19	T: Diprose PG: Sorrell
11 Feb	H	Sale	44-30	T: Grewcock, Shanklin, Hill, Horan, O'Mahony, Cairns C: Sorrell 4 PG: Sorrell 2
24 Feb	A	Leicester	15-56	T: Haughton, O'Mahony C: McRae DG: McRae
11 Mar	H	London Irish	35-22	T: Horan, O'Mahony, Haughton, Roques, Arasa C: McRae 2 PG: Sorrell DG: McRae
18 Mar	H	Bristol	24-13	T: White, Sorrell C: McRae PG: McRae 4
31 Mar	A	Northampton	14-25	T: McRae PG: McRae 2 DG: McRae
15 Apr	H	Newcastle	34-29	T: Diprose, Flatman, Shanklin C: De Beer 2 PG: De Beer 3 DG: De Beer 2

Zurich Championship Record 2000-01

Date	Venue	Opponents	Result	Scorers
28 Apr	A	Northampton (¼-finals)	17-45	T: O'Mahony 2, Bracken C: De Beer

Wasps

Year of formation 1867
Ground Loftus Road Stadium, South Africa Road, Shepherds Bush, London W12 7PA
Contacts Web: www.wasps.co.uk Tel: 0208 740 2545
Colours Black and gold shirts; black shorts
Captain 2000-01 Lawrence Dallaglio
Zurich Premiership League 2000-01 Runners-up
Zurich Championship Record 2000-01 Lost 31-36 to Bath (semi-final)
Tetley's Bitter Cup 2000-01 Lost 17-22 to Bristol (4th round)

League Record 2000-01

Date	Venue	Opponents	Result	Scorers
19 Aug	H	Leicester	22-24	*T:* Lewsey *C:* Logan *PG:* Logan 5
27 Aug	H	Bath	12-36	*PG:* Logan 3 *DG:* Shaw
3 Sep	H	Bristol	23-17	*T:* Logan, Greening *C:* Logan 2 *PG:* Logan 3
6 Sep	A	Saracens	30-24	*T:* Sampson 2, Henderson *C:* Leek 3 *PG:* Leek 3
9 Sep	A	Harlequins	31-18	*T:* Roiser, Henderson, Worsley, Sampson *C:* Leek *PG:* Leek 3
17 Sep	H	Gloucester	43-23	*T:* Henderson 3, Roiser, Shaw *C:* Logan 3 *PG:* Logan 4
23 Sep	A	Newcastle	21-59	*T:* Logan 2, Wood *C:* Logan 3
1 Oct	H	Northampton	53-17	*T:* King 2, Dallaglio, Volley, Lewsey, Reed, Leota *C:* Logan 3 *PG:* Logan 4
18 Nov	A	Leicester	13-28	*T:* Worsley *C:* King *PG:* King 2
26 Nov	H	Sale	33-24	*T:* Roiser, Shaw, Henderson *C:* Logan 3 *PG:* Logan 4
2 Dec	A	Rotherham	30-15	*T:* King, Roiser, Sampson *C:* Logan 3 *PG:* Logan 3
16 Dec	A	London Irish	13-14	*T:* Leota *C:* Logan *PG:* Logan 2
23 Dec	H	Saracens	25-6	*T:* Sampson, Leota, Dallaglio *C:* Logan 2 *PG:* Logan 2
27 Dec	H	London Irish	29-16	*T:* Leota, Sampson *C:* Logan 2 *PG:* Logan 5
30 Dec	A	Northampton	21-18	*T:* Worsley, Sampson *C:* Logan *PG:* Logan, King *DG:* King
10 Feb	A	Gloucester	28-3	*T:* Volley, Worsley, Henderson *C:* Logan 2 *PG:* Logan 3
11 Mar	A	Bristol	24-12	*T:* Lewsey, Worsley, Beardshaw *C:* Logan 3 *PG:* Logan
17 Mar	A	Bath	13-16	*T:* Scrase, Sampson *PG:* King
28 Mar	H	Newcastle	44-7	*T:* King, Denney, Leota, Dallaglio, Logan, Biljon *C:* Logan 4 *PG:* Logan 2
1 Apr	H	Rotherham	58-3	*T:* Logan 3, Sampson 2, Green, pen try, Shaw, Roiser *C:* Logan 5 *PG:* Logan
10 Apr	H	Harlequins	38-19	*T:* King 2, Sampson, Green, Lewsey, Logan *C:* Logan 4
14 Apr	A	Sale	59-29	*T:* Logan 2, Waters, Volley, Dallaglio, Denney, Sampson, Leota *C:* Logan 5 *PG:* Logan 3

Zurich Championship Record 2000-01

Date	Venue	Opponents	Result	Scorers
29 Apr	H	Gloucester (¼-finals)	18-6	*T:* Logan, Sampson *C:* Logan *PG:* Logan 2
6 May	H	Bath (½-final)	31-36	*T:* Henderson, Roiser, Waters *C:* Logan 2 *PG:* Logan 4

NEWCASTLE WIN AT THE BITTER END: TETLEY'S BITTER CUP

John Griffiths and David Llewellyn

24 February 2001, Twickenham
Newcastle 30 (2G 2PG 2T)   **Harlequins 27** (1G 5PG 1T)

For many years the RFU Cup final had marked the end of the fifteen-a-side season in England. How would the crowds – and the players – react to a change to the structured season that brought forward the Cup final by three months to a winter Saturday slap bang in the middle of the Six Nations programme?

The question was fully answered by 71,000 cheerful spectators who demonstrated on the last weekend of February that the winner-takes-all aspect of a Cup-final event remained a highly attractive proposition. To their credit, Newcastle and Harlequins responded with a classic final that underlined the enthusiasm that still exists among the clubs for knock-out rugby in England. Errors there were a few, but the thrill-a-minute entertainment that the sides served up for the crowd's enjoyment showed that there is yet plenty of mileage in this competition for both the RFU and its sponsors.

Newcastle opened the scoring in the 8th minute when Tom May broke a tackle to race over for a try that Jonny Wilkinson converted. Paul Burke, who set a new Cup final record by scoring 22 points, opened Quins' account four minutes later with a penalty before David Wilson put his side in front at 8-7 with a try after 15 minutes. Burke, then Wilkinson, then Burke again gathered penalty points to leave Quins nursing a 14-10 lead at the break.

More penalties in the third quarter took Quins out to 20-13 and even a second try by May, weaving past three defenders, did not dent the Londoners' confidence. Jonny Wilkinson, who uncharacteristically missed four place kicks and a drop at goal, fluffed the conversion and when Burke crossed for a try that he also converted, it looked all over for Newcastle at 18-27 behind with just over 10 minutes to play.

Newcastle threw all they had into those final minutes. Jim Jenner burrowed his way over after Inga Tuigamala, the first player to win Cup winner's medals at both league and union, had created a Newcastle platform. Then, in the third minute of added time, a disputed decision gave Newcastle the throw-in to a lineout near the Quins' line. Television replays showed that Newcastle's Ian Peel had been forced by the defence to carry the ball into touch, but touch-judge Steve Lander awarded the throw to Newcastle. Stuart Grimes won possession and the ball was recycled to the backs where Wilkinson floated a perfectly weighted cut-out pass to May who gave Jamie Noon the space to send Dave Walder slicing through for the winning try. Wilkinson converted and 12,000 Geordie supporters celebrated as Doddie Weir lifted the trophy.

Mark Evans, the Quins' chief executive, admitted afterwards to 'a raging sense of injustice', but added positively, 'there are pluses to be had for the future development of the club.' For Newcastle and rugby union in the North-East of England the win will do much to regenerate interest in the game. 'We'll be showing the Cup to the people all over the region,' said Newcastle's director of rugby, Rob Andrew. 'It's an important part of what we are about.'

Newcastle: D Walder; M Stephenson, J Noon, T May, V Tuigamala; J Wilkinson, G Armstrong; M Ward, R Nesdale, M Hurter, S Grimes, G Weir (*captain*), R Devonshire, J Jenner, A Mower *Substitutions:* I Peel for Ward (49 mins); H Vyvyan for Weir (49 mins); R Arnold for Devonshire (56 mins)

Scorers *Tries:* May (2), Jenner, Walder *Conversions:* Wilkinson (2) *Penalty Goals:* Wilkinson (2)

Harlequins: R O'Neill; N Greenstock, W Greenwood, N Burrows, B Daniel; P Burke, M Powell; J Leonard, K Wood, J Dawson, G Morgan, S White-Cooper, P Sanderson, R Winters, D Wilson (*captain*) *Substitutions:* R Jenkins for Wilson (63 mins); B Starr for Dawson (65 mins); B Gollings for Daniel (67 mins); A Codling for Morgan (78 mins)

Scorers *Tries:* Wilson, Burke *Conversion:* Burke *Penalty Goals:* Burke (5)

Referee E Morrison (RFU)

Earlier rounds

For a competition that apparently no one was all that interested in, the ailing Tetley's Bitter Cup attracted a pretty impressive following throughout. And that despite a change of schedule and, it has to be said, status on the domestic front. The final was demoted from the end of season pinnacle in May to the middle of winter, consequently the early rounds were rather squeezed in at the front of the season.

There was no real romantic run, no real shocks, really, not until the fourth round, anyway, when the big boys from the Premiership joined in the game. Then Bath were hoofed out, on their own ground by Gloucester, and Waterloo, who eventually finished bottom of National League One, trounced Wakefield, outscoring them by four tries to three in the bargain.

Sadly, they were hammered by Sale in the quarter-finals where all four ties went with home advantage. Newcastle were 33-20 winners against London Irish thanks to the all-round brilliance of Jonny Wilkinson, who chipped in with 23 points. His total included a cheeky try scored from a tap-and-go penalty when the opposition were expecting him to kick for goal. Harlequins had a ding-dong battle with Northampton at the Stoop where only a spectacular overhead pass by Garrick Morgan from a late lineout created the chance for big Steve White-Cooper to break the 6-all deadlock with the only try of the game.

The most controversial tie of the entire Cup campaign was undoubtedly the Saracens-Leicester quarter-final at Welford Road. Saracens were well beaten by 41-24, despite a dazzling performance from their young recruit from London Welsh, Tom Shanklin. The controversy emerged after the match when Saracens' chief executive, François Pienaar, cited Martin Johnson for illegal use of the knee. The Tigers and England captain had been involved in an off-the-ball skirmish which left Duncan McRae with broken ribs. At length, video evidence led to Johnson being found guilty on three counts of foul play. He was banned for five weeks and had a subsequent appeal overruled by an RFU disciplinary panel.

Even so, everyone still expected Leicester to pile up the silverware, despite Johnson's absence from the semi-finals. But they too missed out, undone by a former Tiger, Will Greenwood, who had a hand in all three of Harlequins' tries in their 22-18 semi-final. Craig Chalmers had a disappointing afternoon with the boot, missing 17 points in all, but did manage two important conversions and a penalty while the inspirational Keith Wood fired the Quins by storming past Austin Healey for their opening try. In the other semi-final Jonny Wilkinson collected another 22 points as Newcastle had little difficulty in disposing of Sale.

Results

Fourth round: Bath 18, Gloucester 24; Bedford 24, Saracens 54; Birmingham-Solihull 16, Darlington Mowden Park 10; Bristol 22, Wasps 17; Esher 26, Waterloo 27; Exeter 12, London Irish 57; Leicester 83, Otley 11; New Brighton 17, London Welsh 32; Northampton 73, Leeds 35; Plymouth Albion 8, Harlequins 36; Reading 27, Rotherham 46; Rosslyn Park 13, Newcastle 25; Rugby 26, Manchester 38; Sale 37, Coventry 19; Tynedale 12, Worcester 76; Wakefield 31, Bracknell 23

Fifth round: Gloucester 13, Leicester 25; Harlequins 38, Manchester 8; London Welsh 10, London Irish 33; Newcastle 32, Bristol 16; Northampton 47, Birmingham-Solihull 14; Sale 20, Rotherham 12; Saracens 42, Worcester 13; Wakefield 23, Waterloo 35

Quarter-finals: Harlequins 11, Northampton 6; Leicester 41, Saracens 24; Newcastle 33, London Irish 20; Sale 59, Waterloo 12

Semi-finals: Harlequins 22, Leicester 18; Newcastle 37, Sale 25

Final: (at Twickenham) Newcastle 30, Harlequins 27

Previous RFU Cup Finals: 1972 Gloucester 17, Moseley 6; 1973 Coventry 27, Bristol 15; 1974 Coventry 26, London Scottish 6; 1975 Bedford 28, Rosslyn Park 12; 1976 Gosforth 23, Rosslyn Park 14; 1977 Gosforth 27, Waterloo 11; 1978 Gloucester 6, Leicester 3; 1979 Leicester 15, Moseley 12; 1980 Leicester 21, London Irish 9; 1981 Leicester 22, Gosforth 15; 1982 Gloucester 12, Moseley 12 (trophy shared); 1983 Bristol 28, Leicester 22; 1984 Bath 10, Bristol 9; 1985 Bath 24, London Welsh 15; 1986 Bath 25, Wasps 17; 1987 Bath 19, Wasps 12; 1988 Harlequins 28, Bristol 22; 1989 Bath 10, Leicester 6; 1990 Bath 48, Gloucester 6; 1991 Harlequins 25, Northampton 13; 1992 Bath 15, Harlequins 12; 1993 Leicester 23, Harlequins 16; 1994 Bath 21, Leicester 9; 1995 Bath 36, Wasps 16; 1996 Bath 16, Leicester 15; 1997 Leicester 9, Sale 3; 1998 Saracens 48, Wasps 18; 1999 Wasps 29, Newcastle 19; 2000 Wasps 31, Northampton 23; 2001 Newcastle 30, Harlequins 27

All played at Twickenham

DOMESTIC RUGBY IN SCOTLAND 2000-01

Exiles' Triumphant Return: Scottish Inter-District Championship

Bill McMurtrie

Scottish Exiles marked their return to the Inter-District Championship after five years' absence by winning the title. Their success completed a treble, if not a hat trick, as they had won the championship in the two previous seasons they had played in the competition – 1994-95 and 1995-96.

It turned out to be a close, though prolonged championship, starting in January and finishing in May, but it went right to the finishing line before the Exiles could regain the trophy. Going into their final match, a head-to-head duel at Richmond, the Exiles and the Borders Reivers were level. It was a winner-take-all contest from which the Exiles emerged victorious by 26-14, picking up a bonus point by scoring four tries.

For Campbell Aitken the match was a personal triumph. The former Heriot's and Glasgow Hawks full-back scored 16 of the Exiles' points with three conversions and two of his team's four tries. Despite the 4-1 try-count, it was a close-run contest. Exiles led by only 12-11 with time ticking away, and twice Gavin Dalgleish was denied tries for the Borders because of a foot in touch close to the home goal-line. A Cammy Cochrane try also was chalked off for the same reason, and it was only in the final minutes that tries by Campbell Aitken and Ben Hinshelwood secured the game for the Exiles. Their delighted coach, Alastair McHarg, said: 'It was absolutely fantastic. We can say we have been undefeated for seven years.'

Glasgow set the early pace in the championship, winning their first two matches. Albeit with three months between the games, a home victory over Edinburgh by 18-7 in the ancient Inter-City series was followed by a 15-14 win away against Caledonia. Iain Monaghan, Glasgow's replacement scrum half, kicked the winning penalty goal in the dying minutes of that Cupar match. But Glasgow then stumbled to a 20-6 defeat by the Exiles.

A week later, the Borders trounced Glasgow 59-11 at Galashiels and the Exiles squeezed through by 25-22 against Edinburgh at Richmond, results that set up the championship decider.

Results

30 January, Hughenden, Glasgow
Glasgow 18 (1G 2PG 1T)   **Edinburgh 7** (1G)

Glasgow *Tries:* R Good, A Williamson *Conversion:* A Williamson *Penalty Goals:* A Williamson (2)
Edinburgh *Try:* A Warnock *Conversion:* M Duncan

30 January, Bridgehaugh, Stirling
Caledonia 16 (1G 3PG)   Scottish Exiles 18 (1G 2PG 1T)

Caledonia *Try:* J McKenzie *Conversion:* C Sangster *Penalty Goals:* C Sangster (3)
Exiles *Tries:* J Roache, D Whitehead *Conversion:* C Day *Penalty Goals:* C Day, S Dow

25 April, Duffus Park, Cupar
Caledonia 14 (2G)   Glasgow 15 (1G 1PG 1T)

Caledonia *Tries:* A Parsons, S Pearson *Conversions:* B Price (2)
Glasgow *Tries:* A Gibbon, S Petrie *Conversion:* I Monaghan *Penalty Goal:* I Monaghan

2 May, Burnbrae, Milngavie
Glasgow 6 (2PG)   Scottish Exiles 20 (1G 1PG 2T)

Glasgow *Penalty Goals:* I Monaghan (2)
Exiles *Tries:* C Aitken, N Broughton, J Kelly *Conversion:* C Aitken *Penalty Goal:* C Day

2 May, Poynder Park, Kelso
Scottish Borders Reivers 28 (1G 2PG 3T)   Caledonia 25 (1G 1PG 3T)

Borders *Tries:* G Douglas (2), G Hill, S Nichol *Conversion:* S Paterson *Penalty Goals:* S Paterson, C Richards
Caledonia *Tries:* D Adamson, M Fraser, B Price, S Hannah *Conversion:* B Price *Penalty Goal:* B Price

5 May, Murrayfield
Edinburgh 34 (3G 1PG 2T)   Scottish Borders Reivers 29 (2G 3T)

Edinburgh *Tries:* C Dove, M Duncan, B Fisher, C Harrison, G Sharp *Conversions:* M Duncan (3) *Penalty Goal:* M Duncan
Borders *Tries:* R Deans, G Douglas, J Henderson, C Laidlaw, W Mitchell *Conversions:* G Hill (2)

9 May, Netherdale, Galashiels
Scottish Borders Reivers 59 (7G 2T)   Glasgow 11 (2PG 1T)

Borders *Tries:* C Dalgleish (2), S Paterson (2), R Deans, G Douglas, A Hotson, S Nichol, P J Solomon *Conversions:* P J Solomon (7)
Glasgow Try: R Maxton *Penalty Goals:* I Monaghan (2)

9 May, Richmond
Scottish Exiles 25 (2G 2PG 1T)   Edinburgh 22 (2G 1PG 1T)

Exiles *Tries:* N Broughton, C Morley, D Whitehead *Conversions:* C Aitken (2) *Penalty Goals:* C Aitken (2)

Edinburgh *Tries:* C Cusiter, M Murray, D Wilson *Conversions:* P Smith (2) *Penalty Goal:* M Duncan

16 May, Murrayfield
Edinburgh 31 (4G 1PG)   Caledonia 14 (2G)

Edinburgh *Tries:* C Howarth (2), M Clapperton, L Graham *Conversions:* C Howarth (4) *Penalty Goal:* C Howarth
Caledonia *Tries:* K Fraser, C Macdonald *Conversions:* D Adamson (2)

16 May, Richmond
Scottish Exiles 26 (3G 1T)   Scottish Borders Reivers 14 (3PG 1T)

Exiles *Tries:* C Aitken (2), J Brannigan, B Hinshelwood *Conversions:* C Aitken (3)
Borders *Try:* G Dalgleish *Penalty Goals:* S Paterson (3)

Final Table:

	P	W	L	For	Against	Bonus	Pts
Scottish Exiles	4	4	0	89	58	1	17
Scottish Border Reivers	4	2	2	130	96	4	12
Edinburgh	4	2	2	94	86	3	11
Glasgow	4	2	2	50	100	0	8
Caledonia	4	0	4	69	92	4	4

Points: win 4; draw 2; four or more tries, or defeat by seven or fewer points 1

SCOTTISH SUPER DISTRICTS DIRECTORY

Caledonia and Glasgow form the Glasgow Caledonians superdistrict; Edinburgh and Border Reivers amalgamate to form the Edinburgh Reivers. The sides participated in the Heineken European Cup and the Welsh/Scottish League. See those sections for further competition details.

Edinburgh Reivers

Year of formation 1998
Grounds Myreside, Edinburgh, & Netherdale, Galshiels
Contacts Web: www.edinburghrugby.com Tel: Edinburgh (0131) 2266262
Colours Black, red and white
Captain 2000-01 Graham Shiel
Welsh Scottish League 2000-01 8th

Welsh Scottish League Record 2000-01

Date	Venue	Opponents	Result	Scorers
26 Aug	H	Ebbw Vale	43-25	*T:* Murray, Shiel, Officer, Joiner, Hodge, G Dall *C:* Hodge 5 *PG:* Hodge
2 Sep	A	Cardiff	16-80	*T:* Leslie *C:* Paterson *PG:* Hodge 3
6 Sep	H	Llanelli	28-25	*T:* Ross *C:* Ross *PG:* Ross 7
9 Sep	A	Bridgend	3-25	*PG:* Ross
15 Sep	H	Glasgow Caledonians	26-33	*T:* Murray, Shiel *C:* Ross 2 *PG:* Ross 4
23 Sep	A	Swansea	20-69	*T:* D Lee, Officer, Fairley *C:* Ross *PG:* Ross
1 Oct	H	Caerphilly	43-33	*T:* Utterson 2, Paterson, Officer, Ross *C:* Ross 3 *PG:* Ross 3 *DG:* Ross
25 Nov	A	Neath	20-48	*T:* Paterson, Smith *C:* Hodge 2 *PG:* Hodge 2
1 Dec	H	Pontypridd	22-16	*T:* Metcalfe *C:* Hodge *PG:* Hodge 5
6 Dec	A	Ebbw Vale	10-24	*T:* Burns *C:* Hodge *PG:* Hodge
10 Dec	H	Cardiff	29-11	*T:* Officer, Hodge, A Dall *C:* Hodge *PG:* Hodge 4
16 Dec	A	Newport	15-55	*T:* Officer, Joiner *C:* Hodge *PG:* Hodge
22 Dec	H	Bridgend	23-13	*T:* Murray, Fullarton, Mackinnon *C:* Hodge *PG:* Hodge 2
5 Jan	H	Newport	17-15	*T:* Mackinnon *PG:* Hodge 2 *DG:* Officer, Hodge
27 Jan	A	Cross Keys	10-16	*T:* Leslie *C:* Hodge *PG:* Hodge
9 Feb	H	Swansea	16-24	*T:* Paterson *C:* Hodge *PG:* Hodge 3
10 Mar	A	Caerphilly	15-5	*PG:* Hodge 3, Ross 2
23 Mar	A	Glasgow Caledonians	35-32	*T:* Sharman 2, Murray, Jacobsen *C:* Hodge 3 *PG:* Hodge 3
1 Apr	H	Cross Keys	48-12	*T:* Paterson 2, Di Rollo 2, A Dall, Sharman, Smith *C:* Ross, Hodge 4 *PG:* Hodge
21 Apr	A	Llanelli	28-43	*T:* Paterson 2, Sharman, Leslie *C:* Hodge 4
27 Apr	H	Neath	43-19	*T:* Di Rollo, Utterson, Sharman, Sinclair *C:* Hodge 4 *PG:* Hodge 3 *DG:* Hodge, Shiel
5 May	A	Pontypridd	30-44	*T:* Shiel, Joiner, Smith *C:* Hodge 3 *PG:* Hodge, Ross 2

Glasgow Caledonians

Year of formation 1998
Grounds Hughenden, Glasgow, & McDiarmid Park, Perth
Contacts Web: www.glasgowrugby.com Tel: Glasgow (0141) 3533468
Colours Red, dark blue, light blue and white
Captain 2000-01 Andy Nicol
Welsh Scottish League 2000-01 7th

Welsh Scottish League Record 2000-01

Date	Venue	Opponents	Result	Scorers
26 Aug	A	Caerphilly	13-31	*T:* Simpson *C:* Chalmers *PG:* Chalmers 2
3 Sep	H	Cross Keys	52-28	*T:* Reid 3, McKenzie, A Bulloch, Hilton, Griffiths *C:* McKenzie 4 *PG:* McKenzie, Chalmers 2
5 Sep	A	Bridgend	27-49	*T:* Craig, Steel, Reid *C:* McKenzie 3 *PG:* McKenzie 2
8 Sep	H	Neath	36-20	*T:* Waite, Steel, G Bulloch *C:* McKenzie 3 *PG:* McKenzie 5
15 Sep	A	Edinburgh Reivers	33-26	*T:* Stuart, Craig, Hilton, White *C:* Shepherd, McKenzie *PG:* Shepherd, McKenzie *DG:* McKenzie
22 Sep	H	Ebbw Vale	43-37	*T:* Jardine 2, Longstaff, Beveridge *C:* McKenzie 4 *PG:* McKenzie 5
29 Sep	H	Cardiff	27-26	*T:* Hayes, McIlwham *C:* Hayes *PG:* McKenzie, Hayes 4
3 Dec	H	Swansea	22-42	*T:* Steel, Hayes, Stewart *C:* Hayes 2 *PG:* Hayes
9 Dec	A	Cross Keys	54-3	*T:* Nicol 2, McLaren, G Bulloch, MacFadyen, Beveridge, Irving, Longstaff *C:* Hayes 6, Nicol
17 Dec	H	Llanelli	45-35	*T:* MacFadyen 2, Steel, J Stuart *C:* Hayes 2 *PG:* Hayes 7
23 Dec	A	Neath	29-34	*T:* A Bulloch, Beveridge, Reid, MacFadyen, Longstaff *C:* Hayes 2
6 Jan	A	Llanelli	16-10	*T:* Simpson *C:* Hayes *PG:* Hayes 2 *DG:* McLaren
10 Feb	A	Ebbw Vale	10-14	*T:* McLaren *C:* Hayes *PG:* Hayes
10 Mar	A	Cardiff	11-31	*T:* Stott *PG:* Hayes 2
23 Mar	H	Edinburgh Reivers	32-35	*T:* Stuart 2, Simpson, McLaren *C:* Hayes 3 *PG:* Hayes 2
31 Mar	A	Newport	27-6	*T:* McLaren, Stuart, Stott, Irving *C:* Hayes 2 *DG:* Hayes
11 Apr	A	Pontypridd	18-41	*T:* McLaren, Kerr, Hayes *PG:* Hayes
15 Apr	H	Caerphilly	52-15	*T:* Metcalfe 2, Steel, A Bulloch, Kerr, Hayes, Stott, Simpson *C:* Hayes 6
20 Apr	H	Bridgend	15-22	*T:* Simpson, Longstaff *C:* Hayes *PG:* Hayes
27 Apr	H	Pontypridd	45-29	*T:* Irving 2, Petrie 2, Metcalfe, Kerr *C:* Irving 6 *PG:* Irving
1 May	H	Newport	28-20	*T:* McLaren, Kerr, Harrison *C:* Hayes 2 *PG:* Hayes 3
5 May	A	Swansea	10-54	*T:* Henderson *C:* Hayes *PG:* Hayes

ELEVENTH TITLE FOR HAWICK: BT SCOTLAND PREMIERSHIP

Bill McMurtrie

Hawick returned to the peak that they used to climb successfully every year, almost as if by right. Undefeated, they won the 2000-2001 BT Scotland Premier title, the eleventh time they had taken Scottish rugby's club championship in the competition's 28 seasons. It was the first time since 1987 that they tasted championship champagne. Yet in the first 14 years of the competition they had taken the trophy no fewer than 11 times.

Two of Hawick's former Scottish international players, Ian Barnes and Jim Renwick, as coaches, guided the club back to the heady heights. However, even in the moment of final triumph, with a 32-17 victory over Glasgow Hawks at Old Anniesland, the down-to-earth Barnes was not publicly carried away by success. His thoughts were on the hard work that had taken Hawick back up. 'This hasn't happened by accident,' he pointed out. 'It's been three years in the making.' His comments could also have been read as a forecast of more to come.

Certainly, Hawick have youngsters such as Nikki Walker, Morrice Dillon, and Neil Stenhouse for the future . . . unless, of course, they sign professional contracts. A trio of Kiwis – Joe Edwards, Barrie Keown and Craig Dunlea – added mettle to the blend of local youth and experience.

Stenhouse was a notably reliable goal-kicker as the club's top scorer in the league. His 237 points included no fewer than 27 from eight penalty goals and a drop goal in the 32-15 victory over Jed-Forest at Riverside Park.

Hawick, though unbeaten in the league, did not lead the table from start to finish. A 12-all draw with Currie in a try-less match at Malleny Park was no foretaste of what was to come from Hawick.

Heriot's, champions for the two previous seasons, set the early pace with wins against Jed, Gala, and Hawks, but when the Edinburgh club lost at home to Currie by 10-20 Hawick went ahead in the table with a 21-10 win against Jed-Forest at Mansfield Park. It was a lead they were not to relinquish, even though their winning run was interrupted with another draw. Back in Edinburgh – as on the opening day – they were held 23-all, this time at Meggetland against Boroughmuir.

Eventually Hawick were so far ahead that they were even presented with the trophy before they were 100% certain of winning it. That was after their home win against Gala by 31-9 in mid-March, but their celebrations were held back for only a couple of weeks, when they made certain by beating Hawks in Glasgow.

At the end of the campaign, Hawick were 14 points clear of second-placed Melrose. Jed-Forest and Watsonians were relegated.

Final BT Scotland Premiership League Table 2000-01

	P	W	D	L	F	A	Bonus	Pts
Hawick	18	16	2	0	559	244	6	74
Melrose	18	12	1	5	501	288	10	60
Boroughmuir	18	10	2	6	572	365	10	54
Heriot's FP	18	8	1	9	398	377	10	44
Currie	18	8	2	8	350	379	7	43
Glasgow Hawks	18	8	0	10	355	383	8	40
Gala	18	8	0	10	372	433	7	39
Kirkcaldy	18	8	0	10	412	475	7	39
Jed-Forest	18	8	0	10	323	437	5	37
Watsonians	18	0	0	18	251	712	4	4

Four points awarded for a win; two for a draw and none for a defeat.

Previous Scottish League Champions: 1973-74 Hawick; 1974-75 Hawick; 1975-76 Hawick; 1976-77 Hawick; 1977-78 Hawick; 1978-79 Heriot's FP; 1979-80 Gala; 1980-81 Gala; 1981-82 Hawick; 1982-83 Gala; 1983-84 Hawick; 1984-85 Hawick; 1985-86 Hawick; 1986-87 Hawick; 1987-88 Kelso; 1988-89 Kelso; 1989-90 Melrose; 1990-91 Boroughmuir; 1991-92 Melrose; 1992-93 Melrose; 1993-94 Melrose; 1994-95 Stirling County; 1995-96 Melrose; 1996-97 Melrose; 1997-98 Watsonians; 1998-99 Heriot's FP; 1999-2000 Heriot's FP; 2000-01 Hawick.

BOROUGHMUIR'S BACK-TO-BACK SUCCESS: THE BT CELLNET CUP

Bill McMurtrie

28 April 2001, Murrayfield
Boroughmuir 39 (2G 5PG 2T)   **Melrose 15** (1G 1PG 1T)

Boroughmuir re-established themselves in the top flight of Scottish club rugby with victory over Melrose in the BT Cellnet Cup final at Murrayfield. Scoring four tries to two, they became the first club to win the national knock-out competition two years in a row.

A year earlier they had added the cup to the Premiership's second-division title, clearly marking their return after a season out of the top flight. Last season, the cup was more than ample compensation for finishing only third in the league behind Hawick and Melrose.

Final victory was a personal success for Calvin Howarth, Boroughmuir's New Zealand fly-half. Not only did he score 24 points, but he also created much with the precision of his passing. Derek Stark was the last of Boroughmuir's four try-scorers to benefit from Howarth's skills, the fly-half sending the former international wing in at the right corner to complete what was personally an historic day. It was Stark's fourth final, and he had been on the winning side each time – with Melrose in 1997, then Glasgow Hawks a year later as well as the two with Boroughmuir.

Melrose had the final's opening score, a penalty goal by Calum MacRae, and they were in the hunt for much of the first half, leading 8-3 after Alan Kent had rumbled over for a try after 20 minutes. However, Howarth equalised by looping Mark Murray and Malcolm Clapperton to score in the right corner, and the fly-half added his second and third penalty goals before half-time.

Howarth's sleight of hand sent Lindsay Graham through for the holders' second try nine minutes into the second half, and two more penalty goals by the stand-off meant that 'Muir were secure at 27-8 after an hour. Those two goals bracketed the dismissal of Tom Weir, the Melrose No 8, and the short-handed Borderers had no way back, though Bruce Ruthven nipped over from a close-range ruck to cut the 'Muir lead to 27-15 before tries by Murray and Stark in the last 10 minutes put matters beyond doubt.

Boroughmuir played only one of their half-dozen cup-ties at home, and three of those six were against fellow Edinburgh clubs – Royal High, Stewart's Melville, and Heriot's. However, all bar one of the winning margins were in double figures, the exception being the 22-20 victory against Aberdeen Grammar School FP. 'Muir followed up at home with a 30-20 semi-final win against Heriot's. At the same stage Melrose, also at home, edged their fellow Borderers, Hawick, by 23-22.

Boroughmuir: A Sievewright; D Stark, M Clapperton, L Graham, M Murray; C Howarth, C Cusiter; A Green, D Cunningham, S Penman (*captain*),

A Davidson, G McCallum, C Capaldi, B Fisher, O Brown *Substitutions:* D Rutterford for Green (46 mins); A Ness for McCallum (68 mins); N Bruce for Brown (71 mins); R Couper for Murray (76 mins); S Ruddick for Sievewright (78 mins); D Roberts for Cusiter (78 mins); T McGhee for Penman (78 mins)

Scorers *Tries:* Howarth, Graham, Murray, Stark *Conversions:* Howarth (2) *Penalty Goals:* Howarth (5)

Melrose: A Petzer; G Caldwell, B Ruthven, C MacRae, A Clark; S Ruthven, R Chrystie; I Cornwall, K Allan (*captain*), A Kent, R Brown, S Aitken, S Bennet, T Weir, J Dalziel *Substitutions:* M Dungait for Chrystie (53 mins); J Henderson for Bennet (56 mins); K Brown for Aitken (76 mins)

Scorers *Tries:* Kent, B Ruthven *Conversion:* MacRae *Penalty Goal:* MacRae

Referee R Dickson (SRU)

Results

Third round: Aberdeenshire 20, Grangemouth 45; Alloa 0, Peebles 101; Ardrossan Academicals 29, Edinburgh Academicals 5; Berwick 104, Clydebank 0; Biggar 39, Whitecraigs 3; Cambuslang 21, Murrayfield Wanderers 64; Currie 54, Portobello FP 14; Dalziel 3, Watsonians 36; Dundee HSFP 41, Hamilton 17; Duns 15, Kirkcaldy 34; East Kilbride 21, Glenrothes 0; Glasgow Southern 28, Garnock 3; Gordonians 39, Stewartry 25; Haddington 8, Ayr 45; Hawick 50, Irvine 3; Hawick YM 17, Hutchesons'/Aloysians 26; Helensburgh 7, Aberdeen GSFP 40; Hillhead/Jordanhill 11, Perthshire 10; Jed-Forest 34, Madras College FP 10; Kelso 105, Allan Glen's 7; Kilmarnock Falcons 24, Dunfermline 22; Langholm 0, Glasgow Hawks 43; Linlithgow 12, Melrose 58; Lismore 7, Stirling County 68; Livingston 15, Selkirk 32; Musselburgh 19, Annan 3; Preston Lodge FP 11, Corstorphine 20; Royal High 7, Boroughmuir 85; St Andrews University 13, Heriot's FP 75; Stewart's Melville FP 40, St Boswells 7; Strathendrick 5, Gala 7; West of Scotland 37, Ross High 19.

Fourth round: Ardrossan Academicals 10, Gordonians 5; Ayr 12, West of Scotland 6; Biggar 10, Hillhead/Jordanhill 7; Dundee HSFP 5, Selkirk 10; East Kilbride 58, Corstorphine 6; Glasgow Hawks 16, Melrose 26; Glasgow Southern 8, Currie 24; Hawick 18, Kirkcaldy 6; Heriot's FP 55, Peebles 5; Hutchesons'/Aloysians 21, Musselburgh 15; Kelso 19, Gala 32; Kilmarnock Falcons 18, Jed-Forest 15; Murrayfield Wanderers 31, Berwick 22; Stewart's Melville FP 12, Boroughmuir 43; Stirling County 5, Aberdeen GSFP 18; Watsonians 32, Grangemouth 30.

Fifth round: Ardrossan Academicals 13, Aberdeen GSFP 76; Hawick 45, Kilmarnock Falcons 12; Heriot's FP 45, East Kilbride 22; Hutchesons'/Aloysians 0, Boroughmuir 29; Melrose 49, Ayr 13; Murrayfield Wanderers 53, Gala 30; Selkirk 16, Biggar 11; Watsonians 0, Currie 23.

Quarter-finals: Aberdeen GSFP 20, Boroughmuir 22; Currie 12, Hawick 18; Heriot's FP 50, Murrayfield Wanderers 20; Selkirk 16, Melrose 33.

Semi-finals: Boroughmuir 30, Heriot's FP 20; Melrose 23, Hawick 22.

Final: (at Murrayfield) Boroughmuir 39, Melrose 15

Previous SRU Cup Finals: 1996 Hawick 17, Watsonians 15; 1997 Melrose 31, Boroughmuir 23; 1998 Glasgow Hawks 36, Kelso 14; 1999 Gala 8, Kelso 3; 2000 Boroughmuir 35, Glasgow Hawks 10; 2001 Boroughmuir 39, Melrose 15.

All played at Murrayfield

DOMESTIC RUGBY IN IRELAND 2000-01

Three provinces into Europe: Guinness Inter-Pro Championship

Jonathan McConnell

Munster reaffirmed their dominance of Irish provincial rugby by collecting their third consecutive Guinness Interprovincial title and narrowly missed a 100% record when they drew with Leinster in the final game. However, by that stage they had wrapped the title up in emotional circumstances as captain Mick Galwey marked the occasion of his 100th Munster appearance with a 29-21 win over Ulster in the penultimate game.

With only the top two finishers guaranteed a place in the 2001-02 Heineken Cup, the competition was always going to be fierce and the opening round produced two close run encounters. Munster had to rely on the boot of Ronan O'Gara to see them scrape past Ulster in a real forward battle at Ravenhill. In the other game Connacht promised to produce a surprise in Dublin against Leinster, but after the visitors' captain, Mark McConnell, was sent off for foul play the home side were able to turn the screw and won 21-15.

The western province, as so often in the past, were to finish the tournament in last place, but showed some real signs of revival under the control of South African Steph Nel. The high point of their season came when they collected their only win in the return fixture against Leinster. It was Leinster's fifth defeat in six visits to the Galway Sportsground and was to ultimately condemn them to third place. The Dublin-based side had struggled with injuries in the pre-season – most notably at outside-half – and used four different players in the No 10 shirt during the six Interprovincial games.

Leinster's European qualification was to be secured by both themselves and Munster qualifying for the European Cup quarter finals – thus giving Ireland a third place in this year's competition.

Ulster took no chances on awaiting the possibility of a third European qualification place by recovering from a 19-6 defeat against Leinster in Dublin with a much more convincing 26-13 win in the return fixture the following week. This was to be Harry Williams's last season in charge of the 1999 European Champions and they tried to play some attractive rugby throughout the series, with David Humphreys central to their open style. They produced the competition's top two try scorers in James Topping and Andy Ward, and Humphreys was also top points scorer collecting 74 points in the six games.

Champions Munster were again a class above the competition – seemingly able to up their game as necessary. Their side, as always, was built around local players, with Cork Constitution's Mick O'Driscoll ably stepping into the void left by an ankle ligament injury to Australian second-row John Langford in their second game.

Final Irish Interprovincial Championship Table 2000–01

Team	P	W	D	L	For	Against	Bonus	Total
Munster	6	5	1	0	151	99	1	23
Ulster	6	3	0	3	144	119	3	15
Leinster	6	2	1	3	109	111	2	12
Connacht	6	1	0	5	100	175	1	5

Four points for a win, two for a draw and none for a loss.

Previous Irish Interprovincial Champions: 1946-47 Ulster; 1947-48 Munster; 1948-49 Leinster; 1949-50 Leinster; 1950-51 Ulster; 1951-52 Ulster; 1952-53 Ulster & Munster (Shared); 1953-54 Ulster; 1954-55 Munster & Leinster (Shared); 1955-56 Ulster & Connacht (Shared); 1956-57 Ulster & Leinster & Connacht (Shared); 1957-58 Munster; 1958-59 Leinster; 1959-60 Munster; 1960-61 Leinster; 1961-62 Leinster; 1962-63 Munster; 1963-64 Leinster; 1964-65 Leinster; 1965-66 Munster; 1966-67 Ulster & Munster (Shared); 1967-68 Ulster; 1968-69 Munster; 1969-70 Ulster; 1970-71 Ulster; 1971-72 Leinster; 1972-73 Leinster & Ulster & Munster (Shared); 1973-74 Munster; 1974-75 Ulster; 1975-76 Leinster & Ulster & Munster (Shared); 1976-77 Ulster; 1977-78 Leinster & Ulster & Munster (Shared); 1978-79 Munster; 1979-80 Leinster; 1980-81 Leinster; 1981-82 Leinster; 1982-83 Leinster & Ulster & Munster (Shared); 1983-84 Leinster; 1984-85 Ulster; 1985-86 Ulster; 1986-87 Ulster; 1987-88 Ulster; 1988-89 Ulster; 1989-90 Ulster; 1990-91 Ulster; 1991-92 Ulster; 1992-93 Ulster; 1993-94 Leinster & Ulster & Munster (Shared); 1994-95 Munster; 1995-96 Leinster; 1996-97 Munster; 1997-98 Leinster; 1998-99 Munster; 1999-2000 Munster; 2000-01 Munster

IRISH PROVINCES DIRECTORY
(Irish Interprovincial Championship only)

Connacht

Year of formation 1884
Ground The Sports Ground, Galway, Republic of Ireland
Contacts Tel: 00353 91 770236
Colours Green shirts, white shorts
Captain 2000-01 Mark McConnell
Irish Interprovincial Championship 2000-01 4th

Irish Interprovincial Championship Record 2000-01

Date	Venue	Opponents	Result	Scorers
1 Sep	A	Leinster	15-21	*PG:* Elwood 5
8 Sep	H	Ulster	15-39	*T:* Lee, Elwood *C:* Elwood *PG:* Elwood
15 Sep	A	Munster	13-36	*T:* Charlie *C:* Elwood *PG:* Elwood 2
23 Sep	H	Munster	13-23	*T:* Elwood *C:* Elwood *PG:* Elwood 2
30 Sep	H	Leinster	22-20	*T:* Brown, Duignan *PG:* Elwood 4
3 Nov	A	Ulster	22-36	*T:* O'Connor, Munn, Schoemann *C:* Munn 2 *PG:* Munn

Leinster

Year of formation 1879
Ground Donnybrook, Dublin 4, Republic of Ireland
Contacts Tel: 003531 6689599
Colours Blue shirts, white shorts,
Captain 2000-01 Liam Toland
Irish Interprovincial Championship 2000-01 3rd

Irish Interprovincial Championship Record 2000-01

Date	Venue	Opponents	Result	Scorers
1 Sep	H	Connacht	21-15	*T:* Costello, Smith, Hickie *PG:* Dempsey 2
8 Sep	A	Munster	20-26	*T:* D'Arcy, Smith *C:* Dempsey 2 *PG:* Dempsey 2
15 Sep	H	Ulster	19-6	*T:* Hickie *C:* McHugh *PG:* McHugh 2, Dempsey *DG:* O'Meara
22 Sep	A	Ulster	13-26	*T:* McHugh *C:* McHugh *PG:* McHugh *DG:* O'Driscoll
30 Sep	A	Connacht	20-22	*T:* Cullen *PG:* McHugh 4 *DG:* Dunne
3 Nov	H	Munster	16-16	*T:* D'Arcy *C:* Hekenui *PG:* Hekenui 3

Munster

Year of formation 1879
Ground Musgrave Park, Pearse Road, Cork, / Thomond Park, Limerick, Republic of Ireland
Contacts Tel: 00353 214 501533
Colours Red shirts, white shorts
Captain 2000-01 Mick Galwey
Irish Interprovincial Championship 2000-01 Winners

Irish Interprovincial Championship Record 2000-01

Date	Venue	Opponents	Result	Scorers
1 Sep	A	Ulster	21-16	*PG:* O'Gara 5 *DG:* O'Gara 2
8 Sep	H	Leinster	26-20	*T:* Wallace, Kelly *C:* O'Gara 2 *PG:* O'Gara 4

15 Sep	H	Connacht	36-13	T: Crotty, Wallace, McMahon, Foley, Mullins C: O'Gara 2, Staunton 2 PG: Staunton
23 Sep	A	Connacht	23-13	T: Holland PG: Staunton 6
29 Sep	H	Ulster	29-21	T: Crotty, Horgan C: O'Gara 2 PG: O'Gara 5
3 Nov	A	Leinster	16-16	T: Langford C: Staunton PG: Keane 2, Staunton

Ulster

Year of formation 1880
Ground Ravenhill Grounds, 85 Ravenhill Park, Belfast BT6 0DG, Northern Ireland
Contacts Tel: 02890 649141
Colours White shirts with red crest and white shorts
Captain 2000-01 David Humphreys
Irish Interprovincial Championship 2000-01 2nd

Irish Interprovincial Championship Record 2000-01

Date	Venue	Opponents	Result	Scorers
1 Sep	H	Munster	16-21	T: Ward C: Humphreys PG: Humphreys 3
8 Sep	A	Connacht	39-15	T: Nelson, Johns, Bell, J Topping, Stewart C: Humphreys 4 PG: Humphreys 2
15 Sep	A	Leinster	6-19	PG: Humphreys 2
22 Sep	H	Leinster	26-13	T: J Topping, Ward C: Humphreys 2 PG: Humphreys 4
29 Sep	A	Munster	21-29	T: J Topping, Free C: Humphreys PG: Humphreys 3
3 Nov	H	Connacht	36-22	T: Blair 2, J Topping, Humphreys, Ward C: Humphreys 4 PG: Humphreys

CONSTITUTION HEAD THE LEAGUE BUT DUNGANNON TAKE THE TITLE: AIB CHAMPIONSHIP

Jonathan McConnell

Although they ultimately lost to Dungannon in the play off final, Cork Constitution were the class side for much of the 2000-01 AIB All Ireland League campaign, finishing the 15-game campaign seven points clear of nearest rivals Galwegians, who were in their first season in the top division.

Many of the clubs were without their International players for much of the season, as the Irish management imposed an upper limit on Test players' games for their clubs. The season was also thrown into chaos by pre-Christmas postponements owing to bad weather and the subsequent blanket ban on all rugby resulting from the foot-and-mouth epidemic in the United Kingdom. This led to a very congested end to the season with three games for most sides in the final week of the normal league schedule.

Constitution had stated their intentions with an emphatic 43-5 win over newly promoted Belfast Harlequins on the first weekend and maintained an unbeaten record until March when they were beaten at Dungannon. Mid March also saw Galwegians lose for the first time – but not before the Connacht club had taken an impressive series of scalps including eventual champions Dungannon. Galwegians had been promoted alongside Black-rock and Belfast Harlequins and although Blackrock secured mid-table respectability it was a much more difficult season for Harlequins. The recently formed amalgamation of Belfast clubs NIFC and Collegians came close to victory against two former Champions, St Mary's and Shannon, but were never able to string together a strong run which could have secured their future in the top flight.

The 1999-2000 champions, St Mary's, never recovered from opening defeats against Young Munster and at Dungannon, and despite a strong finish ended six points short of the play-off places, while the most prolific AIL side, Shannon, had a disappointing season by their usual standards. They were hit harder than most by the absence of Test players and had a difficult finish to the season. They played their final five games in a 17-day period, defeats by Lansdowne and lowly Old Crescent in the last two games costing them dearly.

The unluckiest side in the battle for the play off places was Ballymena, who had been amongst the leaders for most of the season. André Bester's side defeated Galwegians in a tight battle in early April and looked set to join Dungannon as a second Ulster side in the last four. However, a home defeat by Young Munster was enough to see the Limerick club leap-frog their Ulster rivals into the play-offs.

Final Table

	P	W	D	L	F	A	BP	Pts
Cork Constitution	15	12	0	3	420	265	10	58
Galwegians	15	11	0	4	338	254	7	51
Dungannon	15	10	1	4	435	283	8	50
Young Munster	15	10	0	5	364	241	8	48
Ballymena	15	8	1	6	384	326	10	44
St Mary's College	15	9	1	5	302	276	4	42
Garryowen	15	7	2	6	317	343	4	36
Shannon	15	7	1	7	347	307	5	35
Blackrock College	15	7	1	7	317	302	5	35
Terenure College	15	6	1	8	323	358	4	30
Clontarf	15	6	0	9	343	442	5	29
Lansdowne	15	5	2	8	259	300	4	28
Buccaneers	15	5	0	10	267	334	6	26
D.L.S.P.	15	5	0	10	266	382	4	24
Old Crescent	15	4	0	11	306	422	5	21
Belfast Harlequins	15	3	0	12	265	418	7	19

Four points for a win, two for a draw and none for a loss.

AIB All Ireland League Final

26 May 2001, Lansdowne Road, Dublin
Cork Constitution 12 (3PG 1DG)   **Dungannon 46** (4G 5PG 1DG)

Dungannon became the first Ulster club to win the AIB All Ireland League title when they defeated Cork Constitution, who had been the class act for much of the season, 46-12 at Lansdowne Road in May. The County Tyrone club came into the game on the back of nine league wins out of ten and never permitted their opponents to settle in a high-scoring final.

The first-up tackling by the Ulster back row of Alastair Boyd, Mike Haslett and Tony McWhirter was excellent and they totally disrupted the Cork line-out throughout a first half that they dominated in terms of both possession and points.

Although Conor Mahony, standing in for Lion Ronan O'Gara at outside-half, opened the scoring with an early drop goal, this was soon negated by some excellent place kicking from man-of-the-match David Humphreys, who finished with 26 points. Two penalties from Brian O'Meara left the score line at 9-9 at the end of the first quarter before Dungannon struck the telling blow. Continued pressure forced O'Meara to fumble at a scrum near his line and Stephen Bell pounced on the loose ball for the game's opening try and a 16-9 lead at the break.

Within 10 minutes of the re-start, Humphreys knocked over a penalty and dropped a goal to stretch the lead to 22-9. Constitution were never able to get back on terms as they struggled to contain Dungannon's free flowing three-quarters and a second try for Willie Anderson's side came when Humphreys found Tony McWhirter in midfield. The Ulster No 8 did well to off-load to Jonathan Bell in the tackle and the Test centre strolled in unopposed to open a 20-point margin. Dungannon became increasingly adventurous in the closing stages and tries from Alastair Boyd and Tyrone Howe completed the scoring.

In the semi-finals Constitution had produced a controlled forward display and some solid defending to see off Young Munster 18-10 while Dungannon produced a comfortable 31-29 win over Galwegians.

Cork Constitution: B Walsh; D Dillon, J Kelly (*captain*), R O'Donovan, D O'Dowd; Conor Mahony, B O'Meara; I Murray, F Sheahan, J O'Driscoll, K Murphy, M O'Driscoll, C Taylor, D O'Callaghan, J Murray *Substitutions:* Cian Mahony for O'Donovan (50 mins); U O'Callaghan for Murphy (50 mins); N Kenneally for Dillon (53 mins); R McGrath for O'Driscoll (72 mins); J Fogarty for Murray (72 mins)

Scorers *Penalty Goals:* O'Mera (3) *Drop Goal:* Conor Mahony

Dungannon: B Cunningham; J Cunningham, R Constable, J Bell, T Howe; D Humphreys, S Bell; J Fitzpatrick, N Brady, G Leslie, P Johns (*captain*), A Kearney, A Boyd, T McWhirter, M Haslett *Substitutions:* A Hughes for Haslett (62 mins); R Mackey for Leslie (62 mins); A Clarke for J Bell (75 mins); R Mercer for S Bell (77 mins); S Elkinson for Brady (77 mins); K Walker for Kearney (77 mins)

Scorers *Tries:* S Bell, J Bell, Clarke, Howe *Conversions:* Humphreys (4) *Penalty Goals:* Humphreys (5) *Drop Goal:* Humphreys

Referee A Rolland (IRFU)

Previous All-Ireland Champions: 1990-91 Cork Constitution; 1991-92 Garryowen; 1992-93 Young Munster; 1993-94 Garryowen; 1994-95 Shannon; 1995-96 Shannon; 1996-97 Shannon; 1997-98 Shannon; 1998-99 Cork Constitution; 1999-2000 St Mary's; 2000-01 Dungannon

DOMESTIC RUGBY IN WALES 2000-01

Swansea's Rally Wins Title: The Welsh-Scottish League

John Billot

Cardiff, winners of their opening five games, had an alluring appearance of being the form horses for the title. Swansea, in contrast, stuttered losing three of their first five fixtures while Llanelli limped off with three successive defeats during their initial four matches. Could it be that Bridgend, as outsiders, would follow an impressive launch of five consecutive victories by outpacing the big three? In the event, Swansea's recovery, after critical analysis, brought them top spot in this second season of the Welsh/Scottish league. They incurred just one further failure in the course of their last 17 games and became Welsh/Scottish champions for the first time. No team won a league game at St Helen's.

It was an exceptional turnaround and reward for an exciting team full of tingling pace out wide, menacing midfield penetration and scrum power that hustled most opponents into harassed retreat. There was no shortage of quality possession from a superbly blended pack with Paul Moriarty, almost of 'pensionable age', setting the younger players an inspiring example. Scott Gibbs, retained as captain, was a cagey director of operations, though it was Arwel Thomas, instinctive and artful, who called the tunes. He contributed 172 league points until injury forced him out for much of the second half of the season. Then Swansea enjoyed another talented fly-half in Cerith Rees, recruited from Neath, and, later, Gavin Henson, for whom a glowing future is forecast.

The front-row of Ben Evans, Garin Jenkins and Darren Morris proved a dominating influence while Colin Charvis yet again demonstrated his perception, pugnacity and pace in a back-row of inestimable value. His 13 tries were more than any other forward in the league. Wings Shaun Payne (16 tries) and Matthew Robinson (13) were smooth searchers for overlaps and the tally of 102 tries was 26 more than challengers Cardiff and Llanelli could claim. Swansea also achieved what no other Welsh club accomplished – victories against Glasgow Caledonians and Edinburgh Reivers on Scottish soil. That troubled beginning had been something of a smokescreen!

Cardiff, as runners-up, were always subject to a hiccup or two, as witnessed in losing to Bridgend by 24-19 in their only home defeat and failing by 12-7 at struggling Ebbw Vale. After crushing Llanelli by 65-16 in the Principality Cup, Cardiff returned to Stradey and fell victims by 34-25. Overall, it was considered they had underachieved again.

David Young continued as captain and also led Wales and there was the customary substantial contribution from Neil Jenkins with 235 points. Craig Morgan caught the eye on the wing with 15 tries and Rob Howley was back to his bristling best. New signings included South Africans Pieter Müller, Wayne Fyvie and Kenneth Fourie while Peter Rogers joined from Newport, though he saw little action because of loss of form. Liam Botham left to join Newcastle and others to depart were Leigh Davies (Bristol and then Llanelli), Simon Hill and Lyndon Mustoe (Bridgend), Steve Williams (London Irish) and Paul Burke (Harlequins). Cardiff opened their season with a Champion of Champions fixture against England's top team and defeated Leicester 29-17 at the Arms Park.

Llanelli's bleak start stunned their supporters and another blip occurred during mid-season with four defeats in five games. Inevitably, that put them out of the running; yet their revival was praiseworthy as they won their closing seven matches, including Neath and Cardiff among their victims. Scott Quinnell, as new captain, was always capable of a big performance and Stephen Jones headed the division scoring chart with 279 points. Dafydd James crossed for 13 tries and Llanelli were disappointed to lose him for the current season. Swansea, by 23-22, and Glasgow Caledonians, by 16-10, were the only league rivals to taste victory at Stradey.

Newport kept Gary Teichmann as leader and reinforced the side with Ian Gough (returning from Pontypridd), Ireland wing Matt Mostyn, Natal prop Adrian Garvey, Peter Buxton, from Moseley, Italy full-back Matt Pini and Darren Edwards (London Welsh). Cardiff and Glasgow Caledonians were the only teams to succeed at Rodney Parade, but Newport lost three of their last five games. Fijian Simon Raiwalui, who enjoyed a notable season, followed Teichmann as captain for the current season.

Bridgend made a marked improvement with a new half-back combination of Huw Harries, a commanding scrum-half who was accorded the captaincy, and cool Craig Warlow, from Llanelli, who finished with an impressive 252 points. Josh Taumalolo was an important recruit from Ebbw Vale and a bevy of key players have been signed for the current season, including Dafydd James (from Llanelli), Gareth Thomas (Cardiff), Cerith Rees (Swansea) and Nathan Budgett (Ebbw Vale). They promise a strong challenge.

With their finances in a bit of a tangle, Neath were taken over by a Welsh Rugby Union management team with Union secretary Dennis Gethin as Chairman and Union Chairman Glanmor Griffiths as one of the directors. Gareth Llewellyn returned from Harlequins to lead them. Only Cardiff (by 18-12) and Llanelli (by 10-3) triumphed at the Gnoll.

Pontypridd's decline was disappointing, though their power-base had been steadily eroded by key players leaving for fresh pastures. The irrepressible Paul John, however, remained and captained them again. Lee Jarvis, scorer of 171 points, has joined Neath, but Pontypridd have a highly promising man for the fly-half role in Ceri Sweeney.

Caerphilly, under the command of Nathan Jones, possessed a clever fly-half in Luke Richards, who scored 167 points, and Andrew Williams was a 10-try forward. Their 33-all home draw with Neath was a particularly notable feat and they defeated Ebbw Vale, but it proved a dismal season. Cross Keys, with only one victory, finished bottom of the table and were relegated. Steve Gardner led in lively style, but they lost their record scorer, Ioan Bebb, forced to retire after a punch from Bridgend's Chris Stephens in their opening match caused serious facial and eye injuries. Stephens admitted grievous bodily harm in court proceedings and was ordered to do 200 hours community service and pay £2000 in compensation.

Glasgow Caledonians and Edinburgh Reivers, though failing in Wales, proved stubborn opponents on home territory. Duncan Hodge chalked up 183 points for Edinburgh while Tommy Hayes supplied 153 of Glasgow's points.

Final Welsh–Scottish League Table 2000-01

Team	P	W	D	L	For	Against	Tries	Pts
Swansea	22	18	0	4	844	377	102	54
Cardiff	22	16	0	6	665	410	76	48
Llanelli	22	14	0	8	663	484	76	42
Newport	22	14	0	8	660	388	71	42
Bridgend	22	13	0	9	637	479	71	39
Neath	22	12	1	9	639	543	76	37
Glasgow Caledonians	22	12	0	10	645	608	78	36
Edinburgh Reivers	22	11	0	11	540	667	55	33
Pontypridd	22	10	0	12	635	541	66	30
Caerphilly	22	5	1	16	464	729	52	16
Ebbw Vale	22	5	0	17	428	741	44	15
Cross Keys	22	1	0	21	247	1100	32	3

Three points awarded for a win; one for a draw and none for a defeat.

Previous Welsh–Scottish League Champions: 1999-2000 Cardiff; 2000-01 Swansea

WELSH CLUB DIRECTORY (WELSH–SCOTTISH LEAGUE CLUBS ONLY)

Bridgend

Year of formation 1878
Ground Brewery Field, Tondu Road, Bridgend, Mid Glamorgan, CF31 4JE, Wales
Contacts Web: www.bridgendrfc.com Tel: Bridgend (01656) 652707
Colours Blue and white hoops
Captain 2000-01 Huw Harries
Welsh–Scottish League 2000-01 5th
Principality Cup 2000-01 Lost 21-23 to Neath (quarter-final)

Welsh–Scottish League Record 2000-01

Date	Venue	Opponents	Result	Scorers
26 Aug	A	Cross Keys	37-12	*T:* Taumalolo, Hill, Molitika, Lloyd *C:* Warlow 4 *PG:* Warlow 3
2 Sep	H	Llanelli	41-30	*T:* G Jones, Taumalolo, Hill, Warlow *C:* Warlow 3 *PG:* Warlow 4 *DG:* Warlow
5 Sep	H	Glasgow Caledonians	49-27	*T:* Molitika 2, Durston, G Jones, Taumalolo, Collier, Ringer *C:* Warlow 4 *PG:* Warlow 2
9 Sep	H	Edinburgh Reivers	25-3	*T:* Harries, Molitika, Bryan *C:* Cull, Warlow *PG:* Warlow 2
16 Sep	A	Ebbw Vale	48-15	*T:* G Jones, Taumalolo, Hill, Ferris, Ringer *C:* Warlow 4 *PG:* Warlow 3 *DG:* Warlow 2
23 Sep	A	Cardiff	33-37	*T:* G Jones 2, Hill *C:* Warlow 3 *PG:* Warlow 4
30 Sep	A	Newport	29-34	*T:* D Jones 2, Taumalolo, G Jones *C:* Warlow 3 *PG:* Taumalolo
4 Nov	A	Pontypridd	20-38	*T:* Warlow, pen try *C:* Warlow 2 *DG:* Warlow 2
2 Dec	H	Caerphilly	46-13	*T:* Durston 3, Taumalolo, D Jones, van Rensburg *C:* Warlow 4, Cull *PG:* Warlow 2
5 Dec	H	Cross Keys	67-0	*T:* P Williams 2, O Ford, Taumalolo, G Jones, Durston, Molitika, van Rensburg, Niblo *C:* Cull 8 *PG:* Cull 2
9 Dec	A	Llanelli	27-30	*T:* G Jones, Bryan, van Rensburg *C:* Warlow 3 *PG:* Warlow *DG:* Warlow
16 Dec	H	Neath	28-18	*T:* G Jones, Durston, Molitika *C:* Warlow 2 *PG:* Cull 2 *DG:* Warlow
22 Dec	A	Edinburgh Reivers	13-23	*T:* Mustoe *C:* Cull *PG:* Cull 2
10 Feb	A	Cardiff	24-19	*T:* Peters, Ringer, Molitika *C:* Warlow 3 *DG:* Warlow
20 Feb	H	Ebbw Vale	24-12	*T:* Harries 2, Warlow *C:* Warlow 3 *PG:* Warlow
10 Mar	H	Newport	9-35	*PG:* Warlow 3
31 Mar	H	Pontypridd	16-13	*T:* Mustoe *C:* Warlow *PG:* Warlow 3
20 Apr	A	Glasgow Caledonians	22-15	*T:* Ringer *C:* Warlow *PG:* Warlow 4 *DG:* Warlow
28 Apr	H	Swansea	16-34	*T:* Devereux *C:* Warlow *PG:* Warlow 3
1 May	A	Neath	12-13	*T:* Hewlett, S Ford *C:* P Williams
5 May	A	Caerphilly	31-23	*T:* Warlow 2, G Jones, van Rensburg *C:* Warlow *PG:* Warlow 3
9 May	A	Swansea	20-35	*T:* P Williams, Lloyd *C:* Cull 2 *PG:* Cull 2

Caerphilly

Year of formation 1886
Ground Virginia Park, Pontygwindy Road, Caerphilly, CF83 3JA, Wales
Contacts Web: www.caerphillyrfc.co.uk Tel: Caerphilly (02920) 865077

Colours Green and white hoops
Captain 2000-01 Nathan Jones
Welsh–Scottish League 2000-01 10th
Principality Cup 2000-01 Lost 6-38 to Ebbw Vale (quarter-final)

Welsh–Scottish League Record 2000-01

Date	Venue	Opponents	Result	Scorers
26 Aug	H	Glasgow Caledonians	31-13	*T:* Hawkins, Workman, G Jones *C:* Richards 2 *PG:* Richards 4
2 Sep	A	Swansea	20-59	*T:* Berbillion, Williams *C:* Richards 2 *PG:* Richards 2
9 Sep	H	Cross Keys	36-3	*T:* Berbillion 2, Marshall, Williams, Fonua *C:* Richards 2, John 2 *DG:* Richards
16 Sep	A	Llanelli	26-46	*T:* J Thomas, Hawkins, Marshall, Boobyer *C:* John 3
23 Sep	H	Neath	33-33	*T:* Hawkins, Workman, Williams *C:* Richards 3 *PG:* Richards 4
1 Oct	A	Edinburgh Reivers	33-43	*T:* Marshall, Workman, Williams *C:* John 3 *PG:* John 4
4 Nov	H	Ebbw Vale	45-14	*T:* Berbillion 2, J Thomas, J Hughes, Williams *C:* Richards 4 *PG:* Richards 3 *DG:* Richards
2 Dec	A	Bridgend	13-46	*T:* A Williams *C:* Richards *PG:* Richards 2
9 Dec	H	Swansea	10-48	*T:* Mocelutu, A Williams
16 Dec	A	Pontypridd	7-41	*T:* Richards *C:* Richards
23 Dec	A	Cross Keys	27-11	*T:* A Williams 2, Workman *C:* John 3 *PG:* John 2
26 Dec	H	Llanelli	20-40	*T:* Berbillion, B Watkins *C:* Richards 2 *PG:* Richards 2
27 Jan	H	Pontypridd	12-19	*T:* J Thomas, Jacobs *C:* John
10 Feb	A	Neath	17-22	*T:* J Thomas, Hawkins, B Watkins *C:* John
3 Mar	H	Newport	8-53	*T:* G Evans *PG:* John
10 Mar	H	Edinburgh Reivers	5-15	*T:* Lewis
31 Mar	A	Ebbw Vale	22-16	*T:* G Jones *C:* Richards *PG:* Richards 5
15 Apr	A	Glasgow Caledonians	15-52	*T:* Hawkins, Lewis *C:* Richards *PG:* Richards
21 Apr	H	Cardiff	19-50	*T:* Richards *C:* Richards *PG:* Richards 4
28 Apr	A	Newport	22-31	*T:* Marshall, Bidgood, Jacobs *C:* Richards 2 *PG:* Richards
5 May	H	Bridgend	23-31	*T:* Boobyer, Hawkins *C:* Richards 2 *PG:* Richards *DG:* Richards 2
10 May	A	Cardiff	20-43	*T:* J Thomas, A Williams *C:* Richards 2 *PG:* Richards 2

Cardiff

Year of formation 1876
Ground Cardiff Arms Park, Westgate Street, Cardiff CF10 1JA, Wales
Contacts Web: www.cardiffrfc.co.uk Tel: Cardiff (02920) 302001
Colours Cambridge blue and black
Captain 2000-01 David Young
Welsh–Scottish League 2000-01 Runners-up
Principality Cup 2000-01 Lost 21-28 to Swansea (quarter-final)

Welsh–Scottish League Record 2000-01

Date	Venue	Opponents	Result	Scorers
26 Aug	H	Neath	35-30	*T:* C Morgan, Baugh *C:* Jenkins 2 *PG:* Jenkins 6 *DG:* Jenkins
2 Sep	H	Edinburgh Reivers	80-16	*T:* C Morgan 3, Robinson 2, Jenkins, Young, Walne, Moore, O Williams *C:* Jenkins 7, Rayer 2 *PG:* Jenkins 3 *DG:* Jenkins
9 Sep	A	Pontypridd	28-6	*T:* C Morgan *C:* Jenkins *PG:* Jenkins 6 *DG:* Jenkins

16 Sep	H	Newport	29-16	*T:* C Morgan, Howley *C:* Jenkins 2 *PG:* Jenkins 4 *DG:* Jenkins
23 Sep	A	Bridgend	37-33	*T:* C Morgan 2, John 2, Geraghty *C:* Jenkins 3 *PG:* Jenkins 2
29 Sep	A	Glasgow Caledonians	26-27	*T:* Howley, Walne *C:* Jenkins 2 *PG:* Jenkins 4
4 Nov	A	Swansea	22-29	*T:* P Jones, C Morgan, Walne *C:* Jenkins 2 *PG:* Jenkins
2 Dec	H	Llanelli	22-9	*T:* Rogers *C:* Jenkins *PG:* Jenkins 5
5 Dec	A	Neath	18-12	*T:* Walne 2 *C:* Jenkins *PG:* Jenkins *DG:* Jenkins
10 Dec	A	Edinburgh Reivers	11-29	*T:* Walne *PG:* Davies 2
16 Dec	H	Ebbw Vale	27-16	*T:* C Morgan, Moore, Baugh *PG:* Jenkins 4
23 Dec	H	Pontypridd	21-14	*T:* Walne 2, Jenkins *C:* Jenkins 3
26 Dec	A	Newport	23-16	*T:* Ashman, Jenkins *C:* Jenkins 2 *PG:* Jenkins 2 *DG:* Jenkins
10 Feb	H	Bridgend	19-24	*T:* C Morgan *C:* Jenkins *PG:* Jenkins 4
7 Mar	A	Ebbw Vale	7-12	*T:* Robinson *C:* Rayer
10 Mar	H	Glasgow Caledonians	31-11	*T:* C Morgan 2, R Williams, G Thomas *C:* Jenkins 4 *PG:* Jenkins
28 Mar	A	Cross Keys	33-23	*T:* R Williams 2, Ashman, R Powell *C:* Rayer, Davies *PG:* Rayer, Davies 2
31 Mar	H	Swansea	21-14	*T:* P Jones, Fourie *C:* Jenkins *PG:* Jenkins 3
21 Apr	A	Caerphilly	50-19	*T:* Ashman 2, G Powell, Davies, A Lewis, M Williams, Rayer *C:* Davies 3, Rayer 3 *PG:* Davies
28 Apr	H	Cross Keys	57-0	*T:* C Morgan 2, Quinnell 2, R Williams 2, J Robinson, G Thomas, A Lewis, E Lewis *C:* Davies 2 *PG:* Davies
5 May	A	Llanelli	25-34	*T:* J Robinson, Quinnell, Fyvie *C:* Rayer 2 *PG:* Rayer *DG:* Rayer
10 May	H	Caerphilly	43-20	*T:* G Thomas 4, J Robinson, O Williams, Sowden-Taylor *C:* Rayer 3, N Robinson

Cross Keys

Year of formation 1885
Ground Pandy Park, Cross Keys, Gwent, Wales
Contacts Tel: Ebbw Vale (01495) 270289
Colours Black and white hoops
Captain 2000-01 Steve Gardner
Welsh–Scottish League 2000-01 12th Relegated
Principality Cup 2000-01 Lost 8-31 to Aberavon (6th round)

Welsh–Scottish League Record 2000-01

Date	Venue	Opponents	Result	Scorers
26 Aug	H	Bridgend	12-37	*PG:* Bebb 4
3 Sep	A	Glasgow Caledonians	28-52	*T:* pen try, Stroud, Howarth, Stewart *C:* Webb *PG:* Webb 2
5 Sep	A	Ebbw Vale	10-49	*T:* R Lewis *C:* Webb *PG:* Webb
9 Sep	A	Caerphilly	3-36	*PG:* Webb
16 Sep	H	Pontypridd	12-60	*T:* Reed, L Gardner *C:* Singer
23 Sep	H	Llanelli	7-46	*T:* Bowen *C:* Webb
30 Sep	A	Neath	22-73	*T:* Walsh, L Gardner, Howarth *C:* Bushell 2 *PG:* Bushell
2 Dec	A	Newport	5-53	*T:* Ellis
5 Dec	A	Bridgend	0-67	
9 Dec	H	Glasgow Caledonians	3-54	*PG:* Bushell
16 Dec	A	Swansea	3-55	*PG:* Bushell
23 Dec	H	Caerphilly	11-27	*T:* Gibbs *PG:* Bushell 2
26 Dec	A	Pontypridd	19-59	*T:* Arnold, Reed, Watkins *C:* Reed, Webb
27 Jan	H	Edinburgh Reivers	16-10	*T:* Kelly, Gibbs *PG:* Bushell 2

10 Feb	A	Llanelli	22-53	T: Bai, Walsh, D Davies, Brown C: Bai
10 Mar	H	Neath	12-66	T: Arnold, L Gardner C: Bai
28 Mar	H	Cardiff	23-33	T: pen try, Kelly C: Bai 2 PG: Bai 3
1 Apr	A	Edinburgh Reivers	12-48	T: Bushell 2 C: Bai
21 Apr	H	Ebbw Vale	14-42	T: McCarthy, Hicks C: Bai 2
28 Apr	A	Cardiff	0-57	
2 May	H	Swansea	8-57	T: Arnold PG: Bai
5 May	H	Newport	5-66	T: Crane

Ebbw Vale

Year of formation 1880
Ground Eugene Cross Park, Ebbw Vale, Gwent, NP23 5AZ, Wales
Contacts Web: www.ebbwvalerfc.co.uk Tel: Ebbw Vale (01495) 302995
Colours Red, white and green
Captain 2000-01 11th
Welsh–Scottish League 2000-01 Mark Jones
Principality Cup 2000-01 Lost 12-19 to Newport (semi-final)

Welsh–Scottish League Record 2000-01

Date	Venue	Opponents	Result	Scorers
26 Aug	A	Edinburgh Reivers	25-43	T: Wagstaff 3 C: Strange 2 PG: Strange 2
2 Sep	H	Pontypridd	23-32	T: pen try, John C: Strange, Connor PG: Strange 3
5 Sep	H	Cross Keys	49-10	T: Connor 5, Shorney, M Jones C: Connor 4 PG: Connor 2
9 Sep	A	Newport	24-56	T: John, Connor, Green C: Strange 3 PG: Strange
16 Sep	H	Bridgend	15-48	T: Shorney, Connor C: Strange PG: Strange
22 Sep	A	Glasgow Caledonians	37-43	T: Potter, Hawker, B Morris, Connor C: Strange 2, Connor 2 PG: Strange 3
30 Sep	H	Swansea	6-55	PG: Strange, Connor
4 Nov	A	Caerphilly	14-45	T: Smith PG: Strange 3
2 Dec	H	Neath	10-33	T: Matthews C: Strange PG: Strange
6 Dec	H	Edinburgh Reivers	24-10	T: Matthews, Hawker C: Strange PG: Strange 4
9 Dec	A	Pontypridd	0-54	
16 Dec	A	Cardiff	16-27	T: Smith C: Strange PG: Strange 3
23 Dec	H	Newport	10-19	T: John C: Strange PG: Strange
26 Jan	A	Llanelli	15-42	T: Connor, Penisini C: Connor PG: Connor
10 Feb	H	Glasgow Caledonians	14-10	T: Shorney, L Phillips C: Connor, Strange
20 Feb	A	Bridgend	12-24	PG: Connor 2 DG: Connor 2
7 Mar	H	Cardiff	12-7	PG: Strange 4
10 Mar	A	Swansea	17-68	T: Wagstaff 2 C: Connor 2 PG: Strange
31 Mar	H	Caerphilly	16-22	T: M Jones C: Strange PG: Strange 3
21 Apr	A	Cross Keys	42-14	T: Shorney 3, Matthews, Green C: Strange 4 PG: Strange 2, Connor
28 Apr	H	Llanelli	14-43	T: Shorney, R Smith C: Connor 2
4 May	A	Neath	33-36	T: John, Shorney, Green C: Connor 3 PG: Connor 4

Llanelli

Year of formation 1872
Ground Stradey Park, Llanelli, Dyfed SA15 4BT, Wales
Contacts Web: www.scarlets.co.uk Tel: Llanelli (01554) 783900
Colours Scarlet and white
Captain 2000-01 Scott Quinnell
Welsh–Scottish League 2000-01 3rd
Principality Cup 2000-01 Lost 16-65 to Cardiff (7th round)

Welsh–Scottish League Record 2000-01

Date	Venue	Opponents	Result	Scorers
26 Aug	H	Newport	12-11	PG: S Jones 4
2 Sep	A	Bridgend	30-41	T: James, Quinnell, Lawson C: S Jones 2, Lawson PG: S Jones 3
6 Sep	A	Edinburgh Reivers	25-28	T: G Easterby C: S Jones PG: S Jones 6
9 Sep	A	Swansea	21-28	T: Evans 2, Cardey C: S Jones 3
16 Sep	H	Caerphilly	46-26	T: M Jones 2, N Boobyer 2, Evans, G Easterby, James C: Lawson 4 PG: Lawson
23 Sep	A	Cross Keys	46-7	T: M Jones 2, James, Madden, Gillies, M Thomas C: S Jones 5 PG: S Jones 2
30 Sep	H	Pontypridd	53-20	T: M Jones 2, James, Finau, Evans, D Jones C: S Jones 4 PG: S Jones 5
4 Nov	H	Neath	31-28	T: Quinnell 2, S Jones C: S Jones 2 PG: S Jones 4
2 Dec	A	Cardiff	9-22	PG: S Jones 3
5 Dec	A	Newport	9-20	PG: S Jones 3
9 Dec	H	Bridgend	30-27	T: James 2, pen try, Booth C: S Jones 2 PG: S Jones 2
17 Dec	A	Glasgow Caledonians	35-45	T: Quinnell 2, James, Wyatt C: S Jones 3 PG: S Jones 3
23 Dec	H	Swansea	22-23	T: James 2 PG: S Jones 4
26 Dec	A	Caerphilly	40-20	T: James 2, Proctor, Booth, J Davies, Quinnell C: S Jones 2 PG: S Jones 2
6 Jan	H	Glasgow Caledonians	10-16	T: S Jones C: S Jones PG: S Jones
26 Jan	H	Ebbw Vale	42-15	T: James, Finau, Proctor, Booth, Lawson C: S Jones 3, Lawson PG: S Jones 3
10 Feb	H	Cross Keys	53-22	T: G Evans 2, S Jones 2, Cardey, Proctor, James, L Davies C: Lawson 3, S Jones 2 PG: Lawson
10 Mar	A	Pontypridd	19-15	T: Hodges C: S Jones PG: S Jones 4
31 Mar	A	Neath	10-3	T: I Boobyer C: S Jones PG: S Jones
21 Apr	H	Edinburgh Reivers	43-28	T: James, Madden, Cooper, Hodges, N Boobyer C: S Jones 3 PG: S Jones 4
28 Apr	A	Ebbw Vale	43-14	T: M Jones 2, Booth 2, N Boobyer 2, L Davies C: S Jones 4
5 May	H	Cardiff	34-25	T: Cardey, Finau, C Gillies C: S Jones 2 PG: S Jones 5

Neath

Year of formation 1871
Ground The Gnoll, Gnoll Park Road, Neath, West Glamorgan SA11 3BU, Wales
Contacts Web: www.k-c.co.uk/neathrfc Tel: Neath (01639) 769660
Colours All black with white Maltese cross
Captain 2000-01 Gareth Llewellyn
Welsh–Scottish League 2000-01 6th
Principality Cup 2000-01 Lost 8-13 to Newport (FINAL)

Welsh–Scottish League Record 2000-01

Date	Venue	Opponents	Result	Scorers
26 Aug	A	Cardiff	30-35	T: D Jones, Millward C: S Williams PG: S Williams 5 DG: Brown
2 Sep	A	Newport	13-24	T: S Williams C: S Williams PG: S Williams 2
5 Sep	H	Pontypridd	33-29	T: pen try 3 C: S Williams 3 PG: S Williams 3 DG: Brown
8 Sep	A	Glasgow Caledonians	20-36	T: Tuipulotu PG: S Williams 4 DG: Brown
16 Sep	H	Neath	24-9	T: Tuipulotu, Francis C: S Williams PG: S Williams 4
23 Sep	A	Caerphilly	33-33	T: D Williams 3, S Williams 2 C: S Williams PG: S Williams 2

Date	Venue	Opponents	Result	Scorers
30 Sep	H	Cross Keys	73-22	T: Morris 3, Tuipulotu 3, S Williams 2, Horgan, pen try, Phillips C: S Williams 9
4 Nov	A	Llanelli	28-31	T: Horgan 2, Morris C: C Rees 2 PG: C Rees 3
25 Nov	H	Edinburgh Reivers	48-20	T: Tiueti, Storey, Horgan, Booth, P Jones, S Jones, K James C: Horgan 5 PG: Horgan
2 Dec	A	Ebbw Vale	33-10	T: Tiueti, S Williams, Francis C: S Williams 3 PG: S Williams 4
5 Dec	H	Cardiff	12-18	PG: S Williams 4
9 Dec	H	Newport	36-26	T: T Davies 3, Horgan, Phillips C: S Williams PG: S Williams 3
16 Dec	A	Bridgend	18-28	T: S Williams 2, Storey PG: S Williams
23 Dec	H	Glasgow Caledonians	34-29	T: D Williams, S Williams, Tuipulotu, K James C: S Williams PG: S Williams 4
26 Dec	A	Swansea	23-45	T: K James, S Jones, Bonner-Evans C: S Williams PG: S Williams 2
10 Feb	H	Caerphilly	22-17	T: Tuipulotu C: S Williams PG: S Williams 5
10 Mar	A	Cross Keys	66-12	T: K James 2, Tuipulotu 2, Morris, Storey, S Williams, D Jones, M Davies, Bonner-Evans, pen try C: Miller 4 PG: Miller
31 Mar	H	Llanelli	3-10	PG: Miller
21 Apr	A	Pontypridd	22-21	T: Horgan 2, Storey C: S Williams, Horgan DG: Miller
27 Apr	A	Edinburgh Reivers	19-43	T: Millward C: S Williams PG: S Williams 4
1 May	H	Bridgend	13-12	T: K James, Phillips PG: Miller
4 May	H	Ebbw Vale	36-33	T: K James 2, Storey, Tiueti, Tandy C: S Williams 4 PG: S Williams

Newport

Year of formation 1874
Ground Rodney Parade, Newport, Gwent NP9 0UU, Wales
Contacts Web: www.blackandambers.net Tel: Newport (01633) 670690
Colours Black and amber
Captain 2000-01 Gary Teichmann
Welsh–Scottish League 2000-01 4th
Principality Cup 2000-01 Winners Won 13-8 against Neath (FINAL)

Welsh–Scottish League Record 2000-01

Date	Venue	Opponents	Result	Scorers
26 Aug	A	Llanelli	11-12	T: Mostyn PG: Howarth 2
2 Sep	H	Neath	24-13	T: Mostyn, M Llewellyn C: Howarth PG: Howarth 3 DG: Howarth
6 Sep	H	Swansea	24-13	PG: Howarth 7, E Lewis
9 Sep	H	Ebbw Vale	56-24	T: Mostyn 2, Forster 2, Howarth, Buxton, Young C: Howarth 5, Mitchell PG: Howarth 3
16 Sep	A	Cardiff	16-29	T: Forster C: Howarth PG: Howarth 3
23 Sep	A	Pontypridd	44-22	T: Howarth 2, Pini, Mostyn, M Watkins C: Howarth 5 PG: Howarth 3
30 Sep	H	Bridgend	34-29	T: Jones-Hughes, Snow, Forster C: Howarth 2 PG: Howarth 5
2 Dec	H	Cross Keys	53-5	T: Mostyn 2, Jones-Hughes 2, E Lewis, Pritchard, Garvey, Taylor, Buxton C: Howarth 4
5 Dec	H	Llanelli	20-9	T: Forster PG: Howarth 5
9 Dec	A	Neath	26-36	T: Pini 2, E Lewis C: Howarth PG: Howarth 3
16 Dec	H	Edinburgh Reivers	55-15	T: pen try, Mostyn, Marinos, Jones-Hughes, Breeze, Garvey, Gough, Teichmann C: Howarth 6 PG: Howarth
23 Dec	A	Ebbw Vale	19-10	T: Buxton C: Howarth PG: Howarth DG: Howarth 3

26 Dec	H	Cardiff	16-23	T: Popham C: Howarth PG: Howarth DG: Howarth 2
5 Jan	A	Edinburgh Reivers	15-17	T: Mostyn, Pini C: Howarth PG: Howarth
10 Feb	H	Pontypridd	33-13	T: Pini, Taylor C: Howarth PG: Howarth 6 DG: Pini
3 Mar	A	Caerphilly	53-8	T: Mostyn 3, Howarth, Garvey, Powell, Burn C: Howarth 5, Mitchell PG: Howarth 2
10 Mar	A	Bridgend	35-9	T: Mostyn, Howarth, Teichmann, Forster C: Howarth 3 PG: Howarth 3
31 Mar	H	Glasgow Caledonians	6-27	PG: Howarth 2
21 Apr	A	Swansea	3-19	PG: Howarth
28 Apr	H	Caerphilly	31-22	T: Pini, Garvey, Teichmann C: Mitchell 2 PG: Mitchell 4
1 May	A	Glasgow Caledonians	20-28	T: Pritchard, Raiwalui C: Mitchell 2 PG: Mitchell 2
5 May	A	Cross Keys	66-5	T: E Lewis 3, Marinos 2, Mostyn 2, M Watkins, Forster C: Mitchell 9 PG: Mitchell

Pontypridd

Year of formation 1876
Ground Sardis Road Ground, Pwllgwaun, Pontypridd, CF37 1HA, Wales
Contacts Web: www.pontypriddrfc.co.uk Tel: Pontypridd (01443) 405006
Colours Black and white hoops
Captain 2000-01 Paul John
Welsh–Scottish League 2000-01 9th
Principality Cup 2000-01 Lost 12-45 to Swansea (7th round)

Welsh–Scottish League Record 2000-01

Date	Venue	Opponents	Result	Scorers
26 Aug	H	Swansea	33-22	T: Davey, Johnson, Cockbain C: Jarvis 3 PG: Jarvis 3 DG: Jarvis
2 Sep	A	Ebbw Vale	32-23	T: Woodard, John C: Davey 2 PG: Davey 6
5 Sep	A	Neath	29-33	T: Johnson, Field C: Jarvis 2 PG: Jenkins 5
9 Sep	H	Cardiff	6-28	PG: Jarvis 2
16 Sep	A	Cross Keys	60-12	T: Woodard 2, Johnson 2, Davey, Parker, Parkes, Neville C: Davey 6, Sweeney PG: Davey 2
23 Sep	H	Newport	22-44	T: Jarvis C: Davey PG: Davey 5
30 Sep	A	Llanelli	20-53	T: Parker, Ta'u C: Jarvis 2 PG: Jarvis 2
4 Nov	H	Bridgend	38-20	T: pen try, Davey, Colderley, Jarvis C: Davey, Jarvis 2 PG: Jarvis 4
1 Dec	A	Edinburgh Reivers	16-22	T: Hunte C: Jarvis PG: Jarvis 3
6 Dec	A	Swansea	16-42	T: J Evans C: Davey PG: Davey 3
9 Dec	H	Ebbw Vale	54-0	T: Woodard 2, Parker, Wyatt, Sweeney, Vunipola C: Davey 6 PG: Davey 4
16 Dec	H	Caerphilly	41-7	T: Parker, Bryant, Sweeney, Sidoli, Colderley, James C: Davey 4 PG: Davey
23 Dec	A	Cardiff	14-21	T: Wyatt PG: Davey 3
26 Dec	H	Cross Keys	59-19	T: Jarvis 4, C Williams, Neville, Vunipola, Owen C: Jarvis 8 PG: Jarvis
27 Jan	A	Caerphilly	19-12	T: Ta'u C: Jarvis PG: Jarvis 4
10 Feb	A	Newport	13-33	T: Johnson C: Jarvis PG: Jarvis 2
10 Mar	H	Llanelli	15-19	PG: Jarvis 5
31 Mar	A	Bridgend	13-16	T: Parker C: Jarvis PG: Davey, Jarvis
11 Apr	H	Glasgow Caledonians	41-18	T: Sweeney 2, Johnston, J Evans C: Davey 3 PG: Davey 5
21 Apr	H	Neath	21-22	T: Colderley, Parker, Wyatt C: Davey 3
27 Apr	A	Glasgow Caledonians	29-45	T: Parker, John, Jenkins, Colderley C: Davey 2, Graham PG: Davey

| 5 May | H | Edinburgh Reivers | 44-30 | *T:* Johnston 2, Wyatt 2, C Williams, Sweeney, Field |
| | | | | *C:* Sweeney 3   *PG:* Sweeney |

Swansea

Year of formation 1873
Ground St Helen's Ground, Bryn Road, Swansea, West Glamorgan SA2 0AR, Wales
Contacts Web: www.swansearfc.co.uk Tel: Swansea (01792) 863704
Colours All white
Captain 2000-01 Scott Gibbs
Welsh–Scottish League 2000-01 Winners
Principality Cup 2000-01 Lost 17-26 to Neath (semi-final)

Welsh–Scottish League Record 2000-01

Date	Venue	Opponents	Result	Scorers
26 Aug	A	Pontypridd	22-33	*T:* K Morgan *C:* A Thomas *PG:* A Thomas 5
2 Sep	H	Caerphilly	59-20	*T:* Taylor 2, K Morgan, Gibbs, Moriarty, D Thomas, Charvis, Henson *C:* A Thomas 5 *PG:* A Thomas 3
6 Sep	A	Newport	13-24	*T:* Gibbs *C:* A Thomas *PG:* A Thomas 2
9 Sep	H	Llanelli	28-21	*T:* M Robinson 2, Gibbs *C:* C Rees 2 *PG:* C Rees 2, A Thomas
16 Sep	A	Neath	9-24	*PG:* C Rees 3
23 Sep	H	Edinburgh Reivers	69-20	*T:* Weatherley 2, Taylor 2, M Robinson 2, A Thomas, Payne, Charvis *C:* A Thomas 7, Henson 2 *PG:* A Thomas, Henson
30 Sep	A	Ebbw Vale	55-6	*T:* Payne 3, M Robinson 2, K Morgan, Charvis *C:* A Thomas 5, C Rees 2 *PG:* A Thomas *DG:* A Thomas
4 Nov	H	Cardiff	29-22	*T:* Taylor 2 *C:* A Thomas 2 *PG:* A Thomas 4 *DG:* A Thomas
3 Dec	A	Glasgow Caledonians	42-22	*T:* Charvis 3, Payne, M Robinson *C:* A Thomas 4 *PG:* A Thomas 2 *DG:* A Thomas
6 Dec	H	Pontypridd	42-16	*T:* M Robinson 2, Charvis 2, K Morgan *C:* C Rees 4 *PG:* C Rees 3
9 Dec	A	Caerphilly	48-10	*T:* Griffiths 2, Winn, Gibbs, Charvis, C Rees *C:* A Thomas 6 *PG:* A Thomas 2
16 Dec	H	Cross Keys	55-3	*T:* Payne 3, Winn 2, K Morgan, R Rees, C Rees, H Jenkins *C:* C Rees 5
23 Dec	A	Llanelli	23-22	*T:* Payne, Martens *C:* A Thomas 2 *PG:* A Thomas 3
26 Dec	H	Neath	45-23	*T:* Weatherley 2, R Rees, Maullin, Charvis *C:* A Thomas 4 *PG:* A Thomas 3 *DG:* A Thomas
9 Feb	A	Edinburgh Reivers	24-16	*T:* K Morgan, Lewis *C:* C Rees *PG:* C Rees 4
10 Mar	H	Ebbw Vale	68-17	*T:* Payne 3, K Morgan, R Rees, Gibbs, Lewis, Charvis, R Jones, Weatherley *C:* C Rees 6 *PG:* C Rees 2
31 Mar	A	Cardiff	14-21	*T:* Moriarty *PG:* Henson 3
21 Apr	H	Newport	19-3	*T:* Payne *C:* Henson *PG:* Henson 3 *DG:* Henson
28 Apr	A	Bridgend	34-16	*T:* M Robinson 2, Payne, Charvis *C:* Henson *PG:* Henson 3 *DG:* Henson
2 May	A	Cross Keys	57-8	*T:* L Jones 2, Mason 2, Payne, pen try, Weatherley, M Robinson *C:* C Rees 7 *PG:* C Rees
5 May	H	Glasgow Caledonians	54-10	*T:* Lewis 2, Winn, Payne, Weatherley, M Robinson, Martens, Charvis *C:* C Rees 3, Henson 4
9 May	H	Bridgend	35-20	*T:* R Rees 3, Brailey, Moriarty *C:* C Rees 2 *PG:* Henson, C Rees

NEATH WORRY THE BIG SPENDERS: THE PRINCIPALITY CUP

John Billot

13 May 2001, Millennium Stadium, Cardiff Arms Park
Newport 13 (1G 1PG 1DG)   Neath 8 (1PG 1T)

This was the meeting of the well-heeled against the impecunious. Newport, the big spenders, generously bank-rolled by their owner, Tony Brown, facing Neath, hanging on by their shoe-strings after being rescued by a WRU take-over when debts looked likely to force a great club to fold. This was lords of the manor against peasants, though these were special villains from the Gnoll. This was the team that subdued, shocked and sank Swansea, undisputed favourites for the cup, in a truly memorable semi-final. This was no tatterdemalion Neath side and they promised an unforgettable tussle in front of 37,000 Sunday spectators.

Newport appeared confident it was their destiny to win the cup for their inspirational captain, Gary Teichmann, in his last game for them before returning to South Africa. He had taken them to their first final for 15 years and they expected the cup to be theirs after 24 years. That was how the script was crafted, but Neath very nearly rewrote it in a clash played at a clinking pace. It was Newport's drilled ruck and maul and tactical kicking matched against Neath flair, opportunism and panache.

Shane Williams, who appeared in three positions (wing, full-back and then scrum-half), put Neath in front with a penalty shot before Shane Howarth, the most influential figure and ultimate match-winner, fired over a penalty kick and converted Adrian Garvey's driving maul try. Neath responded with a cracking try from Kevin James, wide out; but Howarth's dropped goal in the 77th minute from barely 10 yards out made sure of matters.

Lyn Jones, the losing coach, reflected dispassionately, 'We came close to qualifying for the Heineken Cup next season and finished second in the Principality Cup – so we have achieved nothing! If I had a £1m budget, I would have won the game!'

He was an unhappy man because he considered Neath suffered the rough end of vital decisions when tries were denied to Shane Williams and Kevin James, and urged the WRU to adopt the Rugby League system of video recording officials to give definitive rulings when referees are uncertain.

There was not much consolation that Neath's James Storey was voted man-of-the-match, or that they were fortunate Gareth Morris, the full-back, escaped the ultimate sanction for a brutal body-check on Howarth that earned a sojourn in the sin-bin. It was a case of the rich getting richer. And Teichmann enjoyed another glory day.

Newport: M Pini; M Mostyn, M Watkins, A Marinos, E Lewis; S Howarth, D Burn; R Snow, J Richards, A Garvey, S Raiwalui, I Gough, P Buxton, G Teichmann (*captain*), J Forster *Substitutions:* S Mitchell for Howarth (18-21 mins); J Pritchard for Mostyn (34 mins); D Edwards for Marinos (52 mins); G Taylor for Gough (67 mins); A Popham for Buxton (67 mins); S Mitchell for Edwards (82 mins)

Scorers *Try:* Garvey *Conversion:* Howarth *Penalty goal:* Howarth *Dropped goal:* Howarth

Neath: G Morris; K James, J Storey, D Tiueti, S Williams; P Horgan, Mark Davies; D Jones, Mefin Davies, A Millward, S Martin, G Llewellyn (*captain*), R Francis, R Phillips, B Sinkinson *Substitutions:* T Davies for Mark Davies (67 mins); A Howell for Millward (67 mins); K Tuipolotu for Francis (67 mins); D Pugh for Horgan (73 mins)

Scorers *Try:* James *Penalty Goal:* S Williams

Referee C Thomas (WRU)

Earlier rounds

Neath's was the tougher trail to the final. They had to win at the Brewery Field in the quarters and that required an all-out effort to squeeze through by 23-21. It was three tries each, but Greg Miller flighted over crucial kicks with two penalty goals and a conversion. Then the semi-final brought the most thrilling match of the tournament. Swansea were cup winners elect in most opinions. Coach Lyn Jones realistically rated his side with just a 30 per cent chance of upsetting the applecart, which was a shrewd psychological factor in raising his forwards' hackles and producing a ferocious performance. Swansea wilted. 'It was our worst display of the season,' said skipper Scott Gibbs bluntly. With little useable possession and even less respite from predators, his side were overawed. Even with wholehearted Rowland Phillips in the bin, Neath added to their score through daring David Tiueti. So Swansea visions of a cup and league double proved a mirage. It was especially disappointing after Swansea had swept Cardiff aside. At 28-21 it would appear a close contest; nothing was further from the truth. The home forwards had Cardiff in a stranglehold from the start.

Anxiety haunted Newport nearly every step of the way in their semi-final tie before they completed victory by 19-12 over defiant Ebbw Vale. Again, Howarth played a key role, kicking four penalty goals and converting Matt Pini's try. Newport won their other ties by handsome margins, including 62 points against Dunvant with 25 points from Howarth; and the same man was on target with 19 points to destroy Division One champions Aberavon by 56-18 in the seventh round.

Llanelli, as holders, were expected to pose Cardiff problems in their seventh round meeting at Stradey. However, there was steel in Cardiff's performance and they dismayed the Scarlets' supporters with an amazing success by 65-16. This was Llanelli's heaviest ever cup defeat. Nine tries to one was wipe-out for the team who had appeared in the three previous finals, winning twice. Dangerous Dan Baugh epitomized the Cardiff spirit of zero tolerance; a Canadian on a one-man crusade to avenge Cardiff's Stradey flop in the Heineken Cup the previous season.

Pontypridd also conceded a record number of cup points. They crashed out by 45-12 to Swansea at Sardis Road. Pontypridd had fallen upon hard times, though skipper Paul John was always a great-hearted worker. Bridgend enjoyed a revived sense of confidence under the command of new scrum-half Huw Harries, recruited from Harlequins. He saw his side raise their record cup score of 89-7 against Cwmllynfell with six tries by Adrian Durston.

Results

Sixth round: Aberavon 31, Cross Keys 8; Bedwas 10, Cardiff 57; Bridgend 89, Cwmllynfell 7; Caerphilly 32, Bonymaen 19; Carmarthen Quins 30, Blackwood 20; Dunvant 23, Abertillery 21; Llandovery 5, Ebbw Vale 27; Llanelli 79, Abercynon 10; Neath 70, Whitland 7; Newbridge 39, Llantrisant 3; Newport 47, UWIC 17; Pontyberem 13, Pontypridd 62; Rumney 10, Swansea 50; Tondu 21, Llanharan 33; Tonmawr 8, Glamorgan Wanderers 18; Tylorstown 15, Rhymney 33.

Seventh round: Caerphilly 43, Glamorgan Wanderers 35; Carmarthen Quins 25, Ebbw Vale 32; Dunvant 41, Llanharan 11; Llanelli 16, Cardiff 65; Newbridge 13, Bridgend 46; Newport 56, Aberavon 18; Pontypridd 12, Swansea 45; Rhymney 3, Neath 63.

Quarter-finals: Bridgend 21, Neath 23; Caerphilly 6, Ebbw Vale 38; Dunvant 14, Newport 62; Swansea 28, Cardiff 21.

Semi-finals: (at the Millennium Stadium) Neath 26, Swansea 17; Newport 19, Ebbw Vale 12.

FINAL: (at Millennium Stadium) Newport 13, Neath 8.

Previous WRU Cup Finals: 1972 Neath 15, Llanelli 9; 1973 Llanelli 30, Cardiff 7; 1974 Llanelli 12, Aberavon 10; 1975 Llanelli 15, Aberavon 6; 1976 Llanelli 16, Swansea 4; 1977 Newport 16, Cardiff 15; 1978 Swansea 13, Newport 9; 1979 Bridgend 18, Pontypridd 12; 1980 Bridgend 15, Swansea 9; 1981 Cardiff 14, Bridgend 6; 1982 Cardiff 12, Bridgend 12 (Cardiff won on most tries rule); 1983 Pontypool 18, Swansea 6; 1984 Cardiff 24, Neath 19; 1985 Llanelli 15, Cardiff 14; 1986 Cardiff 28, Newport 21; 1987 Cardiff 16, Swansea 15; 1988 Llanelli 28, Neath 13; 1989 Neath 14, Llanelli 13; 1990 Neath 16, Bridgend 10; 1991 Llanelli 24, Pontypool 9; 1992 Llanelli 16, Swansea 7; 1993 Llanelli 21, Neath 18; 1994 Cardiff 15, Llanelli 8; 1995 Swansea 17, Pontypridd 12; 1996 Pontypridd 29, Neath 22; 1997 Cardiff 33, Swansea 26; 1998 Llanelli 19, Ebbw Vale 12; 1999 Swansea 37, Llanelli 10; 2000 Llanelli 22, Swansea 12; 2001 Newport 13, Neath 8.

Played at Cardiff Arms Park 1972-1997; at Ashton Gate, Bristol 1998; at Ninian Park, Cardiff 1999; at the Millennium Stadium since 2000.

DOMESTIC RUGBY IN FRANCE 2000-01

Toulouse Toujours: The French Championship

Ian Borthwick

9 June 2001, Stade de France, Paris
Toulouse 34 (1G 6PG 3DG)   **Montferrand 22** (1G 5PG)

For this, the 100th Championship in the history of the French national competition, Montferrand went into the final as favourites. They had won both the earlier contests against Toulouse (28-15 at home and 29-24 away) and, after having lost all six of their finals since 1936, it seemed as though destiny was finally about to smile on the Michelin men from the Auvergne.

Toulouse had largely failed to hit form throughout the season and injuries to their captain Emile Ntamack and their storming former All Black No 8 Isitolo Maka appeared to have weakened them. Once again, however, the Toulouse machine clicked into gear in the final straight. Their big-game temperament saw them through and, while the men in red and black celebrated their sixth national title since 1994, Montferrand went home empty-handed for the seventh time.

They sorely missed Tony Marsh, their Kiwi centre who had been the spearhead of their attack throughout the season, but public expectations and the weight of history also appeared too much for them, with numerous basic errors playing into the hands of the opposition.

Played before a capacity crowd at the Stade de France only hours before the French squad left for its gruelling tour of South Africa and New Zealand, the 2001 final was a triumph for the Toulouse school and their ability to blood promising new players. Full-back Nicolas Jeanjean (20), centre Clément Poitrenaud (19), flanker Jean Bouilhou (22) all had stand-out performances. But it was 18 year-old scrum-half, Frédéric Michalak, who stole the show, combining brilliantly with Yann Delaigue at fly-half and nonchalantly capping off a superb all-round performance with four long-range penalties from 52, 50, 50 and 43 metres respectively.

With 16 national titles to its name, Stade Toulousain is by far the most successful club in the history of French rugby, ahead of Béziers (11), Stade Français (10), Lourdes and Agen (8).

Toulouse: N Jeanjean; X Garbajosa, C Desbrosse, C Poitrenaud, M Marfaing ; Y Delaigue, F Michalak; C Califano, Y Bru, F Tournaire, H Miorin, D Gérard, J Bouilhou, F Pelous (*captain*), C Labit *Substitutions:* C Soulette for Califano (58 mins); F Belot for Gérard (61 mins); S Dispagne for Miorin (61 mins); D Lacroix for Labit (77 mins); S Ougier for Desbrosse (77 mins); A Penaud for Poitrenaud (80 mins); J Cazalbou for Michalak (85 mins)

Scorers *Try:* Marfaing *Conversion:* Marfaing *Penalty Goals:* Michalak (4), Marfaing (2) *Drop Goals:* Delaigue (3)

Montferrand: J Marlu; A Rougerie, J Ngauamo, N Nadau, D Bory; G Merceron, A Troncon; A Tolofua, Y Pedrosa, A Galasso, D Barrier, E Lecomte (*captain*), A Audebert, S Boome, O Magne *Substitutions:* S Viars for Ngauamo (55 mins); J Machacek for Barrier (68 mins); M Caputo for Pedrosa (72 mins); B Reidy for Tolofua (77 mins);

Scorers *Try:* Audebert *Conversion:* Merceron *Penalty Goals:* Merceron (5)

Referee G Borréani (FFR)

Pools One and Two 2000–01

This was an agonising year for many clubs in France, as the decision to reduce the First Division to 16 sides for the 2001-02 season meant that five teams had to be relegated. Consequently, too many matches were dominated by negative tactics and, with teams concentrating more on avoiding defeat at all costs than on adopting expansive tactics, the rugby was often not of a high standard.

Castres and Stade Français took the top two slots in pool one, with Perpignan and Agen coming third and fourth. Castres remained notoriously difficult to beat at home and had the distinct pleasure of scoring a heavy win (29-0) against the reigning champions Stade Français in an early pool round in November. Agen, Béziers and Bourgoin were all threatened with the spectre of relegation at one stage or another, but managed to keep their heads above water towards the end of the season. The same cannot be said about minnows Périgueux (one win from 18 games) nor Mont-de-Marsan, both of whom missed the cut. Pau came desperately close to being relegated and, having finished eighth, was forced to play a cut-throat play-off against Grenoble in order to stay in the First Division.

Pool two, dominated by heavy-weights Montferrand and Toulouse, also had more than its share of heart-stopping games where the whole financial and sporting future of some of France's greatest clubs hung on a single result. Biarritz, who eventually defeated Stade Français in the quarter-finals in Paris, came in third and Colomiers fourth. Narbonne, after sacking their coach Pierre Berbizier, went through a desperate period, but picked up towards the end of the season to finish a creditable fifth. Brive, European champions in 1997, failed to make the grade, however, and, along with Aurillac and Auch, were relegated to Division Two. Grenoble, despite importing several Southern Hemisphere players, also failed to hold their place amongst France's élite, finally succumbing in the rugged play-off against Pau.

Final French Championship Pool Tables 2000-01

Pool One

Team	P	W	D	L	For	Against	Pts
Montferrand	20	15	1	4	633	404	51
Toulouse	20	14	0	6	651	380	48
Biarritz	20	13	1	6	594	408	47
Colomiers	20	11	0	9	474	440	42
Narbonne	20	10	0	10	579	519	40
Dax	20	10	0	10	419	506	40
La Rochelle	20	9	0	11	434	537	38
Grenoble	20	9	0	11	428	479	38
Brive	20	8	0	12	439	563	36
Aurillac	20	7	0	13	464	577	34
Auch	20	3	0	17	320	622	26

Pool Two

Team	P	W	D	L	For	Against	Pts
Castres	18	14	0	4	558	324	46
Stade Français	18	12	2	4	624	409	44
Perpignan	18	11	0	7	492	452	40
Agen	18	10	1	7	480	385	39
Béziers	18	10	0	8	515	414	38
Bourgoin	18	9	1	8	443	379	37
Bègles-Bordeaux	18	8	0	10	402	533	34
Pau	18	8	0	10	427	404	34
Mont-de-Marsan	18	5	0	13	337	481	28
Perigueux	18	1	0	17	279	776	20

Results

Quarter-finals: Castres 37, Colomiers 26; Toulouse 20, Perpignan 15; Biarritz 35, Stade Français 19; Montferrand 33, Agen 21

Semi-finals: Toulouse 32, Castres 21; Montferrand 16, Biarritz 9

Final: (at Stade de France, Paris) Toulouse 34, Montferrand 22

Recent French Championship Finals: 1972 Béziers 9, Brive 0; 1973 Tarbes 18, Dax 12; 1974 Béziers16, Narbonne 14; 1975 Béziers 13, Brive 12; 1976 Agen 13, Béziers10; 1977 Béziers 12, Perpignan 4; 1978 Béziers 31, Montferrand 9; 1979 Narbonne 10, Bagnères 0; 1980 Béziers 10, Toulouse 6; 1981 Béziers 22, Bagnères 13; 1982 Agen 18, Bayonne 9; 1983 Béziers 14, Nice 6; 1984 Béziers 21, Agen 21; 1985 Toulouse 36, Toulon 22; 1986 Toulouse 16, Agen 6; 1987 Toulon 15, RCF 12; 1988 Agen 9, Tarbes 3; 1989 Toulouse 18, Toulon 12; 1990 RCF 22, Agen 12; 1991 Bègles-Bordeaux 19, Toulouse 10; 1992 Toulon 19, Biarritz 14; 1993 Castres 14, Grenoble 11; 1994 Toulouse 22, Montferrand 16; 1995 Toulouse 31, Castres 16; 1996 Toulouse 20, Brive 13; 1997 Toulouse 12, Bourgoin-Jallieu 6; 1998 Stade Français 34, Perpignan 7; 1999 Toulouse 15, Montferrand 11; 2000 Stade Français 28, Colomiers 23; 2001 Toulouse 34, Montferrand 22

DOMESTIC RUGBY IN ITALY 2000-01

Bravo Benetton: The Italian Championship

Giampaolo Tassinari

This was the last tournament to be played under the current league format and, once again, it was Benetton Treviso against the rest. Although the green-and-white-hooped men had struggled the previous season, they were still favourites to win the 2001 title and with their new French coach Alain Teixidor from Perpignan at the helm, they deservedly won the league. Thanks to a good balance of skills in the backs and power among the forwards, the Benetton Treviso side were too strong and superior for their opponents. Despite some losses during the campaign, nobody doubted that they would win the championship. The injection of new blood in the form of Tongan international David Edwards in the back-row with the emerging Mauro Bergamasco enlivened their play in the loose. Other factors in their success were the play of South African Dan Human and the experience and consistency of outside-half Francesco Mazzariol. The youngster Claudio Beltramini in the front-row, moreover, was the revelation of the season.

All of the leading clubs confirmed their pre-season promise, the only uncertainty being in the first round 'A' pool where, after a very tight head to head race, Amatori Calvisano clinched the third spot for the title pool by winning their last match against Rugby Roma in Rome. This left two successful clubs from recent years, Petrarca Padova and Rovigo, struggling for survival in the relegation pool. It was a clear indication that the advent of professionalism has in many ways penalised some teams while at the same time enhancing relatively unknown clubs such as Viadana.

For the 2001-02 season there will be a new 'Super Ten' league with a points system based on the Southern Hemisphere's format. There will also be a chance for all first division teams to play in the two European Cup competitions. Both of these innovations should provide further steps towards a better quality of rugby and speed the development of the game in Italy.

Serie A1

Round Robin First Phase
Final standings

Pool A	P	W	D	L	F	A	Pts
Rugby Roma	10	8	0	2	390	224	39
Viadana	10	7	0	3	349	210	36
Amatori Calvisano	10	6	0	4	247	219	31
Petrarca Padova	10	6	0	4	326	234	30
Piacenza RC	10	3	0	7	245	293	16
Livorno	10	0	0	10	146	523	0

Rugby Roma, Viadana and Amatori Calvisano qualified for title pool.

Petrarca Padova, Piacenza RC and Livorno went into the relegation pool

Pool B	P	W	D	L	F	A	Pts
Benetton Treviso	10	9	0	1	354	162	42
Rugby Parma FC	10	5	1	4	220	192	27
L'Aquila	10	5	1	4	270	229	27
Rovigo	10	4	1	5	184	221	23
Gr A N Rugby	10	4	0	6	177	233	18
San Dona	10	1	1	8	163	331	7

Benetton Treviso, Rugby Parma FC and L'Aquila qualified for title pool

Rovigo, Gr A N Rugby and San Dona went into the relegation pool

Serie A1

Round Robin Second Phase
Final standings

Title Pool	P	W	D	L	F	A	Pts
Benetton Treviso	10	7	0	3	293	189	34
Amatori Calvisano	10	6	1	3	241	199	30
Rugby Roma	10	5	0	5	261	244	26
Viadana	10	5	1	4	267	217	26
Rugby Parma FC	10	5	0	5	223	284	24
L'Aquila	10	1	0	9	202	354	5

Benetton Treviso, Amatori Calvisano, Rugby Roma and Viadana qualified for the semi-finals

Relegation Pool	P	W	D	L	F	A	Pts
Petrarca Padova	10	9	0	1	324	177	39
Gr A N Rugby	18	8	0	2	301	183	37
Rovigo	10	5	0	5	250	192	29
Piacenza RC	10	5	0	5	275	260	26
San Dona	10	3	0	7	208	287	16
Livorno	10	0	0	10	166	425	2

Piacenza RC, San Dona and Livorno relegated to the 2001-02 Serie A2

AS Bologna are promoted from Serie A2 to the 2001-02 Serie A1

Play-off semi-finals: First legs: Viadana 15, Benetton Treviso 23; Rugby Roma 11, Amatori Calvisano 26. Second legs: Benetton Treviso 28, Viadana 11; Amatori Calvisano 24, Rugby Roma 10.

Championship Final

2 June 2001, Stadio Dall'Ara, Bologna
Benetton Treviso 33 (3G 4PG)   **Amatori Calvisano 13** (1PG 2T)

Benetton Treviso and Amatori Calvisano won their semi-finals in contrasting manner. Benetton Treviso overcame Viadana, a little but ambitious club with many foreign players, coming from behind to win a vital away victory in the first leg having been 3-15 down early in the second half. They won the return leg due to Corrado Pilat's boot and an aggressive defensive game plan. Meanwhile, Amatori Calvisano won both their legs handsomely against a poor Rugby Roma side who were a shadow of their former selves. Calvisano were fitter and more creative and deservedly won through for their first ever appearance in the final. For Benetton Treviso, this was their twelfth appearance in fourteen finals since the play-offs began in 1988.

The final itself was not a spectacular match. It was hard fought, the teams were nervous and a strong wind prevailed throughout the game. In the first half, Amatori Calvisano managed to restrain the superior power of the Treviso forwards and went into the break only 6-3 down. After the interval, Benetton immediately increased the pressure with two quick penalties and then virtually won the match with three tries scored within a quarter of an hour. First, a disastrous handling error on Amatori Calvisano's try line enabled Denis Dallan to score the easiest of tries by just picking the ball up and immediately touching it down. This was followed minutes later by a try from the outside-centre Walter Pozzebon before Manuel Dallan added a third. All of the tries were converted by Pilat. Benetton eased up with the score at 33-3 as the game entered its last quarter and allowed Amatori Calvisano to score two late tries by replacement Ivan Merlo, neither of which were converted.

Benetton Treviso did just what was expected of them, but the losers cannot blame themselves. Amatori Calvisano did well to reach the final but clearly could not compete with Benetton in terms of skill and stamina, despite having internationals such as Paolo Vaccari, Massimo Ravazzolo, Luca Mastrodomenico, Andrea de Rossi and Giuseppe Lanzi. For Benetton this was just another national crown and the chance to shine in the next Heineken Cup. For Amatori Calvisano it was confirmation that hard work and team spirit can pay dividends en route to future recognition at national and European level.

Benetton Treviso: C Pilat; M Perziano, W Pozzebon, M Dallan, D Dallan;
F Mazzariol, A P Moore; D C Human, A Moscardi (*captain*), F Properzi Curti,
C Checchinato, W Visser, F Ongaro, D Edwards, M Bergamasco *Substitutions:*
A Gritti for Edwards (41 mins); G Grespan for Properzi Curti (46 mins);
N Mazzucato for D Dallan (57 mins); S Garozzo for Ongaro (67 mins);

C Beltramini for Human (75 mins); G Preo for Mazzariol (77 mins);
M Mazzantini for Moore (77 mins)

Scorers *Tries:* D Dallan, Pozzebon, M Dallan *Conversions:* Pilat (3) *Penalty Goals:*
Pilat (4)

Amatori Calvisano: M Ravazzolo; E Muliero, P Vaccari (*captain*), C Zanoletti,
P Scanziani; L Bordes, P Griffen; D Davo, T Niglio, F Bartolini,
L Mastrodomenico, K Whitley, C Mayerhofler, A De Rossi, J Ricciardo
Substitutions: G Lanzi for Mastrodomenico (56mins); A Cairo for Niglio (62mins);
M Vaghi for Davo (62 mins); J Dragotto for Muliero (74 mins); E Scotuzzi for
Mayerhofler (75 mins); S Macri for Bartolini (75 mins); I Merlo for Ravazzolo
(77mins)

Scorers *Tries:* Merlo (2) *Penalty Goal:* Griffen

Referee G Morandin (FIR)

Previous Italian Championship Finals: 1988 Rovigo 9, Treviso 7 (Rome); 1989
Treviso 20, Rovigo 9 (Bologna); 1990 Rovigo 18, Treviso 9 (Brescia); 1991 Milan
37, Treviso 18 (Parma); 1992 Treviso 27, Rovigo 18 (Padua); 1993 Milan 41,
Treviso 15 (Padua); 1994 L'Aquila 23, Milan 14 (Padua); 1995 Milan 27, Treviso
15 (Padua); 1996 Milan 23, Treviso 17 (Rovigo); 1997 Treviso 34, Milan 29
(Verona); 1998 Treviso 9, Padua 3 (Bologna); 1999 Treviso 23, Padua 14 (Rovigo);
2000 Rome 35, L'Aquila 17 (Rome); 2001 Treviso 33, Calvisano 13 (Bologna).

DOMESTIC RUGBY IN SOUTH AFRICA 2000

Currie Cup Still the Golden Grail: Bankfin Currie Cup

Dan Retief

With each passing South African domestic season the obituaries start to appear for the old Currie Cup, first played for in 1892, and each year it not only survives but the competition it engenders seems to become keener and more vibrant.

The golden cup was presented to South African rugby by Sir Donald Currie, the Chairman of the Castle shipping line, in 1891 through the kind offices of W E (Bill) Maclagan, captain of the British Isles team that toured the union in that year. Maclagan's instructions were to present the cup to the team putting up the best performance against his side and it was duly handed over to the Griqualand West Union who were beaten only by a try to nil by the invincible tourists.

Griqualand West in turn carried out Sir Donald's instructions and presented the "Currie Cup" to the recently formed SA Rugby Board to be used as a floating trophy to be presented to the South African provincial champions. In time it became the golden grail of Springbok rugby, providing intense competition in South African rugby's formative years, a measure by which players could be assessed in the halcyon years of Springbok rugby and, in the troubled seasons of isolation, a substitute for international competition.

In the year 2000, however, an impostor of the modern era was threatening to depose the Currie Cup. The Super 12 was in its fifth year and once again talk was that the Currie Cup would fail to interest the fans or ignite the passions of the teams; especially as it was scheduled after that other product of professionalism and marketing, the Tri Nations. On top of this the competition was to be played according to a complicated new system whereby all 14 provinces would be divided into two sections of seven, each section playing a single round, with the top four teams then going forward to what was dubbed the "Top or Super Eight" competition.

Making the format more confusing was that teams would "take forward" into the Top Eight competition only the points they had gained when playing against each other. The remaining six teams were kept active in a minor competition played for the Bankfin Cup (named after the competition's sponsor) and the big shock was that the once mighty Northern Transvaal, now plying their trade under their old nickname of the Blue Bulls, found themselves in this group.

Crowds at Loftus Versfeld in Pretoria, where once the Currie Cup had been enshrined for season on season fell to below 3000, but the Bulls spared themselves the ultimate humiliation by at least winning the Bankfin Cup by beating Eastern Province who, in the veritable menagerie that has become South African provincial rugby, are now called the Mighty Elephants in the final staged in Port Elizabeth.

At the business end of the contest, however, interest in the Currie Cup was as strong as ever. The Natal Sharks, under new coach Rudolf Straeuli, returned to a basic, safety-first style and always looked assured of qualifying for the semi-finals while Western Province, playing an unorthodox game that often involved full-back Percy Montgomery or wing Pieter Rossouw taking the ball at fly-half to set attacks in motion, resolved to give their coach Alan Solomons a rousing send-off. With Nick Mallett having resigned the post of Springbok coach (just moments before he was asked to!), Solomons's role as his assistant was also snuffed out and he had announced that he would be leaving South Africa to link up with Ulster in Ireland.

A home loss to the Sharks in league play at Newlands meant that Western Province conceded not only top place on the table to the Natalians but also the crucial home advantage in the final if they both won through. Meanwhile two of the traditional "big five", the Gauteng Lions and the Free State Cheetahs, came through to reach the semi-finals after the South Western Districts Eagles and the Falcons (formerly Eastern Transvaal) had at one stage been well-placed to join the play-offs. In the semi-finals the Sharks met the Cheetahs in Durban for the third time in four years and triumphed 29-15 and in Cape Town Western Province saw off the Lions, the defending champions under Laurie Mains, 43-22.

Bankfin Currie Cup Final

28 October 2000, ABSA Stadium, King's Park, Durban
Western Province 25 (2G 2PG 1T)   Natal Sharks 15 (5PG)

The final was played before a full house of 52,000 and if domination of territory and possession were the only yardsticks then the Sharks would have run out convincing winners. The Sharks had the ascendancy for fully three-quarters of the game but a season-long inability to score tries cost them dearly as Western Province, inspired by the unpredictable Pieter Rossouw and mercurial Breyton Paulse, conjured up three long-range tries to take the Cup.

It was Province's third appearance in four finals (having won the Cup in 1997 and lost it the following year) and for the fourth successive year the champions were a team who had failed to reach the semi-finals the previous season – a possible indicator of the value of rest in an overcrowded season. It also meant that Western Province, admirably led by Corné Krige, could boast the unique record of having been the first Currie Cup champions in three successive centuries; having been the first winners of the Currie Cup in

1892, then taking it in 1904 after the Boer War and being crowned champions in 2000. It represented the 30th time that the men in blue-and-white hoops had either won or shared the trophy.

Unsurprisingly, when new Springbok coach Harry Viljoen three days later named his squad to tour Argentina, Ireland, Wales and England there were 14 Western Province men in the team with No 8 Adri Badenhorst the unlucky one to miss out. In the individual stakes Natal's Gaffie du Toit, who mostly played full-back, finished as the leading points-scorer in the competition with 182, with Breyton Paulse the top try-scorer on 12.

Western Province: P C Montgomery; B J Paulse, R F Fleck, A J J van Straaten, P W G Rossouw; C Rossouw, D J van Zyl; A van der Linde, C F Marais, R B Kempson, Q Davids, F H Louw, C P J Krige (*captain*), A Badenhorst, H Gerber *Substitutions:* D W Barry for Rossouw (66 mins); R Brink for Gerber (70 mins); P Dixon for Marais (70 mins); T Stoltz for Louw (75 mins); F Rautenbach for Kempson (77 mins)

Scorers *Tries:* Paulse (2), Rossouw *Conversions:* van Straaten (2) *Penalty Goals:* van Straaten (2)

Natal Sharks: G S du Toit; D J Kayser, C S Terblanche, T M Halstead, S Brink; A James, C Davidson; A-H le Roux, C L C Rossouw, E Fynn, P A van den Berg, M G Andrews (*captain*), W G Brosnihan, S Sowerby, A J Venter *Substitutions:* J W Smit for Rossouw (52 mins); C van Rensburg for Venter (56 mins); R Smith for Brink (78 mins); B S Moyle for Fynn (78 mins)

Scorer *Penalty Goals:* Du Toit (5)

Referee A Watson

Recent Currie Cup Finals: 1990 N Transvaal 12, Natal 18 (Pretoria); 1991 N Transvaal 27 Transvaal 15 (Pretoria); 1992 Transvaal 13, Natal 14 (Johannesburg); 1993 Natal 15, Transvaal 21 (Durban); 1994 Orange Free State 33, Transvaal 56 (Bloemfontein); 1995 Natal 25, Western Province 17 (Durban); 1996 Transvaal 15, Natal 33 (Johannesburg); 1997 Western Province 14, Free State 12 (Cape Town); 1998 Blue Bulls 24, Western Province 20 (Pretoria); 1999 Natal Sharks 9, Golden Lions 32 (Durban); 2000 Natal Sharks 15, Western Province 25 (Durban)

DOMESTIC RUGBY IN NEW ZEALAND 2000

Wellington's Capital Year: NPC Championship

Don Cameron

For a team based on the old Athletic Park – which immodestly labelled itself as the home of New Zealand rugby before it was laid to rest with few mourners last year – Wellington were the under-achievers of the National Provincial Championships which have been the domestic life-blood of New Zealand rugby since their inspired start in 1976.

Wellington had always retained a place in the first of the three divisions, but their trophy-winning fortunes had steadily declined. They won the third championship in 1978, again in 1981 and 1986. They had not won the title since and, in fact, have been so much middle-of-the-road in the 1990s that they had never even qualified for the top-four semi-finals since they were started in 1992.

At the same time, Wellington's record of successful defences of the Ranfurly Shield were seldom mentioned in polite company. They lost their first challenge after winning the shield from Auckland in 1963, they resisted one challenge after good fortune gave them a challenge against lowly-ranked South Canterbury in 1974, and they had four successful challenges in 1984. Since then only Auckland, Canterbury, Waikato and even lowly Taranaki have won the shield.

For a time in the 2000 season, it seemed as if Wellington had finally made a major impact on the NPC first division by staging a splendid launch to what was the 25th birthday of a contest conceived in the early 1970s by an eager Auckland administrator Barry Smith, who dug in his toes until the national administrators took notice.

Wellington started the campaign well with a first win over the title-holders, Canterbury, and followed up with reasonably clear-cut wins over Otago, promoted Northland and Taranaki. They looked so potent, with Christian Cullen, Jonah Lomu, Alama Ieremia, Jason O'Halloran and goal-kicker David Holwell in the backline, and the young loose forwards Jerry Collins and Rodney So'oialo backed by strong experienced tight forwards Dion Waller, Inoke Afeaki, Norm Hewitt and the English prop Kevin Yates. Then Wellington stumbled, 19-24, against Auckland and a week later were humiliated 7-24 by North Harbour, an inconsistent mixture of elderly talent such as Frano Botica and youthful promise in Ron Cribb and Troy Flavell.

On that grim Albany day Wellington played like nervous novices. They and their coaches Graham Mourie and Dave Rennie were scorned, and there was even the suggestion that the super-stars were neither super nor stars and should be replaced by youngsters who would try harder. Either that, or Mourie and Rennie should go.

Mourie, Rennie and their disputatious captain Hewitt held a council of war. The results were spectacular. Wellington roared through the last qualifying matches winning 45-29 over Counties-Manukau, 28-21 over Southland and 48-23 from Waikato, a fortnight after the Ranfurly Shield had departed with Canterbury. So Wellington were in the second semi-final, against the once-powerful Auckland, while Canterbury, the top-ranked side, met Taranaki in the other semi-final. That wet and windy Eden Park night, Wellington ripped Auckland to pieces, five tries to two, and marched confidently into the Christchurch final over a Canterbury side that struggled to qualify against a tenacious Taranaki side.

Final Air New Zealand NPC Round Robin Table 2000

	P	W	D	L	Bonus	For	Against	Pts
Canterbury	9	8	0	1	6	307	155	38
Auckland	9	8	0	1	4	270	147	36
Wellington	9	6	0	3	6	249	190	30
Taranaki	9	5	0	4	3	195	260	23
North Harbour	9	5	0	4	3	197	161	23
Northland	9	4	0	5	6	217	256	22
Waikato	9	4	0	5	5	251	235	21
Otago	9	3	0	6	6	203	182	18
Counties-Manukau	9	1	0	8	5	209	329	9
Southland	9	1	0	8	2	175	358	6

Air New Zealand NPC Grand Final

21 October 2000, Jade Stadium, Lancaster Park, Christchurch
Canterbury 29 (2G 5PG)   **Wellington 34** (4G 2PG)

The script, written in Christchurch, suggested that the final would be the third jewel in Canterbury's crown, following the Crusaders' win in the Super 12 and Canterbury's win of the Ranfurly Shield. The 30,000 red-and-black fans cramming the re-designed Jade Stadium – work had begun on the major grandstand on the western side – spent the first hour in a state of shock. With Christian Cullen leading the way, Wellington pounded Canterbury with stirring combined assaults. Jonah Lomu scored the first try and, 20 minutes after half-time, the fourth. He thus finished the season as the first division's leading try scorer with nine from nine appearances. O'Halloran and Afeaki got the others and Holwell kicked goals from everywhere. Two other Cullen breaks looked like producing tries, but were recalled for minor handling errors.

So Wellington had 34 points, and Canterbury only 15 from five penalty goals at the threequarter-mark. In the 68th minute Andrew Mehrtens finished a long series of Canterbury raids with a try which Ben Blair converted. The Canterbury crowd roared into life and with nine minutes remaining Todd Blackadder, Canterbury's heroic forward leader, scored near the posts and Blair made it 34-29 to Wellington, with the crowd baying for a win.

Tired and obviously nervous, Wellington scraped and scrambled in defence, as Canterbury poured into attacking rucks and scrums near the Wellington line. Then Wellington were down to 14 defenders when Dion Waller was sin-binned for an intentional knock-on. Norm Hewitt was twice injured, but battled on and only an after-match inspection showed he had a broken arm.

Hewitt drew the last ounce of defensive strength from his men, Canterbury could not get through after turning down many chances to kick for penalty goals, and Wellington had one of their best, rarest and most valiant victories. Hewitt was Wellington's special hero for his courage and indomitable leadership – but the do-gooders tut-tutted that he placed his game ahead of the damage to his arm.

Canterbury: B Blair; M Vunibaka, M Mayerhofler, D Gibson (*captain*), C Ralph; A Mehrtens, J Marshall; G Feek, M Hammett, G Somerville, T Blackadder, N Maxwell, R Thorne, S Broomhall, S Robertson *Substitutions:* A So'oalo for Vunibaka; C Jack for Maxwell; D Seymour for Blackadder; M Sexton for Hammett; D Hewett for Feek

Scorers *Tries:* Mehrtens, Blackadder *Conversions:* Blair (2) *Penalty goals:* Blair (4), Mehrtens

Wellington: C Cullen; B Fleming, T Umaga, J O'Halloran, J Lomu; D Holwell, J Spice; K Yates, N Hewitt (*captain*), M van der Merwe, D Waller, I Afeaki, R So'oialo, J Collins, K Vanisi *Substitutions:* A Ieremia for Fleming; R Flutey for Umaga (temp); B Fleming for O'Halloran; S Carter for Yates; M Edwards for van der Merwe; M Ngauamo for Afeaki; P Steinmetz for Fleming

Scorers *Tries:* Lomu (2), O'Halloran, Afeaki *Conversions:* Holwell (4) *Penalty Goals:* Holwell (2)

Referee P G Honiss (NZRFU)

Results

Semi-finals: Auckland 23, Wellington 48 (Eden Park); Canterbury 31, Taranaki 23 (Jade Stadium)

Final: (at Jade Stadium) Canterbury 29, Wellington 34.

Previous NPC Grand Finals: 1992 Waikato 40, Otago 5 (Hamilton); 1993 Auckland 27, Otago 18 (Auckland); 1994 Auckland 22, North Harbour 16 (Takapuna); 1995 Auckland 23, Otago 19 (Auckland); 1996 Auckland 46, Counties Manukau 15 (Auckland); 1997 Canterbury 44, Counties Manukau 13 (Christchurch); 1998 Otago 49, Waikato 20 (Dunedin); 1999 Auckland 24, Wellington 18 (Auckland); 2000 Wellington 34, Canterbury 29 (Christchurch).

DOMESTIC RUGBY IN AUSTRALIA 2000

A Season of Innovation

Peter Jenkins

It was a season of innovation and upheaval for the game's grass roots in Australia. The Australian Rugby Union funded a new competition – the Australian Rugby Shield – designed to provide a meaningful pathway for players in developing and regional areas.

'Just what was needed,' according to David Campese, who has long been calling for the code to be fostered outside the traditional heartlands of Sydney, Brisbane and Canberra. There were six teams contesting the championship – Darwin Mosquitoes, Perth Gold, Adelaide Falcons, Melbourne, NSW Country Cockatoos and the Queensland Country Heelers.

The tournament was played across the country and, from the outset, the NSW Country side stamped itself as the likely winners with an unbeaten run through the round robin section. A major surprise, providing a major fillip for the backwater that has been South Australian rugby, was the 20-19 victory for the Falcons over Queensland Country in Adelaide. Perth almost replicated the boilover, going down narrowly to Queensland Country, 15-13, in the semi-finals.

But if the Heelers had others yapping at their heels on their way to the final, they showed no ill effects from the scares, eventually producing an unexpected victory of their own, when it mattered most, by rolling NSW Country 23-17 in the decider. Full-back Mark Leech scored a try in the final minute to seal victory, with Queensland Country crossing for three tries to two in a match played as a curtain raiser to the Bledisloe Cup Test at Stadium Australia.

Outside of Super 12, the big guns of Queensland, NSW and ACT were also involved in a triangular State of the Union series which was memorable only for the ankle injury sustained by Wallaby full-back Matt Burke during a game for the Waratahs. His mishap ensured in-form Queenslander Chris Latham would start the 2000 international season in the No 15 jumper, and hold it for the remainder of the year.

Queensland won the series, played in June, with successive victories over the Waratahs and the Brumbies, although high-profile Wallabies were missing from all three sides.

On the club front, it was another triumphant season in the NSW competition for Randwick. But it was also a championship win caught up in the swirl of controversy as NSW Rugby Union officials decided to streamline the competition at season end, dumping Canberra and Newcastle from the 2001 premiership. There had been a push that brought the Parramatta and West Harbour clubs, in the western suburbs of Sydney, under threat. But logic prevailed and the two clubs based in rugby league nurseries were saved from execution.

The Randwick win, the 31st title in their illustrious history, was achieved with a try to prop Matt Bowman in the dying stages of a dramatic clash at Concord Oval. There were three minutes remaining, with underdogs Sydney University clinging to a 33-29 lead, when Randwick lock Omar Hassanein won a lineout deep in opposition territory. A rolling maul ensued and Bowman managed to charge over in the corner. Winger Jim Pritchard landed a sideline conversion for a 36-33 victory.

Randwick were forced to come from behind having earlier forfeited what appeared a match-winning lead. The Galloping Greens went to half-time 17-13 ahead and were 29-13 to the good before converted tries to NSW Waratahs centre Luke Inman and hooker Brendan Cannon brought University to within two points.

Fly-half and captain Chris Malone later edged the Students ahead with two penalty goals before Bowman spoiled the party for the varsity side, searching for their first premiership since 1972. Bowman's try was Randwick's fifth. University scored three.

Randwick 36   Sydney University 33

Randwick scorers *Tries:* B Williams 2, A Freier, J Pritchard, M Bowman
Conversions: Pritchard (4) *Penalty Goal:* Pritchard

Sydney University scorers *Tries:* E Carter, L Inman, B Cannon *Conversions:*
C Malone (3) *Penalty Goals:* C Malone (4)

In Brisbane, Souths also pulled off a stunning win in the grand final, downing Wests 34-30. But the Randwick jail escape had nothing on this effort from a Souths side led by fly-half Shane Drahm. Shortly before the interval, Wests led 30-3. But the play-making of Drahm, a strong wind at the backs of the Souths side and a dominant performance from replacement back-rower Toutai Kefu – a hardened Wallaby whose impact off the bench proved decisive – all combined to leave Wests shell-shocked.

Drahm led the revival, embarking on an elusive run to score one try himself and mesmerising the Wests defence on a second occasion to put winger Cam Northcott across for another. Souths were still trailing 30-27 with 12 minutes to play when Drahm, a regular in the Queensland Super 12 squad for the past few seasons but struggling to nail down a starting spot, slipped some shoddy defence and sent Kefu careering to the line.

'I've got no words to describe it. How do you blow that lead?' Wests skipper John Roe told the *Sunday Mail*'s Jim Tucker after a third successive grand final defeat. 'Full wraps to Souths. We played only one half of footy, it was a good one, but still only half a game.'

In the first half, Wests scored five tries, two of them through winger Scott Barton, whose first capped a 70-metre movement in which Test full-back Chris Latham figured twice. Barton also took the final pass from Latham to score his second.

Former Test prop and Souths veteran, Dan Crowley, has been playing grand finals since 1986 and told Tucker he could not remember a greater Houdini act. 'I've never seen a better fight back. Having two Wallabies (Kefu and Mark Connors) come on settled things, but it was the young guys who really put their hands up,' Crowley said.

Souths 34   Wests 30

Souths scorers *Tries:* C Northcott 2, T Mandrusiak, S Drahm, T Kefu *Conversions:* Drahm (3) *Penalty Goal:* Drahm

Wests scorers *Tries:* S Barton 2, C Latham, J Colquhoun, C Hughes *Conversion:* T Walsh *Penalty Goal:* T Walsh

In the ACT Premier Division, Wests defeated Tuggeranong 14-13 in the grand final. Box Hill won the first division title in Victoria, downing Melbourne 8-7. Brighton triumphed in South Australia, defeating Southern Suburbs, who were contesting their first competition decider in the club's 54-year history.

University edged out Palmerston in the Northern Territory championship, University won the state-wide competition in Tasmania and Nedlands again proved the premier club in Western Australia.

FIXTURES 2001-02

Venues and fixtures are subject to alteration. At the time of going to press, only the **weekends** *for which some League, Heineken Cup and European Shield matches had been scheduled were known. See press for which days during weekends matches will be played. Tri Nations and Super Twelve fixtures were not known at time of going to press.*

Thursday, 1 November
SPAIN v AUSTRALIA (Madrid)

Friday, 2 November
Heineken Cup *Fourth round*
Pool 2
Ulster v Stade Francais

Pool 6
Newport v Leinster

Saturday, 3 November
RWC Qualifying Match
DENMARK v POLAND
  (Copenhagen)

PARA Qualifying Match
COLOMBIA v BRAZIL

Heineken Cup *Fourth round*
Pool 1
Leicester v Perpignan
Llanelli v Ghial Amatori & Calvisano

Pool 2
Benetton Treviso v Wasps

Pool 3
Biarritz Olympique v Swansea
Bath v Edinburgh

Pool 4
Castres Olympique v Harlequins
Munster v Bridgend

Pool 6
Newcastle v Toulouse

European Shield *Fourth round*
Pool 1
Agen v Rovigo
Montauban v Ebbw Vale

Pool 2
Colomiers v Petrarca

Pool 3
Beziers v Overmach Parma
Pontypridd v Leeds

Pool 4
RDS Roma v Narbonne
Sale v Connacht

Pool 7
GR A N Parma v La Rochelle
Caerphilly v Gloucester

Pool 8
Bologna v Saracens
Dinamo Bucharest v Begles-Bordeaux

IRU/AIB Division One
Clontarf v Co. Carlow
Cork Constitution v De La Salle
  Palmerston
Dungannon v Buccaneers
Galwegians v Ballymena
Lansdowne v Garryowen
Shannon v Blackrock College
St. Mary's College v UC Dublin
Young Munster v Terenure College

Sunday, 4 November
RWC Qualifying Match
CZECH REPUBLIC v UKRAINE
  (Prague)
Oxford University v Australia

Heineken Cup *Fourth round*
Pool 5
Glasgow v Cardiff
Montferrand v Northampton

European Shield *Fourth round*
Pool 2
Madrid 2012 v Pau

Pool 5
Bourgoin v Neath
Bristol v Arix Viadana

Pool 6
Dax v L'Aquila
London Irish v Valladolid

Tuesday, 6 November
Scotland Development XV v Tonga

Thursday, 8 November
Dubai Sevens (Dubai)

Friday, 9 November
Dubai Sevens (Dubai)

RFU/Zurich Premiership
Northampton v Harlequins

Saturday, 10 November
ENGLAND v AUSTRALIA
(Twickenham)
SCOTLAND v TONGA (Murrayfield)
WALES v ARGENTINA (Cardiff)
FRANCE v SOUTH AFRICA (Paris)
ITALY v FIJI (Treviso)

RWC Qualifying Match
CROATIA v SWITZERLAND
(Makarska)

African Nations Final
MOROCCO v SOUTH AFRICA
under-23 (Casablanca)

RFU/Zurich Premiership
Gloucester v Bristol

Sunday, 11 November
IRELAND v SAMOA (Lansdowne
Road)

RWC Qualifying Match
GERMANY v DENMARK
(Heidelburg)

RFU/Zurich Premiership
Bath v London Irish
Leeds v Leicester
London Wasps v Newcastle
Saracens v Sale

SRU/BT Premiership
Aberdeen GSFP v Kirkcaldy
Currie v Hawick
Glasgow Hawks v Stirling County
Heriot's FP v Gala
Melrose v Boroughmuir

Tuesday, 13 November
Ireland A v New Zealand (Ravenhill,
Belfast)

Wednesday, 14 November
France A v South Africa A (Tarbes)

Friday, 16 November
RFU/Zurich Premiership
Harlequins v Saracens

Saturday, 17 November
ENGLAND v ROMANIA
(Twickenham)
IRELAND v NEW ZEALAND
(Lansdowne Road)
WALES v TONGA (Cardiff)
FRANCE v AUSTRALIA (Marseilles)
ITALY v SOUTH AFRICA (Genoa)

PARA Qualifying Matches
BRAZIL v VENEZUELA
PERU v COLOMBIA
IRB World Sevens Series (Durban)

RFU/Zurich Premiership
Sale v Leicester

Sunday, 18 November
SCOTLAND v ARGENTINA
(Murrayfield)
French Barbarians v Fiji (Toulon)
IRB World Sevens Series (Durban)

RFU/Zurich Premiership
Newcastle v Gloucester
Bristol v Bath
London Irish v Northampton
London Wasps v Leeds

Tuesday, 20 November
Scotland A v New Zealand (Perth)

Friday, 23 November
RFU/Zurich Premiership
Leicester v Harlequins

Saturday, 24 November
ENGLAND v SOUTH AFRICA
(Twickenham)
SCOTLAND v NEW ZEALAND
(Murrayfield)
FRANCE v FIJI (St Etienne)
ITALY v SAMOA (L'Aquila)

RWC Qualifying Matches
BELGIUM v CROATIA (Brussels)
SWITZERLAND v UKRAINE
(Hermance)
KENYA v CAMEROON (Nairobi)

RFU/Zurich Premiership
Gloucester v London Wasps

Sunday, 25 November
WALES v AUSTRALIA (Cardiff)

RWC Qualifying Match
GERMANY v LATVIA (Hanover)

RFU/Zurich Premiership
Bath v Newcastle
Leeds v Sale
Northampton v Bristol
Saracens v London Irish

Wednesday, 28 November
Barbarians v Australia (Cardiff)

Saturday, 1 December
ARGENTINA v NEW ZEALAND
(Buenos Aires)
UNITED STATES v SOUTH AFRICA (Houston)

Celtic League *Quarter Finals*

RFU/Zurich Premiership
Gloucester v Leeds
Harlequins v Sale

SRU/BT Premiership
Boroughmuir v Glasgow Hawks
Gala v Aberdeen GSFP
Hawick v Heriot's FP
Kirkcaldy v Melrose
Stirling County v Currie

IRU/AIB Division One
Ballymena v Lansdowne
Blackrock College v Young Munster
Co. Carlow v Buccaneers
De La Salle Palmerston v Dungannon
Galwegians v Shannon
Garryowen v Terenure College
St. Mary's College v Cork Constitution
UC Dublin v Clontarf

Sunday, 2 December
RFU/Zurich Premiership
Newcastle v Northampton
Bristol v Saracens
London Irish v Leicester
London Wasps v Bath

Saturday, 8 December
Celtic League *Semi Finals*

RFU/Zurich Premiership
Bath v Gloucester
Leicester v Bristol
Northampton v London Wasps
Sale v London Irish

WRU/SRU Welsh/Scottish League
Ebbw Vale v Neath
Edinburgh v Bridgend
Glasgow v Cardiff
Llanelli v Newport
Swansea v Caerphilly

IRU/AIB Division One
Buccaneers v Garryowen
Clontarf v Ballymena
Cork Constitution v Galwegians
Dungannon v Blackrock College
Lansdowne v UC Dublin
Shannon v St. Mary's College
Terenure College v Co. Carlow
Young Munster v De La Salle
 Palmerston

Sunday, 9 December
RFU/Zurich Premiership
Leeds v Harlequins
Saracens v Newcastle

Tuesday, 11 December
**Oxford University v Cambridge
 University** (Twickenham)

Saturday, 15 December
Celtic League *FINAL*

RFU Cup *Sixth Round*

WRU/SRU Welsh/Scottish League
Bridgend v Ebbw Vale
Caerphilly v Newport
Cardiff v Neath
Llanelli v Edinburgh
Swansea v Pontypridd

SRU/BT Premiership
Aberdeen GSFP v Hawick
Currie v Boroughmuir
Gala v Kirkcaldy
Glasgow Hawks v Melrose
Heriot's FP v Stirling County

IRU/AIB Division One
Ballymena v Buccaneers
Blackrock College v Co. Carlow

Cork Constitution v Dungannon
De La Salle Palmerston v Garryowen
Galwegians v Lansdowne
Shannon v Young Munster
St. Mary's College v Clontarf
UC Dublin v Terenure College

Saturday, 22 December
RFU/Zurich Premiership
Harlequins v Leicester
Sale v Leeds

SRU Inter-District Championship
Scottish Borders v Scottish Exiles
Caledonia v Edinburgh District

WRU/SRU Welsh/Scottish League
Bridgend v Cardiff
Caerphilly v Glasgow
Edinburgh v Swansea
Llanelli v Neath
Pontypridd v Ebbw Vale

Sunday, 23 December
RFU/Zurich Premiership
Newcastle v Bath
Bristol v Northampton
London Irish v Saracens
London Wasps v Gloucester

Wednesday, 26 December
WRU/SRU Welsh/Scottish League
Cardiff v Pontypridd
Glasgow v Edinburgh
Neath v Caerphilly
Newport v Ebbw Vale
Swansea v Llanelli

Thursday, 27 December
RFU/Zurich Premiership
Leicester v Sale

SRU Inter-District Championship
Scottish Exiles v Caledonia
Edinburgh District v Glasgow District

Saturday, 29 December
RFU/Zurich Premiership
Bath v Bristol
Gloucester v Newcastle
Northampton v London Irish

SRU Inter-District Championship
Glasgow District v Caledonia
Scottish Borders v Edinburgh District

IRU/Guinness Inter-Provincial Championship
Connacht v Leinster (Galway)

WRU/SRU Welsh/Scottish League
Bridgend v Llanelli
Caerphilly v Edinburgh
Ebbw Vale v Cardiff
Neath v Swansea
Pontypridd v Newport

Sunday, 30 December
RFU/Zurich Premiership
Leeds v London Wasps
Saracens v Harlequins

Thursday, 3 January 2002
SRU Inter-District Championship
Caledonia v Scottish Borders
Scottish Exiles v Glasgow District

Friday, 4 January
IRB World Sevens Series (Punta del Este)

Fri, Sat, Sun, 4/5/6 January
Heineken Cup *Fifth round*
Pool 1
Leicester v Ghial Amatori & Calvisano
Perpignan v Llanelli

Pool 2
Benetton Treviso v Stade Francais
Wasps v Ulster

Pool 3
Biarritz Olympique v Edinburgh
Swansea v Bath

Pool 4
Bridgend v Castres Olympique
Munster v Harlequins

Pool 5
Glasgow v Northampton
Cardiff v Montferrand

Pool 6
Newcastle v Leinster
Toulouse v Newport

European Shield *Fifth round*
Pool 1
Agen v Montauban
Rovigo v Ebbw Vale

Pool 2
Madrid 2012 v Petrarca
Pau v Colomiers

Pool 3
Beziers v Leeds
Overmach Parma v Pontypridd

Pool 4
Connacht v Roma Olimpic
Sale v Narbonne

Pool 5
Bourgoin v Arix Viadana
Neath v Bristol

Pool 6
Dax v Valladolid
L'Aquila v London Irish

Pool 7
Caerphilly v La Rochelle
Gloucester v GR A N Parma

Pool 8
Bologna v Begles-Bordeaux
Saracens v Dinamo Bucharest

Saturday, 5 January
IRB World Sevens Series (Punta del Este)

SRU Inter-District Championship
Edinburgh District v Scottish Exiles
Glasgow District v Scottish Borders

IRU/AIB Division One
Buccaneers v UC Dublin

Clontarf v Galwegians
Co. Carlow v De La Salle Palmerston
Dungannon v Shannon
Garryowen v Blackrock College
Lansdowne v St. Mary's College
Terenure College v Ballymena
Young Munster v Cork Constitution

Friday, 11 January
IRB World Sevens Series (Mar del
Plata)

Fri, Sat, Sun, 11/12/13 January
Heineken Cup *Sixth round*
Pool 1
Ghial Amatori & Calvisano v
Perpignan
Llanelli v Leicester

Pool 2
Stade Francais v Wasps
Ulster v Benetton Treviso

Pool 3
Bath v Biarritz Olympique
Edinburgh v Swansea

Pool 4
Castres Olympique v Munster
Harlequins v Bridgend

Pool 5
Montferrand v Glasgow
Northampton v Cardiff

Pool 6
Newport v Newcastle
Toulouse v Leinster

European Shield *Sixth round*
Pool 1
Ebbw Vale v Agen
Montauban v Rovigo

Pool 2
Colomiers v Madrid 2012
Petrarca v Pau

Pool 3
Leeds v Overmach Parma
Pontypridd v Beziers

Pool 4
Narbonne v Connacht
Roma Olimpic v Sale

Pool 5
Arix Viadana v Neath
Bristol v Bourgoin

Pool 6
London Irish v Dax
Valladolid v L'Aquila

Pool 7
GR A N Parma v Caerphilly
La Rochelle v Gloucester

Pool 8
Begles-Bordeaux v Saracens
Bologna v Dinamo Bucharest

Saturday, 12 January
IRB World Sevens Series (Mar del
Plata)

SRU/BT Premiership
Boroughmuir v Heriot's FP
Hawick v Gala
Kirkcaldy v Glasgow Hawks
Melrose v Currie
Stirling County v Aberdeen GSFP

IRU/AIB Division One
Cork Constitution v Shannon
De La Salle Palmerston v Blackrock
College
Dungannon v Young Munster
Galwegians v St. Mary's College
Garryowen v Co. Carlow
Lansdowne v Clontarf
Terenure College v Buccaneers
UC Dublin v Ballymena

Saturday, 19 January
RFU Cup *Quarter Finals*

**IRU/Guinness Inter-Provincial
Championship**
Connacht v Ulster (Galway)
Munster v Leinster (Limerick)

WRU/SRU Welsh/Scottish League
Caerphilly v Pontypridd
Cardiff v Glasgow
Newport v Llanelli

SRU/BT Premiership
Aberdeen GSFP v Boroughmuir
Currie v Glasgow Hawks
Gala v Stirling County
Hawick v Kirkcaldy
Heriot's FP v Melrose

IRU/AIB Division One
Ballymena v Dungannon
Blackrock College v Buccaneers
Cork Constitution v Clontarf
De La Salle Palmerston v Terenure
   College
Galwegians v Garryowen
Shannon v Lansdowne
St. Mary's College v Co. Carlow
UC Dublin v Young Munster

Fri, Sat, Sun, 25/26/27 January
Heineken Cup *Quarter Finals*

European Shield *Quarter Finals*

Saturday, 26 January
RFU/Zurich Premiership
Leicester v Leeds
Harlequins v Northampton
Sale v Saracens

SRU/BT Premiership
Boroughmuir v Gala
Glasgow Hawks v Heriot's FP
Kirkcaldy v Currie
Melrose v Aberdeen GSFP
Stirling County v Hawick

Sunday, 27 January
RFU/Zurich Premiership
Newcastle v London Wasps
Bristol v Gloucester
London Irish v Bath

Friday, 1 February
Scotland A v England A
France A v Italy A
IRB World Sevens Series (Brisbane)

Saturday, 2 February
**Lloyds TSB Six Nations
   Championship**
SCOTLAND v ENGLAND
   (Murrayfield)
FRANCE v ITALY (Stade de France)
Ireland A v Wales A
IRB World Sevens Series (Brisbane)

Sunday, 3 February
**Lloyds TSB Six Nations
   Championship**
IRELAND v WALES (Lansdowne
   Road)

European Nations Cup
GEORGIA v THE NETHERLANDS
ROMANIA v PORTUGAL
RUSSIA v SPAIN

Friday, 8 February
IRB World Sevens Series (Wellington)

Saturday, 9 February
IRB World Sevens Series (Wellington)

RFU/Zurich Premiership
Bath v Harlequins
Gloucester v London Irish
Northampton v Sale

WRU/SRU Welsh/Scottish League
Caerphilly v Swansea
Ebbw Vale v Llanelli
Edinburgh v Newport
Neath v Bridgend
Pontypridd v Glasgow

IRU/AIB Division One
Buccaneers v De La Salle Palmerston
Clontarf v Shannon
Co. Carlow v Galwegians
Dungannon v UC Dublin
Garryowen v St. Mary's College
Lansdowne v Cork Constitution
Terenure College v Blackrock College
Young Munster v Ballymena

Sunday, 10 February
RFU/Zurich Premiership
Leeds v Newcastle
London Wasps v Bristol
Saracens v Leicester

Friday, 15 February
England A v Ireland A
Wales A v France A
Italy A v Scotland A

Saturday, 16 February
Lloyds TSB Six Nations
Championship
ENGLAND v IRELAND
(Twickenham)
WALES v FRANCE (Cardiff)
ITALY v SCOTLAND (Rome)

Sunday, 17 February
European Nations Cup
PORTUGAL v GEORGIA
ROMANIA v SPAIN
RUSSIA v THE NETHERLANDS

Saturday, 23 February
RFU/Zurich Premiership
Leicester v Northampton
Harlequins v Gloucester
Sale v Bath

SRU/BT Premiership
Aberdeen GSFP v Glasgow Hawks
Gala v Melrose
Hawick v Boroughmuir
Heriot's FP v Currie
Stirling County v Kirkcaldy

IRU/AIB Division One
Ballymena v Blackrock College
Clontarf v Terenure College
Cork Constitution v Garryowen
Galwegians v Young Munster
Lansdowne v Buccaneers
Shannon v Co. Carlow
St. Mary's College v Dungannon
UC Dublin v De La Salle Palmerston

WRU/Principality Cup *Seventh Round*

Sunday, 24 February
RFU/Zurich Premiership
Bristol v Newcastle
London Irish v London Wasps
Saracens v Leeds

Friday, 1 March
Ireland A v Scotland A
France A v England A
Wales A v Italy A

Saturday, 2 March
Lloyds TSB Six Nations
Championship
IRELAND v SCOTLAND
(Lansdowne Road)
FRANCE v ENGLAND (Stade de
France)
WALES v ITALY (Cardiff)

Sunday, 3 March
European Nations Cup
GEORGIA v RUSSIA
PORTUGAL v SPAIN
THE NETHERLANDS v ROMANIA

Saturday, 9 March
RFU Cup *Semi Finals*

RFU/Zurich Premiership
Bath v Leicester
Gloucester v Sale
Northampton v Saracens

WRU/SRU Welsh/Scottish League
Caerphilly v Bridgend
Cardiff v Ebbw Vale
Newport v Glasgow
Pontypridd v Neath
Swansea v Edinburgh

SRU/BT Premiership
Boroughmuir v Stirling County
Currie v Aberdeen GSFP
Glasgow Hawks v Gala
Heriot's FP v Kirkcaldy
Melrose v Hawick

IRU/AIB Division One
Blackrock College v UC Dublin
Buccaneers v Clontarf
Co. Carlow v Cork Constitution
De La Salle Palmerston v Ballymena
Dungannon v Galwegians
Garryowen v Shannon
Terenure College v Lansdowne
Young Munster v St. Mary's College

Sunday, 10 March
RFU/Zurich Premiership
Leeds v Bristol
Newcastle v London Irish
London Wasps v Harlequins

Saturday, 16 March
RFU/Zurich Premiership
Leicester v Gloucester
London Irish v Bristol
Harlequins v Newcastle
Northampton v Leeds
Sale v London Wasps

WRU/SRU Welsh/Scottish League
Bridgend v Edinburgh
Ebbw Vale v Newport
Glasgow v Neath
Llanelli v Caerphilly
Pontypridd v Cardiff

SRU/BT Premiership
Aberdeen GSFP v Heriot's FP
Gala v Currie
Hawick v Glasgow Hawks
Kirkcaldy v Boroughmuir
Stirling County v Melrose

IRU/AIB Division One
Ballymena v Garryowen
Clontarf v Young Munster
Cork Constitution v Terenure College
Galwegians v Blackrock College
Lansdowne v Dungannon
Shannon v Buccaneers
St. Mary's College v De La Salle
   Palmerston
UC Dublin v Co. Carlow

Sat, Sun, 16/17 March
IRB World Sevens Series (Shanghai)

Sunday, 17 March
RFU/Zurich Premiership
Saracens v Bath

Wednesday, 20 March
**IRB/FIRA-AER World Under-19
   Tournament** (Venice)

Friday, 22 March
England A v Wales A
Scotland A v France A
Ireland A v Italy A

IRB World Sevens Series (Hong Kong)

Saturday, 23 March
**Lloyds TSB Six Nations
   Championship**
ENGLAND v WALES (Twickenham)
SCOTLAND v FRANCE
   (Murrayfield)
IRELAND v ITALY (Lansdowne
   Road)

IRB World Sevens Series (Hong Kong)

Sunday, 24 March
European Nations Cup
RUSSIA v ROMANIA
SPAIN v GEORGIA
**THE NETHERLANDS v
   PORTUGAL**

IRB World Sevens Series (Hong Kong)

Saturday, 30 March
RFU/Zurich Premiership
Bath v Northampton
Gloucester v Saracens

IRU/AIB Division One
Blackrock College v St. Mary's College
Buccaneers v Cork Constitution
Carlow v Ballymena
De La Salle Palmerston v Galwegians
Dungannon v Clontarf
Garryowen v UC Dublin
Terenure College v Shannon

WRU/Principality Cup *Quarter Finals*

Sunday, 31 March

RFU/Zurich Premiership
Leeds v London Irish
Newcastle v Sale
Bristol v Harlequins
London Wasps v Leicester

Friday, 5 April

Wales A v Scotland A
France A v Ireland A
Italy A v England A

Saturday, 6 April

Lloyds TSB Six Nations Championship
WALES v SCOTLAND (Cardiff)
FRANCE v IRELAND (Stade de France)
ITALY v ENGLAND (Rome)

RWC Qualifying Matches
LATVIA v DENMARK
POLAND v GERMANY (Sopot)

Sunday, 7 April

European Nations Cup
GEORGIA v ROMANIA
PORTUGAL v RUSSIA
SPAIN v THE NETHERLANDS

Saturday, 13 April

RFU/Zurich Premiership
Bath v Leeds
Leicester v Newcastle
Northampton v Gloucester
Sale v Bristol

WRU/Principality Cup *Semi Finals*

WRU/SRU Welsh/Scottish League
Edinburgh v Ebbw Vale
Neath v Glasgow

Sunday, 14 April

RFU/Zurich Premiership
London Irish v Harlequins
Saracens v London Wasps

Wednesday, 17 April

WRU/SRU Welsh/Scottish League
Cardiff v Caerphilly
Glasgow v Bridgend
Llanelli v Pontypridd
Newport v Neath
Swansea v Ebbw Vale

Friday, 19 April

IRU/Guinness Inter-Provincial Championship
Leinster v Munster (Dublin)
Ulster v Connacht (Ravenhill, Belfast)

Saturday, 20 April

RFU Cup *FINAL* (Twickenham)

IRB World Sevens Series (Singapore)

WRU/SRU Welsh/Scottish League
Edinburgh v Cardiff
Llanelli v Glasgow
Neath v Ebbw Vale
Pontypridd v Bridgend
Swansea v Newport

Sunday, 21 April

IRB World Sevens Series (Singapore)

Friday, 26 April

IRU/Guinness Inter-Provincial Championship
Ulster v Leinster (Ravenhill, Belfast)

Sat, Sun, 27/28 April

IRB World Sevens Series (Kuala Lumpar)
Heineken Cup *Semi Finals*
European Shield *Semi Finals*

Saturday, 27 April

IRU/Guinness Inter-Provincial Championship
Connacht v Munster (Galway)

WRU/SRU Welsh/Scottish League
Bridgend v Swansea
Caerphilly v Llanelli
Ebbw Vale v Glasgow
Newport v Cardiff
Pontypridd v Edinburgh

Saturday, 4 May
RFU/Zurich Premiership
Gloucester v Bath
Harlequins v Leeds

WRU/SRU Welsh/Scottish League
Bridgend v Caerphilly
Edinburgh v Llanelli
Glasgow v Newport
Neath v Pontypridd
Swansea v Cardiff

Sunday, 5 May
RFU/Zurich Premiership
Newcastle v Saracens
Bristol v Leicester
London Irish v Sale
London Wasps v Northampton

Wednesday, 8 May
WRU/SRU Welsh/Scottish League
Cardiff v Bridgend
Ebbw Vale v Caerphilly
Newport v Pontypridd
Swansea v Neath

Saturday, 11 May
RFU/Zurich Premiership
Bath v London Wasps
Leicester v London Irish
Northampton v Newcastle
Leeds v Gloucester
Sale v Harlequins
Saracens v Bristol

WRU/SRU Welsh/Scottish League
Glasgow v Swansea
Cardiff v Llanelli
Neath v Edinburgh
Newport v Bridgend

Monday, 13 May
Womens Rugby World Cup
(Barcelona)

Friday, 17 May
IRU/Guinness Inter-Provincial Championship
Leinster v Connacht

WRU/SRU Welsh/Scottish League
Edinburgh v Glasgow

Saturday, 18 May
WRU/Principality Cup *FINAL*
(Cardiff)

IRU/Guinness Inter-Provincial Championship
Munster v Ulster (Limerick)

Friday, 24 May
IRB World Sevens Series (London)

Saturday, 25 May
Heineken Cup *FINAL*

Womens World Cup *FINAL*
(Barcelona)

IRB World Sevens Series (London)

Sat, Sun, 25/26 May
European Shield *FINAL*

Sunday, 26 May
England v Barbarians (Twickenham)

Friday, 31 May
IRB World Sevens Series (Wales)

Saturday, 1 June
IRB World Sevens Series (Wales)

Sat, Sun 3/4 August
Commonwealth Games Tournament

MEMBER UNIONS OF THE IRB

IRB MEMBER UNIONS

Andorra
Name: Federació Andorrana de Rugby
Address: 31, Baixada pel Molí. Andorra La Vella
– Principat d'Andorra
Phone: (+376) 822232
Fax: (+376) 864564
Website: http://www.vpcrugbyxv.org/
E-mail: mailto:vpc@solucions.ad
IRB Affiliation: 1991
Foundation: 23.04.1986
Chairman: Josep Arasanz Serra
Secretary: Carles Font Rossel
National Coach: Antoni Castillo/Jaume Esteve
Affiliated Clubs: 2
Total Players: 504
Referees: 30
Home Ground: Camp del Micg, 31, Baixada pel
Molí. Andorra La Vella – Principat d'Andorra
Capacity: 600 (seated)
Official Kit (Shirt/Shorts/Stockings):
Blue-Yellow-Red/Blue-Yellow-Red/Red
Most capped player: Jordi Piñero

Arabian Gulf
Name: Arabian Gulf Rugby Football Union
Address: P.O. Box 17123, Jebel Ali, Dubai –
U.A.E.
Phone: (+971) 04 8836827
Fax: (+971) 04 8836810
Website: http://www.AGRFU.com/
E-mail: georgegrant@bblinternational.com
IRB Affiliation: 10.1990
Foundation: 1984
Chairman: Gordon Duncan
Secretary: George Grant
National Coach: Darryl Weir
Affiliated Clubs: 22
Total Players: 2,305
Referees: 15
Home Ground: Dubai, Bahrain & Doha, *Capacity:*
3,000
Official Kit (Shirt/Shorts/Stockings): White (red,
green & Blue stripes)/Black/White
Most capped player: Chris Mathews

Argentina
Name: Union Argentina de Rugby
Address: Avda. Rivadavia 1227, entre piso, 1033
Capital Federal, Buenos Aires
Phone: (+541) 1 43 83 22 11
Fax: (+541) 1 43 83 25 70
Website: http://www.AGRFU.com/
www.uar.com.ar
E-mail: uarugby@uar.com.ar
IRB Affiliation: 1987
Foundation: 1899
President: Luis Chaluleu
Secretary: Federico Fleitas
National Coach: Marcelo Loffreda – Daniel Baetti

Affiliated Clubs: 280
Total Players: 40,000
Referees: 800
Official Kit (Shirt/Shorts/Stockings): Sky
Blue/White
Most capped player: Lisandro Arbizu

Australia
Name: Australian Rugby Union
Address: 12-14 Mount Street, North Sydney
NSW2060 – Australia
Phone: (+61) 29955 3466
Fax: (+61) 2 9955 3299
Website: http://www.rugby.com.au/
E-mail: strath@rugby.com.au
IRB Affiliation: 1949
Foundation: 1949
Chairman: Bob Tuckey
CEO: John O'Neill (managing Director & CEO)
National Coach: Eddie Jones
Affiliated Clubs: 752
Total Players: 163,021
Official Kit (Shirt/Shorts/Stockings):
Gold/Green/Green with Gold hoop
Most capped player: David Campese

Austria
Name: Österreichischer Rugby Verband
Address: c/o Thomas Per Gabriel,
Peter-Jordanstrasse 31, 1190 Wien – Österreich
Phone: (+43) 664 310 91 37
Website: http://www.rugby-austria.com/
E-mail: mailto:thomas.gabriel@rugby.at
IRB Affiliation: 1992
Foundation: 1990
Chairman: Thomas Per Gbariel
Secretary: Paul Duteil
National Coach: Gael Mouysset
Affiliated Clubs: 10
Total Players: 400
Referees: 10
Home Ground: Casino Stadion Hohe Warte, Hohe
Warte/Klabundgasse, 1190 Wien – Österreich
Capacity: 6,000
Official Kit (Shirt/Shorts/Stockings): Black-White
hoops/Black/Black-White hoops
Most capped player: Christian Schwab

Bahamas
Name: Bahamas Rugby Union
Address: P.O. Box N-7213, Nassau – Bahamas
Phone: (+1 242) 323 2165
Fax: (+1 242) 322 8185
E-mail: mailto:stephen@bahamasferries.com
IRB Affiliation: 1996
Foundation: 1973
Chairman: William Mills
Secretary: Matt Adams
National Coach: Garry Markham
Affiliated Clubs: 4
Total Players: 284
Referees: 5

Home Ground: Winton Rugby Pitch, P.O. Box
N-7213, Nassau – Bahamas
Capacity: 300
Official Kit (Shirt/Shorts/Stockings):
Gold/Black/Aqua-Marine
Most capped player: Jon Isaacs

Barbados

Name: Barbados Rugby Football Union
Address: The Plantation Complex, St. Lawrence
Main Road, Christ Church – Barbados
Phone: (+246) 437 3836
Fax: (+246) 437 3838
Website: http://www.rugbybds.com/
E-mail: mailto:brewer@sunbeach.net
IRB Affiliation: 1995
Foundation: 1965
Chairman: Joe Whipple
Secretary: Jason Brewer
Affiliated Clubs: 5
Total Players: 300
Referees: 4
Home Ground: Garrison Savannah, St. Michael –
Barbados
Official Kit (Shirt/Shorts/Stockings): Royal
Blue–Yellow/Black/Royal Blue–Yellow

Belgium

Name: Fédération Belge de Rugby
Address: Avenue de Marathon 135C, Boîte 5,
B-1020 Bruxelles – Belgique
Phone: (+32) 2 479 9332
Fax: (+32) 2 476 2282
E-mail: mailto:fbrb@online.be
IRB Affiliation: 1988
Foundation: 22.09.1931
Chairman: Philippe Damas
Secretary: Eric Willensens
Affiliated Clubs: 46
Total Players: 4,121
Referees: 55
Home Ground: Stadium 'Petit Heysel', Bruxelles –
Belgique, *Capacity:* 4,000
Official Kit (Shirt/Shorts/Stockings):
Black-Yellow-Red/Black/White

Bermuda

Name: Bermuda Rugby Football Union
Address: PO Box HM 1909, Hamilton HM EX –
Bermuda
Phone: (+441) 236 2057
Fax: (+441) 295 3122
E-mail: mailto:bermudarugby@ibl.bm
IRB Affiliation: 1992
Foundation: 1964
President: Dennis Dwyer
Secretary: John Williams
*Affiliated Clubs:*4
Total Players: 120
Official Kit: Blue/Black

Bosnia & Herzegovina

Name: Rugby Football Union of Bosnia &
Herzegovina
Address: Kralja Tvrtka I St. No. 5, PP 45, 72000
Zenica – Bosnia and Herzegovina

Phone: (+387) 32416 323
Fax: (+387) 32416 323
IRB Affiliation: 03.10.1996
Foundation: 13.06.1992
Chairman: Kukolj Bosko
National Coach: Vehbovic Nasir
Affiliated Clubs: 7
Total Players: 594
Referees: 12
Home Ground: Kamberovica polje bb 72000
Zenica – Bosnia & Hercegovina, *Capacity:*
2,000
Official Kit (Shirt/Shorts/Stockings): Sky
Blue/White/White Sky Blue
Most capped player: Karic Husein

Botswana

Name: Botswana Rugby Union
Address: PO Box 632, Francistown – Botswana
Phone: (+267) 212 040
Fax: (+267) 213 761
E-mail: mailto:fnr@info.bw
IRB Affiliation: 1994
Foundation: 1992
President: Andrew Seale
Secretary: Ian White
*Affiliated Clubs:*5
Total Players: 425
Official Kit (Shirt/Shorts/Socks):
Black/White/Blue
Most capped player: Mark Oosthuizen

Brazil

Name: Associação Brasileira de Rugby
Address: R. Dna. Germaine Burchard, 451 – S.53,
Água Branca – São Paulo – SP – Brasil –
CEP: 05002-062
Phone: (+55) 11 3868 1703/11 3864 1336
Fax: (+55) 11 3864 1336
E-mail: mailto:abr@rugbynews.com.br
mailto:abr@ifxbrasil.com.br
IRB Affiliation: 10.1995
Foundation: 20.12.1972
Chairman: Jean-François Teisseire
Secretary: Luis Felipe Monteiro de Barros
National Coach: Flávio Santos
Affiliated Clubs: 14
Total Players: 530
Referees: 4
Official Kit (Shirt/Shorts/Stockings):
Yellow–Green/Green/White
Most capped player: Sebastian Arietti

Bulgaria

Name: Bulgarian Rugby Federation
Address: 75, V. Levski, Sofia 1040 – Bulgaria
Phone: (+359) 2 865 329
Fax: (+359) 2 9815 728
IRB Affiliation: 1992
Foundation: 1962
Chairman: Lubomir Stoitchkov
Secretary: G. Marinkin
National Coach: Ivan Mihailov
Affiliated Clubs: 24
Total Players: 1,645
Referees: 35

Official Kit (Shirt/Shorts/Stockings): Red/Green/White
Most capped player: Ivanov Antonio

Cameroon

Name: Cameroonian Rugby Federation
Address: Sporting Commission of FECARUGBY, PO Box 316, Yaounde – Cameroon
Phone: (+237) 30 53 32
Fax: (+237) 30 53 92
E-mail: mailto:fecarugby@iccnet.cm
IRB Affiliation: 1999
Foundation: 1996
President: René Lej
Affiliated Clubs: 9
Total Players: 400

Canada

Name: Rugby Canada
Address: 2197 Riverside Drive, Ottawa, Ontario – Canada K1H 7X3
Phone: (+613) 521 2466
Fax: (+613) 521 3928
Website: http://www.rugbycanada.ca/
E-mail: mailto:rugbycanada@rugbycanada.ca
IRB Affiliation: 1986
Foundation: 1965
Chairman: Barry Giffen
Secretary: Iain Taylor
National Coach: T B C
Affiliated Clubs: 430
Total Players: 34,500
Referees: 200
Home Ground: Capacity: 5,000 – 10,000
Official Kit (Shirt/Shorts/Stockings): Red with black-red-white stripe & maple leaves on sleeves/ Black/Red – Black
Most capped player: Al Charron

Cayman Islands

Name: Cayman Rugby Football Union
Address: PO Box 1161, Georgetown – Cayman Islands BWI
Phone: (+1345) 949 7960
Fax: (+1345) 949 7004
IRB Affiliation: 1997
Foundation: 1971
President: Sydney Coleman
Secretary: Stuart Diamond
Affiliated Clubs: 6
Total Players: 1247
Official Kit (Shirt/Shorts/Socks): Green/White

Chile

Name: Federación de Rugby de Chile
Address: Av.Lorrain 11095 La Reine, Santiago – Chile
Phone: (+56) 2 275 9341/9315/1082
Fax: (+56) 2 6653191
Website: http://www.feruchi.cl/
E-mail: feruchi@ctcruen.a.cl
IRB Affiliation: 05.11.1991
Foundation: 04.05.1935
Chairman: Miguel A. Mujica
Secretary: Bernardo Santillan
National Coach: Raul Carchio

Affiliated Clubs: 144
Total Players: 13,710
Referees: 80
Home Ground: Centro Alto Pendimiento del Rugby, Av. Larraín 11095, La Reina, Santiago – Chile, *Capacity:* 4,000
Official Kit (Shirt/Shorts/Stockings): Red/Blue/Red-Blue
Most capped player: Rodrigo Lacassie

China

Name: China Rugby Union
Address: No. 9 Tiyuguan Road, Cchongwen District, Beijing 100763 – People's Republic of China
Phone: (+86 10) 8562 6001/6002
Fax: (+86 10) 8582 5994
E-mail: cga_cra@263.net
IRB Affiliation: 1997
Foundation: 1996
Secretary: Li Gaochao
Affiliated Clubs: 30
Total Players: 954
Official Kit (Shirt/Shorts/Socks): Blue/White

Chinese Taipei

Name: Chinese Taipei Rugby Football Union
Address: No. 10 Pa-te Road, Section, Taipei, Taiwan 10560
Phone: (+886) 22 578 7856
Fax: (+886) 22 578 3602
IRB Affiliation: 1986
Foundation: 1946
President: Tsai Cheng
Secretary: Ching-Chung Lin
Affiliated Clubs: 15
Total Players: 1,225
Official Kit (Shirt/Shorts/Socks): Blue/White

Colombia

Name: Federación Colombia de Rugby
Address: Calle 79 # 10-50, Apto. 104, Bogota – Colombia
Phone: (+57) 1 2363617
Fax: (+57) 1 4813099
E-mail: mailto:rianovic@col.net.co
IRB Affiliation: 1999
Chairman: William Nelson Paul
National Coach: Andrew Wright
Affiliated Clubs: 18
Total Players: 460
Referees: 3
Official Kit (Shirt/Shorts/Stockings): Yellow/Dark Blue/Red

Cook Islands

Name: Cook Islands Rugby Union
Address: P.O. Box 898, Rarotonga – Cook Islands
Phone: (+682) 25854
Fax: (+682) 25853
E-mail: mailto:cirugby@cirfu.org.ck
IRB Affiliation: 01.03.1995
Foundation: 01.03.1989
Chairman: Nooroa Tou
Secretary: Antony Turua
National Coach: John McKittrick

Affiliated Clubs: 10
Total Players: 900
Referees: 30
Home Ground: Tereora National Stadium, Nikao, Rarotonga – Cook Islands
Capacity: 5,000
Official Kit (Shirt/Shorts/Stockings): White-Gold-Green/Green/White with Green Band
Most capped player: George George

Croatia

Name: Hrvatski Ragbijaski Savez
Address: Trg sportova 11, 10000 Zagreb – Croatia
Phone: (+385) 013650 250/98318 528
Fax: (+385) 3092 921
E-mail: mailto:cro.rugby@zg.hinet.hr
IRB Affiliation: 12.11.1992
Foundation: 01.04.1962
Chairman: Ivo Jurisic
Secretary: Velimir Juricko
National Coach: Richard Walter Borich
Affiliated Clubs: 9
Total Players: 1,124
Referees: 14
Home Ground: Stadion Nada, Zrinsko Frankopanska 12, 21000 Split – Croatia, *Capacity:* 6,000
Official Kit (Shirt/Shorts/Stockings): Red–White/White/Blue
Most capped player: Pero Prebeg

Czech Republic

Name: Èeská Rugbyová Unie
Address: Mezi stadiony, P.S. 40, 160 17 Praha 6 – Èeská Republika
Phone: (+420) 2 33 35 13 41
Fax: (+420) 2 33 35 13 41
E-mail: mailto:rugby@cstv.cz
IRB Affiliation: 11.1988
Foundation: 05.05.1926
Chairman: Bruno Kudrna
Secretary: Josef Zábransky
National Coach: Václav Horácek
Affiliated Clubs: 21
Total Players: 2,329
Referees: 59
Home Ground: Tatra Smíchov, Praha 5 Podbelohorská ul. – Èeská Republika
Capacity: 5,000
Official Kit (Shirt/Shorts/Stockings): Red-White-blue stripes (from top to tigh) /White/Blue
Most capped player: Bruno Kudrna

Denmark

Name: Dansk Rugby Union
Address: Idrættens Hus, Brøndby Stadion 20, DK 2605 Brøndby – Denmark
Phone: (+45) 43 26 28 00
Fax: (+45) 43 26 28 01
Website: http://www.rugby.dk/
E-mail: mailto:info@rugby.dk
IRB Affiliation: 03.1988
Foundation: 01.04.1950
Chairman: Ole Nielsen

National Coach: Douglas Langley
Affiliated Clubs: 30
Total Players: 2,722
Seniors: 1,947
Referees: 29
Official Kit (Shirt/Shorts/Stockings): Red/White/Red
Most capped player: Jan Andersen

England

Name: The Rugby Football Union
Address: Rugby House, Rugby Road, Twickenham – England
Phone: (+44) 0208 892 2000
Fax: (+44) 0208 891 3814
Website: http://www.rfu.com/
E-mail: mailto:reception@rfu.com
IRB Affiliation: 1890
Foundation: 26.01.1871
CEO: Francis Baron
National Coach: Clive Woodward
Affiliated Clubs: 1,800
Total Players: 634,460
Referees: 5,000
Home Ground: Twickenham Stadium, Rugby Road, Twickenham TWI IDS – England, *Capacity:* 75,000
Official Kit (Shirt/Shorts/Stockings): White red contrast/White/Navy Blue
Most capped player: Jason Leonard

Fiji

Name: Fiji Rugby Union
Address: 35 Gordon Street, Suva, Fiji
Phone: (+679) 302 787
Fax: (+679) 300 936
Website: http://www.teivovo.com
IRB Affiliation: 1987
Foundation: 1913
National Coach: Ifereimi Tawake
Affiliated Clubs: 600
Total Players: 55,130:
Official Kit (Shirt/Shorts/Socks): White/Black
Most capped player: Ifereimi Tawake

Finland

Name: Suomen Rugbyliitto
Address: Laurinniityntie 13 D 18, 00440 Helsinki – Finland
Phone: (+358) 40 500 69 78
Fax: 358 20475 4319
Website: http://www.members.spree.com/sports/finrugby/
E-mail: mailto:peter.eagling@kone.co
IRB Affiliation: 01.03.2001
Foundation: 01.01.1968
Chairman: Peter Eagling
Secretary: Mikko Johansson
National Coach: Thierry Demoulin
Affiliated Clubs: 4
Total Players: 140
Home Ground: Myllypuron Urheilupuisto, Mustapuronpolku 2, 00900 Helsinki – Finland, *Capacity:* 300

Official Kit (Shirt/Shorts/Stockings): Light
Blue/White/Blue-White
Most capped player: Janne Lumme

France

Name: Fédération Française de Rugby
Address: 9 rue de Liège, 75009 Paris – France
Phone: (+33) 0 153 21 15 15
Fax: (+33) 0 145 26 19 19
Website: http://www.ffr.fr/
IRB Affiliation: 16.03.1978
Foundation: 15.05.1919
Chairman: Bernard Lapasset
Secretary: Alain Doucet
National Coach: Bernard Laporte
Affiliated Clubs: 1,699
Total Players: 230,638
Referees: 2,079
Home Ground: Stade de France, Consortium Stade
de France, 93216 La Plaine Saint-Denis cedex
– France, *Capacity:* 80,000
Official Kit (Shirt/Shorts/Stockings):
Blue/White/Red
Most capped player: Philippe Sella

Georgia

Name: Georgian Rugby Union
Address: 49A, Chavchavadze Ave, Sports
Department, Tbilisi – 62 – Georgia
Phone: (+995) 32 294754
Fax: (+995) 32 294763
Website: http://www.chez.com/gru
E-mail: mailto:gru@gol.ge
mailto:choconap@mnet.fr
IRB Affiliation: 27.02.1992
Foundation: 05.09.1964
Chairman: Bidzina Gegidze
Secretary: George Chumburidze
National Coach: Clause Saurel
Affiliated Clubs: 21
Total Players: 1,410
Referees: 12
Home Ground: National Stadium, 2, Cereteli Ave,
Tbilisi – Georgia
Capacity: 74,000
Official Kit (Shirt/Shorts/Stockings):
Black-Bordeaux-Grey/Black/Black
Alternative Kit (Shirt/Shorts/Stockings):
White-Bordeaux-Grey/Black/Black
Most capped player: Levan Tsabadze

Germany

Name: Deutscher Rugby Verband
Address: Ferdinand-Wilhelm-Fricke-Weg 2 A,
30169 Hannover – Deutschland
Phone: (+49) 0511 14 763
Fax: (+49) 0511 1610206
Website: http://www.rugby.de/
E-mail:
mailto:deutscher-rugby-verband@t-online.de
IRB Affiliation: 1988
Foundation: 04.11.1900
Chairman: Ian Mawcliffe
Secretary: Volker Himmer
National Coach: Jim Lowry
Affiliated Clubs: 104

Total Players: 3,900
Referees: 90
Home Ground: Fritz Grunebaum Stadium,
Heidelberg, *Capacity:* 3,000
Official Kit (Shirt/Shorts/Stockings):
White/Black/Yellow
Most capped player: Horst Kemmling

Guam

Name: Guam rugby Football Union
Address: PO Box 7246, Tamuning, Guam
Phone: (+1671) 477 7250
Fax: (+1671) 472 1264
Website: http://www.guaugby.netpci.com
E-mail: mailto:guafu@ambyth.guam.net
IRB Affiliation: 1998
Foundation: 1997
President: Greg David
Secretary: Ken I Cowan
Affiliated Clubs: 2
Total Players: 235
Official Kit (Shirt/Shorts/Socks): White/Black

Guyana

Name: Guyana Rugby Football Union
Address: P.O. Box 101 730, Georgetown – Guyana
Phone: (+592) 226 0082
Fax: (+592) 226 6879/225 9486
E-mail: mailto:guanarugby@yahoo.com
IRB Affiliation: .10.1995
Foundation: 1920
Chairman: Christopher Nascimento
Secretary: Terrence Grant
National Coach: Sherlock Solomon
Affiliated Clubs: 4
Total Players: 240
Referees: 5
Home Ground: National Park, Thomas Lands,
Georgetown – Guyana, *Capacity:* 600
Official Kit (Shirt/Shorts/Stockings):
Green-Gold/White/Green-Gold
Most capped player: Conrad Arjoon

Hong Kong

Name: Hong Kong Rugby Football Union
Address: Room 2001, Sports House, 1 Stadium
Path, So Kon Po, Causeway Bay – Hong Kong
Phone: (+852) 2504 8311
Fax: (+852) 25767237
Website: http://www.hkrugby.com.hk/
E-mail: mailto:info@hkrugby.com.hk
mailto:info@hksevens.com.hk
IRB Affiliation: 1988
Foundation: 1953
Chairman: John Molloy
Secretary: Clement Lau, Secretary
National Coach: T B C
Affiliated Clubs: 14 Full Members, 7 Associate
Members
Total Players: 5,342
Referees: 42
Home Ground: Hong Kong Stadium, No. 55
Eastern Hospital, So Kon Po, Causeway Bay –
Hong Kong, *Capacity:* 40,000

Official Kit (Shirt/Shorts/Stockings):
Blue-Red-White stripes/Blue/Blue-Red-White
Most capped player: David Lewis

Hungary

Name: Magyar Rögbi Szövetség
Address: 1143 Dóza GY. Út 1-3, Budapest –
Hungary
Phone: (+36) 1 251 1222 (ext. 1297)
Fax: (+36) 1 251 1222 (ext. 1297)
Website: http://www.gsz.hu/
E-mail: mailto:vidaszl@mail.datanet.hu
IRB Affiliation: 1991
Foundation: 03.1990
Chairman: Tamás Fehérvári
Secretary: Stuart Durrant
National Coach: András Neuzer
Affiliated Clubs: 15
Total Players: 1,489
Referees: 25
Official Kit (Shirt/Shorts/Stockings):
Red/White/Red
Most capped player: György Ivánfi

India

Name: Indian Rugby Football Union (IRFU)
Address: Nawab House, 2nd Flr, M. Karve Road,
Marine Lines Bombay 400002 – India
Phone: (+91) 22 2086910/22 2096357
Fax: (+91) 22 2091822/22 2044968
E-mail: mailto:irfu_india@hotmail.com
IRB Affiliation: 29.04.2001
Foundation: 15.09.1968
Chairman: Pramod Khanna
National Coach: Takeo Ishizuka
Affiliated Clubs: 28
Total Players: 2,900
Referees: 10
Home Ground: Bombay Gymkhana (BG), Bombay
– India/Calcutta Cricket & Football Club
(CC&FC), 19/1 Gurusaday Road, Calcutta
700019 – India, *Capacity:* 10,000/15,000
Official Kit (Shirt/Shorts/Stockings): Light
Blue-White collar/Dark Blue/Light Blue-Dark
Blue trim
Most capped players: Chaitanya Singh/Nasser
Hussain

Ireland

Name: Irish Rugby Football Union
Address: 62 Lansdowne Road, Ballsbridge, Dublin
4 – Ireland
Phone: (+353) 1 6473800
Fax: (+353) 1 6473801
Website: http://www.irishrugby.ie
E-mail: info:irfu.ie
IRB Affiliation: 1886
Foundation: 14.12.1874
President: Roy Loughead
CEO: Philip Browne
National Coach: Warren Gatland
Affiliated Clubs: 135
Total Players:
Seniors: 55,900
Referees: 700

Home Ground: Lansdowne Road, Dublin – Ireland
Capacity: 49,500
Official Kit (Shirt/Shorts/Stockings):
Green/White/Green
Most capped player: Michael Gibson

Israel

Name: Israel Rugby Union
Address: P.O.Box 560, Raanana 4310 – Israel
Phone: (+972) 9 7422 062
Fax: (+972) 9 7422 062
E-mail: mailto:rugby@netvision.net.il
IRB Affiliation: 01.03.1988
Foundation: 01.03.1971
Chairman: Dave Kaplan
Secretary: Adi Raz
Affiliated Clubs: 20
Total Players: 770
Referees: 10
Official Kit (Shirt/Shorts/Stockings):
Blue-White/White/Blue

Italy

Name: Federazione Italiana Rugby
Address: Stadio Olimpico, Foro Italico, 00194
Roma – Italia
Phone: (+39) 06 36857845
Fax: (+39) 06 36837833
Website: http://www.federugby.it/
E-mail: mailto:federugby@atleticom.it
IRB Affiliation: 1987
Foundation: 09.1928
President: Giancarlo Dondi
Secretary: Giuliano Spingardi
National Coach: Bradley Johnstone
Affiliated Clubs: 500
Total Players: 39,856
Referees: 443
Home Ground: Stadio Flaminio – Italy *Capacity:*
27,000
Official Kit (Shirt/Shorts/Stockings): Sky
Blue/White/Sky Blue
Most capped player: Massimo Cuttitta

Ivory Coast

Name: Federation Ivoirienne De Rugby
Address: 01 BP 2357 Abidjan, 01 Cote d'Ivoire
Phone: (+225) 20 347 102
Fax: (+225) 20 347 107
IRB Affiliation: 1988
Foundation: 1961
President: Zahui Marcellin
Secretary: Anoma Camille
Affiliated Clubs: 40
Total Players: 5962
Official Kit (Shirt/Shorts/Socks):
Orange/White/Green

Jamaica

Name: Jamaica Rugby Union
Address: P.O. Box 144, KIngston 5 – Jamaica,
West Indies
Phone: (+876) 925 6703
Fax: (+876) 931 1743
Website: http://www.jru.org.jm/
E-mail: mailto:thompson@n5.com.jm

IRB Affiliation: 1996
Foundation: 1946
Chairman: Sgt. Jacob Thompson
(chairman)/Major Gen. John I. Simmonds
(ADC)
Secretary: Emertius Richard Guy
National Coach: Harry Shaw
Affiliated Clubs: 10
Total Players: 38
Referees: 25
Home Ground: Caymanas Estate Rugby Field,
Caymanas Estate Garden, St. Catherine –
Jamaica, *Capacity:* 5,000
Official Kit (Shirt/Shorts/Stockings):
Gold-Black-Green/Black/Gold or Green
Most capped player: Rohan Love

Japan

Name: Japan Rugby Football Union
Address: 2 Chome 8-35, Kitaaoyama, Minato-ku,
Tokyo 107, Japan
Phone: (+813) 8401 3321
Fax: (+813) 5410 5523
Website: http://www.rugby-japan.or.jp
E-mail: jrfu@rugby-japan.or.jp
IRB Affiliation: 1987
Foundation: 1926
Chairman: Takayori Tsuboi
Secretary: Koji Tokumasu
*Affiliated Clubs:*4785
Total Players: 140416
Official Kit (Shirt/Shorts/Socks): Red/White
Most capped player: Yukio Motoki

Kazakhstan

Name: Kazakhstan Rugby Union
Address: Str. Kashgarskaya 7, ap. 4, Almaty –
Kazakhstan 480091
Phone: (+3272) 327539
Fax: (+3272) 507357
E-mail: mailto:kaz_rugby@nursat.kz
IRB Affiliation: 07.1997
Foundation: 1993
Chairman: Stanislav Knorr
National Coach: Valeriy Popov/Philippov
Vyacheslav
Affiliated Clubs: 14
Total Players: 950
Referees: 10
Home Ground: Stadium of the Sport Club of
Army, Str. Abai 7, Almaty – Kazakhstan,
Capacity: 10,000
Official Kit (Shirt/Shorts/Stockings):
Yellow/Blue/Blue-Yellow
Most capped player: Mashurov Timur

Kenya

Name: Kenya Rugby Football Union
Address: P.O. Box 48322, GPO Nairobi – Kenya
Phone: (+254) 2 574425/562065/567473
Fax: (+254) 2 574425
Website: http://www.kenyarugby.com/
E-mail: mailto:krfu@iconnect.co.ke
IRB Affiliation: 1990
Foundation: 1923
Secretary: Richard Omwela

National Coach: Kenneth Thimba
Affiliated Clubs: 18
Total Players: 5,050
Referees: 30
Home Ground: Rugby Football Union of East
Africa Grounds (RFUEA), RFUEA Grounds,
Ngong Road, Nairobi – Kenya, *Capacity:* 5,000
Official Kit (Shirt/Shorts/Stockings):
Black-Red-Green/Black/Back-Red top
Most capped player: Felix Ochieng

Korea

Name: Korea Rugby Union
Address: Room #506 Olympic Center, 88
Oryun-Dong, Songpa-Gu, Seoul – Korea
Phone: (+82) 2 420 4244/5
Fax: (+82) 2 420 4246
Website: http://www.rugby.sports.or.kr/
E-mail: mailto:rugby@sports.or.kr
IRB Affiliation: 1998
Foundation: 1945
Chairman: Choo, Kwang-Ho
Affiliated Clubs: 65
Total Players: 1,520
Home Ground: Seoul Rugby Ground, 111-1
Oryu-Dong, Kuro-Gu, Seoul – Korea
Capacity: 3,000
Official Kit (Shirt/Shorts/Stockings): Red-and-Blue
stripes-White/Blue/Red-Blue-White stripes

Latvia

Name: Latvian Rugby Federation
Address: 4 Ternatas Iela, Riga, Latvia
Phone: (+371) 272 92703
IRB Affiliation: 1991
Foundation: 1960
Secretary: Janis Berzins
Affiliated Clubs: 7
Total Players: 790
Official Kit: Dark Red/White

Lithuania

Name: Federation Lithuanienne De Rugby
Address: Zemaites 6, Vilnius 2675, Lithuania
Phone: (+37) 02 335 474
Fax: (+37) 02 235 223
IRB Affiliation: 1992
Foundation: 1961
President: Aleksandras Makarenka
*Affiliated Clubs:*13
Total Players: 1110
Official Kit (Shirt/Short/Socks):
Green/Yellow/Red

Luxembourg

Name: Fédération Luxembourgeoise de Rugby
Address: B.P. 1965, Luxembourg – Gare ou/or 14
Avenue de la GARE L-1410 – Luxembourg
Phone: (+352) 29 75 98
Fax: (+352) 29 75 98
Website: http://www.rugby.lu/
E-mail: luis.moitinho@cec.int
IRB Affiliation: 1991
Foundation: 1974
Chairman: Jean-Philippe de Muyser
Secretary: Luis Moitinho

Affiliated Clubs: 3
Total Players: 295
Referees: 1
Home Ground: "Boy Konen" Sports Complex, 1 Rue des Sports, Luxembourg – Cessange – Luxembourg,
Official Kit (Shirt/Shorts/Stockings): Horizontal sky blue-white stripes/Marine Blue/Red
Most capped player: Nick Edwards

Madagascar

Name: Federation Malgache de Rugby
Address: 12, avenue Lenine. Lot. IVD 26 Ambatomitsangana 101 Antananarivo – Madagascar
Phone: (+261) 20 22 625 60
Fax: (+261) 20 22 623 73
E-mail: mailto:f-rugby@dts.mg
IRB Affiliation: 01.1998
Foundation: 01.1963
Chairman: Rakotoarinirina Tina Rigobert
Secretary: Rakotomamonjy Samuel
National Coach: Rafalimanana Joseph Berthin
Affiliated Clubs: 152
Total Players: 6,000
Referees: 20
Home Ground: Stade Municipal Mahamasina, Rue Rajoelina, Mahamasina, 101 – Antananarivo – Madagascar, *Capacity:* 20,000
Official Kit (Shirt/Shorts/Stockings): White-Green-Red/White/White
Most capped player: Rafalimanana Gilbert

Malaysia

Name: Malaysia Rugby Union
Address: c/o Ipoh City Council, Greentown, Jalan Sultan Abdul Jalil, 30450 Ipoh, Perak, Malaysia
Phone: (+605) 241 1831
Fax: (+605) 253 7396
E-mail: mailto:talaat@mbi.gov.my
IRB Affiliation: 1988
Foundation: 1927
President: Dato' Talaat Hj. Hussain
Secretary: Mohd. Nor Mohd. Tan
Affiliated Clubs: 180
Total Players: 21000
Official Kit (Shirt/Shorts/Socks): Navy/Yellow

Malta

Name: Malta Rugby Football Union
Address: 13, Regent House, Bisazza Street, Sliema SLM 15 – Malta
Phone: (+356) 347704
Fax: (+356) 347703
E-mail: mailto:kevin@jkproperties.com.mt mailto:christopher.martin@megabyte.net
IRB Affiliation: 05.2000
Foundation: 10.04.1991
Chairman: Kevin J. Buttigieg
Secretary: Christopher A. Martin
National Coach: Nigel "Ben" Bennett
Affiliated Clubs: 6
Total Players: 422
Referees: 2

Home Ground: Marsa, Rugby Pitch, Marsa Sports Complex, Marsa – Malta
Official Kit (Shirt/Shorts/Stockings): Black-White-Red/Black/Black
Most capped players: Robert Bonavia/Ian Borda/Christoffel Diamantino

Moldova

Name: Federatia de Rugby din Moldova
Address: Str. Columna 106, Chisinau – R. Moldova
Phone: (+373) 2 222 674
Fax: (+373) 2 222 674
E-mail: mailto:rugbymold@yahoo.com
IRB Affiliation: 04.03.1994
Foundation: 1992
Chairman: Iacob Boris
Secretary: Sadovici Oleg
National Coach: Zbirnea Alexandru
Affiliated Clubs: 4
Total Players: 1,050
Referees: 33
Official Kit (Shirt/Shorts/Stockings): Red/Blue/Yellow
Most capped player: Tabirta Vasile

Monaco

Name: Federation Monegasque de Rugby
Address: Stade Louis II, Avenue des Castelans – 98000 Monaco
Phone: (+377) 607934202
Fax: (+377) 493786270
Website: http://www.monaco-rugby.com/
E-mail: mailto:monacorugby@hotmail.com
IRB Affiliation: 01.1998
Foundation: 10.1996
Chairman: Patrice Pastor
National Coach: André Buonomo
Affiliated Clubs: 2
Total Players: 317
Referees: 5
Home Ground: Stade Louis II, Avenue des Castelans, 98000 – Monaco, *Capacity:* 18,000
Official Kit (Shirt/Shorts/Stockings): White-Red/Red/White-Red stripes
Most capped player: Gilles Parraud

Morocco

Name: Fédération Royale Marocaine de Rugby
Address: c/o Abdelaziz Bougja transports Touristiques-Africabus 26 bld. Felix Houphouet Boigny Casablanca, Morocco
Phone: (+212) 22948247
Fax: (+212) 22369060
E-mail: mailto:abougja@cgea.fr
IRB Affiliation: 10.10.1988
Foundation: 10.10.1956
President: Abdelaziz Bougja
Secretary: Kamal Benjeloune
National Coach: Edmond Jorda, Daniel Dubrocca
Affiliated Clubs: 24
Total Players: 6,800
Referees: 120
Home Ground: Complexe du COC Rugby Casablanca, Avenue des Sports, Ferme Bretonne, Casablanca – Maroc

Capacity: 4,500
Official Kit (Shirt/Shorts/Stockings):
Red-Green/White-Red-Green/Green-Red
Most capped player: El Oula Mohamed Karim

Namibia

Name: Namibia Rugby Union
Address: P.O. Box 138, Windhoek – Namibia
Phone: (+264) 61 251775/251717
Fax: (+264) 61 251028
E-mail: mailto:nru@cyberhost.com.na
IRB Affiliation: 1990
Foundation: 1987
Chairman: Dirk Hendrik Conradie
National Coach: Hendry Pretorius
Affiliated Clubs: 22
Total Players: 13,900
Referees: 100
Home Ground: National Rugby Stadium,
Lichtenstein Strasse, Olympia, Windhoek –
Namibia, *Capacity:* 18,000
Official Kit (Shirt/Shorts/Stockings): Royal Blue
with stripes/Royal Blue/Royal Blue with
stripes
Most capped player: Andries Blaauw

Netherlands

Name: Nederlands Rugby Bond
Address: National Rugby Stadium Amsterdam,
Sportpark de Eendracht, PO Box 8811, 1006
JA Amsterdam
Phone: (+31) 20 4808 100
Fax: (+31) 20 4808 101
Website: http://www.euronet.nl.users.henks.index
IRB Affiliation: 1988
Foundation: 1932
President: Eddie Bicker
Secretary: Leo van Schoonhoven
Affiliated Clubs: 100
Total Players: 6560
Official Kit (Shirt/Shorts/Socks): Orange/White
Most capped player: Mats Marcker

New Zealand

Name: New Zealand Rugby Football Union
Address: P.O. Box 2172, Wellington – New
Zealand
Phone: (+64) 4 994 995
Fax: (+64) 4 994 224
Website: http://www.nzrugby.co.nz/
E-mail: mailto:info@nzrugby.co.nz
IRB Affiliation: 1949
Foundation: 16.04.1892
Chairman: Lane Penn (President)/Murray
McCaw (Chairman)
CEO: David Rutherford
National Coach: John Mitchell
Affiliated Clubs: 520
Total Players: 133,400
Referees: 2,300
Home Ground: Eden Park, Auckland – New
Zealand, *Capacity:* 49,000
Official Kit (Shirt/Shorts/Stockings):
Black/Black/Black
Most capped player: Sean Fitzpatrick

Nigeria

Name: Nigeria Rugby Football Association
(NRFA)
Address: 4 Abibu Oki Close, Adeniran
Ogunsanya, Surulere, Lagos (PO Box 52238
Falomo, Ikoyi) – Nigeria
Phone: (+234) 1 7742637
Fax: (+234) 1 5851555
E-mail: klif@infoweb.abs.net
IRB Affiliation: 2001
Foundation: 1998
President: Ferni Williams
Affiliated Clubs: 16
Total Players: 660
Referees: 8
Official Kit (Shirt/Shorts/Stockings):
Green/Black/White

Niue Island

Name: Niue Rugby Union
Address: P.O. Box 11, Alofi – Niue Island
Phone: (+68) 4153
Fax: (+68) 4322
Website: http://www.nru.virtualave.net/
http://www.okakoa.nu/ www.nru.net
E-mail: mailto:tokes@niue.nu
mailto:niuerugby@email.com
IRB Affiliation: 01.04.1999
Foundation: 01.01.1952
Chairman: Toke T. Talagi
Secretary: Darren Tohovaka
National Coach: Steven McCoy
Affiliated Clubs: 11
Total Players: 800
Referees: 8
Home Ground: Paliati, Alofi – Niue Island,
Capacity: 2,000
Official Kit (Shirt/Shorts/Stockings): Gold
jersey-Navy blue stripes/Blue/Gold-Blue
stripes

Norway

Name: Norwegian Rugby Union
Address: Serviceboks 1, Ullevaan Stadion, N-0840
Oslo – Norway
Phone: (+47) 21029845
Fax: (+47) 21029846
Website: http://www.rugby.no/
E-mail: mailto:rugby@nif.idrett.no
IRB Affiliation: 1993
Foundation: 15.02.1982
Chairman: Per S Modne
Secretary: Kim J. Moore Eriksen
National Coach: Rod Francis
Affiliated Clubs: 12
Total Players: 447
Referees: 8
Home Ground: Ekeberg, Ballslette – Norway
Official Kit (Shirt/Shorts/Stockings): Quarters:
Red-White-LightBlue-Navy Blue /navy
Blue/Red-White turndowns

Papua New Guinea

Name: Papua New Guinea Rugby Football Union
Inc.

Address: Gateway Hotel, Shop Front 2, Morea Tobo Road , 7 mile, Port Moresby, National Capital District – Papua New Guinea
Phone: (+675) 323 4212
Fax: (+675) 323 4211
E-mail: mailto:rugbypng@datec.com.pg
IRB Affiliation: 10.1993
Foundation: 1963
Chairman: Graham Osborne
Secretary: Robert Doko
National Coach: Farell Temata
Affiliated Clubs: 54 clubs located in seven provincial centres
Total Players: 3,100
Referees: 35
Home Ground: The Union does not have a home ground. However when the need arises the Loyd Robson Oval rugby league oval is used. The Oval rugby is managed by the Legends Club – Port Moresby Rugby Football League (Contact: Marc Karcher – General Manager: PO Box 7956, Boroko, National Capital District – Papua New Guinea), *Capacity:* 20,000
Official Kit (Shirt/Shorts/Stockings): Black Jersey-White collar-Yellow & Red stripes on the front left hand side of jersey, red numbering/Black/ Black-Two Yellow stripes and a Red stripe in the middle.
Most capped player: Peter Senat

Paraguay
Name: Union de Rugby Del Paraguay
Address: Independencia Nacional 250 c/ Palma 1er Piso, Asuncion – Paraguay
Phone: (+595) 21 496 390
Fax: (+595) 21496 390
E-mail: mailto:urprugby@pla.net.py
IRB Affiliation: 04.1989
Foundation: 06.09.1970
Chairman: Luis Horacio Amarilla
Secretary: Jorge Benitez
National Coach: Marcelo Gangoiti
Affiliated Clubs: 12
Total Players: 1438
Referees: 40
Official Kit (Shirt/Shorts/Stockings): Red-white stripes/Blue/Red
Most capped player: Pedro Mosciaro

Peru
Name: Unión Peruana de Rugby
Address: Calle Toribio Pacheco 260, Miraflores L18 Lima – Perú
Phone: (+51) 1 4414665
Fax: (+51) 1 2224337
E-mail: mailto:jsilvah@ec-red.com
IRB Affiliation: .04.1999
Foundation: 11.02.1997
Chairman: Jose Luis Silva Hurtado
Secretary: Carlos Hamann Garcia-Belaunde
National Coach: Felix Garcia Hidalgo
Affiliated Clubs: 6
Total Players: 550/24 (F)
Seniors: 280
Referees: 8

Official Kit (Shirt/Shorts/Stockings): White-Red collar/White/Red-White stripes
Most capped player: Erick Marcelo

Poland
Name: Polish Rugby Union
Address: 01-813 Warszawa, ul.Marymoncka 34 – Poland
Phone: (+48) 228353587
Fax: (+48) 228353587
E-mail: mailto:pzrugby@poczta.onet.pl
IRB Affiliation: 1988
Chairman: Jan Kozbowski
Secretary: Grzegorz Borkowski
National Coach: Jerzy Jumas
Affiliated Clubs: 22
Total Players: 2,000
Referees: 18
Official Kit (Shirt/Shorts/Stockings): White/Red/Red
Most capped player: Stanislaw Wiciorek

Portugal
Name: Federação Portuguesa de Rugby
Address: Rua Julieta Ferrão, n°12-3 D Sala 303, 1600-151 Lisboa – Portugal
Phone: (+351) 21 799 16 90
Fax: (+351) 21 793 61 35
E-mail: mailto:geral@fpr.pt
IRB Affiliation: 11.1988
Foundation: 17.12.1926
Chairman: Pedro Sousa Ribeiro
Secretary: Delfim Bernardes Barreira
National Coach: Evan Crawford
Affiliated Clubs: 53 (32 in activity)
Total Players: 3,958
Referees: 49
Home Ground: Estádio Universitário de Lisboa, *Capacity:* 5,000
Official Kit (Shirt/Shorts/Stockings): Green/White/White
Most capped player: João Ferreira Queimado

Romania
Name: Romanian Rugby Federation
Address: Bucharest, bd. Marasati, no. 26, sector 1, cod 7700 – Romania
Phone: (+40) 1 2245482
Fax: (+40) 1 2245481
E-mail: mailto:frr@fx.ro
IRB Affiliation: .11.1987
Foundation: 26.03.1931
Chairman: Dumitru Mihalache
Secretary: Hacic Garabet
National Coach: Mircea Paraschiv
Affiliated Clubs: 53
Total Players: 2,987
Referees: 91
Home Ground: National Stadium, bd. Basarabia, 37.39, Bucharest – Romania, *Capacity:* 80,000
Official Kit (Shirt/Shorts/Stockings): Yellow/Blue/Red
Most capped player: Adrian Lungu

Russia

Name: Rugby Union of Russia
Address: 24 Lenina Street, 660049, Krasnoayarsk
  – Russia
Phone: (+7) 3912 224303
Fax: (+7) 3912 279760
Website: http://www.rugby.ru/
E-mail: mailto:info@rugby.ru
  mailto:rugby@online.ru
IRB Affiliation: 1990
Foundation: 1936
Chairman: Youri Nickolaev
National Coach: Alexandr Pervukhin
  (Russia)/James Younger Stoffberg (South
  Africa)
Affiliated Clubs: 29
Total Players: 7,310
Referees: 40
Home Ground: 'Dinamo', Krasnodar – Russia,
  Capacity: 3,500
Official Kit (Shirt/Shorts/Stockings):
  White/Blue/Red
Most capped player: Igor Mironov

Samoa

Name: Samoa Rugby Football Union
Address: PO Box 618, Apia, Samoa
Phone: (+685) 23 961
Fax: (+685) 25 009
E-mail: mailto:fepuleai@lesamoa.net
IRB Affiliation: 1988
Foundation: 1924
President: Tuiatua Tupua Tamasese Efi
Secretary: Tauiliili Harry Schuster
Affiliated Clubs: 125
Total Players: 14263
Official Kit (Shirt/Short/Socks): Royal Blue/White
Most capped player: To'o Vaega

Scotland

Name: Scottish Rugby Union (SRU)
Address: Murrayfield, Edinburgh EH12 5PJ –
  Scotland
Phone: (+44) 131 346 5000
Fax: (+44) 131 346 5001
Website: http://www.sru.org.uk/
E-mail: mailto:feedback@sru.org.uk
IRB Affiliation: 1886
Foundation: 09.10.1873
Chairman: Graham Young
Secretary: Bill Hogg
National Coach: Ian McGeechan
Affiliated Clubs: 253
Total Players: 33,593
Referees: 440
Home Ground: Murrayfield, Edinburgh EH12 5PJ
  – Scotland, *Capacity:* 67,500
Official Kit (Shirt/Shorts/Stockings): Marine Blue
  with purple stripe & White
  collar/White-Blue/Marine blue with purple
  horizontal stripe
Most capped player: Scott Hastings

Senegal

Name: Fédération Sénégalaise de Rugby
Address: B.P. 2656, Dakar – Sénégal
Phone: (+221) 821 58 58/822 10 75
Fax: (+221) 821 86 51
E-mail: mailto:guedel.ndiaye@sentoo.sn
IRB Affiliation: 11.1999
Foundation: 17.09.1960
Chairman: Guédel Ndiaye
Secretary: Biram Kebe
National Coach: Renaud Puzzenat, Biram Kebe
Affiliated Clubs: 5
Total Players: 438
Referees: 4
Home Ground: Amitié (Dakar), Demba Diop, Iba
  Mar Diop, *Capacity:* Amitié 60,000/Demba
  Diop 20,000/Iba Mar Diop 15,000
Official Kit (Shirt/Shorts/Stockings):
  Green/Yellow/Red
Most capped player: Biram Kebe

Singapore

Name: Singapore Rugby Union (SRU)
Address: 21 Evans Road – Singapore 259 366
Phone: (+65) 467 4038
Fax: (+65) 467 0283
Website: http://www.sru.org.sg/
E-mail: mailto:sru@pacific.net.sg
IRB Affiliation: 1989
Foundation: 1948
Chairman: Dr Chan Peng Mun
Secretary: Mark James
National Coach: Sammuel Chan Kok Wah
Affiliated Clubs: 10
Total Players: 7,200
Referees: 50
Home Ground: Yio Chu Kang Stadium –
  Singapore, *Capacity:* 2,000
Official Kit (Shirt/Shorts/Stockings):
  Red/White/Red-White stripes

Slovenia

Name: Rugby Zveva Slovenije
Address: Pod hribom 55, 1000 Ljubljana –
  Slovenia
Phone: (+386) 1 5076 377
Fax: (+386) 1 5076 377
IRB Affiliation: 10.1996
Foundation: 1989
Chairman: Dušan Gerloviè
Secretary: Nikola Popadiè
National Coach: Jure Mahkota
Affiliated Clubs: 5
Total Players:
Seniors: 820
Referees: 5
Home Ground: Ljubljana Oval, *Capacity:* 1,500
Official Kit (Shirt/Shorts/Stockings):
  Blue/White/Blue
Most capped player: Luka Arko

Solomon Islands

Name: Solomon Islands Rugby Union Federation
  (SIRUF)
Address: C/-P O Box 642, Honiara – Solomon
  Islands
Phone: (+677) 21595
Fax: (+677) 23715
E-mail: mailto:dbsi@welkam.solomon.com.sb

IRB Affiliation: 03.11.1999
Foundation: 15.03.1963
Chairman: Gary Gale
Secretary: Ashley Wickham
National Coach: Josiah Titia
Affiliated Clubs: 42
Total Players: 1,470
Referees: 19
Home Ground: Lawson Tama National Stadium, Lawson Tama Park, Central Honiara – Solomon Islands, *Capacity:* 20,000
Official Kit (Shirt/Shorts/Stockings): Royal Blue-Gold & Emerald Green Stripes with Gold collar/Royal Blue/Royal Blue with Gold stripes
Most capped player: Alfred Soaki

South Africa

Name: South Africa Rugby Football Union
Address: Boundary Road, PO Box 99, Newlands 7725, Cape Town – South Africa
Phone: (+27 21) 685 3038/9
Fax: (+27 21) 685 6771
Website: www.sarugby.net
E-mail: mailto:dbsi@welkam.solomon.com.sb sarfu@icon.co.za
IRB Affiliation: 1949
Foundation: 1889
President: Silas Nkanunu
CEO: Mveleli Ncula
National Coach: Harry Viljoen
Affiliated Clubs: 1080
Total Players: 361,302
Referees: 6,000
Official Kit (Shirt/Shorts/Stockings): Green & Gold /White /Green & Gold
Most capped players: Mark Andrews/Joost van der Westhuizen

Spain

Name: Federacion Espanola De Rugby
Address: Ferraz 16-4 Dcha, 28008, Madrid – Spain
Phone: (+3491) 541 4978
Fax: (+3491) 559 0986
Website: http://www.sportec.com
E-mail: mailto:fed.rugby@teleline.es
IRB Affiliation: 1988
Foundation: 1923
Secretary: Jose Moreno
*Affiliated Clubs:*206
Total Players: 14,500
Official Kit (Shirt/Shorts/Socks): Red/Navy
Most capped player: Francisco Puertas

Sri Lanka

Name: Sri Lanka Rugby Football Union
Address: 28 Longden Place, Colombo 7, Sri Lanka
Phone: (+941) 580 294
Fax: (+941) 580 294
E-mail: mailto:slrfu@dynaweb.lk
IRB Affiliation: 1988
Foundation: 1908
President: Capt. Harsha Mayadunne
Secretary: Shane Dulewe

Affiliated Clubs: 25
Total Players: 9700
Official Kit (Shirt/Shorts/Socks): Green/White
Most capped player: Didacus De Almeida

St. Lucia

Name: St. Lucia Rugby Football Union
Address: PO Box 567, Castries, St. Lucia, West Indies
Phone: (+1758) 453 7194
Fax: (+1758) 452 6001
IRB Affiliation: 1996
Foundation: 1996
President: Kent St Catherine
Secretary: Christopher Wyatt
Affiliated Clubs: 4
Total Players: 70
Official Kit (Shirt/Shorts/Socks): Blue/White/Yellow/Black

Swaziland

Name: Swaziland Rugby Union
Address: P.O. Box 4948, Mbabane – Swaziland
Phone: (+268) 4040740
Fax: (+268) 4040740
E-mail: mailto:lindac@africaonline.co.sz
IRB Affiliation: 1998
Foundation: 1995
President: Michael John Collinson
Secretary: Dion Wade
Affiliated Clubs: 3
Total Players: 350
Home Ground: Malkerns Country Club, Malkerns – Swaziland
Official Kit (Shirt/Shorts/Stockings): White with Blue-Red & yellow stripes on shoulders/White/Blue
Most capped player: Michael Nann

Sweden

Name: Swedish Rugby Federation
Address: Idrottens hus, 123 87 Farsta – Sweden
Phone: (+46) 8 605 65 24
Fax: (+46) 8 605 65 27
Website: www.rugby.se
E-mail: mailto:rugby@rf.se
IRB Affiliation: 01.03.1988
Foundation: 29.03.1932
Chairman: Lars Ohlsson
Secretary: Torbjörn Johansson
National Coach: Guy Dinwoodie
Affiliated Clubs: 48
Total Players: 2,907
Referees: 32
Official Kit (Shirt/Shorts/Stockings): Blue-yellow stripes from chest and down/Blue/Yellow-blue stripes at the top.
Most capped player: Karl Tapper

Switzerland

Name: Fédération Suisse de Rugby (FSR)
Address: P.O. Box 7705, Pavillonweg 3, CH – 3001 Bern – Switzerland
Phone: (+31) 3012388
Fax: (+31) 3012388
Website: http://www.rugby.ch/

E-mail: mailto:fsr@rugby.ch
IRB Affiliation: 1988
Foundation: 1974
Chairman: Luc Baatard
Secretary: Norbert Li-Marchetti
National Coach: Regis Tabarini (ad interim)
Affiliated Clubs: 22
Total Players: 1,400
Referees: 10
Official Kit (Shirt/Shorts/Stockings):
  White/White/Red
Most capped player: Francois Joly

Tahiti

Name: Federation Tahitienne De Rugby De
  Polynesie Francaise
Address: BP 650 Papeete, 98714 Papeete, Tahiti
Phone: (+689) 48 12 28
Fax: (+689) 45 89 42
IRB Affiliation: 1994
Foundation: 1989
President: Charles Tauziet
Secretary: Pique Pascal
Affiliated Clubs: 10
Total Players: 1440
Official Kit (Shirt/Shorts/Socks): Red/White
Most capped player: Apolosi Foliaki

Thailand

Name: Thai Rugby Union
Address: Thephasdin Stadium, National Stadium,
  Rama I Road, Pathumwan, Bangkok 10330 –
  Thailand
Phone: (+66) 2 2153839/2 6124674
Fax: (+66) 2 2141712
Website: http://www.thairugby.com/
E-mail: mailto:info@thairugby.com
  mailto:thai_rugby@thai.com
IRB Affiliation: 1989
Foundation: 1938
Chairman: Air Chief Marshall Pong Maneesilpa
Secretary: Group Captain Somchai Theananant
National Coach: Poj Lakasnasompong/Pol Capt
  Yongyuth Rattanajongjitakon
Total Players: 2,600
Home Ground: Muang Thong Thani Stadium,
  Muang Thong Thani Sports Complex, Muang
  Thong Thani, Bangkok – Thailand, *Capacity:*
  5,000
Official Kit (Shirt/Shorts/Stockings): Yellow/Royal
  Blue/Yellow
Most capped player: Poj Laksanasompong

Tonga

Name: Tonga Rugby Football Union
Address: PO Box 369, Nuku'alofa, Kingdom of
  Tonga
Phone: (+676) 26 045
Fax: (+676) 26 044
E-mail: mailto:tongarfu@kalianet.to
IRB Affiliation: 1987
Foundation: 19
Secretary: Satua Tu'akoi
Affiliated Clubs: 62
Official Kit (Shirt/Shorts/Socks): Scarlet/White
Most capped player: Kuli Faletau

Trinidad & Tobago

Name: Trinidad and Tobago Rugby Football
  Union
Address: P.O. Box 5090 TT Post, Wrightson Road,
  Port of Spain, Trinidad – Trinidad & Tobago
Phone: (+1868) 628 9048
Fax: (+1868) 628 9049
Website: http://www.ttrfu.com/
E-mail: mailto:contact@ttrfu.com
IRB Affiliation: 1992
Foundation: 1928
Chairman: Peter Inglefield
Secretary: Brian Lewis
National Coach: Gregory Rousseau
Affiliated Clubs: 12
Total Players: 1,412
Official Kit (Shirt/Shorts/Stockings):
  Red-Black/Black/Red

Tunisia

Name: Federation Tunisienne De Rugby
Address: Boite Postale 318-1004, El Menzah,
  Tunis, Tunisia
Phone: (+216) 1754 870
Fax: (+216) 1754 870
IRB Affiliation: 1988
Foundation: 1972
President: Aref Belkhiria
Secretary: Bechir Zarbouk
Affiliated Clubs: 36
Total Players: 5220

Uganda

Name: Uganda Rugby Football Union (URFU)
Address: P.O. Box 22108, Kampala – Uganda
Phone: (+256) 41 269 697
Fax: (+256) 41 259 280
Website: http://www.urfu.org/
E-mail: mailto:urfu@africaonline.co.ug
IRB Affiliation: 01.07.1997
Foundation: 01.01.1955
Chairman: Paul Wanyama Sigombe
Secretary: Ojambo Stephen Paul
National Coach: Yayiro Musisis Kasasa/Frank
  Ochieng/Tolbert Onyango
Affiliated Clubs: 12
Total Players: 4,500
Referees: 20
Home Ground: Kampala Rugby Club, P.O. Box
  5094, Kampala – Uganda, *Capacity:* 5,000
Official Kit (Shirt/Shorts/Stockings): Black-Red &
  Yellow stripes/Red/Black-Yellow stripes
Most capped player: Michael Wandera

Ukraine

Name: National Rugby Federation Of Ukraine
Address: 42 Esplanadna, St. Kiev 252023, Ukraine
  Phone: (+380) 44 220 5157
Fax: (+380) 44 220 1294
IRB Affiliation: 1992
Foundation: 1991
Affiliated Clubs: 22
Total Players: 1875
Official Kit (Shirt/Shorts/Socks): Yellow/Blue

Uruguay

Name: Union De Rugby Del Uruguay
Address: Treinta Y Tres 1307, Montevideo, Uruguay
Phone: (+598) 2916 6161
Fax: (+598) 2916 6081
Website: http://www.uru.reduy.com
E-mail: mailto:uru@reduy.com
IRB Affiliation: 1989
Foundation: 1951
President: Andres Sanguinetti
Secretary: Juan Minut
Affiliated Clubs: 12
Total Players: 2646
Official Kit (Shirt/Shorts/Socks): Sky Blue
Most capped player: Diego Ormaechea

United States Of America

Name: USA Rugby Football Union
Address: Football Union (USA Rugby) 3595 E. Fountain Blvd., Colorado Springs, CO 80910 – United States of America
Phone: (+1) 719 637 1022
Fax: (+1) 719 637 1315
Website: http://www.usarugby.org/
E-mail: mailto:info@usarugby.org
IRB Affiliation: 1987
Foundation: 07.06.1975
President: Anne Barry
Secretary: Patrick J. O'Connor
National Coach: Duncan Hall (XVs)/John McKittrick (Sevens)
Affiliated Clubs: 1,246
Total Players: 45,209
Referees: 465
Official Kit (Shirt/Shorts/Stockings): Red W-Blue shoulders/White/Blue
Most capped player: Vaea Anitoni

Vanuatu

Name: Vanuatu Rugby Football Union
Address: P.O. Box 226/1584, Port Vila – Vanuatu
Phone: (+678) 22387
Fax: (+678) 23529/23230
E-mail: mailto:mdunn@vanuatu.com.vu
IRB Affiliation: 01.10.1999
Foundation: 1980
Chairman: David Saul
Secretary: Brian Fong
National Coach: Charles Valentine
Affiliated Clubs: 8
Total Players: 560
Referees: 5
Home Ground: Korman Stadium, Port Vila – Vanuatu, *Capacity:* 5,000
Official Kit (Shirt/Shorts/Stockings): Irish Green-Red-Yellow-Black/Black/ Green-Red-Yellow-Black

Venezuela

Name: Federación Venezolana de Rugby
Address: Urb. Santa Inés, Av. la Terraza, Qta. La Quintana, #85, Baruta 1080, Caracas – Venezuela
Phone: (+58) 212 979 1650/256 1550
Fax: (+58) 212 979 1650/256 1550
E-mail: mailto:rugbyven@hotmail.com mailto:roberto@cantv.net
IRB Affiliation: 1998
Foundation: 1991
Chairman: Jose Victori
Secretary: Rogelio Martinez V
National Coach: Rex Lawrence
Affiliated Clubs: 33
Total Players: 750
Referees: 15
Home Ground: Estadio Olímpico de la Universidad Central de Venezuela, Plaza Venezuela, Caracas – Venezuela, *Capacity:* 8,000
Official Kit (Shirt/Shorts/Stockings): Red wine/Black /Red wine
Most capped player: Mauricio Arevalo

Wales

Name: Welsh Rugby Union
Address: Custom House, Custom House Street, Cardiff, CF10 1RF, Wales
Phone: (+44) 2920 781 700
Fax: (+44) 2920 225 601
Website: http://www.wru.com
IRB Affiliation: 1886
Foundation: 1881
Chairman: Glamour Griffiths
Secretary: Dennis Gethin
National Coach: Graham Henry
Affiliated Clubs: 372
Total Players: 59900
Official Kit (Shirt/Shorts/Socks): Red/White
Most capped player: Neil Jenkins

Yugoslavia

Name: Yougoslav Rugby Union
Address: Terazije 35/III, P.O. Box 1013, 11000 Belgrade – Yugoslavia
Phone: (+381) 11 3245 743
Fax: (+381) 11 3245 743
E-mail: mailto:rugbyoffice@ptt.yu
IRB Affiliation: 31.03.1988
Foundation: 10.07.1954
Chairman: Milos Kostic
National Coach: Dredrag Jerinic
Affiliated Clubs: 12
Total Players: 1,682
Referees: 16
Home Ground: Trudbenik, Oante Sreckovica 66, 11000 Belgrade – Yugoslavia, *Capacity:* 4,000
Official Kit (Shirt/Shorts/Stockings): Blue/White/Red
Most capped player: Dragan Grujic

Zambia

Name: Zambia Rugby Football Union (ZRFU)
Address: 116 Sanlam Building, P.O.Box 21797, Kitwe – Zambia
Phone: (+260) 2 231604
Fax: (+260) 2 231861
E-mail: mailto:zrfu@coppernet.zm
IRB Affiliation: 03.03.1995
Foundation: .06.1975
Chairman: Manuel W Harawa
Secretary: Rodgers Chibuye

National Coach: John Mwanza
Affiliated Clubs: 12
Total Players: 6,000
Referees: 23
Home Ground: Roan Antelope, co ZRFU, Box
21797, Kitwe – Zambia
Capacity: 5,000
Official Kit (Shirt/Shorts/Stockings):
Green-Black-Red-Gold stripes on chest/ Black
/Green
Most capped player: Musonda Kaminsa

Zimbabwe

Name: Zimbabwe Rugby Union
Address: 57 Van Praagh Ave., Milton Park, Harare
– Zimbabwe PO Box 1129
Phone: (+263) 4 251886 /7 /8
Fax: (+263) 4 790914
Website: http://www.ziugby.com/
E-mail: mailto:janice@rugby.co.zw
IRB Affiliation: 03.1987
Foundation: 1895
Chairman: Lawrence Majuru
National Coach: Godwin Murambiwa
Affiliated Clubs: 33
Total Players: 22,770
Referees: 65
Home Ground: Hartsfield, Hartsfield Grounds,
Matabeleland Rugby Board, 1st Ave/Robert
Mugabe Rd, Bulawayo – Zimbabwe, *Capacity:*
20,000
Official Kit (Shirt/Shorts/Stockings): Green-White
hoops/White/Green-White hoops
Most capped player: Iain Buchanan/Brendan
Dawson

IRB ASSOCIATE MEMBER UNIONS

British Virgin Islands

Name: British Virgin Islands Rugby Union
Address: Fort Burt, Road Town, Tortola, British
Virgin Islands
Phone: (+1 284) 494 2868
Fax: (+1 284) 494 7889
E-mail: cmark@surbvl.com
IRB Affiliation: 2001
President: Brian Jackson
Secretary: Mark Chapman

St. Vincents & The Grenadines

Name: St. Vincents & The Grenadines Rugby
Union
Address: PO Box 1034, Kingstown, St. Vincent &
The Grenadines
Phone: (+1 784) 457 5135
Fax: (+1 784) 456 2420
E-mail: mailto:peakcons@caribsurf.com
IRB Affiliation: 2001
President: John Townsend

IRB REGIONAL ASSOCIATIONS

FIRA-AER

Name: Federation Internationale de Rugby
Amateur
Address: FIRA-AER, 33 rue de Liege, 75009 Paris
Phone: (+33 1) 5321 1522
Fax: (+33 1) 4281 004
E-mail: mailto:secretariat@fira-aer-rugby.com
Website: http://www.fira-aer-rugby.com
Secretary General: Jean-Louis Barthes

ARFU

Name: Asian Rugby Football Union
(Associate/Observer Member)
Address: Law Drafting Division, Department of
Justice, Room 825, Eighth Floor, Queensway
Government Offices, 66 Queensway, Hong
Kong
Phone: (+852) 2867 2406
Fax: (+852) 2869 1302
E-mail: mailto:jamiescott@doj.gov.hk
Secretary General: Hon Jamie Scott

CAR

Name: Confederation Africaine de Rugby
Address: c/o Free State Rugby Union, PO Box 15,
BLOEMFONTEIN 9300, South Africa
Phone: (+27 51) 407 1721
Fax: (+27 51) 436 9930
E-mail: jbotes@iafrica.com
Secretary General: Johan Botes

PARA

Name: Pan American Rugby Association
Address: c/oUnion Argentina de Rugby,
Rivadavia 1227, Entre piso (1033) Capital
Federal, Buenos Aires, Argentina
Phone: (+541 1) 43 83 22 11
Fax: (+541 1) 43 83 25 70
President: c/o Carlos Tozzi,

FORU

Name: Federation of Oceanic Rugby Unions
Address: c/o New Zealand RFU, Level 1,
Huddart Parker Building, PO Box 2172,
Wellington, New Zealand
Phone: (+644) 499 4995
Fax: (+644) 499 4224
E-mail: bill.wallace@nzrugby.co.nz
Secretary: Bill Wallace